ANTHROPOLOGICAL THEORY

ANTHROPOLOGICAL THEORY

An Introductory History

FOURTH EDITION

R. Jon McGee

Richard L. Warms

Texas State University–San Marcos

Boston   Burr Ridge, IL   Dubuque, IA   Madison, WI   New York
San Francisco   St. Louis   Bangkok   Bogotá   Caracas   Kuala Lumpur
Lisbon   London   Madrid   Mexico City   Milan   Montreal   New Delhi
Santiago   Seoul   Singapore   Sydney   Taipei   Toronto

The McGraw-Hill Companies

Mc Graw Hill Higher Education

Published by McGraw-Hill, an imprint of The McGraw-Hill Companies, Inc., 1221 Avenue of the Americas, New York, NY 10020. Copyright © 2008. All rights reserved. No part of this publication may be reproduced or distributed in any form or by any means, or stored in a database or retrieval system, without the prior written consent of The McGraw-Hill Companies, Inc., including, but not limited to, in any network or other electronic storage or transmission, or broadcast for distance learning.

1 2 3 4 5 6 7 8 9 0 DOC/DOC 0 9 8 7

ISBN: 978-0-07-340522-3
MHID: 0-07-340522-1

Editor-in-chief: *Emily Barrosse*
Publisher: *Frank Mortimer*
Sponsoring editor: *Monica Eckman*
Developmental editor: *Larry Goldberg*
Marketing manager: *Lori DeShazo*
Managing editor: *David M. Staloch*
Art director: *Jeanne M. Schreiber*
Art manager: *Robin Mouat*
Senior designer: *Violeta Díaz*
Lead production supervisor: *Richard DeVitto*
Production Service: *Matrix Productions Inc.*
Compositor: *Aptara*
Typeface: *10/11.5 Fairfield Medium*
Printing: *R.R. Donnelley & Sons*

Credits: *The credits section for this book begins on page C-1 and is considered an extension of the copyright page.*

Library of Congress Cataloging-in-Publication Data
McGee, R. Jon, 1955-
Anthropological theory: an introductory history / R. Jon McGee, Richard L. Warms.—4th ed.
    p. cm.
  Includes bibliographical references and index.
  ISBN 0-07-340522-1 (alk. paper)
  Anthropology—Philosophy. 2. Anthropology—Methodology. I. Warms, Richard L. II. Title.
GN33.M33 2008
301.101—dc22

2006048088

The Internet addresses listed in the text were accurate at the time of publication. The inclusion of a Web site does not indicate an endorsement by the authors or McGraw-Hill, and McGraw-Hill does not guarantee the accuracy of the information presented at these sites.

www.mhhe.com

CONTENTS

Functionalism   159

Culture and Personality   204

Part Three
THEORY AT MIDCENTURY   226

The Reemergence of Evolutionary Thought   226

Neomaterialism: Evolutionary, Functionalist, Ecological, and Marxist   265

Structuralism   324

Ethnoscience and Cognitive Anthropology   360

Part Four
THE LATE TWENTIETH CENTURY AND BEYOND   406

PREFACE

Theory is the core of anthropology. Theories determine the types of questions anthropologists ask and the sorts of information they collect. Without a solid understanding of the history of theory, anthropological data remain a collection of exotic ethnographic vignettes. With a knowledge of theory, these vignettes become attempts to answer critical philosophical and practical problems. Thus it is critical that anthropologists understand theory and its historical context. Students face two choices, then, if they wish to understand the theoretical perspectives that ultimately drive ethnographic fieldwork: They can read classic theoretical articles or they can read someone's interpretations of those articles. For readers who are not well versed in anthropological theory, neither choice is ideal. We created this volume to provide a more accessible means of introducing students to the past century and a half of theorizing in anthropology.

We believe that it is essential for students to read original essays by the field's important thinkers. Reading original works promotes depth of understanding and opens possibilities of analysis that even the best books describing the history of theory can never provide. What better introduction to Herbert Spencer, Karl Marx, or Lévi-Strauss than actually reading them? Yet many students find reading original essays extremely demanding. The language is sometimes difficult, and the intellectual disputes, references to other thinkers, and historical contexts are often obscure. We have attempted to make the task less onerous by providing detailed commentary, in close proximity to difficult passages in the original essays, to illuminate obscure references, arcane language, and unfamiliar contexts.

As we have repeatedly revised *Anthropological Theory* our goals for the book have grown. *Anthropological Theory* is primarily a textbook designed for students in advanced undergraduate and beginning graduate classes. However, we have increasingly tried to write a reference work that both students and professors will want to keep within easy reach. We have done this by writing extensive footnotes on an enormous variety of individuals and topics and providing an extensive author-written two-level index with well over 1,000 entries. You will find basic information on everyone from Leo Frobenius to Daisy Bates, from Ibn Khaldun to Solly Zuckerman. Of course, no book can possibly include information on everyone and everything, but we believe that there is no other single book in anthropology that has as much basic information about as many different theories and people as the current volume.

APPROACH

We have assembled a diverse collection of essays by some of the most important thinkers in anthropology and have deliberately favored essays that are ethnographic examples of theoretical positions over those that are simply declarations of theory. Wherever possible, we have striven to select essays that are well written, concise, and accessible. The collection begins in the mid-nineteenth century and ends in 2001. It is divided into sections encompassing well-known theoretical positions that are represented by authors generally considered to be the outstanding spokespersons for their points of view, or essays that are especially vivid illustrations of a perspective.

PEDAGOGY

We have provided extensive support material to help students understand the forty-three essays that make up this volume. Each of the fourteen sections begins with an introduction to acquaint readers with some of the most important proponents of a school of thought, the problems they set out to solve, the methods they used, and the dilemmas they faced. Extensive editorial footnotes that provide additional information to help the reader understand and interpret the reading accompany each essay. In addition to providing definitions, translations of foreign phrases, and historical information, the notes help students trace the intellectual connections among thinkers both inside and outside of anthropology. The notes are meant to inform, raise interesting questions, and foster further creative and original thinking. They make essential but sometimes difficult information accessible to students and provide some interesting little-known background details. Anthropological theory, even that of a century ago, is alive and vital. We hope our commentary helps readers see it that way.

No book of theory and commentary can ever be entirely without bias, but we have tried to come as close to this ideal as we can. In our introductions and commentary, we point to both the strengths and weaknesses of each theoretical position. Although astute readers can probably figure out which perspectives we like and which we dislike, we do not intend to promote one theory at the expense of another. In fact, we come from quite different theoretical perspectives, and our ideas have evolved through the years as we teach our theory classes and prepare new editions of this text. Every introductory section and note in this volume was written and rewritten by both of us, and we have been willing to accept substantial criticism of ideas we hold dear.

For us, editing this volume continues to be an exciting process of discovery and interpretation. Research, careful reading, discussion, and argumentation, as well as the comments of numerous reviewers and readers of earlier editions, have greatly deepened our understanding of the works of the great thinkers in anthropology.

Writing this book has forced us to rethink what we believed we knew, and in the process we have become better scholars of theory. Selecting these essays and writing the introductions and commentary for them has been profoundly rewarding for us. We hope that reading the essays and our comments will be as productive for students and colleagues.

NEW TO THIS EDITION

This fourth edition represents the most substantial revision we have undertaken to date. Preparing it has given us a chance to reconsider our selection of essays, the notes we wrote as commentary, and our introductions. We have made substantial improvements in all of these, incorporating new information and bringing an expanded selection of authors and opinions to the volume. Most notably, this edition includes a new section called "Globalization, Power, and Agency," highlighting one of the dominant trends in contemporary anthropology. This section features essays by Arjun Appadurai, Philippe Bourgois, and Aihwa Ong.

In addition to the new final section we have improved existing sections with several new essays. In the section on historical particularism we present Whorf's "The Relation of Habitual Thought and Behavior to Language," a seminal essay in the development of ethnoscience and cognitive and linguistic anthropology. In the section on functionalism we now include one of Radcliffe-Brown's best known essays, "On Joking Relationships." In Part Three we introduce Eric Wolf, one of the most influential Marxist anthropologists of the twentieth century, incorporating his essay "Peasantry and Its Problems"; as in the previous edition we also acquaint the reader with Lévi-Strauss' extensive early work on the relationship between linguistics, cognition, and anthropology, but now represent it with his essay "Linguistics and Anthropology." In Part Four Abu-Lughod's "A Tale of Two Pregnancies" illustrates the postmodern call for new forms of ethnography.

In addition to the new essays, each of the section introductions has been updated. Because it is not possible to have selections from all the great thinkers who have made significant contributions to anthropological thought, we have tried to include as many as possible in the section introductions and the notes. Thus you will find discussions of figures such as Jeremy Bentham, Carl Jung, A. C. Haddon, James Frazer, Antonio Gramsci, Michel Foucault, Pierre Bourdieu, and scores of others whose work has played a major role in anthropological theory. Needless to say, the correction and revision of footnotes has been an ongoing process; we have also revised the index, increasing the level of detail and making the book a more useful research tool.

We have been particularly gratified by the reactions of readers of the first three editions. We have received many letters and e-mails from the United States, Canada, and Europe. Both professors and students have asked questions, sent thoughtful commentary, and offered recommendations. We have been able to incorporate some of these into this edition. We deeply regret that editorial constraints and issues of timing and space have prevented us from including more of these suggestions, but we appreciate your feedback and hope you will continue to advise us. Keep those cards and letters coming! As always, you can contact us at rm08@txstate.edu for McGee and r.warms@txstate.edu for Warms.

ACKNOWLEDGMENTS

Writing this book has involved the labor and forbearance of many people. First and foremost, we would like to thank our families—Stacie, Jacob, and Hannah McGee and Karen, Benjamin, and Nathan Warms. Without their support, this project would have been impossible.

One unintended consequence of writing this kind of book is that we have had the privilege of having contact with several of the scholars whose work appears in this volume. We are indebted to the many people who made suggestions, reviewed, and commented on the text in various stages of preparation. Our work has benefited greatly from their comments, and our ideas were altered by their insights. We deeply appreciate their advice even though we were not always able to follow it. Since the publication of the first edition of this book we have benefited from the insights and advice of numerous individuals. Earlier editions owed a substantial debt to Roy Rappaport, Marvin Harris, Robert Launay, Roy D'Andrade, Joe Heyman, George Marcus, Naomi Quinn, Claudia Strauss, and Ann Stoler. We continue to be thankful for their help, support, and advice. The current edition would not have been possible without the careful analysis and useful suggestions from our reviewers, and we thank them for the time and energy they put into analyzing our work:

Dana A. Cope
College of Charleston

Ben Feinberg
Warren Wilson College

James G. Flanagan
University of Southern Mississippi

Karen Flynn
The University of Akron

Richard R. Jones
Lee University

Christina von Mayrhauser
California State University–Northridge

Diane Mines
Appalachian State University

Janet Rafferty
Mississippi State University

Susan Rasmussen
University of Houston

Clayton Robarchek
Wichita State University

Mary Jo Schneider
University of Arkansas

Emily Schultz
St. Cloud State University

Richard J. Senghas
Sonoma State University

The comments of students in the classes we teach on the history of anthropological thought have also been invaluable, often forcing us to look at problems in new ways. We are thankful to our students for their help. Over the years we have been particularly grateful for the assistance of Ryan Kashanipour, Kiyomi Appleton, Jessica Hurley, and Desserae Shepston. Finally, we are indebted to the people at McGraw-Hill for their steadfast support of our book: Larry Goldberg for guiding the editorial process; Sheri Gilbert for her help in acquiring permissions to reprint articles; Anne Fuzellier for her quality production management; Aaron Downey at Matrix Productions; and our copyeditor, Lauren Root. Their knowledge, editing skills, and many superb suggestions have contributed greatly to this work.

R. Jon McGee
Richard L. Warms

Introduction

Anthropology is concerned with understanding the "other." Typically anthropologists study the behavior, beliefs, and lifestyles of people in other cultures. Some examine current cultures; others study the remains of past societies to re-create the lives of people who disappeared long ago; still others study primates to see what our closest relatives can tell us about being human. What unites this diverse work is a common ground in some fundamental theoretical ideas concerning biological evolution and social behavior.

We teach both undergraduate and graduate courses in anthropological theory at Texas State University. Each spring as the semester begins, we face the same issues: Some students want to know why the theory course is required, and others worry about reading original works by authors and delving into a subject that seems esoteric. Because both matters are important, we begin this book by telling you why we think theory is essential in anthropology and why it is valuable to read original works rather than predigested theoretical summaries.

WHY STUDY THEORY?

Theory is critical because, although anthropologists collect data through fieldwork, data in and of themselves are meaningless. Whether stated explicitly or assumed, theories are the tools anthropologists use to give meaning to their data. Anthropologists' understanding of the artifacts they collect or the events they record in the field is derived from their theoretical perspective. A wink and an eyelid twitch look identical to an observer, but one carries information ("I'm kidding," "you're cute," "that's OK"), whereas the other signifies nothing more than dust in someone's eye. So, to paraphrase Clifford Geertz, a famous cultural anthropologist, how does one differentiate between winks and eyelid twitches? Anthropologists distinguish the two through their understanding of the context in which the action occurs. Theories guide that understanding. They are the tools anthropologists use to sort significant from meaningless information. In fact, one's choice of theory largely determines the data to be collected in the first place. A structuralist interested in the unconscious meaning of mythology probably will not spend too much time studying subsistence patterns. An economic anthropologist might ignore ritual and religion. Without theory, one cannot do anthropology.

Although this is a book about theory in sociocultural anthropology, the different branches of anthropology have always freely borrowed ideas from each other and from other sciences. In the nineteenth century, Herbert Spencer, a sociologist, and Charles Darwin, a naturalist, greatly influenced each other's work. Sigmund Freud was well versed in nineteenth-century evolutionary theories, and his work is imbued with ideas taken from anthropology; anthropology, in turn, has been greatly influenced by his theories. Sociobiologists study human behavior in terms of evolutionary biology and cultural adaptations. Symbolic anthropologists and postmodernists rely on tools developed in the study of literature. In the course of their research, anthropologists today delve into biology, geology, psychology, history, literature, physics, chemistry, medicine, and other subjects.

Modern anthropology is built on the work of earlier generations of theorists. Indeed, anthropologists today ask many of the same questions that occupied scholars in the nineteenth and early twentieth centuries. Nineteenth-century theories continue to resonate in popular culture. Have you ever heard the phrase "survival of the fittest," for example? It was coined by Herbert Spencer in the middle part of the nineteenth century. Do you think that technology is a measure of a society's development? Then you will be comfortable reading Lewis Henry Morgan's *Ancient Society*, first published in 1877. To fully comprehend anthropological writing, you must appreciate the history of the ideas that inform it. These are, ultimately, the principles upon which current work is based.

Anthropological theory is also important because it helps us think about who and what we are as human beings. It does this by forcing us to consider the ways in which we understand the "other." At its most basic level, anthropology asks how we are to understand other people in the world, those who look different from us and have different languages and customs (what anthropologists have come to call different cultures). Are such people inferior to us, superior to us, or just different? Are their cultures unchanging, following their own paths of evolution, or bound to ours in a grand evolutionary scheme? How should we behave toward such people?

At a second level, anthropology forces us to consider the otherness of nature itself. It forces us to ask if we, as human beings, are fundamentally part of the natural world. If so, perhaps we can be studied by the scientific methods and principles used by biologists, physicists, and other scholars in the traditional physical sciences. Alternatively, are human beings sufficiently different from the rest of the world that studying them with these methods will produce only trivial and confusing results? If that is true, the skills needed might be creative insight, imaginative interpretation, and soul-borne empathy—analytic tools traditionally associated with the arts and humanities.

A final level of discourse deals with the otherness of culture itself. By directing us, sometimes only implicitly, to the comparison of cultures, anthropology ultimately points toward the study of universal human nature. If we could strip away the cultural clothing of all peoples, would we be left with some set of basic principles or underlying essence? Would this be equivalent to finding untrammeled human nature before us in the buff? If so, how are we to understand human culture? Is it that which permits the full and satisfying expression of human nature, or that which prevents human nature from destroying human society?

At some level, all theory in anthropology, whether written in the eighteenth, nineteenth, twentieth, or twenty-first centuries, addresses these essential questions. Sometimes, individual theorists take extreme postures and for a time quiet the voices of those who hold alternative positions. However, no definitive conclusion has ever been reached on any of these issues. Perhaps these questions are ultimately unanswerable by their very nature. But the fact that no authoritative conclusion has been reached does not lessen the importance of the debate, for how we answer these questions has practical applications in our world. The answers determine our understanding of ourselves and our behavior toward other individuals and groups. In a world of instantaneous communication and virtually unlimited capacity for violence, in a world of ethnic strife and national warfare, surely these are among the most important questions that face us.

WHY READ ORIGINAL WORKS?

We believe it is important to read original works for several reasons. First, commentary on a theory cannot replace the original work because commentators unavoidably (and frequently intentionally) place their own interpretations on the material. For instance, Robert Lowie's 1937 *History of Ethnological Theory* and Marvin Harris' 1968 *The Rise of Anthropological Theory* are both comprehensive summaries of anthropological theory, but they provide strikingly different perspectives on the field.

Second, part of the importance of classic works in theory is their subtlety and complexity. The creation of theory is part of an ongoing dialogue with earlier thinkers, and these essays (and many others) are a portion of that dialogue. As our understanding changes, we return to these older works. Sometimes we find insights that advance our thinking or perceive errors against which we react. Through this process, new theory is generated. When works are summarized or when we read only analyses, the theoretical dialogue is flattened, simplified, and ultimately impoverished. In this volume, we provide what we believe is useful commentary on the essays we present, but reading such analysis cannot replace careful reading of the original text. As new insights are made, many of our notes may become outdated. The essays themselves have a much longer shelf life.

Finally, a firsthand reading of the original sources helps one avoid inaccuracies. In preparing this text, we have run across numerous cases in which the popularly accepted information passed to us by our professors or found in textbooks was incorrect. Some of the folk wisdom of anthropology consists of half-truths or is frankly inaccurate. We bring this up not to point fingers or assign blame but to suggest that reading original sources can serve as a partial corrective for this problem.

USING THIS TEXTBOOK

This book is designed to help you understand where some of the great minds in anthropology have been before you and to help you formulate your theoretical position in the field today. It is a historical overview of some of the principal developments in culture theory since the 1850s. The book is different from others because it contains our introductions and paragraph-by-paragraph comments to inform your reading and raise interesting points or questions.

Theory texts are problematic because their contents tend to become accepted doctrine. Readers and critics suppose that the authors of such a text have chosen to present those pieces universally considered the most important works in the field. When the editors of such a volume have the audacity to write detailed comments on the essays they have chosen, they seem to elevate the texts they chose to scripture and their work to Talmudic authority. Should you entertain these notions, let us disabuse you of them. No group of

professional anthropologists, however small, will agree on a single set of critical essays. We have selected what we feel are representative articles by individuals traditionally associated with particular theories and works that seem to us to be good examples of theories in practice. We will gladly agree with anyone who claims that better works can be found, but we insist that this will always be the case. An enormous corpus of work in anthropology now exists. We believe that the best way to study anthropological theory is to read as widely as possible. No collection of essays, however artfully chosen, will be able to substitute for years of reading in the field, and that is what is ultimately required for a solid background in theory.

You will find that our commentary on the texts varies from extremely straightforward definitions and explanations to fairly elaborate speculation on the motives of authors and influences upon them. Although it is almost impossible to entirely eliminate mistakes, we have checked our work carefully; when we point to a fact, you may be reasonably certain that it is correct. However, please remember that our interpretations are just that. They are meant to guide your reading, stimulate discussion, call your attention to certain ideas, and get you to think about different issues. You are invited to disagree with them and propose alternatives. If you read through this book and find nothing with which to disagree, you are not reading carefully enough or critically enough.

Although our likes and dislikes may become apparent to the careful reader, we do not intend to promote any particular viewpoint. In fact, we were trained in very different theoretical perspectives (McGee in interpretive-symbolic and Warms in positivist-materialist). We have tried to present the key strengths and weaknesses of each position, but we frequently differ in our interpretations of theory and amuse our students by arguing about them. In short, while we hope that readers will agree with most of what we have written, we have tried to write at least something bound to rile your theoretical sensibilities, no matter who you are. You are invited to disagree with the text and debate us about it if you wish. We can be contacted by e-mail at r.warms@txstate.edu for Warms or rm08@txstate.edu for McGee or by traditional mail at the Department of Anthropology, Texas State University, San Marcos, TX 78666. If, by chance, you reach the end of the book without finding something to offend you, you may contact us at one of the addresses above, and we will try to remedy that situation as well.

THE ARRANGEMENT OF ESSAYS AND THE NOTATIONAL SYSTEM

The arrangement of essays presents a surprising number of problems. Should they be arranged strictly chronologically or by intellectual association or descent? If the text is to be divided into sections, what about those authors who do not quite fit? We have taught our theory course both chronologically and thematically and concluded that a chronological presentation works best. Thus we have chosen to arrange the theories in a rough chronological order to show readers the progression of ideas in cultural anthropology and to demonstrate the relationship between concepts. We have divided our chronology into named sections. Each begins with an introduction describing the theorists represented in the section and the principal ideas presented in their work. However, our scheme is not entirely consistent. Different schools of thought often overlap both intellectually and chronologically. Exploiting these inconsistencies and thinking about other possible arrangements of the text may prove an intellectually useful experience. New arrangements may provide new insights.

Space limitations and, occasionally, copyright regulations have forced us to make difficult decisions about the essays we have reprinted. Essays included in earlier drafts of the book have been removed from the final, and we have added or subtracted essays as our own knowledge base grows. More important, we have occasionally eliminated fairly large passages of some essays or chosen to remove particularly lengthy sets of original footnotes or endnotes. These are not decisions we took lightly, nor do they indicate that we believe the notes and passages removed were of no significance. It was simply a question of choosing between removing notes and passages or losing several entire essays. Although there are good intellectual reasons for selecting either of these options, we believe that most readers are better served by the first. In doing this editing, we have tried to preserve a sense of the original by including notes telling the reader exactly how much text was removed and briefly summarizing the content of the lost passage. We also note how many footnotes appeared in those passages, which allows readers to see the subjects about which the authors wrote notes and those they did not and gives a feel for the frequency and pacing of notes.

Each essay in the volume is accompanied by our notes, which appear as footnotes and are numbered with Arabic numerals. Footnotes or endnotes created by the original authors are indicated by lowercase letters and appear as endnotes to the essays. Where authors have provided references in their work, they appear at the end of the essay. Our own references along with an index appear at the end of the volume.

Nineteenth-Century Evolutionism

In the English-speaking world, the word *anthropologist* first appeared in print in 1805 (Kuklick 1991:6). It was another seventy-nine years before the first university position in anthropology was created. The discipline of anthropology, however, did not just appear but rather combined three long-existing streams of thought. The first was the study of what we have come to call cultural differences among societies. The second dealt with the struggle to explain the antiquity of humans and the artifacts left from these ancient lives. The final line of thought, closely related to the second, was the investigation of the biological origins of humans and other species. All of these areas have been the subject of investigation and speculation for much of the past millennium. Though it is far beyond the scope of this text to analyze all the antecedents of anthropology, we will briefly review some of the principal developments that led to its origin before exploring evolutionary and anthropological thinking in the nineteenth century.

It is probably fair to say that wherever literate civilizations came into contact with members of different societies, something like ethnographic writing occurred. For example, ancient authors such as Herodotus, a Greek historian of the fifth century B.C.E., offered readers fanciful descriptions of other societies. In the fourteenth century, Ibn Khaldun, a Tunisian politician and historian, wrote the *Muqaddimah,* or *Introduction to History,* in which he proposed that the study of human civilization and social organization was an independent science (quoted in Lacoste 1984:169).

In Europe there was a long tradition of interest in the exotic. Writings such as *The Wonders of the East* and *The Travels of Marco Polo* had fascinated Europeans. Until the fifteenth century, however, Europe remained relatively isolated and provincial. Then, developments in sailing technology and advances in weaponry allowed Europeans to expand their influence across the globe. For the first time, they were in frequent contact with people from societies radically different from their own. This exposure raised a host of philosophical problems. Were these other people human in the same way that Europeans were? Did their societies function according to brute natural law, or were they moral beings possessed of a free will? How were social differences to be explained?

From the Renaissance until the eighteenth century, the concept of *degenerationism* provided Europeans with a biblically based explanation of cultural diversity. In this view, prior to the destruction of the Tower of Babel, all people belonged to a single civilization. When God destroyed the Tower, creating differences in language and dispersing the people, however, some degenerated, losing their civilization and eventually becoming savages. Much of the European experience seemed to confirm degenerationism. For example, the recovery of texts and artifacts from ancient Greek and Roman civilizations seemed to show that these were far more advanced than those of later date.

Progressivism was an alternative view of social life. Progressivists believed that, rather than deteriorating from a previously civilized condition, societies had started out primitive but were progressing toward a more advanced state. One proponent of this approach was the British philosopher John Locke (1632–1704). In his *Essay Concerning Government,* published in 1690, Locke proposed that the human mind was a blank slate and that knowledge and reason were derived from experience. The corollary of this was that different sorts of experiences would provide different sorts of ideas. Consequently, individuals growing up in different societies would have varied experiences and the differences between human societies could thus be explained.

The idea that people had progressed rather than degenerated became popular as scientific investigation and empirical observation increasingly yielded both academic and commercial results. By the late 1700s, few Europeans doubted that humankind was making progress, and Europeans generally believed that they were the most advanced of all people.

With the general idea of progress firmly entrenched, philosophers devised various schemes to explain the nature and course of this social evolution. Their goal was generally to construct a universal history of humankind that moved from a primitive past to the development of European nations. One of the most influential of these works was Edward Gibbon's (1737–1794) *The History of the Decline and Fall of the Roman Empire* (1776–1788), but there were others as well. Italian philosopher Giambattista Vico (1668–1744) in his 1744 work *The New Science,* attempted to write a universal history of humanity. Vico believed that human nature was shaped by history and hence changed over time. Thus, he thought that history was a better guide to understanding humanity than the natural sciences. French statesman Anne Robert Jacques Turgot (1727–1781) published his *Plan for Two Discourses on Universal History* in 1750. He argued that, after the biblical flood, humans had passed through stages of savagery and barbarism to agricultural- and urban-based civilization. One last example of this perspective is *Sketch for a Historical Picture of the Progress of the Human Mind,* written by Marie Jean Antoine Nicolas Caritat, the Marquis de Condorcet (1743–1794). Condorcet proposed a ten-stage scheme describing human progress from early tribal society through the founding of the French Republic and beyond, to a future in which human society was perfected. These ideas played pivotal roles in much of later sociocultural evolutionary thinking (Stocking 1987:15).

Condorcet was a *philosophe,* a friend of Turgot and of Voltaire, Franklin, and Paine as well. He was a widely respected mathematician who became the secretary of the Legislative Assembly after the French Revolution. Condorcet supported liberal and rationalist causes but fell out of favor as the radical Montagnard party rose in power. His opposition to the execution of the king and the constitution proposed by the Montagnards led the increasingly powerful radicals to consider him a traitor and call for his arrest. In 1793 Condorcet went into hiding at a friend's home in Paris. *Sketch for a Historical Picture of the Progress of the Human Mind* was written in the months that followed. In 1794, fearing his hiding place was no longer safe, he attempted to flee Paris but was arrested and imprisoned. He was found dead in his cell two days later. Controversy remains over whether he committed suicide or was murdered.

The rise of the violent and radical Montagnards and the death of Condorcet signal an important moment in British, American, and French social thought. The late eighteenth century had been characterized by optimism, progressivism, rationalism, and secularism. The violent overthrow of the social order in France, the increasing disorder and poverty of urban life in England, and the destruction of factories by Luddites in Nottinghamshire and Lancashire led to a retreat from these values. The result was a revival of religion and deep questioning of the notion of progress. There had been clear advances in technology and for many the standard of living had improved. However, the French Revolution and turbulence among the British lower classes suggested that optimism for humanity's future might not be justified. Clearly, if progress was being made, its course was not smooth. How were intellectuals to reconcile ideas of progress and rationalism with an increasingly disordered society?

The European expansion that began in the fifteenth century had a profound effect on the natural sciences as well as philosophy. Explorers' accounts of the flora and fauna of new lands challenged the biblical view of life, which had been based largely on the book of Genesis and the story of the flood. Long before Darwin, naturalists were confronted with distributions and variations in plants and animals that could not be explained in biblical terms. Scholars also struggled to explain evidence of human antiquity that did not correspond to biblical chronologies. This evidence became more widely available in the early nineteenth century as large-scale, nationwide engineering projects, such as the construction of canal and railroad systems, exposed geological strata, fossils, and human artifacts to the study of naturalists and geologists. Scientists were confronted with questions such as why objects of human manufacture were found in association with extinct mammals.

The foundation of biological-evolutionary speculation was laid down in the descriptive writings of seventeenth-century naturalists such as Gilbert White (1720–1793) and John Ray (1627–1705), who attempted to classify and describe the diversity of life-forms they observed (Eiseley 1961). Ray influenced Carolus Linnaeus (1707–1778), best known for his taxonomic categorization of life-forms presented in *Systema Naturae* in 1735. Previously, the naming of plants and animals had been confused. Linnaeus' taxonomic system provided the systematic, organized framework for the classification of life-forms that was necessary for the scientific investigation of biological evolution to take place.

One aspect of Linnaean thought was belief in the *immutability* of species. That is, Linnaeus, along with most scholars believed that life-forms were created separately by God in their present form and could not change. The task of biology was to name and classify them. However, challenges to this position were developed by a number of scholars. For example, in *Telliamed: or Discourses Between an Indian Philosopher and a French Missionary on the Diminution of the Sea, the Formation of the Earth, the Origin of Men and Animals, etc.,* a book widely read in the mid-eighteenth century, Benoit de Maillet (1656–1738) outlined a scheme for biological evolution. He speculated that the age of the earth was much greater than popularly believed, recognized that fossils were the remains of life-forms, and suggested that some of these fossils represented extinct species (Eiseley 1961:29).

Another naturalist, second in importance only to Linnaeus, was Georges Louis Leclerc, Comte de Buffon (1707–1788). The forty-four volumes of Buffon's *Natural History* (1752–1799) outlined an evolutionary theory that he called "degeneration" but which contained many of the elements that Darwin used in his theory of natural selection more than one hundred years later. Some of Buffon's key observations were that physical variation occurred within species; that different animals had underlying structural similarities; that life multiplied faster than its food supply, promoting a struggle for existence; and that some life-forms had become extinct.

Jean Lamarck (1744–1829) and Charles Darwin's grandfather, Erasmus Darwin (1731–1802), were two great evolutionists of the late eighteenth century whose work exerted a profound influence on the development of later evolutionary theory. Although they held similar views, Lamarck's theories were more systematically presented, and his work is better known today. Lamarck believed that changes in geographic and climatic areas placed pressures on plant and animal life. In Lamarck's view, evolutionary changes were due to the effort with which life-forms employed those body parts that were most useful under changed conditions. Thus, physiological need promoted the formation of new organs or alteration of old ones. These acquired characteristics were passed on to future generations. Though various versions of this theory were common in the eighteenth century, Lamarck and the elder Darwin are significant for clearly recognizing the importance of the relationship between organisms and environment.

By the end of the eighteenth century, the philosophical and biological framework for anthropology was in place. Nineteenth-century thinkers, driven by an abundance of new data, from fossil finds in England to explorers' accounts of Africa, built on this framework. They produced new theories of biological and social evolution that were key to the development of anthropology. The insights of Charles Darwin (1809–1882) and Herbert Spencer (1820–1903) were particularly important.

Between 1831 and 1836 Darwin traveled as ship's naturalist on the H.M.S. *Beagle*. When he returned, he published a journal of his voyages (1839) as well as a major multivolume work on coral reefs (1846) and several works on barnacles (1851–1854). In 1837 he also began to write secret notebooks in which he organized his thoughts about evolution. He studied the materials he had collected and gave considerable attention to commercial plant and animal breeders in whose work he saw a practical application of his concepts. He collected data, organized his notes, and in 1844 composed a draft of his ideas that he showed to his close friend, the eminent botanist Joseph Dalton Hooker (1817–1911). However, aware of the controversy his ideas would arouse, he refrained from publishing his work.

Darwin had been refining his ideas for twenty years when he received a letter in June of 1858 from a young naturalist with whom he had been corresponding, Alfred Russell Wallace (1823–1913). From his own observations in Malaysia Wallace had independently formulated the theory that Darwin had been working so diligently to substantiate. Darwin was greatly disheartened by Wallace's letter, but his colleagues Charles Lyell (1797–1875) and Joseph Hooker arranged the joint presentation of the two men's ideas in July 1858, and Darwin was granted the opportunity to publish first. He published *On the Origin of Species by Means of Natural Selection* in November 1859.

Darwin held that change within species must follow natural laws like those found in the physical sciences. In *On the Origin of Species,* he outlined a theory he called *natural selection* and proposed that it was the fundamental principle of biological change. Darwin began with the idea that more organisms were born than survived to adulthood, a widely accepted concept derived from "An Essay on the Principle of Population," published in 1798 by Thomas Malthus (1766–1834), then speculated about the factors that determined which individuals survived and which did not. Darwin observed that no two individuals of any species were precisely alike. Because small variations occur in the appearance or behavioral characteristics of members of any population, Darwin hypothesized that some variations were better than others in that they led those who possessed them to more successfully compete for food, shelter, and mates. These individuals would subsequently produce more offspring who themselves survived and reproduced. Darwin called the characteristics that led to increased numbers of surviving and reproducing offspring "adaptive." Though he did not

have any understanding of the mechanisms of heredity, he observed that parents were capable of passing traits to their offspring and that those possessing the adaptive traits would be "naturally selected" over those who lacked them. Consequently, over a long period, and through the slow, incremental accumulation of these adaptive traits, the appearance of a species could be altered or a new species could develop.

Darwin's theory was extraordinarily important for several reasons. First, it was a scientifically convincing explanation of the ways in which life-forms could change over time and new species emerge. As such, it is the basis of much of modern biology. Additionally, Darwin's theory was a powerful social metaphor. Darwin's theory was capable of explaining how it was possible to have both progress and social disruption. It showed how progress, rather than being a smooth upward climb, was achieved through struggle and conflict.

Natural selection was controversial in religious circles and met with ridicule from the popular press. It was disparaged by French intellectuals (who presented it in seriously flawed mistranslation when it first appeared) and generally rejected in Germany until the turn of the twentieth century. However, in Britain and America, scholars had been moving toward a theory of evolution for half a century. Herbert Spencer, for example, had been working on a theory of human social evolution years before the publication of Darwin's work. Darwin even applied some of the concepts developed in Spencer's work in his own theory of biological evolution. As a result, Darwinian evolution was readily accepted by the scientific community.

Though Herbert Spencer was the son of a schoolmaster, he was largely self-educated. He worked as a civil engineer for the Birmingham and London Railway and then as a subeditor for *The Economist,* a news magazine that promoted free market capitalism. In 1853, having received a small inheritance Spencer was able to leave *The Economist* to devote himself full time to writing.

Spencer was interested in evolution as a general phenomenon, and he applied his evolutionary approach to many fields of study. Garbarino (1977:21) calls him a "philosopher of universal evolution" because Spencer considered evolution to be one of the fundamental natural processes in the universe. His ideas had enormous impact in Britain and the United States, not only on anthropology and sociology but on literature, politics, and popular culture as well (Carneiro 1967:xi). Spencer believed that evolution was progressive and that evolutionary change was from simple to more complex states. He argued that evolutionary progress occurred because life was a struggle for survival in which only those with superior skills and traits succeeded.

Spencer is also famous for his *organic analogy*. As illustrated in the selection reprinted in this book, "The Social Organism," Spencer compared human societies to biological organisms. He used this analogy to link biological and social evolution, implying both followed the same processes and direction. This suggested that social evolution could be studied in the same fashion that one studied biological evolution. Spencer's organic analogy was profoundly influential because it implied that a society was composed of an interconnected set of organs. If this was the case, these organs could be accurately identified and their role and function in maintaining society described. These ideas, in various forms, set the agenda for much of anthropology in the century following the publication of "The Social Organism."

It was Spencer, not Darwin, who coined the phrase "survival of the fittest." Darwin used it as a chapter heading in the fifth edition of *On the Origin of Species* and, in that same edition wrote that, in comparison to natural selection, "the expression often used by Mr. Herbert Spencer of the Survival of the Fittest is more accurate." However, this apparent agreement hid a profound disagreement about the mechanisms of evolution. Although Spencer viewed Darwin's work as supporting his own, there is little evidence Spencer understood what Darwin meant by natural selection. Spencer's vision of evolution had little to do with variation and reproduction. Instead, he believed that evolution was a general moral force pervading the universe and that the mechanisms of evolution on which he focused were Lamarckian, involving the transmission of learned behavior from one generation to the next.

All humans are ethnocentric to one degree or another, and nineteenth-century Europeans and Americans were no exception. Looking with pride at their industrial advances and burgeoning economic and military power, members of Western societies believed they were at the pinnacle of social evolution. One consequence of Spencer's work was the popularization of a point of view called *social darwinism*. Social darwinists interpreted natural selection to mean that if evolution was progress and only the fittest survived, then it was the right of Western powers to dominate those who were less technologically advanced. According to this line of reasoning, the domination of one society by another proved its superiority and its advanced level of fitness. Conquest of an inferior society by a superior one was the result of the action of natural law and hence was not only moral but imperative. This was a convenient philosophy for the rapidly expanding European powers and was used to justify their imperialism, colonialism, and racism. In the United States, social darwinism was invoked as a justification for free enterprise capitalism.

It should be remembered, however, that while most of the evolutionary thinkers represented here thought Western society more highly evolved than any other, they were also highly critical of it. They believed that evolution moved continually toward perfection. Western society might be more advanced than any other, but it was very far from perfect. It is true that Spencer argued, on one hand, that state welfare, education, and public health programs were contrary to the laws of nature and should be avoided because they slowed the evolutionary process that was weeding out the unfit members of society. On the other hand, he also argued against the military, the Church of England, and the perquisites of the landowning class. Despite the use of theories like his to justify colonial conquest, Spencer himself was an adamant opponent of British imperialism who criticized his nation for "picking quarrels with native races and taking possession of their lands" (quoted in Carneiro 1967:xlvi).

Two other nineteenth-century anthropologists interested in the evolution of culture as a general human phenomenon were the American Lewis Henry Morgan (1818–1881) and the Englishman Sir Edward Burnett Tylor (1832–1917). Both men believed there were universal evolutionary stages of cultural development that characterized the transition from primitive to complex societies. Because of this belief, Morgan and Tylor are known as *unilineal* evolutionists. Although Morgan and Tylor shared a similar evolutionary framework, their studies examined different aspects of culture. Morgan focused on the evolution of elements such as the family and subsistence patterns, whereas Tylor's work concentrated on the idea that one could trace the evolution of a society by studying "survivals," a form of cultural remnant. He is best known for his theory of the evolution of religion.

Morgan's early interest in Native American cultures, in particular, patterns of marriage and descent, led to his 1871 book, *Systems of Consanquinity and Affinity,* the first comparative study of kinship, but his most famous work was *Ancient Society,* published in 1877. In this book he attempted to trace the evolution of human society from primeval times to the Victorian era (which he considered the high point of human civilization). Following Turgot and other eighteenth-century writers, he divided human cultural development into three grand stages—savagery, barbarism, and civilization—with the first two stages further subdivided into lower, middle, and upper phases. Morgan accepted Spencer's idea that evolution proceeded from simple to complex and, in *Ancient Society,* outlined this progress by correlating his states of social evolution with specific developments in family structure, subsistence, and technology. For example, in Morgan's scheme, middle savagery begins with the acquisition of fish subsistence, whereas upper savagery is marked by the invention of the bow and arrow. Unlike Spencer, Morgan believed that evolutionary progress was not achieved through competition but was propelled by the "flowering" of "germs of thought." This "flowering" was driven by the development of new subsistence strategies. The increasingly complex technologies produced after such events were markers of evolutionary progress.

E. B. Tylor was a contemporary of Morgan and probably the leading English anthropologist of the nineteenth century. In his principal work, *Primitive Culture* (1871), Tylor outlined two ideas for which he is remembered today. First, he argued that one could reconstruct earlier stages of cultural evolution by studying "survivals." Tylor believed that virtually everything in contemporary society that did not have a function he understood was a survival from a previous stage of cultural evolution. Therefore, one could learn something about past stages of a society's development through the study of these cultural leftovers. His second idea concerned the evolution of religion, Tylor's special interest and the subject of the second volume of *Primitive Culture.* He postulated that the most basic concept underlying the invention of religion was animism. He outlined a developmental sequence for religion that began with animism, evolved into polytheism, and finally progressed into what he viewed as the highest form of religious belief, enlightened monotheism.

Both Morgan and Tylor believed in the fundamental similarity of human thought around the world, a concept called the *psychic unity of humankind.* This belief was the foundation for their unilineal evolutionary views and supported their contention that societies progressed through parallel (but independent) evolutionary stages.

The unilineal evolutionary perspective of the late nineteenth century revolves around several related themes. First, it was generally supposed that all societies evolved through the same stages and were progressing toward civilization. Victorian society represented civilization in its highest currently extant form but would be surpassed by future societies. Second, the whole perspective was rooted in the *comparative method.* In the nineteenth century the term *comparative method* referred to the belief that contemporary "primitive" cultures were like "living fossils," similar to early stages of current advanced cultures. As such, they were clues to cultural evolutionary development. One could study the evolutionary history of Western society by examining contemporary primitive societies. The validity of the comparative method rested on an acceptance of the concept of psychic unity. Simple and complex societies were comparable because human minds were believed to develop along the same lines. If the human mind worked the same way in all cultures, then it was assumed that unrelated societies would develop in a parallel fashion. Beliefs in the comparative method, psychic unity, parallel evolution, and progress were woven together to support the unilineal view of social evolution.

Karl Marx (1818–1883) and his frequent co-author Friedrich Engels (1820–1895) are far better known for their contributions to other disciplines—in particular, economic and political theory—than for their studies in anthropology. Primarily their work focused on the historical development of capitalism. Although they were not anthropologists, their ideas are critical to anthropology and have been the subject of much debate among anthropologists.

Marx derived his theory of social evolution from the theory of dialectical change advanced by the philosopher Georg Wilhelm Friedrich Hegel (1770–1831) and from his own understanding of evolutionary theory. Whereas scholars such as Locke and Tylor believed that cultural institutions were the product of rational thought, Marx thought that all thought was a product of cultural institutions rather than their cause. Marx, a materialist philosopher, gave primacy to the analysis of the conditions of production within society.

Much of the work of Marx and Engels examined the conflict generated by the increasing wealth of the capitalists (bourgeoisie) at the expense of the working class (proletariat), who only sunk deeper into poverty. Marx and Engels viewed social change as an evolutionary process marked by revolution in which new levels of social, political, and economic development were achieved through class struggle. They viewed history as a sequence of evolutionary stages, each marked by a unique mode of production. Just as unilineal evolutionary theorists traced the social

evolution of humans from savagery to civilization, Marx and Engels saw the history of Europe in terms of the transition from feudalism, to capitalism, and on to communism—which they believed was the next inevitable step in this process.

In their later work, Marx and Engels were deeply influenced by the work of Lewis Henry Morgan. In *Ancient Society,* Morgan correlated evolutionary stages of human culture with material achievements and technology. Consequently, Marx and Engels believed his work validated their evolutionary theory. Although Marx despised Spencer (whom he viewed as an apologist for capitalism), both focused on the notion of conflict as the mechanism for social evolution.

Marx's work drew little attention in early twentieth-century anthropology. Although some scholars such as Durkheim were political socialists, until the late 1920s Marx had relatively little effect on ethnographic analysis outside of the Soviet Union. However, since that time, anthropologists have come to depend increasingly on his ideas. Many theories in both cultural anthropology and archaeology have come to rely on Marxist insights. This is particularly true of cultural ecologists, neomaterialist, feminist, and postmodern thinkers discussed in Parts Three and Four of this book. Today, a background in Marxist thought is basic to reading culture theory.

---

1. *The Social Organism*

HERBERT SPENCER (1820–1903)

SIR JAMES MACINTOSH[1] got great credit for the saying, that "constitutions are not made, but grow." In our day the most significant thing about this saying is, that it was ever thought so significant. As from the surprise displayed by a man at

some familiar fact you may judge of his general culture: so from the admiration which an age accords a new thought, its average degree of enlightenment may be safely inferred. That this apothegm of Macintosh should have been quoted

---

From *The Westminster Review* (1860)

---

[1] Sir James Macintosh (1765–1832) was a British philosopher and politician whose works include "Discourse on the Study of the Law of Nature and Nations" (1799). He was a friend of Thomas Malthus.

and requoted as it has, shows how profound has been the ignorance of social science—how a small ray of truth has seemed brilliant, as a distant rushlight looks like a star in the surrounding darkness.

Such a conception could not indeed fail to be startling when let fall in the midst of a system of thought to which it was utterly alien. Universally in Macintosh's day, as by an immense majority in our own day, all things were explained on the hypothesis of manufacture, rather than that of growth. It was held that the planets were severally projected round the sun from the Creator's hand, with exactly the velocity required to balance the sun's attraction. The formation of the earth, the separation of the sea from land, the production of animals, were mechanical works from which God rested as a laborer rests. Man was supposed to be molded after a manner somewhat akin to that in which a modeler makes a clay figure. And of course, in harmony with such ideas, societies were tacitly assumed to be arranged thus or thus by direct interposition of Providence; or by the regulations of law-makers; or by both.[2]

Yet that societies are not artificially put together, is a truth so manifest, that it seems wonderful men should have ever overlooked it. Perhaps nothing more clearly shows the small value of historical studies as they have been commonly pursued. You need but to look at the changes going on around, or observe social organization in its leading peculiarities, to see that these are neither supernatural, nor are determined by the wills of individual men, as by implication historians commonly teach; but are consequent on general natural causes. The one case of the division of labor suffices to show this. It has not been by the command of any ruler that some men have become manufacturers, while others have remained cultivators of the soil. In Lancashire millions have devoted themselves to the making of cotton fabrics;

in Yorkshire, perhaps another million live by producing woollens; and the pottery of Staffordshire, the cutlery of Sheffield, the hardware of Birmingham, severally occupy their hundreds of thousands. These are large facts in the structure of English society; but we can ascribe them neither to miracle, nor to legislation. It is not by "the hero as king," any more than by "collective wisdom," that men have been segregated into producers, wholesale distributors, and retail distributors. The whole of our industrial organization, from its most conspicuous features down to its minutest details, has become what it is, not only without legislative guidance, but, to a considerable extent, in spite of legislative hindrances. It has arisen under the pressure of human wants and activities. While each citizen has been pursuing his individual welfare, and none taking thought about division of labor, or indeed conscious of the need for it, division of labor has yet been ever becoming more complete. It has been doing this slowly and silently; scarcely any having observed it until quite modern times. By steps so small, that year after year the industrial arrangements have seemed to men just what they were before—by changes as insensible as those through which a seed passes into a tree; society has become the complex body of mutually dependent workers which we now see. And this economic organization, mark, is the all-essential organization. Through the combination thus spontaneously evolved it is, that every citizen is supplied with daily necessaries, at the same time that he yields some product or aid to others. That we are severally alive to-day, we owe to the regular working of this combination during the past week; and could it be suddenly abolished, a great proportion of us would be dead before another week was ended. If these most conspicuous and vital arrangements of our social structure have arisen without the devising of any one, but through the individual efforts of citizens severally to satisfy

---

[2] Spencer was a grand proponent of science in an age when the worldview of most of his countrymen was primarily religious. An article he wrote in 1859 asked in the title "What Knowledge Is of Most Worth?"; his emphatic answer was scientific knowledge. Spencer begins this essay by presenting—and then deflating—the popular religious doctrine of creationism. Notice the sarcasm with which he describes how humans were supposed to have been created. This style of writing is typical of Spencer, who can be both obnoxious and smug. Like many other nineteenth-century evolutionary thinkers, Spencer was anti-clerical and deeply skeptical of religion.

their own wants, we may be tolerably certain that all the other less important social arrangements have similarly arisen.[3]

"But surely," it will be said, "the social changes directly produced by law cannot be classed as spontaneous growths. When parliaments or kings dictate this or that thing to be done, and appoint officials to do it, the process is clearly artificial; and society to this extent becomes a manufacture rather than a growth." No, not even these changes are exceptions, if they be real and permanent changes. The true sources of such changes lie deeper than the acts of legislators. To take first the simplest instance:—we all know that the enactments of representative governments ultimately depend on the national will: they may for a time be out of harmony with it, but eventually they have to conform to it. And to say that the national will is that which finally determines them,

is to say that they result from the average of individual desires; or in other words—from the average of individual natures. A law so initiated, therefore, really grows out of the popular character.[4] In the case of a Government representing but a limited class, the same thing still holds, though not so manifestly. For the very existence of a supreme class monopolizing all power, is itself due to certain sentiments in the commonalty. But for the feeling of loyalty on the part of retainers, a feudal system could not exist. We see in the protest of the Highlanders against the abolition of heritable jurisdictions, that they preferred that kind of local rule. And if thus to the popular nature must be ascribed the growth of an irresponsible ruling class; then to the popular nature must be ascribed the social arrangements which that class creates in the pursuit of its own ends. Even where the Government is despotic, the doctrine still holds.[5]

---

[3] Here Spencer claims that societies were not supernaturally manufactured but evolved through a natural process of growth, which he illustrates with examples from the social changes in English society caused by industrialization. Spencer's thinking reflected both evolutionism and the work of economist Adam Smith (1723–1790). Smith held that through pursuit of self-interest, individuals would be guided, as though by an invisible hand, to activities leading to the betterment of society. Spencer presents essentially the same idea here. There is also an evolutionary undercurrent. Like Darwin, Spencer conceived of evolution as operating through the accumulation of minute changes over long periods of time. For Spencer, social evolution was driven by competition among people, through which the best suited to survive were selected. Though this process may have meant misery for some, it led to progress for the society. Spencer believed that the end result of social evolution would be the elimination of social problems and the perfection of society. Following this line of thought, he coined the phrase "survival of the fittest." His ideas, popularized largely by others as social darwinism, were often used to justify the American and English class systems and colonial political system. However, it is important to note that Spencer himself was deeply critical of both imperialism and the landed aristocracy. In America, William Graham Sumner (1840–1910) was one of Spencer's most prominent followers and among the best known promoters of social darwinism. In an essay defending the concentration of wealth, he wrote: "No man can acquire a million without helping a million men to increase their little fortunes. . . . The millionaires are a product of natural selection. . . . They may fairly

be regarded as the naturally selected agents of society for certain work" (1963 [1914]:156–157).

[4] Spencer here suggests that there is some palpable force in a society that conditions its members to act in certain ways. Even actions that appear to be extremely personal are ultimately the result of this social force. This suggestion provides a portion of the foundation for Émile Durkheim's idea of collective consciousness (see essay 6) and A. L. Kroeber's of the superorganic (see essay 10). In fact, Spencer is generally considered the first person to use the term *superorganic*. Notice that he says that actions by rulers or other individuals may disturb evolution's workings, but that the general process is natural and beyond human control.

[5] Believing that social evolution followed natural laws, Spencer writes that rulers rule because it is a reflection of the "national will." Social inequality was ordained by nature in Spencer's view, and movements opposing this inequality were therefore doomed to failure. Spencer cites Oliver Cromwell's revolution against the English Crown, which fell apart after the death of its leader, but he may have had the more recent French revolutions of the 1780s and 1840s in mind. These revolutions and the violence that accompanied them shocked and frightened the English upper classes, who interpreted the mass riots as evidence of the bestiality of the working class. The repeated restoration of monarchy and empire in France was surely a comforting reassurance that the upper class was indeed superior and that the social evolutionary scheme of things had balanced out. As Spencer writes, "other forms suddenly created will not act, but rapidly retrograde to the old form."

It is not simply that the existence of such a form of government is consequent on the character of the people, and that, as we have abundant proof, other forms suddenly created will not act, but rapidly retrograde to the old form; but it is that such regulations as a despot makes, if really operative, are so because of their fitness to the social state. Not only are his acts very much swayed by general opinion—by precedent, by the feeling of his nobles, his priesthood, his army—and are so in part results of the national character; but when they are out of harmony with the national character, they are soon practically abrogated. The utter failure of Cromwell permanently to establish a new social condition, and the rapid revival of suppressed institutions and practices after his death, show how powerless is a monarch to change the type of the society he governs. He may disturb, he may retard, or he may aid the natural process of organization; but the general course of this process is beyond his control.

Thus that which is so obviously true of the industrial structure of society, is true of its whole structure. The fact that constitutions are not made, but grow, is simply a fragment of the much larger fact, that under all its aspects and through all its ramifications, society is a growth and not a manufacture.

A dim perception that there exists some analogy between the body politic and a living individual body, was early reached, and from time to time re-appeared in literature. But this perception was necessarily vague and more or less fanciful. In the absence of physiological science, and especially of those comprehensive generalizations which it has but recently reached, it was impossible to discern the real parallelisms.

[*It is a law of nature, in Spencer's view, that societies change from simple to complex. The purposes of his article are to outline this process of change and to demonstrate the similarities to the corresponding process in biological organisms. In an 850-word passage eliminated from this edition, Spencer discusses analogies similar to his own made by Plato and Thomas Hobbes. Plato, in* The Republic, *compares society to the human psyche. Hobbes, in* Leviathan, *compares it to the human body. Spencer finds that both of these analogies result in inconsistencies. He also faults Plato and Hobbes for suggesting that society was created by man and hence mechanical rather than grown as a human body or mind and hence organic.*]

Notwithstanding errors, however, these speculations have considerable significance. That such analogies, however crudely conceived, should have arrested the attention, not only of Plato and Hobbes, but of many others, is a reason for suspecting that *some* analogy exists. The untenableness of the particular comparisons above instanced is no ground for denying an essential parallelism; for early ideas are usually but vague adumbrations[6] of the truth. Lacking the great generalizations of biology, it was, as we have said, impossible to trace out the real relations of social organizations to organizations of another order. We propose here to show what are the analogies which modern science discloses to us.

Let us set out by succinctly stating the points of similarity and the points of difference. Societies agree with individual organisms in three conspicuous peculiarities:—

1. That commencing as small aggregations they insensibly augment in mass; some of them reaching eventually perhaps a hundred thousand times what they originally were.

2. That while at first so simple in structure as to be almost considered structureless, they assume, in the course of their growth, a continually increasing complexity of structure.

3. That though in their early undeveloped state there exists in them scarcely any mutual dependence of parts, these parts gradually acquire a mutual dependence, which becomes at last so great, that the

---

[6] *Adumbrations:* faint shadows or sketches.

activity and life of each part is made possible only by the activity and life of the rest.[7]

These three parallelisms will appear the more significant the more we contemplate them. Observe that, while they are points in which societies agree with individual organisms, they are points in which all individual organisms agree with each other, and disagree with everything else. In the course of its existence, every plant and animal increases in mass, which, with the exception of crystals, can be said of no inorganic objects. The orderly progress from simplicity to complexity displayed by societies in common with every living body whatever, is a characteristic which substantially distinguishes living bodies from the inanimate bodies amid which they move. And that functional dependence of parts, which is scarcely more manifest in animals or plants than in societies, has no counterpart elsewhere. Moreover, it should be remarked, not only that societies and organisms are alike in these peculiarities, in which they are unlike all other things; but, further, that the highest societies, like the highest organisms, exhibit them in the greatest degree. Looking at the facts in their ensemble, we may observe that the lowest types of animals do not increase to anything like the size of the higher ones; and similarly we see that aboriginal societies are comparatively limited in their growth. In complexity, our large civilized nations as much exceed the primitive savage ones, as a vertebrate animal does a zoophyte. And while in simple communities, as in simple

creatures, the mutual dependence of parts is so slight, that subdivision or mutilation causes but little inconvenience; in complex communities as in complex creatures, you cannot remove or injure any considerable organ without producing great disturbance or death of the rest.[8]

On the other hand, the leading differences between societies and individual organisms are these:—

1. That they have no specific external forms. This, however, is a point of contrast which loses much of its importance, when we remember that throughout the entire vegetal kingdom, as well as in some lower divisions of the animal kingdom, the forms are very indefinite, and are manifestly in part determined by surrounding physical circumstances, as the forms of societies are. If, too, it should eventually be shown, as we believe it will, that the form of every species of organism has resulted from the average play of the external forces to which it has been subject during its evolution as a species; then, that the external forms of societies should depend, as they do, on surrounding conditions, will be a further point of community.[9]

2. That whereas the living tissue whereof an individual organism consists, forms one continuous mass, the living elements which make up a society, do not form a continuous mass, but are more or less widely dispersed over some portion of the earth's surface. This, which at first sight

---

[7] This paragraph contains the fundamental ideas upon which Spencer builds his evolutionary theory. He writes that societies are like organisms in three ways: (1) they grow from small groups to large aggregations; (2) they grow from simple to complex structures; and (3) they grow from a collection of independent units to an organism composed of interdependent parts. The second and third points are particularly important to his theory and were incorporated into most of the evolutionary theories of the nineteenth and twentieth centuries. Durkheim, for example, used the idea of directional movement from simplicity to complexity and relational movement from independence to interdependence in his formulation of the differences between mechanical and organic solidarity (see essay 6).

[8] Here you see illustrated Spencer's belief that social evolution was progressive. Those societies that are large, complex, and integrated are more evolved than those that are not. Industrialized Europe was, in his view, the best society that evolution had thus far created.

[9] Spencer says that the forms of society are, in part, determined by the surrounding physical circumstances. He is using the general evolutionary concept of the influence of environment on selection here, but his application of the idea to human societies provided a grounding that Julian Steward and the cultural ecologists used almost a century later.

appears to be a fundamental distinction, is one which yet to a great extent disappears when we contemplate all the facts.

[*In a 400-word passage, Spencer argues that human society is in this respect similar to several primitive life-forms. He further suggests, though not in these terms, that the environment in which people live must be considered part of the social organism and that, if this is taken into account, societies do form a continuous mass.*]

3. That while the ultimate living elements of an individual organism are mostly fixed in their relative positions, those of the social organism are capable of moving from place to place, seems a marked point of disagreement. But here, too, the disagreement is much less than would be supposed. For while citizens are locomotive in their private capacities, they are fixed in their public capacities. As farmers, manufacturers, or traders, men carry on their businesses at the same spots, often throughout their whole lives; and if they go away for a time, they leave behind others to discharge their functions in their absence. Not only does each great center of production, each manufacturing town or district, continue always in the same place; but many of the firms in such town or district are for generations carried on either by the descendants or successors of those who founded them. Just as in a living body, the individual cells that make up some important organ, severally perform their functions for a time and then disappear, leaving others to supply their vacant places; so in each part of a society, while the organ remains, the persons who compose it change. Thus, in social life, as in the life of an animal, the units as well as the larger agencies composed of them, are in the main stationary as respects the places where they discharge their duties and obtain their sustenance. So that the power of individual locomotion does not practically affect the analogy.[10]

4. That while in the body of an animal only a special tissue is endowed with feeling, in a society all the members are endowed with feeling, is the last and perhaps the most important distinction. Even this distinction, however, is by no means a complete one. For in some lower divisions of the animal kingdom, characterized by the absence of a nervous system, such sensitiveness as exists is possessed by all parts. It is only in the more organized forms that feeling is monopolized by one particular class of vital elements. Moreover, we must not forget that societies, too, are not without a certain differentiation of this kind. Though the units of a community are all sensitive, yet they are so in unequal degrees. The classes engaged in agriculture and laborious occupations in general, are far less susceptible, intellectually and emotionally, than the rest; and especially less so than the classes of highest mental culture. Still we have here a tolerably decided contrast between bodies politic and individual bodies. And it is one which we should keep constantly in view. For it reminds us that while in individual bodies the welfare of all other parts is rightly subservient to the welfare of the nervous system, whose pleasurable or painful activities make up the good or evil of life; in bodies politic the same thing does not hold good, or holds good to but a very slight extent. It is well that the lives of all parts of an animal should be merged in the life of the whole, because the whole has a corporate consciousness capable of happiness or misery. But it is not so with a society; since its living units do not and cannot lose individual consciousness; and since the community as a whole has no general or corporate consciousness distinct from those of its components. And this is an everlasting reason why the welfare of its citizens cannot rightly be sacrificed to some supposed benefit of the State; but why, on the other hand, the State must be regarded as existing solely for the benefit of citizens. The corporate life must here be

---

[10] Spencer writes that social institutions have lives separate from and beyond the lives of the individuals who compose them. He says, "so in each part of a society, while the organ remains, the persons who compose it change." This is an important insight for both anthropology and sociology in the twentieth century, variously echoed in Max Weber's work on bureaucracy, Kroeber's on the superorganic, and Radcliffe-Brown's work on social structure.

subservient to the life of the parts, instead of the life of the parts being subservient to the corporate life.[11]

Such, then, are the points of analogy and the points of difference. May we not say that the points of difference serve but to bring into clearer light the points of analogy? While comparison makes definite the obvious contrast between organisms commonly so called, and the social organism, it shows that even these contrasts are not nearly so decided as was to be expected. The indefiniteness of form, the discontinuity of the parts, the mobility of the parts, and the universal sensitiveness, are not only peculiarities of the social organism which have to be stated with considerable qualifications; but they are peculiarities to which the inferior classes of animals present approximations. Thus we find but little to conflict with the all important analogies. That societies slowly augment in mass; that they progress in complexity of structure; that at the same time their parts become more mutually dependent; and further, that the extent to which they display these peculiarities is proportionate to their vital activity; are traits that societies have in common with all organic bodies. And these traits in which they agree with all organic bodies and disagree with all other things—these traits which in truth constitute the very essence of organization, entirely subordinate the minor distinctions: such distinctions being scarcely greater than those

which separate one half of the organic kingdom from the other. The *principles* of organization are the same; and the differences are simply differences of application.

Thus a general survey of the facts seems quite to justify the comparison of a society to a living body. We shall find that the parallelism becomes the more marked the more closely it is traced. Let us proceed to consider it in detail.

The lowest forms of animal and vegetable life— *Protozoa* and *Protophyta*—are chiefly inhabitants of the water.[12] They are minute bodies, most of which are made individually visible only by the microscope. All of them are extremely simple in structure; and some of them, as the *Amoeba* and *Actinophris,* almost structureless. Multiplying, as they do, by the spontaneous division of their bodies, they produce halves, which may either become quite separate and move away in different directions, or may continue attached. And by the repetition of this process of fission, aggregations of various sizes and kinds are formed. Thus among the *Protophyta* we have some classes, as the *Diatomacea* and the yeast-plant, in which the individuals may be either separate, or attached in groups of two, three, four or more; other classes in which a considerable number of individual cells are united into a thread (*Conferva, Monilia*); others in which they form a network (*Hydrodictyon*); others in which they form plates (*Ulva*); and others in which they form masses (*Laminaria, Agaricus*): all which vegetal forms, having no distinction of root,

---

[11] In this paragraph Spencer clearly expresses his conviction that some classes are superior to others. Much of the negative twentieth-century view of Spencer has focused on statements like this. Because of them, Spencer is sometimes considered the high priest of racism and ethnocentrism, but this criticism may be misleading. Note that, at the end of the paragraph, Spencer tells us that the state exists solely for the benefit of its citizens. Spencer was a self-taught man and a member of the rising middle class. He did not attend a prestigious university and as a result was always, to some extent, an intellectual outsider. The position he presents here pits the rising industrialists against the legal privileges of the landowning aristocracy. Spencer sought to limit the role of the state and believed that a laissez-faire position would best allow for the progress of society. In some ways, his position was fairly close to modern libertarianism.

[12] In this paragraph and below, Spencer makes a highly detailed argument for the analogy between the evolution of biological organisms and that of society. The ideas of simple and complex societies, social structures, and social functions explored here imply a research program. That is, the goal of anthropology (or sociology) should be to identify social "organs" and describe their functioning. Contemporaneously with this essay, Spencer issued a prospectus for a future work, *Principles of Sociology,* in which he proposed to derive empirical generalizations from the comparative study of society (Carneiro 1967). This project was never fully realized, but Spencer's research agenda was central to the development of social anthropology in this century and influenced such thinkers as A. R. Radcliffe-Brown, Julian Steward, and most of all, George Peter Murdock. His ideas continue to be important today.

stem or leaf, are called *Thallogens*. Among the *Protozoa* we find parallel facts.[13] Immense numbers of *Amoeba*-like creatures massed together in a framework of horny fibers, are found in the extensive family of the sponges. In the *Foraminifera* we see smaller groups of such creatures arranged into more definite shapes. Not only do these almost structureless *Protozoa* unite into regular or irregular aggregations of various sizes; but among some of the more organized ones, as the *Vorticellae*, there are also produced clusters of individuals, proceeding from a common stock. But these little societies of monads, or cells, or whatever else we may call them, are societies in the lowest sense: there is no subordination of parts among them—no organization. Each of the component units lives by and for itself, neither giving nor receiving aid; there is no mutual dependence, save that consequent upon mere mechanical union.

Now do we not here clearly discern analogies to the first stages of human societies? Among the lowest races, as the Bushmen, we find but incipient aggregations: sometimes single families, sometimes two or three families wandering about together. The number of associated units is small and variable, and their union inconstant. No division of labor exists except between the sexes; and the only kind of mutual aid is that of joint attack or defence. We have nothing beyond an undifferentiated group of individuals forming the germ of a society; just as in the groups of similar cells above described, we have only the initial stage of animal and vegetal organization.

[In a 1,475-word passage removed from this edition, Spencer elaborates on his analogy. Just as more advanced plants and animals show some specialization of function, more advanced societies show evidence of social structure. Beyond sexual division of labor, government is the first structure to emerge. However, as in lower plants, specialization remains imprecise. Cells can change function and a society's leaders may also do other jobs. The next phase is the spread of similar biological or social units across the landscape. Physical barriers may cause such social units to coalesce into nations. Spencer argues that just as some individuals among a large aggregate of hydra will develop special functions, some communities within a large society will develop specific functions.]

The general doctrine of the progressive division of labor, to which we are here introduced, is more or less familiar to all readers. And further, the analogy between the economical division of labor and the "physiological division of labor" is so striking, as long since to have drawn the attention of scientific naturalists: so striking, indeed, that the expression "physiological division of labor," has been suggested by it. It is not needful, therefore, that we should treat this part of our subject in great detail. We shall content ourselves with noting a few general and significant facts not manifest on a first inspection.

Throughout the whole animal kingdom, from the *Coelenterata* upwards, the first stage of evolution is the same.[14] Equally in the germ of a polype and in the human ovum, the aggregated

---

[13] To modern readers Spencer's writing style may seem highly repetitive. However, he was writing for an audience that was largely unfamiliar with the ideas he was presenting. Further, his readers had time to read and an aesthetic taste for copious examples. Gould (1994) has pointed out that, while modern American museums concentrate on the display of one or a few specimens with elaborate explanation, Victorian museums attempted to overwhelm the senses through the display of the enormous variety of nature but had relatively little explanation. Here Spencer, a model Victorian, does the same thing with words. We have removed about 40 percent of Spencer's original 14,250-word essay, but we have tried to leave enough of what, by modern standards, is excess verbiage for you to get a feel for this sort of writing.

[14] The vocabulary Spencer uses when describing biology is quite technical, especially considering that this essay appeared in a general intellectual journal rather than one specifically devoted to biology. The vocabulary he uses when referring to social formations, on the other hand, is quite simple. The effect of combining the technical language of biology with the rather simple vocabulary of society is to make Spencer's comments on society seem much more scientifically compelling than they actually are. Of course, in a modern sense, Spencer's argument is simply an argument by analogy and is not scientific at all. It is neither an attempt to explore and describe the range of human social organization nor a set of conclusions based on controlled experimentation.

mass of cells out of which the creature is to arise, gives origin to a peripheral layer of cells, slightly differing from the rest which they include; and this layer subsequently divides into two—the inner one lying in contact with the included yolk being commonly called the mucous layer, and the outer exposed to surrounding agencies being called the serous layer: or in the terms used by Professor Huxley,[15] in describing the development of the *Hydrozoa*—the endoderm and the ectoderm. This primary division marks out the fundamental contrast of parts in the future organism. Out of the mucous layer or endoderm is developed the apparatus of nutrition; while out of the serous layer, or ectoderm, is developed the apparatus of external action. From the one arise the organs by which food is prepared and absorbed, oxygen imbibed, and blood purified; while out of the other arise the nervous, muscular, and osseous[16] systems, by whose combined actions the movements of the body as a whole are effected. Though this is not a rigorously correct distinction, seeing that some organs involve both of these primitive membranes, yet the highest authorities agree in stating it as a broad general one. Well, in the evolution of a society we see a primary differentiation of analogous kind, which similarly underlies the whole future structure.[17] As already pointed out, the only contrast of parts which is visible in primitive societies, is that between the government and the governed. In the least organized tribes, the council of chiefs may be a body of men distinguished simply by greater

courage or experience. In more organized tribes, the chief-class is definitely separated from the lower class, and often regarded as different in nature—sometimes as god-descended. And later we find these two becoming respectively freemen and slaves, or nobles and serfs. A glance at their respective functions makes it obvious that the great divisions thus early formed, stand to each other in a relation similar to that in which the primary divisions of the embryo stand to each other. For from its first appearance, the class of chiefs is that by which the external actions of the society are controlled: alike in war, in negotiation, and in migration. As we advance, we see that while the upper class grows distinct from the lower, and at the same time becomes more and more exclusively regulative and defensive in its functions, alike as kings and subordinate rulers, as priests, and as military leaders; the inferior class becomes more and more exclusively occupied in providing the necessaries of life for the community at large. From the soil, with which it comes in most direct contact, the mass of the people takes up and prepares for use the food and such rude articles of manufacture as are known; while the overlying mass of superior men, supplied with the necessaries of life by those below them, deals with circumstances external to the community—circumstances with which, by position, it is more immediately concerned. Ceasing by-and-by to have any knowledge of, or power over, the concerns of the society as a whole, the serf class becomes devoted to the processes of

---

[15] Thomas Henry Huxley (1825–1895) was a prominent biologist famous for his defense of Darwin and the theory of natural selection; his strong advocacy of Darwin's theory earned him the nickname "Darwin's bulldog."

[16] *Osseous*: bony; the osseous system refers to the skeleton.

[17] Here Spencer suggests that just as the first stages of embryonic development are universal for all members of the animal kingdom, so too all societies begin and develop through identical early stages. A key source of this analogy is his reading of the work of the German-Russian embryologist Karl Ernst Von Baer (1792–1876). Von Baer outlined the parallel development of embryological forms but insisted that this did not imply repetition of adult stages. However, the analogy connecting different stages of the development

of human society to the evolution of biological organisms was used by Spencer and was common in nineteenth- and early twentieth-century anthropology. One prominent variation on this theme derived from the work of German biologist Ernst Heinrich Haekel (1834–1919). Haekel claimed that ontogeny recapitulates phylogeny; that is, the growth of individuals repeats the evolutionary history of their phylum. When applied to the evolution of society, this meant that the growth of individuals within advanced societies mirrored the stages through which human social evolution had passed. Someone believing this would conclude that adults in primitive societies were very similar to children in advanced societies. Spencer had frequent recourse to "the child/savage equation" (Stocking 1987:22).

alimentation; while the noble class, ceasing to take any part in the process of alimentation, becomes devoted to the co-ordination and movements of the entire body politic.

Equally remarkable is a further analogy of like kind. After there has taken place in the embryo the separation of the mucous and serous layers, there presently arises between the two, a third, known to physiologists as the vascular layer—a layer out of which is developed the system of blood-vessels. The mucous layer absorbs nutriment from the mass of yolk it encloses; this nutriment has to be transferred to the overlying serous layer, out of which the nervo-muscular system is being developed; and between the two arises the system of vessels by which the transfer is effected—a system of vessels which continues ever after to be the transferrer of nutriment from the places where it is absorbed and prepared, to the places where it is needed for growth and repair. Well, may we not clearly trace a parallel step in social progress? Between the governing and the governed there at first exists no intermediate class; and even in some societies that have reached a considerable size, there are scarcely any but the nobles and their kindred on the one hand, and the serfs on the other: the social structure being such, that the transfer of commodities takes place directly from slaves to their masters. But in societies of a higher type, there grows up between these two primitive classes, another—the trading or middle class. Equally at first as now, we may see that, speaking generally, this middle class is the analogue of the middle layer in the embryo. For all traders are essentially distributors. Whether they be wholesale dealers, who collect into large masses the commodities of various producers; or whether they be retailers, who divide out to those who want them the masses of commodities thus collected together;

all mercantile men are agents of transfer from the places where things are produced to the places where they are consumed. Thus the distributing apparatus of a society answers to the distributing apparatus in a living body, not only in its functions, but in its intermediate origin and subsequent position, and in the time of its appearance.

Without enumerating the minor differentiations which these three great classes afterwards undergo, we will merely note that throughout, they follow the same general law with the differentiations of an individual organism. In a society, as in a rudimentary animal, we have seen that the most general and broadly contrasted divisions are the first to make their appearance; and of the subdivisions it continues true in both cases, that they arise in the order of their generality.[18]

[*In an 875-word passage, Spencer argues that both societies and organisms develop in the direction of increased specialization of function. He compares the development of states to that of segmented worms. Among these, he says, lower forms are composed of many identical segments, while higher forms have organs that transcend segments. Similarly, early states are composed of many similar independent fiefdoms, but larger states have structures that completely transcend them.*]

If, after contemplating these analogies of structure, we inquire whether there are any such analogies between causes and processes of organic growth, the answer is—yes. The causes which lead to the increase of bulk in any part of the body politic, are strictly analogous to those which lead to increase of bulk in any part of an individual body. In both cases the antecedent is greater functional activity consequent on greater demand. Each limb, viscus, gland, or other member of an

---

[18] Here and below Spencer reiterates a basic principle of evolution as he understood it: Evolution invariably proceeds from the simple to the complex, or, in his terminology, from the general to the specialized. This understanding of evolution was shared by most nineteenth-century thinkers and a great many in this century. Today, however, it is hotly contested. Consider, for example, two current popular writers on evolution. E. O. Wilson argues that Spencer was right—the history of biological evolution is essentially one of increasing complexity of organisms and increasing variety of species. Stephen Jay Gould, on the other hand, argues that evolution does not necessarily move in this direction and that the era of life's greatest variety was the Cambrian, some 500 million years ago.

animal, is developed by exercise—by actively discharging the duties which the body at large requires of it; and similarly, any class of laborers or artisans, any manufacturing center, or any official agency, begins to enlarge when the community devolves upon it an increase of work.[19] Moreover, in each case growth has its conditions and its limits. That any organ in a living being may grow by exercise, there needs a due supply of blood: all action implies waste; blood brings the materials for repair; and before there can be growth, the quantity of blood supplied must be more than that requisite for repair only. So is it in a society. If to some district which elaborates for the community particular commodities—say the woollens of Yorkshire—there comes an augmented demand; and if in fulfillment of this demand a certain expenditure and wear of the manufacturing organization are incurred; and if in payment for the extra supply of woollens sent away, there comes back only such quantity of commodities as replaces the expenditure and makes good the waste of life and machinery; there can clearly be no growth. That there may be growth, the commodities obtained in return must be somewhat more than is required for these ends; and just in proportion as the excess is great will the growth be rapid. Whence it is manifest that what in commercial affairs we call *profit*, answers to the excess of nutrition over waste in a living body. To which let us add, that in both cases, where the functional activity is great and the nutrition defective, there results not growth but decay. If in an animal any organ is worked so hard that the channels which bring blood cannot furnish enough for repair, the organ dwindles; and if in the body-politic some part has been stimulated into great productivity, and cannot afterwards get paid for all its produce, certain of its members become bankrupt and it decreases in size.

One more parallelism to be here noted is, that the different parts of the social organism, like the different parts of an individual organism, compete for nutriment; and obtain more or less of it according as they are discharging more or less duty. If a man's brain be suddenly very much excited, it will abstract blood from his viscera and stop digestion; or, digestion actively going on will so affect the circulation through the brain as to cause drowsiness; or great muscular exertion will determine such a quantity of blood to the limbs as to arrest digestion or cerebral action, as the case may be. And in like manner in a society, it frequently happens that great activity in some one direction causes partial arrests of activity elsewhere, by abstracting capital, that is, commodities: as instance the way in which the sudden development of our railway system hampered commercial operations; or the way in which the raising of a large military force temporarily stops the growth of leading industries.

The last few paragraphs naturally introduce the next division of our subject. Almost unawares we have come upon the analogy which exists between the blood of a living body and the circulating mass of commodities in the body-politic. We have now to trace out this analogy from its simplest to its most complex manifestations.

[*In a 2,200-word passage, Spencer compares certain aspects of society to the blood and circulatory system of organisms. Lower animals have no blood or circulatory system; every cell feeds for itself. Similarly, he claims that in primitive tribes there is no system of exchange, and every family fends for itself. Somewhat more complex organisms have extremely simple digestive tracts; likewise, somewhat more complex societies have some trade in agricultural commodities along simple paths. As specialization*

---

[19] Note that the description of the evolution of both organisms and society presented here is Lamarckian rather than Darwinian. Spencer says that organs that are used more grow more. Despite the fact that his use of the phrase "survival of the fittest" and his belief in the virtues of competition tie Spencer to Darwin, his version of evolution was formulated independently of Darwin's and was not based on natural selection. Rather, he believed in the inheritance of acquired characteristics. For example, in 1855, he wrote as follows about the personality traits of members of different societies: "there can be no question that these varieties of disposition, which have a more or less evident relation to the habits of life, have been gradually induced and established in successive generations *and have become* organic" (quoted in Stocking 1987:141, emphasis added).

proceeds in an organism, blood and a circulatory system are required to nourish the now specialized organs. As societies become more complex, the demands for circulation of products between laboring groups similarly increase. Spencer notes that the circulatory material (either blood for organisms or products for societies) increases not only in quantity but in complexity as well. This, of course, fits nicely with his understanding of evolution. As animals evolve, they develop what Spencer calls "blood discs" (corpuscles) to facilitate nutrition. In societies money plays a similar role, elaborated in a sequence of analogies. Like blood cells, money itself is not consumed. Blood cells are found in greatest abundance in large organs, and money in greatest abundance in large cities. Blood in lower animals has no corpuscles, and lower societies have no money. Just as lower animals have minimally organized circulatory systems, countries where civilization is beginning have only rudimentary trails (the paths needed for the exchange of goods) through their countryside. More advanced animals have blood vessels, and more advanced societies have fenced and gravelled roads. In the highest organisms and societies, there are major blood vessels and capillaries or large main roads and small minor ones. The development of railroads that have a track for each direction is analogous to veins and arteries in a body. The analogy between society and organisms includes not only the circulatory system but also the pattern of motion of nutrients through it. In low creatures, the movement is a slow reciprocating motion. Similarly in lower societies there is movement now toward this fair or market, now toward that. In more advanced societies and animals there are "constant currents in definite directions." Moreover, as organisms evolve, they develop hearts that pump blood through the circulatory system, and societies develop large commercial centers. Blood flows more rapidly the closer it is to the heart, and trains move more rapidly and frequently the closer they are to commercial centers.]

Thus, then, we find between the distributing system in living bodies and in the body-politic, wonderfully close parallelisms. In the lowest forms of both there exists neither prepared nutriment nor a distributing apparatus; and in both, these, arising as necessary accompaniments of the differentiation of parts, approach perfection as this differentiation approaches completeness. In animals, as in societies, the distributing agencies begin to show themselves at the same relative period, and in the same relative position. In the one, as in the other, the nutritive materials circulated are at first crude and simple, gradually becoming better elaborated and more heterogeneous, and have eventually added to them a new element facilitating the nutritive processes. The channels of communication pass through similar phases of development which bring them to analogous forms. And the direction, rhythm, and rate of the circulation, progress by like steps to final conditions.[20]

We come at length to the nervous system. Having noticed the primary differentiation of societies into the governing and governed classes, and observed its analogy to the differentiation of the two primary tissues which respectively develop into the organs of alimentation and those of external action; having noticed some of the leading analogies between the development of industrial organization and that of the alimentary apparatus; and having above more fully traced the analogies between the distributing systems, social and individual; we have now to compare the appliances by which a society, as a whole, is regulated, with those by which the movements of an organism are regulated. We shall find here parallelisms equally striking with those already detailed.

The class out of which governmental organization originates is, as we have said, analogous, by origin and position, to the ectoderm of the lowest animals and of embryonic forms. And as this primitive membrane, out of which the nervo-muscular

---

[20] Spencer, like most nineteenth-century evolutionists, saw both biological and social evolution leading to more and more perfect societies. In the twentieth century, this view finds an echo in the work of Leslie White (see essay 18), but few current evolutionists share it.

system is evolved, must, even in the first stage of its differentiation, be slightly distinguished from the rest by that greater impressibility and contractility[21] characterizing the organ to which it gives rise; so, in that superior class which is eventually transformed into the nervo-muscular system of a society (its legislative and defense appliances), does there exist in the beginning a larger endowment of the capacities required for these higher social functions. Always, in rude assemblages of men, there is a tendency for the strongest, most courageous, and most sagacious to become rulers and leaders; and in a tribe of some standing, this results in the establishment of a ruling class characterized on the average by those mental and bodily qualities which fit them for deliberation and vigorous combined action. Very significant, too, is the fact that those units of a society, who from the beginning discharge the directive and executive functions, are those in whom the directive and executive organs predominate: in other words, that what by analogy we call the nervo-muscular apparatus of a society begins to grow out of those units whose nervo-muscular systems are most developed. For the chiefs who, as individuals, or as a class, first separate themselves from the mass of a tribe, and begin to exercise control over their respective dependents and over the society as a whole, are men who have the greatest bodily vigor, the greatest bravery, or the greatest cunning—more powerful limbs, or more powerful brains, or both; while those to whom the industrious processes are chiefly left—in the smallest tribes the women, and in larger ones the least masculine men—are of less nervo-muscular power. Thus that greater impressibility and contractility which in the rudest animal forms characterize the units

of the ectoderm, characterize also the units of the primitive social ectoderm; since impressibility and contractility are the respective roots of intelligence and strength.[22]

Again, in the unmodified ectoderm, as we see it in the Hydra, the units are all endowed both with impressibility and contractility; but as we ascend to higher types of organization, the ectoderm differentiates into classes of units which divide those two functions between them: some, becoming exclusively impressible, cease to be contractile; while some, becoming exclusively contractile, cease to be impressible. Similarly with societies. In an aboriginal tribe the directive and executive functions are more or less equally diffused throughout the whole governing class. Each minor chief not only commands those under him, but, if need be, himself coerces them into obedience. The council of chiefs itself carries out on the battle-field its own decisions. The head chief not only makes laws, but administers justice with his own hands. But in larger and more settled communities, the directive and executive agencies begin to grow distinct from each other. As fast as his duties accumulate, the head chief, or king, confines himself more and more to directing public affairs, and leaves the execution of his will to others: he deputes others to enforce submission, to inflict punishments, or to carry out minor acts of offence and defence; and only on occasions when perhaps the safety of the society and his own supremacy are at stake, does he begin to act as well as direct. As this differentiation establishes itself, we see that the characteristics of the ruler begin to change. No longer, as in an aboriginal tribe, the strongest and most daring man, the tendency is for him to become the man of greatest cunning, foresight, and skill in

---

[21] Spencer uses the words *impressibility* and *contractility* to refer to the ability of the ectoderm, or outer cell layer, in a very simple animal or an embryo to remember (or learn) and to move.

[22] The evolution from simple to complex that Spencer finds across both animal species and societies is repeated within a single complex society. Rural people and the urban underclass are more primitive; the urban elites are more advanced. Rural people and the poor may be compared to people liv-

ing in less complex societies. Evolution is Spencer's overriding metaphor, and he has nested it within several different levels of society in this article. Additionally, note that in Spencer's view men are superior to women. Men do the brain work; women are left with the "industrial processes." Although in his early work Spencer had suggested radical female equality, he later reversed this position and suggested that the needs of reproduction arrested the mental evolution of females at an early age (Stocking 1987:205).

the management of others; for in societies that have advanced beyond the first stage, it is chiefly such qualities that insure success in obtaining supreme power, and holding it against internal and external enemies. That is to say, that individual of the governing class who comes to be the chief directing agent, and so plays the same part that a rudimentary nervous center does in an unfolding organism, is usually one endowed with some superiorities of nervous organization.

When, advancing a stage, we contemplate communities somewhat larger and more complex, in which there have arisen, perhaps, a separate military class, a priesthood, and dispersed masses of population requiring local control, there necessarily grow up subordinate governing agents; who, as their duties accumulate, severally become more directive and less executive in their characters. And when, as commonly happens, the king begins to collect round himself a number of advisors who aid him by communicating information, preparing subjects for his judgement, and issuing his orders; we may say that the form of organization is comparable to one very general among inferior types of animals, in which there exists a chief ganglion with a few dispersed minor ganglia under its control.

The analogies between the evolution of governmental structure in a society, and the evolution of governmental structures in living bodies, are, however, more strikingly displayed during the formation of nations by the coalescence of small communities—a process already shown to be in several respects parallel to the development of those creatures that primarily consist of many like segments. Among the other points of community between the successive rings which make up the body in the lower *Articulata,* is the possession of similar pairs of ganglia. These pairs of ganglia, though united together by nerves, are very incompletely dependent on any general controlling power. Hence it results, that when the body is cut in two, the hinder part continues to move forward under the propulsion of its numerous legs; and that when the chain of ganglia has been divided without severing the body, the hinder limbs may be seen trying to propel the body in one direction, while the fore limbs are trying to propel it in another. Among the higher *Articulata,* however, a number of the anterior pairs of ganglia, besides growing severally much larger, unite into one mass; and this great cephalic ganglion, becoming the coordinator of all the creature's movements, there no longer exists much local independence. Now may we not in the growth of a consolidated kingdom out of petty sovereignties or baronies, observe analogous changes. Like the chiefs and primitive rulers above described, feudal lords, exercising supreme power over their respective groups of retainers, discharge functions analogous to those rudimentary nervous centers; and we know that at first they, like their prototypes, were distinguished by superiority of directive and executive organization. Among these local governing centers, we see in early feudal times very little subordination. They are in frequent antagonism; they are individually restrained chiefly by the influence of large parties in their own class; and are but imperfectly and irregularly subject to that most powerful member of their order who has gained the position of head suzerain or king. Gradually, however, as the growth and organization of the society progresses, we find these local directive centers falling more and more under the control of a chief directive center. Closer commercial and distributive union between the several segments, is accompanied by closer governmental union; and these minor rulers end in being little more than agents who superintend the execution of the commands of the supreme ruler; just as the local ganglia, above described, eventually become agents which enforce in their respective segments the orders of the cephalic ganglion. Note now a further step in which the parallelism equally holds. We remarked above, when speaking of the rise of aboriginal kings, that in proportion as their territories and duties became greater, they were obliged not only to perform their executive functions by deputy, but also to gather round themselves advisers to aid them in their directive functions; and that thus, in place of a solitary governing unit, there grew up a group of governing units, comparable to a ganglion consisting of many cells. Let us here further remark, that the advisers and chief officers who thus form the rudiment of a ministry, tend from the beginning to exercise a certain control over the ruler. By the information they give and the opinions they express, they sway his judgement and affect his commands. To this extent he therefore becomes a channel through which are communicated the directions originating with them; and in course of time, when the advice of ministers becomes the acknowledged source of a king's actions, we see that he assumes very much the character of an automatic center reflecting the impressions made upon him from without.[23]

Beyond this complication in the governmental structure, many societies do not progress; but in some a much further development takes place. Our own case best illustrates this further development, and its further analogies. To kings and their ministries have been added in course of time other great directive centers, exercising a control which, at first small, has been gradually becoming predominant; as with the great governing ganglia that especially distinguish the highest class of living beings. Strange as the assertion will be thought, our Houses of Parliament discharge in the social economy, functions that are in sundry respects comparable to those discharged by the great cerebral masses in a vertebrate animal.[24] As it is in the nature of a single ganglion to be affected only by special stimuli from particular parts of the body; so it is in the nature of a single ruler to be swayed in his acts by exclusive personal or class interests. As it is in the nature of an aggregation of ganglia, closely connected with the primary one, to convey to it a greater variety of influences from more numerous organs, and thus to make its acts conform to more numerous requirements; so it is in the nature of a king surrounded by subsidiary controlling powers to adapt his rule to a greater number of public exigencies. And as it is in the nature of those great and latest developed ganglia which distinguish the highest creatures, to interpret and combine the more numerous and more complex impressions conveyed to them from all parts of the system, and to regulate the actions in such a way as duly to regard them all; so it is in the nature of those great and latest developed legislative bodies which distinguished the most advanced societies, to interpret and combine the wishes and complaints of all classes and localities, and to regulate public affairs as much as possible in harmony with the general wants. It is the function of the cerebrum to coordinate the countless heterogeneous considerations which affect the present and future welfare of the individual as a whole; and it is the function of the House of Commons to coordinate the countless heterogeneous considerations which affect the immediate and remote welfare of the entire community. We may describe the office of the brain as that of *averaging* the interests of life, physical, intellectual, moral, social; and a good brain is one in which the desires answering to these respective interests are so balanced, that the conduct they jointly dictate, sacrifices none of them. Similarly, we may describe the office of a Parliament as that of *averaging* the interests of the various classes in a community; and a good parliament is one in which the parties answering to these respective interests are so balanced, that their united legislation concedes to each class as much as consists with the good of the rest.[25]

---

[23] It is important to remember the historical context within which Spencer wrote. He was writing in Britain's great period of empire building. His discussion refers to the development of British parliamentary government, and readers applied his ideas to the expansion of the British Empire.

[24] Here Spencer claims that the best case to illustrate the highest stages of social evolution is his own society and defends the intricacies of the British parliamentary system. He suggests that one purpose of government is to serve those who could be disenfranchised, but he also writes that Parliament balances out various interests and "concedes to each class as much as consists with the good of the rest." Spencer was strongly influenced by Jeremy Bentham (1748–1832) and John Stuart Mill (1806–1873), two English philosophers who championed Utilitarianism, the key tenet of which was the achievement of the greatest good for the greatest number. Since Spencer and others of his era believed that the greatest good was created through industry and that capitalists were indispensable to industry, in practice, Utilitarian ideas bolstered Victorian support for wealthy capitalists.

[25] Do you notice that throughout the essay Spencer has been comparing simple life-forms like yeast and hydra to primitive societies, but in this paragraph, when discussing the English system of government, his comparison is to the brain?

Besides being comparable in their duties, these great directive centers, social and individual, are also comparable in the processes by which their duties are discharged. It is now a well-understood fact in Psychology, that the cerebrum is not occupied with direct impressions from without, but with the ideas of such impressions: instead of the actual sensations produced in the body, and directly appreciated by the sensory ganglia or primitive nervous centers, the cerebrum receives only the representations of these sensations; and its consciousness is called *representative* consciousness, to distinguish it from the original or *presentative* consciousness. Is it not significant that we have hit upon the same word to distinguish the function of our House of Commons?[26] We call it a representative body, because the interests with which it deals—the pains and pleasures about which it consults—are not directly presented to it, but represented to it by its various members; and a debate is a conflict of representations of the evils or benefits likely to follow from a proposed course—a description which applies with equal truth to a debate in the individual consciousness. Further it should be remarked, that in both cases, these great governing masses take no part in the executive functions. As, after a conflict of motives in the cerebrum, those which finally predominate act on the subjacent ganglia, and through their instrumentality determine the bodily actions; so the parties who, after a parliamentary struggle, finally gain the victory, do not themselves carry out their desires, but get them carried out by the executive divisions of the Government. The fulfillment of all legislative decisions continues still to devolve upon the original directive centers—the impulse passing from the Parliament to the Ministers, and from the Ministers to the King, in whose name everything is done; just as

those smaller first developed ganglia, which in the lowest vertebrata are the chief controlling agents, are still in a man's brain, the agents through which the dictates of the cerebrum are worked out. And yet once more, observe that in both cases these original centers become more and more automatic. In the individual they have now little function beyond that of executing the determinations of the larger centers. In the State we see that the monarch has long been lapsing into a mere passive agent of Parliament; and that now ministries are rapidly falling into the same position. Nay, between the two cases there is a parallelism, even in respect of the exceptions to this automatic action. For in the individual it happens that under circumstances of sudden alarm, as from a loud sound close at hand, an unexpected object starting up in front, or a slip from insecure footing, the danger is guarded against by some quick involuntary jump, or adjustment of the limbs, that takes place before there is time to consider the impending evil, and take deliberate measures to avoid it: the rationale of which is, that these violent impressions produced on the senses are reflected from the sensory ganglia to the spinal cord and muscles, without, as in ordinary cases, first passing through the cerebrum. In like manner on national emergencies calling for prompt action, the king and ministry, not having time to lay the matter before the great deliberative bodies, themselves issue commands for the requisite movements or precautions: the primitive, and now almost automatic directive centers resume for a moment their original uncontrolled power. And then, strangest of all, observe that in either case there is an after-process of approval or condemnation. The individual, on recovering from his automatic start, at once contemplates the cause of his

---

[26] The defense of representative government and executive action in the second half of this paragraph must be read in the context of its time. Recall that Karl Marx's *Communist Manifesto* had been published in 1848, a year in which a series of unsuccessful revolutions had swept through Europe. One of the demands of the communists and other revolutionaries was the abolition of both representative government and monarchies. By his argument, Spencer suggested that the superiority of British parliamentary government (and to some extent the governments of other European nations) was established in natural law.

fright; and, according to the case, concludes that it was well he moved as he did, or condemns himself for his groundless alarm. In like manner the deliberative powers in the State, discuss, as soon as may be, the unauthorized acts of the executive powers; and, deciding that the reasons were or were not sufficient, grant or withhold a bill of indemnity.

Thus far in comparing the governmental organization of the body-politic with that of an individual body, we have considered only the respective co-ordinating centers. We have yet to consider the channels through which these co-ordinating centers receive information and convey commands. In the simplest societies, as in the simplest organisms, there is no "internuncial apparatus," as Hunter styled the nervous system. Consequently, impressions can be but slowly propagated from unit to unit throughout the whole mass. The same progress, however, which in animal organization shows itself in the establishment of ganglia or directive centers, shows itself also in the establishment of nerve-threads, through which the ganglia receive and convey impressions, and so control remote organs. And in societies the like eventually takes place. After a long period during which the directive centers communicate with the various parts of the society through other means, there at length comes into existence an "internuncial apparatus" analogous to that found in individual bodies. The comparison of telegraph wires to nerves is familiar to all. It applies, however, to an extent not commonly supposed. We do not refer to the near alliance between the subtle forces employed in the two cases; though it is now held that the nerve-force, if not literally electric, is still a special form of electric action, related to the ordinary form much as magnetism is. But we refer to the structural arrangements of our telegraph system. Note first the fact that throughout the vertebrate sub-kingdom, we find the great nerve-bundles diverging from the vertebrate axis, side by side with the great arteries; and similarly we see that our groups of telegraph-wires are carried along the sides of our railways. But the most striking parallelism is this,—that into each great bundle of nerves as it leaves the axis of the body along with an artery, there enters a branch of the sympathetic nerve, which branch, accompanying the artery throughout its ramifications, has the function of regulating its diameter and otherwise controlling the flow of blood through it according to the local requirements. In like manner we find that in the group of telegraph wires running alongside each railway, there is one for the purpose of regulating the traffic—for retarding or expediting the flow of passengers and commodities as the local conditions demand. Probably when our now rudimentary telegraph system is fully developed, other analogies will be traceable.[27]

Such, then, is a general outline of the evidence which justifies in detail the comparison of a society to a living organism. The general peculiarities that societies gradually increase in mass, that they become little by little more complex, and that at the same time their parts grow more mutually dependent—these broad peculiarities which societies display in common with all living bodies, and in which they and living bodies differ from everything else; we find to involve minor analogies far closer than might have been expected. To these we would gladly have added others. We had hoped to say something respecting the different types of social organization, and something also on social metamorphoses; but we have reached our assigned limits.

---

[27] For the modern reader one of the most striking things about Spencer is the extraordinary degree of analogical detail he claims. Today, some of his suggestions can sound comic. In another essay ("The Evolution of Society") he compares the transition from guild to factory-based production to processes within the human liver. Here he suggests that like the human nervous system, the telegraph, one of the most spectacular technological achievements of his day, appeared as the result of natural law. Spencer had, incidentally, begun his career as a civil engineer working for the London and Birmingham Railway. One wonders what he might have made of microwave transmission and satellite dishes.

2. *The Science of Culture*

Sir Edward Burnett Tylor (1832–1917)

Culture or civilization, taken in its wide ethnographic sense, is that complex whole which includes knowledge, belief, art, morals, law, custom, and any other capabilities and habits acquired by man as a member of society. The condition of culture among the various societies of mankind, in so far as it is capable of being investigated on general principles, is a subject apt for the study of laws of human thought and action.[1] On the one hand, the uniformity which so largely pervades civilization may be ascribed, in great measure, to the uniform action of uniform causes; while on the other hand its various grades may be regarded as stages of development or evolution each the outcome of previous history, and about to do its proper part in shaping the history of the future. To the investigation of these two great principles in several departments of ethnography, with especial consideration of the civilization of the lower tribes as related to the civilization of the higher nations, the present volumes are devoted.

Our modern investigators in the sciences of inorganic nature are foremost to recognize, both within and without their special fields of work, unity of nature, the fixity of its laws, the definite sequence of cause and effect through which every fact depends on what has gone before it, and acts upon what is to come after it. They grasp firmly the Pythagorean doctrine of pervading order in the universal Kosmos. They affirm, with Aristotle, that nature is not full of incoherent episodes, like a bad tragedy. They agree with Leibnitz in what he calls "my axiom, that nature never acts by leaps (La nature n'agit jamais par saut),"[2] as well as in his "great principle, commonly little employed, that nothing happens without its sufficient reason." Nor, again, in studying the structure and habits of plants and animals, or in investigating the lower functions even of man, are these leading ideas unacknowledged. But when we come to talk of the higher processes of human feeling and action, of thought and language, knowledge and art, a change appears in the prevalent tone of opinion. The world at large is scarcely prepared to accept the general study of human life as a branch of natural science, and to carry out, in a large sense, the poet's injunction to "Account for moral as for natural things." To many educated minds there seems something presumptuous and repulsive in the view that the history of mankind is part and parcel of the history of nature, that our thoughts, wills, and actions accord with laws as definite as those which govern the motion of waves, the combination of acids and bases, and the growth of plants and animals.

The main reasons of this state of the popular judgment are not far to seek. There are many who would willingly accept a science of history if

From *Primitive Culture* (1871)

---

[1] Throughout this essay, Tylor reaffirms his faith in the possibility of a science of human society analogous to the physical sciences. In this he is very much like the other thinkers of his era, particularly Herbert Spencer. The opening sentence of this essay is one of the most frequently quoted definitions of culture in anthropology. Despite this, Tylor's understanding of the meaning of culture is clearly very different from that of most modern anthropologists. Whereas most anthropologists today believe that there are a great many different cultures, Tylor believed that "Culture" was, ultimately, a single body of information of which different human groups had greater or lesser amounts. This understanding was based on his belief in the psychic unity of humankind, here referred to as "the uniform action of uniform causes."

[2] *La nature n'agit jamais par saut*: a French phrase meaning "nature never acts by leaps." Darwin also used this phrase in an 1858 essay on variation in species (in Latin rather than French) to express the gradualism of his evolutionary theory. Tylor frequently uses foreign phrases in this essay. They almost always repeat the sentence that precedes them.

placed before them with substantial definiteness of principle and evidence, but who not unreasonably reject the systems offered to them, as falling too far short of a scientific standard. Through resistance such as this, real knowledge always sooner or later makes its way, while the habit of opposition to novelty does such excellent service against the invasions of speculative dogmatism, that we may sometimes even wish it were stronger than it is. But other obstacles to the investigation of laws of human nature arise from considerations of metaphysics and theology. The popular notion of free human will involves not only freedom to act in accordance with motive, but also a power of breaking loose from continuity and acting without cause,—a combination which may be roughly illustrated by the simile of a balance sometimes acting in the usual way, but also possessed of the faculty of turning by itself without or against its weights. This view of an anomalous action of the will, which it need hardly be said is incompatible with scientific argument, subsists as an opinion patent or latent in men's minds, and strongly affecting their theoretic views of history, though it is not, as a rule, brought prominently forward in systematic reasoning. Indeed the definition of human will, as strictly according with motive, is the only possible scientific basis in such enquiries. Happily, it is not needful to add here yet another to the list of dissertations on supernatural intervention and natural causation, on liberty, predestination, and accountability. We may hasten to escape from the regions of transcendental philosophy and theology, to start on a more hopeful journey over more practicable ground. None will deny that, as each man knows by the evidence of his own consciousness, definite and natural cause does, to a great extent, determine human action. Then,

keeping aside from considerations of extra-natural interference and causeless spontaneity, let us take this admitted existence of natural cause and effect as our standing ground, and travel on it so far as it will bear us. It is on this same basis that physical science pursues, with ever-increasing success, its quest of laws of nature. Nor need this restriction hamper the scientific study of human life, in which the real difficulties are the practical ones of enormous complexity of evidence, and imperfection of methods of observation.[3]

Now it appears that this view of human will and conduct, as subject to definite law, is indeed recognized and acted upon by the very people who oppose it when stated in the abstract as a general principle, and who then complain that it annihilates man's free will, destroys his sense of personal responsibility, and degrades him to a soul-less machine. He who will say these things will nevertheless pass much of his own life in studying the motives which lead to human action, seeking to attain his wishes through them, framing in his mind theories of personal character, reckoning what are likely to be the effects of new combinations, and giving to his reasoning the crowning character of true scientific enquiry, by taking it for granted that in so far as his calculation turns out wrong, either his evidence must have been false or incomplete, or his judgment upon it unsound. Such a one will sum up the experience of years spent in complex relations with society, by declaring his persuasion that there is a reason for everything in life, and that where events look unaccountable, the rule is to wait and watch in hope that the key to the problem may some day be found. This man's observation may have been as narrow as his inferences are crude and prejudiced, but nevertheless he has been an inductive philosopher "more than forty years

---

[3] In this passage, Tylor rejects both religious explanations of social phenomena and objections to social science based on the supposition of human free will. Tylor was stridently anticlerical. He saw human history as proceeding toward increasing rationality. His own religious background is significant in this context. Tylor was from a Quaker family and was highly influenced by Quaker theology. Quakers (members of the Society of Friends) do not believe in the clergy; instead, they believe that God speaks through each individual. This background had important implications for Tylor's work. Since Quakers believed in the essential unity of humankind, they emphasized a degree of tolerance and humanitarianism frequently absent in this era. The Quaker belief in a single spiritual destiny of humankind is reflected in Tylor's understanding of human social evolution.

without knowing it." He has practically acknowledged definite laws of human thought and action, and has simply thrown out of account in his own studies of life the whole fabric of motiveless will and uncaused spontaneity.[4] It is assumed here that they should be just so thrown out of account in wider studies, and that the true philosophy of history lies in extending and improving the methods of the plain people who form their judgments upon facts, and check them upon new facts.[5] Whether the doctrine be wholly or but partly true, it accepts the very condition under which we search for new knowledge in the lessons of experience, and in a word the whole course of our rational life is based upon it.

"One event is always the son of another, and we must never forget the parentage," was a remark made by a Bechuana chief to Casalis the African missionary. Thus at all times historians, so far as they have aimed at being more than mere chroniclers, have done their best to show not merely succession, but connection, among the events upon their record. Moreover, they have striven to elicit general principles of human action, and by these to explain particular events, stating expressly or taking tacitly for granted the existence of a philosophy of history.[6] Should any one deny the possibility of thus establishing historical laws the answer is ready with which Boswell in such a case turned on Johnson:[7] "Then, sir, you would reduce all history to no better than almanack." That nevertheless the labors of so many eminent thinkers should have

as yet brought history only to the threshold of science need cause no wonder to those who consider the bewildering complexity of the problems which come before the general historian. The evidence from which he is to draw his conclusions is at once so multifarious and so doubtful that a full and distinct view of its bearing on a particular question is hardly to be attained, and thus the temptation becomes all but irresistible to garble it in support of some rough and ready theory of the course of events. The philosophy of history at large, explaining the past and predicting the future phenomena of man's life in the world by reference to general laws, is in fact a subject with which, in the present state of knowledge, even genius aided by wide research seems but hardly able to cope. Yet there are departments of it which, though difficult enough, seem comparatively accessible. If the field of inquiry be narrowed from History as a whole to that branch of it which is here called Culture, the history, not of tribes or nations, but of the condition of knowledge, religion, art, custom, and the like among them, the task of investigation proves to lie within far more moderate compass. We suffer still from the same kind of difficulties which beset the wider argument, but they are much diminished. The evidence is no longer so wildly heterogeneous, but may be more simply classified and compared, while the power of getting rid of extraneous matter, and treating each issue on its own proper set of facts, makes close reasoning on the whole more available than in general

---

[4] In this passage Tylor continues his attack on those he considers the enemies of the application of scientific method to social science. His key method is really a call for introspection, which has some roots in the Quaker call to introspective prayer.

[5] Notice that Tylor here refers to his work as creating a philosophy of history. Tylor's anthropology involved re-creation the history of humankind's evolution to civilization. Many later anthropologists rejected such historical re-creation as unscientific or impossible.

[6] In this passage Tylor argues that the success of a philosophy of history depends on restricting the subject matter: by focusing on culture, the historian may ignore specific events in favor of general developmental trends. Because

Tylor understood culture as a unitary phenomenon that characterized peoples to one degree or another, the project was practical. For Tylor, describing culture as an evolutionary phenomenon implied tracing the history of its development. Simple societies could be understood as living history or living fossils. In this century, American followers of Franz Boas, reacting to the evolutionary perspective, also understood the study of culture as the study of history, but for different reasons.

[7] Dr. Samuel Johnson (1709–1784), considered by many to be the greatest eighteenth-century English author, is mentioned several times in this essay. James Boswell (1740–1795) was his biographer and frequent companion.

history. This may appear from a brief preliminary examination of the problem, how the phenomena of Culture may be classified and arranged, stage by stage, in a probable order of evolution.

Surveyed in a broad view, the character and habit of mankind at once display that similarity and consistency of phenomena which led the Italian proverb-maker to declare that "all the world is one country" "tutto il mondo e paese." To general likeness in human nature on the one hand, and to general likeness in the circumstances of life on the other, this similarity and consistency may no doubt be traced, and they may be studied with especial fitness in comparing races near the same grade of civilization. Little respect need be had in such comparisons for date in history or for place on the map; the ancient Swiss lake-dweller may be set beside the medieval Aztec, and the Ojibwa of North America beside the Zulu of South Africa. As Dr. Johnson contemptuously said when he had read about Patagonians and South Sea Islanders in Hawkesworth's Voyages, "one set of savages is like another." How true a generalization this really is, any Ethnological Museum may show. Examine for instance the edged and pointed instruments in such a collection; the inventory includes hatchet, adze, chisel, knife, saw, scraper, awl, needle, spear and arrow-head, and of these most or all belong with only differences of detail to races the most various.[8] So it is with savage occupations; the wood-chopping, fishing with net and line, shooting and spearing game, fire-making, cooking, twisting cord and plaiting baskets, repeat themselves with wonderful uniformity in the museum shelves which illustrate the life of the lower races from Kamchatka to Tierra del Fuego, and from Dahome to Hawaii. Even when it comes to comparing barbarous hordes with civilized nations, the consideration thrusts itself upon our minds, how far item after item of the life of the lower races passes into analogous proceedings of the higher, in forms not too far changed to be recognized, and sometimes hardly changed at all. Look at the modern European peasant using his hatchet and his hoe, see his food boiling or roasting over the log-fire, observe the exact place which beer holds in his calculation of happiness, hear his tale of the ghost in the nearest haunted house, and of the farmer's niece who was bewitched with knots in her inside till she fell into fits and died. If we choose out in this way things which have altered little in a long course of centuries, we may draw a picture where

---

[8] When Tylor speaks here about "comparing races near the same grade of civilization" and placing ethnographic materials next to each other on display, he is probably thinking about actual museum displays. In 1816, Christian Jürgensen Thomsen (1788–1865) became curator of the Museum of Northern Antiquities in Copenhagen (later the National Museum of Denmark). Over the next 20 years, he arranged the museum's collection of artifacts chronologically based on the material and style of their construction. In so doing, he established the sequence of stone to bronze to iron. Thomsen's "Three Age System" became extremely influential in European archaeology and the display of museum collections worldwide. One example of this was the Crystal Palace exhibition of 1851. The Great Exhibition of 1851, held in London in the summer of that year, brought together some 14,000 international exhibitors. It not only showed the latest technology, but archaeological and current artifacts from around the world. Both ancient and modern artifacts were displayed together in order of their presumed technical sophistication. More than six million people attended the exhibition and it had a profound influence on both the general public and scholars of the era. Tylor even had a close personal connection to the exhibition. His friend and mentor the Quaker ethnologist and archaeologist Henry Christi was a juror for the Crystal Palace.

The method of display developed by Thomsen and used in the Crystal Palace showed similarities between ancient European artifacts and current-day items from foraging and tribal societies. It seemed to demonstrate the argument Tylor makes in this passage, that societies could be placed in evolutionary sequence with "Little respect . . . for date in history or place on the map." This idea became a cornerstone of the comparative method in anthropology. Based on the archaeological and ethnographic information available to them, anthropologists of Tylor's day believed that a chronology of human social development could be created by comparing societies around the world. This doctrine drives both Tylor's argument in *Primitive Culture* and the model of cultural evolution L. H. Morgan presented in *Ancient Society* (see essay 3).

there shall be scarce a hand's breadth difference between an English ploughman and a negro of Central Africa. These pages will be so crowded with evidence of such correspondence among mankind, that there is no need to dwell upon its details here, but it may be used at once to override a problem which would complicate the argument, namely, the question of race. For the present purpose it appears both possible and desirable to eliminate considerations of hereditary varieties or races of man, and to treat mankind as homogeneous in nature, though placed in different grades of civilization.[9] The details of the enquiry will, I think, prove that stages of culture may be compared without taking into account how far tribes who use the same implement, follow the same custom, or believe the same myth may differ in their bodily configuration and the color of their skin and hair.

A first step in the study of civilization is to dissect it into details, and to classify these in their proper groups. Thus, in examining weapons, they are to be classed under spear, club, sling, bow and arrow, and so forth; among textile arts are to be ranged matting, netting, and several grades of making and weaving threads; myths are divided under such headings as myths of sunrise and sunset, eclipse-myths, earthquake-myths, local myths which account for the names of places by some fanciful tale, eponymic myths which account for the parentage of a tribe by turning its name into the name of an imaginary ancestor; under rites and ceremonies occur such practices as the various kinds of sacrifice to the ghosts of the dead and to other spiritual beings, the turn-

ing to the east to worship, the purification of ceremonial or moral uncleanness by means of water or fire. Such are a few miscellaneous examples from a list of hundreds, and the ethnographer's business is to classify such details with a view to making out their distribution in geography and history, and the relations which exist among them. What this task is like may be almost perfectly illustrated by comparing these details of culture with the species of plants and animals as studied by the naturalist. To the ethnographer, the bow and arrow is a species, the habit of flattening children's skulls is a species, the practice of reckoning numbers by tens is a species. The geographical distribution of these things, and their transmission from region to region, have to be studied as the naturalist studies the geography of his botanical and zoological species. Just as certain plants and animals are peculiar to certain districts, so it is with such instruments as the Australian boomerang, the Polynesian stick-and-groove for firemaking, the tiny bow and arrow used as a lancet or phleme by tribes about the Isthmus of Panama, and in like manner with many an art, myth, or custom found isolated in a particular field. Just as the catalogue of all the species of plants and animals of a district represents its Flora and Fauna, so the list of all the items of the general life of a people represents that whole which we call its culture. And just as distant regions so often produce vegetables and animals which are analogous, though by no means identical, so it is with the details of the civilization of their inhabitants.[10] How good a working analogy there really is between the

---

[9] Tylor here appears to reject racist explanations of cultural differences. Tylor's Quaker theology committed him to the notion of monogenesis—the belief that all human races belonged to the same species and shared the same evolutionary origins. He wrote: "the facts collected seem to favor the view that the wide differences in the civilization and mental state of the various races of mankind are rather differences of development than of origin, rather of degree than kind" (quoted in Stocking 1987:159). This notion was contested by the Americans Samuel G. Morton (1799–1851) and Louis Agassiz (1807–1873), key promoters of a theory called polygenesis. This theory argued that human races

represented different and unequal species and was used as a "scientific" justification for slavery. Although to modern readers some of Tylor's writing has a decidedly racist cast, he was a liberal by the standards of his day.

[10] Tylor, like Spencer, draws an analogy between cultural and biological evolution. In Tylor's view, the ethnographer's job is to catalog all the practices of humankind and then arrange them into evolutionary and hierarchical order, producing something analogous to the Linnaean classification of plants and animals. We will see this analogy again in other theories found in this book.

diffusion of plants and animals and the diffusion of civilization comes well into view when we notice how far the same causes have produced both at once. In district after district, the same causes which have introduced the cultivated plants and domesticated animals of civilization, have brought in with them a corresponding art and knowledge. The course of events which carried horses and wheat to America carried with them the use of the gun and the iron hatchet, while in return the old world received not only maize, potatoes, and turkeys, but the habit of smoking and the sailor's hammock.[11]

It is a matter worthy of consideration that the accounts of similar phenomena of culture, recurring in different parts of the world, actually supply incidental proof of their own authenticity.[12] Some years since, a question which brings out this point was put to me by a great historian, "How can a statement as to customs, myths, beliefs, &c., of a savage tribe be treated as evidence where it depends on the testimony of some traveller or missionary, who may be a superficial observer, more or less ignorant of the native language, a careless retailer of unsifted talk, a man prejudiced or even wilfully deceitful?" This question is, indeed, one which every ethnographer ought to keep clearly and constantly before his mind. Of course he is bound to use his best judgment as to the trustworthiness of all authors he quotes, and if possible to obtain several accounts to certify each point in each locality. But it is over and above these measures of precaution that the test of recurrence comes in. If two independent visitors to different countries, say a medieval Mohammedan in Tartary and a modern Englishman in Dahome, or a Jesuit missionary in Brazil

and a Wesleyan in the Fiji Islands, agree in describing some analogous art or rite or myth among the people they have visited, it becomes difficult or impossible to set down such correspondence to accident or willful fraud. A story by a bushranger in Australia may, perhaps, be objected to as a mistake or an invention, but did a Methodist minister in Guinea conspire with him to cheat the public by telling the same story there? The possibility of intentional or unintentional mystification is often barred by such a state of things as that a similar statement is made in two remote lands, by two witnesses, of whom A lived a century before B, and B appears never to have heard of A. How distant are the countries, how wide apart the dates, how different the creeds and characters of the observers, in the catalogue of facts of civilization, needs no farther showing to any one who will even glance at the foot-notes of the present work. And the more odd the statement, the less likely that several people in several places should have made it wrongly. This being so, it seems reasonable to judge that the statements are in the main truly given, and that their close and regular coincidence is due to the cropping up of similar facts in various districts of culture. Now the most important facts of ethnography are vouched for in this way. Experience leads the student after a while to expect and find that the phenomena of culture, as resulting from widely-acting similar causes, should recur again and again in the world. He even mistrusts isolated statements to which he knows of no parallel elsewhere, and waits for their genuineness to be shown by corresponding accounts from the other side of the earth, or the other end of history. So strong, indeed, is this means of authentication

---

[11] Unlike modern anthropologists, who tend to see field research as inseparable from the practice of anthropology, Tylor did not believe that it was necessary for anthropologists to be involved in data collection. It was their primary job to compile, organize, and classify data. Despite this view, Tylor did have some field experience. During a year he spent in North America in 1856, he traveled for four months by horseback in Mexico with his friend Christi. He published an account of this trip (*Anahuac: Or Mexico and the Mexicans, Ancient and Modern*) in 1861.

[12] The argument here is tautological. Above, Tylor maintains that the repeated occurrence of cultural traits in widely disparate locations is evidence of the psychic unity of mankind. Here he contends that he can verify or refute claims about the existence of cultural traits by reference to the theory of psychic unity. If a traveler asserted that he found traits different from others around the world, then his claims must be false. The use of this sort of reasoning was one factor that led Franz Boas and his followers to attack the work of Tylor and other evolutionists as unscientific.

that the ethnographer in his library may sometimes presume to decide, not only whether a particular explorer is a shrewd and honest observer, but also whether what he reports is conformable to the general rules of civilization. "Non quis, sed quid."[13]

To turn from the distribution of culture in different countries, to its diffusion within these countries. The quality of mankind which tends most to make the systematic study of civilization possible is that remarkable tacit consensus or agreement which so far induces whole populations to unite in the use of the same language, to follow the same religion and customary law, to settle down to the same general level of art and knowledge. It is this state of things which makes it so far possible to ignore exceptional facts and to describe nations by a sort of general average. It is this state of things which makes it so far possible to represent immense masses of details by a few typical facts, while, these once settled, new cases recorded by new observers simply fall into their places to prove the soundness of the classification. There is found to be such regularity in the composition of societies of men that we can drop individual differences out of sight, and thus can generalize on the arts and opinions of whole nations, just as, when looking down upon an army from a hill, we forget the individual soldier, whom, in fact, we can scarce distinguish in the mass, while we see each regiment as an organized body, spreading or concentrating, moving in advance or in retreat. In some branches of the study of social laws it is now possible to call in the aid of statistics, and to set apart special actions of large mixed communities of men by means of tax-gatherers' schedules, or the tables of the insurance-office. Among modern arguments on the laws of human action, none have had a

deeper effect than generalizations such as those of M. Quetelet,[14] on the regularity, not only of such matters as average stature and the annual rates of birth and death, but the recurrence, year after year, of such obscure and seemingly incalculable products of national life as the numbers of murders and suicides, and the proportion of the very weapons of crime. Other striking cases are the annual regularity of persons killed accidentally in the London streets, and of undirected letters dropped into post-office letterboxes. But in examining the culture of the lower races, far from having at command the measured arithmetical facts of modern statistics, we may have to judge of the condition of tribes from the imperfect accounts supplied by travellers or missionaries, or even to reason upon relics of prehistoric races of whose very names and languages we are hopelessly ignorant. Now these may seem at the first glance sadly indefinite and unpromising materials for a scientific enquiry. But in fact they are neither indefinite nor unpromising, but give evidence that is good and definite, so far as it goes. They are data which, for the distinct way in which they severally denote the condition of the tribe they belong to, will actually bear comparison with the statistician's returns. The fact is that a stone arrow-head, a carved club, an idol, a grave-mound where slaves and property have been buried for the use of the dead, an account of a sorcerer's rites in making rain, a table of numerals, the conjugation of a verb, are things which each express the state of a people as to one particular point of culture, as truly as the tabulated numbers of deaths by poison, and of chests of tea imported, express in a different way other partial results of the general life of a whole community.

That a whole nation should have a special dress, special tools and weapons, special laws of

---

[13] *Non quis, sed quid:* a Latin phrase meaning "not who, but what." It is not who made the report that is important, but rather what they reported.

[14] Adolphe J. Quetelet (1796–1874) was a mathematician who showed that the behavior of large groups of people could be predicted through the analysis of statistics. Quetelet called his theory "social physics," implying that he had created a science of society similar to physics. In Tylor's

time, statistics was a relatively recent and influential discovery. By providing a way to match numbers with social phenomena, statistics seemed to be a method by which natural laws determining human behavior could be ascertained. Here, Tylor tries to show that ethnographic data are comparable to demographic data and can be considered equally valid. This proposition, if accepted, would provide further evidence that a valid science of culture was possible.

marriage and property, special moral and religious doctrines is a remarkable fact, which we notice so little because we have lived all our lives in the midst of it. It is with such general qualities of organized bodies of men that ethnography has especially to deal. Yet, while generalizing on the culture of a tribe or nation, and setting aside the peculiarities of the individuals composing it as unimportant to the main result, we must be careful not to forget what makes up this main result. There are people so intent on the separate life of individuals that they cannot grasp a notion of the action of a community as a whole—such an observer, incapable of a wide view of society, is aptly described in the saying that he "cannot see the forest for the trees." But, on the other hand, the philosopher may be so intent upon his general laws of society as to neglect the individual actors of whom that society is made up, and of him it may be said that he cannot see the trees for the forest. We know how arts, customs, and ideas are shaped among ourselves by the combined actions of many individuals, of which actions both motive and effect often come quite distinctly within our view. The history of an invention, an opinion, a ceremony, is a history of suggestion and modification, encouragement and opposition, personal gain and party prejudice, and the individuals concerned act each according to his own motives, as determined by his character and circumstances. Thus sometimes we watch individuals acting for their own ends with little thought of their effect on society at large, and sometimes we have to study movements of national life as a whole, where the individuals cooperating in them are utterly beyond our observation. But seeing that collective social action is the mere resultant of many individual actions, it is clear that these two methods of enquiry, if rightly followed, must be absolutely consistent.

In studying both the recurrence of special habits or ideas in several districts and their prevalence within each district, there come before us ever reiterated proofs of regular causation producing the phenomena of human life, and of laws of maintenance and diffusion according to which these phenomena settle into permanent standard conditions of society, at definite stages of culture.[15] But, while giving full importance to the evidence bearing on these standard conditions of society, let us be careful to avoid a pitfall which may entrap the unwary student. Of course the opinions and habits belonging in common to masses of mankind are to a great extent the results of sound judgment and practical wisdom. But to a great extent it is not so. That many numerous societies of men should have believed in the influence of the evil eye and the existence of a firmament, should have sacrificed slaves and goods to the ghosts of the departed, should have handed down traditions of giants slaying monsters and men turning into beasts—all this is ground for holding that such ideas were indeed produced in men's minds by efficient causes, but it is not ground for holding that the rites in question are profitable, the beliefs sound, and the history authentic. This may seem at the first glance a truism, but, in fact, it is the denial of a fallacy which deeply affects the minds of all but a small critical minority of mankind. Popularly, what everybody says must be true, what everybody does must be right—"Quod ubique, quod semper, quod ab omnibus creditum est, hoc est vere proprieque Catholicum"—and so forth. There are various topics, especially in history, law, philosophy, and theology, where even the educated people we live among can hardly be brought to see that the cause why men do hold an opinion, or practice a custom, is by no means necessarily a reason why they ought to do so. Now collections of ethnographic evidence, bringing so prominently into view the agreement of immense multitudes of men as to certain traditions, beliefs, and usages, are peculiarly liable to

---

[15] Tylor's goal in *Primitive Culture* was to scientifically examine the development of religion and expose laws underlying its evolution. He aimed to show that the history of religion is characterized by increasing rationality. The path of his argument led him to explain the rational-ity of many "primitive" practices. Here he distinguishes between explaining such practices and defending them; it was important to him that his work was perceived as an explanation of religion rather than a defense of particular beliefs.

be thus improperly used in direct defence of these institutions themselves, even old barbaric nations being polled to maintain their opinions against what are called modern ideas. As it has more than once happened to myself to find my collections of traditions and beliefs thus set up to prove their own objective truth, without proper examination of the grounds on which they were actually received, I take this occasion of remarking that the same line of argument will serve equally well to demonstrate, by the strong and wide consent of nations, that the earth is flat, and nightmare the visit of a demon.

It being shown that the details of Culture are capable of being classified in a great number of ethnographic groups of arts, beliefs, customs, and the rest, the consideration comes next how far the facts arranged in these groups are produced by evolution from one another.[16] It need hardly be pointed out that the groups in question, though held together each by a common character, are by no means accurately defined. To take up again the natural history illustration, it may be said that they are species which tend to run widely into varieties. And when it comes to the question what relations some of these groups bear to others, it is plain that the student of the habits of mankind has a great advantage over the student of the species of plants and animals. Among naturalists it is an open question whether a theory of development from species to species is a record of transitions which actually took place or a mere ideal scheme serviceable in the classification of species whose origin was really independent. But among ethnographers there is no such question as to the possibility of species

of implements or habits or beliefs being developed one out of another, for development in culture is recognized by our most familiar knowledge. Mechanical invention supplies apt examples of the kind of development which affects civilization at large. In the history of fire-arms, the clumsy wheellock, in which a notched steel wheel was turned by a handle against the flint till a spark caught the priming, led to the invention of the more serviceable flintlock, of which a few still hang in the kitchens of our farm-houses, for the boys to shoot small birds with at Christmas; the flintlock in time passed by an obvious modification into the percussion-lock, which is just now changing its old-fashioned arrangement to be adapted from muzzle-loading to breechloading. The medieval astrolabe passed into the quadrant, now discarded in its turn by the seaman, who uses the more delicate sextant, and so it is through the history of one art and instrument after another. Such examples of progression are known to us as direct history, but so thoroughly is this notion of development at home in our minds, that by means of it we reconstruct lost history without scruple, trusting to general knowledge of the principles of human thought and action as a guide in putting the facts in their proper order. Whether chronicle speaks or is silent on the point, no one comparing a longbow and a cross-bow would doubt that the cross-bow was a development arising from the simpler instrument. So among the fire-drills for igniting by friction, it seems clear on the face of the matter that the drill worked by a cord or bow is a later improvement on the clumsier primitive instrument twirled between the hands. That instructive class

---

[16] Tylor was evolutionary and progressivist. He refers in the opening of this passage to the debate between biological evolutionists and creationists, still raging in 1871 when this piece was first published. For Tylor, the proposition that societies evolved from the most simple to most complex was self-evident. He wrote, "the educated world of Europe and America practically settles a standard by simply placing its own nations at one end of the social series and savage tribes at the other, arranging the rest of mankind between these limits according as they correspond more closely to savage or cultured life" (quoted in Stocking

1987:162). For Tylor, the force driving this evolution was the natural development of increasingly rational thinking. Although Tylor's thinking is evolutionary, he downplayed the importance of Darwinian evolution. In the preface to the 1873 edition of *Primitive Culture,* he explained the absence of references to Darwin and Spencer in the work by claiming that his work came "scarcely into contact of detail with the previous works of these eminent philosophers." However, the close connection between the work of Darwin and that of Tylor is shown by Darwin's extensive referencing of Tylor in *The Descent of Man* (1871).

of specimens which antiquaries sometimes discover, bronze celts modelled on the heavy type of the stone hatchet, are scarcely explicable except as first steps in the transition from the Stone Age to the Bronze Age, to be followed soon by the next stage of progress, in which it is discovered that the new material is suited to a handier and less wasteful pattern. And thus, in the other branches of our history, there will come again and again into view series of facts which may be consistently arranged as having followed one another in a particular order of development, but which will hardly bear being turned round and made to follow in reversed order.[17] Such for instance are the facts I have here brought forward in a chapter on the Art of Counting, which tend to prove that as to this point of culture at least, savage tribes reached their position by learning and not unlearning, by elevation from a lower rather than by degradation from a higher state.

Among evidence aiding us to trace the courses which the civilization of the world has actually followed, is that great class of facts to denote which I have found it convenient to introduce the term "survivals."[18] These are processes, customs, opinions, and so forth, which have been carried on by force of habit into a new state of society different from that in which they had their original home, and they thus remain as proofs and examples of an older condition of culture out of which a newer has been evolved. Thus, I know an old Somersetshire woman whose handloom dates from the time before the introduction of the "flying shuttle," which new-fangled appliance she has never even learnt to use, and I have seen her throw her shuttle from hand to hand in true classic fashion; this old woman is not a century behind her times, but she is a case of survival.[19] Such examples often lead us back to the habits of hundreds and even thousands of years ago. The ordeal of the Key and Bible, still in use, is a survival; the Midsummer bonfire is a survival; the Breton peasants' All Souls' supper for the spirits of the dead is a survival. The simple keeping up of ancient habits is only one part of the transition from old into new and changing times. The serious business of ancient society may be seen to sink into the sport of later generations, and its serious belief to linger on in nursery folk-lore, while superseded habits of old-world life may be modified into new-world forms still powerful for good and evil. Sometimes old thoughts and practices will burst out afresh, to the amazement of a world that thought them long since dead or dying; here survival passes into revival, as has lately happened in so remarkable a way in the history of modern spiritualism, a subject full of instruction from the ethnographer's point of view.[20] The study of the principles of survival has, indeed, no small practical importance, for most of what we call superstition is included within survival, and in this way lies open to the attack of its deadliest enemy, a reasonable explanation. Insignificant, moreover, as multitudes of the facts of survival are in themselves, their study is so effective for tracing the course of the historical development through which alone it is possible to understand their meaning, that it becomes a vital point of

---

[17] A popular theory in Tylor's time held that some peoples were primitive because they had degenerated from an earlier state. Tylor rejected this idea and discusses it further on in this essay.

[18] Although other thinkers such as Henry Sumner Maine (see footnote 26) also used the idea of survivals, it is considered one of Tylor's key contributions to anthropology. To him, almost any practice that seemed illogical or smacked of superstition was an example of the survival of the traits and beliefs of an earlier social form. Studying survivals was crucial, since through them—and with the theory of psychic unity—a researcher could trace the course of cultural evolution.

[19] Notice Tylor's frequent references to the customs of English peasantry in this passage. For Tylor and other evolutionists, European peasantry represented a crucial intermediate step between civilization and savagery.

[20] Tylor wrote in an era when the occult was becoming a popular middle-class pastime. He himself had seen and written on psychic phenomena. Although he did not believe in them, he did admit to being very impressed by the demonstrations he witnessed and unable to offer rational explanations of them (Stocking 1987:191).

ethnographic research to gain the clearest possible insight into their nature. This importance must justify the detail here devoted to an examination of survival, on the evidence of such games, popular sayings, customs, superstitions, and the like, as may serve well to bring into view the manner of its operation.

Progress, degradation, survival, revival, modification are all modes of the connexion that binds together the complex network of civilization.[21] It needs but a glance into the trivial details of our own daily life to set us thinking how far we are really its originators, and how far but the transmitters and modifiers of the results of long past ages. Looking round the rooms we live in, we may try here how far he who only knows his own time can be capable of rightly comprehending even that. Here is the "honeysuckle" of Assyria, there the fleur-de-lis of Anjou, a cornice with a Greek border runs round the ceiling, the style of Louis XIV and its parent the Renaissance share the looking-glass between them. Transformed, shifted, or mutilated, such elements of art still carry their history plainly stamped upon them; and if the history yet farther behind is less easy to read, we are not to say that because we cannot clearly discern it there is therefore no history there. It is thus even with the fashion of the clothes men wear. The ridiculous little tails of the German postilion's[22] coat show themselves how they came to dwindle to such absurd rudiments; but the English clergyman's bands no longer so convey their history to the eye, and look unaccountable enough till one has seen the intermediate stages through which they came down from

the more serviceable wide collars, such as Milton wears in his portrait, and which gave their name to the "band-box" they used to be kept in. In fact, the books of costume, showing how one garment grew or shrank by gradual stages and passed into another, illustrate with much force and clearness the nature of the change and growth, revival and decay, which go on from year to year in more important matters of life. In books, again, we see each writer not for and by himself, but occupying his proper place in history; we look through each philosopher, mathematician, chemist, poet, into the background of his education—through Leibnitz into Descartes, through Dalton into Priestley, through Milton into Homer. The study of language has, perhaps, done more than any other in removing from our view of human thought and action the ideas of chance and arbitrary invention, and in substituting for them a theory of development by the co-operation of individual men, through processes ever reasonable and intelligible where the facts are fully known.[23] Rudimentary as the science of culture still is, the symptoms are becoming very strong that even what seem its most spontaneous and motiveless phenomena will, nevertheless, be shown to come within the range of distinct cause and effect as certainly as the facts of mechanics. What would be popularly thought more indefinite and uncontrolled than the products of the imagination in myths and fables? Yet any systematic investigation of mythology, on the basis of a wide collection of evidence, will show plainly enough in such efforts of fancy at once a development from stage to stage, and a production of

---

[21] Here Tylor gives numerous examples of survivals. Tylor's great strength is his ability as a cultural historian; he was a master of the many details of cultural life. This passage also affirms his faith that laws of culture, similar in nature to the cause-and-effect principles of Newtonian physics, could be found. Virtually every paragraph of this essay stresses the ability of rational thinking men to divine cause-and-effect relationships.

[22] *Postilion:* a person who rides the horse on the left of the leading pair when four or more horses are used to draw a carriage, or simply the horse on the left when only one pair is used.

[23] Tylor had an early interest in linguistics and was particularly influenced by Friedrich Max Müller (1823–1900), who used the study of Sanskrit writings to discover the histories of Indo-European languages. Müller identified speakers of Indo-European languages as descendants of an ancient Aryan race. He is generally remembered as a humanist and, late in life, clearly opposed those who used the term *Aryan* as a racial category, but Stocking (1987:59) notes that "many of his more rhapsodic passages are . . . resonant of Aryanist racial ideology," and some of his work was later used in Nazi Germany to construct an intellectual pedigree for that regime's racist philosophy.

uniformity of result from uniformity of cause. Here, as elsewhere, causeless spontaneity is seen to recede farther and farther into shelter within the dark precincts of ignorance; like chance, that still holds its place among the vulgar as a real cause of events otherwise unaccountable, while to educated men it has long consciously meant nothing but this ignorance itself. It is only when men fail to see the line of connexion in events that they are prone to fall upon the notions of arbitrary impulses, causeless freaks, chance and nonsense, and indefinite unaccountability. If childish games, purposeless customs, absurd superstitions are set down as spontaneous because no one can say exactly how they came to be, the assertion may remind us of the like effect that the eccentric habits of the wild rice-plant had on the philosophy of a Red Indian tribe, otherwise disposed to see in the harmony of nature the effects of one controlling personal will. The Great Spirit, said these Sioux theologians, made all things except the wild rice; but the wild rice came by chance.

"Man," said Wilhelm von Humboldt,[24] "ever connects on from what lies at hand (der Mensch Knüpft immer an Vorhandenes an)." The notion of the continuity of civilization contained in this maxim is no barren philosophic principle, but is at once made practical by the consideration that they who wish to understand their own lives ought to know the stages through which their opinions and habits have become what they are. Auguste Comte[25] scarcely overstated the necessity of this study of development, when he declared at the beginning of his "Positive Philosophy" that "no conception can be understood except through its history" and his phrase will bear extension to culture at large. To expect to look modern life in the face and comprehend it by mere inspection is a philosophy whose weakness can easily be tested. Imagine any one explaining the trivial saying, "a little bird told me" without knowing of the old belief in the language of birds and beasts, to which Dr. Dasent, in the introduction to the Norse Tales, so reasonably traces its origin. To ingenious attempts at explaining by the light of reason things which want the light of history to show their meaning, much of the learned nonsense of the world has indeed been due. Sir H. S. Maine,[26] in his "Ancient Law," gives a perfect instance. In all the literature which enshrines the pretended philosophy of law, he remarks, there is nothing more curious than the pages of elaborate sophistry in which Blackstone attempts to explain and justify that extraordinary rule of English law, only recently repealed, which prohibited sons of the same father by different mothers from succeeding to one another's land. To Sir H. S. Maine, knowing the facts of the case, it was easy to explain its real origin from the "Customs of Normandy" where according to the system of agnation, or kinship on the male side, brothers by the same mother but by different fathers were of course no relations at all to one another. But when this rule "was transplanted to England, the English judges, who had no clue to its principle, interpreted it as a general prohibition against the succession of the half-blood, and extended it to consanguineous brothers, that is to sons of the same

---

[24] Wilhelm von Humboldt (1767–1835) was a German diplomat, a humanist, and the founder of the University of Berlin. Humboldt's enduring legacy was his work in language. His appreciation of linguistic differences foreshadowed the work of Edward Sapir (1884–1939) and Benjamin L. Whorf (1897–1941) in this century. In 1820 he wrote: "The differences between languages are not those of sounds and signs but those of differing world view" (1963:246).

[25] Auguste Comte (1798–1857) was one of the architects of the philosophical school of positivism. Comte and other positivists denied the possibility of metaphysical knowledge, asserting that social phenomena were subject to general laws that could be discovered using the scientific method. He proposed a science of society and is often considered a founder of sociology. Comte had a profound influence on the social scientists of Tylor's generation and was a particularly powerful influence on Émile Durkheim and his followers in the early years of this century.

[26] Sir Henry Sumner Maine (1822–1888) was a legal historian and cultural evolutionist whose *Ancient Law* (1863) informed many of the anthropological discussions of Tylor's day. This passage shows an example of Maine's use of survivals.

father by different wives." Then, ages after, Blackstone sought in this blunder the perfection of reason, and found it in the argument that kinship through both parents ought to prevail over even a nearer degree of kinship through but one parent.[a] Such are the risks that philosophers run in detaching any phenomenon of civilization from its hold on past events, and treating it as an isolated fact, to be simply disposed of by a guess at some plausible explanation.

In carrying on the great task of rational ethnography, the investigation of the causes which have produced the phenomena of culture, and the laws to which they are subordinate, it is desirable to work out as systematically as possible a scheme of evolution of this culture along its many lines.[27] In the following chapter [of *Primitive Culture*], on the Development of Culture, an attempt is made to sketch a theoretical course of civilization among mankind, such as appears on the whole most accordant with the evidence. By comparing the various stages of civilization among races known to history, with the aid of archaeological inference from the remains of prehistoric tribes, it seems possible to judge in a rough way of an early general condition of man, which from our point of view is to be regarded as a primitive condition, whatever yet earlier state may in reality have lain behind it. This hypothetical primitive condition corresponds in a considerable degree to that of modern savage tribes, who, in spite of their difference and distance, have in common certain elements of civilization, which seem remains of an early state of the human race at large. If this hypothesis be true, then, notwithstanding the continual interference of degeneration, the main tendency of culture from primeval up to modern times has been from savagery towards civilization.[28] On the problem of this relation of savage to civilized life, almost every one of the thousands of facts discussed in the succeeding chapters has its direct bearing. Survival in Culture, placing all along the course of advancing civilization way-marks full of meaning to those who can decipher their signs, even now sets up in our midst primeval monuments of barbaric thought and life. Its investigation tells strongly in favor of the view that the European may find among the Greenlanders or Maoris many a trait for reconstructing the picture of his own primitive ancestors. Next comes the problem of the Origin of Language. Obscure as many parts of this problem still remain, its clearer positions lie open to the investigation whether speech took its origin among mankind in the savage state, and the result of the enquiry is that, consistently with all known evidence, this may have been the case. From examination of the Art of Counting a far more definite consequence is shown. It may be confidently asserted that not only is this important art found in a rudimentary state among savage tribes, but that satisfactory evidence proves numeration to have been developed by a rational invention from this low stage up to that in which we ourselves possess it. The examination of Mythology contained in the first volume is for the most part made from a special point of view, on evidence collected for a special purpose, that of tracing the relation between the myths of savage tribes and their analogues among more civilized nations. The issue of such enquiry goes far to prove that the earliest myth-maker arose and flourished among savage hordes, setting on foot an art which his more cultured successors would carry on, till its results came to be fossilized in superstition, mistaken for history, shaped and draped in poetry, or cast aside as lying folly.

---

[27] These passages contain numerous examples of the use of the comparative method, which is held together, of course, by the belief in the psychic unity of humankind. If the presumption of psychic unity was incorrect, there would be no reason for societies to have followed the same stages of cultural evolution.

[28] Degenerationism was a popular idea of the eighteenth and early nineteenth centuries that is explained on page 5. Tylor felt that degeneration of particular societies was possible, but he held that the general path of human society was progress, not degeneration.

Nowhere, perhaps, are broad views of historical development more needed than in the study of religion.[29] Notwithstanding all that has been written to make the world acquainted with the lower theologies, the popular ideas of their place in history and their relation to the faiths of higher nations are still of the mediæval type. It is wonderful to contrast some missionary journals with Max Muller's Essays, and to set the unappreciating hatred and ridicule that is lavished by narrow hostile zeal on Brahmanism, Buddhism, Zoroastrism, beside the catholic sympathy with which deep and wide knowledge can survey those ancient and noble phases of man's religious consciousness; nor, because the religions of savage tribes may be rude and primitive compared with the great Asiatic systems, do they lie too low for interest and even for respect. The question really lies between understanding and misunderstanding them. Few who will give their minds to master the general principles of savage religion will ever again think it ridiculous, or the knowledge of it superfluous to the rest of mankind. Far from its beliefs and practices being a rubbish-heap of miscellaneous folly, they are consistent and logical in so high a degree as to begin, as soon as even roughly classified, to display the principles of their formation and development; and these principles prove to be essentially rational, though working in a mental condition of intense and inveterate ignorance. It is with a sense of attempting an investigation which bears very closely on the current theology of our own day, that I have set myself to examine systematically, among the lower races, the development of Animism; that is to say, the doctrine of souls and other spiritual beings in general. More than half of the present work is occupied with a mass of evidence from all regions of the world, displaying the nature and meaning of this great element of the Philosophy of Religion, and tracing its transmission, expansion, restriction, modification, along the course of history into the midst of our own modern thought. Nor are the questions of small practical moment which have to be raised in a similar attempt to trace the development of certain prominent Rites and Ceremonies—customs so full of instruction as to the inmost powers of religion, whose outward expression and practical result they are.

In these investigations, however, made rather from an ethnographic than a theological point of view, there has seemed little need of entering into direct controversial argument, which indeed I have taken pains to avoid as far as possible.[30] The connexion which runs through religion, from its rudest forms up to the status of an enlightened Christianity, may be conveniently treated of with little recourse to dogmatic theology. The rites of sacrifice and purification may be studied in their stages of development without entering into questions of their authority and value, nor does an examination of the successive phases of the world's belief in a future life demand a discussion of the arguments adduced for or against the

---

[29] This and the following paragraphs introduce much of the rest of *Primitive Culture,* which is devoted to an analysis of religion. Many of Tylor's contemporaries suggested that since primitive religion was illogical and irrational, it did not lend itself to scientific study. These included Lewis Henry Morgan, who, though he did write on Iroquois beliefs, considered all primitive religion "to some extent unintelligible" (see essay 3). Tylor, on the other hand, asserted that, properly understood, primitive religious beliefs had rational bases. He further insisted that the development of religion, like most everything else, followed progressive, evolutionary laws. In much of the book that follows, Tylor traced what he believed was the evolution of religion from animism (a term he coined) to "enlightened Christianity."

[30] Tylor is careful to distinguish his ethnographic work from a theological defense of or attack on particular beliefs. However, notice the passage here about his evidence taking its legitimate place. Tylor believed that rational, scientific knowledge had historically displaced religious belief. Although Tylor was certainly no atheist, he implies that many of the religious practices of his own day are survivals of early humans' misunderstanding of the world. Note the anticlerical undercurrents in these passages. Tylor obliquely implies that Christianity itself was a survival and would not survive rational examination.

doctrine itself. The ethnographic results may then be left as materials for professed theologians, and it will not perhaps be long before evidence so fraught with meaning shall take its legitimate place. To fall back once again on the analogy of natural history, the time may soon come when it will be thought as unreasonable for a scientific student of theology not to have a competent acquaintance with the principles of the religions of the lower races, as for a physiologist to look with the contempt of fifty years ago on evidence derived from the lower forms of life, deeming the structure of mere invertebrate creatures matter unworthy of his philosophic study.

Not merely as a matter of curious research, but as an important practical guide to the understanding of the present and the shaping of the future, the investigation into the origin and early development of civilization must be pushed on zealously. Every possible avenue of knowledge must be explored, every door tried to see if it is open. No kind of evidence need be left untouched on the score of remoteness or complexity, of minuteness or triviality. The tendency of modern enquiry is more and more toward the conclusion that if law is anywhere, it is everywhere. To despair of what a conscientious collection and study of facts may lead to, and to declare any problem insoluble because difficult and far off, is distinctly to be on the wrong side in science; and he who will choose a hopeless task may set himself to discover the limits of discovery. One remembers Comte starting in his account of astronomy with a remark on the necessary limitation of our knowledge of the stars: we conceive, he tells us, the possibility of determining their form, distance, size, and movement, whilst we should never by any method be able to study their chemical composition, their mineralogical structure, &c. Had the philosopher lived to see the application of spectrum analysis to this very problem his proclamation of the dispiriting doctrine of necessary ignorance would perhaps have been recanted in favor of a more hopeful view. And it seems to be with the philosophy of remote human life somewhat as with the study of the nature of the celestial bodies. The processes to be made out in the early stages of our mental evolution lie distant from us in time as the stars lie distant from us in space, but the laws of the universe are not limited with the direct observation of our senses. There is vast material to be used in our enquiry; many workers are now busied in bringing this material into shape, though little may have yet been done in proportion to what remains to do; and already it seems not too much to say that the vague outlines of a philosophy of primaeval history are beginning to come within our view.[31]

NOTE

[a]Blackstone, "Commentaries," "As every man's own blood is compounded of the bloods of his respective ancestors, he only is properly of the whole or entire blood with another, who hath (so far as the distance of degrees will permit), all the same ingredients in the composition of his blood that the other hath," etc.

---

[31] Tylor had an important influence on both his generation and future generations of anthropologists, but his attempt to establish anthropology as a university discipline was largely frustrated. Backed by wealthy and influential friends, he held university positions at Oxford from 1884 until his death and received a knighthood in 1912, but a permanent position in anthropology was not established at Oxford during his lifetime. Many American anthropologists, particularly Boas and his students, rejected Tylor's work. However, some, including Leslie White and his students, looked to Tylor for inspiration. Notice the similarity between this paragraph and the last paragraph of White's "Energy and the Evolution of Culture" (essay 18), written more than seventy years later.

3. *Ethnical Periods*

LEWIS HENRY MORGAN (1818–1881)

THE LATEST INVESTIGATIONS respecting the early condition of the human race are tending to the conclusion that mankind commenced their career at the bottom of the scale and worked their way up from savagery to civilization through the slow accumulations of experimental knowledge.[1]

As it is undeniable that portions of the human family have existed in a state of savagery, other portions in a state of barbarism, and still other portions in a state of civilization, it seems equally so that these three distinct conditions are connected with each other in a natural as well as necessary sequence of progress. Moreover, that this sequence has been historically true of the entire human family, up to the status attained by each branch respectively, is rendered probable by the conditions under which all progress occurs, and by the known advancement of several branches of the family through two or more of these conditions.

An attempt will be made in the following pages to bring forward additional evidence of the rudeness of the early condition of mankind, of the gradual evolution of their mental and moral powers through experience, and of their protracted struggle with opposing obstacles while winning their way to civilization. It will be drawn, in part, from the great sequence of inventions and discoveries which stretches along the entire pathway of human progress; but chiefly from domestic institutions, which express the growth of certain ideas and passions.[2]

As we re-ascend along the several lines of progress toward the primitive ages of mankind, and eliminate one after the other, in the order in which they appeared, inventions and discoveries on the one hand, and institutions on the other, we are enabled to perceive that the former stand to each other in progressive, and the latter in unfolding relations. While the former class have had a connection, more or less direct, the latter have been developed from a few primary germs of thought. Modern institutions plant their roots in the period of barbarism, into which their germs were transmitted from the previous period of savagery. They have had a lineal descent through the ages, with the streams of the blood, as well as a logical development.[3]

Two independent lines of investigations thus invite our attention. The one leads through inventions and discoveries, and the other through primary institutions. With the knowledge gained therefrom, we may hope to indicate the principal stages of human development. The proofs to be adduced will be drawn chiefly from domestic

---

From *Ancient Society* (1877)

---

[1] In this first paragraph, Morgan shows that he, like other nineteenth-century anthropologists, viewed cultural evolution as progressive. His statement that humans worked their way up "to civilization through the slow accumulations of experimental knowledge" sounds very much as though he had Charles Darwin's theory of evolution by natural selection on his mind when he wrote this chapter.

[2] A common belief among social scientists of Morgan's day was that cultural evolution referred not only to technological progress but also to moral development. Notice that Morgan speaks of "winning" civilization. The influence of Darwin's concept of evolution as a battle for survival is evident in Morgan's characterization of cultural evolution as a "protracted struggle."

[3] Morgan's comment on the lineal descent of institutions through the ages refers to two different aspects of his thought. Morgan was well acquainted with *The Geological Evidence for the Antiquity of Man* by Sir Charles Lyell (1797–1875) (Tooker 1992). Thus, he was versed in the latest geological evidence demonstrating that the earth and human beings were ancient far beyond biblical projections, and he was able to incorporate this time scale in his evolutionary theory. Second, Morgan's reference to "germs of thought" refers to his belief that there were universal ideas, which, like seeds, would germinate and blossom in the proper environment. Because Morgan, like Tylor, accepted this concept of the psychic unity of humankind, he believed that unilineal evolution was "natural and necessary."

institutions; the references to achievements more strictly intellectual being general as well as subordinate.[4]

The facts indicate the gradual formation and subsequent development of certain ideas, passions, and aspirations. Those which hold the most prominent positions may be generalized as growths of the particular ideas with which they severally stand connected. Apart from inventions and discoveries they are the following:

I. *Subsistence,*	V. *Religion,*
II. *Government,*	VI. *House Life and*
III. *Language,*	*Architecture,*
IV. *The Family,*	VII. *Property.*

First. Subsistence has been increased and perfected by a series of successive arts, introduced at long intervals of time, and connected more or less directly with inventions and discoveries.[5]

Second. The germ of government must be sought in the organization into gentes[6] in the Status of savagery; and followed down, through the advancing forms of this institution, to the establishment of political society.

Third. Human speech seems to have been developed from the rudest and simplest forms of expression. Gesture or sign language, as intimated by Lucretius,[a] must have preceded articulate language, as thought preceded speech. The monosyllabical preceded the syllabical, as the latter did that of concrete words. Human intelligence, unconscious of design, evolved articulate language by utilizing the vocal sounds. This great subject, a department of knowledge by itself, does not fall within the scope of the present investigation.[7]

Fourth. With respect to the family, the stages of its growth are embodied in systems of consanguinity and affinity, and in usages relating to marriage, by means of which, collectively, the family can be definitely traced through several successive forms.

Fifth. The growth of religious ideas is environed with such intrinsic difficulties that it may never receive a perfectly satisfactory exposition. Religion deals so largely with the imaginative and emotional nature, and consequently with such uncertain elements of knowledge, that all primitive religions are grotesque and to some extent

---

[4] Morgan was interested in the evolution of culture as a pan-human event but divides the evidence used in his analysis. He proposed to trace the development of "inventions and discoveries" but considered them subordinate to the development of "primary institutions," such as subsistence, government, language, and property, that were transmitted by germs of thought. Morgan believed that inventions and discoveries were correlated with stages of cultural evolution but developed by different processes. He wrote that inventions and discoveries had a direct, progressive relationship and were connected to developments in subsistence. However, the primary institutions have "unfolding relations." They were seeded as germs of thought in the period of Savagery, germinated in the period of Barbarism, and flowered in Civilization. Although Morgan lists seven of these institutions, the one on which he placed the greatest importance was subsistence. In Morgan's view, it was developments in subsistence that lay behind evolutionary progress.

[5] The keys to cultural evolution, according to Morgan, were techniques of food production, which distinguished humans from other animals. As a result, he devoted a chapter of *Ancient Society* to outlining the development of different types of subsistence and their role in cultural evolution. Morgan speculated that human beings first

subsisted by gathering wild vegetable foods, which meant that people were originally found in tropical climates. His conjecture is surprisingly accurate: modern paleontological research indicates that early human ancestors were foragers on the savannas of Africa. The primary place of subsistence in Morgan's work was adopted later by cultural ecological thinkers such as Julian Steward (essay 19), as well as many contemporary materialists.

[6] *Gentes:* Latin for a patrilineal clan.

[7] As indicated by his reference to the Roman poet and philosopher Lucretius (96?–55 B.C.E.), Morgan subscribed to the popular idea that evolution proceeded from simple to more complex forms. This idea is expressed here in the comment that gestural forms of communication are more primitive than speech. Morgan believed that forms of communication could be ranked and that primitive people spoke primitive languages. This notion survives today in ideas about the linguistic poverty of the poor or the inferiority of nonstandard forms of English. In fact, forms of communication such as American Sign Language are just as complex and expressive as spoken language. Edward Sapir, a student of Boas, attacked the idea of simple and complex languages when he developed the notion of linguistic relativism. For Boasians, all languages were equally evolved.

unintelligible. This subject also falls without the plan of this work excepting as it may prompt incidental suggestions.[8]

Sixth. House architecture, which connects itself with the form of the family and the plan of domestic life, affords a tolerably complete illustration of progress from savagery to civilization. Its growth can be traced from the hut of the savage, through the communal houses of the barbarians, to the house of the single family of civilized nations, with all the successive links by which one extreme is connected with the other. This subject will be noticed incidentally.

Lastly. The idea of property was slowly formed in the human mind, remaining nascent and feeble through immense periods of time. Springing into life in savagery, it required all the experience of this period of barbarism to develop the germ, and to prepare the human brain for the acceptance of its controlling influence. Its dominance as a passion over all other passions marks the commencement of civilization. It not only led mankind to overcome the obstacles which delayed civilization, but to establish political society on the basis of territory and of property. A critical knowledge of the evolution of the idea of property would embody, in some respects, the most remarkable portion of the mental history of mankind.[9]

It will be my object to present some evidence of human progress along these several lines, and through successive ethnical periods, as it is revealed by inventions and discoveries, and by the growth of the ideas of government, of the family, and of property.

It may be here premised that all forms of government are reducible to two general plans, using the word plan in its scientific sense. In their bases the two are fundamentally distinct. The first, in the order of time, is founded upon persons, and upon relations purely personal, and may be distinguished as a society (*societas*). The gens is the unit of this organization; giving as the successive stages of integration, in the archaic period, the gens, the phratry, the tribe, and the confederacy of tribes, which constituted a people or nation (*populus*).[10] At a later period a coalescence of tribes in the same area into a nation took the place of a confederacy of tribes occupying independent areas. Such, through prolonged ages, after the gens appeared, was the substantially universal organization of ancient society; and it remained among the Greeks and Romans after civilization supervened. The second is founded upon territory and upon property, and may be distinguished as a state (*civitas*). The township or ward, circumscribed by metes and bounds, with the property it contains, is the basis or unit of the latter, and political society is the result. Political society is organized upon territorial areas, and deals with property as well as

---

[8] The idea that religion was not fit for scientific study because it was "imaginative and emotional" was common among nineteenth-century anthropologists. However, it was specifically rejected by E. B. Tylor, who attempted to trace the evolutionary history of religion in his book *Primitive Culture* (see essay 2).

[9] Morgan's assertion that the concept of property led to the beginning of civilization as well as the establishment of political organizations may have had its origin in the work of John Locke, but it dovetails nicely with Marxist concerns. One can see why Karl Marx and Friedrich Engels were so interested in Morgan's work. Marx read and extensively annotated *Ancient Society* but died before he was able to publish anything about it. Thus, it was Engels who had the task of integrating Morgan into Marxist theory. Engels believed that, in *Ancient Society*, Morgan had developed a materialist conception of history. Further, Engels claimed that Morgan's comparisons of different societies had led him to the same conclusions as Marx

(Resek 1960:161). In 1884, Engels, working from Marx's annotations, published *The Origin of the Family, Private Property and the State,* which he subtitled *In the Light of the Researches of Lewis Henry Morgan*. There, he claimed Morgan had proven Marx's theory by demonstrating that private property and the state were only passing phases in the continuing evolution of human society. Although Engels believed *Ancient Society* confirmed the truth of Marxist analysis, Morgan was not a Marxist. His ideas of psychic unity and unilineal evolution are very different from Marx's notions that human nature is contingent and created through labor (see pages 57–58).

[10] *Gens* and *gentes* are synonymous terms for patrilineal clans. A *phratry* is a unilineal descent group composed of related clans. Morgan postulated that there were two basic forms of government: those based on kinship and those based on property. He believed that the modern state was founded upon notions of territory and property rather than kinship.

with persons through territorial relations. The successive stages of integration are the township or ward, which is the unit of organization; the county or province, which is an aggregation of townships or wards; and the national domain or territory, which is an aggregation of counties or provinces; the people of each of which are organized into a body politic. It taxed the Greeks and Romans to the extent of their capacities, after they had gained civilization, to invent the deme or township and the city ward; and thus inaugurate the second great plan of government, which remains among civilized nations to the present hour. In ancient society this territorial plan was unknown. When it came in it fixed the boundary line between ancient and modern society, as the distinction will be recognized in these pages.

It may be further observed that the domestic institutions of the barbarous, and even of the savage ancestors of mankind, are still exemplified in portions of the human family with such completeness that, with the exception of the strictly primitive period, the several stages of this progress are tolerably well preserved. They are seen in the organization of society upon the basis of sex, then upon the basis of kin, and finally upon the basis of territory;[11] through the successive forms of marriage and of the family, with the systems of consanguinity thereby created; through house life and architecture; and through progress in usages with respect to the ownership and inheritance of property.[12]

The theory of human degradation to explain the existence of savages and of barbarians is no longer tenable. It came in as a corollary from the Mosaic cosmogony, and was acquiesced in from a supposed necessity which no longer exists. As a theory, it is not only incapable of explaining the existence of savages, but it is without support in the facts of human experience.[13]

The remote ancestors of the Aryan nations presumptively passed through an experience similar to that of existing barbarous and savage tribes. Though the experience of these nations embodies all the information necessary to illustrate the periods of civilization, both ancient and modern, together with a part of that in the Later period of barbarism, their anterior experience must be deduced, in the main, from the traceable connection between the elements of their existing institutions and inventions, and similar elements still preserved in those of savage and barbarous tribes.[14]

---

[11] When Morgan mentions the preservation of earlier stages that can be seen in the organization of society on the basis of sex, then kin, he is referring to the work of Johann J. Bachofen. Bachofen (1815–1887) was a lawyer and a scholar in classical mythology. He and Morgan were intimately familiar with each other's work. Morgan's descriptions of the matrilineal Iroquois in his book *The League of the Iroquois* (1851) provided Bachofen with ethnographic data to support the theory he outlined in his major work *Das Mutterrecht,* or *Mother Right* (1861). In *Mother Right* (1861) Bachofen proposed that in its earliest state, society was organized and controlled by women. Only later did men assert themselves to form patriarchal, patrilineal societies. Following Bachofen's scheme, Morgan assumed that matrilineal societies such as the Iroquois were representative of an earlier stage of political evolution.

[12] Morgan considered primitive societies to be living fossils and assumed that they resembled earlier stages in the development of Western society. Because simple societies, such as foraging bands, are structured by kinship ties, Morgan assumed that similar structures characterized the earliest stages of political evolution in the "archaic" (pre-savagery) period.

[13] The "theory of degradation," or degenerationism, was based on the Old Testament book of Genesis (Morgan's "Mosaic cosmogony"). The theory is explained on page 5. A leading degenerationist, W. Cooke Taylor outlined this view in *Natural History of Society* (1840). He "insisted upon a literal sequence of fall, flood, Babel, and diaspora. Some groups thereafter degenerated in savagery, but others, aided by God, progressed towards new heights of civilization" (Harris 1968:58). The "supposed necessity" Morgan mentions here refers to the view that there had been a relatively brief period of time since creation. He is saying that Lyell's work in geology has discredited degenerationism, making a biblical explanation of civilization unnecessary.

[14] Although he does not make it explicit, Morgan is referring in this paragraph to E. B. Tylor's concept of survivals. For more on survivals, refer to essay 2.

It may be remarked finally that the experience of mankind has run in nearly uniform channels; that human necessities in similar conditions have been substantially the same; and that the operations of the mental principle have been uniform in virtue of the specific identity of the brain of all the races of mankind. This, however, is but a part of the explanation of uniformity in results. The germs of the principal institutions and arts of life were developed while man was still a savage. To a very great extent the experience of the subsequent periods of barbarism and of civilization have been expended in the further development of these original conceptions. Wherever a connection can be traced on different continents between a present institution and a common germ, the derivation of the people themselves from a common original stock is implied.[15]

The discussion of these several classes of facts will be facilitated by the establishment of a certain number of Ethnical Periods; each representing a distinct condition of society, and distinguishable by a mode of life peculiar to itself. The terms "Age of *Stone*," "of *Bronze*," and "of *Iron*," introduced by Danish archaeologists, have been extremely useful for certain purposes, and will remain so for the classification of objects of ancient art; but the progress of knowledge has rendered other and different subdivisions necessary. Stone implements were not entirely laid aside with the introduction of tools of iron, nor of those of bronze. The invention of the process of smelting iron ore created an ethnical epoch, yet we could scarcely date another from the production of bronze. Moreover, since the period of stone implements overlaps those of bronze and of iron, and since that of bronze also overlaps that of iron, they are not capable of a circumscription that would leave each independent and distinct.[16]

It is probable that the successive arts of subsistence which arose at long intervals will ultimately, from the great influence they must have exercised upon the condition of mankind, afford the most satisfactory bases for these divisions. But investigation has not been carried far enough in this direction to yield the necessary information. With our present knowledge the main result can be attained by selecting such other inventions or discoveries as will afford sufficient tests of progress to characterize the commencement of successive ethnical periods. Even though accepted as provisional, these periods will be found convenient and useful. Each of those about to be proposed will be found to cover a distinct culture, and to represent a particular mode of life.[17]

---

[15] The "uniform mental principle" Morgan mentions here reflects his belief in the psychic unity of humankind. Like Tylor before him, Morgan argued that unilineal evolution occurred because human thinking follows a universal course of development. But as the second half of this paragraph shows, Morgan was aware that cross-cultural similarities may imply that people share a common origin or that ideas can spread through diffusion. The concept of diffusion was popularized, at the turn of this century, by the German anthropogeographer Friedrich Ratzel (1844–1904) and his student Leo Froebenius (1873–1938). It was carried to an extreme in the first decades of the twentieth century by such radical diffusionists as the Englishmen Grafton Elliot Smith (1871–1937) and W. J. Perry (1887–1949), who proposed that all world culture had begun in Egypt and diffused from that source (Smith 1928). Additionally, when Morgan wrote that "human necessities in similar conditions have been substantially the same," he anticipated the concept of cultural types outlined in Julian Steward's theory of multilinear evolution sixty years later (see essay 19).

[16] The terms *Stone Age, Bronze Age,* and *Iron Age* were introduced by the first curator of the Danish National Museum, Christian J. Thomesen, in order to chronologically rank European artifacts in an 1807 exhibit. This "three-age system," as it came to be known, was soon widely used throughout Europe (Fagan 1989:34).

[17] Morgan's goal was to outline the stages of cultural evolution. He proposed that the transition between stages could be marked by the acquisition of certain kin patterns and modes of subsistence and the development of certain technological innovations. Half a century later, this insight would be essential in the work of the neoevolutionists Leslie White and Julian Steward, who examined cultural evolution in relation to subsistence and technology (essays 18 and 19). In the next several paragraphs Morgan outlines his design for separating one stage of cultural evolution from another.

The period of savagery, of the early part of which very little is known, may be divided, provisionally, into three subperiods. These may be named respectively the *Older,* the *Middle,* and the *Later* period of savagery; and the condition of society in each, respectively, may be distinguished as the *Lower,* the *Middle,* and the *Upper Status* of savagery.

In like manner, the period of barbarism divides naturally into three sub-periods, which will be called, respectively, the *Older,* the *Middle,* and the *Later* period of barbarism; and the condition of society in each, respectively, will be distinguished as the *Lower,* the *Middle,* and the *Upper Status* of barbarism.

It is difficult, if not impossible, to find such tests of progress to mark the commencement of these several periods as will be found absolute in their application, and without exceptions upon all the continents. Neither is it necessary, for the purpose in hand, that exceptions should not exist. It will be sufficient if the principal tribes of mankind can be classified, according to the degree of their relative progress, into conditions which can be recognized as distinct.

I. LOWER STATUS OF SAVAGERY[18]

This period commenced with the infancy of the human race, and may be said to have ended with the acquisition of a fish subsistence and of a knowledge of the use of fire. Mankind were then living in their original restricted habitat, and subsisting upon fruits and nuts. The commencement of articulate speech belongs to this period. No exemplification of tribes of mankind in this condition remained to the historical period.

II. MIDDLE STATUS OF SAVAGERY

It commenced with the acquisition of a fish subsistence and a knowledge of the use of fire, and ended with the invention of the bow and arrow. Mankind, while in this condition, spread from their original habitat over the greater portion of the earth's surface. Among tribes still existing it will leave in the Middle Status of savagery, for example, the Australians and the greater part of the Polynesians when discovered. It will be sufficient to give one or more exemplifications of each status.

III. UPPER STATUS OF SAVAGERY

It commenced with the invention of the bow and arrow, and ended with the invention of the art of pottery. It leaves in the Upper Status of Savagery the Athapascan tribes of the Hudson's Bay Territory, the tribes of the valley of the Columbia, and certain coast tribes of North and South America; but with relation to the time of their discovery. This closes the period of Savagery.

IV. LOWER STATUS OF BARBARISM

The invention or practice of the art of pottery, all things considered, is probably the most effective and conclusive test that can be selected to fix a boundary line, necessarily arbitrary, between savagery and barbarism. The distinctness of the two conditions has long been recognized, but no criterion of progress out of the former into the latter has hitherto been brought forward. All such tribes, then, as never attained to the art of pottery will be classed as savages, and those possessing this art but who never attained a phonetic alphabet and the use of writing will be classed as barbarians.

---

[18] Here Morgan begins to outline the factors upon which he distinguishes the stages of cultural evolution. Much of the criticism of his theory was based on the fact that Morgan's system created illogical groupings, lumping together societies that we now consider to have vastly different levels of social organization. This critique was first pointed out by Franz Boas in the early part of this century (see footnote 21).

The first sub-period of barbarism commenced with the manufacture of pottery, whether by original invention or adoption. In finding its termination, and the commencement of the Middle Status, a difficulty is encountered in the unequal endowments of the two hemispheres, which began to be influential upon human affairs after the period of savagery had passed. It may be met, however, by the adoption of equivalents. In the Eastern hemisphere, the domestication of animals, and the Western, the cultivation of maize and plants by irrigation, together with the use of adobe-brick and stone in house building have been selected as sufficient evidence of progress to work a transition out of the Lower and into the Middle Status of barbarism. It leaves, for example, in the Lower Status, the Indian tribes of the United States east of the Missouri River, and such tribes of Europe and Asia as practiced the art of pottery, but were without domestic animals.

V. MIDDLE STATUS OF BARBARISM

It commenced with the domestication of animals in the Eastern hemisphere, and in the Western with cultivation by irrigation and with the use of abode-brick and stone in architecture, as shown. Its termination may be fixed with the invention of the process of smelting iron ore. This places in the Middle Status, for example, the Village Indians of New Mexico, Mexico, Central America and Peru, and such tribes in the Eastern hemisphere as possessed domestic animals but were without a knowledge of iron. The ancient Britons, although familiar with the use of iron, fairly belong in this connection. The vicinity of more advanced continental tribes had advanced the arts of life among them far beyond the state of development of their domestic institutions.[19]

VI. UPPER STATUS OF BARBARISM

It commenced with the manufacture of iron, and ended with the invention of a phonetic alphabet, and the use of writing in literary composition. Here civilization begins. This leaves in the Upper Status, for example, the Grecian tribes of the Homeric age, the Italian tribes shortly before the founding of Rome, and the Germanic tribes of the time of Caesar.

VII. STATUS OF CIVILIZATION

It commenced, as stated, with the use of a phonetic alphabet and the production of literary records, and divides into *Ancient* and *Modern*. As an equivalent, hieroglyphical writing upon stone may be admitted.

RECAPITULATION

Periods.	*Conditions.*
I. *Older Period of Savagery,*	I. *Lower Status of Savagery,*
II. *Middle Period of Savagery,*	II. *Middle Status of Savagery,*
III. *Later Period of Savagery,*	III. *Upper Status of Savagery,*
IV. *Older Period of Barbarism,*	IV. *Lower Status of Barbarism,*
V. *Middle Period of Barbarism,*	V. *Middle Status of Barbarism,*
VI. *Later Period of Barbarism,*	VI. *Upper Status of Barbarism,*

---

[19] A society's evolutionary stage was gauged by its technology, subsistence pattern, and kin and family structure together. Consequently, although groups such as the ancient Britons had acquired technological achievements of more advanced societies, such as the use of iron (diagnostic of Upper Barbarism), Morgan believes that the development of their domestic institutions places them squarely in the stage of Middle Barbarism.

VII. *Status of Civilization.*

I. *Lower Status of Savagery,*	*From the Infancy of the Human Race to the commencement of the next Period.*
II. *Middle Status of Savagery,*	*From the acquisition of a fish subsistence and a knowledge of the use of fire, to etc.*
III. *Upper Status of Savagery,*	*From the Invention of the Bow and Arrow, to etc.*
IV. *Lower Status of Barbarism,*	*From the Invention of the Art of Pottery, to etc.*
V. *Middle Status of Barbarism,*	*From the Domestication of animals on the Eastern hemisphere, and in the Western from the cultivation of maize and plants by Irrigation, with the use of adobe-brick and stone, to etc.*
VI. *Upper Status of Barbarism,*	*From the Invention of the process of Smelting Iron Ore, with the use of iron tools, to etc.*
VII. *Status of Civilization,*	*From the Invention of a Phonetic Alphabet, with the use of writing, to the present time.*

Each of these periods has a distinct culture and exhibits a mode of life more or less special and peculiar to itself. This specialization of ethnical periods renders it possible to treat a particular society according to its condition of relative advancement, and to make it a subject of independent study and discussion. It does not affect the main result that different tribes and nations on the same continent, and even of the same linguistic family, are in different conditions at the same time, since for our purpose the *condition* of each is the material fact, the *time* being immaterial.

Since the use of pottery is less significant than that of domestic animals, of iron, or of a phonetic alphabet, employed to mark the commencement of subsequent ethnical periods, the reasons for its adoption should be stated. The manufacture of pottery presupposes village life, and considerable progress in the simple arts.[b] Flint and stone implements are older than pottery, remains of the former having been found in ancient repositories in numerous instances unaccompanied by the latter. A succession of inventions of greater need and adapted to a lower condition must have occurred before the want of pottery would be felt. The commencement of village life, with some degree of control over subsistence, wooden vessels and utensils, finger weaving with filaments of bark, basket making, and the bow and arrow make their appearance before the art of pottery. The Village Indians who were in the Middle Status of barbarism, such as the Zuñians, the Aztecs and the Cholulans, manufactured pottery in large quantities and in many forms of considerable excellence; the partially Village Indians of the United States, who were in the Lower Status of barbarism, such as the Iroquois, the Choctas, and the Cherokees, made it in smaller quantities and in a limited number of forms; but the non-horticultural Indians, who were in the Status of savagery, such as the Athapascans, the tribes of California and of the valley of the Columbia, were ignorant of its use.[c] In Lubbock's *Pre-Historic Times,* in Tylor's *Early History of Mankind,* and in Peschel's *Races of Man,* the particulars respecting this art, and the extent of its distribution, have been collected with remarkable breadth of research. It was unknown in Polynesia (with the exception of the Islands of the Tongans and Fijians), in Australia, in California, and in the Hudson's Bay Territory. Mr. Tylor remarks that "the art of weaving was unknown in most of the Islands away from Asia," and that "in most of the South Sea Islands there was no knowledge of pottery."[d] The Rev. Lorimer Fison, an English missionary residing in Australia, informed the author in answer to inquiries, that "the Australians had no woven fabrics, no pottery, and were ignorant of the bow and arrow."[20] This last fact was also true in general of the Polynesians.[21] The introduction of the ceramic art produced a new epoch in human progress in the direction of an improved living and increased domestic conveniences. While flint and stone implements—which came in earlier and required long periods of time to develop all their uses—gave the canoe, wooden vessels and utensils, and ultimately timber and plank in house architecture,[e] pottery gave a durable vessel for boiling food, which before that had been rudely accomplished in baskets coated with clay, and in ground cavities lined with skin, the boiling being effected with heated stones.[f]

Whether the pottery of the aborigines was hardened by fire or cured by the simple process of drying, has been made a question. Prof E. T. Cox, of Indianapolis, has shown by comparing the analyses of ancient pottery and hydraulic cements, "that so far as chemical constituents are concerned it (the pottery) agrees very well with the composition of hydraulic stones." He remarks further, that "all the pottery belonging to the mound-builders' age, which I have seen, is composed of alluvial clay and sand, or a mixture of the former with pulverized freshwater shells. A paste made of such a mixture possesses in a high degree the properties of hydraulic Puzzuolani and Portland cement, so that vessels formed of it

hardened without being burned, as is customary with modern pottery. The fragments of shells served the purpose of gravel or fragments of stone as at present used in connection with hydraulic lime for the manufacture of artificial stone."[g] The composition of Indian pottery in analogy with that of hydraulic cement suggests the difficulties in the way of inventing the art, and tends also to explain the lateness of its introduction in the course of human experience. Notwithstanding the ingenious suggestion of Prof. Cox, it is probable that pottery was hardened by artificial heat. In some cases the fact is directly attested. Thus Adair, speaking of the Gulf Tribes, remarks that "they make earthen pots of very different sizes, so as to contain from two to ten gallons, large pitchers to carry water, bowls, dishes, platters, basins, and a prodigious number of other vessels of such antiquated forms as would be tedious to describe, and impossible to name. Their method of glazing them is, they place them over a large fire of smoky pitch-pine, which makes them smooth, black and firm."[h]

Another advantage of fixing definite ethnical periods is the direction of special investigation to those tribes and nations which afford the best exemplification of each status, with the view of making each both standard and illustrative. Some tribes and families have been left in geographical isolation to work out the problems of

---

[20] Morgan cites Lubbock and Fison, whose work was an important influence on his own. John Lubbock (1834–1913), also known as Lord Avebury, was an amateur ethnologist and natural historian. A prosperous banker and liberal member of Parliament, Lubbock also served as president of the Royal Anthropological Institute and Ethnological Society of London. His boyhood home was near that of Darwin, and Lubbock became close friends with Darwin and a staunch defender of the *Origin of Species*. Lubbock developed an evolutionary theory of human society based on his study of European and North American archaeology. He proposed a natural progression of social evolution from the primitive to the civilized, and he coined the terms *paleolithic* and *neolithic*. He published his ideas in *Prehistoric Times* (1865) and *The Origin of Civilization* (1870).

Lorimer Fison (1832–1907) was a missionary, journalist, and anthropologist. Morgan's studies of kinship were based on extensive questionnaires sent to European travel-

ers and missionaries throughout the world. While in Fiji in 1869, Fison received one of these questionnaires. It drew his interest to anthropology and he became an ardent follower of Morgan, with whom he corresponded extensively. Fison's research into Australian aboriginal kinship systems, based on interviews with European settlers, provided important data for E. B. Tylor, J. G. Frazer, and Émile Durkheim as well as Morgan.

[21] Morgan's critics cited his placement of the Polynesians in Middle Savagery together with Australian Aborigines as an example of an illogical grouping created by his theory. Aboriginal society was organized by family-based foraging bands. Polynesian society, though without pottery or the technological innovations Morgan mentions here, was composed of highly stratified chiefdoms and was far more complex.

progress by original mental effort; and have, consequently, retained their arts and institutions pure and homogeneous; while those of other tribes and nations have been adulterated through external influence. Thus, while Africa was and is an ethnical chaos of savagery and barbarism, Australia and Polynesia were in savagery, pure and simple, with the arts and institutions belonging to that condition.[22] In like manner, the Indian family of America, unlike any other existing family, exemplified the condition of mankind in three successive ethnical periods. In the undisturbed possession of a great continent, of common descent, and with homogeneous institutions, they illustrated, when discovered, each of these conditions, and especially those of the Lower and of the Middle Status of barbarism, more elaborately and completely than any other portion of mankind. The far northern Indians and some of the coast tribes of North and South America were in the Upper Status of savagery, the partially Village Indians east of the Mississippi were in the Lower Status of barbarism, and the Village Indians of North and South America were in the Middle Status. Such an opportunity to recover full and minute information of the course of human experience and progress in developing their arts and institutions through these successive conditions has not been offered within the historical period. It must be added that it has been indifferently improved. Our greatest deficiencies relate to the last period named.[23]

Differences in the culture of the same period in the Eastern and Western hemispheres undoubtedly existed in consequence of the unequal endowments of the continents; but the condition of society in the corresponding status must have been, in the main, substantially similar.

The ancestors of the Grecian, Roman, and German tribes passed through the stages we have indicated, in the midst of the last of which the light of history fell upon them. Their differentiation from the undistinguishable mass of barbarians did not occur, probably, earlier than the commencement of the Middle Period of barbarism. The experience of these tribes has been lost, with the exception of so much as is represented by the institutions, inventions and discoveries which they had brought with them, and possessed when they first came under historical observation. The Grecian and Latin tribes of the Homeric and Romulian periods afford the highest exemplification of the Upper Status of barbarism.[24] Their institutions were likewise pure and homogeneous, and their experience stands directly connected with the final achievement of civilization.

Commencing, then, with the Australians and Polynesians, following with the American Indian tribes, and concluding with the Roman and Grecian who afford the highest exemplifications respectively of the six great stages of human progress, the sum of their united experiences may be supposed fairly to represent that of the human family from the Middle Status of savagery to the end of ancient civilization. Consequently, the Aryan nations will find the type of the condition of their remote ancestors, when in savagery, in that of the Australians and Polynesians; when in the Lower Status of barbarism in that of the partially Village Indians of America; and when in the Middle Status in that of the Village Indians, with which their own experience in

---

[22] Morgan believed that diffusion confused the evolutionary process. Although he believed all groups evolved along the same path, he did not claim all people were equal. Morgan contended that different races evolved at different speeds. Thus, he talks about "ethnical chaos" because, in his view, diffusion meant that some groups were exposed to other cultures that were far beyond the simpler group's evolutionary development or capabilities.

[23] Morgan had a lifelong interest in Native American culture. He studied the linguistics and kinship systems of Native Americans and as a lawyer was active in the defense of Native American land rights. The recording of Native American culture concerned Morgan, who raises the issue in this paragraph. The fear that these cultures were disappearing motivated Franz Boas and his students to work in Native American societies in the early years of the twentieth century.

[24] The Homeric and Romulian periods refers to the times of Homer, the Greek poet of the eighth century B.C.E., and Romulus, mythological founder of Rome in 753 B.C.E.

the Upper Status directly connects. So essentially identical are the arts, institutions and mode of life in the same status upon all the continents, that the archaic form of the principal domestic institutions of the Greeks and Romans must even now be sought in the corresponding institution of the American aborigines, as will be shown in the course of this volume. This fact forms a part of the accumulating evidence tending to show that the principal institutions of mankind have been developed from a few primary germs of thought; and that the course and manner of their development was predetermined, as well as restricted within narrow limits

of divergence, by the natural logic of the human mind and the necessary limitations of its powers.[25] Progress has been found to be substantially the same in kind in tribes and nations inhabiting different and even disconnected continents, while in the same status, with deviations from uniformity in particular instances produced by special causes. The argument when extended tends to establish the unity of origin of mankind.[26]

In studying the condition of tribes and nations in these several ethnical periods we are dealing, substantially, with the ancient history and condition of our own remote ancestors.

---

[25] One consequence of Morgan's belief that human thought was restricted along certain paths is his contention that all humans had the potential to be equal, even though this equality had not been achieved by all groups. This may explain Morgan's interest in the Iroquois and his relatively enlightened attitude toward Native Americans. Do not mistake this attitude for a belief in racial equality, however. Morgan, like most social scientists of his day, believed Caucasians were superior to other ethnic groups. Despite his respect for Native Americans, he did not consider them equal to people of northern European descent (those he calls "Aryans"). You will note that he consistently identifies the Greek, Roman, and Aryan peoples as evolving first and fastest, consigning the great African and Mesoamerican civilizations to earlier stages in his evolutionary scheme. This notion of Aryan superiority was popularized and given a "scientific" veneer by the German biologist Ernst Heinrich Haekel, most famous for his statement of recapitulation theory, which found political expression during Adolph Hitler's rise to power in Nazi Germany. Applying the theory to ethnic groups, Haekel argued that the "lower races" were like Caucasians during infancy. This idea is also reflected in Freud and his followers' views of people in primitive societies.

In another section of *Ancient Society* Morgan speaks of the inferior brain size of Native Americans and the "preeminent endowment" of the Aryan and Semitic families. This statement is racist, but Morgan was reflecting the scientific opinion of his time, which held that brain size was related to intelligence. Morgan must have been aware of the work of Dr. Samuel G. Morton, who measured the interior capacity of skull samples from different ethnic groups. In his most famous works—*Crania Americana* (1839) and *Crania Aegyptica* (1844)—Morton claimed that whites had bigger brains than any other group, from

which he concluded that they were intellectually and morally superior to those other groups. Morton's data (although not his conclusions) stood unquestioned until 1981 when Harvard biologist Stephen Jay Gould published an analysis of that data. Gould discovered that Morton had committed gross errors in sampling when he chose his selection of skulls for measurement and had incorrectly analyzed his own data. When the sampling errors were corrected and the data reanalyzed, Gould found no significant differences between the skull volumes of different ethnic groups in Morton's collection.

[26] Here Morgan outlines his grand vision of cultural evolution; Australians and Polynesians in savagery, various Native American groups in different stages of barbarism depending on their types of subsistence, and the Greeks and Romans as the first examples of civilization. He supported his theory through the use of the nineteenth-century doctrine of the comparative method and psychic unity. The comparative method proposed that contemporary primitive societies were like living fossils; for example, see Morgan's assertion that the principal institutions of the Greeks and Romans can be seen in archaic form in Native American societies. A clear expression of psychic unity is also found in this paragraph. Morgan states that human development is predetermined by the "natural logic of the human mind," which was based on universal "germs of thought." This doctrine of psychic unity justified the uncritical use of the comparative method, which formed the basis for the belief in unilineal theories of cultural evolution. The logic used in this argument is thus circular: Why are there universals of cultural evolution? Because of the psychic unity of humankind. How do we know psychic unity is a valid concept? Because we see common patterns of cultural development.

NOTES

[a] Et pueros commendarunt mulierbreque saeclum
Vocibus, et gestu, cum balbe significarent,
Imbecillorum esse aequm miserier omnium.
                    —*De Rerum Natura*, lib. v, 1020.

[b] Mr. Edwin B. Tylor observes that Goquet "first propounded, in the last century, the notion that the way in
which pottery came to be made, was that people daubed
such combustible vessels as these with clay to protect
them from fire, till they found that clay alone would answer the purpose, and thus the art of pottery came into
the world."—*Early History of Mankind*, p. 237. Goquet
relates of Capt. Gonneville who visited the southeast
coast of South America in 1503, that he found "their
household utensils of wood, even their boiling pots, but
plastered with a kind of clay, a good finger thick, which
prevented the fire from burning them."—Ib. 273.

[c] Pottery has been found in aboriginal mounds in Oregon within a few years past.—Foster's *Pre-Historic
Races of the United States*, I, 152. The first vessels of
pottery among the Aborigines of the United States
seem to have been made in baskets of rushes or
willows used as moulds which were burned off after
the vessel hardened.—Jones's *Antiquities of Southern
Indians*, p. 461. Prof. Rau's article on *Pottery*. Smithsonian Report, 1866, p. 352.

[d] *Early History of Mankind*, p. 181; *Pre-Historic Times*,
pp. 437, 441, 462, 477, 533, 542.

[e] Lewis and Clarke (1805) found plank in use in
houses among the tribes of the Columbia River.—
Travels, Longman's Ed., 1814, p. 503. Mr. John Keast
Lord found "cedar plank chipped from the solid tree
with chisels and hatchets made of stone," in Indian
houses on Vancouver's Island.—*Naturalist in British
Columbia*, I, 169.

[f] Tylor's *Early History of Mankind*, p. 265, *et seq.*

[g] *Geological Survey of Indiana*, 1873, p. 119. He gives
the following analysis:

Ancient Pottery, "Bone Bank," Posey Co., Indiana.

Moisture at 212°F.,	1.00	Alumina,	5.00
		Peroxide of iron,	5.50
Silica,	36.00	Sulphuric acid,	.20
Carbonate of lime,	25.50	Organic matter (alkalies and loess),	23.60
Carbonate of magnesia,	3.02		100.00

[h] *History of the American Indians*, Lond. ed., 1775,
p. 424. The Iroquois affirm that in ancient times their
forefathers cured their pottery before a fire.

---

4. Feuerbach: Opposition of the Materialist and Idealist Outlook

KARL MARX (1818–1883) AND FRIEDRICH ENGELS (1820–1895)

THE ILLUSIONS OF GERMAN IDEOLOGY

As we hear from German ideologists, Germany
has in the last few years gone through an unparal-
leled revolution.[1] The decomposition of the

Hegelian philosophy, which began with Strauss,
has developed into a universal ferment into which
all the "powers of the past" are swept. In the general chaos mighty empires have arisen only to
meet with immediate doom, heroes have emerged
momentarily only to be hurled back into obscurity

From *The German Ideology* (1845–1846)

---

[1] Marx and Engels, living in exile in Belgium, collaborated
on *The German Ideology* in 1845 and 1846. They sent the
manuscript to Germany for publication, but political crises
prevented it from appearing. Marx later remarked that it had
been abandoned to "the gnawing criticism of the mice." At
the time *The German Ideology* was written, Marx and Engels
were developing a thoroughly materialist worldview, which
separated them from other German philosophers. This work

is the first relatively complete statement of this worldview,
although the materialist position it presents is foreshadowed
in works like "On the Jewish Question" (1963, orig. 1844)
and "The Holy Family" (1975, orig. 1845). The complete
version of *The German Ideology* was not available until
the 1930s. Thus, while European and American theorists of
the early twentieth century were profoundly affected by
Marx, they did not have this particular work.

by bolder and stronger rivals. It was a revolution beside which the French Revolution was child's play, a world struggle beside which the struggles of the Diadochi [successors of Alexander the Great] appear insignificant. Principles ousted one another, heroes of the mind overthrew each other with unheard-of rapidity, and in the three years 1842–45 more of the past was swept away in Germany than at other times in three centuries.

All this is supposed to have taken place in the realm of pure thought.

Certainly it is an interesting event we are dealing with: the putrescence of the absolute spirit. When the last spark of its life had failed, the various components of this *caput mortuum*[2] began to decompose, entered into new combinations and formed new substances. The industrialists of philosophy, who till then had lived on the exploitation of the absolute spirit, now seized upon the new combinations. Each with all possible zeal set about retailing his apportioned share. This naturally gave rise to competition, which, to start with, was carried on in moderately staid bourgeois fashion. Later when the German market was glutted, and the commodity in spite of all efforts found no response in the world market, the business was spoiled in the usual German manner by fabricated and fictitious production, deterioration in quality, adulteration of the raw materials, falsification of labels, fictitious purchases, bill-jobbing and a credit system devoid of any real basis. The competition turned into a bitter struggle, which is now being extolled and interpreted to us as a revolution of world significance, the begetter of the most prodigious results and achievements.

If we wish to rate at its true value this philosophic charlatanry, which awakens even in the breast of the honest German citizen a glow of national pride, if we wish to bring out clearly the pettiness, the parochial narrowness of this whole Young-Hegelian movement and in particular the tragicomic contrast between the illusions of these heroes about their achievements and the actual achievements themselves, we must look at the whole spectacle from a standpoint beyond the frontiers of Germany.

German criticism has, right up to its latest efforts, never quitted the realm of philosophy. Far from examining its general philosophic premises, the whole body of its inquiries has actually sprung from the soil of a definite philosophical system, that of Hegel.[3] Not only in their answers but in their very questions there was a mystification. This dependence on Hegel is the reason why not one of these modern critics has even attempted a comprehensive criticism of the Hegelian system, however much each professes to have advanced beyond Hegel. Their polemics against Hegel and against one another are confined to this—each extracts one side of the Hegelian system and turns this against the whole system as well as against the sides extracted by the others. To begin with they extracted pure unfalsified Hegelian categories such as "substance" and "self-consciousness," later they desecrated these categories with more secular names such as "species," "the Unique," "Man," etc.

The entire body of German philosophical criticism from Strauss to Stirner is confined to criticism of *religious* conceptions. The critics started from real religion and actual theology. What religious consciousness and a religious conception really meant was determined variously as they went along. Their advance consisted in subsuming the allegedly dominant

---

[2] *Caput mortuum:* Latin for the head of death.

[3] Marx, like all German philosophers of the nineteenth century, was profoundly influenced by the work of Georg Wilhelm Friedrich Hegel. Hegel was, among other things, concerned with the relationship of individuals to the state. He saw this as a spiritual process of historical development, fueled by dialectical contradiction and culminating in absolute freedom. He believed this freedom was possible under the Prussian monarchy (which, incidentally, employed him). After Hegel's death, his followers split into two camps: the Right Hegelians and the Young Hegelians. The Right Hegelians stayed very close to Hegel's teaching. The Young Hegelians, with whom Marx associated as a young man, held on to Hegel's ideas of historical progress through contradiction but rejected the notion that freedom was possible under existing forms of the state. They supported political programs varying from liberal democracy to anarchism.

metaphysical, political, juridical, moral and other conceptions under the class of religious or theological conceptions; and similarly in pronouncing political, juridical, moral consciousness as religious or theological, and the political, juridical, moral man—"*man*" in the last resort—as religious. The dominance of religion was taken for granted. Gradually every dominant relationship was pronounced a religious relationship and transformed into a cult, a cult of law, a cult of the State, etc. On all sides it was only a question of dogmas and belief in dogmas. The world sanctified to an ever-increasing extent till at last our venerable Saint Max was able to canonize it *en bloc* and thus dispose of it once for all.[4]

The Old Hegelians had *comprehended* everything as soon as it was reduced to an Hegelian category. The Young Hegelians *criticized* everything by attributing to it religious conceptions or by pronouncing it a theological matter. The Young Hegelians are in agreement with the Old Hegelians in their belief in the rule of religion, of concepts, of a universal principle in the existing world. Only, the one party attacks this dominion as usurpation, while the other extols it as legitimate.

Since the Young Hegelians consider conceptions, thoughts, ideas, in fact all the products of consciousness, to which they attribute an independent existence, as the real chains of men (just as the Old Hegelians declared them the true bonds of human society) it is evident that the Young Hegelians have to fight only against these illusions of consciousness.[5] Since, according to their fantasy, the relationships of men, all their doings, their chains and their limitations are products of their consciousness, the Young Hegelians logically put to men the moral postulate of exchanging their present consciousness for human, critical or egoistic consciousness, and thus of removing their limitations. This demand to change consciousness amounts to a demand to interpret reality in another way, i.e. to recognize it by means of another interpretation. The Young-Hegelian ideologists, in spite of their allegedly "world-shattering" statements, are the staunchest conservatives. The most recent of them have found the correct expression for their activity when they declare they are only fighting against "*phrases.*" They forget, however, that to these phrases they themselves are only opposing other phrases, and that they are in no way combating the real existing world when they are merely combating the phrases of this world. The only results which this philosophic criticism could achieve were a few (and at that thoroughly one-sided) elucidations of Christianity from the point of view of religious history;—all the rest of their assertions are only further embellishments of their claim to have furnished, in these unimportant elucidations, discoveries of universal importance.

It has not occurred to any one of these philosophers to inquire into the connection of German philosophy with German reality, the relation of their criticism to their own material surroundings.

---

[4] Much of *The German Ideology* is a critique of the Young Hegelians from the left. Marx and Engels open with a biting attack on them. David Friedrich Strauss (1808–1874) was an early Young Hegelian. His *Life of Jesus* (1892) held that the gospels were not literally true, but myths about early Christians. The anarchist Max Stirner (1806–1856, born Kaspar Schmidt), ridiculed here as Saint Max, bears the brunt of Marx and Engels' attack. Stirner's influential book, *The Ego and Its Own* (1918), had been published in 1844. In it, Stirner attacks Marx and Engels and calls for a thoroughly idealistic approach to changing the state—he argues that we can change society by changing our ideas about it. For Stirner, oppression and alienation are created through ideas that people accept as holy or sacred (hence Marx and Engels' epithets "holy" and "Saint"); freedom, on the other hand, originates through the ego's creation of its own ideas. Thus people can think their way into a new society, freeing themselves from the oppressive state. For Marx and Engels, this was anathema. They believed that freedom from oppression could only be achieved through changes in the material bases of society.

[5] Much of the controversy over Hegelian philosophy concerned the place of religion within it, but religion was largely a surrogate for discussing politics and the state, taboo subjects for debate within Germany. Marx and Engels were living in Belgium at this time and so could speak a bit more openly about German politics.

FIRST PREMISES OF
MATERIALIST METHOD

The premises from which we begin are not arbitrary ones, not dogmas, but real premises from which abstraction can only be made in the imagination.[6] They are the real individuals, their activity and the material conditions under which they live, both those which they find already existing and those produced by their activity. These premises can thus be verified in a purely empirical way.

The first premise of all human history is, of course, the existence of living human individuals. Thus the first fact to be established is the physical organization of these individuals and their consequent relation to the rest of nature. Of course, we cannot here go either into the actual physical nature of man, or into the natural conditions in which man finds himself—geological, oreohydrographical, climatic and so on. The writing of history must always set out from these natural bases and their modification in the course of history through the action of men.

Men can be distinguished from animals by consciousness, by religion or anything else you like. They themselves begin to distinguish themselves from animals as soon as they begin to *produce* their means of subsistence, a step which is conditioned by their physical organization. By producing their means of subsistence men are indirectly producing their actual material life.[7]

The way in which men produce their means of subsistence depends first of all on the nature of the actual means of subsistence they find in existence and have to reproduce. This mode of production must not be considered simply as being the production of the physical existence of the individuals. Rather it is a definite form of activity of these individuals, a definite form of expressing their life, a definite *mode of life* on their part. As individuals express their life, so they are. What they are, therefore, coincides with their production, both with *what* they produce and with *how* they produce. The nature of individuals thus depends on the material conditions determining their production.[8]

This production only makes its appearance with the *increase of population*. In its turn this presupposes the *intercourse* of individuals with one another. The form of this intercourse is again determined by production.

The relations of different nations among themselves depend upon the extent to which each has developed its productive forces, the division of labour and internal intercourse. This statement is generally recognized. But not only the relation of one nation to others, but also the whole internal structure of the nation itself depends on the stage of development reached by its production and its internal and external intercourse. How far the productive forces of a nation are developed is shown most manifestly by the degree to which the division of labour has been carried. Each new productive force, insofar as it is not merely a quantitative extension of productive forces already known (for instance the bringing into cultivation of fresh land), causes a further development of the division of labour.[9]

---

[6] For Hegel, and most of the Right and Young Hegelians, the world was conditioned by ideas, and history was about the progress of the human spirit. For Marx, human society was based in particular material conditions, and history was driven by conflicts at the core of society. This is the root of Marx and Engels' disagreements with Hegelians. Here and in following paragraphs they lay out a materialist understanding of the world, beginning with real people and the conditions under which they live.

[7] The argument in this paragraph is basic to the Marx-Engels view: the thing that fundamentally distinguishes humans from animals is the manner in which they produce their livelihood, that is, labor. Other characteristics unique to humans are derived from labor.

[8] Here Marx and Engels pursue the importance of labor further: production is more than simply feeding oneself; through labor people create their society. Since human nature is determined by the social conditions under which people live, humans, through labor, create their own nature.

[9] Like the Hegelians, Marx and Engels believed that history had a beginning and an end. It followed a specific, scientifically knowable path. For Marx, this path was tied to modes of production and the necessary forms of property associated with each of them. These follow each other in a historically specific order. Changes in human consciousness are part of this historical progression. There can be no experience of transcendental human nature before the end of history and the emergence of a communist society.

The division of labour inside a nation leads at first to the separation of industrial and commercial from agricultural labour, and hence to the separation of *town* and *country* and to the conflict of their interests.[10] Its further development leads to the separation of commercial from industrial labour. At the same time through the division of labour inside these various branches there develop various divisions among the individuals co-operating in definite kinds of labour. The relative position of these individual groups is determined by the methods employed in agriculture, industry and commerce (patriarchalism, slavery, estates, classes). These same conditions are to be seen (given a more developed intercourse) in the relations of different nations to one another.

The various stages of development in the division of labour are just so many different forms of ownership, i.e. the existing stage in the division of labour determines also the relations of individuals to one another with reference to the material, instrument, and product of labour.[11]

The first form of ownership is tribal ownership. It corresponds to the undeveloped stage of production, at which a people lives by hunting and fishing, by the rearing of beasts or, in the highest stage, agriculture. In the latter case it presupposes a great mass of uncultivated stretches of land. The division of labour is at this stage still very elementary and is confined to a further extension of the natural division of labour existing in the family. The social structure is, therefore, limited to an extension of the family; patriarchal family chieftains, below them the members of the tribe, finally slaves. The slavery latent in the family only develops gradually with the increase of population, the growth of wants, and with the extension of external relations, both of war and of barter.[12]

The second form is the ancient communal and State ownership which proceeds especially from the union of several tribes into a *city* by agreement or by conquest, and which is still accompanied by slavery. Beside communal ownership we already find movable, and later also immovable, private property developing, but as an abnormal form subordinate to communal ownership. The citizens hold power over their labouring slaves only in their community, and on this account alone, therefore, they are bound to the form of communal ownership. It is the communal private property which compels the active citizens to remain in this spontaneously derived form of association over against their slaves. For this reason the whole structure of society based on this communal ownership, and with it the power of the people, decays in the same measure as, in particular, immovable private property evolves. The division of labour is already more developed. We already find the antagonism of town and country; later the antagonism between those states which represent town interests and those which represent country interests, and inside the towns themselves the antagonism between industry and maritime commerce. The

---

[10] This is a critical passage. The developments Marx and Engels outline here are reminiscent of both Adam Smith's work on the division of labor and Herbert Spencer's ideas about the organic growth of societies, but with a key difference. Smith and Spencer saw the division of labor as leading to the achievement of the greatest good for the greatest number. Marx and Engels focus instead on the conflicts and oppression it generates. For them, these conflicts are critical to social development.

[11] The interplay between technology and the social relationships through which technology is put to work is central to Marx and Engels' theory. The idea of ownership is key to this. In these paragraphs, the authors describe history as a progression of different forms of ownership and, hence, different modes of production.

[12] Marx and Engels have stated that humans produce their own nature through labor. However, in this passage they ground their analysis in a claim about the "natural division of labour existing in the family." These assertions seem to contradict each other. Note that Marx and Engels envision the "natural" family as consisting of a patriarch who controls the members of his tribe. Although a powerful male head of the household was a feature of European society of their time, it is hardly a universal aspect of primitive societies. Additionally, Marx and Engels cite no evidence to support their understanding of the family. They were aware of this problem, but almost thirty years would pass before the publication of Morgan's *Ancient Society* in 1877, which they believed resolved this issue.

class relation between citizens and slaves is now completely developed.[13]

With the development of private property, we find here for the first time the same conditions which we shall find again, only on a more extensive scale, with modern private property. On the one hand, the concentration of private property, which began very early in Rome (as the Licinian agrarian law[14] proves) and proceeded very rapidly from the time of the civil wars and especially under the Emperors; on the other hand, coupled with this, the transformation of the plebeian small peasantry into a proletariat, which, however, owing to its intermediate position between propertied citizens and slaves, never achieved an independent development.

The third form of ownership is feudal or estate property. If antiquity started out from the *town* and its little territory, the Middle Ages started out from the *country*. This different starting-point was determined by the sparseness of the population at that time, which was scattered over a large area and which received no large increase from the conquerors. In contrast to Greece and Rome, feudal development at the outset, therefore, extends over a much wider territory, prepared by the Roman conquests and the spread of agriculture at first associated with it. The last centuries of the declining Roman Empire and its conquest by the barbarians destroyed a number of productive forces; agriculture had declined, industry had decayed for want of a market, trade had died out or been violently suspended, the rural and urban population had decreased. From these conditions and the mode of organization of the conquest determined by them, feudal property

developed under the influence of the Germanic military constitution. Like tribal and communal ownership, it is based again on a community; but the directly producing class standing over against it is not, as in the case of the ancient community, the slaves, but the enserfed small peasantry. As soon as feudalism is fully developed, there also arises antagonism to the towns. The hierarchical structure of landownership, and the armed bodies of retainers associated with it, gave the nobility power over the serfs. This feudal organization was, just as much as the ancient communal ownership, an association against a subjected producing class; but the form of association and the relation to the direct producers were different because of the different conditions of production.[15]

This feudal system of landownership had its counterpart in the *towns* in the shape of corporative property, the feudal organization of trades. Here property consisted chiefly in the labour of each individual person. The necessity for association against the organized robber nobility, the need for communal covered markets in an age when the industrialist was at the same time a merchant, the growing competition of the escaped serfs swarming into the rising towns, the feudal structure of the whole country: these combined to bring about the *guilds*. The gradually accumulated small capital of individual craftsmen and their stable numbers, as against the growing population, evolved the relation of journeyman and apprentice, which brought into being in the towns a hierarchy similar to that in the country.[16]

Thus the chief form of property during the feudal epoch consisted on the one hand of

---

[13] One of Marx and Engels' critical ideas is that history is driven by dialectical conflict. Notice the emphasis on conflict and antagonism in this outline of history. This paragraph describes the conflict between the communal action required to control slaves and private ownership of immovable property such as land.

[14] The Licinian law (367 B.C.E.) limited the amount of common land a Roman citizen could hold to about 300 acres.

[15] In Marx and Engels' view, feudal ownership derived from the material conditions of the end of the Roman empire, in particular the collapse of the Roman economy.

Both feudalism and the ancient society that preceded it involved the oppression of those who produced. The differences between these societies resulted from their use of different types of production technology. Once again social form is vitally influenced by production.

[16] Guilds are created as a result of purely material processes. They recapitulate, in the town, the social organization of the countryside. Notice that Marx and Engels understood property as including both material goods and labor. The idea of labor as a commodity that can be bought and sold is crucial to their later analysis of capitalism.

landed property with serf labour chained to it, and on the other of the labour of the individual with small capital commanding the labour of journeymen. The organization of both was determined by the restricted conditions of production—the small-scale and primitive cultivation of the land, and the craft type of industry.[17] There was little division of labour in the heyday of feudalism. Each country bore in itself the antithesis of town and country; the division into estates was certainly strongly marked; but apart from the differentiation of princes, nobility, clergy and peasants in the country, and masters, journeymen, apprentices and soon also the rabble of casual labourers in the towns, no division of importance took place. In agriculture it was rendered difficult by the strip-system, beside which the cottage industry of the peasants themselves emerged. In industry there was no division of labour at all in the individual trades themselves, and very little between them. The separation of industry and commerce was found already in existence in older towns; in the newer it only developed later, when the towns entered into mutual relations.

The grouping of larger territories into feudal kingdoms was a necessity for the landed nobility as for the towns. The organization of the ruling class, the nobility, had, therefore, everywhere a monarch at its head.

The fact is, therefore, that definite individuals who are productively active in a definite way enter into these definite social and political relations.[18] Empirical observation must in each separate instance bring out empirically, and without any mystification and speculation, the connection of the social and political structure with production. The social structure and the State are continually evolving out of the life-process of definite individuals, but of individuals, not as they may appear in their own or other people's imagination, but as they *really* are; i.e. as they operate, produce materially, and hence as they work under definite material limits, presuppositions and conditions independent of their will.

The production of ideas, of conceptions, of consciousness, is at first directly interwoven with the material activity and the material intercourse of men, the language of real life. Conceiving, thinking, the mental intercourse of men, appear at this stage as the direct efflux of their material behaviour. The same applies to mental production as expressed in the language of politics, laws, morality, religion, metaphysics, etc. of a people. Men are the producers of their conceptions, ideas, etc.—real, active men, as they are conditioned by a definite development of their productive forces and of the intercourse corresponding to these, up to its furthest forms. Consciousness can never be anything else than conscious existence, and the existence of men is their actual life-process. If in all ideology men and their circumstances appear upside-down as in a *camera obscura*, this phenomenon arises just as much from their historical life-process as the inversion of objects on the retina does from their physical life-process.[19]

In direct contrast to German philosophy which descends from heaven to earth, here we

---

[17] Marx and Engels give priority to the conditions of production in determining society. It is, however, important to distinguish this stance from ecological determinism. The processes that Marx and Engels list as restricting production are all created by human agency rather than ecological necessity. Production is a human activity.

[18] The next several paragraphs contain a very direct statement of Marx's materialist philosophy. The emphasis is on observable relations and processes. Notice that Marx and Engels make no effort here to document the relationships among social and political structure and production.

Much of Marx's later work was devoted to this task of documentation, particularly *Das Kapital,* the first volume of which appeared in 1867.

[19] To Marx and Engels, ideas, the currency of the Young Hegelians, cannot by themselves have explanatory value. They claim that human thinking is conditioned by the social relations under which people live, which can only be understood with reference to material processes. For example, the fact that ideas in nineteenth-century Germany seemed to have power of their own cannot be understood apart from the social relations of that era.

ascend from earth to heaven.[20] That is to say, we do not set out from what men say, imagine, conceive, nor from men as narrated, thought of, imagined, conceived, in order to arrive at men in the flesh. We set out from real, active men, and on the basis of their real life-process we demonstrate the development of the ideological reflexes and echoes of this life-process. The phantoms formed in the human brain are also, necessarily, sublimates of their material life-process, which is empirically verifiable and bound to material premises. Morality, religion, metaphysics, all the rest of ideology and their corresponding forms of consciousness, thus no longer retain the semblance of independence. They have no history, no development; but men, developing their material production and their material intercourse, alter, along with this their real existence, their thinking and the products of their thinking. Life is not determined by consciousness, but consciousness by life. In the first method of approach the starting-point is consciousness taken as the living individual; in the second method, which conforms to real life, it is the real living individuals themselves, and consciousness is considered solely as *their* consciousness.

This method of approach is not devoid of premises.[21] It starts out from the real premises and does not abandon them for a moment. Its premises are men, not in any fantastic isolation and rigidity, but in their actual, empirically perceptible process of development under definite conditions. As soon as this active life-process is described, history ceases to be a collection of dead facts as it is with the empiricists (themselves still abstract), or an imagined activity of imagined subjects, as with the idealists.

Where speculation ends—in real life—there real, positive science begins: the representation of the practical activity, of the practical process of development of men.[22] Empty talk about consciousness ceases, and real knowledge has to take its place. When reality is depicted, philosophy as an independent branch of knowledge loses its medium of existence. At the best its place can only be taken by a summing-up of the most general results, abstractions which arise from the observation of the historical development of men. Viewed apart from real history, these abstractions have in themselves no value whatsoever. They can only serve to facilitate the arrangement of historical material, to indicate the sequence of its separate strata. But they by no means afford a recipe or schema, as does philosophy, for neatly trimming the epochs of history. On the contrary, our difficulties begin only when we set about the observation and the arrangement—the real depiction—of our historical material, whether of a past epoch or of the present. The removal of these difficulties is governed by premises which it is quite impossible to state here, but which only the study of the actual life-process and the activity of the individuals of each epoch will make evident. We shall select here some of these abstractions, which we use in contradistinction to the ideologists, and shall illustrate them by historical example.

---

[20] In this critical passage, Marx and Engels explain their reversal of Hegelian philosophy. Where Hegelian philosophy gave the driving force of history to the realm of pure thought, Marx and Engels assigned it to the material processes of production. In his critical 1974 article, "Marxism, Structuralism, and Vulgar Materialism," Jonathan Friedman stresses the importance of understanding this passage. He points out that Marx and Engels are not promoting simple materialist determinism (which, following Marx, he calls vulgar materialism) but dialectical materialism, a process of change driven by opposition and contradiction.

[21] One such premise is outlined here: humans, by altering the material conditions of their lives, alter their consciousness.

[22] Notice the emphasis throughout this portion of the text on empiricism and science. Marx and Engels considered their theory to be scientific in the same sense as the physical sciences. They believed that philosophy, in the future, would be replaced by science. Marx devoted much of his later life to writing *Das Kapital,* in which he attempted to use his materialist perspective to explain specific historical developments.

HISTORY: FUNDAMENTAL CONDITIONS

Since we are dealing with the Germans, who are devoid of premises, we must begin by stating the first premise of all human existence and, therefore, of all history, the premise, namely, that men must be in a position to live in order to be able to "make history." But life involves before everything else eating and drinking, a habitation, clothing and many other things. The first historical act is thus the production of the means to satisfy these needs, the production of material life itself. And indeed this is an historical act, a fundamental condition of all history, which today, as thousands of years ago, must daily and hourly be fulfilled merely in order to sustain human life. Even when the sensuous world is reduced to a minimum, to a stick as with Saint Bruno, it presupposes the action of producing the stick.[23] Therefore in any interpretation of history one has first of all to observe this fundamental fact in all its significance and all its implications and to accord it its due importance. It is well known that the Germans have never done this, and they have never, therefore, had an *earthly* basis for history and consequently never an historian. The French and the English, even if they have conceived the relation of this fact with so-called history only in an extremely one-sided fashion, particularly as long as they remained in the toils of political ideology, have nevertheless made the first attempts to give the writing of history a materialistic basis by being the first to write histories of civil society, of commerce and industry.[24]

The second point is that the satisfaction of the first need (the action of satisfying, and the instrument of satisfaction which has been acquired) leads to new needs; and this production of new needs is the first historical act. Here we recognize immediately the spiritual ancestry of the great historical wisdom of the Germans who, when they run out of positive material and when they can serve up neither theological nor political nor literary rubbish, assert that this is not history at all, but the "prehistoric era." They do not, however, enlighten us as to how we proceed from this nonsensical "prehistory" to history proper; although, on the other hand, in their historical speculation they seize upon this "prehistory" with especial eagerness because they imagine themselves safe there from interference on the part of "crude facts," and, at the same time, because there they can give full rein to their speculative impulse and set up and knock down hypotheses by the thousand.

The third circumstance which, from the very outset, enters into historical development, is that men, who daily remake their own life, begin to make other men, to propagate their kind: the relation between man and woman, parents and children, the *family*.[25] The family, which to begin with is the only social relationship, becomes later, when increased needs create new social relations and the increased population new needs, a subordinate one (excepting Germany), and must then be treated and analyzed according to the existing empirical data, not according to "the concept of the family," as is the custom in Germany.[a] These three aspects of social activity

---

[23] Marx and Engels open this section with yet another satirical attack on the Young Hegelians, particularly Bruno Bauer (their "Saint Bruno"). Bauer, one of Marx's colleagues in Berlin in the early 1840s, wrote the three-volume *Critique of the Evangelical Gospels* (1841–1842). Marx and Engels' style is important. Their mixture of name-calling, satirical intellectual humor, polemic, and hyperbole set the tone for much of later writing by Marxists. Their indulgence in these tactics marginalized Marxists within academic discourse. This hyperbole may have been useful for political propaganda, but it made their work easy for others to dismiss.

[24] Marx and Engels claim Germans never had historians because they have relied on spiritual rather than material explanations. History is created by people producing the material goods of subsistence and (in the next paragraph) by the social production of new needs.

[25] Here Marx and Engels turn from production to the reproduction of society. They understood reproduction as including both the biological process of human reproduction and the reproduction of social forms through time. Just as people must produce to live, societies must reproduce themselves to survive.

are not of course to be taken as three different stages, but just as three aspects or, to make it clear to the Germans, three "moments," which have existed simultaneously since the dawn of history and the first men, and which still assert themselves in history today.

The production of life, both of one's own in labour and of fresh life in procreation, now appears as a double relationship: on the one hand as a natural, on the other as a social relationship.[26] By social we understand the co-operation of several individuals, no matter under what conditions, in what manner and to what end. It follows from this that a certain mode of production, or industrial stage, is always combined with a certain mode of co-operation, or social stage, and this mode of co-operation is itself a "productive force." Further, that the multitude of productive forces accessible to men determines the nature of society, hence, that the "history of humanity" must always be studied and treated in relation to the history of industry and exchange. But it is also clear how in Germany it is impossible to write this sort of history, because the Germans lack not only the necessary power of comprehension and the material but also the "evidence of their senses," for across the Rhine you cannot have any experience of these things since history has stopped happening.[27] Thus it is quite obvious from the start that there exists a materialistic connection of men with one another, which is determined by their needs and their mode of production, and which is as old as men themselves. This connection is ever taking on new forms, and thus presents a "history" independently of the

existence of any political or religious nonsense which in addition may hold men together.[28]

Only now, after having considered four moments, four aspects of the primary historical relationships, do we find that man also possesses "consciousness," but, even so, not inherent, not "pure" consciousness. From the start the "spirit" is afflicted with the curse of being "burdened" with matter, which here makes its appearance in the form of agitated layers of air, sounds, in short, of language. Language is as old as consciousness, language *is* practical consciousness that exists also for other men, and for that reason alone it really exists for me personally as well; language, like consciousness, only arises from the need, the necessity, of intercourse with other men. Where there exists a relationship, it exists for me: the animal does not enter into *"relations"* with anything, it does not enter into any relation at all. For the animal, its relation to others does not exist as a relation. Consciousness is, therefore, from the very beginning a social product, and remains so as long as men exist at all.[29] Consciousness is at first, of course, merely consciousness concerning the *immediate* sensuous environment and consciousness of the limited connection with other persons and things outside the individual who is growing self-conscious. At the same time it is consciousness of nature, which first appears to men as a completely alien, all-powerful and unassailable force, with which men's relations are purely animal and by which they are overawed like beasts; it is thus a purely animal consciousness of nature (natural religion) just because nature is

---

[26] Social forms are created by the interaction of the way in which people produce and the way in which they arrange themselves to reproduce their society. Of these, however, production is more important.

[27] In the "across the Rhine" passage, Marx and Engels attack the Hegelians, who believed that history had achieved its culmination with the Prussian monarchy.

[28] A key Marxist doctrine—one later adopted by structural anthropologists—is that the real forces that drive society are hidden from view. For Marxists, specific forms of religion or politics are merely the surface appearances of the

deeper forces of production and reproduction. These forces are visible only through Marxist analysis.

[29] Most other nineteenth-century anthropological writers, perhaps taking their cue from Locke, think of the human mind as evolving through some universal unfolding of natural law. Marx, on the other hand, saw the mind as conditioned by social institutions and claimed there was no such thing as human thought apart from the institutions within which humans do their thinking. However, he did not extend this idea to his own work, maintaining his belief in the truth-generating capacities of science.

as yet hardly modified historically. (We see here immediately: this natural religion or this particular relation of men to nature is determined by the form of society and vice versa. Here, as everywhere, the identity of nature and man appears in such a way that the restricted relation of men to nature determines their restricted relation to one another, and their restricted relation to one another determines men's restricted relation to nature.) On the other hand, man's consciousness of the necessity of associating with the individuals around him is the beginning of the consciousness that he is living in society at all.[30] This beginning is as animal as social life itself at this stage. It is mere herd-consciousness, and at this point man is only distinguished from sheep by the fact that with him consciousness takes the place of instinct or that his instinct is a conscious one. This sheep-like or tribal consciousness receives its further development and extension through increased productivity, the increase of needs, and, what is fundamental to both of these, the increase of population. With these there develops the division of labour, which was originally nothing but the division of labour in the sexual act, then that division of labour which develops spontaneously or "naturally" by virtue of natural predisposition (e.g. physical strength), needs, accidents, etc. etc. Division of labour only becomes truly such from the moment when a division of material and mental labour appears. (The first form of ideologists, *priests*, is concurrent.) From this moment onwards consciousness *can* really flatter itself that it is something other than consciousness of existing practice, that it *really* represents something without representing something real; from now on consciousness is in a position to emancipate itself from the world and to proceed to the formation of "pure" theory, theology, philosophy,

ethics, etc. But even if this theory, theology, philosophy, ethics, etc. comes into contradiction with the existing relations, this can only occur because existing social relations have come into contradiction with existing forces of production; this, moreover, can also occur in a particular national sphere of relations through the appearance of the contradiction, not within the national orbit, but between this national consciousness and the practice of other nations, i.e. between the national and the general consciousness of a nation (as we see it now in Germany).

Moreover, it is quite immaterial what consciousness starts to do on its own: out of all such muck we get only the one inference that these three moments, the forces of production, the state of society, and consciousness, can and must come into contradiction with one another, because the *division of labour* implies the possibility, nay the fact that intellectual and material activity—enjoyment and labour, production and consumption—devolve on different individuals, and that the only possibility of their not coming into contradiction lies in the negation in its turn of the division of labour.[31] It is self-evident, moreover, that "specters," "bonds," "the higher being," "concept," "scruple," are merely the idealistic, spiritual expression, the conception apparently of the isolated individual, the image of very empirical fetters and limitations, within which the mode of production of life and the form of intercourse coupled with it move.

PRIVATE PROPERTY AND COMMUNISM

With the division of labour, in which all these contradictions are implicit, and which in its turn is based on the natural division of labour

---

[30] Particular forms of consciousness arise from specific social arrangements, not vice versa. Cultural ecologists and cultural materialists of the mid and late twentieth century will use this key insight (see essays 18 to 23). According to Marx and Engels, the development of consciousness that is distinctly human is dependent on increased population and division of labor. The implica-

tion is that the most "primitive" human groups have consciousness that is virtually indistinguishable from that of animals.

[31] With the appearance of human society and division of labor comes dialectical conflict. For Marx and Engels, this is the fundamental driving force of history.

in the family and the separation of society into individual families opposed to one another, is given simultaneously the *distribution,* and indeed the *unequal* distribution, both quantitative and qualitative, of labour and its products, hence property: the nucleus, the first form, of which lies in the family, where wife and children are the slaves of the husband.[32] This latent slavery in the family, though still very crude, is the first property, but even at this early stage it corresponds perfectly to the definition of modern economists who call it the power of disposing of the labour-power of others. Division of labour and private property are, moreover, identical expressions: in the one the same thing is affirmed with reference to activity as is affirmed in the other with reference to the product of the activity.

Further, the division of labour implies the contradiction between the interest of the separate individual or the individual family and the communal interest of all individuals who have intercourse with one another. And indeed, this communal interest does not exist merely in the imagination, as the "general interest," but first of all in reality, as the mutual interdependence of the individuals among whom the labour is divided. And finally, the division of labour offers us the first example of how, as long as man remains in natural society, that is, as long as a cleavage exists between the particular and the common interest, as long, therefore, as activity is not voluntarily, but naturally, divided, man's own deed becomes an alien power opposed to him, which enslaves him instead of being controlled by him.[33] For as soon as the distribution of labour comes into being, each man has a particular, exclusive sphere of activity, which is forced upon him and from which he cannot escape. He is a hunter, a fisherman, a shepherd, or a critical critic, and must remain so if he does not want to lose his means of livelihood; while in communist society, where nobody has one exclusive sphere of activity but each can become accomplished in any branch he wishes, society regulates the general production and thus makes it possible for me to do one thing today and another tomorrow, to hunt in the morning, fish in the afternoon, rear cattle in the evening, criticize after dinner, just as I have a mind, without ever becoming hunter, fisherman, shepherd or critic. This fixation of social activity, this consolidation of what we ourselves produce into an objective power above us, growing out of our control, thwarting our expectations, bringing to naught our calculations, is one of the chief factors in historical development up till now.[34]

(And out of this very contradiction between the interest of the individual and that of the community the latter takes an independent form as the *State,* divorced from the real interests of individual and community, and at the same time as an illusory communal life, always based, however, on the real ties existing in every family and tribal conglomeration—such as flesh and blood, language, division of labour on a larger scale, and other interests—and especially, as we shall enlarge upon later, on the classes, already determined by the division of labour, which in every such mass of men separate out, and of which one

---

[32] Notice the concern with gender and the subjugation of women and children present in this paragraph. Because it was a good tool for analyzing relations of inequality between genders, Marxism proved appealing to many feminist scholars. See Eleanor Leacock's essay (33) in this volume for an example of Marxist-feminist scholarship.

[33] Division of labor makes society possible, but it also destroys freedom and creates alienation. Alienation or estrangement, a key Marxist concept, refers to the separation of the individual from either the preconditions or the products of labor, or, in this case, from life's necessities. Alienation was understood by Marx and Engels as antithetical to freedom. Specialization in one activity creates alienation in all others. They believed utopian communist society would end contradiction between the individual and the forces of production and, hence, end alienation.

[34] Marx and Engels claim that alienation is rooted in specialization and here envision a society in which people do not specialize in a single job. But can one be an engineer one day and a doctor the next? Marx and Engels' view of a society without alienation is utopian, but if specialization is an inevitable part of industrial society, their vision cannot be achieved.

dominates all the others.[35] It follows from this that all struggles within the State, the struggle between democracy, aristocracy, and monarchy, the struggle for the franchise, etc. etc. are merely the illusory forms in which the real struggles of the different classes are fought out among one another. Of this the German theoreticians have not the faintest inkling, although they have received a sufficient introduction to the subject in the *Deutsch-Französische Jahrbücher* and *Die Heilige Familie*.[36] Further, it follows that every class which is struggling for mastery, even when its domination, as is the case with the proletariat, postulates the abolition of the old form of society in its entirety and of domination itself, must first conquer for itself political power in order to represent its interest in turn as the general interest, which immediately it is forced to do. Just because individuals seek *only* their particular interest, which for them does not coincide with their communal interest, the latter will be imposed on them as an interest "alien" to them, and "independent" of them, as in its turn a particular, peculiar "general" interest; or they themselves must remain within this discord, as in democracy. On the other hand, too, the *practical* struggle of these particular interests, which constantly *really* run counter to the communal and illusory communal interests, makes *practical* intervention and control necessary through the illusory "general" interest in the form of the State.)

The social power, i.e. the multiplied productive force, which arises through the co-operation of different individuals as it is determined by the division of labour, appears to these individuals, since their cooperation is not voluntary but has come about naturally, not as their own united power, but as an alien force existing outside them, of the origin and goal of which they are ignorant, which they thus cannot control, which on the contrary passes through a peculiar series of phases and stages independent of the will and the action of man, nay even being the prime governor of these.[37]

How otherwise could for instance property have had a history at all, have taken on different forms, and landed property, for example, according to the different premises given, have proceeded in France from parcellation to centralization in the hands of a few, in England from centralization in the hands of a few to parcellation, as is actually the case today?[38] Or how does it happen that trade, which after all is nothing more than the exchange of products of various individuals and countries, rules the whole world through the relation of supply and demand—a relation which, as an English economist[39] says, hovers over the earth like the fate of the ancients, and with invisible hand allots fortune and misfortune to men, sets up empires and overthrows empires, causes nations to rise and to disappear—while with the abolition of the basis of private property, with the communistic regulation of production (and, implicit in this, the destruction of the alien relation between men and what they themselves produce), the power of the relation of supply and

---

[35] This paragraph is a marginal note to the paragraph above it in the original manuscript. Several important Marxist principles are laid out in it. First, all of history is ultimately the history of class struggle (the famous opening of the *Manifesto,* written two years later). Second, this class struggle is the hidden, underlying dynamic driving political and economic history. Third, the state is an instrument of control and oppression. However, seizing control of the state is a necessary step in changing society.

[36] *Deutsch-Französische Jahrbücher* (The German-French Annals, 1844) was a radical periodical edited by Marx and his friend Arnold Ruge. Only one issue of it appeared. *Die Heilige Familie* (*The Holy Family,* 1845) was Marx and Engels' first collaboration. It was a mocking attack on Bruno Bauer and other Young Hegelians.

[37] Marx and Engels argue here that even though people compose society, they are alienated from it. It seems to be something external to them, when in fact, through their production, they create it. Communism will allow the people to break through this form of otherness.

[38] Marx and Engels are very Hegelian in their approach to alienation. Hegel's philosophy dealt with the spirit's alienation from the world, and he viewed history as the process of dissolving this alienation. Marx and Engels here see a human structure—trade and the division of labor—as creating alienation, and communism as providing a way to break through the otherness thus engendered.

[39] Adam Smith.

demand is dissolved into nothing, and men get exchange, production, the mode of their mutual relation, under their own control again?

In history up to the present it is certainly an empirical fact that separate individuals have, with the broadening of their activity into world-historical activity, become more and more enslaved under a power alien to them (a pressure which they have conceived of as a dirty trick on the part of the so-called universal spirit, etc.), a power which has become more and more enormous and, in the last instance, turns out to be the *world market*. But it is just as empirically established that, by the overthrow of the existing state of society by the communist revolution (of which more below) and the abolition of private property which is identical with it, this power, which so baffles the German theoreticians, will be dissolved; and that then the liberation of each single individual will be accomplished in the measure in which history becomes transformed into world history. From the above it is clear that the real intellectual wealth of the individual depends entirely on the wealth of his real connections. Only then will the separate individuals be liberated from the various national and local barriers, be brought into practical connection with the material and intellectual production of the whole world and be put in a position to acquire the capacity to enjoy this all-sided production of the whole earth (the creations of man). *All-round* dependence, this natural form of the *world-historical* co-operation of individuals, will be transformed by this communist revolution into the control and conscious mastery of these powers, which, born of the action of men on one

another, have till now overawed and governed men as powers completely alien to them. Now this view can be expressed again in speculative-idealistic, i.e. fantastic, terms as "self-generation of the species" ("society as the subject"), and thereby the consecutive series of interrelated individuals connected with each other can be conceived as a single individual, which accomplishes the mystery of generating itself. It is clear here that individuals certainly make *one another*, physically and mentally, but do not make themselves.[40]

This "alienation" (to use a term which will be comprehensible to the philosophers) can, of course, only be abolished given two *practical* premises. For it to become an "intolerable" power, i.e. a power against which men make a revolution, it must necessarily have rendered the great mass of humanity "propertyless," and produced, at the same time, the contradiction of an existing world of wealth and culture, both of which conditions presuppose a great increase in productive power, a high degree of its development. And, on the other hand, this development of productive forces (which itself implies the actual empirical existence of men in their *world-historical*, instead of local, being) is an absolutely necessary practical premise because without it *want* is merely made general, and with *destitution* the struggle for necessities and all the old filthy business would necessarily be reproduced; and furthermore, because only with this universal development of productive forces is a *universal* intercourse between men established, which produces in all nations simultaneously the phenomenon of the "propertyless" mass (universal

---

[40] As Hegelians, Marx and Engels saw world history as following an inevitable path. Individual societies may have their own histories, but the destiny of the world was fixed, with communism the ultimate end of this path. Marx and Engels believed that communist revolution must be a worldwide event and that it must happen first in highly industrialized societies. Anything that increased worldwide productivity and industrialization would favor its appearance, hence their seemingly contradictory embrace of British colonialism.

At the time of *The German Ideology,* the authors believed that the preconditions for revolution had been met,

and a communist society was imminent. They altered this belief after the failure of the European revolutions of 1848–1849, which convinced them that the changes they were witness to in Europe were the birth pangs of capitalism rather than its death throes. Although they still believed that dialectical contradictions led history inevitably toward communist society, they now saw this society as still distant. Much greater industrialization and internationalization of the economy would be needed. (This assumption set a conundrum for Marxists after the Russian Revolution: How could the communist revolution have occurred in one of Europe's most technologically backward societies?)

competition), makes each nation dependent on the revolutions of the others, and finally has put *world-historical,* empirically universal individuals in place of local ones. Without this, (1) communism could only exist as a local event; (2) the *forces* of intercourse themselves could not have developed as *universal,* hence intolerable powers: they would have remained home-bred conditions surrounded by superstition; and (3) each extension of intercourse would abolish local communism. Empirically, communism is only possible as the act of the dominant peoples "all at once" and simultaneously, which presupposes the universal development of productive forces and the world intercourse bound up with communism. Moreover, the mass of *propertyless* workers—the utterly precarious position of labour-power on a mass scale cut off from capital or from even a limited satisfaction and, therefore, no longer merely temporarily deprived of work itself as a secure source of life—presupposes the *world market* through competition. The proletariat can thus only exist *world-historically,* just as communism, its activity, can only have a "world-historical" existence. World historical existence of individuals means, existence of individuals which is directly linked up with world history.

Communism is for us not a *state of affairs* which is to be established, an *ideal* to which reality [will] have to adjust itself. We call communism the *real* movement which abolishes the present state of things. The conditions of this movement result from the premises now in existence.[41]

NOTE

[a]The building of houses. With savages each family has as a matter of course its own cave or hut like the separate family tent of the nomads. This separate domestic economy is made only the more necessary by the further development of private property. With the agricultural peoples a communal domestic economy is just as impossible as a communal cultivation of the soil. A great advance was the building of towns. In all previous periods, however, the abolition of individual economy, which is inseparable from the abolition of private property, was impossible for the simple reason that the material conditions governing it were not present. The setting-up of a communal domestic economy presupposes the development of machinery, of the use of natural forces and of many other productive forces—e.g., of water-supplies, of gas-lighting, steam-heating, etc., the removal [of the antagonism] of town and country. Without these conditions a communal economy would not in itself form a new productive force; lacking any material basis and resting on a purely theoretical foundation, it would be a mere freak and would end in nothing more than a monastic economy—What was possible can be seen in the towns brought about by condensation and the erection of communal buildings for various definite purposes (prisons, barracks, etc.). That the abolition of individual economy is inseparable from the abolition of the family is self-evident.

---

[41] Although Marx and Engels believed that the communist revolution would be distant, they also believed that people could speed its arrival. Humans, through production, created their own society. Therefore, they and their followers hoped to use their understanding of the links between material production and the production of consciousness to take actions that would hasten the course of history.

The Foundations of Sociological Thought

Like anthropology, sociology is based on the work of philosophers and scientists of the nineteenth century, and the two disciplines share many ideas in common. Indeed, at the end of the nineteenth century, there was no clear distinction between anthropology and sociology. The theories of the early sociological thinkers are worth exploring because they exerted a profound effect on anthropology that continues to be felt today. In fact, all of the theoreticians discussed here adopted a cross-cultural approach in their work.

One individual central in the creation of modern sociology is Émile Durkheim (1858–1917). Durkheim is responsible for formulating some of the basic concepts of the discipline and training the first generation of French sociologists at the beginning of the twentieth century. Durkheim had studied the works of the positivist philosopher Auguste Comte (1798–1857) as well as those of Herbert Spencer. In agreement with both of these scholars, Durkheim believed that human society followed laws, just like the natural laws of physics or biology, that could be discovered by empirical observation and testing. In 1885 to 1886, Durkheim took a leave of absence from high school teaching to do research in Germany, in the psychological laboratories of Wilhelm Wundt (1832–1920). His experiences with Wundt convinced him that a scientific study of society was possible.

Durkheim wished to substantiate his belief that society was much more than simply a collection of individuals and to discover the laws and principles by which society operated. He began by questioning the nature of social cohesion (the term he used was *social solidarity*): What was it exactly that held societies together? He concluded that social solidarity was primarily the result of a force arising from participation in a shared system of beliefs and values, which molded and controlled individual behavior. Durkheim called this force *l'âme collective*, a phrase usually translated into English as "the collective conscience." However, the French word *âme* can also be translated as "soul," "spirit," "sentiment," or "sensibility," and Durkheim intended all of these meanings.

Durkheim believed that the collective conscience originated in the communal interactions and experiences of members of a society. Because people were born and raised within this shared context of the collective conscience, it determined their values, their beliefs (which he called *collective representations*), and their behaviors. Ultimately, it made life possible and meaningful. For the most part, social cohesion was maintained because everyone in a society shared its set of collective representations. As you can see, Durkheim's collective conscience foreshadowed the modern concept of culture, although he was not familiar with the term and did not use it in his work.

Durkheim believed that the collective conscience was a psychological entity that, although carried by members of a society, superseded individual existence and could not be explained in terms of individual behavior. Once called into existence (through a process Durkheim called *social condensation*) it had a life of its own and operated by its own rules. In other words, the collective conscience was not contained within any individual organism; it was *superorganic*. Given that it was not a material thing, how could the collective conscience be scientifically studied? Durkheim proposed that the appropriate units of analysis were *social facts,* the social and behavioral rules and principles that exist before an individual is born into a society and which that person learns and observes as a member of that society. Social facts can be recognized by their pervasiveness within a society (they are not individualistic) and because they are coercive. People feel obligated to observe their constraints. Durkheim believed that such social facts could be observed in people's actions and studied independently through the use of statistics. His 1897 book, *Suicide,* is a classic example of this form of analysis.

Like the other theorists of his day, Durkheim supposed technologically primitive peoples to be examples of earlier stages of cultural evolution. Though he did no fieldwork himself, he studied reports of primitive societies, in particular the Australian Aborigines, attempting to determine the form and nature of the collective conscience in these societies. In his analysis, he applied the concepts of mechanical and organic solidarity he had developed in his earlier work, *The Division of Labor in Society,* published in 1893. Primitive societies are held together by what Durkheim called *mechanical solidarity.* He believed that in such societies, there are no individuals in the modern sense. Rather, "collective conscience completely envelopes [individual] conscience and coincides with it at every point" (1933[1893]:43). Such societies lack internal differentiation; their parts are interchangeable. Therefore, segments can break away without disrupting the functioning of the entire society. In these societies, kinship forms the primary bond between people.

Industrialized societies, on the other hand, are held together by *organic solidarity.* In such societies collective conscience is at least partially differentiated from individual conscience. One result is occupational specialization—people need each other to function. In this type of society, the primary ties between individuals come from economic and occupational interdependence and cooperation rather than from kinship. Durkheim believed that individual freedom and ultimately happiness were maximized under organic solidarity.

The influence of nineteenth-century evolutionary thought can be clearly seen in Durkheim's study of primitive societies. He believed that societies evolved from mechanical to organic solidarity, that is, from simple undifferentiated groups into more advanced differentiated societies. In this respect, his work developed some of the implications of Herbert Spencer's organic analogy (see essay 1). Unlike Spencer, Darwin, and Marx, who wrote in terms of the human struggle for survival, Durkheim focused on the solidarity within a society. Societies progressed from mechanical to organic solidarity not through competition and strife but rather to achieve greater solidarity at higher levels of population and complexity. Although he certainly did not view complex societies as free from conflict (some of his best known work is on suicide), Durkheim believed that social differentiation and specialization led to increased social cohesion and broadened the possibilities for individuals to achieve their full potential as human beings. Strife in modern society resulted from the incomplete elaboration of organic solidarity. Ultimately, it would greatly diminish. Durkheim and many of his followers had a profound faith in the ability of science and rationality to help people create a better, more peaceful society in the future. This faith was sorely tested as Europe descended into World War I.

Durkheim postulated that all people understood the world through socially created systems of classification. He argued that such systems were not derived from simple observation of nature. Rather, they were social facts. Thus, systems of classification did not reflect the natural world but rather imposed the structure of society upon the natural world. In other words, classification systems were specific to individual societies and reflected the social organization of those societies. Durkheim developed this idea in "Primitive Classification" (Durkheim and Mauss 1963, orig. 1903) and *The Elementary Forms of the Religious Life* (1965, orig. 1912). In these works, Durkheim argues that human societies project their social organization on the material world. In the realm of religion, this classification system becomes sacred. Thus, when societies engage in religious worship, what they are actually praising is their own social order. This act of praise invests society itself with a sacred character and is a critical element in creating and maintaining social solidarity.

Durkheim makes many additional points in these works, but two that are of enduring importance are, first, that the processes he analyzes in Aboriginal society are essentially the same processes that occur in all societies. Thus, primitive societies are not simply living fossils but rather simplified versions of more complex societies in which universal social processes can be seen more clearly. Second, Durkheim proposes that some social facts are universal. For example, he claims that all human thought is dualistic. In all human societies, people have a tendency to classify by dividing everything into things and their opposites (good/bad, day/night, right/left, and so on). Further, he proposed that the most fundamental of these divisions was into the categories of *sacred* and *profane*. Durkheim's emphasis on systems of classification and binary opposition would have enormous effect on later theories, in particular, French structuralism, ethnoscience, and cognitive anthropology.

Durkheim adopted what anthropologists in later decades termed a "functionalist" approach to the analysis of society. His analysis of social institutions and beliefs was often couched in terms of their contribution to promoting and maintaining social solidarity. This aspect of his work is central to the work of many of Durkheim's students and forms the basis of the British functionalist and structural-functionalist schools of anthropological thought exemplified by Bronislaw Malinowski and A. R. Radcliffe-Brown (see essays 13 and 14).

Around 1900, Durkheim's work attracted a very influential group of scholars, some of whom were his relatives. Together, between 1898 and 1912, they published a journal called *L'Année Sociologique*. As a result, they are collectively known as the *L'Année Sociologique* school. Unhappily, World War I exacted a profound toll on Durkheim and his students. Fearing German nationalism and anti-Semitism, Durkheim had supported the war. He was on numerous war-related

committees and wrote several propaganda pamphlets against German expansionism particularly criticizing the work of Heinrich von Treitschke (1834–1896), a profoundly nationalist and anti-Semitic German politician and author. However, a great many of Durkheim's students were killed in the war. These included Maxime David, Antoine Bianconi, Robert Hertz, Jean Reynier, and R. Gelly, all of whom were in their very early thirties. Even more important, Durkheim's only son, André, a promising young linguist, died in 1915 during the retreat from Serbia. André was initially listed as missing, so Durkheim did not definitively know about his death for most of a year. Bereft of his son, Durkheim withdrew into silence. LaCapra writes: "Iron self-discipline remained the dominant force in Durkheim's life, and it finally broke him. In 1917 he died of what has been called a 'broken heart'" (1972:78).

Durkheim's nephew Marcel Mauss (1872–1950), one of the few members of *L'Année Sociologique* to survive the war, was considered one of the school's leading thinkers. In the wake of the disaster that had befallen his friends and colleagues, however, he neglected his own work to concentrate on publishing the work of his mentor, Durkheim, and his deceased colleagues. In 1925, in the first issue of *L'Année Sociologique* to appear after the war, Mauss wrote: "Let us then carry on the work for a few more years. Let us try to do the kind of work which will bring honor to their memory, and which will not be too unworthy of the work begun by our Master" (in Leacock 1954:59). In that same year, he published *Essai sur le don* (*The Gift*), a portion of which is reprinted here. In this essay, Mauss shows that gift-giving in primitive societies is often a part of political and social obligations, reflecting or expressing the society's underlying social structure. He also proposes a special class of social facts called *total social phenomena* and illustrates this concept in his discussion of the potlatch.

The last contributor to this section is the German sociologist Max Weber (1864–1920). Although best known for his work in sociology, Weber was trained in law and history and held academic posts in economics. Unlike Durkheim,

Weber was concerned with the action of individuals as well as social groups. According to Weber, the ultimate base of social action is individual behavior a person undertakes in relation to others; that behavior is best judged by whether the action is rational or not. Weber was relatively poorly versed in the ethnography of "primitive" societies, but he was extremely interested in Asia and wrote extensively on religion in China and India.

Much of Weber's work was influenced by Marx, and he attempted to develop Marx's thoughts on social class. Like Marx, he believed that social class was related to property ownership and control of the means of production. Unlike Marx, he believed that classes, in and of themselves, could not act and that status (or honor) and party could also cut across class lines. In his essay "Class, Status, Party," Weber develops this theory of class stratification and parties (groups that exist to pursue power) and their relationship to the role of the individual in society.

Another critical feature that differentiates Weber's work from Marx's is the prominent place he gave to individual action and ideology. Both Marx and Weber saw these as ultimately grounded in systems of production, but in Weber's work individuals and ideologies take on the capacity for action and culture change that is much less evident in Marx.

The Protestant Ethic and the Spirit of Capitalism, originally published in 1930, is perhaps Weber's best known explanation of the role of ideology. Like Marx, Weber analyzed the rise of capitalism and, like Marx, he saw the roots of capitalism in fundamental changes in relations of production, such as the displacement of peasants. However, unlike Marx, he found these material causes insufficient to explain the emergence and success of capitalism. Instead, he proposed that it was this, coupled with a new Calvinist ethic emphasizing moral accountability and self-discipline, that explained capitalism's rise. It is critical to Weber's point that Calvinism did not emerge from capitalism. It was

aimed at assuring personal salvation, not profits. However, coinciding with changes in relations of production, it greatly favored the emergence of a powerful capitalist bourgeoisie.

Weber believed that individuals could profoundly affect their societies. Prophets could emerge who could change the way people thought. He called the ability of an individual to influence others *charisma,* which he defined in *The Sociology of Religion* (1993, orig. 1920) as an "extraordinary power," a sort of spiritual force possessed by an individual. Weber did not explain the source of charisma, asserting that it simply exists naturally in some people; in others, it is a germ that must be awakened. The power of charisma enables certain individuals to lead their societies and change the thinking of those around them. The notion of charisma gives the individual a place in Weber's work that is lacking in Marx's theory.

Weber's influence on later anthropological work is subtle but significant. His emphasis on individual, rational, social action was incorporated by Bronislaw Malinowski into his theory of psychological functionalism. His work on forms of authority influenced many anthropological thinkers (see Morton Fried, essay 20), as did his analysis of the Protestant ethic and capitalism (see Julian Steward, essay 19, and Clifford Geertz, essay 37). Weber's work on religion influenced Roy Rappaport (Rappaport 1994:167) as well as Anthony F. C. Wallace, Peter Worsley, and Jean and John Comaroff (Erickson 1998:112). Especially important to contemporary anthropologists is his notion of *verstehen,* usually translated as "understanding." Weber used the term to mean the empathetic identification with those you are observing in order to better understand their motives and the meaning of their behavior. This is one of the fundamental concepts of the school of symbolic anthropology. In particular, Clifford Geertz and Renato Rosaldo (essays 37 and 38) illustrate how this principle has been used by anthropologists.

5. *What Is a Social Fact?*

ÉMILE DURKHEIM (1858–1917)

BEFORE INQUIRING INTO the method suited to the study of social facts, it is important to know which facts are commonly called "social." This information is all the more necessary since the designation "social" is used with little precision. It is currently employed for practically all phenomena generally diffused within society, however small their social interest. But on that basis, there are, as it were, no human events that may not be called social. Each individual drinks, sleeps, eats, reasons; and it is to society's interest that these functions be exercised in an orderly manner. If, then, all these facts are counted as "social" facts, sociology would have no subject matter exclusively its own, and its domain would be confused with that of biology and psychology.[1]

But in reality there is in every society a certain group of phenomena which may be differentiated from those studied by the other natural sciences. When I fulfill my obligations as brother, husband, or citizen, when I execute my contracts, I perform duties which are defined, externally to myself and my acts, in law and in custom. Even if they conform to my own sentiments and I feel their reality subjectively, such reality is still objective, for I did not create them; I merely inherited them through my education. How many times it happens, moreover, that we are ignorant of the details of the obligations incumbent upon us, and that in order to acquaint ourselves with

them we must consult the law and its authorized interpreters! Similarly, the church-member finds the beliefs and practices of his religious life ready-made at birth; their existence prior to his own implies their existence outside of himself. The system of signs I use to express my thought, the system of currency I employ to pay my debts, the instruments of credit I utilize in my commercial relations, the practices followed in my profession, etc., function independently of my own use of them. And these statements can be repeated for each member of society. Here, then, are ways of acting, thinking, and feeling that present the noteworthy property of existing outside the individual consciousness.

These types of conduct or thought are not only external to the individual but are, moreover, endowed with coercive power, by virtue of which they impose themselves upon him, independent of his individual will. Of course, when I fully consent and conform to them, this constraint is felt only slightly, if at all, and is therefore unnecessary. But it is, nonetheless, an intrinsic characteristic of these facts, the proof thereof being that it asserts itself as soon as I attempt to resist it. If I attempt to violate the law, it reacts against me so as to prevent my act before its accomplishment, or to nullify my violation by restoring the damage, if it is accomplished and reparable, or to make me expiate it if it cannot be compensated for otherwise.[2]

From *Rules of the Sociological Method* (1895)

---

[1] Durkheim's goal in writing this essay was to show that sociology could be a field of study distinct from other sciences. He wrote at a time when the divisions between anthropology, sociology, and psychology, as we know them today, did not exist. Durkheim was concerned to establish what he considered a new and independent science, which required having something in particular to study, a subject matter that could distinguish it from other sciences. That subject matter, Durkheim proposed, was social facts. As a follower of the French positivist Auguste Comte (1798–1857), Durkheim was vitally concerned

with establishing the reality of social facts. Comte insisted that philosophy (and social science) be based on precise, observable facts subject to general laws. If the existence of such facts could not be demonstrated, sociology had no place in science.

[2] Durkheim argues that social facts are real because their effects can be felt. People are compelled to live according to the rules of their society and violate them at their peril. Fertile ground for discovering examples of social facts can be found in a society's general rules of behavior, such as

In the case of purely moral maxims; the public conscience exercises a check on every act which offends it by means of the surveillance it exercises over the conduct of citizens, and the appropriate penalties at its disposal. In many cases the constraint is less violent, but nevertheless it always exists. If I do not submit to the conventions of society, if in my dress I do not conform to the customs observed in my country and in my class, the ridicule I provoke, the social isolation in which I am kept, produce, although in an attenuated form, the same effects as a punishment in the strict sense of the word. The constraint is nonetheless efficacious for being indirect. I am not obliged to speak French with my fellow-countrymen nor to use the legal currency, but I cannot possibly do otherwise. If I tried to escape this necessity, my attempt would fail miserably. As an industrialist, I am free to apply the technical methods of former centuries; but by doing so, I should invite certain ruin. Even when I free myself from these rules and violate them successfully, I am always compelled to struggle with them. When finally overcome, they make their constraining power sufficiently felt by the resistance they offer. The enterprises of all innovators, including successful ones, come up against resistance of this kind.[3]

Here, then, is a category of facts with very distinctive characteristics: it consists of ways of acting, thinking, and feeling, external to the individual, and endowed with a power of coercion, by reason of which they control him. These ways of thinking could not be confused with biological phenomena, since they consist of representations and of actions; nor with psychological phenomena, which exist only in the individual consciousness and through it. They constitute, thus, a new

variety of phenomena; and it is to them exclusively that the term "social" ought to be applied. And this term fits them quite well, for it is clear that, since their source is not in the individual, their substratum can be no other than society, either the political society as a whole or some one of the partial groups it includes, such as religious denominations, political, literary, and occupational associations, etc. On the other hand, this term "social" applies to them exclusively, for it has a distinct meaning only if it designates exclusively the phenomena which are not included in any of the categories of facts that have already been established and classified. These ways of thinking and acting therefore constitute the proper domain of sociology. It is true that, when we define them with this word "constraint," we risk shocking the zealous partisans of absolute individualism. For those who profess the complete autonomy of the individual, man's dignity is diminished whenever he is made to feel that he is not completely self-determinant. It is generally accepted today, however, that most of our ideas and our tendencies are not developed by ourselves but come to us from without. How can they become a part of us except by imposing themselves upon us? This is the whole meaning of our definition. And it is generally accepted, moreover, that social constraint is not necessarily incompatible with the individual personality.[a]

Since the examples that we have just cited (legal and moral regulations, religious faiths, financial systems, etc.) all consist of established beliefs and practices, one might be led to believe that social facts exist only where there is some social organization. But there are other facts without such crystallized form which have the same objectivity and the same ascendancy over

---

the informal rules about what is appropriate to eat and how to eat. Most readers of this book probably have an aversion to eating insects—not because there is a law against eating them but because of informal rules that shape behavior. Even thinking about eating insects probably disgusts most Americans, which is how the effects of the social fact can be observed.

[3] Although Durkheim refers to social facts as "laws" and speaks of "executing contracts," he is not just thinking of laws in the legal sense. He was referring to the general

rules of behavior that people unconsciously follow; rules we internalize through growing up in a society—what he calls "moral maxims." He argues that public opinion also controls people's conduct, in particular, through mechanisms such as shaming, ridicule, and ostracism. For instance, it is not illegal to pick your nose in public, but it does violate an informal rule of behavior. Taking this action provokes reactions of disgust from onlookers, and the offender would feel embarrassed or ashamed and probably not repeat the action.

the individual. These are called "social currents." Thus the great movements of enthusiasm, indignation, and pity in a crowd do not originate in any one of the particular individual consciousnesses. They come to each one of us from without and can carry us away in spite of ourselves. Of course, it may happen that, in abandoning myself to them unreservedly, I do not feel the pressure they exert upon me. But it is revealed as soon as I try to resist them. Let an individual attempt to oppose one of these collective manifestations and the emotions that he denies will turn against him. Now, if this power of external coercion asserts itself so clearly in cases of resistance, it must exist also in the first-mentioned cases, although we are unconscious of it. We are then victims of the illusion of having ourselves created that which actually forced itself from without. If the complacency with which we permit ourselves to be carried along conceals the pressure undergone, nevertheless it does not abolish it. Thus, air is no less heavy because we do not detect its weight. So, even if we ourselves have spontaneously contributed to the production of the common emotion, the impression we have received differs markedly from that which we would have experienced if we had been alone. Also, once the crowd has dispersed, that is, once these social influences have ceased to act upon us and we are alone again, the emotions which have passed through the mind appear strange to us, and we no longer recognize them as ours. We realize that these feelings have been impressed upon us to a much greater extent than they were created by us. It may even happen that they horrify us, so much were they contrary to our nature. Thus, a group of individuals, most of whom are perfectly inoffensive, may, when gathered in a crowd, be drawn into acts of atrocity. And what we say of these transitory outbursts applies similarly to those more permanent currents of opinion on religious, political, literary, or artistic matters which are constantly being formed around us, whether in society as a whole or in more limited circles.[4]

To confirm this definition of the social fact by a characteristic illustration from common experience, one need only observe the manner in which children are brought up. Considering the facts as they are and as they have always been, it becomes immediately evident that all education is a continuous effort to impose on the child ways of seeing, feeling, and acting which he could not have arrived at spontaneously. From the very first hours of his life, we compel him to eat, drink, and sleep at regular hours; we constrain him to cleanliness, calmness, and obedience; later we exert pressure upon him in order that he may learn proper consideration for others, respect for customs and conventions, the need for work, etc. If, in time, this constraint ceases to be felt, it is because it gradually gives rise to habits and to internal tendencies that render constraint unnecessary; but nevertheless it is not abolished, for it is still the source from which these habits were derived. It is true that, according to Spencer, a rational education ought to reject such methods, allowing the child to act in complete liberty; but as this pedagogic theory has never been applied by any known people, it must be accepted only as an expression of personal opinion, not as a fact which can contradict the aforementioned observations. What makes these facts particularly instructive is that the aim of education is, precisely, the socialization of the human being; the process of education, therefore,

---

[4] Durkheim differentiates social facts, which are enduring, from transitory social currents. Social currents, such as the momentary emotions sweeping a crowd, give a taste of the power of social facts. As members of a crowd, we are clearly capable of emotions (and actions) beyond our own capabilities or desires.

Issues of crowd behavior were very much on the minds of writers of this era. The unsuccessful European revolutions of 1848 and the Paris Commune of 1871 had included striking displays of mob and government violence. In 1894, a year before the publication of this essay, Alfred Dreyfus (1859–1935), the only Jewish officer in the French army's General Staff, was wrongly convicted of spying for the Germans. The affair inflamed mob passions against Jews, socialists, and other minorities. The protofascist politician and author Maurice Barrès (1862–1923) called for a leader who would be an embodiment of the collective will of the masses. Durkheim, as a secular, Jewish socialist, must have been deeply impressed and concerned.

gives us in a nutshell the historical fashion in which the social being is constituted. This unremitting pressure to which the child is subjected is the very pressure of the social milieu which tends to fashion him in its own image, and of which parents and teachers are merely the representatives and intermediaries.[5]

It follows that sociological phenomena cannot be defined by their universality. A thought which we find in every individual consciousness, a movement repeated by all individual manifestations, is not thereby a social fact. If sociologists have been satisfied with defining them by this characteristic, it is because they confused them with what one might call their reincarnation in the individual. It is, however, the collective aspects of the beliefs, tendencies, and practices of a group that characterize truly social phenomena. As for the forms that the collective states assume when refracted in the individual, these are things of another sort. This duality is clearly demonstrated by the fact that these two orders of phenomena are frequently found dissociated from one another. Indeed, certain of these social manners of acting and thinking acquire, by reason of their repetition, a certain rigidity which on its own account crystallizes them, so to speak, and isolates them from the particular events which reflect them. They thus acquire a body, a tangible form, and constitute a reality in their own right, quite distinct from the individual facts which produce it. Collective habits are inherent not only in the successive acts which they determine but, by a privilege of which we find no

example in the biological realm, they are given permanent expression in a formula which is repeated from mouth to mouth, transmitted by education, and fixed even in writing. Such is the origin and nature of legal and moral rules, popular aphorisms and proverbs, articles of faith wherein religious or political groups condense their beliefs, standards of taste established by literary schools, etc. None of these can be found entirely reproduced in the applications made of them by individuals, since they can exist even without being actually applied.[6]

No doubt, this dissociation does not always manifest itself with equal distinctness, but its obvious existence in the important and numerous cases just cited is sufficient to prove that the social fact is a thing distinct from its individual manifestations. Moreover, even when this dissociation is not immediately apparent, it may often be disclosed by certain devices of method. Such dissociation is indispensable if one wishes to separate social facts from their alloys in order to observe them in a state of purity. Currents of opinion, with an intensity varying according to the time and place, impel certain groups either to more marriages, for example, or to more suicides, or to a higher or lower birthrate, etc. These currents are plainly social facts. At first sight they seem inseparable from the forms they take in individual cases. But statistics furnish us with the means of isolating them. They are, in fact, represented with considerable exactness by the rates of births, marriages, and suicides, that is, by the number obtained by dividing the average

---

[5] Modern anthropologists call this process *enculturation* and believe that it is largely unconscious. In other words, we think and act the way we do largely because of the unconscious internalization of cultural constraints imposed on us during childhood, not because of conscious, rational choice. Durkheim's citation of Herbert Spencer here is strange because the name that would come to the mind of any French intellectual reading this passage is Jean-Jacques Rousseau (1712–1778), whose 1762 book *Émile* proposed a similar theory of "natural" education. So why does Durkheim, writing in French, cite Spencer, an Englishman, and not Rousseau, who was French? Probably because he considered Spencer a scientist and Rousseau a philosopher and wished to emphasize the scientific nature of his work.

[6] Since they are beyond the individual, social facts must have an existence apart from their individual manifestations. Indeed, individual behavior can only approximate the rules of behavior. Durkheim was familiar with Platonic philosophy and his argument parallels that perspective. Plato, in his *Republic*, proposed that objects on earth are imperfect representations of ideal forms existing beyond human consciousness; Durkheim suggests that actual behavior is the imperfect representation of crystallized social facts existing beyond individual awareness. A problem with this view is that a social fact must somehow be teased out of a myriad of individual manifestations, none of which accurately reflects it. Will all observers find the same social facts?

annual total of marriages, births, suicides, by the number of persons whose ages lie within the range in which marriages, births, and suicides occur.[b] Since each of these figures contains all the individual cases indiscriminately, the individual circumstances which may have had a share in the production of the phenomenon are neutralized and, consequently, do not contribute to its determination. The average, then, expresses a certain state of the group mind (*l'âme collective*).[7]

Such are social phenomena, when disentangled from all foreign matter. As for their individual manifestations, these are indeed, to a certain extent, social, since they partly reproduce a social model. Each of them also depends, and to a large extent, on the organopsychological constitution of the individual and on the particular circumstances in which he is placed. Thus they are not sociological phenomena in the strict sense of the word. They belong to two realms at once; one could call them sociopsychological. They interest the sociologist without constituting the immediate subject matter of sociology. There exist in the interior of organisms similar phenomena, compound in their nature, which form in their turn the subject matter of the "hybrid sciences," such as physiological chemistry, for example.

The objection may be raised that a phenomenon is collective only if it is common to all members of society, or at least to most of them—in other words, if it is truly general. This may be true; but it is general because it is collective (that is, more or less obligatory), and certainly not collective because general. It is a group condition repeated in the individual because imposed on him. It is to be found in each part because it exists in the whole, rather than in the whole because it exists in the parts.[8] This becomes conspicuously evident in those beliefs and practices which are transmitted to us ready-made by previous generations; we receive and adopt them because, being both collective and ancient, they are invested with a particular authority that education has taught us to recognize and respect. It is, of course, true that a vast portion of our social culture is transmitted to us in this way; but even when the social fact is due in part to our direct collaboration, its nature is not different. A collective emotion which bursts forth suddenly and violently in a crowd does not express merely what all the individual sentiments had in common; it is something entirely different, as we have shown. It results from their being together, a product of the actions and reactions which take place between individual consciousnesses; and if each individual consciousness echoes the collective sentiment, it is by virtue of the special energy resident in its collective origin. If all hearts beat in unison, this is not the result of a spontaneous and pre-established harmony but rather because an identical force propels them in the same direction. Each is carried along by all.[9]

---

[7] The use of statistics to predict behavior was of relatively recent origin when Durkheim wrote this article. The astronomer-turned-statistician Adolphe J. Quetelet published two volumes, *On Man and the Development of His Faculties* (1835) and *Of the Social System and the Laws Which Rule It* (1848), in which probability theory was first applied to population characteristics (Tylor also refers to Quetelet in essay 2). Because the behavioral characteristics of a population are predictable through statistical analysis, Durkheim saw statistics as a scientific method for identifying social facts. In this paragraph he mentions their use in analyzing suicide rates. One of Durkheim's most influential works was *Suicide: A Study in Sociology* (1897), which appeared two years after this essay and makes extensive use of statistics.

[8] Although the wording may be confusing, Durkheim makes an important point at the outset of this paragraph.

He thought that a belief or behavior held in common by members of a society was prevalent *because* it was a collective phenomenon. Everyone shares social facts because they are collective; they are not collective simply because everyone shares them. Social facts precede individuals and are imposed upon them.

[9] In this paragraph, Durkheim returns once again to the problem of the crowd. He suggests that by virtue of coming together, people create a "special energy," which in *The Elementary Forms of the Religious Life* (1965 [1912]), he called "*l'âme collective*." The use of the term *energy* is important. Durkheim wished to show that sociology was a science and borrowed some of the vocabulary of physics to make his point. Just as the physicists of his day were concerned with the discovery of laws of energy, Durkheim wanted to uncover the laws underlying the behavior of this "social energy."

We thus arrive at the point where we can formulate and delimit in a precise way the domain of sociology.[10] It comprises only a limited group of phenomena. A social fact is to be recognized by the power of external coercion which it exercises or is capable of exercising over individuals, and the presence of this power may be recognized in its turn either by the existence of some specific sanction or by the resistance offered against every individual effort that tends to violate it. One can, however, define it also by its diffusion within the group, provided that, in conformity with our previous remarks, one takes care to add as a second and essential characteristic that its own existence is independent of the individual forms it assumes in its diffusion. This last criterion is perhaps, in certain cases, easier to apply than the preceding one. In fact, the constraint is easy to ascertain when it expresses itself externally by some direct reaction of society, as is the case in law, morals, beliefs, customs, and even fashions.[11] But when it is only indirect, like the constraint which an economic organization exercises, it cannot always be so easily detected. Generality combined with externality may, then, be easier to establish. Moreover, this second definition is but another form of the first; for if a mode of behavior whose existence is external to individual consciousnesses becomes general, this can only be brought about by its being imposed upon them.[c]

But these several phenomena present the same characteristic by which we defined the others. These "ways of existing" are imposed on the individual precisely in the same fashion as the "ways of acting" of which we have spoken. Indeed, when we wish to know how a society is divided politically, of what these divisions themselves are composed, and how complete is the fusion existing between them, we shall not achieve our purpose by physical inspection and by geographical observations; for these phenomena are social, even when they have some basis in physical nature. It is only by a study of public law that a comprehension of this organization is possible, for it is this law that determines the organization, as it equally determines our domestic and civil relations. This political organization is, then, no less obligatory than the social facts mentioned above. If the population crowds into our cities instead of scattering into the country, this is due to a trend of public opinion, a collective drive that imposes this concentration upon the individuals. We can no more choose the style of our houses than of our clothing—at least, both are equally obligatory. The channels of communication prescribe the direction of internal migrations and commerce, etc., and even their extent.[12] Consequently, at the very most, it should be necessary to add to the list of phenomena which we have enumerated as presenting the distinctive criterion of a social fact only one additional category, "ways of existing"; and as this enumeration was not meant to be rigorously exhaustive, the addition would not be absolutely necessary.

Such an addition is perhaps not necessary, for these "ways of existing" are only crystallized "ways of acting." The political structure of a society is merely the way in which its component segments have become accustomed to live with

---

[10] In this paragraph, Durkheim summarizes the characteristics of social facts: They are external to individuals and coercive. Sometimes social facts are enshrined in law or can be recognized by the negative reaction of others when a principle is violated. Frequently they can be determined by the statistical analysis of a population's behavior.

[11] Durkheim says that the constraint exercised by social facts is easily recognized when expressed "externally by some direct reaction of society, as is the case in law, morals, beliefs, customs and even fashions." Compare this statement to Tylor's famous definition of culture, which opens *Primitive Culture* (1871; see essay 2): "Culture or civilization, taken in its wide ethnographic sense, is that complex whole which includes knowledge, belief, art, morals, law, custom, and any other capabilities and habits acquired by man as a member of society." Although not cited, it appears Durkheim's formulation was influenced by Tylor's definition. He may well have conceived of society as a collection of social facts.

[12] Durkheim contends in this paragraph that social movements, such as the change from rural to predominantly urban lifestyles, are driven by collective opinion, revealing himself as a strict idealist. Unlike Marxists, cultural ecologists, and cultural materialists, he attributes social changes to changes in ideas and opinions rather than changes in material structures such as the development of industrial capitalism.

one another. If their relations are traditionally intimate, the segments tend to fuse with one another, or, in the contrary case, to retain their identity. The type of habitation imposed upon us is merely the way in which our contemporaries and our ancestors have been accustomed to construct their houses. The methods of communication are merely the channels which the regular currents of commerce and migrations have dug, by flowing in the same direction. To be sure, if the phenomena of a structural character alone presented this permanence, one might believe that they constituted a distinct species. A legal regulation is an arrangement no less permanent than a type of architecture, and yet the regulation is a "physiological" fact. A simple moral maxim is assuredly somewhat more malleable, but it is much more rigid than a simple professional custom or a fashion. There is thus a whole series of degrees without a break in continuity between the facts of the most articulated structure and those free currents of social life which are not yet definitely molded. The differences between them are, therefore, only differences in the degree of consolidation they present. Both are simply life, more or less crystallized.[13] No doubt, it may be of some advantage to reserve the term "morphological" for those social facts which concern the social substratum, but only on condition of not overlooking the fact that they are of the same nature as the others. Our definition will then include the whole relevant range of facts if we say: *A social fact is every way of acting, fixed or not, capable of exercising on the individual an external constraint; or again, every way of acting which is general throughout a given society, while at the same time existing in its own right independent of its individual manifestations.*[d]

NOTES

[a]We do not intend to imply, however, that all constraint is normal. We shall return to this point later.

[b]Suicides do not occur at every age, and they take place with varying intensity at the different ages in which they occur.

[c]It will be seen how this definition of the social fact diverges from that which forms the basis of the ingenious system of M. Tarde. First of all, we wish to state that our researches have nowhere led us to observe that preponderant influence in the genesis of collective facts which M. Tarde attributes to imitation. Moreover, from the preceding definition, which is not a theory but simply a résumé of the immediate data of observation, it seems indeed to follow, not only that imitation does not always express the essential and characteristic features of the social fact, but even that it never expresses them. No doubt, every social fact is imitated; it has, as we have just shown, a tendency to become general, but that is because it is social, i.e., obligatory. Its power of expansion is not the cause but the consequence of its sociological character. If, further, only social facts produced this consequence, imitation could perhaps serve, if not to explain them, at least to define them. But an individual condition which produces a whole series of effects remains individual nevertheless. Moreover, one may ask whether the word "imitation" is indeed fitted to designate an effect due to a coercive influence. Thus, by this single expression, very different phenomena, which ought to be distinguished, are confused.

[d]This close connection between life and structure, organ and function, may be easily proved in sociology because between these two extreme terms there exists a whole series of immediately observable intermediate stages which show the bond between them. Biology is not in the same favorable position. But we may well believe that the inductions on this subject made by sociology are applicable to biology and that, in organisms as well as in societies, only differences in degree exist between these two orders of facts.

---

[13] It is easy to see the coercive element in illegal or immoral acts, whereby violation of a rule results (at least theoretically) in punishment. However, coercion is also present in ways of behaving that are outside of the individual and general throughout society, such as participation in the capitalist economic system or living in a certain type of house. Durkheim calls these phenomena "ways of existing." He further suggests that ways of existing and acting are variable in degree of fixity. There is, for example, a continuum of rigidity between custom and law, but both are still included in Durkheim's famous definition of social facts presented at the end of the paragraph.

6. *The Cosmological System of Totemism and the Idea of Class*

ÉMILE DURKHEIM (1858–1917)

WE ARE BEGINNING to see that totemism is a much more complex religion than it first appeared to be. We have already distinguished three classes of things which it recognizes as sacred, in varying degrees: the totemic emblem, the animal or plant whose appearance this emblem reproduces, and the members of the clan.[1] However, this list is not yet complete. In fact, a religion is not merely a collection of fragmentary beliefs in regard to special objects like those we have just been discussing. To a greater or less extent, all known religions have been systems of ideas which tend to embrace the universality of things, and to give us a complete representation of the world. If totemism is to be considered as a religion comparable to the others, it too should offer us a conception of the universe. As a matter of fact, it does satisfy this condition.

1

The fact that this aspect of totemism has generally been neglected is due to the too narrow notion of the clan which has been prevalent. Ordinarily it is regarded as a mere group of human beings. Being a simple subdivision of the tribe, it seems that like this, it is made up of nothing but men. But in reasoning thus, we substitute our European ideas for those which the primitive has of man and of society. For the Australian, things themselves, everything which is in the universe, are a part of the tribe; they are constituent elements of it and, so to speak, regular members of it; just like men, they have a determined place in the general scheme of organization of the society. "The South Australian savage," says Fison, "looks upon the universe as the Great Tribe, to one of whose divisions he himself belongs—and all things, animate and inanimate, which belong to his class are parts of the body corporate whereof he himself is a part."[a] As a consequence of this principle, whenever the tribe is divided into two phratries,[2] all known things are distributed between them. "All nature," says Palmer, in speaking of the Bellinger River tribe, "is also divided into class [phratry] names. . . . The sun and moon and stars are said . . . to belong to classes [phratries] just as the blacks themselves."[b] The Port Mackay tribe in Queensland has two phratries with the names Yungaroo and Wootaroo, as do the neighboring tribes. Now as Bridgmann says, "all things, animate and inanimate, are divided by

From *The Elementary Forms of the Religious Life* (1912)

---

[1] Durkheim was concerned with the mechanisms that held societies together. He believed that social cohesion was maintained because people in a society shared the same values and beliefs and reinforced those beliefs through rituals or communal action. For example, cohesion in simple societies was achieved through totemic beliefs (modeled on their own social relationships) and religious rituals (which reinforced those beliefs through communal action).

Sigmund Freud, in *Totem and Taboo*, first published in 1913, used totems to establish a link between psychoanalysis and anthropology and used psychoanalytic concepts to explain anthropological data. Durkheim, on the other hand, discussed how totemic beliefs structure society, contribute to social solidarity, and ultimately represent society. According to him, because totems are the fundamental form of kinship division, and these divisions compose the basic structure of society, the worship of totem ancestors represents the worship of society itself.

[2] Lorimer Fison (1832–1907) was a missionary, journalist, and anthropologist. He was a follower of Lewis Henry Morgan, and they corresponded extensively. Fison's research into Australian Aboriginal kinship systems, based on interviews with European settlers, provided important data for Morgan, Tylor, and James George Frazer, as well as Durkheim.

A *phratry* is a unilineal descent group composed of two or more clans.

these tribes into two classes, named Yungaroo and Wootaroo."[c] Nor does the classification stop here. The men of each phratry are distributed among a certain number of clans; likewise, the things attributed to each phratry are in their turn distributed among the clans of which the phratry is composed. A certain tree, for example, will be assigned to the Kangaroo clan, and to it alone; then, just like the human members of the clan, it will have the Kangaroo as totem; another will belong to the Snake-clan; clouds will be placed under one totem, the sun under another, etc. All known things will thus be arranged in a sort of tableau or systematic classification embracing the whole of nature.

We have given a certain number of these classifications elsewhere,[d] at present we shall confine ourselves to repeating a few of these as examples. One of the best known of these is the one found in the Mount Gambier tribe. This tribe includes two phratries, named respectively the Kumite and the Kroki; each of these, in its turn, is subdivided into five clans. Now "everything in nature belongs to one or another of these ten clans";[e] Fison and Howitt say that they are all "included" within it. In fact, they are classified under these ten totems just like species in their respective classes. This is well shown by the following table based on information gathered by Curr and by Fison and Howitt.[f]

[*The next several paragraphs of Durkheim's article (about 280 words) are given to describing examples of totems in a variety of Australian aboriginal tribes. His basic point is that the Australian Aborigines subdivide themselves and all the objects in their world into related totems. The passage includes 4 footnotes.*]

If we remember that there are many other clans (Howitt names twelve and Mathews fourteen and adds that his list is incomplete[g]), we will understand how all the things in which the native takes an interest find a natural place in these classifications.

Similar arrangements have been observed in the most diverse parts of the Australian continent; in South Australia, in Victoria, and in New South Wales (among the Euahlayi[h]); very clear traces of it are found in the central tribes.[i] In Queensland,

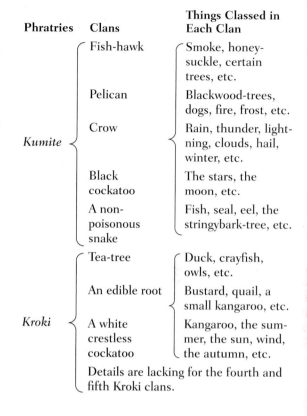

Phratries	Clans	Things Classed in Each Clan
Kumite	Fish-hawk	Smoke, honey-suckle, certain trees, etc.
	Pelican	Blackwood-trees, dogs, fire, frost, etc.
	Crow	Rain, thunder, lightning, clouds, hail, winter, etc.
	Black cockatoo	The stars, the moon, etc.
	A non-poisonous snake	Fish, seal, eel, the stringybark-tree, etc.
Kroki	Tea-tree	Duck, crayfish, owls, etc.
	An edible root	Bustard, quail, a small kangaroo, etc.
	A white crestless cockatoo	Kangaroo, the summer, the sun, wind, the autumn, etc.
	Details are lacking for the fourth and fifth Kroki clans.	

where the clans seem to have disappeared and where the matrimonial classes are the only subdivisions of the phratry, things are divided up among these classes. Thus the Wakelbura are divided into two phratries, Mallera and Wutaru; the classes of the first are called Kurgilla and Banbe, those of the second, Wungo and Obu. Now to the Banbe belong the opossum, the kangaroo, the dog, honey of little bees, etc.; to the Wungo are attributed the emu, the bandicoot, the black duck, the black snake, the brown snake; to the Obu, the carpet snake, the honey of stinging bees, etc., to the Kurgilla, the porcupine, the turkey of the plains, water, rain, fire, thunder, etc.[j]

This same organization is found among the Indians of North America. The Zuni have a system of classification which, in its essential lines, is in all points comparable to the one we have just described. That of the Omaha rests on the same principles as that of the Wotjobaluk.[k] An echo of these same ideas survives even into the more advanced societies. Among the Haida, all the gods and mythical beings who are placed in charge of the different phenomena of nature are classified in one or the other of the two phratries which make up the tribe just like men; some are Eagles, the others, Crows.[l] Now the gods of things are only another aspect of the things which they govern.[m] This mythological classification is therefore merely another form of the preceding one. So we may rest assured that this way of conceiving the world is independent of all ethnic or geographic particularities; and at the same time it is clearly seen to be closely united to the whole system of totemic beliefs.[3]

2

In the paper to which we have already made allusion several times, we have shown what light these facts throw upon the way in which the idea of kind or class was formed in humanity.[4] In fact, these systematic classifications are the first we meet with in history, and we have just seen that they are modeled upon the social organization, or rather that they have taken the forms of society as their framework. It is the phratries which have served as classes, and the clans as species. It is because men were organized that they have been able to organize things, for in classifying these latter, they limited themselves to giving them places in the groups they formed themselves.[5] And if these different classes of things are not merely put next to each other, but are arranged according to a unified plan, it is because the social groups with which they commingle themselves are unified and, through their union, form an organic whole, the tribe. The unity of these first logical systems merely reproduces the unity of the society. Thus we have an occasion for verifying the proposition which we laid down at the commencement of this work, and for assuring ourselves that the fundamental notions of the intellect, the essential categories of thought, may be the product of social factors.[6] The above-mentioned facts show clearly that this is the case with the very notion of category itself.

---

[3] Durkheim was concerned with documenting the universality of his theory through the use of cross-cultural ethnographic data. He cites a wide variety of examples from different parts of the world and concludes that totemism exists "independent of ethnic and geographic particularities." This issue is important because he believed totemism was one of the fundamental elements of primitive social organization. Writing at the same time as Durkheim, Franz Boas challenged the use of cross-cultural comparison (see essay 9). Boas believed that every society was the product of its own historical development. To understand a society, one needed to study the environmental and historical circumstances under which it developed.

[4] Although Durkheim does not specify what paper he is referring to in this passage, it is probably the article *"De quelques formes primitives de classification"* ("Primitive Forms of Classification"), co-authored with Mauss, which appeared in *L'Année Sociologique* in 1903.

[5] Durkheim asserted that totemic classification of the objects in the world was based on the social classification of people. Thus, totemic classification was derived from a model of social structure. Compare the very different treatment Freud accorded to totemism in *Totem and Taboo* (1950 [1913]), in which totemism originated in the memorialization of the primal father who was killed and eaten by his sons. Thus, in Freud's view, social classification was derived from totemism.

[6] In this paragraph Durkheim writes that "the fundamental notions of the intellect" and "the essential categories of thought" are the products of social factors, not individual invention. In the introduction to his book Durkheim wrote:

> Collective representations are the result of an immense co-operation, which stretches out not only into space but into time as well; to make them, a multitude of minds have associated, united and combined their ideas and sentiments; for them, long generations have accumulated their experience and knowledge. A special intellectual activity is therefore concentrated in them which is infinitely richer and complexer than that of the individual. (1965 [1912]:29)

In the final sentence of this paragraph in the essay, Durkheim notes that the very notion of a category of classification is itself a social construction. This is one of the critical insights upon which ethnoscience and cognitive anthropology were constructed in the 1950s and 1960s (see essays 27–29). Durkheim reiterates his belief that society is the model from which categories of classification are derived and that these shared models are the foundation of social solidarity. He writes that the unity of categories reproduces the unity of society.

However, it is not our intention to deny that the individual intellect has of itself the power of perceiving resemblances between the different objects of which it is conscious. Quite on the contrary, it is clear that even the most primitive and simple classifications presuppose this faculty. The Australian does not place things in the same clan or in different clans at random. For him as for us, similar images attract one another, while opposed ones repel one another, and it is on the basis of these feelings of affinity or of repulsion that he classifies the corresponding things in one place or another.

There are also cases where we are able to perceive the reasons which inspired this. The two phratries were very probably the original and fundamental bases for these classifications, which were consequently bifurcate at first. Now, when a classification is reduced to two classes, these are almost necessarily conceived as antitheses; they are used primarily as a means of clearly separating things between which there is a very marked contrast. Some are set at the right, the others at the left.[7] As a matter of fact this is the character of the Australian classifications. If the white cockatoo is in one phratry, the black one is in the other; if the sun is on one side, the moon and the stars of night are on the opposite side.[n] Very frequently the beings which serve as the totems of the two phratries have contrary colours.[o] These oppositions are even met with outside of Australia. Where one of the phratries is disposed to peace, the other is disposed to war,[p] if one has water as its totem, the other has earth.[q] This is undoubtedly the explanation of why the two phratries have frequently been thought of as naturally antagonistic to one another. They say that there is a sort of rivalry or even a constitutional hostility between them.[r] This opposition of

things has extended itself to persons; the logical contrast has begotten a sort of social conflict.[s]

It is also to be observed that within each phratry, those things have been placed in a single clan which seem to have the greatest affinity with that serving as totem. For example, the moon has been placed with the black cockatoo, but the sun, together with the atmosphere and the wind, with the white cockatoo. Or again, to a totemic animal has been united all that serves him as food,[t] as well as the animals with which he has the closest connection.[u] Of course, we cannot always understand the obscure psychology which has caused many of these connections and distinctions, but the preceding examples are enough to show that a certain intuition of the resemblances and differences presented by things has played an important part in the genesis of these classifications.

But the feeling of resemblances is one thing and the idea of class is another. The class is the external framework of which objects perceived to be similar form, in part, the contents. Now the contents cannot furnish the frame into which they fit. They are made up of *vague and fluctuating* images, due to the superimposition and partial fusion of a *determined number of individual images,* which are found to have common elements; the framework, on the contrary, is a *definite form,* with fixed outlines, but which may be applied to an *undetermined number of things,* perceived or not, actual or possible. In fact, every class has possibilities of extension which go far beyond the circle of objects which we know, either from direct experience or from resemblance. This is why every school of thinkers has refused, and not without good reason, to identify the idea of class with that of a generic image. The generic image is only the indistinctly-bounded residual representation left in us by similar representations, when

---

[7] Durkheim's belief that human systems of classification were dualistic is expressed in this paragraph. One of the first studies suggesting the dualistic nature of human thought was the 1909 article "The Pre-eminence of the Right Hand: A Study in Religious Polarity" by Durkheim's student Robert Hertz (1881–1915). In this essay he examined the values placed on right- and left-handedness and analyzed the social function of these beliefs in society.

Hertz said that the valuation of right- over left-handedness was a social fact that reflected the fundamental religious dichotomy between sacred and profane. Durkheim draws from Hertz's article in the next few paragraphs. Durkheim's ideas on dual classification form one of the principal assumptions underlying French structuralism as practiced by Claude Lévi-Strauss (see essays 24 and 25).

they are present in consciousness simultaneously; the class is a logical symbol by means of which we think distinctly of these similarities and of other analogous ones. Moreover, the best proof of the distance separating these two notions is that an animal is able to form generic images though ignorant of the art of thinking in classes and species.[8]

The idea of class is an instrument of thought which has obviously been constructed by men. But in constructing it, we have at least had need of a model; for how could this idea ever have been born, if there had been nothing either in us or around us which was capable of suggesting it to us? To reply that it was given to us *a priori*[9] is not to reply at all; this lazy man's solution is, as has been said, the death of analysis. But it is hard to see where we could have found this indispensable model except in the spectacle of the collective life. In fact, a class is not an ideal, but a clearly defined group of things between which internal relationships exist, similar to those of kindred. Now the only groups of this sort known from experience are those formed by men in associating themselves. Material things may be able to form collections of units, or heaps, or mechanical assemblages with no internal unity, but not groups in the sense we have given the word. A heap of sand or a pile of rock is in no way comparable to that variety of definite and organized society which forms a class. In all probability, we would never have thought of uniting the beings of the universe into homogeneous groups, called classes, if we had not had the example of human societies before our eyes, if we had not even commenced by making

things themselves members of men's society, and also if human groups and logical groups had not been confused at first.[v]

It is also to be borne in mind that a classification is a system whose parts are arranged according to a hierarchy. There are dominating members and others which are subordinate to the first; species and their distinctive properties depend upon classes and the attributes which characterize them; again, the different species of a single class are conceived as all placed on the same level in regard to each other. Does someone prefer to regard them from the point of view of the understanding? Then he represents things to himself in an inverse order: he puts at the top the species that are the most particularized and the richest in reality, while the types that are most general and the poorest in qualities are at the bottom. Nevertheless, all are represented in a hierarchic form. And we must be careful not to believe that the expression has only a metaphorical sense here: there are really relations of subordination and coordination, the establishment of which is the object of all classification, and men would never have thought of arranging their knowledge in this way if they had not known beforehand what a hierarchy was. But neither the spectacle of physical nature nor the mechanism of mental associations could furnish them with this knowledge. The hierarchy is exclusively a social affair. It is only in society that there are superiors, inferiors and equals. Consequently, even if the facts were not enough to prove it, the mere analysis of these ideas would reveal their origin. We have taken them from society, and projected them into our

---

[8] In this section, Durkheim is discussing how humans classify things into groups. He begins by talking about the classification of people and objects into totems. He says the contents of a class do not construct the boundaries of that class but that the class framework is external: Humans impose these class boundaries on the objects in the world. The obvious question then is, what are the origins of these classes? In the next paragraph he tries to answer this question. Durkheim carefully distinguishes between generic images and ideas of class. The generic image is based on a vague feeling of affinity, whereas a class is a fixed framework in which an indefinite number of objects

can be categorized. This idea is critical in the development of ethnoscience and is implicit in the concept of domains (see essays 27 and 28). In the final statement in this paragraph, Durkheim says the best proof of the distinction between generic images and classes is that an animal is able to form generic images but not think in classes! We find this intriguing. This statement is probably based on the experimental psychology of Durkheim's time, but as he provides no citation, we do not really know what he was referring to.

[9] *A priori:* Latin for without or before examination.

conceptions of the world. It is society that has furnished the outlines which logical thought has filled in.[10]

3

But these primitive classifications have a no less direct interest for the origins of religious thought.

They imply that all the things thus classed in a single clan or a single phratry are closely related both to each other and to the thing serving as the totem of this clan or phratry. When an Australian of the Port Mackay tribe says that the sun, snakes, etc., are of the Yungaroo phratry, he does not mean merely to apply a common, but none the less a purely conventional, nomenclature to these different things; the word has an objective signification for him. He believes that "alligators really *are* Yungaroo and that kangaroos are Wootaroo. The sun *is* Yungaroo, the moon Wootaroo, and so on for the constellations, trees, plants, etc."[w] An internal bond attaches them to the group in which they are placed; they are regular members of it. It is said that they belong to the group,[x] just exactly as the individual men make a part of it; consequently, the same sort of a relation unites them to these latter. Men regard the things in their clan as their relatives or associates; they call them their friends and think that they are made out of the same flesh as themselves.[y] Therefore, between the two there are elective affinities and quite special relations of

agreement. Things and people have a common name, and in a certain way they naturally understand each other and harmonize with one another. For example, when a Wakelbura of the Mallera phratry is buried, the scaffold upon which the body is exposed "must be made of the wood of some tree belonging to the Mallera phratry."[z] The same is true for the branches that cover the corpse. If the deceased is of the Banbe class, a Banbe tree must be used. In this same tribe, a magician can use in his art only those things which belong to his own phratry;[aa] since the others are strangers to him, he does not know how to make them obey him. Thus a bond of mystic sympathy unites each individual to those beings, whether living or not, which are associated with him; the result of this is a belief in the possibility of deducing what he will do or what he has done from what they are doing. Among these same Wakelbura, when a man dreams that he has killed an animal belonging to a certain social division, he expects to meet a man of this same division the next day.[bb] Inversely, the things attributed to a clan or phratry cannot be used against the members of this clan or phratry. Among the Wotjobaluk, each phratry has its own special trees. Now in hunting an animal of the Gurogity phratry, only arms whose wood is taken from trees of the other phratry may be used, and *vice versa*; otherwise the hunter is sure to miss his aim.[cc] The native is convinced that the arrow would turn of itself and refuse, so to speak, to hit a kindred and friendly animal.[11]

---

[10] Durkheim emphasized the idea that systems of classification reflect the social categories a group imposes on its members. There is an additional level at which imposition may be at work in this essay—one of which Durkheim was unaware. Is it possible that Durkheim is projecting his own Eurocentric vision of a hierarchical world onto the Australian Aboriginal worldview? His statement that the object of all classification is to rank elements in relations of subordination or domination may tell us more about the society in which Durkheim lived than Aboriginal society.

[11] Although Durkheim makes no specific citations, his comments closely follow an earlier work by his fellow French scientist Lucien Levy-Bruhl (1857–1939), who is best known for his discussion of primitive mentality. In an

article published in 1910, "Fonctions mentales dans les sociétés inférieures" (published in translation in 1966 as *How Natives Think*), Levy-Bruhl used information on the Bororo of central Brazil to support his theory that thought in primitive societies was less advanced than that in civilized societies. He writes

> The Bororo . . . boast that they are red araras (parakeets). This does not merely signify that after their death they become araras, nor that araras are metamorphosed Bororos, and must be treated as such. . . . It is not a name they give themselves, nor a relationship that they claim. What they desire to express by it is actual identity. . . . All communities which are totemic in form admit of collective representations of

Thus the men of the clan and the things which are classified in it form by their union a solid system, all of whose parts are united and vibrate sympathetically. This organization, which at first may have appeared to us as purely logical, is at the same time moral. A single principle animates it and makes its unity: this is the totem. Just as a man who belongs to the Crow clan has within him something of this animal, so the rain, since it is of the same clan and belongs to the same totem, is also necessarily considered as being "the same thing as a crow"; for the same reason, the moon is a black cockatoo, the sun a white cockatoo, every black-nut tree a pelican, etc. All the beings arranged in a single clan, whether men, animals, plants or inanimate objects, are merely forms of the totemic being. This is the meaning of the formula which we have just cited and this is what makes the two really of the same species: all are really of the same flesh in the sense that all partake of the nature of the totemic animal. Also, the qualifiers given them are those given to the totem.[dd] The Wotjobaluk give the name *Mir* both to the totem and to the things classed with it.[ee] It is true that among the Arunta, where visible traces of classification still exist, as we shall see, different words designate the totem and the other beings placed with it; however, the name given to these latter bears witness to the close relations which unite them to the totemic animal. It is said that they are its *intimates*, its *associates*, its *friends*; it is believed that they are inseparable from it.[ff] So there is a

feeling that these are very closely related things.[12]

But we also know that the totemic animal is a sacred being. All the things that are classified in the clan of which it is the emblem have this same character, because in one sense, they are animals of the same species, just as the man is. They, too, are sacred, and the classifications which locate them in relation to the other things of the universe, by that very act give them a place in the religious world. For this reason, the animals or plants among these may not be eaten freely by the human members of the clan. Thus in the Mount Gambier tribe, the men whose totem is a certain non-poisonous snake must not merely refrain from eating the flesh of this snake; that of seals, eels, etc., is also forbidden to them.[gg] If, driven by necessity, they do eat some of it, they must at least attenuate the sacrilege by expiatory rites, just as if they had eaten the totem itself.[hh] Among the Euahlayi, where it is permitted to use the totem, but not to abuse it, the same rule is applied to the other members of the clan.[ii] Among the Arunta, the interdictions protecting the totemic animal extend over the associated animals;[jj] and in any case, particular attention must be given to these latter.[kk] The sentiments inspired by the two are identical.[ll]

[In an 870-word section (with 15 footnotes) Durkheim discusses the process by which new totems are formed. He says that as clans undergo division or as already existing subdivisions within a

---

this kind, implying similar identity of the individual members of a totemic group and their totem (quoted in Crocker 1977:165).

Although Durkheim and Levy-Bruhl discuss the features of totemic classification for different purposes, the work of both men influenced the later thoughts of the French structuralist Claude Lévi-Strauss. Levy-Bruhl says the Bororo think they are parrots to prove his point that primitive people have a primitive mentality; Durkheim believes the Bororo say they are parrots as a way of understanding and classifying their world. Building a theory based on the work of both men, Lévi-Strauss argued that the Bororo think they are parrots because the human brain is organized in such a way that classifying the world in this fashion is naturally appealing.

[12] In the first sentence of this paragraph, Durkheim writes that the men of a clan and all the things classified with it form a system whose parts "are united and vibrate sympathetically." This is very close to the concept of mechanical solidarity, which Durkheim used to refer to social cohesion based on kinship. Durkheim appears to say that the concept of totemism is the central unifying symbol of a society with mechanical solidarity. In large, industrial societies, however, different social groups may have different sets of rules—the collective conscience is no longer the sole regulator of action. Social cohesion in this situation is maintained through professional and social ties created by the interdependence of classes, professions, and services necessary to maintain a complex society. Durkheim called this form of cohesion organic solidarity.

clan become more pronounced, subtotems are formed. When a subclan splits completely from its parent clan, the subtotem becomes a new totem. This discussion is followed by a number of ethnographic examples.]

So the field of religious things extends well beyond the limits within which it seemed to be confined at first. It embraces not only the totemic animals and the human members of the clan; but since no known thing exists that is not classified in a clan and under a totem, there is likewise nothing which does not receive to some degree something of a religious character. When, in the religions which later come into being, the gods properly so-called appear, each of them will be set over a special category of natural phenomena, this one over the sea, that one over the air, another over the harvest or over fruits, etc., and each of these provinces of nature will be believed to draw what life there is in it from the god upon whom it depends. This division of nature among the different divinities constitutes the conception which these religions give us of the universe. Now so long as humanity has not passed the phase of totemism, the different totems of the tribe fulfill exactly the same functions that will later fall upon the divine personalities. In the Mount Gambier tribe, which we have taken as our principal example, there are ten clans; consequently the entire world is divided into ten classes, or rather into ten families, each of which has a special totem as its basis. It is from this basis that the things classed in the clan get all their reality, for they are thought of as variant forms of the totemic being; to return to our example, the rain, thunder, lightning, clouds, hail and winter are regarded as different sorts of crows. When brought together, these ten families of things make up a complete and systematic representation of the world; and this representation is religious, for religious notions furnish its basis. Far from being limited to one or two categories of beings, the domain of totemic religion extends to

the final limits of the known universe. Just like the Greek religion, it puts the divine everywhere; the celebrated formula πάντα πλήρη θεων (everything is full of the gods), might equally well serve it as motto.[13]

However, if totemism is to be represented thus, the notion of it which has long been held must be modified on one essential point. Until the discoveries of recent years, it was made to consist entirely in the cult of one particular totem, and it was defined as the religion of the clan. From this point of view, each tribe seemed to have as many totemic religions, each independent of the others, as it had different clans. This conception was also in harmony with the idea currently held of the clan; in fact, this was regarded as an autonomous society,[mmm] more or less closed to other similar societies, or having only external and superficial relations with these latter. But the reality is more complex. Undoubtedly, the cult of each totem has its home in the corresponding clan; it is there, and only there, that it is celebrated; it is members of the clan who have charge of it; it is through them that it is transmitted from one generation to another, along with the beliefs which are its basis. But it is also true that the different totemic cults thus practised within a single tribe do not have a parallel development, though remaining ignorant of each other, as if each of them constituted a complete and self-sufficing religion. On the contrary, they mutually imply each other; they are only the parts of a single whole, the elements of a single religion. The men of one clan never regard the beliefs of neighboring clans with that indifference, skepticism or hostility which one religion ordinarily inspires for another which is foreign to it; they partake of these beliefs themselves. The Crow people are also convinced that the Snake people have a mythical serpent as ancestor, and that they owe special virtues and marvelous powers to this origin. And have we not seen that at least in certain conditions, a man may eat a totem that is not his own only after he has observed

---

[13] This is a crucial paragraph. Durkheim says that the original form of religion was totemism, which is modeled on human society and integrates all humans, animals, and ob-

jects into one system of religious classification. As the gods of later religions replace the roles held by totems in simpler societies, the gods, too, are modeled after human society.

certain ritual formalities? Especially, he must demand the permission of the men of this totem, if any are present. So for him also, this food is not entirely profane; he also admits that there are intimate affinities between the members of a clan of which he is not a member and the animal whose name they bear. Also, this community of belief is sometimes shown in the cult. If in theory the rites concerning a totem can be performed only by the men of this totem, nevertheless representatives of different clans frequently assist at them. It sometimes happens that their part is not simply that of spectators; it is true that they do not officiate, but they decorate the officiants and prepare the service. They themselves have an interest in its being celebrated; therefore, in certain tribes, it is they who invite the qualified clan to proceed with the ceremonies.[nn] There is even a whole cycle of rites which must take place in the presence of the assembled tribe: these are the totemic ceremonies of initiation.[oo]

Finally, the totemic organization, such as we have just described it, must obviously be the result of some sort of an indistinct understanding between all the members of the tribe. It is impossible that each clan should have made its beliefs in an absolutely independent manner; it is absolutely necessary that the cults of the different totems should be in some way adjusted to each other, since they complete one another exactly. In fact, we have seen that normally a single totem is not repeated twice in the same tribe, and that the whole universe is divided up among the totems thus constituted in such a way that the same object is not found in two different clans. So methodical a division could never have been made without an agreement, tacit or

planned, in which the whole tribe participated.[14] So the group of beliefs which thus arise are partially (but only partially) a tribal affair.[pp]

To sum up, then, in order to form an adequate idea of totemism, we must not confine ourselves within the limits of the clan, but must consider the tribe as a whole. It is true that the particular cult of each clan enjoys a very great autonomy; we can now see that it is within the clan that the active ferment of the religious life takes place. But it is also true that these cults fit into each other and the totemic religion is a complex system formed by their union, just as Greek polytheism was made by the union of all the particular cults addressed to the different divinities. We have just shown that, thus understood, totemism also has its cosmology.[15]

NOTES

[a] *Kamilaroi and Kurnai*, p. 170.

[b] *Notes on Some Australian Tribes, J.A.I.,* XIII, p. 300.

[c] In Curr, *Australian Race,* III, p. 45; Brough Smyth, *The Aborgines of Victoria,* I, p. 91; Fison and Howitt, *Kamilaroi and Kurnai,* p. 168.

[d] Durkheim and Mauss, *De quelques formes primitives de classification,* in Année Sociol., VI, pp. 1 ff.

[e] Curr, III, p. 461.

[f] Curr and Fison were both informed by the same person, D. S. Stewart.

[g] The tables of Mathews and Howitt disagree on many important points. It even seems that clans attributed by Howitt to the Kroki phratry are given to the Gamutch phratry by Mathews, and inversely. This proves the great difficulties that these observations present. But these differences are without interest for our present question.

[h] Mrs. Langloh Parker, *The Euahlayi Tribe,* pp. 12 ff.

---

[14] Durkheim presents an extremely interesting idea here. He says that the universe is divided among the totems, with each totem having a set of elements identified as part of its totemic classification. As the same object is not found in two different totems, the systems complement each other. Thus, when all the clans assemble, an observer is presented with a complete model of the Aboriginal universe.

[15] Durkheim focused on totems because he believed them to be the most elementary form of religion and therefore simple to analyze and understand. However, he did not

believe that totemic religions were different in kind from the religions of complex societies. His argument was revolutionary in that he asserted that all religions, including Christianity, were based on fundamentally similar patterns. Furthermore, Durkheim believed that all religions were fundamentally equal. In the introduction to *The Elementary Forms of the Religious Life* he wrote, "In reality, then, there are no religions which are false. All are true in their own fashion; all answer, though in different ways, to the given conditions of human existence. . . . They respond to the same needs, they play the same role, they depend upon the same causes" (1965 [1912]:15).

[i] The facts will be found below.

[j] Carr, III, p. 27. Cf. Howitt, *Nat. Tr.*, p. 112. We are merely mentioning the most characteristic facts. For details, one may refer to the memoir already mentioned on *Les classifications primitives.*

[k] *Ibid.*, pp. 34 ff.

[l] Swanton, *The Haida*, pp. 13–14, 17, 22.

[m] This is especially clear among the Haida. Swanton says that with them every animal has two aspects. First, it is an ordinary animal to be hunted and eaten; but it is also a supernatural being in the animal's form, upon which men depend. The mythical beings corresponding to cosmic phenomena have the same ambiguity (Swanton, *ibid.*, 16, 14, 25).

[n] See above, p. 166. This is the case among the Gournditch-mara (Howitt, *Nat. Tr.*, p. 124), in the tribes studied by Cameron near the Dead Lake, and among the Wotjobaluk (*ibid.*, pp. 125, 250).

[o] J. Mathews, *Two Representative Tribes*, p. 139; Thomas, *Kinship and Marriage*, pp. 53 f.

[p] Among the Osage, for example, see Dorsey, *Siouan Sociology*, in *XVth Rep.*, pp. 233 ff.

[q] At Mabuiag, an island in Torrès' Strait (Haddon, *Head Hunters*, p. 132), the same opposition is found between the two phratries of the Arunta: one includes the men of a water totem, the other those of earth (Strehlow, I, p. 6).

[r] Among the Iroquois there is a sort of tournament between the two phratries (Morgan, *Ancient Society*, p. 94). Among the Haida, says Swanton, the members of the two phratries of the Eagle and the Crow "are frequently considered as avowed enemies. Husband and wife (who must be of different phratries) do not hesitate to betray each other" (*The Haida*, p. 62). In Australia this hostility is carried into the myths. The two animals serving the phratries as totems are frequently represented as in a perpetual war against each other (see J. Mathews, *Eaglehawk and Crow, a Study of Australian Aborigines*, pp. 14 ff). In games, each phratry is the natural rival of the other (Howitt, *Nat. Tr.*, p. 770).

[s] So Thomas has wrongly urged against our theory of the origin of the phratries its inability to explain their opposition (*Kinship and Marriage*, p. 69). We do not believe that it is necessary to connect this opposition to that of the profane and the sacred (see Hertz, *La prééminence de la main droite*, in the *Revue Philosophique*, Dec., 1909, p. 559). The things of one phratry are not profane for the other; both are a part of the same religious system (see below, p. 181).

[t] For example, the clan of the Tea-tree includes the grasses, and consequently herbivorous animals (see *Kamilaroi and Kurnai*, p. 169). This is undoubtedly the explanation of a particularity of the totemic emblems of North America pointed out by Boas. "Among the Tlinkit," he says, "and all the other tribes of the coast, the emblem of a group includes the animals serving as food to the one whose name the group bears" (*Fifth Rep. of the Committee, etc. British Association for the Advancement of Science*, p. 25).

[u] Thus, among the Arunta, frogs are connected with the totem of the gumtree, because they are frequently found in the cavities of this tree; water is related to the water-hen; with the kangaroo is associated a sort of parrot frequently seen flying about this animal (Spencer and Gillen, *Nat. Tr.*, pp. 146–147, 448).

[v] One of the signs of this primitive lack of distinction is that territorial bases are sometimes assigned to the classes just as to the social divisions with which they were at first confounded. Thus, among the Watjobaluk in Australia and the Zuñi in America, things are ideally distributed among the different regions of space, just as the clans are. Now this regional distribution of things and that of the clans coincide (see *De quelques formes primitives de classification*, pp. 34 ff.). Classifications keep something of this special character even among relatively advanced peoples, as for example, in China (*ibid.*, pp. 55 ff.).

[w] Bridgmann, in Brough Smyth, *The Aborigines of Victoria*, I, p. 91.

[x] Fison and Howitt, *Kamilaroi and Kurnai*, p. 168; Howitt, *Further Notes on the Australian Class Systems*, *J.A.I.*, XVIII, p. 60.

[y] Curr, III, p. 461. This is about the Mount Gambier tribe.

[z] Howitt, *On Some Australian Beliefs*, *J.A.I.*, XIII, p. 191, n. 1.

[aa] Howitt, *Notes on Australian Message Sticks*, *J.A.I.*, XVIII, p. 326; *Further Notes*, *J.A.I.*, XVIII, p. 61, n. 3.

[bb] Curr, III, p. 28.

[cc] Mathews, *Ethnological Notes on the Aboriginal Tribes of N.S. Wales and Victoria*, in *Journ. and Proceed. of the Royal Soc. of N.S. Wales*, XXXVIII, p. 294.

[dd] Cf. Curr, III, p. 461; and Howitt, *Nat. Tr.*, p. 146. The expressions *Tooman* and *Wingo* are applied to the one and the other.

[ee] Howitt, *Nat. Tr.*, p. 123.

[ff] Spencer and Gillen, *Nat. Tr.*, pp. 447 ff.; cf. Strehlow, III, pp. xii ff.

[gg] Fison and Howitt, *Kamilaroi and Kurnai*, p. 169.

[hh] Turr, III, p. 462.

[ii] Mrs. Parker, *The Euahlayi Tribe*, p. 20.

[jj] Spencer and Gillen, *Nor. Tr.*, p. 151; *Nat. Tr.*, p. 447; Strehlow, III, p. xii.

[kk] Spencer and Gillen, *Nat. Tr.*, p. 449.

[ll] However, there are certain tribes in Queensland where the things thus attributed to a social group are

not forbidden for the members of the group: this is notably the case with the Wakelbura. It is to be remembered that in this society, it is the matrimonial classes that serve as the framework of the classification (see above, p. 169). Not only are the men of one class allowed to eat the animals attributed to this class, but *they may eat no others*. All other food is forbidden them (Howitt, *Nat. Tr.*, p. 113; Curr, III, p. 27).

But we must not conclude from this that these animals are considered profane. In fact, it should be noticed that the individual not only has the privilege of eating them, but that he is compelled to do so, for he cannot nourish himself otherwise. Now the imperative nature of this rule is a sure sign that we are in the presence of things having a religious nature, only this has given rise to a positive obligation rather than the negative one known as an interdiction. Perhaps it is not quite impossible to see how this deviation came about. We have seen above (p. 163) that every individual is thought to have a sort of property-right over his totem and consequently over the things dependent upon it. Perhaps, under the influence of special circumstances, this aspect of the totemic relation was developed, and they naturally came to believe that only the members of the clan had the right of disposing of their totem and all that is connected with it, and that others, on the contrary, did not have the right of touching it. Under these circumstances, a tribe could nourish itself only on the food attributed to it.

ᵐᵐ Thus it comes about that the clan has frequently been confounded with the tribe. This confusion, which frequently introduces trouble into the writings of ethnologists, has been made especially by Curr (I, pp. 61 ff.).

ⁿⁿ This is the case especially among the Warramunga (*Nor. Tr.*, p. 298).

ᵒᵒ See, for example, Spencer and Gillen, *Nat. Tr.*, p. 380 and *passim*.

ᵖᵖ One might even ask if tribal totems do not exist sometimes. Thus, among the Arunta, there is an animal, the wild cat, which serves as totem to a particular clan, but which is forbidden for the whole tribe; even the people of other clans can eat it only very moderately (*Nat. Tr.*, p. 168). But we believe that it would be an abuse to speak of a tribal totem in this case, for it does not follow from the fact that the free consumption of an animal is forbidden that this is a totem. Other causes can also give rise to an interdiction. The religious unity of the tribe is undoubtedly real, but this is affirmed with the aid of other symbols. We shall show what these are below (Bk. II, ch. ix).

---

7. *Excerpts from* The Gift

Marcel Mauss (1872–1950)

[*Our reprint of Mauss' work opens with sections three of Chapter 2. In sections one and two of that chapter, comprising about 5,000 words, Mauss describes the rules of generosity on the Andaman Islands and the Kula trade in Melanesia, as well as other associated exchange practices. These exchanges, he believes, are the material expressions of Émile Durkheim's social facts. They are used to forge and maintain alliances, and they replicate the divisions between the people involved in them. The interdependence of the exchange network increases social solidarity. He continues here with a discussion of potlatch among Native Americans.*]

3. HONOUR AND CREDIT (NORTH-WEST AMERICA)

From these observations on Melanesian and Polynesian peoples our picture of gift economy is already beginning to take shape.[1] Material and moral life, as exemplified in gift exchange, functions

---

From Chapters 2 and 4 of *The Gift* (1925)

---

[1] The parts of Mauss' essay reproduced here contain more than one hundred notes. Space limitations prevent us from reproducing them here, but asterisks have been included to give the reader an idea of the volume of notes Mauss wrote. The intrepid reader can look them up in a complete version of *The Gift*.

there in a manner at once interested and obligatory. Furthermore, the obligation is expressed in myth and imagery, symbolically and collectively; it takes the form of interest in the objects exchanged; the objects are never completely separated from the men who exchange them; the communion and alliance they establish are well-nigh indissoluble. The lasting influence of the objects exchanged is a direct expression of the manner in which subgroups within segmentary societies of an archaic type are constantly embroiled with and feel themselves in debt to each other.

Indian societies of the American North-West have the same institutions, but in a more radical and accentuated form.[2] Barter is unknown there. Even now after long contact with Europeans it does not appear that any of the considerable and continual transfers of wealth take place otherwise than through the formality of the potlatch.* We now describe this institution as we see it.

First, however, we give a short account of these societies.[3] The tribes in question inhabit the North-West American coast—the Tlingit and Haida of Alaska,* and the Tsimshian and Kwakiutl of British Columbia.* They live on the sea or on the rivers and depend more on fishing than on hunting for their livelihood; but in contrast to the Melanesians and Polynesians they do not practice agriculture. Yet they are very wealthy, and even at the present day their fishing, hunting and trapping activities yield surpluses which are considerable even when reckoned on the European scale. They have the most substantial houses of all the American tribes, and a highly evolved cedar industry. Their canoes are good; and although they seldom venture out on to the open sea they are skillful in navigating around their islands and in coastal waters. They have a high standard of material culture. In particular, even back in the eighteenth century, they collected, smelted, molded and beat local copper from Tsimshian and Tlingit country. Some of the copper in the form of decorated shields they used as a kind of currency. Almost certainly another form of currency was the beautifully embellished Chilkat blanket-work still used ornamentally, some of it being of considerable value.* The peoples are excellent carvers and craftsmen. Their pipes, clubs and sticks are the pride of our ethnological collections. Within broad limits this civilization is remarkably uniform. It is clear that the societies have been in contact with each other from very early days, although their languages suggest that they belong to at least three families of peoples.*

Their winter life, even with the southern tribes, is very different from their summer life. The tribes have a two-fold structure: at the end of spring they disperse and go hunting, collect berries from the hillsides and fish the rivers for salmon; while in winter they concentrate in what are known as towns. During this period of concentration they are in a perpetual state of effervescence.[4] The social life becomes intense in the extreme, even more so than in the concentrations of tribes that manage to form in the summer. This life consists of continual movement. There are constant visits of whole tribes to others, of clans to clans and families to families. There is feast upon feast, some of long duration. On the occasion of a marriage, on various ritual occasions,

---

[2] Mauss implies here that the purpose of these practices cannot be explained simply by economics. If their root purposes were economic, they would have disappeared with European contact.

[3] The next several paragraphs provide a broad ethnographic description of the potlatch customs of several Northwest Native American groups, much of which is drawn from Franz Boas' work. Mauss' description is a catalog of material culture, but his real interests lie in examining patterns of social interaction.

[4] For Durkheim and his followers, members of the *L'Année Sociologique* school, the idea of periods of "effervescence" was critical in the binary separation of sacred and profane. For example, discussing the Australian Aborigines in *The Elementary Forms of the Religious Life,* Durkheim wrote that sacred times, when people assemble, were marked by "a sort of electricity . . . which transports them to exaltation. Every sentiment expressed finds a place without resistance in all the minds . . . each re-echoes the others, and is re-echoed by the others. . . . How could such experiences as these . . . fail to leave [an individual convinced] that there really exist two heterogeneous and mutually incomparable worlds?" (1965:245–50).

and on social advancement, there is reckless consumption of everything which has been amassed with great industry from some of the richest coasts of the world during the course of summer and autumn. Even private life passes in this manner; clansmen are invited when a seal is killed or a box of roots or berries opened; you invite everyone when a whale runs aground.

Social organization, too, is fairly constant throughout the area though it ranges from the matrilineal phratry (Tlingit and Haida) to the modified matrilineal clan of the Kwakiutl; but the general characters of the social organization and particularly of totemism are repeated in all the tribes. They have associations like those of the Banks Islanders of Melanesia, wrongly called "secret societies," which are often inter-tribal; and men's and women's societies among the Kwakiutl cut across tribal organization. A part of the gifts and counter-prestations[5] which we shall discuss goes, as in Melanesia,* to pay one's way into the successive steps* of the associations. Clan and association ritual follows the marriage of chiefs, the sale of coppers, initiations, shamanistic seances and funeral ceremonies, the latter being more particularly pronounced among the Tlingit and Haida. These are all accomplished in the course of an indefinitely prolonged series of potlatches. Potlatches are given in all directions, corresponding to other potlatches to which they are the response. As in Melanesia the process is one of constant give-and-take.

The potlatch, so unique as a phenomenon, yet so typical of these tribes, is really nothing other than gift-exchange.[6] The only differences are in the violence, rivalry and antagonism aroused, in a lack of jural[7] concepts, and in a simpler structure. It is less refined than in Melanesia, especially as regards the northern tribes, the Tlingit and the Haida,* but the collective nature of the contract is more pronounced than in Melanesia and Polynesia.* Despite appearances, the institutions here are nearer to what we call simple total prestations. Thus the legal and economic concepts attached to them have less clarity and conscious precision. Nevertheless, in action the principles emerge formally and clearly.

There are two traits more in evidence here than in the Melanesian potlatch or in the more evolved and discrete institutions of Polynesia: the themes of credit and honour.*

As we have seen, when gifts circulate in Melanesia and Polynesia the return is assured by the virtue of the things passed on, which are their own guarantees. In any society it is in the nature of the gift in the end to being its own reward. By definition, a common meal, a distribution of *kava,*[8] or a charm worn, cannot be repaid at once. Time has to pass before a counterprestation can be made. Thus the notion of time is logically implied when one pays a visit, contracts a marriage or an alliance, makes a treaty, goes to organized games, fights or feasts of others, renders ritual and honorific service and "shows respect," to use the Tlingit term.* All these are things exchanged side by side with other material objects, and they are the more numerous as the society is wealthier.

On this point, legal and economic theory is greatly at fault.[9] Imbued with modern ideas,

---

[5] Mauss' work deals with a class of phenomena he calls *prestations,* which are a type of gift exchange between groups. They appear "disinterested and spontaneous" but are, in reality, neither. Rather, they are obligatory and enacted under a highly specific system of reciprocity.

[6] Mauss followed Durkheim's idea of social evolution from mechanical to organic solidarity. Simple societies, such as those he is describing, are characterized by mechanical solidarity, which means that their social institutions are not separated, as in complex society. Instead, a few phenomena—called *total social phenomena*—simultaneously express a great many institutions. Pot-

latch exchange, as Mauss details below, is such a phenomenon.

[7] *Jural:* legal.

[8] *Kava:* a Polynesian ritual beverage consumed to produce a euphoric state. Made from the roots of the kava plant, *Piper methysticum.*

[9] Here Mauss takes aim at simple linear evolutionary schemes. Durkheim and Mauss were hostile to Darwinian models of social evolution, which stressed conflict and competition. In Durkheim's model, social evolution is driven by the need to achieve social solidarity at greater levels of population density and complexity.

current theory tends towards *a priori* notions of evolution,* and claims to follow a so-called necessary logic; in fact, however, it remains based on old traditions. Nothing could be more dangerous than what Simiand[10] called this "unconscious sociology." For instance, Cuq could still say in 1910: "In primitive societies barter alone is found; in those more advanced, direct sale is practiced. Sale on credit characterizes a higher stage of civilization; it appears first in an indirect manner, a combination of sale and loan."* In fact the origin of credit is different. It is to be found in a range of customs neglected by lawyers and economists as uninteresting: namely the gift, which is a complex phenomenon especially in its ancient form of total prestation which we are studying here. Now a gift necessarily implies the notion of credit. Economic evolution has not gone from barter to sale and from cash to credit. Barter arose from the system of gifts given and received on credit, simplified by drawing together the moments of time which had previously been distinct. Likewise purchase and sale—both direct sale and credit sale—and the loan, derive from the same source. There is nothing to suggest that any economic system which has passed through the phase we are describing was ignorant of the idea of credit, of which all archaic societies around us are aware. This is a simple and realistic manner of dealing with the problem, which Davy[11] has already studied, of the "two moments of time" which the contract unites.*

No less important is the role which honour plays in the transactions of the Indians. Nowhere else is the prestige of an individual as closely bound up with expenditure, and with the duty of returning with interest gifts received in such a way that the creditor becomes the debtor. Consumption and destruction are virtually unlimited.

In some potlatch systems one is constrained to expend everything one possesses and to keep nothing.* The rich man who shows his wealth by spending recklessly is the man who wins prestige.[12] The principles of rivalry and antagonism are basic. Political and individual status in associations and clans, and rank of every kind, are determined by the war of property, as well as by armed hostilities, by chance, inheritance, alliance or marriage.* But everything is conceived as if it were a war of wealth.* Marriage of one's children and one's position at gatherings are determined solely in the course of the potlatch given and returned. Position is also lost as in war, gambling,* hunting and wrestling.* Sometimes there is no question of receiving return; one destroys simply in order to give the appearance that one has no desire to receive anything back.* Whole cases of candlefish or whale oil,* houses, and blankets by the thousand are burnt; the most valuable coppers are broken and thrown into the sea to level and crush a rival. Progress up the social ladder is made in this way not only for oneself but also for one's family. Thus in a system of this kind much wealth is continually being consumed and transferred. Such transfers may if desired be called exchange or even commerce or sale;* but it is an aristocratic type of commerce characterized by etiquette and generosity; moreover, when it is carried out in a different spirit, for immediate gain, it is viewed with the greatest disdain.*

We see, then, that the notion of honour, strong in Polynesia, and present in Melanesia, is exceptionally marked here. On this point the classical writings made a poor estimate of the motives which animate men and of all that we owe to societies that preceded our own. Even as informed a scholar as Huvelin felt obliged to

---

[10] François Simiand (1873–1935) was a French economic historian. A student of Durkheim and a socialist, he was critical of scholars of his day and suggested that history could not be studied apart from social and economic structures.

[11] Georges Davy (1883–1955) was a member of the *L'Année Sociologique* school and a specialist in the sociology of law. He made extensive use of Mauss' analysis of the potlatch in describing the transition from statute to contractual law.

[12] For Mauss, neither psychology nor economics could explain the vast destruction of property caused by the potlatch or the seemingly illogical behavior of its participants. Instead, he believed that potlatch was about the status of groups, their maintenance of internal cohesion, and their relations with each other.

deduce the notion of honour—which is reputedly *without* efficacy—from the notion of magical efficacy.* The truth is more complex. The notion of honor is no more foreign to these civilizations than the notion of magic.* Polynesian *mana* itself symbolizes not only the magical power of the person but also his honour, and one of the best translations of the word is "authority" or "wealth."* The Tlingit or Haida potlatch consists in considering mutual services as honours.* Even in really primitive societies like the Australian, the "point of honor" is as ticklish as it is in ours; and it may be satisfied by prestations, offerings of food, by precedence or ritual, as well as by gifts.* Men could pledge their honor long before they could sign their names.[13]

The North-West American potlatch has been studied enough as to the form of the contract. But we must find a place for the researches of Davy and Adam in the wider framework of our subject. For the potlatch is more than a legal phenomenon; it is one of those phenomena we propose to call "total." It is religious, mythological and shamanistic because the chiefs taking part are incarnations of gods and ancestors, whose names they bear, whose dances they dance and whose spirits possess them.* It is economic; and one has to assess the value, importance, causes and effects of transactions which are enormous even when reckoned by European standards. The potlatch is also a phenomenon of social morphology; the reunion of tribes, clans, families and nations produces great excitement. People fraternize but at the same time remain strangers; community of interest and opposition are revealed constantly in a great whirl of business.* Finally,

from the jural point of view, we have already noted the contractual forms and what we might call the human element of the contract, and the legal status of the contracting parties—as clans or families or with reference to rank or marital condition; and to this we now add that the material objects of the contracts have a virtue of their own which causes them to be given and compels the making of counter-gifts.

It would have been useful, if space had been available, to distinguish four forms of American potlatch: first, potlatch where the phratries and chiefs' families alone take part (Tlingit); second, potlatches in which phratries, clans, families and chiefs take more or less similar roles (Haida); third, potlatch with chiefs and their clans confronting each other (Tsimshian); and fourth, potlatch of chiefs and fraternities (Kwakiutl). But this would prolong our argument, and in any case three of the four forms (with the exception of the Tsimshian) have already been comparatively described by Davy.* But as far as our study is concerned all the forms are more or less identical as regards the elements of the gift, the obligation to receive and the obligation to make a return.

4. THE THREE OBLIGATIONS: GIVING, RECEIVING, REPAYING[14]

THE OBLIGATION TO GIVE

This is the essence of potlatch. A chief must give a potlatch for himself, his son, his son-in-law or daughter* and for the dead.* He can keep his

---

[13] Here, and in other passages, Mauss attacks simplistic understandings of primitive people as morally inferior to Europeans. Although optimistic about the future of civilization, he was highly critical of his own society and, to some degree, romanticized the primitive. In the conclusion to *The Gift,* he wrote, "Hence, we should return to the old and elemental. Once again we shall discover . . . the joy of giving in public, the delight in generous artistic expenditure, the pleasure of hospitality in the public or private feast. . . . We can visualize a society in which these principles obtain. . . . For honour, disinterestedness and corporate solidarity are not

vain words, nor do they deny the necessity for work" (1967:67).

[14] In this section, Mauss describes what he believes is a fundamental pattern underlying prestations. Since prestations are total social phenomena, this same pattern must also underlie other aspects of society. This insight was of crucial importance in the development of Lévi-Strauss' French structural anthropology (see essay 25). Lévi-Strauss said, on reading *The Gift,* that his mind was "overcome by the certainty as yet undefinable of assisting in a decisive event in the evolution of science" (quoted in Harris 1968:484).

authority in his tribe, village and family, and maintain his position with the chiefs inside and outside his nation,* only if he can prove that he is favorably regarded by the spirits, that he possesses fortune* and that he is possessed by it.* The only way to demonstrate his fortune is by expending it to the humiliation of others, by putting them "in the shadow of his name."* Kwakiutl and Haida noblemen have the same notion of "face" as the Chinese mandarin or officer.* It is said of one of the great mythical chiefs who gave no feast that he had a "rotten face."* The expression is more apt than it is even in China; for to lose one's face is to lose one's spirit, which is truly the "face," the dancing mask, the right to incarnate a spirit and wear an emblem or totem. It is the veritable *persona* which is at stake, and it can be lost in the potlatch* just as it can be lost in the game of gift-giving,* in war,* or through some error in ritual.* In all these societies one is anxious to give; there is no occasion of importance (even outside the solemn winter gatherings) when one is *not* obliged to invite friends to share the produce of the chase or the forest which the gods or totems have sent;* to redistribute everything received at a potlatch; or to recognize services* from chiefs, vassals or relatives* by means of gifts. Failing these obligations—at least for the nobles—etiquette is violated and rank is lost.*

The obligation to invite is particularly evident between clans or between tribes. It makes sense only if the invitation is given to people other than members of the family, clan or phratry.* Everyone who can, will or does attend the potlatch must be invited.* Neglect has fateful results.* An important Tsimshian myth* shows the state of mind in which the central theme of much European folklore originated: the myth of the bad fairy neglected at a baptism or marriage.[15] Here the institutional fabric in which it is sewn appears clearly, and we realize the kind of civilization in which it functioned. A princess of one of the Tsimshian villages conceives in the "Country of the Otters" and gives birth miraculously to "Little Otter." She returns with her child to the village of her father, the chief. Little Otter catches halibut with which her father feeds all the tribal chiefs. He introduces Little Otter to everyone and requests them not to kill him if they find him fishing in his animal form: "Here is my grandson who has brought for you this food with which I serve you, my guests." Thus the grandfather grows rich with all manner of wealth brought to him by the chiefs when they come in the winter hunger to eat whale and seal and the fresh fish caught by Little Otter. But one chief is not invited. And one day when the crew of a canoe of the neglected tribe meets Little Otter at sea the bowman kills him and takes the seal. The grandfather and all the tribes search high and low for Little Otter until they hear about the neglected tribe. The latter offers its excuses; it has never heard of Little Otter. The princess dies of grief; the involuntarily guilty chief brings the grandfather all sorts of gifts in expiation. The myth ends: "That is why the people have great feasts when a chief's son is born and gets a name; for none may be ignorant of him."* The potlatch—the distribution of goods—is the fundamental act of public recognition in all spheres, military, legal, economic and religious. The chief or his son is recognized and acknowledged by the people.

Sometimes the ritual in the feasts of the Kwakiutl and other tribes in the same group expresses this obligation to invite.* Part of the ceremonial opens with the "ceremony of the dogs." These are represented by masked men who come out of one house and force their way into another. They commemorate the occasion on which the people of the three other tribes of Kwakiutl proper neglected to invite the clan which ranked highest among them, the Guetela who, having no desire to remain outsiders, entered the dancing house and destroyed everything.*

---

[15] The comparison of the Tsimshian myth to European folklore here presupposes an evolutionary framework. Mauss, like many other social thinkers, saw primitive cultures as living fossils. Given this premise, it followed that current Tsimshian myths were equivalent to ancient European folktales.

THE OBLIGATION TO RECEIVE

This is no less constraining.[16] One does not have the right to refuse a gift or a potlatch.* To do so would show fear of having to reply, and of being abased in default. One would "lose the weight" of one's name by admitting defeat in advance.* In certain circumstances, however, a refusal can be an assertion of victory and invincibility.* It appears at least with the Kwakiutl that a recognized position in the hierarchy, or a victory through previous potlatches, allows one to refuse an invitation or even a gift without war ensuing. If this is so, then a potlatch must be carried out by the man who refuses to accept the invitation. More particularly, he has to contribute to the "fat festival" in which a ritual of refusal may be observed.* The chief who considers himself superior refuses the spoonful of fat offered him: he fetches his copper and returns with it to "extinguish the fire" (of the fat). A series of formalities follow which mark the challenge and oblige the chief who has refused to give another potlatch or fat festival.* In principle, however, gifts are always accepted and praised.* You must speak your appreciation of food prepared for you.* But you accept a challenge at the same time.* You receive a gift "on the back." You accept the food and you do so because you mean to take up the challenge and prove that you are not unworthy.* When chiefs confront each other in this manner they may find themselves in odd situations and probably they experience them as such. In like manner in ancient Gaul and Germany, as well as nowadays in gatherings of French farmers and students, one is pledged to swallow quantities of liquid to "do honor" in grotesque fashion to the host. The obligation stands even although one is only heir to the man who bears the challenge.* Failure to give or receive,* like failure to make return gifts, means a loss of dignity.*

THE OBLIGATION TO REPAY

Outside pure destruction the obligation to repay is the essence of potlatch.* Destruction is very often sacrificial, directed towards the spirits, and apparently does not require a return unconditionally, especially when it is the work of a superior clan chief or of the chief of a clan already recognized as superior.* But normally the potlatch must be returned with interest like all other gifts. The interest is generally between 30 and 100 per cent a year. If a subject receives a blanket from his chief for a service rendered he will return two on the occasion of a marriage in the chief's family or on the initiation of the chief's son. But then the chief in his turn redistributes to him whatever he gets from the next potlatch at which rival clans repay the chief's generosity.

The obligation of worthy return is imperative.* Face is lost for ever if it is not made or if equivalent value is not destroyed.*

The sanction for the obligation to repay is enslavement for debt. This is so at least for the Kwakiutl, Haida and Tsimshian. It is an institution comparable in nature and function to the Roman *nexum*.[17] The person who cannot return a loan or potlatch loses his rank and even his status of a free man. If among the Kwakiutl a man of poor credit has to borrow he is said to "sell a slave." We need not stress the similarity of this expression with the Roman one.* The Haida say, as if they had invented the Latin phrase independently, that a girl's mother who gives a betrothal payment to the mother of a young chief "puts a thread on him."

Just as the Trobriand *kula* is an extreme case of gift exchange, so the potlatch in North-West America is the monster child of the gift system. In societies of phratries, amongst the Tlingit and Haida, we find important traces of a former total prestation (which is characteristic of the Athabascans, a related group). Presents are exchanged on

---

[16] Notice that, while Mauss has said that prestations do sometimes serve an economic role, his discussion of potlatch is not economic. Instead, the potlatch is seen as symbolic of social relations between groups, which is why he can say that the obligation to receive is "no less constraining" than the obligation to give.

[17] The *nexum* was a system of contracting a loan in ancient Rome in which the loan was made in the presence of five witnesses. Debtors could be held in bondage for failure to repay.

any pretext for any service, and everything is returned sooner or later for redistribution.* The Tsimshian have almost the same rules.* Among the Kwakiutl these rules, in many cases, function outside the potlatch.* We shall not press this obvious point; old authors described the potlatch in such a way as to make it doubtful whether it was or was not a distinct institution.* We may recall that with the Chinook, one of the least known tribes but one which would repay study, the word "potlatch" means "gift."*

5. THE POWER IN OBJECTS OF EXCHANGE

Our analysis can be carried farther to show that in the things exchanged at a potlatch there is a certain power which forces them to circulate, to be given away and repaid.

To begin with, the Kwakiutl and Tsimshian, and perhaps others, make the same distinction between the various types of property as do the Romans, Trobrianders and Samoans. They have the ordinary articles of consumption and distribution and perhaps also of sale (I have found no trace of barter). They have also the valuable family property—talismans, decorated coppers, skin blankets and embroidered fabrics.* This class of articles is transmitted with that solemnity with which women are given in marriage, privileges are endowed on sons-in-law, and names and status are given to children and daughters' husbands.* It is wrong to speak here of alienation, for these things are loaned rather than sold and ceded.[18] Basically they are *sacra*[19] which the family parts with, if at all, only with reluctance.

Closer observation reveals similar distinctions among the Haida. This tribe has in fact sacralized, in the manner of Antiquity, the no-

tions of property and wealth.[20] By a religious and mythological effort of a type rare enough in the Americas they have managed to reify an abstraction: the "Property Woman," of whom we possess myths and a description.* She is nothing less than the mother, the founding goddess of the dominant phratry, the Eagles. But oddly enough—a fact which recalls the Asiatic world and Antiquity—she appears identical with the "queen," the principal piece in the game of tip-cat, the piece that wins everything and whose name the Property Woman bears. This goddess is found in Tlingit* country and her myth, if not her cult, among the Tsimshian* and Kwakiutl.*

Together these precious family articles constitute what one might call the magical legacy of the people; they are conceived as such by their owner, by the initiate he gives them to, by the ancestor who endowed the clan with them, and by the founding hero of the clan to whom the spirits gave them.* In any case in all these clans they are spiritual in origin and nature.* Further, they are kept in a large ornate box which itself is endowed with a powerful personality, which speaks, is in communion with the owner, contains his soul, and so on.*

Each of these precious objects and tokens of wealth has, as amongst the Trobrianders, its name,* quality and power.* The large *abalone* shells,* the shields covered with them, the decorated blankets with faces, eyes, and animal and human figures embroidered and woven into them, are all personalities.* The houses and decorated beams are themselves beings.* Everything speaks—roof, fire, carvings and paintings; for the magical house is built not only by the chief and his people and those of the opposing phratry but also by the gods and ancestors; spirits and young initiates are welcomed and cast out by the house in person.*

Each of these precious things has, moreover, a productive capacity within it.* Each, as well as

---

[18] Mauss' comment on alienation illustrates his insistence that the transactions he describes are not economic—that is, they are not driven by the desire to maximize material profit or minimize loss. Therefore, he believed that the term *alienation* (frequently used by Marxist economists) was not appropriate.

[19] *Sacra:* Latin for objects of devotion.

[20] Durkheim and his followers divided the cultural world into the sacred and profane. Here, Mauss demonstrates the sacred nature of gift-giving. Twenty years later, Lévi-Strauss and his followers emphasized the binary division of sacred and profane employed by *L'Année Sociologique* thinkers, along with the use of binary opposition by structural linguists (see essays 24–26).

being a sign and surety of life, is also a sign and surety of wealth, a magico-religious guarantee of rank and prosperity.* Ceremonial dishes and spoons decorated and carved with the clan totem or sign of rank, are animate things.* They are replicas of the never ending supply of tools, the creators of food, which the spirits gave to the ancestors. They are supposedly miraculous. Objects are confounded with the spirits who made them, and eating utensils with food. Thus Kwakiutl dishes and Haida spoons are essential goods with a strict circulation and are carefully shared out between the families and clans of the chiefs.

6. MONEY OF RENOWN (RENOMMIERGELD)*

Decorated coppers* are the most important articles in the potlatch, and beliefs and a cult are attached to them. With all these tribes copper, a living being, is the object of cult and myth.* Copper, with the Haida and Kwakiutl at least, is identified with salmon, itself an object of cult.* But in addition to this mythical element each copper is by itself an object of individual belief.* Each principal copper of the families of clan chiefs has its name and individuality;* it has also its own value,* in the full magical and economic sense of the word which is regulated by the vicissitudes of the potlatches through which it passes and even by its partial or complete destruction.*

Coppers have also a virtue which attracts other coppers to them, as wealth attracts wealth and as dignity attracts honours, spirit-possession and good alliances.* In this way they live their own lives and attract other coppers.* One of the Kwakiutl coppers is called "Bringer of Coppers" and the formula describes how the coppers gather around it, while the name of its owner is "Copper-Flowing-Towards-Me."* With the Haida and Tlingit, coppers are a "fortress" for the princess who owns them; elsewhere a chief who owns them is rendered invinci-

ble.* They are the "flat divine objects" of the house.* Often the myth identifies together the spirits who gave the coppers, the owners and the coppers themselves.* It is impossible to discern what makes the power of the one out of the spirit and the wealth of the other; a copper talks and grunts, demanding to be given away or destroyed;* it is covered with blankets to keep it warm just as a chief is smothered in the blankets he is to distribute.*

From another angle we see the transmission of wealth and good fortune.* The spirits and minor spirits of an initiate allow him to own coppers and talismans which then enable him to acquire other coppers, greater wealth, higher rank and more spirits (all of these being equivalents). If we consider the coppers with other forms of wealth which are the object of hoarding and potlatch—masks, talismans and so on—we find they are all confounded in their uses and effects.* Through them rank is obtained; because a man obtains wealth he obtains a spirit which in turn possesses him, enabling him to overcome obstacles heroically. Then later the hero is paid for his shamanistic services, ritual dances and trances. Everything is tied together; things have personality, and personalities are in some manner the permanent possession of the clan. Titles, talismans, coppers and spirits of chiefs are homonyms and synonyms, having the same nature and function.* The circulation of goods follows that of men, women and children, of festival ritual, ceremonies and dances, jokes and injuries. Basically they are the same. If things are given and returned it is precisely because one gives and returns "respects" and "courtesies." But in addition, in giving them, a man gives himself, and he does so because he owes himself—himself and his possessions—to others.[21]

7. PRIMARY CONCLUSION

From our study of four important groups of people we find the following: first, in two or three of the groups, we find the potlatch, its leading

---

[21] In this paragraph, Mauss claims that the goods given in potlatch are, in essence, indistinguishable from the people giving them. The goods have personalities and are members of households. Giving them is then spiritually the same as the movement of people from household to household. Later, in his first major work, *Les Structures Élémentaires de la Parenté* (1949) *(The Elementary Structures of Kinship)*, Lévi-Strauss expanded this line of argument by analyzing the exchange of women between groups as a fundamental social phenomenon.

motive and its typical form. In all groups we see the archaic form of exchange—the gift and the return gift. Moreover, in these societies we note the circulation of objects side by side with the circulation of persons and rights. We might stop at this point. The amount, distribution and importance of our data authorize us to conceive of a regime embracing a large part of humanity over a long transitional phase, and persisting to this day among peoples other than those described. We may then consider that the spirit of gift exchange is characteristic of societies which have passed the phase of "total prestation" (between clan and clan, family and family) but have not yet reached the stage of pure individual contract, the money market, sale proper, fixed price, and weighed and coined money.[22]

[The Gift, *in its entirety, is a reasonably short essay (only about 80 pages plus extensive notes in the Norton Library edition). The passage you have just read is the conclusion of Chapter 2. Chapter 3, titled "Survivals in Early Literature," discusses written evidence for Mauss' theory of gift-giving from ancient Roman law, ancient Hindu legal documents, early Germanic society, and, very briefly, Chinese law. Chapter 4 is titled "Conclusions." The first two sections, which we have excluded here, are moral conclusions and political and economic conclusions. They consist of about 4,750 words and 23 footnotes. We rejoin the text with the sociological and ethical conclusions with which Mauss ends his essay.*]

3. SOCIOLOGICAL AND ETHICAL CONCLUSIONS

We may be permitted another note about the method we have used. We do not set this work up as a model; it simply proffers one or two suggestions. It is incomplete: the analysis could be pushed farther.* We are really posing questions for historians and anthropologists and offering possible lines of research for them rather than resolving a problem and laying down definite answers. It is enough for us to be sure for the moment that we have given sufficient data for such an end.

This being the case, we would point out that there is a heuristic element in our manner of treatment.[23] The facts we have studied are all "total" social phenomena. The word "general" may be preferred although we like it less. Some of the facts presented concern the whole of society and its institutions (as with potlatch, opposing clans, tribes on visit, etc.); others, in which exchanges and contracts are the concern of individuals embrace a large number of institutions.

These phenomena are at once legal, economic, religious, aesthetic, morphological and so on. They are legal in that they concern individual and collective rights, organized and diffuse morality; they may be entirely obligatory, or subject simply to praise or disapproval. They are at once political and domestic, being of interest both to classes and to clans and families. They are religious; they concern true religion, animism, magic and diffuse religious mentality. They are economic, for the notions of value, utility, interest, luxury, wealth, acquisition, accumulation, consumption and liberal and sumptuous expenditure are all present, although not perhaps in their modern senses. Moreover, these institutions have an important aesthetic side which we have left unstudied; but the dances performed, the songs and shows, the dramatic representations given between camps or partners, the objects made, used, decorated, polished, amassed and transmitted with affection, received with joy, given away in triumph, the feasts in which everyone participates—all these,

---

[22] This conclusion points once again to the evolutionary nature of Mauss' thinking.

[23] In this paragraph and below, Mauss provides a comprehensive definition of total social phenomena, suggesting that the investigation of such phenomena provides an outstanding pathway for developing an understanding of society in general. Mauss claims that total social phenomena are morphological. That is, they reveal the underlying structure of the groups practicing them.

the food, objects and services, are the source of aesthetic emotions as well as emotions aroused by interest.* This is true not only of Melanesia but also, and particularly, of the potlatch of North-West America and still more true of the market-festival of the Indo-European world. Lastly, our phenomena are clearly morphological. Everything that happens in the course of gatherings, fairs and markets or in the feasts that replace them, presupposes groups whose duration exceeds the season of social concentration, like the winter potlatch of the Kwakiutl or the few weeks of the Melanesian maritime expeditions. Moreover, in order that these meetings may be carried out in peace, there must be roads or water for transport and tribal, intertribal or international alliances—*commercium and connubium.**[24]

We are dealing then with something more than a set of themes, more than institutional elements, more than institutions, more even than systems of institutions divisible into legal, economic, religious and other parts. We are concerned with "wholes," with systems in their entirety. We have not described them as if they were fixed, in a static or skeletal condition, and still less have we dissected them into the rules and myths and values and so on of which they are composed. It is only by considering them as wholes that we have been able to see their essence, their operation and their living aspect, and to catch the fleeting moment when the society and its members take emotional stock of themselves and their situation as regards others. Only by making such concrete observation of social life is it possible to come upon facts such as those which our study is beginning to reveal. Nothing in our opinion is more urgent or promising than research into "total" social phenomena.[25]

The advantage is twofold. Firstly there is an advantage in generality, for facts of widespread occurrence are more likely to be universal than local institutions or themes, which are invariably tinged with local color. But particularly the advantage is in realism. We see social facts in the round, as they really are. In society there are not merely ideas and rules, but also men and groups and their behaviours. We see them in motion as an engineer sees masses and systems, or as we observe octopuses and anemones in the sea. We see groups of men, and active forces, submerged in their environments and sentiments.[26]

Historians believe and justly resent the fact that sociologists make too many abstractions and separate unduly the various elements of society.[27] We should follow their precepts and observe what is given. The tangible fact is Rome or Athens or the average Frenchman or the Melanesian of some island, and not prayer or law as such. Whereas formerly sociologists were obliged to analyze and abstract rather too much, they should now force themselves to reconstitute the whole. This is the way to reach incontestable facts. They will also find a way of

---

[24] *Commercium and connubium:* Latin for commerce and intermarriage.

[25] Here Mauss seems to emphasize the holism that was part of American anthropology of his era, particularly Boas' thought. Mauss cites Boas' work many times in the present article. However, the application of holism to total social phenomena is distinctly his own. Boas and his followers did not believe that total social phenomena existed; they tended to believe that the different aspects of culture were of equal importance.

[26] Mauss relies on Durkheim's idea of a social fact. For Durkheim, sociology was the analysis of social facts. He defines these as "every way of acting, fixed or not, capable of exercising on the individual an external constraint; or again, every way of acting which is general throughout a given society, while at the same time existing in its own right independent of its individual manifestations" (see essay 5).

[27] At the turn of the century, academic disciplines were not divided the same way they are today. One of Durkheim's concerns, here echoed by Mauss, was to show that sociology is a discipline with its own area of study and is distinct from history or psychology. The concern of modern anthropologists is frequently the reverse. Recent theorists such as Renato Rosaldo have explored how history and psychology provide fundamental insights into anthropology (see essay 38).

satisfying psychologists who have a pronounced viewpoint, and particularly psycho-pathologists, since there is no doubt that the object of their study is concrete. They all observe, or at least ought to, minds as wholes and not minds divided into faculties. We should follow suit. The study of the concrete, which is the study of the whole, is made more readily, is more interesting and furnishes more explanations in the sphere of sociology than the study of the abstract. For we observe complete and complex beings. We too describe them in their organisms and *psychai* as well as in their behavior as groups, with the attendant psychoses: sentiments, ideas and desires of the crowd, of organized societies and their sub-groups. We see bodies and their reactions, and their ideas and sentiments as interpretations or as motive forces. The aim and principle of sociology is to observe and understand the whole group in its total behavior.

It is not possible here—it would have meant extending a restricted study unduly—to seek the morphological implications of our facts. It may be worth while, however, to indicate the method one might follow in such a piece of research.

All the societies we have described above with the exception of our European societies are segmentary. Even the Indo-Europeans, the Romans before the Twelve Tables, the Germanic societies up to the *Edda,* and Irish society to the time of its chief literature, were still societies based on the clan or on great families more or less undivided internally and isolated from each other externally. All these were far removed from the degree of unification with which historians have credited them or which is ours today. Within these groups the individuals, even the most influential, were less serious, avaricious and selfish than we are; externally at least they were and are generous and more ready to give. In tribal feasts, in ceremonies of rival clans, allied families or those that assist at each other's initiation, groups visit each other; and with the development of the law of hospitality in more advanced societies, the rules of friendship and the contract are present—along with the gods—to ensure the peace of markets and villages; at these times men meet in a curious frame of mind with exaggerated fear and an equally exaggerated generosity which appear stupid in no one's eyes but our own. In these primitive and archaic societies there is no middle path. There is either complete trust or mistrust. One lays down one's arms, renounces magic and gives everything away, from casual hospitality to one's daughter or one's property. It is in such conditions that men, despite themselves, learnt to renounce what was theirs and made contracts to give and repay.

But then they had no choice in the matter. When two groups of men meet they may move away or in case of mistrust or defiance they may resort to arms; or else they can come to terms. Business has always been done with foreigners, although these might have been allies. The people of Kiriwina said to Malinowski:[28] "The Dobu man is not good as we are. He is fierce, he is a man-eater. When we come to Dobu, we fear him, he might kill us! But see! I spit the charmed ginger root and their mind turns. They lay down their spears, they receive us well."* Nothing better expresses how close together lie festival and warfare.

Thurnwald describes with reference to another Melanesian tribe, with genealogical material, an actual event which shows just as clearly how these people pass in a group quite suddenly from a feast to a battle.* Buleau, a chief, had invited Bobal, another chief, and his people to a feast which was probably to be the first of a long series. Dances were performed all night long. By morning everyone was excited by the sleepless night of song and dance. On a remark

---

[28] Mauss refers to anthropologist Bronislaw Malinowski, best known for his work in the Trobriand Islands. We present an extract from Malinowski's *Argonauts of the Western Pacific* (1922) in essay 13. Richard Thurnwald (1869–1954), mentioned in the next paragraph, led research expeditions to the South Pacific in the early twentieth century. He was the founder of the journal *Sociologus* and a key voice in midcentury German anthropology.

made by Buleau one of Bobal's men killed him; and the troop of men massacred and pillaged and ran off with the women of the village. "Buleau and Bobal were more friends than rivals," they said to Thurnwald. We all have experience of events like this.

It is by opposing reason to emotion and setting up the will for peace against rash follies of this kind that peoples succeed in substituting alliance, gift and commerce for war, isolation and stagnation.

The research proposed would have some conclusion of this kind.[29] Societies have progressed in the measure in which they, their sub-groups and their members, have been able to stabilize their contracts and to give, receive and repay. In order to trade, man must first lay down his spear. When that is done he can succeed in exchanging goods and persons not only between clan and clan but between tribe and tribe and nation and nation, and above all between individuals. It is only then that people can create, can satisfy their interests mutually and define them without recourse to arms. It is in this way that the clan, the tribe and nation have learnt—just as in the future the classes and nations and individuals will learn—how to oppose one another without slaughter and to give without sacrificing themselves to others. That is one of the secrets of their wisdom and solidarity.

There is no other course feasible. The *Chronicles of Arthur** relate how King Arthur, with the help of a Cornish carpenter, invented the marvel of his court, the miraculous Round Table at which his knights would never come

to blows. Formerly because of jealousy, skirmishes, duels and murders had set blood flowing in the most sumptuous of feasts. The carpenter says to Arthur: "I will make thee a fine table, where sixteen hundred may sit at once, and from which none need be excluded . . . And no knight will be able to raise combat, for there the highly placed will be on the same level as the lowly." There was no "head of the table" and hence no more quarrels. Wherever Arthur took his table, contented and invincible remained his noble company. And this today is the way of the nations that are strong, rich, good and happy. Peoples, classes, families and individuals may become rich, but they will not achieve happiness until they can sit down like the knights around their common riches. There is no need to seek far for goodness and happiness. It is to be found in the imposed peace, in the rhythm of communal and private labor, in wealth amassed and redistributed, in the mutual respect and reciprocal generosity that education can impart.

Thus we see how it is possible under certain circumstances to study total human behavior; and how that concrete study leads not only to a science of manners, a partial social science, but even to ethical conclusions—"civility," or "civics" as we say today. Through studies of this sort we can find, measure and assess the various determinants, aesthetic, moral, religious and economic, and the material and demographic factors, whose sum is the basis of society and constitutes the common life, and whose conscious direction is the supreme art—politics in the Socratic sense of the word.

---

[29] According to Durkheim's ideas about evolution, primitive mechanistic solidarity gives way to modern organic solidarity. In this scheme, there is constant progress toward interdependence, and society reaches ever higher levels of integration. Rather than segments of society being opposed to each other in class warfare, as Marxist analysts claim, or engaged in a Malthusian struggle for survival, as Spencerians believed, every part of society should be seen as working for the peace and benefit of the whole.

Although Durkheim believed that social evolution would be characterized by a progression of ever better social forms, Mauss' life was tragic. His mentor Durkheim died in 1917. Few of the members of *L'Année Sociologique*, many of whom were his close friends, survived World War I. When *The Gift* was published, in 1925, conditions in Europe were far from stable. These concluding paragraphs to *The Gift* must be read in this context. They are, at the same time, an affirmation of Durkheim's belief in progress and a plea for peace and harmony in the aftermath of war.

8. *Class, Status, Party*

MAX WEBER (1864–1920)

1: ECONOMICALLY DETERMINED POWER AND THE SOCIAL ORDER[a]

Law exists when there is a probability that an order will be upheld by a specific staff of men who will use physical or psychical compulsion with the intention of obtaining conformity with the order, or of inflicting sanctions for infringement of it. The structure of every legal order directly influences the distribution of power, economic or otherwise, within its respective community. This is true of all legal orders and not only that of the state. In general, we understand by "power" the chance of a man or of a number of men to realize their own will in a communal action even against the resistance of others who are participating in the action.[1]

"Economically conditioned" power is not, of course, identical with "power" as such. On the contrary, the emergence of economic power may be the consequence of power existing on other grounds. Man does not strive for power only in order to enrich himself economically. Power, including economic power, may be valued "for its own sake." Very frequently the striving for power is also conditioned by the social "honor" it entails. Not all power, however, entails social honor: The typical American Boss, as well as the typical big speculator, deliberately relinquishes social honor. Quite generally, "mere economic" power, and especially "naked" money power, is by no means a recognized basis of social honor. Nor is power the only basis of social honor. Indeed, social honor, or prestige, may even be the basis of political or economic power, and very frequently has been. Power, as well as honor, may be guaranteed by the legal order, but, at least normally, it is not their primary source. The legal order is rather an additional factor that enhances the chance to hold power or honor; but it cannot always secure them.[2]

The way in which social honor is distributed in a community between typical groups participating in this distribution we may call the "social order." The social order and the economic order are, of course, similarly related to the "legal order." However, the social and the economic order are not identical. The economic order is for us merely the way in which economic goods and services are distributed and used. The social order is of course conditioned by the economic order to a high degree, and in turn it reacts upon it.[3]

From *Economy and Society* (1922)

---

[1] This essay was part of Weber's massive posthumous work, *Wirtschaft und Gesellschaft (Economy and Society)*. Probably written between 1915 and 1920, it was first published in 1922. *Wirtschaft und Gesellschaft* was one volume of an extensive series of studies in the social sciences that Weber organized for the German publishing house Siebeck. Much of Weber's work was written in response to Karl Marx (see essay 4), and the relationship between the two is complex. The first section of the essay sets Weber's argument. In contrast to Marx, Weber insists that individual identity is not subsumed by class identity. Status and party may, and frequently do, cut across class membership. In this essay, he presents and discusses each of these forms of identity.

[2] Social thinkers and political activists (and Weber was both) in the Germany of Weber's time were extreme conservatives (generally members of the landowning upper class) or radicals who often espoused Marxist ideals (generally those identified with industrial workers). Weber—from a family whose wealth was based in textile manufacturing—identified with neither the conservative landowners nor the radical workers, but was a political liberal trying to sit midway between the two.

[3] Weber felt that Marx's methods of analysis produced valuable insights. However, he believed that they leaned too heavily on economics and dialectical conflict between forces of production and relations of production as the motor driving social evolution. Weber incorporated much Marxist thought into his theories, yet he was not a Marxist and did not believe in a communist utopia. In the days of the cold war, this might have been a factor in his appeal to American sociologists and anthropologists.

Now: "classes," "status groups," and "parties" are phenomena of the distribution of power within a community.

2: DETERMINATION OF CLASS-SITUATION BY MARKET-SITUATION

In our terminology, "classes" are not communities; they merely represent possible, and frequent, bases for communal action. We may speak of a "class" when (1) a number of people have in common a specific causal component of their life chances, in so far as (2) this component is represented exclusively by economic interests in the possession of goods and opportunities for income, and (3) is represented under the conditions of the commodity or labor markets.[4] [These points refer to "class situation," which we may express more briefly as the typical chance for a supply of goods, external living conditions, and personal life experiences, in so far as this chance is determined by the amount and kind of power, or lack of such, to dispose of goods or skills for the sake of income in a given economic order. The term "class" refers to any group of people that is found in the same class situation.]

It is the most elemental economic fact that the way in which the disposition over material property is distributed among a plurality of people, meeting competitively in the market for the purpose of exchange, in itself creates specific life chances. According to the law of marginal utility this mode of distribution excludes the non-owners from competing for highly valued goods; it favors the owners and, in fact, gives to them a monopoly to acquire such goods. Other things being equal, this mode of distribution monopolizes the opportunities for profitable deals for all those who, provided with goods, do not necessarily have to exchange them. It increases, at least generally, their power in price wars with those who, being propertyless, have nothing to offer but their services in native form or goods in a form constituted through their own labor, and who above all are compelled to get rid of these products in order barely to subsist. This mode of distribution gives to the propertied a monopoly on the possibility of transferring property from the sphere of use as a "fortune," to the sphere of "capital goods"; that is, it gives them the entrepreneurial function and all chances to share directly or indirectly in returns on capital. All this holds true within the area in which pure market conditions prevail. "Property" and "lack of property" are, therefore, the basic categories of all class situations. It does not matter whether these two categories become effective in price wars or in competitive struggles.

Within these categories, however, class situations are further differentiated: on the one hand, according to the kind of property that is usable for returns; and, on the other hand, according to the kind of services that can be offered in the market. Ownership of domestic buildings; productive establishments; warehouses; stores; agriculturally usable land, large and small holdings—quantitative differences with possibly qualitative consequences—; ownership of mines; cattle; men

---

[4] Weber's definition of class overlapped Marx's, yet differed from it. For Marx, class signified a specific relationship to the means of production. In a class society, one class has ownership or control of the means of production, and another is employed producing surplus for that owner class. Further, classes are born in the struggle for control of the means of production. For Marx, understanding the role of class was key to the analysis of society; all other identifications were secondary. Although focused on ownership of property as the constitutive element of class, he downplayed other elements of Marx's analysis. In particular, Weber suggested that class does not necessarily have analytic primacy—other elements of identity may be of equal or greater importance.

Moreover, Weber gave conflict less of a role in generating and maintaining class relationships than Marx did. For Marx, this conflict was critical since it drove history (recall *The Communist Manifesto* (1972 [1848]:241): "The history of all hitherto existing society is the history of class struggles"). For Weber, other forces are of much greater importance in social change. For example, Weber saw social evolution as a generalized process toward increased rationalization and bureaucratization that necessarily entailed the destruction of individual liberties. He believed that charisma acted in opposition to this force. Through strength of personality, the charismatic individual was able to break the bonds of routine and radically redirect society.

(slaves); disposition over mobile instruments of production, or capital goods of all sorts, especially money or objects that can be exchanged for money easily and at any time; disposition over products of one's own labor or of others' labor differing according to their various distances from consumability; disposition over transferable monopolies of any kind—all these distinctions differentiate the class situations of the propertied just as does the "meaning" which they can and do give to the utilization of property, especially to property which has money equivalence. Accordingly, the propertied, for instance, may belong to the class of rentiers or to the class of entrepreneurs.

Those who have no property but who offer services are differentiated just as much according to their kinds of services as according to the way in which they make use of these services, in a continuous or discontinuous relation to a recipient. But always this is the generic connotation of the concept of class: that the kind of chance in the *market* is the decisive moment which presents a common condition for the individual's fate. "Class situation" is, in this sense, ultimately "market situation." The effect of naked possession *per se* which among cattle breeders gives the non-owning slave or serf into the power of the cattle owner, is only a forerunner of real "class" formation. However, in the cattle loan and in the naked severity of the law of debts in such communities, for the first time mere "possession" as such emerges as decisive for the fate of the individual. This is very much in contrast to the agricultural communities based on labor. The creditor-debtor relation becomes the basis of "class situations" only in those cities where a "credit market," however primitive, with rates of interest increasing according to the extent of dearth and a factual monopolization of credits, is developed by a plutocracy. Therewith "class struggles" begin.

Those men whose fate is not determined by the chance of using goods or services for themselves on the market, e.g., slaves, are not, however, a "class" in the technical sense of the term. They are, rather, a "status group."

3: COMMUNAL ACTION FLOWING FROM CLASS INTEREST

According to our terminology, the factor that creates "class" is unambiguously economic interest, and indeed, only those interests involved in the existence of the "market." Nevertheless, the concept of "class-interest" is an ambiguous one: even as an empirical concept it is ambiguous as soon as one understands by it something other than the factual direction of interests following with a certain probability from the class situation for a certain "average" of those people subjected to the class situation. The class situation and other circumstances remaining the same, the direction in which the individual worker, for instance, is likely to pursue his interests may vary widely, according to whether he is constitutionally qualified for the task at hand to a high, to an average, or to a low degree. In the same way, the direction of interests may vary according to whether or not a *communal* action of a larger or smaller portion of those commonly affected by the "class situation," or even an association among them, e.g., a "trade union," has grown out of the class situation from which the individual may or may not expect promising results. [Communal action refers to that action which is oriented to the feeling of the actors that they belong together. Societal action, on the other hand, is oriented to a rationally motivated adjustment of interests.] The rise of societal or even of communal action from a common class situation is by no means a universal phenomenon.[5]

The class situation may be restricted in its effects to the generation of essentially *similar* reactions, that is to say, within our terminology, of "mass actions." However, it may not have even

---

[5] Underlying Weber's analysis is a concern for the issues of action and abstraction. For Weber, a class was an abstraction and therefore, in and of itself, could perform no action; thus the actions that flow from class interest were problematic. In order to act, any group must be organized. In this passage, Weber shows that the actions of classes must be mediated by individuals. However, individual variation within a class may be so great that it prevents the emergence of any generalized class consciousness or class struggle. Parties and status groups, discussed below, play key roles in organizing classes.

this result. Furthermore, often merely an amorphous communal action emerges. For example, the "murmuring" of the workers known in ancient oriental ethics: the moral disapproval of the work-master's conduct, which in its practical significance was probably equivalent to an increasingly typical phenomenon of precisely the latest industrial development, namely, the "slow down" (the deliberate limiting of work effort) of laborers by virtue of tacit agreement. The degree in which "communal action" and possibly "societal action," emerges from the "mass actions" of the members of a class is linked to general cultural conditions, especially to those of an intellectual sort. It is also linked to the extent of the contrasts that have already evolved, and is especially linked to the *transparency* of the connections between the causes and the consequences of the "class situation." For however different life chances may be, this fact in itself, according to all experience, by no means gives birth to "class action" (communal action by the members of a class). The fact of being conditioned and the results of the class situation must be distinctly recognizable.[6] For only then the contrast of life chances can be felt not as an absolutely given fact to be accepted, but as a resultant from either (1) the given distribution of property, or (2) the structure of the concrete economic order. It is only then that people may react against the class structure not only through acts of an intermittent and irrational protest, but in the form of rational association. There have been "class situations" of the first category (1), of a specifically naked and transparent sort, in the urban centers of Antiquity and during the Middle Ages; especially then, when great fortunes were

accumulated by factually monopolized trading in industrial products of these localities or in foodstuffs.[7] Furthermore, under certain circumstances, in the rural economy of the most diverse periods, when agriculture was increasingly exploited in a profit-making manner. The most important historical example of the second category (2) is the class situation of the modern "proletariat."

4: TYPES OF CLASS STRUGGLE

Thus every class may be the carrier of any one of the possibly innumerable forms of "class action," but this is not necessarily so. In any case, a class does not in itself constitute a community. To treat "class" conceptually as having the same value as "community" leads to distortion. That men in the same class situation regularly react in mass actions to such tangible situations as economic ones in the direction of those interests that are most adequate to their average number is an important and after all simple fact for the understanding of historical events. Above all, this fact must not lead to that kind of pseudo-scientific operation with the concepts of "class" and "class interests" so frequently found these days and which has found its most classic expression in the statement of a talented author, that the individual may be in error concerning his interests but that the "class" is "infallible" about its interests.[8] Yet, if classes as such are not communities, nevertheless class situations emerge only on the basis of communalization. The communal action that brings forth class situations, however, is not basically

---

[6] Like the Marxists, Weber saw ideology as frequently masking the true nature of relations among people. Society could be understood by debunking the myths and ideological assertions that often cover economically or politically motivated action. Here he suggests that in order for class action to take place, class consciousness must already exist. However, various ideological structures may prevent classes from becoming aware of the true nature of their oppression and hence prevent the formation of class consciousness.

[7] Although Weber wrote on India and China, by far his primary interest was European history and society, and most of his analysis was driven by his understanding of these.

His original scholarly interest was in history, and he wrote his doctoral thesis on trading companies during the Middle Ages. He later wrote essays on the social structure of ancient society. He refers frequently to both the European Middle Ages and to ancient Greece and Rome throughout his writing.

[8] The talented author Weber refers to in this passage is, of course, Marx. The point here is to highlight his disagreement with the Marxists. Marxism is a theory of class and group action in which the individual plays little role. For Weber, on the other hand, individuals and their relationships to social groups were of great importance. For

action between members of the identical class; it is an action between members of different classes. Communal actions that directly determine the class situation of the worker and the entrepreneur are: the labor market, the commodities market, and the capitalistic enterprise. But, in its turn, the existence of a capitalistic enterprise presupposes that a very specific communal action exists and that it is specifically structured to protect the possession of goods *per se* and especially the power of individuals to dispose, in principle freely, over the means of production. The existence of a capitalistic enterprise is preconditioned by a specific kind of "legal order." Each kind of class situation, and above all when it rests upon the power of property *per se*, will become most clearly efficacious when all other determinants of reciprocal relations are, as far as possible, eliminated in their significance. It is in this way that the utilization of the power of property in the market obtains its most sovereign importance.

Now "status groups" hinder the strict carrying through of the sheer market principle. In the present context they are of interest to us only from this one point of view. Before we briefly consider them, note that not much of a general nature can be said about the more specific kinds of antagonism between "classes" (in our meaning of the term). The great shift, which has been going on continuously in the past, and up to our times, may be summarized, although at the cost of some precision: the struggle in which class situations are effective has progressively shifted from consumption credit toward, first, competitive struggles in the commodity market and, then, toward

price wars on the labor market. The "class struggles" of antiquity—to the extent that they were genuine class struggles and not struggles between status groups—were initially carried on by indebted peasants, and perhaps also by artisans threatened by debt bondage and struggling against urban creditors. For debt bondage is the normal result of the differentiation of wealth in commercial cities, especially in seaport cities. A similar situation has existed among cattle breeders. Debt relationships as such produced class action up to the time of Cataline.[9] Along with this, and with an increase in provision of grain for the city by transporting it from the outside, the struggle over the means of sustenance emerged. It centered in the first place around the provision of bread and the determination of the price of bread. It lasted throughout antiquity and the entire Middle Ages. The propertyless as such flocked together against those who actually and supposedly were interested in the dearth of bread. This fight spread until it involved all those commodities essential to the way of life and to handicraft production. There were only incipient discussions of wage disputes in antiquity and in the Middle Ages. But they have been slowly increasing up into modern times. In the earlier periods they were completely secondary to slave rebellions as well as to fights in the commodity market.[10]

The propertyless of antiquity and of the Middle Ages protested against monopolies, preemption, forestalling, and the withholding of goods from the market in order to raise prices. Today the central issue is the determination of the price of labor.

Marxists, conflict between social groups was the key force that drives history. Weber suggests that such conflict can only exist when classes and groups are organized under quite specific conditions. A class, in the example here, cannot be infallible about its interests because a class is an abstraction and cannot have interests outside of a very particular context. In this passage he illustrates some of the conditions under which class interests and struggle are likely to exist or historically did exist.

[9] Cataline: Lucius Sergius Catilina (108–62 B.C.E.) was a soldier and politician in the Roman Republic.

[10] In this passage Weber presents a very rough outline of the history of European class struggles. Weber viewed

sociology as the background information necessary to do history. The goal of his sociology was to propose general principles, but he believed that the actual unfolding of history was predicated on individual action and thus beyond any law. He wrote that "The reduction of empirical reality . . . to 'laws' is meaningless" and that "A systematic science of culture . . . would be senseless in itself" (quoted in Ritzer 1992:114). Franz Boas was probably quite familiar with Weber's work and had a similar understanding of the role of the individual. He, too, was suspicious of any attempt to make anthropology a science of culture based on the discovery of natural laws.

This transition is represented by the fight for access to the market and for the determination of the price of products. Such fights went on between merchants and workers in the putting-out system of domestic handicraft during the transition to modern times. Since it is quite a general phenomenon we must mention here that the class antagonisms that are conditioned through the market situation are usually most bitter between those who actually and directly participate as opponents in price wars. It is not the rentier, the share-holder, and the banker who suffer the ill will of the worker, but almost exclusively the manufacturer and the business executives who are the direct opponents of workers in price wars. This is so in spite of the fact that it is precisely the cash boxes of the rentier, the share-holder, and the banker into which the more or less "unearned" gains flow, rather than into the pockets of the manufacturers or of the business executives.[11] This simple state of affairs has very frequently been decisive for the role the class situation has played in the formation of political parties. For example, it has made possible the varieties of patriarchal socialism and the frequent attempts—formerly, at least—of threatened status groups to form alliances with the proletariat against the "bourgeoisie."

5: STATUS HONOR

In contrast to classes, *status groups* are normally communities.[12] They are, however, often of an amorphous kind. In contrast to the purely economically determined "class situation" we wish to designate as "status situation" every typical component of the life fate of men that is determined by a specific, positive or negative, social estimation of *honor*. This honor may be connected with any quality shared by a plurality, and, of course, it can be knit to a class situation: class distinctions are linked in the most varied ways with status distinctions. Property as such is not always recognized as a status qualification, but in the long run it is, and with extraordinary regularity. In the subsistence economy of the organized neighborhood, very often the richest man is simply the chieftain. However, this often means only an honorific preference. For example, in the so-called pure modern "democracy," that is, one devoid of any expressly ordered status privileges for individuals, it may be that only the families coming under approximately the same tax class dance with one another. This example is reported of certain smaller Swiss cities. But status honor need not necessarily be linked with a "class situation." On the contrary, it normally stands in sharp opposition to the pretensions of sheer property.

Both propertied and propertyless people can belong to the same status group, and frequently they do with very tangible consequences. This "equality" of social esteem may, however, in the long run become quite precarious. The "equality" of status among the American "gentlemen," for instance, is expressed by the fact that outside the subordination determined by the different functions of "business," it would be considered strictly repugnant—wherever the old tradition still prevails—if even the richest "chief," while playing billiards or cards in his club in the evening, would not treat his "clerk" as in every

---

[11]Here Weber points out that class struggles are often misdirected, a significant critique of the Marxist view. If class struggles were truly between classes, owners such as rentiers, shareholders, and bankers should suffer the wrath of the working class as much as manufacturers and business executives. Weber claims, however, that they do not because they are less likely to be in direct contact with the workers.

[12] Above, Weber has described the operation of class within society. Here and below, he adds what he considers two other forces that cut across class identification and compete with it for prominence in social action: status and party. For Weber, class, status, and party are overlapping identifications. None of them has universal analytic priority, but rather identification with one or the other is dependent on circumstances. This idea of overlapping identities anticipates much of current interpretive and postmodern anthropology.

sense fully his equal in birthright. It would be repugnant if the American "chief" would bestow upon his "clerk" the condescending "benevolence" marking a distinction of "position," which the German chief can never dissever from his attitude. This is one of the most important reasons why in America the German "clubby-ness" has never been able to attain the attraction that the American clubs have.[13]

6: GUARANTEES OF STATUS STRATIFICATION

In content, status honor is normally expressed by the fact that above all else a specific *style of life* can be expected from all those who wish to belong to the circle. Linked with this expectation are restrictions on "social" intercourse (that is, intercourse which is not subservient to economic or any other of business's "functional" purposes). These restrictions may confine normal marriages to within the status circle and may lead to complete endogamous closure. As soon as there is not a mere individual and socially irrelevant imitation of another style of life, but an agreed-upon communal action of this closing character, the "status" development is under way.

In its characteristic form, stratification by "status groups" on the basis of conventional styles of life evolves at the present time in the United States out of the traditional democracy.[14] For example, only the resident of a certain street ("the street") is considered as belonging to "society," is qualified for social intercourse,

and is visited and invited. Above all, this differentiation evolves in such a way as to make for strict submission to the fashion that is dominant at a given time in society. This submission to fashion also exists among men in America to a degree unknown in Germany. Such submission is considered to be an indication of the fact that a given man *pretends* to qualify as a gentleman. This submission decides, at least *prima facie*,[15] that he will be treated as such. And this recognition becomes just as important for his employment chances in "swank" establishments, and above all, for social intercourse and marriage with "esteemed" families, as the qualification for dueling among Germans in the Kaiser's day. As for the rest: certain families resident for a long time, and, of course, correspondingly wealthy, e.g., "F.F.V., i.e., First Families of Virginia," or the actual or alleged descendants of the "Indian Princess" Pocahontas, of the Pilgrim fathers, or of the Knickerbockers,[16] the members of almost inaccessible sects and all sorts of circles setting themselves apart by means of any other characteristics and badges . . . all these elements usurp "status" honor. The development of status is essentially a question of stratification resting upon usurpation. Such usurpation is the normal origin of almost all status honor. But the road from this purely conventional situation to legal privilege, positive or negative, is easily traveled as soon as a certain stratification of the social order has in fact been "lived in" and has achieved stability by virtue of a stable distribution of economic power.

---

[13] Weber's 1904 visit to America made a profound and lasting impression on him. Though greatly disturbed by the position of African Americans and immigrants, in many respects he viewed America as, for better and worse, the model of a new society. He felt that in America, rationalization and bureaucratization had proceeded to the greatest extent. The example of boss and worker treating each other as equals may appear fanciful to the modern reader, but for Weber, it illustrated the compartmentalization and bureaucratization of American life.

[14] Although Weber recognized a link between economic position and status, he also believed that there were many

other ways to acquire status. The examples he uses here are drawn from American society but reflect the extremely status-conscious German society. Weber himself came from a family of factory owners. He had trained in law at Heidelberg and been a member of his father's prestigious dueling fraternity. He had scars from the dueling he refers to in this passage. After his studies and a year of military training, he was commissioned as an officer in the German army.

[15] *Prima facie:* Latin for at first sight.

[16] *Knickerbockers* refers to the descendants of the Dutch settlers of New York.

7: "ETHNIC" SEGREGATION AND "CASTE"

Where the consequences have been realized to their full extent, the status group evolves into a closed "caste."[17] Status distinctions are then guaranteed not merely by conventions and laws, but also by *rituals*. This occurs in such a way that every physical contact with a member of any caste that is considered to be "lower" by the members of a "higher" caste is considered as making for a ritualistic impurity and to be a stigma which must be expiated by a religious act. Individual castes develop quite distinct cults and gods.

In general, however, the status structure reaches such extreme consequences only where there are underlying differences which are held to be "ethnic." The "caste" is, indeed, the normal form in which ethnic communities usually live side by side in a "societalized" manner. These ethnic communities believe in blood relationship and exclude exogamous marriage and social intercourse. Such a caste situation is part of the phenomenon of "pariah" peoples and is found all over the world. These people form communities, acquire specific occupational traditions of handicrafts or of other arts, and cultivate a belief in their ethnic community. They live in a "diaspora" strictly segregated from all personal intercourse, except that of an unavoidable sort, and their situation is legally precarious. Yet, by virtue of their economic indispensability, they are tolerated, indeed, frequently privileged, and they live in interspersed political communities. The Jews are the most impressive historical example.

A "status" segregation grown into a "caste" differs in its structure from a mere "ethnic" segregation: the caste structure transforms the horizontal and unconnected coexistences of ethnically segregated groups into a vertical social system of super- and subordination. Correctly formulated: a comprehensive societalization integrates the ethnically divided communities into specific political and communal action.[18] In their consequences they differ precisely in this way: ethnic coexistences condition a mutual repulsion and disdain but allow each ethnic community to consider its own honor as the highest one; the caste structure brings about a social subordination and an acknowledgment of "more honor" in favor of the privileged caste and status groups. This is due to the fact that in the caste structure ethnic distinctions as such have become "functional" distinctions within the political societalization (warriors, priests, artisans that are politically important for war and for building, and so on). But even pariah people who are most despised are usually apt to continue cultivating in some manner that which is equally peculiar to ethnic and to status communities: the belief in their own specific "honor." This is the case with the Jews.

Only with the negatively privileged status groups does the "sense of dignity" take a specific deviation. A sense of dignity is the precipitation in individuals of social honor and of conventional demands which a positively privileged status group raises for the deportment of its members. The sense of dignity that characterizes positively privileged status groups is naturally related to their "being" which does not transcend itself, that is, it is to their

---

[17] Weber developed his notions of caste more fully in his work on the Indian caste system, but he clearly believed the term *caste* applied to a wide variety of social systems. He spends a good deal of time discussing caste here because he sees it as an extreme manifestation of status differences. One of Weber's contributions to sociology is the idea of the ideal type, a "one-sided accentuation of one or more points of view" (quoted in Ritzer 1992). Weber uses *ideal* in the sense of the most extreme logical possibility rather than in the sense of best. He looked for, or logically constructed, extreme examples to gain insight into more typical social forms. Although the use of ideal types pro-

vides clear examples amenable to analysis, it may also obscure the complexity of social life.

[18] Notice Weber's use of the words *society* and *societalization*. He theorized that there were three basic types of social structure: the community, the association, and the society (Gerth and Mills 1946:57). To some degree, he understood history as a progression from community to society, with society marked by increased rationalization and bureaucratization. In Weber's usage, society is what modern anthropologists might refer to as state-level society. For Weber, when a group became societalized, it also became bureaucratized.

"beauty and excellence" (καλο-κάγαθια). Their kingdom is "of this world." They live for the present and by exploiting their great past. The sense of dignity of the negatively privileged strata naturally refers to a future lying beyond the present, whether it is of this life or of another. In other words, it must be nurtured by the belief in a providential "mission" and by a belief in a specific honor before God. The "chosen people's" dignity is nurtured by a belief either that in the beyond "the last will be the first," or that in this life a Messiah will appear to bring forth into the light of the world which has cast them out the hidden honor of the pariah people. This simple state of affairs, and not the "resentment" which is so strongly emphasized in Nietzsche's much admired construction in the *Genealogy of Morals,* is the source of the religiosity cultivated by pariah status groups. In passing, we may note that resentment may be accurately applied only to a limited extent; for one of Nietzsche's main examples, Buddhism, it is not at all applicable.[19]

Incidentally, the development of status groups from ethnic segregations is by no means the normal phenomenon. On the contrary, since objective "racial differences" are by no means basic to every subjective sentiment of an ethnic community, the ultimately racial foundation of status structure is rightly and absolutely a question of the concrete individual case.[20] Very frequently a status group is instrumental in the production of a thoroughbred anthropological type. Certainly a status group is to a high degree effective in producing extreme types, for they select personally

qualified individuals (e.g., the Knighthood selects those who are fit for warfare, physically and psychically). But selection is far from being the only, or the predominant, way in which status groups are formed: Political membership or class situation has at all times been at least as frequently decisive. And today the class situation is by far the predominant factor, for of course the possibility of a style of life expected for members of a status group is usually conditioned economically.

8: STATUS PRIVILEGES

For all practical purposes, stratification by status goes hand in hand with a monopolization of ideal and material goods or opportunities, in a manner we have come to know as typical.[21] Besides the specific status honor, which always rests upon distance and exclusiveness, we find all sorts of material monopolies. Such honorific preferences may consist of the privilege of wearing special costumes, of eating special dishes taboo to others, of carrying arms—which is most obvious in its consequences—the right to pursue certain non-professional dilettante artistic practices, e.g., to play certain musical instruments. Of course, material monopolies provide the most effective motives for the exclusiveness of a status group; although, in themselves, they are rarely sufficient, almost always they come into play to some extent. Within a status circle there is the question of intermarriage: the interest of the

---

[19] The work of Friedrich Wilhelm Nietzsche (1844–1900) was extremely influential for German social thinkers of the late nineteenth century. He was concerned, among other things, with the benefit that people gained from holding certain types of ideas. Simply put, his resentment theory (from *On the Genealogy of Morals* (1956 [1887]) states that, because they cannot bear the psychological burden of low position, oppressed people turn the characteristics of their subjugation into sources of honor. Thus, Nietzsche believed that ascetic Christian morality reflected the resentment of early Christians who were often slaves (Gerth and Mills 1946:62). Although Weber is concerned with individual psychology, he understands the attribution of elevated moral status to oppressed peoples as a group function—one that maintains the status differentials

of the caste system—rather than as an individual psychological coping mechanism. Weber probably considered resentment theory inapplicable to Buddhism because that religion's founder, the Indian prince Siddhartha Gautama (563?–483? B.C.E.), was a man of high status.

[20] Note that Weber argues that caste groups may be separated by perceived racial distinctions but are not *created* by these. Rather, differential status may, in time, create distinctions that are then *perceived* as racial. This is a fairly radical point.

[21] Weber suggests that while economic privileges are frequently one important aspect of status, they are rarely sufficient to explain stratification. Other, less material privileges may well be more important.

families in the monopolization of potential bride-grooms is at least of equal importance and is parallel to the interest in the monopolization of daughters. The daughters of the circle must be provided for. With an increased enclosure of the status group, the conventional preferential opportunities for special employment grow into a legal monopoly of special offices for the members. Certain goods become objects for monopolization by status groups. In the typical fashion these include "entailed estates" and frequently also the possessions of serfs or bondsmen and, finally, special trades. This monopolization occurs positively when the status group is exclusively entitled to own and to manage them; and negatively when, in order to maintain its specific way of life, the status group must *not* own and manage them.

The decisive role of a "style of life" in status "honor" means that status groups are the specific bearers of all "conventions."[22] In whatever way it may be manifest, all "stylization" of life either originates in status groups or is at least conserved by them. Even if the principles of status conventions differ greatly, they reveal certain typical traits, especially among those strata which are most privileged. Quite generally, among privileged status groups there is a status disqualification that operates against the performance of common physical labor. This disqualification is now "setting in" in America against the old tradition of esteem for labor. Very frequently every rational economic pursuit, and especially "entrepreneurial activity," is looked upon as a disqualification of status. Artistic and literary activity is also considered as degrading work as soon as it is exploited for income, or at least when it is connected with hard physical exertion. An example is the sculptor working like a mason in his dusty smock as over against the painter in his salon-like "studio" and those forms of musical practice that are acceptable to the status group.

9: ECONOMIC CONDITIONS AND EFFECTS OF STATUS STRATIFICATION

The frequent disqualification of the gainfully employed as such is a direct result of the principle of status stratification peculiar to the social order, and of course, of this principle's opposition to a distribution of power which is regulated exclusively through the market. These two factors operate along with various individual ones, which will be touched upon below.

We have seen above that the market and its processes "knows no personal distinctions": "functional" interests dominate it. It knows nothing of "honor." The status order means precisely the reverse, viz.: stratification in terms of "honor" and of styles of life peculiar to status groups as such. If mere economic acquisition and naked economic power still bearing the stigma of its extra-status origin could bestow upon anyone who has won it the same honor as those who are interested in status by virtue of style of life claim for themselves, the status order would be threatened at its very root. This is the more so as, given equality of status honor, property *per se* represents an addition even if it is not overtly acknowledged to be such. Yet if such economic acquisition and power gave the agent any honor at all, his wealth would result in his attaining more honor than those who successfully claim honor by virtue of style of life. Therefore all groups having interests in the status order react with special sharpness precisely against the pretensions of purely economic acquisition. In most cases they react the more vigorously the more they feel themselves threatened.[23] Calderon's respectful treatment of the peasant, for instance, as opposed to Shakespeare's simultaneous and ostensible disdain of the *canaille*

---

[22] In his emphasis on consumption as a marker of status, Weber may have been strongly influenced by the economic and social theorist Thorstein Veblen (1857–1929). Veblen's *The Theory of the Leisure Class* (1912 [1899]) suggested that there was a conflict between making goods and making money: Monied classes increasingly freed themselves from any involvement in labor. Weber expands upon this topic in the section below.

[23] To a modern American reader, this passage may sound terribly anachronistic. For most of us, enormous wealth is likely to confer status almost instantly. In Weber's nineteenth-century world, quick wealth was often considered to be tainted, and the old rich had little respect for those who acquired their money more recently. To Weber—member of a dueling society, officer, and nationalist—honor and the acquisition of status played a role that is, for most of us today, quite alien.

illustrates the different way in which a firmly structured status order reacts as compared with a status order that has become economically precarious.[24] This is an example of a state of affairs that recurs everywhere. Precisely because of the rigorous reactions against the claims of property *per se* the "parvenu"[25] is never accepted, personally and without reservation, by the privileged status groups, no matter how completely his style of life has been adjusted to theirs. They will only accept his descendants who have been educated in the conventions of their status group and who have never besmirched its honor by their own economic labor.

As to the general *effect* of the status order, only one consequence can be stated, but it is a very important one: the hindrance of the free development of the market occurs first for those goods which status groups directly withheld from free exchange by monopolization.[26] This monopolization may be effected either legally or conventionally. For example, in many Hellenic cities during the epoch of status groups, and also originally in Rome, the inherited estate (as is shown by the old formula for indiction against spendthrifts) was monopolized just as were the estates of knights, peasants, priests, and especially the clientele of the craft and merchant guilds. The market is restricted, and the power of naked property *per se* which gives its stamp to "class formation," is pushed into the background. The results of this process can be most varied. Of course, they do not necessarily weaken the contrasts in the economic situation. Frequently they strengthen these contrasts, and in any case, where stratification by status permeates a community as strongly as was the case in all political communities of antiquity and of the Middle Ages, one can never speak of a genuinely free market competition as we understand it today. There are wider effects than this direct exclusion of special

goods from the market. From the contrariety between the status order and the purely economic order mentioned above, it follows that in most instances the notion of honor peculiar to status absolutely abhors that which is essential to the market: higgling. Honor abhors higgling among peers and occasionally it taboos higgling for the members of a status group in general. Therefore, everywhere some status groups, and usually the most influential, consider almost any kind of overt participation in economic acquisition as absolutely stigmatizing.

With some over-simplification, one might thus say that "classes" are stratified according to their relations to the production and acquisition of goods; whereas "status groups" are stratified according to the principles of their *consumption* of goods as represented by special "styles of life."

An "occupational group" is also a status group. For normally, it successfully claims social honor only by virtue of the special style of life which may be determined by it. The differences between classes and status groups frequently overlap. It is precisely those status communities most strictly segregated in terms of honor (viz. the Indian castes) who today show, although within very rigid limits, a relatively high degree of indifference to pecuniary income. However, the Brahmins seek such income in many different ways.

As to the general economic conditions making for the predominance of stratification by "status," only very little can be said.[27] When the bases of the acquisition and distribution of goods are relatively stable, stratification by status is favored. Every technological repercussion and economic transformation threatens stratification by status and pushes the class situation into the foreground. Epochs and countries in which the naked class situation is of predominant significance are regularly the periods of technical and economic

---

[24] *Calderon* refers to Spanish playwright Pedro Calderon de la Barca (1600–1681). A *canaille* is a mob.

[25] *Parvenu:* people with manners that ill-fit their new-found wealth.

[26] In this paragraph, Weber provides a concise summary of his understanding of class and status.

[27] Compare the conception of change here with Marx's understanding of change caused by conflict between classes. In both cases, conflict between ideological superstructure and technological base plays a crucial role.

transformations. And every slowing down of the shifting of economic stratifications leads, in due course, to the growth of status structures and makes for a resuscitation of the important role of social honor.

10: PARTIES

Whereas the genuine place of "classes" is within the economic order, the place of "status groups" is within the social order, that is, within the sphere of the distribution of "honor." From within these spheres, classes and status groups influence one another and they influence the legal order and are in turn influenced by it. But "parties" live in a house of "power."

Their action is oriented toward the acquisition of social "power," that is to say, toward influencing a communal action no matter what its content may be. In principle, parties may exist in a social "club" as well as in a "state." As over against the actions of classes and status groups, for which this is not necessarily the case, the communal actions of "parties" always mean a societalization. For party actions are always directed toward a goal which is striven for in planned manner. This goal may be a "cause" (the party may aim at realizing a program for ideal or material purposes), or the goal may be "personal" (sinecures, power, and from these, honor for the leader and the followers of the party). Usually the party action aims at all these simultaneously. Parties are, therefore, only possible within communities that are societalized, that is, which have some rational order and a staff of persons available who are ready to enforce it. For parties aim precisely at influencing this staff, and if possible, to recruit it from party followers.[28]

In any individual case, parties may represent interests determined through "class situation" or "status situation," and they may recruit their following respectively from one or the other. But they need be neither purely "class" nor purely "status" parties. In most cases they are partly class parties and partly status parties, but sometimes they are neither.[29] They may represent ephemeral or enduring structures. Their means of attaining power may be quite varied, ranging from naked violence of any sort to canvassing for votes with coarse or subtle means: money, social influence, the force of speech, suggestion, clumsy hoax, and so on to the rougher or more artful tactics of obstruction in parliamentary bodies.

The sociological structure of parties differs in a basic way according to the kind of communal action which they struggle to influence. Parties also differ according to whether or not the community is stratified by status or by classes. Above all else, they vary according to the structure of domination within the community. For their leaders normally deal with the conquest of a community. They are, in the general concept which is maintained here, not only products of specially modern forms of domination. We shall also designate as parties the ancient and medieval "parties," despite the fact that their structure differs basically from the structure of modern parties. By virtue of these structural differences of domination it is impossible to say anything about the structure of parties without discussing the structural forms of social domination *per se*. Parties, which are always structures struggling for domination, are very frequently organized in a very strict "authoritarian" fashion.

Concerning "classes," "status groups," and "parties," it must be said in general that they necessarily presuppose a comprehensive societal-

---

[28] Weber understood parties very broadly as any group committed to using power to achieve a certain goal. Thus, his understanding of party was not limited to official state political parties. For Weber, two things separated parties from classes and status groups: They existed to pursue power, and they strove to achieve a specific goal or cause. These gave them much more definite

shape than Weber perceives in either class or status groups.

[29] Just as class and status sometimes coincide, party may as well. However, such overlapping cannot be assumed. Class, status, and party are often different and contradictory institutions.

ization, and especially a political framework of communal action, within which they operate. This does not mean that parties would be confined by the frontiers of any individual political community. On the contrary, at all times it has been the order of the day that the societalization (even when it aims at the use of military force in common) reaches beyond the frontier of politics.[30] This has been the case in the solidarity of interests among the oligarchs and among the democrats in Hellas, among the Guelfs and among Ghibellines in the Middle Ages, and within the Calvinist party during the period of religious struggles.[31] It has been the case up to the solidarity of the landlords (international congress of agrarian landlords), and has continued among princes (holy alliance,

Karlsbad decrees), socialist workers, conservatives (the longing of Prussian conservatives for Russian intervention in 1850). But their aim is not necessarily the establishment of new international political, i.e., *territorial*, dominion. In the main they aim to influence the existing dominion.

[*The posthumously published text breaks off here. We omit an incomplete sketch of types of "warrior estates."*]

NOTE

[a] *Wirtschaft und Gesellschaft*, part III, chap. 4, pp. 631–40. The first sentence in paragraph one and the several definitions in this chapter which are in brackets do not appear in the original text. They have been taken from other contexts of *Wirtschaft und Gesellschaft*.

---

[30] Weber's description of parties reaching across political communities must be considered in the context of the debate between Weber and the Marxists. Communist parties of Weber's era were aimed precisely at political action across international boundaries. Unlike the Marxists, Weber does not view these parties as historically unique and is equivocal about their chances for success.

[31] Hellas refers to classical Greece. The Guelfs and the Ghibellines were the major political factions of twelfth- and thirteenth-century Italy. The Guelfs defeated the Ghibellines in 1268.

Historical Particularism

A great deal of ethnographic writing took place in late nineteenth-century America. We have already discussed the anthropological theorist Lewis Henry Morgan, who published his major works between 1851 and 1881 (see essay 3). In addition to Morgan, early ethnologists such as Alice Fletcher (1838–1923) were actively pursuing ethnographic investigations. The Bureau of American Ethnology (BAE) together with the Smithsonian also sponsored the work of many scholars, including Otis Mason (1838–1908), James Mooney (1861–1921), and Frank Cushing (1857–1900). The BAE was a division of the Smithsonian Institution created in 1879 to organize anthropological research in America. Its first director was John Wesley Powell (1834–1902), better known as the explorer of the Grand Canyon. Despite this variety of anthropological activity, it was not until the turn of the twentieth century that anthropology coalesced as an academic discipline in America. When it did, the ideas of a single individual, Franz Boas (1858–1942), had enormous impact. The method of research Boas pioneered, later labeled *historical particularism,* is widely considered the first American-born school of anthropological thought, and he is considered one of the founders of American anthropology.

Boas was born to a secular and intellectual German Jewish family. His father was a merchant of liberal political views and his mother a radical freethinker, the founder of a kindergarten devoted to the "consciousness of mutual interdependence" in children (Frank 1997:733). Boas described his home as a place in which "the ideals of the revolution of 1848 were a living force (1974 [1938]:41)." His upbringing emphasized the freedom, dignity, and fundamental equality of all peoples, and Boas remained

deeply devoted to these ideas throughout his life.

Boas' education emphasized the physical sciences of his day. After graduating from gymnasium in 1877, he went first to the University of Heidelberg, then to Bonn, and finally to Kiel, where he received his Ph.D. His examination subjects were geography, physics, and philosophy and his dissertation was titled *Contribution to the Understanding of the Color of Water.* Although his training emphasized quantitative data, he later wrote that these studies caused him to realize that "there are domains of our experience in which the concepts of quantity . . . are not applicable" (1974 [1938]:42). Although Boas believed in a science of anthropology, he recognized a distinction between the social and natural sciences.

As a Jewish liberal, Boas had few opportunities for academic employment in late nineteenth-century Germany and, by 1882, he had begun contemplating immigration to the United States. In 1883, he seized an opportunity to do research on migration patterns and seawater among the Eskimo on Baffin Island. Boas spent fifteen months in "the sublime loneliness of the arctic" (quoted in Stocking 1974:22), and the experience changed him from a geographer to an ethnographer. Living among the Eskimo convinced him that the liberal and humanistic values of his childhood could be applied to the study of human society.

Not long before Boas left for Baffin Island, he had become engaged to Marie Krackoweiser. During his fieldwork, he kept a diary in the form of a single long letter to her. In an oft-quoted passage written on December 23, 1883, he wrote:

> I believe, if this trip has for me (as a thinking person) a valuable influence, it lies in the

strengthening of the viewpoint of the relativity of all cultivation and that the evil as well as the value of a person lies in the cultivation of the heart, which I find or do not find here just as much as amongst us, and that all service, therefore, which a man can perform for humanity must serve to promote truth. (quoted in Cole 1983)

A month later, on January 22, 1884, he wrote:

I do not want a German professorship because I know I would be restricted to my science and to teaching, for which I have little inclination. I should much prefer to live in America in order to be able to further those ideas for which I live. . . . What I want to live and die for, is equal rights for all, equal possibilities to learn and work for poor and rich alike! Don't you believe that to have done even the smallest bit for this, is more than all science taken together? (quoted in Cole 1983)

After spending the winter of 1884–1885 in New York, Boas returned to Germany in 1885 to take positions at the Berlin Ethnological Museum (the *Musuum fur Volkenkunde*) and the University of Berlin. However, he soon left Germany once more, this time to visit the Kwakiutl and other tribes on Northern Vancouver Island in Canada, groups he was to study for the rest of his life. In 1886, after a brief return to Germany, he decided to immigrate to the United States.

His first position in America was at Clark University, where he taught from 1888 to 1892. Boas left Clark during a faculty strike in 1892 and accepted a job with the Columbian Exposition of 1893, a fair held in Chicago to celebrate the four hundredth anniversary of Columbus' arrival in America. The Field Museum of Anthropology grew out of this exhibition. Boas briefly served as the curator of anthropology there but left after quarreling with the museum's administration. In 1896 he moved to Columbia University as a lecturer in physical anthropology and in 1899 became a professor of anthropology. Boas spent the rest of his career at Columbia. He retired in 1936 but remained extremely active in anthropology until his death six years later.

Boas began his career at a time when anthropology was not recognized as a science or even as a field of university study. With his training in the physical sciences, he brought a rigorous approach to ethnographic fieldwork. Boas' emphasis on the careful collection of ethnographic data and his rejection of nineteenth-century evolutionary theories in favor of ethnographic field experience were, in part, a reaction to the uncritical use of the comparative method by the unilineal evolutionists of his day.

Though Boas recognized that humans and other primates shared common ancestry, he was also deeply influenced by Rudolph Virchow, one of his mentors, who was skeptical of Darwinian evolution. Boas seems never to have fully understood or accepted the Darwinian process of natural selection (Caspari 2003:68). Boas strongly repudiated the social Darwinism and evolutionary speculation of his day. These beliefs may have influenced his views of natural selection. In fact, his famous study of changing head size among immigrants and their children (1912) was more Lamarckian than Darwinian. According to Boas, children, because they had better nutrition, had larger head sizes than their immigrant parents. Thus they had acquired a trait that might be passed to future generations.

Boas maintained that the sweeping generalizations of the unilineal social evolutionists were not scientifically valid. He based much of his attack on the distinction between convergent and parallel evolution. Evolutionists assumed that similar cultural traits were the result of parallel development driven by universal evolutionary law. Boas showed that it was possible for the same characteristics to come about through different processes. In "The Limitations of the Comparative Method in Anthropology" (1896), he demonstrated that cultures may have similar traits for a variety of reasons, including diffusion and trade. Corresponding environments or historical accident may produce similar cultural traits independent of any universal evolutionary process. Thus, the existence of such traits could not be used as evidence for universal stages of cultural evolution.

Boas believed that to explain cultural customs, one must examine them from three fundamental perspectives: the environmental conditions under which they developed, psychological factors, and historical connections. Of these, the third was the most important. He felt that societies were created by their own historical circumstances. Thus the best explanations of cultural phenomena were to be acquired by studying the historical development of the societies in which they were found. Because Boas focused on the specific histories of individual societies, his approach to anthropology is called historical particularism, although he never used this label. It was coined by Marvin Harris in the 1960s.

Boas advocated a four-field perspective that included studying prehistory, linguistics, and physical anthropology in addition to the observation of culture. This idea shaped the anthropology department Boas created at Columbia and the departments his students founded at other universities. The hallmark of Boasian-style anthropology became the intensive study of specific cultures through long periods of fieldwork. Boas argued that it was only through living with a people and learning their language that one could develop an accurate understanding of a culture.

Boas and his students were driven by the belief that "primitive" societies were rapidly disappearing. In particular, the situation of Native Americans, forced onto reservations and their populations decimated, gave Boas and his students a sense of urgency. They believed that if these cultures were not recorded immediately, knowledge of them would be lost entirely. The sense that anthropology was an urgent salvage operation conditioned much of the theory and method in American anthropology and caused it to develop in a very different direction than anthropology in Britain and France.

Boas also pioneered the concept that has become known as *cultural relativism.* He himself never used the term, which was coined in the 1950s, but, like historical particularism, it accurately describes his position. As we have noted above, cultural evolutionists had argued that all societies were following the same path of development from savagery to civilization. If this was so, then it was perfectly reasonable to say that some societies were more or less advanced, more or less savage than others. Boas rejected parallel evolution and argued that societies were the result of their own unique histories. If this was the case, then there could be no universal yardstick by which to judge them. Their traits were the result of their historical and environmental

circumstance and could only be understood within that context. Consequently, terms such as *primitive, inferior,* and *superior* could not apply.

Because Boas discredited the unilineal evolutionary schemes popular in his day and insisted that societies were the result of their particular histories and could not be compared, he is often perceived as antitheoretical. Some of Boas' students argued that this was not the case; he recognized the need for new theoretical perspectives but believed that more general theories of human behavior would become obvious once enough data had been collected (for example, see Lesser 1981). However, it is clear that Boas was uninterested in theory building, and the central tenet of historical particularism, that cultures are primarily the result of their unique histories, is inimical to any general theory of culture.

Though he did not leave a coherent theory, Boas had a profound effect on the development of anthropology. He almost single-handedly trained the first generation of American anthropologists and directed their initial field studies. Individuals such as Alfred Louis Kroeber (1876–1960), Robert Lowie (1883–1957), Edward Sapir (1884–1939), Margaret Mead (1901–1978), Melville Herskovits (1895–1963), Paul Radin (1883–1959), Ruth Fulton Benedict (1887–1948), Clark Wissler (1870–1947), Ashley Montagu (1905–1999), and many others, were his students. Several of these researchers have works that appear or are mentioned later in this text.

In addition to training students, Boas lived his life as a citizen scientist, true to the ideals he had expressed in his Baffin Island letter-diary. He was an indefatigable campaigner for justice, equality, and the rights of individuals. He spoke out against World War I and the xenophobia and jingoism the war had triggered in America. A staunch champion of the rights of immigrants and African Americans, he fought against the poll tax, racial discrimination, the intimidation of teachers in colleges and high schools, and the rise of Nazism in Europe.

In particular, Boas was deeply involved in the early years of the NAACP. He contributed the lead article for the second issue of that organization's journal, *The Crisis,* and spoke out on the subject of race and racism repeatedly throughout his life. Boas died in 1942 at a luncheon in honor of Paul Rivet, a founder of French anthropology, whose escape from Nazi-occupied France Boas had championed. Rivet reported that Boas' last words were, "One must never tire of repeating that racism is a monstrous error or an impudent lie" (in Lewis 2001:456).

Boas and his students dominated American anthropology from about 1911 until after World War II (Stocking 1992:117), but he was not unopposed. In the late nineteenth century, anthropology in America was controlled by scholars from Harvard (sometimes called the Maya Group, after their interest in Mayan Studies) and the Smithsonian (called the Washington Group). Academics from these institutions, drawn largely from old WASP families, subscribed to programs of evolutionary anthropology. Many were devoted to race-science attempts to prove the superiority of Northern Europeans. Anthropologists in the Maya and Washington Groups objected to Boas and his students, most of whom were either immigrants themselves or the sons and daughters of immigrants, and many of whom were Jewish. They opposed Boas' notions of cultural relativism and racial equality. Boas' most virulent enemies were members of the anthropology division of the National Research Council (an organization founded to promote American aims in World War I) and the Galton Society, which promoted racial science and eugenics. Key members of both organizations included Charles B. Davenport (1866–1944), Madison Grant (1865–1937), and Ales Hrdlicka (1869–1943) (Stocking 1968:289).

Boas was also deeply disturbed by the race-based anthropology practiced by physical anthropologists in the late nineteenth and early twentieth centuries. Virchow taught Boas anthropometrics, or techniques of human measurement, which he later put to use in his studies, debunking the notion that race was a factor in cultural development (Caspari 2003:68).

Boas' conflicts with other anthropologists over cultural relativism, racism, eugenics, and opposition to immigrants were intensified by his pacifism and opposition to World War I. In 1919, Boas wrote a letter to *The Nation* castigating unnamed anthropologists for working as spies for the American government. He wrote that such actions undermined belief in the "truthfulness of science" and "raised a new barrier" against international scientific cooperation (quoted in Stocking 1968:274). Additionally, he called President Woodrow Wilson a hypocrite. The letter brought a series of old grievances and resentments against Boas to the surface at the American Anthropological Association (AAA) meeting ten days after its publication. The Harvard and Smithsonian anthropologists moved successfully to have Boas censured by the AAA and stripped of membership in its governing council; he was also pressured to resign from the National Research Council (Stocking 1968:273). Despite these setbacks, Boas and his students already controlled key positions in anthropology departments around the country and were the most important group of scholars shaping the direction of American anthropology. Although the place of Boas and his students in American anthropology was assured by the 1920s, the AAA censure of Boas stood for ninety-six years. In 2005, by a vote of 1245 to 73, the organization finally rescinded and repudiated its 1919 motion of censure.

Next to Boas, the most influential figure in American anthropology during the first half of the last century was A. L. Kroeber. Kroeber was the first of Boas' students at Columbia to receive a doctorate in anthropology, which he earned in 1901. In that same year, Kroeber was hired by the University of California at Berkeley. At the age of twenty-five, he became the first instructor in the newly created anthropology program and the curator for the university's museum of anthropology. Kroeber stayed at Berkeley for the rest of his career, retiring in 1946. He stayed active in research and writing until his death in 1960.

Throughout his life Kroeber maintained a Boasian perspective. Both Kroeber and Boas were antievolutionists, believed in integrating the four subfields of anthropology, and taught that a historical perspective was necessary to understand other cultures. However, Kroeber split from Boas over two critical issues. Their first disagreement concerned Kroeber's rejection of Boas' idea that anthropology was ultimately a discipline devoted to the study of humankind's origins. Their second disagreement is more significant to contemporary anthropology. Boas believed that individuals played a significant role in a culture's development and change. Kroeber argued that this was not the case, adopting a view of culture very close to that expressed by the French sociologist Émile Durkheim (see essays 5 and 6). The Kroeber essay we have chosen for this volume consists of a series of statements or "professions" about the nature of anthropology. Kroeber argues that although culture came from and is carried by human beings, it cannot be reduced to individual psychology. He maintains that culture is a pattern that transcends and controls individuals and plays a powerful determining role in individual human behavior. This idea is very similar to Durkheim's "collective conscience." In Kroeber's view, individual accomplishment results from historical trends within society rather than anything important about the individual. These ideas are further developed in Kroeber's 1917 essay "The Superorganic."

Kroeber also pursued the Boasian notion of studying cultures in relation to their environmental surroundings. Much of his research consisted of surveys of culture traits among Native Americans in California and on the Great Plains. Unlike Boas, who advocated the intensive study of individual societies, Kroeber was more interested in mapping the distribution of cultural traits into larger geographic patterns (Jacknis 2002:525). As early as 1903, he had already conceived of the ethnological survey that would become his 1925 volume, the *Handbook of the Indians of California*. In his study *Cultural and Natural Areas of Native North America* (1939), he mapped geographic, climatological, and vegetation distribution in relation to Native American cultures. This work was influential among his students, particularly Julian Steward, who went on to develop the cultural ecological approach to the analysis of culture.

Whereas Kroeber believed that the individual was unimportant in cultural analysis, other students of Boas saw individuals as of paramount importance to anthropology. Among them Paul Radin, in particular, typified this approach. The selection of his work we have chosen demonstrates his focus on the relationship between specific men and women and their own culture. Another good example is Radin's 1926 book *Crashing Thunder: The Autobiography of a Winnebago Indian*—an

ethnography in the form of a single individual's life history. Like Boas, Radin believed that it was only through long-term intensive study, including the mastery of language, that an anthropologist could fully comprehend another culture. Following this principle, Radin studied Winnebago society for fifty years, producing a comprehensive record of the culture. Curiously, Radin's focus on the individual distanced him from Boas' own conviction that anthropology was a natural science. His emphasis on life histories moved anthropology in the direction of biography and literature.

The final essay in this section is the work of one of the best known linguists of the Boasian era, Benjamin Lee Whorf (1897–1941). Whorf earned a degree in chemical engineering at the Massachusetts Institute of Technology in 1918, then worked for the Hartford Fire Insurance Company in Connecticut. He pursued his interests in language primarily as a hobby. Although Whorf received several offers of professorships, he refused them, claiming that his work with the insurance company provided him with greater freedom and more money than an academic position could (Lavery 2001). In 1931, Whorf began to study linguistics at Yale University with Edward Sapir (1884–1939), one of the leading linguists of the period.

Whorf's main area of interest was the languages of Mesoamerica. However, he is most remembered for his work on the Hopi language and the *Sapir-Whorf hypothesis*, which he developed with his mentor, Sapir. The Sapir-Whorf hypothesis contains two basic elements: linguistic determinism and linguistic relativity. The first deals with the manner in which the structure of a language affects cognition. Sapir and Whorf proposed that the grammatical and lexical categories of the language a person speaks organize the way they think and shape their behavior. Linguistic relativity is the idea that the grammatical and lexical categories of a language are unique to that language and thus speakers of different languages inhabit separate conceptual worlds. Sapir was a student of Boas and you can see how the notion of linguistic relativity reflects the Boasian view of culture.

The work of Sapir and Whorf inspired research on the relationship between language and culture for almost two decades. Through the 1950s and 1960s, linguists and psychologists sought to test the notion of linguistic determinism. The concept of linguistic relativity was instrumental in the development of the ethnoscience and cognitive anthropology schools. In particular, the influence of the Sapir-Whorf hypothesis is evident in the studies of subjects such as ethnobotany and ethnomedicine in the 1960s and in work such as Conklin's (see essay 27).

The essay chosen for this volume is Whorf's "The Relation of Habitual Thought and Behavior to Language." It is one of Whorf's best known statements of linguistic determinism, containing many examples derived from his investigative work for the Hartford Insurance Company and his study of the Hopi language.

In most European universities, archaeology and linguistics are separate departments from social anthropology, and biological anthropology is typically a part of biology. The four-field focus of anthropology departments in American universities today is a reflection of Boas and his students' view of anthropology.

Though anthropologists today rarely identify themselves as historical particularists, it is almost impossible to overestimate the influence of Boas and historical particularism on mainstream American anthropology. The effects of Boas' critical insights are seen most clearly in the work of his students in the first half of this century, but clear echoes of Boasian thought are present in ethnoscience and cognitive anthropology, as well as in the symbolic and postmodern approaches to the study of culture.

9. *The Methods of Ethnology*

Franz Boas (1858–1942)

DURING THE LAST ten years the methods of inquiry into the historical development of civilization have undergone remarkable changes. During the second half of the last century evolutionary thought held almost complete sway and investigators like Spencer, Morgan, Tylor, Lubbock, to mention only a few, were under the spell of the idea of a general, uniform evolution of culture in which all parts of mankind participated. The newer development goes back in part to the influence of Ratzel, whose geographical training impressed him with the importance of diffusion and migration. The problem of diffusion was taken up in detail particularly in America, but was applied in a much wider sense by Foy and Graebner, and finally seized upon in a still wider application by Elliot Smith and Rivers, so that at the present time, at least among certain groups of investigators in England and also in Germany, ethnological research is based on the concept of migration and dissemination rather than upon that of evolution.[1]

(1920)

---

[1] In this essay, Boas attacks evolutionary theorists such as those represented in this volume. He also attacks diffusionists, whom we have discussed in notes only (see essay 3, footnote 15, for example). He mentions some particularly eminent diffusionists here. Fritz Graebner (1877–1934) and Friedrich Ratzel (1844–1904) were founders of the German *Kulturkreis* ("culture circle") school of diffusionism. *Kulturkreis* members were tightly linked to the Catholic church, and in much of their work they attempted to make newly available ethnographic data correspond with prevailing biblical interpretation (Harris 1968:379). In Cologne, Graebner worked as assistant to museum director Willy Foy (1873–1929). Graebner and Foy collaborated on Graebner's book *Die Methode der Ethnologie* (1911), which Boas brutally critiqued in an essay in *Science* that same year. Grafton Elliot Smith (1871–1937) and William Halse Rivers Rivers (that's right, Rivers Rivers) (1864–1922) were radical English diffusionists who believed that all civilization had diffused from Egypt.

A critical study of these two directions of inquiry shows that each is founded on the application of one fundamental hypothesis.[2] The evolutionary point of view presupposes that the course of historical changes in the cultural life of mankind follows definite laws which are applicable everywhere, and which bring it about that cultural development is, in its main lines, the same among all races and all peoples. This idea is clearly expressed by Tylor in the introductory pages of his classic work "Primitive Culture." As soon as we admit that the hypothesis of a uniform evolution has to be proved before it can be accepted, the whole structure loses its foundation. It is true that there are indications of parallelism of development in different parts of the world, and that similar customs are found in the most diverse and widely separated parts of the globe. The occurrence of these similarities, which are distributed so irregularly that they cannot readily be explained on the basis of diffusion, is one of the foundations of the evolutionary hypothesis, as it was the foundation of Bastian's[3] psychologizing treatment of cultural phenomena. On the other hand, it may be recognized that the hypothesis implies the thought that our modern Western European civilization represents the highest cultural development towards which all other more primitive cultural types tend, and that, therefore, retrospectively, we construct an orthogenetic[4] development towards our own modern civilization. It is clear that if we admit that there may be different ultimate and co-existing types of civilization, the

hypothesis of one single general line of development cannot be maintained.

Opposed to these assumptions is the modern tendency to deny the existence of a general evolutionary scheme which would represent the history of the cultural development the world over.[5] The hypothesis that there are inner causes which bring about similarities of development in remote parts of the globe is rejected and in its place it is assumed that identity of development in two different parts of the globe must always be due to migration and diffusion. On this basis historical contact is demanded for enormously large areas. The theory demands a high degree of stability of cultural traits such as is apparently observed in many primitive tribes, and it is furthermore based on the supposed correlation between a number of diverse and mutually independent cultural traits which reappear in the same combinations in distant parts of the world. In this sense, modern investigation takes up anew Gerland's theory of the persistence of a number of cultural traits which were developed in one center and carried by man in his migrations from continent to continent.

It seems to me that if the hypothetical foundations of these two extreme forms of ethnological research are broadly stated as I have tried to do here, it is at once clear that the correctness of the assumptions has not been demonstrated, but that arbitrarily the one or the other has been selected for the purpose of obtaining a consistent picture of cultural development.[6] These methods

---

[2] Boas' attack on the evolutionists rested on what he considered a logical flaw in their argument. According to him, their argument assumes what it is trying to prove: that historical changes in human culture follow general laws. Boas supported the Darwinian model of biological evolution but was hostile to its application to social evolution.

[3] Adolf Bastian (1826–1905) was a German theorist of psychic unity who believed that a few fundamental ideas, common to humankind, were the building blocks of culture. Bastian was acquainted with Boas in Berlin in the early 1880s.

[4] *Orthogenetic:* evolution along definite, predetermined lines.

[5] Above, Boas has focused his assault on cultural evolutionists. Here he turns his attack to the diffusionists.

[6] This paragraph is typical of Boas' method of attack: He does not attack particular examples but looks for flaws in methodology. Trained in physics, mathematics, and geography, Boas brought a striving for meticulous scientific methodology to anthropology. Essentially, he faults his opponents for sloppy thinking. Writing in this way, he seems to imply that a rigorously scientific presentation of the data might allow the construction of an evolutionary model of human society. In fact Boas staunchly opposed evolutionary explanations. He believed profoundly in human equality and viewed social evolutionary theories as undermining this position. Thus, while Boas couches his arguments against social evolution in methodological terms, his ultimate reasons for making such arguments are deeply held moral convictions.

are essentially forms of classification of the static phenomena of culture according to two distinct principles, and interpretations of these classifications as of historical significance, without, however, any attempt to prove that this interpretation is justifiable. To give an example: It is observed that in most parts of the world there are resemblances between decorative forms that are representative and others that are more or less geometrical. According to the evolutionary point of view, their development is explained in the following manner: the decorative forms are arranged in such order that the most representative forms are placed at the beginning. The other forms are so placed that they show a gradual transition from representative forms to purely conventional geometric forms. This order is then interpreted as meaning that geometric designs originated from representative designs which gradually degenerated. This method has been pursued, for instance, by Putnam, Stolpe, Balfour, and Haddon, and by Verworn and, in his earlier writings, by von den Steinen. While I do not mean to deny that this development may have occurred, it would be rash to generalize and to claim that in every case the classification which has been made according to a definite principle represents an historical development. The order might as well be reversed and we might begin with a simple geometric element which, by the addition of new traits, might be developed into a representative design, and we might claim that this order represents an historical sequence. Both of these possibilities were considered by Holmes[7] as early as 1885. Neither the one nor the other theory can be established without actual historical proof.

The opposite attitude, namely, origin through diffusion, is exhibited in Heinrich Schurtz's attempt to connect the decorative art of Northwest America with that of Melanesia. The simple fact that in these areas elements occur that may be interpreted as eyes, induced him to assume that both have a common origin, without allowing for the possibility that the pattern in the two areas—each of which shows highly distinctive characteristics—may have developed from independent sources. In this attempt Schurtz followed Ratzel, who had already tried to establish connections between Melanesia and Northwest America on the basis of other cultural features.

While ethnographical research based on these two fundamental hypotheses seems to characterize the general tendency of European thought, a different method is at present pursued by the majority of American anthropologists. The difference between the two directions of study may perhaps best be summarized by the statement that American scholars are primarily interested in the dynamic phenomena of cultural change, and try to elucidate cultural history by the application of the results of their studies; and that they relegate the solution of the ultimate question of the relative importance of parallelism of cultural development in distant areas, as against worldwide diffusion, and stability of cultural traits over long periods to a future time when the actual conditions of cultural change are better known.[8] The American ethnological methods are analogous to those of European, particularly of Scandinavian, archaeology, and of the researches into the prehistoric period of the eastern Mediterranean area.

It may seem to the distant observer that American students are engaged in a mass of detailed investigations without much bearing upon the solution of the ultimate problems of a philosophic history of human civilization. I think this interpretation of the American attitude would be unjust because the ultimate questions

---

[7] Notice Boas' passing reference to William Henry Holmes (1846–1933), who was John Wesley Powell's successor at the Bureau of American Ethnology. In 1919, the year before this essay was published, Holmes led the American Anthropological Association's successful effort to censure Boas.

[8] When Boas speaks here of American anthropologists, he is really referring to himself and the many students he trained. The particular issue of cultural change with which they were concerned was the acculturation and disappearance of Native American groups. Despite Boas' claim that American anthropologists analyze culture change, he and his followers were often faulted for producing an essentially static anthropology unable to deal effectively with change.

are as near to our hearts as they are to those of other scholars, only we do not hope to be able to solve an intricate historical problem by a formula.[9]

First of all, the whole problem of cultural history appears to us as an historical problem. In order to understand history it is necessary to know not only how things are, but how they have come to be. In the domain of ethnology, where, for most parts of the world, no historical facts are available except those that may be revealed by archaeological study, all evidence of change can be inferred only by indirect methods. Their character is represented in the researches of students of comparative philology.[10] The method is based on the comparison of static phenomena combined with the study of their distribution. What can be done by this method is well illustrated by Dr. Lowie's[11] investigations of the military societies of the Plains Indians, or by the modern investigation of American mythology. It is, of course, true that we can never hope to obtain incontrovertible data relating to the chronological sequence of events, but certain general broad outlines can be ascertained with a high degree of probability, even of certainty.

As soon as these methods are applied, primitive society loses the appearance of absolute stability which is conveyed to the student who sees a certain people only at a certain given time. All cultural forms rather appear in a constant state of flux and subject to fundamental modifications.

It is intelligible why in our studies the problem of dissemination should take a prominent position. It is much easier to prove dissemination than to follow up developments due to inner forces, and the data for such a study are obtained with much greater difficulty. They may, however, be observed in every phenomenon of acculturation in which foreign elements are remodeled according to the patterns prevalent in their new environment, and they may be found in the peculiar local developments of widely spread ideas and activities. The reason why the study of inner development has not been taken up energetically is not due to the fact that from a theoretical point of view it is unimportant, it is rather due to the inherent methodological difficulties.[12] It may perhaps be recognized that in recent years attention is being drawn to this problem as is manifested by the investigations on the processes of acculturation and of the interdependence of cultural activities which are attracting the attention of many investigators.

The further pursuit of these inquiries emphasizes the importance of a feature which is common to all historic phenomena. While in natural sciences we are accustomed to consider a given number of causes and to study their effects, in historical happenings we are compelled to consider every phenomenon not only as effect but also as cause.[13] This is true even in the particular application of the laws of physical nature, as, for instance, in the study of astronomy in which the position of certain heavenly bodies at a given moment may be considered as the effect of gravitation, while, at the same time, their particular arrangement in space determines future changes. This relation appears much more clearly in the history of human civilization. To give an example:

---

[9] Boas was concerned with methodology rather than theory. European anthropologists often accused Boas and his students of producing an atheoretical anthropology concerned only with the collection of data. In the following paragraphs, he attempts to answer this charge.

[10] *Philology:* the study of written records, their authenticity and original form, and the determination of their meaning.

[11] Robert Lowie (1883–1957), a student of Boas and, later, professor of anthropology at Berkeley, was an influential voice in American anthropology in the 1930s and 1940s.

Boas' reference here is to Lowie's 1913 article, "Military Societies of the Crow Indians."

[12] Note that Boas does not claim his opponents' conclusions are necessarily wrong, simply that they are not supported by competent research.

[13] Boas here defines the position that came to be called historical particularism: Rather than operating under the constraints of some universal law, cultures are *sui generis* (that is, they create themselves). Thus, cultures can only be understood with reference to their particular historical development.

a surplus of food supply is liable to bring about an increase of population and an increase of leisure, which gives opportunity for occupations that are not absolutely necessary for the needs of everyday life. In turn the increase of population and of leisure, which may be applied to new inventions, gives rise to a greater food supply and to a further increase in the amount of leisure, so that a cumulative effect results.

Similar considerations may be made in regard to the important problem of the relation of the individual to society, a problem that has to be considered whenever we study the dynamic conditions of change.[14] The activities of the individual are determined to a great extent by his social environment, but in turn his own activities influence the society in which he lives, and may bring about modifications in its form. Obviously, this problem is one of the most important ones to be taken up in a study of cultural changes. It is also beginning to attract the attention of students who are no longer satisfied with the systematic enumeration of standardized beliefs and customs of a tribe, but who begin to be interested in the question of the way in which the individual reacts to his whole social environment, and to the differences of opinion and of mode of action that occur in primitive society and which are the causes of far-reaching changes.

In short then, the method which we try to develop is based on a study of the dynamic changes in society that may be observed at the present time. We refrain from the attempt to solve the fundamental problem of the general development of civilization until we have been able to unravel the processes that are going on under our eyes.[15]

Certain general conclusions may be drawn from this study even now. First of all, the history of human civilization does not appear to us as determined entirely by psychological necessity that leads to a uniform evolution the world over. We rather see that each cultural group has its own unique history, dependent partly upon the peculiar inner development of the social group, and partly upon the foreign influences to which it has been subjected. There have been processes of gradual differentiation as well as processes of leveling down differences between neighboring cultural centers, but it would be quite impossible to understand, on the basis of a single evolutionary scheme, what happened to any particular people. An example of the contrast between the two points of view is clearly indicated by a comparison of the treatment of Zuñi civilization by Frank Hamilton Cushing[16] on the one hand, on the other by modern students, particularly by Elsie Clews Parsons, A. L. Kroeber and Leslie Spier.[17] Cushing believed that it was possible to explain Zuñi culture entirely on the basis of the reaction of the Zuñi mind to its geographical environment, and that the whole of Zuñi culture could be explained as the development which followed necessarily from the

---

[14] Notice Boas' focus on the effects of an individual on society. During his life, Boas moved from a position that gave individuals little importance to one that gave them much more. The issue split Boas' followers. Kroeber argued that individuals had little importance (see essay 10); Radin contended that anthropology should concentrate on individual life histories (see essay 11).

[15] In other words, Boas' approach was to be purely inductive. Theoretical claims, he believed, could not be supported without the collection of large amounts of data. He is generally understood to have believed that the attempt to formulate a general theory was not wrong, just extremely premature. However, Boas insisted that cultures could only be understood with respect to their unique historical development. Building theory, on the other hand, necessarily involves comparison and generalization. Thus, it seems unlikely that Boasian-style anthropology could ever generate broad theoretical propositions. Harris has noted that Boas "could never . . . feel at ease in the presence of a generalization" (1968:260).

[16] Frank Hamilton Cushing (1857–1900) spent five years with the Zuñi people (1879–1884) and was initiated into their Bow Priest Society. He wrote extensively on Zuñi religion and technology. Here, Boas critiques Cushing's work as ahistorical.

[17] Kroeber and Leslie Spier (1893–1961) were trained by Boas. Elsie Clews Parsons (1875–1941) worked extensively with him (one of his monographs is dedicated to her).

position in which the people were placed. Cushing's keen insight into the Indian mind and his thorough knowledge of the most intimate life of the people gave great plausibility to his interpretations. On the other hand, Dr. Parsons' studies prove conclusively the deep influence which Spanish ideas have had on Zuñi culture, and, together with Professor Kroeber's investigations, give us one of the best examples of acculturation that have come to our notice. The psychological explanation is entirely misleading, notwithstanding its plausibility; and the historical study shows us an entirely different picture, in which the unique combination of ancient traits (which in themselves are undoubtedly complex) and of European influences has brought about the present condition.

Studies of the dynamics of primitive life also show that an assumption of long continued stability such as is demanded by Elliot Smith[18] is without any foundation in fact. Wherever primitive conditions have been studied in detail, they can be proved to be in a state of flux, and it would seem that there is a close parallelism between the history of language and the history of general cultural development. Periods of stability are followed by periods of rapid change. It is exceedingly improbable that any customs of primitive people should be preserved unchanged for thousands of years. Furthermore, the phenomena of acculturation prove that a transfer of customs from one region into another without concomitant changes due to acculturation is very rare. It is, therefore, very unlikely that ancient Mediterranean customs could be found at the present time practically unchanged in different parts of the globe, as Elliot Smith's theory demands.

While on the whole the unique historical character of cultural growth in each area stands out as a salient element in the history of cultural development, we may recognize at the same time that certain typical parallelisms do occur. We are, however, not so much inclined to look for these similarities in detailed customs but rather in certain dynamic conditions which are due to social or psychological causes that are liable to lead to similar results. The example of the relation between food supply and population to which I referred before may serve as an example. Another type of example is presented in those cases in which a certain problem confronting man may be solved by a limited number of methods only. When we find, for instance, marriage as a universal institution, it may be recognized that marriage is possible only between a number of men and a number of women; a number of men and one woman; a number of women and one man; or one man and one woman. As a matter of fact, all these forms are found the world over and it is, therefore, not surprising that analogous forms should have been adopted quite independently in different parts of the world, and, considering both the general economic conditions of mankind and the character of sexual instinct in the higher animals, it also does not seem surprising that group marriage and polyandrous marriages should be comparatively speaking rare. Similar considerations may also be made in regard to the philosophical views held by mankind. In short, if we look for laws, the laws relate to the effects of physiological, psychological, and social conditions, not to sequences of cultural achievement.[19]

---

[18] As mentioned above, the diffusionist Grafton Elliot Smith had theorized that all complex cultural traits diffused from Egypt. The radical diffusionists believed that humans were not inherently inventive, and as a result, societies remained static for long periods. Boas disagreed with this contention.

[19] Equifinality is a key aspect of Boas' theoretical position. He argues that the presence of similar traits in many societies is not necessarily evidence either for psychic unity or large-scale diffusion. They may be the result of convergent evolution and independent invention. Note also a key point in this passage: Boas says that one reason for the development of similar institutions is that logically, certain things can only be done in a limited number of ways. Thus, in his example here, one reason for similarities in marriage patterns is the low number of ways it is possible to construct an institution such as marriage.

In some cases a regular sequence of these may accompany the development of the psychological or social status. This is illustrated by the sequence of industrial inventions in the Old World and in America, which I consider as independent. A period of food gathering and of the use of stone was followed by the invention of agriculture, of pottery and finally of the use of metals. Obviously, this order is based on the increased amount of time given by mankind to the use of natural products, of tools and utensils, and to the variations that developed with it. Although in this case parallelism seems to exist on the two continents, it would be futile to try to follow out the order in detail. As a matter of fact, it does not apply to other inventions. The domestication of animals, which, in the Old World must have been an early achievement, was very late in the New World, where domesticated animals, except the dog, hardly existed at all at the time of discovery. A slight beginning had been made in Peru with the domestication of the llama, and birds were kept in various parts of the continent.[20]

A similar consideration may be made in regard to the development of rationalism. It seems to be one of the fundamental characteristics of the development of mankind that activities which have developed unconsciously are gradually made the subject of reasoning.[21] We may observe this process everywhere. It appears, perhaps, most clearly in the history of science which has gradually extended the scope of its inquiry over an ever-widening field and which has raised into consciousness human activities that are automatically performed in the life of the individual and of society.

I have not heretofore referred to another aspect of modern ethnology which is connected with the growth of psycho-analysis. Sigmund Freud has attempted to show that primitive thought is in many respects analogous to those forms of individual psychic activity which he has explored by his psycho-analytical methods. In many respects his attempts are similar to the interpretation of mythology by symbolists like Stucken. Rivers has taken hold of Freud's suggestion as well as of the interpretations of Graebner and Elliot Smith, and we find, therefore, in his new writings a peculiar disconnected application of a psychologizing attitude and the application of the theory of ancient transmission.[22]

While I believe some of the ideas underlying Freud's psycho-analytic studies may be fruitfully applied to ethnological problems, it does not seem to me that the one-sided exploitation of this method will advance our understanding of the development of human society. It is certainly true that the influence of impressions received during the first few years of life has been entirely underestimated and that the social behavior of man depends to a great extent upon the earliest habits which are established before the time when connected memory begins, and that many so-called racial or hereditary traits are to be considered rather as a result of early exposure to a certain form of social conditions. Most of these habits do not rise into consciousness and are, therefore, broken with difficulty

---

[20] This paragraph is an attack on Morgan (see essay 3), who used the presence of specific technologies or items of material culture to mark eras in his scheme of cultural evolution.

[21] It is curious that, having attacked the principle of psychic unity, Boas here relies on a statement about the universal nature of humankind.

[22] Freud's psychoanalytic theory was extremely popular in the 1920s. Although Boas and his students were pro-foundly affected by portions of Freud's work, they entirely rejected his treatment of the origins and development of society. However, for many of Boas' students, some of Freud's other insights were critical. Margaret Mead and Ruth Benedict developed their views on culture and personality partially in reaction to Freud's ideas. Others, such as Cora Du Bois (1903–1991) and Abram Kardiner (1891–1981), attempted to apply Freudian psychology to anthropology (see the section "Culture and Personality" in this volume).

only. Much of the difference in the behavior of adult male and female may go back to this cause. If, however, we try to apply the whole theory of the influence of suppressed desires to the activities of man living under different social forms, I think we extend beyond their legitimate limits the inferences that may be drawn from the observation of normal and abnormal individual psychology. Many other factors are of greater importance. To give an example: The phenomena of language show clearly that conditions quite different from those to which psycho-analysts direct their attention determine the mental behavior of man.[23] The general concepts underlying language are entirely unknown to most people. They do not rise into consciousness until the scientific study of grammar begins. Nevertheless, the categories of language compel us to see the world arranged in certain definite conceptual groups which, on account of our lack of knowledge of linguistic processes, are taken as objective categories and which, therefore, impose themselves upon the form of our thoughts. It is not known what the origin of these categories may be, but it seems quite certain that they have nothing to do with the phenomena which are the subject of psycho-analytic study.

The applicability of the psycho-analytic theory of symbolism is also open to the greatest doubt. We should remember that symbolic interpretation has occupied a prominent position in the philosophy of all times. It is present not only in primitive life, but the history of philosophy and of theology abounds in examples of a high development of symbolism, the type of which depends upon the general mental attitude of the philosopher who develops it. The theologians who interpreted the Bible on the basis of religious symbolism were no less certain of the correctness of their views, than the psycho-analysts are of their interpretations of thought and conduct based on sexual symbolism. The results of a symbolic interpretation depend primarily upon the subjective attitude of the investigator who arranges phenomena according to his leading concept. In order to prove the applicability of the symbolism of psycho-analysis, it would be necessary to show that a symbolic interpretation from other entirely different points of view would not be equally plausible, and that explanations that leave out symbolic significance or reduce it to a minimum would not be adequate.[24]

While, therefore, we may welcome the application of every advance in the method of psychological investigation, we cannot accept as an advance in ethnological method the crude transfer of a novel, one-sided method of psychological investigation of the individual to social phenomena the origin of which can be shown to be historically determined and to be subject to influences that are not at all comparable to those that control the psychology of the individual.[25]

---

[23] Linguistics was a particular interest of Boas and his students. In this paragraph, Boas refers to the idea that language determines the categories we use to think. This line of reasoning was pursued by Boas' student Edward Sapir (1884–1939) and Sapir's student and colleague, Benjamin Lee Whorf (1897–1941). Today, it is known as the Sapir-Whorf hypothesis.

[24] Boas' assault on psychoanalysis is similar to his attack on evolutionists and diffusionists: He faults it on methodological grounds. All of Boas' criticisms are intended to reinforce his call for an inductive methodology in anthropology. He insisted that it was only through the meticulous collection of empirical data that anthropologists could hope to understand cultures.

[25] The particular attacks Boas makes in this essay are repeated frequently in anthropology. For example, Boas' criticism of psychology as dependent on "[the] subjective attitude of the investigator who arranges phenomena according to his leading concept" is repeated almost word for word by ethnoscientists and cognitive anthropologists in the 1950s and 1960s in their critique of other forms of anthropology (see essays 27 and 28) and in slightly different form by postmodernists as well (see essays 38 and 39).

10. *Eighteen Professions*[1]

A. L. KROEBER (1876–1960)

ANTHROPOLOGY TODAY INCLUDES two studies which fundamental differences of aim and method render irreconcilable. One of these branches is biological and psychological; the other, social or historical.[2]

There is a third field, the special province of anthropology, concerned with the relation of biological and social factors. This is no-man's-land, and therefore used as a picnic-ground by whosoever prefers pleasure excursions to the work of cultivating a patch of understanding. Some day this tract will also be surveyed, fenced, and improved. Biological science already claims it; but the title remains to be established. For the present, the labor in hand is the delimitation of the scope of history from that of science.[3]

In what follows, historical anthropology, history, and sociology are referred to as history. Physical anthropology and psychology are included in biology.[4]

1. *The aim of history is to know the relations of social facts to the whole of civilization.*

(1915)

---

[1] Readers expecting an excursion into the uses of anthropology in the early twentieth century are bound to be disappointed by this essay. Kroeber uses the word *professions* to mean items of belief rather than jobs that an anthropologist might do. Most Boasian anthropologists prided themselves on replacing what they considered the empty theorizing of nineteenth-century scholars such as Morgan and Tylor with the scientific reasoning of Franz Boas. They often reminded students that Boas was trained in the physical sciences. By using the word *professions,* Kroeber is emphasizing the notion that he considers these points to be the bedrock of anthropology.

Kroeber's early training was in English, and he held both a B.A. and an M.A. in that subject. Even though he earned a Ph.D. in anthropology (his doctoral dissertation was a twenty-eight-page paper on Arapaho art that attacked nineteenth-century evolutionary assumptions about the meaning and form of symbols), he retained a deep interest in history and the humanities throughout his life. He believed that anthropology should be objective, but he differed with Boas on its subject matter. Boas believed that anthropologists should focus on the intensive study of a single society. Kroeber was more interested in regional surveys of general traits (Jacknis 2002:525).

[2] Anthropologists today often bemoan the collapse of the four-field approach, the notion that they should be trained in physical, archaeological, linguistic, and cultural anthropology. We tend to look at the early American anthropologists as masters of all of these fields. However, tension among the fields dates from the early twentieth century, and even Boas and his students argued about whether all of these areas could be covered in a single field of study. Kroeber devoted his life to the study of cultural anthropology, archaeology, and linguistics but did little with physical anthropology.

[3] At the time this essay was published in *American Anthropologist* (1915) very little was known of human evolution and the biology of human variation. In this paragraph, Kroeber is making fun of the physical anthropology of his era. Much anthropology of this time was devoted to showing that people other than Europeans were biologically, intellectually, and socially inferior. Here he pokes fun at this work but his comments indicate that he considers biology's claim to physical anthropology to be an open issue.

[4] Like Boas, Kroeber understands anthropology as a type of cultural history. Cultures are created by their own histories, and therefore understanding them is a form of historical research.

Civilization means civilization itself, not its impulses. Relation is actual connection, not cause.[5]

> 2. *The material studied by history is not man, but his works.*

It is not men, but the results of their deeds, the manifestations of their activities, that are the subject of historical inquiry.[6]

> 3. *Civilization, though carried by men and existing through them, is an entity in itself, and of another order from life.*

History is not concerned with the agencies producing civilization, but with civilization as such. The causes are the business of the psychologist. The entity civilization has intrinsically nothing to do with individual men nor with the aggregates of men on whom it rests. It springs from the organic, but is independent of it. The mental processes of groups of men are, after all, only the collected processes of individuals reacting under certain special stimuli. Collective psychology is therefore ultimately resolvable into individual human psychology, just as this in turn is resolvable into organic psychology and physiology. But history deals with material which is essentially non-individual and integrally social. History is not concerned with the relations of civilization to men or organisms, but with the interrelations of civilization. The psychic organization of man in the abstract does not exist for it, save as something given directly and more or less completely to the student's consciousness. The uncivilized man does not exist; if he did, he would mean nothing to the historian. Even civilized man is none of history's business; its sphere is the civilization of which man is the necessary basis but which is inevitable once this basis exists.[7]

> 4. *A certain mental constitution of man must be assumed by the historian, but may not be used by him as a resolution of social phenomena.*

The historian can and should obtain for himself the needed interpretation of man's mind from familiarity with social facts and the direct application to them of his own psychic activities. This interpretation is likely to be of service in proportion as it emanates immediately from himself and not from the formulated laws of the biological psychologist. Whether an understanding

---

[5] Kroeber uses the term *social facts* in his first profession. In doing so, he is referencing Durkheim (see essay 5). Kroeber looked to both Durkheim and Spencer as critical nineteenth-century thinkers in anthropology and sociology. To some extent, this essay and Durkheim's are designed to serve similar ends. In both, the authors try to delineate anthropology or sociology as particular fields of study separate from other fields. However, there are several critical differences. First, Kroeber uses the term *social fact* without defining it. This makes its meaning much broader than that given to it by Durkheim. Second, Durkheim set out to model sociology on the natural sciences, but Kroeber was opposed to such modeling.

[6] In this profession Kroeber is emphasizing the Boasian focus on fieldwork and patterns of diffusion between areas. Further, although we do not remember Kroeber as a museum curator today, a major part of his early work at Berkeley was setting up the anthropology museum there, collecting material for exhibits, and curating those collections. The focus on material works in the second profession reflects Kroeber's background in museum work and emphasis on the diffusion of cultural traits in his research.

[7] In professions 3 and 4, Kroeber proclaims that civilization is totally separate from the individuals who compose it. Like Durkheim, he rejects the notion that culture or society can be reduced to the actions of human minds, working either separately or as a group. One of the key tenants of Kroeber's anthropology (and one that he will develop further in this essay) is that individuals count for little or nothing in culture. Following Spencer and Durkheim, Kroeber claims that culture is superorganic; that is, that it has an existence separate from the human beings who compose it, and follows a pattern of its own.

Kroeber also argues here that the focus of anthropological research should be on wide cultural patterns that could be demonstrated by studying the diffusion of cultural traits. Despite Boas' urgings for him to settle down and study one group, Kroeber was more interested in conducting comparative surveys of data over large geographic areas (Jacknis 2002:525–526). These interests are the background for his statements about "civilization," by which he means culture, as an entity in itself.

of civilization will or will not help the psychologist is for the latter to determine.[8]

> 5. *True instincts lie at the bottom and origin of social phenomena, but cannot be considered or dealt with by history.*

History begins where instincts commence to be expressed in social facts.

> 6. *The personal or individual has no historical value save as illustration.*

Ethnological genealogies are valuable material. So are the actions of conspicuous historical personages. But their dramatic, anecdotic, or biographic recital is biographic or fictional art, or possibly psychology, not history.[9]

> 7. *Geography, or physical environment, is material made use of by civilization, not a factor shaping or explaining civilization.*

Civilization reacts to civilization, not to geography. For the historian, geography does not act on civilization, but civilization incorporates geographical circumstances. Agriculture presupposes a climate able to sustain agriculture, and modifies itself according to climatic conditions. It is not caused by climate. The understanding of agricultural activity is to be sought in the other phenomena of civilization affecting it.[10]

---

[8] There are two very important aspects of this statement. First, note the primacy that Kroeber gives to social facts and culture. He notes that psychology, "man's mind," cannot explain culture, but rather culture, social facts, can be used to help explain human psychology. Second, note that Kroeber advises historians to examine their own minds. In so doing, he reflects his own experience and the dictates of Freudian psychoanalysis. This essay was written in 1915, in the years that Kroeber called his "Hegira," a word generally used to refer to the prophet Mohammad's years of exile from Mecca. It was a tragic era in Kroeber's life that began with the death of his first wife, Henriette Rothschild, in 1913. There were numerous calamities in the years that followed, including the death of Ishi, a Yana Indian who had lived and worked with Kroeber. Throughout it all, Kroeber had an ear infection that was misdiagnosed as "neurasthenia," a nineteenth- and early twentieth-century term for a neurotic mental disorder. This, combined with an apparent midlife crisis, led Kroeber to psychoanalysis in 1917. After undergoing analysis by a student of Freud, he returned to California and practiced for several years as a Freudian psychoanalyst, taking partial leave from his university position to do so.

[9] Here again, Kroeber stresses the importance of the social and cultural above the individual. Kroeber and many other American anthropologists arrayed themselves against the Great Man theory of history. Much of history was then (and still is) taught as biography. Historians and students tend to understand policies and practices as the result of the ideas and will of single individuals. Thus, books about the American presidents are extraordinarily popular and people debate whether or not World War II would have happened without Hitler. Kroeber and others such as Leslie White (1949) argued that such individuals made no difference at all; they were merely placeholders, representing trends and tendencies in their social and cultural systems.

Kroeber's radical deemphasis of the individual led him away from Boas and others such as Sapir and Radin, who believed that culture was the result of the interplay of individuals and their society. Kroeber's condemnation of the use of the individual to explain history raises another issue: Kroeber himself developed a close personal and research relationship with a single individual, Ishi, and relied primarily on information from Ishi in his work on the Yana. If culture was really superorganic and "ethnological genealogies" are not history, i.e., anthropology, then why did Kroeber go to such great lengths to cultivate and maintain his relationship with Ishi?

[10] In profession 7, Kroeber rejects any role of environment in shaping culture. In this he follows his mentor Boas. The idea that environment determined culture was popular in the late nineteenth and early twentieth centuries. Europeans and white Americans often explained cultural differences by reference to climate and geography. One typical example was the notion that northern Europeans were hardworking and hardy because they had to deal with harsh winters, whereas Africans, Mexicans, etc., were uncivilized because tropical climates made them lazy. The Boasians rejected formulations such as this. In the 1880s, Boas was interested in the relationship between environment, geography, and society, but this interest clearly waned after his experiences on Baffin Island. According to his student Gladys A. Reichard (1893–1955), Boas came to believe that the Eskimo "did things in spite of rather than because of the environment" (quoted in Herskovitz 1957:115). Most Boasians followed this line of reasoning and saw very little connection between culture and environment.

Kroeber's student Julian Steward (see essay 19), was an important exception. Steward formulated a theory in which the relationship between environment and culture was the cornerstone of anthropological study.

8. *The absolute equality and identity of all human races and strains as carriers of civilization must be assumed by the historian.*

The identity has not been proved nor has it been disproved. It remains to be established, or to be limited, by observations directed to this end, perhaps only by experiments. The historical and social influences affecting every race and every large group of persons are closely intertwined with the alleged biological and hereditary ones, and have never yet been sufficiently separated to allow demonstration of the actual efficiency of either. All opinions on this point are only convictions falsely fortified by subjectively interpreted evidence. The biologist dealing with man must assume at least some hereditary differences, and often does assume biological factors as the only ones existent. The historian, until such differences are established and exactly defined, must assume their non-existence. If he does not base his studies on this assumption, his work becomes a vitiated mixture of history and biology.[11]

9. *Heredity cannot be allowed to have acted any part in history.*

Individual hereditary differences undoubtedly exist, but are not historical material because they are individual. Hereditary differences between human groups may ultimately be established, but like geography must in that event be converted into material acted upon by the force of civilization, not treated as causes of civilization.

10. *Heredity by acquirement is equally a biological and historical monstrosity.*

This naive explanation may be eliminated on the findings of biology; but should biology ever determine that such heredity operates through a mechanism as yet undiscovered, this heredity must nevertheless be disregarded by history together with congenital heredity. In the present stage of understanding, heredity by acquirement is only too often the cherished inclination of those who confuse their biological thinking by the introduction of social aspects, and of those who confound history by deceiving themselves that they are turning it into biology.[12]

11. *Selection and other factors of organic evolution cannot be admitted as affecting civilization.*

It is actually unproved that the processes of organic evolution are materially influencing civilization or that they have influenced it. Civilization obviously introduces an important factor which is practically or entirely lacking in the existence of animals and plants, and which must at least largely neutralize the operation of any kind of selection. Prehistoric archaeology shows with certainty that civilization has changed profoundly without accompanying material alterations in the human organism. Even so far as biological evolution may ultimately be proved in greater or less degree for man, a correspondence between organic types and civilizational forms will have to be

---

[11] The complete rejection of biologically based racism was one of the most critical achievements of Boas and his students. Boas fought long and hard against the idea of race and the practice of racism. He attracted students sympathetic to his notions about race and imbued them with a passion for the idea that all human differences are the result of culture rather than biology. In this profession and the several following, Kroeber summarizes and reiterates this Boasian belief.

Kroeber's discussion of profession 8 closely resembles the argument that Boas made when attacking theories of unilineal evolution (essay 9). Like Boas, Kroeber says that the evidence is inadequate to conclude whether or not the human races and their cultures are equal or not, and until better data can be gathered, one must assume their equality.

[12] This profession was more controversial in 1915 than it sounds today. Kroeber is not typically remembered for his political or social activism, but this statement was a major stand on his part. In Kroeber's day, Lamarckian evolution (the inheritance of acquired characteristics, or "heredity by acquirement") was a common belief. Mendel's laws of genetics had been rediscovered only recently and were not very widely known. It was popularly believed that undesirable behaviors such as crime, prostitution, and alcoholism were hereditary and that certain classes and ethnic groups were predisposed to these behaviors. This belief in part fed the American eugenics movement of the first decades of the twentieth century during which there was a call for the involuntary sterilization of "undesirables." It is this sort of public policy that Kroeber is calling "monstrous."

definitely established before history can concern itself with these organic types or their changes.[13]

12. *The so-called savage is no transition between the animal and the scientifically educated man.*

All men are totally civilized. All animals are totally uncivilized because they are almost totally uncivilizable. The connecting condition which it is universally believed must have existed, is entirely unknown. If ever it becomes known, it can furnish to the historian only an introduction to history. There is no higher and lower in civilization for the historian. The ranging of the portions of civilization in any sequence, save the actual one of time, place, and connection, is normally misleading and always valueless. The estimation of the adult savage as similar to the modern European child is superficial and prevents

his proper appreciation either biologically or historically.[14]

13. *There are no social species or standard cultural types or stages.*

A social species in history rests on false analogy with organic species. A stage in civilization is merely a preconception made plausible by arbitrarily selected facts.[15]

14. *There is no ethnic mind, but only civilization.*

There are only individual minds. When these react on each other cumulatively, the process is merely physiological. The single ethnic or social existence is civilization, which biologically is resolvable purely into a product of physiological forces, and historically is the only and untranscendable entity.[16]

---

[13] Like those above it, this profession continues Kroeber's direct attack on scientific racism and the notion that there were superior or inferior cultures. Much of anthropology (particularly physical anthropology) between the Civil War and the 1920s was aimed at proving the hereditary and biological superiority of northern Europeans. Social Darwinists of Kroeber's day argued that the technological superiority of the industrialized nations was proof that they were evolutionarily superior. Kroeber, like Boas, rejects all notions of biological superiority or inferiority.

[14] This profession is a resounding statement of Boasian cultural relativism and an attack on the social evolutionary theories of the nineteenth and early twentieth centuries. Throughout this essay, Kroeber has used the term *civilization* as synonymous with culture. He does so to shock the reader and make a point. In Kroeber's day, readers would have been surprised by the usage because scholars equated civilization with either ancient state-level society or the fine arts. The notion that technologically simple societies were civilized would strike them as incongruous. Today, the usage is equally surprising but for a different reason. Now, anthropologists generally equate civilization with state-level societies and use the term *culture* to speak of all societies. However, by insisting that all human societies are civilizations and all humans are equally civilized, Kroeber proposes radical equality, not only of societies but, by implication, of individual human beings as well. This was a touchstone of Boasian anthropology.

Note too that in profession 12, Kroeber explicitly rejects the unilineal evolutionary theories popular in the

late nineteenth century and the "ontogeny recapitulates phylogeny" argument that was common in the fields of biology, psychology, and medicine in the nineteenth and early twentieth centuries. This is discussed in greater detail in the notes on pages 19 and 53.

The notion that an adult savage was equivalent to a European child was widely popularized by Freud's 1913 book, *Totem and Taboo*. In that work, Freud proposed a psychoanalytic theory for the origin of culture that depended on the notion that primitive people were similar to European children and neurotics. Given his deep involvement in psychoanalysis, it is curious that Kroeber so willingly attacked one of Freud's cherished ideas.

[15] In this profession, Kroeber provides a one-sentence summary of Boas' argument against evolutionism. Boas charged that evolutionist thinking was unscientific because evolutionists chose facts without regard to their historical and ethnographic context in order to fit their theories (see essay 9).

[16] In other words, culture is superorganic. It generates itself and cannot be reduced to the group thinking of the individuals who compose it. However, it is interesting that while many of Kroeber's statements closely track Durkheim's notions of social facts and *l'âme collective*, here he makes a decisive break. Durkheim proposed that the origin of culture was a process of "social condensation" created by a critical mass of individuals coming together. Here Kroeber says that when minds react cumulatively the result is purely physiological. He is unwilling to speculate on the origin of culture.

15. *There are no laws in history similar to the laws of physico-chemical science.*

All asserted civilizational laws are at most tendencies, which, however determinable, are not permanent quantitative expressions. Nor are such tendencies the substitute which history has for the laws of science. History need not deny them and may have to recognize them, but their formulation is not its end.[17]

16. *History deals with conditions sine qua non, not with causes.*

The relations between civilizational phenomena are relations of sequence, not of effect. The principles of mechanical causality, emanating from the underlying biological sciences, are applicable to individual and collective psychology. Applied to history, they convert it into psychology. An insistence that all treatment of civilizational data should be by the methods of mechanical causality is equivalent to a denial of the valid existence of history as a subject of study. The only antecedents of historical phenomena are historical phenomena.[18]

17. *The causality of history is teleological.*

Psychological causes are mechanical. For history, psychology is assumable, not demonstrable. To make the object of historical study the proving of the fundamental identity of the human mind by endless examples is as tedious as barren. If the process of civilization seems the worthwhile end of knowledge of civilization, it must be sought as a process distinct from that of mechanical causality, or the result will be a reintegration that is not history. Teleology of course does not suggest theology to those free from the influence of theology. The teleology of history involves the absolute conditioning of historical events by other historical events. This causality of history is as completely unknown and unused as chemical causality was a thousand and physical causality three thousand years ago.[19]

---

[17] In many of the earlier professions, Kroeber's ideas seem similar to Durkheim's: Kroeber mentions social facts and he talks about the existence of something that sounds very much like Durkheim's notion of *l'âme collective* (in 1917, two years after this paper, Kroeber published a famous essay called "The Superorganic" in which he described his notion of culture in greater detail). However, in profession 15 he breaks from Durkheim and from the British social anthropologists who followed Durkheim. For Durkheim, the point of describing social facts and *l'âme collective* was to search for the laws by which societies happen. Durkheim believed that a science of society similar to the natural sciences could be developed. Kroeber rejects these notions entirely. In professions 15 and 16, he claims that though laws might exist, anthropologists should not be interested in finding them. Like Boas, Kroeber believes that cultures are understandable only in the context of their own historical and environmental circumstances.

[18] Here Kroeber says that the cause-and-effect relationships seen in the biological sciences do not apply to cultural phenomena. It is interesting that Kroeber rejects the notion that anthropology can be scientific but supports the idea that psychology is scientific. On the one hand, in the nineteenth century, Wilhelm Wundt and others developed a psychology that was based on laboratory experiments. Clearly, using such a technique was not possible for anthropologists. On the other hand, the form of psychology to which Kroeber was personally drawn was Freudian psychoanalysis, one of the least scientific theories of psychology imaginable.

[19] In this profession, Kroeber uses the word *teleology* in an interesting fashion. Teleology is the study of ultimate causes and is often linked to some religious conception of the world; the search for ultimate causes usually implies a series of beliefs about human destiny. Thus, Herbert Spencer's theory that evolution was a universal force driving everything to a destiny of perfection was teleological. Echoing Boas, Kroeber says that the cause of history is history, or in other words, culture is *sui generis* (see page 124). In the last sentence of the profession, Kroeber declares himself to be at the dawn of a new era of study. History has been dominated by studies of great men and the acts of literate nation-states. Now that we understand that history is anthropology and that it is not the biography of the great or the property of technologically advanced nations, Kroeber says, we can begin to document and understand it. For Kroeber, the goal of anthropology was to be knowledge itself—understanding for understanding's sake. In 1959, only a year before his death, Kroeber wrote: "The pursuit of anthropology must often have seemed strange and useless to many people, but no one has ever called it an arid or a toneless or a dismal science" (1959:404).

18. *In fine, the determinations and methods of biological, psychological, or natural science do not exist for history, just as the results and the manner of operation of history are disregarded by consistent biological practice.*

Most biologists have implicitly followed their aspect of this doctrine, but their consequent success has tempted many historians, especially sociologists, anthropologists, and theorists, to imitate them instead of pursuing their proper complementary method.[20]

---

[20] Kroeber and most other Boasians maintained a strong stance against a scientific anthropology throughout their lives. In the same essay quoted above, Kroeber writes:

> Now, maturity has stolen upon us. The times and utilitarianism have caught up with us, and we find ourselves classified and assigned to the social sciences. . . . As our daily bread, we invent hypotheses in order to test them, as we are told is the constant practice of the high tribe of physicists. If at times some of you, like myself, feel somewhat ill at ease in the house of social science, do not wonder; we are changelings therein; our true paternity lies elsewhere. (1959:404)

---

11. *Right and Wrong*

PAUL RADIN (1883–1959)

ON NO SUBJECT connected with primitive people does so much confusion exist in the mind of the general public and have so many ill-considered statements been made as on the nature of their behavior to one another.[1] The prevalent view today among laymen is that they are at all times the plaything of their passions, and that self-control and poise are utterly alien to their character, if not, indeed, quite beyond their reach. We have seen in fact that even so open-minded and sympathetic a scholar as Jung apparently still accepts this view (c.f. 39). That an example like the one used by Jung should in all good faith be given as representative of the normal or even the abnormal reaction of a

primitive man to a given emotional situation, shows the depth of ignorance that still exists on this subject. Now quite apart from the manifest absurdity involved in the belief that any parent in a primitive group would wreak his rage at his lack of success in hunting, in this murderous fashion upon the first object that came within his reach, even if it be his innocent and beloved child, there are a hundred and one reasons that would have deterred him, even had he been the uncontrolled animal the illustration assumes him to have been. However, let that pass. The illustration has its uses, for it permits the contrast between the generally accepted belief and the true nature of the facts to emerge all the

---

From *Primitive Man as Philosopher* (1927)

---

[1] One of Franz Boas' most important principles was cultural relativism, and among his students, Radin was one of its most vociferous supporters. For Radin, the intrinsic sophistication, wisdom, and value of culture was evident from the details of the lives of his informants. Radin's anthropology focused on extensive fieldwork among the Winnebago Indians, and his association with them lasted fifty years. He spoke excellent Winnebago and was widely considered one of the best fieldworkers among Boas' students.

more definitely. Actually the situation is quite different.[2]

Briefly stated, the underlying idea of conduct among most primitive tribes is self-discipline, self-control and a resolute endeavor to observe a proper measure of proportion in all things. I am well aware that in some tribes this is more definitely expressed than in others and that not infrequently certain excrescences[3] in their ceremonial life seem to contradict this assertion. Yet I think most field ethnologists would agree with me. Since in the face of so formidable a body of opinion apparently to the contrary, incontrovertible evidence will be demanded of me to substantiate so broad and explicit a statement, I shall confine myself in my presentation of the facts to a tribe which I know personally and where the material which I use can be definitely controlled. The data upon which I rely come from the Winnebago Indians of Wisconsin and Nebraska and are to be found in two monographs published by me. Only statements made by the Winnebago themselves in accounts either actually written by themselves or contained in verbatim descriptions of the rituals obtained in the original Winnebago are used in order to obviate all inaccuracy.

I can think of no better method of introducing the subject than by quoting appropriate passages from the Winnebago texts secured[4] and then discussing them in the light of the knowledge they throw upon the system of ethics enunciated and, more specifically, upon the type of self-control implied. For facility of reference I shall number these passages:[a]

1. It is always good to be good.
2. What does life consist of but love?
3. Of what value is it to kill?
4. You ought to be of some help to your fellow men.
5. Do not abuse your wife; women are sacred.
6. If you cast off your dress for many people, they will be benefitted by your deed.
7. For the good you do every one will love you.
8. Never do any wrong to children.
9. It is not good to gamble.
10. If you see a helpless old man, help him if you have anything at all.
11. If you have a home of your own, see to it that whoever enters it obtains something to eat. Such food will be a source of death to you if withheld.
12. When you are recounting your war deeds on behalf of the departed soul, do not try to add to your honor by claiming more for yourself than you have actually accomplished. If you tell a falsehood then and exaggerate your achievements you

---

[2] Carl Gustave Jung (1875–1961) was a Swiss psychologist and early follower of Freud who broke with him over the role of sexuality in the development of neuroses. For anthropologists, among Jung's most important ideas are his concepts of the collective unconscious and archetypes. The reference to Jung in this paragraph concerns an example of what Jung called "primitive mentality" that Radin took from Jung's *Psychological Types* (1971 [1923]). Jung had written an account of a Bushman who, enraged at having caught nothing while fishing, strangled his young son who ran out to greet him and then mourned for the boy with "the same abandon and lack of comprehension as had before made him strangle him" (Radin 1957[1927]:39).

Radin wished to show that "primitive" thinking was similar to that of modern, "civilized" people—that it is sophisticated, profound, and self-aware. This was central to his life's work. In claiming that primitive peoples can be philosophers, as he does in the title of the book from which this extract is taken, he is attacking cultural evolutionism, particularly the idea that ontogeny recapitulates phylogeny. This idea, perhaps most forcefully stated by Freud, suggests that primitive people are childlike and hence lack self-discipline and self-control.

[3] *Excrescences:* normal or abnormal growths or appendages such as horns or bunions. Radin uses the term to refer to Native American practices such as ecstatic trances.

[4] Radin's method was to try to stay very close to "pure" ethnographic material. In many of his works, translated folklore or ethnographic observations are presented with little or no commentary. Some good examples are "Description of a Winnebago Funeral" (1911) and "Ojibwa Ethnological Chit Chat" (1924).

will die beforehand. The telling of truth is sacred. Tell less than you did. The old men say it is wiser.

13. Be on friendly terms with every one and then every one will love you.

14. Marry only one person at a time.

15. Do not be haughty with your husband. Kindness will be returned to you and he will treat you in the same way in which you treat him.

16. Do not imagine that you are taking your children's part if you just speak about loving them. Let them see it for themselves.

17. Do not show your love for other people so that people notice it. Love them but let your love be different from that for your own.

18. As you travel along life's road, never harm any one or cause any one to feel sad. On the contrary, if at any time you can make a person feel happy, do so. If at any time you meet a woman away from your village and you are both alone and no one can see you, do not frighten her or harm her.

19. If you meet any one on the road, even if it is only a child, speak a cheering word before you pass on.

20. If your husband's people ever ask their own children for something when you are present, assume that they had asked it of you. If there is anything to be done, do not wait till you are asked to do it but do it immediately.

21. Never think a home is yours until you have made one for yourself.

22. If you have put people in charge of your household, do not nevertheless act as though the home were still yours.

23. When visiting your husband's people, do not act as if you were far above them.

Obviously we are here in the presence of a fairly well elaborated system of conduct. To those who consistently deny to primitive man any true capacity for abstract thinking or objective formulation of an ethical code—and their number is very large both among scholars and laymen—the injunctions given above would probably be interpreted as having a definitely concrete significance. That is, they are not to be regarded as attempts at generalization in any true sense of the word but merely as inherently wise saws and precepts of a practical and personal application. Now there is sufficient justification for such a view to warrant our discussing it before we proceed any further.[5]

A number of the precepts given avowedly allow a concrete practical and personal application. In 5, for example, we are told, "If you abuse your wife you will die in a short time. Our grandmother Earth is a woman and in abusing your wife you will be abusing her. Since it is she who takes care of us, by your actions you will be practically killing yourself." To precept 10 is added the following: "If you happen to possess a home, take him (the old man) there and feed him for he may suddenly make uncomplimentary remarks about you. You will be strengthened thereby."

We thus do indeed seem to obtain the impression that a Winnebago in being good to a helpless old man is guided by motives secondary to those implied in the precept as quoted. And what follows would seem to strip our apparently generous precept of whatever further altruistic value still attaches to it, for there it is stated that perhaps the old man is carrying under his arm a box of medicines that he cherishes very much and which he will offer to you. Similarly in precept 11 we find, "If you are stingy about giving food someone may kill you." Indeed, I think we shall have to admit that in the majority of cases none of the Winnebago virtues or actions are extolled for their own sake, and that in every instance they have reference to and derive their validity from whatever relation they possess to the

---

[5] Childish, and hence primitive, thinking was supposed to be tied to specific, immediate stimulus; primitives were supposed to be incapable of abstraction. Therefore, Radin wants to show that the points he has outlined are general and abstract.

preponderatingly practical needs of human intercourse. "Don't be a fool," precept 5 seems to imply "and don't treat your wife badly, because if you do, you'll run the risk of having the woman's protecting deity, the Earth, punish you." I should not even be surprised if, in concrete instances, the moral was further emphasized by giving examples of how men were punished who had abused their wives. We are fairly obviously told to be guided by the practical side of the question, i.e., take no risks and get the most out of every good action you perform.

Now all this sounds extremely cynical and practical. But we must be fair and not too hasty in drawing our inferences. First of all it should be asked if the Winnebago in actual practice give the impression of always being guided by egotistical and ulterior motives, and second it should be borne in mind that if we can really prove that the ideal of human conduct is on a high plane, we need not concern ourselves needlessly with the apparent nature of the motives prompting individual acts. As a matter of fact primitive people are much less guided by consciously selfish and ulterior motives than we are, not because of any innate superiority over ourselves in this regard but because of the conditions under which they live.[6] But, quite apart from this consideration, ought we in fact to lay undue stress on illustrations following what is clearly a general principle? Are we not after all, in our illustrations, merely dealing with a statement of what happens when some general principle of the ethical code is transgressed, and not primarily with an explanation of the principle? I do not feel, therefore, that even those instances which seem superficially to corroborate the prevalent assumption of primitive man's inability to formulate an abstract ethical creed, actually bear out, when more carefully examined, the contention of its advocates.

Now the question of the capacity of the Winnebago to formulate an ethical code in a fairly abstract fashion is of fundamental importance for the thesis of this chapter and that is why I am laying so much stress on it; for if it were not true our precepts would have to be regarded in the nature of mere proverbs and practical folk wisdom, as nothing higher indeed than crystallized maxims of conduct.

There are, however, in our list certain precepts where the abstract formulation is undeniable, where, in fact, reference to the particular context in which the precepts occur not only shows no secondary concrete significance, but, on the contrary, a reinforcement of their abstract and general connotation. In precept 1 the full statement is this: "If you hear of a person traveling through your country and you want to see him, prepare your table and send for him. In this manner you will do good and it is always good to do good, it is said." Similarly in precept 2. Here it is in the course of a speech delivered at a ceremony that the phrase occurs: "what does life consist of but love?" "All the members of the clan have given me counsel," the speaker says, "and all the women and children have pleaded in my behalf with the spirits. What love that was! And of what does life consist but of love?"

Here we have no concrete practical implications. The statements are meant to be taken as general propositions. They are very remarkable enunciations and we may legitimately draw from their existence the inference that even in so-called "primitive" tribes, certain individuals have apparently felt within themselves the same moral truths that are regarded as the glory of our great moralists, and that they have formulated these truths in general terms.

So much for the actual formulation. What, however, does this Winnebago creed tell us about the idea of conduct itself? Does it teach us that love and forbearance are to be practiced for their own sake and is the love of which they speak identical with or even comparable to our idea of love?

When a Western European speaks of love, forbearance, remorse, sorrow, etc., he generally

---

[6] Note Radin's point that the conditions under which people live, rather than any innate fundamental differences, determine their understanding of the world. This is basic to Boasian cultural relativism. Boas used his experience on Baffin Island to support his deeply held belief in human equality. Radin used his long experience with the Winnebago to similar ends.

understands by these terms some quality belonging to an individual and for the possession of which he is to be honored and praised.[7] We do not ask whether the love or the virtue in question is of an intelligent nature, whether it does harm or good, or whether we have any right to it. Who among us would speak of an individual not being entitled to his remorse or sorrow? We assume that the mere expression of remorse and sorrow is somehow ethically praiseworthy. If we see a man of manifestly weak character but of a loving disposition, even if his actions are inconsistent with a true love for his fellow men, insist that he loves them, while we may condemn him, we are inclined to overlook much in recognition of his enunciation of the principle that love of mankind is the highest ideal of life. In much the same way do we look upon any manifestation of sincere remorse or sorrow. We simply regard love, remorse, sorrow, etc., as inalienable rights of man, quite independent of any right, as it were, he may possess to express them. In other words, the Western European ethics is frankly egocentric and concerned primarily with self-expression. The object toward which love, remorse, repentance, sorrow, is directed is secondary. Christian theology has elevated them all to the rank of virtues as such, and enjoins their observance upon us because they are manifestations of God's, if not of man's way.

Among primitive people this is emphatically not true. Ethics there is based upon behavior. No mere enunciation of an ideal of love, no matter how often and sincerely repeated, would gain an individual either admiration, sympathy, or respect. Every ethical precept must be submitted to the touchstone of conduct. The Winnebago moralist would insist that we have no right to preach an ideal of love or to claim that we love, unless we have lived up to its practical implications. That is the fundamental basis of all primitive education and is unusually well expressed among the Winnebago. "When you are bringing up children," runs the injunction to a young mother, "do not imagine that you are taking their part if you merely speak of loving them. Let them see it for themselves; let them know what love is by seeing you give away things to the poor. Then they will see your good deeds and then they will know whether you have been telling the truth or not." An exactly similar attitude is taken toward remorse. "If you have always loved a person, then when he dies you will have the right to feel sorrow." No amount of money spent upon the funeral of a person with whom you had been quarreling will make amends.

But it is not merely love, remorse, etc., to which you have no right as such. You have equally no right to the glory attendant upon joining a war party unless it is done in the right spirit. In the document from which most of our statements have been taken—the autobiography of a Winnebago Indian[8]—a man is represented as being about to embark on a war party because his wife has run away from him. "Such a man," the author insists, "is simply throwing away his life. If you want to go on the warpath, do not go because your wife has been taken away from you but because you feel courageous enough to go."

In consonance with such an attitude is the differentiation in the degree of love insisted upon. Love everybody, it is demanded, but do not love them all equally. Above all do not love your neighbor as you love those of your own blood. "Only if you are wicked," the injunction says, "will you love other people's children more than your own." The injunction certainly says that we must love everybody but this must be humanly understood, and

---

[7] In this paragraph and below, Radin turns the tables on Jung's argument. He suggests (at least implicitly) that as regards questions of morality, so-called primitive thinking is, in fact, more sophisticated than our own. There is a subtext here. Radin, from a particularly rationalistic Jewish background and son of a rabbi, critiques Christian theology.

[8] The document referred to here is *Crashing Thunder: The Autobiography of an American Indian.* Originally published in 1926, this autobiography of Radin's key informant has been frequently reprinted and remains popular both among anthropologists and the general public. Radin's interest in autobiography was guided by his belief that the individual was of paramount importance and that an individual in a primitive society had a total understanding of his or her culture. Thus, a thorough understanding of an individual gave the anthropologist complete understanding of the culture to which that person belonged.

humanly understood you cannot, of course, love everyone alike. The Winnebago would contend that such a statement would be untrue and that any attempt to put it into practice must manifestly lead to insincerity. It would, moreover, be definitely unjust in that it might make for the neglect of those whom primarily you ought to love most. Here the difference between the attitude of primitive man and that of Western Europe is most clearly brought out. According to primitive standards you deserve neither credit nor discredit, neither praise nor condemnation, for giving expression to a normal human emotion. It is the manner in which, in your relations to the other members of the tribe, you *distribute* this emotion and the degree to which it is felt by others to be sincere, that calls forth respect and admiration.[9] It is wicked to love other people's children as much as your own; it is wicked to love your wife to the detriment of your family and yourself; it is wicked to love your enemy while he is your enemy. An excellent illustration of this conviction—that it is fundamentally wicked and unintelligent to make the expression of even a socially commendable emotion like love an end in itself—is contained in the following passage taken from the autobiography quoted above:

> When you get married do not make an idol of the woman you marry; do not worship her. If you worship a woman she will insist upon greater and greater worship as time goes on. It may be that when you get married you will listen to the voice of your wife and you will refuse to go on the warpath. Why should you thus run the risk of being ridiculed? After a while you will not be allowed to go to a feast. In time even your sisters will not think anything of you. (You will become jealous) and after your jealousy has developed to its highest pitch your wife will run away. You have let her know by your actions that you worship a woman and one alone. As a result she will run away from you. If you think that a woman

(your wife) is the only person you ought to love, you have humbled yourself. You have made the woman suffer and have made her feel unhappy. You will be known as a bad man and no one will want to marry you again. (Perhaps afterwards) when people go on the warpath you will join them because you feel unhappy at your wife's desertion. You will then, however, simply be throwing away your life.

A complete insight is afforded by this example into every phase of Winnebago ethics. You are to love your wife, for instance, but it is to be kept within personally and socially justifiable limits. If not, the whole adjustment of an individual to his environment is disturbed and injustice is eventually done to every one concerned—to his family, to his wife, and to himself. Marked exaggeration and disproportion would, from a practical point of view, be unthinkable in a primitive community. The result, in the hypothetical case we discussed above, is clear; loss of life and suicide, and possibly even the dragging of innocent people into your calamity—those, for instance, who are going on a warpath properly prepared spiritually.

The psychology expressed here is unimpeachable. To have analyzed the situation so completely and so profoundly and to have made this analysis the basis of social behavior is not a slight achievement, and this achievement is to be evaluated all the more highly because the Winnebago was predominantly a warrior culture. The objectivity displayed is altogether unusual, the husband's, the wife's, the tribal viewpoints, all are presented fairly and clearly.[10]

NOTE

[a]All these passages, with the exception of 3, 18, 19, and 20, come from *Crashing Thunder: The Autobiography of an American Indian*, edited by Paul Radin; 3 comes from the myth given on page 79 of *Primitive Man as Philosopher*, and the others from the 37th *Report of the Bureau of American Ethnology.*

---

[9] It is interesting that Radin stressed the logical, rational element of Winnebago thinking. These are elements that Radin's contemporaries saw in his personality.

[10] Radin was not openly political. However, he was an eloquent spokesman for native and minority people and frequently published articles in the popular press. In this, he carried on Boas' commitment to moral engagement in the social sciences.

12. *The Relation of Habitual Thought and Behavior to Language*

BENJAMIN L. WHORF (1897–1941)

> *Human beings do not live in the objective world alone, nor alone in the world of social activity as ordinarily understood, but are very much at the mercy of the particular language which has become the medium of expression for their society. It is quite an illusion to imagine that one adjusts to reality essentially without the use of language and that language is merely an incidental means of solving specific problems of communication or reflection. The fact of the matter is that the "real world" is to a large extent unconsciously built up on the language habits of the group. . . . We see and hear and otherwise experience very largely as we do because the language habits of our community predispose certain choices of interpretation.*
>
> —*Edward Sapir*[1]

THERE WILL PROBABLY be general assent to the proposition that an accepted pattern of using words is often prior to certain lines of thinking and forms of behavior, but he who assents often sees in such a statement nothing more than a platitudinous recognition of the hypnotic power of philosophical and learned terminology on the one hand or of catchwords, slogans, and rallying cries on the other. To see only thus far is to miss the point of one of the important interconnections which Sapir saw between language, culture, and psychology, and succinctly expressed in the introductory quotation. It is not so much in these special uses of language as in its constant ways of arranging data and its most ordinary everyday analysis of phenomena that we need to recognize the influence it has on other activities, cultural and personal.[2]

(1939)

THE NAME OF THE SITUATION AS AFFECTING BEHAVIOR

I came in touch with an aspect of this problem before I had studied under Dr. Sapir, and in a field usually considered remote from linguistics. It was in the course of my professional work for a fire insurance company, in which I undertook the task of analyzing many hundreds of reports of circumstances surrounding the start of fires, and in some cases, of explosions. My analysis was directed toward purely physical conditions, such as defective wiring, presence or lack of air spaces between metal flues and woodwork, etc., and the results were presented in these terms. Indeed it was undertaken with no thought that any other significances would or could be revealed. But in due course it became evident that not only a

---

[1] Whorf opens this essay with a quote from his friend and mentor, Edward Sapir, that is a strong statement of linguistic relativity and determinism, the principles underlying the Sapir-Whorf hypothesis. This essay, written in 1939, was first published in Language, Culture, and Personality (Spier, Hallowell, and Newman, eds.), a 1941 memorial volume dedicated to Sapir, who died in 1939. The fundamental point of the essay is to demonstrate some ways in which grammatical categories in language unconsciously influence the ways in which people interpret the world around them and thus direct their behavior

(linguistic determinism). Whorf argues that speakers of different languages think and act differently because their languages create different conceptual worlds (linguistic relativity).

[2] Whorf begins by noting that there "will probably be general assent" to the notion that language precedes thought. This is, in fact, a very controversial proposition (see Pinker 1994). To some degree, by claiming "general assent," Whorf assumes what he is trying to prove, that language asserts a controlling influence on thought and action.

physical situation *qua* physics, but the meaning of that situation to people, was sometimes a factor, through the behavior of the people, in the start of the fire. And this factor of meaning was clearest when it was a *linguistic meaning*, residing in the name or the linguistic description commonly applied to the situation. Thus, around a storage of what are called "gasoline drums," behavior will tend to a certain type, that is, great care will be exercised; while around a storage of what are called "empty gasoline drums," it will tend to be different-careless, with little repression of smoking or of tossing cigarette stubs about. Yet the "empty" drums are perhaps the more dangerous, since they contain explosive vapor. Physically the situation is hazardous, but the linguistic analysis according to regular analogy must employ the word "empty," which inevitably suggests lack of hazard. The word "empty" is used in two linguistic patterns: (1) as a virtual synonym for "null and void, negative, inert," (2) applied in analysis of physical situations without regard to, e.g., vapor, liquid vestiges, or stray rubbish, in the container. The situation is named in one pattern (2) and the name is then "acted out" or "lived up to" in another (1), this being a general formula for the linguistic conditioning of behavior into hazardous forms.[3]

In a wood distillation plant the metal stills were insulated with a composition prepared from limestone and called at the plant "spun limestone." No attempt was made to protect this covering from excessive heat or the contact of flame. After a period of use, the fire below one of the stills spread to the "limestone," which to everyone's great surprise burned vigorously. Exposure to acetic acid fumes from the stills had converted part of the limestone (calcium carbonate) to calcium acetate. This when heated in a fire decomposes, forming inflammable acetone. Behavior that tolerated fire close to the covering was induced by use of the name "limestone," which because it ends in "-stone" implies noncombustibility.

A huge iron kettle of boiling varnish was observed to be overheated, nearing the temperature at which it would ignite. The operator moved it off the fire and ran it on its wheels to a distance, but did not cover it. In a minute or so the varnish ignited. Here the linguistic influence is more complex; it is due to the metaphorical objectifying (of which more later) of "cause" as contact or the spatial juxtaposition of "things"—to analyzing the situation as "on" versus "off" the fire. In reality, the stage when the external fire was the main factor had passed; the overheating was now an internal process of convection in the varnish from the intensely heated kettle, and still continued when "off" the fire.

An electric glow heater on the wall was little used, and for one workman had the meaning of a convenient coathanger. At night a watchman entered and snapped a switch, which action he verbalized as "turning on the light." No light appeared, and this result he verbalized as "light is burned

---

[3] Whorf is an unusual figure in the history of anthropology in that he is a widely known theorist who never held a regular academic position. Although he was an honorary research fellow at Yale in the mid-1930s, He was educated as a chemical engineer and he spent his career working for the Hartford Fire Insurance Company. Whorf began his studies with Sapir in 1931 during the Great Depression, at a time when academic jobs were difficult to find and did not pay well. Apparently Whorf considered himself lucky to have had a lucrative job that allowed him time to pursue his intellectual interests. Whorf became aware of the effect of language on thought, as he says at the start of this section, while investigating the causes of fires. In this section Whorf provides a series of examples from his work as an insurance inspector. He claims that in these cases, fires started because the language people used did not adequately describe physical reality. He proposes that the "empty" gasoline drums were not really empty and the "spun limestone" was not stone. The implication is that the language we use for things can affect our actions because it influences the way we think about things. However, Whorf's examples are somewhat troubling. We really don't know how much of the workers' behavior was actually driven by the data and how much of it was Whorf's interpretation. For example, was the "spun limestone" allowed to catch fire because workers thought of it as stone, or did they and the owners who bought the metal stills simply assume that the manufacturer provided safe equipment? Did the workers know the name of the insulation at all? Since Whorf does not provide us with his interview data, we don't know the answer to these questions.

out." He could not see the glow of the heater because of the old coat hung on it. Soon the heater ignited the coat, which set fire to the building.

A tannery discharged waste water containing animal matter into an outdoor settling basin partly roofed with wood and partly open. This situation is one that ordinarily would be verbalized as "pool of water." A workman had occasion to light a blowtorch near by, and threw his match into the water. But the decomposing waste matter was evolving gas under the wood cover, so that the setup was the reverse of "watery." An instant flare of flame ignited the woodwork, and the fire quickly spread into the adjoining building.

A drying room for hides was arranged with a blower at one end to make a current of air along the room and thence outdoors through a vent at the other end. Fire started at a hot bearing on the blower, which blew the flames directly into the hides and fanned them along the room, destroying the entire stock. This hazardous setup followed naturally from the term "blower" with its linguistic equivalence to "that which blows," implying that its function necessarily is to "blow." Also its function is verbalized as "blowing air for drying," overlooking that it can blow other things, e.g., flames and sparks. In reality, a blower simply makes a current of air and can exhaust as well as blow. It should have been installed at the vent end to *draw* the air over the hides, then through the hazard (its own casing and bearings), and thence outdoors. Beside a coal-fired melting pot for lead reclaiming was dumped a pile of "scrap lead"—a misleading verbalization, for it consisted of the lead sheets of old radio condensers, which still had paraffin paper between them. Soon the paraffin blazed up and fired the roof, half of which was burned off.

Such examples, which could be greatly multiplied, will suffice to show how the cue to a certain line of behavior is often given by the analogies of the linguistic formula in which the situation is spoken of, and by which to some degree it is analyzed, classified, and allotted its place in that world which is "to a large extent unconsciously built up on the language habits of the group." And we always assume that the linguistic analysis made by our group reflects reality better than it does.

GRAMMATICAL PATTERNS AS INTERPRETATIONS OF EXPERIENCE

The linguistic material in the above examples is limited to single words, phrases, and patterns of limited range. One cannot study the behavioral compulsiveness of such material without suspecting a much more far-reaching compulsion from large-scale patterning of grammatical categories, such as plurality, gender and similar classifications (animate, inanimate, etc.), tenses, voices, and other verb forms, classifications of the type of "parts of speech," and the matter of whether a given experience is denoted by a unit morpheme, an inflected word, or a syntactical combination. A category such as number (singular vs. plural) is an attempted interpretation of a whole large order of experience, virtually of the world or of nature; it attempts to say how experience is to be segmented, what experience is to be called "one" and what "several." But the difficulty of appraising such a far-reaching influence is great because of its background character, because of the difficulty of standing aside from our own language, which is a habit and a cultural *non est disputandum*, and scrutinizing it objectively.[4] And if we take a very dissimilar language, this language becomes a part of nature, and we even do to it what we have already done to nature. We tend to think in our own language in order to examine the exotic language. Or we find the task of unraveling the purely morphological intricacies so gigantic that it seems to absorb all else. Yet the

---

[4] *Non est disputandum* is Latin for indisputable. Whorf is suggesting that it is very difficult to understand the effects of language on culture because we perceive all cultures through our own language, which is filled with fundamental assumptions about the nature of the world. In other words, it is difficult to study the linguistic categories of another language because we must ultimately perceive these through the linguistic categories of our own language. Whorf suggests that the way around this problem is to examine an exotic language, since becoming familiar with such a language can give us a new point of view from which to examine our own.

problem, though difficult, is feasible; and the best approach is through an exotic language, for in its study we are at long last pushed willy-nilly out of our ruts. Then we find that the exotic language is a mirror held up to our own.

In my study of the Hopi language, what I now see as an opportunity to work on this problem was first thrust upon me before I was clearly aware of the problem. The seemingly endless task of describing the morphology did finally end. Yet it was evident, especially in the light of Sapir's lectures on Navaho, that the description of the *language* was far from complete. I knew for example the morphological formation of plurals, but not how to use plurals. It was evident that the category of plural in Hopi was not the same thing as in English, French, or German. Certain things that were plural in these languages were singular in Hopi. The phase of investigation which now began consumed nearly two more years. The work began to assume the character of a comparison between Hopi and western European languages. It also became evident that even the grammar of Hopi bore a relation to Hopi culture, and the grammar of European tongues to our own "Western" or "European" culture. And it appeared that the interrelation brought in those large subsummations of experience by language, such as our own terms "time," "space," "substance," and "matter." Since, with respect to the traits compared, there is little difference between English, French, German, or other European languages with the *possible* (but doubtful) exception of Balto-Slavic and non-Indo-European, I have lumped these languages into one group called SAE, or "Standard Average European."[5]

That portion of the whole investigation here to be reported may be summed up in two questions: (1) Are our own concepts of "time," "space," and "matter" given in substantially the same form by experience to all men, or are they in part conditioned by the structure of particular languages? (2) Are there traceable affinities between (a) cultural and behavioral norms and (b) large-scale linguistic patterns? (I should be the last to pretend that there is anything so definite as "a correlation" between culture and language, and especially between ethnological rubrics such as "agricultural, hunting," etc., and linguistic ones like "inflected," "synthetic," or "isolating."[a] When I began the study, the problem was by no means so clearly formulated, and I had little notion that the answers would turn out as they did.

PLURALITY AND NUMERATION IN SAE AND HOPI

In our language, that is SAE, plurality and cardinal numbers are applied in two ways: to real plurals and imaginary plurals. Or more exactly if less tersely: perceptible spatial aggregates and metaphorical aggregates. We say "ten men" and also "ten days." Ten men either are or could be objectively perceived as ten, ten in one group perception[b]—ten men on a street corner, for instance. But "ten days" cannot be objectively experienced. We experience only one day, today; the other nine (or even all ten) are something conjured up from memory or imagination. If "ten days" be regarded as a group it must be as an "imaginary," mentally constructed group. Whence comes this mental pattern? Just as in the case of the fire-causing errors, from the fact that our language confuses the two different situations, has but one pattern for both. When we speak of "ten steps forward, ten strokes on a bell," or any similarly described cyclic sequence, "times" of any sort, we are doing the same thing as with "days." *Cyclicity* brings the response of

---

[5] European scholars have been speculating about the nature of language and cognition and the differences between languages since the late seventeenth century. Echoing the Boasian rejection of unilineal evolutionary thinking and the related ranking of races that was common at the time, Sapir and Whorf rejected the ranking of cultures or languages. Here Whorf begins to use his concept of linguistic relativity, the notion that different languages reflect different cultural conceptions of reality. He aims to demonstrate here that European concepts of time, space, and matter are not universal, but take different conceptual forms in different cultures and that these differences are the result of differences in language.

imaginary plurals. But a likeness of cyclicity to aggregates is not unmistakably given by experience prior to language, or it would be found in all languages, and it is not.[6]

Our *awareness* of time and cyclicity does contain something immediate and subjective—the basic sense of "becoming later and later." But, in the habitual thought of us SAE people, this is covered under something quite different, which though mental should not be called subjective. I call it *objectified*, or imaginary, because it is patterned on the *outer* world. It is this that reflects our linguistic usage. Our tongue makes no distinction between numbers counted on discrete entities and numbers that are simply "counting itself." Habitual thought then assumes that in the latter the numbers are just as much counted on "something" as in the former. This is objectification. Concepts of time lose contact with the subjective experience of "becoming later" and are objectified as counted *quantities,* especially as lengths, made up of units as a length can be visibly marked off into inches. A "length of time" is envisioned as a row of similar units, like a row of bottles.[7]

In Hopi there is a different linguistic situation. Plurals and cardinals are used only for entities that form or can form an objective group. There are no imaginary plurals, but instead ordinals used with singulars. Such an expression as "ten days" is not used. The equivalent statement is an operational one that reaches one day by a suitable count. "They stayed ten days" becomes "they stayed until the eleventh day" or "they left after the tenth day." "Ten days is greater than nine days" becomes "the tenth day is later than the ninth." Our "length of time" is not regarded as a length but as a relation between two events in lateness. Instead of our linguistically promoted objectification of that datum of consciousness we call "time," the Hopi language has not laid down any pattern that would cloak the subjective "becoming later" that is the essence of time.[8]

NOUNS OF PHYSICAL QUANTITY IN SAE AND HOPI

We have two kinds of nouns denoting physical things: individual nouns, and mass nouns, e.g., water, milk, wood, granite, sand, flour, meat. Individual nouns denote bodies with definite outlines: a tree, a stick, a man, a hill. Mass nouns denote homogeneous continua without implied boundaries. The distinction is marked by linguistic form; e.g., mass nouns lack plurals,[c] in English drop articles, and in French take the partitive article *du, de la, des.* The distinction is more widespread in language than in the observable appearance of things. Rather few natural occurrences present themselves as unbounded extents; air of course, and often water, rain, snow, sand, rock, dirt, grass. We do not encounter butter, meat, cloth, iron, glass, or most "materials" in such kind of manifestation, but in bodies small or large with definite outlines. The distinction is somewhat forced upon our description of events by an unavoidable pattern in language. It is so

---

[6] In this section Whorf argues that SAE speakers use the same grammatical construction for physical things that we can experience at a single time such as "ten men" and things that we can only experience as a sequence such as ten days. He refers to the first of these as "real" plurals and the second as "imaginary" plurals.

[7] Whorf claims that because SAE speakers treat the abstract concept of numbers, particularly numbers of days, as if they were physical objects, SAE speakers have constructed a linear concept of time as a line of units that stretches out before us into the future and behind us in the past. He makes this point because he is preparing readers for a discussion of the cyclical nature of time in Hopi thought.

[8] In other words while speakers of SAE think of time as an imaginary plural "ten days" speakers of Hopi think of it as a series of concrete events, day following day, getting later. This makes sense to McGee, because a similar situation exists in Lacandon Maya. When speaking in Maya, the Lacandon talk of time in terms of phases of the moon. For example, if McGee is staying in a community for two weeks, he describes this as "half a moon." Two weeks is an imaginary plural, fourteen days lined up in front of us that we will experience one day at a time. But the phases of the moon are something that can be concretely experienced. One can see when the moon is halfway through its cycle.

inconvenient in a great many cases that we need some way of individualizing the mass noun by further linguistic devices. This is partly done by names of body-types: stick of wood, piece of cloth, pane of glass, cake of soap; also, and even more, by introducing names of containers though their contents be the real issue: glass of water, cup of coffee, dish of food, bag of flour, bottle of beer. These very common container formulas, in which "of" has an obvious, visually perceptible meaning ("contents"), influence our feeling about the less obvious type-body formulas: stick of wood, lump of dough, etc. The formulas are very similar: individual noun plus a similar relator (English "of"). In the obvious case this relator denotes contents. In the inobvious one it "suggests" contents. Hence the lumps, chunks, blocks, pieces, etc., seem to contain something, a "stuff," "substance," or "matter" that answers to the water, coffee, or flour in the container formulas. So with SAE people the philosophic "substance" and "matter" are also the naïve idea; they are instantly acceptable, "common sense." It is so through linguistic habit. Our language patterns often require us to name a physical thing by a binomial that splits the reference into a formless item plus a form.

Hopi is again different. It has a formally distinguished class of nouns. But this class contains no formal subclass of mass nouns. All nouns have an individual sense and both singular and plural forms. Nouns translating most nearly our mass nouns still refer to vague bodies or vaguely bounded extents. They imply indefiniteness, but not lack, of outline and size. In specific statements, "water" means one certain mass or quantity of water, not what we call "the substance water." Generality of statement is conveyed through the verb or predicator, not the noun. Since nouns are individual already, they are not individualized by either type-bodies or names of containers, if there is no special need to emphasize shape or container. The noun itself implies a suitable type-body or container. One says, not "a glass of water" but *kə·yi* "a water," not "a pool of water" but *pa·hə*,[d] not "a dish of cornflour" but *nəmni* "a (quantity of) cornflour," not "a piece of meat" but *sik^wi* "a meat." The language has neither need for nor analogies on which to build the concept of existence as a duality of formless item and form. It deals with formlessness through other symbols than nouns.[9]

PHASES OF CYCLES IN SAE AND HOPI

Such terms as summer, winter, September, morning, noon, sunset are with us nouns, and have little formal linguistic difference from other nouns. They can be subjects or objects, and we say "at" sunset or "in" winter just as we say at a corner or in an orchard.[e] They are pluralized and numerated like nouns of physical objects, as we have seen. Our thought about the referents of such words hence becomes objectified. Without objectification, it would be a subjective experience of real time, i.e. of the consciousness of "becoming later and later"—simply a cyclic phase similar to an earlier phase in that ever-later-becoming duration. Only by imagination can such a cyclic phase be set beside another and another in the manner of a spatial (i.e., visually perceived) configuration. But such is the power of linguistic analogy that we do so objectify cyclic phasing. We do it even by saying "a phase" and "phases" instead of, e.g., "phasing." And the pattern of individual and mass nouns, with the resulting binomial formula of formless item plus form, is so general

---

[9] In this section Whorf says that SAE has mass nouns such as "glass" and "water" that require us to individualize them by adding a qualifier such as "pane of glass" or a container such as "glass of water." However, he claims that Hopi has no mass nouns; rather, Hopi nouns for indefinite objects such as water imply outline size or quantity. It is curious that Whorf chooses the example of water to illustrate this point, because water is a case in English in which one can construct nouns in the same manner as Hopi. The nouns *puddle, pond,* and *lake* all imply a certain size and quantity of water. *Twig, stick,* and *board* are other examples in the case of wood. Maybe the differences between SAE and Hopi noun construction are not as absolute as Whorf claims.

that it is implicit for all nouns, and hence our very generalized formless items like "substance," "matter," by which we can fill out the binomial for an enormously wide range of nouns. But even these are not quite generalized enough to take in our phase nouns. So for the phase nouns we have made a formless item, "time." We have made it by using "a time," i.e. an occasion or a phase, in the pattern of a mass noun, just as from "a summer" we make "summer" in the pattern of a mass noun. Thus with our binomial formula we can say and think "a moment of time," "a second of time," "a year of time." Let me again point out that the pattern is simply that of "a bottle of milk" or "a piece of cheese." Thus we are assisted to imagine that "a summer" actually contains or consists of such-and-such a quantity of "time."

In Hopi however all phase terms, like summer, morning, etc., are not nouns but a kind of adverb, to use the nearest SAE analogy. They are a formal part of speech by themselves, distinct from nouns, verbs, and even other Hopi "adverbs." Such a word is not a case form or a locative pattern, like "des Abends" or "in the morning." It contains no morpheme like one of "in the house" or "at the tree."f It means "when it is morning" or "while morning-phase is occurring." These "temporals" are not used as subjects or objects, or at all like nouns. One does not say "it's a hot summer" or "summer is hot"; summer is not hot, summer is only *when* conditions are hot, *when* heat occurs. One does not say "*this* summer," but "summer now" or "summer recently." There is no objectification, as a region, an extent, a quantity, of the subjective duration-feeling. Nothing is suggested about time except the perpetual "getting later" of it. And so there is no basis here for a formless item answering to our "time."[10]

TEMPORAL FORMS OF VERBS IN SAE AND HOPI

The three-tense system of SAE verbs colors all our thinking about time. This system is amalgamated with that larger scheme of objectification of the subjective experience of duration already noted in other patterns—in the binomial formula applicable to nouns in general, in temporal nouns, in plurality and numeration. This objectification enables us in imagination to "stand time units in a row." Imagination of time as like a row harmonizes with a system of *three* tenses; whereas a system of *two,* an earlier and a later, would seem to correspond better to the feeling of duration as it is experienced. For if we inspect consciousness we find no past, present, future, but a unity embracing complexity. *Everything* is in consciousness, and everything in consciousness *is,* and is together. There is in it a sensuous and a nonsensuous. We may call the sensuous—what we are seeing, hearing, touching—the "present" while in the nonsensuous the vast image-world of memory is being labeled "the past" and another realm of belief, intuition, and uncertainty "the future"; yet sensation, memory, foresight, all are in consciousness together-one is not "yet to be" nor another "once but no more." Where real time comes in is that all this in consciousness is "getting later," changing certain relations in an irreversible manner. In this "latering" or "durating" there seems to me to be a paramount contrast between the newest, latest instant at the focus of attention and the rest—the earlier. Languages by the score get along well with two tenselike forms answering to this paramount relation of later to earlier. We can of course *construct and contemplate in thought* a system of past, present, future, in the objectified

---

[10] Building on his discussions of plurality and mass nouns, Whorf proposes here that SAE terminology for phases of time such as summer or morning quantify these imaginary nouns as if they were a quantity of concrete, observable items. In fact, in the Western calendar the seasons are specific series of days that disregard local environmental conditions. This is another example of the Western objectification of time. In contrast, he says the Hopi use phase terms in the manner of adverbs. For example, summer is not hot (because summer is not a concrete thing that contains heat). Summer for the Hopi is when conditions are hot. From Whorf's description we can see that, in general, Hopi is a concrete language that reflects people's physical experience. This is a point that is dealt with in greater detail in the next section in the discussion of verb forms.

configuration of points on a line. This is what our general objectification tendency leads us to do and our tense system confirms.

In English the present tense seems the one least in harmony with the paramount temporal relation. It is as if pressed into various and not wholly congruous duties. One duty is to stand as objectified middle term between objectified past and objectified future, in narration, discussion, argument, logic, philosophy. Another is to denote inclusion in the sensuous field: "I *see* him." Another is for nomic, i.e. customarily or generally valid, statements: "We *see* with our eyes." These varied uses introduce confusions of thought, of which for the most part we are unaware.[11]

Hopi, as we might expect, is different here too. Verbs have no "tenses" like ours, but have validity-forms ("assertions"), aspects, and clause-linkage forms (modes), that yield even greater precision of speech. The validity-forms denote that the speaker (not the subject) reports the situation (answering to our past and present) or that he expects it (answering to our future)[8] or that he makes a nomic statement (answering to our nomic present). The aspects denote different degrees of duration and different kinds of tendency "during duration." As yet we have noted nothing to indicate whether an event is sooner or later than another when both are *reported*. But need for this does not arise until we have two verbs: i.e., two clauses. In that case the "modes" denote relations between the clauses, including relations of later to earlier and of simul-

taneity. Then there are many detached words that express similar relations, supplementing the modes and aspects. The duties of our three-tense system and its tripartite linear objectified "time" are distributed among various verb categories, all different from our tenses; and there is no more basis for an objectified time in Hopi verbs than in other Hopi patterns; although this does not in the least hinder the verb forms and other patterns from being closely adjusted to the pertinent realities of actual situations.[12]

[*Because of space constraints we have skipped a 590-word section of Whorf's essay called "Duration, Intensity, and Tendency in SAE and Hopi." In this section Whorf discusses how duration, intensity, and tendency are expressed metaphorically in SAE. For example, an event that concludes quickly is "short." Someone with an injury may suffer a "sharp" pain, and as the oil market reacts to shifting supplies of crude oil caused by political and environmental events the price of gasoline "rises" and "falls." Whorf concludes that this is part of the whole process in SAE of objectifying or spatializing qualities and events that are not concrete or spatial. He says that we can hardly refer to the simplest nonspatial situation without using physical metaphors. For example, do you "grasp" this point, or is it "over your head"? Whorf concludes this section by saying that the Hopi language does not use these physical metaphors because Hopi has "tensors," a class of words that denotes intensity, tendency and duration.*]

---

[11] Whorf points out that SAE requires one to think and speak in a three-tense system. However, there is no past, present, or future in our consciousness. We live in a continual present and experience our memories (past), sensations (present), and anticipation of things (future) all together in "real time." This is another example of the way that SAE steers its speakers toward the Western objectification of time. Hopi, however, is different, as Whorf explains later. Besides outlining how he thinks Hopi speakers understand the world, Whorf's claim has much larger implications. Whorf is saying that the physical phenomenon of consciousness can be divided into two categories: the sensuous, that is, what we are experiencing at this instant, and the nonsensuous, everything else (memories, anticipations, anxieties, and so on). Because of the structure of our language, we carve three tenses out of this phenomenon: past, present, and future. In fact, as a

physical phenomenon, the only thing that actually exists is the process of getting later. In this, Whorf understands consciousness in a fashion that is consistent with Boasian thinking. Consciousness is essentially undifferentiated . . . a blank slate, or tabula rasa. Understandings are created by culture and environment rather than by any preexisting tendency of the brain to work in particular ways. Here, Whorf focuses on an important, and very Boasian, debate: Are notions such as past, present, and future related to aspects of human physiology or is human behavior virtually completely flexible? Are they learned, cultural phenomena?

[12] As Whorf indicates, many languages like Hopi have two tense forms (past and present) and numerous aspect forms that indicate duration or whether an action is about to happen, is ongoing, or has been completed.

HABITUAL THOUGHT IN SAE AND HOPI

The comparison now to be made between the habitual thought worlds of SAE and Hopi speakers is of course incomplete. It is possible only to touch upon certain dominant contrasts that appear to stem from the linguistic differences already noted. By "habitual thought" and "thought world" I mean more than simply language, i.e., than the linguistic patterns themselves. I include all the analogical and suggestive value of the patterns (e.g., our "imaginary space" and its distant implications), and all the give-and-take between language and the culture as a whole, wherein is a vast amount that is not linguistic but yet shows the shaping influence of language. In brief, this "thought world" is the microcosm that each man carries about within himself, by which he measures and understands what he can of the macrocosm.[13]

The SAE microcosm has analyzed reality largely in terms of what it calls "things" (bodies and quasibodies) plus modes of extensional but formless existence that it calls "substances" or "matter." It tends to see existence through a binomial formula that expresses any existent as a spatial form plus a spatial formless continuum related to the form, as contents is related to the outlines of its container. Nonspatial existents are imaginatively spatialized and charged with similar implications of form and continuum.

The Hopi microcosm seems to have analyzed reality largely in terms of *events* (or better "eventing"), referred to in two ways, objective and subjective. Objectively, and only if perceptible physical experience, events are expressed mainly as outlines, colors, movements, and other perceptive reports. Subjectively, for both the physical and nonphysical, events are considered the expression of invisible intensity factors, on which depend their stability and persistence, or their fugitiveness and proclivities.[14] It implies that existents do not "become later and later" all in the same way; but some do so by growing like plants, some by diffusing and vanishing, some by a procession of metamorphoses, some by enduring in one shape till affected by violent forces. In the nature of each existent able to manifest as a definite whole is the power of its own mode of duration: its growth, decline, stability, cyclicity, or creativeness. Everything is thus already "prepared" for the way it now manifests by earlier phases, and what it will be later, partly has been, and partly is in act of being so "prepared." An emphasis and importance rests on this preparing or being prepared aspect of the world that may to the Hopi correspond to that "quality of reality" that "matter" or "stuff" has for us.[15]

---

[13] Up to this point Whorf has spent his time (whoops, another metaphor objectifying time as a quantity) discussing how SAE and Hopi grammatical categories are different. In this section he now turns his attention to the relationship between language, thought, and behavior. Whorf will argue that cultural differences are not simply reflected in language. Rather, the cultural differences "stem from" linguistic differences. He proposes that each person carries within themselves a "thought world," shaped by language, through which they understand the world around them. In the discussion that follows, Whorf is proposing that language and culture are homogeneous phenomena. An individual is born into both and they are largely responsible for shaping that person's worldview. In fact, this notion of the thought world is similar to Ruth Benedict's concept of a cultural configuration (see essay 16). Although he does not cite Benedict in his essay, both Whorf and Benedict were close friends of Edward Sapir and shared his interests in the relationship between psychology and culture. Romanucci-

Ross reports that Sapir was "intimately friendly with Ruth [Benedict] and even more involved with Margaret [Mead]" (2001:1176). Benedict's *Patterns of Culture* was published in 1934, just at the time Whorf was first formulating his thoughts on the role of language in anthropology. It is clear here that Whorf was familiar with Benedict's work.

[14] Fugitiveness and proclivities: in this context, instabilities and tendencies.

[15] In other words, whereas SAE is characterized by "being," Hopi is characterized by "becoming." This is an interesting point, because Whorf's concerns here dovetail key interests of philosophers of his era, particularly the phenomenologists. Edmund Husserl and his student Martin Heidegger had both published works on the nature of time in the 1920s. Heidegger published *Being and Time* in 1927 and Husserl *Lectures on the Phenomenology of Internal Time Consciousness* in 1928. In these works they explore various objective and subjective experiences of time.

HABITUAL BEHAVIOR FEATURES
OF HOPI CULTURE

Our behavior, and that of Hopi, can be seen to be coordinated in many ways to the linguistically conditioned microcosm. As in my fire casebook, people act about situations in ways which are like the ways they talk about them. A characteristic of Hopi behavior is the emphasis on preparation. This includes announcing and getting ready for events well beforehand, elaborate precautions to insure persistence of desired conditions, and stress on good will as the preparer of right results. Consider the analogies of the day-counting pattern alone. Time is mainly reckoned "by day" (*taLk, -tala*) or "by night" (*tok*), which words are not nouns but tensors, the first formed on a root "light, day," the second on a root "sleep." The count is by *ordinals*. This is not the pattern of counting a number of different men or things, even though they appear successively, for, even then, they *could* gather into an assemblage. It is the pattern of counting successive reappearances of the *same* man or thing, incapable of forming an assemblage. The analogy is not to behave about day-cyclicity as to several men ("several days"), which is what *we* tend to do, but to behave as to the successive visits of the *same man*. One does not alter several men by working upon just one, but one can prepare and so alter the later visits of the same man by working to affect the visit he is making now. This is the way the Hopi deal with the future—by working within a present situation which is expected to carry impresses, both obvious and occult, forward into the future event of interest. One might say that Hopi society understands our proverb "Well begun is half done," but not our "Tomorrow is another day." This may explain much in Hopi character.[16]

This Hopi preparing behavior may be roughly divided into announcing, outer preparing, inner preparing, covert participation, and persistence. Announcing, or preparative publicity, is an important function in the hands of a special official, the Crier Chief. Outer preparing is preparation involving much visible activity, not all necessarily directly useful within our understanding. It includes ordinary practicing, rehearsing, getting ready, introductory formalities, preparing of special food, etc. (all of these to a degree that may seem overelaborate to us), intensive sustained muscular activity like running, racing, dancing, which is thought to increase the intensity of development of events (such as growth of crops), mimetic and other magic, preparations based on esoteric theory involving perhaps occult instruments like prayer sticks, prayer feathers, and prayer meal, and finally the great cyclic ceremonies and dances, which have the significance of preparing rain and crops. From one of the verbs meaning "prepare" is derived the noun for "harvest" or "crop": *na'twani* "the prepared" or the "in preparation."[h]

Inner preparing is use of prayer and meditation, and at lesser intensity good wishes and good will, to further desired results. Hopi attitudes stress the power of desire and thought. With their "microcosm" it is utterly natural that they should. Desire and thought are the earliest, and therefore the most important, most critical and crucial, stage of preparing. Moreover, to the Hopi, one's desires and thoughts influence not only his own actions, but all nature as well. This too is wholly natural. Consciousness itself is aware of work, of the feel of effort and energy, in desire and thinking. Experience more basic than language tells us that, if energy is expended, effects are produced. *We* tend to believe that our bodies can stop up this energy,

---

[16] In this section Whorf seeks to make the connection between Hopi language and behavior. He says that as with the insurance cases he has investigated, the Hopi act in ways that are similar to the way they talk and he provides several examples that contrast the Hopi point of view with that of SAE speakers. The examples speak for themselves and do not need our explanation. It is worth pointing out that Whorf is firmly Boasian in using Hopi language as a way of explaining the Hopi worldview. This was a position Boas first formulated in 1911 in the introduction to his *Handbook of American Indian Languages*. However, unlike Boas and following Sapir, Whorf believed that psychology (rather than history) provided the explanatory tools that anthropology needed to analyze the relationship between humans and culture, and he saw linguistics as the bridge between anthropology and psychology.

prevent it from affecting other things until we will our *bodies* to overt action. But this may be so only because we have our own linguistic basis for a theory that formless items like "matter" are things in themselves, malleable only by similar things, by more matter, and hence insulated from the powers of life and thought. It is no more unnatural to think that thought contacts everything and pervades the universe than to think, as we all do, that light kindled outdoors does this. And it is not unnatural to suppose that thought, like any other force, leaves everywhere traces of effect. Now, when *we* think of a certain actual rosebush, we do not suppose that our thought goes to that actual bush, and engages with it, like a searchlight turned upon it. What then do we suppose our consciousness is dealing with when we are thinking of that rosebush? Probably we think it is dealing with a "mental image" which is not the rosebush but a mental surrogate of it. But why should it be *natural* to think that our thought deals with a surrogate and not with the real rosebush? Quite possibly because we are dimly aware that we carry about with us a whole imaginary space, full of mental surrogates. To us, mental surrogates are old familiar fare. Along with the images of imaginary space, which we perhaps secretly know to be imaginary only, we tuck the thought-of actually existing rosebush, which may be quite another story, perhaps just because we have that very convenient "place" for it. The Hopi thought-world has no imaginary space. The corollary to this is that it may not locate thought dealing with real space anywhere but in real space, nor insulate real space from the effects of thought. A Hopi would naturally suppose that his thought (or he himself) traffics with the actual rosebush—or more likely, corn plant—that he is thinking about. The thought then should leave some trace of itself with the plant in the field. If it is a good thought, one about health and growth, it is good for the plant; if a bad thought, the reverse.[17]

The Hopi emphasize the intensity-factor of thought. Thought to be most effective should be vivid in consciousness, definite, steady, sustained, charged with strongly felt good intentions. They render the idea in English as "concentrating," "holding it in your heart," "putting your mind on it," "earnestly hoping." Thought power is the force behind ceremonies, prayer sticks, ritual smoking, etc. The prayer pipe is regarded as an aid to "concentrating" (so said my informant). Its name, *na'twanpi*, means "instrument of preparing."

Covert participation is mental collaboration from people who do not take part in the actual affair, be it a job of work, hunt, race, or ceremony, but direct their thought and good will toward the affair's success. Announcements often seek to enlist the support of such mental helpers as well as of overt participants, and contain exhortations to the people to aid with their active good will.[i] A similarity to our concepts of a sympathetic audience or the cheering section at a football game should not obscure the fact that it is primarily the power of directed thought, and not merely sympathy or encouragement, that is expected of covert participants. In fact these latter get in their deadliest work before, not during, the game! A corollary to the power of thought is the power of wrong thought for evil; hence one purpose of covert participation is to obtain the mass force of many good wishers to offset the harmful thought of ill wishers. Such attitudes greatly favor cooperation and community spirit. Not that the Hopi community is not full of rivalries and colliding interests. Against the tendency to social disintegration in such a small, isolated group, the theory of "preparing" by the power of thought, logically leading to the great power of the combined, intensified, and harmonized thought of the whole community, must help vastly toward the rather remarkable degree of cooperation that, in spite of much private bickering, the Hopi

---

[17] This section is a brilliant example of culturally relativistic writing, and we want to draw your attention to the skill with which Whorf explains how a Hopi views his place in the world. Boas believed that one of the goals of anthropology was to understand the "native" worldview. Here Whorf not only explains the Hopi view of things, he does it in such a way that highlights the contrasts between Hopi and SAE and makes Hopi seem reasonable. It is good to point out here that the clarity of Whorf's presentation does not mean he was correct. Linguists and psychologists have been experimenting with different aspects of Whorf's ideas for half a century without reaching any definitive conclusions.

village displays in all the important cultural activities.

Hopi "preparing" activities again show a result of their linguistic thought background in an emphasis on persistence and constant insistent repetition. A sense of the cumulative value of innumerable small momenta is dulled by an objectified, spatialized view of time like ours, enhanced by a way of thinking close to the subjective awareness of duration, of the ceaseless "latering" of events. To us, for whom time is a motion on a space, unvarying repetition seems to scatter its force along a row of units of that space, and be wasted. To the Hopi, for whom time is not a motion but a "getting later" of everything that has ever been done, unvarying repetition is not wasted but accumulated. It is storing up an invisible change that holds over into later events.[j] As we have seen, it is as if the return of the day were felt as the return of the same person, a little older but with all the impresses of yesterday, not as "another day," i.e. like an entirely different person. This principle joined with that of thought-power and with traits of general Pueblo culture is expressed in the theory of the Hopi ceremonial dance for furthering rain and crops, as well as in its short, piston-like tread, repeated thousands of times, hour after hour.[18]

SOME IMPRESSES OF LINGUISTIC HABIT IN WESTERN CIVILIZATION

It is harder to do justice in few words to the linguistically conditioned features of our own culture than in the case of the Hopi, because of both vast scope and difficulty of objectivity—because of our deeply ingrained familiarity with the attitudes to be analyzed. I wish merely to sketch certain characteristics adjusted to our linguistic binomialism of form plus formless item or "substance," to our metaphoricalness, our imaginary space, and our objectified time. These, as we have seen, are linguistic.

From the form-plus-substance dichotomy the philosophical views most traditionally characteristic of the "Western world" have derived huge support. Here belong materialism, psychophysical parallelism, physics at least in its traditional Newtonian form—and dualistic views of the universe in general. Indeed here belongs almost everything that is "hard, practical common sense." Monistic,[19] holistic, and relativistic views of reality appeal to philosophers and some scientists, but they are badly handicapped in appealing to the "common sense" of the Western average man—not because nature herself refutes them (if she did, philosophers could have discovered this much), but because they must be talked about in what amounts to a new language. "Common sense," as its name shows, and "practicality" as its name does not show, are largely matters of talking so that one is readily understood. It is sometimes stated that Newtonian space, time, and matter are sensed by everyone intuitively, whereupon relativity is cited as showing how mathematical analysis can prove intuition wrong. This, besides being unfair to intuition, is an attempt to answer offhand question (1) put at the outset of this paper, to answer which this research was undertaken. Presentation of the findings now nears its end, and I think the answer is clear. The offhand

---

[18] Here Whorf uses his discussion of the Hopi conception of time and their views on the physical power of thought to make sense of Hopi ritual activity. He says that because their language treats time fundamentally differently than SAE, repetition, for the Hopi, is an essential part of their ceremonies. However, Whorf claims that SAE speakers as a result of their language cannot conceive of time in this "becoming later" fashion and therefore do not see the same value to repetition as do the Hopi. We are not in a position to quibble with Whorf over his observations of the Hopi, but we feel that Whorf overlooked the history of traditional Christian religious ceremony all over Europe.

Much Christian ritual activity involves repetition. It would be hard to look at the life of people in Catholic monastic orders, for example, and not see that the lives of monks and nuns are structured around a repetitive prayer and ritual cycle. Catholic penance may involve repeated sayings of specific prayers. The last line in this paragraph could apply equally well to Christian pilgrims, whose every footstep may be considered a prayer in exactly the same way.

[19] Monism is the philosophical principle that mind and matter are essentially the same.

answer, laying the blame upon intuition for our slowness in discovering mysteries of the Cosmos, such as relativity, is the wrong one. The right answer is: Newtonian space, time, and matter are no intuitions. They are recepts [*sic*] from culture and language. That is where Newton got them.[20]

Our objectified view of time is, however, favorable to historicity and to everything connected with the keeping of records, while the Hopi view is unfavorable thereto. The latter is too subtle, complex, and ever-developing, supplying no ready-made answer to the question of when "one" event ends and "another" begins. When it is implicit that everything that ever happened still is, but is in a necessarily different form from what memory or record reports, there is less incentive to study the past. As for the present, the incentive would be not to record it but to treat it as "preparing." But *our* objectified time puts before imagination something like a ribbon or scroll marked off into equal blank spaces, suggesting that each be filled with

an entry. Writing has no doubt helped toward our linguistic treatment of time, even as the linguistic treatment has guided the uses of writing. Through this give-and-take between language and the whole culture we get, for instance:

1. Records, diaries, bookkeeping, accounting, mathematics stimulated by accounting.
2. Interest in exact sequence, dating, calendars, chronology, clocks, time wages, time graphs, time as used in physics.
3. Annals, histories, the historical attitude, interest in the past, archaeology, attitudes of introjection toward past periods, e.g., classicism, romanticism.[21]

Just as we conceive our objectified time as extending in the future in the same way that it extends in the past, so we set down our estimates of the future in the same shape as our records

---

[20] Because he studied engineering Whorf had a better background in the physical sciences than most of his colleagues, and he continued to follow developments in the sciences throughout his career. He was familiar with Einstein's work on relativity and saw a link between relativity in physics and cultural relativity in the study of human societies, namely, that "reality" depends on the positioning of the observer. Here this leads him to an extremely radical claim: that we experience Newtonian physics (things such as the effects of gravity, the consistency of time, or mass) not because these things are "real" but because our language and culture cause us to perceive and believe them. By implication, if we had a different language and culture (like the Hopi) we might perceive what SAE speakers call time, gravity, and mass differently. It's an intriguing notion, and one needs to be careful not to misunderstand his point. Whorf is not arguing here that the physical laws that govern the universe are different in different cultures because people speak differently, but that the cultural reality or how events are defined may be different.

Whorf is arguing a linguistic version of cultural relativity. However, his work is closer than most Boasians to *hermeneutics,* the study of the interpretation of meaning. Hermeneutics was developed in Europe in the early twentieth century by philosophers such as Martin Heidegger and Hans-Georg Gadamer. Hermeneuticists argued that one could not have objective knowledge about the world because people necessarily understood the world through their cultural, linguistic, and intellectual models.

In American anthropology Boas and his students used the notion of cultural relativity to argue against racism and discrimination and to support the notion of cultural equality. Unfortunately, in post–World War I Germany political leaders used ideas from hermaneutics to argue for German cultural superiority that lead to a rise in nationalism, anti-Semitism, and the ascendance of Hitler and the National Socialist Party.

[21] Whorf here mentions the influence of writing on our objectified concept of time. Some more recent authors argue that writing has a profound influence on the way people think and communicate. For example, in *Orality and Literacy* (1982) Ong argues that literacy transforms thought in ways possible only after the technology of writing has been adopted. Whereas Whorf believed the differences he found between SAE and Hopi speakers were due to the grammar of the languages, a generation later scholars such as Ong and Goody argued that these differences were due to literacy and writing. Goody in particular chides Whorf for failing to see that the features of SAE are shared in common in part because they are written languages (1977:161).

Beyond this, note that Whorf's notion of society is thoroughly idealist. It is entirely determined by thinking. Most modern theorists would probably link the development of record keeping to commerce, taxation, and the emergence of state-level society. For Whorf, it is a function of language. Whereas Hopi language seems to virtually prohibit record keeping, SAE compels it.

of the past, producing programs, schedules, budgets. The formal equality of the spacelike units by which we measure and conceive time leads us to consider the "formless item" or "substance" of time to be homogeneous and in ratio to the number of units. Hence our prorata[22] allocation of value to time, lending itself to the building up of a commercial structure based on time-prorata values: time wages (time work constantly supersedes piece work), rent, credit, interest, depreciation charges, and insurance premiums. No doubt this vast system, once built, would continue to run under any sort of linguistic treatment of time; but that it should have been built at all, reaching the magnitude and particular form it has in the Western world, is a fact decidedly in consonance with the patterns of the SAE languages. Whether such a civilization as ours would be possible with widely different linguistic handling of time is a large question—in our civilization, our linguistic patterns and the fitting of our behavior to the temporal order are what they are, and they are in accord. We are of course stimulated to use calendars, clocks, and watches, and to try to measure time ever more precisely; this aids science, and science in turn, following these well-worn cultural grooves, gives back to culture an ever-growing store of applications, habits, and values, with which culture again directs science. But what lies outside this spiral? Science is beginning to find that there is something in the Cosmos that is not in accord with the concepts we have formed in mounting the spiral. It is trying to frame a NEW LANGUAGE by which to adjust itself to a wider universe.[23]

It is clear how the emphasis on "saving time" which goes with all the above and is very obvious objectification of time, leads to a high valuation of "speed," which shows itself a great deal in our behavior.

Still another behavioral effect is that the character of monotony and regularity possessed by our image of time as an evenly scaled limitless tape measure persuades us to behave as if that monotony were more true of events than it really is. That is, it helps to routinize us. We tend to select and favor whatever bears out this view, to "play up to" the routine aspects of existence. One phase of this is behavior evincing a false sense of security or an assumption that all will always go smoothly, and a lack in foreseeing and protecting ourselves against hazards. Our technique of harnessing energy does well in routine performance, and it is along routine lines that we chiefly strive to improve it—we are, for example, relatively uninterested in stopping the energy from causing accidents, fires, and explosions, which it is doing constantly and on a wide scale. Such indifference to the unexpectedness of life would be disastrous to a society as small, isolated, and precariously poised as the Hopi society is, or rather once was.

Thus our linguistically determined thought world not only collaborates with our cultural idols and ideals, but engages even our unconscious personal reactions in its patterns and gives them certain typical characters. One such character, as we have seen, is *carelessness,* as in reckless driving or throwing cigarette stubs into waste paper. Another of different sort is *gesturing* when we talk. Very many of the gestures made by English-speaking people at least, and probably by all SAE

---

[22] *Prorata*: on a proportional basis.

[23] Here Whorf suggests that language directs our scientific thinking and that scientific thinking in turn reinforces our "well-worn cultural grooves." Although Whorf here is talking about SAE-speaking society and not the Hopi, following this reasoning implies that the Hopi could never have come up with ideas such as payment for hourly labor or either Einsteinian or Newtonian physics. Their language would have prevented them from seeing the world in the way necessary for these concepts. At the time Whorf wrote, relativity was a fairly new concept (Whorf published this piece in 1941, Einstein published the theory of specific relativity in 1905). Whorf argues that language had not yet adapted to Einstein's discoveries.

Relativity creates an interesting problem for Whorf. If language controls thought to the degree that Whorf suggests, then how could Einstein discover concepts for which there were no words (that required a "NEW LANGUAGE")? Whorf attempts to solve this problem by proposing a feedback loop. Language creates science, which, in turn creates new vocabularies.

speakers, serve to illustrate, by a movement in space, not a real spatial reference but one of the nonspatial references that our language handles by metaphors of imaginary space. That is, we are more apt to make a grasping gesture when we speak of grasping an elusive idea than when we speak of grasping a doorknob. The gesture seeks to make a metaphorical and hence somewhat unclear reference more clear. But, if a language refers to nonspatials without implying a spatial analogy, the reference is not made any clearer by gesture. The Hopi gesture very little, perhaps not at all in the sense we understand as gesture.

It would seem as if kinesthesia, or the sensing of muscular movement, though arising before language, should be made more highly conscious by linguistic use of imaginary space and metaphorical images of motion. Kinesthesia is marked in two facets of European culture: art and sport. European sculpture, an art in which Europe excels, is strongly kinesthetic, conveying great sense of the body's motions; European painting likewise. The dance in our culture expresses delight in motion rather than symbolism or ceremonial, and our music is greatly influenced by our dance forms. Our sports are strongly imbued with this element of the "poetry of motion." Hopi races and games seem to emphasize rather the virtues of endurance and sustained intensity. Hopi dancing is highly symbolic and is performed with great intensity and earnestness, but has not much movement or swing.

Synesthesia, or suggestion by certain sense receptions of characters belonging to another sense, as of light and color by sounds and *vice versa*, should be made more conscious by a linguistic metaphorical system that refers to nonspatial experiences by terms for spatial ones, though undoubtedly it arises from a deeper source. Probably in the first instance metaphor arises from synesthesia and not the reverse; yet metaphor

need not become firmly rooted in linguistic pattern, as Hopi shows. Nonspatial experience has one well-organized sense, *hearing*—for smell and taste are but little organized. Nonspatial consciousness is a realm chiefly of thought, feeling, and *sound*. Spatial consciousness is a realm of light, color, sight, and touch, and presents shapes and dimensions. Our metaphorical system, by naming nonspatial experiences after spatial ones, imputes to sounds, smells, tastes, emotions, and thoughts qualities like the colors, luminosities, shapes, angles, textures, and motions of spatial experience. And to some extent the reverse transference occurs; for, after much talking about tones as high, low, sharp, dull, heavy, brilliant, slow, the talker finds it easy to think of some factors in spatial experience as like factors of tone. Thus we speak of "tones" of color, a gray "monotone," a "loud" necktie, a "taste" in dress: all spatial metaphor in reverse. Now European art is distinctive in the way it seeks deliberately to play with synesthesia. Music tries to suggest scenes, color, movement, geometric design; painting and sculpture are often consciously guided by the analogies of music's rhythm; colors are conjoined with feeling for the analogy to concords and discords. The European theater and opera seek a synthesis of many arts. It may be that in this way our metaphorical language that is in some sense a confusion of thought is producing, through art, a result of far-reaching value—a deeper esthetic sense leading toward a more direct apprehension of underlying unity behind the phenomena so variously reported by our sense channels.[24]

HISTORICAL IMPLICATIONS

How does such a network of language, culture, and behavior come about historically? Which was first: the language patterns or the cultural

---

[24] Earlier in the essay Whorf pointed out that SAE speakers typically use physical metaphors to talk about nonphysical things. For example, the phrase "I take your point." Here Whorf makes the interesting suggestion that this phenomenon developed from synesthesia. Yet if we accept Whorf's idea, this raises an interesting (and

presumably unsolvable) problem. Whorf says that linguistic metaphor perhaps arose from the experience of synesthesia, which, presumably, all humans are capable of having. An interesting question, then, is why certain metaphors become "rooted" in one language but not others.

norms? In main they have grown up together, constantly influencing each other. But in this partnership the nature of the language is the factor that limits free plasticity and rigidifies channels of development in the more autocratic way. This is so because a language is a system, not just an assemblage of norms. Large systematic outlines can change to something really new only very slowly, while many other cultural innovations are made with comparative quickness. Language thus represents the mass mind; it is affected by inventions and innovations, but affected little and slowly, whereas to inventors and innovators it legislates with the decree immediate.[25]

The growth of the SAE language-culture complex dates from ancient times. Much of its metaphorical reference to the nonspatial by the spatial was already fixed in the ancient tongues, and more especially in Latin. It is indeed a marked trait of Latin. If we compare, say Hebrew, we find that, while Hebrew has some allusion to not-space as space, Latin has more. Latin terms for nonspatials, like *educo, religio, principia, comprehendo,* are usually metaphorized physical references: lead out, tying back, etc. This is not true of all languages—it is quite untrue of Hopi. The fact that in Latin the direction of development happened to be from spatial to nonspatial (partly because of secondary stimulation to abstract thinking when the intellectually crude Romans encountered Greek culture) and that later tongues were strongly stimulated to mimic Latin, seems a likely reason for a belief, which still lingers on among linguists, that this is the natural direction of semantic change in all languages, and for the persistent notion in Western learned circles (in strong contrast to Eastern ones) that objective experience is prior to subjective. Philosophies make out a weighty case for the reverse, and certainly the direction

of development is sometimes the reverse. Thus the Hopi word for "heart" can be shown to be a late formation within Hopi from a root meaning think or remember. Or consider what has happened to the word "radio" in such a sentence as "he bought a new radio," as compared to its prior meaning "science of wireless telephony." In the Middle Ages the patterns already formed in Latin began to interweave with the increased mechanical invention, industry, trade, and scholastic and scientific thought. The need for measurement in industry and trade, the stores and bulks of "stuffs" in various containers, the type-bodies in which various goods were handled, standardizing of measure and weight units, invention of clocks and measurement of "time," keeping of records, accounts, chronicles, histories, growth of mathematics and the partnership of mathematics and science, all cooperated to bring our thought and language world into its present form.

In Hopi history, could we read it, we should find a different type of language and a different set of cultural and environmental influences working together. A peaceful agricultural society isolated by geographic features and nomad enemies in a land of scanty rainfall; arid agriculture that could be made successful only by the utmost perseverance (hence the value of persistence and repetition), necessity for collaboration (hence emphasis on the psychology of teamwork and on mental factors in general), corn and rain as primary criteria of value, need of extensive *preparations* and precautions to assure crops in the poor soil and precarious climate, keen realization of dependence upon nature favoring prayer and a religious attitude toward the forces of nature, especially prayer and religion directed toward the ever-needed blessing, rain—these things interacted with Hopi linguistic patterns to mold them, to be

---

[25] Here Whorf outlines a view of language that parallels his Boasian colleagues' view of culture. He refuses to speculate on whether language or culture came first, saying only that they form a network of factors that developed together and influenced each other. One can also see Whorf's linguistic determinism in the conclusion of this paragraph where he says that while language is little affected by inventions and changes slowly, it has an immediate power over the inventors.

molded again by them, and so little by little to shape the Hopi world outlook.[26]

To sum up the matter, our first question asked in the beginning (p. 144) is answered thus: Concepts of "time" and "matter" are not given in substantially the same form by experience to all men but depend upon the nature of the language or languages through the use of which they have been developed. They do not depend so much upon *any one system* (e.g., tense, or nouns) within the grammar as upon the ways of analyzing and reporting experience which have become fixed in the language as integrated "fashions of speaking" and which cut across the typical grammatical classifications, so that such a "fashion" may include lexical, morphological, syntactic, and otherwise systemically diverse means coordinated in a certain frame of consistency. Our own "time" differs markedly from Hopi "duration." It is conceived as like a space of strictly limited dimensions, or sometimes as like a motion upon such a space, and employed as an intellectual tool accordingly. Hopi "duration" seems to be inconceivable in terms of space or motion, being the mode in which life differs from form, and consciousness *in toto* from the spatial elements of consciousness. Certain ideas born of our own time-concept, such as that of absolute simultaneity, would be either very difficult to express or impossible and devoid of meaning under the Hopi conception, and would be replaced by operational concepts. Our "matter" is the physical subtype of "substance" or "stuff," which is conceived as the formless extensional item that must be joined with form before there can be real existence. In Hopi there seems to be nothing corresponding to it; there are no formless extensional items; existence may or may not have form, but what it also has, with or without form, is intensity and duration, these being nonextensional and at bottom the same.

But what about our concept of "space," which was also included in our first question? There is no such striking difference between Hopi and SAE about space as about time, and probably the apprehension of space is given in substantially the same form by experience irrespective of language. The experiments of the Gestalt psychologists with visual perception appear to establish this as a fact. But the *concept* of *space* will vary somewhat with language, because, as an intellectual tool,[k] it is so closely linked with the concomitant employment of other intellectual tools, of the order of "time" and "matter," which are linguistically conditioned. We see things with our eyes in the same space forms as the Hopi, but our idea of space has also the property of acting as a surrogate of nonspatial relationships like time, intensity, tendency, and as a void to be filled with imagined formless items, one of which may even be called "space." Space as sensed by the Hopi would not be connected mentally with such surrogates, but would be comparatively "pure," unmixed with extraneous notions.

As for our second question (p. 144): There are connections but not correlations or diagnostic correspondences between cultural norms and linguistic patterns. Although it would be impossible to infer the existence of Crier Chiefs from the lack of tenses in Hopi, or vice versa, there is a relation between a language and the rest of the culture of the society which uses it. There are cases where the "fashions of speaking" are closely integrated with the whole general culture, whether or not this be universally true, and there are connections within this integration, between the kind of linguistic analyses employed and various behavioral reactions and also the shapes taken by various cultural developments. Thus the importance of Crier Chiefs does have a connection, not with tenselessness itself, but with a system of thought in which categories different from our tenses are natural. These connections are to be found not so much by focusing attention on the typical rubrics of linguistic, ethnographic, or sociological description as by examining the culture and the language (always and only when the two have been together historically for a considerable time) as a whole in

---

[26] Here Whorf summarizes how language and culture developed together and influenced each other to produce Western society as we know it, and how a different language and different set of cultural and environmental influences produced a very different type of culture among the Hopi. This is classic statement of the historical-particularistic view of culture.

which concatenations that run across these departmental lines may be expected to exist, and, if they do exist, eventually to be discoverable by study.[27]

NOTES

[a]We have plenty of evidence that this is not the case. Consider only the Hopi and the Ute, with languages that on the overt morphological and lexical level are as similar as, say, English and German. The idea of "correlation" between language and culture, in the generally accepted sense of correlation, is certainly a mistaken one.

[b]As we say, "ten at the *same time*," showing that in our language and thought we restate the fact of group perception in terms of a concept "time," the large linguistic component of which will appear in the course of this paper.

[c]It is no exception to this rule of lacking a plural that a mass noun may sometimes coincide in lexeme with an individual noun that of course has a plural; e.g., "stone" (no pl.) with "a stone" (pl. "stones"). The plural form denoting varieties, e.g., "wines" is of course a different sort of thing from the true plural; it is a curious outgrowth from the SAE mass nouns, leading to still another sort of imaginary aggregates, which will have to be omitted from this paper.

[d]Hopi has two words for water quantities; kə·yi and pa·hə. The difference is something like that between "stone" and "rock" in English, pa·hə implying greater size and "wildness"; flowing water, whether or not outdoors or in nature; is pa·hə; so is "moisture." But, unlike "stone" and "rock," the difference is essential, not pertaining to a connotative margin, and the two can hardly ever be interchanged.

[e]To be sure, there are a few minor differences from other nouns, in English for instance in the use of the articles.

[f]"Year" and certain combinations of "year" with name of season, rarely season names alone, can occur with a locative morpheme "at," but this is exceptional. It appears like historical detritus of an earlier different patterning, or the effect of English analogy, or both.

[g]The expective and reportive assertions contrast according to the "paramount relation." The expective expresses anticipation existing *earlier* than objective fact, and coinciding with objective fact *later* than the status quo of the speaker, this status quo, including all the subsummation of the past therein, being expressed by the reportive. Our notion "future" seems to represent at once the earlier (anticipation) and the later (afterwards, what will be), as Hopi shows. This paradox may hint of how elusive the mystery of real time is, and how artificially it is expressed by a linear relation of past-present-future.

[h]The Hopi verbs of preparing naturally do not correspond neatly to our "prepare"; so that na'twani could also be rendered "the practiced-upon," "the tried-for," and otherwise.

[i]See, e.g., Ernest Beaglehole, *Notes on Hopi economic life* (Yale University Publications in Anthropology, no. 15, 1937), especially the reference to the announcement of a rabbit hunt, and on p. 30, description of the activities in connection with the cleaning of Toreva Spring—announcing, various preparing activities, and finally, preparing the continuity of the good results already obtained and the continued flow of the spring.

[j]This notion of storing up power, which seems implied by much Hopi behavior, has an analog in physics: acceleration. It might be said that the linguistic background of Hopi thought equips it to recognize naturally that force manifests not as motion or velocity, but as cumulation or acceleration. Our linguistic background tends to hinder in us this same recognition, for having legitimately conceived force to be that which produces change, we then think of change by our linguistic *metaphorical* analog, motion, instead of by a pure motionless changingness concept, i.e. accumulation or acceleration. Hence it comes to our naïve feeling as a shock to find from physical experiments that it is not possible to define force by motion, that motion and speed, as also "being at rest," are wholly relative, and that force can be measured only by acceleration.

[k]Here belong "Newtonian" and "Euclidean" space, etc.

[27] In this essay Whorf supplies a series of linguistic examples that seem to be compelling evidence in support of linguistic determinism. He concludes however, that what he has demonstrated are "connections but not correlations or diagnostic correspondences between cultural norms and linguistic patterns." Whorf the scientist recognized that his work was not proof of his ideas in a scientific sense. Reviewing almost fifty years of work on different aspects of the Sapir-Whorf hypothesis, Lucy argues that there has been no sustained program of empirical research that supports it (1997:291–292). He points out that work such as Whorf's typically highlights features of a language that the researcher assumes to be relevant to a behavior. However, even though the feature of the language may stand out to the observer, it may not be structurally or functionally important in the language. One doesn't know unless there is a formal analysis of the language (Lucy 1997:302). More particularly, Whorf's knowledge and understanding of Hopi have been questioned. In 1983, Ekkehart Malotki argued that Whorf simply got it wrong and that claims that Hopi do not use expressions such as "ten days" are incorrect. Malotki argued that the Hopi conception of time was not radically different from our own (1983: 529–530). Still, Whorf and Sapir's notion that there is a relationship between language, thought, and behavior seems intuitively obvious and retains a strong presence in some branches of anthropological thinking.

Functionalism

In the first thirty years of the twentieth century, Franz Boas and his students were clearly the dominant anthropological thinkers in America, and the evolutionary model was temporarily abandoned. In Britain, on the other hand, the reaction to cultural evolution did not occur with the same force. With no single figure comparable to Boas, British anthropologists were divided into two camps: the diffusionists and the functionalists. It is the latter group that concerns us here.

In the 1880s and 1890s, a new group of anthropological thinkers, led by Alfred Cort Haddon (1855–1940) emerged in Britain. Haddon was trained in anatomy and zoology but was deeply influenced by Tylor, Frazer, and Spencer. In the 1880s, he held a position at the Royal College of Science in Dublin. In 1888, dissatisfied with life in Dublin, Haddon journeyed to the Torres Straits, between New Guinea and Australia, in the hopes that an important expedition might get him a better job (Stocking 1992:21). Haddon went primarily to study coral reefs, but once there, he became fascinated by the tales of the local elders, and by the time he returned he was committed to anthropology.

Haddon brought several works of anthropology along on his trip, including *Notes and Queries on Anthropology for the Use of Travelers and Residents in Uncivilized Lands.* This was a book-length questionnaire designed to help untrained observers collect information of use to anthropologists. *Notes and Queries* was a collaborative work by many anthropologists, but Tylor was the primary author of the nineteenth-century editions.

Once back in England, Haddon moved to Cambridge University, where he became the first lecturer in physical anthropology. He published some of the data he had collected in the Torres Straits but soon became convinced that another expedition was essential. He hoped to make a comprehensive study of native body types, psychology, language, and material culture. To this end, he enlisted an interdisciplinary team of scholars, including the physician Charles Seligman (1873–1940), the experimental psychologist W. H. R. (William Halse Rivers) Rivers (1864–1922), and his students, William McDougall (1871–1938) and C. S. Myers (1873–1946). Other team members included linguist S. H. Ray and A. Wilkin, who served as photographer and studied land tenure issues. The team arrived in the Torres Straits in April 1898. Group members stayed for varying lengths of time, but all left within six months.

Despite its relative brevity, the Torres Straits expedition was a defining moment in the development of both anthropology and psychology in Britain. Most expedition members went on to hold important professorships in England and the United States. Haddon and Rivers were at Cambridge, Seligman at the London School of Economics. Myers worked first as an assistant to Rivers at Cambridge but then moved to London, founding the Institute of Industrial Psychology in 1921. McDougall taught at Oxford, then at Harvard and Duke.

Haddon and his colleagues made fieldwork a critical component of British anthropology. While on the expedition they worked largely by summoning people to speak with them through translators, but they encouraged their students to learn local languages and live in far closer proximity to those they studied. After their return to England, they published extensive accounts of their research. Perhaps more important, Haddon, Rivers, and Seligman were critical in the training of the key thinkers of British functionalist anthropology.

Although Haddon and his colleagues were profoundly affected by Tylor and the evolutionism of the nineteenth century, the focus of their research was different. They were less interested in determining the course of human social evolution than in describing the material, social, physiological, and psychological characteristics of different people. Their students absorbed this emphasis on fieldwork and description. However, also strongly influenced by Spencer and Durkheim, in a sense the students of Haddon and his colleagues attempted to carry out the research agenda implied by Spencer's organic analogy and Durkheim's *Rules of Sociological Method*. If, as Spencer claimed, society was like an organism, anthropologists should be able to describe the different social "organs" that composed a society. If, as Durkheim claimed, a positivist science of society was possible, then anthropologists should be able to find social facts and discover the laws that determine how they operate. The functionalists set out to accomplish just these things.

Functionalism in anthropology is generally divided into two schools of thought, each associated with a key personality. Psychological functionalism is linked to Bronislaw Malinowski (1884–1942). For the psychological functionalists, cultural institutions function to meet the basic physical and psychological needs of people in a society. Like Boas, Malinowski's method was based on extensive in-depth fieldwork during which he gathered evidence to support his theoretical position. The second school, structural functionalism, is associated with A. R. Radcliffe-Brown (1881–1955). Structural functionalists, who drew heavily on Durkheim's work, sought to understand how cultural institutions maintained the equilibrium and cohesion of a society.

Though Bronislaw Malinowski was interested in religion and folklore and had read Frazer's *The Golden Bough* as a young man, he was trained in the physical sciences and received a Ph.D. in physics and mathematics in 1908. The following year, he did advanced studies in Leipzig, where he, like Durkheim, was deeply influenced by Wilhelm Wundt and took classes with Karl Bücher (1847–1930), an economist who specialized in gift-and-exchange economies. His time

with Wundt and Bücher led him to an interest in folk psychology, and from there, to anthropology (Gross 1986). In 1910 Malinowski traveled to England and enrolled in the London School of Economics (LSE), where he studied anthropology under Charles Seligman. At the outbreak of World War I, Malinowski was traveling in the British-controlled South Pacific. He had intended that the trip, undertaken for ethnographic research, be relatively brief. However, Malinowski was from Krakow, in a part of Polish Galicia that had been controlled by Austria since 1849. Thus he was considered an enemy national, and the British forbade his return to Europe. They did permit him to stay in the Trobriand Islands from 1915 to 1918, and he conducted ethnographic research there for almost two years. Malinowski's intensive day-to-day contact with his informants and his familiarity with the local language set a high standard for modern ethnographic fieldwork. After the war, Malinowski returned to England and accepted a teaching position at the LSE, where he spent most of his career, training many of the finest English anthropologists of his era. These included E. E. Evans-Pritchard (1902–1973), Isaac Schapera (1905–2003), Audrey Richards (1899–1984), Raymond Firth (1901–2002), Meyer Fortes (1906–1983), Lucy Mair (1901–1986), and S. F. Nadel (1903–1956).

At the time functionalism emerged, anthropology did not have a particularly good reputation. Traveling to distant locations to study natives was exciting and exotic, but also uncouth. It probably didn't help that Seligman, as well as many of his students (and those of Haddon and Rivers) were Jewish. As a result, in the early years of the century, anthropology languished at Oxford and Cambridge, the most prestigious universities. Cambridge anthropologists Haddon and Rivers (1864–1922) were considered ungentlemanly by other members of the faculty (Leach 1984:5). However, anthropology prospered at the LSE, an institution founded by members of the socialist Fabian Society. While Malinowski built the anthropology program at the LSE, at Cambridge his books *Sex and Repression in Savage Society*, first published in 1927, and *The Sexual Life of Savages in Northwestern Melanesia* (1929b) were kept in a special section of the library and could only be read with the permission of a senior college official (Leach 1984:8).

Malinowski was concerned with how individuals pursued their own ends within the constraints of their culture. He believed that culture existed to satisfy seven basic human needs: nutrition, reproduction, bodily comforts, safety, relaxation, movement, and growth (1939). He wished to demonstrate how various cultural beliefs and practices contributed to the smooth functioning of society while providing individual biological or psychological benefits. For example, in his 1925 essay, "Magic, Science, and Religion," Malinowski discussed the nature of thought in primitive societies and demonstrated the psychological functions served by supernatural beliefs such as magic. By basing his theory on physiological and biopsychological needs, Malinowski gave his theory of culture a universal character. Because these needs were satisfied through cultural institutions, he was able to identify particular cultural and societal formations set up to fulfill them (Applebaum 1987:1–12). Malinowski was famous for his ethnographic reporting, and he was skilled at weaving theoretical ideas into his ethnographic discussions. His concept of psychological functionalism is represented by "The Essentials of the Kula," chapter 3 of his groundbreaking ethnography, *Argonauts of the Western Pacific* (1922). In this chapter, Malinowski offers a description of the trade in kula valuables that has become a classic of anthropology. The chapter showcases Malinowski's skill as an ethnographer but also illustrates many of his fundamental ideas.

Radcliffe-Brown, who studied anthropology at Cambridge under Haddon and Rivers, was heavily influenced by the work of Durkheim. Although he did fieldwork in the Andaman Islands and Australia, Radcliffe-Brown was more interested in deriving social laws governing behavior from the comparative study of different cultures than in cultural description based on intensive fieldwork in one culture. Durkheim's influence is evident in Radcliffe-Brown's attempts to illustrate how cultural systems function to maintain a society's equilibrium.

Although he used the term *culture* in his early work, Radcliffe-Brown rejected the concept later in his career. He believed that culture was an abstract concept and that, because the values and norms of a society could not be observed, a science of culture was impossible (Garbarino 1977:58). Radcliffe-Brown preferred to limit his research to social structures—to the principles that organize persons in a society (such as kinship) and to the actual roles and relationships that can be observed firsthand. To illustrate this perspective, Radcliffe-Brown used Spencer's organic analogy (and acknowledged his debt to Spencer). In 1935, he wrote:

> An animal organism is an agglomeration of cells and interstitial fluids arranged in relation to one another not as an aggregate but as an integrated living whole. The system of relations by which these units are related is the organic structure. As the terms are here used the organism is not itself the structure; it is a collection of units (cells or molecules) arranged in a structure, i.e., in a set of relations; the organism has a structure. The structure is thus to be defined as a set of relations between entities. Over a period its constituent cells do not remain the same. But the structural arrangement of the constituent units does remain similar. (Radcliffe-Brown 1965b [1935]:178–179)

Applying this analogy to anthropological data, Radcliffe-Brown argued that it is more useful to study kinship systems than to study the individuals in a society because, although people die, the kin structure remains the same from generation to generation. In Radcliffe-Brown's view, Malinowski's focus on individuals led nowhere. To use a cliché, Radcliffe-Brown thought that Malinowski did not see the forest for the trees.

We have chosen two articles to represent structural functionalism. In the first, "On Joking Relationships (1940)," Radcliffe-Brown argues that structural relations between people in certain positions in kinship systems lead to conflicts of interest. Such conflict could threaten the stability of society. However, this problem is solved through ritualized joking or avoidance between people in such positions. Thus, when conflict threatens stability, society develops social institutions to mediate oppositions and preserve social solidarity.

The second structural-functionalist essay, "The Licence in Ritual," is by Max Gluckman. Gluckman (1911–1975) was born in South Africa and trained there. He studied at the University of Witwatersrand under Winnifred Hoernle (1885–1960) and Isaac Schapera, both of whom had studied with Radcliffe-Brown at Oxford. Additionally, Hoernle studied psychology with Wundt and sociology with Durkheim (Stocking 1995). From South Africa, Gluckman went to Oxford, where he studied with Robert Marett (1866–1943). Marett was a student of Tylor but turned against his evolutionary ideas and became one of the first British intellectuals to use Durkheim's work in social analysis (Stocking 1995:169). Besides doing extensive fieldwork among South African groups, including the Zulu (1936–1938) and the Barotse (1939–1941), Gluckman held a series of important academic positions. He was head of the Rhodes-Livingstone Institute from 1941 to 1947 and then served for two years as a lecturer at Oxford. In 1949 he moved to Manchester, where he founded the Department of Social Anthropology at the University of Manchester. Gluckman brought a group of outstanding scholars to Manchester, including Elizabeth Colson, Victor Turner, Frederick Bailey, Edmund Leach, and Fredrik Barth. Together they forged a distinctive anthropological style focusing on process, change, and the maintenance of social order. The department became known as the Manchester School, and although the ideas and scholars associated with Manchester have changed over the past few decades, it continues to exert a powerful influence.

In many ways Gluckman's work represents the culmination of British functionalist thought. A specialist in political anthropology, he is especially known for his analysis of political systems among different groups in Africa, especially the functions of feuds and conflicts. Two of Gluckman's most famous books on this theme are *Rituals of Rebellion in South-East Africa* (1954) and *Custom and Conflict in Africa* (1956). His essay in this volume is an example of this type of work. In "The Licence in Ritual" Gluckman shows how ritualized reversals of social roles, seemingly acts of rebellion, act instead to support a society's social order and political systems.

We stated in the first section of this book that scientific theories are a product of the social and cultural context in which they are conceived. Functionalism was conceived and practiced largely by European anthropologists in territories that were European colonial possessions such as the Trobriand Islands, Australia, India, and East Africa. Given this context, it is surely no accident that these thinkers studied the function of cultural institutions in relation to the maintenance of social order and the smooth working of society. This focus was precisely the aspect of non-Western societies in which colonial governments were most interested.

The nature of the relationship between anthropology and colonialism is highly equivocal. It is certain that British anthropologists often thought about their usefulness to colonial administrations. From the turn of the twentieth century until World War II, most anthropologists wanted to provide their expertise to governments. A. C. Haddon, for example, campaigned persistently (but unsuccessfully) for an "imperial bureau of ethnology," designed to help the state deal with "conflicts derived from racial and cultural variation that arose both in the colonies and at home" (Kuklick 1991:44). Radcliffe-Brown held positions in Cape Town and Sydney, in which he was responsible for training officials to govern indigenous peoples (Max Gluckman was one notable exception to this trend. A political activist, he campaigned openly against colonialism and apartheid policies of his native South Africa). Both Radcliffe-Brown and Malinowski often pointed out ways in which anthropology could be useful to the colonial enterprise. Governments, however, were not particularly interested in either funding or listening to anthropologists. Most of the money that supported the functionalists came from the Rockefeller Foundation and other charitable organizations. The British government provided almost nothing (Goody 1995). Additionally, governments were deeply suspicious of anthropologists. Colonial officials were most often political conservatives, whereas anthropologists tended to be liberals. Officials generally believed that anthropologists were too close to the natives and were more likely to see their efforts as undermining than supporting colonialism.

One other observation about functionalism is warranted: the functionalists typically were only marginally interested in history. Whereas American anthropology at this time was based largely on reconstructing cultures from interviews with informants, British anthropologists were directly observing native societies in action (or thought they were). Under these circumstances, they believed that issues of the functioning of the current system were of primary importance. They asserted that historical reconstruction did little to clarify the current functioning of social institutions—indeed, they were deeply skeptical of historical reconstructions. Many functionalists held that since most of the societies they studied lacked writing, such reconstructions could be little more than fictions. As a result, they examined societies as if they were timeless and thus were unable to account for social change.

Functionalism lost its place of theoretical prominence after World War II. Because of the massive social, cultural, and political transformations that resulted from the war, interest in how societies maintained social stability declined, to be replaced by concern with cultural change. Despite this, the work of Malinowski, Radcliffe-Brown, and their students Fortes, Gluckman, Schapera, Richards, and others, continues to be widely read and to provide inspiration for modern anthropologists. Although few people would refer to themselves as structural-functionalist anthropologists today, and virtually no explicitly functionalist theoretical papers are being published, key functionalist concepts are still implicit in a great deal of anthropology. Functionalism continues to be a powerful idea, and most anthropologists are probably more functionalist than is generally acknowledged.

---

13. *The Essentials of the Kula*

Bronislaw Malinowski (1884–1942)

I

Having thus described the scene, and the actors, let us now proceed to the performance.[1] The Kula is a form of exchange, of extensive, intertribal character; it is carried on by communities inhabiting a wide ring of islands, which form a closed circuit. This circuit can be seen on Map V, where it is represented by the lines joining a number of islands to the North and East of the East end of New Guinea. Along this route, articles of two kinds, and these two kinds only, are constantly travelling in opposite directions.

In the direction of the hands of a clock, moves constantly one of these kinds—long necklaces of red shell, called *soulava*. . . . In the opposite direction moves the other kind—bracelets of white shell called *mwali*. . . . Each of these articles, as it travels in its own direction on the closed circuit, meets on its way articles of the other class, and is constantly being exchanged for them. Every movement of the Kula articles, every detail of the transactions is fixed and regulated by a set of traditional rules and conventions, and some acts of the Kula are accompanied by an elaborate magical ritual and public ceremonies.

From *Argonauts of the Western Pacific* (1922)

---

[1] "The Essentials of the Kula" is the third chapter of Malinowski's 1922 monograph *Argonauts of the Western Pacific*. In the introduction and first two chapters of the work, Malinowski discusses his research methods, the geography of the region, and the different "races" of people who inhabit it, as well as their notions of magic, sorcery, and power. Here he begins his discussion of the Kula, perhaps the thing for which this book is best remembered.

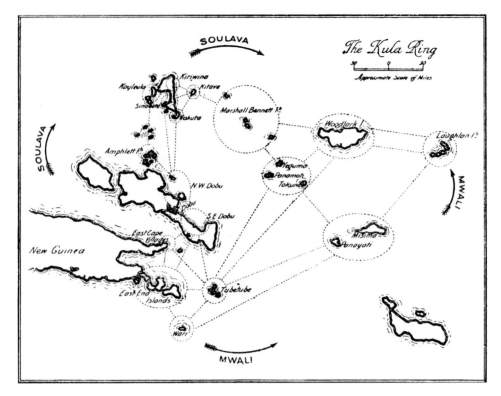

MAP V. The Kula ring

On every island and in every village, a more or less limited number of men take part in the Kula—that is to say, receive the goods, hold them for a short time, and then pass them on. Therefore every man who is in the Kula, periodically though not regularly, receives one or several *mwali* (arm-shells), or a *soulava* (necklace of red shell discs), and then has to hand it on to one of his partners, from whom he receives the opposite commodity in exchange. Thus no man ever keeps any of the articles for any length of time in his possession. One transaction action does not finish the Kula relationship, the rule being "once in the Kula, always in the Kula," and a partnership between two men is a permanent and lifelong affair. Again, any given *mwali* or *soulava* may always be found travelling and changing hands, and there is no question of its ever settling down, so that the principle "once in a Kula, always in a Kula" applies also to the valuables themselves.

The ceremonial exchange of the two articles is the main, the fundamental aspect of the Kula. But associated with it, and done under its cover, we find a great number of secondary activities and features.[2] Thus, side by side with the ritual exchange of arm-shells and necklaces, the natives carry on ordinary trade, bartering from one island to another a great number of utilities, often unprocurable in the district to which they are imported, and indispensable there. Further, there

---

[2] Malinowski's theoretical position is known as psychological functionalism. In a 1939 essay "The Group and The Individual in Functionalist Analysis," Malinowski argued that there were seven universal biological and psychological needs. These individual needs were converted to cultural behavior through the use of symbols, which also served to mold individual behavior to group standards. The task of the psychological functionalist was to describe these symbols and demonstrate how social institutions operated to fill psychological needs. However, it is not

are other activities, preliminary to the Kula, or associated with it, such as the building of sea-going canoes for the expeditions, certain big forms of mortuary ceremonies, and preparatory taboos.

The Kula is thus an extremely big and complex institution, both in its geographical extent, and in the manifoldness of its component pursuits. It welds together a considerable number of tribes, and it embraces a vast complex of activities, interconnected, and playing into one another, so as to form one organic whole.[3]

Yet it must be remembered that what appears to us an extensive, complicated, and yet well ordered institution is the outcome of ever so many doings and pursuits, carried on by savages, who have no laws or aims or characters definitely laid down.[4] They have no knowledge of the *total outline* of any of their social structure. They know their own motives, know the purpose of individual actions and the rules which apply to them, but how, out of these, the whole collective institution shapes, this is beyond their mental range. Not even the most intelligent native has any clear idea of the Kula as a big, organized social construction, still less of its sociological function and implications. If you were to ask him what the Kula is, he would answer by giving a few details, most likely by giving his personal experiences and subjective views on the Kula, but nothing approaching the definition just given here. Not even a partial coherent account could be obtained. For the integral picture does not exist in his mind; he is in it, and cannot see the whole from the outside.

The integration of all the details observed, the achievement of a sociological synthesis of all the various, relevant symptoms, is the task of the Ethnographer. First of all, he has to find out that certain activities, which at first sight might appear incoherent and not correlated, have a meaning. He then has to find out what is constant and relevant in these activities and what accidental and inessential, that is, to find out the laws and rules of all the transactions. Again, the Ethnographer has to *construct* the picture of the big institution, very much as the physicist constructs his

---

clear to what extent Malinowski had worked out these ideas when he wrote *Argonauts* and his other book-length accounts of the Trobriand Islands, most of which were published in the 1920s. In these he seems far more interested in portraying the experiences of the Trobrianders in ways that make them comprehensible to audiences in Europe and America than in examining the ways in which institutions such as the Kula fill specific psychological needs. The degree to which psychological functionalism is actually represented in *Argonauts* is unclear. On the one hand, it is true that the Kula does serve at least some of the seven psychological functions Malinowski enumerated in 1939: It increases their safety by setting up networks of trading partners and allies and may allow for movement and growth. On the other hand, Malinowski does not address these issues anywhere in *Argonauts,* and there is little evidence he had them in mind as he was writing this book.

[3] Malinowski takes pains throughout this chapter to emphasize the size and complexity of the Kula. His understanding of it was conditioned by Spencer's notion of the social organism as a complex system of interrelated parts.

[4] Notice Malinowski's characterization of the Trobriand Islanders in this and the next paragraph as aware of their individual actions and motives but unable to see their entire system. It takes an outsider, the ethnographer according to Malinowski, to conduct an objective analysis of a society and its institutions—a point that Victor Turner echoed half a century later (see essay 36). Malinowski is not denigrating the intelligence of the Trobriand Islanders here, for he believed the same principle to be true for people in Western societies. The point that a person cannot objectively analyze the system in which he or she participates is a central tenet of psychoanalytic thought. A selection of Freud's work was made available to Malinowski in the field by his professor Charles G. Seligman (1873–1940), and Malinowski's opinion on the issue may have been influenced by Freud's writings. Seligman, a medical doctor, was a member of the Torres Straits expedition and wrote the groundbreaking *The Melanesians of British New Guinea* (1910), which set the stage for Malinowski's research. Seligman found Freud useful in his work with victims of shell shock during World War I. Malinowski, on the other hand, became a key critic of Freud and used data from the Trobriands to attack Freud's Oedipal theory in *Sex and Repression in Savage Society* (1955 [1927]). Note also the analogy Malinowski makes between ethnography and the physical sciences.

theory from the experimental data, which always have been within reach of everybody but which needed a consistent interpretation. I have touched on this point of method in the Introduction (Divisions V and VI), but I have repeated it here, as it is necessary to grasp it clearly in order not to lose the right perspective of conditions as they really exist among the natives.

II

In giving the above abstract and concise definition, I had to reverse the order of research, as this is done in ethnographic field-work, where the most generalised inferences are obtained as the result of long inquiries and laborious inductions. The general definition of the Kula will serve as a sort of plan or diagram in our further concrete and detailed descriptions. And this is the more necessary as the Kula is concerned with the exchange of wealth and utilities, and therefore it is an economic institution, and there is no other aspect of primitive life where our knowledge is more scanty and our understanding more super ficial than in Economics. Hence misconception is rampant, and it is necessary to clear the ground when approaching any economic subject.

Thus in the Introduction we called the Kula a "form of trade," and we ranged it alongside other systems of barter. This is quite correct, if we give the word "trade" a sufficiently wide interpretation, and mean by it any exchange of goods. But the word "trade" is used in current Ethnography

and economic literature with so many different implications that a whole lot of misleading, preconceived ideas have to be brushed aside in order to grasp the facts correctly. Thus the *a priori* current notion of primitive trade would be that of an exchange of indispensable or useful articles, done without much ceremony or regulation, under stress of dearth or need, in spasmodic, irregular intervals—and this done either by direct barter, everyone looking out sharply not to be done out of his due, or, if the savages were too timid and distrustful to face one another, by some customary arrangement, securing by means of heavy penalties compliance in the obligations incurred or imposed.[a5] Waiving for the present the question how far this conception is valid or not in general—in my opinion it is quite misleading—we have to realise clearly that the Kula contradicts in almost every point the above definition of "savage trade." It shows us primitive exchange in an entirely different light.

The Kula is not a surreptitious and precarious form of exchange. It is, quite on the contrary, rooted in myth, backed by traditional law, and surrounded with magical rites. All its main transactions are public and ceremonial, and carried out according to definite rules. It is not done on the spur of the moment, but happens periodically, at dates settled in advance, and it is carried on along definite trade routes, which must lead to fixed trysting places. Sociologically, though transacted between tribes differing in language, culture, and probably even in race, it is based on a fixed and permanent status, on a partnership

---

[5] In his first footnote, Malinowski references the German economist Carl Bücher (1847–1930), whose *Industrial Evolution*, first published in Germany in 1893, was enormously influential in Europe, and by 1901 had been translated into English, French, and Russian. Bücher developed a three-stage view of economic evolution, proposing that households led to towns, which led to national economies. The factor that differentiated these stages was the role of exchange. He believed that contemporary primitive societies represented a preeconomic stage of society (Firth 1964:210). Bücher writes that "primitive man lives only for the present. . . shuns all regular work . . . has not the conception of duty, not of a vocation as a moral function

in life" (1968 [1901]:82). These views influenced the work of scholars such as Max Weber (see essay 8) and Marcel Mauss (see essay 7). Malinowski—though sympathetic to Bücher's attempts to understand primitive economy—wrote *Argonauts* as a reaction to this view of primitive humans, using the Kula as a counterexample. Later in *Argonauts* he wrote, "Now I hope that whatever the meaning of the Kula might be for Ethnology, for the general science of culture, the meaning of the Kula will consist in being instrumental to dispel such crude, rationalistic conceptions of primitive mankind, and to induce both the speculator and the observer to deepen the analysis of economic facts" (1922:516).

which binds into couples some thousands of individuals. This partnership is a lifelong relationship, it implies various mutual duties and privileges, and constitutes a type of inter-tribal relationship on an enormous scale. As to the economic mechanism of the transactions, this is based on a specific form of credit, which implies a high degree of mutual trust and commercial honour—and this refers also to the subsidiary, minor trade, which accompanies the Kula proper. Finally, the Kula is not done under stress of any need, since its main aim is to exchange articles which are of no practical use.

From the concise definition of Kula given at the beginning of this chapter, we see that in its final essence, divested of all trappings and accessories, it is a very simple affair, which at first sight might even appear tame and unromantic. After all it only consists of an exchange, interminably repeated, of two articles intended for ornamentation, but not even used for that to any extent. Yet this simple action—this passing from hand to hand of two meaningless and quite useless objects—has somehow succeeded in becoming the foundation of a big inter-tribal institution, in being associated with ever so many other activities. Myth, magic and tradition have built up

around it definite ritual and ceremonial forms, have given it a halo of romance and value in the minds of the natives, have indeed created a passion in their hearts for this simple exchange.[6]

The definition of the Kula must now be amplified, and we must describe one after the other its fundamental characteristics and main rules, so that it may be clearly grasped by what mechanism the mere exchange of two articles results in an institution so vast, complex, and deeply rooted.

III

First of all, a few words must be said about the two principal objects of exchange, the arm-shells (*mwali*) and the necklaces (*soulava*). The arm-shells are obtained by breaking off the top and the narrow end of a big, cone-shaped shell (*Conus millepunctatus*) and then polishing up the remaining ring. These bracelets are highly coveted by all the Papuo-Melanesians of New Guinea, and they spread even into the pure Papuan district of the Gulf.[b] The manner of wearing the arm-shells is illustrated by Plate XVII, where the men have put them on on purpose to be photographed.[7]

---

[6] Malinowski believed that technologically primitive peoples were fully rational and just as intelligent as "civilized" people, but the point of the economic discussion in *Argonauts* is to critique the concept of "economic man." This is the notion that human beings rationally deploy limited resources to competing ends in such a way as to increase their personal benefit. This idea lies behind Adam Smith's *Wealth of Nations* (1976 [1776]) and most of Western economics. Malinowski's attack at its most vitriolic is found on page 60 of *Argonauts,* where he writes,

> Another notion which must be exploded, once and forever, is that of the Primitive Economic Man of some current economic textbooks. This fanciful, dummy creature, who has been very tenacious of existence in popular and semi-popular economic literature and whose shadow haunts even the minds of competent anthropologists, blighting their outlook with a preconceived idea, is an imaginary, primitive man, or savage, prompted in all his actions by a rationalistic concept of self-interest, and achieving his aims directly with the minimum of effort.

Malinowski wanted "rational man" but not "economic man," and he needed to show that it was possible to have one without the other. In large part, this is the goal of the Kula discussion. To Malinowski, the Kula is a highly elaborate and rational system of exchange that has an economically irrational end: the distribution of goods that have no utilitarian value. Much of later substantivist economics treated Malinowski's attack as virtually a founding document of their form of analysis. On the other hand, Firth says Malinowski's attack was essentially against a straw man (1964:217).

[7] Unusually for the period in which this was written, Malinowski tells the reader about the conditions under which the photograph (not included in this volume) was taken. This is a level of ethnographic reporting that did not become common until the 1970s and 1980s. Ellipses throughout this section indicate the deletion of other references to photographs.

The use of the small discs of red spondylus shell out of which the *soulava* are made, is also of very wide diffusion. There is a manufacturing centre of them in one of the villages in Port Moresby, and also in several places in Eastern New Guinea, notably in Rossell Island, and in the Trobriands. I have said "use" on purpose here, because these small beads, each of them a flat, round disc with a hole in the centre, coloured anything from muddy brown to carmine red, are employed in various ways for ornamentation. They are most generally used as part of earrings, made of rings of turtle shell, which are attached to the ear lobe, and from which hang a cluster of the shell discs. These earrings are very much worn, and, especially among the Massim, you see them on the ears of every second man or woman, while others are satisfied with turtle shell alone, unornamented with the shell discs. Another everyday ornament, frequently met with and worn, especially by young girls and boys, consists of a short necklace, just encircling the neck, made of the red spondylus discs, with one or more cowrie shell pendants. These shell discs can be, and often are, used in the make-up of the various classes of the more elaborate ornaments, worn on festive occasions only. Here however, we are more especially concerned with the very long necklaces, measuring from two to five metres, made of spondylus discs, of which there are two main varieties, one, much the finer, with a big shell pendant, the other made of bigger discs, and with a few cowrie shells or black banana seeds in the centre. . . .

The arm-shells on the one hand, and the long spondylus shell strings on the other, the two main Kula articles, are primarily ornaments. As such, they are used with the most elaborate dancing dress only, and on very festive occasions such as big ceremonial dances, great feasts, and big gatherings, where several villages are represented. . . . Never could they be used as everyday ornaments, nor on occasions of minor importance such as a small dance in the village, a harvest gathering, a love-making expedition, when facial painting, floral decoration and smaller though not quite everyday ornaments are worn. . . . But even though usable and sometimes used, this is not the main function of these articles. Thus, a chief may have several shell strings in his possession, and a few arm-shells. Supposing that a big dance is held in his or in a neighbouring village, he will not put on his ornaments himself if he goes to assist at it, unless he intends to dance and decorate himself, but any of his relatives, his children or his friends and even vassals, can have the use of them for the asking. If you go to a feast or a dance where there are a number of men wearing such ornaments, and ask anyone of them at random to whom it belongs, the chances are that more than half of them will answer that they themselves are not the owners, but that they had the articles lent to them. These objects are not owned in order to be used; the privilege of decorating oneself with them is not the real aim of possession.

Indeed—and this is more significant—by far the greater number of the arm-shells, easily ninety percent, are of too small a size to be worn even by young boys and girls. A few are so big and valuable that they would not be worn at all, except once in a decade by a very important man on a very festive day. Though all the shell-strings can be worn, some of them are again considered too valuable, and are cumbersome for frequent use, and would be worn on very exceptional occasions only.

This negative description leaves us with the questions: why, then, are these objects valued, what purpose do they serve? The full answer to this question will emerge out of the whole story contained in the following chapters, but an approximate idea must be given at once. As it is always better to approach the unknown through the known, let us consider for a moment whether among ourselves we have not some type of objects which play a similar role and which are used and possessed in the same manner. When, after a six years' absence in the South Seas and Australia, I returned to Europe and did my first bit of sight-seeing in Edinburgh Castle, I was shown the Crown Jewels. The keeper told many stories of how they were worn by this or that king or queen on such and such occasion, of how some of them had been taken over to London, to the great and just indignation of the whole Scottish nation, how they were restored, and how now everyone can be pleased, since they are safe under lock and key, and no one can touch them. As I was looking at them and thinking how ugly, useless, ungainly, even tawdry they were, I had the feeling that something similar had been told to me of late, and that I had seen many other objects of this sort, which made a similar impression on me.[8]

And then arose before me the vision of a native village on coral soil, and a small, rickety platform temporarily erected under a pandanus thatch, surrounded by a number of brown, naked men, and one of them showing me long, thin red strings, and big, white, worn-out objects, clumsy to sight and greasy to touch. With reverence he also would name them, and tell their history, and by whom and when they were worn, and how they changed hands, and how their temporary possession was a great sign of the importance and glory of the village. The analogy between the European and the Trobriand *vaygu'a* (valuables) must be delimited with more precision. The Crown Jewels, in fact, any heirlooms too valuable and too cumbersome to be worn, represent the same type as *vaygu'a* in that they are merely possessed for the sake of possession itself, and the ownership of them with the ensuing renown is the main source of their value. Also both heirlooms and *vaygu'a* are cherished because of the historical sentiment which surrounds them. However, ugly, useless, and—according to current standards—valueless an object may be, if it has figured in historical scenes and passed through the hands of historic persons, and is therefore an unfailing vehicle of important sentimental associations, it cannot but be precious to us. This historic sentimentalism, which indeed has a large share in our general interest in studies of past events, exists also in the South Seas. Every really good Kula article has its individual name, round each there is a sort of history and romance in the traditions of the natives. Crown Jewels or heirlooms are insignia of rank and symbols of wealth respectively, and in olden days with us, and in New Guinea up till a few years ago, both rank and wealth went together. The main point of difference is that the Kula goods are only in possession for a time, whereas the European treasure must be permanently owned in order to have full value.[9]

Taking a broader, ethnological view of the question, we may class the Kula valuables among the many "ceremonial" objects of wealth; enormous, carved and decorated weapons, stone implements, articles of domestic and industrial nature, too well decorated and too clumsy for use. Such things are usually called "ceremonial," but this word seems to cover a great number of meanings and much that has no meaning at all. In fact, very often, especially on museum labels, an article is called "ceremonial" simply because nothing is known about its uses and general nature. Speaking only about museum exhibits from New Guinea, I can say that many so-called ceremonial objects are nothing but simply overgrown objects of use, which preciousness of material and amount of labour expended have transformed into reservoirs of condensed economic value. Again, others are used on festive occasions, but play no part whatever in rites and ceremonies, and serve for decoration only, and these might be

---

[8] Malinowski is considered one of the great ethnographers in anthropological history in part because of his gift for ethnographic reportage. He believed it was important to understand how natives perceived their world and passed this understanding on to his readers by comparisons such as that presented here between *vaygu'a* and the crown jewels of Scotland. Like the jewels, *vaygu'a* do not have a practical utility; rather their value is symbolic, derived from their age and history. In making this comparison, Malinowski uses a nontechnical example easily accessible to a popular audience. *Argonauts,* like many of Malinowski's other works, was designed to be read by educated laypersons as well as professional anthropologists.

[9] In the passage above, Malinowski tries to give us a native's perspective when he explains what the Kula items mean to their recipients. Malinowski's writing style gave him a reputation as a man with great personal empathy for the people he studied. Admirers of Malinowski were greatly disillusioned when his diaries were published in 1967 *(A Diary in the Strict Sense of the Term).* The diaries showed that Malinowski was intensely unhappy and lonely much of the time, was constantly preoccupied with his health, and often spoke of the Trobriand Islanders in racist terms. In other words, he reacted like most people of his era (and perhaps our own) when forced into unfamiliar circumstances for a long period of time.

called *objects of parade* (compare Chap. VI, Div. I). Finally, a number of these articles function actually as instruments of a magical or religious rite, and belong to the intrinsic apparatus of a ceremony. Such and such only could be correctly called *ceremonial.* During the *So'i* feasts among the Southern Massim, women carrying polished axe blades in fine carved handles, accompany with a rhythmic step to the beat of drums, the entry of the pigs and mango saplings into the village. . . . As this is part of the ceremony and the axes are an indispensable accessory, their use in this case can be legitimately called "ceremonial." Again, in certain magical ceremonies in the Trobriands, the *towosi* (garden magician) has to carry a mounted axe blade on his shoulders, and with it he delivers a ritual blow at a *kamkokola* structure. . . .

The *vaygu'a*—the Kula valuables—in one of their aspects are overgrown objects of use. They are also, however, *ceremonial* objects in the narrow and correct sense of the word. This will become clear after perusal of the following pages, and to this point we shall return in the last chapter.

It must be kept in mind that here we are trying to obtain a clear and vivid idea of what the Kula valuables are to the natives, and not to give a detailed and circumstantial description of them, nor to define them with precision. The comparison with the European heirlooms or Crown Jewels was given in order to show that this type of ownership is not entirely a fantastic South Sea custom, untranslatable into our ideas. For— and this is a point I want to stress—the comparison I have made is not based on purely external, superficial similarity. The psychological and sociological forces at work are the same, it is really the same mental attitude which makes us value our heirlooms, and makes the natives in New Guinea value their *vaygu'a.*

IV

The exchange of these two classes of *vaygu'a,* of the arm-shells and the necklaces, constitutes the main act of the Kula. This exchange is not done freely, right and left, as opportunity offers, and where the whim leads. It is subject indeed to strict limitations and regulations. One of these refers to the sociology of the exchange, and entails that Kula transactions can be done only between partners. A man who is in the Kula—for not everyone within its district is entitled to carry it on—has only a limited number of people with whom he deals. This partnership is entered upon in a definite manner, under fulfillment of certain formalities, and it constitutes a life-long relationship. The number of partners a man has varies with his rank and importance. A commoner in the Trobriands would have a few partners only, whereas a chief would number hundreds of them. There is no special social mechanism to limit the partnership of some people and extend that of the others, but a man would naturally know to what number of partners he was entitled by his rank and position. And there would be always the example of his immediate ancestors to guide him. In other tribes, where the distinction of rank is not so pronounced, an old man of standing, or a headman of a hamlet or village would also have hundreds of Kula associates, whereas a man of minor importance would have but few.

Two Kula partners have to *kula* with one another, and exchange other gifts incidentally; they behave as friends, and have a number of mutual duties and obligations, which vary with the distance between their villages and with their reciprocal status. An average man has a few partners near by, as a rule his relations-in-law or his friends, and with these partners, he is generally on very friendly terms. The Kula partnership is one of the special bonds which unite two men into one of the standing relations of mutual exchange of gifts and services so characteristic of these natives. Again, the average man will have one or two chiefs in his or in the neighbouring districts with whom he *kulas.* In such a case, he would be bound to assist and serve them in various ways, and to offer them the pick of his *vaygu'a* when he gets a fresh supply. On the other hand he would expect them to be specially liberal to him.

The overseas partner is, on the other hand, a host, patron and ally in a land of danger and insecurity. Nowadays, though the feeling of danger still persists, and natives never feel safe and comfortable in a strange district, this danger is rather felt as a magical one, and it is more the fear of foreign sorcery that besets them. In olden days, more tangible dangers were apprehended, and the partner was the main guarantee of safety. He also provides with food, gives presents, and his house, though never used to sleep in, is the place in which to foregather while in the village. Thus the Kula partnership provides every man within its ring with a few friends near at hand, and with some friendly allies in the far-away, dangerous, foreign districts. These are the only people with whom he can *kula,* but, of course, amongst all his partners, he is free to choose to which one he will offer which object.

Let us now try to cast a broad glance at the cumulative effects of the rules of partnership. We see that all around the ring of Kula there is a network of relationships, and that naturally the whole forms one interwoven fabric. Men living at hundreds of miles' sailing distance from one another are bound together by direct or intermediate partnership, exchange with each other, know of each other, and on certain occasions meet in a large inter-tribal gathering. . . . Objects given by one, in time reach some very distant indirect partner or other, and not only Kula objects, but various articles of domestic use and minor gifts. It is easy to see that in the long run, not only objects of material culture, but also customs, songs, art motives and general cultural influences travel along the Kula route. It is a vast, inter-tribal net of relationships, a big institution, consisting of thousands of men,—all bound together by one common passion for Kula exchange, and secondarily, by many minor ties and interests.[10]

Returning again to the personal aspect of the Kula, let us take a concrete example, that of *an average man* who lives, let us assume, in the village of Sinaketa, an important Kula centre in the Southern Trobriands. He has a few partners, near and far, but they again fall into categories, those who give him arm-shells, and those who give him necklaces. For it is naturally an invariable rule of the Kula that arm-shells and necklaces are never received from the same man, since they must travel in different directions. If one partner gives the arm-shells, and I return to him a necklace, all future operations have to be of the same type. More than that, the nature of the operation between me, the man of Sinaketa, and my partner, is determined by our relative positions with regard to the points of the compass. Thus I, in Sinaketa, would receive from the North and East only arm-shells; from the South and West, necklaces are given to me. If I have a near partner next door to me, if his abode is North or East of mine, he will always be giving me arm-shells and receiving necklaces from me. If, at a later time, he were to shift his residence within the village, the old relationship would obtain, but if he became a member of another village community on the other side of me the relationship would be reversed. The partners in villages to the North of Sinaketa, in the district of Luba, Kulumata, or Kiriwina all supply me with arm-shells. These I hand over to my partners in the South, and receive from them necklaces. The South in this case means the southern districts of Boyowa, as well as the Amphletts and Dobu.

Thus every man has to obey definite rules as to the geographical direction of his transactions. At any point in the Kula ring, if we imagine him turned towards the centre of the circle, he receives the arm-shells with his left hand, and the necklaces with his right, and then hands them both on. In other words, he constantly passes the arm-shells from left to right, and the necklaces from right to left.

Applying this rule of personal conduct to the whole Kula ring, we can see at once what the aggregate result is. The sum total of exchanges will not result in an aimless shifting of the two classes of article, in a fortuitous come and go of the arm-shells and necklaces. Two continuous streams will constantly flow on, the one of necklaces

---

[10] Following Spencer's organic analogy, functionalists tended to see societies as collections of interrelated parts that worked together to promote the society's smooth functioning and equilibrium. Malinowski's emphasis on the Kula as a mechanism for establishing ties between people on different islands is apparent in the previous few paragraphs. He characterizes the Kula as a "vast, intertribal net of relationships."

following the hands of a clock, and the other, composed of the arm-shells, in the opposite direction. We see thus that it is quite correct to speak of the *circular* exchange of the Kula, of a ring or circuit of moving articles (comp. Map V). On this ring, all the villages are placed in a definitely fixed position with regard to one another, so that one is always on either the arm-shell or on the necklace side of the other.

Now we pass to another rule of the Kula, of the greatest importance. As just explained "the arm-shells and shellstrings always travel in their own respective directions on the ring, and they are never, under any circumstances, traded back in the wrong direction. Also, they never stop. It seems almost incredible at first, but it is the fact, nevertheless, that no one ever keeps any of the Kula valuables for any length of time. Indeed, in the whole of the Trobriands there are perhaps only one or two specially fine armshells and shell necklaces permanently owned as heirlooms, and these are set apart as a special class, and are once and for all out of the Kula. 'Ownership,' therefore, in Kula, is quite a special economic relation. A man who is in the Kula never keeps any article for longer than, say, a year or two. Even this exposes him to the reproach of being niggardly, and certain districts have the bad reputation of being 'slow' and 'hard' in the Kula. On the other hand, each man has an enormous number of articles passing through his hands during his life time, of which he enjoys a temporary possession, and which he keeps in trust for a time. This possession hardly ever makes him use the articles, and he remains under the obligation soon again to hand them on to one of his partners. But the temporary ownership allows him to draw a great deal of renown, to exhibit his article, to tell how he obtained it, and to plan to whom he is going to give it. And all this forms one of the favourite

subjects of tribal conversation and gossip, in which the feats and the glory in Kula of chiefs or commoners are constantly discussed and re-discussed."[c] Thus every article moves in one direction only, never comes back, never permanently stops, and takes as a rule some two to ten years to make the round.[11]

This feature of the Kula is perhaps its most remarkable one, since it creates a new type of ownership, and places the two Kula articles in a class of their own. Here we can return to the comparison drawn between the *vaygu'a* (Kiriwinian valuables) and the European heirlooms. This comparison broke down on one point: in the European objects of this class, permanent ownership, lasting association with the hereditary dignity or rank or with a family, is one of its main features.

In this the Kula articles differ from heirlooms, but resemble another type of valued object, that is, trophies, gauges of superiority, sporting cups, objects which are kept for a time only by the winning party, whether a group or an individual. Though held only in trust, only for a period, though never used in any utilitarian way, yet the holders get from them a special type of pleasure by the mere fact of owning them, of being entitled to them. Here again, it is not only a superficial, external resemblance, but very much the same mental attitude, favoured by similar social arrangements. The resemblance goes so far that in the Kula there exists also the element of pride in merit, an element which forms the main ingredient in the pleasure felt by a man or group holding a trophy. Success in Kula is ascribed to special, personal power, due mainly to magic, and men are very proud of it. Again, the whole community glories in a specially fine Kula trophy, obtained by one of its members.

All the rules so far enumerated—looking at them from the individual point of view—limit the social range and the direction of the

---

[11] Malinowski was concerned with differentiating his brand of functionalism from that of A. R. Radcliffe-Brown (see essay 14). Malinowski's theory was derived from his personal experiences in the field and was concerned with behavior within a cultural context, whereas Radcliffe-Brown studied social structure as an abstract representation that he believed existed independent of human beings. One of the most important differences between the two theorists was that Malinowski believed in the importance of individuals within a culture. Here he speaks of the Kula as many individual transactions taking place simultaneously. Radcliffe-Brown, on the other hand, believed that the study of culture as individual human behavior was impossible.

transactions as well as the duration of owner-ship of the articles. Looking at them from the point of view of their integral effect, they shape the general outline of the Kula, give it the char-acter of the double-closed circuit. Now a few words must be said about the nature of each in-dividual transaction, in so far as its *commercial technicalities* are concerned. Here very definite rules also obtain.

V

The main principle underlying the regulations of actual exchange is that the Kula consists in the bestowing of a ceremonial gift, which has to be repaid by an equivalent counter-gift, after a lapse of time, be it a few hours or even minutes, though sometimes as much as a year or more may elapse between payments.[d] But it can never be exchanged from hand to hand with the equivalence between the two objects discussed, bargained about and computed. The decorum of the Kula transaction is strictly kept, and highly valued. The natives sharply distinguish it from barter, which they practise extensively, of which they have a clear idea, and for which they have a settled term—in Kiriwinian: *gimwali*. Often, when criticising an incorrect, too hasty, or indecorous procedure of Kula, they will say: "He conducts his Kula as if it were *gimwali*."

The second very important principle is that the equivalence of the counter-gift is left to the giver, and cannot be enforced by any kind of co-ercion. A partner who has received a Kula gift is expected to give back fair and full value, that is, to give as good an arm-shell as the necklace he receives, or vice versa. Again, a very fine article must be replaced by one of equivalent value, and not by several minor ones, though intermediate gifts may be given to mark time before the real repayment takes place.[12]

If the article given as counter-gift is not equivalent, the recipient will be disappointed and angry, but he has no direct means of re-dress, no means of coercing his partner, or of putting an end to the whole transaction. What then are the forces at work which keep the part-ners to the terms of the bargain? Here we come up against a very important feature of the na-tive's mental attitude towards wealth and value. The great misconception of attributing to the savage a pure economic nature, might lead us to reason incorrectly thus: "The passion of acquir-ing, the loathing to lose or give away, is the fun-damental and most primitive element in man's attitude to wealth. In primitive man, this primi-tive characteristic will appear in its simplest and purest form. *Grab and never let go* will be the guiding principle of his life."[e] The fundamental error in this reasoning is that it assumes that "primitive man," as represented by the present-day savage, lives, at least in economic matters, untrammeled by conventions and social restric-tions. Quite the reverse is the case. Although, like every human being, the Kula native loves to possess and therefore desires to acquire and dreads to lose, the social code of rules, with re-gard to give and take by far overrides his natural acquisitive tendency.[13]

---

[12] Malinowski's Kula description is considered one of the seminal works in the development of economic anthro-pology and had a major impact on scholars of his day. Mauss, for example, believed the Kula was similar to the potlatch, and he frequently references *Argonauts of the Western Pacific* in *The Gift,* which was published three years after *Argonauts.* The first two principles of the Kula outlined at the start of this section are fundamental ele-ments of prestation adopted and discussed by Mauss in his work (see essay 7).

[13]Structural functionalists such as Radcliffe-Brown trace their intellectual descent directly from Durkheim. Malinowski

was a bitter rival of Radcliffe-Brown, but he too was influ-enced by the French sociologist. In one article Malinowski called social structure a "vast conditioning apparatus" (Malinowski 1939), and here he says it overrides a person's natural acquisitiveness. In some respects these comments seem to echo Durkheim's definition of a social fact (essay 5), but there are critical differences. Durkheim emphasized the independent nature of the collective conscience, which he believed had an existence apart from any individual and operated by its own laws. Malinowski, on the other hand, believed that culture existed to serve human needs and that, ultimately, these needs were individual physiological and psychological requirements.

This social code, such as we find it among the natives of the Kula is, however, far from weakening the natural desirability of possession; on the contrary, it lays down that to possess is to be great, and that wealth is the indispensable appanage of social rank and attribute of personal virtue. But the important point is that with them to possess is to give—and here the natives differ from us notably. A man who owns a thing is naturally expected to share it, to distribute it, to be its trustee and dispenser. And the higher the rank the greater the obligation. A chief will naturally be expected to give food to any stranger, visitor, even loiterer from another end of the village. He will be expected to share any of the betel-nut or tobacco he has about him. So that a man of rank will have to hide away any surplus of these articles which he wants to preserve for his further use. In the Eastern end of New Guinea a type of large basket, with three layers, manufactured in the Trobriands, was specially popular among people of consequence, because one could hide away one's small treasures in the lower compartments. Thus the main symptom of being powerful is to be wealthy, and of wealth is to be generous. Meanness, indeed, is the most despised vice, and the only thing about which the natives have strong moral views, while generosity is the essence of goodness.

This moral injunction and ensuing habit of generosity, superficially observed and misinterpreted, is responsible for another wide-spread misconception, that of the *primitive communism of savages*. This, quite as much as the diametrically opposed figment of the acquisitive and ruthlessly tenacious native, is definitely erroneous, and this will be seen with sufficient clearness in the following chapters.[14]

Thus the fundamental principle of the natives' moral code in this matter makes a man do his fair share in Kula transaction and the more important he is, the more will he desire to shine by his generosity. *Noblesse oblige*[15] is in reality the social norm regulating their conduct. This does not mean that people are always satisfied, and that there are no squabbles about the transactions, no resentments and even feuds. It is obvious that, however much a man may want to give a good equivalent for the object received, he may not be able to do so. And then, as there is always a keen competition to be the most generous giver, a man who has received less than he gave will not keep his grievance to himself, but will brag about his own generosity and compare it to his partner's meanness; the other resents it, and the quarrel is ready to break out. But it is very important to realise that there is no actual haggling, no tendency to do a man out of his share. The giver is quite as keen as the receiver that the gift should be generous, though for different reasons. Then, of course, there is the important consideration that a man who is fair and generous in the Kula will attract a larger stream to himself than a mean one.[16]

The two main principles, namely, first that the Kula is a gift repaid after an interval of time by a counter-gift, and not a bartering; and second, that the equivalent rests with the giver, and cannot be enforced, nor can there be any haggling or going back on the exchange—these underlie all the transactions. A concrete outline of how they are carried on, will give a sufficient preliminary idea.

"Let us suppose that I, a Sinaketa man, am in possession of a pair of big arm-shells. An overseas expedition from Dobu in the d'Entrecasteaux

---

[14] Malinowski was writing just a few years after the Russian Revolution, when communist rhetoric was fashionable in Europe and the United States. This comment on primitive communism is a critique of the Marxist five-stage theory of history—Marx had suggested that European society had evolved through stages of primitive communism, ancient slave societies, feudalism, and capitalism. He believed that this evolution would end with the stage of socialism-communism. Many Marxists believed these stages could be found in all societies.

[15] *Noblesse oblige:* benevolent and honorable behavior, originally thought to be an obligation of persons of high rank.

[16] Notice how Malinowski acknowledges the presence of conflict but minimizes its effect. For him, conflict exists but does not drive the system; rather, it is an aberration in what is generally a smoothly functioning organism.

Archipelago, arrives at my village. Blowing a conch shell, I take my arm-shell pair and I offer it to my overseas partner, with some words as 'This is a *vaga* (opening gift)—in due time, thou returnest to me a big *soulava* (necklace) for it!' Next year, when I visit my partner's village, he either is in possession of an equivalent necklace, and this he gives to me as *yotile* (return gift), or he has not a necklace good enough to repay my last gift. In this case he will give me a small necklace—avowedly not equivalent to my gift—and he will give it to me as *basi* (intermediary gift). This means that the main gift has to be repaid on a future occasion, and the *basi* is given in token of good faith—but it, in turn, must be repaid by me in the meantime by a gift of small arm-shells. The final gift, which will be given to me to clinch the whole transaction, would then be called *kudu* (clinching gift) in contrast to *basi*" (loc. cit., p. 99).

Although haggling and bargaining are completely ruled out of the Kula, there are customary and regulated ways of bidding for a piece of *vaygu'a* known to be in the possession of one's partner. This is done by the offer of what we shall call solicitary gifts, of which there are several types. "If I, an inhabitant of Sinaketa, happen to be in possession of a pair of arm-shells more than usually good, the fame of it spreads, for it must be remembered that each one of the first-class arm-shells and necklaces has a personal name and a history of its own, and as they circulate around the big ring of the Kula, they are all well known, and their appearance in a given district always creates a sensation. Now, all my partners—whether from overseas or from within the district—compete for the favour of receiving this particular article of mine, and those who are specially keen try to obtain it by giving me *pokala* (offerings) and *kaributu* (solicitary gifts). The former (*pokala*) consist as a rule of pigs, especially fine bananas, and yams or taro; the latter (*kaributu*) are of greater value: the valuable, large axe blades (called *beku*), or lime spoons of whale bone are given" (loc. cit., p. 100). The further complication in the repayment of these solicitary gifts and a few more technicalities and technical expressions connected herewith will be given later on in Chapter IV.

VI

I have enumerated the main rules of the Kula in a manner sufficient for a preliminary definition, and now a few words must be said about the associated activities and secondary aspects of the Kula. If we realise that at times the exchange has to take place between districts divided by dangerous seas, over which a great number of people have to travel by sail, and do so keeping to appointed dates, it becomes clear at once that considerable preparations are necessary to carry out the expedition. Many preliminary activities are intimately associated with the Kula. Such are, particularly, the building of canoes, preparation of the outfit, the provisioning of the expedition, the fixing of dates and social organisation of the enterprise. All these are subsidiary to the Kula, and as they are carried on in pursuit of it, and form one connected series, a description of the Kula must embrace an account of these preliminary activities. The detailed account of canoe-building, of the ceremonial attached to it, of the incidental magical rites, of the launching and trial run, of the associated customs which aim at preparing the outfit—all this will be described in detail in the next few chapters.

Another important pursuit inextricably bound up with the Kula, is that of the *secondary trade*. Voyaging to far-off countries, endowed with natural resources unknown in their own homes, the Kula sailors return each time richly laden with these, the spoils of their enterprise. Again, in order to be able to offer presents to his partner, every outward bound canoe carries a cargo of such things as are known to be most desirable in the overseas district. Some of this is given away in presents to the partners, but a good deal is carried in order to pay for the objects desired at home. In certain cases, the visiting natives exploit on their own account during the journey some of the natural resources overseas. For example, the Sinaketans dive for the spondylus in Sanaroa Lagoon, and the Dobuans fish in the Trobriands on a beach on the southern end of the island. The second trade is complicated still more by the fact that such big Kula centres as, for instance, Sinaketa, are not efficient in any of the industries of special value to the Dobuans. Thus,

Sinaketans have to procure the necessary store of goods from the inland villages of Kuboma, and this they do on minor trading expeditions preliminary to the Kula. Like the canoe-building, the secondary trading will be described in detail later on, and has only to be mentioned here.[17]

Here, however, these subsidiary and associated activities must be put in proper relation with regard to one another and to the main transaction. Both the canoe-building and the ordinary trade have been spoken of as secondary or subsidiary to the Kula proper. This requires a comment. I do not, by thus subordinating the two things in importance to the Kula mean to express a philosophical reflection or a personal opinion as to the relative value of these pursuits from the point of view of some social teleology. Indeed, it is clear that if we look at the acts from the outside, as comparative sociologists and gauge their real utility, trade and canoe-building will appear to us as the really important achievements, whereas we shall regard the Kula only as an indirect stimulus, impelling the natives to sail and to trade. Here, however, I am not dealing in sociological, but in pure ethnographical description and any sociological analysis I have given is only what has been absolutely indispensable to clear away misconceptions and to define terms.[f,18]

By ranging the Kula as the primary and chief activity, and the rest as secondary ones, I mean that this precedence is implied in the institutions themselves. By studying the behaviour of the natives and all the customs in question, we see that the Kula is in all respects the main aim: the dates are fixed, the preliminaries settled, the expeditions arranged, the social organisation determined, not with regard to trade, but with regard to Kula. On an expedition, the big ceremonial feast, held at the start, refers to the Kula; the final ceremony of reckoning and counting the spoil refers to Kula, not to the objects of trade obtained. Finally, the magic, which is one of the main factors of all the procedure, refers only to the Kula, and this applies even to a part of the magic carried out over the canoe. Some rites in the whole cycle are done for the sake of the canoe itself, and others for the sake of Kula. The construction of the canoes is always carried on directly in connection with a Kula expedition. All this, of course, will become really clear and convincing only after the detailed account is given. But it was necessary at this point to set the right perspective in the relation between the main Kula and the trade.

Of course not only many of the surrounding tribes who know nothing of the Kula do build canoes and sail far and daringly on trading expeditions, but even within the Kula ring, in the Trobriands for instance, there are several villages who do not *kula,* yet have canoes and carry on energetic overseas trade. But where the Kula is practiced, it governs all the other allied activities, and canoe-building and trade are made subsidiary to it. And this is expressed both by the nature of the institutions and the working of all the arrangements on the one hand, and by the

---

[17] Later theorists were critical of Malinowski's comments on the nature of primitive economies. Malinowski insisted that the Kula was a rational system directed toward nonrational ends, that is, the exchange of items with only symbolic value. Because of this he gives little weight to the fact that the offerings given to induce a partner to part with good *vaygu'a* are utilitarian items such as pigs, bananas, yams, and axe blades. Although this secondary trade is repeatedly mentioned, Malinowski does not analyze it to see if participants gain an economic benefit. Critics suggest that in insisting that his perspective on the Kula is the right one, Malinowski ignores the data that disprove his theory.

[18] Malinowski's footnote is important because it is directed at the diffusionists and the Boasians, whose ideas were popular at this time. Participant observation and the integration of culture were central aspects of the work of Franz Boas (see essay 9), and Malinowski's work consistently incorporates these ideas. However, Boas and Malinowski disagreed on the importance of history. Boas believed that the current state of a culture could only be understood through the study of its history. Malinowski vehemently disagreed. In this note, Malinowski says that reconstructing history is an "unpardonable sin" and that he is unconcerned with searching for origins of institutions, preferring to spend his time working out the interrelations of elements within a society. Similarly, Malinowski dismissed popular diffusionists such as W. H. R. Rivers and Grafton Elliot Smith (1871–1937), who were trying to prove that all culture began in ancient Egypt and diffused from there.

behaviour and explicit statements of the natives on the other.

The Kula—it becomes, I hope, more and more clear—is a big, complicated institution, insignificant though its nucleus might appear. To the natives, it represents one of the most vital interests in life, and as such it has a ceremonial character and is surrounded by magic. We can well imagine that articles of wealth might pass from hand to hand without ceremony or ritual, but in the Kula they never do. Even when at times only small parties in one or two canoes sail overseas and bring back *vaygu'a*, certain taboos are observed, and a customary course is taken in departing, in sailing, and in arriving; even the smallest expedition in one canoe is a tribal event of some importance, known and spoken of over the whole district. But the characteristic expedition is one in which a considerable number of canoes take part, organised in a certain manner, and forming one body. Feasts, distributions of food and other public ceremonies are held, there is one leader and master of the expedition, and various rules are adhered to, in addition to the ordinary Kula taboos and observances.

The ceremonial nature of the Kula is strictly bound up with another of its aspects—magic. "The belief in the efficiency of magic dominates the Kula, as it does ever so many other tribal activities of the natives. Magical rites must be performed over the sea-going canoe when it is built, in order to make it swift, steady and safe; also magic is done over a canoe to make it lucky in the Kula. Another system of magical rites is done in order to avert the dangers of sailing. The third system of magic connected with overseas expeditions is the *mwasila* or the Kula magic proper. This system consists in numerous rites and spells, all of which act directly on the mind

(*nanola*) of one's partner, and make him soft, unsteady in mind, and eager to give Kula gifts" (loc. cit., p. 100).[19]

It is clear that an institution so closely associated with magical and ceremonial elements, as is the Kula, not only rests on a firm, traditional foundation, but also has its large store of legend. "There is a rich mythology of the Kula in which stories are told about far-off times when mythical ancestors sailed on distant and daring expeditions. Owing to their magical knowledge they were able to escape dangers to conquer their enemies, to surmount obstacles, and by their feats they established many a precedent which is now closely followed by tribal custom. But their importance for their descendants lies mainly in the fact that they handed on their magic, and this made the Kula possible for the following generations" (loc. cit., p. 100).

The Kula is also associated in certain districts, to which the Trobriands do not belong, with the mortuary feasts called *so'i*. The association is interesting and important and in Chapter XX an account of it will be given.

The big Kula expeditions are carried on by a great number of natives, a whole district together. But the geographical limits, from which the members of an expedition are recruited, are well defined. Glancing at Map V, "we see a number of circles, each of which represents a certain sociological unit which we shall call a Kula community. A Kula community consists of a village or a number of villages, who go out together on big overseas expeditions, and who act as a body in the Kula transactions, perform their magic in common, have common leaders, and have the same outer and inner social sphere, within which they exchange their valuables. The Kula consists, therefore, first of the small, internal transactions within a Kula community or contiguous communities, and secondly, of

---

[19] Magic plays an important role in Trobriand Island society, and Malinowski discusses the subject in other chapters of *Argonauts* and in his later works *Magic, Science, and Religion* (1954 [1925]) and *Coral Gardens and Their Magic* (1935). Malinowski was reacting against the theory of one of his mentors, Sir James Frazer. Frazer, a popular theorist of anthropology and religion, argued that people in primitive societies had magical beliefs and other superstitions because they had some form of primitive mentality and were incapable of scientific thought. Concerned with presenting people in simple societies as rational, Malinowski was careful to distinguish the contexts in which magic was used. He argued that the Trobrianders were just as intelligent as anyone else and used magic in circumstances that were beyond rational control. Thus, magic had a psychological function: to reassure individuals in unpredictable situations.

the big overseas expeditions in which the exchange of articles takes place between two communities divided by the sea. In the first, there is a chronic, permanent trickling of articles from one village to another, and even within the village. In the second, a whole lot of valuables, amounting to over a thousand articles at a time, are exchanged in one enormous transaction, or, more correctly, in ever so many transactions taking place simultaneously" (loc. cit., p. 101).[20] "The Kula trade consists of a series of such periodical overseas expeditions, which link together the various island groups, and annually bring over big quantities of *vaygu'a* and of subsidiary trade from one district to another. The trade is used and used up, but the *vaygu'a*—the arm-shells and necklets—go round and round the ring" (loc. cit., p. 105).

In this chapter, a short, summary definition of the Kula has been given. I enumerated one after the other its most salient features, the most remarkable rules as they are laid down in native custom, belief and behaviour. This was necessary in order to give a general idea of the institution before describing its working in detail. But no abridged definition can give to the reader the full understanding of a human social institution. It is necessary for this, to explain its working concretely, to bring the reader into contact with the people, show how they proceed at each successive stage, and to describe all the actual manifestations of the general rules laid down in abstract.

As has been said above, the Kula exchange is carried on by enterprises of two sorts; first there are the big overseas expeditions, in which a more or less considerable amount of valuables are carried at one time. Then there is the inland trade in which the articles are passed from hand to hand, often changing several owners before they move a few miles.

The big overseas expeditions are by far the more spectacular part of the Kula. They also contain much more public ceremonial, magical ritual, and customary usage. They require also, of course, more of preparation and preliminary activity. I shall therefore have a good deal more to say about the overseas Kula expeditions than about the internal exchange.

As the Kula customs and beliefs have been mainly studied in Boyowa, that is, the Trobriand Islands, and from the Boyowan point of view, I shall describe, in the first place, the typical course of an overseas expedition, as it is prepared, organized, and carried out from the Trobriands. Beginning with the construction of the canoes, proceeding to the ceremonial launching and the visits of formal presentation of canoes, we shall choose then the community of Sinaketa, and follow the natives on one of their overseas trips, describing it in all details. This will serve us as a type of a Kula expedition to distant lands. It will then be indicated in what particulars such expeditions may differ in other branches of the Kula, and for this purpose I shall describe an expedition from Dobu, and one between Kiriwina and Kitava. An account of inland Kula in the Trobriands, of some associated forms of trading and of Kula in the remaining branches will complete the account.

In the next chapter I pass, therefore, to the preliminary stages of the Kula, in the Trobriands, beginning with a description of the canoes.

NOTES

[a] By "current view," I mean such as is to be found in textbooks and in passing remarks, scattered through economic and ethnological literature. As a matter of fact, Economics is a subject very seldom touched upon either in theoretical works or Ethnology, or in accounts of field-work. I have enlarged on this deficiency in the article on "Primitive Economics," published in the *Economic Journal*, March, 1921.

The best analysis of the problem of savage economy is to be found, in spite of its many shortcomings, in K. Bücher's "Industrial Evolution," English translation, 1901. On primitive trade, however, his views are inadequate. In accordance with his general view that savages have no national economy, he maintains that any spread of goods among natives is achieved by non-economic means, such as robbery, tributes and gifts. The information contained in the present volume is incompatible with Bücher's views, nor could he have maintained them had he been acquainted with

---

[20] The above paragraphs demonstrate Malinowski's belief that culture was a system of interrelated parts. One cannot study the Kula alone, because it is interconnected with other aspects of Trobriand life such as canoe-building, magic, and family structure. Spencer's organic analogy can be seen behind Malinowski's model of the Kula. The Kula is a system in a physical sense; it can be diagrammed like the circulatory system of the body.

[a]Barton's description of the Hiri (contained in Seligman's "Melanesians").

A summary of the research done on Primitive Economics, showing, incidentally, how little real, sound work has been accomplished, will be found in Pater W. Kopper's "Die Ethnologische Wirtschaftsforschung" in *Anthropos*, X–XI, 1915–16, pp. 611–651, and 971–1079. The article is very useful, where the author summarises the views of others.

[b]Professor C. G. Seligman, op. cit., p. 93, states that arm-shells, *toea*, as they are called by the Motu, are traded from the Port Moresby district westward to the Gulf of Papua. Among the Motu and Koita, near Port Moresby, they are highly valued, and nowadays attain very high prices, up to £30, much more than is paid for the same article among the Massim.

[c]This and the following quotations are from the Author's preliminary article on the Kula in *Man*, July, 1920. Article number 51, p. 100.

[d]In order not to be guilty of inconsistency in using loosely the word "ceremonial" I shall define it briefly. I shall call an action ceremonial, if it is (1) public; (2) carried on under observance of definite formalities; (3) if it has sociological, religious, or magical import, and it carries with it obligations.

[e]This is not a fanciful construction of what an erroneous opinion might be, for I could give actual examples proving that such opinions have been set forth, but as I am not giving here a criticism of existing theories of Primitive Economics, I do not want to overload this chapter with quotations.

[f]It is hardly necessary perhaps to make it quite clear that all questions of origins of development or history of the institutions have been rigorously ruled out of this work. The mixing up of speculative or hypothetical views with an account of facts is, in my opinion an unpardonable sin against ethnographic method.

---

14. *On Joking Relationships*[a]

A. R. RADCLIFFE-BROWN (1881–1955)

THE PUBLICATION OF Mr. F. J. Pedler's note[b] on what are called "joking relationships", following on two other papers on the same subject by Professor Henri Labouret[c] and Mademoiselle Denise Paulme,[d] suggests that some general theoretical discussion of the nature of these relationships may be of interest to readers of Africa[e,1]

What is meant by the term "joking relationship" is a relation between two persons in which one is by custom permitted, and in some instances required, to tease or make fun of the other, who in turn is required to take no offence. It is important to distinguish two main varieties. In one the relation is symmetrical; each of the two persons teases or makes fun of the other. In

---

(1940)

[1]Radcliffe-Brown begins his essay, which first appeared in the journal *Africa* by mentioning several other anthropologists of his era. F. J. Pedler (1908–1991), later Sir Frederick Pedler, was a colonial administrator and diplomat who became the director of the United Africa Company and wrote several books on Africa. In the note referenced here, Pedler reports on a legal case involving a joking relationship called *utani*. We will return to that case below. Henri Labouret (1878–1959) was a soldier, colonial administrator, linguist, and ethnographer who played a critical role in West African ethnography in the early twentieth century. Denise Paulme (1909–1998) was a student of Marcel Mauss who became one of the leading French Africanist scholars. Her book *Femmes d'Afrique Noire* (1960), a volume of essays about African women written entirely by female anthropologists, is an early classic of feminist anthropology. All of the work cited by Radcliffe-Brown, as well as this essay itself, appeared in the journal *Africa: Journal of the International Africa Institute*. National traditions in anthropology tended to be located in specific places. Much American anthropology was done among Native American groups in the United States or among people living on American controlled territories, particularly in the Pacific Islands. British and French anthropology tended to focus on Africa or Southeast Asia, where these nations had colonial possessions.

the other variety the relation is asymmetrical; A jokes at the expense of B and B accepts the teasing good humouredly but without retaliating; or A teases B as much as he pleases and B in return teases A only a little. There are many varieties in the form of this relationship in different societies. In some instances the joking or teasing is only verbal, in others it includes horse-play; in some the joking includes elements of obscenity, in others not.

Standardized social relationships of this kind are extremely widespread, not only in Africa but also in Asia, Oceania and North America. To arrive at a scientific understanding of the phenomenon it is necessary to make a wide comparative study. Some material for this now exists in anthropological literature, though by no means all that could be desired, since it is unfortunately still only rarely that such relationships are observed and described as exactly as they might be.[2]

The joking relationship is a peculiar combination of friendliness and antagonism. The behavior is such that in any other social context it would express and arouse hostility; but it is not meant seriously and must not be taken seriously. There is a pretence of hostility and a real friendliness. To put it in another way, the relationship is one of permitted disrespect. Thus any complete theory of it must be part of, or consistent with, a theory of the place of respect in social relations and in social life generally. But this is a very wide and very important sociological problem; for it is evident that the whole maintenance of a social order depends upon the appropriate kind and degree of respect being shown towards certain persons, things and ideas or symbols.[3]

Examples of joking relationships between relatives by marriage are very commonly found in Africa and in other parts of the world. Thus Mademoiselle Paulme[f] records that among the

Dogon a man stands in a joking relationship to his wife's sisters and their daughters. Frequently the relationship holds between a man and both the brothers and sisters of his wife. But in some instances there is a distinction whereby a man is on joking terms with his wife's younger brothers and sisters but not with those who are older than she is. This joking with the wife's brothers and sisters is usually associated with a custom requiring extreme respect, often partial or complete avoidance, between a son-in-law and his wife's parents.[8]

The kind of structural situation in which the associated customs of joking and avoidance are found may be described as follows. A marriage involves a readjustment of the social structure whereby the woman's relations with her family are greatly modified and she enters into a new and very close relation with her husband. The latter is at the same time brought into a special relation with his wife's family, to which, however, he is an outsider. For the sake of brevity, though at the risk of over-simplification, we will consider only the husband's relation to his wife's family. The relation can be described as involving both attachment and separation, both social conjunction and social disjunction, if I may use the terms. The man has his own definite position in the social structure, determined for him by his birth into a certain family, lineage or clan. The great body of his rights and duties and the interests and activities that he shares with others are the result of his position. Before the marriage his wife's family are outsiders for him as he is an outsider for them. This constitutes a social disjunction which is not destroyed by the marriage. The social conjunction results from the continuance, though in altered form, of the wife's relation to her family, their continued interest in her and in her children. If the wife were really bought

---

[2] Note that Radcliffe-Brown says his goal is to provide a scientific understanding of joking relationships. He hoped to make anthropology a science and believed that it was possible to discover universal laws and principles underlying the structure of human society. These laws were to be discovered through the comparative analysis of social structure.

[3] Following Durkheim, and using the concept of the organic analogy developed by Spencer, Radcliffe-Brown's key concern was the maintenance of social order. He understood society as composed of a series of institutions, each of which could be understood in terms of its function (hence functionalism). Its function was the role it played in maintaining social order.

and paid for, as ignorant persons say that she is in Africa, there would be no place for any permanent close relation of a man with his wife's family. But though slaves can be bought, wives cannot.[4]

Social disjunction implies divergence of interests and therefore the possibility of conflict and hostility, while conjunction requires the avoidance of strife. How can a relation which combines the two be given a stable, ordered form? There are two ways of doing this. One is to maintain between two persons so related an extreme mutual respect and a limitation of direct personal contact. This is exhibited in the very formal relations that are, in so many societies, characteristic of the behavior of a son-in-law on the one side and his wife's father and mother on the other. In its most extreme form there is complete avoidance of any social contact between a man and his mother-in-law.

This avoidance must not be mistaken for a sign of hostility. One does, of course, if one is wise, avoid having too much to do with one's enemies, but that is quite a different matter. I once asked an Australian native why he had to avoid his mother-in-law, and his reply was, "Because she is my best friend in the world; she has given me my wife". The mutual respect between son-in-law and parents-in-law is a mode of friendship. It prevents conflict that might arise through divergence of interest.

The alternative to this relation of extreme mutual respect and restraint is the joking relationship, one, that is, of mutual disrespect and licence. Any serious hostility is prevented by the playful antagonism of teasing, and this in its regular repetition is a constant expression or reminder of that social disjunction which is one of the essential components of the relation, while the social conjunction is maintained by the friendliness that takes no offence at insult.[5]

The discrimination within the wife's family between those who have to be treated with extreme respect and those with whom it is a duty to be disrespectful is made on the basis of generation and sometimes of seniority within the generation. The usual respected relatives are those of the first ascending generation, the wife's mother and her sisters, the wife's father and his brothers, sometimes the wife's mother's brother. The joking relatives are those of a person's own generation; but very frequently a distinction of seniority within the generation is made; a wife's older sister or brother may be respected while those younger will be teased.

In certain societies a man may be said to have relatives by marriage long before he marries and indeed as soon as he is born into the world. This is provided by the institution of the required or preferential marriage. We will, for the sake of brevity, consider only one kind of such organisations. In many societies it is regarded as preferable that a man should marry the daughter of his mother's brother; this is a form of the custom known as cross-cousin marriage. Thus his female cousins of this kind, or all those women whom by the classificatory system he classifies as such, are potential wives for him, and their brothers are his potential brothers-in-law. Among the Ojibwa Indians of North America, the Chiga of Uganda, and in Fiji and New Caledonia, as well as elsewhere, this form of marriage is found and is accompanied by a joking relationship between a man and the sons and daughters of his mother's brother. To quote one instance of these, the following is recorded for the Ojibwa. "When cross-cousins meet they must try to embarrass one another. They 'joke' one another, making the most vulgar allegations, by their standards as well as ours. But being 'kind' relations, no one can take offence. Cross-cousins who do not joke in this

---

[4] Radcliffe-Brown sees a critical contradiction at the core of marriage. A husband does not become part of his wife's family but neither is he entirely separate from them. A wife does not become part of her husband's family, and her family of origin continues to have interest in her and her children. This contradiction creates the preconditions for conflict between the two families. For society to function

smoothly there must be an institution to resolve this conflict.

[5] Thus, society functions smoothly because the contradiction between husband and wife's family is resolved either by avoidance or joking. Radcliffe-Brown shows that these are two related phenomena.

way are considered boorish, as not playing the social game."[h]

The joking relationship here is of fundamentally the same kind as that already discussed. It is established before marriage and is continued, after marriage, with the brothers- and sisters-in-law.

In some parts of Africa there are joking relationships that have nothing to do with marriage. Mr. Pedler's note, mentioned above, refers to a joking relationship between two distinct tribes, the Sukuma and the Zaramu, and in the evidence it was stated that there was a similar relation between the Sukuma and the Zigua and between the Ngoni and the Bemba. The woman's evidence suggests that this custom of rough teasing exists in the Sukuma tribe between persons related by marriage, as it does in so many other African tribes.[i,6]

While a joking relationship between two tribes is apparently rare, and certainly deserves, as Mr. Pedler suggests, to be carefully investigated, a similar relationship between clans has been observed in other parts of Africa. It is described by Professor Labouret and Mademoiselle Paulme in the articles previously mentioned, and amongst the Tallensi it has been studied by Dr. Fortes, who will deal with it in a forthcoming publication.[j,7]

The two clans are not, in these instances, specially connected by intermarriage. The relation between them is an alliance involving real friendliness and mutual aid combined with an appearance of hostility.

The general structural situation in these instances seems to be as follows. The individual is a member of a certain defined group, a clan, for example, within which his relations to others are defined by a complex set of rights and duties, referring to all the major aspects of social life, and supported by definite sanctions. There may be another group outside his own which is so linked with his as to be the field of extension of jural and moral relations of the same general kind. Thus, in East Africa, as we learn from Mr. Pedler's note, the Zigua and the Zaramu do not joke with one another because a yet closer bond exists between them since they are ndugu (brothers). But beyond the field within which social relations are thus defined there lie other groups with which, since they are outsiders to the individual's own group, the relation involves possible or actual hostility. In any fixed relations between the members of two such groups the separateness of the groups must be recognised. It is precisely this separateness which is not merely recognised but emphasised when a joking relationship is established. The show of hostility, the perpetual disrespect, is a continual expression of that social disjunction which is an essential part of the whole structural situation, but over which, without destroying or even weakening it, there is

---

[6] Be sure to read Radcliffe-Brown's original footnote here. Pedler had reported a court case involving a joking relationship. Radcliffe-Brown uses this as a springboard to argue that anthropology should be involved in colonial administration. He had been a colonial administrator himself (director of education in Tonga from 1916 to 1920) and like other functionalists, saw service to the colonial administrations as one aim of their work. Malinowski argued, in an article entitled "Practical Anthropology" (1929a), that such service should be a key goal. Then (as today) access to funding was an important reason for stressing the applied aspects of anthropological research: Much of the money that funded research projects came from the Colonial Social Science Research Council. In general, functionalists did not question the basic fact of colonization or the subservient position of the colonized. Both paternalism and social evolutionism were implied in their writings. They believed that benev-

olent colonialism offered native societies the chance for progress. On the other hand, they considered themselves friends of those they studied and argued on their behalf before colonial administrations. Colonial administrations, for their part, were deeply suspicious of anthropologists, considering them too liberal and too close to the natives (Goody 1995). The same Malinowski who authored "Practical Anthropology" also authored the preface to Jomo Kenyatta's *Facing Mount Kenya: The Traditional Life of the Gikuyu* (1979 [1938]). Kenyatta, a student of Malinowski, is better remembered as a leader of Kenya's fight for independence and that nation's first president.

[7] Fortes (1906–1983) was a member of the group of students who gathered around Malinowski and Radcliffe-Brown in the years between World War I and II. He is discussed more fully in the next essay in this volume.

provided the social conjunction of friendliness and mutual aid.

The theory that is here put forward, therefore, is that both the joking relationship which constitutes an alliance between clans or tribes, and that between relatives by marriage, are modes of organising a definite and stable system of social behaviour in which conjunctive and disjunctive components, as I have called them, are maintained and combined.[8]

To provide the full evidence for this theory by following out its implications and examining in detail its application to different instances would take a book rather than a short article. But some confirmation can perhaps be offered by a consideration of the way in which respect and disrespect appear in various kinship relations, even though nothing more can be attempted than a very brief indication of a few significant points.[9]

In studying a kinship system it is possible to distinguish the different relatives by reference to the kind and degree of respect that is paid to them.[k] Although kinship systems vary very much in their details there are certain principles which are found to be very widespread. One of them is that by which a person is required to show a marked respect to relatives belonging to the generation immediately preceding his own. In a majority of societies the father is a relative to whom marked respect must be shown. This is so even in many so-called matrilineal societies, i.e. those which are organised into matrilineal clans or lineages. One can very frequently observe a tendency to extend this attitude of respect to all relatives of the first ascending generation and, further, to persons who are not relatives. Thus in those tribes of East Africa that are organised into age-sets a man is required to show special respect to all men of his father's age-set and to their wives.[10]

The social function of this is obvious. The social tradition is handed down from one generation to the next. For the tradition to be maintained it must have authority behind it. The authority is therefore normally recognised as possessed by members of the preceding generation and it is they who exercise discipline. As a result of this the relation between persons of the two generations usually contains an element of inequality, the parents and those of their generation being in a position of superiority over the children who are subordinate to them. The unequal relation between a father and his son is maintained by requiring the latter to show respect to the former. The relation is asymmetrical.

When we turn to the relation of an individual to his grandparents and their brothers and sisters we find that in the majority of human societies relatives of the second ascending generation are treated with very much less respect than those of the first ascending generation, and instead of a marked inequality there is a tendency to approximate to a friendly equality.

Considerations of space forbid any full discussion of this feature of social structure, which is one of very great importance. There are many instances in which the grandparents and their grandchildren are grouped together in the social

---

[8] Thus, that which is true within a group, is also true between groups. Just as the potential conflicts between husband's and wife's families are resolved by avoidance and joking, so too potential conflicts between related tribes may be resolved by avoidance or joking.

[9] Passages such as this are very typical of Radcliffe-Brown's work. He frequently claims that the idea he wishes to demonstrate or the theory he wishes to prove would require a substantial body of work, but he never provides that work. Radcliffe-Brown constructs his arguments based almost exclusively on his reading of the ethnographic reports of others. His own fieldwork is rarely mentioned. He had done fieldwork among the Andaman Islanders and among the Kariera in Australia but he was

not known for his ethnographic talents and had little interest in writing ethnography. Almost the whole of his work consists of relatively brief essays such as this one, and addresses. He published one full-length ethnography *The Andaman Islanders,* his account of his 1906–1908 fieldwork, but even this was not published until 1922, well over a decade after his return from the field.

[10] Much of Radcliffe-Brown's work focused on kinship. He was guided in this in part by his mentor, W. H. R. Rivers. Rivers, a medical doctor who had joined the 1898 Torres Straits expedition, devised what he called the "genealogical method." He suggested that a truly scientific anthropology could be achieved through the study of kinship (Rivers 1910).

structure in opposition to their children and parents. An important clue to the understanding of the subject is the fact that in the flow of social life through time, in which men are born, become mature and die, the grandchildren replace their grandparents.

In many societies there is an actual joking relationship, usually of a relatively mild kind, between relatives of alternate generations. Grandchildren make fun of their grandparents and of those who are called grandfather and grandmother by the classificatory system of terminology, and these reply in kind.

Grandparents and grandchildren are united by kinship; they are separated by age and by the social difference that results from the fact that as the grandchildren are in process of entering into full participation in the social life of the community the grandparents are gradually retiring from it. Important duties towards his relatives in his own and even more in his parents' generation impose upon an individual many restraints; but with those of the second ascending generation, his grandparents and collateral relatives, there can be, and usually is, established a relationship of simple friendliness relatively free from restraint. In this instance also, it is suggested, the joking relationship is a method of ordering a relation which combines social conjunction and disjunction.

This thesis could, I believe, be strongly supported if not demonstrated by considering the details of these relationships. There is space for only one illustrative point. A very common form of joke in this connection is for the grandchild to pretend that he wishes to marry the grandfather's wife, or that he intends to do so when his grandfather dies, or to treat her as already being his wife. Alternatively the grandfather may pretend that the wife of his grandchild is, or might be, his wife.[1] The point of the joke is the pretence at

ignoring the difference of age between the grandparent and the grandchild.[11]

In various parts of the world there are societies in which a sister's son teases and otherwise behaves disrespectfully towards his mother's brother. In these instances the joking relationship seems generally to be asymmetrical. For example the nephew may take his uncle's property but not vice versa; or, as amongst the Nama Hottentots, the nephew may take a fine beast from his uncle's herd and the uncle in return takes a wretched beast from that of the nephew.[m]

The kind of social structure in which this custom of privileged disrespect to the mother's brother occurs in its most marked forms, for example the Thonga of South-East Africa, Fiji and Tonga in the Pacific, and the Central Siouan tribes of North America, is characterised by emphasis on patrilineal lineage and a marked distinction between relatives through the father and relatives through the mother.

In a former publication[n] I offered an interpretation of this custom of privileged familiarity towards the mother's brother. Briefly it is as follows. For the continuance of a social system children require to be cared for and to be trained. Their care demands affectionate and unselfish devotion; their training requires that they shall be subjected to discipline. In the societies with which we are concerned there is something of a division of function between the parents and other relatives on the two sides. The control and discipline are exercised chiefly by the father and his brothers and generally also by his sisters; these are relatives who must be respected and obeyed. It is the mother who is primarily responsible for the affectionate care; the mother and her brothers and sisters are therefore relatives who can be looked to for assistance and indulgence. The mother's brother is called "male

---

[11] Once again, Radcliffe-Brown alludes to evidence but fails to present anything more than anecdote. At this point, his thesis seems to be that joking is found in relationships where there is conjuncture and disjuncture. As with in-laws and in his examples of other groups, grandchildren are conjoined to their grandparents by being members of the same family but disjoined because they are separated by the generation of parents. This may be true but raises a problem: because we are all individuals, no two human beings have exactly the same interests. Therefore, couldn't any two individuals be said to have both conjoined and disjoined interests? The question highlights the difficulties in trying to explain the behavior of groups of individuals through abstract and generalized theoretical constructs.

mother" in Tonga and in some South African tribes.[12]

I believe that this interpretation of the special position of the mother's brother in these societies has been confirmed by further field work since I wrote the article referred to. But I was quite aware at the time it was written that the discussion and interpretation needed to be supplemented so as to bring them into line with a general theory of the social functions of respect and disrespect.

The joking relationship with the mother's brother seems to fit well with the general theory of such relationships here outlined. A person's most important duties and rights attach him to his paternal relatives, living and dead. It is to his patrilineal lineage or clan that he belongs. For the members of his mother's lineage he is an outsider, though one in whom they have a very special and tender interest. Thus here again there is a relation in which there is both attachment, or conjunction, and separation, or disjunction, between the two persons concerned.

But let us remember that in this instance the relation is asymmetrical.° The nephew is disrespectful and the uncle accepts the disrespect. There is inequality and the nephew is the superior. This is recognised by the natives themselves. Thus in Tonga it is said that the sister's son is a "chief" (eiki) to his mother's brother, and Junod[p] quotes a Thonga native as saying "The uterine nephew is a chief! He takes any liberty he likes with his maternal uncle". Thus the joking relationship with the uncle does not merely annul the usual relation between the two generations, it reverses it. But while the superiority of the father and the father's sister is exhibited in the respect that is shown to them the nephew's superiority to his mother's brother takes the opposite form of permitted disrespect.

It has been mentioned that there is a widespread tendency to feel that a man should show respect towards, and treat as social superiors, his relatives in the generation preceding his own, and the custom of joking with, and at the expense of, the maternal uncle clearly conflicts with this tendency. This conflict between principles of behaviour helps us to understand what seems at first sight a very extraordinary feature of the kinship terminology of the Thonga tribe and the VaNdau tribe in South-East Africa. Amongst the Thonga, although there is a term malume (= male mother) for the mother's brother, this relative is also, and perhaps more frequently, referred to as a grandfather (kokwana) and he refers to his sister's son as his grandchild (ntukulu). In the VaNdau tribe the mother's brother and also the mother's brother's son are called "grandfather" (tetekulu, literally "great father") and their wives are called "grandmother" (mbiya), while the sister's son and the father's sister's son are called "grandchild" (muzukulu).

This apparently fantastic way of classifying relatives can be interpreted as a sort of legal fiction whereby the male relatives of the mother's lineage are grouped together as all standing towards an individual in the same general relation. Since this relation is one of privileged familiarity on the one side, and solicitude and indulgence on the other, it is conceived as being basically the one appropriate for a grandchild and a grandfather. This is indeed in the majority of human societies the relationship in which this pattern of behaviour most frequently occurs. By this legal fiction the mother's brother ceases to belong to the first ascending generation, of which it is felt that the members ought to be respected.[13]

---

[12] The former publication is "Mother's Brother in South Africa," found in the earlier editions of this book. In that essay, in addition to making the point he just described, Radcliffe-Brown argues that matrilineal kinship systems are not survivals of earlier stages of human evolution (as Morgan, Junod, and Bachofen had argued) but a fully functioning part of current-day societies. In the present essay he attempts to place "Mother's Brother" in a more general theory of kin relations.

[13] Keep in mind that in kinship studies (particularly those by functionalist authors) kin names such as "grandfather" or "male mother" refer primarily to behavioral expectations rather than biological linkages. So, if a Thonga youth calls his mother's brother "grandfather," he behaves to him as he behaves to his father's father (whom he also calls "grandfather").

It may be worth while to justify this interpretation by considering another of the legal fictions of the VaNdau terminology. In all these south-eastern Bantu tribes both the father's sister and the sister, particularly the elder sister, are persons who must be treated with great respect. They are also both of them members of a man's own patrilineal lineage. Amongst the VaNdau the father's sister is called "female father" (tetadji) and so also is the sister.[q] Thus by the fiction of terminological classification the sister is placed in the father's generation, the one that appropriately includes persons to whom one must exhibit marked respect.

In the south-eastern Bantu tribes there is assimilation of two kinds of joking relatives, the grandfather and the mother's brother. It may help our understanding of this to consider an example in which the grandfather and the brother-in-law are similarly grouped together. The Cherokee Indians of North America probably numbering at one time about 20,000, were divided into seven matrilineal clans.[r] A man could not marry a woman of his own clan or of his father's clan. Common membership of the same clan connects him with his brothers and his mother's brothers. Towards his father and all his relatives in his father's clan of his own or his father's generation he is required by custom to show a marked respect. He applies the kinship term for "father" not only to his father's brothers but also to the sons of his father's sisters. Here is another example of the same kind of fiction as described above; the relatives of his own generation whom he is required to respect and who belong to his father's matrilineal lineage are spoken of as though they belonged to the generation of his parents. The body of his immediate kindred is included in these two clans, that of his mother and his father. To the other clans of the tribe he is in a sense an outsider. But with two of them he is connected, namely with the clans of his two grandfathers, his father's father and his mother's father. He speaks of all the members of these two clans, of whatever age, as "grandfathers" and "grandmothers". He stands in a joking relationship with all of them. When a man marries he must respect his wife's parents but jokes with her brothers and sisters.

The interesting and critical feature is that it is regarded as particularly appropriate that a man should marry a woman whom he calls "grandmother", i.e. a member of his father's father's clan or his mother's father's clan. If this happens his wife's brothers and sisters, whom he continues to tease, are amongst those whom he previously teased as his "grandfathers" and "grandmothers". This is analogous to the widely spread organisation in which a man has a joking relationship with the children of his mother's brother and is expected to marry one of the daughters.[14]

It ought perhaps to be mentioned that the Cherokee also have a one-sided joking relationship in which a man teases his father's sister's husband. The same custom is found in Mota of the Bank Islands. In both instances we have a society organised on a matrilineal basis in which the mother's brother is respected, the father's sister's son is called "father" (so that the father's sister's husband is the father of a "father"), and there is a special term for the father's sister's husband. Further observation of the societies in which this custom occurs is required before we can be sure of its interpretation. I do not remember that it has been reported from any part of Africa.

What has been attempted in this paper is to define in the most general and abstract terms the kind of structural situation in which we may expect to find well-marked joking relationships. We have been dealing with societies in which the basic social structure is provided by kinship. By reason of his birth or adoption into a certain position in the social structure an individual is connected with a large number of other persons. With some of them he finds himself in a definite and specific jural relation, i.e. one which can be denned in terms of rights and duties. Who these persons will be and what will be the rights and duties

---

[14] In other words, in this example, a man jokes with his potential marriage partners and their families. He continues to joke with their families after his marriage.

depend on the form taken by the social structure. As an example of such a specific jural relation we may take that which normally exists between a father and son, or an elder brother and a younger brother. Relations of the same general type may be extended over a considerable range to all the members of a lineage or a clan or an age-set. Besides these specific jural relations which are defined not only negatively but also positively, i.e. in terms of things that must be done as well as things that must not there are general jural relations which are expressed almost entirely in terms of prohibitions and which extend throughout the whole political society. It is forbidden to kill or wound other persons or to take or destroy their property. Besides these two classes of social relations there is another, including many very diverse varieties, which can perhaps be called relations of alliance or consociation. For example, there is a form of alliance of very great importance in many societies, in which two persons or two groups are connected by an exchange of gifts or services.[s] Another example is provided by the institution of blood-brotherhood which is so widespread in Africa.

The argument of this paper has been intended to show that the joking relationship is one special form of alliance in this sense. An alliance by exchange of goods and services may be associated with a joking relationship, as in the instance recorded by Professor Labouret.[t] Or it may be combined with the custom of avoidance. Thus in the Andaman Islands the parents of a man and the parents of his wife avoid all contact with each other and do not speak; at the same time it is the custom that they should frequently exchange presents through the medium of the younger married couple.[15]

But the exchange of gifts may also exist without either joking or avoidance, as in Samoa, in the exchange of gifts between the family of a man and the family of the woman he marries or the very similar exchange between a chief and his "talking chief".

So also in an alliance by blood-brotherhood there may be a joking relationship as amongst the Zande;[u] and in the somewhat similar alliance formed by exchange of names there may also be mutual teasing. But in alliances of this kind there may be a relation of extreme respect and even of avoidance. Thus in the Yaralde and neighbouring tribes of South Australia two boys belonging to communities distant from one another, and therefore more or less hostile, are brought into an alliance by the exchange of their respective umbilical cords. The relationship thus established is a sacred one; the two boys may never speak to one another. But when they grow up they enter upon a regular exchange of gifts, which provides the machinery for a sort of commerce between the two groups to which they belong.

Thus the four modes of alliance or consociation, (1) through intermarriage, (2) by exchange of goods or services, (3) by blood-brotherhood or exchanges of names or sacra, and (4) by the joking relationship, may exist separately or combined in several different ways. The comparative study of these combinations presents a number of interesting but complex problems. The facts recorded from West Africa by Professor Labouret and Mademoiselle Paulme afford us valuable material. But a good deal more intensive field research is needed before these problems of social structure can be satisfactorily dealt with.

What I have called relations by alliance need to be compared with true contractual relations.

---

[15] Radcliffe-Brown was very deeply influenced by his reading of Durkheim and Durkheim's followers. This is evident in many ways in this essay. First, Radcliffe-Brown makes very heavy use of the ideas of Marcel Mauss and Mauss' student, Paulme. Beyond this, his overriding concern is the same as Durkheim's. Durkheim was particularly concerned with the ways in which social solidarity is developed and maintained. In other words, he focused on the mechanisms that held societies together. He found these in notions of the collective conscience, social facts, and collective represen- tations. Radcliffe-Brown has similar concerns. For him, kinship is the critical institution holding societies together (and this is consistent with his mentor Rivers' ideas as well as a general concern within Anglo-American anthropology). Within kinship, the relations of law and alliance that he discusses here function to hold society together and maintain it. Notice that the system is very neat: Where there are possibilities of disjuncture and rupture, society creates institutions such as joking and avoidance relationships to smooth the disjunctures over and avoid conflict.

The latter are specific jural relations entered into by two persons or two groups, in which either party has definite positive obligations towards the other, and failure to carry out the obligations is subject to a legal sanction. In an alliance by blood-brotherhood there are general obligations of mutual aid, and the sanction for the carrying out of these, as shown by Dr. Evans-Pritchard, is of a kind that can be called magical or ritual. In the alliance by exchange of gifts failure to fulfil the obligation to make an equivalent return for a gift received breaks the alliance and substitutes a state of hostility and may also cause a loss of prestige for the defaulting party. Professor Mauss[v] has argued that in this kind of alliance also there is a magical sanction, but it is very doubtful if such is always present, and even when it is it may often be of secondary importance.

The joking relationship is in some ways the exact opposite of a contractual relation. Instead of specific duties to be fulfilled there is privileged disrespect and freedom or even licence, and the only obligation is not to take offence at the disrespect so long as it is kept within certain bounds defined by custom, and not to go beyond those bounds. Any default in the relationship is like a breach of the rules of etiquette; the person concerned is regarded as not knowing how to behave himself.

In a true contractual relationship the two parties are conjoined by a definite common interest in reference to which each of them accepts specific obligations. It makes no difference that in other matters their interests may be divergent. In the joking relationship and in some avoidance relationships, such as that between a man and his wife's mother, one basic determinant is that the social structure separates them in such a way as to make many of their interests divergent, so that conflict or hostility might result. The alliance by extreme respect, by partial or complete avoidance, prevents such conflict but keeps the parties conjoined. The alliance by joking does the same thing in a different way.

All that has been, or could be, attempted in this paper is to show the place of the joking relationship in a general comparative study of social structure. What I have called, provisionally, relations of consociation or alliance are distinguished from the relations set up by common membership of a political society which are defined in terms of general obligations, of etiquette, or morals, or of law. They are distinguished also from true contractual relations, defined by some specific obligation for each contracting party, into which the individual enters of his own volition. They are further to be distinguished from the relations set up by common membership of a domestic group, a lineage or a clan, each of which has to be defined in terms of a whole set of socially recognised rights and duties. Relations of consociation can only exist between individuals or groups which are in some way socially separated.[16]

This paper deals only with formalised or standardised joking relations. Teasing or making fun of other persons is of course a common mode of behaviour in any human society. It tends to occur in certain kinds of social situations. Thus I have observed in certain classes in English-speaking countries the occurrence of horse-play between young men and women as a preliminary to courtship, very similar to the way in which a Cherokee Indian jokes with his "grandmothers". Certainly these

---

[16] Radcliffe-Brown's goal was to create a science of society. He proposes that this essay is a step toward a science of social structure. Functionalist anthropology in general (and Radcliffe-Brown in particular) were scathingly critiqued by American anthropologists for their failure (so the Americans believed) to effectively do this. In 1951 George Peter Murdock wrote an essay cataloging the sins of functionalism. Of Radcliffe-Brown's attempts at scientific theorizing, he says:

> Radcliffe-Brown is responsible for two serious distortions of scientific method from which his followers

have never freed themselves, namely (1) the notion that universal "laws" are discoverable from the intensive study of a very few societies without reference to their representativeness and (2) the misconception that such laws can be adequately expressed by verbal statements which do not specify the concomitant behavior of variables (1951:469).

Later in the same essay, he accuses functionalist anthropologists of having a "predilection" for "'sociologistic' verbalisms as a substitute for scientific laws" (1951:472).

unformalised modes of behaviour need to be studied by the sociologist. For the purpose of this paper it is sufficient to note that teasing is always a compound of friendliness and antagonism.

The scientific explanation of the institution in the particular form in which it occurs in a given society can only be reached by an intensive study which enables us to see it as a particular example of a widespread phenomenon of a definite class. This means that the whole social structure has to be thoroughly examined in order that the particular form and incidence of joking relationships can be understood as part of a consistent system. If it be asked why that society has the structure that it does have, the only possible answer would lie in its history. When the history is unrecorded, as it is for the native societies of Africa, we can only indulge in conjecture, and conjecture gives us neither scientific nor historical knowledge.[w,17]

NOTES

[a]Reprinted from *Africa,* Vol. XIII, No. 3, 1940, pp. 195–210.

[b]"Joking Relationships in East Africa", *Africa,* Vol. XIII, p. 170.

[c]"La Parenté à Plaisanteries en Afrique Occidentale", *Africa,* Vol. II, p. 244.

[d]"Parenté à Plaisanteries et Alliance par le Sang en Afrique Occidentale", *Africa,* Vol. XII, p. 433.

[e]Professor Marcel Mauss has published a brief theoretical discussion of the subject in the *Annuaire de l'École Pratique des Hautes Etudes, Section des Sciences religieuses,* 1927–8. It is also dealt with by Dr. F. Eggan in *Social Anthropology of North American Tribes,* 1937, pp. 75–81.

[f]*Africa,* Vol. XII, p. 438.

[g]Those who are not familiar with these widespread customs will find descriptions in Junod, *Life of a South African Tribe,* Neuchatel, Vol. I, pp. 220–37, and in *Social Anthropology of North American Tribes,* edited by F. Eggan, Chicago, 1937. pp. 55–7.

[h]Ruth Landes in Mead, *Co-operation and Competition among Primitive Peoples,* 1937, p. 103.

[i]Incidentally it may be said that it was hardly satisfactory for the magistrate to establish a precedent whereby the man, who was observing what was a permitted and may even have been an obligatory custom, was declared guilty of common assault, even with extenuating circumstances. It seems quite possible that the man may have committed a breach of etiquette in teasing the woman in the presence of her mother's brother, for in many parts of the world it is regarded as improper for two persons in a joking relationship to tease one another (particularly if any obscenity is involved) in the presence of certain relatives of either of them. But the breach of etiquette would still not make it an assault. A little knowledge of anthropology would have enabled the magistrate, by putting the appropriate questions to the witnesses, to have obtained a fuller understanding of the case and all that was involved in it.

[j]Fortes, M., *The Dynamics of Clanship among the Tallensi.* Oxford University Press, 1945.

[k]See, for example, the kinship systems described in *Social Anthropology of North American Tribes,* edited by Fred Eggan, University of Chicago Press, 1937; and Margaret Mead, "Kinship in the Admiralty Islands", *Anthropological Papers of the American Museum of Natural History,* Vol. XXXIV, pp. 243–56.

[l]For examples see Labouret, *Les Tribus du Rameau Lobi,* 1931, p. 248 and Sarat Chandra Roy, *The Oraons of Chota Nagpur,* Ranchi, 1915, pp. 352–4.

[m]A. Winifred Hoernle, "Social Organisation of the Nama Hottentot", *American Anthropologist,* N.s., Vol. XXVII, 1925, pp. 1–24.

[n]"The Mother's Brother in South Africa", *South African Journal of Science,* Vol. XXI, 1924. See Chapter I.

[o]There are some societies in which the relation between a mother's brother and a sister's son is approximately symmetrical, and therefore one of equality. This seems to be so in the Western Islands of Torres Straits, but we have no information as to any teasing or joking, though it is said that each of the two relatives may take the property of the other.

---

[17] In this last paragraph, Radcliffe-Brown attacks Boasian anthropologists. The Boasians insisted that societies were the *sui generis* results of their own historical development. They had a strong distaste for general theories of society. Radcliffe-Brown argues that the histories of nonliterate societies are unknowable (and therefore, Boasian anthropology essentially groundless). Earlier, he had written that those who hold that laws of human society do not exist (i.e., Boas and his followers) must hold that "in the field of social phenomena, in contradistinction to physical and biological phenomena, any attempt at the systematic testing of existing generalizations or toward the discovery and verification of new ones is, for some unexplained reason, futile, or as Dr. Radin puts it, 'crying for the moon'" (1965b [1935]:187). He viewed this as a clearly irrational belief and suggested that arguing against such lack of logic was a waste of time.

[p] *Life of a South African Tribe,* Vol. I, p. 255.

[q] For the kinship terminology of the VaNdau see Boas, "Das Verwandtschafts system der Vandau", in *Zeitschrift für Ethnologie.* 1922, pp. 41–51.

[r] For an account of the Cherokee see Gilbert, in *Social Anthropology of North American Tribes,* pp. 285–338.

[s] See Mauss, "Essai sur le Don", *Année Sociologique,* Nouvelle Série, tome I, pp. 30–186.

[t] *Africa.* Vol. II, p. 245.

[u] Evans-Pritchard, "Zande Blood-brotherhood", *Africa,* Vol. VI, 1933, pp. 369–401.

[v] "Essai sur le Don".

[w] The general theory outlined in this paper is one that I have presented in lectures at various universities since 1909 as part of the general study of the forms of social structure. In arriving at the present formulation of it I have been helped by discussions with Dr. Meyer Fortes.

15. *The Licence in Ritual*

MAX GLUCKMAN (1911–1975)

IN CERTAIN ARMED services at Christmas, and at Christmas only, the officers wait at table on the men. This kind of reversal of role is well-known in ceremonial and ritual. It was one of the problems which lay at the heart of Sir James Frazer's monumental study, *The Golden Bough.* In his attempt to interpret the situation of the Roman priest-king who had to defend his life against his would-be successor, Frazer went on to consider ceremonies in which people of lower social categories are made temporary kings, in which women act as men and men act as women, and so forth.[1] These rites of reversal obviously include a protest against the established order. Yet they are intended to preserve and even to strengthen the established order; and in many rituals their performance is believed to achieve success and prosperity for the group which practices them. Therefore they fall squarely within the general problem which I am discussing in this series of lectures—the problem of how custom in Africa emphasizes conflicts in certain ranges of social relationship and yet establishes cohesion in the wider society or over a longer period of time. It is with this problem in mind that I am going to try to interpret ceremonies in which women don men's clothing and do things normally prohibited to them, such as herding cattle, and also to

Custom and Conflict in Africa (1956)

[1] Gluckman begins this essay with a brief example of a custom from the British military to prepare his readers for his discussion of comparable rituals in the African societies that are the subject of his essay. This was a common technique of many functionalists who looked for universal cultural patterns or laws that were true for any society. Another technique of these anthropologists was to make customs that appear strange more familiar by comparing them with customs of British society (for example, in essay 13 Malinowski compares kula items with the crown jewels of Scotland).

This opening paragraph mentions Sir James George Frazer (1854–1941), a towering figure in British anthropology in the late nineteenth and early twentieth centuries. Frazer was a key influence on British anthropologists of Gluckman's generation. He is best known for his comparative study of religion and folklore, *The Golden Bough* (1890). The purpose of this book was to trace the evolutionary development of thought from magical to religious thinking to the rational/scientific thought of civilized societies. Frazer's evolutionary thinking was soon replaced by diffusionist and functionalist theories, but his work synthesized a huge volume of cross-cultural material that influenced the work of later generations of anthropologists. For example, Gluckman here refers to Frazer's work on the rituals of divine kingships in African societies.

interpret great political feasts in which kings are pitied and insulted and threatened.[2]

Before I go on with this description and its interpretation, I must stress that African ritual and religion form a vast field of study. Many psychological and sociological—indeed physiological—combinations are required for a full analysis. I am not attempting this impossible task. I am discussing only one aspect of ritual—how its protest against the established order is licensed and even encouraged. This encouragement must be explained by some theory which demonstrates that the ritual is socially valuable. And I am going to deal mainly with rituals which contain this element of protest—which are organized to exhibit rebellion. There are many rituals which are not organized thus.[3]

I start from the empirical fact that African rituals are frequently organized to exhibit rebellion and protest, and to emphasize the conflicts which exist between those who participate in the rituals. Thus there are descriptions of Zulu agricultural rites—no longer performed—in which women and girls committed public obscenities and acted as if they were men. More strikingly, the ceremonies were said to be performed in order to propitiate a certain goddess named Nomkubulwana. She is described 'as being robed with light as a garment and having come down from heaven to teach people to make beer, to plant, to harvest, and all the useful arts. . . . She is a maiden and she makes her visit to the earth in the Spring of the year. She is also described as presenting the appearance of a beautiful landscape with verdant forests on some parts of her body, grass-covered slopes on others, and cultivated slopes on others. She is said to be the maker of the rain.' The cere-

monies to supplicate a good harvest from the goddess were comparatively simple. I describe only their core. The young unmarried girls donned men's garments and carried shields and assagais.[4] They drove the cattle out to pasture and milked them, though cattle were normally taboo to females. Meanwhile their mothers planned a garden for the goddess far out in the veld, and poured a libation of beer to her. Thereafter this garden was neglected. At various stages of the ceremonies women and girls went naked, and sang lewd songs. Men and boys hid inside the huts, and might not go near the women. If they did, the women and girls could attack them.

This goddess and her ceremonies are interesting for many reasons. The Zulu and other South African tribes have very little mythology and have not elaborated descriptions of any other of their spirits—of their High-God who, after making the world, withdrew from direct interest in it, or of the power of the Sky, or of ancestral spirits. Why should there be this clearer idea of an unusual naturalistic anthropomorphic goddess, connected with rites in which women behaved both lewdly and as if they were men? A search for the information on the surrounding tribes produced no similar goddess, but I found in them items of these lewd and other protests by women against established rules. To the south, the Tembu women behaved thus when they were celebrating a girl's puberty; to the north, Tsonga women went naked and sang lewd songs and maltreated any man they might meet, when they were trying to get rid of a crop-pest. These obscene and domineering acts by the women were encouraged, for they were believed to achieve a blessing for the community—good crops, the fertility and good health of a nubile

---

[2] Gluckman mentions a "series of lectures." This essay is a written version of one of six lectures that were presented on BBC radio in Britain in 1955. This was the fifth such lecture. The titles of the others are: (1) "The Peace in the Feud," (2) "The Frailty in Authority," (3) "Estrangement in the Family," (4) "The Logic in Witchcraft," and (6) "The Bonds in the Color-Bar." The lectures were published in book form under the title *Custom and Conflict in Africa* (1956). This volume became one of Gluckman's best known works. In the preface, he writes that he has published the lectures as he delivered them.

[3] Note here another central tenet of structural functionalism: Society is composed of institutions such as religion. These institutions exist because they serve functions for society, thus, they are socially valuable. In this series of essays, Gluckman takes as his task to show that rituals that appear to be disruptive of society actually serve to support it.

[4] An *assagai* is a light spear or javelin.

girl, the riddance of crop-pest. I am recounting here the personal experience which first brought me up against the problem of how the customary exaggeration of conflict achieves a social blessing; and beyond that, the problem of how conflicts are built into a system of social order.[5]

I set out to trace the roles of women in all other social situations. I found that there were a whole series of beliefs and customs which emphasized that women as such were ritually ambivalent for the Zulu—that is, they had in them power for evil, and power for good. The power for evil existed in them independently of their conscious volition. Whenever they menstruated they threatened danger to warriors, crops, and cattle, by what we call supernatural means. They became witches harming others, by attracting to themselves sexual familiars. As ancestral-spirits, they were capriciously evil, while male spirits sent merited misfortune. These beliefs were extended into the wider world, for dangerous forked lightning was female, and sheet lightning was male. And so forth. On the other hand, their menstrual blood was important for it helped to make children, and their pregnant condition was magically fertilizing. The striking fact was that these capacities for good and for evil were inherent in being a female. Men had no such conflicting capacities, in their very nature as men. Men had deliberately to seek to do magical evil, by performing actions of sorcery. They could learn to be good magicians. But for women to become good magicians they had to undergo a painful illness ascribed to possession by a spirit. This was the ritual difference between men and women.[6]

After surveying Zulu culture, I worked out that a woman was in law—in law, not always in practice—subject to the control of some man—either her father or brother, or after marriage her husband. The prime effect of this subordination was to give these men control over the woman's capacities as wife and as child-bearer. In exchange for transferring to the husband a woman's capacity as a wife, including her work in the gardens, and her capacity as a bearer of children, the husband handed over to her male relatives cattle which were taboo to her—she could not touch them or go into their corral. Here there seemed to me to be a fundamental conflict involved in the social position of a woman in Zulu society, a conflict which I've described in earlier lectures, but which I sharpen now in order to focus the problems of ritual. Zulu kinship groups are built on the principle of descent from men going on through men; succession to office and inheritance of property pass in this line, and the line of descent through women is completely excluded. That is, the line of descent through women as sisters and as daughters transmitted neither power nor property. But in practice the line of a man descends to his sons through his wife or wives. The Romans had a similar system, and they have a paradoxical legal maxim which sums up admirably this conflict which centres on the woman: *mulier et origo et finis familiae est*—a woman is the beginning and the end of a family. In Roman and Zulu society a woman as wife perpetuates her husband's line, as a daughter she is the end of her father's line. And her transference to the position of wife from that of daughter is achieved by the wedding-ceremony, in which she carries a man's shield and assagai, and by the handing-over of cattle.[7]

Other evidence showed strongly that the approach of marriage was a period of great distress

---

[5] The way that Gluckman poses his problem is very different from the way that a Boasian anthropologist might. Whereas Boasians insisted that anthropology was fundamentally about cultural description, British social anthropologists looked for general principles underlying human society. Thus, Gluckman is drawn to these rituals because similar events seem to appear in different societies. Most of Boas' students probably would have argued that such superficial similarities may mask profound differences, thus events in each society must be understood in their context. Gluckman assumes that, in southern Africa at least, if there are similar customs in different groups, they are likely to have similar causes and meanings.

[6] Gluckman seems to be saying that the ability of women to perform rituals of reversal is related to their ambivalent position in society. Men are viewed as having a single nature, whereas women are conflicted. By their nature they bring both good and ill.

[7] British social anthropology frequently focused on systems of kinship (see Radcliffe-Brown, essay 14), and it is there that Gluckman identifies a central issue in Zulu society. The kinship system fictionally excludes women, passing

for Zulu girls: they were subject to frequent attacks of hysteria which were ascribed to the love-magic of their suitors. Marriage itself was a difficult relation, requiring adjustment to a strange family where the girl was hedged with many taboos. She had to avoid important parts of her husband's home village and even parts of her own hut. She had to alter her language so as not to use any word containing the root of her husband's name or the names of her senior male relatives-in-law. Her stressed function was to be a dutiful, hard-working, faithful, and decorous wife, bearing children for her husband, and caring for those children. Only when they grew up, could she become independent, as the mother of grown sons. And after her death it was believed that her spirit would send them capricious misfortune, not deserved by evil deeds; nor would she withdraw it after sacrifice, as a male spirit did. But in fulfilling her duty as a wife, she weakened her husband's group as well as strengthening it. On the one hand she gave her husband's group more members, fresh recruits; and on the other hand she produced competitors for power and for property in the group. Here is a second conflict in the position of a woman in these groups. These conflicts centering on the position of woman as wife and as child-bearer both hinge on the cattle which regulate Zulu marriage—Zulu say, therefore, 'cattle beget children.' Hence it seemed to me that cattle, and the herding of cattle, might well symbolize the whole legal subordination of women. Allowing them to herd the cattle would be a reward and a release, especially while they were also allowed to go naked and sing lewd songs and attack wandering men. This statement, that performing these normally

tabooed actions is a reward and release, seems to be justified by the descriptions we have. But part of its interpretation involves psychological analysis for which there is no evidence.[8]

Socially, the lifting of the normal taboos and restraints obviously serves to emphasize them. It is this aspect of the ceremony which most interests me. Zulu custom emphasizes the difference between men and women, beyond their biological differences. Women cannot approach cattle; women must be decorous in public; women do not take part in national life or national ceremonies; women, when they menstruate, are full of mystical danger. This is part of woman's social position, and the customs and beliefs emphasize her distinction and her separateness from men. For men herd cattle, they can be forward in national life and in national ceremonies, they do not menstruate and are not full of this mystical danger. But on one occasion in the year—the time of planting when they begin their arduous agricultural labours—women are allowed to act as if they were men. They are not only licensed to do so, but they are encouraged and even enjoined to do so in the interests of the community. When I was working in Zululand in 1937 these ceremonies were no longer performed: old men told me that therefore crops were poor. Hence the lifting of the taboos not only rewarded the women but it also brought benefits to the men who allowed this lifting and subjected themselves to the temporarily dominant women. I suggest that this was possible, and effective in ways we do not yet fully understand, because the women as well as the men accepted the general nature of Zulu society—as good and valuable. That is, this particular ritual, by allowing people to behave in normally prohibited ways,

---

property and power from father to son. However, women, of course, are necessary to procreation. Thus, the ritual in Zulu society must somehow reconcile the conflict between women excluded from kinship but central to its composition. Gluckman's job is now to show what the handing over of cattle and the wearing of men's clothing have to do with this conflict.

[8] There are, of course, two classic forms of functionalism: psychological and structural, the former promoted by Malinowski, the latter by Radcliffe-Brown. Gluckman was influenced far more by Radcliffe-Brown and Evans-

Pritchard than by Malinowski. In fact, Gluckman attacked Malinowski for psychologizing culture and abstracting it from its historical and political context (Gluckman 1947, 1949). In this paragraph, he suggests that allowing the women to herd cattle might serve a psychological function: the release of tension caused by the conflict between women and their marriage families. However, he ends the paragraph by dismissing psychological analysis in general, suggesting there is no evidence for it. It is not clear what sort of evidence Gluckman has in mind.

gave expression, in a reversed form, to the normal rightness of a particular kind of social order. And the ritual would continue to be effective in this sense, and yet be rewarding to the women, so long as the women accepted Zulu arrangements as good. They were not suffragettes and feminists seeking to alter Zulu society in order to strengthen their own position. Had they been in revolt against Zulu rules, the ritual could not be effective in stating moral principles by reversal, with the belief that this reversal would bring the social blessing of rich harvests.[9]

My analysis of the deeper social alignments affecting the position of women in this ritual is supported when we examine other rites among these peoples. Take this description of the Tsonga ritual which organizes the moving of a village. A Tsonga village is inhabited by a headman, with his wives and children, and the wives and children of his married sons. When they are ready to move, the headman goes first to examine some spots where he would like to build. He breaks small twigs from various trees and these are tested by the divining bones to see which spot will be prosperous. Building material is then collected at the chosen spot, and the headman and his principal wife leave the old village finally. They have ritual sexual relations on the new site and in the morning tie a knot in grass over which all the villagers should step. This ties the village to the headman and his principal wife. Now begins a month of taboo, especially on sexual relations by the villagers. Breach of this taboo may make the headman ill; it does not make the offender ill. The huts of the old village are carried to the new site by the men, who sing obscene songs insulting the women. Later when the women smear the floors of the huts with mud

they retaliate with obscene songs at the men's expense. A Tsonga said of these songs: 'The village is broken to pieces, so are the ordinary laws. The insults which are taboo are now allowed.' The village is fenced with magical substances to obstruct the entry of witches. Finally the new home is ready. All couples have ritual sexual relations in order of precedence, and then the final rite of establishing the headman has to be performed. The headman's principal wife takes his assagai and shield and closes the gate of the village. She makes an offering to the ancestral spirits and prays for the people: 'Be not tied by the village! Bring forth children; live and be happy and get everything. You gods, see! I have no bitterness in my heart. It is pure. I was angry because my husband abandoned me, he said I was not his wife; he loved his younger wives. Now, this is finished in my heart. We shall have friendly relations together.' They then feast together.[10]

This ceremony again requires that in the ritual there should be an emphatic statement of those conflicts within the village which are likely to lead to its break-up. In the end, indeed, over time these conflicts do lead to the splitting of the village. The conflicts centre on the marital relations of the different men in the village; for through these marital relations each man gets children who may eventually enable him to set up his own village. Sexual relations are therefore banned during the period when the old village is deserted but the new village is not yet built—the period when dissident villagers may decide to leave. Normal restraints are lifted and obscenity is allowed. And a breach of the taboo on marital relations does not lead to mystical punishment of the wrongdoer, but to mystical threats to the headman. For it is his authority which is threatened

---

[9] This paragraph contains the center of Gluckman's argument, and it displays some of the weaknesses and strengths of structural-functionalist thinking. He begins by stating that it is obvious that the lifting of taboos serves to emphasize them. Is this in fact obvious? Gluckman then observes that the reversals of taboos can serve to strengthen society. Thus, he proposes to explain that rituals that seemingly disrupt society in fact support it and lead to its continuation. British structural anthropologists

were often masterful in showing that apparent contradictions were surface manifestations of underlying agreements. Things were not necessarily what they seemed.

[10] Note in this description of ritual that individuals who break taboos do not themselves suffer; it is the headman who suffers. Thus, the villagers are declaring their support of their headman and affirming the structure of the village despite the ceremonies in which they publically revile each other.

by the marriages which lead to the independence of each man from the group. Finally, the principal wife takes the place of her husband, carrying his weapons, to symbolize the unity of the group of males and their wives, despite the fact that it is through the wives, who bear children, that the group will ultimately split. Women and men are shown to be identified in the interests of village unity. In her prayer the principal wife states the conflicts which exist between herself and other wives of the headman. She says they are jealous for his attentions; but it is also because they are jealous for the rights of their own children. The general opposition of the group of male kin to the stranger women whom they marry, and who bring dissension into the village, is stated in the obscene songs. This ritual again emphasizes conflicts which threaten the unity of the village. And it is carried out even if in practice everyone lives together harmoniously. But by this statement of the conflicts, the ritual emphasizes that the conflicts exist, and indeed it may exaggerate them. Yet the Tsonga believe that the effect of the ceremony is to bless the village with fertility and prosperity. This belief can be held so long as the members of the village accept the unity of the village as a good thing. These same conflicts appear in many other rituals of these tribes. The desire of each group of male kin for wives, and yet their rejection of the wives as trouble-makers between them, is clearly stated in Zulu wedding ceremonies. The two intermarrying groups insult one another and threaten one another with weapons, they dance competitively against one another, the bride attempts to run away and has to be captured by her husband. Most clearly, this symbolism appears in the bride's carrying a small shield and a knife or assagai, as if she were a man, an enemy threatening her husband's group. And for long periods of the ceremony she has to sit with downcast head while her husband's kin insult her as a lazy good-for-nothing, of bad family, who is

going to introduce quarrels into their happy home. Again, the ritual of marriage states in advance the conflicts that will hinge on her position, and this statement is believed to bless the marriage. Open expression of conflict within the group is believed to bring success, and to achieve the unity and prosperity of the wider group.[11]

These rituals contain the belief that if people perform certain actions they will influence the course of events so that their group be made richer, more prosperous, more successful, and so forth. Some of us therefore call these actions 'ritual,' and say that they contain 'mystical notions'—notions that their performance will in some mysterious way affect the course of events. 'Ritual' in this definition is contrasted with 'ceremonial' which consists of similar actions but has no such mystical notions associated with it.

Rituals of this kind, in which people perform actions in terms of their social roles, are very widespread in the so-called primitive societies. They occur in the round of agriculture, in hunting and herding and manufacturing, and in military operations. They also occur when villages are moved or established and persons of authority are installed, and at different stages during the growing-up of individuals—at birth, puberty, marriage. Finally, they are important in funerals. We find that different societies ritualize these events to very different degrees, and different societies seize on different occasions to perform ritual. But overall a high ritualization of these social occasions is characteristic of the simpler societies, when compared with developed industrial civilizations. This rule is general, not absolute: for many simple societies, including those which belong to Islam, are not thus full of ritual.

The characteristic feature of this type of ritualization is that it makes use of the details of particular social relationships—of relationships between parents and children, maternal uncle and

---

[11] In several ways, this passage expresses the critical points made above. The rebellious acts expressed in rituals are real in that they are about points of conflict in society: Women really do hold conflicted positions that are necessary to the survival of the lineage, but as outsiders they are also dangerous to it; villages do eventually split up over conflicts between different families. But allowing the expression of these real conflicts in ritual somehow controls them and promotes the stability of the village rather than its destruction.

sister's son, men and women, king and princes and subjects. Indeed, the performance of specific ritual acts by persons in a particular kind of relationship with one another, is an essential element of that relationship. In many patriarchal societies, for example, it is the mother's brother who offers support to a lad at certain crises, by assisting him through initiation and other rituals. And provision of this ritual support, or the performance of any rite in a ceremony involving some related person, is strongly enforced. Failure to conform is believed to lead to severe mystical penalties. Thus these ritual obligations are a very significant part of each relationship, and mark it off from other relationships. The varying ritual role of any person marks out his or her particular relationship with the person concerned; and the mystical penalties ensure that attention shall be paid to this role.[12]

This being so, the ritual of each African tribe is built about the framework of its own forms of organization. Generally each tribe has distinctive sets of rituals for particular occasions, and in these rituals persons appear according to their relationships with one another in secular life. What happens is, that the various persons involved act out their roles, either directly or by reversal of normal behaviour or by special symbolic rites. The Zulu bride carries shield and assagai, but she also carries a child of her husband's village on her back. She aggressively hurls an assagai into her husband's cattle-kraal; but she also meekly and ceremoniously collects firewood, cooks, and sweeps. In one set of rites she reverses her role, in the other set of rites she performs her future duties. The rites thus exhibit the ambivalence of her total role. In national ceremonies the king is insulted; but he is also lauded as all-powerful.[13]

To say that African rituals have this high degree of particularism is not to deny that they deal with some of the general problems of social and human existence which have faced men everywhere. Some problems are universal. What is man? Whence does he come and whither does he go? Why should there be good and evil, prosperity and misfortune? How is human society set in the world of nature? What of the relations of men and women, parents and children, magistrates and people? What of the dealings of different groups with one another? These problems may be summed up, perhaps, in the general question: What is man's place, as a member of society, in the world? The answer is given partly in myth and legend, partly in dogma, and largely in rituals, like the Zulu ritual of women propitiating the goddess Nomkubulwana.

Africans have not worked out elaborate dogmas to explain the nature of the universe, though there are important exceptions to this generalization. Partly, they lack professional theologians. Hence, too, they do not strive to make their dogmas consistent. Their different rituals often embody inconsistent, and even contradictory, principles and values. For they reflect the existence in social life of different principles of social organization, which work out against each other, as we have seen. A wife is a blessing and a danger. These different principles compensate for one another, so that after a period of time or in a wider range of social relations conflicts in particular relationships are redressed, and the social pattern is re-established or duplicated. The village remains united, or two similar villages are built. This repetitive process in African social life allows the use of ritual statement of conflict. For social processes are working through quarrels and disputes to produce the same kind of social relationships, and not different new relationships. After their orgy of cattle-herding, Zulu women return to their daily tasks:

---

[12] Here Gluckman is outlining a function of ritual that is lifted straight from Durkheim via Radcliffe-Brown. He says that certain ritual roles are prescribed for individuals with specific relationships to each other and are sanctioned by mystical penalties. Thus the rituals emphasize certain kin ties and reinforce the social order.

[13] Note the emphasis in this passage on the roles that individuals fill. People do not act out their personal rebellions in these ceremonies, but rather they play parts that are dictated by their social roles. Structural functionalists tended to think of society as a series of social roles standing in particular relationships to each other. Personalities of individuals were not relevant to their analysis. This was not a denial that people in primitive societies had emotions and were able to rebel; rather, the structural functionalists understood these as psychological factors and not part of anthropological understandings.

they do not seek for a different set of feminist laws. The rituals are statements of rebellion, and never of revolution.[14]

This tendency appears very markedly in the great national ceremonies of the tribes who dwell in Southeast Africa. At sowing, first fruits and harvest, and before war, the Zulu nation performed, and the Swazi still perform, great military rituals. These rituals are believed to strengthen the nation, and to ensure national prosperity and victory. Yet they consist largely of statements of rebellion against the king, by his brother-princes and by his subjects, and of affirmations that he is unworthy of his high office. Dr. Hilda Kuper[15] has brought this out in a brilliant description and analysis of the Swazi ceremonies. She also brings out the smallness of the universe within which Swazi cosmology is established, and the particularistic nature of their answer to the problem, what is man? The world is seen as a setting for the Swazi, in competition with neighbouring nations, and not for humanity in general. The king has to race the sun by beginning the first fruits ceremony before the sun reaches the Tropic of Capricorn; but he has also to begin the ceremony at the last wane of the moon when man's powers go into decline, in order that a fortnight later the ritual climax may occur at the full moon when man's powers are at their height.

The ceremony itself is strikingly an acting out of the whole of Swazi political relations, so that Dr. Kuper calls it 'a drama of kingship.' The king and queen-mother and queens, princes and councillors, men in their regiments, commoner chiefs, women, all have specific roles in the ritual which are related to their roles in everyday life. But the rites affirm not only the unity of the nation about the kingship, but also all the conflicts around the person of the reigning king: the resentment of his subjects against authority, the jealousy of his brother-princes who covet the throne, and so forth. Indeed, the ritual exaggerates the conflicts. Whether or not princes covet the throne they are made to act as if they do so covet it. At critical points when loyalty to the king is being affirmed, they have to leave the arena. And even their unborn children are also involved in the conflict—for the pregnant wife of a prince must also withdraw. At particular points in the ceremony a black bull is required: these bulls are stolen from commoner subjects who are thus made "angry and proud," say the Swazi—an apt description of the ambivalent attitudes involved in being a member of an authoritative nation.[16] There are, of course, also rites which affirm the support of the king both by princes and by subjects, but the general tone is as much one of rejection of the king as of triumph in his might. Here are typical songs:

> You hate the child king,
> You hate the child king;

and

> You hate him,
> Mother, the enemies are the people.
> You hate him,
> The people are wizards.
> Admit the treason of Mabedla—
> You hate him,

---

[14] This passage does two critical things. First, it reminds us that although the rituals Gluckman has been discussing are intended to strike the Western audience for whom the lecture was planned as exotic, the people performing them are dealing with fundamental issues that are faced by people everywhere; hence we should be able to think about similar rituals in our society. Second, Gluckman once again emphasizes that while the rituals have the appearance of rebellion, they are really nothing of the kind. In fact, they support the societies in which they are found and reproduce the same social forms they critique.

[15] Hilda Kuper (1911–1992), like Gluckman, was an African-born anthropologist. She was from Bulawayo in Rhodesia (now Zimbabwe). Like Gluckman, she studied anthropology at the University of Witwatersrand under A. Winnifred Hoernle and Isaac Schapera. Kuper did extensive fieldwork among the Swazi and in the slums of South Africa. Like Gluckman, she was concerned with racism and the problems of apartheid.

[16] It would have been hard to read this last sentence in the 1950s without thinking of both Nazi Germany and the Soviet Union, authoritarian nations with angry and proud citizens. Gluckman is trying to make his anthropology germane to the daily concerns of his audience.

You have wronged,
Bend great neck,
Those and those they hate him,
They hate the king;

and

King, alas for thy fate,
King, they reject thee,
King, they hate thee.

Those who hate the king are those who reject him: enemies within the tribe, not external enemies, his brothers and his discontented subjects. His fate is sad because he carries the burden of office, and the hatred that is the lot of office.

This theme of rejection and hatred of the king is so built into this great national ceremony that we have to ask, again, how the affirmation of rebellion can be so strong in a ritual which the people believe unifies and blesses their nation. And the king not only allows them to reject, and also to insult him; by doing so they are believed to support him in his arduous office.

Obviously there may be high psychological catharsis and relief in the princes and subjects who are required thus publicly to express hidden resentments. This problem lies outside my province. But again, as a sociologist, I am interested in the fact that this affirmation of rebellion goes on within an accepted order. The kingship is sacred, and its sacred strength is necessary for the nation—not only for its political strength, but also for the fertility of its women, fields, and cattle. The acceptance of the established order as right and good, and even sacred, seems to allow unbridled licence, very rituals of rebellion, for the order itself keeps this rebellion within bounds. Hence to act the conflicts, whether directly or by inversion or in other symbolical forms, emphasizes the social cohesion within which the conflicts exist. As the social order always contains a division of rights and duties, and of privileges and powers as against responsibilities, the ritual enactment of the order states its rightness. The ritual states that in virtue of their social position princes and people hate the king, but nevertheless they support him. They support him despite the conflicts between them. Or, at least, if they don't support the particular king, they support the kingship. For in the conditions of Swazi polity, as I've explained in an earlier lecture, malcontents did not attempt to subvert the social order, but to install a new king in the old kingship. Swazi were rebels, never revolutionaries. Should a particular king be a tyrant, his people's redress was not to seek to establish a republic, but to find some good prince in the king's family; for only a member of that family could hold the sacred kingship.[17]

I myself believe that in the undeveloped Swazi economy, with its poor communications, different territorial sections of the nation developed strong autonomous tendencies, and tendencies to break out of the national hegemony. But these tendencies to fragment were canalized into a struggle to put particular princes on to the throne: the sections fought for the sacred kingship, and not for independence from it. Hence I have argued that in these African states periodic rebellions strengthened, and did not weaken, the political system. If this argument is acceptable, it is possible to see that the Swazi may be right when they say their great ceremony, so openly affirming conflicts, is a source of unity and strength—of cohesion. For the 'drama of kingship' states a process that is present in actual political life. It affirms the acceptance of kingship as such, as the source of law and moral order for the Swazi, against internal traitors and external foes. It does so by stating that those who are hostile to the ruling king, nevertheless support him because they support the kingship. And the possibility that the king

---

[17] Note two ideas drawn directly from Durkheim in this passage: First, ritual is about social cohesion. Much of Durkheim's work focused on the problem of social cohesion: How exactly were societies held together? Both Durkheim and Gluckman agree that the process has a great deal to do with the rituals that the society conducts. Second: Consider that what Gluckman is really saying in this passage is that when society conducts these religious rituals, it is really, in fact, worshiping itself, or more specifically its social order, a central point of Durkheim's *The Elementary Forms of Religious Life* (1965 [1912]).

may be personally inadequate, and may desecrate the values of the kingship, is admitted in the insults he suffers. This does not invalidate the kingship itself.[18]

The general theme I have been putting forward emerges with great force from an account by Delegorgue, an early French traveller, of the Zulu ceremony.[19] His account is the more telling because he did not understand what he was looking at. He described the Zulu government as despotic, and commented on the ceremony: 'It is at the time of the general assembly of warriors (towards December 8th) when the maize ripens, that lively discussion takes place. There are free interrogations which the king must immediately answer, and in a manner which will satisfy the people. I have seen at that time ordinary warriors come leaping out of their ranks, transformed into orators full of spirit, extremely excited, not only returning the fiery glance of the king, but even denouncing him before everyone, blaming his actions, stigmatizing them as base and cowardly, obliging him to explain, destroying the reasoning in his answers, dissecting them and unmasking their falsehood; then proudly threatening him and ending with a gesture of contempt. I have also seen, after such discussions,' Delegorgue goes on, 'I have also seen the king's party and that of the opposition on the point of hurling themselves upon one another. I have seen that the voice of the despot was no longer heeded, and

that a revolution could have exploded then and there had a single ambitious man come forward to profit by the indignation of the party opposed to the king. But what surprised me no less, was the order which succeeded the end of this kind of popular tribunal.' It is the surprise of M. Delegorgue that I am trying to explain away. Clearly no revolutionary leader could come forward at that point. The attack on the king was demanded by tradition and it naturally culminated in the warriors exhorting the king to lead them to war. For the attack must have been on the king, as shown by Delegorgue's words, for failing to live up to the standards of kingship—it exhibited the conflict between the kingship and the human frailty of the king, between subjects and king. But it affirmed the value of kingship.[20]

I could demonstrate the extent to which conflict is thus used in ritual in many other political ceremonies, both in states and in societies without governmental institutions. A remarkable example among a people without government occurs among the Tallensi of the Gold Coast. Professor Fortes has shown there that different groups are involved in a series of rites, so that each group must perform its part of a cycle of rituals if all are to be prosperous.[21] One lot of groups is responsible for rain, another for fertility of the crops. And what is important for my purpose is that when each lot performs its rites the other must remain shut up in its homes, under pain of

---

[18] Note again that what is ritually supported and reinforced is not the individuals who hold social roles (as Gluckman points out, these may be either good or bad) but the roles themselves.

[19] Adulphe Delegorgue (1814–1850) was a French explorer and naturalist who visited South Africa between 1838 and 1844. His two-volume *Travels in Southern Africa,* originally published in 1847, is a classic of exploration literature.

[20] Delegorgue misunderstands the actions he witnesses because he puts them in European social context: He thinks he is witnessing a potential revolution. He explains them in a way that was probably both ethnocentric and racist: The Zulu lack the incentive and ambition to change their system. Gluckman provides an alternative explanation that he believes is neither ethnocentric nor racist:

Delegorgue wasn't witnessing a rebellion at all; what he saw was a ceremony confirming and reinforcing the values of the Zulu kingship.

[21] Meyer Fortes (1906–1983) was another of the African-born anthropologists around Gluckman. He was trained at the University of Capetown and later under Malinowski, who wrote that "for sheer brilliancy and real capacity and intelligence [he is] the best pupil I have ever had" (quoted in Goody 1995:28). However, like Gluckman, Fortes was ultimately more drawn to the structural side of functionalism than the psychological.

Also note that Gluckman points out that the Tallensi are a people without governmental institutions. The maintenance of order in societies without government was a central problem for the British structural-functionalist anthropologists (and not unrelated to British colonization).

mystical punishment. Unity and interdependence are again stressed by mutual exclusion, to achieve prosperity for all. For this unity and this interdependence are made up by the separateness of the component groups. It is significant, too, that marriages are banned in this period, for marriages establish special links between the independent groups and conflicts within each group which I've already discussed. Herein, I venture to suggest, lies the origin of the ban on Christian marriages in Lent, and of Jewish marriages at the same period. This, in the Mediterranean, is the period between first fruits and harvest, and the period of great national rites in the ancient civilizations. Marriages, as the source of unity across division, were taboo.

These rebellious rituals thus occur in national ceremonies and in domestic ceremonies. At the installation of a village headman in many Central African tribes he is insulted and told he is unworthy of office: the Yao strike him on the head to knock him out, ritually to kill him. Here successors to headmanship are also tested for witchcraft, because it is believed they may have killed their predecessor and their rivals. In these small political groups the struggle for power cuts deep into personal relations, and this is used in the ritual to cleanse the headman and to install him so that he may rule wisely and to the benefit of the villagers. But the statement of conflict in ritual is not carried into the smallest grouping of society, and that a very important one—the elementary family. No ceremony that I know allows the open statement of hostility by children to parents, by parents to children, or by brothers and sisters to one another. Psychologists will probably say that may be because the conflicts here cut too near the bone: the relationship could not be re-established if the conflicts repressed in these most intimate sentiments were exhibited. As a social anthropologist I seek for an explanation of a different kind. The rites I have been considering all go on in groups which endure despite the life and death of members, or their geographical movements. They are on the whole enduring groups—nations, interlinked political groups, villages, local districts of women in the Zulu goddess's ritual. The family is not such an enduring group: it breaks up with the death of the parents and with the marriages of the children. It has not the same sort of cohesion as the other groups. And the basis of my argument is that the licensed ritual of protest and of rebellion is effective so long as there is no querying of the order within which the ritual of protest is set, and the group itself will endure.[22]

But family relationships are altered when children grow up and when they marry. Here the ritual which involves their separation from their parents does not state that the parents resent the adulthood of their children or their marriages. Commonly, the parents may abstain from being present. When a Tsonga girl reaches puberty, her mother does not attend the rites: she is looked after by a substitute mother. This in itself signifies a breaking away from her mother's apron-strings. Barotse parents do not attend their children's marriages. Absence in this way may be ritually effective in symbolizing a change of relationships; in the Tallensi political ceremonies I've quoted (where political groups which are interlinked hide when their peers are performing their ceremonies) absence is effective in allowing the ceremony to achieve the blessing of prosperity for all. Prescribed absence from a ritual is thus a form of participation in it: though it is not a protest, it states that there is a conflict present in the social process.

I myself was fortunate to observe this process vividly in certain boys' circumcision ceremonies in North-western Rhodesia.[23] There are many

[22] In this passage, Gluckman once again dismisses psychological explanations. He says that the kinds of rituals he discusses do not happen in the nuclear family because it is changing, whereas the broader social structure is permanent. Note the tendency throughout this essay to view society as unchanging. The functionalists were strongly criticized, particularly by American anthropologists, for painting a static portrait of society. If, as Gluckman argues in this essay, personal psychological factors are irrelevant to social analysis and acts of rebellion within the social system can be interpreted as supporting that system, it is hard to see what dynamic might drive change in society.

[23] Northwestern Rhodesia is now Zambia.

similar rituals throughout South-central Africa. Earlier descriptions of these rituals all just stressed that they were taboo to women, who had to remain away. I found that the absence of the women was part of their contribution to the ritual which aimed to help their sons grow up. By not being present they assisted their sons to break away from them, and become men, associated with their fathers. But through the ritual as a whole, the women had to abstain for periods, and then join actively in certain rites. The rites involved a symbolic marriage of men and women to give rebirth to the boys as complete men. This symbolic marriage was based on the idea that the mating of sexes for procreation involves the union of two opposed but complementary persons— man and woman. Male and female symbols were linked throughout the camp where the boys were isolated. And men and women successively fought one another, separated, united in joy at the growing-up of their sons. The ceremony was compared for me with marital relations—a "fighting with joy," a union fraught with conflict, but a union which would be successful if the proper rites were observed, as ordained by the ancestors. Again, the open statement, the exaggeration of conflict, was believed to achieve a generally desired end—the maturity and fruitfulness of the boys. It did so because women agreed in wanting their sons to become men, like their husbands. There was no division over the ultimate rightness of the social order.

I have been arguing that the emphatic dramatizing of conflict within a particular type of social order may be believed to bless that order, so long as it is unquestioned. People are required to express their hostilities to one another so as to secure a blessing: they assert acceptance of common goals despite these hostilities. I have also suggested reasons why rituals of licence do not occur inside the elementary family. But I have still to deal with other rituals where the element of conflict is not expressed, and the aim of the ritual is secured by straightforward affirmations of unity and identity of purpose. This is a complex problem, but I believe the clue to the answer was given by Delegorgue's description of the Zulu national ceremonies. In all the ceremonies I've been describing this evening, despite the conflicts, there is no division about the desired end, and no doubt about which is the dominant moral rule or social relationship. The Zulu and Swazi states were strong and unquestioned. In domestic life, the Zulu had a very strong patriarchy, under the dominance of the eldest son of a man's chief wife. It was difficult for men to leave their paternal kin, or for women to leave their husbands. The strength of this system may allow the women's licence in ritual; as the strength of the army structure allows the Christmas reversal of roles when officers wait on men. Similarly, in the Polish ghettoes, where the rabbis were powerful, once a year a sermon attacking them was preached in the synagogue by a wastrel; this was not found where the rabbinate was weak.[24] In Swaziland, if the king was still a boy, the rites of rebellion were not practised. I don't know the full answer to this, but I am suggesting that where the relationships involved are weak, there cannot be licence in ritual.[25]

The weakness of a relationship may lie in its own structure. But it may also be weak because it

---

[24] Gluckman was Jewish, like many of his colleagues in British social anthropology, including Charles Seligman (a member of the Torres Straits expedition), Isaac Schapera, Meyer Fortes, S. F. Nadel, Hortense Powdermaker, and Ashley Montague. Many of Gluckman's essays contain references to Jewish history and Jewish law.

[25] Once again, Gluckman is proposing but not elaborating on a general law of social behavior: There is an inverse relationship between the strength of a social relationship and the existence of rebellious ritual. Where social relationships are strong, such rituals are likely; where they are weak, such rituals are unlikely. Now, near the end of his essay, Gluckman returns to a Durkheimian theme. In this passage, Gluckman is arguing that the societies he has been describing are held together by mechanical solidarity (see pages 69–70). In these societies, "a man does everything with the same set of fellows" and the social order is unquestioned and unquestionable. Gluckman argues that a ritual of rebellion is most effective under these circumstances. Since the social order is ultimately unquestionable, such rituals bless it rather than threaten it.

involves conflicts of social principles which are immediately obvious and which cannot be reconciled. Then, I think, the ritual will affirm the principles separately, and it will not stress the conflict between them. Finally, another profitable line of inquiry seems to lie in the contrast of ritual handling of conflict with the secular handling of conflict. For example, the political conflicts which I described for the Zulu and Swazi, are also present in Barotse life. Yet the Barotse do not have rituals of rebellion. But their political system is so organized—as the systems of Zulu and Swazi are not—that all these conflicts are built into an elaborate series of councils. The conflicts are exhibited and expressed in differentiated secular relationships. And here, I believe, lies an important clue to understanding why rituals are so few in our own society. There must be many reasons for this, but I put only the lessons of rites of protest.

I have been advancing two lines of argument in my attempt to understand these rites. First, in Africa, on the whole, a man does everything with the same set of fellows—he works with them, plays with them, acts politically with them, worships with them. An intricate set of relationships is woven in which every interest for the people depends on right relationship with the same lot of their fellows. A quarrel with your brother or your wife upsets your subsistence activities, for example. Wider ties in the society are developed by extending the ties inside the family: and the result is an intricate mesh of relationships in which the same people depend on one another for many things. Custom marks out the individuality of different relationships within the whole. And the customs of ritual are used to indicate any change in the relationships, or change in the activities within them. So that the birth of a child, or a boy's attainment of maturity or marriage, a man's going hunting or the taking in of harvest, and so forth—all these change the whole pattern of social life. The intricate set of relationships is disturbed, and thus the moral order of the society. This has to be righted. And it is righted by reaffirming the general moral order, through stating both the cohesion and the conflicts which exist within that cohesion. The conflicts can be stated openly wherever the social order is unquestioned and indubitable—where there are rebels, and not revolutionaries. In such a system, the licensed statement of conflict can bless the social order.[26]

This hypothesis of how rituals of protest can occur in certain societies, also implies why they cannot exist in other types of society, such as our own. First, we have revolutionaries as well as rebels, suffragettes as well as good wives and mothers—indeed, good wives and mothers are often suffragettes. Once there is questioning of the social order, the ritual of protest is inappropriate, since the purpose of the ritual is to unite people who do not or cannot query their social roles. And beyond this, our society is composed of highly fragmented and divided relationships—our interests lead us into association with a whole variety of different persons, in the family, schools, pubs, workplaces, churches, political organizations, recreational clubs, and so on. The dissatisfied person can change his membership of groups, vote for a new government, join a new club, seek work in a new factory, move away from his family when he marries. In African society, a man could not do this so easily; and my impression is that rites of protest are less developed in those societies where some movement is possible. Hence, I suggest—the problem is too complex for a strong affirmation—hence, I suggest, we do not have the many rituals of Africa. They are inappropriate in the family, our single many-interest

---

[26] Continuing the Durkheimian theme, Gluckman proposes that modern society is held together by organic solidarity: It is composed of many groups with different interests that both collaborate and compete. Because, in such a situation, revolution is a distinct possibility, rituals that emphasize conflicts pose a danger to the entire system. They are also, to a great extent, unnecessary. Rather than experience conflict, an individual can, in many cases, move to a different social group. Durkheim believed that systems of organic solidarity were preferable to systems of mechanical solidarity because the former allowed for a greater development of human individuality and the human spirit. Gluckman seems to share this belief.

group. They are inappropriate in the state, because we have revolutionaries as well as rebels. All our other groups have voluntary and not compelled membership. And many differentiated secular institutions, with great freedom of movement, allow for the temporary solution of personal and sectional conflicts.

We don't have rituals in the sense that we believe that the acting of social roles will in some supernatural manner affect our prosperity and unity in this way. But, of course, we have many ceremonials expressing unity. And a few of these are recognized to state conflicts. Yet I am also sometimes tempted to regard as 'ceremonies' other squabbling actions in our social life, which are usually assumed to be realistic. Parliamentary debates and election campaigns are full of dispute: I wonder how realistic much of this is, and what relation it bears to the actual taking of political decisions. Periodic scandals, say about the actions of the Civil Service, may lead to the affirmation of general principles about how the country should be run, as if there were not posed impossible reconciliations of different interests. These inquiries may not alter what actually happens, but they affirm an ideal condition of unity and justice. Even some strikes appear to be ceremonials of rebellion in the national industrial system. For some of them end, and apparently for a time happily, without changing conditions; and others lead to a change which might have been achieved without the demonstration. Yet the demonstration appears to be a preliminary necessity. African society was not changing in its structure, and rituals of rebellion worked because ultimate values, some contradictory, were put on a mystical plane where they could not be questioned. Ours is a rapidly changing society. Nevertheless, I am not sure that these processes which are like those we find in Africa, may not act to persuade us that there is great persistence notwithstanding the change.[27]

---

[27] In closing the essay, Gluckman revises what he has said above, arguing that perhaps some actions in modern society are like rituals of rebellion. He is trying to make his essay relevant to his audience, but given his background as a social activist it is a rather cynical point of view. It seems unlikely that union members on strike or candidates fighting elections believe that their actions are designed to preserve the status quo. However, it is a profoundly functionalist point of view: The purpose of elections is not to choose among candidates (for that ultimately makes little difference) but to celebrate, and thus perpetuate, the political system of our society.

Culture and Personality

The fact that British functionalists relied on Spencer's organic analogy and Durkheim's notion of the collective conscience necessarily gave their work a holistic quality. In America, Franz Boas insisted that anthropology was holistic but lacked any compelling unifying theory that either required or demonstrated this feature. Although Boas used the rhetoric of holism, many of the historical particularists tended to treat culture as a chance association of disparate features. In 1920, Boas' student Robert Lowie (1883–1957) concluded *Primitive Society* with an attack on the notion of historical laws of cultural evolution. Quoting Gilbert and Sullivan's operetta *The Mikado*, he wrote: "To that planless hodge-podge, that thing of shreds and patches called civilization, its historian can no longer yield superstitious reverence." Lowie later wrote that he was critiquing American civilization in the post–World War I years, not proposing that all cultures were things of shreds and patches (Lowie 1946:119). However, many took his words as a general statement on the impossibility of finding coherent regularities in culture. Whatever Lowie's intentions, Boas and his followers were certainly open to this critique.

One way that several of Boas' students sought to circumvent this problem without challenging the bases of historical particularism was through ideas borrowed from psychoanalysis and Gestalt psychology. Gestalt psychologists examined personality as an interrelated psychological pattern rather than a collection of separate elements. This insight particularly influenced the work of Ruth Fulton Benedict (1887–1948), who focused on the psychological concept of personality as her unifying theme. However, many of the other great culture and personality theorists took

their lead from the work of Sigmund Freud. Margaret Mead (1901–1978), for example, was keenly interested in the effect of early childhood influences on adult personality and behavior.

Sigmund Freud (1856–1939) was an Austrian physician and neurologist who founded the field of psychoanalysis. Psychoanalytic theory, with its emphasis on unconscious psychological processes and psychological defense mechanisms such as repression, projection, and sublimation, captured the popular imagination of his day and became an important part of anthropological thought in the first decades of the twentieth century. Freud proposed that the mind consisted of "mental organs" (id, ego, and superego) that struggled for control over behavior (Bock 1988:24). He postulated that certain psychological processes and responses were innate and universal, believing, for example, that all humans evolved through a universal series of psychosexual phases he named the oral, anal, genital, latency, and genital primacy stages of development.

Freud is best known for his study and treatment of neurosis through psychoanalysis and his work on dreams. The latter is summarized in his first book, *On Dreams* (1963, orig. 1900). Here, Freud challenged the popular European view that dreams were insignificant, calling them the "royal road to the unconscious" and outlining his method for examining their symbolic and unconscious meanings.

Freud, also fascinated by history and anthropology, was familiar with anthropological theory of the nineteenth century. Starting about 1910 on a quest that would occupy him for the rest of his life, Freud wrote a series of books and articles attempting to demonstrate how psychoanalysis could explain the origins of cultural institutions.

Two of the most famous are *Totem and Taboo* (1950, orig. 1913) and *Civilization and Its Discontents* (1961, orig. 1930). Freud believed that he could analyze cultural institutions in a way that was analogous to his method of analyzing the neurotic symptoms of his patients. In fact, the subtitle of *Totem and Taboo* is *Some Points of Agreement Between the Mental Lives of Savages and Neurotics.*

Although very few people today would describe themselves as Freudian anthropologists, Freud's influence on the discipline was profound. His evolutionary ideas, in particular the notion that adults in primitive tribes were similar to children in civilized society, were widely popularized. The antievolutionary ideas of Boasian anthropology of the early twentieth century were designed, in part, to counter Freud's theories.

Although anthropologists rejected Freud's evolutionism, they were interested in the relationship between culture and the individual and were drawn to his ideas about the importance of early childhood and the significance of sexual symbolism. They believed that psychoanalysis was a powerful tool for probing the human psyche. Kroeber, though not a culture and personality theorist, actually practiced psychoanalysis in San Francisco from 1921 to 1923. Following Freud, many American anthropologists from the 1920s through the 1950s focused attention on the importance of weaning and toilet training in the development of adult personalities and cultural institutions. More recently, symbolic and interpretive anthropologists of the 1960s, 1970s, and 1980s were attracted to the Freudian notion that many cultural ideas and symbols reflected unconscious impulses or deep-seated sexual tensions (see, for example, Obeyesekere 1981).

Boasians Benedict, Mead, Edward Sapir, Abram Kardiner (1891–1981), and Cora Du Bois (1903–1991) examined different aspects of the problem of how humans acquired culture and culture's relationship to individual personality. Because they focused on the interaction between individual personality and culture, they became known as founding members of the culture and personality school. There are two broad themes within this perspective: the relationship between culture and individual personality (represented

here by Benedict's essay "Psychological Types in the Cultures of the Southwest") and the relationship between culture and human nature (represented here by Mead's introduction to her 1935 book, *Sex and Temperament in Three Primitive Societies*).

The major figures associated with the founding of the culture and personality school all had close ties to Boas and to each other. For example, Edward Sapir was one of Boas' most gifted students. Although primarily known for his work in linguistics (see pages 120–121), Sapir was well versed in psychoanalytic literature and was good friends with Benedict, who taught at Columbia University with Boas. Their correspondence played an important role in shaping Benedict's theories. Mead was one of Benedict's first students and also studied under Boas.

Benedict came to anthropology from literature. She had taught secondary-school English and published numerous poems of her own before starting her career in anthropology. Her interest in the interplay between culture and personality was encouraged by her friend Sapir and her mentor, Boas. Benedict was an ardent cultural relativist. For example, in "Anthropology and the Abnormal" (1934), she argued that normal and abnormal were culturally determined and that what was abnormal in one culture might be perfectly acceptable in another. The most comprehensive expression of Benedict's ideas was her book *Patterns of Culture* (1934). Here, Benedict proposed that each culture had a unique pattern, called a *cultural configuration,* which determined the fundamental personality characteristics of its members. To illustrate this concept, Benedict selected three societies: Zuni, Dobu, and Kwakiutl. Relying on her own and Elsie Clews Parsons' (1875–1941) observations among the Zuni, Reo Fortune's (1903–1979) work with the people of Dobu, and Boas' writings on the Kwakiutl, she described the configuration for each society based on the dominant personality characteristics observed in those cultures. Thus, she argued that culture was "personality writ large." Although this idea was a guiding principle in her work, Benedict offered little explanation of why a culture or its members should have a particular personality or how it was passed from generation to generation.

Margaret Mead and later culture and personality theorists largely accepted Benedict's notion of cultural configuration and focused on discovering its sources. Their investigations centered on the interplay of biological and cultural factors, most significantly on Freud's notion that child-rearing practices had profound effects on adult personality. Margaret Mead's work clearly illustrates this theme. In a series of studies, starting with *Coming of Age in Samoa* (1928) and continuing with *Growing up in New Guinea* (1930) and one of her more controversial books, *Sex and Temperament in Three Primitive Societies* (1935), Mead attempted to separate the biological and cultural factors that control human behavior and personality development. Together with Benedict's *Patterns of Culture* (1934b), Mead's trilogy firmly established the cultural configuration and national character approaches in American psychological anthropology (Hsu 1980:349).

Mead was also one of the most colorful figures in American anthropology. She was born in Philadelphia, the daughter of a professor at the Wharton School of the University of Pennsylvania. Like her mentor, Ruth Benedict, she had an early interest in literature. During her undergraduate career at Barnard College in New York City, she was a member of a literary group called the Ash Can Cats (Lutkehaus 1995:189).

In 1923, Mead began her graduate career at Columbia University, working with both Ruth Benedict and Franz Boas. Her relationship with her mentor Benedict was particularly intense. Mead and Benedict became lovers after the completion of her dissertation, a relationship that continued until Benedict's death in 1948 (Bateson 1984:117).

In 1925 Mead did her first fieldwork in Samoa. Her Samoan experience was the only fieldwork she was to undertake alone, and it became the basis of her first book, *Coming of Age in Samoa*. This book was an immediate hit and launched Mead on a long career as one of anthropology's most prolific authors. She published thirty-nine books (fifteen of them collaborations) and almost fourteen hundred other pieces of various kinds. Many of these were brief essays designed for popular consumption. She wrote regularly for *The Nation* and *The New York Times*.

For seventeen years, with her collaborator, Rhoda Metraux (1914–2003), she wrote a monthly column for the women's magazine *Redbook*. In addition to this she made films and appeared frequently on radio and television. By the late 1950s her regular appearances on television talk shows made her one of the best known academics in American life, and certainly the best known anthropologist. Publication in the popular press placed Mead squarely in the tradition of Franz Boas, who frequently wrote for a general, rather than professional, audience.

Mead's personal life was particularly tumultuous. In addition to her long affair with Benedict, she was married three times. Her first marriage to her childhood sweetheart, Luther Cressman, began in 1923. Cressman was ordained an Episcopal priest that same year but also studied sociology and anthropology at Columbia, receiving a Ph.D. in sociology in 1928. In 1925, Cressman left New York to continue his studies in theology in Europe, and Mead began her fieldwork in Samoa. On the way back from Samoa, she met and fell in love with the Australian anthropologist and psychologist Reo Fortune. She divorced Cressman and married Fortune in 1928. Cressman went on to found the anthropology department at the University of Oregon and conducted some of the first research in the history and prehistory of the Northwest.

In the late 1920s and early 1930s Fortune and Mead continued to do fieldwork together in New Guinea. In 1932, while working on the Sepik River in New Guinea, they met British anthropologist and psychologist Gregory Bateson. From 1932 to 1935, Mead, Fortune, and Bateson worked together and occasionally lived together. During this time, Mead fell in love with Bateson. When the three returned from the field in 1935, Mead divorced Fortune and in 1936 married Bateson. Soon after, they left to conduct research together in Bali. Mead's only child, Mary Catherine Bateson, was born to the couple in 1939. Catherine Bateson is today a linguist and anthropologist specializing in Middle Eastern culture. Mead and Gregory Bateson divorced in 1950.

In 1942 Mead began a professional collaboration with her research assistant, Rhoda Metraux. In 1955, after Metraux's divorce, Mead and

Metraux began to share the same residence. This relationship continued for twenty-three years until Mead's death in 1978. In addition to their columns for *Redbook,* Mead and Metraux collaborated on several books.

We are often asked why we choose to present Mead's personal life in these pages. After all, we don't tell you about Radcliffe-Brown's or Boas' family, so why should we talk about Mead and Benedict? There are several reasons. First, all serious students of anthropology will surely hear something of Mead's private life and, because of this, it is important that the outline of her life be presented clearly. There is a complex relationship between Mead's sexual and family life and her work, which focused extensively on family and sexual roles in different societies. Clearly, readers of Mead should ask to what extent her personal life colored her research and vice versa. For example, the research Mead did for *Sex and Temperament in Three Primitive Societies,* the introduction of which we reprint here, was done while she, Fortune, and Bateson lived together in New Guinea. Mead's daughter later wrote:

> It is not accidental that when Margaret was on the Sepik, struggling with the question of diversity in herself and in her ways of loving, she was formulating the contrasts between three New Guinea peoples who dealt very differently with maleness and femaleness, with assertion and creativity. (Bateson 1984:160)

The introduction to *Sex and Temperament* clearly shows Mead's interest in culture as a primary factor determining masculine and feminine social characteristics and behavior. The book, written for a popular rather than a professional audience, aimed to demonstrate the range of cultural diversity (McDowell 1980:278).

Mead was always a controversial scholar, both within anthropology and outside of it. Books such as *Coming of Age in Samoa* were intended as a critique of American culture and read as such. Mead was involved in politics for much of her life and consistently stood for liberal causes. Wilton Dillon wrote that "perhaps no citizen in modern times has testified on so many different topics before more different professional committees as Mead" (1980:327). Although Mead

posthumously received the Presidential Medal of Freedom in 1979, she also made many enemies in the course of her life, particularly among conservative thinkers. *Coming of Age in Samoa* figures prominently on several lists put together by conservative organizations featuring, the worst books of the twentieth century. In fact, the arch-conservative Intercollegiate Studies Institute named it the number one worst book of the century. Within academia, Mead's work, as well as Benedict's, also faced criticism. Benedict was critiqued for ignoring aspects of culture that did not fit her cultural configuration model, such as the drunkenness affecting Pueblo Indians and the calculating self-control practiced by the Kwakiutl. In 1983, five years after Mead's death, Australian anthropologist Derek Freeman (1916–2001) ignited a controversy with the publication of *Margaret Mead and Samoa: The Making and Unmaking of an Anthropological Myth,* in which he claimed that Mead's *Coming of Age in Samoa* was factually incorrect. Freeman charged that Mead's informants, embarrassed by her questions about intimate matters, deceived her with wild tales of sexual abandon. Debate over Freeman's assertions was a major issue in anthropology in the 1980s and early 1990s and still remains unresolved.

Essentially, culture and personality theorists of the 1930s were interested in learning more about the specific ways in which a culture determined the personality of its members. Psychoanalyst Abram Kardiner, in collaboration with anthropologists Du Bois, Sapir, and Ralph Linton (1893–1953), among others, developed a neo-Freudian approach to the study of this issue. According to Langness (1987), Kardiner was influenced by reading *The Future of an Illusion,* first published in 1928, in which Freud proposed that children's early life experiences determine their later religious beliefs. For example, children raised in a household with a strict authoritarian father conceptualized their deities as demanding, always observant, and strict disciplinarians. In accord with this line of thought, Kardiner advanced a theory that explained the mechanism by which culture determined personality.

Kardiner proposed what he called the *basic personality structure,* a collection of fundamental personality traits shared by the normal members of a society. Following Freud, he hypothesized that the foundations of personality development were set in early childhood. He argued that since child-rearing procedures such as disciplining, weaning, and toilet training (what Kardiner termed *primary institutions*) are generally standardized within a society, all members of that society are subjected to the same basic influences on their personality development. Consequently, a society's primary institutions lead to the formation of its basic personality structure. Personality, in turn, influences culture through the creation of secondary institutions. These are cultural institutions, such as religion, created to satisfy the needs of personality through the psychological mechanism of projection.

Organizing a series of seminars in 1936 and 1937, Kardiner tested his theory with data supplied by his anthropologist colleagues. It soon became apparent to Kardiner that no data had been collected specifically for the sort of analysis he proposed. To resolve this issue, anthropologist Cora Du Bois traveled to the island of Alor in the Dutch East Indies to gather the appropriate types of information. Du Bois collected a variety of ethnographic and psychological data (such as Rorschach tests, life histories, and reports of dreams) from Alorese informants. After her return in 1939, Du Bois, Kardiner, and other independent analysts reviewed the data; they all reached the same fundamental conclusions concerning the basic characteristics of Alorese personality.

A weakness in Kardiner's theory was that the basic personality structure could not account for the variation in personality present in even the smallest society. To finesse this problem, Du Bois proposed the *modal personality*, the personality type that was statistically most common in a society. Like Kardiner, Du Bois hypothesized that primary institutions would lead to the formation of a basic set of personality characteristics (as illustrated by her research on the Alorese) but that there would also exist individual variation in how personalities developed and were expressed. Thus the concept of modal personality provided a theoretical tool for examining the interplay of personality and culture while allowing for the psychological variation that invariably exists among the members of a given society.

The outbreak of World War II provided anthropologists with opportunities to push culture and personality research still further. In the 1940s and during the cold war, the United States became vitally interested in studying the psychology of the citizens of the nations with which it was in conflict. The culture and personality theorists responded with *national character studies*. These studies differed from the modal personality work in scale and methodology. First, the national character studies dealt with industrial nation-states rather than simple societies. Second, culture and personality theorists typically worked with small numbers of people and relied on information gathered through participant observation. However, national character studies involved nations with millions of people and because the nations being studied were sometimes hostile, participant observation was inappropriate and often impractical. To find their way around these problems, anthropologists interviewed immigrants, analyzed literature and films, and searched government records. The results were mixed.

Two of the most famous national character studies are Benedict's *The Chrysanthemum and the Sword* (1946), a study of the Japanese, and Geoffrey Gorer (1905–1985) and John Rickman's (1891–1951) *The People of Great Russia: A Psychological Study* (1949). Both followed a neo-Freudian approach, attempting to relate childrearing practices to adult personality types. Benedict, for example, examined Japanese toilet-training practices in relation to the alleged Japanese preoccupation with obedience and order. Gorer and Rickman hypothesized that the Russian national character (supposedly a manic-depressive personality type) resulted from the practice of swaddling infants. It is easy to see how this study fit into the politics of the cold war.

The *Chrysanthemum and the Sword,* though it undoubtedly contains many inaccuracies and was strongly critiqued by both American and Japanese scholars (for example Bennett and Nagai 1953, Lummis 1982), proved highly influential. The book played an important role in determining the nature of the American occupation of Japan (1945–1952) and has been much discussed and debated since, particularly in Japan.

In 1999 Fukui reported that over 2.3 million copies of the book had been sold in Japan and its pocket-size Japanese edition, first published in 1967, has gone through more than 100 printings (Ryang 2004). Gorer and Rickman's work has not fared nearly so well. As with most national character studies, subsequent research has shown it to be inaccurate. The practice of swaddling, for example, was not widespread in Russia; thus it could not explain the Russian personality type—if such a thing existed. Such errors cast doubts on whether or not anthropological techniques could ever be appropriate to the analysis of large-scale societies, and played a large part in the declining popularity of culture and personality studies. By the 1960s, most anthropologists had moved away from the examination of enculturation and its relationship to personality development. Though Benedict's work continued to be read and Mead became increasingly popular with the public, within anthropology, their work was sidelined.

Despite their lack of scholarly acceptance, culture and personality studies, and national character studies in particular, remain keen areas of popular interest. Introductory textbooks in cultural anthropology still reference Mead's and Benedict's work. Numerous books, such as Harrison and Huntington's *Culture Matters: How Values Shape Human Progress* (2001), continue to be published detailing aspects of the cultural personality of this or that group. As in the case of Copeland's *Going International: How to Make Friends and Deal Effectively in the Global Marketplace* (1985) or Thomas and Inkson's *Cultural Intelligence: People Skills for Global Business* (2004), these works are usually marketed as guides for businesspeople.

16. *Psychological Types in the Cultures of the Southwest*

Ruth Fulton Benedict (1887–1948)

THE CULTURE OF the Pueblo Indians is strongly differentiated from that of surrounding peoples.[1] Most obviously, all aspects of their life are highly ritualized, highly formalized. No one has lived among them who has not been struck by the importance of the formal detail in rite and dance, the intricate interrelations of the ceremonial organization, the lack of concern with personal religious experience or with personal prestige or exploit. The emphasis in their all-absorbing ceremonial routine is placed where it was in the medieval Roman church of certain periods, on the formal observance, the ritualistic detail for its own sake.

This is so conspicuously true for the Southwest peoples that in descriptions of their culture we have been content to let the matter rest with this characterization. Yet in a civilization such as that of the North American Indians high ritualistic development sets no group off in any

(1930)

---

[1] Benedict did fieldwork among the Zuñi, Cochiti, and Pima throughout the mid-1920s. This paper, presented in 1928, was her first major analysis of her experiences there. In it, she develops themes later elaborated in *Patterns of Culture,* published in 1934. Perhaps because it was designed for a popular audience and written in an engaging style, *Patterns of Culture* became an enduring classic of anthropology—one still frequently read by students in introductory courses. Despite frequent criticism, Benedict's descriptions of Native American cultures and her theoretical position have had an important effect on American anthropology.

definitive fashion from the vast majority of peoples. The ritual of the sun dance, the peace pipe ceremonies, the cult groups, and age-societies of the Plains, or the winter ceremonial of the Northwest Coast bulk perhaps slightly less prominently in the total life of these people than the calendric dances and retreats of the Southwest, but it is not by any such matter of gradation that the Southwest is set off from other American Indian cultures. There is in their cultural attitudes and choices a difference in psychological type fundamentally to be distinguished from that of surrounding regions. It goes deeper than the presence or the absence of ritualism; ritualism itself is of a fundamentally different character within this area, and without the understanding of this fundamental psychological set among the Pueblo peoples we must be baffled in our attempts to understand the cultural history of this region.[a]

It is Nietzsche who has named and described, in the course of his studies in Greek tragedy, the two psychological types which have established themselves in the region of the Southwest in the cultures of the Pueblo.[2] He has called them the Dionysian and the Apollonian. He means by his classification essentially confidence in two diametrically different ways of arriving at the values of existence.[b] The Dionysian pursues them through "the annihilation of the ordinary bounds and limits of existence"; he seeks to attain in his most valued moments escape from the boundaries imposed upon him by his five senses, to break through into another order of experience. The desire of the Dionysian, in personal experience or in ritual, is to press beyond, to reach a certain psy-

chological state, to achieve excess. The closest analogy to the emotions he seeks is drunkenness, and he values the illuminations of frenzy. With Blake,[3] he believes "the path of excess leads to the palace of wisdom." The Apollonian distrusts all this, if by chance he has any inkling of the occurrence of such experiences; he finds means to outlaw them from his conscious life. He "knows but one law, measure in the Hellenic sense." He keeps the middle of the road, stays within the known map, maintains his control over all disruptive psychological states. In Nietzsche's fine phrase, even in the exaltation of the dance, "he remains what he is, and retains his civic name."[c]

The Southwest Pueblos are, of course, Apollonian, and in the consistency with which they pursue the proper valuations of the Apollonian they contrast with very nearly the whole of aboriginal America. They possess in a small area, islanded in the midst of predominantly Dionysian cultures, an *ethos* distinguished by sobriety, by its distrust of excess, that minimizes to the last possible vanishing point any challenging or dangerous experiences. They have a religion of fertility without orgy, and absorption in the dance without using it to arrive at ecstasy. They have abjured torture. They indulge in no wholesale destruction of property at death. They have never made or bought intoxicating liquors in the fashion of other tribes about them, and they have never given themselves up to the use of drugs. They have even stripped sex of its mystic danger. They allow to the individual no disruptive role in their social order. Certainly in all of these traits they stand so strikingly over against their neighbors that it is necessary to seek some

---

[2] Benedict derives her categories of Apollonian and Dionysian from *The Birth of Tragedy* (published in 1872), a study of the origins of Greek drama by German philosopher Friedrich Nietzsche (1844–1900). Some biographers have suggested that Benedict's intellectual preference for this classification scheme was related to her experience as a very young child, when, at her father's open-casket funeral, she experienced the contrast between her mother's open grief and her father's calm, tragic corpse (Modell 1983:1).

[3] The reference is to William Blake (1757–1827), an English poet, painter, and visionary. Benedict, who had studied English literature at Vassar College, was a more artful writer than most anthropologists. In addition to her anthropological works, Benedict wrote poetry under the pen name of Anne Singleton, a name that may be revealing of her personality. Her poems appeared in literary magazines, but she was unable to get a collection of them published. Thankfully for anthropology, her inability to find a publisher for her book dissuaded her from a career in poetry.

explanation for the cultural resistances of the Pueblos.[4]

The most conspicuous contrast, in the Pueblos, is their outlawry of the divine frenzy and the vision. Now in North America at large the value of ecstatic experience in religion is a cornerstone of the whole religious structure. It may be induced by intoxicants and drugs; it may be self-induced— which may include such means as fasting and torture—or it may be achieved in the dance.

We may consider first the ecstasy induced by intoxicants and drugs.[5] For the neighboring Pima, who share the culture of the primitive tribes of northern Mexico, intoxication is the visible mirroring of religion, it is the symbol of its exaltation, the pattern of its mingling of clouded vision and of insight. Theory and practice are explicitly Dionysian.

> "And I was made drunk and given the sacred songs;"
>
> "He breathed the red liquor into me,"

are in their songs common forms of reference to the shamanistic experience. Their great ceremony is the drinking of the "tizwin," the fermented juice of the fruit of the giant cactus. The ceremony begins with all religious formality and the recitation of ritual, but its virtue lies in the intoxication itself; the desired state is that of roused excitement, and they accept even extreme violence more readily than a state of lethargy. Their ideal is to stave off the final insensibility indefinitely while achieving the full excitation of the intoxicant. This is of course a form of fertility and health magic and is in complete accord with the Dionysian slant of their culture.

It is much commoner, north of Mexico, to use drugs rather than intoxicants for religious ends. The peyote or mescal bean of northern Mexico has been traded up the Mississippi Valley as far as the Canadian border, and has been the occasion of serious religious movements among many tribes. It gives supernormal experiences with particularly strong affect, no erotic excitation, very often brilliant color images. The cult is best described for the Winnebago[d] where the peyote is identified with the supernatural. "It is the only holy thing I have been aware of in all my life"; "this medicine alone is holy and has rid me of all evil."[e] It was eaten everywhere with the object of attaining the trance or supernormal sensations which the drug can give. The Arapaho ate it in an all-night ceremony after which the effects of the drug prolonged themselves throughout the following day.[f] The Winnebago speak of eating it for four days and nights without sleep.

The *datura* is a more drastic poison. I have been told by the Serrano[6] and Cahuilla of boys who have died as a result of the drink, and the Luiseño tell also the same story.[g] It was used by the tribes of Southern California, and north including the Yokuts, for the initiation of boys at puberty. Among the Serrano the boys were overcome by the drug during the night and lay in a comatose condition through the next day and night, during

---

[4] Benedict speaks here of seeking explanation for Pueblo Apollonian behavior, but offers none. Benedict saw culture as personality writ large. She believed that societies were able to choose their cultures out of the full range of human variability, but she was not concerned with understanding why a society would choose one type of culture rather than another. Although Benedict's work offered many examples of Pueblo Apollonian behavior, it provided no historical context—she made no attempt to explain the origins of the cultural personalities she documented. The lack of history is surprising, since Franz Boas, her teacher, placed such an emphasis on historical reconstruction. Despite their Boasian backgrounds, culture and personality writers were generally ahistorical.

[5] Benedict's anthropology is psychological, but it is not Freudian. Like other Boasians, she rejected Freud's notions of cultural evolution as nonscientific and ethnocentric. She traced her intellectual descent from the German psychologist Wilhelm Dilthey (1883–1911), who believed that the goal of psychology was to understand the inner life of the mind. He also proposed the existence of different *weltanshauungen,* or worldviews, which were categories much like Benedict's Apollonian and Dionysian cultures.

[6] Although Benedict here mentions her own 1922 study of the Serrano, she did little fieldwork, preferring instead to draw on studies from many sources.

which time they were granted visions. On the following day they ran a race.[h] Among the Luiseño it seems to have been the same, four nights of trance being spoken of as excessive.[i] The Diegueño reckon only one night of complete stupefaction.[j] The Mohave drank *datura* in order to gain luck in gambling; they were said to be unconscious for four days,[k] during which time they received their power in a dream.

None of these alcohol- and drug-induced excitations have gained currency among the Pueblos.[7] The Pima are the nearest settled neighbors of the Zuñi to the southwest and easily accessible; tribes of the Plains with which the eastern Pueblos came in contact are the very ones in which peyote practices are important; and to the west the tribes of Southern California share certain characteristic traits of this very Pueblo culture. The absence of these traits in the Pueblos is therefore not due to the cultural isolation of impassable barriers. We know too that the period of time during which the Pueblos and their neighbors have been settled relatively near to one another is of considerable antiquity. But the Pueblos have defended themselves against the use of drugs and intoxicants to produce trance or excitement even in cases where the drugs themselves are known among them. Any Dionysian effect from them is, we may infer, repulsive to the Pueblos, and if they receive cultural recognition at all it is in a guise suited to Apollonian sobriety. They did not themselves brew any native intoxicant in the old days, nor do they now. Alone among the Indian reservations, the whiskey of the whites has never been a problem in the Southwest. When, in 1912, drinking seemed to be making some headway among the younger generation in Zuñi, it was the Pueblo elders themselves who took the matter in hand. It is not that it is a religious taboo; it is deeper than that, it is uncongenial. The peyote has been introduced only in Taos, which is in many ways marginal to Pueblo culture.

Datura is used in Zuñi as it was in ancient Mexico[l] in order to discover a thief, and Mrs. Stevenson[8] gives an account of the manner of its use.[m] Read in connection with her quotations on *datura* poisoning and the two to four day trances of the Mohave and Mission Indians, it is a classic example of the Apollonian recasting of a Dionysian technique. In Zuñi the man who is to take the drug has a small quantity put in his mouth by the officiating priest, who then retires to the next room and listens for the incriminating name from the lips of the man who has taken the *datura*. He is not supposed to be comatose at any time; he alternately sleeps and walks about the room. In the morning he is said to have no memory of the insight he has received. The chief care is to remove every trace of the drug and two common desacratizing techniques are employed: first, he is given an emetic, four times, till every vestige of the drug is supposed to be ejected; then his hair is washed in yucca suds.[9] The other Zuñi use of *datura* is even further from any connection with a Dionysian technique; members of the

---

[7] Benedict started her career in ethnology as a student of Elsie Clew Parsons (1875–1941) at the New School for Social Research but soon went to study under Franz Boas at Columbia. After the completion of her dissertation, she remained with Boas until his retirement in 1936; she herself continued at Columbia until her death in 1948. The particularly close relationship between Boas and Benedict gave her exceptional access to the work and friendship of his other students, particularly Sapir, Mead (essay 17), and Kroeber (see essay 10). Both their work, and her conversations and correspondence with them, had a profound influence on Benedict's anthropology. Note the strong reliance on work by Boas, his students, and friends in Benedict's notes to this essay.

[8] Matilda Stevenson (1849–1915) was a pioneering American ethnographer who did extensive fieldwork among the Zuñi between 1879 and 1915 and published several monographs on them. Stevenson, founder and first president of the Women's Anthropological Society, was one of the first ethnographers to do work that centered on women and children.

[9] Two aspects of Boasian thought exerted particularly strong influences on Benedict. The first was cultural relativism. Notice that her language describing the use of hallucinogens, an exotic and possibly offensive cultural practice, is matter-of-fact and nonjudgmental. Although Apollonian culture traits might seem more desirable to

priestly orders go out at night to plant prayer sticks on certain occasions "to ask the birds to sing for rain," and at such times a minute quantity of the powdered root is put into the eyes, ears, and mouth of each priest. Here any connections with the physical properties of the drug are lost sight of.

Much more fundamental in North America than any use of drugs or alcohol to induce ecstasy was the cult of the self-induced vision. This was a near-universality from ocean to ocean, and everywhere it was regarded as the source of religious power. The Southwest is by no means beyond the southern limits of its distribution, but it is the one outstanding area of North America where the characteristic development of the vision is not found. This experience has several quite definite characteristics for North America: it is achieved characteristically in isolation, and it gives to the successful individual a personal manitou or guardian spirit who stands to him in a definite life-long relationship. Though west of the Rockies it is often regarded as an involuntary blessing available only for those of a particular psychological make-up, throughout the great extent of the continent it is sought by isolation and fasting, and in the central part of the continent often by self-torture. This "vision," from which supernatural power was supposed to flow, did not by any means signify only supernormal or Dionysian experiences, but it provided always a pattern within which such an experience had peculiar and institutionalized value; and in the great majority of cases it was these more extreme experiences that were believed to give the greater blessing.

The absence of this vision complex in the Southwest is one of the most striking cases of cultural resistance or of cultural reinterpretation that we know in North America. The formal elements are found there: the seeking of dangerous places, the friendship with a bird or animal, fasting, the belief in special blessings from supernatural encounters. But they are no longer instinct with the will to achieve ecstasy. There is complete reinterpretation. In the pueblos they go out at night to feared or sacred places and listen for a voice, not that they may break through to communication with the supernatural, but that they may take the omens of good luck and bad. It is regarded as a minor ordeal during which you are badly frightened, and the great taboo connected with it is that you must not look behind you on the way home no matter what seems to be following you. The objective performance is much the same as in the vision quest; in each case, they go out during the preparation for a difficult undertaking—in the Southwest often a race—and make capital of the darkness, the solitariness, the appearance of animals. But the significance is utterly different.[10]

Fasting, the technique most often used in connection with the self-induced vision, has received the same sort of reinterpretation in the Southwest. It is no longer utilized to dredge up experiences that normally lie below the level of consciousness; it is here a requirement for ceremonial cleanness. Nothing could be more unexpected to a Pueblo Indian than any theory of a connection between fasting and any sort of exaltation. Fasting is required during all retreats, before participation in a dance, in a race, etc., etc., but it is never followed

---

upper-middle-class intellectual Americans (her primary audience), her writing here and in *Patterns of Culture* describes Apollonian and Dionysian cultures as equally attractive.

The second Boasian influence was an emphasis on holism. Boas suggested that cultures were integrated; Benedict pushed this idea further. She saw culture as having internal logical consistency and being characterized by a single dominant trend or pattern. This essay is largely an exercise in the demonstration of the holism that she saw in culture in general and among the Pueblo peoples in particular. Throughout the essay, she tries to show that all Pueblo practices, even the use of hallucinogenic drugs, fit the restrained, Apollonian worldview.

[10] Benedict's focus here is not on the actions performed, but on how the actors interpret their actions. Boas wanted to build anthropology on a scientific, empirical model; Benedict came to see anthropology as an interpretive art, as much a humanity as a social science. At the end of her life, she wrote that anthropology stood at the boundary between science and the humanities (1948:585). This view has made her an important figure for many interpretive and postmodern anthropologists.

by power-giving experience; it is never Dionysian. Fasting, also, like drugs and visions, has been revamped to the requirements of the Apollonian.

Torture, on the contrary, has been much more nearly excluded.[11] It is important only in the initiations and dances of certain curing societies[n] and in these cases there is no suggestion of any states of self-oblivion. It is interesting that the Pueblos have been exposed to self-torture practices, both in the aboriginal culture of the Plains, and in European-derived practices of the Mexican Penitentes.[12] The eastern Pueblos are in the very heart of the Santa Fe Penitentes country and these Mexicans attend their dances and ceremonies regularly and without hindrance. Much in their practice they have in common with the Indians: the retreats in the ceremonial house, the organization of the brotherhood (priesthood, for the Indian), the planting of crosses. But the self-lashing with cactus whips, the crucifixion on Good Friday, are alien; torture has not penetrated Pueblo life either from these practices or from those of the Plains or of California. Among the Pueblos, every man's hand has its five fingers,[13] and unless he has been tortured as a witch, he is unscarred.

No more than the Pueblos have allowed ecstasy as induced by alcohol or drugs, or under the guise of the vision, have they admitted it as induced by the dance. Perhaps no people in North America spend more time in dance than the Southwest Pueblos. But its use as the most direct technique at our command for the inducement of supernormal experience is alien to them. With the frenzy of a Nootka bear dance, of a Kwakiutl cannibal dance, of a ghost dance, of a Mexican whirling dance, their dancing has nothing in common. It is rather a technique of monotonous appeal, of unvarying statement; always, in the phrase of Nietzsche's I used before, "they remain as they are and retain their civic names." Their theory seems to be that by the reiteration of the dance they can exercise compulsion upon the forces they wish to influence.

There are several striking instances of the loss, for the Pueblos, of the Dionysian significance of specific dance behavior, the objective aspects of which they still share with their neighbors. The best is probably the dance upon the altar. For the Cora of northern Mexico the climax of the whirling dance is reached in the dancer's ecstatic, and otherwise sacrilegious, dancing upon the ground altar itself. In his madness it is destroyed, trampled into the sand again.[o] But this is also a Pueblo pattern. Especially the Hopi at the climax of their dances in the kivas dance upon the altar destroying the ground painting. Here there is no ecstasy; it is raw material used to build up one of the common Pueblo dance patterns where two "sides" which have previously come out alternately from opposite sides, now come out together for the dance climax. In the snake dance, for instance,[p] in the first set Antelope (dancer of Antelope society) dances, squatting, the circuit of the altar, retires; Snake (dancer of Snake society) repeats. In the second set Antelope receives a vine in his mouth and dances before the initiates trailing it over their knees; retires; Snake repeats with a live rattlesnake held in the same fashion. In the final set Antelope and Snake come out together, dancing together upon the altar, still in the squatting position, and destroy the ground painting. It is a formal sequence, like a Morris dance.[14]

---

[11] Notice that Benedict offers no reason why the Pueblo have rejected torture. It is simply an aspect of their culture, and culture is an independent force creating itself.

[12] *Penitentes* are individuals who, at Easter, imitate the suffering of Jesus by whipping themselves and imitating his crucifixion.

[13] *Five fingers* refers to a common Plains Indian practice of chopping off a finger joint in mourning or for spiritual purposes.

[14] Critics have frequently accused Benedict of being so guided by her vision of the logical constancy of culture that she distorted her data. They point out that, Benedict's claims to the contrary, alcoholism was common on the Pueblo reservations during her fieldwork (and is so today). In this passage, Benedict suggests that a dance done with a live rattlesnake in the mouth is not an ecstatic ritual, but rather like a Morris dance, a rather staid and orderly form of British folk dancing. Perhaps so, but this assertion raises important questions of interpretation. Most observers would consider dancing with live rattlesnakes an ecstatic rite. However, few members of any religion would use such words to describe their actions. So, is it or is it not ecstatic? If we accept that dancing with live rattlesnakes is not an ecstatic ritual, does the phrase have any meaning;

It is evident that ecstatic experience is not recognized in the Southwest and that the techniques associated with it in other areas are reinterpreted or refused admittance. The consequence of this is enormous: it rules out shamanism. For the shaman, the religious practitioner whose power comes from experiences of this type, is everywhere else in North America of first rate importance. Wherever the authority of religion is derived from his solitary mental aberrations and stress experiences and his instructions derived therefrom are put into practice by the tribe as a sacred privilege, that people is provided with a technique of cultural change which is limited only by the unimaginativeness of the human mind.[15] This is a sufficient limitation; so much so that it has never been shown that cultures which operate on this basic theory are more given to innovation than those which disallow such disruptive influences. This should not blind us to the fact, however, that the setting in these two cultures for the exercise of individuality is quite different; individual initiative which would be fully allowed in the one case[q] would in the other be suspect, and these consequences are fully carried out in the Southwest. They have hardly left space for an impromptu individual act in their closely knit religious program; if they come across such an act they label the perpetrator a witch. One of the Zuñi tales I have recorded tells of the chief priest of Zuñi who made prayer sticks and went out to deposit them. It was not the time of the moon when prayer sticks must be planted by members of the curing societies, and the people said, "Why does the chief priest plant prayer sticks? He must be conjuring." As a matter of fact he was calling an earthquake for a private revenge. If this is so in the most personal of Zuñi religious acts, that of planting prayer sticks, it is doubly so of more formal activities like retreats, dances, etc. Even individual prayers of the most personal sort—those where cornmeal is scattered—must be said at sunrise, or over a dead animal, or at a particular point in a program, etc.; the times and seasons are always stipulated. No one must ever wonder why an individual was moved to pray.

Instead therefore of shamans with their disruptive influence upon communal practices and settled traditions, the Southwest has religious practitioners who become priests by rote memorizing and by membership in societies and cult groups. This membership is determined by heredity and by payment[r] for though in their own theory serious illness or an accident like snake bite or being struck by lightning are the accepted reasons for membership in certain societies, there are always alternative ways of joining even the curing societies so that no man with interest and sufficient means remains outside. In Zuñi heredity is the chief factor in membership in the priestly groups, payment in the curing societies; in neither is individual supernatural power ever claimed by any member as a result of personal illumination. Those who practice curing in Zuñi are merely those who by payment and by knowledge of ritual have reached the highest orders of the curing societies and received the personal corn fetish, the *mili*.

If the ecstasy of the Dionysian has been rejected in the Southwest with all its implications, so too has the orgy.[16] There is no doubt that the idea of fertility bulks large in the religious

---

can any ritual be described as ecstatic? Such issues of interpretation became the subject of intense anthropological debate in the 1950s and 1960s and to some extent remain so today.

[15] Benedict comments in passing on the "unimaginativeness of the human mind." Like Boas, Benedict believed that within a culture, most traits originated by diffusion rather than independent invention. However, neither agreed at all with the radical European diffusionist thinkers.

[16] Throughout this essay, but particularly here and below, the examples given are quite sensational, even risqué. This is typical of much of the anthropology of Benedict's time and, in her case, there were at least two reasons for it. First, she often wrote for a popular audience, and like Freud, Mead, and Malinowski, used the lure of the discussion of forbidden topics such as sex to attract and hold her audience. Second, she was a firm believer in cultural relativism. Showing exotic cultural practices that were unacceptable to her audience in a calm and rational light helped build the case for the acceptance of all cultures as equally valid. In this connection, it should be noted that Benedict practiced what she preached. She was a bitter opponent of racism and a forceful advocate for tolerance within her own society.

practices of the Southwest,[s] and with fertility rites we almost automatically couple orgy, so universally have they been associated in the world. But the Southwest has a religion of fertility founded on other associations. Haeberlin's study gives a useful summary of the type of ritual that is here considered to have this efficacy.[t] The cylinders the men carry and the amulets carried by the women in ceremonies are sex symbols and are thrown by them into springs or onto ground paintings; or in the women's dance two are dressed as male dancers and shoot arrows into a bundle of cornhusks; or a line of women with yucca rings run in competition with a line of men with kicking sticks. In Peru in a race of exactly similar import, men racing women, the men ran naked and violated every woman they overtook.[u] The pattern is self-evident and common throughout the world, but not in the Southwest. In Zuñi there are three occasions on which laxness is countenanced. One of these is in the retreat of the Tlewekwe society, which has power over cold weather. The priestesses of the medicine bundle of this society (*te etone*) and the associated bundle (*mu etone*) during one night receive lovers, and they collect a thumb's length of turquoise from their partners to add to the decorations of their bundles. It is an isolated case in Zuñi and the society can no longer be very satisfactorily studied. The other two cases are rather a relaxation of the customary strict chaperonage of the young people, and occur at the ceremonial rabbit hunt[v] and on the nights of the scalp dance; children conceived on these nights are said to be exceptionally vigorous. Doctor Bunzel[17] writes, "These occasions on which boys and girls dance together or are out together at night provide an opportunity for sweethearts. There is no promiscuity, and they are never, never orgiastic in character. There is amiable tolerance of sexual laxity; a 'boys will be boys' attitude." It is all very far indeed from the common Dionysian sex practices for the sake of fertility.

It is not only in connection with fertility and sex that orgy is common among the peoples of America. In the region immediately surrounding the Southwest, there is on the one hand the orgy of sun dance torturing to the east and the orgy of wholesale destruction in the mourning ceremonies to the west. As I have said, torture plays a very slight role in the Southwest, orgiastic or otherwise. Mourning is made oppressive by fear of the dead, but there is no trace of abandon. Mourning here is made into the semblance of an anxiety complex; it is a completely different thing from the wild scenes of burning the dead in a bonfire of offered property and of clothes stripped from the mourner's backs that the Mohave practice[w] and that is found in such Dionysian fullness commonly in California, where among the Maidu mourners have to be forcibly restrained from throwing themselves into the flames,[x] and among the Pomo they snatch pieces of the corpse and devour them.[y]

One Dionysian ceremony of wide American distribution has established itself in the Southwest—the scalp dance.[18] This is the victory dance of the Plains, or the women's dance, and the position of honor given to women in it, the four-circle coil danced around the encampment, the close-fitting war bonnet, certain treatments of the scalp, are the same in the Southwest as on the Plains. The wilder abandons of the Plains dance are, as we should expect, omitted, but there occurs in this dance, at least in Zuñi, one of the few ritual Dionysian acts of the Southwest—the washing and biting of the scalp. For the repulsion against contact with bones or a corpse is intense among these people, so that it makes an occasion for horror out of placing a scalp between the teeth, whereas placing a snake between the teeth in the snake dance is no such matter. The woman who carries the scalp in the dance—the position of honor—must rise to this pitch and every girl is said to dread being called out for the role.

---

[17] Like many of those that Benedict mentions, Ruth Bunzel (1898–1990) was a student of Boas and a member of Benedict's own circle. She is particularly remembered for her studies of Zuñi pottery making.

[18] In this passage, Benedict seems to allow that an Apollonian society can include some Dionysian practices. However, this apparent contradiction is resolved by the fact that those who perform the Dionysian act dread participating in it.

Ecstasy and orgy, therefore, which are characteristic of America at large are alien in the Southwest. Let me illustrate this fundamental Apollonian bent in the Southwest by certain specific examples of the way in which it has worked itself out in their culture.

There is considerable emphasis in North America upon the ritualistic eating of filth and it is in this category that the very slightly developed cannibalistic behavior of the Northwest Coast belongs.[19] That is, the emphasis there is never, as so often in cannibalism, upon the feast, nor on doing honor to or reviling the dead. The cannibal dance of the Kwakiutl is a typically Dionysian ritual.[z] It is not only that it is conceived as a dramatization of a condition of ecstasy which the main participant must dance to its climax before he can be restored to normal life; every ritualistic arrangement is designed—I do not mean consciously—to heighten the sense of the anti-natural act. A long period of fasting and isolation precedes the rite, the dance itself is a crouching, ecstatic pursuit of the prepared body held outstretched toward him by a woman attendant. With the required ritualistic bites the anti-natural climax is conceived to be attained, and prolonged vomiting and fasting and isolation follows.

In the filth eating of the Southwest, which is the psychological equivalent to this initiation of the Kwakiutl cannibal, the picture is entirely different. The rite is not used to attain horror, nor to dramatize a psychological climax of tension and release. Captain Bourke has recorded the Newekwe feast he attended with Cushing, at which gallon jars of urine were consumed by the members of the society. The picture is as far from that of the Kwakiutl rite as any buffoonery of our circus clowns. The atmosphere was one of coarse joviality, each man trying to outdo the others. "The dancers swallowed

huge decanters, smacked their lips, and amid the roaring merriment of the spectators, remarked that it was very, very good. The clowns were now upon their mettle, each trying to surpass his neighbors in feats of nastiness."[aa]

The same comment is true not only of filth eating but of clowning in the Southwest in general.[20] I take it that the true Dionysian use of clowning is as comic relief in sacred ceremonial where the release from tension is as full of meaning as the preceding tension, and serves to accentuate it. This use of clowning seems to have been developed, for instance, in the ancient Aztec rites. Now I have never seen any clowning in the Pueblos that seemed to me remotely even to partake of this character, and I do not know of any description which would indicate its presence. Clowning can be buffoonery with no Dionysian implications, as we know well enough from the examples in our own civilization. It is this same use that is most prominent in the Southwest, but clowning is used there also for social satire, as in the take-offs of agents, churches, Indian representatives, etc., and it is common too as a substitute for the joking-relationship, which is absent here, and its license for very personal public comment.

Another striking example of the Southwest Apollonian bent is their interpretation of witch power. The Southwest has taken the European witch complex with all its broomsticks and witches' animal suits and eyes laid on a shelf, but they have fitted it into their own *Weltanschauung*. The most articulate statement that I know of a widespread attitude is still in manuscript in Doctor Parson's monograph on Isleta.[21] The difference, for Isleta, between witch power and good power is simply that good supernatural power is always removed from you as soon as you have put it to the use you intended; witch power

---

[19] Here, as in *Patterns of Culture,* Benedict uses the Kwakiutl as her chief example of a Dionysian culture. In so doing, she relied almost entirely on the work of Boas. She had access not only to Boas' published work, but also to his notebooks and journals. More important, she worked closely with Boas for almost twenty years.

[20] Notice Benedict's use of the first person in this paragraph and below. Her reporting of Pueblo clowning is not

couched in neutral, scientific language; rather she focuses on how things seemed to her. This articulates well with her view of anthropology as an interpretive art.

[21] Benedict draws much of her information on the Pueblos from the work of Parsons, her first teacher, who worked extensively among the Pueblos and published many books on them. Boas and Parsons were very close friends and did some of their research together.

is nonremovable, it rides you for life. Their practice perfectly agrees with this; after every sacred investiture every participant in any rite is de-sacratized, the unwanted mysterious power is laid aside. Nothing could conceptualize more forcibly their discomfort in the face of mystery. Even the best supernatural power is uncanny.

Their lack of comprehension of suicide is, I think, another specific Apollonian trait. The Pima tell many stories of men who have killed themselves for women, and the Plains made suicide a ceremonial pattern; fundamentally their vows to assume the slit sash were suicide pledges in order to raise their rank. But the Pueblos tell the most inept stories[bb] which are obvious misunderstandings of the concept. Again and again I have tried to convey the general idea of suicide to different Pueblo Indians, either by story or by exposition. They always miss the point. Yet in their stories they have the equivalent. There are a number of Zuñi stories[cc] which tell of a man or woman whose spouse has been unfaithful—or of priests whose people have been unruly; they send messengers, often birds, to the Apache and summon them against their pueblo. When the fourth day has come—nothing ever happens in the Southwest till the fourth day—they wash themselves ceremonially and put on their finest costumes and go out to meet the enemy that they may be the first to be killed. When I have asked them about suicide no one has ever mentioned these stories, though they had perhaps been told that very day, and indeed they do not see them in that light at all. They are ritual revenge and the Dionysian gesture of throwing away one's life is not in question.

The cultural situation in the Southwest is in many ways hard to explain.[22] With no natural barriers to isolate it from surrounding peoples, it presents probably the most abrupt cultural break that we know in America. All our efforts to trace out the influences from other areas are impressive for the fragmentariness of the detail; we find bits of the weft or woof of the culture, we do not find any very significant clues to its pattern. From the point of view of the present paper this clue is

to be found in a fundamental psychological set which has undoubtedly been established for centuries in the culture of this region, and which has bent to its own uses any details it imitated from surrounding peoples and has created an intricate cultural pattern to express its own preferences. It is not only that the understanding of this psychological set is necessary for a descriptive statement of this culture; without it the cultural dynamics of this region are unintelligible. For the typical choices of the Apollonian have been creative in the formation of this culture, they have excluded what was displeasing, revamped what they took, and brought into being endless demonstrations of the Apollonian delight in formality, in the intricacies and elaborations of organization.

NOTES

Proceedings of the Twenty-third International Congress of Americanists, September 1928 (New York, 1930), 572–81.

[a] For the theoretical justification of this position in the study of culture see Benedict, Ruth, "Cultures and Psychological Types," *American Anthropologist*, N. S., in press.

[b] I have not followed Nietzsche's definitions in their entirety; I have used that aspect which is pertinent to the problems of the Southwest.

[c] *Birth of Tragedy*, p. 68.

[d] Radin, Paul, "The Winnebago Tribe," *Thirty-seventh Annual Report, Bureau of American Ethnology*, Washington, 1923, 388–426.

[e] Ibid., pp. 408; 392.

[f] Kroeber, A. L., "The Arapaho," *Bulletin, American Museum of Natural History*, vol. 18, New York, 1907, p. 398.

[g] Kroeber, A. L., "Handbook of the Indians of California," *Bulletin 78, Bureau of American Ethnology*, Washington, 1925, p. 669.

[h] Benedict, Ruth, "A Brief Sketch of Serrano Culture," *American Anthropologist*, N. S., vol. 26, pp. 366–392, 1924, p. 383.

[i] Kroeber, A. L., "Handbook," p. 669.

[j] Ibid.

[k] Ibid., p. 779.

---

[22] In conclusion, Benedict again declares the fundamental inexplicability of culture. In *Patterns of Culture,* she used a Digger Indian myth to explain cultural origins and differences: "God gave to every people . . . a cup of clay, and from this cup they drank their life. . . . They all dipped in the water but their cups were different" (1934b:33).

[l] Safford, William E., "Narcotic Daturas of the Old and New World; an Account of Their Remarkable Properties and Their Uses as Intoxicants and in Divination," *Annual Report, Smithsonian Institution for 1920*, pp. 537–567, Washington, 1922, p. 551.

[m] Stevenson, Matilda C., "The Zuñi Indians, Their Mythology, Esoteric Fraternities and Ceremonies," *Twenty-third Annual Report, Bureau of American Ethnology*, Washington, 1904, p. 89.

[n] Cushing, F. H., "My Experience in Zuñi," *Century Magazine*, N. S., 4, p. 31; Stevenson, M. A., *The Zuñi Indians*, p. 503. "All are filled with the spirit of good nature."

[o] Preuss, K. T., *Die Nayarit-Expedition*. Leipzïg, 1912, p. 55.

[p] Voth, H. R., "Oraibi Summer Snake Ceremony," *Field Columbian Museum, Publication 83*. Chicago, 1903, p. 299.

[q] See Radin, Paul, *Primitive Man as Philosopher*. New York and London, 1927, pp. 257–275, for discussion of the wide limits of individualism among the Winnebago.

[r] Except for the war chiefs' societies where it was necessary to have taken a scalp.

[s] Haeberlin, H. K., "The Idea of Fertilization in the Culture of the Pueblo Indians," *Memoirs, American Anthropological Association*, vol. 3, no. 1, 1916.

[t] Ibid., especially p. 39 ff.

[u] Arriaga, P. J., *Extirpacion de la Idolotria del Peru*. Lima, 1621, p. 36 sq.

[v] Information from Dr. Ruth Bunzel.

[w] Kroeber, "Handbook," p. 750.

[x] Ibid., p. 431.

[y] Ibid., p. 253.

[z] Boas, Franz, "The Social Organization and Secret Societies of the Kwakiutl," *Report, United States National Museum for 1895*, Washington, 1897, p. 537 sq.

[aa] Bourke, John G., *Compilation of Notes and Memoranda Bearing on the Use of Human Ordure and Human Urine in Rites of a Religious or Semi-religious Character among Various Nations*. Washington, 1888, p. 9.

[bb] Parsons, Elsie Clews, "A Zuñi Detective," *Man*, vol. 16, pp. 168–170, London, 1916, p. 169.

[cc] Benedict, R., Mss.

17. *Introduction to Sex and Temperament in Three Primitive Societies*

Margaret Mead (1901–1978)

WHEN WE STUDY the simpler societies, we cannot but be impressed with the many ways in which man has taken a few hints and woven them into the beautiful imaginative social fabrics that we call civilizations.[1] His natural environment provided him with a few striking periodicities and contrasts—day and night, the change of seasons, the untiring waxing and waning of the moon, the spawning of fish and the migration-times of animals and birds. His own physical

From *Sex and Temperament in Three Primitive Societies* (1935)

---

[1] Mead was influenced by Ruth Benedict in her writing style, her strong emphasis on cultural relativism, and her belief in patterns in human culture. Note the psychological emphasis placed in the first paragraph. According to Mead, social stratification developed out of personal differences between individuals. Humans select their cultures, choosing some traits and ignoring others. In the last line of this paragraph, she even paraphrases Benedict's cultural configuration concept. Although *Patterns of Culture* was published only one year before Mead's book, Mead had read an early draft of Benedict's work while conducting the field research upon which *Sex and Temperament* was based (Sanday 1980:342). Compare the opening quotation in Benedict's book—"In the beginning God gave to every people a cup of clay, and from this cup they drank their life"—to Mead's "man made for himself a fabric of culture within which each human life was dignified by form and meaning."

nature provided other striking points—age and sex, the rhythm of birth, maturation, and senescence, the structure of blood-relationship. Differences between one animal and another, between one individual and another, differences in fierceness or in tenderness, in bravery or in cunning, in richness of imagination or plodding dullness of wit—these provided hints out of which the ideas of rank and caste, of special priesthoods, of the artist and the oracle, could be developed. Working with clues as universal and as simple as these, man made for himself a fabric of culture within which each human life was dignified by form and meaning. Man became not merely one of the beasts that mated, fought for its food, and died, but a human being, with a name, a position, and a god. Each people makes this fabric differently, selects some clues and ignores others, emphasizes a different sector of the whole arc of human potentialities. Where one culture uses as a main thread the vulnerable ego, quick to take insult or perish of shame, another selects uncompromising bravery and even, so that there may be no admitted cowards, may like the Cheyenne Indians invent a specially complicated social position for the overfearful. Each simple, homogeneous culture can give scope to only a few of the varied human endowments, disallowing or penalizing others too antithetical or too unrelated to its major emphases to find room within its walls. Having originally taken its values from the values dear to some human temperaments and alien to others, a culture embodies these values more and more firmly in its structure, in its political and religious systems, in its art and its literature; and each new generation is shaped, firmly and definitely, to the dominant trends.

Now as each culture creates distinctively the social fabric in which the human spirit can wrap itself safely and intelligibly, sorting, reweaving, and discarding threads in the historical tradition that it shares with many neighboring peoples, it may bend every individual born within it to one type of behavior, recognizing neither age, sex, nor special disposition as points for differential elaboration. Or a culture may seize upon the very obvious facts of difference in age, in sex, in strength, in beauty, or the unusual variations, such as a native propensity to see visions or dream dreams, and make these dominant cultural themes. So societies such as those of the Masai and the Zulus make a grading of all individuals by age a basic point of organization, and the Akikiyu of East Africa make a major drama out of the ceremonial ousting of the older generation by the younger. The aborigines of Siberia dignified the nervously unstable individual into the shaman, whose utterances were believed to be supernaturally inspired and were a law to his more nervously stable fellow tribesmen. Such an extreme case as this, where a whole people bows down before the word of an individual whom we would classify as insane, seems clear enough to us. The Siberians have imaginatively and from the point of view of our society unjustifiably, elevated an abnormal person into a socially important one. They have built upon a human deviation that we would disallow, or if it became troublesome, imprison.[2]

If we hear that among the Mundugumor people of New Guinea children born with the umbilical cord wound around their necks are singled out as of native and indisputable right artists, we feel that here is a culture which has not merely institutionalized a kind of temperament that we regard as abnormal—as in the case of the Siberian shaman—but also a culture that has arbitrarily associated, in an artificial and imaginative way, two completely unrelated points: manner of birth and an ability to paint intricate designs upon pieces of bark. When we learn further that

---

[2] In this paragraph, Mead makes a strong statement of cultural relativism. In particular, she emphasizes Benedict's contention that what is abnormal in one culture may be celebrated in another and provides a series of ethnographic examples to illustrate this point. Along with the issue of cultural relativity, Mead introduces the major point of this work. She says that cultures choose to emphasize issues like sex, age, or beauty, or ignore them. In other words, these factors are culturally rather than biologically determined.

so firmly is this association insisted upon that only those who are so born can paint good pictures, while the man born without a strangulating cord labours humble and unarrogant, and never attains any virtuosity, we see the strength that lies in such irrelevant associations once they are firmly embedded in the culture.

Even when we encounter less glaring cases of cultural elaboration, when we read of a people in which the first-born son is regarded as different in kind from his later-born brethren, we realize that here again the human imagination has been at work, re-evaluating a simple biological fact. Although our own historical tradition hints to us that the first-born is "naturally" a little more important than the others, still when we hear that among the Maori the first-born son of a chief was so sacred that only special persons could cut his infant locks without risking death from the contact, we recognize that man has taken the accident of order of birth and raised a superstructure of rank upon it. Our critical detachment, our ability to smile over these imaginative flights of fancy—which see in the first-born or the last-born, the seventh child of the seventh child, the twin, or the infant born in a caul[3] a being specially endowed with precious or maleficent powers—remains undisturbed. But if we turn from these "self-evident" primitive constructs to points of elaboration that we share with primitive peoples, to points concerning which we are no longer spectators, but instead are deeply involved, our detachment vanishes. It is no doubt purely imaginative to attribute ability to paint to birth with the cord about the neck, or the power to write poetry to one born a twin. To choose leaders or oracles from aberrant and unusual temperaments that we brand as insane is not wholly imaginative, but at least is based on a very different premise, which selects a natural

potentiality of the human race that we neither use nor honour. But the insistence upon a thousand and one innate differences between men and women, differences many of which show no more immediate relationship to the biological facts of sex than does ability to paint to manner of birth, other differences which show a congruence with sex that is neither universal nor necessary—as is the case in the association of epileptic seizure and religious gift—this indeed we do not regard as an imaginative creation of the human mind busy patterning a bare existence with meaning.[4]

This study is not concerned with whether there are or are not actual and universal differences between the sexes, either quantitative or qualitative. It is not concerned with whether women are more variable than men, which was claimed before the doctrine of evolution exalted variability, or less variable, which was claimed afterwards. It is not a treatise on the rights of women, nor an inquiry into the basis of feminism. It is, very simply, an account of how three primitive societies have grouped their social attitudes towards temperament about the very obvious facts of sex difference. I studied this problem in simple societies because here we have the drama of civilization writ small, a social microcosm alike in kind, but different in size and magnitude, from the complex social structures of peoples who, like our own, depend upon a written tradition and upon the integration of a great number of conflicting historical traditions. Among the gentle mountain-dwelling Arapesh, the fierce cannibalistic Mundugumor, and the graceful head-hunters of Tchambuli, I studied this question. Each of these tribes had, as has every human society, the point of sex-difference to use as one theme in the plot of social life, and each of these three peoples has developed that

---

[3] *Caul:* an infant in a caul is born partially covered with membrane from the uterus.

[4] Mead continues her attack on biological determinism in this paragraph. She says that Westerners can accept that there is great variation in beliefs and customs between cultures but inappropriately resist the notion that almost

all the differences we identify between men and women are also cultural. The biological facts of man- and womanhood, she argues, cannot explain the variation in gender behavior across cultures. In this and many other works, Mead focused on childrearing as one of the processes by which people learn their culture's patterns (McDowell 1980:283).

theme differently. In comparing the way in which they have dramatized sex-difference, it is possible to gain a greater insight into what elements are social constructs, originally irrelevant to the biological facts of sex-gender.[5]

Our own society makes great use of this plot. It assigns different roles to the two sexes, surrounds them from birth with an expectation of different behaviour; plays out the whole drama of courtship, marriage, and parenthood in terms of types of behaviour believed to be innate and therefore appropriate for one sex or for the other. We know dimly that these roles have changed even within our history. Studies like Mrs. Putnam's *The Lady*[a] depict woman as an infinitely malleable lay figure upon which mankind has draped ever varying period-costumes, in keeping with which she wilted or waxed imperious, flirted or fled. But all discussions have emphasized not the relative social personalities assigned to the two sexes, but rather the superficial behavior-patterns assigned to women, often not even to all women, but only to women of the upper class. A sophisticated recognition that upper-class

women were puppets of a changing tradition blurred rather than clarified the issue. It left untouched the roles assigned to men, who were conceived as proceeding along a special masculine road, shaping women to their fads and whims in womanliness. All discussion of the position of women, of the character and temperament of women, the enslavement or the emancipation of women, obscures the basic issue—the recognition that the cultural plot behind human relations is the way in which the roles of the two sexes are conceived, and that the growing boy is shaped to a local and special emphasis as inexorably as is the growing girl.[6]

The Vaërtings attacked the problem in their book *The Dominant Sex*[b] with their critical imagination handicapped by European cultural tradition.[7] They knew that in some parts of the world there had been and still were matriarchal institutions which gave to women a freedom of action, endowed women with an independence of choice that historical European culture granted only to men. By simple sleight-of-hand they reversed the European situation, and built up an interpretation

---

[5] It may be hard to conceptualize the climate in which Mead was writing, but it is useful to remember that women had only been given the right to vote fifteen years before the publication of this book. Biological theories about the place of men and women in society were still strong. Consequently, Mead is disingenuous in this passage. She is careful to claim her book is not about women's rights or feminism but simply offers an objective description of men and women in three different societies. Of course, it *is* about women's rights and feminism, and she is attacking the common theories that stated that women were inherently inferior to men, but Mead makes her argument indirectly. She demonstrates that the ways we categorize men and women as masculine and feminine are cultural, not biological. She steers the reader to this conclusion obliquely by showing how American beliefs are different from beliefs in other cultures. Notice also the whack she takes at the evolutionists and their thoughts on feminism in the second sentence. It's a good line.

[6] Contrary to Putnam, Mead argues that gender stereotyping is as inexorable for boys as it is for girls. The determination of maleness and femaleness is arbitrary. Thus, the question is not only the "enslavement or emancipation of women" but also of men. Mead may have been trying to make her argument more palatable to men.

[7] Mathilde and Mathis Vaërting published their book in 1923, resurrecting the "mother-right" school of thought that had been popular in Europe off and on since the middle of the nineteenth century. In *Das Mutterrecht* (*Mother Right,* 1861), the evolutionist Johann Jakob Bachofen popularized the idea that the earliest human civilizations were governed by women, who were eventually overthrown and subjugated by men. Since Bachofen, this theory has appeared in a number of guises. For example, in *The Witch-Cult in Western Europe* (1921), Margaret Murray (1863–1963) proposed a similar argument in relation to the witchcraft persecutions of the Renaissance. Murray argued that pre-Christian religion took the form of a fertility cult centered on the goddess Diana, who had a horned consort. According to Murray, male-dominated Christianity perverted this religion by twisting the cult's nature symbolism into devil worship and instigating the witch trials of the Renaissance. Another incarnation of this idea was expressed in Robert Graves' *The White Goddess* (1948). Mead uses this discussion of the Vaërtings' book not only to criticize their point of view but also to condemn the tendency to view situations as dichotomous extremes (if women are dominant, then men must be submissive; if men are strong, then women must be weak).

of matriarchal societies that saw women as cold, proud, and dominant, men as weak and submissive. The attributes of women in Europe were foisted upon men in matriarchal communities— that was all. It was a simple picture, which really added nothing to our understanding of the problem, based as it was upon the limiting concept that if one sex is dominating in personality, the other sex must be ipso facto submissive. The root of the Vaërtings' mistake lies in our traditional insistence upon contrasts between the personality of the two sexes, in our ability to see only one variation upon the theme of the dominant male, and that the hen-pecked husband. They did conceive, however, of the possibility of a different arrangement of dominance from our traditional one, mainly because to thinking based upon patriarchal institutions the very existence of a matriarchal form of society carries with it an implication of an imaginary reversal of the temperamental position of the two sexes.

But recent studies of primitive peoples have made us more sophisticated.[c] We know that human cultures do not all fall into one side or the other of a single scale and that it is possible for one society to ignore completely an issue which two other societies have solved in contrasting ways. Because a people honour the old may mean that they hold children in slight esteem, but a people may also, like the Ba Thonga of South Africa, honour neither old people nor children or, like the Plains Indians, dignify the little child and the grandfather; or, again, like the Manus and parts of modern America, regard children as the most important group in society. In expecting simple reversals—that if an aspect of social life is not specifically sacred, it must be specifically secular; that if men are strong, women must be weak—we ignore the fact that cultures exercise far greater

licence than this in selecting the possible aspects of human life which they will minimize, overemphasize, or ignore. And while every culture has in some way institutionalized the roles of men and women, it has not necessarily been in terms of contrast between the prescribed personalities of the two sexes, nor in terms of dominance or submission. With the paucity of material for elaboration, no culture has failed to seize upon the conspicuous facts of age and sex in some way, whether it be the convention of one Philippine tribe that no man can keep a secret, the Manus assumption that only men enjoy playing with babies, the Toda prescription of almost all domestic work as too sacred for women, or the Arapesh insistence that women's heads are stronger than men's. In the division of labour, in dress, in manners, in social and religious functioning—sometimes in only a few of these respects, sometimes in all—men and women are socially differentiated, and each sex, as a sex, forced to conform to the role assigned to it. In some societies, these socially defined roles are mainly expressed in dress or occupation, with no insistence upon innate temperamental differences. Women wear long hair and men wear short hair, or men wear curls and women shave their heads; women wear skirts and men wear trousers, or women wear trousers and men wear skirts. Women weave and men do not, or men weave and women do not. Such simple tie-ups as these between dress or occupation and sex are easily taught to every child and make no assumptions to which a given child cannot easily conform.[8]

It is otherwise in societies that sharply differentiate the behaviour of men and of women in terms which assume a genuine difference in temperament. Among the Dakota Indians of the Plains, the importance of an ability to stand any degree of danger or hardship was frantically

---

[8] Here you see a strong statement of the cultural nature of sex roles. Interestingly, Mead reversed this argument in her 1949 book *Male and Female*. There she argued that variability in sex roles was conditioned by biology, specifically, the reproductive functions and anatomical differences between men and women (Sanday 1980:340).

Additionally, she directly attacks the French sociologist Émile Durkheim in this paragraph. Durkheim had

suggested that cultural dichotomies (sacred-profane, right-left, and so on) were a fundamental human method of conceptualizing the world. Here she says that the sacred-profane distinction does not exist and that seeing things in terms of dichotomies ignores all the possibilities in between.

insisted upon as a masculine characteristic. From the time that a boy was five or six, all the conscious educational effort of the household was bent towards shaping him into an indubitable male. Every tear, every timidity, every clinging to a protective hand or desire to continue to play with younger children or with girls, was obsessively interpreted as proof that he was not going to develop into a real man. In such a society it is not surprising to find the berdache, the man who had voluntarily given up the struggle to conform to the masculine role and who wore female attire and followed the occupations of a woman. The institution of the berdache in turn served as a warning to every father; the fear that the son might become a berdache informed the parental efforts with an extra desperation, and the very pressure which helped to drive a boy to that choice was redoubled. The invert who lacks any discernible physical basis for his inversion has long puzzled students of sex, who when they can find no observable glandular abnormality turn to theories of early conditioning or identification with a parent of opposite sex. In the course of this investigation, we shall have occasion to examine the "masculine" woman and the "feminine" man as they occur in these different tribes, to inquire whether it is always a woman of dominating nature who is conceived as masculine, or a man who is gentle, submissive, or fond of children or embroidery who is conceived as feminine.[9]

In the following chapters we shall be concerned with the patterning of sex behaviour from the standpoint of temperament, with the cultural assumptions that certain temperamental attitudes are "naturally" masculine and others "naturally" feminine. In this matter, primitive people seem to be, on the surface, more sophisticated than we are. Just as they know that the gods, the food habits, and the marriage customs of the next tribe differ from those of their own people, and do not insist that one form is true or natural while the other is false or unnatural, so they often know that the temperamental proclivities which they regard as natural for men or for women differ from the natural temperaments of the men and women among their neighbours. Nevertheless, within a narrower range and with less of a claim for the biological or divine validity of their social forms than we often advance, each tribe has certain definite attitudes towards temperament, a theory of what human beings, either men or women or both, are naturally like, a norm in terms of which to judge and condemn those individuals who deviate from it.[10]

Two of these tribes have no idea that men and women are different in temperament. They allow them different economic and religious roles, different skills, different vulnerabilities to evil magic and supernatural influences. The Arapesh believe that painting in colour is appropriate only to men, and the Mundugumor consider fishing an essentially feminine task. But any idea that temperamental traits of the order of dominance, bravery, aggressiveness, objectivity, malleability, are inalienably associated with one sex (as opposed to the other) is entirely lacking. This may seem strange to a civilization which in its sociology, its medicine, its slang, its poetry, and its obscenity accepts the socially defined differences between the sexes as having an innate basis in temperament

---

[9] Mead uses the term *invert* to refer to *berdache* in Native American societies. Her references to the "feminine man" and "masculine woman" make it clear she is referring to homosexuality. Her mention of "early conditioning or identification with a parent of opposite sex" is a reference to the psychoanalytic explanation for homosexuality. Although Mead is specifically addressing these topics in a discussion of peoples in New Guinea, she must also have been struggling with issues of sexuality and gender roles in her personal life. Mead—a strong, outspoken woman in a field dominated by men—was intimately involved with another woman, Ruth Benedict. Furthermore, while conducting the research upon which this book was based with Reo Fortune, her second husband, she had met and become interested in Gregory Bateson, who later became her third husband.

[10] Along with cultural relativism, a persistent strain in American anthropology has been to romanticize primitive peoples as being inherently wise or somehow living closer to and more in tune with nature. This theme is very strong in Mead's work. In *Coming of Age in Samoa* (1928), for example, Mead presents Samoan life as almost utopian.

and explains any deviation from the socially determined role as abnormality of native endowment or early maturation. It came as a surprise to me because I too had been accustomed to use in my thinking such concepts as "mixed type," to think of some men as having "feminine" temperaments, of some women as having "masculine" minds.[11] I set as my problem a study of the conditioning of the social personalities of the two sexes, in the hope that such an investigation would throw some light upon sex-differences. I shared the general belief of our society that there was a natural sex-temperament which could at the most only be distorted or diverted from normal expression. I was innocent of any suspicion that the temperaments which we regard as native to one sex might instead be mere variations of human temperament, to which the members of either or both sexes may, with more or less success in the case of different individuals, be educated to approximate.

NOTES

[a] E. J. S. Putnam, *The Lady,* Sturgis and Walton, 1910.

[b] Mathilde and Mathis Vaërting, *The Dominant Sex,* Doran, 1923.

[c] See especially Ruth Benedict, *Patterns of Culture,* Houghton Mifflin, 1934.

---

[11] Once again, note Mead's style. In this last paragraph she shifts from a third-person description to a first-person confession. This is important since she ultimately bases her theory on her personal experiences in New Guinea and the authority these experiences give her as an ethnographer. By reading the book, she hopes, you will be converted as she was.

The Reemergence of Evolutionary Thought

A major theoretical shift occurred in American anthropology in the late 1940s and the 1950s. For the first half of the century, the principal work in American anthropology was based on the Boasian tradition or the neo-Freudian approach of the culture and personality school. Beginning in the 1930s, the antievolutionary perspective of the Boasian tradition had once again to compete with new and more sophisticated evolutionary approaches proposed by Julian Steward (1902–1972), Leslie White (1900–1975), and George Peter Murdock (1897–1985).

Steward and White developed a techno-environmental approach to cultural change and both were influenced by Marxist thought. Steward's ecological approach focused on the adaptation of individual cultures to specific environmental circumstances. White is best known for his formulation of a general evolutionary theory of culture, an approach that had been abandoned after Boas thrashed unilineal evolutionary theory at the turn of the century. George Peter Murdock was influential in resurrecting the sort of large-scale cross-cultural comparisons that had been the basis of the work of nineteenth-century anthropologists such as Lewis Henry Morgan and E. B. Tylor. He is best known for his creation of the Human Relations Area Files, or HRAF. Harris (1968:606) credits Murdock, Steward, and White's revival of cross-cultural comparison with the "mid-century collapse of historical particularism." Although Harris' eulogy for historical particularism was premature, these three men set the foundation for the formulation of ecological anthropology and cultural materialism, two of the most influential forms of anthropological analysis since the 1960s.

Julian Steward grew up in Washington, D.C., but at age sixteen went to the newly founded Deep Springs Preparatory School (today Deep Springs College). Deep Springs almost surely had a profound affect on Steward. It was then, as today, an extremely small school (about twenty students) where intense study and debate was combined with strenuous physical labor. Deep Springs is also in an extraordinarily spectacular physical setting in the deserts and mountains of Eastern California. At Deep Springs, Steward became interested in the local Paiute and Shoshoni communities and may well have been impressed with the way in which these groups had survived in this beautiful but harsh environment. After completing his undergraduate education at the University of California–Berkeley and Cornell University, Steward studied anthropology at Berkeley, as a student of A. L. Kroeber. Since Steward was interested in discovering the causes of cultural traits and Kroeber insisted that such causes were not "a proper concern of anthropology" (Manners 1973:889) their relationship was contentious. Steward devoted most of his energy to the study of the environmental adaptation of specific societies. His first research was in archaeology, but he then moved to ethnography and worked with the Shoshoni, the Pueblo, and later the Carrier Indians in British Columbia. Steward also devoted a great deal of energy to the investigation of parallel developmental sequences in the evolution of civilizations in the New and Old Worlds.

Steward proposed that cultures in similar environments would tend to follow the same developmental sequences and formulate similar responses to their environmental challenges. He termed those cultural features most closely associated with subsistence practices the *cultural core* (1955). Cultures that shared similar core features belonged to the same *culture type*. Having identified these culture types, he compared and sorted them into a hierarchy arranged by complexity. Steward's original ranking was family, multifamily, and state-level societies. His followers later refined these categories into the now familiar classifications of band, tribe, chiefdom, and state.

Steward did not believe that cultures followed a single universal sequence of development. He proposed instead that cultures could evolve in any number of distinct patterns depending on their environmental circumstances. He called his theory *multilinear evolution* to distinguish it from nineteenth-century unilineal evolutionary theories. The methodology Steward outlined for multilinear evolution involved a field of study he called *cultural ecology*—that is, the examination of the cultural adaptations formulated by human beings to meet the challenges posed by their environments. The selection of Steward's work we have chosen, "The Patrilineal Band," clearly shows how he viewed culture as an evolutionary adaptation to the environment.

Leslie White studied at the University of Chicago under Edward Sapir, a student of Boas. White was thus trained in Boasian historical particularism but found this approach intellectually unsatisfying. At his first teaching post at the University of Buffalo, he read the work of nineteenth-century evolutionists such as Herbert Spencer and particularly Lewis Henry Morgan. Morgan had been vilified by Boas and was the target of attacks by many of Boas' students. White, however, argued that much of what Morgan wrote was correct. Specifically, White agreed that cross-cultural comparison showed that cultural evolution did exist and that this evolution was in the direction of increasing complexity. The problem with the evolutionary thinkers of the nineteenth century, White argued, was that they failed to develop a nonethnocentric, scientific method of accurately assessing cultural complexity. Therefore, although their general idea was correct, many of their specific examples were in error. White proposed to remedy this by developing a quantifiable, universal standard of measurement. In his 1943 essay, "Energy and the Evolution of Culture," White proposed that the control of energy was a key factor in

cultural evolution and could serve as the standard by which to measure evolutionary progress. He traced the history of human culture, arguing that changes in technology marked evolutionary stages. White understood culture as the means by which humans adapted to nature. As members of societies learned to capture energy, they were able to make their lives increasingly secure and so culture advanced. White proposed a grand, universal law of cultural evolution: Culture advances as the amount of energy harnessed per capita per year increases, or as the efficiency with which energy is utilized increases.

Inspired by his reading of Marx, White separated culture into three analytical levels: technological, sociological, and ideological. Like Marx, he believed that all the institutions of society contributed to the evolution of culture; however, technology played the primary role in social evolution and changes in technology affected a society's institutions and value systems.

George Peter Murdock was another important anthropologist deeply influenced by the work of Spencer and Morgan. He received his undergraduate and graduate degrees at Yale University and taught there for thirty-two years. He also rejected the Boasian approach to anthropology. Murdock was interested in the statistical testing of cross-cultural hypotheses, in direct opposition to Boas' avoidance of cross-cultural generalizations. Toward this end he established the Cross-Cultural Survey in 1937, which a decade later formed the basis of the Human Relations Area Files (HRAF), a huge bank of ethnographic data on more than one thousand societies indexed according to standardized categories. Using this information, one can conduct cross-cultural quantitative analyses and test cultural hypotheses in a wide variety of societies.

In addition to creating the HRAF, Murdock is remembered for his 1949 book *Social Structure*. He believed that a universal set of principles governed the relationship between family structure, kinship, and marriage practices. In *Social Structure* Murdock attempted to determine these principles through quantitative analysis and, using comparative data from 250 societies, he was able to demonstrate the utility of the HRAF.

Murdock generally saw his work as deriving from the positivist approach of Spencer, but he recognized that Morgan's (1871) study of kinship was instrumental in shaping the quantitative-comparative approach he developed in *Social Structure*. On the opening page of his chapter on kinship, Murdock wrote, "The scientific significance of kinship systems was first appreciated by Morgan in what is perhaps the most original and brilliant single achievement in the history of anthropology" (1960:61). Additionally, Morgan is one of the anthropologists to whom *Social Structure* is dedicated.

Although White, Steward, and Murdock were evolutionists, they had very different ideas of what cultural evolution meant and how it happened. Steward did not focus on any general, overall pattern of cultural evolution. His vision of evolution was specific and relativistic; he viewed a society's core features as cultural adaptations to their specific environment. On the other hand, White, like L. H. Morgan, looked at evolution as a general overall pattern of technological development. White argued that cultural progress can be measured by specific, absolute standards and can be ranked on a universal scale. He proposed that the key factor driving evolutionary change was revolutionary changes in technology. In the 1960s, Marshall Sahlins (b. 1930) and Elman Service (1915–1996) attempted to reconcile these two approaches. Based on yet another analogy with biological evolution, they suggested that evolution follows two paths. The first is general evolution, a grand movement from simple to complex. The second is specific evolution, the change of individual cultures in response to their particular environmental circumstances (Sahlins and Service 1960).

Murdock's cross-cultural comparisons of cultural traits in many ways paralleled Steward's theory of multilinear evolution, and his attempts to statistically demonstrate universal principles of kin relations resembled White's effort to formulate a universal theory of cultural evolution. However, Murdock focused his efforts on the evolution of aspects of social structure such as kin terminology, family structure, and marriage patterns.

No theoretical viewpoint is immune to the political context in which it develops, and cultural ecology is a particularly good example of this point. The cultural ecologists relied heavily on the insights of Marxist analysis, but given the virulently anticommunist political climate of the United States at the time, they generally did not cite Marx openly. Steward made no reference at all to the influence of Marx in his work and was thus able to avoid controversy. White, to the contrary, often courted controversy.

Like many American scholars of the 1920s, White was drawn to Soviet communism. He visited the Soviet Union for eight weeks in the summer of 1929 and by the time he returned, he was convinced that "the Russian Revolution was the most significant event in modern history" (Peace 1998:85). When the American Association for the Advancement of Science met in 1930, White gave an address, called "An Anthropological Appraisal of the Russian Revolution," praising the Soviet Union and predicting disaster for capitalist nations. The address received front-page attention in *The New York Times* and *Pravda* (the official state newspaper of the Soviet Union), and created a firestorm. Burnt by this experience, White became much more cautious in expressing his political views. He concealed his political activities and avoided public statements of his attachment to either authors or individuals associated with the left. In the 1930s, as the nature of Stalin's dictatorship became apparent, White became a fierce opponent and critic of Soviet communism but he remained a committed socialist. He wrote articles and letters for *The Weekly People,* the newspaper of the Socialist Labor Party of America, under the pseudonym of John Steele (Shankman and Dino 2001).

We should note that many anthropologists have paid a heavy price for their political activism. Boas, as you will recall, was censured for criticizing the government. Other anthropologists were followed and harassed by the FBI. These include Melville Jacobs, Paul Radin, Elman Service, Oscar Lewis, Margaret Mead, and Cora Du Bois. The Boasian Ashley Montagu was fired from Rutgers University after giving a speech condemning Senator Joseph McCarthy (Price 2004 [1960]). Boas' student Gene Weltfish (1902–1980) was a specialist on the Pawnee and author, with Ruth Benedict, of an extremely influential antiracist pamphlet *The Races of Mankind* distributed to troops during World War II (but recalled because it suggested that northern blacks were intellectually superior to southern whites). Weltfish was called to testify before McCarthy and the House Committee on Un-American Activities. *The Races of Mankind* was declared subversive material, and Weltfish's teaching position at Columbia not renewed (Shipp 1980, Pathe 1988).

White was pleased by the attention his views generated, but he was also worried for his position at the University of Michigan. His ideas were repeatedly attacked, and attempts to have him fired were a recurring theme of his career. The university denied him promotion and pay raises for thirteen years. Nevertheless, White remained there and at the end of his career felt that he owed a great debt to the university. He wrote that the university's "devotion to its own ideals made it possible for a nonconformist to stay there and keep being a nonconformist" (in Peace 1998:89; see also Peace and Price 2001).

Eventually, White's work was widely acclaimed. In the late '50s and '60s, he received numerous awards, two honorary degrees, and was elected president of the American Anthropological Association. His prominence allowed him to be politically active once more. In 1957, just after the Russians launched the satellite Sputnik, White said, "A cultural system that can launch earth satellites can dispense with gods entirely." This statement was quoted by the *New York Times,* and clergy in Michigan responded by calling for

White's dismissal from the university. White later responded to the situation by asking whether God "need[ed] a protective clergyman to defend Him" (in Carneiro 1981).

Although a materialist, Murdock was at the opposite end of the political spectrum from White and thus avoided the kinds of public political controversies in which White became embroiled. However, in recent years Murdock has come under scrutiny for his political activities during the 1940s and 1950s. Based on files recovered under the Freedom of Information Act, David Price discovered that Murdock, as an informant for the FBI, reported on the activities of many of his professional colleagues. For example, in 1949 he corresponded directly with J. Edgar Hoover, naming a dozen anthropologists who he was convinced were communists (Price 2004).

Murdock's research has also not escaped the critical appraisal of other anthropologists. One of the most telling criticisms of Murdock's work is the same as that which Boas leveled at the nineteenth-century evolutionists in his 1896 article, "The Limitations of the Comparative Method in Anthropology." That is, the data on which Murdock's analyses were based were taken out of their appropriate cultural contexts, thus invalidating the reliability of the analysis. Murdock's popularity was largely limited to American anthropologists. Many British social anthropologists considered Murdock's work to be nothing more than classification of data.

---

18. *Energy and the Evolution of Culture*

LESLIE WHITE (1900–1975)

EVERYTHING IN THE universe may be described in terms of energy.[a] Galaxies, stars, molecules and atoms may be regarded as organizations of energy. Living organisms may be looked upon as engines which operate by means of energy

derived directly or indirectly from the sun. The civilizations, or cultures of mankind, also, may be regarded as a form of organization of energy. Culture is an organization of phenomena—material objects, bodily acts, ideas, and sentiments—which

(1943)

consists of or is dependent upon the use of symbols. Man, being the only animal capable of symbol-behavior, is the only creature to possess culture.[b] Culture is a kind of behavior. And behavior, whether of man, mule, plant, comet or molecule, may be treated as a manifestation of energy. Thus we see, on all levels of reality,[c] that phenomena lend themselves to description and interpretation in terms of energy. Cultural anthropology is that branch of natural science[d] which deals with matter-and-motion, i.e., energy, phenomena in cultural form, as biology deals with them in cellular, and physics in atomic, form.[1]

The purpose of culture is to serve the needs of man. These needs are of two kinds: (1) those which can be served or satisfied by drawing upon resources within the human organism alone. Singing, dancing, myth-making, forming clubs or associations for the sake of companionship, etc., illustrate this kind of needs and ways of satisfying them. (2) The second class of needs can be satisfied only by drawing upon the resources of the external world, outside the human organism. Man must get his food from the external world. The tools, weapons, and other materials with which man provides himself with food, shelter from the elements, protection from his enemies, must likewise come from the external world. The satisfaction of spiritual and aesthetic needs through singing, dancing, myth-making, etc., is possible, however, only if man's bodily needs for food, shelter, and defense are met. Thus the whole cultural structure depends upon the material, mechanical means with

which man articulates himself with the earth. Furthermore, the satisfaction of human needs from "inner resources" may be regarded as a constant,[e] the satisfaction of needs from the outer resources a variable. Therefore, in our discussion of cultural development we may omit consideration of the constant factor and deal only with the variable—the material, mechanical means with which man exploits the resources of nature.

The articulation-of-man-with-the-earth process may be analyzed and resolved into the following five factors: (1) the human organism, (2) the habitat, (3) the amount of energy controlled and expended by man, (4) the ways and means in which energy is expended, and (5) the human-need-serving product which accrues from the expenditure of energy. This is but another way of saying that human beings, like all other living creatures, exploit the resources of their habitat, in one way or another in order to sustain life and to perpetuate their kind.

Of the above factors, we may regard the organic factor as a constant. Although peoples obviously differ from each other physically, we are not able to attribute differences in culture to differences in physique (or "mentality"). In our study of culture, therefore, we may regard human race as of uniform quality, i.e., as a constant, and, hence, we eliminate it from our study.[2]

No two habitats are alike; every habitat varies in time. Yet, in a study of culture as a whole,[f] we may regard the factor of habitat as a constant: we simply reduce the need-serving, welfare-promoting resources of particular habitats to an average. (In

---

[1] This arresting opening passage reveals several aspects of White's thinking at this stage of his career. Because he saw anthropology as a branch of natural science, he believed that the research methods used in the sciences, when applied to anthropology, would reveal the laws of culture. Later in this essay, White provides a materialist and functionalist basis for the analysis of culture. His "functions and needs" approach is reminiscent of Bronislaw Malinowski, whom he admired (see essay 13), and Herbert Spencer (see essay 1). However, his emphasis on "material, mechanical means" reflects his grounding in Karl Marx (see essay 4).

White was trained in the Boasian tradition. He studied at the New School for Social Research under Alexander

Goldenweiser (1880–1940), a student of Franz Boas and the mentor of Ruth Benedict. At Chicago, where he received his Ph.D., he worked with Edward Sapir, another of Boas' students. However, his theoretical work diverged sharply from that of the Boasians.

[2] As a teenager, White was interested in astronomy and intended to become a physicist. His style of writing and of argument reflect this background. White argues in a scientific idiom—defining and eliminating or analyzing variables and describing laws. Like other Boasians, he discounts the effects of race.

a consideration of particular manifestations of culture we would of course have to deal with their respective particular habitats.) Since we may regard habitat as a constant, we exclude it, along with the human organism, from our study of the development of culture.[3]

This leaves us, then, three factors to be considered in any cultural situation: (1) the amount of energy per capita per unit of time harnessed and put to work within the culture, (2) the technological means with which this energy is expended, and (3) the human-need-serving product that accrues from the expenditure of energy.[4] We may express the relationship between these factors in the following simple formula: $E \times T = P$ in which E represents the amount of energy expended per capita per unit of time, T the technological means of its expenditure, and P the magnitude of the product per unit of time. This may be illustrated concretely with the following simple example: A man cuts wood with an axe. Assuming the quality of the wood and the skill of the workman to be constant, the amount of wood cut in a given period of time, say an hour, depends, on the one hand upon the amount of energy the man expends during this time: the more energy expended, the more wood cut. On the other hand, the amount of wood cut in an hour depends upon the kind of axe used. Other things being equal, the amount of wood cut varies with the quality of the axe: the better the axe the more wood cut. Our workman can cut more wood with an iron, or steel, axe than with a stone axe.

The efficiency with which human energy is expended mechanically depends upon the bodily skills of the persons involved, and upon the nature of the tools employed. In the following discussion we shall deal with skill in terms of averages.[5] It is obvious, of course, that, other things being equal, the product of the expenditure of human energy varies directly as the skill employed in the expenditure of this energy. But we may reduce all particular skills, in any given situation, to an average which, being constant, may be eliminated from our consideration of culture growth. Hereafter, then, when we concern ourselves with the efficiency with which human energy is expended mechanically, we shall be dealing with the efficiency of tools only.

With reference to tools, man can increase the efficiency of the expenditure of his bodily energy in two ways: by improving a tool, or by substituting a better tool for an inferior one. But with regard to any given kind of tool, it must be noted that there is a point beyond which it cannot be improved. The efficiency of various tools of a certain kind varies; some bows are better than others. A bow, or any other implement, may vary in efficiency between 0 per cent and 100 per cent. But there is a maximum, theoretically as well as actually, which cannot be exceeded. Thus, the efficiency of a canoe paddle can be raised or lowered by altering its length, breadth, thickness, shape, etc. Certain proportions or dimensions would render it useless, in which case its efficiency would be 0 per cent. But, in the direction of improvement, a point is reached, ideally as well as practically, when no further progress can be made—any further change would be a detriment. Its efficiency is now at its maximum (100 per cent). So it is with a canoe, arrow, axe, dynamo, locomotive, or any other tool or machine.

---

[3] Although White was concerned with the relationship between humans and nature, he did not share Steward's interest in the effects of specific environments on culture (see essay 19).

[4] The concerns upon which White focuses in this essay, especially technology, reflect the influence of Marx on his works. White visited the Soviet Union in 1929 and, while there, was inspired by his reading of Marx and Engels. He later corresponded briefly with the communist Leon Trotsky (Beardsley 1976:619). He told one of his students that

he had profitably read the last chapter of Marx's work *Capital* sixteen times (Carneiro 1981).

[5] Here and later, White refers to numbers and writes equations, suggesting that he is measuring attributes that can be quantified, perhaps with relative ease. However, White and his followers had great trouble actually providing agreed-on, concrete, quantitative measures of the variables they discussed. As a result, critics considered their work pseudoscientific.

We are now ready for some generalizations about cultural development.[6] Let us return to our formula, but this time let us write it $E \times F = P$, in which E and P have the same values as before— E, the amount of energy expended; P the product produced—while F stands for the efficiency of the mechanical means with which the energy is expended. Since culture is a mechanism for serving human needs, cultural development may be measured by the extent to which, and the efficiency with which, need-serving goods or services are provided. P, in our formula, may thus stand for the total amount of goods or services produced in any given cultural situation. Hence P represents the status of culture, or, more accurately, the degree of cultural development. If, then, F, the efficiency with which human energy is expended, remains constant, then P, the degree of cultural development, will vary as E, the amount of energy expended per capita per year[8] varies:

$$\frac{E_1 \times F}{E_2 \times F} = \frac{P_1}{P_2}$$

Thus we obtain the first important law of cultural development: *Other things being equal, the degree of cultural development varies directly as the amount of energy per capita per year harnessed and put to work.*[7]

Secondly, if the amount of energy expended per capita unit of time remains constant, then P varies as F:

$$\frac{E \times F_1}{E \times F_2} = \frac{P_1}{P_2}$$

and we get the second law of cultural development: *Other things being equal, the degree of cultural development varies directly as the efficiency of the technological means with which the harnessed energy is put to work.*

It is obvious, of course, that E and F may vary simultaneously, and in the same or in opposite directions. If E and F increase simultaneously P will increase faster, naturally, than if only one increased while the other remained unchanged. If E and F decrease simultaneously P will decrease more rapidly than if only one decreased while the other remained constant. If E increases while F decreases, or vice versa, then P will vary or remain unchanged, depending upon the magnitude of the changes of these two factors and upon the proportion of one magnitude to the other. If an increase in E is balanced by a decrease in F, or vice versa, then P will remain unchanged. But should E increase faster than F decreases or vice versa, then P would increase; if E decreases faster than F increases, or vice versa, then P would decrease.

We have, in the above generalizations *the* law of cultural evolution: *culture develops when the amount of energy harnessed by man per capita per year is increased; or as the efficiency of the technological means of putting this energy to work is increased; or, as both factors are simultaneously increased.*

All living beings struggle to live, to perpetuate their respective kinds.[8] In the human species the struggle for survival assumes the cultural form. The human struggle for existence expresses itself in a never-ending attempt to make of culture a more effective instrument with which to provide security of life and survival of the species. And one of the ways of making culture a more powerful instrument is to harness and to put to work

---

[6] In this passage, White writes of degrees of cultural development. This places him in direct opposition to most Boasians, who held that comparing cultures in this manner was impossible and came dangerously close to ethnocentrism.

[7] Here and later, White offers several laws of culture. These occasioned a dispute between White and Steward. Steward's critique was that White's laws were so general as to be virtually self-evident and told nothing about the specifics of change within a culture. White responded that this, while true, was the fundamental nature of universal laws. Supporting White's defense of his laws, Harris (1968:649) asks, "Does the law of gravitation tell us nothing about particulars? When one predicts a particular eclipse on a particular planet . . . has this no relation to the general law?"

[8] White's emphasis on struggle reflects his reading of both Darwin and Marx. Compare his statement here to Marx's famous dictum that all history is the history of class struggle. In Marx, social classes struggle for control of the means of production. For White, the struggle is for increased control of energy and increased efficiency of energy usage.

within it more energy per capita per year. Thus, wind, and water and fire are harnessed; animals are domesticated, plants cultivated; steam engines are built. The other way of improving culture as an instrument of adjustment and control is to invent new and better tools and improve old ones. Thus energy for culture-living and culture-building is augmented in quantity, is expended more efficiently, and culture advances.

Thus we know, not only *how* culture evolves, but *why*, as well. The urge, inherent in all living species, to live, to make life more secure, more rich, more full, to insure the perpetuation of the species, seizes upon, when it does not produce, better[h] (i.e., more effective) means of living and surviving. In the case of man, the biological urge to live, the power to invent and to discover, the ability to select and use the better of two tools or ways of doing something—these are the factors of cultural evolution.[9] Darwin could tell us the consequences of variations, but he could not tell us how these variations were produced. We know the motive force as well as the means of cultural evolution. The culturologist[10] knows more about cultural evolution than the biologist, even today, knows about biological evolution.[i]

A word about man's motives with regard to cultural development. We do not say that man deliberately set about to improve his culture. It may well have been, as Morgan[j] suggested, decades before Lowie[k] emphasized the same point, that animals were first domesticated through whim or caprice rather than for practical, utilitarian reasons. Perhaps agriculture came about through accident. Hero's steam engine was a plaything. Gunpowder was first used to make pretty fireworks. The compass began as a toy. More than this, we know that peoples often resolutely oppose technological advances with a passionate devotion to the past and to the gods of their fathers. But all of this does not alter the fact that domesticated animals and cultivated plants have been used to make life more secure. Whatever may have been the intentions and motives (if any) of the inventors or discoverers of the bow and arrow, the wheel, the furnace and forge, the steam engine, the microscope, etc., the fact remains that these things have been seized upon by mankind and employed to make life more secure, comfortable, pleasant, and permanent. So we may disregard the psychological circumstances under which new cultural devices were brought into being. What is significant to the cultural evolutionist is that inventions and discoveries have been made, new tools invented, better ways of doing things found, and that these improved tools and techniques are kept and used until they are in turn replaced.

So much for the laws, or generalizations, derived from our basic formula. Let us turn now to concrete facts and see how the history of culture is illuminated and made intelligible by these laws.

---

[9] Much of American anthropology has denied the existence of any but the most rudimentary human instincts. White goes against this trend. Here he relies on the existence of a biologically based drive to use culture to make life "more rich, more full."

[10] As this essay shows, White was much given to inventing new words and phrases. He called his work *culturology* rather than anthropology and proposed that culturology was a science and that it treated cultural phenomena as obeying their own laws, distinct from human biology or individual psychology. In this, he was clearly influenced by Kroeber's idea of the superorganic (see essay 10) and Durkheim's notion of the collective conscience (see essays 5 and 6). White once wrote that great men were no more

personally effective in shaping the general course of culture than a "sack of sawdust" (1949:279).

White's insistence that culture follows its own path independent of individual humans, however, seems to contradict his notion that culture exists to make life more secure for humans. At the end of his life, he confronted this problem. White's emphasis on the notion of culture as a system and evidence that culture was often maladaptive led him to reject the idea that culture exists to serve people's needs. In his last work he wrote, "We no longer think of culture as designed to serve the needs of man; culture goes its own way in accordance with laws of its own. Man lives within the embrace of cultural systems, and enjoys or suffers whatever they mete out to him" (1975:159).

In the beginning of culture history, man had only the energy of his own body under his control and at his disposal for culture-living and culture-building. And for a very long period of time this was almost the only source of energy available to him. Wind, water, and fire were but rarely used as forms of energy. Thus we see that, in the first stage of cultural development, the only source of energy under man's control and at his disposal for culture-building was, except for the insignificant and limited use of wind, water and fire, his own body.

The amount of energy that could be derived from this source was very small. The amount of energy at the disposal of a community of 50, 100, 300 persons would be 50, 100, or 300 times the energy of the average member of the community, which, when infants, the sick, the old and feeble are considered, would be considerably less than one "man-power" per capita. Since one "manpower" is about one-tenth of one horsepower, we see that the amount of energy per capita in the earliest stage of cultural development was very small indeed—perhaps 1/20th horsepower per person.

Since the amount of energy available for culture-building in this stage was finite and limited, the extent to which culture could develop was limited. As we have seen, when the energy factor is a constant, cultural progress is made possible only by improvements in the means with which the energy is expended, namely, the technology. Thus, in the human-energy stage of cultural development progress is achieved only by inventing new tools—the bow and arrow, harpoon, needle, etc., by improving old ones—new techniques of chipping flint implements, for example. But when man has achieved maximum efficiency in the expenditure of energy, and when he has reached the limits of his finite bodily energy resources, then his culture can develop no further. Unless he can harness additional quantities of energy—by tapping new sources—cultural development will come to an end. Man would have remained on the level of savagery[1] indefinitely if he had not learned to augment the amount of energy under his control and at his disposal for culture-building by harnessing new sources of energy. This was first accomplished by the domestication of animals and by the cultivation of plants.[11]

Man added greatly to the amount of energy under his control and at his disposal for culture-building when he domesticated animals and brought plants under cultivation.[12] To be sure, man nourished himself with meat and grain and clothed himself with hides and fibers long before animal husbandry and agriculture came into being. But there is a vast difference between merely exploiting the resources of nature and harnessing the forces of nature. In a wild food economy, a person, under given environmental conditions, expends a certain amount of energy (we will assume it is an average person so that the question of

[11] White's description of the relationship between technology and culture was heavily influenced by Marx's idea of a mode of production. Marxists understand different societies as being determined by particular combinations of relations of production and forces of production (see essays 4, 23, and 33). White's analysis is similar but perhaps less complex. He sees different types of society as fundamentally conditioned by the different types of technology they use.

[12] The evolutionary perspective of the nineteenth century had been largely abandoned by American cultural anthropologists, but after World War I it was rehabilitated by archaeologists and European anthropologists. Although they explicitly rejected the ethnocentric and racist formulations of nineteenth-century evolutionary theory, they retained and elaborated its basic elements. White saw little resemblance between his work and that of V. Gordon Childe (1892–1957), but this passage, and much of White's analysis later, shows that influence (Service 1976:613). Childe was an Australian-born archaeologist and culture theorist who lived and worked largely in Great Britain. Openly Marxist, he is remembered for, among other things, coining the term *Neolithic Revolution*. He and others conducted studies of cultural evolution based on archaeological data for a number of years before White published this essay. White, along with Steward, returned the evolutionary element to American cultural anthropology. The evolutionary materialism of these thinkers is reflected in much of American archaeology in the second half of the twentieth century.

skill may be ignored) and in return he will secure, on the average, so much meat, fish, or plant food. But the food which he secures is itself a form and a magnitude of energy. Thus the hunter or wild plant-food gatherer changes one magnitude of energy for another: m units of labor for n calories of food. The ratio between the magnitude of energy obtained in the form of food and the magnitude expended in hunting and gathering may vary. The amount obtained may be greater than, less than (in which case the hunter-gatherer would eventually perish), or equal to, the amount expended. But although the ratio may vary from one situation to another, it is in any particular instance fixed: that is, the magnitude of energy-value of the game taken or plant-food gathered remains constant between the time that it is obtained and the time of its consumption. (At least it does not increase, it may in some instances decrease through natural deterioration.)

In a wild food economy, an animal or a plant is of value to man only after it has ceased to be an animal or a plant, i.e., a living organism. The hunter kills his game, the gatherer digs his roots and bulbs, plucks the fruit and seeds. It is different with the herdsman and the farmer. These persons make plants and animals work for them.[13]

Living plants and animals are biochemical mechanisms which, of themselves, accumulate and store up energy derived originally from the sun. Under agriculture and animal husbandry these accumulations can be appropriated and utilized by man periodically in the form of milk, wool, eggs, fruits, nuts, seeds, sap, and so on. In the case of animals, energy generated by them may be utilized by man in the form of work, more or less continuously throughout their lifetime. Thus, when man domesticated animals and brought plants under cultivation, he harnessed powerful forces of nature, brought them under his control, and made them work for him just as he has harnessed rivers

and made them run mills and dynamos, just as he has harnessed the tremendous reservoirs of solar energy that are coal and oil. Thus the difference between a wild plant and animal economy and a domestic economy is that in the former the return for an expenditure of human energy, no matter how large, is fixed, limited, whereas in agriculture and animal husbandry the initial return for the expenditure of human labor, augments itself indefinitely. And so it has come about that with the development and perfection of the arts of animal husbandry and agriculture—selective breeding, protection from their competitors in the Darwinian struggle for survival, feeding, fertilizer, irrigation, drainage, etc.—a given quantity of human labor produces much more than it could before these forces were harnessed. It is true, of course, that a given amount of human labor will produce more food in a wild economy under exceptionally favorable circumstances,—such, e.g., as in the Northwest Coast of America where salmon could be taken in vast numbers with little labor, or in the Great Plains of North America where, after the introduction of the horse and in favorable circumstances, a large quantity of bison meat could be procured with but little labor,—than could be produced by a feeble development of agriculture in unfavorable circumstances. But history and archaeology prove that, by and large, the ability of man to procure the first necessity of life, food, was tremendously increased by the domestication of animals and by the cultivation of plants. Cultural progress was extremely rapid after the origin of agriculture.[m] The great civilizations of China, India, Mesopotamia, Egypt, Mexico, and Peru sprang up quickly after the agricultural arts had attained to some degree of development and maturity. This was due, as we have already observed, to the fact that, by means of agriculture man was able to harness, control, and put to work for himself powerful forces of nature. With greatly

---

[13] In these passages White, following Childe (1942)—who followed Morgan (see essay 3)—provides criteria for distinguishing savagery, barbarism, and civilization. Compare White's criteria with Childe's comment that "upper Paleolithic societies must be designated savage inasmuch as they relied for a livelihood on hunting, fishing, and collecting" (1942:37) or his statement that the development of agriculture was the first step in the Neolithic Revolution and distinguishes barbarism from savagery (1942:48).

augmented energy resources man was able to expand and develop his way of life, i.e., his culture.[14]

In the development of culture, agriculture is a much more important and powerful factor than animal husbandry." This is because man's control over the forces of nature is more immediate and more complete in agriculture than in animal husbandry. In a pastoral economy man exerts control over the animals only, he merely harnesses solar energy in animal form. But the animals themselves are dependent upon wild plants. Thus pastoral man is still dependent to a great extent upon the forces and caprices of nature. But in agriculture, his control is more intimate, direct, and, above all, greater. Plants receive and store up energy directly from the sun. Man's control over plants is direct and immediate. Further independence of nature is achieved by means of irrigation, drainage, and fertilizer. To be sure, man is always dependent upon nature to a greater or less extent; his control is never complete. But his dependence is less, his control greater, in agriculture than in animal husbandry. The extent to which man may harness natural forces in animal husbandry is limited. No matter how much animals are improved by selective breeding, no matter how carefully they are tended—defended from beasts of prey, protected from the elements—so long as they are dependent upon wild plant food, there is a limit, imposed by nature, to the extent to which man can receive profitable returns from his efforts expended on his herds. When this limit has been reached no further progress can be made. It is not until man controls also the growth of the plants upon which his animals feed that progress in animal husbandry can advance to higher levels. In agriculture, on the other hand, while there may be a limit to the increase of yield per unit of human labor, this limit has not yet been reached, and, indeed it is not yet even in sight. Thus there appears to be a limit to the return from the expenditure of a given amount of human labor in animal husbandry. But in agriculture this technological limit, if one be assumed to exist, lies so far ahead of us that we cannot see it or imagine where it might lie.

Added to all of the above, is the familiar fact that a nomadic life, which is customary in a pastoral economy, is not conducive to the development of advanced cultures. The sedentary life that goes with agriculture is much more conducive to the development of the arts and crafts, to the accumulation of wealth and surpluses, to urban life.

Agriculture increased tremendously the amount of energy per capita available for culture-building, and, as a consequence of the maturation of the agricultural arts, a tremendous growth of culture was experienced. Cultural progress was very slow during Eolithic and Paleolithic times. But after a relatively brief period in the Neolithic age, during which the agricultural arts were being developed, there was a tremendous acceleration of culture growth and the great cultures of China, India, Mesopotamia, Egypt, Mexico, and Peru, came rapidly into being.

The sequence of events was somewhat as follows: agriculture transformed a roaming population into a sedentary one. It greatly increased the food supply, which in turn increased the population. As human labor became more productive in agriculture, an increasing portion of society became divorced from the task of food-getting, and was devoted to other occupations. Thus society becomes organized into occupational groups: masons, metal workers, jade carvers, weavers, scribes, priests. This has the effect of accelerating progress in the arts, crafts, and sciences (astronomy,

---

[14] As these passages illustrate, for White, human cultural evolution was best understood as a process of increasing human control over the natural environment. This is a teleological vision of evolution, much like that of the nineteenth-century evolutionists. For White, cultural evolution has a single goal: virtually complete human control of the environment. This vision accords very well with the times in which White wrote. In the 1940s and (particularly) the 1950s, people foresaw a not-too-distant future of domed, climate-controlled cities. Childe, for example, wrote in 1942 that the development of agriculture turned humans into "active partners with nature instead of parasites on nature" (1942:48). Today, our understanding of human ability to exert control over nature, as well as its desirability, is considerably different. Would a modern textbook, for example, refer to hunters and gatherers as parasites on nature? The theories we produce today tend to emphasize the limits of human abilities and the impossibility of determining the direction of biological or cultural evolution. Perhaps our vision of the world is conditioned by the economics and politics of our own day just as White's was by events of his era.

mathematics, etc.), since they are now in the hands of specialists, rather than jacks-of-all-trades. With an increase in manufacturing, added to division of society into occupational groups, comes production for exchange and sale (instead of primarily for use as in tribal society), mediums of exchange, money, merchants, banks, mortgages, debtors, slaves. An accumulation of wealth and competition for favored regions provoke wars of conquest, and produce professional military and ruling classes, slavery and serfdom. Thus agriculture wrought a profound change in the life-and-culture of man as it had existed in the human-energy stage of development.[15]

But the advance of culture was not continuous and without limit. Civilization had, in the main, reached the limit of its development on the basis of a merely agricultural and animal husbandry technology long before the next great cultural advance was initiated by the industrial revolution. As a matter of fact, marked cultural recessions took place in Mesopotamia, Egypt, Greece, Rome, perhaps in India, possibly in China. This is not to say that no cultural progress whatsoever was made; we are well aware of many steps forward from time to time in various places. But so far as general type of culture is concerned, there is no fundamental difference between the culture of Greece during the time of Archimedes and that of Western Europe at the beginning of the eighteenth century.

After the agricultural arts had become relatively mature, some six, eight or ten thousand years before the beginning of the Christian era, there was little cultural advance until the nineteenth century A.D. Agricultural methods in Europe and the United States in 1850 differed very little from those of Egypt of 2000 B.C. The Egyptians did not have an iron plow, but otherwise there was little difference in mode of production. Even today in many places in the United States and in Europe we can find agricultural practices which, the use of iron excepted, are essentially like those of dynastic Egypt. Production in other fields was essentially the same in western Europe at the beginning of the eighteenth (we might almost say nineteenth) century as in ancient Rome, Greece, or Egypt. Man, as freeman, serf, or slave, and beasts of burden and draft animals supplemented to a meager extent by wind and water power, were the sources of energy. The Europeans had gunpowder whereas the ancients did not. But gunpowder cannot be said to be a culture-builder.° There was no essential difference in type of social–political and economic–institutions. Banks, merchants, the political state, great land-owners, guilds of workmen, and so on were found in ancient Mesopotamia, Greece, and Rome.

Thus we may conclude that culture had developed about as far as [it] could upon the basis of an agricultural-animal husbandry economy, and that there were recessions from peaks attained in Mesopotamia, Egypt, Greece and Rome long before the beginning of the eighteenth century A.D. We may conclude further, that civilization would never have advanced substantially beyond the levels already reached in the great cultures of antiquity if a way had not been found to harness a greater magnitude of energy per capita per unit of time, by tapping a new source of energy: fuel.[16]

The invention of the steam engine, and of all subsequent engines which derive power from fuels, inaugurated a new era in culture history.

---

[15] In this passage, White presents an evolutionary model that derives from Childe (1942: chapters 3 and 4) but is ultimately based upon Spencer. He saw cultural evolution as a process of increasing differentiation and specialization. White's evolutionism, like that of other twentieth-century thinkers, lacks the explicit ethnocentrism and racism of nineteenth-century evolutionists. A key difference is probably the experience of World Wars I and II. (White fought in World War I.) It was, perhaps, easy for an English intellectual at the end of the nineteenth century to maintain that the Victorian Age represented the pinnacle of currently achieved evolution. To continue to hold this position after the carnage of battles like the Somme, where the British took 60,000 casualties on the first day of fighting and where there were a total of more than 1.2 million casualties, however, required considerable mental gymnastics.

[16] White's evolutionism was modified by his reading of Marx. Most nineteenth-century evolutionists saw evolution as a process of gradual incremental change without major breaks, but Marx saw cultural evolution as proceeding by revolution: long periods of relative stasis broken by cataclysmic upheaval. White's vision in these passages is close to this view: He saw long epochs without change broken by quantum changes in energy production and consumption.

When man learned to harness energy in the form of fuel he opened the door of a vast treasure house of energy. Fuels and engines tremendously increased the amount of energy under man's control and at his disposal for culture-building. The extent to which energy has been thus harnessed in the modern world is indicated by the eminent physicist, Robert A. Millikan[17] (1939:211) as follows:[p]

> In this country [the U.S.A.] there is now expended about 13.5 horsepower hours per day per capita—the equivalent of 100 human slaves for each of us; in England the figure is 6.7, in Germany 6.0, in France 4.5, in Japan 1.8, in Russia 0.9, China, 0.5.

Let us return now, for a moment, to our basic principle—culture develops as (1) the amount of energy harnessed and put to work per capita per unit of time increases, and (2) as the efficiency of the means with which this energy is expended increases—and consider the evolution of culture from a slightly different angle. In the course of human history various sources of energy are tapped and harnessed by man and put to work at culture-living and culture-building. The original source of energy was, as we have seen, the human organism. Subsequently, energy has been harnessed in other forms—agriculture, animal husbandry, fire,[q] wind, water, fuel. Energy is energy, and from the point of view of technology it makes no difference whether the energy with which a bushel of wheat is ground comes from a free man, a slave,[r] an ox, the flowing stream or a pile of coal. But it makes a big difference to human beings where the energy comes

from,[s] and an important index of cultural development is derived from this fact.

To refer once more to our basic equation: On the one hand we have energy expended; on the other, human-need-serving goods and services are produced. Culture advances as these two factors increase, hand in hand. But the energy component is resolvable into two factors: the human energy, and the non-human energy, factors. Of these, the human energy factor is a constant; the non-human energy factor, a variable. The increase in quantity of need-serving goods goes hand in hand with an increase in the amount of non-human energy expended. But, since the human energy factor remains constant, an increase in amount of goods and services produced means more goods and services per unit of human labor. Hence, we obtain the law: *Other things being equal, culture evolves as the productivity of human labor increases.*[18]

In Savagery (wild food economy) the productivity of human labor is low; only a small amount of human-need-serving goods and services are produced per unit of human energy. In Barbarism (agriculture, animal husbandry), this productivity is greatly increased. And in Civilization (fuels, engines) it is still further increased.

We must now consider another factor in the process of cultural development, and an important one it is, viz., *the social system within which energy is harnessed and put to work.*

We may distinguish two kinds of determinants in social organization, two kinds of social groupings.[19] On the one hand we have social groupings

---

[17] White had an interest in physics and would certainly have been aware of quantum mechanics. Although there is no direct link between White's theories here and quantum theory, which developed in the late 1920s and the 1930s, the parallel is suggestive. Quantum mechanics described abrupt changes in the levels of energy of subatomic particles; White describes abrupt changes in the levels of energy available to cultures.

He quotes Robert Millikan twice in this article. Millikan (1868–1953) won the Nobel Prize in 1923, primarily for his famous oil drop experiment. Using a simple but ingenious apparatus, Millikan determined the electrical charge of an electron and discovered that it was constant. The experiment is a classic of scientific literature,

and its results were fundamental building blocks of quantum mechanics.

[18] In *Capital* (1930 [1867]), Marx argues that it is human labor that gives value to goods and services. White may have considered that as he wrote this passage.

[19] White distinguished three components in the analysis of culture: technological, sociological, and ideational-attitudinal. He gave priority to the technological. He saw social organization and beliefs as arising primarily from the constraints and possibilities of technology (1959:18–28). These ideas are variations on Marx's analytical divisions: forces of production, relations of production, base, and superstructure.

which serve those needs of man which can be fed by drawing upon resources within man's own organism: clubs for companionship, classes or castes in so far as they feed the desire for distinction, will serve as examples. On the other hand, social organization is concerned with man's adjustment to the external world; social organization is the way in which human beings organize themselves for the three great processes of adjustment and survival—food-getting, defense from enemies, protection from the elements. Thus, we may distinguish two factors in any social system, those elements which are *ends in themselves,* which we may call E; and elements which are *means to ends* (food, defense, etc.) which we may term M.

In any social system M is more important than E, because E is dependent upon M. There can be no men's clubs or classes of distinction unless food is provided and enemies guarded against. In the development of culture, moreover, we may regard E as a constant: a men's club is a men's club whether among savage or civilized peoples. Being a constant, we may ignore factor E in our consideration of cultural evolution and deal only with the factor M.

M is a variable factor in the process of cultural evolution.[20] It is, moreover, a dependent variable, dependent upon the technological way which energy is harnessed and put to work. It is obvious, of course, that it is the technological activities of hunting people that determine, in general, their form of social organization (in so far as that social organization is correlated with hunting rather than with defense against enemies). We of the United States have a certain type of social system (in part) because we have factories, railroads, automobiles, etc.; we do not possess these things as a consequence of a certain kind of social system. Technological systems engender social systems rather than the reverse. Disregarding the factor E, social organization is to be regarded as the way in which human beings

organize themselves to wield their respective technologies. Thus we obtain another important law of culture: *The social organization (E excluded) of a people is dependent upon and determined by the mechanical means with which food is secured, shelter provided, and defense maintained.* In the process of cultural development, *social evolution is* [a] *consequence of technological evolution.*

But this is not the whole story. While it is true that social systems are engendered by, and dependent upon, their respective underlying technologies, it is also true that social systems condition the operation of the technological systems upon which they rest; the relationship is one of mutual, though not necessarily equal, interaction and influence. A social system may foster the effective operation of its underlying technology or it may tend to restrain and thwart it. In short, in any given situation the social system may play a progressive role or it may play a reactionary role.

We have noted that after the agricultural arts had attained a certain degree of development, the great civilizations of China, India, Egypt, the Near East, Central America and Peru came rapidly into being as a consequence of the greatly augmented energy resources of the people of these regions. But these great civilizations did not continue to advance indefinitely. On the contrary they even receded from maximum levels in a number of instances. Why did they not continue progressively to advance? According to our law culture will advance, other things being equal, as long as the amount of energy harnessed and put to work per capita per unit of time increases. The answer to our question, Why did not these great cultures continue to advance? is, therefore, that the amount of energy per capita per unit of time, *ceased to increase,* and furthermore, the efficiency of the means with which this energy was expended *was not advanced beyond a*

---

[20] Here, without crediting Marx, White lays out some principles of materialist thinking. Marx had written that the mode of economic production determines the general character of the social, political, and spiritual processes of life. White uses American society in an example of precisely this sort of thinking. Marx believed that the ultimate result of the thwarting of technology by society was revolution and the emergence of new social structures. In the passages below, White echoes this belief.

certain limit.[21] In short, there was no fundamental improvement in the agricultural arts from say 2000 B.C. to 1800 A.D.

The next question is, Why did not the agricultural arts advance and improve during this time? We know that the agricultural arts are still capable of tremendous improvement, and the urge of man for plenty, security and efficiency was as great then as now. Why, then, did agriculture fail to progress beyond a certain point in the great civilizations of antiquity? The answer is, The social system, within which these arts functioned, curbed further expansion, thwarted progress.

All great civilizations resting upon intensive agriculture are divided into classes: a ruling class and the masses who are ruled.[22] The masses produced the means of life. But the distribution of these goods is in accordance with rules which are administered by the ruling class. By one method of control or another—by levies, taxes, rents, or some other means—the ruling class takes a portion of the wealth produced by the masses from them, and consumes it according to their liking or as the exigencies of the time dictate.

In this sort of situation cultural advancement may cease at a certain point for lack of incentive. No incentive to progress came from the ruling class in the ancient civilizations of which we are speaking. What they appropriated from their subjects they consumed or wasted. To obtain more wealth the ruling class merely increased taxes, rents, or other levies upon the producers of wealth. This was easier, quicker, and surer than increasing the efficiency of production and thereby augmenting the total product. On the other hand, there was no incentive to progress among the masses—if they produced more by increasing efficiency it would only mean more for

the tax-gatherers of the ruling class. The culture history of China during the past few centuries, or indeed, since the Han dynasty, well illustrates situations of this sort.

We come then to the following conclusion: *A social system may so condition the operation of a technological system as to impose a limit upon the extent to which it can expand and develop. When this occurs, cultural evolution ceases.* Neither evolution nor progress in culture is inevitable (neither Morgan nor Tylor ever said, or even intimated, that they are). When cultural advance has thus been arrested, it can be renewed only by tapping some new source of energy and by harnessing it in sufficient magnitude to burst asunder the social system which binds it. Thus freed the new technology will form a new social system, one congenial to growth, and culture will again advance until, perhaps, the social system once more checks it.[23]

It seems quite clear that mankind would never have advanced materially beyond the maximum levels attained by culture between 2000 B.C. and 1700 A.D. had it not tapped a new source of energy (fuel) and harnessed it in substantial magnitudes. The speed with which man could travel, the range of his projectiles, and many other things, could not have advanced beyond a certain point had he not learned to harness more energy in new forms. And so it was with culture as a whole.

The steam engine ushered in a new era. With it, and various kinds of internal combustion engines, the energy resources of vast deposits of coal and oil were tapped and harnessed in progressively increasing magnitudes. Hydroelectric plants contributed a substantial amount from rivers. Populations grew, production expanded, wealth increased. The limits of growth of the new technology have not yet been reached; indeed, it

---

[21] Many of White's theories stay close to Marx, but his use of energy to explain social change is not found in Marx's work.

[22] Notice, here and below, the direct use of class analysis. White does not quote Marx directly, but the Marxist view of history as class struggle is very much evident in these passages.

[23] Here White diverges critically from Marx. Marx believed that social evolution toward communism was inevitable, though its rate might be affected by human action. White claims that "neither evolution nor progress in culture is inevitable."

is probably not an exaggeration to say that they have not even been foreseen, so vast are the possibilities and so close are we still to the beginning of this new era. But already the new technology has come into conflict with the old social system.[24] The new technology is being curbed and thwarted. The progressive tendencies of the new technology are being held back by a social system that was adapted to pre-fuel technology. This fact has become commonplace today.

In our present society, goods are produced for sale at a profit. To sell one must have a market. Our market is a world market, but it is, nevertheless, finite in magnitude. When the limit of the market has been reached production ceases to expand: no market, no sale; no sale, no profit; no profit, no production. Drastic curtailment of production, wholesale destruction of surpluses follow. Factories, mills, and mines close; millions of men are divorced from industrial production and thrown upon relief. Population growth recedes. National incomes cease to expand. Stagnation sets in.

When, in the course of cultural development, the expanding technology comes into conflict with the social system, one of two things will happen: either the social system will give way, or technological advance will be arrested. If the latter occurs, cultural evolution will, of course, cease. The outcome of situations such as this is not preordained. The triumph of technology and the continued evolution and progress of culture are not assured merely because we wish it or because it would be better thus.[25] In culture as in mechanics, the greater force prevails. A force is applied to a boulder. If the force be great enough,

the rock is moved. If the rock be large enough to withstand the force, it will remain stationary. So in the case of technology-institutions conflicts: if the force of the growing technology be great enough, the restraining institutions will give way; if this force is not strong enough to overcome institutional opposition, it must submit to it.

There was undoubtedly much institutional resistance to the expanding agricultural technology in late Neolithic times. Such staunch institutions as the tribe and clan which had served man well for thousands of years did not give way to the political state without a fight; the "liberty, equality and fraternity" of primitive society were not surrendered for the class-divided, serf and lord, slave and master, society of feudalism without a struggle.[26] But the ancient and time-honored institutions of tribal society could not accommodate the greatly augmented forces of the agricultural technology. Neither could they successfully oppose these new forces. Consequently, tribal institutions gave way and a new social system came into being.

Similarly in our day, our institutions have shown themselves incapable of accommodating the vast technological forces of the Power Age. What the outcome of the present conflict between modern fuel technology and the social system of an earlier era will be, time alone will tell. It seems likely, however, that the old social system is now in the process of destruction. The tremendous forces of the Power Age are not to be denied. The great wars of the twentieth century derive their chief significance from this fact: they are the means by which an old social order is to be scrapped, and a new one to be brought into being.[27] The first World War wiped out the old

---

[24] White's distaste for capitalism is evident in passages such as this. When White wrote this essay in 1943, World War II was raging, and the memory of the Depression was still very fresh in people's minds. White believed that capitalism inevitably entailed a cycle of depression and destructive warfare. Although he was appalled by Stalin's policies in Russia and considered the members of the American Communist Party "a bunch of stooges for Stalin" (quoted in Peace 1998), he was a committed socialist.

[25] White's absolute faith in the desirability of technological progress is characteristic of the era in which he

wrote. Modern anthropologists have lost much of this faith.

[26] White again echoes Marx's dictum that change comes about through revolutionary struggle rather than gradual evolutionary progress.

[27] Remember that this essay was written during World War II. White had served in the Navy in World War I and was greatly shaken by his wartime experiences. He later wrote that these experiences inspired his move from the physical to the social sciences (Barnes 1960).

ruling families of the Hapsburgs, Romanoffs, and Hohenzollerns, hulking relics of Feudalism, and brought Communist and Fascist systems into being. We do not venture to predict the social changes which the present war will bring about. But we may confidently expect them to be as profound and as far-reaching as those effected by World War I.

Thus, in the history of cultural evolution, we have witnessed one complete cultural revolution, and the first stage of a second. The technological transition from a wild food economy to a relatively mature agricultural and animal husbandry economy was followed by an equally profound institutional change: from tribal society to civil society. Thus the first fundamental and all-inclusive cultural change, or revolution, took place. At the present time we are entering upon the second stage of the second great cultural revolution of human history. The Industrial Revolution was but the first stage, the technological stage, of this great cultural revolution. The Industrial Revolution has run its course, and we are now entering upon the second stage, one of profound institutional change, of social revolution. Barring collapse and chaos, which is of course possible, a new social order will emerge. It appears likely that the human race will occupy the earth for some million years to come. It seems probable, also, that man, after having won his way up through Savagery and Barbarism, is not likely to stop, when at last he finds himself upon the very threshold of Civilization.[28]

The key to the future, in any event, lies in the energy situation. If we can continue to harness as much energy per capita per year in the future as we are doing now, there is little doubt but that our old social system will give way to a new one, a new era of civilization. Should, however, the amount of energy that we are able to harness diminish materially, then culture would cease to advance or

even recede. A return to a cultural level comparable to that of China during the Ming dynasty is neither inconceivable nor impossible. It all depends upon how man harnesses the forces of nature and the extent to which this is done.

At the present time "the petroleum in sight is only a twelve year supply, . . . and new discoveries [of oil] are not keeping pace with use."[t] Coal is more abundant. Even so, many of the best deposits in the United States—which has over half of the world's known coal reserves—will some day be depleted.[29] "Eventually, no matter how much we conserve, this sponging off past ages for fossil energy must cease . . . What then?"[u] The answer is, of course, that culture will decline unless man is able to maintain the amount of energy harnessed per capita per year by tapping new sources.

Wind, water, waves, tides, solar boilers, photochemical reactions, atomic energy, etc., are sources which might be tapped or further exploited. One of the most intriguing possibilities is that of harnessing atomic energy. When the nucleus of an atom of uranium (U235) is split it "releases 200,000,000 electron volts, the largest conversion of mass into energy that has yet been produced by terrestrial means."[v] Weight for weight, uranium (as a source of energy produced by nuclear fission) is 5,000,000 times as effective as coal.[w] If harnessing sub-atomic energy could be made a practical success, our energy resources would be multiplied a thousand fold. As Dr. R. M. Langer,[x] research associate in physics at California Institute of Technology, has put it:

> The face of the earth will be changed. . . . Privilege and class distinctions will become relics because things that make up the good life will be so abundant and inexpensive. War will become obsolete because of the disappearance of those economic stresses that immemorially have caused it. . . . The kind of civilization we

---

[28] Notice a strong utopian thread in White's writing here and later. Provided enough energy can be found, the destiny of humanity is civilization and a new social order. It follows from White's logic that the new social order, since it is better matched to technology, will be superior to the old. Progress is our most important product.

[29] Fears about limits of the world's energy supplies are nothing new. The estimates White cites here are similar to some of those given during the energy crisis thirty years later.

might expect . . . is so different in kind from anything we know that even guesses about it are futile.

To be able to harness sub-atomic energy would, without doubt, create a civilization surpassing sober imagination of today. But not everyone is as confident as Dr. Langer that this advance is imminent. Some experts have their doubts, some think it a possibility. Time alone will tell.[30]

But there is always the sun, from which man has derived all of his energy, directly or indirectly, in the past. And it may be that it will become, directly, our chief source of power in the future. Energy in enormous amounts reaches the earth daily from the sun. "The average intensity of solar energy in this latitude amounts to about 0.1 of a horse power per square foot" (Furnas 1941:426). "Enough energy falls on about 200 square miles of an arid region like the Mojave Desert to supply the [present needs of the] United States" (Furnas 1941:427). But the problem is, of course, to harness it effectively and efficiently.[y] The difficulties do not seem insuperable. It will doubtless be done, and probably before a serious diminution of power from dwindling resources of oil and coal overtakes us. From a power standpoint the outlook for the future is not too dark for optimism.

We turn now to an interesting and important fact, one highly significant to the history of anthropology: The thesis set forth in the preceding pages is substantially the same as that advanced by Lewis H. Morgan and E. B. Tylor many decades ago.[31] We have expounded it in somewhat different form and words; our presentation is, perhaps, more systematic and explicit. At one point we have made a significant change in their theoretical scheme: we begin the third great stage of cultural evolution with engines rather than with writing. But essentially our thesis is that of the Evolutionist school as typified by Morgan and Tylor.

According to Morgan, culture developed as man extended and improved his control over his environment, especially with regard to the food supply.[32] The "procurement of subsistence" is man's "primary need" (p. 525).[z]

> The important fact that mankind commenced at the bottom of the scale and worked up, is revealed in an expressive manner by their successive arts of subsistence. Upon their skill in this direction, the whole question of human supremacy on the earth depended. Mankind are the only beings who may be said to have gained an absolute control over the production

---

[30] White wrote this before the invention of the atomic bomb and the nuclear power plant. In the 1950s, his writing seemed almost prescient. Many people then believed that nuclear energy would result in electric power so inexpensive it would not be worth metering. White, and others, pointed out that such a development would have profound effects on social structure. Langer (quoted here) is perhaps disingenuous when he writes that guesses are futile; the type of society he describes is precisely that predicted by Marx.

[31] You may have caught many references to Morgan's and Tylor's scheme of cultural evolution in the preceding passages. Here, White makes their contribution to his work explicit. White's detailed acknowledgment of Morgan and Tylor must be seen as an attack on most of American anthropology of his time—much of Boasian anthropology was a reaction against the evolutionism of nineteenth-century writers such as Morgan and Tylor. Boas and his students dismissed their work as logically flawed, insufficiently scientific, and implicitly racist. White's rehabilita-

tion of Morgan and Tylor in the pages of *American Anthropologist* (where this essay first appeared) must have seemed audacious to his contemporaries. His repeated quotation of them in these passages was a goad to established anthropological opinion. White later wrote, "I was ridiculed and scoffed at. Everyone knew that evolutionism was dead." He quotes Ralph Linton (1893–1953), an eminent anthropologist of the time, as saying that he, White, "ought to be given the courtesy extended to suspected horse thieves and shady gamblers in the days of the Wild West, namely, to allow them to get out of town before sundown" (quoted in Carneiro 1981:229).

[32] White's first teaching post was at Buffalo, Morgan's hometown. While there, he read Morgan's work and was profoundly affected by it. He later edited Morgan's letters and journals and produced a definitive edition of Morgan's *Ancient Society*. He was certainly the greatest scholar of Morgan's work of his era. Harris has written, "In every respect, White's *The Evolution of Culture* is the modern equivalent of Morgan's *Ancient Society*" (1968:643).

of food; which at the outset they did not possess above other animals. Without enlarging the basis of subsistence, mankind could not have propagated themselves into other areas not possessing the same kinds of food, and ultimately over the whole surface of the earth; and, lastly, without obtaining an absolute control over both its variety and amount, they could not have multiplied into populous nations. It is accordingly probable that the great epochs of human progress have been identified, more or less directly, with the enlargement of the sources of subsistence (p. 19). When the great discovery was made that the wild horse, cow, sheep, ass, sow and goat might be tamed, and, when produced in flocks and herds, become a source of permanent subsistence, it must have given a powerful impulse to human progress (p. 534).

And

the acquisition of farinaceous food by cultivation must be regarded as one of the greatest events in human experience (p. 42).

Morgan is much concerned with the significance of technology and its development:

"The domestic animals supplementing human muscle with animal power, contributed a new factor of the highest value" (p. 26). The bow and arrow, "the first deadly weapon for the hunt, . . . must have given a powerful upward influence to ancient society," since it made man more effective in the food quest (pp. 21–22). "The plow drawn by animal power may be regarded as inaugurating a new art" (p. 26). The "production of iron gave the plow with an iron point and a better spade and axe" (p. 26). Many other inventions, such as pottery, adobe brick, metallurgy—when man "had invented the furnace, and produced iron from ore, nine tenths of the battle for civilization was won" (p. 43)—are emphasized as motive forces of cultural development. "The most advanced portion of the human race were halted, so to express it, at certain stages of progress, until some great invention or discovery, such as the domestication of animals or the smelting of iron ore, gave a new and powerful impulse forward" (pp. 39–40).

Morgan shows how technological advance brings about social change: technological evolu-

tion produces social evolution. In many places, but particularly in Part IV of *Ancient Society*, he shows how property, which accumulates through "an enlargement of the means of subsistence" and through a development of the individual arts, affects and changes the constitution of society. "Property and office were the foundations upon which aristocracy planted itself" (p. 551). Also,

From . . . the increased abundance of subsistence through field agriculture, nations began to develop, numbering many thousands under one government. . . . The localization of tribes in fixed areas and in fortified cities, with the increase of the numbers of the people, intensified the struggle for the possession of the most desirable territories. It tended to advance the art of war, and to increase the rewards of individual prowess. These changes of condition and of the plan of life indicate the approach of civilization which was to overthrow gentile and establish political society (p. 540).

We find essentially the same ideas in Tylor. Like Morgan, Tylor declares that man's "first need is to get his daily food" (p. 206).[aa] Culture develops as man's control over his environment, especially over the food supply, increases. Mankind advanced from savagery to barbarism when they took to agriculture: "With the certain supply of food which can be stored until next harvest, settled village and town life is established, with immense results in the improvement of arts, knowledge, manners and government" (p. 24). "Those edible grasses," says Tylor, "which have been raised by cultivation into the cereals, such as wheat, barley, rye, and by their regular and plentiful supply have become the mainstay of human life and the *great moving power of civilization*" (p. 215; emphasis ours).

A pastoral economy, according to Tylor, is superior to that of a hunting and gathering (wild food) economy, but inferior to an agricultural economy. A combination of agriculture and animal husbandry is superior to either way of life by itself (pp. 24, 220).

Social evolution comes as a consequence of technological development: To this "change of habit [i.e., from a wild food economy to agriculture] may be plainly in great part traced the expansion of industrial arts and the creation of higher social and political institutions" (p. 118; article "Anthropology," in Encyclopaedia Britannica, 11th ed.).

With the development of agriculture and the industrial arts comes a struggle for the most desirable territories (as Morgan puts it) and warfare "for gain" rather than "for quarrel or vengeance" (Tylor, p. 225). The consequences of this warfare for gain are tremendous: ". . . captives, instead of being slain, are brought back for slaves, and especially set to till the ground. By this agriculture is much increased, and also a new division of society takes place . . . Thus we see how in old times the original equality of men broke up, a nation dividing into an aristocracy of warlike freemen, and an inferior laboring caste" (p. 225). "It was through slave labor that agriculture and industry increased, that wealth accumulated, and leisure was given to priests, scribes, poets, philosophers, to raise the level of men's minds" (p. 435). Furthermore, according to Tylor, warfare, among culturally advanced peoples, produces "two of the greatest facts in history—the organized army . . . and the confederation of tribes . . ." (pp. 432–433); tribes become states, primitive society gives way to civil society.

Tylor is much interested in the ways in which man harnesses the forces of nature and the extent to which energy is harnessed. "It was a great movement in civilization," he says, when man harnessed water power (p. 204). He speaks of the "civilized world . . . drawing an immense supply of power from a new source, the coal burnt in the furnace of the steam-engine, which is already used so wastefully that economists are uneasily calculating how long this stored-up fossil force will last, and what must be turned to next—tide force or sun's heat—to labor for us" (pp. 204–205).

Tylor clearly recognizes the problem we have dealt with in this essay when he speculates: "It is an interesting problem in political economy to reckon the means of subsistence in our country during the agricultural and pastoral period, and to compare them with the resources we now gain from coal, in doing home-work and manufacturing goods to exchange for foreign produce. Perhaps the best means of realizing what coal is to us, will be to consider, that of three Englishmen now [1881], one at least may be reckoned to live by coal, inasmuch as without it the population would have been so much less" (p. 272). The energy significance of modern civilization lies in the fact that "in modern times, man seeks more and more to change the laborer's part he played in early ages, for the higher duty of director or controller of the world's forces" (p. 205).

Thus, we see that our essay is substantially a systematic exposition of the ideas of Morgan and Tylor.[33] Man is an animal. His first and greatest need is food. Control over habitat in general and food supply in particular is effected by means of tools (of all kinds, weapons included). Through invention and discovery the technological means of control are extended and improved. Social evolution follows upon technological evolution.

At one point we have made an innovation. Both Morgan (p. 12) and Tylor (p. 24) use the origin of writing to mark the beginning of the third great era of cultural development, "Civilization." In our scheme, "civilization" begins with the invention of the steam engine as a practical means of harnessing energy.[34]

---

[33] White's portrayal of Morgan and Tylor conceals a very important difference between their thinking and his own. Morgan and Tylor, like many other nineteenth-century evolutionists, generally saw social change as driven by psychic unity. Although the material aspects of a society may indicate the level of evolution it had attained, progress was ultimately dependent on the organic unfolding of germs of thought. White, on the other hand, proposed that humans' biologically based need to make life secure was the force driving cultural evolution.

[34] White's appreciation of Morgan was enhanced by the importance given him by Marx and Engels, who saw Morgan's *Ancient Society* as providing independent confirmation of their model of social and historical development. For this reason, Soviet communists in the first half of this century often had an unusually detailed understanding of Morgan. White would have been exposed to this on his trip to the Soviet Union in 1929.

Although Morgan and Tylor both deal directly with the energy factor in cultural development, they lose sight of it when they consider writing. Writing is not a motive force. What change would writing have effected in the culture of the Arunta, or the Eskimo, or the Iroquois? It would not have altered their way of life in any essential respect. The culture of the ancient Peruvians, which lacked writing, was quite as advanced as that of the Aztecs who had writing. And in our own culture, writing has served to preserve and perpetuate—when it has not sanctified—the ignorance and superstitions of our barbaric ancestors quite as much as it has promoted progress and enlightenment.

But, if writing is not to be considered a motive force in cultural development, the human organism, domesticated animals, cultivated plants, water wheels, windmills, steam engines, etc., are motive forces (or the means of harnessing energy). What we have done is to reduce all specific, concrete motive forces in cultural development to a single, abstract, common term: energy. To classify cultures as "wild food, domestic food, and literate," as Morgan and Tylor did, is illogical; it is like classifying vehicles as "three-wheeled, four-wheeled, and pretty." We classify cultures according to the way, or ways, in which they harness energy and the manner in which it is put to work to serve human needs.

In the foregoing we have, we believe, a sound and illuminating theory of cultural evolution. We have hold of principles, fundamental principles, which are operative in all cultures at all times and places. The motive force of cultural evolution is laid bare, the mechanisms of development made clear. The nature of the relationship between social institutions on the one hand and technological instruments on the other is indicated.

Understanding that the function of culture is to serve the needs of man, we find that we have an objective criterion for evaluating culture in terms of the extent to which, and the efficiency with which, human needs are satisfied by cultural means. We can measure the amounts of energy expended; we can calculate the efficiency of the expenditure of energy in terms of measurable quantities of goods and services produced. And, finally, as we see, these measurements can be expressed in mathematical terms.[35]

The theory set forth in the preceding pages was, as we have made clear, held by the foremost thinkers of the Evolutionist school of the nineteenth century, both in England and in America. Today they seem to us as sound as they did to Tylor and Morgan, and, if anything, more obvious. It seems almost incredible that anthropologists of the twentieth century could have turned their backs upon and repudiated such a simple, sound, and illuminating generalization, one that makes the vast range of tens of thousands of years of culture history intelligible. But they have done just this.[bb] The anti-evolutionists, led in America by Franz Boas, have rejected the theory of evolution in cultural anthropology and have given us instead a philosophy of "planless hodge-podge-ism."[36]

It is not surprising, therefore, to find at the present time the most impressive recognition of the significance of technological progress in cultural evolution in the writings of a distinguished physicist, the Nobel prize winner, Robert A. Millikan:[cc]

> The changes that have occurred within the
> past hundred years not only in the external
> conditions under which the average man, at
> least in this western world, passes life on earth,
> but in his superstitions . . . his fundamental

---

[35] Boas and most of his students believed that universal laws of the evolution of human culture could not be formulated and that thinkers such as Morgan and Tylor were ethnocentric. However, Boas' specific criticism of the evolutionists was based on flaws in their method—he claimed that they were insufficiently scientific. Here, White answers this criticism by showing what he believes are objective, empirical criteria for the comparison of cultures.

[36] The "planless hodge-podge-ism" refers to a frequently quoted passage in the work of Robert Lowie (1883–1957), a student of Boas. In the final paragraph of his widely read *Primitive Society*, Lowie wrote, "To that planless hodge-podge, that thing of shreds and patches called civilization, its historian can no longer yield superstitious reverence" (1920:441). Although it stands at variance with much of Lowie's other work, this statement has often been used to caricature historical particularism.

beliefs, in his philosophy, in his conception of religion, in his whole world outlook, are probably greater than those that occurred during the preceding four thousand years all put together. Life seems to remain static for thousands of years and then shoot forward with amazing speed. The last century has been one of those periods of extraordinary change, the most amazing in human history. If, then, you ask me to put into one sentence the cause of that recent rapid and enormous change I should reply: "It is found in the discovery and utilization of the means by which heat energy can be made to do man's work for him."

Tucked away in the pages of Volume II of a manual on European archaeology, too, we find a similar expression from a distinguished American scholar, George G. MacCurdy:[dd]

> The *degree of civilization* of any epoch, people, or group of peoples *is measured by ability to utilize energy for human advancement or needs.* Energy is of two kinds, internal and external or free. Internal energy is that of the human body or machine, and its basis is food. External energy is that outside the human body and its basis is fuel. Man has been able to tap the great storehouse of external energy. Through his internal energy and that acquired from external sources, he has been able to overcome the opposing energy of his natural environment. *The difference between these two opposing forces is the gauge of civilization* (emphasis ours).

Thus, this view is not wholly absent in anthropological theory in America today although extremely rare and lightly regarded. The time will come, we may confidently expect, when the theory of evolution will again prevail in the science of culture as it has in the biological and the physical sciences. It is a significant fact that in cultural anthropology alone among the sciences is a philosophy of anti-evolutionism respectable— a fact we would do well to ponder.[37]

NOTES

[a] By "energy" we mean "the capacity for performing work."

[b] Cf. Leslie A. White, *The Symbol: The Origin and Basis of Human Behavior* (Philosophy of Science, Vol. 7, October, 1940), pp. 451–463.

[c] See Leslie A. White, *Science Is Sciencing* (Philosophy of Science, Vol. 5, October, 1938), pp. 369–389, for a discussion of this general point of view.

[d] "Natural science" is a redundancy. All science is natural; if it is not natural it is not science.

[e] Actually, of course, it is not wholly constant; there may be progress in music, myth-making, etc., regardless of technology. A men's club, however, is still a men's club, whether the underlying technology be simple and crude or highly developed. But, since the overwhelming portion of cultural development is due to technological progress, we may legitimately ignore that small portion which is not so dependent by regarding it a constant.

[f] "There is only one cultural reality that is not artificial, to wit: the culture of all humanity at all periods and in all places," R. H. Lowie, *Cultural Anthropology: A Science* (American Journal of Sociology, Vol. 42, 1936), p. 305.

[g] We say "per year" although "per unit of time" would serve as well, because in concrete cultural situations a year would embrace the full round of the seasons and the occupations and actions appropriate thereto.

[h] The cultural evolutionists have been criticized for identifying progress with evolution by pointing out that these two words are not synonymous. It is as true as it is obvious that they are not synonymous—in the dictionary. But by and large, in the history of human culture, progress and evolution *have gone hand in hand.*

[i] See Tylor, *Primitive Culture*, Vol. I, p. 14 (London, 1929 printing) for another respect in which, in the theory of evolution, "the student of the habits of mankind has a great advantage over the student of the species of plants and animals."

[j] "Commencing probably with the dog . . . followed . . . by the capture of the young of other animals and rearing them, not unlikely, *from the merest freak of fancy*, it required time and experience to discover the utility of each . . ." (emphasis ours). Morgan, *Ancient Society*, p. 42 (Holt ed.).

[k] *Introduction to Cultural Anthropology* (New York, 1940 ed.), pp. 51–52. In this argument Lowie leans

---

[37] Despite his rejection by the Boasians, White had a profound effect on many younger scholars. He spent almost all of his forty-year academic career at the University of Michigan and was known as a brilliant and challenging teacher. Through his students, he had a powerful impact not only on cultural anthropology but on archaeology and physical anthropology as well. His students include cultural anthropologists Robert Carneiro, David Kaplan, and Napoleon Chagnon; archaeologists Louis Binford and Jeffrey Parsons; and physical anthropologists Frank Livingston, George Armelagos, and Jack Kelso, as well as many others in each of these fields.

heavily upon Eduard Hahn, whose work, incidentally, appeared many years after *Ancient Society* ("Subsistence," p. 303, in *General Anthropology*, F. Boas, ed., New York, 1938; *History of Ethnological Theory*, p. 112 ff., New York, 1937).

[l] Following Morgan and Tylor, we use "savagery" to designate cultures resting upon a wild-food basis, "barbarism" for cultures with a domestic food basis. Our use of "civilization," however, differs from that of Tylor and Morgan (see p. 355).

[m] "Finds in the Near East seem to indicate that the domestication of plants and animals in that region was followed by an extraordinary flowering of culture," Ralph Linton, *The Present Status of Anthropology* (Science, Vol. 87, 1938), p. 245.

[n] But this does not mean that agriculture *must be preceded* by a pastoral economy in the course of cultural development. Contrary to a notion current nowadays, none of the major evolutionists ever maintained that farming must be preceded by herding.

[o] It is true, of course, that powder is used in blasting in quarries, etc., and is to this extent a motive force in culture-building. But energy employed in this way is relatively insignificant quantitatively. The bow and arrow inaugurated cultural advance because in its economic context it provided man with food in greater quantity or with less effort. The gun, in its hunting context, has had the opposite effect, that of reducing the food supply by killing off the game. In their military contexts, neither the bow and arrow or the gun has been a culture-builder. The mere conquest or extermination of one tribe or nation by another, the mere change from one dynasty or set of office holders to another, is not culture-building.

[p] *Science and the World Tomorrow* (Scientific Monthly, Sept. 1939) p. 211. These figures do not, however, tell the whole story for they ignore the vast amount of energy harnessed in the form of cultivated plants and domesticated animals.

[q] We may be permitted thus to distinguish two different ways of harnessing energy although each involves fire and fuel. By "fire" we indicate such energy uses of fire which preceded the steam engine—clearing forests, burning logs to make dugout canoes, etc. By "fuel" we designate energy harnessed by steam, gasoline, etc., engines.

[r] Technologically a freeman and a slave are equal, both being energy in homo sapiens form. Sociologically, there is, of course, a vast difference between them. Sociologically, a slave is not a human being; he is merely a beast of burden who can talk.

[s] According to E. H. Hull, of the General Electric Research Laboratory, the power equivalent of "a groaning and sweating slave" is "75 watts of electricity, which most of us can buy at the rate of two-fifths of a cent an hour." *Engineering: Ancient and Modern* (Scientific Monthly, November, 1939), p. 463.

[t] C. C. Furnas, *Future Sources of Power* (Science, Nov. 7, 1941), p. 425.

[u] Ibid., p. 426.

[v] Herbert L. Anderson, *Progress in Harnessing Power from Uranium* (Scientific Monthly, June 1940).

[w] Robert D. Potter, *Is Atomic Power at Hand?* (Scientific Monthly, June, 1940), p. 573.

[x] *Fast New World* (Collier's, July 6, 1940).

[y] See C. C. Abbot, *Utilizing Heat from the Sun* (Smithsonian Miscellaneous Collections, Vol. 98, No. 5, March 30, 1939).

[z] The page references are to Morgan's *Ancient Society*, Henry Holt edition.

[aa] Page references are to Tylor's *Anthropology* (New York, Appleton & Co. edition of 1916).

[bb] One distinguished anthropologist has gone so far as to declare that "the theory of cultural evolution [is] to my mind the most inane, sterile, and pernicious theory ever conceived in the history of science . . ." B. Laufer, in a review of Lowie's *Culture and Ethnology* (American Anthropologist, Vol. 20, 1918), p. 90.

[cc] Op. cit., p. 211.

[dd] *Human Origins* (New York, 1933), Vol. II, pp. 134–135.

19. *The Patrilineal Band*[a]

Julian Steward (1902–1972)

Loose aggregates of comparatively independent families such as those of the Shoshoni occur only rarely because in most parts of the world subsistence patterns required sufficient regularity of co-operation and leadership to give definite form and stability to multifamily social groups. There are many kinds of such multifamily groups of which the patrilineal band is but one.

The patrilineal band illustrates several concepts. First, it is a cultural type whose essential features—partrilineality, patrilocality, exogamy, land ownership, and lineage composition—constituted a cultural core which recurred cross-culturally with great regularity, whereas many details of technology, religion, and other aspects of culture represent independent variables, the nature of which was determined by diffusion or by unique local circumstances. Second, its cultural core resulted from ecological adaptations which, under the recurrent conditions of environment and subsistence technology, could vary only within minor limits. Third, it represents a level of sociocultural integration slightly higher than that of the Shoshoni family; for its multifamily aggregates found cohesion not only in kinship relations but in co-operative hunting, in common landownership, and to some extent in joint ceremonies.[1]

I shall analyze the cultures of these bands as they occurred among the Bushmen of South Africa, some of the Congo Negritos of Central Africa, some Philippine Negritos, the Australians, the Tasmanians, some southern California Shoshonean-speaking groups, and the Ona of Tierra del Fuego. Other tribes besides those covered in the present survey no doubt had the same pattern.

The essential features of these bands are most readily explained as the independent product of similar patterns of adaptation of technology and certain social forms to the environment. There are only two other possible explanations of

the patrilineal band. First, that the pattern was borrowed from neighboring tribes. This explanation is untenable since their neighbors did not have the pattern. Second, that the pattern is the heritage of some archaic culture which developed at an early period of human history and has been preserved ever since. Perhaps some social patterns do have great persistence, but they must meet some need. It would be stretching credulity much too far to suppose that a pattern which is closely adapted to a special kind of subsistence had persisted for thousands of years among tribes who had wandered through dozens of unlike environments to the remotest corners of the earth, especially when other hunting and gathering tribes had lost these patterns and acquired types of society appropriate to their mode of life. Moreover, like most cultural historical theories, neither the hypothesis of diffusion nor of archaic heritage provides an explanation of how and why the patrilineal band developed in the first place. The cultural ecological hypothesis on the other hand is not only explanatory but it is by far the simplest and most consistent with the facts.[2]

The cultural ecological explanation of the patrilineal band hinges on an identity of exploitative patterns rather than of technology or environment. Technology and environment were similar in crucial respects, but they were not identical in their totality. Cultures do not exploit their entire environments, and it is, therefore, necessary to consider only those features which bear upon the

---

[1] Steward's preoccupation with the causes of culture is immediately evident in this first passage. Unlike the historical particularists, Steward was interested in discovering general laws of culture.

Steward divided culture into core and secondary features. He probably got the division from his professor A. L. Kroeber, who divided culture into value and utility components—Steward's *culture core* was similar to Kroeber's *utility culture*. It consisted of those cultural traits that Steward felt were closest to subsistence activities and economic arrangements. A key difference between the two men is that Kroeber thought the value culture more interesting and important than the utility culture, whereas Steward focused his studies on the utility features. Collections of elements of the culture core that regularly occur

cross-culturally, such as the patrilineal band described here, he termed *culture types*.

[2] In this passage, Steward differentiates his own cultural ecological approach from that of the historical particularists, which he claims has little explanatory power. He further distinguished himself from the nineteenth-century evolutionists such as Morgan and Tylor, who saw the existence of such bands as survivals of some preexisting social form, precisely the second possibility that Steward mentions and discounts here. Unlike other Boasians, Steward's research emphasized cross-cultural comparison, but his rejection of the idea of psychic unity separates his work from the comparative method of the nineteenth-century evolutionists.

productive patterns.[3] The environments of the patrilineal bands were similar in that, first, they had limited and scattered food resources, which not only restricted population to a low density but which prevented it from assembling in large, permanent aggregates. Second, the principal food resource was game, which unlike wild seeds, may be profitably taken collectively. Third, the game occurred in small, nonmigratory bands rather than in large, migratory herds. This kind of game can support only small aggregates of people, who remain within a restricted territory. Large herds, on the other hand, support much larger aggregates who can remain together as they follow the herds. These latter aggregates were bilateral or composite bands.

Dispersed and small game herds are, therefore, a condition of patrilineal bands, but this does not mean identity of environment, for deserts, jungles, and mountains tend to limit the number of game and the distance it could wander.[4] Of the tribes examined here, the Bushmen, Australians, and southern California Shoshoneans lived in areas which had sparse game because of extreme aridity. Moreover, all were affected by the limited sources of water. In Tierra del Fuego, the habitat is one of wet plains but guanaco[5] and small rodents, the principal foods, were scattered and nonmigratory. The Congo Negritos[6] and the

Philippine Negritos lived in the tropical rain forests, the former in lowlands and the latter in mountains.

Exploitative technology of these societies varied considerably in detail, but in all cases it included weapons of about equal efficiency and hunting patterns which entailed as much cooperation as circumstances permitted. The Bushmen used bows, poisoned arrows, clubs, pitfalls, poisoned springs, grass fires, dogs, and surrounds. The Congo Negritos employed bows, poisoned and nonpoisoned arrows, spears, knives, and long game nets. The Shoshoneans had bows, thrown clubs, traps, nets, surrounds, and drives. The Ona used bows, spears, clubs, slings, and spring pole nooses. Australian technology may have been less efficient in that it lacked the bow, but it included clubs, spears, and the spear-thrower. The sociological effect of hunting scattered game individually or collectively was the same everywhere.

The interaction between a bow-spear-club technology and a small, nonmigratory herd food resource tended to produce the patrilineal band. This type of band was the normal result of the adaptive processes of cultural ecology, and though various factors constantly operated to destroy the ideal pattern, as will be shown, interaction of technology and environment was such as to restore it.

---

[3] Steward's cultural ecology is often misunderstood as a sort of ecological determinism, but his emphasis was on the process of human labor within the environment. Steward was concerned with the technological process by which people exploited their environment, and his analysis focused on how different subsistence strategies required different social structures. This emphasis derives from Steward's reading of Marx.

[4] Here and below, Steward focuses on the interplay between environment and technology. The idea that environment determined culture—a position known as geographical determinism—was not new. One prominent advocate was the British historian Henry Thomas Buckle (1821–1862), who believed history to be governed by laws of nature. The development of nations could be explained by the general effect of nature upon the human mind as well as the specific effects of climate, food, soil, and so on. American anthropologist Clark Wissler

(1870–1947), a student of Boas, was also interested in environment and culture. His research convinced him that there was a relationship between the two. In a series of works, including *The Relation of Nature to Man in Aboriginal America* (1926), Wissler attempted to map American cultural areas based on the principal modes of food production. Steward was not a geographic determinist such as Buckle, and his formulation was more sophisticated than that of Wissler. He believed that certain types of society are extremely likely to occur under particular conditions of technology and environment.

[5] *Guanaco:* a South American ruminant, of which the llama and alpaca are domesticated varieties.

[6] *Negrito:* in Steward's day, the parlance of racial classification included the term *Negrito,* used for short, dark-skinned peoples. These included people in Africa, India, the Philippines, and the Malay Peninsula. The term is rarely used today.

Only a basic change in environment or technology could have eliminated the patrilineal band. The inevitability of such bands under the given conditions is shown by its persistence along with clans, moieties, and other special patterns in the different groups, and, in the case of the Congo, an interdependence of the hunting Negritos and farming Bantu tribes who inhabited the same area.

With a given population density, the size of the territory and of the band which owns it are direct variables. If the group is enlarged the territory must also be increased in order to support it. Among the ethnic groups in question, however, the population is sparse, ranging from a maximum which seldom exceeds one person per 5 square miles to one person per 50 or more square miles. This prevents indefinite enlargement of the band because there would be no means of transporting the food to the people or the people to the food. The area which the band can conveniently forage averages some 100 square miles and seldom exceeds 500 square miles, a tract roughly 20 miles to a side. Consequently, the band averages 50 individuals and seldom exceeds 100.[b] Only in regions of unusual resources—for example, where there are herds of migratory game—does the group size surpass these figures.

We now have to consider why these bands are patrilineal. First, it is characteristic of hunters in regions of sparse population for postmarital residence to be patrilocal. This has several causes. If human beings could be conceived stripped of culture, it is not unreasonable to suppose that innate male dominance would give men a commanding position.[c] If, in addition to native dominance, however, the position of the male is strengthened by his greater economic importance, as in a hunting culture,[d] or even if women are given greater economic importance than men, it is extremely probable that postmarital residence will be patrilocal.[7]

But in these small bands patrilocal residence will produce the fact or fiction that all members of the band are patrilineally related[e] and hence matrimonially taboo. Band exogamy—that is local exogamy—is therefore required. Probably at one time or another such bands have actually consisted of relatives with traceable connection. Genealogical data on the tribes of southern California, for example, show that more often than not the band comprises a true patrilineal lineage. Because life is so precarious that increase of the total population is impossible and budding collateral lineages often become extinct, the possibility is small that several independent families which have no traceable connection will develop in any band. Such families will occur only if the band is extraordinarily large. And even in this case, the fiction of relationship may be perpetuated after the connection is forgotten if group unity is reinforced by patronymy, myths, and other factors.[f,8]

---

[7] Rather than arguing that material conditions (hunting) give rise to social forms (patrilineality), Steward here relies on the supposition of biological differences between males and females to explain the origins of patrilineality. It is an uncharacteristically weak explanation, especially given the last line of this paragraph, when he asserts the adoption of patrilocality regardless of whether males or females are relatively more influential in a society.

[8] Notice that Steward's explanation is generally materialist. Cultural fictions (the name of the patrilineage for example) are necessitated by ecological conditions.

This materialist basis was influenced by Marx (see essay 4). The intellectual climate of his day prevented Steward from referencing Marx, but he had read Marx's work. Despite this, Steward cannot be considered a Marxist,

nor was he as heavily influenced by Marx as was Leslie White, the other major American materialist of this era (see essay 18). Unlike Steward, White's work was concerned with establishing an overall evolutionary scheme for society and with the roles of conflict and class within society; these are typically Marxist issues. Steward's work lacks the characteristically Marxist emphasis on conflict as a motor of evolution. He was far more interested in showing the specific interrelations among technology, environment, and society. Further, as Harris (1968) notes, although Steward's division of culture into core and secondary features sounds superficially like Marx's division of society into base and superstructure, it is quite different. Marx saw superstructure as arising from base; Steward generally saw secondary features as virtually unrelated to the core.

For these reasons, the bands of hunters who live in sparsely populated areas must ordinarily be patrilineal. But special factors may make them temporarily composite. Thus, if unrelated and hence intermarriageable families exist within a band, local exogamy and patrilocal residence with respect to the band are unnecessary. This will occur when parallel-cousin marriage is permitted or where bands have, for various reasons, become unusually large and lack any factor that would create or perpetuate a fiction of relationship between its members. Occasionally, matrilocal residence will introduce families which are not related patrilineally into a band. This will prevent strictly patrilineal inheritance of band territory and tend to weaken the fiction of relationship between band members. For these reasons, patrilineal bands at certain times or places deviate from the ideal pattern and consist of unrelated families. In this respect, they resemble composite bands, but whereas the latter normally must remain composite, patrilineal bands tend to return to their typical pattern. The factors which produce composite bands will be analyzed subsequently.

Political unity in all bands is very similar. Centralized control exists only for hunting, for rituals, and for the few other affairs that are communal. Consequently, the leader has temporary and slight authority. In patrilineal bands, he is usually the head of the lineage, which, being a status based on kinship, is usually not formally institutionalized. The shaman, however, controls many collective activities, and he is feared and respected for his supernatural power, which often gives him more influence than the other leaders. Bands which are ordinarily autonomous may temporarily unite for special occasions such as Australian and Fuegian initiation ceremonies. Although the reason for this larger unity is religious and social, food supply strictly limits the duration of multiband gatherings.

The occurrence of clans among Australians, Ojibway, and others, of moieties in Australia and in southern California, and of other social forms in no way affects the cause-and-effect relationships involved in the formation of the patrilineal band.[9] Such institutions are variables with respect to the pattern we have analyzed. Their presence or absence is to be explained by diffusion or by some special local factors and not by adaptations of technology to environment.[10]

TRIBES WITH THE PATRILINEAL BAND

In the following pages some patrilineal bands will be discussed in detail, showing reasons in each case for departures from the ideal pattern.[11]

The Bushmen[g]

A hunting and gathering culture imposed upon an arid and unproductive native environment produced a sparse population among the Bushmen. Population aggregates were necessarily small[h] and the group that co-operated in various undertakings was a politically autonomous patrilineal lineage. Although the band or lineage split seasonally into smaller units, probably family groups, it owned and communally utilized a definite territory. Some hunting required joint effort of all band members, and game was often shared by all.

The bands of the Northwestern Bushmen, including the Heikum, were ordinarily patrilineal owing to patrilocal residence and local or band exogamy. The Naron bands, however, were sometimes composite because matrilocal residence, which was practiced occasionally in order that

[9] When the members of a tribe are divided into two groups, these divisions are called *moieties*.

[10] Critics of Steward's work point out that he explained away those things that did not fit the patterns he outlined by suggesting, as he does here, that they were secondary features resulting from diffusion or the specific history of the group under study.

[11] In this section of the essay, Steward cites evidence from a wide variety of societies to support his contention that certain environmental and technological constraints lead to the formation of patrilineal bands.

the wife's mother might help the wife with her children, introduced families which were not related patrilineally into the same band. This weakened patrilineal inheritance of the estate and tended to obviate the necessity of band exogamy, which, however, was preferred (Schapera, 1930: 81–85). The Cape, Namib, and !Okung bands also tended to be composite because, although band exogamy was preferred, matrilocal residence, for a reason which has not been revealed, was sometimes practiced. Band endogamy, moreover, was facilitated by cousin marriage, parallel or cross, which was barred among the Northwestern groups (Schapera, 1930:82–83;102–07).[12]

Schebesta (1931) reports what appears to be an identical pattern. The Bambuti, Efe, Bac'wa, and Batwa of the Belgian Congo had exogamous, patrilocal, and generally autonomous sibs ("sippe") or families of male relatives numbering sixty to sixty-five persons each. Apparently, the "totemic clans" of these people were the same as lineages, that is, they were localized clans or sibs.

Central African Negritos

Several scattered groups of Negritos or pygmies living in the dense tropical rain forests of the Congo in equatorial Africa also belonged to the patrilineal band type. The bands were predominantly hunters, and the exploitative patterns produced the features typical of the patrilineal band despite the fact that the pygmies lived in a close dependency relationship with the Bantu Negroes.[13]

In the Ituri Forest (Putnam, 1948:322–42), a Negro village and a pygmy band jointly owned about 100 square miles of country. The Negroes were largely farmers, and the pygmies were entirely hunters, the latter supplying the former with meat in exchange for vegetable foods. The dependence of the pygmy upon the Negro might account for the cohesion of the pygmy band and for the pattern of land-tenure, but it would not account for the patrilineality and exogamy, which must be explained by the low population density, the small band size, and the predominance of hunting.

The bands ranged in size from 100 to 200 persons, 150 being the average. All families were normally related through the male line, and the band, therefore, constituted a locally exogamous and patrilocal group. The cohesion of the lineage or band was reinforced by the belief that a totemic animal was the ancestor of the band and by myths. The band contained unrelated families only when exceptional circumstances introduced a man from some other band, for example, when a man could not get along in his own band or when he had trouble with his Negro group. The patrilineal features resulted from the hunting pattern. The men spent all their time hunting for game which was normally scattered. They used nets in collective drives or else bows, spears, and knives in individual stalking. The game was varied and included turtles, rats, antelope, buffalo, and elephants. Hunting was restricted to the band's territory, the size of which must be interpreted as the optimum which can be exploited. Had the territory been substantially larger, the band would have surpassed a kin group in size and therefore ceased to be exogamous and patrilocal. However, the sparse population, the limitations upon the area which could be hunted, and the patrilocality after marriage produced localized lineages.

These bands sometimes tended to be composite for two reasons. First, it was customary at marriage for the husband's band to furnish a woman who married a member of his wife's band.

---

[12] Harris (1968:667) claims that Steward's listing of factors responsible for patrilineal, complex, or matrilineal band formation are "fortuitous and quixotic." Note the reliance in this passage and later in this essay on "a reason which has not been revealed" and other such devices.

[13] The fact that hunting bands of pygmies lived in close proximity to agricultural Bantus was critical for Steward.

Traditional evolutionary schemes had placed agriculture far above hunting and gathering. If diffusion alone could account for cultural traits and agriculture was superior to hunting and gathering, why had the pygmies not adopted it? Steward felt he could solve this problem using a cultural-ecological approach.

When no woman was available, the man lived with his wife's people. Second, band endogamy, that [is], marriage between related members of the band, though felt to be a breach of incest laws, was often practiced when other bands were remote and inaccessible (Schmidt, 1910:173).

The Negritos of Gabon in French Equatorial Africa were grouped in some 100 or 150 villages, each of which usually comprised one family "rangée sous l'autorité d'un seul chef, le père du clan, généralement de 30 à 35 individus mâles."[14] These seemed to be independent, patrilocal, and exogamous, and therefore true patrilineal bands. But they belonged to some kind of larger patrilineal totemic clans, which were preferably, but not always, exogamous (Trilles, 1932:20–23, 143–51, 409–18).[15]

Semang

The more or less inadequate information now available indicates that many of the Negritos of the Malay peninsula possessed the patrilineal band. Largely hunters and gatherers and more or less isolated in the sparsely settled mountain forests, the Semang groups were small, ranging, according to fragments of evidence recorded by Schebesta (1929), from individual families which were probably temporary subdivisions to groups of 50 or more persons. These seem to have been politically autonomous, landowning bands. Skeat and Blagden (1900:495–97) say that the Kedah Semang band often amounted to an enlarged family and, somewhat obscurely, that the chief was practically "the head of a family, which in this case is represented by a larger family, the tribe." It may be, however, that band territory was sometimes further subdivided among bilateral families so that each owned an area for

its durian trees. Schebesta says (1929:83, 234, 279) that "the individual groups wander within the tribal boundaries but always return to their family territory, especially at the time of the durian crop" and that the trees are owned by men as family heads. These family tracts were, perhaps, comparable to the Algonkian and Althabaskan beaver-trapping territories.

That these bands were truly patrilineal is indicated by Schebesta's statement (1929) that the unit of society was the "sib" like that of the Congo Negritos, but he does not particularize its characteristics. Elsewhere he observes that there was considerable band exogamy and patrilocal residence, although he recorded one band that was composite. One reason for the occurrence of the latter among the Kenta Semang was that durian trees were sometimes inherited matrilineally. This would, of course, favor matrilocal residence and tend to set up a composite band.

Philippine Negritos

The predominantly hunting and gathering Philippine Negritos lived in comparative isolation from the Malaysians. They were clustered in bands which Vanoverbergh (1925:430–33), says comprise "a certain group of families." These remained in the same portion of the forest and seasonally exploited different parts of an area which had a radius of not over twenty miles. Trespass on the land of neighboring bands was not forbidden but was avoided. The land was hunted communally by its owners, but cultivated trees and honey nests were privately owned. It is not recorded, however, how trees were inherited. Bands seem to have been politically autonomous, but the lack of an institutionalized band chief is implied by the

---

[14] *"rangée . . . mâles"*: The French comment means "placed under the authority of a single leader, usually the eldest of the clan, and consisting of thirty to thirty-five men."

[15] In assembling his cases, Steward relied on historical accounts as well as then-current ethnography. The use of these sources was important for him since his intellectual achievement was to explain the presence of the band in

very different and widely distributed locales. Use of historical accounts was problematic, however, since it led him to use sources that were not very reliable and to discuss groups, such as the Tasmanians, which had disappeared by his era. Further, much of the information he presents here, for example, his description of the Central African Negritos, has since been shown to be invalid, or, at best, only partially correct. Does this invalidate his argument?

somewhat vague statement that authority rested in the father of the family.

There is some indication that Philippine Negrito bands have recently changed from patrilineal to composite.[16] Schmidt (1910:72–73), quoting Blumentritt on the Zambales-Bataam, says that the bands are now endogamous but at the end of the eighteenth century were exogamous. Present-day endogamy is further shown by the presence of unrelated families in the same band.[i] Nevertheless, patrilocal residence is recorded, although it is not clear whether residence is patrilocal with respect to the band or the family.

There is, therefore, some doubt as to the frequency of the two types of bands and the customs concerning residence and other matters which would produce them. It appears, however, that some factor has tended to produce a change from patrilineal to composite bands during the past century. At least one important cause of composite bands today is the practice of marrying cousins. Although marriage was preferably between cross-cousins, parallel-cousins were eligible for matrimony (Vanoverbergh, 1925:425–28).[17]

Australians[j]

The relatively low productivity of Australia permitted but a sparse population which averaged only 1 person per 12 square miles for the entire continent.[k] The population was grouped into relatively small, autonomous bands which Radcliffe-Brown calls hordes. Each band comprised 20 to 50 individuals and owned 100 to 150 square miles of land. The male members of the band inherited and communally hunted their tract, which was definitely bounded and protected from trespass.[l]

These bands were truly patrilineal, and they approximated male lineages. They were almost universally exogamous and patrilocal. The idea of relationship between band members was further reinforced by kinship terminology. Even those ethnic groups which had moieties, sections (formerly called "marriage classes"), and matrilineal clans and totems had not, except in a portion of western Australia, lost the patrilineal band (Radcliffe-Brown, 1931:438).

Tasmanians

Information on the Tasmanians, though incomplete, indicates the aboriginal presence of the patrilineal band. The scant population[m] was divided into autonomous bands of 30 to 40 persons each. Each band owned a tract of land on which it wandered seasonally in search of food. It protected its hunting rights against trespass, which was a common cause of war (Roth, 1899:58–59, 104–07).

The Tasmanian band must have been patrilineal, for evidence assembled by Roth indicates, although it does not prove beyond question, that the band was exogamous and marriage patrilocal.

The Ona of Tierra del Fuego

The Ona of Tierra del Fuego fall strictly into the patrilineal band pattern. The low subsistence level, based largely upon guanaco hunting, produced a population of only one individual to 4.5 or 5 square miles. This was grouped in politically independent bands of 40 to 120 persons, each owning an average of 410 square miles. Gusinde (1931) believes that the manner of life would not have supported larger aggregates.

---

[16] Tracing out the ways in which culture changed was to become one of Steward's key concerns. He is known as the creator of multilinear evolutionism, which he contrasted with nineteenth-century unilineal evolution and his contemporary Leslie White's universal evolution. He argued that unlike White and his nineteenth-century predecessors, he was not interested in formulating a general, universal plan of evolution but rather with showing how particular cultures changed and developed (1955:11–19).

[17] Steward's is an uneasy evolutionism. It is perhaps best seen as a compromise between his historical-particularist training and his goal of creating an anthropology based in the discovery of causal principles. He placed societies in an essentially unilineal evolutionary scheme from family to multifamily to state civilization. He then focused on the multiple pathways that societies may take between evolutionary stages.

Each territory was named, band rights to it were sanctioned by myths, and hunting privileges were protected against trespass. Although each band was politically autonomous, there was no institution of chief.

The band was patrilineal because it was exogamous and patrilocal. Local exogamy was required even among the large bands in which relationship between members was not traceable, for native theory held that each band was a male lineage.

Tehuelche of Patagonia

The Tehuelche of Patagonia, although very incompletely known, are instructive when compared with the Ona. Also dependent largely upon herds of guanaco, their economic life appears formerly to have resembled that of the Fuegians. There is evidence that they were divided into bands, each having some degree of localization[n] and led in its travels, etc., by a patrilineal chief (Outes and Bruch, 1910:126; Beerbohn, 1881:93) who was called "father" (Musters, 1873:194). The band chief, however, acknowledged a general cacique, who, according to Musters, had very little authority. The institution of general or tribal cacique[18] may easily have developed subsequent to the arrival of the European.

The introduction of the horse about a century and a half ago completely altered ecological conditions in Patagonia. It enabled people to move widely in pursuit of guanaco herds and to transport foods considerable distances. This would, of course, have tended to eliminate band ownership of small parcels of territory, even had it existed. It also permitted enlargement of population aggregates far beyond the size of the usual lineage. Further motivation for amalgamation of formerly separate bands was provided by internecine strife, which was stimulated by competition for foods and war against the white man. The political unit consequently increased in size and had a single, although not absolute, chief. Thus, in 1871, bands numbered as many as 400 or 500 persons, although they occasionally split into smaller groups (Musters, 1873:64, 70, 96–97, 117, 188). As there is no mention of exogamy of any form, it must be assumed that these bands were composite. This is common elsewhere in bands of such size.[19]

Southern Californians

The Shoshonean-speaking Serrano, Cahuilla, and Luiseño, and some of the Yuman-speaking Diegueño of southern California were divided into patrilineal bands.[20] This region is exceptional in that abundance of acorns and other wild seeds permitted the unusually dense native population of one person per square mile. But this great density was accompanied by small territory size rather than large band size, probably because

---

[18] *Cacique* refers to a leader in Mesoamerican Indian communities.

[19] Here Steward gives an example of the effect of technological change on social structure: The introduction of the horse led to an increase in band size. Examples linking technology and social structure were essential because they were the sort of things that would leave traces in the archaeological record, which meant that archaeological data could be used to bolster Steward's theoretical position. This connection between theory in cultural anthropology and archaeology was one of the factors leading to the emergence of the new archaeology in the 1960s. Steward had, in fact, begun his career as an archaeologist working in the Columbia River valley.

[20] Steward's most protracted fieldwork was among the Shoshoni in Utah, and here, as he describes Southern California peoples, he is closest to his own fieldwork interests. His fieldwork experiences were important for two reasons. First, working among the traditional Shoshoni, he was struck by the small group size and the extremely demanding environment they inhabited. In the deserts of the Great Basin, the powerful influences of environment and technology might have been more evident than they were in many other places. Second, Steward was known for his fieldwork technique. He was highly critical of ethnographic studies that used material collected from people no longer engaged in aboriginal lifestyles. He encouraged an ethnography based on recording actual behavior rather than one based on what people said about past behavior. It is ironic that in developing multilinear evolution, he, of necessity, had to rely on secondhand data collected under conditions that were not well known, precisely the type of information he distrusted.

the very few and small sources of water prevented greater concentration of people. Therefore, bands averaged only fifty individuals and the territory only fifty square miles.

The other factors producing the patrilineal bands were those which operated elsewhere. Because of patrilocal residence coupled with the small size of the bands, most of them were actual patrilineal lineages so local exogamy was required. In addition, a band chief, "priest," ceremonies, ceremonial house and bundle, and myths contributed to group cohesion (Strong, 1927, 1929; Gifford, 1918, 1926, 1931; Kroeber, 1925, 1934). This strongly fortified patrilineal pattern may also have served to maintain the band at lineage size.

The culturally similar neighboring Cupeño provide an illuminating contrast to these groups. Because the local abundance of food and water permitted greater concentration, they were able to live in two permanent towns, each numbering some 250 persons. Each village contained several lineages and had a chief. Bands were, therefore, of the composite type (Gifford, 1926:394–96; Strong, 1929:188–90, 233).

CAUSAL FORMULATION FOR PATRILINEAL BANDS

In any society there are certain cultural factors which potentially give cohesion to aggregates of several families: marriage, extension of kinship ties and corollary extensions of incest taboos, group ceremonies, myths, games, and other features. These features may be derived from cultural heritage of the group or they may be borrowed from neighboring tribes. In each group they are integrated in a total sociocultural system, but the nature of this system is not explained merely by tracing the diversified history of the features or by describing the functional interdependency of the parts. These features must be adjusted to the subsistence patterns that are established through the exploitation of a particular habitat by means of a particular technology; and the subsistence patterns are only partly explainable in terms of culture history. The use of bows and arrows, traps, hunting nets, game drives, or grass firing can generally be traced to diffusion, but the hunting patterns and the social effect of these patterns are quite unlike in areas of sparse and scattered game and in areas of large herds of migratory game. Among societies which devote a very great portion of their time and energy to food-getting, these differences in hunting patterns will greatly affect the size, permanency, composition, and general behavior patterns of the group. The extent and degree to which subsistence patterns affect the total structure of the society and the functional integration of its various parts are questions to be answered by empirical procedure.[21]

The patrilineal band represents a social type the principal features of which are determined within exceedingly narrow limits by the cultural ecology—by the interaction of technology and environment. Other features, such as clans, moieties, age-grades, men's tribal societies, group ceremonialism, totemism, and mythology may or may not also be present. If they do form part of the cultural inventory of the band, they are integrated to the patrilineal pattern. A causal formulation of the factors producing the patrilineal band may therefore omit these various historically-derived features, for the latter are of interest only when attention is shifted to the uniqueness of each culture and they do not help explain the patrilineal features which are the subject of inquiry.

---

[21] This passage contains a critique of historical particularism and functionalism and outlines Steward's theoretical position. Staking out this position brought him into direct conflict with many other Boasians. For example, in this passage, Steward discards unique historically derived features as having no explanatory value. However, it was precisely these unique features that Kroeber and many other historical particularists were interested in documenting. They believed these showed the creative genius of human-kind. Unsurprisingly, the relationship between Kroeber and Steward was not close. Kroeber considered Steward a promising but not particularly interesting student. Steward respected Kroeber but was fundamentally at odds with most of what he stood for (Wolf 1981:63).

The factors which produce the patrilineal band are:[22]

1. A population density of one person or less—usually much less—per square mile, which is caused by a hunting and gathering technology in areas of scarce wild foods;
2. An environment in which the principal food is game that is nonmigratory and scattered, which makes it advantageous for men to remain in the general territory of their birth;
3. Transportation restricted to human carriers;
4. The cultural-psychological fact, which cannot be explained by local adaptation, that groups of kin who associate together intimately tend to extend incest taboos from the biological family to the extended family thus requiring group exogamy.

These four factors interact as follows: The scattered distribution of the game, the poor transportation, and the general scarcity of the population make it impossible for groups that average over 50 or 60 persons and that have a maximum of about 100 to 150 persons to associate with one another frequently enough and to carry out sufficient joint activities to maintain social cohesion. The band consists of persons who habitually exploit a certain territory over which its members can conveniently range. Customary use leads to the concept of ownership. Were individual families to wander at will, hunting the game in neighboring areas, competition would lead to conflict. Conflict would call for alliance with other families,

allies being found in related families. As the men tend to remain more or less in the territory in which they have been reared and with which they are familiar, patrilineally related families would tend to band together to protect their game resources. The territory would therefore become divided among these patrilineal bands.

It is worth noting that the nature of Great Basin Shoshonean land-use precluded the banding together of patrilineal families and landownership. For two reasons, the pine nut, which was the principal food, had a very different sociological effect than game hunting. First, good crops were so abundant that there was never competition for it. Second, abundant crops occurred each year in very different localities and they brought different groups together each time.[23]

Among the patrilineal bands, the component biological families associated together sufficiently often to permit an extension of incest taboos to all members. Prohibition of marriage within the immediate biological family is universal among mankind. There are generally extensions of marriage restrictions to collateral relatives of the second or third degree, though cross-cousins may marry in certain cultures. The patrilineal bands were so small that they usually consisted of known relatives who commonly fall within the prohibited degrees of relationship, and cross-cousins—the father's sister's daughter or the mother's brother's daughter—would normally be in another band. Band exogamy is therefore required.

The several features of the patrilineal band reinforce one another. Patrilocal residence after marriage because the male wishes to remain in country he knows causes an area to be habitually

---

[22] Although Steward rejected much of what his professors believed, his work was not unprecedented in American anthropology. Earlier, members of the culture area school attempted to map North and South America into a series of areas of similar cultures, which, they noted, tended to overlap with ecological zones. Otis Mason (1838–1908) formulated one such version in the 1890s, but Boas and his students Kroeber and Wissler created a more definitive mapping in the teens and early twenties (see Mason 1895, Holmes 1914, Wissler 1917). The culture area theorists tended to see environment as a passive factor placing broad restrictive limits on cultural possibilities.

Steward saw the combination of technology and environment as playing a far more causal role in determining social systems.

[23] Steward was also influenced by his work with Carl Sauer (1889–1975), a geographer interested in anthropology and archaeology who stressed an approach to geography based on the interaction of humans and environment. Sauer, who was at Berkeley during Steward's time there, had an important impact on Kroeber and his students. Sauer, incidentally, is also infamous for his belief that Irish monks visited North America before the Vikings.

occupied, utilized, and defended by patrilineally-related families. Local exogamy prevents the introduction into the band of unrelated families, so that the band becomes in fact, a patrilineal lineage.[24]

The requirement that the band be exogamous may persist after traceable kinship relations in the group are forgotten if the patrilineal complex is reinforced by other features, such as names, kinship terminology, myths, ceremonies, totems, and the like. Thus, the bands of Australia, southern California, and Tierra del Fuego conform more rigidly to the pattern because they possess such supports. Among the Bushmen and Negritos patrilineal bands may often temporarily become composite bands when special conditions exist.

A theory of the patrilineal band which sought its origin in purely cultural-historical terms would be confronted by insuperable difficulties.[25] Such a theory would have to assume either that the band inherited the basic patrilineal pattern from some archaic world-wide culture or that it borrowed it from some neighboring tribes. As we have seen, primitive nonagricultural peoples in areas of seed resources, of fish, or of large game herds do not have the patrilineal band because these areas are not conducive to the exploitation of a certain restricted territory by small groups of men in the manner found among the patrilineal band peoples. It is inconceivable that this pattern could have survived the migrations of mankind over dozens of unlike environments during thousands of years. The theory of borrowing from neighbors will not stand up because the neighbors of these tribes simply do not have patrilineal bands.

A holistic or functional explanation minimizes the importance of cultural ecology by insisting that all features of the culture are equally cause

and effect.[26] This simply evades the issue of causality. As we have seen, the clans, moieties, men's tribal societies, and other special features occur with only some of the patrilineal patterns and they also occur among quite different kinds of societies. There is a functional interrelationship between hunting in a restricted area, the male's continued residence in that area, patrilocality, and local exogamy. Exogamy within a localized patrilineal group causes the men to hunt scattered game in certain ways. The groups hunt what is available with devices at their command; men best remain in the territory where they were raised; their wives come to their territory after marriage; and the bands are so small that people are related and, given concepts of incest, local exogamy is practiced. It is not claimed that the cultural ecological factors explain everything about the patrilineal band. They explain why these bands differ from other bands which have a similar technology and similar potentialities for extending incest taboos outward from the biological family.

A common explanation of the patrilineal band is that it is merely a localized clan, and diffusionists seek to trace its source to clans elsewhere. Societies which have clans may influence patrilineal bands in two ways; first, borrowed clans may crosscut the bands but fail to change their basic patterns; second, clan myths, ceremonies, and other features may be borrowed by the band and reinforce its local unity. But diffused unilateral structure and exogamy cannot explain the adjustment of male lineages to exploitative activities. In fact, the concept of the patrilineal band has greater value in explaining the clan than vice versa. If, for reasons stated here, a localized patrilineal group develops, it is in effect

---

[24] Steward's approach is oriented toward technology and environment, but he frequently refers to psychology as an important factor (as here, where he discusses the male's wishes). Steward's work is contemporaneous with the culture and personality school (see essays 16 and 17), which relied heavily on psychological explanations.

[25] In this passage and later, Steward attacks the other prominent theoretical positions of his time. This paragraph dismisses historical particularism; later he takes on functionalism and diffusionism.

[26] When Steward presented the first version of this paper in 1936, British functionalism was growing increasingly important in this country. A. R. Radcliffe-Brown, then at the University of Chicago, was a loud and eloquent critic of the Boasians. This passage is aimed directly at his thinking. Radcliffe-Brown identified an ecological-adaptive aspect of social structure but assigned it no particular importance. Steward argues that because of this, Radcliffe-Brown's system describes but does not explain culture.

a localized clan. Whether it should properly be called a clan, however, would depend upon whether it is exogamous regardless of locality. Those groups which have reinforcing features, such as the southern California Shoshoneans, the Australians, and others, would be clans if exogamy continued after they were dislocated from their territories and the different bands mixed up. Evidently this has happened often in human history and clans have developed in many places. We shall subsequently show how the data of archaeology and ethnography support such an interpretation of the origin of clans among the Pueblo Indians of the Southwest.[27]

CULTURAL VARIABLES AND THE PATRILINEAL BAND

The features of the patrilineal band which must be explained by ecological factors are patrilineality, patrilocality, exogamy, landownership, and informal and limited leadership.[28] Many other features however, were fairly variable in form despite this basic pattern. A substantial range of possible alternatives made diffusion a more direct explanation of their presence.

Some of the technological traits secondary to the main hunting patterns were extremely variable. Containers used in transporting, preparing, and storing food, for example, could not be elaborate, heavy, or numerous because of the nomadic life, but the materials of which they were made, their specific forms, and their decorations were quite variable. The Congo Negritos, Semang, Shoshoneans, and Ona used basketry of various weaves, shapes, and ornamentation; the Bushmen and Congo Negritos employed some pottery; the other areas utilized skins, shells, bark, or other convenient materials. Fire was made with the wooden drill by the Bushmen and Shoshoneans, with the fire saw by the Semang, and with pyrite and stone by the Ona. The Congo Negritos had no means of making fire and were forced to borrow it if their own went out. Shelters were limited by the requirement that they be quickly and easily put together of materials available. These bands used natural shelters, such as caves, when possible. Otherwise, they built mere windbreaks, brush- or skin-covered conical lodges, or dome-shaped brush houses. Similar huts are found scattered throughout the world among primitive peoples, and it would be rather profitless to speculate as to whether they diffused or not, for they are so elementary that it would require no great ingenuity to invent them. Clothing was scant and made with simple skills, but styles varied locally: string skirts or aprons, wrap-around skin skirts, breechclouts, robes, and the like, or perhaps nothing but a few smudges of paint.

Musical instruments and games were generally simple, for extensive paraphernalia was out of the question. The former were generally learned from neighboring tribes. For example, the Semang used flutes, jew's-harps, guitars, and drums borrowed from their Malay neighbors; and the Bushmen had musical bows, flutes, cocoon rattles, and drums, all probably acquired from the Bantu; while the southern California Shoshoneans used only flutes and rattles; the Australians swung bull-roarers and pounded sticks on rolled-up hides; the Ona struck sticks together; and the African Negritos thumped hollow logs.

---

[27] Kroeber had done important work in tracing the diffusion of cultural traits throughout the Southwest. Additionally, radical diffusionist theories were popular in Britain and Germany when Steward wrote. Steward's point is that while diffusion of traits can be shown to exist, the traits are always modified to fit the ecological conditions of the society accepting them.

[28] In this section, Steward explores cultural variables that he considers secondary features, those aspects of culture not closely tied to the cultural core and determined by purely cultural-historical factors such as random innovation and diffusion. This section of the essay is fairly long (more than 1,300 words), but much of it is a simple cataloging of cultural traits with little or no analysis of them. This presentation reflects two factors: first, Steward's training in historical particularism (the collection and cataloging of cultural traits was precisely the sort of anthropology Kroeber urged on his followers) and, second, the likelihood that Steward placed little importance on the information he presents here. From the lack of analysis and the fact that this section is only weakly articulated with the rest of the essay, it appears that Steward considered this material a collection of virtually random facts of no particular interest.

A certain distinctiveness is evident in many features of social organization. While the formal aspects of these are attributable to diffusion, their functional significance was very similar because of their role in the total culture. Several of the bands had men's tribal societies—religious organizations into which young men were initiated during rites from which women and children were barred. The neophytes were scarified, given hunting tests, and made to observe food taboos while religion was explained to them. The Australian societies used bull-roarers in their ceremonies, whereas the Ona used masks and special huts and had rites based on the concept of death and resurrection of the initiate. Southern California Shoshoneans lacked such societies, but their group fetish bundle, ritual, and ceremonial leader had a similar function in reinforcing group cohesion. These and other social features, however, were not necessary to existence of the patrilineal band pattern, and they can hardly constitute the primary basis of cultural typology. The Semang have no men's society.

The presence in any society of the patrilineal band and the tribal society must be "explained" in different terms. The secret society is scattered throughout the world in many kinds of cultures and there is little doubt that it represents a very ancient pattern which has fitted certain psychological-cultural needs as well as a variety of cultural functions so well that it has persisted in spite of tremendous cultural change and that it has even diffused from one type of culture to another. The secret society can in no way be considered a cause of the patrilineal pattern or of the type of land use that underlies this pattern.[29]

There were other social features which, from the point of view of the patrilineal pattern, were secondary or variable and which were found also among tribes lacking the patrilineal band. Some of the northern Australians had matrilineal moieties, which were probably diffused from Melanesia. The combination of these with localized patrilineal, exogamous groups created a very complex organization. The uniqueness of this organization—the fact that it consisted of functionally interrelated parts—does not mean that the origin of its parts cannot be treated separately and in causal terms. The southern California Shoshoneans had moieties which cut across localized patrilineal bands, but these functioned primarily at death ceremonies.

The religious patterns of these tribes were affected by the ecological adjustments principally in a negative sense: they lacked complicated and institutionalized worship of the kinds found among more developed cultures, there being little ceremonialism dedicated to group purposes. Rites were concerned primarily with birth, puberty, sickness, death, and other crisis situations of individuals. The patterns of these crisis rites and of shamanism show certain general similarity to one another and very probably they represent in large part an ancient heritage which survived throughout the world in cultures of many kinds. That is, these rites show a great deal of stability, their basic patterns persisting in many cultural contexts which are quite dissimilar. This fact makes it obviously quite absurd to conceive that religion could be the starting point, the primary factor, in an investigation of the origin of social forms and economic patterns. Religion was a functional part of each culture, but from the point of view of the basic social types and cultural ecological determinants its form was a relatively independent variable.[30]

The local forms and functions of the puberty rites are an illustration of the considerable range

---

[29] Here and later, Steward attempts to demonstrate that the cultural features he believes are secondary have little causal significance for the cultural core: subsistence, technology, and social structure.

[30] Here Steward reaffirms his basic materialism: Material conditions condition ideas, not vice versa. This passage seems to be a direct attack on Tylor, who saw the progressive rationalization of religion as one of the fundamental processes driving cultural change (see essay 2). But why would Steward attack Tylor more than a half century after the publication of *Primitive Culture* and two decades after the latter's death? It is more likely that he was thinking of Max Weber. The English translation of Weber's highly influential *The Protestant Ethic and the Spirit of Capitalism* had been published in 1930, not many years before the first appearance of Steward's essay. In this book Weber argued that Protestant theology was critical to the advent of capitalism in Europe.

TABLE 1   Patrilineal Bands

	Number of persons per square mile	Average size of band	Average number of square miles in band territory	Permanent residence patrilocal with respect to band	Exogamy of band, i.e., locality, required	Band politically autonomous, weak chief	References and remarks
N. W. Bushmen	?	50–60	?	X	X	X	Schapera, 1926, 1930; Dornan, 1925:85; Stow, 1905:33, 229–30; Dunn, 1931:7, 22
Congo Negritos— Bambuti, Efe, Bac'wa, Batwa	?	60–65	?	X	X	X	Schebesta, 1931; Schmidt, 1910
Negritos—Gabon	?	20–70	?	X	X	X	Trilles, 1932
Semang	½–⅛	35?	?		(X)	X	Schebesta, 1929; Skeat and Blagden, 1900
Australia—W	⅕	30	150	X	X	X	Radcliffe-Brown, 1930:688
—S	?	40–	?	X	X	X	Radcliffe-Brown, 1930:690
Victoria	1/15	50+	750	X	X	X	Radcliffe-Brown, 1930:691
Queensland	3/10	30	100	X	X	X	Radcliffe-Brown, 1930:694
Herbert R.	⅕	20–25	100	X	X	X	Radcliffe-Brown, 1930:696
Average	1/12	35	420	X	X	X	
Tasmania	⅛–1/13	30–40	350	X	X	X	Radcliffe-Brown, 1930:695; Roth, 1899
Ona	¼–⅕	40–120	410	X	X	X	Gusinde, 1931
California: Miwok, Luiseño, Serrano, Cahuilla, Cupeño	1	50	50	X	X	X	Gifford, 1926; Kroeber, 1925:883, 58; Strong, 1927, 1929; Gifford, 1926
Diegueño (N & S)	½	50?	50?	X	X	X	Gifford, 1926

of variations that could be woven into the basic pattern of the patrilineal band.[31] We have already seen how puberty rites stressed the maturing of young men among the Northwest Bushmen, the Australians, and the Ona to the extent that the adult males constituted a secret organization. The Congo Negritos may also have had such societies; at least, it is clear that in the Ituri Forest young Pygmy men together with the sons of their Negro overlords were circumcised in groups

[31] Steward turns the historical particularists' practice of cataloging cultural traits against them. Here, his style of writing is significant. By presenting a seemingly random listing of traits, he draws the reader to the conclusion that such a presentation, and hence the historical-particularist research program, can have little explanatory value.

every few years, each group becoming an age-grade society. The other tribes wholly lacked any such formal grouping of their males. Among the Semang, children of both sexes were merely inducted into the status of puberty by a simple rite at which they were painted, tattooed, scarified, and had their teeth filed. The Shoshoneans of southern California, like their nonpatrilineal neighbors, had observances for both sexes. Pubescent girls were "roasted" in a pit and required to race each day, to scratch themselves only with a stick, and to refrain from drinking cold water. Boys were drugged, lectured on tribal lore and morality, subjected to biting ants, and required to dance. Among the Semang both sexes were painted, scarified, and tattooed at adolescence.

In all these tribes, as in hundreds of others throughout the world, the shaman's chief function was to cure disease by supernatural means, generally through singing and sucking out the supposed cause of disease. He had certain other functions, however, which varied with the special local patterning of religion. Among the Bushmen, for example, he officiated at puberty ceremonies, and among the Semang he mediated between mankind and the thunder god.

Death observances were matters of private ritual among most of these bands, but the Shoshoneans of southern California developed them into a ceremony which greatly strengthened group cohesion. An annual mourning ceremony was held under the direction of a special ceremonial leader, while images of the deceased were burned and myths were recited to commemorate the dying god. This ceremony seems to have contributed greatly to the cohesion of Shoshonean bands, and it may partly explain why the bands continued to regard themselves as kin groups and to practice exogamy after they became dislocated from their territories, scattered, and lost genealogical knowledge of their relationship to one another.[32]

NOTES

[a] This is an adaptation and expansion of the article, "The Economic and Social Basis of Primitive Bands," in *Essays in Honor of A. L. Kroeber* (University of California Press, 1936), pp. 331–50.

[b] Wilhelm Koppers observes that 15 to 20 individuals is common and about 100 the probable limit. See Wilhelm Koppers, *Die Anfänge des menschlichen Gemeinschaftslebens* (Vienna, 1921), p. 72.

[c] Bingham observed gorillas in a state of nature in groups of eight to twenty-two individuals, each group under a dominant male; chimpanzees are said to be similar; and it is probable that the males among the baboons observed in nature by Zuckerman had a comparable dominance. See Harold C. Bingham, *Gorillas in a Native Habitat*. Report Joint Expedition of 1929–1932 by Yale University and Carnegie Institution of Washington for Psychobiological Study of Mountain Gorillas (*Gorilla berengei*) in Parc National Albert, Belgian Congo Africa (1932). Also see S. Zuckerman, *The Social Life of Monkeys and Apes* (New York: Harcourt, Brace and Company, 1932).

[d] E.g., the extraordinarily low status of women in the arduous hunting area of northern Canada. Radcliffe-Brown has observed that Australian hunters would be much less successful in territory which was not known to them from childhood.

[e] Relationship is seldom traced beyond three generations among these people.

[f] I make no effort to solve the very difficult problem of why there are incest laws at all. Marriage with relatives to the third generation, i.e., cousins, is taboo in most of these cases, although cross-cousin and even parallel-cousin marriage is permitted among several.

[g] This section is based on I. Schapera, "A Preliminary Consideration of the Relationship between the Hottentots and the Bushmen," *South African Journal of Science*, XXIII (1926), 833–66; I. Schapera, *The Khoisan Peoples of South Africa* (London, 1930); S. S. Dornan, *Pygmies and Bushmen of the Kalahari* (London, 1925); E. J. Dunn, *The Bushman* (London, 1931); George W. Stow, *The Native Races of South Africa* (New York, 1905); S. Passarge, *Die Buschmanner der Kalahari* (Berlin, 1907).

[h] Schapera, *The Khoisan Peoples of South Africa*, pp. 67–81, has gleaned a few figures on band size from

---

[32] Steward's work had a profound effect on the anthropologists of his day. Although his career, unlike that of Boas or White, was characterized by many short stays at different universities, he was a charismatic professor and attracted an important following. Among the students of Steward who later became prominent anthropologists were Stanley Diamond (1922–1991), Morton H. Fried (1923–1986) (see essay 20), Sidney Mintz (b. 1922), Elman Service (1915–1996), Elliott Skinner (b. 1924), and Eric Wolf (1923–1999).

various sources: Cape Bushmen, who were seriously affected by foreign contacts, 100 to 150, according to one estimate, and 3 to 4 families each, according to a more recent figure; Heichware, 20; Kalahari, 30; !Okung, not exceeding 30; Northwestern Bushmen, ranging from 20 to 150 and probably averaging 50 to 60 each.

[i] Morice Vanoverbergh, "Negritos of Northern Luzon," *Anthropos*, XXV (1930), 538–39, found that some bands contained related males and also that related males occurred in different bands.

[j] This material is largely from A. R. Radcliffe-Brown, "Former Numbers and Distribution of the Australian Aborigines," *Official Yearbook of the Commonwealth of Australia*, No. 23 (1930), pp. 671–96, and Radcliffe-Brown, "The Social Organization of Australian Tribes, I–III," *Oceania* I (1930, 1931) 34–63, 204–46, 426–56 (especially pp. 436–39, 455).

[k] Radcliffe-Brown, *Official Yearbook of the Commonwealth of Australia*, No. 23 (1930), p. 696. The population range was 1 person per 2 square miles in the most fertile section to 1 per 38 square miles in the more arid regions.

[l] D. Sutherland Davidson, "The Family Hunting Territory in Australia," *American Anthropologist*, n.s., XXX (1928), 614–32. Davidson has collected evidence that in some localities the landowning group was the bilateral family. It is the opinion of Radcliffe-Brown, *Oceania*, I (1931), 438, however, that "the particularism of the family whereby it might tend to become an isolated unit is neutralized by the horde [i.e., band] solidarity."

[m] Radcliffe-Brown, *Official Yearbook of the Commonwealth of Australia*, No. 23 (1930), p. 695, gives the aboriginal total as probably 2,000 or 3,000, which is one person to 8 or 13 square miles.

[n] Antonio Serrano, *Los Primitivos Habitantes del Territorio Argentina* (Buenos Aires, 1930), p. 157. Nuñoz, quoted by Serrano, says that among the Northern Tehuelche the head chief owned the land and that the lesser chiefs could not change their land without giving notice to him.

REFERENCES

Beerbohm, Julius. 1881. *Wanderings in Patagonia or Life Among the Ostrich-Hunters*. London.

Dornan, S. S. 1925. *Pygmies and Bushmen of the Kahlahari*. London.

Dunn, E. J. 1931. *The Bushman*. London.

Gifford, E. W. 1918. "Clans and Moieties in Southern California," *University of California Publications in American Archaeology and Ethnology*, XIV, 155–219.

———. 1926. "Miwok Lineages and the Political Unit in Aboriginal California," *American Anthropologist*, n.s., XXVIII, 389–401.

———. 1931. "The Kamia of the Imperial Valley," *Bureau of American Ethnology Bulletin* 97.

Gusinde, Martin. 1931. "Die Feuerland Indianer. Bande I. Die Selk'nam. Verlag der Internationalen Zeitschrift," *Anthropos*, pp. 302–06.

Kroeber, A. L. 1925. "Handbook of the Indians of California," *Bureau of American Ethnology Bulletin* 78.

———. 1934. "Native American Population," *American Anthropologist*, n.s., XXXVI, No. 1, pp. 1–25.

Musters, George C. 1873. *At Home with the Patagonians. A Year's Wandering over Untrodden Ground from the Straits of Magellan to the Rio Negro*. London.

Outes, Felix, F., and Carlos Bruch. 1910. *Los Aborigines de la Republica Argentina*. Buenos Aires.

Putnam, Patrick. 1948. "The Pygmies of the Ituri Forest," in Carleton S. Coon, *A General Reader in Anthropology*. New York: H. Holt and Company, pp. 322–342.

Radcliffe-Brown, A. R. 1930. "Former Numbers and Distribution of the Australian Aborigines," *Official Yearbook of the Commonwealth of Australia* No. 23, pp. 671–96.

———. 1931. "The Social Organization of Australian Tribes, III," *Oceania*, I, 426–56.

Roth, H. Ling. 1899. *The Aborigines of Tasmania*. Halifax (England): F. King and Sons.

Schapera, I. 1926. "A Preliminary Consideration of the Relationship between the Hottentots and the Bushmen." *South African Journal of Science*, XXIII, 833–66.

———. 1930. *The Khosian Peoples of South Africa*. London.

Schebesta, Paul. 1929. *Among the Forest Dwarfs of Malaya*. London.

———. 1931. "Erste Mitteilungen uber die Ergebnisse meiner Forschungsreise bei den Pygmaen in Belgische-Kongo," *Anthropos*, XXVI, 1–17.

Schmidt, P. W. 1910. "Die Stellung der Pygmaenvolker in der Entwicklungsgeschichte des Menschen," *Studien u. Forschungen zur Menschen-u. Volkerkunde*. Stuttgart.

Skeat, W. W., and C. O. Blagden. 1900. *Pagan Races of the Malay Peninsula*. London and New York: The Macmillan Company.

Strong, W. D. 1927. "An Analysis of Southwestern Society," *American Anthropologist*, n.s., XXIX, 1–61.

———. 1929. "Aboriginal Society in Southern California," *University of California Publications in American Archaeology and Ethnology*, XXVI, 1–358.

Trilles, R. P. 1932. "Les Pygmées de la Forêt Equatorial," *Anthropos*, III, 1–530.

Vanoverbergh, Morice. 1925. "Negritos of Northern Luzon," *Anthropos*, XX, 148–99, 399–443.

Neomaterialism: Evolutionary, Functionalist, Ecological, and Marxist

Julian Steward and Leslie White set the stage for ecological anthropology and materialist cultural analysis, but it was the next generation of anthropologists who really developed these fields of inquiry. By midcentury, two types of materialism were becoming popular in anthropology: ecological-materialist approaches and neo-Marxist approaches.

The ecological-materialist approach to anthropology was heavily influenced by general systems theory and the growing science of ecology (Orlove 1980). Ecological materialists also borrowed from cybernetics. They commonly assumed that societies were homeostatic, that is, that cultural institutions functioned as feedback mechanisms (like thermostats) to maintain a balance between energy production and expenditure and the productive capacity of the environment. Typically, ecological materialists examined culture using an equilibrium model that traced energy flow within an ecosystem. For example, a society might be analyzed in terms of its food production and the caloric expenditure of human energy required to maintain the society in equilibrium.

In addition, ecological-materialist studies differed from those of Steward and White in that the former tended to take local populations rather than cultures as their units of analysis. Ecological materialists examined the interactions between populations and environments rather than treating the environment as a passive background that shapes culture but is not influenced by it.

Ecological materialism can be subdivided into two different approaches: neoevolutionism and neofunctionalism (Orlove 1980). Like Lewis Henry Morgan (see essay 3), neoevolutionists were primarily interested in the origins of cultural phenomena and in particular, the rise of civilization. Examples of this work include Morton H. Fried's (1923–1986) *The Evolution of Political Society* (1967), Elman Service's (1915–1996) *Primitive Social Organization: An Evolutionary Perspective* (1962), and Kent Flannery's (b. 1934) "The Cultural Evolution of Civilizations" (1972). (Archaeological research has been a major part of this field as well but is beyond the scope of this book.)

The neoevolutionists were often concerned with the identification of stages through which cultural phenomena developed. For instance, the famous bands-tribes-chiefdoms-states sequence of cultural development was proposed by Service (1962), a student of both White and Steward. The essay we chose to represent this school of thought is by Morton Fried. Fried was first a graduate student and then a professor at Columbia University. He was deeply affected by classes he took from Julian Steward as well as by his fellow students, including Elman Service, Stanley Diamond (1922–1991), Eric Wolf (1923–1999), and Robert Manners (1913–1996). He also credited Leslie White and V. Gordon Childe with making major contributions to his understanding of social evolution (Service 1988). Fried's principal area of field research was China; he made numerous trips to the mainland as well as to Chinese communities in other parts of the world.

In the essay presented here, Fried examines the evolution of social stratification in relation to the control and distribution of resources, a perspective he develops more fully in *The Evolution of Political Society.* There, Fried examined the development of social inequality, proposing the evolutionary stages of egalitarian, ranked, stratified, and state societies.

Like the psychological and structural functionalists of the first half of the twentieth century, neofunctionalists were interested in the function and purpose of institutions and beliefs. However, whereas the functionalists described institutions in terms of their contribution to individual needs or social stability, neofunctionalists were interested in adaptation. They focused on the ways in which particular cultural beliefs, practices, and institutions allowed populations to maintain and reproduce themselves successfully within specific physical, political, and economic environments. The dominant perspective within neofunctionalism is called cultural materialism, and Marvin Harris (1927–2001) was its leading proponent.

Harris did both his undergraduate and graduate training at Columbia University, where he also served as a professor from 1953 to 1980. His mentor was Charles Wagley (1913–1991), a student of Boas. Harris took courses from Steward and was attracted by White's critique of the Boasians, but during his career as a student, these experiences did not have a very profound effect on him. He moved decisively toward materialism after his fieldwork in Mozambique. His experiences of Portuguese colonialism there convinced him that systems of production were fundamental to any understanding of culture (Harris: 1994:75–76).

Harris' work followed the Marxist perspective resurrected by Leslie White. Marx (see essay 4) believed that production played the primary role in social evolution, influencing the sociological and ideological levels of society. While rejecting Marxist dialectics, cultural materialists firmly insist on the primacy of modes of production and reproduction—what Harris (1979) called "infrastructure"—in determining behaviors and beliefs within a society. Much of Harris' work was an attack on what he considered to be the obscurant, spiritualized explanations of symbolic and interpretive anthropology, as well as religion and various "consciousness" movements. Harris

wrote that Americans have "been taught to value elaborate "spiritualized" explanations of cultural phenomena. . . ." He, on the other hand, intended to show

> that even the most bizarre-seeming beliefs and practices turn out on closer inspection to be based on ordinary, banal, one might say "vulgar" conditions, needs, and activities. What I mean by a banal or vulgar solution is that it rests on the ground and that it is built up out of guts, sex, energy, wind, rain, and other palpable and ordinary phenomena. (1974:2–3)

Cultural materialism has been one of the most powerful and enduring theoretical positions within modern American anthropology, partly because Harris himself was an extremely successful and indefatigable promoter of it. Generations of graduate students have read Harris' classic *The Rise of Anthropological Theory* (1968). You may have noticed that we frequently refer to it in this volume. Harris' book is a comprehensive analysis of the history of anthropology, but it is also a polemic promoting cultural materialism.

In addition to copious work designed for professional consumption, Harris also wrote many books for popular audiences, including *Cows, Pigs, Wars and Witches: The Riddles of Culture* (1974), *Cannibals and Kings: The Origins of Culture* (1977), *Good to Eat: Riddles of Food and Culture* (1985), and many others. These books, which give cultural-materialist explanations of cultural phenomena, are written in an extremely accessible and engaging style and had enormous popular success.

Cultural-materialist analysis was extremely popular in the 1970s and 1980s and continues to command a large following today. However, it is also frequently attacked as naive positivism, "rooted in a mechanical, naturalistic mode that fails to reckon with the fact that the mind is more than a tabula rasa" (Murphy 1994:58). Harris vehemently resisted such charges, while insisting that an objective, positivist science of society is not only possible but necessary. His position is perhaps best summed up in the title of one of his essays, "Cultural Materialism Is Alive and Well and Won't Go Away Until Something Better Comes Along" (1994).

Our example of cultural materialism is Harris' 1966 article, "The Cultural Ecology of India's Sacred Cattle." Writing for a technical audience, Harris argues that the Hindu prohibition on killing cattle should be understood in relation to the role that cattle play in the production of food crops, fuel, and fertilizer. He convincingly demonstrates the material and ecological importance of cattle to Indian society and argues that this, rather than Hindu religious doctrine, is the ultimate basis of the ban on killing and eating cattle. In fact, in line with Marx's and Harris' thought, the sacredness of cattle can be seen as a result of their productive importance.

A second orientation in neofunctionalist materialism comes from the work of Roy Rappaport (1926–1997). Whereas Fried and Harris drew their inspiration from Marx, Rappaport was more deeply affected by the work of ecological biologists. Like Fried and Harris, Rappaport was a student at Columbia. However, although he was influenced by White's notions concerning cultural evolution, Rappaport was more deeply affected by classes he took with Harold Conklin (b. 1926) and Conrad Arensburg (1912–1997), and fieldwork seminars with Margaret Mead (Rappaport 1994:166). His deep reading in biological ecology led to doing research for his dissertation under Andrew P. Vayda, an anthropologist vitally interested in ecology. Rappaport and Vayda believed that general laws of biological ecology could be used to study human populations, a belief they sought to substantiate in their fieldwork.

Rappaport and other neofunctionalist anthropologists adopted the concept of feedback from cybernetics to explain cultural stability. In the essay reproduced here, "Ritual Regulation of Environmental Relations Among a New Guinea People," Rappaport proposes that the sacrifice of pigs in the *kaiko* ritual of the Tsembaga of New Guinea is a feedback mechanism that regulates the ecological relationship between men, pigs, local food supplies, and warfare. He outlined this point of view in greater detail in his 1967 work, *Pigs for the Ancestors*.

The Neomarxist approach was developed in Europe at about the same time that neoevolutionism and neofunctionalism were becoming popular in the United States. Neofunctionalism and neoevolutionism were primarily American theoretical developments that, despite their reliance on insights from Marxist scholarship, rejected key elements of Marxist doctrine, particularly the dialectic. Neo-Marxism was centered in Europe, where political conditions made strictly Marxist anthropology more feasible. There, a tradition of rigorously Marxist research already existed. Much of this was inspired by Soviet ethnographers, who generally reflected Stalinist and Leninist interpretations of Marx. However, in the 1960s, particularly in France, a group of Marxist thinkers emerged that challenged Soviet ethnographic hegemony. This group, including Claude Meillassoux (1925–2005) and Maurice Godelier (b. 1934) suggested that Marx's work provided the basic insights for the analysis of traditional society but that, because his writings had focused primarily on the development of capitalism in Europe, they could not be applied directly to ethnographic analysis. The neo-Marxists modified Marx's work to adapt it for this purpose. In particular, they described new modes of production and proposed new evolutionary sequences. Unlike almost all other anthropologists of their era, they had a keen critical eye for the effects of colonialism and international economic exchanges.

Whereas American materialists tended to focus on feedback mechanisms and stable adaptations, the neo-Marxists directed their attention to dialectical contradiction. They viewed society in terms of the struggle of different social groups (which they frequently insisted were classes) for control and power. They were often brutally critical of American materialist approaches that minimized the role of conflict or ignored the dialectic. A particularly good example of this criticism is the essay "Marxism, Structuralism, and Vulgar Materialism" (1974), in which Jonathan Friedman provides an extensive critique of Harris' ideas on Indian cattle worship and Rappaport's understanding of the ecological importance of pigs and ritual. Friedman argues that, by ignoring the dialectic, American anthropologists transform subtle and sophisticated Marxist analysis to mechanistic "vulgar materialism." As a result, they misunderstand the insights Marxist analysis can provide.

Neo-Marxist analysis is represented in this section by an essay from Eric Wolf (1923–1999). Wolf was one of the most influential neo-Marxist thinkers in the United States. Born in Vienna, he emigrated first to England, then, in 1940, to New York. After service in World War II during which he was decorated for bravery, he went on to earn his Ph.D. at Columbia, where he studied with Ruth Benedict, Stanley Diamond, Sidney Mintz, Morton Fried, and Julian Steward.

Because of his contact with Fried, Steward, and others, Wolf's work was informed by Marx's notion of society as a historical and material process. His first book, *Sons of the Shaking Earth* (1959), explored the rise of Mesoamerican cultures in relation to the geography, ecology, and ethnic diversity of the area and examined effects of the Spanish conquest.

Wolf began to conduct cultural analysis in openly Marxist terms in *Peasants* (1966), the first chapter of which is presented here. In *Peasants* Wolf examines the structure of peasant societies and their relation to industrialized states. *Peasants* was followed in 1969 by *Peasant Wars of the Twentieth Century,* a book that applied Marxist thinking to a series of conflicts in Mexico, Russia, China, Algeria, and Cuba. Wolf was a strong critic of the war in Vietnam. Along with Marshal Sahlins, he helped start the "teach-in" movement at the University of Michigan (Wolf and Jorgensen 1970). Teach-ins were part of the 1960s and early 1970s protest against the Vietnam War and soon spread to many universities. Students and faculty would meet to debate, question, challenge assumptions and learn about the Vietnam War. Wolf intended *Peasant Wars* to be a text used at such meetings. As a result of their activism, Wolf and Sahlins both came under FBI scrutiny in the late 1960s, as did Morton Fried (Price, 2004).

Wolf's most influential book was *Europe and the People Without History* (1982). Wolf was deeply influenced by the economist Andre Gunder Frank (1929–2005) and the sociologist Immanuel Wallerstein (b. 1930), who were leading thinkers of dependency theory and World System theory. In the 1960s, economists such as W. W. Rostow proposed that poor nations could become wealthy by repeating the historical experience of wealthy nations—the premise of what came to be called modernization theory. Frank and others argued that modernization in undeveloped nations could not succeed because their wealth and labor had been systematically siphoned from them by Europe and the United States. Poor nations had not simply failed to modernize and develop. They had been systematically underdeveloped by wealthy nations.

In *Europe and the People Without History* Wolf takes the expansion of European capitalism as his central subject. He shows how the mercantile and capitalist expansion of Europe affected and undermined indigenous cultural systems throughout the Third World and how this process produced great wealth and great suffering. The book is critical because it moved American neo-Marxists and neofunctionalists away from the study of small-scale isolated systems to large-scale social analysis. However, Wolf's analysis had effects well beyond neo-Marxist circles. His revisionist approach to world history championed the voices of the poor and oppressed. He cast doubt on the coherence of ethnic groupings and identities, pointing out that these were often created by the forces of capital. He reminded readers that the dominant narrative of history was generally told only from the point of view of the wealthy and powerful, which was a very biased perspective. Wolf attempted to give voice to the poor and oppressed in his telling of history.

Wolf's work was particularly influential because it combined the concern for the downtrodden that was an important element of Boasian thinking with a powerful neo-Marxist analysis. At a time when postmodernism was emerging as an important force within anthropology, Wolf drew attention to the issue of voice, of who has the authority to tell history and how that authority is constituted, and to the historical and contingent nature of identity.

20. *On the Evolution of Social Stratification and the State*

MORTON H. FRIED (1923–1986)

*The evolutionists never discussed in detail—still less observed—what
actually happened when a society in Stage A changed into a society at
Stage B; it was merely argued that all Stage B societies must somehow
have evolved out of the Stage A societies.*

—E. R. Leach, 1954, p. 283

To SOME EXTENT E. R. Leach's charge, which relates to the evolution of political organization, is unfair. The climate in which pristine systems of state organization took shape no longer exists. The presence of numerous modern states and the efficiency of communications have converted all movements toward state level organization into acculturation phenomena of some degree. In fact, it seems likely that the only truly pristine states—those whose origin was *sui generis*,[1] out of local conditions and not in response to pressures emanating from an already highly organized but separate political entity—are those which arose in the great river valleys of Asia and Africa and the one or two comparable developments in the Western Hemisphere. Elsewhere the development of the state seems to have been "secondary" and to have depended upon pressures, direct or indirect, from existing states. Where such pressures exist, the process of development is accelerated, condensed, and often warped, so that a study of contemporary state for-

mation is a murky mirror in which to discern the stages in the development of the pristine states.

Further, the conditions of emergence of rank and stratification as pristine phenomena are similarly obscured when the impetus to change is the introduction of aspects of a market economy, money as a medium of exchange, rationalization of production, and the transformation of labor into a commodity. It would be extremely gratifying to actually observe societies in transition from a "Stage A" (egalitarian organization) to a "Stage B" (rank society) and from there to a "Stage C" (stratification society) and finally from that stage to a "Stage D" (state society).[2] Indeed, some of these observations have been made, though no one has yet been able to follow a single society or even selected exemplars from a group of genetically related societies through all these stages. Instead a variety of unrelated societies are selected, each representing one or another of the several possible transitions. Mr. Leach himself has contributed one of the most valuable

(1960)

---

[1] *Sui generis:* Latin for of its own kind, meaning here "unique" or "individual."

[2] In this article, Fried proposes an evolutionary model of society. Ever since Morgan, cultural-evolutionary studies have tended to be synchronic—comparing contemporary societies at different levels of development to try to reconstruct the process by which simple societies evolved into more complex forms. (On the other hand, archaeological studies of cultural evolution tend to be diachronic—studying the development of one society in

a specific area through time.) Fried posits that state-level societies are the final product of an evolutionary sequence that begins with egalitarian bands and progresses first to ranked and then to stratified societies. The mechanisms that propel societies through this evolutionary sequence are material factors such as economy, population, and environment. Fried also points out that the evolutionary sequence he is proposing has never actually been observed. Pristine traditional systems no longer exist.

of the accounts dealing with this matter in his analysis of the movement from *gumlao* to *gumsa* organization among the Kachin of northern Burma.[3]

Following leads supplied in the data of such accounts as that of Leach, just mentioned, of Douglas Oliver (1955), and others, it is our intention to discuss in detail the things which it seems to us must have occurred in order to make the previous transitions possible. Since the data are largely contemporary, the statements are to be viewed as hypotheses in their application to pristine situations beyond even archaeological recall.

Here then is what we seek to accomplish: (1) to suggest some specific institutional developments, the occurrences of which are normal and predictable in viable societies under certain conditions, and in the course of which the whole society perforce moves into a new level of sociocultural organization; (2) to suggest some of the conditions under which these institutional developments occurred and came to florescence; (3) to indicate as a by-product, that the movement occurs without conscious human intervention, the alterations taking place slowly enough and with such inevitability that the society is revolutionized before the carriers of the culture are aware of major changes.[4]

In approaching this task, it seems wise, if only to head off needless argument, to deny any intention of supplying a single master key to a lock that has defied the efforts of great talents from the time of the Classical civilizations to the present. It seems obvious that other sequences of events than those sketched here could, under proper circumstances, have had similar results. Indeed, the writer is eager to entertain other possibilities and hopes hereby to stimulate others to offer counter suggestions. It will also be obvious to the reader that substantial trains of thought herein stated are merely borrowed and not created by the writer. The recent strides in economic anthropology, and I refer primarily to the work of Polanyi, Arensberg, and Pearson (1957), the clarification of some basic concepts in the study of social organization, and the incentives provided by a seminal paper by Paul Kirchhoff (1935) have all been combined in the present effort.[5]

---

[3] Fried cites Edmund Leach's (1911–1989) classic 1954 study, *Political Systems of Highland Burma,* which describes the evolution of a political system. A weakness of the functionalists was their tendency to view cultures as static. *Political Systems of Highland Burma* was a structural-functionalist study, but Leach saw Kachin political structure as dynamic, alternating between egalitarian and stratified forms. His book emphasized the evolution of political systems in relation to ecology and subsistence. This work, coming just six years before Fried's, had a major impact on Fried's own analysis of social stratification. Fried in fact used Leach's data in formulating his own theory. Note that the quotation at the opening of this article is from Leach's book.

[4] Note the third goal listed in this paragraph. Fried's comments are reminiscent of the nineteenth-century Spencerian view of social evolution. Recall that Spencer described evolution as superorganic, occurring without the conscious awareness or intervention of the members of society. The evolutionary process was inevitable and resulted from the slow accumulation of social changes. The course of evolution was from simple undifferentiated societies to increasingly complex and specialized societies. Similarly, in Fried's evolutionary model, egalitarian bands evolve into increasingly complex societies with internal social differentiation.

[5] The 1957 work by Polanyi, Arensberg, and Pearson, *Trade and Market in the Early Empires,* was a seminal document in economic anthropology. Karl Polanyi (1886–1964), a historian, suggested that economies could be organized by ideas other than the market and that the rules of economic analysis developed for use in capitalist societies did not apply to other societies. This perspective came to be known as substantivism and was important in the economic anthropology of the 1960s. According to Polanyi, societies could be organized either by reciprocity, redistribution, or some form of market. Fried makes great use of this theory later in this article. You should also remember the principles of prestation Marcel Mauss outlined in *The Gift* (see essay 7) when reading Fried's discussion of Polanyi.

Paul Kirchhoff (1900–1972) was an ethnologist who studied theology, comparative religion, and psychology as well as anthropology. Kirchhoff spent the majority of his career working in Mexico. His primary work was on the Indians of North and South America, and he was a co-founder of the Escuela Nacional de Anthropología e Historia. It was he who first coined the term *Mesoamerica.* The work Fried refers to is a manuscript called "The Principles of Clanship in Human Society."

THE NON-RANK, NON-STRATIFIED SOCIETY

Every human society differentiates among its members and assigns greater or less prestige to individuals according to certain of their attributes. The simplest and most universal criteria of differential status are those two potent axes of the basic division of labor, age and sex. Beyond are a host of others which are used singly or in combination to distinguish among the members of a category otherwise undifferentiated as to sex or age group. Most important of the characteristics used in this regard are those which have a visible relation to the maintenance of subsistence, such as strength, endurance, agility, and other factors which make one a good provider in a hunting and gathering setting. These characteristics are ephemeral; moreover, the systems of enculturation prevalent at this level, with their emphasis upon the development of subsistence skills, make it certain that such skills are well distributed among the members of society of the proper sex and age groups.

The major deviation from this system of subsistence-oriented statuses is associated with age. However, it makes no difference to the argument of this paper whether the status of the old is high or low since the basis of its ascription is universal. Anyone who is of the proper sex and manages to live long enough automatically enters into its benefits or disabilities.

Given the variation in individual endowment which makes a chimera[6] of absolute equality, the primitive societies which we are considering are sufficiently undifferentiated in this respect to permit us to refer to them as "egalitarian societies." An egalitarian society can be defined more precisely: it is one in which there are as many positions of prestige in any given age-sex grade as there are persons capable of filling them. If within a certain kin group or territory there are four big men, strong, alert, keen hunters, then there will be four "strong men"; if there are six, or three, or one, so it is. Eskimo society fits this general picture. So do many others. Almost all of these societies are founded upon hunting and gathering and lack significant harvest periods when large reserves of food are stored.

There is one further point I wish to emphasize about egalitarian society. It accords quite remarkably with what Karl Polanyi has called a reciprocal economy.[a]

Production in egalitarian society is characteristically a household matter. There is no specialization; each family group repeats essentially similar tasks. There may be individuals who make certain things better than do others, and these individuals are often given recognition for their skills, but no favored economic role is established, no regular division of labor emerges at this point, and no political power can reside in the status (Leacock, 1958). Exchange in such a society takes place between individuals who belong to different small-scale kin groups; it tends to be casual and is not bound by systems of monetary value based upon scarcity. Such exchanges predominate between individuals who recognize each other as relatives or friends, and may be cemented by such procedures as the provision of hospitality and the granting of sexual access to wives.

Within the local group or band the economy is also reciprocal, but less obviously so. Unlike the exchanges between members of different local groups which, over the period of several years, tend to balance, the exchanges within a group may be quite asymmetrical over time. The skilled and lucky hunter may be continually supplying others with meat; while his family also receives shares from the catch of others, income never catches up with the amounts dispensed. However, the difference between the two quantities is made up in the form of prestige, though, as previously mentioned, it conveys no privileged economic or political role. There frequently is a feeling of transience as it is understood that the greatest hunter can lose his luck or his life, thereby making his family dependent on the largesse of others.

In all egalitarian economies, however, there is also a germ of redistribution. It receives its

---

[6] *Chimera:* something unreal or imaginary.

simplest expression in the family but can grow no more complex than the pooling and redisbursing of stored food for an extended family. In such an embryonic redistributive system the key role is frequently played by the oldest female in the active generation, since it is she who commonly coordinates the household and runs the kitchen.

THE RANK SOCIETY

Since a truly egalitarian human society does not exist, it is evident that we are using the word "rank" in a somewhat special sense. The crux of the matter, as far as we are concerned, is the structural way in which differential prestige is handled in the rank society as contrasted with the way in which egalitarian societies handle similar materials. If the latter have as many positions of valued status as they have individuals capable of handling them, the rank society places additional limitations on access to valued status. The limitations which are added have nothing to do with sex, age group, or personal attributes. Thus, the rank society is characterized by having fewer positions of valued status than individuals capable of handling them. Furthermore, most rank societies have a fixed number of such positions, neither expanding them nor diminishing them with fluctuations in the populations, save as totally new segmented units originate with fission or disappear as the result of catastrophe or sterility.

The simplest technique of limiting status, beyond those already discussed, is to make succession to status dependent upon birth order. This principle, which is found in kinship-organized societies, persists in many more complexly organized societies. At its simplest, it takes the form of primogeniture or ultimogeniture on the level of the family, extended family, or lineage.[7] In more complex forms it may be projected through time so that only the first son of a first son of a first son

enjoys the rights of succession, all others having been excluded by virtue of ultimate descent from a positionless ancestor. There are still other variants based on the theme: the accession to high status may be by election, but the candidates may come only from certain lineages which already represent selection by birth order.

The effects of rules of selection based on birth can be set aside by conscious action. Incompetence can be the basis for a decision to by-pass the customary heir, though it would seem more usual for the nominal office to remain vested in the proper heir while a more energetic person performed the functions of the status. A strategic murder could also accomplish the temporary voiding of the rule, but such a solution is much too dangerous and extreme to be practical on the level which we are considering. It is only in rather advanced cultures that the rewards associated with such statuses are sufficient to motivate patricide and fratricide.

Whether accomplished by a rule of succession or some other narrowing device, the rank society as a framework of statuses resembles a triangle, the point of which represents the leading status hierarchically exalted above the others. The hierarchy thus represented has very definite economic significance, going hand in hand with the emergence of a superfamilial redistributive network. The key status is that of the central collector of allotments who also tends to the redistribution of these supplies either in the form of feasts or as emergency seed and provender in time of need. Depending on the extent and maturity of the redistributive system, there will be greater or lesser development of the hierarchy. Obviously, small-scale networks in which the members have a face-to-face relationship with the person in the central status will have less need of a bureaucracy.[8]

In the typical ranked society there is neither exploitative economic power nor genuine political power. As a matter of fact, the central status closely resembles its counterpart in the embryonic

---

[7] *Primogeniture* is inheritance by the firstborn son; *ultimogeniture* is inheritance by the lastborn.

[8] In Fried's theory one can see Marx's idea that modes of production determine the ideological features of society. Fried believes that the force that drives political evolution

is the control over production and distribution of resources. Egalitarian societies are marked by universal access to prestige and reciprocity of resources. A key feature of rank societies is that their members have unequal access to prestige that results from the power of high-prestige individuals to control the distribution of resources.

redistributive network that may be found even in the simplest societies. This is not surprising, for the system in typical rank societies is actually based upon a physical expansion of the kin group and the continuation of previously known kinship rights and obligations. The kingpin of a redistributive network in an advanced hunting and gathering society or a simple agricultural one is as much the victim of his role as its manipulator. His special function is to collect, not to expropriate; to distribute, not to consume. In a conflict between personal accumulation and the demands of distribution it is the former which suffers. Anything else leads to accusations of hoarding and selfishness and undercuts the prestige of the central status; the whole network then stands in jeopardy, a situation which cannot be tolerated. This, by the way, helps to explain that "anomaly" that has so frequently puzzled students of societies of this grade: why are their "chiefs" so often poor, perhaps poorer than any of their neighbors? The preceding analysis makes such a question rhetorical.[9]

It is a further characteristic of the persons filling these high status positions in typical rank societies that they must carry out their functions in the absence of political authority. Two kinds of authority they have: familial, in the extended sense, and sacred, as the redistributive feasts commonly are associated with the ritual life of the community. They do not, however, have access to the privileged use of force, and they can use only diffuse and supernatural sanctions to achieve their ends. Indeed, the two major methods by which they operate are by setting personal examples, as of industriousness, and by utilizing the principles of reciprocity to bolster the emergent redistributive economy.[b]

Despite strong egalitarian features in its economic and political sectors, the developing rank society has strong status differentials which are marked by sumptuary specialization and ceremonial function.[10] While it is a fact that the literature abounds in references to "chiefs" who can issue no positive commands and "ruling classes" whose members are among the paupers of the realm, it must be stated in fairness that the central redistributive statuses *are* associated with fuss, feathers, and other trappings of office. These people sit on stools, have big houses, and are consulted by their neighbors. Their redistributive roles place them automatically to the fore in the religious life of the community, but they are also in that position because of their central kinship status as lineage, clan,[c] or kindred heads.[11]

FROM EGALITARIAN TO RANK SOCIETY

The move from egalitarian to rank society is essentially the shift from an economy dominated by reciprocity to one having redistribution as a major device. That being the case, one must look for the causes of ranking (the limitation of statuses such that they are fewer than the persons capable of handling them) in the conditions which enable the redistributive economy to emerge from its position of latency in the universal household economy, to dominate a network of kin groups which extend beyond the boundaries of anything known on the reciprocal level.

Though we shall make a few suggestions relating to this problem, it should be noted that the focus of this paper does not necessitate immediate disposition of this highly complicated question. In view of the history of our topic, certain negative conclusions are quite significant. Most important of all is the deduction that the roots of ranking do not lie in features of human personality.

---

[9] Fried, although strongly influenced by Marx, does not believe in revolutionary dialectical change. Instead, he says that the transition from egalitarian to rank societies is characterized by the continuation of previously known rights and obligations. Like Darwin and Spencer, Fried believed that evolutionary change occurred in slow incremental stages. Further, in his discussion of "mature" and "embryonic" redistributive networks, Fried's terminology harkens back to the organic analogy of the nineteenth century.

[10] *Sumptuary specialization:* specialized clothing marking one's status.

[11] Max Weber conducted some of the early work on the distinction between types of authority and power. Fried's distinction between political versus familial and sacred authority is clearly part of the same tradition.

The structural approach obviates, in this case, psychological explanations. To be precise, we need assume no universal human drive for power[d] in comprehending the evolution of ranking.[12]

It is unthinkable that we should lead a reader this far without indicating certain avenues whereby the pursuit of the problem may be continued. We ask, therefore, what are the circumstances under which fissioning kin or local groups retain active economic interdigitation,[13] the method of interaction being participation in the redistributive network?

In a broad sense, the problem may be seen as an ecological one. Given the tendency of a population to breed up to the limit of its resources and given the probably universal budding of kin and local groups which have reached cultural maxima of unit size, we look into different techno-geographical situations for clues as to whether more recently formed units will continue to interact significantly with their parent units, thereby extending the physical and institutional range of the economy. Such a situation clearly arises when the newer group moves into a somewhat different environment while remaining close enough to the parent group to permit relatively frequent interaction among the members of the two groups. Given such a condition, the maintenance of a redistributive network would have the effect of diversifying subsistence in both units and also providing insurance against food failures in one or the other. This is clearly something of a special case; one of its attractions is the amount of work that has been done upon it by another student of the problem (Sahlins, 1957, 1958).[14]

It is possible to bring to bear upon this problem an argument similar to that employed by Tylor in the question of the incest taboo (Tylor, 1888, p. 267; White, 1948), to wit: the redistributive network might appear as a kind of random social mutation arising out of nonspecific factors difficult to generalize, such as a great personal dependence of the members of the offspring unit upon those they have left behind. Whatever the immediate reason for its appearance, it would quickly show a superiority over simple reciprocal systems in (a) productivity, (b) timeliness of distribution, (c) diversity of diet, and (d) coordination of mundane and ceremonial calendars (in a loose cyclical sense). It is not suggested that the success of the institution depends upon the rational cognition of these virtues by the culture carriers; rather the advantages of these institutions would have positive survival value over a long period of time.[15]

We should not overlook one other possibility that seems less special than the first one given above. Wittfogel has drawn our attention on numerous occasions to the social effects of irrigation (see Wittfogel, 1957, for a summation of his latest thinking). The emergence of the superfamilial

---

[12] Here Fried rejects all psychological explanations for the evolutionary shift from egalitarian to rank societies, pointing instead to the change from one form of economic distribution to another. By linking the evolution from egalitarian to rank society to the shift from a reciprocal economy to one dominated by redistribution, Fried echoes the Marxist-materialist perspective as interpreted in Polanyi's work.

[13] *Interdigitation:* interlocking, like the fingers of both hands.

[14] Fried attempts here to expand the scientific basis for his argument (which is essentially a hypothetical reconstruction) by incorporating the field of cultural ecology, which was relatively new at this time. Notice that the reader is taken from a discussion of kin groups, economies, and prestige to breeding populations and ecology. In particular, he cites Marshall Sahlins (b. 1930), a fellow evolutionist and a leading proponent of cultural ecology. See, for example, Sahlins' article "Culture and Environment: The Study of Cultural Ecology" (1964).

[15] Fried cannot definitively outline the rationale behind the transition from egalitarian to rank society, so he offers three possibilities. The first is the fissioning of related kin groups in expanded redistributive networks. The second is an argument borrowed from evolutionary biology: The development of ranking may be a random "social mutation" that conveyed a selective advantage or "positive survival value" on those who adopted the trait. The third is Wittfogel's hydro-agriculture hypothesis, which is discussed in the next paragraph. Karl A. Wittfogel (1896–1988) was an archaeologist who proposed that irrigation was a primary factor in the development of stratified societies. Briefly, Wittfogel felt that the origins of social stratification and the state lay in the formation of a body of ruler-managers who oversaw the construction and maintenance of large-scale irrigation systems necessary for intensive agriculture. As a universal explanation, this theory was refuted by Adams (1966) and Carneiro (1970).

redistributive network and the rank society seem to go well with the developments he has discussed under the rubric "hydro-agriculture," in which some supervision is needed in order to control simple irrigation and drainage projects yet these projects are not large enough to call into existence a truly professional bureaucracy.

It may be wondered that one of the prime explanations for the emergence of ranking, one much favored by notable sociologists of the past, has not appeared in this argument. Reference is to the effects of war upon a society. I would like in this article to take a deliberately extreme stand and assert that military considerations serve to institutionalize rank differences only when these are already implicit or manifest in the economy. I do not believe that pristine developments in the formalization of rank can be attributed to even grave military necessity.[16]

THE STRATIFIED SOCIETY

The differences between rank society and stratified society are very great, yet it is rare that the two are distinguished in descriptive accounts or even in the theoretical literature. Briefly put, the essential difference is this: the rank society operates on the principle of differential status for members with similar abilities, but these statuses are devoid of privileged economic or political power, the former point being the essential one for the present analysis. Meanwhile, the stratified society is distinguished by the differential relationships between the members of the society and its subsistence means—some of the members of the society have unimpeded access to its strategic resources[e] while others have various impediments in their access to the same fundamental resources.[17]

With the passage to stratified society man enters a completely new area of social life. Whereas the related systems of redistribution and ranking rest upon embryonic institutions that are as universal as family organization (*any* family, elementary or extended, conjugal or consanguineal, will do equally well), the principles of stratification have no real foreshadowing on the lower level.

Furthermore, the movement to stratification precipitated many things which were destined to change society even further, and at an increasingly accelerated pace. Former systems of social control which rested heavily on enculturation, internalized sanctions, and ridicule now required formal statement of their legal principles, a machinery of adjudication, and a formally constituted police authority. The emergence of these and other control institutions were associated with the final shift of prime authority from kinship means to territorial means and describes the evolution of complex forms of government associated with the state. It was the passage to stratified society which laid the basis for the complex division of labor which underlies modern society. It also gave rise to various arrangements of socio-economic classes and led directly to both classical and modern forms of colonialism and imperialism.[18]

---

[16] The most notable of the sociologists referred to by Fried was Spencer, whose views on stratification and war he quotes several times in *The Evolution of Political Society*. The role of warfare in the evolution of society has long been a contentious issue among anthropologists. Here and in *The Evolution of Political Society* Fried argues emphatically that warfare was not a primary catalyst in the formation of stratified societies, an opinion based on his belief that primitive societies are not typically warlike. He cites several ethnographic examples supporting this view in his book. In contrast, Robert Carneiro (b. 1927) is one of the strongest advocates for the role of warfare in the origin of state-level societies (Carneiro 1970).

[17] The description Fried gives in this paragraph stands today as the standard definition of social stratification. It can be found virtually verbatim in most introductory cultural anthropology texts.

[18] For Fried, the development of stratification was a revolutionary step that defined the transition to state-level societies. The influence of nineteenth-century evolutionary thought is evident in this paragraph. Like the Spencerians, Fried focuses on increasing complexity, specialization, and the shift from autonomous individuals to interdependency of occupations and classes. The shift from kin-based to property-based authority is derived from Marx and Morgan. In Morgan's view, the modern state was founded on the notions of territory and property (see essay 3).

THE TRANSITION TO STRATIFIED SOCIETY

The decisive significance of stratification is not that it sees differential amounts of wealth in different hands but that it sees two kinds of access to strategic resources. One of these is privileged and unimpeded; the other is impaired, depending on complexes of permission which frequently require the payment of dues, rents, or taxes in labor or in kind. The existence of such a distinction enables the growth of exploitation, whether of a relatively simple kind based upon drudge slavery or of a more complex type associated with involved divisions of labor and intricate class systems. The development of stratification also encourages the emergence of communities composed of kin parts and non-kin parts which, as wholes, operate on the basis of non-kin mechanisms.[19]

So enormous is the significance of the shift to stratification that previous commentators have found it essential that the movement be associated with the most powerful people in the society. Landtman, for example, says:

"It is in conjunction with the dissimilarity of individual endowments that inequality of wealth has conduced to the rise of social differentiation. As a matter of course the difference as regards property in many cases goes hand in hand with difference in personal qualities. A skillful hunter or fisher, or a victorious warrior, has naturally a better prospect of acquiring a fortune than one who is inferior to him in these respects" (Landtman, 1938, p. 68).

If our analysis is correct, however, such is definitely not the case. The statuses mentioned by Landtman are not those which stand to make great accumulations but rather stand to make great give-aways. Furthermore, the leap from distribution to power is unwarranted by the ethnographic evidence.[20]

There are unquestionably a number of ways in which secondary conditions of stratification can emerge. That is, once the development of stratification proceeds from contact with and tutelage by cultures which are at the least already stratified and which may be the possessors of mature state organization, there are many specific ways in which simpler cultures can be transformed into stratified societies. The ways which come quickest to mind include the extension of the complex society's legal definitions of property to the simpler society, the introduction of all-purpose money and wage labor, and the creation of an administrative system for the operation of the simpler society on a basis which is acceptable to the superordinate state. Often the external provenance of these elements is obvious in their misfit appearance. A sharper look may reveal, indeed, that the stratified system is a mere facade operated for and often by persons who have no genuine local identities, while the local system continues to maintain informally, and sometimes in secrecy, the older organization of the society. Put more concretely, this means that "government" appointed chiefs are respected only in certain limited situations and that the main weight of social control continues to rest upon traditional authorities and institutions which may not even be recognized by the ruling power.[21]

An excellent climate for the development of stratification in a simple society can be supplied in

---

[19] Although Fried, like most materialists at this time, did not cite Marx, the Marxist view of stratification and class exploitation is clearly expressed in this paragraph. This is particularly evident in his use of the term *exploitation,* the meaning of which is different for Marxists and non-Marxists. For non-Marxists, exploitation refers to receiving unfair returns for labor. To Marxists, exploitation is the appropriation of the surplus value of labor, which is inherently unfair. Fried is using the term in the Marxist sense.

[20] Fried explicitly rejects the claim that social stratification is founded on the differences between people's personal qualities and skills, an idea reminiscent of nineteenth-century social darwinism. He provides ethnographic evidence in his discussion of redistribution in rank societies to refute this doctrine.

[21] Remember that Fried is writing at the end of the period of European colonialism in the Pacific, Africa, and Asia and the beginning of the "development" of the Third World. His comments about local systems operating in secrecy and government-appointed chiefs refer to this situation. These remarks are an early example of the anthropological critique of colonialism; earlier theorists had often discussed how their work was useful to colonial administrators. Fried says that colonialism does not work.

a relatively indirect way by a society of advanced organization. Let us take the situation in which a culture has no concept of nuclear family rights to land. The economy is based upon hunting, trapping, and fishing, with the streams and forests being associated in a general way with weakly organized bands which have a decided tendency to fragment and reconstitute, each time with potentially different membership. Subvert this setup with an external market for furs and a substantial basis for stratification has been laid. This system, like the direct intervention of a superordinate state, also seems to have certain limitations for there is ample evidence that the development of private property in such a system as that just mentioned is confined to trapping lines and does not extend to general subsistence hunting and fishing in the area (see Leacock, 1958).

Another situation that bears study is one in which important trade routes linking two or more advanced societies traverse marginal areas in which simple societies are located. Certain geographical conditions make it possible for the relatively primitive folk to enhance their economies with fruits derived from the plunder of this trade or, in a more mature system, by extorting tribute from the merchants who must pass by. The remoteness of these areas, the difficulty of the terrain and the extreme difficulties and costs of sending a punitive force to pacify the area often enables the simpler people to harass populations whose cultural means for organized violence far exceeds their own. Be this as it may, the combination of the examples of organization presented by the outposts of complexly organized societies and the availability of commodities which could not be produced in the simple culture may combine to lay the basis for an emergence of stratification. Precisely such conditions seem partially responsible for the political developments described for the Kachin (Leach, 1954, esp. pp. 235, 247 ff.).

None of this seems to apply to the pristine emergence of stratification. As a matter of fact, it is not even particularly suggestive. There is, however, one particular ecological condition that appears in highland Burma which also has been noted elsewhere, each time in association with rather basic shifts in social organization paralleling those already sketched in the previous section of this paper. We refer to the shift from rainfall to irrigation farming, particularly to the construction of terraced fields. This is admittedly a restricted ethnographic phenomenon and as such it cannot bear the weight of any general theory. It is the suggestive character of these developments and the possibility of extrapolating from them to hypothetical pristine conditions that makes them so interesting.[22]

In brief, the shift to irrigation and terracing is from swiddens or impermanent fields to plots which will remain in permanent cultivation for decades and generations. Whereas we have previously stressed the possible role of hydro-agriculture in the transition from egalitarian to rank society, we now note its possible role in the transition to stratification. This it could accomplish by creating conditions under which access to strategic resources, in this case land and water, would be made the specific prerogative of small-scale kin groups such as minimal lineages or even stem families. Through the emergence of hydro-agriculture a community which previously acknowledged no *permanent* association between particular component units and particular stretches of land now begins to recognize such permanent and exclusive rights. Incidentally, the evidence seems to indicate that the rank-forming tendencies of hydro-agriculture need not occur prior to the tendencies toward stratification: both can occur concomitantly. This in turn suggests that we must be cautious in constructing our theory not to make stratification emerge from ranking, though under particular circumstances this is certainly possible.[23]

---

[22] The passage refers back to Wittfogel's hydraulic hypothesis, discussed above. Fried wrote this article at a time when Wittfogel's hypothesis was popular, before major criticisms of the theory had been published.

[23] An important point is being made here. Although Fried has proposed a materialist analysis of the relationship between stratification (differential access to prestige and wealth) and ranking, he allows for the possibility that ranking precedes stratification. In other words, he hedges on a strictly Marxist interpretation. Do you see how nicely this statement ties into Julian Steward's views on multilinear evolution? In fact, Steward's *Theory of Culture Change: The Methodology of Multilinear Evolution* had been published in 1955, just five years before this article.

A point of considerable interest about hydro-agriculture is that it seems to present the possibility of an emergence of stratification in the absence of a problem of overpopulation or resource limitation. We need a great deal of further thought on the matter. Studies of the last two decades, in which a considerably higher degree of agricultural expertise on the part of the fieldworkers has been manifested than was formerly the case, have increasingly tended to show that hydro-agriculture does not invariably out-produce slash and burn and that, other things being equal, a population does not automatically prefer hydro-agriculture as a more rationalized approach to agricultural subsistence. Here we can introduce a factor previously excluded. The hydro-agricultural system invariably has a higher degree of settlement concentration than swiddens. Accordingly, it would seem to have considerable value in the maintenance of systems of defense, given the presence of extensive warfare. Here then, is a point at which military considerations would seem to play an important if essentially reinforcing role in the broad evolutionary developments which we are considering.

The writer is intrigued with another possibility for the emergence of stratification. Once again, the conditions involved seem a little too specific to serve the purpose of a single unified theory. It requires the postulation of a society with a fixed rule of residence, preferably one of the simpler ones such as patrilocality/virilocality or matrilocality/uxorilocality[f] and a fixed rule of descent, preferably one parallel to the residence rule.[24] It further postulates a condition of population expansion such that, given slash and burn agriculture, the society is very near the limits of the carrying capacity of the system. Such conditions are very likely to develop at varying speeds within an area of several hundred miles due to obvious imbalances in reproductive rates and to micro-ecological variation.

Now, as long as there is no notable pressure of people on the land, deviation in residence and even in descent will be expectable though quite unusual and lacking in motivation. As the situation grows grave in one area but remains relatively open in another, there may be a tendency for a slight readjustment in residence rules to occur. For example, in a normally virilocal society, the woman who brings her husband back to her natal group transgresses a few customary rules in doing so but presents her agnates with no basic problems in resource allocation since she, as a member of the agnatic group, has her own rights of access which may be shared by the spouse during her lifetime. The complication arises at her death when her husband and all of her children discover themselves to be in an anomalous position since they are not members of the kin community. Where local land problems are not severe and where such breaches of the residence pattern are yet uncommon, it is not unlikely that the aliens will be accepted as *de facto* members of the community with the expectation that future generations will revert to custom, the unorthodox switch of residence fading in memory with the passage of time. Here we have a crude and informal *ambil-anak*.[25] But as the local community enters worsening ecological circumstances and as the exceptional residence becomes more frequent, the residence and descent rules, particularly the latter, assume greater and greater importance. As the situation continues, the community is slowly altered, though the members of the community may be unable to state exactly what the changes are. The result, however, is clear. There are now two kinds of people in the village where formerly there was only one. Now there are kernel villagers, those who have unimpaired access to land, and those whose tenure rests upon other conditions, such as loyalty to a patron, or tribute, or even a precarious squatter's right.[26]

---

[24] *Virilocality:* customary residence with the husband's father's kin after marriage; *uxorilocality:* customary residence with the wife's kin after marriage.

[25] *Ambil-anak:* a form of marriage occurring among the otherwise patrilocal Batak people of Indonesia. There, under certain conditions, rather than paying bridewealth, a man may move in with his wife's family. The children

of such a marriage will be members of the wife's father's lineage.

[26] In this paragraph Fried is trying to describe an ecological scenario in which population pressure in an area of limited resources leads to the formation of stratification within a formerly egalitarian society. He proposes that stratification may evolve in a society of swidden horticulturalists when

THE STATE SOCIETY

The word should be abandoned entirely . . . after this chapter the word will be avoided scrupulously and no severe hardship in expression will result. In fact, clarity of expression demands this abstinence (Easton, 1953, p. 108).

The word was "state" and the writer, a political scientist, was reacting to some of the problems in his own field in making this judgment, but it does look as if he was pushed to drastic action by the work of some anthropologists in whose hands the concept of state lost all character and utility, finally ending as a cultural universal. E. Adamson Hoebel, one of the few United States anthropologists to make a serious specialization in the field of law and the state, formerly introduced students to this question by remarking that

> where there is political organization there is a state. If political organization is universal, so then is the state. One is the group, the other an institutionalized complex of behavior (Hoebel, 1949, p. 376).[27]

In a revision of the same book after a few years, Hoebel's treatment of the subject seems to indicate that he is in the process of rethinking the matter. His summary words, however, repeat the same conclusion:

> Political organization is characteristic of every society. . . . That part of culture that is recognized as political organization is what constitutes the state (Hoebel, 1958, p. 506).

This is a far cry from the approach of evolutionists to the state as exemplified in Sumner and Keller (1927, I, p. 700):

> The term state is properly reserved for a somewhat highly developed regulative organization. . . . It is an organization with authority and discipline essential to large-scale achievements, as compared with the family, for example, which is an organization on the same lines but simpler and less potent.

Without making a special issue of the definition of the state (which would easily consume the entire space of this article, if not the volume) let me note one used by the jurist Léon Duguit which conveys the sense most useful to the point of view of this paper:

> En prenant le mot dans son sens le plus général, on peut dire qu'il y a un Etat toutes les fois qu'il existe dans une société donnée une différenciation politique, quelque rudimentaire ou quelque compliquée et developée qu'elle soit. Le mot Etat designe soit les gouvernants où le pouvoir politique, soit la société elle même, où existe cette différenciation entre gouvernants et gouvernés et où existe par là même une puissance politique (Duguit, 1921, p. 395).[28]

The difference between Hoebel and Duguit seems to be in the clear statement of power. Reviewing our own paper in the light of this difference we note our previous emphasis on the absence of coercive economic or political power in the egalitarian and rank societies. It is only in the

---

an expanding population taxes the carrying capacity of the local environment. The change is propelled by the potential conflict between the patrilineal inheritance of land and the demand for land by people who are related matrilineally to those in the village. This is a very Marxist view: A change in the structure of society is a result of this conflict.

[27] E. Adamson Hoebel (1907–1993) was an American anthropologist who specialized in the study of politics and law in primitive societies. He was a student of Franz Boas, author of a famous ethnography of the Cheyenne, and president of the American Anthropology Association. Hoebel represents the Boasian relativism to which Fried is reacting. The source of the first quotation is the first edition

of Hoebel's book, *Man in the Primitive World* (1949); the quotation that follows is from a revised edition.

[28] Leon Duguit (1859–1928) was a French political scientist whose work focused on the government and the state. The translation of his quotation is:

> Taking the word in its most general sense, one could say that there is a state every time a political disparity, however simple or however complex and well developed, exists within a given society. The word state can refer either to governments or political power or to the society itself, where there is a difference between governors and governed and where, accordingly, political power exists.

stratified society that such power emerges from embryonic and universal foreshadowings in familial organization.[29]

The maturation of social stratification has manifold implications depending on the precise circumstances in which the developments take place. All subsequent courses, however, have a certain area of overlap; the new social order, with its differential allocation of access to strategic resources, must be maintained and strengthened. In a simple stratified society in which class differentials are more implicit than explicit the network of kin relations covers a sufficient portion of the total fabric of social relations so that areas not specifically governed by genuine kinship relations can be covered by their sociological extensions. The dynamic of stratification is such that this situation cannot endure. The stratified kin group emphasizes its exclusiveness: it erodes the corporative economic functions formerly associated with stipulated kinship and at every turn it amputates extensions of the demonstrated kin unit. The result of this pruning is that the network of kin relations fails more and more to coincide with the network of personal relations. Sooner or later the discrepancy is of such magnitude that, were non-kin sanctions and non-kin agencies absent or structured along customary lines only, the society would dissolve in uncomposable conflict.

The emergent state, then, is the organization of the power of the society on a supra-kin basis. Among its earliest tasks is the maintenance of general order but scarcely discernible from this is its need to support the order of stratification. The defense of a complete system of individual statuses is impossible so the early state concentrates on a few key statuses (helping to explain the tendency to convert any crime into either sacrilege or *lèse majesté*) and on the basic principles of organization, e.g., the idea of hierarchy, property, and the power of the law.

The implementation of these primary functions of the state gives rise to a number of specific and characteristic secondary functions, each of which is associated with one or more particular institutions of its own. These secondary functions include population control in the most general sense (the fixing of boundaries and the definition of the unit; establishment of categories of membership; census). Also a secondary function is the disposal of trouble cases (civil and criminal laws moving toward the status of codes; regular legal procedure; regular officers of adjudication). The protection of sovereignty is also included (maintenance of military forces; police forces and power; eminent domain). Finally, all of the preceding require fiscal support, and this is achieved in the main through taxation and conscription.[30]

In treating of this bare but essential list of state functions and institutions the idea of the state as a universal aspect of culture dissolves as a fantasy. The institutions just itemized may be made to appear in ones or twos in certain primitive societies by exaggeration and by the neglect of known history. In no egalitarian society and in no rank society do a majority of the functions enumerated appear regardless of their guise. Furthermore there is no indication of their appearance as a unified functional response to basic socio-cultural needs except in those stratified societies which are verging upon statehood.

THE TRANSITION TO STATE

Just as stratified society grew out of antecedent forms of society without the conscious awareness of the culture carriers, so it would seem that the state emerged from the stratified society in a similar, inexorable way.[31] If this hypothesis is correct, then such an explanation as the so-called

---

[29] Fried says that social stratification is foreshadowed in "familial organization"; that is, it lies in differential access to resources between small-scale kin groups.

[30] At the time Fried wrote this article there was a controversy over how to define a state. Archaeologists argued that features such as monumental architecture, urban pop-

ulations, and large-scale public works were indicative of state-level societies. Here Fried is defining a state by complexity of social organization and stratification.

[31] When Fried talks about the inexorability of the emergence of the state, can there be any doubt about the influence of nineteenth-century evolutionism on his thinking?

"conquest theory" can be accepted only as a special case of "secondary-state" formation. The conquests discussed by such a theorist as Franz Oppenheimer (1914) established not stratification but super-stratification, either the conqueror or the conquered, or perhaps even both, already being internally stratified.[32]

The problem of the transition to state is so huge and requires such painstaking application to the available archaeological and historical evidence that it would be foolish to pursue it seriously here. Let us conclude, therefore, by harking back to statements made at the outset of this paper, and noting again the distinction between pristine and secondary states. By the former term is meant a state that has developed *sui generis* out of purely local conditions. No previous state, with its acculturative pressures, can be discerned in the background of a pristine state. The secondary state, on the other hand, is pushed by one means or another toward a higher form of organization by an external power which has already been raised to statehood.

The number of pristine states is strictly limited; several centuries, possibly two millennia, have elapsed since the last one emerged in Meso-America, and there seems to be no possibility that any further states of the pristine type will evolve, though further research may bring to light some of the distant past of which we yet have no positive information. In all, there seems to have been some six centers at which pristine states emerged, four in the Old World and two in the New: the Tigris-Euphrates area, the region of the lower Nile, the country drained by the Indus and the middle course of the Huang Ho where it is joined by the Han, Wei, and Fen. The separate areas of Peru-Bolivia and Meso-America complete the roster.

If there is utility in the concept of the pristine state and if history has been read correctly in limiting the designation to the six areas just enumerated, then we discover a remarkable correlation between areas demanding irrigation or flood control and the pristine state. Certainly this is no discovery of the author. It is one of the central ideas of Wittfogel's theory and has received extensive treatment from Julian Steward and others (see Steward, 1955, pp. 178–209; Steward *et al.*, 1955). The implication of the "hydraulic theory" for this paper, however, is that the development of the state as an internal phenomenon is associated with major tasks of drainage and irrigation. The emergence of a control system to ensure the operation of the economy is closely tied to the appearance of a distinctive class system and certain constellations of power in the hands of a managerial bureaucracy which frequently operates below a ruler who commands theoretically unlimited power.

It is an interesting commentary on nineteenth-century political philosophy that the starting point of so many theories was, of necessity, the Classical world of Greece and Rome. According to the present hypothesis, however, both of these great political developments of antiquity were not pristine but secondary formations which built on cultural foundations laid two thousand years and more before the rise of Greece. Furthermore, it would seem that the active commercial and military influences of the truly ancient pristine states, mediated through the earliest of the secondary states to appear in Asia Minor and the eastern Mediterranean littoral, were catalysts in the events of the northern and western Mediterranean.

CONCLUSION

The close of a paper like this, which moves like a gadfly from time to time, place to place, and subject matter to subject matter, and which never pauses long enough to make a truly detailed inquiry or supply the needed documentation, the close of such a paper requires an apology perhaps more than a conclusion.

---

[32] Franz Oppenheimer (1864–1943) was a German sociologist best known for his book *The State: Its History and Development Viewed Sociologically* (1914). In this essay Fried is concerned with the evolution of stratification in pristine states, not stratification imposed on a society through conquest. Thus he dismisses work like Oppenheimer's.

I have been led to write this paper by my ignorance of any modern attempt to link up the contributions which have been made in many sub-disciplines into a single unified theory of the emergence of social stratification and the state. That the theory offered here is crude, often too special, and by no means documented seems less important than that it may be used as a sitting duck to attract the fire and better aim of others.[33]

NOTES

[a]The reader may object to crediting Polanyi with the concept of a reciprocal economy. While it is true that Thurnwald and Malinowski earlier expressed similar concepts, and Durkheim, with his distinction between segmental and organic societies, also foreshadows this development, it awaited Polanyi's analysis to place reciprocal economies into systematic harmony with other, more complex types of economy, such as the redistributive type discussed later on, and the market kind as well. For Polanyi's definitions of each of these types see Polanyi, Arensberg and Pearson, 1957, pp. 250–56.

[b]For an ethnographic illustration of this point see Oliver, 1955, pp. 422 ff.

[c]These, of course, would be ranked lineages or ranked clans. Cf. Fried, 1957, pp. 23–26.

[d]As does Leach, 1954, p. 10.

[e]Strategic resources are those things which, given the technological base and environmental setting of the culture, maintain subsistence. See Fried, 1957, p. 4.

[f]Our residence terms follow usage suggested by J. L. Fischer, 1958.

---

[33] When Fried speaks of linking the contributions of many subdisciplines into a single unified theory, he refers, in particular, to the exchange between archaeology and cultural ecology and materialism. The transfer of ideas between these areas resulted in the publication of numerous works on cultural evolution for almost two decades.

---

21. *The Cultural Ecology of India's Sacred Cattle*

MARVIN HARRIS (1927–2001)

IN THIS PAPER I attempt to indicate certain puzzling inconsistencies in prevailing interpretations of the ecological role of bovine cattle in India. My argument is based upon intensive reading—I have never seen a sacred cow, nor been to India. As a non-specialist, no doubt I have committed blunders an Indianist would have avoided. I hope these errors will not deprive me of that expert advice and informed criticism which alone can justify so rude an invasion of unfamiliar territory.[1]

I have written this paper because I believe the irrational, non-economic, and exotic aspects of the Indian cattle complex are greatly overemphasized at the expense of rational, economic, and mundane interpretations.

My intent is not to substitute one dogma for another, but to urge that explanation of taboos,

(1966)

---

[1] In the 1960s ethnographic experience was the cornerstone of authority in American anthropology (and to some extent still is today). Harris' upfront admission that he had never been to India was a challenge to this prevailing anthropological opinion and is related to his views on the emic-etic debate that was raging within the profession at this time. (For more on emics and etics, see footnote 5.)

customs, and rituals associated with management of Indian cattle be sought in "positive-functioned" and probably "adaptive" processes of the ecological system of which they are a part,[a] rather than in the influence of Hindu theology.[2]

Mismanagement of India's agricultural resources as a result of the Hindu doctrine of *ahimsa*,[b] especially as it applies to beef cattle, is frequently noted by Indianists and others concerned with the relation between values and behavior. Although different antirational, dysfunctional, and inutile aspects of the cattle complex are stressed by different authors, many agree that *ahimsa* is a prime example of how men will diminish their material welfare to obtain spiritual satisfaction in obedience to non-rational or frankly irrational beliefs.

A sample opinion on this subject is here summarized: According to Simoons (1961:3), "irrational ideologies" frequently compel men "to overlook foods that are abundant locally and are of high nutritive value, and to utilize other scarcer foods of less value." The Hindu beef-eating taboo is one of Simoons' most important cases. Venkatraman (1938:706) claims, "India is unique in possessing an enormous amount of cattle without making profit from its slaughter." The Ford Foundation (1959:64) reports "widespread recognition not only among animal husbandry officials, but among citizens generally, that India's cattle population is far in excess of the available supplies of fodder and feed . . . At least ⅓, and possibly as many as ½, of the Indian cattle population may be regarded as surplus in relation to feed supply." Matson (1933:227) writes it is a commonplace of the "cattle question that vast numbers of Indian

cattle are so helplessly inefficient as to have no commercial value beyond that of their hides." Srinivas (1952:222) believes "Orthodox Hindu opinion regards the killing of cattle with abhorrence, even though the refusal to kill the vast number of useless cattle which exist in India today is detrimental to the nation."

According to the Indian Ministry of Information (1957:243), "The large animal population is more a liability than an asset in view of our land resources." Chatterjee (1960) calculates that Indian production of cow and buffalo milk involves a "heavy recurring loss of Rs 774 crores. This is equivalent to 6.7 times the amount we are annually spending on importing food grains." Knight (1954:141) observes that because the Hindu religion teaches great reverence for the cow, "there existed a large number of cattle whose utility to the community did not justify economically the fodder which they consumed." Das and Chatterji (1962:120) concur: "A large number of cattle in India are old and decrepit and constitute a great burden on an already impoverished land. This is due to the prejudice among the Hindus against cow killing." Mishra (1962) approvingly quotes Lewis (1955:106): "It is not true that if economic and religious doctrines conflict the economic interest will always win. The Hindu cow has remained sacred for centuries, although this is plainly contrary to economic interest." Darling (1934:158) asserts, "By its attitude to slaughter Hinduism makes any planned improvement of cattle breeding almost impossible." According to Desai (1959:36), "The cattle population is far in excess of the available fodder and feeds."[3]

---

[2] Harris makes his materialist and neofunctionalist position clear in the opening paragraphs of this essay. As a materialist, Harris presumes that Indian beliefs about the sacredness of cattle have a rational economic explanation that takes precedence over references to Hindu theology. Additionally, Harris' statement that the explanation for Indian cattle management can be found in the "adaptive processes of the ecological system of which they are a part" clearly demonstrates the influence of the cultural ecology of Julian Steward (see essay 19). His claim that he does not wish to substitute one dogma for another is disingenuous—Harris is brilliant, but he is one of the more polemic writers in anthropology.

[3] Harris' materialist point of view has been so successful in the last few decades that it should be noted that Westerners really used to think that Indian cattle usage was irrational. In fact, the view that non-Western people's traditional practices were irrational formed one of the cornerstones of colonial ethnocentrism. From the Western point of view, the irrationality of Indian culture was demonstrated by the failure of Indians to conform to European notions of animal husbandry, a failure that confirmed the British in their self-perceived civilizing mission. So, while Harris is doing a cultural-materialist analysis, he is also working in a form of analysis that would have made Franz Boas proud.

[*In a 400-word passage eliminated from this edition, Harris continues his catalog of experts and government agencies that have declared Indian cattle practices uneconomic.*]

In spite of the sometimes final and unqualified fashion in which "surplus," "useless," "uneconomic," and "superfluous" are applied to part or all of India's cattle, contrary conclusions seem admissible when the cattle complex is viewed as part of an *eco-system* rather than as a sector of a national price market. Ecologically, it is doubtful that any component of the cattle complex is "useless," i.e., the number, type, and condition of Indian bovines do not per se impair the ability of the human population to survive and reproduce. Much more likely the relationship between bovines and humans is symbiotic[c] instead of competitive. It probably represents the outcome of intense Darwinian pressures acting upon human and bovine population, cultigens, wild flora and fauna, and social structure and ideology. Moreover presumably the degree of observance of taboos against bovine slaughter and beef-eating reflect the power of these ecological pressures rather than *ahimsa*; in other words, *ahimsa* itself derives power and sustenance from the material rewards it confers upon both men and animals.[4] To support these hypotheses, the major aspects of the Indian cattle complex will be reviewed under the following headings: (1) Milk Production, (2) Traction, (3) Dung, (4) Beef and Hides, (5) Pasture, (6) Useful and Useless Animals, (7) Slaughter, (8) Anti-Slaughter Legislation, (9) Old-Age Homes, and (10) Natural Selection.

MILK PRODUCTION

In India the average yield of whole milk per Zebu cow is 413 pounds, compared with the 5,000-pound average in Europe and the U.S.[d]

(Kartha 1936:607; Spate 1954:231). In Madhya Pradesh yield is as low as 65 pounds, while in no state does it rise higher than the barely respectable 1,445 pounds of the Punjab (Chatterjee 1960:1347). According to the 9th Quinquennial Livestock Census (1961) among the 47,200,000 cows over 3 years old, 27,200,000 were dry and/or not calved (Chaudri and Giri 1963:598).

These figures, however should not be used to prove that the cows are useless or uneconomic, since milk production is a minor aspect of the sacred cow's contribution to the *eco-system*. Indeed, most Indianists agree that it is the buffalo, not the Zebu, whose economic worth must be judged primarily by milk production. Thus, Kartha (1959:225) writes, "the buffalo, and not the Zebu, is the dairy cow." This distinction is elaborated by Mamoria (1953:255):

> Cows in the rural areas are maintained for producing bullocks rather than for milk. She-buffaloes, on the other hand, are considered to be better dairy animals than cows. The male buffaloes are neglected and many of them die or are sold for slaughter before they attain maturity.

Mohan (1962:47) makes the same point:

> For agricultural purposes bullocks are generally preferred, and, therefore, cows in rural areas are primarily maintained for the production of male progeny and incidentally only for milk.

It is not relevant to my thesis to establish whether milk production is a primary or secondary objective or purpose of the Indian farmer. Failure to separate emics from etics (Harris 1964) contributes greatly to confusion surrounding the Indian cattle question.[5] The significance of the preceding quotations lies in the agreement that cows contribute to human material welfare

---

[4] Harris' debt to the cultural ecology of Steward is clear in this paragraph. Although Harris' materialism is derived from Karl Marx via Leslie White, his statement that the features of the cattle complex are the consequence of Darwinian pressures within an ecological system sounds very much like Steward's concept of the cultural core. Harris doesn't spell

out exactly how these pressures operate, but the invocation of Darwin increases the scientific feel of the article by associating it with a well-established scientific position.

[5] The terms *emic* and *etic* were coined in 1954 by the missionary-linguist Kenneth Pike (1912–2000). Emic

in more important ways than milk production. In this new context, the fact that U.S. cows produce 20 times more milk than Indian cows loses much of its significance. Instead, it is more relevant to note that, despite the marginal status of milking in the symbiotic syndrome, 46.7% of India's dairy products come from cow's milk (Chatterjee 1960:1347). How far this production is balanced by expenditures detrimental to human welfare will be discussed later.

TRACTION

The principal positive ecological effect of India's bovine cattle is in their contribution to production of grain crops, from which about 80% of the human calorie ration comes. Some form of animal traction is required to initiate the agricultural cycle, dependent upon plowing in both rainfall and irrigation areas. Additional traction for hauling, transport, and irrigation is provided by animals, but by far their most critical kinetic contribution is plowing.

Although many authorities believe there is an overall surplus of cattle in India, others point to a serious shortage of draught animals. According to Kothavala (1934:122), "Even with . . . overstocking, the draught power available for land operations at the busiest season of the year is inadequate. . . ."For West Bengal, the National Council of Applied Economic Research (1962:56) reports:

> However, despite the large number of draught animals, agriculture in the State suffers from a shortage of draught power. There are large numbers of small landholders entirely dependent on hired animal labour.

Spate (1954:36) makes the same point, "there are too many cattle in the gross, but most individual farmers have too few to carry on with." Gupta (1959:42) and Lewis and Barnouw (1958:102) say a pair of bullocks is the minimum technical unit for cultivation, but in a survey by Diskalkar (1960:87), 18% of the cultivators had only 1 bullock or none. Nationally, if we accept a low estimate of 60,000,000 rural households (Mitra 1963:298) and a high estimate of 80,000,000 working cattle and buffaloes (Government of India 1962:76), we see at once that the allegedly excess number of cattle in India is insufficient to permit a large portion, perhaps as many as ⅓, of India's farmers to begin the agricultural cycle under conditions appropriate to their techno-environmental system.

Much has been made of India's having 115 head of cattle per square mile, compared with 28 per square mile for the U.S. and 3 per square mile for Canada. But what actually may be most characteristic of the size of India's herd is the low ratio of cattle to people. Thus, India has 44 cattle per 100 persons, while in the U.S. the ratio is 58 per 100 and in Canada, 90 (Mamoria 1953:256). Yet, in India cattle are employed as a basic instrument of agricultural production.

Sharing of draught animals on a cooperative basis might reduce the need for additional animals. Chaudhri and Giri point out that the "big farmer manages to cultivate with a pair of bullock a much larger area than the small cultivators" (1963:596). But, the failure to develop cooperative forms of plowing can scarcely be traced to *ahimsa*. If anything, emphasis upon independent, family-sized farm units follows intensification of individual land tenure patterns

---

statements refer to meaning as it is perceived by the natives of a culture, and emic anthropologists tried to outline the models by which natives understood their society. By definition, emic understanding is culture-bound. In contrast, etic meanings are those arrived at by empirical investigation. Etic anthropologists aim at producing generalizations that are cross-culturally valid using methods of investigation that can be verified and replicated by anyone using a similar investigative process. Etic analyses are typically perceived to be more scientific, and Harris'

analysis of cattle in India is an etic study. Harris believes that many studies mix etic and emic data together, thus confounding the analysis. Here he says the same problem "contributes greatly to confusion surrounding the Indian cattle question." Harris claims that when the situation is examined from an etic perspective (energy contribution of cows versus energy expenditures of cows within an overall ecosystem), it is clear that the treatment of cattle in India is adaptive.

and other property innovations deliberately encouraged by the British (Bhatia 1963:18 on). Under existing property arrangements, there is a perfectly good economic explanation of why bullocks are not shared among adjacent households. Plowing cannot take place at any time of the year, but must be accomplished within a few daylight hours in conformity with seasonal conditions. These are set largely by summer monsoons, responsible for about 90% of the total rainfall (Bhatia 1963:4). Writing about Orissa, Bailey (1957:74) notes:

> As a temporary measure, an ox might be borrowed from a relative, or a yoke of cattle and a ploughman might be hired . . . but during the planting season, when the need is the greatest, most people are too busy to hire out or lend cattle.

According to Desai (1948:86):

> . . . over vast areas, sowing and harvesting operations, by the very nature of things, begin simultaneously with the outbreak of the first showers and the maturing of crops respectively, and especially the former has got to be put through quickly during the first phase of the monsoon. Under these circumstances, reliance by a farmer on another for bullocks is highly risky and he has got, therefore, to maintain his own pair.

Dube (1955:84) is equally specific:

> The cultivators who depend on hired cattle or who practice cooperative lending and borrowing of cattle cannot take the best advantage of the first rains, and this enforced wait results in untimely sowing and poor crops.

Wiser and Wiser (1963:62) describe the plight of the bullock-short farmer as follows, "When he needs the help of bullocks most, his neighbors are all using theirs." And Shastri (1960:1592) points out, "Uncertainty of Indian farming due to dependence on rains is the main factor creating obstacles in the way of improvements in bullock labor."

It would seem, therefore, that this aspect of the cattle complex is not an expression of spirit and ritual, but of rain and energy.[6]

DUNG

In India cattle dung is the main source of domestic cooking fuel. Since grain crops cannot be digested unless boiled or baked, cooking is indispensable. Considerable disagreement exists about the total amount of cattle excrement and its uses, but even the lowest estimates are impressive. An early estimate by Lupton (1922:60) gave the BTU equivalent of dung consumed in domestic cooking as 35,000,000 tons of coal or 68,000,000 tons of wood. Most detailed appraisal is by National Council of Applied Economic Research (1959:3), which rejects H. J. Bhabha's estimate of 131,000,000 tons of coal and the Ministry of Food and Agriculture's 112,000,000 tons. The figure preferred by the NCAER is 35,000,000 tons anthracite or 40,000,000 tons bituminous, but with a possible range of between 35–45,000,000 of anthracite dung-coal equivalent. This calculation depends upon indications that only 36% of the total wet dung is utilized as fuel (p. 14), a lower estimate than any reviewed by Saha (1956:923). These

---

[6] Harris was taking a fairly radical position at this time, therefore he presents quotation after quotation supporting his views when one or two would suffice. Note that he relies almost exclusively on statistical rather than ethnographic data. True to his etic perspective, Harris provides the reader with a statistical portrait of Indian society. It is also instructive to examine Harris' writing style. Although not as polemical an author as Marx, who called one of his opponents "Saint Max" (see essay 4), Harris undercuts his opponents through rhetorical style as well as scientific argument. Throughout this section— as he does here—Harris concludes points by saying, in effect, you do not need religion to explain this. The cumulative effect is to make the position he is opposing look silly.

vary from 40% (Imperial Council on Agricultural Research) to 50% (Ministry of Food and Agriculture) to 66.6% (Department of Education, Health and Lands). The NCAER estimate of a dung-coal equivalent of 35,000,000 tons is therefore quite conservative; it is nonetheless an impressive amount of BTU's to be plugged into an energy system.

Kapp (1963:144 on), who discusses at length the importance of substituting tractors for bullocks, does not give adequate attention to finding cooking fuel after the bullocks are replaced. The NCAER (1959:20) conclusion that dung is cheaper than coke seems an understatement. Although it is claimed that wood resources are potentially adequate to replace dung the measures advocated do not involve *ahimsa* but are again an indictment of a land tenure system not inspired by Hindu tradition (NCAER 1959:20 on; Bansil 1958:97 on). Finally, it should be noted that many observers stress the slow burning qualities of dung and its special appropriateness for preparation of *ghi* and deployment of woman-power in the household (Lewis and Barnouw 1958:40; Mosher 1946:153).[7]

As manure, dung enters the energy system in another vital fashion. According to Mujumdar (1960:743), 300,000,000 tons are used as fuel, 340,000,000 tons as manure, and 160,000,000 tons "wasted on hillsides and roads." Spate (1954:238) believes that 40% of dung production is spread on fields, 40% burned, and 20% "lost." Possibly estimates of the amount of dung lost are grossly inflated in view of the importance of "roads and hillsides" in the grazing pattern (see Pasture). Similarly artificial and culture- or even class-bound judgments refer to utilization of India's night soil. It is usually assumed that

Chinese and Indian treatment of this resource are radically different, and that vast quantities of nitrogen go unused in agriculture because of Hindu-inspired definitions of modesty and cleanliness. However, most human excrement from Indian villages is deposited in surrounding fields; the absence of latrines helps explain why such fields raise 2 and 3 successive crops each year (Mosher 1946:154, 33; Bansil 1958:104). More than usual caution, therefore, is needed before concluding that a significant amount of cattle dung is wasted. Given the conscious premium set on dung for fuel and fertilizer, thoughtful control maintained over grazing patterns (see Pasture), and occurrence of specialized sweeper and gleaner castes, much more detailed evidence of wastage is needed than is now available. Since cattle graze on "hillsides and roads," dung dropped there would scarcely be totally lost to the *eco-system,* even with allowance for loss of nitrogen by exposure to air and sunlight. Also, if any animal dung is wasted on roads and hillsides it is not because of *ahimsa* but of inadequate pasturage suitable for collecting and processing animal droppings. The sedentary, intensive rainfall agriculture of most of the subcontinent is heavily dependent upon manuring. So vital is this that Spate (1954:239) says substitutes for manure consumed as fuel "must be supplied, and lavishly, even at a financial loss to government." If this is the case, then old, decrepit, and dry animals might have a use after all, especially when, as we shall see, the dung they manufacture employs raw materials lost to the culture-energy system unless processed by cattle, and especially when many apparently moribund animals revive at the next monsoon and provide their owners with a male calf.[8]

---

[7] Harris' statement about "a land tenure system not inspired by Hindu tradition" is an allusion to British colonialism. As Friedman points out in his 1974 critique of Harris' analysis, Harris never really deals with the cultural context in which the traditions he analyzes take place— that is, centuries of British colonial rule.

Ghi, or *ghee,* is clarified butter made from the butterfat of milk.

[8] Since the publication of Leslie White's "Energy and the Evolution of Culture" in 1943, energy has had a significant role in American anthropology. Harris' discussion of dung as an energy source is an early example of the type of analysis that became a mainstay of the ecological and evolutionary approaches in cultural anthropology.

BEEF AND HIDES[9]

Positive contributions of India's sacred cattle do not cease with milk-grazing, bullock-producing, traction, and dung-dropping. There remains the direct protein contribution of 25,000,000 cattle and buffalo which die each year (Mohan 1962:54). This feature of the eco-system is reminiscent of the East African cattle area where, despite the normal taboo on slaughter, natural deaths and ceremonial occasions are probably frequent enough to maintain beef consumption near the ecological limit with dairying as the primary function (Schneider 1957:278 on). Although most Hindus probably do not consume beef, the *eco-system* under consideration is not confined to Hindus. The human population includes some 55,000,000 "scheduled" exterior or untouchable groups (Hutton 1961:vii), many of whom will consume beef if given the opportunity (Dube 1955:68–69), plus several million more Moslems and Christians. Much of the flesh on the 25,000,000 dead cattle and buffalo probably gets consumed by human beings whether or not the cattle die naturally. Indeed, could it be that without the orthodox Hindu beef-eating taboo, many marginal and depressed castes would be deprived of an occasional, but nutritionally critical, source of animal protein?

It remains to note that the slaughter taboo does not prevent depressed castes from utilizing skin, horns and hoofs of dead beasts. In 1956 16,000,000 cattle hides were produced (Randhawa 1962:322). The quality of India's huge leather industry—the world's largest—leaves much to be desired, but the problem is primarily outmoded tanning techniques and lack of capital, not *ahimsa.*

PASTURE

The principal positive-functioned or useful contributions of India's sacred cattle to human survival and well-being have been described. Final evaluation of their utility must involve assessment of energy costs in terms of resources and human labor input which might be more efficiently expended in other activities.

Direct and indirect evidence suggests that in India men and bovine cattle do not compete for existence. According to Mohan (1962:43 on):

> . . . the bulk of the food on which the animals subsist . . . is not the food that is required for human consumption, i.e., fibrous fodders produced as incidental to crop production, and a large part of the crop residues or byproducts of seeds and waste grazing.

On the contrary, "the bulk of foods (straws and crop residues) that are ploughed into the soil in other countries are converted into milk" (p. 45).

The majority of the Indian cattle obtain their requirements from whatever grazing is available from straw and stalk and other residues from human foodstuffs, and are starved seasonally in the dry months when grasses wither.

In Bengal the banks and slopes of the embankments of public roads are the only grazing grounds and the cattle subsist mainly on paddy straw, paddy husks and . . . coarse grass. . . . (Mamoria 1953:263–64).

According to Dube (1955:84, ". . . the cattle roam about the shrubs and rocks and eat whatever fodder is available there." This is confirmed by Moomaw (1949:96): "Cows subsist on the pasture and any coarse fodder they can find. Grain is fed for only a day or two following parturition." The character of the environmental

---

[9] This section may be the weakest in Harris' argument. Notice the absence of statistical support in his discussion of beef eating and the leather industry. He writes, "The quality of India's huge leather industry—the world's largest—leaves much to be desired, but the problem is primarily outmoded tanning techniques and lack of capital, not *ahimsa.*" But one could easily argue that it is precisely *ahimsa* that keeps the industry outmoded since, because of *ahimsa,* no one with prestige or capital will invest in tanning. Treating hides is the domain of the lowest castes. This point does not really damage his argument, but it is typical of Harris' dogmatism: He will allow no explanatory power to *ahimsa* at all.

niche reserved for cattle nourishment is described by Gourou (1963:123), based on data furnished by Dupuis (1960) for Madras:

> If faut voir clairement que le faible rendement du bétail indien n'est pas un gaspillage: ce bétail n'entre pas en concurrence avec la consommation de produits agricoles . . . ils ne leur sacrifient pas des surfaces agricoles, ou ayant un potential agricole.[10]

NCAER (1961:57) confines this pattern for Tripura: "There is a general practice of feeding livestock on agricultural by-products such as straw, grain wastes and husks"; for West Bengal (NCAER 1962:59): "The state has practically no pasture or grazing fields, and the farmers are not in the habit of growing green fodders . . . livestock feeds are mostly agricultural by-products"; and for Andhra Pradesh (NCAER 1962:52): "Cattle are stall-fed, but the bulk of the feed consists of paddy straw. . . . "

The only exceptions to the rural pattern of feeding cattle on waste products and grazing them on marginal or unproductive lands involve working bullocks and nursing cows:

> The working bullocks, on whose efficiency cultivation entirely depends, are usually fed with chopped bananas at the time of fodder scarcity. But the milch cows have to live in a semi-starved condition, getting what nutrition they can from grazing on the fields after their rice harvest (Gangulee 1935:17). At present cattle are fed largely according to the season. During the rainy period they feed upon the grass which springs up on the *uncultivated* hillsides. . . . But in the dry season there is hardly any grass, and cattle wander on the *cropless* lands in an often halfstarved condition. True there is some fodder at these times in the shape of rice-straw and dried copra, but it is not generally sufficient, and is furthermore given mainly to the animals actually *working* at the time (Mayer 1952:70, italics added).

There is much evidence that Hindu farmers calculate carefully which animals deserve more food and attention. In Madras, Randhawa, et al. (1961:117) report: "The cultivators pay more attention to the male stock used for ploughing and for draft. There is a general neglect of the cow and the female calf even from birth . . . " Similar discrimination is described by Mamoria (1953:263 on):

> Many plough bullocks are sold off in winter or their rations are ruthlessly decreased whenever they are not worked in full, while milch cattle are kept on after lactation on poor and inadequate grazing. . . . The cultivator feeds his bullocks better than his cow because it pays him. He feeds his bullocks better during the busy season, when they work, than during the slack season, when they remain idle. Further, he feeds his more valuable bullocks better than those less valuable. . . . Although the draught animals and buffaloes are properly fed, the cow gets next to nothing of stall feeding. She is expected to pick up her living on the bare fields after harvest and on the village wasteland. . . .

The previously cited NCAER report on Andhra Pradesh notes that "Bullocks and milking cows during the working season get more concentrates. . . . "(1962:52). Wiser and Wiser (1963:71) sum up the situation in a fashion supporting Srinivas' (1958:4) observation that the Indian peasant is "nothing if he is not practical":

> Farmers have become skillful in reckoning the minimum of food necessary for maintaining animal service. Cows are fed just enough to assure their calving and giving a little milk. They are grazed during the day on lands which yield very little vegetation, and are given a very sparse meal at night.

Many devout Hindus believe the bovine cattle of India are exploited without mercy by greedy

---

[10] The translation of this passage is: "One needs to see clearly that the small return of Indian cattle is not waste: these beasts do not compete for the consumption of agricultural produce . . . neither fields nor areas that could be used for agriculture are sacrificed to them."

Hindu owners. *Ahimsa* obviously has little to do with economizing which produces the famous *phooka* and *doom dev* techniques for dealing with dry cows.[11] Not to Protestants but to Hindus did Gandhi (1954:7) address lamentations concerning the cow:

> How we bleed her to take the last drop of milk from her, how we starve her to emaciation, how we ill-treat the calves, how we deprive them of their portion of milk, how cruelly we treat the oxen, how we castrate them, how we beat them, how we overload them. . . . I do not know that the condition of the cattle in any other part of the world is as bad as in unhappy India.

USEFUL AND USELESS ANIMALS

How then, if careful rationing is characteristic of livestock management, do peasants tolerate the widely reported herds of useless animals? Perhaps "useless" means one thing to the peasant and quite another to the price-market-oriented agronomist. It is impossible at a distance to judge which point of view is ecologically more valid, but the peasants could be right more than the agronomists are willing to admit.

Since non-working and non-lactating animals are thermal and chemical factories which depend on waste lands and products for raw materials, judgment that a particular animal is useless cannot be supported without careful examination of its owner's household budget. Estimates from the cattle census which equate useless with dry or non-working animals are not convincing. But even if a given animal in a particular household is of less-than-marginal utility, there is an additional factor whose evaluation would involve long-range bovine biographies. The utility of a particular animal to its owner cannot be established simply by its performance during season or an animal cycle. Perhaps the whole system of Indian bovine management is alien to costing procedures of the West. There may be a kind of low-risk sweep-stakes which drags on for 10 or 12 years before the losers and winners are separated.

As previously observed, the principal function of bovine cows is not their milk-producing but their bullock-producing abilities. Also established is the fact that many farmers are short of bullocks. Cows have the function primarily to produce male offspring, but when? In Europe and America, cows become pregnant under well-controlled, hence predictable, circumstances and a farmer with many animals can count on male offspring in half the births. In India, cows become pregnant under quite different circumstances. Since cows suffer from malnutrition through restriction to marginal pasture, they conceive and deliver in unpredictable fashion. The chronic starvation of the inter-monsoon period makes the cow, in the words of Mamoria (1953:263), "an irregular breeder." Moreover, with few animals, the farmer may suffer many disappointments before a male is born. To the agriculture specialist with knowledge of what healthy dairy stock look like, the hot weather herds of walking skeletons "roaming over the bare fields and dried up wastes" (Leake 1923:267) must indeed seem without economic potential. Many of them, in fact, will not make it through to the next monsoon. However, among the survivors are an unknown number still physically capable of having progeny. Evidently neither the farmer nor the specialist knows which will conceive, nor when. To judge from Bombay city, even when relatively good care is bestowed on a dry cow, no one knows the outcome: "If an attempt is made to salvage them, they have to be kept and fed for a long time. Even then, it is not known whether they will conceive or not" (Nandra, *et al.* 1955:9).

In rural areas, to judge a given animal useless may be to ignore the recuperative power of these breeds under conditions of erratic rainfall and unpredictable grazing opportunities. The difference of viewpoint between the farmer and the expert is apparent in Moomaw's (1949) incomplete attempt to describe the life history of an informant's cattle. The farmer in question had 3 oxen,

---

[11] The "famous" *phooka* and *doom dev* techniques Harris refers to are procedures Indians use to stimulate a cow's flow of milk. As described by Harris in his 1974 book *Cows, Pigs, Wars, and Witches, phooka* is blowing air into the cow's uterus through a hollow pipe; *doom dev* refers to stuffing the cow's tail into its vagina.

2 female buffaloes, 4 head of young cattle and 3 "worthless" cows (p. 23). In Moomaw's opinion, "the three cows . . . are a liability to him, providing no income, yet consuming feed which might be placed to better use." Yet we learn, "The larger one had a calf about once in three years"; moreover 2 of the 3 oxen were "raised" by the farmer himself. (Does this mean that they were the progeny of the farmer's cows?) The farmer tells Moomaw, "The young stock get some fodder, but for the most part they pasture with the village herd. The cows give nothing and I cannot afford to feed them." Whereupon Moomaw's *non sequitur*: "We spoke no more of his cows, for like many a farmer he just keeps them, without inquiring whether it is profitable or not" (p. 25).

The difficulties in identifying animals that are definitely uneconomic for a given farmer are reflected in the varying estimates of the total of such animals. The Expert Committee on the Prevention of Slaughter of Cattle estimated 20,000,000 uneconomic cattle in India (Nandra, *et al.* 1953:62). Roy (1955:14) settles for 5,500,000, or about 3.5%. Mamoria (1953:257), who gives the still lower estimate of 2,900,000, or 2.1%, claims most of these are males. A similarly low percentage—2.5%—is suggested for West Bengal (NCAER 1962:56). None of these estimates appears based on bovine life histories in relation to household budgets; none appears to involve estimates of economic significance of dung contributions of older animals.[12]

Before a peasant is judged a victim of Oriental mysticism, might it not be well to indicate the devastating material consequences which befall a poor farmer unable to replace a bullock lost through disease, old age, or accident? Bailey (1957:73) makes it clear that in the economic life of the marginal peasantry, "Much the most devastating single event is the loss of an ox (or a plough buffalo)." If the farmer is unable to replace the animal with one from his own herd, he must borrow money at usurious rates. Defaults on such loans are the principal causes of transfer of land titles from peasants to landlords. Could this explain why the peasant is not overly perturbed that some of his animals might turn out to be only dung-providers? After all, the real threat to his existence does not arise from animals but from people ready to swoop down on him as soon as one of his beasts falters. Chapekar's (1960:27) claim that the peasant's "stock serve as a great security for him to fall back on whenever he is in need" would seem to be appropriate only in reference to the unusually well-established minority. In a land where life expectancy at birth has only recently risen to 30 years (Black 1959:2), it is not altogether appropriate to speak of security. The poorest farmers own insufficient stock. Farm management studies show that holdings below ⅔ of average area account for ⅔ of all farms, but maintain only ¼ of the total cattle on farms. "This is so, chiefly because of their limited resources to maintain cattle" (Chaudhri and Giri 1963:598).

SLAUGHTER

Few, if any, Hindu farmers kill their cattle by beating them over the head, severing their jugular veins or shooting them. But to assert that they do not kill their animals when it is economically important for them to do so may be equally false. This interpretation escapes the notice of so many observers because the slaughtering process receives recognition only in euphemisms. People will admit that they "neglect" their animals, but will not openly accept responsibility for the *etic* effects, i.e., the more or less rapid death which ensues. The strange result of this euphemistic pattern is evidenced in the following statement by Moomaw (1949:96): "All calves born, however inferior, are allowed to live until they die of neglect." In the light of many similar but, by Hindu standards, more vulgar observations,

---

[12] Harris' concern is for the economics of cattle at the level of the Indian peasant household, but the statistics he cites are national or state-level figures. Millions of starving cattle wandering around might present state-level problems not experienced by an individual farmer—the level at which a problem is examined affects one's analysis. Both Harris and the government figures he cites may be correct, but in different ways. The only macro-level view Harris takes is farther down, when he discusses the political significance of cattle slaughter bans.

it is clear that this kind of statement should read, "Most calves born are not allowed to live, but are starved to death."

This is roughly the testimony of Gourou (1963:125), "Le paysan conserve seulement les veaux qui deviendront boeufs de labour ou vaches laitières; les autres sont écartés . . . et meurent d'épuisement."[13] Wiser and Wiser (1963:70) are even more direct:

> Cows and buffaloes too old to furnish milk are not treated cruelly, but simply allowed to starve. The same happens to young male buffaloes. . . . The males are unwanted and little effort is made to keep them alive.

Obviously, when an animal, undernourished to begin with, receives neither food nor care, it will not enjoy a long life (compare Gourou 1963: 124). Despite claims that an aged and decrepit cow "must be supported like an unproductive relative, until it dies a natural death" (Mosher 1946: 124), ample evidence justifies belief that "few cattle die of old age"[e] (Bailey 1957:75). Dandekar (1964:352) makes the same point: "In other words, because the cows cannot be fed nor can they be killed, they are neglected, starved and left to die a 'natural' death."

The farmer culls his stock by starving unwanted animals and also, under duress, sells them directly or indirectly to butchers. With economic pressure, many Indians who will not kill or eat cows themselves:

> are likely to compromise their principles and sell to butchers who slaughter cows, thereby tacitly supporting the practice for other people. Selling aged cows to butchers has over the centuries become an accepted practice along side the *mos* that a Hindu must not kill cattle (Roy 1955:15)

Determining the number of cattle slaughtered by butchers is almost as difficult as determining the number killed by starvation. According to Dandekar (1964:351), "Generally it is the useless animals that find their way to the slaughter house." Lahiry (n.d.:140) says only 126,900 or .9% of the total cattle population is slaughtered per year. Darling (1934:158) claims:

> All Hindus object to the slaughter and even to the sale of unfit cows and keep them indefinitely. . . . rather than sell them to a cattle dealer, who would buy only for the slaughter house, they send them to a *gowshala* or let them loose to die. Some no doubt sell secretly, but this has its risks in an area where public opinion can find strong expression through the *panchayat*.[14]

Such views would seem to be contradicted by Sinha (1961:95): "A large number of animals are slaughtered privately and it is very difficult to ascertain their numbers." The difficulty of obtaining accurate estimates is also implied by the comment of the Committee on the Prevention of Slaughter that "90% of animals not approved for slaughter are slaughtered stealthily outside of municipal limits" (Nandra, *et al.* 1955:11).[15]

An indication of the propensity to slaughter cattle under duress is found in connection with the food crisis of World War II. With rice imports cut off by Japanese occupation of Burma (Thirumalai 1954:38; Bhatia 1963:309 on), increased consumption of beef by the armed forces, higher prices for meat and foodstuffs generally, and famine conditions in Bengal, the doctrine of *ahimsa* proved to be alarmingly ineffectual. Direct military intervention was required to avoid destruction of animals needed for plowing, milking, and bullock-production:

> During the war there was an urgent need to reduce or to avoid the slaughter for food of animals useful for breeding or for agricultural work. For the summer of 1944 the slaughter

---

[13] The translation of this quotation is "The peasant only saves those cows that will become traction animals or milk cows. The others are taken away and die of starvation."

[14] *Gowshala*: an "old age home" for cattle; *panchayat*: a village council.

[15] One thing to keep in mind while reading all these statements is that cattle slaughter is a sensitive political topic in India; those making the statements may be politically motivated to take one or another position. It is possible that such statements are more revealing of Indian politics than the conditions of Indian cattle. Currently, in most Indian states cattle slaughter is illegal.

was prohibited of: 1) Cattle below three years of age; 2) Male cattle between two and ten years of age which were being used or were likely to be used as working cattle; 3) All cows between three and ten years of age, other than cows which were unsuitable for bearing offspring; 4) All cows which were pregnant or in milk (Knight 1954:141).

Gourou (1963:124–25), aware that starvation and neglect are systematically employed to cull Indian herds, nonetheless insists that destruction of animals through starvation amounts to an important loss of capital. This loss is attributed to the low price of beef caused by the beef-eating taboo, making it economically infeasible to send animals to slaughter. Gourou's appraisal, however, neglects deleterious consequences to the rural tanning and carrion-eating castes if increased numbers of animals went to the butchers. Since the least efficient way to convert solar energy into comestibles is to impose an animal converter between plant and man (Cottrell 1955), it should be obvious that without major technical and environmental innovations or drastic population cuts, India could not tolerate a large beef-producing industry. This suggests that insofar as the beef-eating taboo helps discourage growth of beef-producing industries, it is part of an ecological adjustment which maximizes rather than minimizes the calorie and protein output of the productive process.

ANTI-SLAUGHTER LEGISLATION AND GOWSHALAS[16]

It is evident from the history of anti-slaughter agitation and legislation in India that more than *ahimsa* has been required to protect Indian cattle from premature demise. Unfortunately, this legislation is misinterpreted and frequently cited as

evidence of the anti-economic effect of Hinduism. I am unable to unravel all the tangled economic and political interests served by the recent anti-slaughter laws of the Indian states. Regardless of the ultimate ecological consequences of these laws, however, several points deserve emphasis. First it should be recalled that cow protection was a major political weapon in Gandhi's campaign against both British and Moslems. The sacred cow was the ideological focus of a successful struggle against English colonialism; hence the enactment of total anti-slaughter legislation obviously had a relational base, at least among politicians who seized and retained power on anti-English and anti-Moslem platforms. It is possible that the legislation will now backfire and upset the delicate ecological balance which now exists. The Committee on the Prevention of Slaughter claimed that it

> actually saw in Pepsu (where slaughter is banned completely) what a menace wild cattle can be. Conditions have become so desperate there, that the State Government have got to spend a considerable sum for catching and redomesticating wild animals to save the crops (Nandra, *et al.* 1955:11).

According to Mayadas (1954:29):

> The situation has become so serious that it is impossible in some parts of the country to protect growing crops from grazing by wandering cattle. Years ago it was one or two stray animals which could either be driven off or sent to the nearest cattle pound. Today it is a question of constantly being harassed day and night by herds which must either feed on one's green crops, or starve. How long can this state of affairs be allowed to continue?

Before the deleterious effects of slaughter laws can be properly evaluated, certain additional evolutionary and functional possibilities must

---

[16] Having discussed the utility of *ahimsa* to Indian peasant farmers, Harris turns to a discussion of the social and political ramifications of the practice. Here he injects an element of class conflict into his argument. Discussing the disparity between wealthy landowners and the landless he writes, "To have one's cow eat other people's crops may be a very fine solution to the subsistence problem of those with no crops of their own." However, while Harris sees conflict, he doesn't make it the engine of cultural change. The system he describes is essentially static. A true Marxist would bring this conflict to the center of the analysis.

be examined. For example, given the increasing growth rate of India's human population, the critical importance of cattle in the *eco-system*, and the absence of fundamental technical and environmental changes, a substantial increase in cattle seems necessary and predictable, regardless of slaughter legislation. Furthermore, there is some indication, admittedly incomplete but certainly worthy of careful inquiry, that many who protest most against destructiveness of marauding herds of useless beasts may perceive the situation from very special vantage points in the social hierarchy. The implications of the following newspaper editorial are clear:

> The alarming increase of stray and wild cattle over wide areas of Northern India is fast becoming a major disincentive to crop cultivation. . . . Popular sentiment against cow slaughter no doubt lies at the back of the problem. People prefer to let their aged, diseased, and otherwise useless cattle live at the expense of *other people's crops* (Indian Express, New Delhi, 7 February 1959, italics added).

Evidently we need to know something about whose crops are threatened by these marauders. Despite post-independence attempts at land reform, 10% of the Indian agricultural population still owns more than ½ the total cultivated area and 15,000,000, or 22%, of rural households own no land at all (Mitra 1963:298). Thorner and Thorner (1962:3) call the land reform program a failure, and point out how "the grip of the larger holder serves to prevent the lesser folk from developing the land. . . ." Quite possibly, in other words, the anti-slaughter laws, insofar as they are effective, should be viewed as devices which, contrary to original political intent, bring pressure to bear upon those whose lands are devoted to cash crops of benefit only to narrow commercial, urban, and landed sectors of the population. To have one's cows eat other people's crops may be a very fine solution to the subsistence problem of those with no crops of their own. Apparently, in the days when animals could be driven off or sent to the pound with impunity, this could not happen, even though *ahimsa* reigned supreme then as now.

Some form of anti-slaughter legislation was required and actually argued for, on unambiguously rational, economic, and material grounds. About 4% of India's cattle are in the cities (Mohan 1962:48). These have always represented the best dairy stock, since the high cost of feeding animals in a city could be offset only by good milking qualities. A noxious consequence of this dairy pattern was the slaughter of the cow at the end of its first urban lactation period because it was too expensive to maintain while awaiting another pregnancy. Similarly, and by methods previously discussed, the author calf was killed after it had stimulated the cow to "let down." With the growth of urban milk consumption, the best of India's dairy cattle were thus systematically prevented from breeding, while animals with progressively poorer milking qualities were preserved in the countryside (Mohan 1962:48; Mayadas 1954:29; Gandhi 1954:13 on). The Committee on the Prevention of Slaughter of Cattle (Nandra, *et al.* 1955:2) claimed at least 50,000 high-yielding cows and she-buffaloes from Madras, Bombay, and Calcutta were "annually sent to premature slaughter" and were "lost to the country." Given such evidence of waste and the political potential of Moslems being identified as cow-butchers and Englishmen as cow-eaters (Gandhi 1954:16), the political importance of *ahimsa* becomes more intelligible. Indeed, it could be that the strength of Gandhi's *charisma* lay in his superior understanding of the ecological significance of the cow, especially in relation to the underprivileged masses, marginal low caste and out caste farmers. Gandhi (p. 3) may have been closer to the truth than many a foreign expert when he said:

> Why the cow was selected for apotheosis is obvious to me. The cow was in India the best companion. She was the giver of plenty. Not only did she give milk but she also made agriculture possible.

OLD-AGE HOMES

Among the more obscure aspects of the cattle complex are bovine old-age homes, variously identified as *gowshalas, pinjrapoles,* and, under the Five-Year Plans, as *gosadans*. Undoubtedly some of these are "homes for cows, which are supported by public charity, which maintain the old and derelict animals till natural death occurs" (Kothavala 1934:123). According to Gourou (1963:125), however, owners of cows sent to these religious institutions pay rent with the understanding that if the cows begin to lactate they will be returned. The economics of at least some of these "charitable" institutions is, therefore, perhaps not as quaint as usually implied. It is also significant that, although the 1st Five-Year Plan called for establishment of 160 *gosadans* to serve 320,000 cattle, only 22 *gosadans* servicing 8,000 cattle were reported by 1955 (Government of India Planning Commission 1956:283).

NATURAL SELECTION

Expert appraisers of India's cattle usually show little enthusiasm for the typical undersized breeds. Much has been made of the fact that 1 large animal is a more efficient dung, milk, and traction machine than 2 small ones. "Weight for weight, a small animal consumes a much larger quantity of food than a bigger animal" (Mamoria 1953:268). "More dung is produced when a given quantity of food is consumed by one animal than when it is shared by two animals" (Ford Foundation 1959:64). Thus it would seem that India's smaller breeds should be replaced by larger, more powerful, and better milking breeds. But once again, there is another way of looking at the evidence. It might very well be that if all of India's scrub cattle were suddenly replaced by an equivalent number of large, high-quality European or American dairy and traction animals, famines of noteworthy magnitude would immediately ensue. Is it not possible that India's cattle are undersized precisely because

other breeds never could survive the atrocious conditions they experience most of the year? I find it difficult to believe that breeds better adapted to the present Indian *eco-system* exist elsewhere.

> By nature and religious training, the villager is unwilling to inflict pain or to take animal life. But the immemorial grind for existence has hardened him to an acceptance of survival of the fittest (Wiser and Wiser 1963).

Not only are scrub animals well adapted to the regular seasonal crises of water and forage and general year-round neglect, but long-range selective pressures may be even more significant. The high frequency of drought-induced famines in India (Bhatia 1963) places a premium upon drought-resistance plus a more subtle factor: A herd of smaller animals, dangerously thinned by famine or pestilence, reproduces faster than an equivalent group of larger animals, despite the fact that the larger animal consumes less per pound than 2 smaller animals. This is because there are 2 cows in the smaller herd per equivalent large cow. Mohan (1962:45) is one of the few authorities to have grasped this principle, including it in defense of the small breeds:

> Calculations of the comparative food conversion efficiency of various species of Indian domestic livestock by the writer has revealed, that much greater attention should be paid to small livestock than at present, not only because of their better conversion efficiency for protein but also because of the possibilities of bringing about a rapid increase in their numbers.

CONCLUSION[17]

The probability that India's cattle complex is a positive-functioned part of a naturally selected

---

[17] At the time Harris wrote this essay, an approach called ethnoscience, or the new ethnography, was very popular. With a focus on the emic perspective, an underlying assumption of ethnoscience was that culture was a mental model that people acted out. One goal of ethnoscience was to re-create these models so that anthropologists could understand the world in the same way as their informants. Harris, however, disagrees strongly with this view of culture, arguing against it in *The Rise of Anthropological Theory* (1968). According to Harris, culture should be defined as behavior that is determined by techno-environmental factors. Harris' article is both an example of a materialist perspective and a challenge to ethnoscience.

eco-system is at least as good as that it is a negative-functioned expression of an irrational ideology. This should not be interpreted to mean that no "improvements" can be made in the system, nor that different systems may not eventually evolve. The issue is not whether oxen are more efficient than tractors. I suggest simply that many features of the cattle complex have been erroneously reported or interpreted. That Indian cattle are weak and inefficient is not denied, but there is doubt that this situation arises from and is mainly perpetuated by Hindu ideology. Given the techno-environmental base, Indian property relationships, and political organization, one need not involve the doctrine of *ahimsa* to understand fundamental features of the cattle complex. Although the cattle population of India has risen by 38,000,000 head since 1940, during the same period, the human population has risen by 120,000,000. Despite the anti-slaughter legislation, the ratio of cattle to humans actually declined from 44:100 in 1941 to 40:100 in 1961 (Government of India 1962:74; 1963:6). In the absence of major changes in environment, technology or property relations, it seems unlikely that the cattle population will cease to accompany the rise in the human population. If *ahimsa* is negative-functioned, then we must be prepared to admit the possibility that all other factors contributing to the rapid growth of the Indian human and cattle populations, including the germ theory of disease, are also negative-functioned.[18]

NOTES

[a] The author (1960) suggested that the term "adaptive" be restricted to traits, biological or cultural, established and diffused in conformity with the principle of natural selection. Clearly, not all "positive-functioned," i.e., useful, cultural traits are so established.

[b] *Ahimsa* is the Hindu principle of unity of life, of which sacredness of cattle is principal sub-case and symbol.

[c] According to Zeuner (1954:328), "Symbiosis includes all conditions of the living together of two different species, provided both derive advantages therefrom. Cases in which both partners benefit equally are rare." In the symbiosis under consideration, men benefit more than cattle.

[d] The U.S. Census of Agriculture (1954) showed milk production averaging from a low of 3,929 pounds per cow in the Nashville Basin sub-region to 11,112 pounds per cow in the Southern California sub-region.

[e] Srinivas (1962:126) declared himself properly skeptical in this matter: "It is commonly believed that the peasant's religious attitude to cattle comes in the way of the disposal of useless cattle. Here again, my experience of Rampura makes me skeptical of the general belief. I am not denying that cattle are regarded as in some sense sacred, but I doubt whether the belief is as powerful as it is claimed to be. I have already mentioned that bull-buffaloes are sacrificed to village goddesses. And in the case of the cow, while the peasant does not want to kill the cow or bull himself he does not seem to mind very much if someone else does the dirty job out of his sight."

---

[18] Harris is certainly one of the most colorful and polemical figures in contemporary anthropology. For the last thirty years, while other perspectives have come and gone, Harris has stood firm as one of the leading proponents of cultural materialism and the etic approach. Starting as an intellectual approach to cultural analysis, his advocacy of cultural materialism has taken on a moral-ideological dimension. For example, in the introduction to his book *America Now,* Harris writes:

> The task of this book is to reassert the primacy of rational endeavor and objective knowledge in the struggle to save and renew the American dream. . . . Anthropologists regard it as their solemn duty to represent the hopes and fears, values and goals, beliefs and rituals of different groups and communities seen from within, the way people who belong to these groups and communities perceive them to be, and the way they want to be seen by others. But that can be only half the job. The other half is to describe and explain what people are actually saying and doing from the standpoint of the objective study of culture and history (Harris 1981:15).

22. *Ritual Regulation of Environmental Relations Among a New Guinea People*[a]

Roy A. Rappaport (1926–1997)

Most functional studies of religious behavior in anthropology have as an analytic goal the elucidation of events, processes, or relationships occurring within a social unit of some sort.[1] The social unit is not always well defined, but in some cases it appears to be a church, that is, a group of people who entertain similar beliefs about the universe, or a congregation, a group of people who participate together in the performance of religious rituals. There have been exceptions. Thus Vayda,[2] Leeds, and Smith (1961) and O. K. Moore (1957) have clearly perceived that the functions of religious ritual are not necessarily confined within the boundaries of a congregation or even a church. By and large, however, I believe that the following statement by Homans (1941:172) represents fairly the dominant line of anthropological thought concerning the functions of religious ritual:

> Ritual actions do not produce a practical result on the external world—that is one of the reasons why we call them ritual. But to make this statement is not to say that ritual has no function. Its function is not related to the world external to the society but to the internal constitution of the society. It gives the members of

(1967)

the society confidence, it dispels their anxieties, it disciplines their social organization.

No argument will be raised here against the sociological and psychological functions imputed by Homans, and many others before him, to ritual. They seem to me to be plausible. Nevertheless, in some cases at least, ritual does produce, in Homans' terms, "a practical result on the world" external not only to the social unit composed of those who participate together in ritual performances but also to the larger unit composed of those who entertain similar beliefs concerning the universe. The material presented here will show that the ritual cycles of the Tsembaga, and of other local territorial groups of Maring speakers living in the New Guinea interior, play an important part in regulating the relationships of these groups with both the nonhuman components of their immediate environments and the human components of their less immediate environments, that is, with other similar territorial groups.[3] To be more specific, this regulation helps to maintain the biotic communities existing within their territories, redistributes land among people and people over land, and limits

---

[1] In the opening passage of this essay, Rappaport critiques functionalism in much the same way Julian Steward did almost thirty years previously. That is, holistic functional explanations do not generally show causes, only interrelations among parts within a system. Functionalists suppose that social systems are only weakly connected with their environments. Rappaport, following the cultural-ecology model, wishes to show that religion, at least among those he studies, is articulated with, and has a profound effect upon, the natural world.

[2] Andrew P. Vayda (b. 1931) was Rappaport's dissertation advisor at Columbia and was in New Guinea with Rappaport when the fieldwork that formed the basis for this essay was done.

[3] One of the principal influences on Rappaport and many other social scientists of the 1960s was general systems theory. This approach, developed primarily by Austrian biologist Ludwig von Bertalanffy (1901–1972), was a way of providing a mathematical description of a physical system. It encouraged anthropologists to examine cultures as systems composed of both human and nonhuman elements. It presumed that the normal state of a system was equilibrium and described the various methods by which systems deviated from states of balance and were returned to them. In this essay, Rappaport describes Tsembaga culture as just such a system, highlighting the role of religious practices as mechanisms that return the system to equilibrium.

the frequency of fighting. In the absence of authoritative political statuses or offices, the ritual cycle likewise provides a means for mobilizing allies when warfare may be undertaken. It also provides a mechanism for redistributing local pig surpluses in the form of pork throughout a large regional population while helping to assure the local population of a supply of pork when its members are most in need of high quality protein.

Religious ritual may be defined, for the purposes of this paper, as the prescribed performance of conventionalized acts manifestly directed toward the involvement of nonempirical or supernatural agencies in the affairs of the actors. While this definition relies upon the formal characteristics of the performances and upon the motives for undertaking them, attention will be focused upon the empirical effects of ritual performances and sequences of ritual performances. The religious rituals to be discussed are regarded as neither more nor less than part of the behavioral repertoire employed by an aggregate of organisms in adjusting to its environment.[4]

The data upon which this paper is based were collected during fourteen months of field work among the Tsembaga, one of about twenty local groups of Maring speakers living in the Simbai and Jimi Valleys of the Bismarck Range in the Territory of New Guinea. The size of Maring local groups varies from a little over 100 to 900. The Tsembaga, who in 1963 numbered 204 persons, are located on the south wall of the Simbai Valley. The country in which they live differs from the true highlands in being lower, generally more rugged, and more heavily forested. Tsembaga territory rises, within a total surface area of 3.2 square miles, from an elevation of 2,200 feet at the Simbai river to 7,200 feet at the ridge crest. Gardens are cut in the secondary forests up to between 5,000 and 5,400 feet, above which the area remains in primary forest. Rainfall reaches 150 inches per year.

The Tsembaga have come into contact with the outside world only recently; the first government patrol to penetrate their territory arrived in 1954.[5] They were considered uncontrolled by the Australian government until 1962, and they remain unmissionized to this day.

The 204 Tsembaga are distributed among five putatively patrilineal clans, which are, in turn, organized into more inclusive groupings on two hierarchical levels below that of the total local group.[b] Internal political structure is highly egalitarian. There are no hereditary or elected chiefs nor are there even "big men" who can regularly coerce or command the support of their clansmen or coresidents in economic or forceful enterprises.

It is convenient to regard the Tsembaga as a population in the ecological sense, that is, as one of the components of a system of trophic[6] exchanges taking place within a bounded area. Tsembaga territory and the biotic community existing upon it may be conveniently viewed as an ecosystem. While it would be permissible arbitrarily to designate the Tsembaga as a population and their territory with its biota as an ecosystem, there are also nonarbitrary reasons for doing so.[7] An ecosystem is a system of material exchanges, and the Tsembaga maintain against other human groups exclusive access to the resources within

---

[4] Notice Rappaport's style—he writes in a scientific trope, frequently referring to those he studies as "biological organisms" rather than people or individuals. His goal is to analyze human behavior in a fashion analogous to that used by biologists examining animal behavior. Ethology, the study of animal behavior, was becoming an increasingly important field within biology at this time. Austrian ethologist Konrad Lorenz (1901–1989) published his popular account of animal behavior, *King Solomon's Ring*, in 1952. This had an important impact on many scholars in this era.

[5] A criticism sometimes made of this essay (and this style of analysis) is that it makes very little reference to history. This brief paragraph is virtually the only reference to the history of the Tsembaga or their relations with outside (European) powers.

[6] *Trophic:* relating to nutrition.

[7] Notice that Rappaport again treats humans simply as organisms within an ecosystem. Given this, how would Rappaport define culture? See the epilogue to the second edition of Rappaport's book-length treatment of this material, *Pigs for the Ancestors* (1984:371–403).

their territorial borders. Conversely, it is from this territory alone that the Tsembaga ordinarily derive all of their foodstuffs and most of the other materials they require for survival. Less anthropocentrically, it may be justified to regard Tsembaga territory with its biota as an ecosystem in view of the rather localized nature of cyclical material exchanges in tropical rainforests.

As they are involved with the nonhuman biotic community within their territory in a set of trophic exchanges, so do they participate in other material relationships with other human groups external to their territory. Genetic materials are exchanged with other groups, and certain crucial items, such as stone axes, were in the past obtained from the outside. Furthermore, in the area occupied by the Maring speakers, more than one local group is usually involved in any process, either peaceful or warlike, through which people are redistributed over land and land redistributed among people.

The concept of the ecosystem, though it provides a convenient frame for the analysis of interspecific trophic exchanges taking place within limited geographical areas, does not comfortably accommodate intraspecific exchanges taking place over wider geographic areas. Some sort of geographic population model would be more useful for the analysis of the relationship of the local ecological population to the larger regional population of which it is a part, but we lack even a set of appropriate terms for such a model. Suffice it here to note that the relations of the Tsembaga to the total of other local human populations in their vicinity are similar to the relations of local aggregates of other animals to the totality of their species occupying broader and more or less continuous regions. This larger, more inclusive aggregate may resemble what geneticists mean by the term population, that is, an aggregate of interbreeding organisms persisting through an indefinite number of generations

and either living or capable of living in isolation from similar aggregates of the same species. This is the unit which survives through long periods of time while its local ecological (*sensu stricto*)[8] subunits, the units more or less independently involved in interspecific trophic exchanges such as the Tsembaga, are ephemeral.

Since it has been asserted that the ritual cycles of the Tsembaga regulate relationships within what may be regarded as a complex system, it is necessary, before proceeding to the ritual cycle itself, to describe briefly, and where possible in quantitative terms, some aspects of the place of the Tsembaga in this system.[9]

All gardens are mixed, many of them containing all of the major root crops and many greens. Two named garden types are, however, distinguished by the crops which predominate in them. "Taro-yam gardens" were found to produce, on the basis of daily harvest records kept on entire gardens for close to one year, about 5,300,000 calories[c] per acre during their harvesting lives of 18 to 24 months; 85 percent of their yield is harvested between 24 and 76 weeks after planting. "Sugar-sweet potato gardens" produce about 4,600,000 calories per acre during their harvesting lives, 91 percent being taken between 24 and 76 weeks after planting. I estimated that approximately 310,000 calories per acre is expended on cutting, fencing, planting, maintaining, harvesting, and walking to and from taro-yam gardens. Sugar-sweet potato gardens required an expenditure of approximately 290,000 calories per acre.[d] These energy ratios, approximately 17:1 on taro-yam gardens and 16:1 on sugar-sweet potato gardens, compare favorably with figures reported for swidden cultivation in other regions.[e]

Intake is high in comparison with the reported dietaries of other New Guinea populations. On the basis of daily consumption records kept for ten

---

[8] *Sensu stricto:* Latin for strictly speaking.

[9] Rappaport's description focuses on those aspects of Tsembaga life that are of direct concern to his theoretical approach, particularly gardening. Within this framework, he discusses the Tsembaga as calorie producers and consumers. Note also Rappaport's quantification of data,

which reflects his desire to make his work scientifically rigorous. Subsistence activities form the basis of his analysis. Other cultural features arise as a result of this core or are historically particular and of less analytic importance. Rappaport's treatment is similar to Steward's idea of the culture core.

months on four households numbering in total six-teen persons, I estimated the average daily intake of adult males to be approximately 2,600 calories, and that of adult females to be around 2,200 calories.[10] It may be mentioned here that the Tsembaga are small and short-statured.[11] Adult males average 101 pounds in weight and approximately 58.5 inches in height; the corresponding averages for adult females are 85 pounds and 54.5 inches.[f]

Although 99 percent by weight of the food consumed is vegetable, the protein intake is high by New Guinea standards. The daily protein consumption of adult males from vegetable sources was estimated to be between 43 and 55 grams, of adult females 36 to 48 grams. Even with an adjustment for vegetable sources, these values are slightly in excess of the recently published WHO/FAO daily requirements (Food and Agriculture Organization of the United Nations 1964). The same is true of the younger age categories, although soft and discolored hair, a symptom of protein deficiency, was noted in a few children. The WHO/FAO protein requirements do not include a large "margin for safety" or allowance for stress; and, although no clinical assessments were undertaken, it may be suggested that the Tsembaga achieve nitrogen balance at a low level. In other words, their protein intake is probably marginal.[12]

Measurements of all gardens made during 1962 and of some gardens made during 1963 indicate that, to support the human population, between .15 and .19 acres are put into cultivation per capita per year. Fallows range from 8 to 45 years. The area in secondary forest comprises approximately 1,000 acres, only 30 to 50 of which are in cultivation at any time. Assuming calories to be the limiting factor, and assuming an unchanging population structure, the territory could support—with no reduction in lengths of fallow and without cutting into the virgin forest from which the Tsembaga extract many important items—between 290 and 397 people if the pig population remained minimal. The size of the pig herd, however, fluctuates widely. Taking Maring pig husbandry procedures into consideration, I have estimated the human carrying capacity[13] of the Tsembaga territory at between 270 and 320 people.

Because the timing of the ritual cycle is bound up with the demography of the pig herd, the place of the pig in Tsembaga adaptation must be examined.[14]

First, being omnivorous, pigs keep residential areas free of garbage and human feces. Second,

---

[10] Rappaport is giving many figures here, but they are based on observation of a small number of people: 16 in four families. In most studies in biology or ecology, this would be a very small sample indeed. What sort of questions does this raise about his conclusions? Despite the small numbers, it should be noted that, at the time this essay was published, it was probably the most detailed and comprehensive body of data ever collected on swidden agriculturalists. In keeping with the biological model on which he based this work, all of the data is available for inspection in the appendices to *Pigs for the Ancestors* (1967).

[11] In *Pigs for the Ancestors* (1967), a picture shows the five-foot, ten-inch Rappaport towering over the Tsembaga.

[12] Rappaport's analysis, clearly materialist, is functionalist rather than Marxist; there is no reference to the evolution of culture in this essay. Further, for Marxists, conflict drives progressive change, but for Rappaport, conflict is a feature that returns the cultural system to a state of equilibrium.

[13] Rappaport again uses a concept borrowed from biology—carrying capacity, which is the number of individuals of a species that a given ecosystem can support without suffering degradation. Notice that for humans, the technology of food production must be taken into account, a point also discussed by Steward.

[14] When Rappaport did his graduate training at Columbia, thinking there was dominated by the ideas of White and Steward. Rappaport thus went into the field with a background in cultural ecology. Once there, his experiences compelled him to take a position in some ways more extreme than these classic cultural ecologists. Steward had supposed that, though environment had a profound impact on human society, humans were, in fundamental ways, so different from other creatures that natural laws that applied to populations of other animals could not be applied to them. (This view was consistent with his training in historical particularism.) Rappaport, on the other hand, came to believe that while the human possession of culture does separate us from other animals, as biological organisms we are subject to the same fundamental laws. In this essay he repeatedly compares humans to other species.

limited numbers of pigs rooting in secondary growth may help to hasten the development of that growth. The Tsembaga usually permit pigs to enter their gardens one and a half to two years after planting, by which time second-growth trees are well established there. The Tsembaga practice selective weeding; from the time the garden is planted, herbaceous species are removed, but tree species are allowed to remain. By the time cropping is discontinued and the pigs are let in, some of the trees in the garden are already ten to fifteen feet tall. These well-established trees are relatively impervious to damage by the pigs, which, in rooting for seeds and remaining tubers, eliminate many seeds and seedlings that, if allowed to develop, would provide some competition for the established trees. Moreover, in some Maring-speaking areas swiddens are planted twice, although this is not the case with the Tsembaga. After the first crop is almost exhausted, pigs are penned in the garden, where their rooting eliminates weeds and softens the ground, making the task of planting for a second time easier. The pigs, in other words, are used as cultivating machines.

Small numbers of pigs are easy to keep. They run free during the day and return home at night to receive their ration of garbage and substandard tubers, particularly sweet potatoes. Supplying the latter requires little extra work, for the substandard tubers are taken from the ground in the course of harvesting the daily ration for humans. Daily consumption records kept over a period of some months show that the ration of tubers received by the pigs approximates in weight that consumed by adult humans, i.e., a little less than three pounds per day per pig.

If the pig herd grows large, however, the substandard tubers incidentally obtained in the course of harvesting for human needs become insufficient, and it becomes necessary to harvest especially for the pigs. In other words, people must work for the pigs and perhaps even supply them with food fit for human consumption. Thus, as Vayda, Leeds, and Smith (1961:71) have pointed out, there can be too many pigs for a given community.

This also holds true of the sanitary and cultivating services rendered by pigs. A small number of pigs is sufficient to keep residential areas clean, to suppress superfluous seedlings in abandoned gardens, and to soften the soil in gardens scheduled for second plantings. A larger herd, on the other hand, may be troublesome; the larger the number of pigs, the greater the possibility of their invasion of producing gardens, with concomitant damage not only to crops and young secondary growth but also to the relations between the pig owners and garden owners.

All male pigs are castrated at approximately three months of age, for boars, people say, are dangerous and do not grow as large as barrows. Pregnancies, therefore, are always the result of unions of domestic sows with feral males. Fecundity is thus only a fraction of its potential. During one twelve-month period only fourteen litters resulted out of a potential 99 or more pregnancies. Farrowing generally takes place in the forest and mortality of the young is high. Only 32 of the offspring of the above mentioned fourteen pregnancies were alive six months after birth. This number is barely sufficient to replace the number of adult animals which would have died or been killed during most years without pig festivals.

The Tsembaga almost never kill domestic pigs outside of ritual contexts. In ordinary times, when there is no pig festival in progress, the rituals are almost always associated with misfortunes or emergencies, notably warfare, illness, injury, or death. Rules state not only the contexts in which pigs are to be ritually slaughtered, but also who may partake of the flesh of the sacrificial animals. During warfare it is only the men participating in the fighting who eat the pork. In cases of illness or injury, it is only the victim and certain near relatives, particularly his co-resident agnates and spouses, who do so.

It is reasonable to assume that misfortune and emergency are likely to induce in the organisms experiencing them a complex of physiological changes known collectively as "stress." Physiological stress reactions occur not only in organisms which are infected with disease or traumatized, but also in those experiencing rage or fear (Houssay et al. 1955:1096), or even prolonged anxiety (National Research Council 1963:53). One important aspect of stress is the increased catabolization of protein (Houssay et al. 1955:451; National Research Council

1963:49), with a net loss of nitrogen from the tissues (Houssay et al. 1955:450).[15] This is a serious matter for organisms with a marginal protein intake. Antibody production is low (Berg 1948:311), healing is slow (Large and Johnston 1948:352), and a variety of symptoms of a serious nature are likely to develop (Lund and Levenson 1948:349; Zintel 1964:1043). The status of a protein-depleted animal, however, may be significantly improved in a relatively short period of time by the intake of high quality protein, and high protein diets are therefore routinely prescribed for surgical patients and those suffering from infectious diseases (Burton 1959:231; Lund and Levenson 1948:350; Elman 1951:85ff.; Zintel 1964:1043ff.).

It is precisely when they are undergoing physiological stress that the Tsembaga kill and consume their pigs, and it should be noted that they limit the consumption to those likely to be experiencing stress most profoundly.[8] The Tsembaga, of course, know nothing of physiological stress. Native theories of the etiology and treatment of disease and injury implicate various categories of spirits to whom sacrifices must be made. Nevertheless, the behavior which is appropriate in terms of native understandings is also appropriate to the actual situation confronting the actors.

We may now outline in the barest of terms the Tsembaga ritual cycle. Space does not permit a description of its ideological correlates. It must suffice to note that the Tsembaga do not necessarily perceive all of the empirical effects which the anthropologist sees to flow from their ritual behavior. Such empirical consequences as they may perceive, moreover, are not central to their rationalizations of the performances. The Tsembaga say that they perform the rituals in order to rearrange their relationships with the supernatural world. We may only reiterate here that behavior undertaken in reference to their "cognized environment"—an environment which includes as very important elements the spirits of ancestors—seems appropriate in their "operational environment," the material environment specified by the anthropologist through operations of observation, including measurement.[16]

Since the rituals are arranged in a cycle, description may commence at any point.[17] The operation of the cycle becomes clearest if we begin with the rituals performed during warfare. Opponents in all cases occupy adjacent territories, in almost all cases on the same valley wall. After hostilities have broken out, each side performs certain rituals which place the opposing side in the formal category of "enemy." A number of taboos prevail while hostilities continue. These include prohibitions on sexual intercourse and on the ingestion of certain things—food prepared by women, food grown on the lower portion of the territory, marsupials, eels, and while actually on the fighting ground, any liquid whatsoever.

---

[15] One element of Rappaport's argument is that pig consumption is driven by exceptional demand for protein. This is based on the idea that humans in crisis situations or about to do strenuous work experience a physiological need for protein. Even when this article was written, in 1967, this was a controversial position, and there was evidence in the scientific literature pointing against it (see Keys 1943, 1946; Mayer and Bullen 1960). Today, most nutritionists would probably agree that what people in these conditions need is not protein but carbohydrates. Rappaport reconsidered the protein issue in the appendix of the 1984 edition of *Pigs for the Ancestors* and suggested that he was probably mistaken about protein intake, but for a different reason—further fieldwork revealed that the stressed person generally does not get to eat much of the pig sacrificed for him.

[16] The focus of much of Rappaport's work is the relationship between the cognized and operational environments. This distinction is similar to the one Marvin Harris and others have made between etic and emic analysis (see essay 21, footnote 5). Although this essay focuses on describing the Tsembaga in ecosystem terms, *Pigs for the Ancestors* contains an extensive treatment of the Tsembaga's understanding of their environment.

[17] The idea of a cycle is quite important and again relates to developments in biology in the 1960s. Biologists viewed ecosystems in terms of nutrient cycles. Rappaport applies the same sort of logic to the system he describes here. Note, however, that Rappaport was in the field for only fourteen months, from October 1962 to December 1963. He was thus unable to observe a single complete cycle, which takes place over a period of a decade or more.

One ritual practice associated with fighting which may have some physiological consequences deserves mention. Immediately before proceeding to the fighting ground, the warriors eat heavily salted pig fat. The ingestion of salt, coupled with the taboo on drinking, has the effect of shortening the fighting day, particularly since the Maring prefer to fight only on bright sunny days. When everyone gets unbearably thirsty, according to informants, fighting is broken off.

There may formerly have been other effects if the native salt contained sodium (the production of salt was discontinued some years previous to the field work, and no samples were obtained). The Maring diet seems to be deficient in sodium. The ingestion of large amounts of sodium just prior to fighting would have permitted the warriors to sweat normally without a lowering of blood volume and consequent weakness during the course of the fighting. The pork belly ingested with the salt would have provided them with a new burst of energy two hours or so after the commencement of the engagement. After fighting was finished for the day, lean pork was consumed, offsetting, at least to some extent, the nitrogen loss associated with the stressful fighting (personal communications from F. Dunn, W. McFarlane, and J. Sabine, 1965).

Fighting could continue sporadically for weeks. Occasionally it terminated in the rout of one of the antagonistic groups, whose survivors would take refuge with kinsmen elsewhere. In such instances, the victors would lay waste to their opponents' groves and gardens, slaughter their pigs, and burn their houses. They would not, however, immediately annex the territory of the vanquished. The Maring say that they never take over the territory of an enemy for, even if it has been abandoned, spirits of their ancestors remain to guard it against interlopers. Most fights, however, terminated in truces between the antagonists.

With the termination of hostilities a group which has not been driven off its territory performs a ritual called "planting the *rumbim*." Every man puts his hand on the ritual plant, rumbim (*Cordyline fruticosa* (L.), A. Chev; C. *terminalis*, Kunth), as it is planted in the ground. The ancestors are addressed, in effect, as follows:[18]

> We thank you for helping us in the fight and permitting us to remain on our territory. We place our souls in this *rumbim* as we plant it on our ground. We ask you to care for this *rumbim*. We will kill pigs for you now, but they are few. In the future, when we have many pigs, we shall again give you pork and uproot the *rumbim* and stage a *kaiko* (pig festival). But until there are sufficient pigs to repay you the *rumbim* will remain in remain the ground.

This ritual is accompanied by the wholesale slaughter of pigs. Only juveniles remain alive. All adult and adolescent animals are killed, cooked, and dedicated to the ancestors. Some are consumed by the local group, but most are distributed to allies who assisted in the fight.

Some of the taboos which the group suffered during the time of fighting are abrogated by this ritual. Sexual intercourse is now permitted, liquids may be taken at any time, and food from any part of the territory may be eaten. But the group is still in debt to its allies and ancestors. People say it is still the time of the *bamp ku*, or "fighting stones," which are actual objects used in the rituals associated with warfare. Although the fighting ceases when *rumbim* is planted, the concomitant obligations, debts to allies and ancestors, remain outstanding; and the fighting stones may not be put away until these obligations are fulfilled. The time of the fighting stones is a time of debt and danger which lasts until the *rumbim* is uprooted and a pig festival (*kaiko*) is staged.

---

[18] Notice that Rappaport does not report what people *said* on a particular occasion, but rather the kind of thing they are *likely to say*. He cannot report verbatim because he was not present at a *rumbim* planting. Anthropologists who view culture in primarily mentalistic terms, such as structuralists and ethnoscientists, would have trouble with such a reconstruction. They would most likely be concerned with the specifics of *rumbim* symbolism and would see such a reconstruction as doing violence to the data. Because Rappaport's view of culture is primarily materialistic, the reconstruction adds a bit of ethnographic interest and is largely irrelevant to the data.

Certain taboos persist during the time of the fighting stones. Marsupials, regarded as the pigs of the ancestors of the high ground, may not be trapped until the debt to their masters has been repaid. Eels, the "pigs of the ancestors of the low ground," may neither be caught nor consumed. Prohibitions on all intercourse with the enemy come into force. One may not touch, talk to, or even look at a member of the enemy group, nor set foot on enemy ground. Even more important, a group may not attack another group while its ritual plant remains in the ground, for it has not yet fully rewarded its ancestors and allies for their assistance in the last fight. Until the debts to them have been paid, further assistance from them will not be forthcoming. A kind of "truce of god" thus prevails until the *rumbim* is uprooted and a *kaiko* completed.[19]

To uproot the *rumbim* requires sufficient pigs. How many pigs are sufficient, and how long does it take to acquire them? The Tsembaga say that, if a place is "good," this can take as little as five years; but if a place is "bad," it may require ten years or longer. A bad place is one in which misfortunes are frequent and where, therefore, ritual demands for the killing of pigs arise frequently. A good place is one where such demands are infrequent. In a good place, the increase of the pig herd exceeds the ongoing ritual demands, and the herd grows rapidly. Sooner or later the substandard tubers incidentally obtained while harvesting become insufficient to feed the herd, and additional acreage must be put into production specifically for the pigs.

The work involved in caring for a large pig herd can be extremely burdensome. The Tsembaga herd just prior to the pig festival of 1962–63, when it numbered 169 animals, was receiving 54 percent of all the sweet potatoes and 82 percent of all the manioc harvested. These comprised 35.9 percent by weight of all root crops harvested. This figure is consistent with the difference between the amount of land under cultivation just previous to the pig festival, when the herd was at maximum size, and that immediately afterwards, when the pig herd was at minimum size. The former was 36.1 percent in excess of the latter.[20]

I have estimated, on the basis of acreage yield and energy expenditure figures, that about 45,000 calories per year are expended in caring for one pig 120–150 pounds in size. It is upon women that most of the burden of pig keeping falls. If, from a woman's daily intake of about 2,200 calories, 950 calories are allowed for basal metabolism, a woman has only 1,250 calories a day available for all her activities, which include gardening for her family, child care, and cooking, as well as tending pigs. It is clear that no woman can feed many pigs; only a few had as many as four in their care at the commencement of the festival; and it is not surprising that agitation to uproot the *rumbim* and stage the *kaiko* starts with the wives of the owners of large numbers of pigs.

A large herd is not only burdensome as far as energy expenditure is concerned; it becomes increasingly a nuisance as it expands. The more numerous pigs become, the more frequently are gardens invaded by them. Such events result in

---

[19] Rappaport's description of the relationship between ritual and environment is heavily influenced by cybernetics, which was considered an important new field at the time the essay was written. Cybernetics had begun in the 1940s and was concerned with environmental feedback to automatic devices, specifically antiaircraft guns. By the time Rappaport was writing, the principles of cybernetics were being applied to computers and the human nervous system as well. Here, the ritual planting of the *rumbim* is understood as a switch that turns hostilities off.

[20] Rappaport goes to lengths to prove that the Tsembaga hold festivals when the burden of caring for pigs becomes excessive. Critics ask why the Tsembaga don't control herd size simply by killing and eating pigs when they are too numerous. Rappaport does not address these issues here, preferring to concentrate on the functioning of the *kaiko* rather than its origin, but he did respond to such questions at length in the epilogue to the 1984 edition of *Pigs for the Ancestors*. Functionalism did, of course, have an important effect on Steward and other key thinkers in cultural ecology. They criticized it because it did not give enough attention to the relation between people and their environment (see essay 19) and because it did not produce empirically testable hypotheses. Rappaport's work is, in part, a functional analysis that attempts to respond to these problems.

serious disturbances of local tranquility. The garden owner often shoots, or attempts to shoot, the offending pig; and the pig owner commonly retorts by shooting, or attempting to shoot, either the garden owner, his wife, or one of his pigs. As more and more such events occur, the settlement, nucleated when the herd was small, disperses as people try to put as much distance as possible between their pigs and other people's gardens and between their gardens and other people's pigs. Occasionally this reaches its logical conclusion, and people begin to leave the territory, taking up residence with kinsmen in other local populations.

The number of pigs sufficient to become intolerable to the Tsembaga was below the capacity of the territory to carry pigs. I have estimated that, if the size and structure of the human population remained constant at the 1962–1963 level, a pig population of 140 to 240 animals averaging 100 to 150 pounds in size could be maintained perpetually by the Tsembaga without necessarily inducing environmental degradation. Since the size of the herd fluctuates, even higher cyclical maxima could be achieved. The level of toleration, however, is likely always to be below the carrying capacity, since the destructive capacity of the pigs is dependent upon the population density of both people and pigs, rather than upon population size. The denser the human population, the fewer pigs will be required to disrupt social life. If the carrying capacity is exceeded, it is likely to be exceeded by people and not by pigs.

The *kaiko* or pig festival, which commences with the planting of stakes at the boundary and the uprooting of the *rumbim*, is thus triggered by either the additional work attendant upon feeding pigs or the destructive capacity of the pigs themselves. It may be said, then, that there are sufficient pigs to stage the *kaiko* when the relationship of pigs to people changes from one of mutualism to one of parasitism or competition.[21]

A short time prior to the uprooting of the *rumbim*, stakes are planted at the boundary. If the enemy has continued to occupy its territory, the stakes are planted at the boundary which existed before the fight. If, on the other hand, the enemy has abandoned its territory, the victors may plant their stakes at a new boundary which encompasses areas previously occupied by the enemy. The Maring say, to be sure, that they never take land belonging to an enemy, but this land is regarded as vacant, since no *rumbim* was planted on it after the last fight. We may state here a rule of land redistribution in terms of the ritual cycle: *If one of a pair of antagonistic groups is able to uproot its rumbim before its opponents can plant their rumbim, it may occupy the latter's territory.*[22]

Not only have the vanquished abandoned their territory; it is assumed that it has also been abandoned by their ancestors as well. The surviving members of the erstwhile enemy group have by this time resided with other groups for a number of years, and most if not all of them have already had occasion to sacrifice pigs to their ancestors at their new residences. In so doing they have invited these spirits to settle at the new locations of the living, where they will in the future receive sacrifices. Ancestors of vanquished groups thus relinquish their guardianship over the territory, making it available to victorious groups. Meanwhile, the *de facto* membership of the living in the groups with which they have taken refuge is converted eventually into *de jure* membership.[23] Sooner or later the groups with which they have taken up residence will have occasion to plant *rumbim*, and the refugees, as co-residents, will participate, thus ritually validating their connection to the new territory and the new group. *A rule of population redistribution*

---

[21] Here Rappaport again relies on the vocabulary of biology. *Mutualism* is a relationship between any two species in which both species benefit. *Parasitism* is such a relationship in which only one benefits.

[22] In this paragraph and below, Rappaport builds a formal model (or part of one) by stating a series of rules. This is similar to White's style of writing (see essay 18). Unlike White, whose rules are evolutionary and intended to apply to all cultures, however, Rappaport's rules are specific to Tsembaga culture and say nothing about the long-term direction of cultural change.

[23] *De facto* means "in actuality," *de jure* means "in law."

may thus be stated in terms of ritual cycles: A man becomes a member of a territorial group by participating with it in the planting of rumbim.[24]

The uprooting of the *rumbim* follows shortly after the planting of stakes at the boundary. On this particular occasion the Tsembaga killed 32 pigs out of their herd of 169. Much of the pork was distributed to allies and affines outside of the local group.

The taboo on trapping marsupials was also terminated at this time.[25] Information is lacking concerning the population dynamics of the local marsupials, but it may well be that the taboo which had prevailed since the last fight—that against taking them in traps—had conserved a fauna which might otherwise have become extinct.

The *kaiko* continues for about a year, during which period friendly groups are entertained from time to time. The guests receive presents of vegetable foods, and the hosts and male guests dance together throughout the night.

These events may be regarded as analogous to aspects of the social behavior of many non-human animals. First of all, they include massed epigamic,[26] or courtship, displays (Wynne-Edwards 1962:17). Young women are presented with samples of the eligible males of local groups with which they may not otherwise have had the opportunity to become familiar. The context, moreover, permits the young women to discriminate amongst this sample in terms of both endurance (signaled by how vigorously and how long a man dances) and wealth (signaled by the richness of a man's shell and feather finery).

More importantly, the massed dancing at these events may be regarded as epideictic display,[27] communicating to the participants information concerning the size or density of the group (Wynne-Edwards 1962:16). In many species such displays take place as a prelude to actions which adjust group size or density, and such is the case among the Maring. The massed dancing of the visitors at a *kaiko* entertainment communicates to the hosts, while the *rumbim* truce is still in force, information concerning the amount of support they may expect from the visitors in the bellicose enterprises that they are likely to embark upon soon after the termination of the pig festival.

Among the Maring there are no chiefs or other political authorities capable of commanding the support of a body of followers, and the decision to assist another group in warfare rests with each individual male. Allies are not recruited by appealing for help to other local groups as such. Rather, each member of the groups primarily involved in the hostilities appeals to his cognatic and affinal kinsmen in other local groups. These men, in turn, urge other of their co-residents and kinsmen to "help them fight." The channels through which invitations to dance are extended are precisely those through which appeals for military support are issued. The invitations go not from group to group, but from kinsman to kinsman, the recipients of invitations urging their co-residents to "help them dance."

Invitations to dance do more than exercise the channels through which allies are recruited; they provide a means for judging their effectiveness. Dancing and fighting are regarded as in some sense equivalent. This equivalence is expressed in the similarity of some pre-fight and pre-dance rituals, and the Maring say that those who come to dance come to fight. The size of a visiting dancing contingent is consequently taken as a measure of the size of the contingent of warriors whose assistance may be expected in the next round of warfare.[28]

---

[24] In a personal communication Rappaport noted that participating in the planting of a *rumbim* is how the Tsembaga themselves understand becoming a member of a territorial group. What is important for Rappaport's approach, however, is that participation in this ceremony provides a clear operational and behavioral way of determining group membership, whether perceived that way by the Tsembaga or not.

[25] Notice that Rappaport suggests that other aspects of the system he has identified also serve ecological functions.

[26] *Epigamic:* related to the mating of animals and particularly the use of color to attract the opposite sex.

[27] *Epideictic:* in ornithology, this refers to collective displays and other conventional behaviors, which are believed to have evolved from the need to control population.

[28] Notice that the flow of information is important in Rappaport's description. Information theory, developed in the 1950s, provided a way of expressing the transmission of certain types of information in energy terms. It was

In the morning the dancing ground turns into a trading ground. The items most frequently exchanged include axes, bird plumes, shell ornaments, an occasional baby pig, and, in former times, native salt. The *kaiko* thus facilitates trade by providing a market-like setting in which large numbers of traders can assemble. It likewise facilitates the movement of two critical items, salt and axes, by creating a demand for the bird plumes which may be exchanged for them.

The *kaiko* concludes with major pig sacrifices. On this particular occasion the Tsembaga butchered 105 adult and adolescent pigs, leaving only 60 juveniles and neonates alive. The survival of an additional fifteen adolescents and adults was only temporary, for they were scheduled as imminent victims. The pork yielded by the Tsembaga slaughter was estimated to weigh between 7,000 and 8,500 pounds, of which between 4,500 and 6,000 pounds were distributed to members of other local groups in 163 separate presentations. An estimated 2,000 to 3,000 people in seventeen local groups were the beneficiaries of the redistribution. The presentations, it should be mentioned, were not confined to pork. Sixteen Tsembaga men presented bridewealth or child-wealth, consisting largely of axes and shells, to their affines at this time.[29]

The *kaiko* terminates on the day of the pig slaughter with the public presentation of salted pig belly to allies of the last fight. Presentations are made through the window in a high ceremonial fence built specially for the occasion at one end of the dance ground. The name of each honored man is announced to the assembled multitude as he charges to the window to receive his hero's portion. The fence is then ritually torn down, and the fighting stones are put away. The pig festival and the ritual cycle have been completed, demonstrating, it may be suggested, the ecological and economic competence of the local population. The local population would now be free, if it were not for the presence of the government, to attack its enemy again, secure in the knowledge that the assistance of allies and ancestors would be forthcoming because they have received pork and the obligations to them have been fulfilled.[30]

Usually fighting did break out again very soon after the completion of the ritual cycle. If peace still prevailed when the ceremonial fence had rotted completely—a process said to take about three years, a little longer than the length of time required to raise a pig to maximum size—*rumbim* was planted as if there had been a fight, and all adult and adolescent pigs were killed. When the pig herd was large enough so that the *rumbim* could be uprooted, peace could be made with former enemies if they were also able to dig out their *rumbim*. To put this in formal terms: *If a pair of antagonistic groups proceeds through two ritual cycles without resumption of hostilities their enmity may be terminated.*[h]

The relations of the Tsembaga with their environment have been analyzed as a complex system composed of two subsystems. What may be called the "local subsystem" has been derived from the relations of the Tsembaga with the nonhuman components of their immediate or territorial environment. It corresponds to the ecosystem in which the Tsembaga participate. A second subsystem, one which corresponds to the larger regional

---

useful because, in principle, when combined with nutritional analysis, it provided a way of measuring the flow of both food and information through a cultural system in terms of energy. In practice, it proved extremely difficult to apply.

[29] Rappaport, here and above, briefly mentions the economic functions of the *kaiko* but does not elaborate upon them, and below he mentions some specifics about how pork is distributed. Rappaport frequently supplies ethnographic details, like Steward, but they play a different role for each researcher. For Steward, details of ceremonies are generally secondary cultural

features determined by the specific history of the group and therefore not meaningful for analysis. For Rappaport, they are part of the critical interface between culture and environment.

[30] The Tsembaga were under the administration of the Australian government when Rappaport worked among them, and the government had suppressed fighting among the different groups. Rappaport describes a *kaiko* festival he witnessed. However, he was unable to witness the cycle of warfare that led to it, which took place before his arrival. This element of his description is thus reconstructed from the memories of informants he interviewed.

population of which the Tsembaga are one of the constituent units and which may be designated as the "regional subsystem," has been derived from the relations of the Tsembaga with neighboring local populations similar to themselves.[31]

It has been argued that rituals, arranged in repetitive sequences, regulate relations both within each of the subsystems and within the larger complex system as a whole. The timing of the ritual cycle is largely dependent upon changes in the states of the components of the local subsystem. But the *kaiko*, which is the culmination of the ritual cycle, does more than reverse changes which have taken place within the local subsystem. Its occurrence also affects relations among the components of the regional subsystem. During its performance, obligations to other local populations are fulfilled, support for future military enterprises is rallied, and land from which enemies have earlier been driven is occupied. Its completion, furthermore, permits the local population to initiate warfare again. Conversely, warfare is terminated by rituals which preclude the reinitiation of warfare until the state of the local subsystem is again such that a *kaiko* may be staged and completed. Ritual among the Tsembaga and other Maring, in short, operates as both transducer, "translating" changes in the state of one subsystem into information which can effect changes in a second subsystem, and homeostat, maintaining a number of variables which in sum comprise the total system within ranges of viability. To repeat an earlier assertion, the operation of ritual among the Tsembaga and

other Maring helps to maintain an undegraded environment, limits fighting to frequencies which do not endanger the existence of the regional population, adjusts man-land ratios, facilitates trade, distributes local surpluses of pig throughout the regional population in the form of pork, and assures people of high quality protein when they are most in need of it.[32]

Religious rituals and the supernatural orders toward which they are directed cannot be assumed *a priori* to be mere epiphenomena.[33] Ritual may, and doubtless frequently does, do nothing more than validate and intensify the relationships which integrate the social unit, or symbolize the relationships which bind the social unit to its environment. But the interpretation of such presumably *sapiens*-specific phenomena as religious ritual within a framework which will also accommodate the behavior of other species shows, I think, that religious ritual may do much more than symbolize, validate, and intensify relationships. Indeed, it would not be improper to refer to the Tsembaga and the other entities with which they share their territory as a "ritually regulated ecosystem," and to the Tsembaga and their human neighbors as a "ritually regulated population."[34]

NOTES

[a]The field work upon which this paper is based was supported by a grant from the National Science Foundation, under which Professor A. P. Vayda was principal investigator. Personal support was received by the author from the National Institutes of Health. Earlier versions of this paper were presented at the 1964

---

[31] In this paper, due to space limitations imposed by the original publication format, Rappaport tells us little about data collection. In his book-length treatment of this material, however, he includes a good deal of information on data collection and extensive appendices with raw data. Rappaport was unusual for his time. Most ethnographic work of this era did not include this sort of information and was strongly criticized on that basis by anthropologists in the 1970s and 1980s.

[32] When Rappaport's work on the Tsembaga was published in the late 1960s, it fell on fertile ground. It seemed to many to demonstrate the ecological soundness and wisdom of traditional society. This idea was appealing in the late 1960s

and the 1970s, when many in academia were concerned with ecology and the value of traditional communities and folks were busy developing communes. As these ideas fell out of popularity and political conservatism became increasingly dominant, criticism of his work grew.

[33] *Epiphenomena:* secondary events.

[34] The functions Rappaport identifies for religion here fit well with those Bronislaw Malinowski noted in his work among the people of the Trobriand Islands. Although Rappaport's work is limited to the Maring, it may suggest to readers that ecological, homeostatic functions be looked for in other religions as well.

annual meeting of the American Anthropological Association in Detroit, and before a Columbia University seminar on Ecological Systems and Cultural Evolution. I have received valuable suggestions from Alexander Alland, Jacques Barrau, William Clarke, Paul Collins, C. Glen King, Marvin Harris, Margaret Mead, M. J. Meggitt, Ann Rappaport, John Street, Marjorie Whiting, Cherry Vayda, A. P. Vayda and many others, but I take full responsibility for the analysis presented herewith.

[b] The social organization of the Tsembaga will be described in detail elsewhere.

[c] Because the length of time in the field precluded the possibility of maintaining harvest records on single gardens from planting through abandonment, figures were based, in the case of both "taro-yam" and "sugar-sweet potato" gardens, on three separate gardens planted in successive years. Conversions from the gross weight to the caloric value of the yield were made by reference to the literature. The sources used are listed in Rappaport (1966: Appendix VIII).

[d] Rough time and motion studies of each of the tasks involved in making, maintaining, harvesting, and walking to and from gardens were undertaken. Conversion to energy expenditure values was accomplished by reference to energy expenditure tables prepared by Hipsley and Kirk (1965:43) on the basis of gas exchange measurements made during the performance of garden tasks by the Chimbu people of the New Guinea highlands.

[e] Marvin Harris, in an unpublished paper, estimates the ratio of energy return to energy input on Dyak (Borneo) rice swiddens at 10:1. His estimates of energy ratios on Tepoltzlan (Meso-America) swiddens range from 13:1 on poor land to 29:1 on the best land.

[f] Heights may be inaccurate. Many men wear their hair in large coiffures hardened with pandanus grease, and it was necessary in some instances to estimate the location of the top of the skull.

[g] The possible significance of pork consumption by protein-short people during periods of physiological stress was unknown to me while I was in the field. I did not, therefore, investigate this matter in full detail. Georgeda Bick and Cherry Vayda, who visited the Maring area in 1966, have investigated the circumstances surrounding pork consumption further, and will publish their more detailed materials elsewhere.

[h] After this article had gone to press in *Ethnology*, where it was originally published, I learned from A. P. Vayda, who spent the summer of 1966 in the Maring area, that he received somewhat different accounts of peace-making mechanisms, both from informants in other Maring local groups and from the Tsembaga man who had supplied me with the only full account which I was able to obtain (details of his account were, however, corroborated by information obtained from other Tsem-

baga men). According to Vayda's account, when the ceremonial fence had rotted away completely, some, but not all, adult and adolescent pigs were slain and offered to certain ancestral spirits to insure the health and fecundity of the remaining pigs, and no *rumbim* was planted. When the herds of the erstwhile antagonists again reached maximum size peace could be made.

It is important to note here that the other rituals treated in this paper were either observed by me or described by a number of informants who had participated in them, but none of either Vayda's informants or mine had ever participated in peace-making procedures, for none had taken place during the adult life of any of them. They were only reporting what they remembered from their childhood or what they had heard from their fathers or grandfathers. It is likely, therefore, that none of the informants are particularly well-versed in the details of the procedure. However, it is also important to note that all of the informants are in basic agreement upon what is in the present context the most important aspects of peace-making: that the rituals were not performed until pig herds of the erstwhile antagonists had reached maximum size. The rule which I have proposed would seem to stand if it is understood that the second ritual cycle of the sequence may differ from the first in that *rumbim* might not be planted, and if it is understood that the truce may not be sanctified during the second cycle of the sequence.

REFERENCES

Berg, C. 1948. Protein deficiency and its relation to nutritional anemia, hypoproteinemia, nutritional edema, and resistance to infection. *In* Protein and amino acids in nutrition, ed. M. Sahyun, pp. 290–317. New York: Reinhold.

Burton, B. T., ed. 1959. The Heinz handbook of nutrition. New York: McGraw-Hill.

Elman, R. 1951. Surgical Care. New York: Appleton-Century-Crofts.

Food and Agriculture Organization of the United Nations. 1964. Protein: At the heart of the world food problem. World Food Problems 5. Rome: FAO.

Hipsley, E., and N. Kirk. 1965. Studies of the dietary intake and energy expenditure of New Guineans. South Pacific Commission, Technical Paper 147. Noumea: South Pacific Commission.

Homans, G. C. 1941. Anxiety and ritual: The theories of Malinowski and Radcliffe-Brown. American Anthropologist 43:164–172.

Houssay, B. A., et al. 1955. Human physiology, 2nd ed. New York: McGraw-Hill.

Large, A., and C. G. Johnston. 1948. Proteins as related to burns. *In* Proteins and amino acids in nutrition, ed. M. Sahyun, pp. 386–396. New York: Reinhold.

Lund, C. G., and S. M. Levenson. 1948. Protein nutrition in surgical patients. *In* Proteins and amino acids in nutrition, ed. M. Sahyun, pp. 349–363. New York: Reinhold.

Moore, O. K. 1957. Divination—a new perspective. American Anthropologist 59:69–74.

National Research Council. 1963. Evaluation of protein quality. National Academy of Sciences—National Research Council Publication 1100. Washington: NAS/NRC.

Rappaport, R. A. 1966. Ritual in the ecology of a New Guinea people. Unpublished doctoral dissertation. Columbia University.

Vayda, A. P., A. Leeds, and D. B. Smith. 1961. The place of pigs in Melanesian subsistence. In proceedings of the 1961 Annual Spring Meeting of the American Ethnological Society, ed. V. E. Garfield, pp. 69–77. Seattle: University of Washington Press.

Wynne-Edwards V. C. 1962. Animal dispersion in relation to social behavior. Edinburgh and London: Oliver & Boyd.

Zintel, Harold A. 1964. Nutrition in the care of the surgical patient. *In* Modern nutrition in health and disease. ed. M. G. Wohl and R. S. Goodhart, pp. 1043–1064, 3rd ed. Philadelphia: Lea and Febiger.

23. *Peasantry and Its Problems*

ERIC WOLF (1923–1999)

THIS BOOK IS about peasants; its approach is anthropological. Although anthropology had its beginnings in the investigation of the so-called primitive peoples of the world, in recent years anthropologists have become increasingly interested in rural populations that form part of larger, more complex societies. Where an anthropologist previously examined the life-ways of a roaming band of desert hunters or of migratory cultivators occupying a hamlet in some tropical forest, now he often sets himself the task of investigating a village in Ireland, in India, or in China, in areas of the world that have long supported a variegated and rich cultural tradition carried on by many different kinds of people. Among these, rural cultivators constitute only one—though an important—segment. Thus, the people now under anthropological scrutiny are in continuous interaction and communication with other social groups. What goes on in Gopalpur, India or Alcala de la Sierra in Spain cannot be explained in terms of that village alone; the explanation must include consideration both of the outside forces impinging on these villages and of the reactions of villagers to these forces.[1]

From *Peasants* (1966)

---

[1] This essay is the opening chapter of a brief book called *Peasants* (1966). It appeared as part of a series called *The Foundations of Modern Anthropology,* which also included books on hunters, tribesmen, the formation of the state, and numerous other subjects. The series was published for the college market in the mid-1960s and designed to introduce undergraduate students to then current thinking in anthropology. By current-day standards, the opening paragraph seems unexceptional, even commonsensical in its insistence that anthropologists be concerned with outside forces impinging on village life. In its era, however, this statement was considerably more radical. Anthropology in the first half of the twentieth century did have precisely this problem. Anthropologists tended to study communities as if they were self-contained. Although in beginning chapters or forewords ethnographers often referred to the broader setting of the society they were studying, they then tended to focus entirely on the social dynamics within that community. A good example of this is Robert Redfield's work on Chan Kom, a Maya village in the Yucatan. Wolf's work, and other neo-Marxist work from the 1960s to the current day, focuses on the connections and exchanges that bind the local community to the economic aspects of the wider world. Wolf's book is ostensibly aimed at introductory students, but his references show that he clearly has a professional audience in mind as well—the examples in this paragraph are anything but random. Golpalpur refers to Alan R. Beals' 1962 book *Gopalpur: A South Indian Village* (1962), and Alcala de la Sierra refers to Julian Pitt-Rivers' *The People of the Sierra* (1961); both are important and, at that time, recently published ethnographies.

PEASANTS AND PRIMITIVES

Our first question, then, is to ask what distinguishes peasants from the primitives more often studied by anthropologists. We have spoken of peasants as rural cultivators; that is, they raise crops and livestock in the countryside, not in greenhouses in the midst of cities or in aspidistra boxes on the windowsill.[2] At the same time they are not *farmers,* or agricultural entrepreneurs as we know them in the United States. The American farm is primarily a business enterprise, combining factors of production purchased in a market to obtain a profit by selling advantageously in a products market. The peasant, however, does not operate an enterprise in the economic sense; he runs a household, not a business concern. But there are also primitive peoples who live in the countryside and raise crops and livestock. What then is the distinguishing mark of the peasant, as opposed to the primitive cultivator?

One way of approaching this question has been to say that peasants form part of a larger, compound society, whereas a primitive band or tribe does not. But this answer hardly does justice to the question. For primitives seldom live in isolation. There are exceptions, like the Polar Eskimos who were cut off from all outside contact until rediscovered for the larger world by Admiral Peary in his attempt to reach the North Pole. But much more frequently, primitive tribes also entertain relations with their neighbors. Even the simple hunters and gatherers of the Australian deserts maintain ties which bring together groups of people, often widely dispersed, into systematic economic and ritual exchanges. The tribes of the Amazon basin, apparently isolated in separate pockets of the tropical forest, trade with one another, or marry one another, or fight one another—for warfare is indeed also a kind of relationship. We owe to anthropologists like Bronislaw Malinowski, the author of *Argonauts of the Western Pacific* (1922) descriptions and analyses of the trade uniting the east end of New Guinea and the adjacent archipelagoes into a network of ceremonial and commercial transactions. Similarly, the Plains Indians of the United States, we now see, were part and parcel of American history, influenced by the advancing frontier and influencing its advance in turn.

The distinction between primitives and peasants thus does not lie in the greater or lesser outside involvement of one or the other, but in the character of that involvement. Marshall D. Sahlins has characterized the economic and social world of primitives as follows:

> In primitive economies, most production is geared to use of the producers or to discharge of kinship obligations, rather than to exchange and gain. A corollary is that de facto control of the means of production is decentralized, local, and familial in primitive society. The following propositions are then implied: (1) economic relations of coercion and exploitation and the corresponding social relations of dependence and mastery are not created in the system of production; (2) in the absence of the incentive given by exchange of the product against a great quantity of goods on a market, there is a tendency to limit production to goods that can be directly utilized by the producers.[a]

Thus, in primitive society, producers control the means of production, including their own labor, and exchange their own labor and its products for the culturally defined equivalent goods and services of others. In the course of cultural evolution, however, such simple systems have been superseded by others in which control of the means of production, including the disposition of human labor, passes from the hands of the primary producers into the hands of groups that do not carry on the productive process themselves, but assume instead special executive and administrative functions, backed by the use of force. The constitution of society in such a case is no longer based on the equivalent and direct exchanges of goods and services between one group and another; rather, goods and services are first furnished to a center and only later redirected. In primitive society, surpluses are exchanged directly among groups or members of groups; peasants, however, are rural cultivators whose surpluses are

---

[2] *Aspidistra* is a popular indoor plant.

transferred to a dominant group of rulers that uses the surpluses both to underwrite its own standard of living and to distribute the remainder to groups in society that do not farm but must be fed for their specific goods and services in turn.[3]

CIVILIZATION

The development of a complex social order based on a division between rulers and food-producing cultivators is commonly referred to as the development of civilization. Civilization has a long and involved history; the archaeological record indicates a great diversity in the processes which allowed men in different parts of the world to make the transition from primitives to peasants. Nevertheless, gross features of the process stand out. In the Old World, for example, cultivation and animal domestication seem to have been under way in Southwestern Asia as early as 9000 B.C., and it is probable that sedentary farming villages were established in the same area by 6000 B.C. Similarly,

finds in Northeastern Mexico suggest that experiments with food production were begun around 7000 B.C., with full-fledged cultivation firmly established around 1500 B.C. From these or similar original centers, cultivation spread out with variable speed in different directions, being adapted to the demands of new climates and new social exigencies. But not all areas of the world were caught up equally in this process. The people in some areas never accepted cultivation or accepted it only reluctantly, while others forged ahead to attain the new levels of productivity and social organization which permitted the unfolding of the functional division of labor between cultivators and rulers which we have defined as the hallmark of civilization.[4]

CALORIC MINIMA AND SURPLUSES

It is sometimes said that the capacity to sustain a functional division of labor between cultivators and rulers is a simple consequence of the capacity of a society to produce a surplus above and

---

[3] Wolf does not refer directly to Marx in this passage. Nevertheless, it would be difficult to find a more solidly Marxist approach to anthropology in America in this era. In this passage, Wolf clearly defines the peasantry as a specific mode of production. You will recall that the notion of a mode of production is central to Marxist thinking. A mode of production is briefly defined as the set of material factors and social relations that any society uses to produce its sustenance. In this passage Wolf identifies three modes of production: (1) The American farmer whose goal is to use resources to create a profit represents the capitalist mode of production. (2) The primitive who uses resources to supply the family and satisfy kinship demands represents what Marshal Sahlins will call the familial or domestic mode of production (1968). (3) The peasant is defined by a mode of production in which surpluses are siphoned away to rulers with higher standards of living and, largely through them, to nonfarming specialists.

Wolf relies here on the work of Marshal Sahlins (b. 1930). A student of Leslie White, Sahlins was also deeply influenced by Julian Steward. He was one of the co-authors of the critical volume *Evolution and Culture* (1960), which attempted to synthesize the work of Steward and White. Like Wolf, he was deeply affected by Marxist ideas as well as the work of the economist Karl Polanyi (1886–1964; see footnote 6). Sahlins wrote the volume

Tribesman for the "Foundations of Modern Anthropology Series," though this did not appear until 1968, two years after Wolf's volume. He is probably best known for his 1972 book *Stone Age Economics,* in which he presents a materialist analysis of band and tribal societies based on the notion of the domestic mode of production.

[4] Wolf's use of the concept of civilization is striking here and differentiates him clearly from Boasian anthropologists and culture and personality theorists. For Wolf, civilization is a distinct mode of production involving plant and animal domestication and a division of society into social levels. Boasians and culture and personality theorists tended to use *civilization* as synonymous with *culture.* They spoke frequently of "primitive civilization" (for example, Boas 1901:8; Goldenweiser 1917:449; Sapir 1924:416). For them the separation of societies into the primitive and civilized was dangerously ethnocentric. Even current-day anthropologists often prefer the term *state-level-society* to *civilization,* perhaps for this reason. Wolf clearly has no qualms about describing certain types of societies as civilizations. However, for Wolf, as for other neo-Marxists, *civilization* refers to a society with specific social and political characteristics. A principal characteristic of civilization is not that it is superior to other forms of society but that it is more oppressive, as you will see in Wolf's examples below.

beyond the minimum required to sustain life. This minimum can be defined quite rigorously in physiological terms as the daily intake of food calories required to balance the expenditures of energy a man incurs in his daily output of labor. This amount has been put at roughly between 2000 and 3000 calories per person per day. It is probably not amiss to point out that this daily minimum is still not met in most parts of the world. About half the population of the world has an average daily per capita ration of less than 2250 calories. This category includes Indonesia (with 1750 calories), China (with 1800 calories) and India (with 1800 calories). Two-tenths of the world's population fall into the category receiving an average daily per capita ration between 2250 and 2750 calories. This group includes Mediterranean Europe and the Balkan countries. Only three-tenths of the world's population—the United States, the British dominions, Western Europe, and the Soviet Union—attain figures higher than 2750.[b] Even this last achievement must be seen in historical perspective. In the seventeenth century for example, France—now among the fortunate three-tenths—attained the amount of 3000 daily calories per person (represented by half a loaf of bread per day) in only one out of every five years. In the eighteenth century, this accomplishment became possible in one out of four years. In the off years, the average daily ration clearly fell below minimum requirements.[c]

Cultivators must not only furnish themselves with minimal caloric rations; they must also raise enough food beyond this caloric minimum to provide sufficient seed for next year's crop, or to provide adequate feed for their livestock. Thus, for example, a 40-acre farm in Mecklenburg northeastern Germany, during the fourteenth and fifteenth centuries produced 10,200 pounds of grain crops, of which 3400 pounds had to be set aside for seed and 2800 pounds to feed four

horses. More than half of the total yield was thus committed in advance to seed and feed.[d] This amount is therefore not absolute surplus, but an amount destined for the upkeep of the instruments of production. The cultivator had to set aside time and effort to repair his tools, to sharpen his knives, to caulk his storage bin, to fence his yard, to shoe his work animals, perhaps to make and set up a scarecrow to keep the eager birds out of his fields. Moreover, he had to replace such things as a leaky roof, a broken pot, or his clothing when it became too tattered and torn. The amount needed to replace his minimum equipment for both production and consumption was his *replacement fund.*[5]

It is important that we think of this replacement fund not merely in purely technical terms, but in cultural terms as well. The instruments and techniques of a particular technology are the product of a prolonged process of cultural accumulation in the past. There are technologies without pottery or storage bins or work animals. Once a technology has come to include these items, however, they become part and parcel of everyday existence, and hence culturally necessary. Like the Greek philosopher Diogenes, a man can rid himself of his last cup, since he need not suffer thirst as long as he can make a cup of his hands. But once pottery cups are a part of a man's cultural expectations, they become more than that— they become something he must commit himself to obtain. Hence, a drought or an invasion of locusts or any other misfortune which endangers the replacement fund threatens not only a man's minimal biological existence but also his capacity to meet his cultural necessities.

It is conceivable that a cultivator might cease his productive efforts on the land once his caloric minimum and his replacement fund are assured. Thus, for example, the Kuikuru Indians of the Amazon are able to reach their caloric

---

[5] Note Wolf's interest in the caloric production of societies. In "Energy and the Evolution of Culture" (1943), White had argued that culture evolves as the amount of energy it produces increases. For White's students and others, one way of accessing this was through counting how many calories a society could produce. A second of Wolf's concerns is

evident in this passage. He is deeply concerned with world history. In particular, he is concerned with correcting the misapprehension that European societies have always been wealthy and technologically advanced in comparison to the rest of the world. This theme is explored in much greater depth in *Europe and the People Without History* (1982).

minimum and replacement requirements by working only three-and-a-half hours each day, and do not work beyond this time. There are neither technical nor social reasons why they should add additional hours to their daily labor budget.[e] Production beyond the level of the caloric minimum and the replacement level obeys social incentives and dictates. At stake is a major issue in economic anthropology. There are some who argue that the appearance of surpluses generates further development; others hold that potential surpluses are universal and what counts is the institutional means for mobilizing them.[6]

SOCIAL SURPLUSES

Ceremonial Fund

There are two such sets of social imperatives. The first of these occurs in any society. Even where men are largely self-sufficient in food and goods, they must entertain social relations with their fellows. They must, for example, marry outside the household into which they were born, and this requirement means that they must have social contacts with people who are their potential or actual in-laws. They must also join with their fellow men in keeping order, in ensuring the rudimentary acceptances of certain rules of conduct so as to render life predictable and livable. They may be required to help each other in some phase of the food quest. But social relations of any kind are never completely utilitarian and instrumental. Each is always surrounded

with symbolic constructions which serve to explain, to justify, and to regulate it. Thus, a marriage does not involve merely the passage of a spouse from one house to another. It also involves gaining the goodwill of the spouse-to-be and of her kinfolk; it involves a public performance in which the participants act out, for all to see, both the coming of age of the marriage partners and the social realignments which the marriage involves; and it involves also the public exhibition of an ideal model of what marriages—all marriages—ought to do for people and how people should behave once they have been married. All social relations are surrounded by such ceremonial, and ceremonial must be paid for in labor, in goods, or in money. If men are to participate in social relations, therefore, they must also work to establish a fund against which these expenditures may be charged. We shall call this the *ceremonial fund*.

The ceremonial fund of a society—and hence the ceremonial fund of its members—may be large or small. Size is once again a relative matter. The ceremonial funds of Indian villages in Mexico and Peru, for example, are very large when compared to their caloric budgets and their replacement funds, for there a man must expend a great deal of effort and goods in the sponsorship of ceremonials that serve to underline and exemplify the solidarity of the community to which he belongs.[f] Ceremonial expenditures are a matter of cultural tradition, and will vary from culture to culture. Yet everywhere the need to establish and maintain such a ceremonial fund will result in the production of surpluses beyond the replacement fund discussed above.

---

[6] Thus, Wolf argues, biological reproduction is different from cultural reproduction. Reproducing a society is not just providing enough calories for people to live, but enough calories for people to recreate the social and material conditions of their own society. This concern with social reproduction is central to Marxist thought.

In the final two sentences, Wolf refers to a major issue in economic anthropology. This probably refers to the then-current debate between "formalist" and "substantivist" economic anthropologists. Formalists (such as Harold Schneider and Scott Cook) held that the principles of new-

classical Western economics could be used to understand all economic systems ("the appearance of surpluses generates further development"). Substantivists (such as Paul Bohannan and George Dalton) held that economics was conditioned by social institutions ("what counts is the institutional means for mobilizing it"). Substantivist thinkers were deeply influenced by the socialist economic historian Karl Polanyi, whose book *The Great Transformation* (1944) argued that the development of capitalism and free market economics were linked to the historic rise of the nation-state.

It is important at this point, however, to remember that the efforts of a peasantry are not governed wholly by the exigencies internal to its own way of life. A peasantry always exists within a larger system. Hence the size of the effort which it must put forward to replace its means of production or to cover its ceremonial costs is also a function of the ways in which labor is divided within the society to which the peasant belongs, and of the regulations governing that division of labor. Thus, in some societies, the amount of effort required to meet these needs may be quite small. This is true, for example, in a society where a man grows his own food and makes his own basic equipment. For him the amount of surplus required to obtain articles from the outside is reduced; indeed, it is identical with his replacement fund. This is also true in societies where different households manufacture different objects or provide different services that are exchanged in equivalent reciprocal relations. If I grow grain, but do not make my own blankets, I may exchange a given amount of grain for a given number of blankets; the blanket-maker thus gets food in return for his labor. In such situations men obtain goods through exchanges, but—and this is an important but—the amount of food they must grow to get needed blankets or pots is still chargeable to their replacement fund, even though the manner by which they replace goods they do not make themselves is indirect. But it is possible, and increasingly so as societies have grown more complex, that the exchange ratios between units of food produced by the cultivator and units of goods produced are not exchanged in equivalencies determined by the face-to-face negotiation of producer and consumer, but according to asymmetrical ratios of exchange determined by external conditions. Where the networks of exchange are restricted and localized,

the participants must adjust the prices of their goods to the purchasing power of their potential customers. But where exchange networks are far-flung and obey pressures which take no account of the purchasing power of a local population, a cultivator may have to step up his production greatly to obtain even the items that are required for replacement. Under such conditions, a considerable share of the peasant's replacement fund may become somebody else's fund of profit.[7]

Funds of Rent

There is yet a second set of social imperatives which may produce surpluses beyond the caloric minimum and replacement level. The relation of the cultivator to other craft specialists may be symmetrical, as we have seen above. They may exchange different products, but at traditional and long-established ratios. However, there exist in more complex societies social relations which are not symmetrical, but are based, in some form, upon the exercise of power. In the case of the Mecklenburg farm mentioned above, for example, the 4000 pounds of grain left over after the cultivator had subtracted his committed replacement fund for seed and feed were not consumed by the cultivator's household alone. Twenty-seven hundred pounds, or more than half of the effective yield, went in payment of dues to a lord who maintained jurisdiction, or domain, over the land. Only 1300 pounds remained to feed the cultivator and his family, yielding a per capita daily ration of 1600 calories.[8] To sustain minimal caloric levels, therefore, the cultivator was forced to seek additional sources of calories, such as he could derive from his garden or from livestock of his own. This peasant, then, was subject to asymmetrical power relations which made a

---

[7] Here, Wolf once again reminds us of the ways that communities articulate with the outside world. A farmer can exchange food with a blanket maker in a simple system at rates that are equitable for both and which both parties agree too. What happens, however, if, because of global connections, the blanket maker has an opportunity to sell

his wares to wealthy collectors? The price of blankets rises and the farmer is placed in competition with the wealthy collector. The blanket maker has opportunities that are not available (or not equally available) to the farmer, and the producers of blankets will find that their livelihoods will be affected by external forces outside of their control.

permanent charge on his production. Such a charge, paid out as the result of some superior claim to his labor on the land, we call rent, regardless of whether that rent is paid in labor, in produce, or in money. Where someone exercises an effective superior power, or domain, over a cultivator, the cultivator must produce a fund of rent.

It is this production of a fund of rent which critically distinguishes the peasant from the primitive cultivator. This production in turn is spurred by the existence of a social order in which some men can through power demand payments from others, resulting in the transfer of wealth from one section of the population to another. The peasant's loss is the power-holder's gain, for the fund of rent provided by the peasant is part of the fund of power on which the controllers may draw.

It is important to note, though, that there are many different ways in which this fund of rent is produced, and many different ways in which it is siphoned from the peasant stratum into the hands of the controlling group. Since the distinctions in the exercise of this power have important structural effects on the way the peasantry is organized, there are consequently many kinds of peasantry, not just one. So far, then, the term "peasant" denotes no more than an asymmetrical structural relationship between producers of surplus and controllers; to render it meaningful, we must still ask questions about the different sets of conditions which will maintain this structural relationship.

THE ROLE OF THE CITY

The development of civilization has commonly been identified with the development of cities, hence the peasant has commonly been defined as a cultivator who has an enduring relationship with the city. It is certainly true that, in the course of cultural evolution, the rulers have commonly settled in special centers which have often become cities. Yet, in some societies, the rulers merely "camped" among the peasantry, as the Watusi rulers did until very recently among the Bahutu peasantry of Ruanda Urundi. Or the rulers may have lived at religious centers such as tombs or shrines to which produce was brought by the peasantry. In ancient Egypt, the Pharaoh set up his temporary capital near the pyramid being built in his honor; the role of cities remained insignificant. Among the Peten Maya, political integration appears to have been achieved without the emergence of densely settled urban zones.[h] The city is therefore a likely, but not an inevitable, product of the increasing complexity of society. I should like to think of it as a settlement in which a combination of functions are exercised, and which becomes useful because in time greater efficiency is obtained by having these functions concentrated in one site.[8]

Yet there remain very different kinds of cities. In India, until recently, some large settlements contained the castle and power apparatus of military rulers, and served as administrative centers. Others, the sites of famous shrines, functioned primarily as religious centers, attracting devotees in periodic pilgrimages to its temples. Still others were settlements of literati, specialists in elaborating some aspect of the intellectual tradition of the country.[i] It is only where one or another of these functions comes to overshadow all the others and exerts a powerful attraction on others that these come to be concentrated under one roof or in one site. But there are areas where no such dominant centers arise, where political, religious, or intellectual functions remain dispersed in the countryside. Wales, for instance, and Norway are areas in which many functions

---

[8] In twentieth-century anthropology, there was often much debate over what exactly was necessary for a society to be considered a civilization or state-level society. Cities being widely considered a central feature of civilizations, their presence was one classic diagnostic tool. In fact, the word *civilization* has its roots in the Latin word for city (*civis*).

Wolf's neo-Marxist position is reflected in his insistence here that the presence or absence of cities is incidental to civilization; rather, civilization is defined by social relations of production. Critical to those are the relations of exploitation that link the peasant to the landowner and to the state (in Wolf's words, "to power holders outside his social stratum").

remain dispersed over the countryside, and the development of cities is weak. The presence or absence of cities will certainly affect the pattern of a society but the particular seat for the apparatus of power and influence is only one phase in the establishment of power and influence, not its totality. A piano is an instrument for making polyphonic music; but it is possible to make polyphonic music without pianos. Similarly, the city is but one—though common—form in the orchestration of power and influence, but not its exclusive or even decisive form.

Thus, it is the crystallization of executive power which serves to distinguish the primitive from the civilized, rather than whether or not such power controls are located in one kind of place or another. Not the city, but the state is the decisive criterion of civilization and it is the appearance of the state which marks the threshold of transition between food cultivators in general and peasants. Thus, it is only when a cultivator is integrated into a society with a state—that is, when the cultivator becomes subject to the demands and sanctions of power-holders outside his social stratum—that we can appropriately speak of peasantry.

It is, of course, difficult to place this threshold of civilization in terms of time and space. Nevertheless, on the basis of such data as we now possess, we may mark the beginnings of the state and hence of a peasantry at around 3500 B.C. in the Near East and around 1000 B.C. in Middle America. We must emphasize that the processes of state-building are multiple and complex. Different areas were integrated into states in markedly different ways and at different times. In some areas of the world these processes have not yet run their course, and in a few places we can still witness the encounter between primitive cultivators and state societies which impinge on the primitive and try to bring them within control.

THE PLACE OF PEASANTRY IN SOCIETY

Not only does our world contain both primitives on the verge of peasantry and full-fledged peasants, but it also contains both societies in which the peasant is the chief producer of the store of social wealth and those in which he has been relegated to a secondary position. There are still large areas of the world in which peasants who cultivate the land with their traditional tools not only form the vast majority of the population, but also furnish the funds of rent and profit which underwrite the entire social structure. In such societies, all other social groups depend upon peasants both for their food and for any income that may accrue to them. There are other societies, however, in which the Industrial Revolution has created vast complexes of machines that produce goods quite independently of peasants. If there are any peasants left in such societies, they occupy a secondary position in the creation of wealth. Moreover, the vast and growing numbers of industrial workers who man the wealth-creating machines must also be fed. More often than not the provision of food for these workers is no longer in the hands of peasants who work small units of land with traditional techniques, but in the hands of new "factories in the field," which apply the technology of the Industrial Revolution to the growing of food on large, heavily capitalized, scientifically operated farms.[j] Such farms are staffed not by peasants, but by agricultural workers who are paid wages for their work much as an industrial worker is paid for running a blast furnace or a spinning machine. Both kinds of society contain threats to the peasant, whether these threats emanate from demands for surplus, or from competition which may render the peasant economically useless.[9]

---

[9] This passage mirrors the one above it. In the previous passage, Wolf reminded us that cities were not essential to a state. Here he reminds us that people are not peasants just because they cultivate the land. It is the social relations of production that are critical to understanding the mode of production. People who are paid wages to cultivate the land are capitalist workers—members of the proletariat. People who work the land and pay rents to absentee landowners and the state are more likely to be peasants.

THE PEASANT DILEMMA

The outsider may look down upon the peasant as upon a sheep to be shorn periodically of its wool: "three bags full—one for my master, one for my dame, and one for the little boy who lives down the lane." But to the peasant, his caloric minimum and his replacement fund will be primary, together with such ceremonial payments as he must make to maintain the social order of his narrow peasant world. These needs, as we have indicated above, are culturally relative; they will differ in China from what they are in Puerto Rico. Yet they are both functionally and logically prior to the demands of the outsider, whether lord or merchant. This attitude is neatly implied in the old song, sung during the peasant uprisings of the late European Middle Ages:

When Adam delved and Eve span,
Who was then the gentleman?

Peasant needs—the requirement to maintain a caloric minimum, a replacement fund, and a ceremonial fund—will often conflict with the requirements imposed by the outsider.

Yet if it is correct to define the peasantry primarily in terms of its sub-ordinate relationships to a group of controlling outsiders, it is also correct to assert as a corollary of this definition that a peasantry will be forced to maintain a balance between its own demands and the demands of the outsiders and will be subject to the tensions produced by this struggle to keep the balance. The outsider sees the peasant primarily as a source of labor and goods with which to increase his fund of power. But the peasant is at once an economic agent and the head of a household. His holding is both an economic unit and a home.[10]

The peasant unit is thus not merely a productive organization constituted of so many "hands" ready to labor in the fields; it is also a unit of consumption, containing as many mouths as there are workers. Moreover, it does not merely feed its members; it also supplies them with many other services. In such a unit children are raised and socialized to the demands of the adult world. Old people may be cared for until their death, and their burial paid for from the unit's stock of wealth. Marriage provides sexual satisfaction, and relationships within the unit generate affection which ties the members to each other. Using its ceremonial fund, such a unit pays "the costs of representation" incurred by its members within the larger community. Hence, labor is contributed as needed in a great number of different contexts; its expenditure is not prompted directly by the existence of an economic system governed by prices and profits.

We are, of course, familiar with this kind of economic behavior in our own society. A mother will also sit up all night with a sick child or cook a meal for the family, without reckoning the cost of her labor. A father may do minor repairs around the house; a teen-age son may mow the lawn. Purchased in the open market, such services would cost a good deal. It has been estimated, for example, that in our society a man can save annually $6000–$8000 in payments for economic services if he gets married, rather than paying for their performance by specialists at prices current in the open market. Within the family, such labors of love are performed readily, without the need for cost accounting.

Peasant households function similarly. Certainly peasants are aware of the price of labor

---

[10] A critical feature that differentiates Marxist analysis in all of its forms is an emphasis on conflict. Up until now, Wolf has described the fundamental relations of production for the peasantry. Here and below, he delves into sources of conflict. If the peasant considers his replacement fund and ceremonial fund to have priority over payments to landowners and states, these later will rarely share that opinion—and are generally armed as well. Thus, a fundamental conflict of interests shapes the livelihoods of peasants. Most other forms of anthropology (particularly functionalism) consider conflict to be mediated by ritual. According to Wolf, it is more likely to be mediated by armed uprising. Wolf explored this theme in substantial detail in his subsequent book, *Peasant Wars of the Twentieth Century* (1969).

and goods in the market—their economic and social survival depends on it. The shrewdness of peasants is proverbial. Certainly many anthropologists would second Sol Tax, who concluded in a study of Indian peasants in Guatemala that "the purchasers of goods make a choice of markets according to what they want to buy and how much time they are willing to spend to get it more cheaply and closer to its source."[k] However, to the extent that a peasant holding serves to provision a group of people, every decision made in terms of the external market also has its internal, domestic aspect.[11]

This fact has caused the Russian economist A. V. Chaianov to speak of a special kind of peasant economics. He explains this concept in the following terms:

> The first fundamental characteristic of the farm economy of the peasant is that it is a family economy. Its whole organization is determined by the size and composition of the peasant family and by the coordination of its consumptive demands with the number of its working hands. This explains why the conception of profit in peasant economy differs from that in capitalist economy and why the capitalistic conception of profit cannot be applied to peasant economy. The capitalistic profit is a net profit computed by subtracting all the expenses of production from the total income. The computation of profit in this manner is inapplicable in a peasant economy because in the latter the elements entering into expenses of production are expressed in units incomparable to those in a capitalist economy.
>
> In peasant economy, as in capitalist economy, gross income and material expenditures can be expressed in rubles; but labor expended can neither be expressed in, nor measured by, rubles of paid wages, but only in the labor effort of the peasant family itself. These efforts cannot be subtracted from, or added to, money units; they can merely be confronted with rubles. The comparison of the value of a certain effort of the family with the value of a ruble would be very subjective; it would vary with the degree to which the demands of the family were satisfied and with the hardships involved in the working effort itself, as well a with other conditions.
>
> So long as the requirements of the peasant family are unsatisfied, since the subjective significance of its satisfaction is valued more highly than the burden of labor necessary for such satisfaction, the peasant family will work for a small remuneration that would be definitely unprofitable in a capitalistic economy. Since the principal object of peasant economy is the satisfaction of the yearly consumption budget of the family, the fact of most interest is not the remuneration of the labor unit (the working day), but the remuneration of the whole labor year. Of course, if there is an abundance of land any working unit expended by the family will tend to receive the maximum wage for that unit, whether it be a peasant or capitalistic economy. Under such conditions, peasant economy often results in more extensive cultivation than the economy of privately (entrepreneurially) owned land. There will be a smaller income from a unit of land but higher wages for a unit of work. But when the amount of available land is limited and is under a normal degree of intensity of cultivation, the peasant family cannot use all its labor forces on its own land if it practices extensive cultivation. Having a surplus of these forces and being unable to secure all its necessities with the income derived from the annual wage of its members, the

---

[11] Sol Tax (1907–1995) was an influential American anthropologist of the mid-twentieth century. He studied at the University of Chicago under the Boasian Ralph Linton. One of the founders of the journal *Current Anthropology*, he was also known for promoting "action anthropology," (1960) which was based on the notion that anthropologists should discover and promote the interests of the communities in which they work. Tax believed that anthropology should increase scientific knowledge but also improve community welfare (Rylko-Bauer, Singer, and Van Willigen 2006). Rather than providing reports to government authorities, anthropologists should provide indigenous communities with alternative courses of action and help them pursue those they choose. A great many anthropologists today would subscribe to this position, but it was radical in the 1950s when Tax promoted it.

peasant family can utilize the surplus of labor in a more intensive cultivation of its land. In this way it can increase the yearly income of its working members, though the remuneration for each unit of their work will be lower. . . . For the same reason the peasant family often rents land at an exceedingly high price, unprofitable from a purely capitalistic standpoint, and buys land for a price considerably exceeding the capitalized rent. This is done in order to find a use for the surplus labor of the family, which (otherwise) could not be utilized under conditions of land scarcity.[1,12]

The perennial problem of the peasantry thus consists in balancing the demands of the external world against the peasants' need to provision their households. Yet in meeting this root problem peasants may follow two diametrically opposed strategies. The first of these is to increase production; the second, to curtail consumption.

If a peasant follows the first strategy, he must step up the output of labor upon his own holding, in order to raise its productivity and to increase the amount of produce with which to enter the market. His ability to do so depends largely on how easy it is for him to mobilize the needed factors of production—land, labor, capital (whether in the form of savings, ready cash, or credit)—and, of course, on the general condition of the market. Let us remember that among peasants factors of production are usually heavily encumbered with prior commitments, especially in the form of committed surpluses for ceremonial expenditure and for the payment of rent. It is very rare, if not impossible, for a man to raise himself singlehandedly by his economic bootstraps to a level of productivity above and beyond that demanded by the mandatory payments. It is also difficult for most peasants to see their possessions in an economic context divorced from the provisioning of the household. A piece of land, a house, are not merely factors of production; they are also loaded with symbolic values. Family jewelry is not merely a form of cold cash; it is often an heirloom, encumbered with sentiments. Yet our analysis can tell us also when we may expect increasing numbers of peasants to follow the strategy of increasing production.

First, this becomes possible when traditional liens on the peasants' funds of rent have weakened—a condition likely to occur when the power structure through which funds have been siphoned off to traditional overlords has become ineffective. Second, we may expect to find this phenomenon where it has become possible for the peasant to escape the demands placed on him to underwrite with ceremonial expenditures the traditional social ties with his fellows. If he can refuse to commit his surplus to ceremonial outlays, he can use the funds so released to support his economic ascent. The two changes

---

[12] Wolf uses this long Chayanov quote to support his contention that the primary interest of peasant households is their own support and sustenance. Alexander Chayanov (also, less commonly, spelled Chaianov (1888–1937?) was an influential Soviet economist, essayist, and author. As seen in this passage, he argued that peasant economic behavior was fundamentally different from capitalist behavior. Peasants were vitally concerned with supplying their own needs, which are, in part, a function of the family cycle. Children are unproductive but must be fed. Therefore peasants will work very hard, often buying resources at unattractive prices and toiling at extremely low effective rates of pay. In other words, they end up exploiting themselves. Contrary to Lenin and other Soviet thinkers, Chayanov argued that these activities did not represent protocapitalism. Surplus could not be easily extracted from the peasantry. Any surplus generated would ultimately not be reinvested in productive resources. Rather, as children grew up and married, resources would be split up and the cycle would begin again. Chayanov's theories drew him into conflict with the Stalinist state in the 1930s. Stalin persecuted wealthier peasants *(kuluks)* as emerging capitalists and therefore enemies of the state. Chayanov's theory of cyclical accumulation went against this interpretation. He was repeatedly arrested in the Stalinist purges of the 1930s and probably executed in either 1937 or 1939. Though Wolf cites a Chayanov essay that had been published in 1931, Chayanov's *Theory of Peasant Economy,* originally published in Russian in 1926, was first available in English translation in 1966, the year of Wolf's essay. Chayanov was increasingly influential in the economic anthropology of the late 1960s and 1970s.

frequently go together. As the overarching power structure weakens, many traditional social ties also lose their particular sanctions. The peasant community, under such circumstances, may see the rise of wealthy peasants who shoulder aside their less fortunate fellows and move into the power vacuum left by the retreating superior holders of power. In the course of their rise, they frequently violate traditional expectations of how social relations are to be conducted and symbolized—frequently they utilize their newly won power to enrich themselves at the cost of their neighbors. Such men were the rising *yeomen* of sixteenth century England, the rich peasants of China, the *kulaki* or "fists" of pre-revolutionary Russia. In other cases, large numbers of peasants may end their ceremonial commitments, as happened among many Middle American Indian groups who have abandoned their traditional Catholic folk rituals—with their great costs paid out in the support of religious organizations and events—and have turned to a sober Protestantism for which such expenditures are not required.[m,13]

The alternative strategy is to solve the basic peasant dilemma by curtailing consumption. The peasant may reduce his caloric intake to the most basic items of food; he may cut his purchases in the outside market to a few essential items only. Instead, he may rely as much as possible on the labor of his own domestic group to produce both food and needed objects, within the confines of his own homestead. Such efforts to balance accounts by underconsumption go a long way towards explaining why peasants tend to cleave to their traditional way of life, why they fear the new as they would fear temptation: Any novelty may undermine their precarious balance. At the same time, such peasants will also support

the maintenance of traditional social relations and the expenditure of ceremonial funds required to sustain them. As long as these can be upheld, a peasant community can ward off the further penetration of outside demands and pressures, while at the same time forcing its more fortunate members to share some of their labor and goods with their less fortunate neighbors.

In many parts of the world, therefore—even in those where the peasantry has been relegated to a secondary role in the total social order—we shall encounter the phenomenon of peasants striving to stay alive without undue commitments to the larger system. At the same time, it must be remembered that in many situations—especially during wartime and depressions—peasant holdings represent sanctuaries from the ravages which afflict people in cities and industrial centers. A man with 40 acres and a mule has a hard row to hoe; at the same time he has at least some measure of probable caloric output when others may have to seek their sustenance in the garbage cans of crumbling towns. The peasant retains—in his control of land and his capacity to raise crops on it—both his autonomy and his capacity to survive when others, more delicately dependent upon the larger society, find such survival difficult.

While the two strategies of peasant operations point in entirely different directions, we must not, however, think of them as mutually exclusive. We have seen that their relative dominance is largely a function of the larger social order within which the peasant must make his living. To the extent, then, that a social order grows in strength or weakens, the peasants will favor one or the other, sometimes playing both at the same time in different contexts. Periods in which the first strategy is strongly favored may be

---

[13] The subtext here is probably economic development. In the 1950s and 1960s, many anthropologists were concerned with cultural change and the "modernization" of "traditional" society. Here, Wolf explains how in the peasant context such modernization may occur. Note additionally the contrast with Max Weber's notions. In *The Protestant Ethic and the Spirit of Capitalism,* (1958 [1930])

Weber argued that the move from Catholicism to Protestantism encouraged the development of a work ethic that led to capitalism. Here, Wolf the materialist argues that economic interests may influence a peasant's move from Catholicism to Protestantism because the latter places fewer economic demands upon him.

followed by others when the peasant retrenches and renews his social fabric within a narrower orbit. Similarly, at any given time, there will be some individuals who will risk the social ostracism involved in testing the limits of traditional social ties, while others prefer the security involved in following the norm that has been tried, and is therefore thought to be true. Literary clichés about the immovable peasantry to the contrary, a peasantry is always in a dynamic state, moving continuously between two poles in the search for a solution of its basic dilemma.[14]

The existence of a peasantry thus involves not merely a relation between peasant and nonpeasant, but a type of adaptation, a combination of attitudes and activities designed to sustain the cultivator in his effort to maintain himself and his kind within a social order which threatens that maintenance. In this study, we shall attempt to outline both the kinds of relations peasants entertain with outsiders and the strategies they follow in modifying or neutralizing the effects of these relations.

NOTES

[a] Marshall D. Sahlins, "Political Power and the Economy in Primitive Society," in *Essays in the Science of Culture: In Honor of Leslie A. White*, eds. Gertrude E. Dole and Robert L. Cameiro (New York: Thomas Y. Crowell Company, 1960), p. 408.

[b] Jean Fourastié, *The Causes of Wealth* (Glencoe: The Free Press, 1960), pp. 102–103.

[c] *Ibid.*, p. 41.

[d] Wilhelm Abel, *Geschichte der deutschen Landwirtschaft vom frühen Mittelalter bis zum 19. Jahrhundert*, Deutsche Agrargeschichte II (Stuttgart: Eugen Ulmer, 1962), p. 95.

[e] Robert L. Cameiro, "Slash-and-Burn Cultivation among the Kuikuru and its Implications for Cultural Development in the Amazon Basin," in *The Evolution of Horticultural Systems in Native South America: Causes and Consequences*, ed. Johannes Wilbert, *Antropologica*, Supplement, No. 2 (1961), p. 49.

[f] Evidence from Middle America indicates that a man may have to expend at least the equivalent of one year's local wages to act as a sponsor in a community ceremonial. Expenditures of two to twenty times this amount are noted for particular communities. For examples, see Ralph Beals, *Cherán, a Sierra Tarascan Village*, Smithsonian Institution Institute of Social Anthropology, Publication No. 2 (Washington D.C.: United States Government Printing Office, 1946), p. 85; Calixta Guiteras-Holmes, *Perils of the Soul: The World View of a Tzotzil Indian* (New York: The Free Press, 1961), p. 58; Sol Tax, *Penny Capitalism: A Guatemalan Indian Economy*, Smithsonian Institution, Institute of Social Anthropology, Publication No. 16 (Washington, D.C.: United States Government Printing Office, 1953), pp. 177–178. For the Andes, see William W. Stein, *Hualcan: Life in the Highlands of Peru* (Ithaca: Cornell University Press, 1961), p. 52, 236, 255.

[g] Abel, *Geschichte der deutschen Landwirtschaft*, p. 95.

[h] On Watusi and Bahutu settlement pattern, see Pierre B. Gravel, *The Play for Power: Description of a Community in Eastern Ruanda* (Ann Arbor: Department of Anthropology, University of Michigan, Ph.D. Thesis, 1962). On Egypt, see Henri Frankfort, *The Birth of Civilization in the Near East* (Garden City, N.Y.: Doubleday and Company, 1956), pp. 97–98, and John A. Wilson, *The Culture of Ancient Egypt* (Chicago: University of Chicago Press, 1951), p. 37, pp. 97–98. On the Maya, see Gordon R. Willey, "Mesoamerica," in *Courses Toward Urban Life*, eds. Robert J. Braidwood and Gordon R. Willey (Chicago: Aldine Publishing Company, 1962), p. 101, and Michael Coe, "Social Typology and the Tropical Forest Civilizations,"

---

[14] In these final paragraphs, Wolf portrays the peasant world as a dialectical system, characterized by a set of embedded contradictions: the contradiction between the production of surplus (at the expense of community) and the necessity to curtail consumption, is set within the contradiction between the interests of peasants (to retain as much of their surplus as possible) and those of the landlords (to strip the peasantry of as much surplus as possible). Wolf portrays this as a dynamic but continuous state of affairs. In other words, peasants negotiate and renegotiate their livelihoods within a more or less stable framework of peasant-landlord relations. However, it is also a potentially revolutionary state of affairs. The peasantry as a class may rise against the landlords as a class in an attempt at revolutionary change. Elsewhere, Wolf argues that such revolt was particularly likely to occur as the spread of capitalism from North America and Europe weakened the power of preexisting elites, opened new possibilities for peasants, and made the structures that protected them from risk less dependable.

Comparative Studies in Society and History, IV, No. 1 (1961), p. 66.

[i] McKim Mariott and Bernard C. Cohn, "Networks and Centers in the Integration of Indian Civilization," *Journal of Social Research* (Ranchi, Bihar, India), I, No. 1 (1958).

[j] For a discussion of the plantation see Eric R. Wolf and Sidney W. Mintz, "Hadendas and Plantations in Middle America and the Antilles," *Social and Economic Studies,* VI, No. 3 (1957), and *Plantation Systems of the New World.* Papers and discussion summaries of the Seminar held in San Juan, Puerto Rico, Social Science Monographs, VII, Pan American Union, Washington, D.C., 1959. For a good case study of the replacement of peasants by plantations see Ramiro Guerra y Sánchez, *Sugar and Society in the Caribbean* (New Haven: Yale University Press, 1964).

[k] Sol Tax, *Penny Capitalism,* p. 14.

[l] A. V. Chaianov, "The Socio-economic Nature of Peasant Farm Economy," in *A Systematic Source Book in Rural Sociology,* eds. Pitirim A. Sorokin, Carle C. Zimmerman, and Charles J. Galpin (Minneapolis: The University of Minnesota Press, 1931) II, pp. 144–145.

[m] See, for instance, June Nash, "Protestantism in an Indian Village in the Western Highlands of Guatemala," *The Alpha Kappa Deltan,* XXX, No. 1 (1960), p. 50.

Structuralism

Claude Lévi-Strauss (b. 1908) almost single-handedly founded the field of structuralism. He began with the assumption that culture was, first and foremost, a product of the mind. Since all human brains are biologically similar, he reasoned, there must be deep-seated similarities among cultures. The goal he set for anthropology was to discover the fundamental structure of human cognition, the underlying patterns of human thought that produce the great variety of current and historical cultures. Pursuing this quest, he has spent his career conducting cross-cultural studies of kinship, myths, and religion.

Lévi-Strauss believes that the underlying processes tying cultures together are to be found in bits of information that provide messages about the structuring of society. However, each culture is also the product of its own history and its technological adaptation to the world. These processes have combined, altered, transfigured, and modified the original bits of information. Transmitting culture is rather like playing "telephone" or "whispering down the alley" in a crowded bus station. Messages are apt to get jumbled. This jumble is the result of the particular history and technological adaptation of each culture. Lévi-Strauss hoped that by breaking down cultures into their elemental parts he could get beyond this "noise" and return to the original message.

Lévi-Strauss' structuralism was heavily influenced by the great French scholars of the previous generation, particularly Émile Durkheim and Marcel Mauss. In fact, the title of his first major work, *The Elementary Structures of Kinship* (1949), echoes the title of Durkheim's great work on religion, *The Elementary Forms of the Religious Life* (1965, orig. 1912). The Prague School of structural linguistics, organized in 1926, also played a major role in the conception of his theory. This group of scholars, led by the linguists Roman Jakobson (1896–1982) and Nikolai Troubetzkoy (1890–1938), emphasized the synchronic (descriptive) rather than diachronic (historical) study of language and promoted the theory that linguistic meaning was built upon contrasts between sounds, or phonemes. Members of the Prague School defined and characterized the phonemic study of languages. This work, and his study of Durkheim, provided Lévi-Strauss with the concept of binary contrasts that was fundamental to his formulation of structuralism.

Perhaps the simplest way to explain the theoretical basis of structuralism is to compare it to linguistics. All languages are composed of arbitrary groups of sounds called *phonemes.* Phonemes by themselves are meaningless. It is only when they are combined into larger units (morphemes, words, phrases, and so on) according to certain patterns (the rules of syntax and grammar) that phonemes form meaningful units (speech). Most speakers of a language cannot articulate the underlying rules that structure their use of phonemes in creating meaningful communication, yet all are able to use language to communicate successfully with one another. Therefore, at a subconscious level we must all "know" the rules that structure our use of language. The job of a linguist is to analyze the outward use of language in such a way as to discover these unconscious principles. In the same fashion, Lévi-Strauss tried to design a technique for studying the unconscious principles that structure human culture.

To Lévi-Strauss, culture, like language, is essentially a collection of arbitrary symbols. He is not interested in the specific meaning of the symbols any more than a linguist is interested in the phonemes of a language. Rather, he is concerned with the patterning of elements, the way cultural elements relate to one another to form the overall system (Lévi-Strauss 1963:208).

A key insight of the Prague School was that words were built upon contrasts (binary oppositions) between phonemes rather than simply being groups of sounds. Following this linguistic model, Lévi-Strauss proposed that the fundamental pattern of human thought also uses binary contrasts such as black-white, night-day, and hot-cold. This insight dovetailed nicely with Durkheim's and Hertz's proposition that distinctions such as sacred-profane and right-left were fundamental manifestations of the collective conscious.

Lévi-Strauss used the notion of the binary structure of human thought to analyze kinship, applying the work of Marcel Mauss, who in *The Gift* (1967, orig. 1925) had tried to demonstrate that exchange in primitive societies was driven not by economic motives but by rules of reciprocity upon which the solidarity of society depended. In *Elementary Structures of Kinship* (1969, orig. 1949) Lévi-Strauss took Mauss' concept of reciprocity and applied it to marriage in primitive societies, arguing that in those societies women were a commodity that could be exchanged. Lévi-Strauss contended that one of the first and most important distinctions a human makes is between self and others. This "natural" binary distinction then leads to the formation of the incest taboo, which necessitates choosing spouses from outside of one's family. In this fashion, the binary distinction between kin and nonkin is resolved in primitive societies by the reciprocal exchange of women and the formation of kin networks.

Lévi-Strauss is best known today for his analysis of myth. His interest in mythology lies in his belief that studying the mythologies of primitive peoples allows him to examine the unconscious universal patterning of human thought in its least contaminated form. In Lévi-Strauss' view, the mythology of primitive peoples is closer to these universal principles than are Western beliefs because the training we receive in Western society buries the logical structure he seeks under layers of "cultural interference" created by our social environment.

In his work on myths, folktales, and religion, Lévi-Strauss elaborated on the notion that binary oppositions were the basis of human cognition. He proposed that a fundamental characteristic of human thought was the desire to find a midpoint between such oppositions, a category that transcends and somehow resolves them. In Lévi-Strauss' view, the elements of myth, like the phonemes of a language, acquire meaning only as a consequence of certain structural relations. Therefore, to uncover the unconscious meaning of myth, the structuralist must break myth into its constituent elements and examine the rules that govern their relationships. This hidden structural core will reveal the essential patterns and processes of human thought.

The articles we have chosen for this section are examples of the application of structural analysis to different areas of study over several decades. "Linguistics and Anthropology" is a transcription of a talk Lévi-Strauss gave at a conference in 1952, in which he describes his understanding of the relationship between culture and language and proposes a series of problems on which anthropologists and linguists might find room for cooperation. In the essay "Four Winnebago Myths: A Structural Sketch," published in 1960, Lévi-Strauss outlines the fundamental aspects of his methodology by comparing four Native American myths collected by Paul Radin.

Our final selection in this section is a structural analysis of gender stratification by the American anthropologist Sherry Ortner (b. 1941). Although her first work was in symbolic anthropology, in the last few decades Ortner has become known for her contributions to the field of feminist anthropology. In particular, her volume *Sexual Meanings: The Cultural Construction of Gender and Sexuality*, (edited with Harriet Whitehead and originally published in 1974), is considered a classic in the field. Ortner's essay, drawn from this volume, examines the issue of gender inequality. Echoing Lévi-Strauss, Ortner suggests that gender stratification is based on the fundamental opposition between nature and culture. Women, she proposes, because of pregnancy and childbirth, are universally associated with nature. Men, because they are unable to bear children, create in the realm of culture and are thus accorded higher status.

Structuralism had a profound effect on American anthropology. In particular, it influenced symbolic anthropology, which was popular in the 1970s, cognitive anthropology, and postmodernism, which achieved notoriety in the 1980s.

24. *Linguistics and Anthropology*[a]

CLAUDE LÉVI-STRAUSS (b. 1908)

PROBABLY FOR THE first time, anthropologists and linguists have come together on a formal basis and for the specific purpose of confronting their respective disciplines.[1] However, the problem was not a simple one, and it seems to me that some of the many difficulties which we have met with can be referred to the fact we were not only trying to make a confrontation of the theme of linguistics and of anthropology, but that this confrontation itself could be and had to be undertaken on several different levels, and it was extremely difficult to avoid, in the midst of the same discussion, shifting from one level to another. I shall try first of all to outline what these different levels are.

In the first place, we have spoken about the relation between a language and a culture. That is, how far is it necessary, when we try to study a culture, to know the language, or how far is it necessary to understand what is meant by the

population, to have some knowledge of the culture besides the language.[2]

There is a second level, which is not the relationship between a language and a culture, but the relationship between language and culture. And though there are also many important problems on this level, it seems to me that our discussions have not so often been placed on the second level as on the first one. For instance, I am rather struck by the fact that at no moment during our discussions has any reference been made to the behavior of culture as a whole toward language as a whole. Among us, language is used in a rather reckless way—we talk all the time, we ask questions about many things. This is not at all a universal situation. There are cultures—and I am inclined to say most of the cultures of the world—which are rather thrifty in relation to language. They don't believe that language should be used indiscriminately, but only in certain specific frames of reference and

(1952)

[1] As Lévi-Strauss' footnote tells you, this essay was transcribed from a presentation at the 1952 Conference of Anthropologists and Linguists. The conference, sponsored by the Wenner-Gren Society, the Linguistic Society of America, and Indiana University, brought together (by invitation) nineteen preeminent scholars in the two disciplines. In addition to Lévi-Strauss other notable invitees were Roman Jakobson (who gave the keynote address), Joseph Casagrande, and Gene Weltfish. Numerous other participants are mentioned by name in the essay.

[2] The degree to which language is separable from culture, a then-current topic of considerable debate in both an-

thropology and linguistics, was the central topic at this conference. Sapir and Whorf, you will recall, had argued that language and culture are inseparable and that the first has a powerful influence over the second (see essay 12). Margaret Mead and other Boasians had argued that thorough knowledge of native languages was essential to fieldwork (see, for example, Mead 1939). Other anthropologists, such as A. P. Elkin (1941), had argued against this position. Within linguistics this issue had also been fraught with difficulty. Jakobson and the Prague School linguists had argued that language can be studied without reference to anything but itself.

somewhat sparingly. Problems of this kind have, to be sure, been mentioned in our discussions, but certainly they have not been given the same importance as the problems of the first type.[3]

And there is a third level, which has received still less attention. It is the relation, not between a language or language and a culture or culture, but the relation between linguistics as a scientific discipline and anthropology. And this, which to my mind would be probably the most important level, has remained somewhat in the background during our discussions.

Now how can this be explained? The relationship between language and culture is an exceedingly complicated one. In the first place language can be said to be a result of culture: The language which is spoken by one population is a reflection of the total culture of the population. But one can also say that language is *part* of culture. It is one of those many things which make up a culture—and if you remember Tylor's famous definition of culture, culture includes a great many things, such as tools, institutions, customs, beliefs, and also, of course, language. And from this point of view the problems are not at all the same as from the first one. In the third place, language can be said to be a *condition* of culture and this in two different ways: First, it is a condition of culture in a diachronic way, because it is mostly through the language that we learn about our own culture—we are taught by our parents, we are scolded, we are congratu-

lated, with language. But also, from a much more theoretical point of view, language can be said to be a condition of culture because the material out of which language is built is of the same type as the material out of which the whole culture is built: logical relations, oppositions, correlations, and the like. Language, from this point of view, may appear as laying a kind of foundation for the more complex structures which correspond to the different aspects of culture.[4]

This is how I see our problem from an objective point of view. But there is also a subjective point of view, which is no less important. During the discussion it appeared to me that the reasons for anthropologists' and linguists' being so eager to get together are of an entirely different nature, and that their motivations are practically contradictory. Linguists have told us over and over again during these sessions that they are somewhat afraid of the trend which is becoming predominant in their discipline—that they have felt more and more unrelated; that they have been dealing more and more with abstract notions, which many times have been very difficult to follow for the others; and that what they have been mainly concerned with, especially in structural linguistics, has no relation whatsoever to the whole culture, to the social life, to the history, of the people who speak the language; and so on. And the reason, it seems to me, for the linguists' being so eager to get closer to the anthropologists is precisely that they expect the anthropologists

---

[3] In this paragraph Lévi-Strauss proposes that rather than looking at the relationship between a culture and a language of that culture, anthropologists and linguists should examine the relationship between culture and language as universal human phenomena. However, his description of the problem seems somewhat ill formed. He seems to refer more to cultural attitudes toward the use of language—for example, whether speaking or silence is prized (something specific to individual cultures)—than to any universal principle. In the following paragraph he states that the relationship between linguistics and anthropology has received even less attention. In Lévi-Strauss' view this is the most significant issue, and it is the main subject of this essay.

[4] The second half of this paragraph presents a neat encapsulation of much of Lévi-Strauss' theoretical perspective.

He mentions (but is not really interested in) the fact that language is part of and reflects culture. He then focuses on what he believes are two absolutely critical facts. First, language is the means through which culture is transmitted. Second, both language and culture are visible (or audible) manifestations of the same underlying processes. Ultimately for Lévi-Strauss both language and culture are mental processes; both are thus conditioned by the ways in which human brains work. Lévi-Strauss' contention is that linguistics, specifically the linguistics of the Prague School theorists, has given us scientific tools to analyze mental processes. Since culture is the result of the same mental processes as language, the tools of linguistics can be used to analyze culture.

to be able to give back to them some of this concreteness which seems to have disappeared from their own methodological approach. And now, what about the anthropologists? The anthropologists are in a very peculiar situation in relation to linguistics. For many years they have been working very closely with the linguists, and all of a sudden it seems to them that the linguists are vanishing, that they are going on the other side of the borderline which divides the exact and natural sciences on the one hand from the human and social sciences on the other. All of a sudden the linguists are playing their former companions this very nasty trick of doing things as well and with the same sort of rigorous approach that was long believed to be the privilege of the exact and natural sciences. Then, on the side of the anthropologist there is some, let us say, melancholy, and a great deal of envy. We should like to learn from the linguists how they succeeded in doing it, how we may ourselves in our own field, which is a complex one—in the field of kinship, in the field of social organization, in the field of religion, folklore, art, and the like—use the same kind of rigorous approach which has proved to be so successful for linguistics.[5]

And I should like to elaborate—since the point of view that I am expected to explain here is the point of view of the anthropologist—how important this is to us. I have learned a great deal during this Conference, but it was not only during the sessions of the Conference: I was extremely impressed, as a non-linguist anthropologist, in attending some of the classes in field work, led by C. F. Voegelin and Henry L. Smith, to witness the precision, the care, the rigor which

is used in a field that, after all, belongs to the social sciences to the same extent as the other fields of anthropology. And this is not all. During the past three or four years we have been impressed not only by the theoretical but by the practical connection which has been established between linguistics and communication engineering—by the fact that now, when you have a problem, it is possible not only to use a method more rigorous than our own to solve it, but to have a machine built by an engineer and to make a kind of experiment, completely similar to a natural-science experiment, and to have the experiment tell you if the hypothesis is worthwhile or not. For centuries the humanities and the social sciences have resigned themselves to contemplating the world of the natural and exact sciences as a kind of paradise which they will never enter. And all of a sudden there is a small door which is being opened between the two fields, and it is linguistics which has done it. So you may see that the motivations of the anthropologists, insofar as I am able to interpret them correctly, are rather contradictory to the motivations of the linguists. The linguists try to join the anthropologists in order to make their study more concrete, while the anthropologists are trying to rejoin the linguists precisely because the linguists appear to show them a way to get out of the confusion resulting from too much acquaintance and familiarity with concrete and empirical data. Sometimes it seems to me this has resulted, during this Conference, in a somewhat—shall I call it—unhappy merry-go-round, where the anthropologists were running after the linguists while the linguists were running after the anthropologists,

---

[5] Lévi-Strauss certainly considered linguistics to be the most advanced of the social sciences. By advanced, he meant the most able to successfully apply scientific method to its field of study. Elsewhere he wrote that linguistics was probably the only social science "which can truly claim to be a science and which has achieved both the formulation of an empirical method and an understanding of the nature of data submitted to its analysis" (1963:31). Lévi-Strauss claims here that anthropologists are envious of linguistics' scientific success. This may well have been true at the time he presented this paper in 1952. The 1950s and 1960s were the era of ethnoscience, when American anthropologists hoped to develop an ethnographic method that produced testable and replicable results like that produced in the natural sciences. It's also interesting that, in this passage, Lévi-Strauss, in 1952, predicts a future in which linguistics was increasingly a natural science, disassociated from the social sciences. This prediction has largely been borne out. However, most linguistics today builds only indirectly on the Prague School favored by Lévi-Strauss. Chomsky and his followers and critics have proved more important.

each group trying to get from the other precisely what it was trying itself to get rid of. And this, I think, deserves some kind of attention. Why this basic misunderstanding? In the first place, because the task is extremely difficult. I was particularly struck by the session where Mary Haas tried to write on the board formulas to analyze a problem as apparently simple as that of bilingualism— very simple, since it might seem from the outside that there are only two terms, two languages, though the number of possible permutations was enormous. And enormous as it was, during the discussion new types of permutation were discovered. It was also admitted that, besides these permutations, other dimensions could be introduced which would complicate the problem still more. This is what I believe to be one of the main lessons of this Conference—that whenever we try to express in the same language linguistic problems and cultural problems, the situation becomes tremendously complicated and we shall always have to keep this in mind.[6]

In the second place, we have been behaving as if there were only two partners—language on the one hand, culture on the other—and as if the problem should be set up in terms of the causal relations: "Is it language which influences culture? Is it culture which influences language?" But we have not been sufficiently aware of the fact that both language and culture are the products of activities which are basically similar. I am now referring to this uninvited guest which has been seated during this Conference beside us and which is *the human mind.* The fact that the psychologist C. E. Osgood is here and the many occasions when he was literally compelled to intervene in order to call our attention to this basic fact are the best proofs of the point I am trying to make.[7]

---

[6] C. F. Voegelin (1906–1986), Mary Haas (1910–1996), and Henry L. Smith (1913–1972) were also participants at the conference. The first two were anthropologists who specialized in Native American languages; Smith established the Foreign Service Institute Language School. Lévi-Strauss refers in this passage to communications engineering and rigorous scientific methodologies, as he was also deeply influenced by the work of Norbert Wiener (1884–1964) and Claude Shannon (1916–2001). Wiener is considered one of the founders of the field of cybernetics. He published *Cybernetics or Control and Communication in the Animal and the Machine* in 1948. Shannon published his seminal description of information theory, *A Mathematical Theory of Communication,* that same year. Information theory is a branch of mathematics concerned with the amount of energy and storage required to transmit or preserve units of information (conceived of as binary bits). Shannon developed information theory at Bell Labs, which provides the mathematics behind much of modern telephonic communication and data storage. Lévi-Strauss was captivated by cybernetics and ideas such as information theory for two reasons: First, they offered a scientific way of analyzing the flow of information. Lévi-Strauss conceived of culture as information flowing from generation to generation. Therefore the insights of information theory would seem particularly germane. Second, the use Wiener and Shannon made of binary logic seemed to parallel Durkheim's notion that all human thinking (and hence, both language and culture) was patterned on dualistic lines. Lévi-Strauss mentions computers and information theory frequently in his work but nowhere does he display a deep technical understanding of these subjects. He treats them more as metaphors, never, for example, providing an applied mathematical model of the transmission of culture. Strangely, Lévi-Strauss and Shannon had apartments in the same building in New York in the early 1940s, though they did not know one another (Bucher and Lévi-Strauss 1985:367).

[7] Charles E. Osgood (1916–1991) was a psychologist best known for the notion of "semantic differential." He developed a technique to map the connotations of words and used it to measure the psychological distance between words. This passage is important because it identifies Lévi-Strauss' key concern—that is, the nature of human thinking. Lévi-Strauss' structuralism has a very different purpose than most other forms of anthropology. Most anthropological theories point to methods of describing cultures or methods of determining the relationships between different parts of culture. However, in Lévi-Strauss' view, the purpose of structuralism is to examine the relationships among elements of culture and ultimately to describe the nature of the human mind itself. Lévi-Strauss contends that all cultures (and languages) are products of human thinking. In his view differences in cultures and languages are superficial and mask deep-seated similarities that are ultimately biologically based. Through "decoding" and comparing different cultures, Lévi-Strauss hopes to accurately describe the fundamental nature of human thought.

If we try to formulate our problem in purely theoretical terms, then it seems to me that we are entitled to affirm that there should be some kind of relationship between language and culture, because language has taken thousands of years to develop, and culture has taken thousands of years to develop, and both processes have been taking place side by side within the same minds. Of course, I am leaving aside for the moment cases where a foreign language has been adopted by a society that previously spoke another language. We can, for the sake of argument, consider only those cases where, in an undisturbed fashion, language and culture have been able to develop together. Is it possible to conceive of the human mind as consisting of compartments separated by rigid bulkheads without anything being able to pass from one bulkhead to the other? Though, when we try to find out what these connections or correlations are, we are confronted with a very serious problem, or, rather, with two very serious problems.[8]

The first problem has to do with the level at which to seek the correlations between language and culture, and the second one, with the things we are trying to correlate. I shall now give some attention to these basic distinctions.[9]

I remember a very striking example which was given to us by F. G. Lounsbury, about the use of two different prefixes for womankind among the Oneida. Lounsbury was telling us he paid great attention to what was going on on the social level, but he could find no correlation whatsoever. Indeed, no correlation can be found on the level of behavior, because behavior, on the one hand, and categories of thought, on the other (such as would be called for to explain the use of these two different prefixes), belong to two entirely different levels. It would not be possible to try to correlate one with the other.[10]

But I can hardly believe it a pure coincidence that this strange dichotomy of womankind should appear precisely in a culture where the maternal principle has been devel-

---

[8] Here Lévi Strauss develops his idea that language and culture arise from the same source. With rhetorical flourish, he asks whether it is possible that the linguistic and cultural spheres of the brain are separated by "rigid bulkheads." The reader, of course, is drawn to Lévi-Strauss' position. However, most current day linguists would argue that at least as far as learning language and the fundamental structure of language is concerned, the answer is emphatically yes. Language capabilities are, in fact, a very specific faculty of the brain located in very specific parts of the brain. Of course, this was not as well established when Lévi-Strauss wrote this essay.

[9] In the rest of this essay, Lévi-Strauss presents four examples of areas in which he believes that linguists and anthropologists might have something to learn from each other. The first concerns two ways the Oneida have of referring to women; the second concerns the fundamental structure of kinship systems; the third deals with the relationship between kinship and mythology among the Hopi, Zuni, and Acoma/Laguna; and the fourth compares Indo-European kinship and language to Sino-Tibetan kinship and language. The examples are brief and impressionistic rather than detailed and precise,

showing some of the range of Lévi-Strauss' interests in language, logic, kinship, and mythology. They are intended as ideas for future collaboration rather than problems whose solutions were currently within reach. It's not clear that other anthropologists and linguists took up Lévi-Strauss' challenge, perhaps because his examples are so vague that it is difficult to specify the precise research needed.

[10] Floyd Lounsbury (1914–1998) was an anthropological linguist who worked primarily with the Oneida. In the 1970s and 1980s, he turned to the analysis of Mayan hieroglyphics, and his work was critical in deciphering them. In this paragraph, Lévi-Strauss presents a seemingly odd notion: that behavior and categories of thought belong to two different "levels," and therefore we should expect no correlation between them. This idea emphasizes the degree to which Lévi-Strauss believes culture to be a mental phenomenon. His position was precisely opposite to that of the cultural ecologists, such as Julian Steward, and neofunctionalists, such as Marvin Harris. These anthropologists believed that categories of thought were irrelevant. What people said didn't matter so much as how they behaved.

oped in such an extreme way as among the Iroquois. It is as if the culture had to pay a price for giving women an importance elsewhere unknown, the price being an inability to think of women as belonging to only one logical category. To recognize women, unlike most other cultures of the world, as full social beings would thus compel the culture, in exchange, to categorize that part of womankind as yet unable to play the important maternal role—such as young girls—as animals and not as humans. However, when I suggest this interpretation, I am not trying to correlate language and behavior, but two parallel ways of categorizing the same data.[11]

Let me now give you another example. We reduce the kinship structure to the simplest conceivable element, the atom of kinship, if I may say so, when we have a group consisting of a husband, a woman, a representative of the group which has given the woman to the man—since incest prohibitions make it impossible in all societies for the unit of kinship to consist of one family, it must always link two families,

two consanguineous groups—and one offspring.[12] Now it can be shown that, if we divide all the possible behavior between kin according to a very simple dichotomy, positive behavior and negative behavior (I know this is very unsatisfactory, but it will help me to make my point), it can be shown that a great many different combinations can be found and illustrated by specific ethnographical observations. When there is a positive relationship between husband and wife and a negative one between brother and sister, we note the presence of two correlative attitudes: positive between father and son, negative between maternal uncle and nephew. We may also find a symmetrical structure, where all the signs are inverted. It is therefore common to find arrangements of the type $\left(\begin{smallmatrix}+&-\\+&-\end{smallmatrix}\right)$ or $\left(\begin{smallmatrix}-&+\\-&+\end{smallmatrix}\right)$, that is, two permutations. On the other hand, arrangements of the type $\left(\begin{smallmatrix}-&+\\-&+\end{smallmatrix}\right)$, $\left(\begin{smallmatrix}-&+\\+&-\end{smallmatrix}\right)$ occur frequently but often are poorly developed, while those of the type $\left(\begin{smallmatrix}+&-\\+&-\end{smallmatrix}\right)$, $\left(\begin{smallmatrix}-&+\\+&-\end{smallmatrix}\right)$ are rare, or perhaps impossible, because they would lead to the breakdown of the group,

[11] Note that Lévi-Strauss contends that because there are two linguistic categories for women in Oneida, speakers of this language are unable to think of women as "belonging to one logical category." Thus, he follows Sapir and Whorf (and precedes the cognitive anthropologists and ethnoscientists) in assuming that categories of language indeed represent categories of thought.

[12] Much of structuralism is built on an analogy with the discoveries of the Prague School of linguistics. Lévi-Strauss was particularly influenced by Nikolai Troubetzkoy (1890–1938) and Roman Jakobson (1896–1982), the founders of the school. Lévi-Strauss and Jakobson were colleagues at the New School for Social Research in New York City in the 1940s. Key to Prague school theory were the insights of the Swiss linguist Ferdinand de Saussure (1857–1913). In contrast to nineteenth-century linguists, who had emphasized the history of languages, Saussure studied language as a self-sufficient system existing at a given time. He distinguished between the set of abstract rules governing the production of language, which he called *langue,* and the act of speech, which he termed *parole.* Saussure focused on *langue* and was the

first to identify *phonemes*—the basic units of sound in a language that can be characterized by the physiology required for their production (the position of lips, tongue, and so on). Following Saussure, the Prague School emphasized the study of phonemes, concerning itself with the form of an utterance rather than its meaning. In studying the ways each language builds the system of phonemes of which it is composed, the Prague School theorists discovered that such systems were built on contrasts and oppositions, rather than simply being catalogs of sounds. Lévi-Strauss believed that Saussure and the Prague School linguists had discovered in the phoneme the "atom," or basic building block, of language and the rules by which systems of phonemes are constructed. He wanted to do the same for anthropology. Here he declares that one of the "atoms" of culture is a particular set of kin relations. Below, he tries to determine the oppositions characterizing different kinship systems, using the basic relations he has identified. Much of this paragraph is a very brief summary of the material in his groundbreaking 1949 book *The Elementary Structures of Kinship.*

diachronically in the first case, synchronically in the second.[b,13]

Now, what connections are possible with linguistics? I cannot see any whatsoever, except only one, that when the anthropologist is working in this way he is working more or less in a way parallel to that of the linguist. They are both trying to build a structure with constituent units. But, nevertheless, no conclusions can be drawn from the repetition of the signs in the field of behavior and the repetition, let us say, of the phonemes of the language, or the grammatical structure of the language; nothing of the kind—it is perfectly hopeless.

Now let us take a somewhat more elaborate way of approaching a problem of that kind, Whorf's approach, which has been discussed so many times and which certainly must have been at the back of our minds during this discussion.[c] Whorf has tried to establish a correlation between certain linguistic structures and certain cultural structures. Why is it that the approach is unsatisfactory? It is, it seems to me, because the linguistic level as he considers it is the result of a rather sophisticated analysis—he is not at all trying to correlate an empirical impression of the language, but, rather, the result of true linguistic work (I don't know if this linguistic work is satisfactory from the point of view of the linguists, I'm just assuming it for the sake of argument)—what he is trying to correlate with this linguistic structure is a crude, superficial, empirical view of the culture itself. So he is really trying to correlate things which belong to entirely different levels.[14]

---

[13] So far so good. However, if you begin to feel confused at this point, you're not alone. Lévi-Strauss' arguments can be extremely difficult to follow. We will attempt to paraphrase some of them as best we can. Here, Lévi-Strauss presents us with elements of kinship systems based on contrasts, working (as he points out in the next paragraph) in a way that he believes is analogous with the methods of the Prague School. To simplify his argument, in an admittedly "unsatisfactory" way, he says that relations among individuals in kin systems can be either positive or negative, without specifying exactly what he means by this "dichotomy" or how to measure it. One common possibility is that a husband's relationship with his wife is positive and his relationship with his son is positive, but the wife's relationship with her brother and the son's relationship with the wife's brother are negative. He claims the reverse of this is also common. That is, a husband's relationship with his wife is negative and his relationship with his son is negative, but the wife has a positive relationship with her brother and the son has a positive relationship with his mother's brother. These two possibilities roughly correspond to the relationships in strong patrilineal and matrilineal societies, respectively. The relationships he claims are frequent but poorly developed are, first, that the husband has a positive relationship with his wife but a negative relationship with his son; the wife has a negative relationship with her brother, but the son has a positive relationship with his mother's brother. The second is that a husband has a negative relationship with his wife but a positive relationship with his son; the wife has a positive relationship with her brother, but the son has a negative relationship with his mother's brother. The first of these possibilities would create a society that is weakly matrilineal, the second a society that is weakly patrilineal. Are you still with us? Finally, Lévi-Strauss proposes two relationships that he says are rare or perhaps impossible. In the first, a man has a positive relationship with his wife but a negative relationship with his son; the wife has a positive relationship with her brother, but the son has a negative relationship with his mother's brother. Lévi-Strauss says this is impossible because it would lead to the breakup of the group across time (that is, the son would have neither the positive relationship with his father necessary for patrilineal descent nor the positive relations with his mother's brother necessary for matrilineal descent). The second almost impossible possibility is that a husband has negative relations with his wife but positive relations with his son; the wife has negative relations with her brother, but the son has positive relations with his mother's brother. Lévi-Strauss claims that a kinship system constructed this way would be unstable (the wife would have no positive relations but the son would be torn between his father and his mother's brother).

Still there? Good, because this is the really critical part. What you have just seen is Lévi-Strauss' fundamental method of working. He has identified an "atom" of society (the husband, wife, son, and wife's brother) and explored *all* of the logically possible relationships that could connect these people (assuming that their relations can be characterized as positive or negative). He has suggested that some of these relationships are common, some frequent, and some rare or impossible. Thus, he has shown that all kinship systems are really various permutations of a single underlying pattern. The "atom" of kinship is the group consisting of husband, wife, son, and wife's brother. All possible systems of descent can be derived by arranging the members of the group in ways that can be characterized by binary opposition.

[14] Although structuralism is clearly not a Marxist theory, Lévi-Strauss was influenced by Marx and the theory does

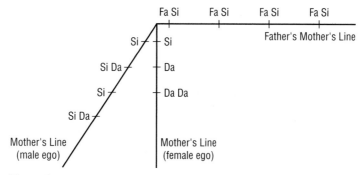

Figure 3.

When we now turn to study the communication system, there are two statements that can be made.[15] The first is that in order to build a model of the Hopi kinship system one has to use a block model, tri-dimensional. It is not possible to use a two-dimensional model. And this, incidentally, is characteristic of all the Crow-Omaha systems. Now, why is that so? Because the Hopi system makes use of three different time continuums. We have the first one, which corresponds to the mother's line (female Ego), which is a kind of time dimension that we use ourselves, that is, progressive and continuative: We have the grandmother, mother, Ego, daughter, granddaughter, and so on; it is really genealogical. (See Figure 3.) Now, when we consider other lines, there is a different time dimension: For instance, if we take the father's mother's line, we find that, although people do belong to generations which are consecutive to each other, the same terms are consistently applied to

them—that is, a woman is called "father's sister" and her daughter is still "father's sister," and so on indefinitely; this is a kind of empty time, with no change taking place whatsoever. And there is also a third dimension, which is found in the mother's line for male Ego, where individuals are alternately called "sibline" and "nephew."

Now if we consider the Zuni kinship system, these three dimensions still exist, but they are considerably reduced; they have a somewhat abortive form. And what is important is that the "straight" time framework that we have in the mother's line is replaced by a kind of "circular" framework, where we have only three terms, a term which equally means "grandmother" and "granddaughter," and then a term for "mother" and a term for "daughter"—a woman would call by the same term her grandmother and her granddaughter.

If we look now at another Pueblo system, let us say Acoma or Laguna, which are Keresan and

---

show some elements of Marxist thinking. In Marxist analysis, the everyday patterns of society are taken to be the surface manifestation of an underlying pattern, the dialectic, which propels the society over the course of time. Lévi-Strauss' theory is timeless. That is to say that, unlike Marxist analysts, he has no interest in history as such. However, like Marxists he believes that society is the surface manifestation of an underlying pattern. The patterns underlying individual cultures are, in their turn, manifestations of a deeper, universal patterning that ultimately resides in the human mind. Thus, talk of levels of analysis is germane to structuralism.

[15] In the next several paragraphs Lévi-Strauss compares the Hopi, Zuni, and Acoma/Laguna kinship systems. He tries

to establish that the patternings present in these systems are also present in the systems of mythology of these groups. He argues that the Hopi system is primarily genealogical (by which he means that, irrespective of other dimensions, Hopi time, represented genealogically, is much the same as ours: grandmother, mother, self, daughter, granddaughter). Zuni kinship and time, is, on the other hand, circular (grandmother/granddaughter, mother, self, daughter, grandmother/granddaughter.) The Acoma/Laguna system is unlike either of these. Instead, people refer to each other by their relation to a third person. Thus, in summary, Hopi kinship systems are linear, Zuni kinship systems are circular, and Acoma/Laguna kinship systems are planar.

belong to a different linguistic stock, then we find a completely new picture: the development of symmetrical terms. Two individuals who occupy symmetrical positions in relation to a third individual will call each other by the same term. This is usually called a "self-reciprocal" terminology.

When we pass from Hopi to Acoma, we have a change from a block model to a flat model, but we have other significant changes. We have a change from a time framework which has a threefold quality, through the Zuni, which is intermediate, to something quite different; it is no longer a time continuum, it is a time-space continuum, since in order to conceive of the system one individual has to think of the other individual through the intermediary of a third one.

This can be very well correlated with the different aspects of the same myths among the Hopi, Zuni, and Acoma.[16] When we consider one myth, let us say the emergence myth, the very striking thing is that among the Hopi the entire structure of the myth is organized in a genealogical way. The different gods are conceived as husband, wife, father, grandfather, daughter, and so on, to one another, more or less as it occurs in the Greek pantheon. Among the Zuni we do not find such a developed genealogical structure. Instead we find a kind of cyclical historical structure. The history is divided into periods, and each period repeats to some extent the preceding period. Now, with the Acoma the striking fact is that most of the characters which among the Hopi or the Zuni are conceived as one person are dichotomized into different persons with antithetic attributes. This is made clear by the fact that the emergence scene, which is so obvious in the first two cases, is preceded, and to some extent replaced, by a dual operation, in which the power from above and the power from below cooperate to create mankind. It is no longer a progressive linear movement, it is a system of polar oppositions, such as we find in the kinship system. Now if it is true that these features of the kinship system can be correlated with systems belonging to a completely different field, the field of mythology, we are entitled to ask the linguist whether or not something of the same kind does not show up in the field of language. And it would be very surprising if something—I do not know exactly what, because I am not a linguist—could not be found to exist, because if the answer should be in the negative we should have to assume that, while fields that are so wide apart as kinship and mythology nevertheless succeed in remaining correlated, language and mythology, which are much more closely related, show no connection or no communication whatsoever.

This new formulation of the problem is, it seems to me, on a level with what the linguists are doing. The linguists are dealing in grammar with the time aspect. They discover the different ways of expressing the idea of time in a language. And we might try to compare the way of expressing time on a linguistic level with the way of expressing time on the kinship level. I do not know what the answer will be, but it is possible to discuss the problem, and it is possible in a meaningful way to answer it by "yes" or "no."[17]

Permit me to give you another, and much more elaborate, example of the kind of analysis the anthropologist could perform to try to find common ground with the linguist. I am going to consider two social developments which have taken place in widely different parts of the world, the first in an area extending roughly from India to Ireland, the second in an area extending from Manchuria to Assam. I am certainly not saying

---

[16] In the passage that follows, Lévi-Strauss argues that the patterning of genealogy and time he has just explained is reflected in the mythologies of the three groups he has described. Thus, he suggests that there is a level of patterning that exists prior to and is generative of both the systems of kinship and the mythologies of these three groups.

[17] Lévi-Strauss has drawn his insight from linguistics. Here he challenges linguists to draw some insight from anthropology. He poses his question in interesting terms. Much

of the conference at which this presentation was made was clearly devoted to arguments for and against the Sapir-Whorf hypothesis. Whorf had argued that the Hopi language did not permit the perception of past, present, and future. Here Lévi-Strauss presents precisely the opposite point of view, claiming that Hopi perceptions are linear and genealogical. His challenge to linguists is to discover some aspect of language that reflects the linear, cyclical, and spatial patternings of Hopi, Zuni, and Acoma/Laguna kinship and mythology.

	Indo-European Area	Sino-Tibetan Area
Marriage Rules	Circular systems, either resulting directly from explicit rules or indirectly from the fact that the choice of a mate is left to probability	Circular systems, present in juxtaposition with systems of symmetrical exchange
Social Organization	Numerous social units, with a complex structure (extended family type)	Few social units, with a simple structure (clan or lineage type)
Kinship System	(1) subjective	(1) objective
	(2) few terms	(2) numerous terms

that each of these two areas has shown exactly one kind of development, and only one. I am saying only that the developments I am referring to are well illustrated within these very vague boundaries, which, as you are well aware, correspond to some extent to the boundaries of the Indo-European languages on the one hand and the Sino-Tibetan languages on the other.

I propose to consider from three different points of view what has taken place. First, the marriage rules; next, social organization; and third, the kinship system.

Now let us consider first the marriage rules, for the sake of clarity. What we find in the Indo-European area are various systems which in order to be properly interpreted have to be referred to a very simple type of marriage rule called the generalized form of exchange, or circular system, because any number of groups can be connected by using this rule.[18] This corresponds roughly to what the anthropologists have called marriage with mother's brother's daughter: Group A is taking wives from Group B, Group B from Group C, and Group C again from Group A; so it is a kind of circle; you can have two groups, three groups, four, five, any number of groups; they can always be organized according to this system. This does not mean that Indo-European-speaking groups have necessarily, at one time or another, practiced

marriage with mother's brother's daughter, but that most of the marriage systems in their area of occupancy belong directly or indirectly to the same family as the simpler type.

Now, in the field of social organization, what do we have? We have, as distinctive of the Indo-European area, something we know by the name of "extended family." What is an extended family? An extended family consists of several collateral lines; but the collateral lines should remain to some extent distinguished from one another, because if they did not—if, for instance, Extended Family A were marrying into B, and Extended Family B into C, then there would be no distinction whatsoever between an extended family and a clan. The extended family would become a kind of clan. And what keeps the different collateral lines distinct in an extended family is that there cannot exist a rule of marriage applicable to all the lines. Now this has been followed up in Indo-European kinship systems in many different ways. Some systems, which are still working in India, state that it is only the senior line which follows a rule, and that all the other lines can marry exactly as they wish within the sole limitation of prohibited degrees. When one studies certain curious features of the old Slavic kinship system, the interpretation is somewhat different: It seems that what may be called the "exemplary

---

[18] Lévi-Strauss was profoundly affected by both Durkheim and Mauss. From Durkheim (as well as the Prague School linguists) he derives the notion that all human thinking is characterized by binary division. From Mauss he derives the idea that the giving and receiving of gifts is a basic human social interaction. He puts these

ideas into play in *Elementary Structures of Kinship* (1969 [1949]), where he analyzes marriage patterns based on the hypothesis that for all people the social world is divided into two categories—my group and not my group—and that women, as marriage partners, are the gifts given and received between these groups.

line" was more or less diagonal to the main one; that is, if a man married according to a given rule, then at the next generational level it would be a man of a different line, and then in the next generation a man of another different line. This does not matter. The point is that with an extended family system it is not possible for all the groups to marry according to the same rule and that a great many exceptions to any conceivable rule should take place.

Now the kinship system itself calls for very few terms and it is a subjective system. This means that all the relatives are described in relation to the subject, and the further the relative is from the subject the vaguer the terms are. We can accurately describe our relationship to our father, mother, son, daughter, brother, and sister, but even aunt or uncle is slightly vague; and when it comes to more distant relationships, we have no terms at all at our disposal; it is an egocentric system.[19]

Let us now compare some features in the Sino-Tibetan area. Here we find two types of marriage rules: one which is the same as the one previously described, generalized exchange; and another one, which is a special form of exchange, usually called "exchange marriage," a special form because, instead of making it possible to organize any number of groups, it can work only with two, four, six, eight—an even number—the system could not work with an odd number. And these two rules exist side by side within the area.

Now about the social organization. We do not have extended families in our second area, but we do find very simple types of the clan system, which can become complicated quantitatively (when the clan system divides into lineages), but never qualitatively, as is the case with the extended family.

As regards the kinship system, the terms are very numerous. You know, for instance, that in the Chinese kinship system the terms number several hundreds; and it is even possible to create an indefinite number of terms; any relationship can be described with accuracy, even if it is very far away from the subject. And this makes the system completely objective; as a matter of fact, Kroeber a long time ago noticed that no kinship systems are so completely different from each other than the Indo-European on the one hand and the Chinese on the other.[20]

If we try to interpret this picture, what do we find? We find that in the Indo-European case we have a very simple structure (marriage rules), but that the elements (social organization) which must be arranged in this structure are numerous and complicated, whereas in the Sino-Tibetan case the opposite prevails: We have a very complicated structure (marriage rules), with two different sets of rules, and the elements (social organization) are few. And to the separation between the structure and the elements correspond, on the level of terminology—which is a linguistic level—antithetic features as to the framework (subjective versus objective) and to the terms themselves (numerous versus few). Now it seems to me that if we formulate the situation in these terms, it is at least possible to start a useful discussion with the linguists. While I was making this chart, I could not but remember what R. Jakobson said at yesterday's session about the structure of the Indo-European language: a great discrepancy between form and substance, a great many irregularities in relation to the rules, and considerable freedom regarding the choice of means to express

---

[19] So, to summarize: (1) We can divide the world into two great areas, one corresponding to the Indo-European world, the other to the Sino-Tibetan world. (2) Indo-European marriage systems link any number of separate groups. (3) Indo-European family systems are characterized by extended families but cannot operate according to a set rule fixed and eternal for all members of all groups. (4) Indo-European kinship systems are egocentric. The more distant an individual is from a person, the less well that person will be able to describe their relationship.

[20] To summarize again, in the Sino-Tibetan area: (1) Marriage systems are either the same as in the Indo-European area or link only even numbers of groups. (2) This area is characterized by clans rather than extended families. (3) Sino-Tibetan kin systems have a great many terms whereby people can describe relationships at large genealogical distances.

the same idea. Are not all of these traits similar to those we have singled out with respect to social structure?[21]

Finally, I would say that between culture and language there cannot be *no* relations at all, and there cannot be 100 percent correlation either. Both situations are impossible to conceive. If there were no relations at all, that would lead us to assume that the human mind is a kind of jumble—that there is no connection at all between what the mind is doing on one level and what the mind is doing on another level. But, on the other hand, if the correlation were 100 percent, then certainly we should know about it and we should not be here to discuss whether it exists or not. So the conclusion which seems to me the most likely is that some kind of correlation exists between certain things on certain levels, and our main task is to determine what these things are and what these levels are. This can be done only through a close cooperation between linguists and anthropologists. I should say that the most important results of such cooperation will not be for linguistics alone or for anthropology alone, or for both; they will mostly be for an anthropology conceived in a broader way—that is, a knowledge of man that incorporates all the different approaches which can be used and that will provide a clue to the way according to which our uninvited guest, the human mind, works.

NOTES

[a]Transcribed from a tape recording of a paper read at the Conference of Anthropologists and Linguists, Bloomington, Indiana, 1952, and first published in *Supplement to International Journal of American Linguistics*, XIX, No. 2.

[b]For examples and a more intensive analysis, see Chapter II of this book.

[c]Benjamin L. Whorf, *Collected Papers on Metalinguistics* (Washington: 1952); *Language, Thought, and Reality*, ed. John B. Carroll (New York:1956).

---

[21] Here again, Lévi-Strauss argues that there is a patterned homology. Language requires grammar: an unconscious set of rules by which utterances are ordered. Kinship is a sort of grammar: a more-or-less unconscious set of rules by which we order relations. Lévi-Strauss believes that, at some level, the rules underlying both are the same. Lévi-Strauss closes this paragraph with a rhetorical question. He believes he has shown that the differences between Indo-European and Sino-Tibetan languages are similar to the differences between the kinship systems common in these areas. However, his example is beset with profound difficulties, some of which he recognizes. First, as he points out, both Indo-European and Sino-Tibetan areas include many different kinship systems. Second, it is in no way self-evident that Jakobson's characteristics (discrepancy between form and substance, many irregularities, and much freedom of choice) are the same as his own (linkage of many groups, numerous and complex social units, subjective/few terms). No doubt, the intrepid scholar can find connections between Jakobson's list and Lévi-Strauss, but that's precisely the problem. Such an individual could, no doubt, find some connections between any two sets of three ideas. Are those connections actually in any way demonstrable or are they simply created by the scholar's thinking? Third, at times, one must wonder if Lévi-Strauss knows what Lévi-Strauss means. For example, you have just read:

What we find in the Indo-European area are various systems which in order to be properly interpreted have to be referred to a very simple type of marriage rule called the generalized form of exchange. . . . This corresponds roughly to what the anthropologists have called marriage with mother's brother's daughter.

A year earlier, speaking of Sino-Tibetan kinship, he had written "They belong to or derive directly from the simplest form of general reciprocity, namely mother's brother's daughter marriage (1951:161)." Thirty years later, Bernadette Bucher asked Lévi-Strauss to reflect back on his work. He replied:

I think that of my theoretical positions as they have been formulated in my first articles, in my first books, I have absolutely nothing to change. However, many things I wrote in the beginning I would not write now, or at least not that way. I realize that many were unwise and not sufficiently grounded in facts, certain parallels between linguistics and anthropology for instance. Let's say that I went a bit too far or too fast. I would now express myself more carefully but with the same basic convictions. (Bucher and Lévi-Strauss 1985:368)

25. *Four Winnebago Myths: A Structural Sketch*

CLAUDE LÉVI-STRAUSS (b. 1908)

AMONG THE MANY talents which make him one of the great anthropologists of our time, Paul Radin has one which gives a singular flavor to his work. He has the authentic esthetic touch, rather uncommon in our profession. This is what we call in French *flair*: the gift of singling out those facts, observations, and documents which possess an especially rich meaning, sometimes undisclosed at first, but likely to become evident as one ponders the implications woven into the material. A crop harvested by Paul Radin, even if he does not choose to mill it himself, is always capable of providing lasting nourishment for many generations of students.[1]

This is the reason why I intend to pay my tribute to the work of Paul Radin by giving some thought to four myths which he has published under the title *The Culture of the Winnebago: As Described by Themselves*.[a] Although Radin himself pointed out in the Preface: "In publishing these texts I have only one object in view, to put at the disposal of students, authentic material for the study of Winnebago culture," and although the four myths were each obtained from different informants, it seems that, on a structural level, there was good reason for making them the subject of a single publication. A deep unity underlies all four, notwithstanding the fact that one myth, as Radin has shown in his introduction and notes, appears to differ widely in content, style, and structure from the other three. My purpose will be to analyze the structural relationships between the four myths and to suggest that they can be grouped together not only because they

are part of a collection of ethnographic and linguistic data referring to one tribe, which Radin too modestly claimed as his sole purpose, but because they are of the same genre, i.e., their meanings logically complement each other.[2]

The title of the first myth is "The Two Friends Who Became Reincarnated: The Origin of the Four Nights' Wake." This is the story of two friends, one of them a chief's son, who decide to sacrifice their lives for the welfare of the community. After undergoing a series of ordeals in the underworld, they reach the lodge of Earthmaker, who permits them to become reincarnated and to resume their previous lives among their relatives and friends.

As explained by Radin in his commentary,[b] there is a native theory underlying the myth: every individual is entitled to a specific quota of years of life and experience. If a person dies before his time, his relatives can ask the spirits to distribute among them what he has failed to utilize. But there is more in this theory than meets the eye. The unspent life-span given up by the hero, when he lets himself be killed by the enemies, will be added to the capital of life, set up in trust for the group. Nevertheless, his act of dedication is not entirely without personal profit: by becoming a hero an individual makes a choice, he exchanges a full life-span for a shortened one, but while the full life-span is unique, granted once and for all, the shortened one appears as a kind of lease taken on eternity. That is, by giving up one full life, an indefinite succession of half-lives is gained. But since all the unlived halves will increase the life expectancy of the ordinary people, everybody gains in the

(1960)

---

[1] This article first appeared in a volume called *Culture in History: Essays in Honor of Paul Radin* (1960), published soon after Radin's death.

[2] "Four Winnebago Myths" is a short example of Lévi-Strauss' structural analysis of myth. His goal is to understand the unconscious structure of the human mind and thought processes. In his opinion, myths of aboriginal so-

cieties are the perfect vehicles for that endeavor because such mythology has less "cultural interference" to filter out than stories in Western industrial societies. The outward story line of the myth is irrelevant, but by analyzing the logical relationships between elements of the myth Lévi-Strauss believes he can arrive at the unconscious message the myth conveys.

process: the ordinary people whose average life expectancy will slowly but substantially increase generation after generation, and the warriors with shortened but indefinitely renewable lives, provided their minds remain set on self-dedication.

It is not clear, however, that Radin pays full justice to the narrator when he treats as a "secondary interpretation" the fact that the expedition is undertaken by the heroes to show their appreciation of the favors of their fellow villagers.[c] My contention is that this motive of the heroes deserves primary emphasis, and it is supported by the fact that there are two war parties. The first one is undertaken by the warriors while the heroes are still in their adolescent years, so they are neither included in, nor even informed of it; they hear about the party only as a rumor[d] and they decide to join it uninvited. We must conclude then that the heroes have no responsibility for the very venture wherein they distinguish themselves, since it has been instigated and led by others. Moreover, they are not responsible for the second war party, during which they are killed, since this latter foray has been initiated by the enemy in revenge for the first.[3]

The basic idea is clear: the two friends have developed into successful social beings;[e] accordingly, they feel obliged to repay their fellow tribesmen who have treated them so well.[f] As the story goes, they set out to expose themselves in the wilderness; later they die in an ambush prepared by the enemy in revenge for the former defeat. The obvious conclusion is that the heroes have willingly died for the sake of their people. And because they died without responsibility of their own, but instead that of others, those will inherit the unspent parts of their lives, while the heroes themselves will be permitted to return to earth and the same process will be repeated all over again. This interpretation is in agreement with information given elsewhere by Radin: i.e., in order to pass the test of

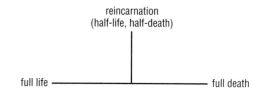

DIAGRAM 1.

the Old Woman who rids the soul of all the recollections belonging to its earthly life, each soul must be solicitous not of its own welfare but of the welfare of the living members of the group.

Now at the root of this myth we find—as the phonologist would say—a double opposition. First there is the opposition between *ordinary life* and *heroic life,* the former realizing a full life-span, not renewable, the latter gambling with life for the benefit of the group. The second opposition is between two kinds of death, one "straight" and final, although it provides a type of unearthly immortality in the villages of the dead; the other "undulating," and swinging between life and death. Indeed one is tempted to see the reflection of this double fate in the Winnebago symbol of the ladder of the afterworld as it appears in the Medicine Rite. One side is "like a frog's leg, twisted and dappled with light-and-life. The other [is] like a red cedar, blackened from frequent usage and very smooth and shiny."[g,4]

To sum up the meaning of the myth so far: if one wants a full life one gets a full death; if one renounces life and seeks death, then one increases the full life of his fellow-tribesmen, and, moreover, secures for oneself a state composed of an indefinite series of half-lives and half-deaths. Thus we have a triangular system.

The second myth, entitled "The Man Who Brought His Wife Back from Spiritland," is a variation on the same theme, although there is a significant difference involved. Here too, we find

---

[3] Like the Freudian analyst, Lévi-Strauss is searching for unconscious meaning, freeing him to interpret the motives of the myth's characters and place emphasis on the elements of the story he feels are significant regardless of the storyline. As Lévi-Strauss pointed out in the previous essay, the structural analyst is not interested in individual story elements but combinations of those elements. Examining the relationship between combinations of elements provides the analyst with the unconscious meaning the myth.

[4] Lévi-Strauss believes in the Hegelian idea that the structure of human perception is dialectical. In his structural analyses of myth he looks for binary oppositions within the elements of the story and the factors that mediate them. For example, in the Winnebago myth described here, the opposition between life and death is mediated by reincarnation. The myth's message is derived from the logical relationships between patterns of such oppositions.

a hero—the husband—ready to sacrifice his un-spent life-span; not, as in the first myth, for the benefit of the group, but rather for the benefit of only one individual, his beloved wife. Indeed, the hero is not aware at first that by seeking death he will secure a new lease on life for both his dead wife and himself. Had he been so aware, and this holds equally for the protagonists in the first myth, the essential element of sacrifice would have been missing. In both cases the result is similar: an altruistic loss of life means life re-gained, not only for the self-appointed victim, but also for the one or more persons to whom the sacrifice was consecrated.

The third myth, "The Journey of the Ghost to Spiritland, as Told in the Medicine Rite," be-longs, as the title suggests, to a religious society. It explains how the members of the Medicine Rite, after death, undergo (as do the protagonists of the other myths) several tests in Spiritland, which they overcome, thus gaining the right to become reincarnated.[5]

At first sight this situation seems to differ from the others, since nobody sacrificed his life. However, the members of the Medicine Rite ac-tually spend their lives in symbolic sacrifice. As Radin has shown, in *The Road of Life and Death* and elsewhere, the Medicine Rite follows the fa-miliar pattern of letting oneself be "killed" and then "revived." Thus the only departure consists in the fact that whereas in the first and second myths the heroes are willing to die once and, so they anticipate, permanently, the heroes of the third myth (the members of the Rite) repeatedly, though symbolically, have trained themselves to self-sacrifice. They have, so to speak, mithrida-tized[6] themselves against a full death by re-nouncing a full ordinary life which is replaced, in ritual practice, by a lifelong succession of half-lives and half-deaths. Therefore we are entitled to assume that, in this case too, the myth is made up of the same elements, although Ego—and not another person, nor the group as a whole—is conceived as the primary beneficiary.

Let us now consider the fourth myth, "How an Orphan Restored the Chief's Daughter to Life," a tale which has given Radin some con-cern. This myth, he says, is not only different from the other three, its plot appears unusual rel-ative to the rest of Winnebago mythology. After recalling that in his book *Method and Theory of Ethnology*[h] he suggested that this myth was a version, altered almost beyond recognition, of a type which he then called village-origin myths, he proceeds to explain in *The Culture of the Win-nebago*[i] why he can no longer support his earlier interpretation.

It is worthwhile to follow closely Radin's new line of reasoning. He begins by recapitulating the plot—such a simple plot, he says, that there is practically no need for doing so: "The daughter of a tribal chief falls in love with an orphan, dies of a broken heart and is then restored to life by the orphan who must submit to and overcome cer-tain tests, not in spiritland but here, on earth, in the very lodge in which the young woman died."[j]

If this plot is "simplicity itself," where do the moot points lie? Radin lists three which he says every modern Winnebago would question: (1) the plot seems to refer to a highly stratified society; (2) in order to understand the plot one should as-sume that in that society women occupied a high position and that, possibly, descent was reckoned in the matrilineal line; (3) the tests which in

---

[5] Notice that Lévi-Strauss writes in the tradition of the French sociological school that preceded him: His method is com-parative. He chooses those pieces of traditions or beliefs from different societies that fit his view regardless of the cul-tural context in which these elements are found. Lévi-Strauss interprets these myths for his readers without giving them the full text of the stories or providing any background infor-mation about Winnebago society. This is a typical French structuralist approach: Because the unconscious structure of human thought is universal, the cultural context of the myths is superficial and irrelevant to the myths' underlying mes-sage. For this kind of analysis, he says, the meaning of the myths is not found in the history or culture of the Win-nebago. The only context Lévi-Strauss requires is the myths themselves. American anthropologists, as inheritors of the Boasian tradition, are inclined to place more emphasis on the specific cultural contexts in which events occur.

[6] *Mithridatized:* To develop a tolerance or immunity to something by taking small doses of it, from the Greek myth of King Mithridates, who in this way developed an immunity to poison.

Winnebago mythology take place, as a rule, in the land of ghosts occur, in this instance, on earth.

After dismissing two possible explanations—that we are dealing here with a borrowed European tale or that the myth was invented by some Winnebago radical—Radin concludes that the myth must belong to "a very old stratum of Winnebago history." He also suggests that two distinct types of literary tradition, divine tales on the one hand and human tales on the other, have merged while certain primitive elements have been reinterpreted to make them fit together.[k]

I am certainly not going to challenge this very elegant reconstruction backed by an incomparable knowledge of Winnebago culture, language, and history. The kind of analysis I intended to offer is no alternative to Radin's own analysis. It lies on a different level, logical rather than historical. It takes as its context the three myths already discussed, not Winnebago culture, old or recent. My purpose is to explicate the structural relationship—if any—which prevails between this myth and the other three.

First, there is a theoretical problem which should be noted briefly. Since the publication of Boas' *Tsimshian Mythology,* anthropologists have often simply assumed that a full correlation exists between the myths of a given society and its culture. This, I feel, is going further than Boas intended. In the work just referred to, he did not suppose that myths automatically reflect the culture, as some of his followers seem always to anticipate. Rather, he tried to find out how much of the culture actually did pass into the myths, if any, and he convincingly showed that *some* of it does. It does not follow that whenever a social pattern is alluded to in a myth this pattern must correspond to something real which should be attributed to the past if, under direct scrutiny, the present fails to offer an equivalent.[7]

There must be, and there is, a correspondence between the unconscious meaning of a myth—the problem it tries to solve—and the conscious content it makes use of to reach that end, i.e., the plot. However, this correspondence should not always be conceived as a kind of mirror-image, it can also appear as a *transformation.*[8] If the problem is presented in "straight" terms, that is, in the way the social life of the group expresses and tries to solve it, the overt content of the myth, the plot, can borrow its elements from social life itself. But should the problem be formulated, and its solution sought for, "upside down," that is *ab absurdo,* then the overt content will become modified accordingly to form an inverted image of the social pattern actually present to the consciousness of the natives.

If this hypothesis is true, it follows that Radin's assumption that the pattern of social life referred to in the fourth myth must belong to a past stage of Winnebago history, is not inescapable.

We may be confronted with the pattern of a nonexistent society, contrary to the Winnebago traditional pattern, only because the structure of that particular myth is itself inverted, in relation to those myths which use as overt content the traditional pattern. To put it simply, if a certain correspondence is assumed between A and B, then if A is replaced by −A, B must be replaced by −B, without implying that, since B corresponds to an external object, there should exist another external object −B, which must exist somewhere: either in another society (borrowed element) or in a past stage of the same society (survival).

---

[7] Franz Boas was a vehement cultural relativist. Here Lévi-Strauss tries to reconcile French structuralism with Boasian particularism.

[8] In his first great book, *The Elementary Structures of Kinship* (1949), Lévi-Strauss postulated that there was a universal psychological need to give and receive gifts. He believed that this was based on a fundamental dialectic of the human mind—the distinction between self and others. He devoted an entire chapter to child psychology in an attempt to justify this claim (Harris 1968:491). Here Lévi-Strauss once again resorts to psychological theory, in this case psychoanalysis, to justify his point of view. He states that there must be some agreement between a myth's underlying meaning and its plot. However, the correspondence between meaning and plot may appear as a "transformation," or an "upside down" version of the apparent meaning. There is no question that this is an important insight for both psychology and myth analysis, but it offers dangers as well. If used carelessly, this concept can be used to justify any flight of imagination that may occur to the interpreter.

Obviously the problem remains: why do we have three myths of the A type and one of the −A type? This could be the case because −A is older than A, but it can also be because −A is one of the transformations of A which is already known to us under three different guises: A_1A_2, A_3, since we have seen that the three myths of the assumed A type are not identical.

We have already established that the group of myths under consideration is based upon a fundamental opposition: on the one hand, the lives of ordinary people unfolding towards a natural death, followed by immortality in one of the spirit villages—; and, on the other hand, heroic life, self-abridged, the gain being a supplementary life quota for the others as well as for oneself. The former alternative is not envisaged in this group of myths which, as we have seen, is mostly concerned with the latter. There is, however, a secondary difference which permits us to classify the first three myths according to the particular end assigned to the self-sacrifice in each. In the first myth the group is intended to be the immediate beneficiary, in the second it is another individual (the wife), and in the third it is oneself.

When we turn to the fourth myth, we may agree with Radin that it exhibits "unusual" features in relation to the other three. However, the difference seems to be of a logical more than of a sociological or historical nature. It consists in a new opposition introduced within the first pair of opposites (between "ordinary" life and "extraordinary" life). Now there are two ways in which an "extraordinary" phenomenon may be construed as such; it may consist either in a *surplus* or in a *lack*. While the heroes of the first three myths are all overgifted, through social success, emotions or wisdom, the heroes of the fourth myth are, if one may say so, "below standard," at least in one respect.

The chief's daughter occupies a high social position; so high, in fact, that she is cut off from the rest of the group and is therefore paralyzed when it comes to expressing her feelings. Her exalted position makes her a defective human being, lacking an essential attribute of life. The boy is also defective, but socially, that is, he is an orphan and very poor. May we say, then, that the myth reflects a stratified society? This would compel us to overlook the remarkable symmetry which prevails between our two heroes, for it would be wrong to say simply that one is high and the other low: as a matter of fact, each of them is high in one respect and low in the other, and this pair of symmetrical structures, wherein the two terms are inverted relative to each other, belongs to the realm of ideological constructs rather than of sociological systems. We have just seen that the girl is "socially" above and "naturally" below. The boy is undoubtedly very low in the social scale; however, he is a miraculous hunter, i.e. he entertains privileged relations with the natural world, the world of animals. This is emphasized over and over again in the myth.[1]

Therefore may we not claim that the myth actually confronts us with a polar system consisting in two individuals, one male, the other female, and both exceptional insofar as each of them is overgifted in one way (+) and undergifted in the other (−).[9]

The plot consists in carrying this disequilibrium to its logical extreme; the girl dies a *natural* death, the boy stays alone, i.e. he also dies, but in a *social* way. Whereas during their ordinary lives the girl was overtly above, the boy overtly below, now that they have become segregated (either from the living or from society) their positions are inverted: the girl is below (in her grave), the boy above (in his lodge). This, I think, is clearly implied in a detail stated by the narrator which seems to have puzzled Radin: "On top of the grave they then piled loose dirt, placing everything in such a way that nothing could seep through."[m] Radin comments: "I do not understand why piling the dirt loosely would prevent seepage. There must be something else involved that has not been mentioned."[n] May I suggest that this detail be correlated with a similar detail about the building of the young man's lodge: ". . . the bottom was piled high with dirt so that, in this fashion, they

---

[9] The opposition of nature and culture illustrated in the figure and explained later is one of the fundamental principles in French structuralist thought and finds expression in a variety of forms. See for example, Lévi-Strauss' book *The Raw and the Cooked* (1969).

	Nature	Culture
Boy	+	−
Girl	−	+

DIAGRAM 2.

could keep the lodge warm."[o] There is implied here, I think, not a reference to recent or past custom but rather a clumsy attempt to emphasize that, relative to the earth's surface, i.e. dirt, the boy is now above and the girl below.

This new equilibrium, however, will be no more lasting than the first. *She who was unable to live cannot die*; her ghost lingers "on earth." Finally she induces the young man to fight the ghosts and take her back among the living. With a wonderful symmetry, the boy will meet, a few years later, with a similar, although inverted, fate; "Although I am not yet old, he says to the girl (now his wife), I have been here (lasted) on earth as long as I can. . . ."[p] *He who overcame death, proves unable to live.* This recurring antithesis could develop indefinitely, and such a possibility is noted in the text (with an only son surviving his father, he too an orphan, he too a sharpshooter) but a different solution is finally reached. The heroes, equally unable to die or to live, will assume an intermediate identity, that of twilight creatures living under the earth but also able to come up on it; they will be neither men nor gods, but wolves, that is, ambivalent spirits combining good and evil features. So ends the myth.

If the above analysis is correct, two consequences follow: first, our myth makes up a consistent whole wherein the details balance and fit each other nicely; secondly, the three problems raised by Radin can be analyzed in terms of the myth itself; and no hypothetical past stage of Winnebago society need be invoked.

Let us, then, try to solve these three problems, following the pattern of our analysis.

1. The society of the myth appears stratified, only because the two heroes are conceived as a pair of opposites, but they are such both from the point of view of nature *and* of culture. Thus, the so-called stratified society should be interpreted not as a sociological

vestige but as a projection of a logical structure wherein everything is given both in opposition and correlation.

2. The same answer can be given to the question of the assumed exalted position of the women. If I am right, our myths state three propositions, the first by implication, the second expressly stated in myths 1, 2 and 3, the third expressly stated in myth 4.

These propositions are as follow:

a. Ordinary people live (their full lives) and die (their full deaths).

b. Positive extraordinary people die (earlier) and live (more).

c. Negative extraordinary people are able neither to live nor to die.

Obviously proposition c offers an inverted demonstration of the truth of a and b. Hence, it must use a plot starting with protagonists (here, man and woman) in inverted positions. This leads us to state that a plot and its component parts should neither be interpreted by themselves nor relative to something outside the realm of the myth proper, but as *substitutions* given in, and understandable only with reference to *the group made up of all the myths of the same series.*

3. We may now revert to the third problem raised by Radin about myth 4, that is, the contest with the ghosts takes place on earth instead of, as was usually the case, in spiritland. To this query I shall suggest an answer along the same lines as the others.

It is precisely because our two heroes suffer from a state of *under-life* (in respect either to culture or nature) that, in the narrative, the ghosts become a kind of *super-dead*. It will be recalled that the whole myth develops and is resolved on an intermediary level, where humans become underground animals and ghosts linger on earth. It tells about people who are, from the start, half-alive and half-dead while, in the preceding myths, the opposition between life and death is strongly emphasized at the beginning, and overcome only at the end. Thus, the integral meaning of the four myths is that, in order to be overcome the opposition between life and death

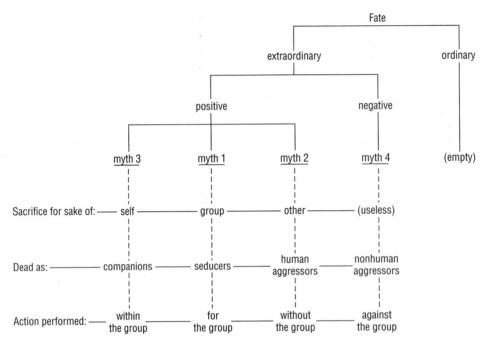

DIAGRAM 3.

should be first acknowledged, or else the ambiguous state will persist indefinitely.[10]

I hope to have shown that the four myths under consideration all belong to the same *group* (understood as in *group theory*) and that Radin was even more right than he supposed in publishing them together. In the first place, the four myths deal with extraordinary, in opposition to ordinary, fate. The fact that ordinary fate is not illustrated here and thus is reckoned as an "empty" category, does not imply, of course, that it is not illustrated elsewhere. In the second place, we find an opposition between two types of extraordinary fate, positive and negative. This new dichotomy which permits us to segregate myth 4 from myths 1, 2 and 3 corresponds, on a logical level, to the discrimination that Radin makes on psychological, sociological, and historical grounds. Finally, myths 1, 2 and 3 have been classified according to the purpose of the sacrifice which is the theme of each.[11]

Thus the four myths can be organized in a dichotomous structure of correlations and oppositions. But we can go even further and try to order them on a common scale. This is suggested by the curious variations which can be observed in each myth with respect to the kind of test the hero is put to by the ghosts. In myth 3 there is no test at all, so

---

[10] Lévi-Strauss presents his analysis with unquestioned skill, but is erudition the same as accuracy? One of the principal criticisms of Lévi-Strauss' structuralism is that he presents masterful analyses that seem to be based in his own fantastic imagination and forceful writing style. Attempts to replicate his analyses usually fail or arrive at different conclusions.

[11] Lévi-Strauss has done anthropology a tremendous service by outlining a methodology for the sorting of anthropological data. As a method of analysis, structuralism can lead to valuable interpretive insights where other theoretical perspectives may fail. But as a means for proving the binary structure of the mind, structuralism has failed. Lévi-Strauss is no closer to proving his hypothesis about the unconscious structure of human thought than Sigmund Freud had been almost a century ago. In spite of the dialectical nature of Lévi-Strauss' theory and his self-professed allegiance to Marxist thought, materialists have provided some of the most telling critiques of structuralism. Those who view anthropology as a science generally discount Lévi-Strauss' structuralism because the reality he claims to present is an unconscious one and thus unverifiable (Malefijt 1974:330). Marvin Harris, for example, says that a "paralysis of reality"

far as the ghosts are concerned. The tests consist in overcoming material obstacles while the ghosts themselves figure as indifferent fellow travelers. In myth 1 they cease to be indifferent without yet becoming hostile. On the contrary, the tests result from their overfriendliness, as inviting women and infectious merry-makers. Thus, from *companions* in myth 3 they change to seducers in myth 1. In myth 2 they still behave as human beings, but they now act as *aggressors,* and permit themselves all kinds of rough play. This is even more evident in myth 4, but here the human element vanishes; it is only at the end that we know that ghosts, not crawling insects, are responsible for the trials of the hero. We have thus a twofold progression, from a *peaceful* attitude to an *aggressive* one, and from *human* to *nonhuman* behavior.

This progression can be correlated with the kind of relationship which the hero (or heroes) of each myth entertain with the social group. The hero of myth 3 belongs to a ritual brotherhood: he definitely assumes his (privileged) fate as a member of a group, he acts with and in his group.

The two heroes of myth 1 have resolved to part from the group, but the text states repeatedly that this is in order to find an opportunity to achieve something beneficial for their fellow tribesmen. They act, therefore, for the group. But in myth 2 the hero is only inspired by his love for his wife. There is no reference to the group. The action is undertaken independently for the sake of another individual. Finally, in myth 4, the negative attitude toward the group is clearly revealed; the girl dies of her "uncommunicativeness," if one may say so. Indeed she prefers to die rather than speak; death is her "final" exile. As for the boy, he refuses to follow the villagers when they decide to move away and abandon the grave. The segregation is thus willfully sought on all sides; the action unrolls against the group.

The accompanying chart summarizes our discussion. I am quite aware that, in order to be fully convincing, the argument should not be limited to the four myths considered here, but include more of the invaluable Winnebago mythology which Radin has given us. But I hope that by integrating more material the basic structure outlined has become richer and more complex, without being impaired. By singling out one book which its author would perhaps consider a minor contribution, I have intended to emphasize, in an indirect way, the fecundity of the method followed by Radin, and the lasting value of the problems he poses for the anthropologist.[12]

NOTES

[a] Paul Radin, *The Culture of the Winnebago: As Described by Themselves* Special Publication of the Bollingen Foundation (also published as Memoir 2 of the *International Journal of American Linguistics,* 1949, pp. iv, 1–119).

[b] *Ibid.,* p. 41, para. 32.

[c] *Ibid.,* p. 37, para. 2.

[d] *Ibid.,* paras. 11–14.

[e] *Ibid.,* paras. 66–70.

[f] *Ibid.,* para. 72.

[g] *Ibid.,* p. 71, paras. 91–93; see also Paul Radin, *The Road of Life and Death,* Bollingen Series, Vol. V (New York, 1945), especially the author's illuminating comments on pp. 63–65.

[h] Paul Radin, *Method and Theory of Ethnology* (New York, 1933), pp. 238–45.

[i] Radin, *The Culture of the Winnebago,* pp. 74 ff.

[j] *Ibid.,* p. 74.

[k] *Ibid.,* pp. 74–77.

[l] *Ibid.,* see paras. 10–14, 17–18, 59–60, 77–90.

[m] *Ibid.,* p. 87, para. 52.

[n] *Ibid.,* p. 100, n. 40.

[o] *Ibid.,* p. 87, para. 74.

[p] *Ibid.,* p. 4, para. 341.

---

spreads over his entire work (1968:497). Even one of Lévi-Strauss' greatest admirers, Edmund Leach, says:

> I am ready to concede that the structures which he displays are products of an unconscious mental process, but I can see no reason to believe that they are human universals. Bereft of Lévi-Strauss' resourceful special pleading they appear to be local, functionally determined attributes of particular individuals or of particular cultural groups. (Leach 1976:126)

[12] It is ironic that in the last paragraph of this essay Lévi-Strauss states he intended to emphasize the "fecundity of the method followed by Radin." Radin was the quintessential historical particularist who spent much of his career studying the Winnebago in extensive detail. With its emphasis on universal structures of the mind and large-scale cross-cultural comparisons, nothing could be further from Radin's approach than Lévi-Strauss' structuralism. Lévi-Strauss was perhaps aware of this irony.

26. *Is Female to Male as Nature Is to Culture?*

Sherry B. Ortner (b. 1941)

Much of the creativity of anthropology derives from the tension between two sets of demands: that we explain human universals, and that we explain cultural particulars. By this canon, woman provides us with one of the more challenging problems to be dealt with. The secondary status of woman in society is one of the true universals, a pan-cultural fact. Yet within that universal fact, the specific cultural conceptions and symbolizations of woman are extraordinarily diverse and even mutually contradictory. Further, the actual treatment of women and their relative power and contribution vary enormously from culture to culture, and over different periods in the history of particular cultural traditions. Both of these points—the universal fact and the cultural variation—constitute problems to be explained.[1]

My interest in the problem is of course more than academic: I wish to see genuine change come about, the emergence of a social and cultural order in which as much of the range of human potential is open to women as is open to men. The universality of female subordination, the fact that it exists within every type of social and economic arrangement and in societies of every degree of complexity, indicates to me that we are up against something very profound, very stubborn, something we cannot rout out simply by rearranging a few tasks and roles in the social system, or even by reordering the whole economic structure. In this paper I try to expose the underlying logic of cultural thinking that assumes the inferiority of women; I try to show the highly persuasive nature of the logic, for if it were not so persuasive, people would not keep subscribing to it. But I also try to show the social and cultural sources of that logic, to indicate wherein lies the potential for change.[2]

(1974)

---

[1] Early feminist critiques assumed the universal subordination of women; for instance, in her opening paragraph, Ortner states that the secondary status of women is a "pan-cultural fact." The purpose of the article is to formulate a theory that explains this universal gender asymmetry.

Feminist scholars dealt with the question of gender asymmetry in a variety of ways. Leacock (essay 33 in this volume), for example, approached the issue from a Marxist perspective, claiming that gender subordination was a product of external factors—namely, the introduction of capitalism and men's control of the forces of production in society. Ortner's answer to this issue turns inward. Rather than finding the answer to her questions in the material factors of society, she looks for the answer in the structure of human thought.

Structuralists believe that cultural phenomena are the product of universal logical processes that organize human thought. And a fundamental characteristic of human thought, according to structuralists, is to sort data into binary oppositions. Therefore, one should be able to identify cross-cultural patterns of oppositions associated with men and women. This is exactly what Ortner sets out to do in this essay.

A decade later, theorists abandoned the view that women were everywhere and always subordinate to men in favor of a more sophisticated view that examined the cultural construction of relationships between men and women. But in the 1970s, within the political context of the women's movement, the domination of women by men was accepted doctrine for feminist anthropologists.

[2] Most anthropological theory, though influenced by prevailing political events or philosophies, is not written with an openly political objective. With rare exceptions, such as Gorer and Rickman's *The People of Great Russia* (1962 [1949]), it was not until the 1970s, when college campuses were extremely politicized, that anthropologists such as Ortner started writing politically charged work.

Ortner talks about exposing the "underlying logic of cultural thinking." The notion that a hidden logic underlies human thought is basic to structuralism. The fundamental dichotomy she has constructed for analysis is male-power versus female-subordination. Ortner's argument is based directly on the work of Lévi-Strauss, whose books *The Elementary Structures of Kinship* (1969 [1949]) and *The Raw and the Cooked* (1969) are cited in her paper. In fact, the title of one section of her essay ("Nature and Culture") is a direct reference to Lévi-Strauss' proposition that a fundamental opposition through which humans conceptualize the world is between nature and culture.

It is important to sort out the levels of the problem. The confusion can be staggering. For example, depending on which aspect of Chinese culture we look at, we might extrapolate any of several entirely different guesses concerning the status of women in China. In the ideology of Taoism, *yin*, the female principle, and *yang*, the male principle, are given equal weight; "the opposition, alternation, and interaction of these two forces give rise to all phenomena in the universe" (Siu, 1968:2). Hence we might guess that maleness and femaleness are equally valued in the general ideology of Chinese culture.[a] Looking at the social structure, however, we see the strongly emphasized patrilineal descent principle, the importance of sons, and the absolute authority of the father in the family. Thus we might conclude that China is the archetypal patriarchal society. Next, looking at the actual roles played, power and influence wielded, and material contributions made by women in Chinese society—all of which are, upon observation, quite substantial—we would have to say that women are allotted a great deal of (unspoken) status in the system. Or again, we might focus on the fact that a goddess, Kuan Yin, is the central (most worshiped, most depicted) deity in Chinese Buddhism, and we might be tempted to say, as many have tried to say about goddess-worshiping cultures in prehistoric and early historical societies, that China is actually a sort of matriarchy. In short, we must be absolutely clear about *what* we are trying to explain before explaining it.

We may differentiate three levels of the problem:

1. The universal fact of culturally attributed second-class status of women in every society. Two questions are important here. First, what do we mean by this; what is our evidence that this is a universal fact? And second, how are we to explain this fact, once having established it?

2. Specific ideologies, symbolizations, and socio-structural arrangements pertaining to women that vary widely from culture to culture. The problem at this level is to account for any particular cultural complex in terms of factors specific to that group—the standard level of anthropological analysis.

3. Observable on-the-ground details of women's activities, contributions, powers, influence, etc., often at variance with cultural ideology (although always constrained within the assumption that women may never be officially preeminent in the total system). This is the level of direct observation, often adopted now by feminist-oriented anthropologists.

This paper is primarily concerned with the first of these levels, the problem of the universal devaluation of women. The analysis thus depends not upon specific cultural data but rather upon an analysis of "culture" taken generically as a special sort of process in the world. A discussion of the second level, the problem of cross-cultural variation in conceptions and relative valuations of women, will entail a great deal of cross-cultural research and must be postponed to another time. As for the third level, it will be obvious from my approach that I would consider it a misguided endeavor to focus only upon women's actual though culturally unrecognized and unvalued powers in any given society, without first understanding the overarching ideology and deeper assumptions of the culture that render such powers trivial.[3]

---

[3] Ortner's choice of level follows from her structuralist theoretical position. A basic principle of structuralism is that a single universal cultural patterning underlies all individual cultures. Therefore, structuralism should be a good method for explaining universal cultural characteristics. It would be less effective at explaining the specifics of cultural symbols (Ortner's second level). In fact, structuralists do not generally consider the meanings of individual symbols important. It is their pattern that is critical. The third level is of even less interest for structuralists. Since they believe that culture is a mental model, structuralists are much more concerned with what people think and say than what they do.

THE UNIVERSALITY OF FEMALE SUBORDINATION

What do I mean when I say that everywhere, in every known culture, women are considered in some degree inferior to men? First of all, I must stress that I am talking about *cultural* evaluations; I am saying that each culture, in its own way and on its own terms, makes this evaluation. But what would constitute evidence that a particular culture considers women inferior?

Three types of data would suffice: (1) elements of cultural ideology and informants' statements that *explicitly* devalue women, according them, their roles, their tasks, their products, and their social milieux less prestige than are accorded men and the male correlates; (2) symbolic devices, such as the attribution of defilement, which may be interpreted as *implicitly* making a statement of inferior valuation; and (3) social structural arrangements that exclude women from participation in or contact with some realm in which the highest powers of the society are felt to reside.[b] These three types of data may all of course be interrelated in any particular system, though they need not necessarily be. Further, any one of them will usually be sufficient to make the point of female inferiority in a given culture. Certainly, female exclusion from the most sacred rite or the highest political council is sufficient evidence. Certainly, explicit cultural ideology devaluing women (and their tasks, roles, products, etc.) is sufficient evidence. Symbolic indicators such as defilement are usually sufficient, although in a few cases in which, say, men and women are equally polluting to one another, a

further indicator is required—and is, as far as my investigations have ascertained, always available.

On any or all of these counts, then, I would flatly assert that we find women subordinated to men in every known society.[4] The search for a genuinely egalitarian, let alone matriarchal, culture has proved fruitless. An example from one society that has traditionally been on the credit side of this ledger will suffice. Among the matrilineal Crow, as Lowie[5] (1956) points out, "Women . . . had highly honorific offices in the Sun Dance; they could become directors of the Tobacco Ceremony and played, if anything, a more conspicuous part in it than the men; they sometimes played the hostess in the Cooked Meat Festival; they were not debarred from sweating or doctoring or from seeking a vision" (p. 61). Nonetheless, "Women [during menstruation] formerly rode inferior horses and evidently this loomed as a source of contamination, for they were not allowed to approach either a wounded man or men starting on a war party. A taboo still lingers against their coming near sacred objects at these times" (p. 44). Further, just before enumerating women's rights of participation in the various rituals noted above, Lowie mentions one particular Sun Dance Doll bundle that was not supposed to be unwrapped by a woman (p. 60). Pursuing this trail we find: "According to all Lodge Grass informants and most others, the doll owned by Wrinkled-face took precedence not only of other dolls but of all other Crow medicines whatsoever. . . . This particular doll was not supposed to be handled by a woman" (p. 229).[c]

In sum, the Crow are probably a fairly typical case. Yes, women have certain powers and rights,

---

[4] In this paragraph, Ortner sets out the basic criteria that she believes prove a culture considers women inferior. Below, she provides examples of these different classes of evidence from different societies. However, she doesn't give the reader all three types of evidence for any single society. Ortner says that although the three types of data may all be found in one system, any single one of them is sufficient to prove female inferiority in a given culture.

If one accepts the structuralist premise that cultural patterns originate in the way the brain processes informa-

tion, this is an acceptable methodological technique. However, her methods seem little different from those of the nineteenth-century evolutionists who validated their cross-cultural comparative analyses using the concept of psychic unity.

[5] Austrian-born anthropologist Robert Lowie (1883–1957) was a student of Franz Boas. Lowie wrote extensively on the Crow as well as other Plains Indians. Be sure to read Ortner's footnote "c" (page 358) about Lowie and his doll.

in this case some that place them in fairly high positions. Yet ultimately the line is drawn: menstruation is a threat to warfare, one of the most valued institutions of the tribe, one that is central to their self-definition; and the most sacred object of the tribe is taboo to the direct sight and touch of women.

Similar examples could be multiplied ad infinitum, but I think the onus is no longer upon us to demonstrate that female subordination is a cultural universal; it is up to those who would argue against the point to bring forth counter examples. I shall take the universal secondary status of women as a given, and proceed from there.[6]

NATURE AND CULTURE[d]

How are we to explain the universal devaluation of women? We could of course rest the case on biological determinism. There is something genetically inherent in the male of the species, so the biological determinists would argue, that makes them the naturally dominant sex; that "something" is lacking in females, and as a result women are not only naturally subordinate but in general quite satisfied with their position, since it affords them protection and the opportunity to maximize maternal pleasures, which to them are the most satisfying experiences of life. Without going into a detailed refutation of this position, I think it fair to say that it has failed to be established to the satisfaction of almost anyone in academic anthropology. This is to say, not that biological facts are irrelevant, or that men and women are not different, but that these facts and differences only take on significance of superior/inferior within the framework of culturally defined value systems.[7]

If we are unwilling to rest the case on genetic determinism, it seems to me that we have only

one way to proceed. We must attempt to interpret female subordination in light of other universals, factors built into the structure of the most generalized situation in which all human beings, in whatever culture, find themselves. For example, every human being has a physical body and a sense of nonphysical mind, is part of a society of other individuals and an inheritor of a cultural tradition, and must engage in some relationship, however mediated, with "nature," or the nonhuman realm in order to survive. Every human being is born (to a mother) and ultimately dies, all are assumed to have an interest in personal survival, and society/culture has its own interest in (or at least momentum toward) continuity and survival, which transcends the lives and deaths of particular individuals. And so forth. It is in the realm of such universals of the human condition that we must seek an explanation for the universal fact of female devaluation.

I translate the problem, in other words, into the following simple question. What could there be in the generalized structure and conditions of existence, common to every culture, that would lead every culture to place a lower value upon women? Specifically, my thesis is that woman is being identified with—or, if you will, seems to be a symbol of—something that every culture devalues, something that every culture defines as being of a lower order of existence than itself. Now it seems that there is only one thing that would fit that description, and that is "nature" in the most generalized sense. Every culture, or, generically, "culture," is engaged in the process of generating and sustaining systems of meaningful forms (symbols, artifacts, etc.) by means of which humanity transcends the givens of natural existence, bends them to its purposes, controls them in its interest. We may thus broadly equate culture with the notion of human consciousness, or with the products of human consciousness (i.e., systems of

---

[6] Ortner says that even in societies in which women may hold high status and powerful positions, one can still find evidence indicating that they are inferior to men. She declares her case to be proven and places the burden of disproof on those who disagree. Are you convinced? Does the Crow example she provides bear this out?

[7] The reference to biological determinism in this paragraph is an allusion to theories popular at the time this essay was written. Additionally, books such as Ardrey's 1961 *African Genesis,* which emphasized the aggressive nature of men, had captured the popular imagination.

thought and technology), by means of which humanity attempts to assert control over nature.[8]

Now the categories of "nature" and "culture" are of course conceptual categories—one can find no boundary out in the actual world between the two states or realms of being. And there is no question that some cultures articulate a much stronger opposition between the two categories than others—it has even been argued that primitive peoples (some or all) do not see or intuit any distinction between the human cultural state and the state of nature at all. Yet I would maintain that the universality of ritual betokens an assertion in all human cultures of the specifically human ability to act upon and regulate, rather than passively move with and be moved by, the givens of natural existence. In ritual, the purposive manipulation of given forms toward regulating and sustaining order, every culture asserts that proper relations between human existence and natural forces depend upon culture's employing its special powers to regulate the overall processes of the world and life.[9]

One realm of cultural thought in which these points are often articulated is that of concepts of purity and pollution. Virtually every culture has some such beliefs, which seem in large part (though not, of course, entirely) to be concerned with the relationship between culture and nature (see Ortner, 1973, n.d.). A well-known aspect of purity/pollution beliefs cross-culturally is that of the natural "contagion" of pollution; left to its own devices, pollution (for these purposes grossly equated with the unregulated operation of natural energies) spreads and overpowers all that it comes in contact with. Thus a puzzle—if pollution is so strong, how can anything be purified? Why is the purifying agent not itself polluted? The answer, in keeping with the present line of argument, is that purification is effected in a ritual context; purification ritual, as a purposive activity that pits self-conscious (symbolic) action against natural energies, is more powerful than those energies.[10]

In any case, my point is simply that every culture implicitly recognizes and asserts a distinction

---

[8] The idea that all humans make a fundamental distinction between culture and nature, and that in every society, culture is believed to be superior to nature, is basic to the work of Lévi-Strauss. In the two paragraphs you have just read, Ortner paraphrases him. In *The Elementary Structures of Kinship* Lévi-Strauss wrote:

> . . . it is easy to recognize universality as the criterion of nature, for what is constant in man falls necessarily beyond the scope of customs, techniques, and institutions. . . . Let us suppose that everything universal in man relates to the natural order . . . and that everything subject to a norm is cultural and is both relative and particular. (quoted in Boyne 1966:200)

Ortner's comments here directly reflect Lévi-Strauss' statement. She reasons from this passage that if everything universal relates to nature, and if female subordination is universal, then female subordination must relate to nature.

[9] A critical element of structuralist thought is expressed in this passage. Ortner notes that there is no boundary in the physical world between nature and culture. The boundary is a product of human thinking. Structuralists believe that the human mind imposes order by *parsing,* or breaking down, the world into culturally meaningful bits. Structuralists try to

discover the fundamental principles by which humans accomplish this parsing.

[10] Having rejected biological foundations for the universal subordination of women, Ortner must formulate a cultural explanation. Following Lévi-Strauss, she chooses ritual as the focus of her analysis, as the place where cultures attempt to regulate and sustain order. Lévi-Strauss authored two studies of mythology—*The Raw and the Cooked* (1969) and *From Honey to Ashes* (1973)—based on what he claimed to be a fundamental opposition between nature and culture. Following Lévi-Strauss, Ortner states that humans transcend and control nature through the use of symbols. In particular, we distinguish ourselves from the natural world and regulate it through the use of ritual. It is through ritual that the natural, dangerous, and unacceptable are transformed into the cultural, acceptable, and safe.

The focus on ritual symbols and their power is not new for Ortner. In 1973, the year before the publication of this essay, Ortner published an article in *American Anthropologist* called "On Key Symbols," in which she discusses how symbols operate in ritual thought and action. Ortner is also not a strict structuralist. Then in 1975 she published another analysis titled "Gods' Bodies, Gods' Food: A Symbolic Analysis of Sherpa Ritual," which was inspired by the work of Clifford Geertz (see essay 37).

between the operation of nature and the operation of culture (human consciousness and its products); and further, that the distinctiveness of culture rests precisely on the fact that it can under most circumstances transcend natural conditions and turn them to its purposes. Thus culture (i.e., every culture) at some level of awareness asserts itself to be not only distinct from but superior to nature, and that sense of distinctiveness and superiority rest precisely on the ability to transform— to "socialize" and "culturalize"—nature.[11]

Returning now to the issue of women, their pan-cultural second-class status could be accounted for, quite simply, by postulating that women are being identified or symbolically associated with nature, as opposed to men, who are identified with culture. Since it is always culture's project to subsume and transcend nature, if women were considered part of nature, then culture would find it "natural" to subordinate, not to say oppress, them. Yet although this argument can be shown to have considerable force, it seems to oversimplify the case. The formulation I would like to defend and elaborate on in the following section, then, is that women are seen "merely" as being *closer* to nature than men. That is, culture (still equated relatively unambiguously with men) recognizes that women are active participants in its special processes, but at the same time sees them as being more rooted in, or having more direct affinity with, nature.

The revision may seem minor or even trivial, but I think it is a more accurate rendering of cul-tural assumptions. Further, the argument cast in these terms has several analytic advantages over the simpler formulation; I shall discuss these later. It might simply be stressed here that the revised argument would still account for the pan-cultural devaluation of women, for even if women are not equated with nature, they are nonetheless seen as representing a lower order of being, as being less transcendental of nature than men are. The next task of the paper, then, is to consider why they might be viewed in that way.[12]

WHY IS WOMAN SEEN AS CLOSER TO NATURE?

It all begins of course with the body and the natural procreative functions specific to women alone. We can sort out for discussion three levels at which this absolute physiological fact has significance: (1) woman's *body and its functions,* more involved more of the time with "species life," seem to place her closer to nature, in contrast to man's physiology, which frees him more completely to take up the projects of culture; (2) woman's body and its functions place her in *social roles* that in turn are considered to be at a lower order of the cultural process than man's; and (3) woman's traditional social roles, imposed because of her body and its functions, in turn give her a different *psychic structure,* which, like her physiological nature and her social roles, is seen as being closer to nature. I shall discuss

---

[11] Lévi-Strauss' ideas, like those of other theorists, were not uniformly accepted. Anthropologist Carol MacCormack (1934–1997), for example, criticized Lévi-Strauss' nature-culture formulation. Whereas he saw the nature-culture contrast as timeless and value-free, MacCormack concluded that such ideas were culturally specific. MacCormack wrote:

> There is no way to absolutely verify that the nature-culture opposition exists as an essential feature of universal unconscious structure, and there is ethnographic evidence to suggest that in the form in which Europeans now conceive it, the contrast is not a universal feature of consciously-held folk models. (1980:10)

[12] Ortner's distinction between women as identified with nature and women as "merely" closer to nature is subtle and performs two tasks in this essay. First, it makes her case more compelling but less amenable to testing. If Ortner said that women were identified wholly with nature, one or two counterexamples could easily disprove her point. However, she suggests that women are merely closer to nature than men. This means that in every case where anthropologists find women associated with culture rather than nature, they must ask, "Well, are men even more associated with culture?" This is a difficult proposition to test. Second, it opens the possibility that women mediate between culture and nature. This issue is discussed further below (see esp. notes 17, 18, and 20).

each of these points in turn, showing first how in each instance certain factors strongly tend to align woman with nature, then indicating other factors that demonstrate her full alignment with culture, the combined factors thus placing her in a problematic intermediate position. It will become clear in the course of the discussion why men seem by contrast less intermediate, more purely "cultural" than women. And I reiterate that I am dealing only at the level of cultural and human universals. These arguments are intended to apply to generalized humanity; they grow out of the human condition, as humanity has experienced and confronted it up to the present day.

1. *Woman's physiology seen as closer to nature.* This part of my argument has been anticipated, with subtlety, cogency, and a great deal of hard data, by De Beauvoir (1953).[13] De Beauvoir reviews the physiological structure, development, and functions of the human female and concludes that "the female, to a greater extent than the male, is the prey of the species" (p. 60). She points out that many major areas and processes of the woman's body serve no apparent function for the health and stability of the individual; on the contrary, as they perform their specific organic functions, they are often sources of discomfort, pain, and danger. The breasts are irrelevant to personal health; they may be excised at any time of a woman's life. "Many of the ovarian secretions function for the benefit of the egg, promoting its maturation and adapting the uterus to its requirements; in respect to the organism as a whole, they make for disequilibrium rather than for regulation—the woman is adapted to the needs of the egg rather than to her own requirements" (p. 24). Menstruation is often uncomfortable, sometimes painful; it frequently has negative emotional correlates and in any case involves bothersome tasks of cleansing and waste disposal; and—a point that De Beauvoir does not

mention—in many cultures it interrupts a woman's routine, putting her in a stigmatized state involving various restrictions on her activities and social contacts. In pregnancy many of the woman's vitamin and mineral resources are channeled into nourishing the fetus, depleting her own strength and energies. And finally, childbirth itself is painful and dangerous (pp. 24–27 *passim*). In sum, De Beauvoir concludes that the female "is more enslaved to the species than the male, her animality is more manifest" (p. 239).

While De Beauvoir's book is ideological, her survey of woman's physiological situation seems fair and accurate. It is simply a fact that proportionately more of woman's body space, for a greater percentage of her lifetime, and at some—sometimes great—cost to her personal health, strength, and general stability, is taken up with the natural processes surrounding the reproduction of the species.

De Beauvoir goes on to discuss the negative implications of woman's "enslavement to the species" in relation to the projects in which humans engage, projects through which culture is generated and defined. She arrives thus at the crux of her argument (pp. 58–59):

> Here we have the key to the whole mystery. On the biological level a species is maintained only by creating itself anew; but this creation results only in repeating the same Life in more individuals. But man assures the repetition of Life while transcending Life through Existence [i.e., goal-oriented, meaningful action]; by this transcendence he creates values that deprive pure repetition of all value. In the animal, the freedom and variety of male activities are vain because no project is involved. Except for his services to the species, what he does is immaterial. Whereas in serving the species, the human male also remodels the face of the earth, he creates new instruments, he invents, he shapes the future.

---

[13] Simone de Beauvoir (1908–1986) was a French existentialist author of plays and novels and the companion of the philosopher Jean-Paul Sartre (1905–1980). The reference is to her book *The Second Sex* (1952), which analyzes women's inferior positions in society. In *The Second Sex*, de Beauvoir used existential argument and ethnographic data to compare women to oppressed minorities and proposed that women's status was the result of social conditions rather than biological factors. Today, *The Second Sex* is considered a fundamental document of modern feminism.

In other words, woman's body seems to doom her to mere reproduction of life; the male, in contrast, lacking natural creative functions, must (or has the opportunity to) assert his creativity externally, "artificially," through the medium of technology and symbols. In so doing, he creates relatively lasting, eternal, transcendent objects, while the woman creates only perishables—human beings.

This formulation opens up a number of important insights. It speaks, for example, to the great puzzle of why male activities involving the destruction of life (hunting and warfare) are often given more prestige than the female's ability to give birth, to create life. Within De Beauvoir's framework, we realize it is not the killing that is the relevant and valued aspect of hunting and warfare; rather, it is the transcendental (social, cultural) nature of these activities, as opposed to the naturalness of the process of birth: "For it is not in giving life but in risking life that man is raised above the animal; that is why superiority has been accorded in humanity not to the sex that brings forth but to that which kills" (*ibid.*).

Thus if male is, as I am suggesting, everywhere (unconsciously) associated with culture and female seems closer to nature, the rationale for these associations is not very difficult to grasp, merely from considering the implications of the physiological contrast between male and female. At the same time, however, woman cannot be consigned fully to the category of nature, for it is perfectly obvious that she is a full-fledged human being endowed with human consciousness just as a man is; she is half of the human race, without whose cooperation the whole enterprise would collapse. She may seem more in the possession of nature than man, but having consciousness, she thinks and speaks; she generates, communicates, and manipulates symbols, categories, and values. She participates in human dialogues not only with other women but also with men. As Lévi-Strauss says, "Woman could never become just a sign and nothing more, since even in a man's world she is still a person, and since insofar as she is defined as a sign she must [still] be recognized as a generator of signs" (1969a:496).[14]

Indeed, the fact of woman's full human consciousness, her full involvement in and commitment to culture's project of transcendence over nature, may ironically explain another of the great puzzles of "the woman problem"—woman's nearly universal unquestioning acceptance of her own devaluation. For it would seem that, as a conscious human and member of culture, she has followed out the logic of culture's arguments and has reached culture's conclusions along with the men. As De Beauvoir puts it (p. 59):

> For she, too, is an existent, she feels the urge to surpass, and her project is not mere repetition but transcendence towards a different future— in her heart of hearts she finds confirmation of the masculine pretensions. She joins the men in the festivals that celebrate the successes and victories of the males. Her misfortune is to have been biologically destined for the repetition of Life, when even in her own view Life does not carry within itself its reasons for being, reasons that are more important than life itself.

In other words, woman's consciousness—her membership, as it were, in culture—is evidenced in part by the very fact that she accepts her own devaluation and takes culture's point of view.

I have tried here to show one part of the logic of that view, the part that grows directly from the physiological differences between men and women. Because of woman's greater bodily involvement with the natural functions surrounding reproduction, she is seen as more a part of nature than man is. Yet in part because of her consciousness and participation in human social dialogue, she is recognized as a participant in

---

[14] Lévi-Strauss' comments on women and signs are from his 1949 book *The Elementary Structures of Kinship*. There, he uses the notion of sign taken from the turn-of-the-century Swiss structural linguist Ferdinand de Saussure (1857–1913). Contrary to the popular views of his time, Saussure argued that the meanings of the majority of words in a language are derived from the arbitrary association of sound and meaning. Each idea in language is arbitrarily associated with a sound. The sound, Saussure called the "signifier"; the idea, the "signified." Together they form, in Saussure's terminology, a linguistic "sign." So, Ortner is saying that although devalued, women are still "generators of signs."

culture. Thus she appears as something interme-diate between culture and nature, lower on the scale of transcendence than man.[15]

2. *Woman's social role seen as closer to nature.* Woman's physiological functions, I have argued, may tend in themselves to motivate[e] a view of woman as closer to nature, a view she herself, as an observer of herself and the world, would tend to agree with. Woman creates naturally from within her own being, whereas man is free to, or forced to, create artificially, that is, through cultural means, and in such a way as to sustain culture. In addition, I now wish to show how woman's physiological functions have tended universally to limit her social movement, and to confine her universally to certain social contexts which *in turn* are seen as closer to nature. That is, not only her bodily processes but the social situation in which her bodily processes locate her may carry this significance. And insofar as she is permanently associated (in the eyes of culture) with these social milieux, they add weight (perhaps the decisive part of the burden) to the view of woman as closer to nature. I refer here of course to woman's confinement to the domestic family context, a confinement moti-vated, no doubt, by her lactation processes.

Woman's body, like that of all female mam-mals, generates milk during and after pregnancy for the feeding of the newborn baby. The baby can-not survive without breast milk or some similar formula at this stage of life. Since the mother's body goes through its lactation processes in direct relation to a pregnancy with a particular child, the relationship of nursing between mother and child is seen as a natural bond, other feeding arrange-ments being seen in most cases as unnatural and makeshift. Mothers and their children, according to cultural reasoning, belong together. Further, children beyond infancy are not strong enough to engage in major work, yet are mobile and unruly and not capable of understanding various dangers; they thus require supervision and constant care. Mother is the obvious person for this task, as an extension of her natural nursing bond with the children, or because she has a new infant and is al-ready involved with child-oriented activities. Her own activities are thus circumscribed by the limi-tations and low levels of her children's strengths and skills:[f] she is confined to the domestic family group; "woman's place is in the home."[16]

Woman's association with the domestic circle would contribute to the view of her as closer to nature in several ways. In the first place, the sheer fact of constant association with children plays a role in the issue; one can easily see how infants and children might themselves be consid-ered part of nature. Infants are barely human and utterly unsocialized; like animals they are unable to walk upright, they excrete without control, they do not speak. Even slightly older children are clearly not yet fully under the sway of culture. They do not yet understand social duties, respon-sibilities, and morals; their vocabulary and their range of learned skills are small. One finds im-plicit recognition of an association between chil-dren and nature in many cultural practices. For example, most cultures have initiation rites for adolescents (primarily for boys; I shall return to

---

[15] Although Lévi-Strauss proposed that human thinking al-ways parsed the world into binary oppositions, he also be-lieved that the mind was dissatisfied with such oppositions and always searched for a mediator for them. A mediating category was a category that was not subsumed by either part of the binary but somehow transcended them. He ar-gued that this mediator was always problematic. It was privileged, special, or ambiguous. In positioning women as "merely" closer to nature than men, and in insisting that women, while identified with nature, are in truth part of society's cultural project, Ortner is beginning to build a case that women are the mediating element in the culture-nature binary.

[16] Ortner, like all authors, writes within a historical and political context. Her remarks on mother-child bonds and mother's nursing are an interesting reflection of this. American middle-class women "rediscovered" breast-feeding in the 1970s. Nursing became part of a political movement that included campaigns against corpora-tions such as Nestlé, which sold infant formula, espe-cially in poor nations. There was also much popular writing on the importance of mother-infant bonding. Ortner may have had these things in mind as she wrote these passages.

this point below), the point of which is to move the child ritually from a less than fully human state into full participation in society and culture; many cultures do not hold funeral rites for children who die at early ages, explicitly because they are not yet fully social beings. Thus children are likely to be categorized with nature, and woman's close association with children may compound her potential for being seen as closer to nature herself. It is ironic that the rationale for boys' initiation rites in many cultures is that the boys must be purged of the defilement accrued from being around mother and other women so much of the time, when in fact much of the woman's defilement may derive from her being around children so much of the time.[17]

The second major problematic implication of women's close association with the domestic context derives from certain structural conflicts between the family and society at large in any social system. The implications of the "domestic/public opposition" in relation to the position of women have been cogently developed by Rosaldo (1974), and I simply wish to show its relevance to the present argument. The notion that the domestic unit—the biological family charged with reproducing and socializing new members of the society—is opposed to the public entity—the superimposed network of alliances and relationships that is the society—is also the basis of Lévi-Strauss's argument in the *Elementary Structures of Kinship*

(1969a). Lévi-Strauss argues not only that this opposition is present in every social system, but further that it has the significance of the opposition between nature and culture. The universal incest prohibition[g] and its ally, the rule of exogamy (marriage outside the group), ensure that "the risk of seeing a biological family become established as a closed system is definitely eliminated; the biological group can no longer stand apart, and the bond of alliance with another family ensures the dominance of the social over the biological, and of the cultural over the natural" (p. 479). And although not every culture articulates a radical opposition between the domestic and the public as such, it is hardly contestable that the domestic is always subsumed by the public; domestic units are allied with one another through the enactment of rules that are logically at a higher level than the units themselves; this creates an emergent unit—society—that is logically at a higher level than the domestic units of which it is composed.[18]

Now, since women are associated with, and indeed are more or less confined to, the domestic context, they are identified with this lower order of social/cultural organization. What are the implications of this for the way they are viewed? First, if the specifically biological (reproductive) function of the family is stressed, as in Lévi-Strauss's formulation, then the family (and hence woman) is identified with nature pure and simple,

---

[17] Ortner has constructed an elegant argument, but like Lévi-Strauss before her, has based her logic on a set of arbitrary assumptions. Why, for example, is the link between women and nature assumed as fact? As she herself states, women socialize children into cultural beings and turn raw substances into edible meals. So why are women not closer to culture? She answers by saying that socialization activities are taken over by men in adolescence. But why should this time period be inherently more important than earlier childhood in determining the relation of men and women to culture? Further, Ortner does not deal with activities that seem to place men close to nature. Shouldn't adult men, who are presumably out in nature hunting and killing, be closer to nature than women?

[18] Ortner is referring here to Lévi-Strauss' contention that one of the most basic of binary oppositions is between us

and them, kin and nonkin. This relates to the nature-culture opposition because of the universal rules of incest (see essay 24).

Additionally, Ortner mentions Michelle Rosaldo's (1944–1981) article on gender inequality. There, Rosaldo presented a structuralist argument, but one that relied on a sociocultural rather than a biological explanation. She focused on the domestic-public opposition between men and women. She argued that men are typically associated with higher prestige public activities, while women, because they raise children, are limited to less prestigious domestic tasks.

Michelle Rosaldo, the wife of Renato Rosaldo, was killed in an accident during field research in October 1981. Renato Rosaldo's attempt to deal with his wife's death forms the core of his article "Grief and a Headhunter's Rage" (essay 38).

as opposed to culture. But this is obviously too simple; the point seems more adequately formulated as follows: the family (and hence woman) represents lower-level, socially fragmenting, particularistic sort of concerns, as opposed to interfamilial relations representing higher-level, integrative, universalistic sorts of concerns. Since men lack a "natural" basis (nursing, generalized to child care) for a familial orientation, their sphere of activity is defined at the level of interfamilial relations. And hence, so the cultural reasoning seems to go, men are the "natural" proprietors of religion, ritual, politics, and other realms of cultural thought and action in which universalistic statements of spiritual and social synthesis are made. Thus men are identified not only with culture, in the sense of all human creativity, as opposed to nature; they are identified in particular with culture in the old-fashioned sense of the finer and higher aspects of human thought—art, religion, law, etc.[19]

Here again, the logic of cultural reasoning aligning woman with a lower order of culture than man is clear and, on the surface, quite compelling. At the same time, woman cannot be fully consigned to nature, for there are aspects of her situation, even within the domestic context, that undeniably demonstrate her participation in the cultural process. It goes without saying, of course, that except for nursing newborn infants (and artificial nursing devices can cut even this biological tie), there is no reason why it has to be mother—as opposed to father, or anyone else— who remains identified with child care. But even assuming that other practical and emotional reasons conspire to keep woman in this sphere, it is possible to show that her activities in the domestic context could as logically put her squarely in the category of culture.

In the first place, one must point out that woman not only feeds and cleans up after children in a simple caretaker operation; she in fact is the primary agent of their early socialization. It is she who transforms newborn infants from

mere organisms into cultured humans, teaching them manners and the proper ways to behave in order to become fullfledged members of the culture. On the basis of her socializing functions alone, she could not be more a representative of culture. Yet in virtually every society there is a point at which the socialization of boys is transferred to the hands of men. The boys are considered, in one set of terms or another, not yet "really" socialized; their entree into the realm of fully human (social, cultural) status can be accomplished only by men. We still see this in our own schools, where there is a gradual inversion in the proportion of female to male teachers up through the grades: most kindergarten teachers are female; most university professors are male.[h]

Or again, take cooking. In the overwhelming majority of societies cooking is the woman's work. No doubt this stems from practical considerations—since the woman has to stay home with the baby, it is convenient for her to perform the chores centered in the home. But if it is true, as Lévi-Strauss has argued (1969b), that transforming the raw into the cooked may represent, in many systems of thought, the transition from nature to culture, then here we have woman aligned with this important culturalizing process, which could easily place her in the category of culture, triumphing over nature. Yet it is also interesting to note that when a culture (e.g., France or China) develops a tradition of *haute cuisine*—"real" cooking, as opposed to trivial ordinary domestic cooking—the high chefs are almost always men. Thus the pattern replicates that in the area of socialization—women perform lower-level conversions from nature to culture, but when the culture distinguishes a higher level of the same functions, the higher level is restricted to men.

In short, we see once again some sources of woman's appearing more intermediate than man with respect to the nature/culture dichotomy. Her "natural" association with the domestic context (motivated by her natural lactation functions)

---

[19] When Ortner talks of culture in the old-fashioned sense, she is referring to Tylor's nineteenth-century definition of culture (arts, laws, morals, etc.; see essay 2) as opposed to a Boasian notion of culture.

tends to compound her potential for being viewed as closer to nature, because of the animal-like nature of children, and because of the infrasocial connotation of the domestic group as against the rest of society. Yet at the same time her socializing and cooking functions within the domestic context show her to be a powerful agent of the cultural process, constantly transforming raw natural resources into cultural products. Belonging to culture, yet appearing to have stronger and more direct connections with nature, she is once again seen as situated between the two realms.

[*We have omitted most of the last two sections of Ortner's article, about 3,000 words, called "Woman's Psyche Seen as Closer to Nature" and "The Implications of Intermediacy." In the first section she argues that women not only have a different body and a different social importance than men but also a different psychic structure. In support of this view she relies mainly on an argument developed by Chodorow (1974), who claimed that men are more objective than women and communicate in terms of relatively abstract categories whereas women are subjective and relate in terms of relatively concrete phenomena. She argued that these differences are not innate but are due to the fact that "women, universally, are largely responsible for early care and for (at least) later female socialization" (1974:43).*

The last section, "The Implications of Intermediacy," summarizes the essay's main points and discusses the implications of women's mediation between nature and culture. Ortner says that women are universally seen as occupying a middle status on a hierarchy of being from culture to nature. As a result they are lower than men and less capable of achieving transcendence of nature. Ortner believes that this position assigns them greater symbolic ambiguity. She says,

> *Thus we can account easily for both the subversive feminine symbols (witches, evil eye, menstrual pollution, castrating mothers) and the feminine symbols of transcendence (mother goddesses, merciful dispensers of salvation, female symbols of justice, and the strong presence of feminine symbolism in the realms of art, religion, ritual, and law). Feminine symbolism, far more often than masculine*

> *symbolism, manifests this propensity toward polarized ambiguity—sometimes utterly exalted, sometimes utterly debased, rarely within the normal range of human possibilities.*

Ortner concludes this section as follows:]

In short, the postulate that woman is viewed as closer to nature than man has several implications for further analysis, and can be interpreted in several different ways. If it is viewed simply as a *middle* position on a scale from culture down to nature, then it is still seen as lower than culture and thus accounts for the pan-cultural assumption that woman is lower than man in the order of things. If it is read as a *mediating* element in the culture-nature relationship, then it may account in part for the cultural tendency not merely to devalue woman but to circumscribe and restrict her functions, since culture must maintain control over its (pragmatic and symbolic) mechanisms for the conversion of nature into culture. And if it is read as an *ambiguous* status between culture and nature, it may help account for the fact that, in specific cultural ideologies and symbolizations, woman can occasionally be aligned with culture, and in any event is often assigned polarized and contradictory meanings within a single symbolic system. Middle status, mediating functions, ambiguous meaning—all are different readings, for different contextual purposes, of woman's being seen as intermediate between nature and culture.

CONCLUSIONS

Ultimately, it must be stressed again that the whole scheme is a construct of culture rather than a fact of nature. Woman is not "in reality" any closer to (or further from) nature than man—both have consciousness, both are mortal. But there are certainly reasons why she appears that way, which is what I have tried to show in this paper. The result is a (sadly) efficient feedback system: various aspects of woman's situation (physical, social, psychological) contribute to her being seen as closer to nature, while the view of her as closer to nature is in turn embodied in institutional forms that reproduce her situation. The implications for social change are similarly circular: a different cultural view can only grow out of a different social actuality; a different social actuality can only grow out of a different cultural view.

It is clear, then, that the situation must be attacked from both sides. Efforts directed solely at changing the social institutions—through setting quotas on hiring, for example, or through passing equal-pay-for-equal-work laws—cannot have far-reaching effects if cultural language and imagery continue to purvey a relatively devalued view of women. But at the same time efforts directed solely at changing cultural assumptions—through male and female consciousness-raising groups, for example, or through revision of educational materials and mass-media imagery—cannot be successful unless the institutional base of the society is changed to support and reinforce the changed cultural view. Ultimately, both men and women can and must be equally involved in projects of creativity and transcendence. Only then will women be seen as aligned with culture, in culture's ongoing dialectic with nature.[20]

NOTES

The first version of this paper was presented in October 1972 as a lecture in the course "Women: Myth and Reality" at Sarah Lawrence College. I received helpful comments from the students and from my co-teachers in the course: Joan Kelly Gadol, Eva Kollisch, and Gerda Lerner. A short account was delivered at the American Anthropological Association meetings in Toronto, November 1972. Meanwhile, I received excellent critical comments from Karen Blu, Robert Paul, Michelle Rosaldo, David Schneider, and Terence Turner, and the present version of the paper, in which the thrust of the argument has been rather significantly changed, was written in response to those comments. I, of course, retain responsibility for its final form. The paper is dedicated to Simone De Beauvoir, whose book *The Second Sex* (1953), first published in French in 1949, remains in my opinion the best single comprehensive understanding of "the woman problem."

[a] It is true of course that *yin*, the female principle, has a negative valence. Nonetheless, there is an absolute complementarity of *yin* and *yang* in Taoism, a recognition that the world requires the equal operation and interaction of both principles for its survival.

[b] Some anthropologists might consider this type of evidence (social-structural arrangements that exclude women, explicitly or de facto, from certain groups, roles, or statuses) to be a subtype of the second type of evidence (symbolic formulations of inferiority). I would not disagree with this view, although most social anthropologists would probably separate the two types.

[c] While we are on the subject of injustices of various kinds, we might note that Lowie secretly bought this doll, the most sacred object in the tribal repertoire, from its custodian, the widow of Wrinkled-face. She asked $400 for it, but this price was "far beyond [Lowie's] means," and he finally got it for $80 (p. 300).

[d] With all due respect to Lévi-Strauss (1969a, b, and *passim*).

[e] Semantic theory uses the concept of motivation of meaning, which encompasses various ways in which a meaning may be assigned to a symbol because of certain objective properties of that symbol, rather than by arbitrary association. In a sense, this entire paper is an inquiry into the motivation of the meaning of woman as a symbol, asking why woman may be unconsciously assigned the significance of being closer to nature. For a concise statement on the various types of motivation of meaning, see Ullman (1963).

[f] A situation that often serves to make her more child-like herself.

[g] David M. Schneider (personal communication) is prepared to argue that the incest taboo is not universal, on the basis of material from Oceania. Let us say at this point, then, that it is virtually universal.

[h] I remember having my first male teacher in the fifth grade, and I remember being excited about that—it was somehow more grown up.

---

[20] In the final paragraph Ortner seems to be caught on the horns of a dilemma. She advocates political action to end what she considers the universal subordination of women but cannot accommodate this notion within structuralism. Structuralism is designed to find consistencies within different cultures in order to reconstruct fundamental patterns of human thought. Because of this, culture change is irrelevant to structuralist analysis. Additionally, Ortner has located the source of female oppression in the fact that members of societies universally parse their worlds into nature and culture and universally assign women to a mediating category between them. One can easily imagine political action designed to improve the conditions of women in a society, but how can one ever change a culturally universal pattern of thought?

REFERENCES

Carlson, Rae. 1971. "Sex Differences in Ego Functioning: Exploratory Studies of Agency and Communion," *Journal of Consulting and Clinical Psychology,* 37:267–77.

De Beauvoir, Simone. 1953. *The Second Sex.* New York.

Lévi-Strauss, Claude. 1969a. *The Elementary Structures of Kinship.* Trans. J. H. Bell and J. R. von Sturmer; ed. R. Needham. Boston.

———. 1969b. *The Raw and the Cooked.* Trans. J. and D. Weightman. New York.

Lowie, Robert. 1956. *The Crow Indians.* New York. Originally published in 1935.

Ortner, Sherry B. 1973. "Sherpa Purity," *American Anthropologist,* 75:49–63.

———. n.d. "Purification Beliefs and Practices," *Encyclopedia Britannica,* forthcoming.

Pitt-Rivers, Julian. 1961. People of the Sierra. Chicago.

Rosaldo, Michelle. 1974. "Women, Culture, and Society: A Theoretical Overview," Michelle Rosaldo and Louise Lamphere, eds., *Women, Culture, and Society,* pp. 14–42. Palo Alto, Calif.: Stanford University Press.

Siu, R. G. H. 1968. *The Man of Many Qualities.* Cambridge, Mass.

Ullman, Stephen. 1963. "Semantic Universals," in Joseph H. Greenberg, ed., *Universals of Language.* Cambridge, Mass.

Ethnoscience and Cognitive Anthropology

It has long been evident that a major weakness in anthropology is the underdeveloped condition of ethnographic method. Typologies and generalizations abound, but their descriptive foundations are insecure. Anthropology is in the natural history stage of development rather than the "stage of deductively formulated theory" (Northrup 1947).

What is needed is the improvement of ethnographic method, to make cultural descriptions replicable and accurate, so that we know what we are comparing. Ethnoscience shows promise as the New Ethnography required to advance the whole of cultural anthropology. (Sturtevant 1987:131–132)

Beginning in the mid-1950s, ethnographers constructed a new methodological program for conducting fieldwork: ethnoscience, or the new ethnography. Ethnoscience was based on a critique of traditional fieldwork. Ethnoscientists claimed that for several reasons, ethnography had been unscientific. They complained that there was no single way of doing ethnography. Each anthropologist studied and wrote in their own, idiosyncratic way. As a result, ethnographies contained different sorts of information and were not analytically comparable to each other. Further, ethnographers tried to describe native society and native understandings, but they did so using the conceptual categories of Western society. Critics claimed that this distorted the results. To make anthropology more scientific and ethnographic descriptions more accurate, ethnoscientists argued, anthropologists should attempt to reproduce cultural reality as it was perceived and lived by members of society. To this end, they urged that descriptions of culture be couched in terms of native thought. Understanding native conceptual categories was key to this task. The ideal ethnoscientific ethnography would include all the rules, principles, and categories that natives must know in order to understand and act appropriately in social situations within their cultures.

The underlying theoretical assumption of ethnoscience was that a culture was a set of mental models. It was the job of ethnographers to duplicate the features of those cognitive models so that they could "think like a native." An ethnographer's model was presumed correct if it allowed him or her to replicate the way a native categorized phenomena.

Because no one has direct access to another person's mind, the cognitive principles and codes drawn by ethnographers were based on what informants told them. Thus, the new ethnography drew heavily on the techniques of linguistic analysis. In particular, they adopted the methodology developed in the 1920s by members of the Prague School of linguistics. Members of the Prague School such as Jakobson and Troubetzkoy were interested in the structure of languages, in particular, phonology. They studied the phonetic structure of languages by contrasting sounds in order to analyze the features that made sounds distinct. Ethnoscientists incorporated this idea into their research by creating diagrams in which contrasts of meaning could be outlined and the features of native conceptual categories distinguished.

Another set of linguistic principles upon which ethnoscience is based: can be traced to the 1930s and the work of Edward Sapir and Benjamin L.

Whorf. As we have seen (essay 12) Sapir and Whorf were interested in the relationship between language and thought. Together they formulated the Sapir-Whorf hypothesis, proposing that language was not just a means of communication but also shaped people's perceptions of the world. Whorf wrote:

> We dissect nature along lines laid down by our native languages. . . . We cut nature up, organize it into concepts, and ascribe significances as we do, largely because we are parties to an agreement to organize it in this way—an agreement that holds throughout our speech community and is codified in the patterns of our language. (1956:213)

Sapir and Whorf's emphasis on the linguistic determinism of perception was one element that led the ethnoscientists to see a close connection between culture and language. They reasoned that replicating the classification system of any language would give them the ability to view the world in the same way as native speakers of that language.

William Sturtevant outlined the fundamental principles of this new approach in his 1964 article, "Studies in Ethnoscience," published in *American Anthropologist.* However, other ethnoscientists were already outlining the new research methodologies. Individuals such as Ward Goodenough and Charles Frake described specific ways to conduct fieldwork and analyze data (Goodenough 1956, Frake 1962). The key instrument to be used in fieldwork was the highly structured interview, aimed specifically at eliciting native conceptual categories, which ethnoscientists called *domains.* They then used a technique called *componential analysis* to determine the definitive characteristics by which the objects and ideas in each domain were sorted. Ethnoscientists believed that the members of domains (and domains themselves) were organized following one of several logical possibilities, including the paradigm, the taxonomy, the congerie, and the type-token. In theory, data collection in this manner was more systematic and replicable and thus, followers claimed, more scientific. Once the appropriate model was selected, the ethnographer could classify information according to

native conceptual categories. Some ethnoscientists claimed that this allowed them to think like a native member of that culture.

Early attempts at this form of classification, such as Lounsbury's (1956), concentrated on kin terminologies, but the methodology was easily applicable to other areas and soon applied in a variety of research situations. Notable examples of this are Conklin's study of Hanunóo color categories reprinted in this section, Metzger and Williams' study of Tzeltal Maya categories of firewood (1966), Berlin, Breedlove, and Raven's 1974 analysis of Tzeltal Maya plant terminology, and a more contemporary example, Holland and Skinner's 1987 study of the cultural models behind American gender types.

The ethnoscientists' focus on the native point of view was not new. In the introduction to *Argonauts of the Western Pacific,* Bronislaw Malinowski had written that the final goal of ethnography was "to grasp the native's point of view, his relation to life, to realise *his* vision of his world" (1922:25, emphasis in original). The search for the native viewpoint also had strong resonances with Boasian historical particularism. Franz Boas and his students insisted on the uniqueness of each culture. They collected masses of physical data on the material and behavioral existence of the people they studied, and made the doctrine of cultural relativism an item of faith among American anthropologists. Ethnoscientists continued the Boasian insistence on culture being *sui generis* and extended the search for data from the material to the mental, something Boas had first suggested half a century previously.

Ethnoscience, like Boasian anthropology, implied an extreme cultural relativism—an approach that presented problems. Critics maintained that this approach made cross-cultural comparison impossible. If each culture had a unique way of conceptualizing the world and could only be described in its own terms, how could cultures be compared? Lévi-Strauss' structuralism was seen by some as the answer to this dilemma, but skeptics argued that it was impossible for either ethnoscientists or structuralists to get inside another's head and see how they think or what they believe. A further problem concerned individual variation within society. When ethnoscientists said they were trying to re-create cultural reality from a native's point of view, an obvious question to ask was, "Which native?" (Kaplan and Manners 1972:185). Despite these criticisms, ethnoscience was an important factor in the development of at least two other theoretical approaches—cognitive anthropology and symbolic anthropology—that both achieved major prominence in the following decades.

In the late 1960s and early 1970s the focus of ethnoscientific work shifted. Instead of simply outlining native categories of thought, anthropologists proposed that by analyzing these, one could learn how the human mind functioned. They called this approach *cognitive anthropology*. Like structuralists and most linguists, cognitive anthropologists of the 1970s believed that there were universal cognitive processes that reflect an innate structure of the human brain. Taking their cue from the ethnoscientists, they proposed that linguistic analysis was the best way to understand these structures and gain insight into human thought and culture. Cognitive anthropologists attempted to understand the abstract thinking patterns of people in various cultures, studying not only the content of cognition but also the mental processes by which ideas and symbols were related (Applebaum 1987:407).

Anthropologists have long debated the nature of their field. Some argue that anthropology should be an empirical science similar to biology or physics. Others think that anthropology is an interpretive art. Cognitive anthropologists such as Stephen A. Tyler (b. 1932) conceptualized culture as a mental model and focused on the rules by which things were categorized. They believed that anthropology should be more like philosophy or mathematics, with anthropologists searching for formal logical models.

Although cognitive anthropology never achieved the prominence hoped for by its practitioners, the anthropological study of cognition remains an active field of research that has moved far from its ethnoscientific beginnings. By the mid-1970s, advances in anthropology, psychology, and the field of artificial intelligence had made it apparent that human cognition was much more complex than the models of native classification derived from

componential analysis. The earlier focus on domains and taxonomies has given way to work in schema theory and connectionism.

A fundamental part of ethnoscience and early cognitive anthropology was the idea that people classified objects in their world by checking off a mental list of essential features (apple = red, round, stem). Cognitive anthropologists today argue that people conceptualize by reference to general mental prototypes called *schemas*, or *schemata*. Cognitive psychologist George Mandler describes schema in the following manner:

> The schema that is developed as a result of prior experiences with a particular kind of event is not a carbon copy of that event; schemas are abstract representations of environmental regularities. We comprehend events in terms of the schemas they activate.
>
> Schemas are also processing mechanisms; they are active in selecting evidence, in parsing the data provided by our environment, and in providing appropriate general or specific hypotheses. Most, if not all, of the activation processes occur automatically and without awareness on the part of the perceiver-comprehender. (Mandler in D'Andrade 1995a:122)

Thus, according to schema theory, a child will recognize an object that is green, round, and has no stem as an apple because it activates an "appleness" schema, rather than because it matches an exact list of traits.

Contrary to the view assumed by Tyler in essay 28 in this volume, it is now understood that much knowledge is nonlinguistic and is not governed by the linear logic of language. Thinking, in the view of Tyler (1969) and his contemporaries, involved a process whereby one element followed another in a linear sequence much like a computer program. However, this model does not account for the speed and efficiency with which we process information and perform tasks. To explain nonsequential thought processes in areas where thinking is nonlinguistic, contemporary cognitive anthropologists and psychologists have turned to the notion of *connectionism*. Connectionism suggests that knowledge is linked, networked, and widely distributed by "processing units" that work like neurons (Strauss and Quinn 1994:286) and that we access and analyze information through these processing units. Because these units are connected and work simultaneously, we can process information much faster than any computer.

Looking at thinking and knowledge using the connectionist model has two advantages over the old ethnoscientific view. First, it acknowledges that information and knowledge do not have to be language-based, and second, it is compatible with our ability to perform commonplace but complex actions rapidly and without conscious thought.

The experience of learning to drive a car illustrates the difference between language-based rule learning and nonverbal connectionist learning based on the networking of schemas (D'Andrade 1995). Driving involves both connectionist networks and verbally based knowledge. One can be told that the brake pedal is on the left, gas pedal on the right, and that in the United States one drives on the right side of the road. This type of learning is rapid and easy to change. However, verbal instruction is very different from the physical process of driving. It may require hundreds of driving experiences to make basic driving actions such as shifting gears smooth and automatic. The automatic driving reactions that come from practice and experience are based on schema networks that are set down and interconnected through observation and trial and error, not verbal instruction. If you learned to drive as McGee did, in a car with a manual transmission, you remember the practice it took to shift smoothly, something that no amount of verbal instruction could help. It is connectionist networks based on experience that allow you to drive without conscious thought, reacting quickly and automatically to situations around you. For example, if a child runs out into the street in front of your car, you do not go through a thought process that ends with the conclusion that it would be logical in this situation to slow your vehicle. You simply automatically apply the brakes.

A major consequence of the development of schema and connectionist theories of cognition was a shift in how cognitive anthropologists looked at the concept of culture. For the ethnoscientists of the 1950s and 1960s, culture was a mental model in the heads of native informants that could be diagrammed and replicated using the proper interviewing techniques. However, schema theorists have argued that a great deal of what goes on in the minds of human beings is certainly cultural, but not verbal, not conscious, and not able to be elicited through questioning. Thus the old definition of culture is inadequate. A solution to this problem proposed by Hutchins (1994) is to define culture as a process. In this view, culture is not simply mental content; rather, it involves the process of thinking and interacting in and with the physical world. These interactions build the schemas and create the mental connections in the brain that make cognition possible.

The articles chosen for this section reflect the development of ethnoscientific and cognitive anthropological thought through the last half century. The first article, Harold C. Conklin's 1955 study, is a classic piece of ethnoscientific work in which he outlines the features by which the Hanunóo categorize colors. The second essay is the introduction from Stephen A. Tyler's 1969 edited volume *Cognitive Anthropology*. There, he describes some of the conceptual models that he proposes underlie human thought. Though he has since changed his mind, at the time he wrote this introduction, he believed he was examining the fundamental processes by which people classify information. Claudia Strauss' essay, published in 1992, is an ethnographic application of schema theory in which she outlines a more sophisticated view of schemas and how they motivate behavior. Strauss argues that a general shared work/success schema of a small group of blue-collar factory workers forms just one level of their thinking, and she discusses three other forms of cognitive representation that had a motivational effect on their career choices.

With their emphasis on brain structure and cognitive processes, today's cognitive anthropologists have moved away from traditional notions of cultural anthropology and closer to the field of evolutionary psychology.

27. *Hanunóo Color Categories*[a]

HAROLD C. CONKLIN (b. 1926)

IN THE FOLLOWING brief analysis of a specific Philippine color system I shall attempt to show how various ethnographic field techniques may be combined profitably in the study of lexical sets relating to perceptual categorization.[1]

Recently, I completed more than a year's field research on Hanunóo folkbotany.[b] In this type of work one soon becomes acutely aware of problems connected with understanding the local system of color categorization because plant determinations so often depend on chromatic differences in the appearance of flowers or vegetative structures—both in taxonomic botany and in popular systems of classification. It is no accident that one of the most detailed accounts of native color terminology in the Malayo-Polynesian area was written by a botanist.[c] I was, therefore, greatly concerned with Hanunóo color categories during the entire period of my ethnobotanical research. Before summarizing the specific results of my analysis of the Hanunóo material, however, I should like to draw attention to several general considerations.[2]

1. Color, in a western technical sense, is not a universal concept and in many languages such as Hanunóo there is no unitary terminological equivalent. In our technical literature definitions state that color is the evaluation of the visual sense of that quality of light (reflected or transmitted by some substance) which is basically determined by its spectral composition. The spectrum is the range of visible color in light measured in wave lengths (400 [deep red] to 700 [blue-violet] millimicrons).[d] The total color sphere—holding any set of external and surface conditions constant—includes two other dimensions, in addition to that of spectral position or hue. One is saturation or intensity (chroma), the other brightness or brilliance (value). These three perceptual dimensions are usually combined into a coördinate system as a cylindrical continuum known as the color solid. Saturation diminishes toward the central axis which forms the achromatic core of neutral grays from the white at the end of greatest brightness to black at the opposite extremity. Hue varies with circumferential position. Although technically speaking *black* is the absence of any "color," *white*, the presence of all visible color wave lengths, and neutral *grays* lack spectral distinction, these achromatic positions within the color solid are often included with spectrally-defined positions in the categories distinguished in popular color systems.

2. Under laboratory conditions, color *discrimination* is probably the same for all human populations, irrespective of language; but the manner in which different languages classify the millions[e] of "colors" which every normal individual can discriminate *differ*. Many stimuli are classified

(1955)

---

[1] The focus of ethnoscientific studies were usually *domains*, which are patterns of classification of objects in a society. For example, sofas, chairs, and desks fall within the domain of furniture. Most of the early ethnoscientific studies concentrated on outlining the domains of limited phenomena such as native conceptions of disease or ethnobotany. Conklin's essay is a classic example of such a study.

[2] In the two numbered paragraphs, Conklin is setting up the framework on which he is going to build his presentation of Hanunóo color categories. He first provides a scientific definition of color, states that all humans are equally able to discriminate between colors, and postulates that color vocabulary influences the perception of color. Note here that Conklin is not saying that color vocabularies determine color perception, an implication of the Sapir-Whorf hypothesis described in the introduction to this section. Rather, he sets out to prove that color vocabularies influence color classification and thus the criteria by which people define colors. He wants to show the culturally specific criteria by which the Hanunóo classify color.

as equivalent, as extensive, cognitive—or perceptual—screening takes place.[f] Requirements of specification may differ considerably from one cuituraiiy-defined situation to another. The largest collection[g] of English color names runs to over 3,000 entries, yet only eight of these occur very commonly.[h] Recent testing by Lenneberg and others[i] demonstrates a high correlation in English and in Zuñi between ready color vocabulary and *ease in recognition of colors.* Although this is only a beginning it does show how the structure of a lexical set may affect color perception. It may also be possible to determine certain nonlinguistic correlates for color terminology. Color terms are a part of the vocabulary of particular languages and only the intracultural analysis of such lexical sets and their correlates can provide the key to their understanding and range of applicability. The study of isolated and assumed translations in other languages can lead only to confusion.[j]

In the field I began to investigate Hanunóo color classification in a number of ways, including the eliciting of linguistic responses from a large number of informants to painted cards, dyed fabrics, other previously prepared materials,[k] and the recording of visual-quality attributes taken from descriptions of specific items of the natural and artificial surroundings. This resulted in the collection of a profusion of attributive words of the nonformal—and therefore in a sense "color"—type. There were at first many inconsistencies and a high degree of overlap for which the controls used did not seem to account. However, as the

work with plant specimens and minute floristic differentiation progressed, I noted that in *contrastive* situations this initial confusion and incongruity of informants' responses did not usually occur. In such situations, where the "nonformal (i.e., not spatially organized) visible quality"[l] of one substance (plant part, dyed thread, or color card) was to be related to and contrasted with that of another, both of which were either at hand or well known, terminological agreement was reached with relative ease. Such a defined situation seemed to provide the frame necessary for establishing a known level of specification. Where needed, a greater degree of specification (often employing different root morphemes) could be and was made. Otherwise, such finer distinctions were ignored. This hint of terminologically significant levels led to a reexamination of all color data and the following analysis emerged.[3]

Color distinctions in Hanunóo are made at two levels of contrast. The first, higher, more general level consists of an all-inclusive, coordinate, four-way classification which lies at the core of the color system. The four categories are mutually exclusive in contrastive contexts, but may overlap slightly in absolute (i.e., spectrally, or in other measurable) terms. The second level, including several sublevels, consists of hundreds of specific color categories, many of which overlap and interdigitate. Terminologically, there is "unanimous agreement"[m] on the designations for the four Level I categories, but considerable lack of unanimity—with a few explainable exceptions—in the use of terms at Level II.[4]

---

[3] Ethnoscience is primarily based on linguistic analysis of information elicited from informants in highly structured interviews. The data is then subjected to componential analysis. In componential analysis one identifies the defining attributes of a cultural category (in Conklin's case, colors) by discovering and describing contrasts within the category (Spradley 1980:133). In the following pages, Conklin describes the criteria used by the Hanunóo to classify different colors.

[4] Conklin says that the Hanunóo classify colors at two levels. The more general level of classification, upon which there is a high level of agreement, is a set of four terms—darkness, lightness, redness, and greenness—that are mut-

ually exclusive contrasts. At the second level, hundreds of specific color names can overlap, and there is a lack of exact agreement. We have found an analogous situation during tests in our large classes. We color-code exams, asking students to identify the color of their exam on their answer sheets. Students easily distinguish between red, green, yellow, and blue (Conklin's Level I categorization) because these terms are mutually exclusive contrasts—if something is red, it cannot be blue. But there is a great deal of disagreement about softer pastel colors. For example, students typically do not differentiate well between gold and orange. Although all agree they are different colors, where does gold end and orange begin? This situation is analogous to Conklin's Level II Hanunóo color distinctions.

The four Level I terms are:

1. *(ma) biru*[n] "relative darkness (of shade of color); blackness" (black)
2. *(ma) lagti*[?] "relative lightness (or tint of color); whiteness" (white)
3. *(ma) rara*[?] "relative presence of red; redness" (red)
4. *(ma) latuy* "relative presence of light greenness; greenness" (green).

The three-dimensional color solid is divided by this Level I categorization into four unequal parts; the largest is *mabiru,* the smallest *malatuy.* While boundaries separating these categories cannot be set in absolute terms, the focal points (differing slightly in size, themselves) within the four sections, can be limited more or less to black, white, orange-red, and leaf-green respectively. In general terms, *mabiru* includes the range usually covered in English by black, violet, indigo, blue, dark green, dark gray, and deep shades of other colors and mixtures; *malagti*[?], white and very light tints of other colors and mixtures; *marara*[?], maroon, red, orange, yellow, and mixtures in which these qualities are seen to predominate; *malatuy,* light green, and mixtures of green, yellow, and light brown. All color terms can be reduced to one of these four but none of the four is reducible. This does not mean that other color terms are synonyms, but that they designate color categories of greater specification within four recognized color realms.

The basis of this Level I classification appears to have certain correlates beyond what is usually considered the range of chromatic differentiation, and which are associated with nonlinguistic phenomena in the external environment. First, there is the opposition between light and dark, obvious in the contrasted ranges of meaning of *lagti*[?] and *biru*. Second, there is an opposition between dryness or desiccation and wetness or freshness (succulence) in visible components of the natural environment which are reflected in the terms *rara*[?] and *latuy* respectively. This distinction is of particular significance in terms of plant life. Almost all living plant types possess some fresh, succulent, and often "greenish" parts. To eat any kind of raw, uncooked food, particularly fresh fruits or vegetables, is known as *pag-laty-un* (< *latuy*). A shiny, wet, *brown*-colored section of newly-cut bamboo is *malatuy* (not *marara*[?]). Dried-out or matured plant material such as certain kinds of yellowed bamboo or hardened kernels of mature or parched corn are *marara*[?]. To become desiccated, to lose all moisture, is known as *mamara*[?] (< *para*[?] "desiccation"; and parenthetically, I might add that there are morphological and historical reasons—aside from Hanunóo folk etymologizing—to believe that at least the final syllables of these two forms are derived from a common root). A third opposition, dividing the two already suggested, is that of deep, unfading, indelible, and hence often more desired material as against pale, weak, faded, bleached, or "colorless" substance, a distinction contrasting *mabiru* and *marara*[?] with *malagti*[?] and *malatuy.* This opposition holds for manufactured items and trade goods as well as for some natural products (e.g., red and white trade beads, red being more valuable by Hanunóo standards; indigo-dyed cotton sarongs, the most prized being those dyed most often and hence of the deepest indigo color—sometimes obscuring completely the designs formed originally by *white* warp yarns; etc.). Within each of these Level I categories, increased esthetic value attaches as the focal points mentioned above are approached. There is only one exception: the color which is most tangibly visible in their jungle surroundings, the green (even the focal point near light- or yellow-green) of the natural vegetation, is *not* valued decoratively. Green beads, for example, are "unattractive," worthless. Clothing and ornament are valued in proportion to the sharpness of contrast between, and the intensity (lack of mixture, deep quality) of "black," "red," and "white."[5]

---

[5] Ethnoscientists asserted that their method of analysis helped anthropologists see how people in different cultures conceptualize their world. Hanunóo color categories incorporate distinctions that are not made in the American definition of color. For example, a factor that influences Hanunóo color identification is the perceived moisture content of the object. Conklin says the Hanunóo also pay attention to the texture and shine of the object's surface.

Level II terminology is normally employed only when greater specification than is possible at Level I is required, or when the name of an object referred to happens also to be a "color" term (e.g., *bulawon* "gold; golden [color]"). Level II terms are of two kinds: relatively specific color words like *(ma)dapug* "gray" (< *dapug* "hearth; ashes"), *(ma)ʔarum* "violet," *(ma)dilaw* "yellow" (< *dilaw* "tumeric"); and constructions, based on such specific terms—or on Level I names—but involving further derivations, such as *mabirubiru* "somewhat *mabiru*" (more specific than *mabiru* alone only in that a color which is *not* a solid, deep, black is implied, i.e., a color classed within the *mabiru* category at Level I, but not at or near the focal point), *mabiru (gid)* "very *mabiru*" (here something close to the focal center of jet black is designated), and *madilawdilaw* "weak yellow." Much attention is paid to the texture of the surface referred to, the resulting degree and type of reflection (iridescent, sparkling, dull), and to admixture of other nonformal qualities. Frequently these noncolorimetric aspects are considered of primary importance, the more spectrally-definable qualities serving only as secondary attributes. In either case polymorphemic descriptions are common.

At Level II there is a noticeable difference in the ready color vocabulary of men as compared to women. The former excel (in the degree of specification to which they carry such classification terminologically) in the ranges of "reds" and "grays" (animals, hair, feather, etc.); the latter, in "blues" (shades of indigo-dyed fabrics). No discernible similar difference holds for the "greens" or "whites."

In short, we have seen that the apparent complexity of the Hanunóo color system can be reduced at the most generalized level to four basic terms which are associated with lightness, darkness, wetness, and dryness. This intracultural analysis demonstrates that what appears to be color "confusion" at first may result from an inad-equate knowledge of the internal structure of a color system and from a failure to distinguish sharply between sensory reception on the one hand and perceptual categorization on the other.[6]

NOTES

[a] Fieldwork among the Hanunóo on Mindoro Island (1952–1954) was supported by grants from the Social Science Research Council, the Ford Foundation, and the Guggenheim Foundation.

[b] Conklin, 1954a, 1954b.

[c] Bartlett, 1929.

[d] Osgood, 1953, p. 137.

[e] Estimates range from 7,500,000 to more than 10,000,000 (Optical Society of America, 1953; Evans, 1948, p. 230).

[f] Lounsbury, 1953.

[g] Maerz and Paul, 1930.

[h] Thorndike and Lorge, 1944.

[i] Lenneberg, 1953, pp. 468–471; Lenneberg and Roberts, 1954; Brown and Lenneberg, 1954.

[j] Lenneberg, 1953, pp. 464–466; Hjelmslev, 1953, p. 33.

[k] Cf. Ray, 1952, 1953.

[l] The lack of a term similar in semantic range to our word "color" makes abstract interrogation in Hanunóo about such matters somewhat complicated. Except for leading questions (naming some visual-quality attribute as a possibility), only circumlocutions such as *kabitay tida nu pagbantayun?* "How is it to look at?" are possible. If this results in a description of spatial organization or form, the inquiry may be narrowed by the specification *bukun kay ʔ anyu ʔ* "not its shape (or form)."

[m] Lenneberg, 1953, p. 469.

[n] These forms occur as attributes with the prefix *ma* "exhibiting, having" as indicated above in parentheses, or as free words (abstracts).

REFERENCES

Bartlett, Harley Harris. 1929. *Color Nomenclature in Batak and Malay.* (Papers, Michigan Academy of Science, Arts, and Letters, vol. 10, pp. 1–52, Ann Arbor).

---

[6] Conklin's conclusion is a classic ethnoscientific statement: What researchers had considered "color confusion" by the Hanunóo is actually a lack of understanding of the criteria by which the Hanunóo distinguish colors. Although ethnoscientists soon realized that complete descriptions of all the domains of a society would be impossible to achieve, studies such as Conklin's, though limited in scale, provided valuable information about the beliefs of people in other societies. Ethnoscientists believed they had developed a method for the analysis of society that provided scientific results that could be replicated. One can see how much promise the first ethnoscientists saw in their method and why they called it the new ethnography.

Brown, Roger W., and Eric H. Lenneberg. 1954. A Study in Language and Cognition. (*Journal of Abnormal and Social Psychology*, vol. 49, pp. 454–462).

Conklin, Harold C. 1954a. *The Relation of Hanunóo Culture to the Plant World* (Doctoral dissertation, Yale University, New Haven).

———.1954b. *An Ethnoecological Approach to Shifting Agriculture* (Transactions, New York Academy of Sciences, ser. II, vol. 17, pp. 133–142, New York).

Evans, Ralph M. 1948. *An Introduction to Color* (New York: Wiley).

Hjelmslev, Louis. 1953. *Prolegomena to a Theory of Language* (Indiana University Publications in Anthropology and Linguistics, Memoir 7 of the International Journal of American Linguistics [translated by Francis J. Whitfield], Bloomington).

Lenneberg, Eric H. 1953. *Cognition in Ethnolinguistics* (Language, vol. 29, pp. 463–471, Baltimore).

Lenneberg, Eric H., and John M. Roberts. 1954. *The Language of Experience, a Case Study* (Communications Program, Center of International Studies,

Massachusetts Institute of Technology, Cambridge: hectographed, 45 pp. and 9 figs.).

Lounsbury, Floyd G. 1953. "Introduction" [section on Linguistics and Psychology] (in *Results of the Conference of Anthropologists and Linguists*, pp. 47–49, Memoir 8, International Journal of American Linguistics, Baltimore).

Maerz, A., and M. R. Paul. 1930. *A Dictionary of Color* (New York: McGraw-Hill).

Optical Society of America, Committee on Colorimetry. 1953. *The Science of Color* (New York: Crowell).

Osgood, Charles E. 1953. *Method and Theory in Experimental Psychology* (New York: Oxford University Press).

Ray, Verne F. 1952. *Techniques and Problems in the Study of Human Color Perception* (Southwestern Journal of Anthropology, vol. 8, pp. 251–259).

———. 1953. *Human Color Perception and Behavioral Response* (Transactions, New York Academy of Sciences, ser. II, vol. 16, pp. 98–104, New York).

Thorndike, E. L., and I. Lorge. 1944. *The Teacher's Word Book of 30,000 Words* (Teacher's College, Columbia University, New York).

28. *Introduction to Cognitive Anthropology*

Stephen A. Tyler (b.1932)

THE OLD AND THE NEW[a]

The history of all scientific disciplines is marked by periods of intense theoretical innovation followed by relatively quiescent periods of consolidation and refinement. When the descriptive facts of science no longer fit the older explanatory models, it becomes necessary to discover new theories which will more adequately explain the accumulated data. Anthropology is currently in one of these periods of innovation.

On every hand, the various subdisciplines of anthropology are astir with new formulations challenging and supplementing established concepts and methods. The very lexicon of anthropology reflects this ferment. The journals are full of articles on *formal analysis, componential analysis, taxonomy, ethnoscience, ethnosemantics,* and *sociolinguistics,* to list but a few. Nearly all of these topics have appeared in the brief span of approximately ten years, with increasing frequency in the last three or four years.[1]

Cognitive Anthropology (1969)

---

[1] The model of science that Tyler outlines here resembles that in Thomas Kuhn's *The Structure of Scientific Revolutions.* This book, which first appeared in 1962, had a substantial impact on American science and social science. Kuhn proposed that paradigms—models used to describe the natural world—shifted when scientific explanation no longer accounted accurately for data. Tyler suggests that such a paradigm shift was happening in anthropology. The "scientific" approach he takes throughout this essay evokes Kuhn's ideas.

Assessment of such new departures is always difficult. What are their historical antecedents and what do they augur for the future of anthropology? Are these genuinely viable reformulations or are they simply short-lived fads and blind alleys, detrimental in the long run to significant research?

Enough has been presented in symposia and journals for us to feel that we are witnessing a quiet revolution in anthropology—quiet because the new departures are firmly rooted in the past. Formal analysis derives in part from the work of such anthropological titans as Radcliffe-Brown, Lévi-Strauss, and Nadel. Folk taxonomies are foreshadowed in the writings of Mauss, Boas, and Evans-Pritchard.[2] That great ethnographer Malinowski would have been no stranger to recent developments in sociolinguistics. The concern for psychological validity is congruent with much of Sapir's work and, to a lesser extent, with some of Kroeber's. And, perhaps, most relevant of all is the work of Bateson.[3]

Yet, these developments constitute more than a disconnected reworking of disparate themes from out of the past. These new formulations contrast sharply with many of the aims, assumptions, goals, and methods of an earlier anthropology. Previous theoretical orientations in anthropology can in a very general way be classed into two types—those concerned primarily with change and development and those concerned with static descriptions. Thus, the evolutionists and the diffusionists concentrated on patterns of change, while the functionalists eschewed this work as mere "speculative history," and focused on the internal organization and comparison of systems, hoping thereby to discover general laws of society. Some culture and personality studies attempted to characterize whole cultures with such concepts as "national character" and "modal personality type," while other culture and personality studies utilized a comparative approach in an attempt to correlate psychological and cultural features.

These formulations were attempts to construct universal organizational types which were linked either by similar processes of change or by similarities of internal structure. In order to achieve this goal, only certain kinds of information were accepted as relevant, and concrete ethnographic data had to be elevated to more abstract forms such as index variables and typological constructs. Consequently, abstract definitions of these features were necessary, and much of the discussion in books and journals concerned the adequacy of these definitions.[4] Once a corporate lineage, for example, had been

---

[2] Later in the essay, Tyler will elaborate on formal analysis. A formal analysis is a set of logical principles. A good example would be a set of postulates and their implications applied to a proof in geometry.

[3] Tyler positions his work as a logical extension of many strands of theory in anthropology, but most of the theorists he mentions here, some of whom have essays in this volume, probably would not have supported his ideas. Tyler gives particular credit to Gregory Bateson, calling his ideas "most relevant of all." Bateson studied anthropology at Cambridge under Alfred Cort Haddon and did fieldwork in New Guinea. *Naven* (1958 [1936]), an important anthropological study of the religion and culture of the Iatmul of New Guinea, came from this field work *Naven* is crucial to Tyler because Bateson proposed a definition of culture very close to the one Tyler uses in this essay. Bateson defined culture as "a collective term for the coherent 'logical' system which may be constructed by the scientist, fitting together the various premises of

the culture" (1958:218). He further specified that "we must expect to find different systems of logic, different modes of building together of premises, in different cultures" (1958:219).

[4] Ethnoscientists and cognitive anthropologists were concerned with problems of classification. Their critique of earlier anthropology was really much like Boas' attack on unilineal evolution half a century earlier. Boas had criticized evolutionists for theorizing in advance of data; the ethnoscientists criticized the methods by which anthropological data was obtained. The cornerstone of their critique was that the ethnographic method was fundamentally subjective because anthropologists applied their own classification systems to the societies they studied. Therefore, the categories used in traditional ethnographic analysis were incommensurate. The proliferation of categories Tyler mentions here is an artifact of that problem—evidence, to him, that anthropological theories no longer fit the data being collected.

defined in a particular way, it was only a matter of time before some fieldworker returned to his desk and elatedly reported that his tribe did not conform to the received definition. One way around this problem was to construct more types and subtypes, and broader, more abstract definitions. It was generally accepted that neither the types nor the definitions actually corresponded to anything in the "real world." They were merely convenient methods of ordering the data at hand. Proliferation of types, however, was dangerous, for as the types proliferated, so did the processes linking the types and their constituents. Contrary to expectations, anthropology became more and more particularistic rather than more general and universal.

This concern with typology and definition is an index to another feature characteristic of this period in anthropology. Anthropologists were really much more concerned with discovering what anthropology was than, for example, what an Eskimo was.[5] In a sense anthropologists were studying only one small culture—the culture of anthropology.

Aside from the diffusionists, these earlier theories can be characterized as attempts to construct monolithic, unitary systems which purported to either explain cultures or their development. Such concepts as cultural core, cultural norm, structure, modal structure, pattern, and others were used to describe these systems. These ideas are symptomatic of a quest for the typical, the normal, the usual, for those definitely bounded phenomena which would systematically differentiate one culture from another. In fact the very concept of culture is but another of these labels for some arbitrarily bounded unit within which certain types of behavior, norms, artifacts, and emotions are typical (cf. Sapir 1932:515;

1934:593–595). The atypical, especially as expressed in patterns of variation, were either simply dismissed or artificially worked into the scheme as indices of change, diffusion, survival, innovation, dysfunction, abnormality, cultural disintegration, opportunities for the exercise of social control and the like. The only important variations were variations between cultures.

In contrast to these approaches, cognitive anthropology constitutes a new theoretical orientation. It focuses on *discovering* how different people organize and use their cultures. This is not so much a search for some generalized unit of behavioral analysis as it is an attempt to understand the *organizing principles underlying* behavior. It is assumed that each people has a unique system for perceiving and organizing material phenomena—things, events, behavior, and emotions (Goodenough 1957). The object of study is not these material phenomena themselves, but the way they are organized in the minds of men. Cultures then are not material phenomena; they are cognitive organizations of material phenomena.[b] Consequently cultures are neither described by mere arbitrary lists of anatomical traits and institutions such as house type, family type, kinship type, economic type and personality type, nor are they necessarily equated with some over-all integrative pattern of these phenomena. Such descriptions may tell us something about the way an anthropologist thinks about a culture, but there is little, if any, reason to believe that they tell us anything of how the people of some culture think about their culture.[6]

In essence, cognitive anthropology seeks to answer two questions: What material phenomena are significant for the people of some culture; and, how do they organize these phenomena? Not only do cultures differ among one another in their

---

[5] The idea that traditional ethnology is really anthropology studying itself rather than making objective statements about others is a crucial insight of postmodern theorists. Many of them see themselves as direct descendants of the ethnoscientists. In his critique Tyler explains that in traditional ethnography, culture is a creation of the anthropologists rather than the people they are studying. By defining some aspects of behavior as *culture core* (a term from Julian Steward and the cultural ecologists) or *modal culture* (a term from the culture and personality theorists), anthro-

pologists inappropriately classify behavior according to their own idiosyncratic standards.

[6] Although Tyler does not use the term, ethnoscientists and cognitive anthropologists proposed an *emic* approach to anthropology. The critical distinction between emics and etics was first made by the linguist Kenneth Pike in 1954 based on the use of the words *phonetics* and *phonemics* in linguistics. Phonetics is the study of the production and transmission of language sounds in general. Phonemics is

organization of material phenomena, they differ as well in the kinds of material phenomena they organize. The people of different cultures may not recognize the same kinds of material phenomena as relevant, even though from an outsider's point of view the same material phenomena may be present in every case. For example, we distinguish between dew, fog, ice, and snow, but the Koyas of South India do not. They call all of these *mancu*. Even though they can perceive the differences among these if asked to do so, these differences are not significant to them. On the other hand, they recognize and name at least seven different kinds of bamboo, six more than I am accustomed to distinguish. Similarly, even though I know that my cousin George is the son of my mother's sister, while my cousin Paul is the son of my mother's brother, this objective difference is irrelevant to my system of classification. They are both "cousins." If I were a Koya, however, this difference would be highly important. I would call my mother's brother's son *baaTo* and my mother's sister's son *annaal*. Even though the same material phenomena are objectively present, they are subjectively perceived and organized differently by Koyas than they are by Americans.[c] Furthermore, there is no apparent over-all integrative pattern which relates the classification of bamboo to the classification of relatives. These are separate classes of phenomena with distinctive and unrelated principles of organization.

Not only may the same phenomena be organized differently from culture to culture, they may also be organized in more than one way in the same culture. There is, then, *intracultural* variation as well as *intercultural* variation. Some intracultural variations may be idiosyncratic, but more important from the anthropologist's point of view are those variations which are used by different classes of people and/or occur in different situations and contexts (cf. Goodenough 1963:257–264). For example, if we are interested in describing the way people classify colors we may discover that there are variant patterns dependent upon the sex or age of our informant as well as his general experience with colors. Thus, females in our culture can generally discriminate and name more colors than males. Or, to take another example, the classification of relatives may be partially dependent on the social statuses of the people talking about relatives, the relationship between them, and the social context in which they are conversing. A Telugu refers to his younger sister as *celli* when talking to another member of his family, but when speaking to a person outside his family group, he uses the term *cellelu*, which may mean younger sister, or mother's sister's daughter, or father's brother's daughter.[7]

---

the study of the ways in which sounds are organized within a language—that is, it analyzes units of sound that are psychologically distinct for speakers of a language. In anthropology, those studying emics strive to reproduce the meanings and understandings of the members of a culture. Those studying etics strive to analyze culture in terms meaningful to the scientific community though not necessarily to the members of the culture under observation. Cognitive anthropologists and ethnoscientists thus viewed culture as a mental construct or template. The principal tool they used to examine culture was linguistic analysis. They based their use of language on the work of Edward Sapir, a student of Boas best known for his work on Native American languages and cognition. Sapir argued that language determined those things people habitually noticed and, by extension, the manner in which they organized their worlds. An analysis of language could then be used to examine how people understood their worlds. In the later passages, Tyler points out several examples of distinctions between linguistic classification and empirical reality.

[7] Tyler's discussion of variation within cultures reflects the concern of ethnoscientists and their descendants with describing the precise nature of a culture. That culture is not a unitary phenomenon is a critical insight that distinguishes cognitive anthropology from many traditional approaches. However, it also leads to several logical problems. If culture is a mental template and can be approached through linguistic classification, then in what sense can individuals who have different systems of classification be said to be members of the same culture? Additionally, can one draw valid conclusions about a culture based on data from only a few informants?

These sorts of problems could lead to two distasteful possibilities. On the one hand, since no two people have exactly the same system of classification, each person may be a culture unto himself. On the other hand, if we look for the "average" system of classification, that shared by most people, we are back once again with a modal culture, precisely what Tyler says cognitive anthropology avoids.

A consequence of this interest in variation is the idea that cultures are not unitary phenomena, that is, they cannot be described by only one set of organizing principles. For each class of relevant phenomena there may be several alternative organizations. The realization or choice of one alternative to the exclusion of some other is dependent upon a variety of factors. For example, some people have more or less knowledge of some phenomena, or certain alternatives may be acceptable only in particular contexts (cf. Hymes 1964b:41). If these variants are used only in certain identified situations, or if there is a hierarchy of choice so that variants are ordered on the basis of their relative desirability, we can say that they are in complementary distribution and do not conflict with one another. In such a situation it is possible for a large number of variants to coexist. But, if the variants conflict in their organization and the situations in which they occur, there must be some means of harmonizing the contrast. This can be achieved by some change in the principles of organization or in the situation in which they occur. For example, among the Koyas, the pig is classed as an edible animal, but among neighboring Muslims the pig is classed as inedible and defiling. Suppose a Koya woman were married to a Muslim man.[8] While in her husband's home she could not act on her classification of pig as an edible by eating pork; while visiting her parents in the absence of her husband she could. So long as the two systems of classification can be realized in these isolated contexts there is no necessary conflict between them, and both may persist. If these contexts were not in complementary distribution, some rearrangement of the two contrasting systems of classification would have to take place if the marriage were to persist.[d]

In fact, this is an argument for a different kind of unitary description which sees unity as emerging from the ordered relations between variants and contexts. Variants are not mere deviations from some assumed basic organization; with their rules of occurrence *they are the organization.* (Wallace 1961:29–41; Hymes 1964a:386–387). It must be emphasized, however, that such a unitary description can be achieved only by the anthropologist. It is highly unlikely that the members of a culture ever see their culture as *this kind of* unitary phenomenon. Each individual member may have a unique unitary model of his culture, but is not necessarily cognizant of all unique, unitary models held by other members of his culture. He will be aware of and use some, but it is only the anthropologist who completely transcends these particular models and constructs a single, unitary model.[9] This cognitive organization exists solely in the mind of the anthropologist (cf. Bateson 1958:294). Yet, to the extent that it will generate concept models used by the people of a particular culture, it is a model of their cognitive systems.[e]

The "theory" here is not so much a THEORY OF CULTURE as it is *theories of cultures,* or a theory of descriptions. The aim of such a theory is to provide answers to the questions: How would the people of some other culture expect me to behave if I were a member of their culture; and what are the rules of appropriate behavior in their culture? Answers to these questions are provided by an adequate description of the rules used by people in that culture. Consequently, this description itself constitutes "theory" for that culture, for it represents the conceptual model of organization used by its members. Such a theory is validated by our ability to predict how these people would expect us to behave if we were members of the culture.

---

[8] Another problem Tyler faces is that a single person, such as the Koya woman mentioned here, might hold more than one system of classification. This presents a problem because ethnoscience, as a logical system, should have no inconsistencies. Tyler deals with this by suggesting that an individual may hold differing systems of classification as long as these are used in different situations, but a person may not hold two conflicting classification systems in the same situation. However, it is worth asking if people *do* simultaneously hold conflicting ideas.

[9] Tyler is extremely equivocal about the ability of cognitive anthropologists to think like natives. In this passage he first states that models generated by cognitive anthropologists exist only in their own minds. This would seem to suggest that an anthropologist might learn to speak and behave as a native but not actually think like one. However, Tyler then asserts that to the extent that such a model generates conceptual models used by the people of a culture, it is a model of *their* (emphasis added) cognitive systems. This claim comes perilously close to claiming to think like the natives.

ORDER OUT OF CHAOS

In a sense, cognitive anthropology is not a new departure. Many anthropologists have expressed an interest in how the natives see their world. Yet, there is a difference of focus between the old and the new. Where earlier anthropologists sought categories of description in their native language, cognitive anthropologists seek categories of description in the language of their natives.[f] Ultimately, this is the old problem of what do we describe and how do we describe it? Obviously, we are interested in the mental codes of other peoples, but how do we infer these mental processes? Thus far, it has been assumed that the easiest entry to such processes is through language, and most of the recent studies have sought to discover codes that are mapped in language.[10] Nearly all of this work has been concerned with how other peoples "name" the "things" in their environment and how these names are organized into larger groupings. These names are thus both an index to what is significant in the environment of some other people, and a means of discovering how these people organize their perceptions of the environment. Naming is seen as one of the chief methods for imposing order on perception.[g]

In a very real sense, the anthropologist's problem is to discover how other people create order out of what appears to him to be utter chaos. Imagine, for a moment, a being from another planet equipped with all our sensory apparatus who perceives for the first time the infinite variety of sight and sound in which we live. Suppose further that he is attempting to describe this world in a scientific report for his colleagues at home. At first, everything would be chaotic. Each sound and object would seem to be unlike any other. His experience would be similar to what we feel the first time we hear a language we have never heard before. But, with infinite time and patience, let us assume that he is able to describe everything he perceives—that is, the total environment of earth. Probably he would eventually be able to organize his report around concepts acceptable to his world or devise new ones as he saw fit. Yet, would anyone of us accept his report as an accurate account of the world as we see and live in it? If he in fact describes everything, we would not. Nor would we accept his organization of the things he perceived, for they would almost certainly not fit our own system of organization. Unlike this mythical creature, we do not live in a world in which we discriminate among all the possible sensory stimuli in our environment, nor do we react to each stimulus as if it were totally new and foreign. In effect, we choose to ignore many of those perceptual differences which make each object unique. In large part, we do this by naming. By naming we classify and put objects which to us are similar into the same category, even though we can perceive differences among them (cf. Boas 1938: 208–214). For example, the chair in which I sit has a nick in the left leg, yet I class it as a "straight chair" no different from others like it in the room.[11]

---

[10] At the core of ethnoscience and cognitive anthropology is an analogy between culture and language. One key source of this insight was Sapir, who has already been mentioned. Another was the work of Lévi-Strauss and, through him, that of the Prague School linguistic theorists, described in the notes to essay 24. Many social scientists working in the 1950s and 1960s considered linguistics to be the most advanced of all the social sciences and believed that it could provide a model for other social sciences.

[11] A key insight of cognitive anthropology, derived from Sapir and Lévi-Strauss (who in his turn was inspired by Durkheim and Mauss), was that humans order their world through classification. The world presents us with chaos. We make sense of it by noticing some phenomena and ignoring others or by grouping some things together and excluding others. Both French and American thinkers arrived at this conclusion, but it implied different things to each of them. Working in the tradition of Durkheim and the evolutionists, Lévi-Strauss and his followers understood classification as reflecting underlying universal principles of organization, perhaps rooted in human biology.

Working in the tradition of Boasian cultural relativism, ethnoscientists and cognitive anthropologists attempted no such search for universal laws or generalizations. Instead, they viewed the classification system of each culture as more or less unique, reflecting that culture's specific history. Thus, as Tyler noted earlier, cognitive anthropology produces not a theory of culture, but essentially incommensurate theories of culture. Cognitive anthropologists proposed that ultimately, universal laws of culture might be derived from their work, but like Boas, they believed that this goal required massive data collection and could only be attained in the distant future. Moreover, they presented no logical framework in which to move from such theories of culture to one overarching theory.

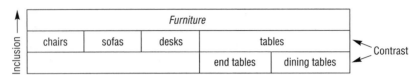

FIGURE 1 Taxonomy of furniture

We classify because life in a world where nothing was the same would be intolerable. It is through naming and classification that the whole rich world of infinite variability shrinks to manipulable size and becomes bearable. Our methods of classification are entirely arbitrary and subjective. There is nothing in the external world which demands that certain things go together and others do not. It is our perception of similarities and differences together with a set of hierarchical cues that determine which things go together. We not only react to certain discriminable stimuli as if they were the same, we name them and organize them into groupings. Thus, for example, there are objects with a seat, a back and four legs which we label *chairs,* even though no two of these objects are exactly alike. The word *chair* then stands as a sign for a whole class of objects with a seat, a back, and four legs. This sign, too, is arbitrary—we might as well call these objects *argoboos.* Just as there is no inherent quality in an object that forces us to perceive it in exactly one way, neither is there an intrinsic characteristic associating an object with its name. Consequently, with the passage of time, a class of objects may be renamed, but the class of objects denoted by this name does not change, or, conversely, the class of objects denoted by a name may change, but the name does not.

Thus, we subjectively group the phenomena of our perceptual world into named classes. These classes are not disparate and singular. They are organized into larger groupings.[12] To the extent that these groupings are hierarchically arranged by a process of inclusion, they form a taxonomy. To continue the example of chairs, there are other objects in our homes which are not chairs. There are sofas, tables, desks, cabinets, and the like. Each of these constitutes a separate class, some with many subclasses. For example there are end tables, dining tables, and coffee tables, but each of these is also a member of some more inclusive class—the class of things called "furniture." A portion of this taxonomy is shown in Fig. 1.

Figure 1 illustrates two processes characteristic of taxonomies: (1) items at the same level contrast with one another; (2) items at different levels are related by inclusion. At the bottom level are the more highly discriminated classes, at the top is the most inclusive class. Thus, end tables are kinds of tables as tables are kinds of furniture; end tables are not the same as dining tables just as tables are not the same as chairs. These relationships could also be represented in a branching diagram as in Fig. 2.

This particular taxonomy constitutes one *semantic domain* in our culture. A semantic domain consists of a class of objects all of which

---

[12] As noted in footnote 1, essay 27, the work of ethnoscience has generally consisted of describing *domains*—categories of cultural meaning that include other, smaller categories. Tyler, as he notes later, conceives of culture as consisting of a collection of domains. One has described a culture completely when one has outlined all of its domains.

A domain must be organized by some logical principle. Here and in later passages, Tyler provides three differ-

ent examples of this: taxonomy, paradigm, and tree. These are the most common principles of data organization used by ethnoscientists, but elsewhere Tyler lists more including key, partonomy, congeries, type-token, and several others (Tyler 1978:255).

Note that when Tyler uses these terms (particularly *taxonomy* and *paradigm*), he is assigning new meanings to them that are specific to cognitive anthropology.

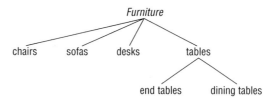

FIGURE 2   Branching diagram

share at least one feature in common which differentiates them from other semantic domains. Chairs, sofas, desks, end tables, and dining tables have in common the designation *furniture*.

Note that Fig. 2 tells us nothing of the things which distinguish a chair from a table. It tells us only that they are different. Suppose you had to tell someone how you know that one object is a chair and the other is a table. In the process of doing this, you might describe certain underlying features, some of which both chairs and tables share and some of which they do not. For example, you might say a chair has four legs, a seat, and a back, but a table has four legs and a top. Chairs would thus differ from tables by the presence of two features—a seat and a back, and the absence of one feature—a top. These underlying features are *components* or *features* of meaning. They are some of the dimensions of meaning underlying the general domain of *furniture*. That these are not the only dimensions is apparent in the contrasts between desk and table. Both pieces of furniture have four legs and a top. Using only the two features you have isolated, it is not possible to say how a table differs from a desk. Should you wish to show how each of these items differs from the other you would have to discover other features of meaning.[13]

Semantic features, like labels, are also organized. A part of the taxonomy of "animals" in American English consists of the following lexemes: cow, bull, heifer, calf, steer, mare, stallion, filly, foal, colt, gelding, sow, boar, gilt, barrow, shoat, piglet, ewe, ram, wether, lamb, livestock, cattle, swine, horse, sheep. This taxonomy is arranged in Table 1.

On even casual examination the items occurring in the lowest level of Table 1 seem to be related in some way. Closer inspection reveals that similar distinctions are made under each major category of livestock. The contrast between cow and bull, for example, is the same as the contrast between boar and sow; ram and ewe; stallion and mare. We can readily identify this contrast as one of sex or gender, male versus female. Similarly, there is an identical contrast between bull and steer; ram and wether; stallion and gelding; boar and barrow. Again, we would identify this as a contrast between male animals versus neutered animals. In addition to this sex-contrast there is a further contrast between mature and immature animals. A calf is an immature cow or bull and a heifer is an "adolescent" cow. All the lexemes in the lowest level of Table 1 reflect the two semantic features of sex and maturity. Each of these has three values: sex (male, female, neuter); maturity (adult, adolescent, child). Note, however, that horse and pig have an additional

---

[13] Once a domain has been identified, ethnoscientists and cognitive anthropologists attempted to perform componential analyses, which James P. Spradley (1933–1982) defined as "the systematic search for the attributes (components of meaning) associated with cultural categories" (1980:130). To do componential analysis, ethnoscientists search for how items in a domain systematically differ from each other. They construct a series of categories on which elements of the domain contrast. Tyler uses the example of horse and swine below. The contrasting categories are related to the sex of the animal. He calls the diagrams showing these contrasts *paradigms*.

TABLE 1   Taxonomy of "Livestock"

ANIMAL			
LIVESTOCK			
cattle	horse	sheep	swine
cow	mare	ewe	sow
bull	stallion	ram	boar
steer	gelding	wether	barrow
heifer	filly	lamb	gilt
calf	colt		shoat
	foal		piglet

feature of maturity denoting "newborn" or "baby" (piglet and foal).

Using symbols: $\male$—male; $\female$—female; $\varnothing$—neuter; M^{-1} adult; M^{-2} adolescent; M^{-3} child; M^{-4} baby; H—horse; P—swine; C—cattle; S—sheep; the distribution of features for each label can be stated in formulae as follows:

stallion	H $\male$ M^{-1}	boar	P $\male$ M^{-1}
mare	H $\female$ M^{-1}	sow	P $\female$ M^{-1}
gelding	H $\varnothing$ $M^{-1}M^{-2}$	barrow	P $\varnothing$ $M^{-1}M^{-2}$
filly	H $\female$ M^{-2}	gilt	P $\female$ M^{-2}
colt	H $\male\female$ M^{-3}	shoat	P $\male\female$ M^{-3}
foal	H $\male\female$ M^{-4}	piglet	P $\male\female$ M^{-4}

The first formula reads: a stallion is a horse, male, adult, or more appropriately, a stallion is an adult male horse. Such formulae are simply expressions of the distribution of features for each separate label. A box figure shows how these features distribute across the whole set of labels.

Reading from the diagram, a stallion is an adult male horse and a mare is an adult female horse. The features "adult" and "male" *intersect* at the space containing the label "stallion," while the features "adult" and "female" intersect at the space containing the label "mare." Since this diagram has two major features (maturity and sex) which cut across (intersect) one another, it is a *paradigm*. Features are paradigmatically arranged when they are: (1) multiple; (2) intersect.[h]

Paradigms and taxonomies are different kinds of semantic arrangements. In contrast to a paradigm, a taxonomy orders its labels by contrast and inclusion. A taxonomy typically asserts that items in lower levels are *kinds* of items in higher levels. A horse, for example, is a *kind* of livestock. A paradigm makes no such assertion. In Fig. 3 for example, a shoat is not necessarily a kind of boar.[14]

In addition to taxonomies and paradigms semantic features may be arranged on a branching diagram called a *tree*.[15] Features in a tree are ordered by sequential contrast of only one feature at a time. Trees are thus based on successive choices between only two alternatives. Such a semantic arrangement is most frequently encountered in zoological or botanical texts. Figure 4 is a simplified example of a tree.

A reading of Fig. 4 would be: Are the flowers spurred? If yes, are the flowers regular? If they are regular, then this is a delphinium. Unlike a paradigm, the features of a tree do not intersect, and unlike a taxonomy items at lower levels are not included in higher levels. Consequently, paradigms, taxonomies and trees are fundamentally different kinds of semantic arrangements. Each semantic domain of a culture may be ordered by one or more of these arrangements.

A culture consists of many semantic domains organized around numerous features of meaning, and no two cultures share the same set of semantic domains or features of meaning, nor do they share the same methods of organizing

---

[14] Although paradigms and taxonomies are different, they are not mutually exclusive. The same lexical elements may be arranged into both paradigms and taxonomies.

[15] Binary distinctions underlie many forms of organization but are most evident in trees. This emphasis on duality and opposition reflects the influence of Prague School linguistics, perhaps largely as filtered by Lévi-Strauss (see essay 24), a powerful influence on ethnoscientists.

		Sex		
		male ♂	female ♀	neuter ∅
	adult M^{-1}	stallion boar	mare sow	gelding barrow
Maturity	adolescent M^{-2}		filly gilt	
	child M^{-3}	colt shoat		
	baby M^{-4}	foal piglet		

FIGURE 3   Paradigm of features for "horse" and "swine." For cattle and sheep the contrast between baby and child would be omitted. Sheep also omits the adolescent distinction. There is however an archaic form for newborn sheep *viz.* "Yeanling."

these features. The problem for the anthropologist is to discover these semantic domains and their features, for an anthropologist in the field is much like our interplanetary visitor. There is no familiar order to the way these strange people organize their world. But, unlike our visitor, the anthropologist must avoid imposing his own semantic categories on what he perceives. He must attempt to discover the semantic world in which these people live. There are, then, two ways of bringing order out of apparent chaos—*impose* a preexisting order on it, or *discover* the order underlying it.[i] Nearly all of earlier anthropology was characterized by the first method. By contrast, cognitive anthropology seeks to develop methods which can be used for discovering and describing these principles of organization.[16]

Since such semantic systems are implicit in our use of language, they constitute one of the most significant features of human communication. Yet, what can be communicated and how it is communicated is not solely determined by this kind of semantic feature. Other semantic features deriving from the context of communication are equally important. Context includes the manner of communication (for example, verbal and written), the social setting, and the linguistic repertories of speaker and hearer. Contextual semantic features and their mutual interdependence are as much a part of the cognitive system as taxonomies and semantic domains.

---

[16] The ethnoscientists' key critique of earlier anthropology was that it artificially imposed order on the data. Interestingly, at the same time that ethnoscience was emerging, George Peter Murdock was developing the Human Relations Area Files (HRAF). Begun in 1937, the HRAF project was (and continues to be) a massive effort to provide a universal index to anthropological literature. Using the HRAF, a researcher may look up a single topic, say friendship, and find information indexed as friendship in ethnographies on many different societies. Murdock's statistical comparative approach was favored by materialists such as Marvin Harris and modern evolutionists such as Morton Fried.

Ethnoscientists and cognitive anthropologists were very critical of Murdock's approach on two levels: First, it was not clear that a classification such as friendship has the same meaning from culture to culture. Second, it was not clear that the various people who indexed the work had the same ideas about the meaning of friendship. Thus, critics claimed that the index compared apples to oranges, which meant that reliable generalizations could not be drawn.

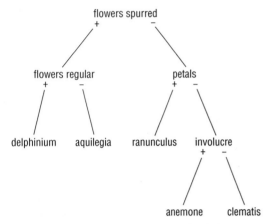

FIGURE 4 A tree arrangement. Plus (+) indicates presence of the feature, minus (−) its absence. Thus, if a flower is not spurred, has no petals, and no involucre, it is a clematis.

There still remains the question of how we discover features in cultures other than our own. If you will attempt to complete the statement of semantic features for the taxonomy of furniture, you will see that the discovery of these features is difficult enough in your native language. It is even more difficult in a strange language. As a consequence, new fieldwork techniques and methods have had to be devised. Most important among these are techniques of *controlled eliciting* and methods of *formal analysis.*[17]

Controlled eliciting utilizes sentence frames derived from the language of the people being studied. The aim of such eliciting is to enable the ethnographer to behave linguistically in ways appropriate to the culture he is studying. This involves the use of linguistically correct questions which relate concepts meaningful in that culture. Suppose you are a foreigner attempting to learn something about American culture. On seeing an object for which you do not know an English term, one possible sequence of related questions and responses might be:

Q: What is this?

A: This is a sow.

Q: Is that a sow, too?

A: No, that's a boar.

Q. Is a boar a kind of sow?

A: No, a boar is a kind of livestock.

Q: Is a sow a kind of livestock?

A: Yes.

Q: How many kinds of livestock are there?

A: There are pigs, horses, mules, sheep, goats, and others.

This sequence indicates that sows and boars are conceptually linked and that there are numerous other things grouped with them in the taxonomy of livestock. Note that decisions concerning the inclusion of items within this taxonomy are made by the informant, not by the investigator. Contrast this procedure with a familiar questionnaire technique derived from

---

[17]Ethnoscientists and cognitive anthropologists criticized early anthropology in general and Murdock in particular for their lack of systematic methods of data collection.

It is certainly true that, until recently, graduate-level texts or courses that dealt with field methods were few and far between. Michael Agar (1980) tells the story of a student of Kroeber who went to ask the grand old man for advice on the ways to do fieldwork. "After several passes by the open door, she entered and nervously cleared her throat. Kroeber was typing (naturally) and did not look up for a minute or so. When he did, the student . . . asked for advice. 'Well,' said Kroeber, returning to his typing, 'I suggest that you buy a notebook and a pencil.'"

The key point made by cognitive anthropologists and ethnoscientists was that since ethnographers did not use consistent data collection techniques, and since they used categories from their own cultures that they defined imprecisely, they could neither accurately reflect native understandings of the world nor make useful generalizations across cultures. They claimed that Murdock's HRAF was meaningless because it implied the existence of "natural" domains, that is, domains that have the same boundaries in every culture. Ethnoscientists and cognitive anthropologists believed that such things were theoretically possible but not likely to exist. Their position mirrors Boas' ideas on natural laws pertaining to cultures.

handbooks on social science methodology. Is the cow ___ very like; ___ somewhat like; ___ only a little like; ___ not at all like a god (check one). Aside from the spurious scaling, this question would be meaningful only in societies of English speakers in which there were: (a) cows, (b) gods, (c) some evidence that gods and cows were conceptually linked, or (d) sociologists. In this technique, the investigator has already made all the decisions about conceptual relevance. The informant's responses can only be replications in one way or another of the investigator's judgments about conceptual relevance. In a sense, such a method merely tells you what you already know. Controlled eliciting, on the other hand, is designed to provide the ethnographer with not only the answers, but also to assist him in discovering the relevant questions. It clearly derives from the fact that the questioning process is itself the dominant factor in scientific investigation (Collingwood 1929:29–43). Where the procedures and results of controlled eliciting are contained in the report, two things are achieved: (1) there is an explicit record of how the data were gathered; (2) a public record of the results is available.

Formal analysis is simply one method of stating the results of such controlled eliciting. It differs from other methods in its emphasis on internal consistency, completeness, and form. A particular set of data relating to some semantic domain must be explained by the relationship between units comprising that domain—not by determinants outside it.[18] The problem of external determinants is delayed until internal determinants are analyzed. For example, the question of whether I call my mother's sister's son "cousin" determined until I know the system of relations between cousin, brother, and all the other kin terms in the English system. A formal analysis is complete when the relations among all the units comprising a semantic domain are described.

THE NEW ORDER

The aims and methods of cognitive anthropology have important implications for cultural anthropology. They entail a rethinking of the culture concept, the comparative method, and of ethnography.

In this discussion culture has been identified with cognition. This must strike some cultural anthropologists as a truncated version of the culture concept, for it neglects many of their traditional interests. They might well ask, What about process? What about behavior? What about motivation? Implicit in these questions is an assumption that in addition to cognitive systems a theory of culture must explain cultures as systems emerging from patterned frequencies of observed behavior and processes of development and change (cf. Goodenough 1964). *As a general statement of anthropological goals, these are relevant considerations, but they are not relevant to a theory of culture.* There is no necessity to assume that the cognitive order is either systematically a derivative of or a predictor of substantive actions.[19] Just as the grammar of a language provides no information on what all individual speakers will say on any given occasion, so too a cognitive description of a culture does not pretend to predict the actual behavior of any individual.

---

[18] In many ways, cognitive anthropology and ethnoscience represent an extreme logical end of Boasian thinking. In this paragraph, for example, notice the restatement of Boasian cultural relativism in ethnoscientific terms: Semantic domains may only be explained with reference to themselves. Like Boasian culture, they are *sui generis*.

[19] The theoretical battles of the 1950s and 1960s crystallized a profound division in American anthropology—that between materialist and idealist thinkers. This division had been present in anthropology from the beginning but is probably best seen in this era. Tyler and the cognitive and ethnoscientific anthropologists, who represent one extreme, conceive of culture in purely mentalistic terms. It is created *sui generis* and has no predictable effect on the "real world." The other pole is represented by Harris and the functional materialists and ecologists, who view culture as adaptive. They were concerned with observable behavior and generally less interested in the underlying thoughts of the actors.

The formal analysis of culture, like a grammar, is concerned only with what is expected and appropriate. And just as an adequate grammar is neither contingent upon prior assumptions concerning developmental processes nor necessarily explains them, a grammar of culture need make no assumptions about nor attempt to explain these processes. So construed, neither prediction of actual events nor specification of developmental process is a necessary component of a theory of culture.[j] To paraphrase Collingwood (1956:217), cultural anthropology is not a description of events or an account of change. The cultural anthropologist is only concerned with those events which are expressions of underlying thoughts. His aim is to penetrate beyond mere material representation to the logical nexus of underlying concepts.

Culture, conceived as the totality of human behavior, ideas, history, institutions and artifacts has never been particularly useful as a meaningful method of explaining ethnographic facts.[20] Such a conception merely asserts that culture is equivalent to the whole of human knowledge. As a device which purports to explain all of man's learned behavior, motivations, prehistoric record, ecological adaptations, biological limitations, and evolution it attempts too much. What we need is a more limited notion of culture which stresses *theories of culture*. Rather than attempt to develop a general THEORY OF CULTURE, the best we can hope for at present is particular theories of cultures. These theories will constitute complete, accurate descriptions of particular cognitive systems. Only when such particular descriptions are expressed in a single metalanguage with known logical properties will we have arrived at a general theory of culture. Such a general theory will be equivalent to the language in which we describe cultures (Kay 1965:112). In effect we already have a pseudometalanguage. It is for this reason that nearly all ethnographies have similar chapter headings. The problem with this metalanguage is that is assumes universality without prior demonstration.[21] Its universality inheres in the language of description and not necessarily in the object being described.[k]

At issue here are two contrasting views of cultural anthropology. The central issue is, is cultural anthropology a *natural* or *formal* science? Traditional cultural anthropology is based on the assumption that its data are discrete material phenomena which can be analyzed like the material phenomena of any other natural science. Cognitive anthropology is based on the assumption that its data are mental phenomena which can be analyzed by formal methods similar to those of mathematics and logic.[l] Each particular culture consists of a set of logical principles which order relevant material phenomena. To the cognitive anthropologist these logical principles rather than the material phenomena are the object of investigation. For the cognitive anthropologist cultural anthropology is a formal science. It seems likely that the logical operations underlying principles of ordering are finite and universal, but capable of generating an infinite number of possible specific orderings (cf. Lévi-Strauss 1966:268). In this limited sense, cognitive anthropology constitutes a return to Bastian's search for the "psychic unity of mankind."[22]

---

[20] Tyler here takes aim at E. B. Tylor's classic definition of culture (see essay 2). What he proposes is, in fact, similar to what Boas proposed; that is, detailed descriptions of individual cultures rather than any single overarching analysis of culture. The difference is that Boas did not propose a specific methodology, and Tyler does. In theory, this means that Tyler's theories of culture will be expressed in a consistent manner that might allow a general theory to emerge.

[21] The metalanguage Tyler refers to here is the language that would describe the structure of the domains outlined by cognitive anthropology and ethnoscience. He claims that current metalinguistic categories, such as kinship, religion, political system, and so on, are inadequate because it has not been shown that they describe cross-culturally consistent domains. He calls these *pseudometalanguage*.

[22] Tyler here describes anthropology as a formal science, not only like math and logic but also like structural linguistics. He opens the possibility that some of the logical principles that will be discovered by cognitive anthropology are universals.

The implications for the comparative method follow directly from the above. The central issue in comparative analysis is, What is the unit of comparison? There have been many attempts to specifically delimit the unit of comparison. Yet most so-called cross-cultural comparisons have really been nothing more than cross-tribal or cross-community comparisons. Obviously, if a culture is the unit of comparison, then we must compare whole systems which are bounded in space and time or demonstrate that the parts of systems we are comparing are justifiably isolable (cf. Boas 1940:275). Since most ethnographies are not sufficiently complete for either of these possibilities, the whole comparative approach based on substantive variables must be abandoned if our aim is indeed cultural comparison.[23] Those who insist that no fact has meaning except by comparison are right, but the implication that comparison can occur only between similar facts from different systems does not follow. It is much more pertinent to compare similar, but not identical facts within the same system. This is not so much a total abandonment of the comparative method; it is a matter of priorities. Comparisons between systems can only be useful if the facts compared are truly comparable, and we cannot know what facts are comparable until the facts themselves are adequately described. When this is achieved, the units of comparison will be formal features rather than substantive variables.

PROBLEMS AND PROSPECTS

[*Tyler concludes his essay with a 2,000-word discussion of the problems and prospects of his approach. He discusses research problems in the following areas: arrangements, perception and conception, discourse analysis, propositional analysis, metamessages, historical linguistics, and semantic ontogenesis. Tyler views the problems he has identified as indicative of the vitality of cognitive anthropology rather than as fatal flaws in its theory. He closes with the following passage.*]

These comments are intended as speculations on the possible areas of future development in cognitive anthropology. They do not pretend to be exhaustive nor even representative. Nonetheless, they do indicate that cognitive anthropology has moved into a secondary stage of development. We have a few tentative answers, some new questions, and a host of old questions still unanswered. Fresh ground has been broken and new areas occupied, but still more remote territories have opened up for further research.

Explicit here is a view of culture derived from a kind of ethnography in which the methods of description are public and replicable, and the results predictive of expectations of appropriate behavior.[24] Implicit is the cognitive reorganization of our categories of description and analysis. Cognitive anthropology entails an ethnographic technique which describes cultures from the inside out rather than from the outside in. Categories of description are initially derived from relevant features in a culture rather than from the lexicon of anthropology.

Cognitive reorganization is a familiar process in the history of anthropology—in fact of any scientific discipline. The history of science is but the record of constant reexamination of assumptions, methods, and data. Such new developments in science do not take place in a vacuum. Innovations in one branch of science are

---

[23] In this passage, Tyler returns to his critique of traditional ethnography. He touches on a topic that became crucial to anthropologists in the late 1980s—defining the boundaries of cultural groups or subgroups. Tyler suggests that traditional ethnography has not done this in a consistent way that would make comparison possible. Some anthropologists in the 1980s suggested that such definition was by nature an impossible task.

[24] Tyler emphasizes that, in his view, anthropology is a scientific and not an interpretive discipline (though a formal and not a natural science). Its goal is to produce logical, consistent, and public descriptions of culture that will withstand what Tyler considers rigorous testing.

complemented by convergent developments in other branches.[25]

The psychologist's renewed interest in cognition, the linguist's rediscovery of semantics, the biologist's recent emphasis on taxonomy and species specific behavior, and the sociologist's concern with the presentation of the self all reflect a set of recent developments complementary to one another and to those in anthropology. To be sure, among these disciplines there are differences in emphasis and method, yet each shares with the other a common orientation—the discovery of the organizing principles used by individuals, cultures, and species in manipulating and adapting to their particular life-space.

NOTES

[a] I wish to thank the following people who commented on previous versions of this paper: Brent Berlin, Mary Black, Charles Frake, John Gumperz, Dell Hymes, Paul Kay, Floyd Lounsbury, Ronald Rohner, George and Louise Spindler. I hope it is evident that the views in this chapter are those of the editor and do not necessarily represent a consensus of opinion among the above nor among those whose papers comprise subsequent chapters.

[b] In this, and in much of what follows, there is a pronounced neo-Kantian flavor.

[c] For an instance of a similar distinction between "objective environment" and "perceived life-space," see von Uexküll (1957).

[d] The processes involved in this example are related to theories of cognitive dissonance (cf. Festinger 1957).

[e] The line of argument here derives mainly from Russell (1929:92–98), but see also Bateson (1958:294) and Sapir (1932:515–519).

[f] The most notable exception to this statement is Boas.

[g] It is probably not true that all named things are significant, just as it is not the case that all significant things are named. Yet, as a point of departure, named categories are of primary importance.

[h] Note the two empty spaces in Fig. 3. These indicate that this is not a perfect paradigm. The empty spaces

are the result of incomplete combination of semantic components. The combinations $\male M^{-2}; \varnothing M^{-3}; \varnothing M^{-4}$ do not occur. In a perfect paradigm all possible combinations would be realized. Perfect paradigms occur less frequently than imperfect paradigms. It should also be noted that in some contexts the lexemes "boar" and "stallion" denote not only $\male M^{-1}$ but $\male M^{-1} M^{-2}$. For "horse" the lexeme "yearling" may sometimes denote $\male M^{-2}; \female M^{-2}; \varnothing M^{-2}$. Historically it is interesting to note that all the lexemes denoting "newborn" ($\male \female M^{-4}$) except piglet are derived from verbs denoting "to give birth to." A cow "calves," a mare "foals," a ewe "lambs," or "yeans," but a sow "farrows." As might be expected the archaic term for a newborn pig is "farrow." The lexeme piglet is recent. Also relevant is the fact that the "wild animal" category denoted by the lexeme "deer" has, except for the neuter category, the same semantic features as the category denoted by cattle. Formerly deer denoted "animal." Finally the features male, female, neuter correspond to the generalized Indo-European classification of nouns as masculine, feminine, neuter.

[i] This distinction between a priori and a posteriori models is difficult to maintain, for it impinges directly on the philosophical problem of "other minds." If the mind imposes its own order on the disorderly happenings of the universe, then the investigator of necessity imposes his own logical constructs on the world he believes he is exploring. From this point of view there is no evidence for a belief in the existence of other minds except by analogy. Yet, granted the existence of other minds it is possible to assume that since the logical constructs of an informant and of an investigator are both products of a mind, these constructs are knowable insofar as they are communicable. Hence, the cognitive anthropologist's emphasis on language as both a method of discovery and an object of investigation (cf. Russell 1929:99–103).

[j] This is not to imply that such a theory is incompatible with the study of change and development. The point is that a theory of description constitutes a different order of theory than that required for processes of change (for a discussion of this point, see Bateson 1958:296–300). A theory of change emphasizing cognitive organization would probably demonstrate that most anthropological data on change relate not to cultural change, but merely to epiphenomenal fluctuations.

---

[25] In closing, Tyler returns once again to Kuhn's idea of paradigm shift. He views cognitive anthropology and ethnoscience as new paradigms that will revolutionize anthropology. This assessment of the place of cognitive anthropology was overoptimistic, however. It certainly did not have a revolutionary effect that rendered competing paradigms obsolete. In fact, Tyler later abandoned this approach in favor of postmodernism. Nevertheless, ethnoscience and cognitive anthropology did have powerful impacts on anthropology in the 1960s and 1970s and were crucial to the development of postmodernist thinking in the 1980s.

[k]This is misleading. Scientific laws are of necessity statements of universals in the language of description. All talk of "objects" and an hypothesized relation between "objects" and the language of description is symptomatic of a pernicious kind of dualism. The point is that our current language of description is inadequate either for the description of particular cultures or the development of universals simply because its assumptions are implicit and its operations (when specified) are contradictory. The continuing argument in descent "theory" is a classic example of the inadequacy of our current "metalanguage." The misleading statement reflects my own vacillation between an "intuitionist" (conceptualist) and "logicist" (realist) point of view (cf. Quine 1952). In general, this chapter is intuitionist with occasional logicist lapses. The lapses create problems like the one referred to above. My assertion that the description of a culture is really a description of the anthropologist's cognitive ordering is pure intuitionism which does not square directly with the Lévi-Straussian quest for a universal pan-human logic expressed in other sections. In a sense, the psychological reality problem is a confrontation between intuitionism and realism or perhaps formalism (nominalism). My belief in the relevance of relevance as an aspect of cognitive anthropology is probably creeping realism.

[l]Leach (1961:6–21) makes a similar point, but with different emphasis. For two discussions of the distinction between formal and factual or natural sciences, see Carnap (1953) and Quine (1960:270–276). The distinction may be somewhat overdrawn, but this should not obscure the fact that cultural anthropology has traditionally emulated a model of scientific method derived from a rather naive nineteenth century scientific materialism. Harris's (1962) quest for elementary units of cultural "matter" is a recent example of this attitude.

REFERENCES

Bateson, Gregory. 1958. *Naven*, 2d ed. Stanford: Stanford University Press.

Boas, Franz. 1938. *The Mind of Primitive Man*. London: Macmillan.

———. 1940. *Race, Language and Culture*. New York: Macmillan.

Carnap, Rudolf. 1953. Formal and factual science. In H. Feigl and M. Brodbeck, eds., *Readings in the philosophy of science*. New York: Appleton.

Collingwood, R. G. 1929. *An Autobiography*. New York: Oxford University Press.

———. 1956. *The Idea of History*. New York: Oxford University Press.

Festinger, Leon. 1957. *A Theory of Cognitive Dissonance*. New York: Harper and Row.

Goodenough, Ward H. 1957. Cultural anthropology and linguistics. In Paul Garvin, ed., Report of the seventh annual round table meeting on linguistics and language study. Georgetown University Monograph Series on Language and Linguistics No. 9.

———. 1963. *Cooperation in Change*. New York: Russell Sage.

———. 1964. Introduction. In W. H. Goodenough, ed., *Explorations in Cultural Anthropology*. New York: McGraw-Hill.

Harris, Marvin. 1964. *The Nature of Cultural Things*. New York: Random House.

Harris, Zellig. 1952. Discourse analysis. *Language* 28:1–30.

Hymes, Dell, ed. 1964a. *Language in Culture and Society*. New York: Harper and Row.

———. 1964b. Directions in (ethno-) linguistic theory. *American Anthropologist* 66 Pt. 2, No. 3:656.

Kay, Paul. 1965. Does anthropology need a metalanguage? Paper presented at the Southwestern Anthropological Association Annual Meeting, 1965.

Leach, E. R. 1961. *Rethinking Anthropology*. London School of Economics Monographs on Social Anthropology No. 22. London: University of London Press.

Lévi-Strauss, Claude. 1966. *The Savage Mind*. Chicago: University of Chicago Press.

Quine, Willard Van Orman. 1960. *Word and Object*. New York: Wiley.

———. 1952. On what there is. In L. Linsky, ed., *Semantics and the Philosophy of Language*. Urbana: University of Illinois Press.

Russell, Bertrand. 1929. *Our Knowledge of the External World*. New York: Norton.

Sapir, Edward. 1932. Cultural anthropology and psychiatry. In D. G. Mandelbaum, ed., *Selected Writings of Edward Sapir*. Berkeley: University of California Press.

———. 1934. The emergence of the concept of personality in a study of cultures. In D. G. Mandelbaum, ed., *Selected Writings of Edward Sapir*. Berkeley: University of California Press.

Uexküll, Jakob Von. 1957. A stroll through the world of animals and men: A picture book of invisible worlds. In C. H. Schiller and K. S. Lashley, eds., *Instinctive Behavior: The Development of a Modern Concept*. New York: International Universities.

Wallace, A. F. C. 1961. *Culture and Personality*. New York: Random House.

Woodger, J. H. 1952. *Biology and Language: An Introduction to the Methodology of the Biological Sciences Including Medicine*. Cambridge: University Press.

29. *What Makes Tony Run? Schemas as Motives Reconsidered*

Claudia Strauss (b. 1953)

IT IS OBVIOUS that people's wants are shaped, to a large extent, by their culture. There are probably few goals shared by !Kung hunter-gatherers, United States businesspeople, and Hindu renouncers. But how, exactly, does culture shape motivation?

Following some recent work by Roy D'Andrade (1984, 1990, 1992), I assume that insight into this problem can be provided by looking at the cognitive representation of cultural knowledge. Unlike D'Andrade, however, I argue that cognitive representations can differ in the kind of motivational force they provide. This paper focuses on five Rhode Island male blue-collar workers' talk about "getting ahead." I also know about some significant choices they have made in their work lives. What I found is that their choices have been directed by three types of knowledge. These three types of knowledge differ not just in content, but also in form of cognitive representation, manner of verbal expression, and type of motivational effect.[1]

SCHEMAS AND DIRECTIVE FORCE

D'Andrade's central thesis[a] is that culturally formed cognitive schemas not only determine our interpretation of the world but also direct our actions in it, often serving as goals. To appreciate this claim it is necessary to understand what a cognitive schema is.

Casson (1983) provides a helpful review of the cognitive science literature on schemas. Although this notion has received different treatments by different theorists, and has even been presented under different names (e.g., "scripts," "frames," and "scenarios"), the core concept is that

> Schemata are conceptual abstractions that mediate between stimuli received by the sense organs and behavioral responses . . . not all stimuli are stored in memory; rather, schemata are employed to provide "a general impression of the whole" and to construct (or reconstruct) "probable details." (1983:430)

Rumelhart provides a similar explanation:

> According to schema theories, all knowledge is *packaged into units*. These units are the schemata. Embedded in these *packets of knowledge* is, in addition to the knowledge itself, information about how this knowledge is to be used. A schema, then, is a data structure for representing the generic concepts stored in memory. (1980:34; emphasis mine)

One famous example of a schema is our knowledge of the typical sequence of events when we eat at a restaurant. This schema organizes our perceptions of ongoing restaurant experiences and our memories of earlier ones. It is also the

(1992)

---

[1] Strauss introduces her essay by asking the question, "How does culture shape motivation?" She then proposes that insight can be gained by examining the "cognitive representation of cultural knowledge," or schema, that underlies people's thoughts about work and success. However, she begins her argument by setting up a contrast between her work and earlier studies conducted by Roy D'Andrade (b. 1931). D'Andrade, a professor at the University of California–San Diego, is one of the leading figures in cognitive anthropology (see essay 40). D'Andrade claims that schemas are more than models by which we interpret the world. He believes that they can motivate or direct actions. Strauss calls these "goal-embedded" schemas. One of the points of Strauss' essay is to demonstrate that D'Andrade's model is too limited. She claims that the motivational power of schemas depends on other elements of thought. Her purpose is to demonstrate the cognitive elements that motivated the career choices of the men in her study.

basis for interpreting others' discourse, because speakers in this society can leave most of this background knowledge unsaid when talking about particular dining-out experiences (Schank and Abelson 1977). Finally, this schema clearly has directive force for us: if we are eating in a restaurant, we generally feel motivated to follow the restaurant "script" (i.e., pick choices from a menu, tell them to a waiter or waitress, eat, wait for a check, pay it, leave a tip, and go out). To put it as D'Andrade does, the restaurant schema has goals "embedded" in it.

Gerber (1985) provides another good example of a schema with directive force. The Samoan term *alofa,* loosely equivalent to our "love," is linked to the following scenario:

> an old person, often portrayed as a stranger, is seen walking along the road, carrying a heavy burden. It is hot, and perhaps the elder seems ill or tired. The appropriate response in this instance is a feeling of *alofa,* which implies helpful or giving actions such as taking over the burden or providing a cool drink and a place to rest. (Gerber 1985:145)

In other words Samoans have an *alofa* schema, which links this term to the above scenario. The Samoan *alofa* schema, like our restaurant schema, has embedded in it certain goals for action: if one sees an old person who is hot, tired, and overburdened, one should offer refreshment or help. Thus, the Samoan *alofa* schema is a good example of a cultural model with directive force.[2]

The goal-embedded schema model of motivation has many advantages over previous approaches. D'Andrade notes that earlier motivational research searched for a small, cross-culturally applicable set of measurable motives that worked like the drives of hunger and sex. If goals are seen as embedded in schemas, on the other hand, there is room for cross-cultural variation and no need to specify a single, fixed list of human motives. The fact that the goals embedded in any schema are not always activated—as D'Andrade points out, we know chairs are for sitting in, but we do not feel motivated to sit just because we see a chair—can be explained by seeing at what level a schema contributes to the interpretation of a situation. Thus,

> One recognizes some chair as part of the "finding a seat" schema, which is part of the "attending a lecture" schema, which is part of the "finding out what's going on" schema, which may be for some people part of the "doing anthropology" schema. (1992:30)

D'Andrade proposes that the schemas at higher levels of interpretation (e.g., doing anthropology or getting ahead) will trigger their embedded goals more than those at lower levels of interpretation: *"a person's most general interpretations of what is going on will function as important goals for that person"* (1992:30).

I agree with D'Andrade that a goal-embedded schema theory of motivation has the advantages he cites over earlier motivational research. My own study of five working men's success discourse has led me, however, to the conclusion that high-level cultural schemas do not necessarily serve as important goals. The motivational effect of cultural knowledge depends on other features of its cognitive representation. My interviewees' discourse about getting ahead, and the career choices they have made, reflect three different types of

---

[2] The ethnoscientists proposed that people classified objects by matching things with a mental checklist and that if an anthropologist could learn these lists of features, they could think like a native. However, cognitive anthropologists today propose that people conceptualize their world through mental prototypes called schemas, or *schemata*. Action follows the activation of one schema or a set of schemas. In his article "Schemata in Anthropology," Ronald Casson describes schemas this way:

> Schemata are conceptual abstractions that mediate between stimuli received by the sense organs and

behavioral responses. They are abstractions that serve as the basis for all human information processing. (1983:430)

Here Strauss, following D'Andrade, gives us two examples of schemas that have directive power, the restaurant schema and the *alofa* schema. D'Andrade claims that goals are embedded within the schema. Thus within the *alofa* schema is information that triggers behavior associated with the schema.

cognitive representation, each of which has qualitatively different motivational effects.[3]

Consider first the widely shared, easily verbalized values that underpin the "American Dream": with hard work anyone in America can get ahead, and everyone should strive to do so. Although my interviewees voiced this success model, they appear to hold it in a bounded way. By "bounded" I mean these ideas are only weakly linked to the rest of the belief-holder's knowledge structure. Furthermore, my interviewees were able to see these values as values. Their discourse shows not only an acceptance of success values, but also an awareness that these values are dominant ones in our society. Success values are a good example of what D'Andrade calls "a person's most general interpretations," which are supposed to act as motivators. Yet success values did not greatly influence the career choices most of my interviewees made. This surprising finding is discussed in the next section.

In the following section I turn to a more class- and gender-specific schema held by my interviewees. Much of their discourse about being a breadwinner suggests that they are not aware of these values as values, seeing them instead as inescapable reality. Breadwinner values, unlike success values, *did* direct my interviewees' routine behavior.[4]

Although my interviewees share many beliefs about work and success, each also has a unique outlook stored not in the bounded way of the success model, but as an unbounded network linking key symbols, emotionally salient experiences, and ideas about himself. These personal semantic networks, the third form of belief discussed below, have had a still different sort of directive force, guiding each man toward idiosyncratic self-defining goals and general styles of behavior. This is illustrated, in the penultimate section, with the discourse of one interviewee, Tony D'Abrosca.[b] Tony's accomplishments as a runner fit into a personal semantic network linking athletic achievement to childhood memories, feelings of distance from others, and current political values.[5]

The final section speculates that these different forms of cognition are the products of different sorts of cultural messages and briefly considers the implications of these findings for a theory of culture.

AMERICAN SUCCESS VALUES

D'Andrade (1984) has used American beliefs about success as an example of a cultural model with strong directive force. He notes that from some interview data he has collected:

> It seems to be the case that Americans think that if one has ability, and if, because of competition or one's own strong drive, one works hard at achieving high goals, one will reach an

---

[3] D'Andrade argues that higher-level schemas trigger their embedded goals more than lower-level schemas. However, Strauss claims that her own study has led her to conclude that high-level cultural schemas do not necessarily direct goal-seeking behavior. In this essay she outlines three types of thinking about success and work that were held by her interview subjects but which did not motivate them all to the same degree. These three forms of cognitive representation are, first, *success values*, the kind of generalized interpretation that D'Andrade believes should act to motivate people. Second are *breadwinner values*, which Strauss claims directed her subjects' behavior. Finally there are what Strauss calls *personal semantic networks*, which linked the men's values, life experiences, and personal ideas. According to Strauss, these personal semantic networks directed her subjects' self-defined goals and behaviors.

[4] Here Strauss furthers her distinction between success values and breadwinner values. She claims that her interviewees understood success values as a *value,* in other words, a belief that one should strive for. Breadwinner values were more deeply embedded, that is, the men in the study saw breadwinner values as the way the world was, and these beliefs directed their behavior.

[5] In this paragraph Strauss provides a description of *personal semantic networks,* the third cognitive model through which the men in the study viewed their world. Although these five men knew the success model and to differing degrees shared the breadwinner model, personal semantic networks are individual belief systems created from the men's life experiences. These beliefs motivated men in personal ways, such as the importance that one subject, Tony D'Abrosca, placed on running.

outstanding level of accomplishment. And when one reaches this level one will be recognized as a success, which brings prestige and self-satisfaction. (1984:95)

He adds about the American emphasis on success:

There are external sanctions involving money and employment, there are conformity pressures of many kinds, and there are the direct personal rewards and value satisfactions already mentioned. Perhaps what is surprising is that anyone can resist the directive force of such a system—that there are incorrigibles. (1984:98)

I found that in certain contexts, several of my interviewees voiced the same ideas about success as D'Andrade's interviewees. The main difference is that D'Andrade's interviewees seem to have had a model that transcended purely economic criteria, whereas most of my informants, like the white-collar managers and professionals interviewed by Robert Bellah and his colleagues (1985), associate high goals and hard work with upward mobility.

In 1985 I conducted a series of semistructured interviews with four neighbors (two male, two female) and six union and management employees (all male) of a batch-processing chemical plant in Cranston, Rhode Island. This plant, owned by Ciba-Geigy Ltd., a multinational pharmaceutical and chemical company, had been a source of local controversy, first for its noxious discharges, later for its decision to close and leave the state. Over the course of six to seven lengthy interview sessions we talked about the Ciba-Geigy controversy, the role of business in American society, current events, general political and economic questions, and their own work experiences and life histories. The first five interview sessions with each person

were very loosely structured around a common set of topics that got covered sooner or later with each interviewee. In the sixth interview session I asked a series of open-ended but standardized questions about our social system. The interviews were tape-recorded and transcribed.[c,6]

This analysis focuses on the responses of the five working-class men in the interview group. Four were employees and one was a neighbor of the Cranston Ciba-Geigy plant. The men are all native Rhode Islanders in their forties or fifties, are married and have children, had between nine and twelve years of schooling, and have (or had—some are now retired) skilled or semiskilled blue-collar occupations. All are white and their ethnic backgrounds cover the four most common Rhode Island ethnic groups: Italian-American, French-Canadian, Irish, and Yankee.[d]

The questions that most reliably elicited shared American success values came from the standardized series used in the last interview. At one point I asked (one at a time): "What things keep people from getting ahead in the world?" "Who or what is to blame for this?" "What things help people to get ahead?" and "Is the system fair? Does everyone pretty much have the same chance to get ahead?" Later in the same interview I asked each man if he agreed strongly, agreed somewhat, disagreed somewhat, or disagreed strongly with the statement, "Anybody can get ahead if they just work hard enough." Here are the answers four of the men gave to one of those questions. (Underscore indicates my emphasis; italics the speaker's.)[e]

1. CS: If people can't get ahead in the world, who is to blame for that?

Jim Lovett: I don't know that you could *blame* any one. You, you are the one to blame. It's you.

---

[6] Here Strauss tells readers how her data were collected, through semistructured interviews. Although cognitive anthropologists do not discuss data in terms of "domains" or "thinking like natives," they are just as dependent on linguistics and the structured interview as the ethnoscientists of the 1950s and 1960s. Practitioners of this school of thought interview subjects and create cultural models of how their informants think about the world just as the ethnoscientists of the 1950s attempted to create models of

native thought. One difference is that the ethnoscientists tended to just identify categories of classifications, whereas cognitive anthropologists understand schemas as processors of information and examine how schemas motivate behavior. Casson calls schemas "prototypes," or "generic representations of concepts" (1983:434), as opposed to the ethnoscientists' "checklist theories of meaning" derived from componential analysis (quoted in Casson 1983:435).

Because . . . you can achieve anything your mind can conceive. If you can think, if you have an idea. [del] And if you think about it hard enough. And you want it bad enough. Then you can achieve it. There's nothing on this, in this country or on earth that if you were willing enough to work at it, that you cannot achieve it. So we all have the potential of being a millionaire, if that is your goal. You've got to have a goal. And if you're willing to work at it, *hard* enough, then you can achieve it. So, it goes right back down to you. [del] If it's your own personal *drive* if you will or your goals. Goals. Everyone should have a goal. (6:17–18)

2. George Gauvin [responding to "Anybody can get ahead if they just work hard enough"]: I would say that's true. You've got to work, you've got to really try to better yourself. Even if you're not—you don't have to be on top, but improve your job, improve your class. You start off as a helper, you become good, you become a journeyman—have to work hard at it. (6:24)

3. Daniel Collins [responding to "Anybody can get ahead if they just work hard enough"]: I *strongly* agree with that … I believe if you put an effort into *anything,* you can get ahead. Just [like] myself, where I have to put the effort into learning, again. You know. If I want to succeed, I'll succeed. It has to be, come from within here. Nobody else is going to make you succeed but yourself … And, if anybody disagrees with that, there's something wrong with them. (6:27–8)

4. CS: "What things keep people from getting ahead in the world?"

Anthony Gallucci: Brains and . . . not having any initiative or . . . money. Some people don't want to get ahead. Too much responsibility, I guess, you know, in some [cases?]. [del] It could be laziness. [In answer to later questions, he adds] I would think if you were trying to bring your kids up properly and . . . show them, I mean,

try to show them what the advantages of having a good job—or disadvantages of digging a ditch. [del] It all depends how bad you want something. Your kids going to school now, pump gas and work at hamburger places and everything else, trying to save a few bucks, help pay their way to college, anyway. I think if you want it bad enough, there's ways. (6:12–13)

Each of these men claims that anyone can get ahead and either states or implies that one should want to.

Only one man, Tony D'Abrosca, seriously disputed in response to these questions[f] the premise that anyone can get ahead and the value of doing so:

5. CS: "Does everyone pretty much have the same chance to get ahead?"

D'Abrosca: [del] That's the old saw, you know. "Anybody can get ahead." "Lot of opportunities." Nah. There is for some . . . There is for some. They get the opportunity to skin the small guys. That's how I look at it. (6:32)

One thing that is distinctive about the way these ideas were held by my interviewees, compared to many of their other beliefs, is that they could see them as values. This is obvious from D'Abrosca's statement ("That's the old saw, you know" [5.]), but the values embedded in this model were not accessible only to someone who disputed it. Every man but one spoke at some point as if he were aware that he might be judged by the criteria of the success model and found wanting.[7]

Some particularly clear examples of this awareness come from Jim Lovett's speech:

6. I'm happily married. And I've got three terrific kids and wonderful grandchildren. I feel so, that with my education, which was only to the ninth grade, <u>I've been fairly successful, um,[8] raising my family.</u> (1:2)

7. So I was always able to provide a decent living for my family. We never had a lot of—my own,

---

[7] Here Strauss is making the distinction between her model and that outlined by D'Andrade. In D'Andrade's understanding the schema of success should motivate action. Strauss says that the men are aware of the schema but some dispute it.

my *own* family—a lot of *elaborate* things perhaps. We always were the last one in the, in my group that I grew up with or went to school with, to have a new car. *But.* We—our children never went without clothing. They never went hungry. And Irene and I would probably not get to go to the movies or go out to dinner as often as the others did, but our *children* never went without. So we were in a sense good parents or providers or whatever. And we look back on it now with the others that did afford, could afford themselves nightclubs and, and restaurants and new cars. That their children, because of it, have to've been left with a babysitter a lot more than my children because we did stay with them. We were *involved* with them and they weren't. So . . . their children have grown up and gotten married and divorced where—and fallen away a little bit because maybe they weren't attended to by their family, or, or afforded their parents as they grew up as much as my children were. (5:18)

What is the meaning of the pause in 6. after Lovett says he was "fairly successful"? The construction of "I feel so, that with my education, which was only to the ninth grade, I've been fairly successful," which implicitly contrasts his "success" with his education, suggests that Lovett was starting to say something about his success in monetary terms. Probably he was starting to say that even though he dropped out after the ninth grade, he still made a fairly good living. But then he stopped, perhaps realizing that most people would not say that he has made a good living, would not judge him to have been successful in those terms. (When I interviewed Lovett, he had been out of work for seven years with a crippling occupational disability. His workers' compensation payments, frozen at a rate determined by his wages when he left work, put him just over the poverty line.) So in 6. Lovett pauses, then com-

pletes the thought by saying that he was successful at raising his family. Passage 7. shows the same realization that others (perhaps the friends who can afford the new cars and movies and nightclubs) might judge him to have been a failure by the goals of the success model.[8]

A similar awareness is apparent in the following remarks by Anthony Gallucci:

8. CS: Is there anything about your life that you would do over, if you could?

Gallucci: [del] I had a good time at Ciba-Geigy. I mean, I wouldn't, if I could find something better, naturally, I would do something better, but if I—for a poor working man, I had a good time there, over the years, for the most part. (5:20)

9. [Gallucci mentioned that some workers at Ciba-Geigy can get enough overtime and holiday pay to make a salary of $40,000. He added] Which isn't bad for, you know, nobodies. (5:32)

Gallucci, more than anyone else I interviewed, used terms like the ones highlighted above to put himself and fellow workers down. It may be that he actually is embarrassed to be a working man or it might be something more complicated—that he anticipates that I will look down on him and so talks about himself and his fellow workers from what he imagines is my point of view, which is not one he shares necessarily.[h] In any case, Gallucci shows an awareness that the dominant social judgment is that one should strive to be more than a "poor working man."

Even D'Abrosca anticipated and reacted to the social judgment that he had not made enough money:

10. CS: "What things keep people from getting ahead in the world?"

D'Abrosca: [del] like me, I'm not cut out for business. I couldn't charge a guy ten bucks for something I paid five for. You know. And . . .

---

[8] In this paragraph Strauss tries to interpret Lovett's motivations instead of going back to ask him how he feels about his choices. She writes, "Probably he was starting to say . . . but then he stopped, perhaps realizing that most people would not say that he has made a good living." This passage outlines a fundamental weakness of the cognitive-anthropological approach even in its most sophisticated

form. Like Conklin in the 1950s, Strauss is still dependent on drawing models of thought from what her informants say, but ultimately this record is incomplete. It is axiomatic in anthropology that what people say is often different from what they do, and the moods and thoughts of informants shift. As Stephen Tyler, following Bateson, points out in essay 28, the anthropologist's models are still the anthropologists.

There's a certain makeup there you [?] have to be, to be a businessman. I did the best I could with my education and knowledge and skills. I'm not rich, I'm not poor. I'm happy with what I have. I've got a home and the kids have grown up pretty good. (6:15)

Daniel Collins spoke with greater pride and less defensiveness than some of the others about a key decision that kept him from getting ahead. Twice he was offered promotions into management at Ciba-Geigy, and both times he turned the offers down. The second refusal came when Collins held an elected position in his union's local. He felt he could not betray the men who had elected him by becoming a foreman. At one point Collins recollected a conversation with the plant manager who had offered him that promotion:

11. He said, "You stupe," he said, "You could have been a boss there." I said, "Well, I chose to do what I'm doing." I said, "Maybe in later life," I said, "It might haunt me." [laughs] [del] I look back and I'm not mad at myself. I'm happy that I, you know, didn't take that type of job instead of what I had to contribute to my fellow workers and the union and international. [del] I don't kick myself in the fanny as some people would say for not taking it. (2:12)

Collins had spoken earlier of how much more money he could have made as a foreman than as a worker, especially in severance benefits from the plant closing. So this statement, too, is a reply to the judgment that he did not make the smartest moves he could have to get ahead.

Collins's decision to remain in the union may seem surprising, given his explicit assertion of success values. (Later he said that he agreed with the statement, "I usually admire successful businessmen," adding, "I do, anybody who succeeds, I admire him" [6:32].) In fact, of the four men who endorsed success values in response to my questions about getting ahead, only one made career choices consistent with those values.[9]

The one man whose behavior was strongly directed by the goals of the success model was George Gauvin. Gauvin presented his life history as a success story, stressing how he overcame a physical handicap, learned a trade, and was able to support his family fairly well through a strategic series of job moves when he was young. He said that when he was young, his friends never knew where he was working, because if he learned he could make a few more dollars somewhere else, he would be there. Even after he had settled in at Ciba-Geigy, he persistently applied for the position of lead man in his department in an effort to get ahead.

Jim Lovett, like George Gauvin, learned a trade so that he could make more money than an unskilled worker would. Unlike Gauvin, however, Lovett stayed at a job that did not pay especially well and did not pursue promotions. He considered but decided against moving to another state where his skills would have brought a higher income, because he and his wife felt they should remain near their aging parents.

Gallucci, like Collins, turned down an opportunity to take a foreman's position at Ciba-Geigy. Collins had been interested, however, in advancing in the ranks of his union's international. Gallucci, on the other hand, consistently placed working conditions and personal relationships above economic advancement. He left a better-paying job with the railroads to begin working at the chemical plant because the hours of his first job did not leave him enough time to date the woman he later married. At Ciba-Geigy he turned down at least one opportunity for a promotion into management and then moved to a position in the company that promised to pay less well, but had better hours and less supervision. After moving to this department he avoided overtime assignments and promotion into a higher rank with better pay, but more unpleasant work duties. Since Ciba-Geigy's closing, although Gallucci is only fifty-six, he has retired.

Tony D'Abrosca, the only man who thoroughly rejected the success model (elsewhere he said,

---

[9] Here again Strauss is pointing out that the men she interviewed seem to hold the success schema but that they did not try to follow this model in their career choices. Later in the essay she discusses breadwinner values, which she says had a major impact on the men's behavior.

"Small things make me happy. Not money" [5:5]), in fact worked harder than anyone else in this group to earn a good living. This is not as inconsistent as it sounds, because D'Abrosca also had a larger family to support than any of the other men did. Still, in 1985 D'Abrosca reported an income significantly higher than that of my other blue-collar interviewees. Unlike Gallucci, D'Abrosca worked two jobs much of his life and chose a career path at Ciba-Geigy that gave him many overtime opportunities, which he took. Also unlike Gallucci, who retired when Ciba-Geigy closed, D'Abrosca, at sixty-one, went back to work.

In sum, explicit belief or disbelief in American success values is only weakly correlated with the actual behaviors of these five working men.[i] Why is this?

My explanation turns on the way success values were internalized as cognitive schemas by my interviewees. For most of them success values seem to be held as a relatively isolated, compact package of ideas that is only weakly linked to a larger picture of reality or sense of self. Connections of the latter sort may be necessary to motivate action.[10]

Some evidence for the supposition that my interviewees hold the success model in a bounded way comes from the fact that their beliefs could be stated compactly, in the space of a few sentences. This suggests a correspondingly compact form of storage.[j]

Further evidence for the bounded way in which these beliefs were held comes from two men who stated the same ideas earlier in the course of the interviews. The earlier expressions of the model are given . . . first . . . , the later expressions (from above) are given . . . second. . . . Notice how similar they are.

12. [Jim Lovett is talking about the Amway sales organization, which he and his wife have been part of for many years] There's a, we used to

have a little saying that *if your mind can conceive you can achieve. It's like, you know, whatever your mind can conceive, you can achieve.* But you only get out of *anything* what you're *willing* to put into it. And if you're going to lazy around, then you're going to lazy, that's what you're going to earn, is lazying around. But if you're going to *work*, you're going to earn something. (4:21)

[From 1. above] You, you are the one to blame. It's you. *Because . . . you can achieve anything your mind can conceive.* If you can think, if you have an idea. [del] And if you think about it hard enough. And you want it bad enough. Then you can achieve it. There's nothing on this, in this country or on earth that if you were *willing* enough to *work* at it, that you cannot achieve it. (6:17)

13. [Collins is talking about his plans to go to college for training in a new field] I see on TV where people sixty-five, sixty-eight years old, graduating from college, so that kind of inspires me to say, Yea, I can do it. If they can do it, I can do it . . . You know, it's just a matter of applying yourself. And *wanting to succeed.* (6:3)

[From 3. above] I believe if you put an effort into *anything*, you can get ahead. Just [like] myself, where I have to put the effort into learning, again. You know. *If I want to succeed*, I'll succeed. (6:27–8).

The largely unchanged way Collins and Lovett repeated their views is further evidence for a bounded form of storage.

An illuminating description of bounded storage was once given by Robert Abelson. He proposed the following:

> Let us postulate the existence of self-contained cognitive units called opinion *molecules* . . . [which] give you something to say and think when the topic comes up . . . These sorts of

---

[10] Strauss proposes that the success schemas, of which all the men were aware, were "bounded," that is, they were isolated ideas poorly connected to more powerfully motivating ideas. This follows the insight by Casson (1983:430–431) and others that schemas occur at different levels of abstraction and schemas at one level may not be sensitive to schemas at other levels. Schemas at low levels of abstraction, for example, might be those for perceiving geometric figures and colors, while some at higher levels are for understanding complex activities.

opinions are often quite impervious to other levels of argumentation because of their complete, closed, molecular character. It is as if the opinion-holder were saying, "What else could there possibly be to add?" (1968a:27)

The bounded, packaged quality of this kind of knowledge was earlier described by Mikhail Bakhtin as a feature of "authoritative discourse": "It remains sharply demarcated, compact and inert . . . It enters our verbal consciousness as a compact and indivisible mass; one must either totally affirm it, or totally reject it" (1981:343).[11]

Abelson's "opinion molecules" and Bakhtin's "authoritative discourse" are examples of knowledge that is held in an isolated, encapsulated, bounded way. Both theorists also describe knowledge that is less bounded.[k] Similarly, Rumelhart, quoted above from a 1980 publication as asserting the building blocks of cognition to be "packets of knowledge," is one of the propounders of a new theory of cognition, connectionism, which proposes the building blocks of cognition to be not large packets of knowledge but smaller units modeled after neurons (Rumelhart, McClelland, and the PDP Research Group 1986). Units can be joined in many different configurations, from bounded packages to unbounded networks. I argue below that beliefs represented in the latter

way—especially when they include links to key childhood memories and self-understandings—do embed strongly motivating goals.[12]

Before turning to unbounded beliefs, however, we should consider some beliefs that contrast with my interviewees' success values in a different way. As discussed above, their talk about getting ahead indicated a metaawareness that these values are dominant social values. This contrasts with much of their discourse about their duties as the breadwinner in the family. The latter talk suggests that breadwinner values typically come to consciousness not as values, but as an inescapable reality.

WORKING MEN'S BREADWINNER ASSUMPTIONS

These ideas were expressed in statements like the following:

14. [Collins is discussing the workers' fight against Ciba-Geigy's proposal mandating Sunday work] But when that changed and it was negotiated through a contract that you would work, so you <u>had to</u> change or keep losing that eight hours pay. With three children, I couldn't afford

---

[11] Mikhail Bakhtin (1895–1975) was a Russian literary theorist and philosopher best known for his theory of "dialogics." Writing in the Soviet Union in the 1920s, Bakhtin was immersed in Marxist theory. He proposed that language was a part of the material world, constituted by the subjects who used it. He argued that the fundamental linguistic activity was the utterance, which acquires meaning only within the sociocultural context of a dialogue. Bahktin's theory focused on the concept of the dialogue, and the notion that any form of speech or writing is always a dialogue. Bahktin wrote that a dialogue consisted of three elements: a speaker/writer, a listener/respondent/reader, and the relationship between the two. Language and what language says were the products of the interactions between these elements.

[12] In this paragraph Strauss mentions "a new theory of cognition, connectionism." Connectionism is an important innovation in schema theory because it has forced theorists to examine schemas in a different light. Schemas were originally conceived as fixed cognitive structures

that were recognition devices, but connectionist theory suggests that rather than being recognition devices, schemas are units for processing information. Supporters of connectionist theory argue that if schemas were just recognition devices, then the brain would have to process the world in a serial, stepwise fashion, much like a computer. However, it is clear that this processing method would be time consuming and would not allow for the split-second decisions and actions that are involved in activities such as playing a piano or driving a car. Thus, connectionist theory has forced cognitive anthropologists and psychologists to expand their notions of schemas and how they operate. Donald Norman writes:

> . . . Schemas are flexible configurations, mirroring the regularities of experience, providing automatic completion of missing components, automatically generalizing from the past, but also continually in modification, continually adapting to the current state of affairs. (in D'Andrade 1995a:142)

it. So I <u>had to go with the flow</u> and work the Sundays. (1:7)

15. [D'Abrosca is talking about why he worked at Ciba-Geigy] Lot of people getting cancer there. So—over the years. And . . . it's a risk. We know it. And—but the money's good. This state doesn't have too many good-paying jobs. So. <u>We're sort of trapped.</u> So. I wouldn't want my kid going there. <u>If he had a choice.</u> (1:5)

16. [Lovett is explaining why more workers don't report hazards at the workplace] And if you're making good money, <u>you're not going to</u> make no waves. Even if your buddy next to you is dying with whatever that caused it, that you *know.* You're still <u>not going to</u> make waves. I mean, if a guy's making a living, you now, <u>he's just not going to do that,</u> unless he's ready to make a move. (1:15)

17. [Gauvin is sixty-two and would like to stop working, but Ciba-Geigy has made it difficult for him to retire] <u>they keep me there, they keep me there,</u> and I want to leave, and now they want me to stay. (6:5)

Unlike the individualistic success model expressed in 1.–4., passages 14.–17. assume that the interests of the family come ahead of the interests of any individual, including the father/husband/breadwinner. Bellah et al. (1985) found that some of their white-collar informants carried their individualism to the extreme of not being sure they had any responsibility for their families. The individualistic focus on my interviewees' success model was also clear. Thus, Lovett said, "You can achieve anything your mind can conceive" (1.); Gauvin urged, "You've got to really try to better yourself" (2.); and Collins stated, "If you put an effort into anything, you can get ahead" (3.). By contrast, see 14. in this section, and 7. and 10. in the last, where Collins, Lovett, and D'Abrosca state explicitly their responsibility for their families, especially their children. The same assumption is implicit in 15.–17. above. Gauvin, for example, went on to say that he has to have Blue Cross coverage because his wife is sick.

Furthermore, this is not, as in the success model, a matter of putting upward mobility ahead of all else. The men were not talking about the possibility of upward mobility so much as the pitfall of downward mobility. Each man was considering a situation in which he or someone like him held a job that paid well—and the question was whether or not to keep it. If the alternative is another manufacturing job, this could easily mean, at least for the Ciba-Geigy workers, a much lower income. In 1985 most of the Ciba-Geigy workers I interviewed had incomes between $20,000 and $25,000. In Rhode Island as a whole, the average manufacturing wage in 1985 was only $15,860.[1] So it is not a question of striving for wealth above all, but of avoiding near-poverty.

These working men's breadwinner values have in common with middle-class gender-role expectations the idea that an adult male's income should be his family's primary source of support. My interviewees' norms differ from white-collar versions of these gender-role expectations, however, in three ways. First, it is not necessary for the breadwinner to advance his family's fortunes; it is sufficient if he has a steady paycheck that covers the bills. Furthermore, unlike the middle-class man's version, which is closely linked to the success model, the focus in the working man's model is not on the individual, but on the family. In the working man's model, the interests of the family come ahead of the interests of any one individual in the family.[m] It follows that getting and keeping a job that pays well enough (in wages and benefits) to ensure that his family is secure is more important than the breadwinner's self-fulfillment or personal needs. Also part of this model is the knowledge—for Rhode Islanders with a high school education or less—that there are not many jobs in the state for men of their skills that pay a decent wage.

Thus far I have discussed only the content of this model. In comparing the way my interviewees talked about success in 1.–4. with passages 14.–17. above, I was also struck by the use of constructions in the former passages that indicated a sense of choice between values, as compared with constructions in the latter passages that indicated a sense of constraints imposed by inescapable realities.

Thus, in answering my questions about getting ahead, Lovett said, "if you're <u>willing</u> to work at it . . ." and "Everyone <u>should</u> have a goal"

(1.). Collins said, "If I <u>want</u> to succeed, I'll succeed" (3.). Gallucci said, "Some people don't <u>want</u> to get ahead" (4.). Finally, Gauvin exhorted a generalized "you" to "improve your job" (2.).

By contrast, in talking about the sorts of situations they or others have faced as breadwinners, Collins said, "<u>I had to go with the flow</u>" (14.). D'Abrosca said, "We're sort of <u>trapped.</u>" Lovett asserted flatly that unless a worker is ready to leave the job, "You're <u>not going to</u> make no waves" (16.). And Gauvin said that the company "<u>keeps me</u> there" (17.).

Of course, these men are not literally trapped, without any choice, in jobs that are tiring, dangerous, and interfere with family life. They could report hazards on the job. But to do so would probably mean a drastic loss of income. The metaphors of necessity these men use hide the implicit value premise that downward mobility is bad, highlighting instead the day-to-day realities of their work lives.[13]

This does not mean that these men are unable to see that they have a choice. On another occasion Collins was talking about how his life had become very routine:

18. No, boredom did set in, I believe, after twelve or fourteen years, I was kind of getting edgy and said, Wish I would go somewhere else or go look for something. But I never did, the one factor was that the money was too good to, you know, to say, I'm going to go somewhere else for $3 [an hour] less. So, I guess you get married to the job after a while . . . And I guess, that's kind of why you like to stay in that field because the money, the money is there. You know, you get to say, Well, I like putting a few

dollars in the bank account and doing what I like to do. But if you go down and do some different type of work, especially in this state, the money isn't there. (6:5)

The first part of this statement shows a sense of constraint, similar to that exhibited in 14.–17. above ("you get married to the job after a while"). Then, however, Collins pauses and indicates that he *could* have left the job; it is just that he liked the wage scale there, which gave him the money for "doing what I like to do."

Similarly, a few minutes after Gauvin said that the company "keeps me there" (17.), he spoke in a different vein about making choices rather than being held against his will:

19. And they want to keep me there? I'll stay. Okay. Otherwise, if I go, I lose my severance pay and my Blue Cross. (6:6)

So it is not quite the case that my interviewees cannot see that they have a choice. What is at stake is how they tend to think. Their tendency, as shown by the way they usually talked, is not to see the value of avoiding downward mobility as a value. This is quite different from the way they talked about success, which they consistently treated as a value.[14]

There is also a clear difference between success and breadwinner values in their directive force. Knowing that the success model represents widely shared values led several men to respond verbally—defensively in some cases, with pride in others—to the imagined judgment that they had not been very successful. It may be that awareness of their failure to live up to these values has affected their self-esteem. However, this

---

[13] Here again Strauss is following the method pioneered by the ethnoscientists of the 1950s. Although she is not filling in box diagrams or drawing taxonomies, she is interpreting models of meaning from her informants' comments, "getting inside their heads," if you will. Previous notes have already discussed the weaknesses of the ethnoscientific approach and the difficulties of applying it to any more than the few people who were interviewed.

[14] Here Strauss's informants are talking about the clear material consequences of changing jobs: less money,

poorer lifestyle, etc. Although she recognizes that material factors influence people's choices, Strauss defines these statements in terms of mental models and values. This is an excellent example of how cognitive anthropologists tend to see culture as a mental rather than material phenomena. However, critics also see this as an example of the weakness of the approach. A materialist would argue that people's choices are compelled by the possibility of real, tangible gains and losses rather than their values and mental models. So how can one differentiate between material and mental motivations?

model was less effective than the breadwinner model at motivating action: only one of the blue-collar interviewees who endorsed the model acted on it consistently in his work life. Every man who spoke of breadwinner role expectations as an inescapable reality, on the other hand, assumed primary responsibility for supporting his family, subordinating his own interests to the need to keep a steady paycheck coming. For these four men at least, the values they felt constrained by were usually seen not as values, but as simple reality.[n]

Only Gallucci—the one man for whom I did not find a quote comparable to 14.–17. above—seems to have seen and acted on the belief that downward mobility is a real choice. In one sense Gallucci did subordinate his interests by going to work in as dangerous an environment as a chemical plant. (Although the long-term health effects of these chemicals were not publicized until recently, the risks of fire, toxic leaks, and explosion were obvious all along.) On the other hand, even though Gallucci had a family to support, he moved to a position in the plant that paid less well but allowed him to escape the close contact with chemicals, rotating shifts, and strict supervision he had faced as a chemical operator. This is consistent with his initial decision to work at the chemical plant, where he made less money initially than he had in his previous job but had more time to court the woman he married.

PERSONAL SEMANTIC NETWORKS

My understanding of "semantic networks" relies on the significant insight of symbolic anthropologists that symbols draw their force from their links with concepts from diverse realms of experience (Good 1977).[o] The webs of significance that can stretch from house layouts to kinship structures and cosmology are good examples of outlooks represented in an unbounded way rather than as bounded "packets of knowledge." (Unbounded networks can be composed of smaller, bounded sets of beliefs; although the constituents may be bounded, the whole is not.)

Personal semantic networks are the idiosyncratic webs of meaning carried by each person, linking individually salient verbal symbols[p] to memories of significant life experiences and conscious self-understandings (Quinn, 1992). Everyone I interviewed had a different cognitive network of this sort. Each man's personal semantic network has directed him toward an idiosyncratic pattern of self-defining goals and styles of behavior.[15]

How are cognitive links expressed in discourse? The following aspects of discourse may be indicative of strong associations in cognition:

> *Contiguity.* In the absence of any interruptions that change the topic of the conversation, if idea B follows idea A in a person's discourse, then B and A are linked for them.
>
> *Significant terms.* If a person talks about A and B using the same significant terms, then A and B are linked for them.
>
> *Shared "voice."* If a person talks about A and B using the same "voice" (Bakhtin 1981), i.e., with the same outlook and mode of expression, then A and B are linked for them. (In this paper lexical rather than paralinguistic features are used as the primary indicator of "voice.")[q]

These clues can help us construct part of Tony D'Abrosca's personal semantic network.

Tony D'Abrosca was fifty-nine when I interviewed him, married, with children and grandchildren. He had been working at Ciba-Geigy for twenty-five years, first as a chemical operator, then as a maintenance mechanic. His discourse

---

[15] In this paragraph Strauss comes to the last of the three types of thinking that she claims motivates the men in her study. These personal semantic networks are unbounded, that is, they are connected to a wide variety of experiences. They are personal and linked to the individual's significant life events, self-understanding, and memories. Below, Strauss reconstructs the personal semantic network of one of her subjects, Tony D'Abrosca, the Tony in the title of this essay. He seems different from the other men in the study, not only because he runs marathons but because he is interested in issues of politics and ideology and writes frequent articulate and cynical letters to his local newspaper.

revealed a personal semantic network that links up the following ideas: memories of growing up poor, concerns about social injustice in America, the conviction that his views about social injustice are very different from most people's, the idea that his values and beliefs are different from his siblings' and parents', the sense that his childhood asthma helped make him different, and the realization that his childhood asthma makes him now want to compete in marathons.

D'Abrosca, the oldest in a family of eleven children, grew up poor. His parents, immigrants from Italy, both worked in Rhode Island's textile mills, where D'Abrosca, too, worked for many years before taking a job at Ciba-Geigy. Although D'Abrosca has worked hard and had the highest income of the working men I talked to, he still identifies with the "poor."

20. [CS asks for TD's overall attitudes about business.]

TD: Well, businessmen I think would sell us for a buck. [del] And . . . well all my sisters and brothers are all in business. Most of them are and I shouldn't feel that way, but . . . [del] That's my attitude on businessmen. Businessmen are, to me, are a shady bunch. That, that's my feeling, so. And . . . I can't see soaking a poor guy. Because I was poor. I was one of eleven kids. The oldest. And we were all poor. (1:4)

21. CS: What do you think of the free enterprise system?

TD: Well here I go. Free enterprise. I think . . . too many guys have too much greed in them. And . . . they want all they can get for—at the expense of others. You know? The businessman is out for one thing—money. (3:13–14)

D'Abrosca connects his criticism of businesspeople to a more general critique of American society. He is not hesitant to voice these opinions—whether in discussions at work or in his frequent, caustic letters to the editor of the Providence paper. The following letter, written after Ronald Reagan's reelection, is representative in both content and tone:

22. The results of the recent elections indicate to me that either there are 52 million rich Ameri-

cans or else we have become a nation of insensitive, uncaring dolts with no social or moral conscience. Since this majority is so concerned with only number one and so infatuated with greed, superficiality, and tinsel, I wouldn't be surprised to see the following changes made soon:

1. Move the US Capital to America's Mecca, Disneyworld.
2. Redesign the American flag to a facsimile of the dollar bill and pledge allegiance to same.
3. Change the National Anthem to that inspiring tune, "Hooray for Hollywood" complete with chorus line and soft-shoe dance.

The use of the word "greed" and the references to money in this letter connect these ideas to D'Abrosca's criticism of businesspeople like his siblings (20., 21.). It is evident from 22. that D'Abrosca sees himself as different not only from his siblings, but also from most Americans. This theme, the consciousness of being different, was repeated often in the context of talking about his politics:

23. [CS asked who would agree with the statement, "People on top in society don't really care about the little guy." TD agreed, then CS asked who else would agree with that.]

TD: I don't know, I'm unique I think in a lot of these thoughts. I mean . . . Who would agree with me? [del] The working man is so busy working that he doesn't think about these things. Seems to me. (laughs) I don't know what it is. They've got no opinions—there's a vacuum in their head. The working guys . . . Like I told you, they voted Reagan in. That's—they don't think it out. (6:31–2)

24. [CS mentioned that TD has taken "different stands on certain issues."]

TD: Yea, I'm different.
CS: Yea.
TD: I'm one of a kind maybe. I don't know. (6:6)

As 23. indicates, D'Abrosca has particular scorn for his fellow working men: "There's a vacuum in their head." This theme, how uninformed his work-mates and other working men are, was also repeated often:

25. I'm not a Communist. I'm just a socialist. I'm not Communist. I like—I want the people to have a fair deal, so—fair break. I'm against what these people are doing here for the rich, you know. The rich get richer and the poor get poorer. Like the old saying goes, and it's true. And . . . I'm called Communist. At work. By a few guys. That's their scape word, you know. Copout. Try to talk to these guys and forget it. I may as well [just] talk Red Sox to them. (2:33)

D'Abrosca sees himself as being different from others (e.g., more bookish) since his childhood. He explains this as being the result, in part, of his severe childhood asthma:

26. [CS asked if TD "went with the crowd" more as a child.]

TD: I never did. I had my own way of thinking. If they want to jump off a bridge somewhere, I wouldn't do it. Unless I'd want to do it. When I was a kid I had asthma. Real bad. And when I was about nine I couldn't even walk. (6:10)

27. [CS asked if it was tough being a young boy and not being athletic.]

TD: I could never play. You know, with the other kids. So I took to books. (6:12)

D'Abrosca also connects his childhood asthma to his desire to compete in marathons now:

28. TD: It's different. Test yourself. I had asthma as a boy. I still have it and I wanted to see what I could do. Wanted to prove to myself I could do something because as a young boy I'd dream about Boston [Marathon]. Impossible dream then, you know? 'Cause of the asthma. Now I've done it three times.(2:12)

Finally, D'Abrosca links up his interest in running marathons to his critique of his family's concerns with money, closing the circle to the ideas with which we began:

29. CS: Do you think you pretty much lived up to your parent's expectations for you? What they would've hoped for you?

TD: I don't know. The boy—the other kids did. Went in <u>business.</u> They're all proud of them and bragging about them. Which is normal I guess. I'm not sure if they ever bragged about me or not. They never did in front of me. One time I was so proud, I ran in that 50-mile race, I won the New England championship. I called up, I was all excited you know? "Are you crazy? You're an old man. You should be in a rocking chair." That shot me down. But . . . that's my mother. My father was dead. He died back in '68 I think. And . . . that was the end of that. That was one thing I was really proud about, but . . . no one else was I guess. Well my wife and kids were. It's a sense of values I guess. I guess if I told them I made a million dollars they'd be out of their minds but, it was only a race, so it didn't count. It counted to me. I was happy with it. So. I was happy when my kid ran his first marathon. You know. Small things make me happy. Not <u>money.</u> (5:5)

Fig. 1 summarizes the connections I have discussed above. Some of these connections were indicated by contiguity of topics within a passage (e.g., marathon running and making money in 29. or attitudes toward businessmen and attitudes toward his siblings in 20.). Cognitive links were also indicated by shared significant verbal symbols in different passages (e.g., "money" in 21. and 29. or "greed" in 21. and 22.). Finally, there is a shared "voice"—the same embattled, sarcastic tone—expressed in many of these passages (e.g., 22., 23., and 25.). These aspects of discourse, especially when they occur in combination, strongly suggest cognitive links.

Note how different this whole network of ideas is from the bounded success model each interviewee was able to express compactly in response to my standardized interview questions about getting ahead. There was no time in the interviews when D'Abrosca compactly described this whole set of ideas, indeed, he may never at any one time be aware of the whole set. The extensiveness of the ideas encompassed (and I could have described further linkages with, for example, his ideas about war or about family roles) probably makes it impossible to capture the whole within awareness. What we have here is not a bounded opinion, but

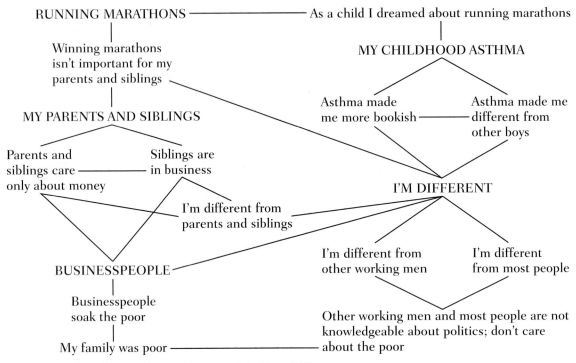

FIGURE 1 Partial personal semantic network for Tony D'Abrosca.

an unbounded network (containing within it, to be sure, many bounded opinions).[16]

Two elements of this unbounded network have acted as strong motives for D'Abrosca. He has published his political views in frequent letters to the editor—so many, that for the last two years he has been invited to attend the *Providence Journal*'s annual dinner for frequent contributors of letters to the editor. He has continued writing letters like the one quoted in 22. despite threatening phone calls, vandalism to his home, and hostile reactions from his workmates.

D'Abrosca has also continued with his marathon running. His extraordinary accomplishments as a runner show just how powerful that goal has been for him. When D'Abrosca was a child he was so severely asthmatic that he could not walk more

than a few yards without collapsing. His asthma improved as he grew older, but because he worked two jobs on rotating shifts most of his adult life, he did not have much time left for physical fitness programs. He did not begin running until he was fifty and his work was mostly on the day shift. Within two years he was running marathons, then ultramarathons, that is, races 50 miles or longer. Recently he won the New England Championship for his age group in a 50-mile race. In 1986 he was one of only six Americans to compete in a 40-mile race through the Swiss Alps.

Idiosyncratic networks are not important just for people who, like D'Abrosca, consider themselves to be unique. Everyone I interviewed had a personal semantic network that contained strong goals.

---

[16] Strauss characterizes Tony D'Abrosca's set of ideas as an unbounded network, by which she means an extensively connected set of ideas that are not held in a compact form.

In Strauss' view, D'Abrosca's unbounded network shifts from basic ideas about oppression and the working class to rather specific thoughts about asthma and marathons.

George Gauvin, like Tony D'Abrosca, had physical problems as a child. Unlike D'Abrosca, however, the memory of his disability is linked for Gauvin to pride in the skills that have enabled him to earn a steady living despite his problems, and to the belief that people should just do their best and not complain. He was quite contemptuous of the "radicals" at Ciba-Geigy who bad-mouthed the company. I mentioned above that Gauvin is the only working man I interviewed for whom (at least when he was young) making more money was a consistent, strong goal. In his case, the bounded, shared American success model seems to have been reinforced by the unbounded personal network of ideas just described.

Jim Lovett has a personal semantic network that links the key terms "responsibility" and "caring" to family concerns and unhappy memories of the absence of his father's companionship as a child. This family-centered model is in turn linked to Lovett's politics: many of his views about business and society can be paraphrased by saying that people should always treat each other as they would inside a family. The motivational force of these ideas can be seen in the energy he has devoted to his family and to caring for others. When Lovett was working he learned first aid and assumed responsibility for treating fellow workers' injuries. Now, although Lovett is out of work with an occupational disability, he has very little free time left in days devoted to providing assistance to his parents, inlaws, and children.

Anthony Gallucci's networks are very different. His views cannot be summed up easily, but one theme he expressed quite explicitly:

30. [Thinking about who influenced him when he was growing up.] I really hated any kind of authority. (5:4)

This general dislike of authorities continued into adulthood, and is linked to specific views about his bosses at work and governmental authority in society. The directive force of these views can be seen in pranks that undermined authorities in the workplace. These ideas also influenced his decision to switch to a position at Ciba-Geigy where he earned less money than he had made as a chemical operator but was freer of supervision.

David Collins, by contrast, believes in the need for strong leadership. His network links this idea to his concerns about working people's welfare, opposition to "selfishness" and "complacency," and remembrance of his mother's admonition to "speak your piece." These ideas have had strong motivational force for him. Until Ciba-Geigy announced its closing, Collins devoted much of his free time to the union local at the plant. He has also put aside concerns about his safety and welfare to "speak his piece" whenever he thought it necessary, whether to fellow workers, bosses, state bureaucrats, military commanders, or neighborhood toughs.

In sum, each man's personal semantic networks contain strongly motivating goals. The directive force of these goals is not just stronger than the force of the goals attached to other sorts of beliefs, however. Each of the three types of belief I have described has had a different sort of directive force for my interviewees. The bounded success schema, which they were aware of as a widely shared value, may have had potent effects as an internalized social judgment affecting each man's self-esteem. Success values were much less potent, however, in determining career choices for most of them. Their breadwinner assumptions were likewise internalized social judgments, failure to satisfy which would also have affected their self-esteem. However, because these values were generally seen not as a matter of choice but rather as an inescapable fact of life, they were much more effective than the success schema in shaping the men's routine behavior. Finally, the goals contained in personal semantic networks, which are linked to emotionally salient individual experiences, have pushed each man to out-of-the-ordinary, self-defining efforts.[17]

---

[17] Casson writes that schemata are hierarchical. Schemata at the higher levels represent general concepts, lower-level schemata represent more specific concepts (1983:437). Strauss' discussion of success values, breadwinner values, and personal semantic networks reflects Casson's insight. All the men in her study knew the general model of success but were motivated more by breadwinner values and their specific life circumstances.

CONCLUSIONS

The main argument of this paper is that cultural models differ in not only the extent but also the kind of directive force they provide. American success values, though endorsed by four of the working men I talked to, motivated the actions of only one of the men who stated them. This is not to say that this ideology had no effect on the rest. The one man who thoroughly rejected success values may have been influenced in a less conscious way by them.[r] The others might be moved by political rhetoric that appeals to this model. Finally, the fact that success values can be seen as shared values meant that my interviewees all judged themselves by that standard. These recognized social values, however, did not determine their practice.

Working men's breadwinner values were apprehended differently by most of my interviewees. In talking about choices faced by breadwinners, they tended to speak not of what people should do, but of what they have no choice but to do. This is the form of belief that Clifford Geertz has called "the native's point of view":

> People use experience-near concepts spontaneously, unselfconsciously . . . they do not, except fleetingly and on occasion, recognize that there are any "concepts" involved at all. That is what experience-near means—that ideas and the realities they inform are naturally and indissolubly bound up together. What else could you call a hippopotamus? Of course the gods are powerful, why else would we fear them? (1984:125)

Shweder (1992) has developed this argument, pointing out that when experience is seen in this way, directive force naturally follows out of commonsensical adherence to the reality principle. Indeed, for the four men who saw the constraints of the breadwinner model as the constraints of

reality, these ideas were a powerful predictor of their actions.

Geertz and Shweder overlook, however, the fact that "the native's point of view" is not at all uniform.[s] Some cultural constructs are indeed used in the "unselfconscious" way Geertz talks about. Others, however, such as the shared success model, are apprehended with a greater meta-awareness of the status of the constructs as cultural values.[t]

Parts of the personal semantic networks I traced were, like the success model and unlike the breadwinner model, seen as values. The unbounded cognitive storage of these networks, however, means that they are difficult to apprehend in their entirety. These networks embed self-defining goals consciously chosen and acted on by my interviewees (cf. Quinn, 1992) as well as less conscious personal styles of action.

Each of these three kinds of beliefs was expressed differently in discourse. The bounded, cognitively accessible success model was expressed fairly explicitly, as compact generalizations. This made my interviewees' statements of the ideology very similar to analysts' statements of the ideology. When repeated by two men, major elements of this model were preserved largely intact. The breadwinner model, on the other hand, was present more often in an implicit form. Its premises were just assumed in what Bourdieu has called a "discourse of familiarity, [which] leaves unsaid all that goes without saying" (1977:18).[18] It is true that most of the statements of the success model quoted above were elicited by questions that asked for compact generalizations, while no questions of the sort that would have elicited a compact, explicit statement of the breadwinner model were asked. Yet, two informants also volunteered explicit statements of the success model (12. and 13.) before being asked the questions about getting ahead. Furthermore,

---

[18] Pierre Bourdieu (1930–2002) was a French sociologist and philosopher. He held the chair of sociology at the Collège de France, one of that nation's premier research institutions. Bourdieu was interested in exploring the roots of class distinctions and power structures. The quote Strauss uses here is from Bourdieu's 1972 book, *Outline of a Theory of Practice,* in which he discusses the notion of reflexivity, a fundamental concept in the postmodern school of thought developing at that time (see essays 38 and 39). He was a critic of capitalist society and helped found the French antiglobalization movement.

as a member of this culture, I would have felt foolish asking something like, "What are the obligations of an adult man?" The mere fact that it would not have occurred to me to ask such a question, whereas it seemed reasonable to my interviewees and me to ask, "What things keep people from getting ahead in the world?" is itself some indication that success values and breadwinner role expectations are different types of culturally shaped beliefs.[19]

Some elements in personal semantic networks were expressed in a similarly explicit, compact form in my interviewees' discourse. Explicit self-descriptions (e.g., "I'm unique I think, in a lot of these thoughts" [23.] or "I really hated any kind of authority" [30.]) are examples of this. The cognitive connections between these elements, however, can be seen only by tracing the order of topics in a speaker's discourse and the links between ideas expressed with the same significant terms or in the same "voice."

Some further points can be made about these three forms of belief. First, they were probably acquired by my interviewees in different ways. While they may have observed many people who tried to get ahead and even some who succeeded at it, their explicit verbal formulation of shared success values suggests acquisition from an explicit verbal source. Such sources are readily available in U.S. society in the mass media, advice books, fictional accounts, and popular discussion. Lovett mentioned another source: the slogans he learned at Amway sales meetings (12.). As evidence for the supposition that the success model is learned largely from verbal formulations, notice that when D'Andrade summarized his informants' ideas about success, he used several key terms ("drive," "works hard," and

"goals") that also turned up in one or more of my interviewees' statements. The importance of these terms as explicit verbal symbols can also be seen in the way my interviewees emphasized them through repetition within a statement, verbal stress, or use as a one-word sentence (e.g., "Goals. Everyone should have a goal" [1.]).

These working men's breadwinner assumptions, on the other hand, were likely to have been acquired more through observation than explicit statements. Some aspects of this model are common enough in popular discussion (e.g., that men should be the main income earners in a family), but others (e.g., the need to sacrifice one's interests to keep a steady paycheck coming) were probably learned simply by observing other working men staying at boring or dangerous jobs.[u]

Personal semantic networks contain elements learned both in the explicit verbal manner of success values and the implicit, observational manner of breadwinner assumptions. Particularly important here, however, are the ideas and experiences that each man came to take as self-defining ones—often because they contrasted with the values of others with whom he interacted.

Each of these models represents different forms of knowledge and awareness—different *ways of believing*. These ways of believing are not reducible to differences in content, but involve different forms of cognitive representation and conscious apprehension. Thus, for most of my interviewees, success values are stored as the packets of knowledge postulated in traditional schema theory, while their wide-ranging personal semantic networks are stored in a less packaged way. The success model comes to their consciousness as a set of values, while the breadwinner model (though it contains values as well) often comes to

---

[19] Strauss proposes that because success values and breadwinner role expectations are "different types of culturally shaped beliefs," this influenced the kind of questions she asked, or didn't think to ask. We suggest that another possible element that may have directed the questions she chose to ask her informants was gender. That she did not ask questions to elicit a compact statement about breadwinner values may be related to being a woman and her own thoughts on these values rather than indicating the "cognitively diffuse" nature of the

breadwinner model. Gender may explain why she felt more comfortable asking what keeps people from getting ahead in the world, rather than what they thought an adult man's obligations were. After all, what it means to be a man was an important question in the United States in the mid-1980s when Strauss conducted this work. It also seems that in this paragraph Strauss comes perilously close to saying that her success and breadwinner model are simply a function of the questions she asked or failed to ask.

their consciousness in a different way, as knowledge of reality.

It was also interesting that these three models are shared by increasingly narrow segments of American society—from the widely shared success model, to the more class- and gender-specific working man's breadwinner model, to personal semantic networks, which contain many culturally given elements, but include unique life events and, in any case, represent idiosyncratic combinations of shared elements. This is not surprising. The success model is acquired from ideological sources that are widely available in our society; the working man's breadwinner model is learned from observation of other working men; and personal semantic networks are shaped by the particular combination of experiences and ideas to which each individual is exposed, which are never exactly the same for any two people.

A few warnings are in order about the extent to which my findings could be generalized beyond my interviewees and the particular sets of ideas I described.[20]

First, the separate effects of these different kinds of beliefs were probably easier to see with my blue-collar informants than they would have been with white-collar informants. In a white-collar working environment behaviors probably conform to the success model more than they do on the factory floor. Thus, observation learning would reinforce explicit ideological learning, making their separate effects harder to distinguish. In general, it is doubtless the case that differences between distinct kinds of cultural models will be easier to observe in the discourse and behaviors of non-dominant than of dominant social groups. (Furthermore, this paper has downplayed interactions, which did exist, between these different levels of belief. One example of this is the way the success model was reinforced for George Gauvin by the particular configuration of experiences and linked explanatory concepts in his personal semantic network.)

It is also possible that the distinct effects of these different models were enhanced by two peculiarities of industrialized western cultures. In the liberal western tradition there is a distinction between values, adherence to which is a matter of choice, and "hard" reality. Other cultures would not make the same distinction. Perhaps peculiar to western cultures is our metaphysical and moral construct of the self. I claimed that elements of personal semantic networks are strongly motivating. I do not know if this is because they are stored in an extensive, unbounded cognitive network (which would be the case in any culture) or because these ideas are attached to a distinct, valued self-construct more limited to the West. (Probably both explanations are partly correct.)

Finally, although the focus of my argument has been on ways of believing, it has a bearing on what we assume culture to be. If we conceive of culture monistically—everything is symbols or discourses, which differ only in meaning and position in the ordering of experience—then it is difficult to talk about different *kinds* of cultural values and motivational force. As D'Andrade has noted (n.d.), we will not make progress in anthropological theory without a more differentiated model of culture.[21]

---

[20] In the paragraphs above Strauss proposes that the three forms of belief expressed by her informants were probably acquired in different ways. She suggests that the shared success model was acquired from an "explicit verbal source" such as the mass media. Breadwinner assumptions were acquired by observation of other working men. Personal semantic networks were learned both verbally and observationally. She emphasizes that each of the three models are different forms of knowledge and awareness. In the final three paragraphs of her essay Strauss discusses the problems with generalizing her findings beyond the five men she interviewed. First, she believes that a white-collar working environment would reflect stronger adherence to the success model than she found among her working-class sample. She also believes that a "Western" distinction between values and reality enhances the effect of the different belief systems and that this effect would not be seen in other cultures. Her final point concerns the weakness of the mental/symbolic definition of culture, which is predominant in cognitive and symbolic anthropology, but she does not expand on this point.

[21] Contemporary cognitive anthropologists call cognitive models "schemas," but are schemas all that different from the paradigms and taxonomies of the new ethnographers? In the cognitive-anthropology literature schemas

ACKNOWLEDGMENTS

An earlier version of this paper was presented at the 85th Annual Meeting of the American Anthropological Association, Philadelphia, PA, December 1986, in an invited session, "The Directive Force of Cultural Models." I am grateful to Roy D'Andrade and Naomi Quinn for organizing this session. The two discussants in this session, Robert Weller and Edwin Hutchins, had comments that were helpful in rewriting my material. This paper has also benefited from comments by Ellen Basu, Bradley Levinson, Naomi Quinn, Robert Strauss, and Kathryn Woolard. My biggest debt is to the five men quoted here.

NOTES

[a]D'Andrade does not take credit for the insight that schema theory can subsume motivation theory, citing Schank and Abelson (1977), Mandler (1984), and Gallistel (1985), among others, as sources for this idea.

[b]Tony D'Abrosca asked that I use his real name. All other interviewee names here are pseudonyms.

[c]Most of these questions came from Kornhauser (1965).

[d]Every interviewee but one chose a pseudonym consistent with his ethnicity.

[e]My other transcript conventions are the following:
[?] unintelligible
[word?] uncertain transcription
. . . long pause
[del] deletion
[ ] paraphrase
" " my reading of a standardized interview question
(X:Y) utterance citation from my transcripts, where X is the interview number and Y the page number
(X.) utterance citation from previous use in this paper

Punctuation reflects the speaker's intonation rather than rules of grammar, and transcripts were regularized for stammers, stutters, and verbal pauses.

[f]Elsewhere, D'Abrosca stated that he and his siblings had all "turned out fairly good. Moneywise or otherwise." He added, "I hope my kids do well" (5:3, 4). Conversely, the other four men, who endorsed the success model in response to my standardized questions, expressed doubts about the moral worth of riches and discussed inequality of opportunity in other discourse contexts. So their beliefs are more complicated than it would appear here (Strauss 1988, 1990).

[g]I did not usually transcribe verbal pauses. This one seemed especially significant, however.

[h]There were several examples of this speech in another's "voice" in Gallucci's discourse.

[i]This is not to say that success values are rarely linked to action for working men in general. Beyond the obvious difficulty of generalizing from a sample of five people, there is the less obvious factor that some of these men fell into the working-class part of my interview group precisely because they had not been motivated by the success model. Two of the white-collar workers I interviewed started out life in circumstances much like these five, but then sought education and promotions that put them into management positions.

[j]Gauvin's belief structure is the only exception here. His references to starting as a helper, then becoming a journeyman (2.) show that the general statements quoted are intimately linked to a broader set of ideas he has about his own career.

[k]See Bakhtin on "internally persuasive discourse" (1981:345–6) and Abelson's cognitive consistency theories (1968b).

---

are discussed as if they were concrete entities rather than conceptual abstractions. However, no one has ever seen a schema. They are not biological entities, and they cannot be found by dissecting the brain or measured with medical equipment. Instead, the evidence for them, which is largely linguistic rather than biological, is primarily elicited through interviews. Because of this, many of the problems that plagued the ethnoscientists in the 1960s still apply to cognitive anthropology.

The ethnoscientists derived their models of native thought through a concrete methodology that could be copied by anyone. But what are the criteria by which schemas are determined? Strauss identifies success and breadwinner schemas by examining her interview data. However, other analysts might see different schemas at work. How is one to judge the accuracy of one anthropologist's schema identifications over another's? Further, are the

results of Strauss' study generalizable to a wider population, or do they apply only to the five men she interviewed? If people's behavior is ultimately driven by *personal semantic networks* created by individual experience, as Strauss demonstrates in this study, then the incommensurate nature of groups that was implied by Boasian cultural relativity reaches its ultimate form in this type of work. Does cognitive anthropology become the study of individual cultural models derived from an individual's personal experience? If that is the case, how is cognitive anthropology to be distinguished from psychology?

On the other hand, unlike many forms of ethnography, Strauss provides us with the actual commentary of real people rather than generalizations about anonymous natives. This places her work in a tradition of life history ethnography that goes back to the work of anthropologists such as Paul Radin.

[1]Based on $305 average weekly earnings in Rhode Island manufacturing industries (1987 Providence Journal-Bulletin *Rhode Island Almanac*).

[m]This model is based primarily on my research. However, it fits with other accounts of American working-class culture, e.g., Halle (1984), Komarovsky (1987), and Miller and Riessman (1961).

[n]However, in some contexts (see 7. and 10.) some of the men talked as if they were being judged by the breadwinner model. This was especially true when, as in the above two cases, the breadwinner model overlaps with the success model.

[o]Good's "semantic network analysis" (Good 1977) captures at the cultural level what my "personal semantic networks" try to capture at the individual level.

[p]In finding these symbols I used the methods outlined by Agar (1979).

[q]For a more detailed discussion of all three criteria, see Strauss (1988).

[r]In D'Abrosca's case the example provided by his hardworking immigrant parents may have been more significant than the success model as an explicit ideology.

[s]Geertz's own view is not uniform either. Earlier works of his suggest a much more sophisticated understanding of different forms of belief.

[t]These different forms of awareness are usually referred to as the difference between "overt" and "covert" or "explicit" and "implicit" culture (LeVine 1984). (See also Bourdieu's [1977] doxa/dogma distinction.) These terms do not capture all the degrees of opacity and transparency that exist, however (see Strauss 1988).

[u]The process here is much as Bourdieu (1977) describes for the formation of the habitus.

REFERENCES

Abelson, Robert P. 1968a. Computers, Polls, and Public Opinion—Some Puzzles and Paradoxes. *Transaction* 5(9):20–7.

———.1968b. Psychological Implication. In *Theories of Cognitive Consistency: A Sourcebook,* R. P. Abelson et al., eds. Skokie, IL: Rand-McNally.

Agar, Michael. 1979. Themes Revisited: Some Problems in Cognitive Anthropology. *Discourse Processes* 2:11–31.

Bakhtin, Mikhail M. 1981. Discourse in the Novel. In *The Dialogic Imagination: Four Essays by M. M. Bakhtin,* Michael Holquist, ed., Caryl Emerson and Michael Holquist, trans. Austin: University of Texas Press. Pp. 259–422.

Bellah, Robert N., Richard Madsen, William M. Sullivan, Ann Swidler, and Steven M. Tipton. 1985. *Habits of the Heart: Individualism and Commitment in American Life.* Berkeley and Los Angeles: University of California Press.

Bourdieu, Pierre. 1977. *Outline of a Theory of Practice,* Richard Nice, trans. Cambridge: Cambridge University Press.

Casson, Ronald W. 1983. Schemata in Cognitive Anthropology. *Annual Reviews in Anthropology* 12:429–62.

D'Andrade, Roy G. 1984. Cultural Meaning Systems. In *Culture Theory: Essays on Mind, Self, and Emotion,* Richard A. Shweder and Robert A. LeVine, eds. Cambridge: Cambridge University Press. Pp. 88–119.

———. 1990. Some Propositions about the Relations between Culture and Human Cognition. In *Cultural Psychology: Essays on Comparative Human Development,* James W. Stigler, Richard A. Shweder, and Gilbert Herdt, eds. Cambridge: Cambridge University Press. Pp. 65–129.

D'Andrade, Roy G., and Claudia Strauss 1992. *Human Motives and Cultural Models.* Cambridge: Cambridge University Press.

———. n.d. Anthropological Theory: Where Did It Go? (How Can We Get It Back?). Unpublished manuscript.

Gallistel, Charles R. 1985. Motivation, Intention, and Emotion: Goal-Directed Behavior from a Cognitive-Neuroethological Perspective. In *Goal-Directed Behavior: The Concept of Action in Psychology,* M. Frese and J. Sabini, eds. Hillsdale, NJ: Lawrence Erlbaum.

Geertz, Clifford. 1984. "From the Native's Point of View": On the Nature of Anthropological Understanding. In *Culture Theory: Essays on Mind, Self, and Emotion,* Richard A. Shweder and Robert A. LeVine, eds. Cambridge: Cambridge University Press. Pp. 123–36.

Gerber, Eleanor R. 1985. Rage and Obligation: Samoan Emotion in Conflict. In *Person, Self, and Experience: Exploring Pacific Ethnopsychologies,* Geoffrey M. White and John Kirkpatrick, eds. Berkeley: University of California Press. Pp. 121–67.

Good, Byron J. 1977. The Heart of What's the Matter. *Culture, Medicine and Psychiatry* 1:25–58.

Halle, David. 1984. *America's Working Man: Work, Home, and Politics among Blue-Collar Property Owners.* Chicago: University of Chicago Press.

Holland, Dorothy, and Naorni Quinn, eds. 1987. *Cultural Models in Language and Thought.* Cambridge: Cambridge University Press.

Komarovsky, Mirra. 1987. *Blue-Collar Marriage,* 2nd ed. New Haven: Yale University Press.

Kornhauser, Arthur. 1965. *Mental Health of the Industrial Worker: A Detroit Study.* New York: John Wiley.

LeVine, Roben A. 1984. Properties of Culture: An Ethnographic View. In *Culture Theory: Essays on Mind,*

Self, and Emotion, Richard A. Shweder and Robert A. LeVine, eds. Cambridge: Cambridge University Press. Pp. 67–87.

Mandler, George. 1984. *Mind and Body: Psychology of Emotion and Stress.* New York: W. W. Norton.

Miller, S. M., and Frank Riessman. 1961. The Working Class Subculture: A New View. *Social Problems* 9:86–97.

Providence Journal-Bulletin, comp. 1987. *Rhode Island Almanac,* 101st edn. Providence Journal-Bulletin.

Quinn, Naomi. 1992. The Motivational Force of Self-Understanding. In *Human Motives and Cultural Models,* R. D'Andrade and C. Strauss, eds. Cambridge: Cambridge University Press.

Quinn, Naomi, and Dorothy Holland. 1987. Culture and Cognition. In *Cultural Models in Language and Thought,* Dorothy Holland and Naomi Quinn, eds. Cambridge: Cambridge University Press. Pp. 3–40.

Rumelhart, David E. 1980. Schemata: The Building Blocks of Cognition. In *Theoretical Issues in Reading Comprehension: Perspectives from Cognitive Psychology, Linguistics, Artificial Intelligence, and Education,* Rand

J. Spiro, Bertram C. Bruce, and William F. Brewer, eds. Hillsdale, NJ: Lawrence Erlbaum. Pp. 33–58.

Rumelhart, David E., Jarnes L. McClelland, and the PDP Research Group. 1986. *Parallel Distributed Processing: Explorations in the Microstructure of Cognition,* Vol. II: *Psychological and Biological Models.* Cambridge, MA: MIT Press.

Schank, Roger C., and Robert P. Abelson. 1977. *Scripts, Plans, Goals, and Understanding: An Enquiry into Human Knowledge Structures.* Hillsdale, NJ: Lawrence Erlbaum.

Shweder, Richard. 1992. Ghost Busters in Anthropology. In *Human Motives and Cultural Models,* R. D'Andrade and C. Strauss, eds. Cambridge: Cambridge University Press.

Strauss, Claudia. 1988. Culture, Discourse, and Cognition: Forms of Belief in Some Rhode Island Working Men's Talk about Success. Ph.D. dissertation, Harvard University.

———. 1990. Who Gets Ahead? Cognitive Responses to Heteroglossia in American Political Culture. *American Ethnologist* 17(2):312–28.

Sociobiology, Evolutionary Psychology, and Behavioral Ecology

Unlike most other twentieth-century anthropological perspectives, sociobiology, evolutionary psychology, and behavioral ecology seek to explain human behavior in terms of Darwinian evolutionary theory. (In the remainder of this introductory essay, we will use the term *sociobiology* to stand for all three of these fields, except as needed to differentiate viewpoints.) Just as Charles Darwin proposed the theory of natural selection to account for the biological evolution of physical characteristics, sociobiologists propose that differential reproductive success shapes the evolution of social behavior of all organisms, including humans. The basis of Darwinian evolution is that individuals with those variations best adapted to their environment reproduce more than those lacking such variations. As a result, each subsequent generation will include a higher percentage of such individuals. Sociobiologists argue that because humans are biological organisms, they are subject to the same evolutionary laws as other life-forms. Given that there is a genetic component to behavior, they say, those behavior patterns that improve an organism's adaptation to its environment will be selected for and reproduced in future generations.

Cultural analogies to evolution are not new in anthropology. As outlined in the first section of this text, many nineteenth-century thinkers believed that the goal of anthropology was to describe and illustrate how culture evolved from primitive to civilized and simple to complex. New work in sociobiology differs from this in fundamental ways. Most important, nineteenth-century thinkers viewed evolution as a metaphor

or analogy. Spencer, for example, focused on what he termed the *organic analogy*. For these scholars, the history of society was like the evolution of biological organisms. Theirs was an argument by comparison, a literary argument. Further, to the extent that they focused at all on the mechanisms of evolution, they understood these in Lamarckian terms; that is, they believed that cultural innovations were developed in one generation and passed on to the next.

Nineteenth-century evolutionists believed that societies evolved in the direction of increased size, complexity, and interdependence. They did so through competition that led to increases in technology and power that could be passed culturally to the next generation. Their vision of evolution had little to do with Darwin's notion of natural selection through reproductive success. In fact, they feared the reproductive success of some segments of society (the poor, the infirm, various minority groups), viewing it as a force that could undermine the evolutionary progress of society. Modern-day sociobiologists, to the contrary, are very specifically concerned with Darwinian fitness. They understand individual cultural traits to be evolving under the pressure of reproductive success: Natural selection favors those behaviors that lead to greater numbers of offspring. This belief points to another important distinction between contemporary sociobiologists and nineteenth-century evolutionists. The work of nineteenth-century scholars was strongly teleological. They believed that the process of evolution created increasingly perfect societies, whereas sociobiologists see no such teleology. The fact that a behavior leads to reproductive success does not, in itself, make that behavior morally superior or inferior to other behaviors. Further, most sociobiologists argue that the evolution of human behavioral characteristics must have happened when humans lived in foraging societies. Social organization above the band level has only existed for a few thousand years, and this is probably not enough time for biological evolution to occur. Consequently, many social problems we experience happen because we live in the twenty-first century with behaviors adapted to ancient foraging lifestyles. Whether this speculation is true or not remains an open question.

Sociobiology grew out of the work of evolutionary biologists, geneticists, ethologists, and anthropologists studying primate behavior. The animal behavior specialists Konrad Lorenz, Karl Von Frisch (1906–1982), and Nikolas Tinbergen (1907–1988) were particularly influential. These three published widely in the 1950s and 1960s and shared a Nobel Prize in 1973. Although some anthropologists and biologists, including Lionel Tiger and Robin Fox, had been publishing on sociobiological themes since the 1960s, the publications that brought sociobiology to the critical attention of anthropologists and the general public were two books published in 1975 and 1976—Harvard biologist E. O. Wilson's (b. 1929) *Sociobiology: The New Synthesis* and *The Selfish Gene* by Richard Dawkins (b. 1941). These authors adopted an approach that saw social behavior as controlled, in principle, by particular genes. In Wilson and Dawkin's view, evolutionary selection for behavior occurred at this level because reproductive success amounted to increasing the frequency of certain genes in future generations. In effect, they proposed that humans were little more than the vehicles genes use to reproduce themselves.

The notion that human cultural behavior could be reduced to genetics violated the fundamental tenets of Boasian anthropology and produced enormous hostility among cultural anthropologists. Of the many criticisms most focused on three points: First, sociobiological studies looked at behavior in terms of reproductive success and population genetics but ignored the effects of culture and learning, which most anthropologists claim are extremely powerful influences on human society. Second, virtually all sociobiological research was conducted on animals and insects rather than humans. Wilson's own work, for example, was concerned with ants. Anthropologists doubted that research findings based on insect behavior were applicable to human behavior. Finally, sociobiology was critically dependant on the notion that specific human behaviors could be linked to specific biological genes. Selection for the behaviors was, in fact, selection for the genes that produced them. These genes and thus the behavior they produced would be inherited by future generations. However, no conclusive link between a specific gene and a specific behavior has ever been demonstrated in "normal" human beings (clearly people with genetic abnormalities such as Down syndrome do show such gene-specific behaviors). In fact, most anthropologists argued that although genetically based predispositions to behavior may exist, the very diversity of human behavior makes a direct connection between a specific behavior and a particular gene very unlikely (Sahlins 1976, Montagu 1980).

Even though many of the flaws of the early work have been corrected, sociobiology remains one of the most contentious areas within anthropology—so contentious that each time this book is reviewed for a new edition, several reviewers encourage us to remove this section. You are reading this over their objections. Part of the hostility is a continuing reaction to the extreme claims sociobiologists made in the 1970s and early 1980s, when they frequently asserted that sociobiology would render all forms of social science obsolete. Today, it would be hard to find a sociobiologist who would support this radical notion. Beyond this, sociobiology is inimical to some of the most dearly held principles of American cultural anthropology. The insistence of sociobiologists on grounding at least some behavior in universal human genetic predispositions runs contrary to cultural anthropologists' emphasis on the primacy of culture itself as the determinant of human social life.

Because of the high level of hostility, the word *sociobiology* has been almost entirely dropped from anthropological discourse, and much of the study of the relationship between biology and human behavior has moved into other academic disciplines, notably psychology. Sociobiology also remains a strong field of study in biology.

Several distinct approaches can be distinguished in current-day sociobiology. Among them are evolutionary psychology, human behavioral ecology, and the study of human universals. Evolutionary psychology is concerned primarily with the analysis of the mind as a device formed by natural selection. Evolutionary psychologists hypothesize that the mind is composed of a large number of functionally specialized neural circuits. These circuits were designed by natural selection to solve adaptive problems faced by our foraging ancestors. Evolutionary psychologists attempt to describe brain circuits, show how they work, what information they are designed to process, and what they were designed to accomplish in a foraging context (Cosmides and Tooby 1997).

A second focus, human behavioral ecology, looks to integrate earlier forms of cultural ecology with more recent understandings of biological ecology. It emphasizes populations rather than cultures (Kormondy and Brown 1998). Rather than focusing on the mind, human behavioral ecologists focus on testing the hypothesis that culturally patterned traits actually enhance fitness.

A third current approach involves the search for human universals (Brown 1991, Fessler 1995, Shapiro 2004, Wierzbica 2005). Followers of this approach concentrate on discovering the characteristics found in all human societies. They presume that ultimately such traits must be primarily based in human evolutionary biology and adaptation but do not focus their studies there.

The articles chosen for this section show some of the evolution of the sociobiological approach. The first selection, the introduction from E. O. Wilson's classic *Sociobiology: The New Synthesis* (1975), is an example of early sociobiology. Wilson's approach is extremely reductionist. His essay here is a polemical statement in support of the idea that all human cultural behavior ultimately will come to be understood as a reflection of underlying genetic forces. The second essay, "The Hunting Handicap" by Rebecca Bliege Bird, Eric Alden Smith, and Douglas W. Bird, takes an approach based in behavioral ecology. It tries to explain how evolution might select for a behavior that is wasteful, in this case the hunting of fish and turtles by means that are more difficult and inefficient than necessary.

Although sociobiology in all of its forms continues to be rejected by most cultural anthropologists, it has increased in popularity, both among anthropologists and the general public, in the last several years. At least two factors help to explain this increasing acceptance. First, recent medical successes and high-profile research such as the Human Genome Project have generally focused attention on the role of genetic inheritance in human life. As evidence emerges that things as diverse as cancers and religious sentiments may have genetic and biochemical bases, people are more willing to examine the connection between biology and behavior (see Sloane 2006). Second, many anthropologists have reacted vehemently against postmodernism and the notion that no objective description of culture (or anything else) is possible. They turn to sociobiology as the branch of anthropology that most resembles the natural sciences. A good example of this is James Lett, whose book *Science, Reason, and Anthropology* is largely an attack on postmodernism. Lett takes postmodern anthropologists to task for their polemic approach to debate and goes on to define anthropology as "the scientific study of human evolution" (1997:121).

30. *The Morality of the Gene*

EDWARD O. WILSON (b. 1929)

CAMUS SAID THAT the only serious philosophical question is suicide. That is wrong even in the strict sense intended. The biologist, who is concerned with questions of physiology and evolutionary history, realizes that self-knowledge is constrained and shaped by the emotional control centers in the hypothalamus and limbic system of the brain. These centers flood our consciousness with all the emotions—hate, love, guilt, fear, and others—that are consulted by ethical philosophers who wish to intuit the standards of good and evil. What, we are then compelled to ask, made the hypothalamus and limbic system? They evolved by natural selection. That simple biological statement must be pursued to explain ethics and ethical philosophers, if not epistemology and epistemologists, at all depths. Self-existence, or the suicide that terminates it, is not the central question of philosophy. The hypothalamic-limbic complex automatically denies such logical reduction by countering it with feelings of guilt and altruism. In this one way the philosopher's own emotional control centers are wiser than his solipsist consciousness, "knowing" that in evolutionary time the individual organism counts for almost nothing. In a Darwinist sense the organism does not live for itself. Its primary function is not even to reproduce other organisms; it reproduces genes, and it serves as their temporary carrier. Each organism generated by sexual reproduction is a unique, accidental subset of all the genes constituting the species. Natural selection is the process whereby certain genes gain representation in the following generations superior to that of other genes located at the same chromosome positions. When new sex cells are manufactured in each generation, the winning genes are pulled apart and reassembled to manufacture new organisms that, on the average, contain a higher proportion of the same genes. But the individual organism is only their vehicle, part of an elaborate device to preserve and spread them with the least possible biochemical perturbation. Samuel Butler's famous aphorism, that the chicken is only an egg's way of making another egg, has been modernized: the organism is only DNA's way of making more DNA. More to the point, the hypothalamus and limbic system are engineered to perpetuate DNA.[1]

In the process of natural selection, then, any device that can insert a higher proportion of certain genes into subsequent generations will come to characterize the species. One class of such devices promotes prolonged individual survival. Another promotes superior mating performance and care of the resulting offspring. As more complex social behavior by the organism is added to the genes' techniques for replicating themselves, altruism becomes increasingly prevalent and eventually appears in exaggerated forms. This brings us to the central theoretical problem of sociobiology: how can altruism, which by definition reduces personal fitness, possibly evolve by natural selection? The answer

From *Sociobiology: The New Synthesis* (1975)

---

[1] This electrifying paragraph, which opens the first chapter of Wilson's book, makes immediately clear why it was so controversial. Wilson begins by quoting Albert Camus (1913–1960), the French existential philosopher and novelist, and then immediately reduces the philosopher's statement to a biological issue. In *Sociobiology*, Wilson proposes a theory in which all human social activity is reduced to evolutionary genetics. Wilson's attempt to tackle what Camus believed was the ultimate problem of human existence is a powerful rhetorical device. It is intended to grab the reader's attention by radically reducing philosophy to a subfield of evolutionary biology. However, the book does not fulfill the promise of this first chapter. Most of it is devoted to animal and insect behavior. Wilson does not return to human sociobiology again until the final chapter, 27. There he explores issues such as culture, religion, ethics, and esthetics, but these together account for five pages of a book of almost 700 pages.

is kinship: if the genes causing the altruism are shared by two organisms because of common descent, and if the altruistic act by one organism increases the joint contribution of these genes to the next generation, the propensity to altruism will spread through the gene pool. This occurs even though the altruist makes less of a solitary contribution to the gene pool as the price of its altruistic act.[2]

To his own question, "Does the Absurd dictate death?" Camus replied that the struggle toward the heights is itself enough to fill a man's heart. This arid judgment is probably correct, but it makes little sense except when closely examined in the light of evolutionary theory. The hypothalamic-limbic complex of a highly social species, such as man, "knows," or more precisely it has been programmed to perform as if it knows, that its underlying genes will be proliferated maximally only if it orchestrates behavioral responses that bring into play an efficient mixture of personal survival, reproduction, and altruism. Consequently, the centers of the complex tax the conscious mind with ambivalences whenever the organisms encounter stressful situations. Love joins hate; aggression, fear; expansiveness, withdrawal; and so on; in blends designed not to promote the happiness and survival of the individual, but to favor the maximum of the controlling genes.

The ambivalences stem from counteracting pressures of natural selection. Their genetic consequences will be explored formally later in this book. For the moment suffice it to note what is good for the individual can be destructive to the family; what preserves the family can be harsh on both the individual and the tribe to which its family belongs; what promotes the tribe can weaken the family and destroy the individual;

and so on upward through the permutations of levels of organization. Counteracting selection on these different units will result in certain genes being multiplied and fixed, others lost, and combinations of still others held in static proportions. According to the present theory, some of the genes will produce emotional states that reflect the balance of counteracting selection forces at the different levels.

I have raised a problem in ethical philosophy in order to characterize the essence of sociobiology. Sociobiology is defined as the systematic study of the biological basis of all social behavior. For the present it focuses on animal societies, their population structure, castes, and communication, together with all of the physiology underlying the social adaptations. But the discipline is also concerned with the social behavior of early man and the adaptive features of organization in the more primitive contemporary human societies. Sociology *sensu stricto*,[3] the study of human societies at all levels of complexity, still stands apart from sociobiology because of its largely structuralist and nongenetic approach. It attempts to explain human behavior primarily by empirical description of the outermost phenotypes and by unaided intuition, without reference to evolutionary explanations in the true genetic sense. It is most successful, in the way descriptive taxonomy and ecology have been most successful, when it provides a detailed description of particular phenomena and demonstrates first-order correlations with features of the environment. Taxonomy and ecology, however, have been reshaped entirely during the past forty years by integration into neo-Darwinist evolutionary theory—the "Modern Synthesis," as it is often called—in which each phenomenon is weighed for its adaptive significance and then

---

[2] Altruism was a problem for sociobiology. If behavior is dictated by natural selection, how can altruistic acts (which may cost the organism food, reproductive potential, living space, and even its life) exist? The answer is called *kin selection theory*, which Wilson explains in this paragraph. The question of altruism came into focus for Wilson through his study of ant colonies. Only queen ants reproduce, and the vast majority of individuals are workers who give up their reproductive potential to support the queen and the colony. Why should these workers forgo reproduction to facilitate that of the queen? Wilson discovered that a worker ant actually passes on a greater percentage of its genetic material to future generations by supporting the queen, with whom it shares genetic material, rather than by reproducing itself.

[3] *Sensu stricto:* Latin for in a strict sense.

related to the basic principles of population genetics. It may not be too much to say that sociology and the other social sciences, as well as the humanities, are the last branches of biology waiting to be included in the Modern Synthesis. One of the functions of sociobiology, then, is to reformulate the foundations of the social sciences in a way that draws these subjects into the Modern Synthesis. Whether the social sciences can be truly biologized in this fashion remains to be seen.[4]

This book makes an attempt to codify sociobiology into a branch of evolutionary biology and particularly of modern population biology. I believe that the subject has an adequate richness of detail and aggregate of self-sufficient concepts to be ranked as coordinate with such disciplines as molecular biology and developmental biology. In the past its development has been slowed by too close an identification with ethology and behavioral physiology. In the view presented here, the new sociobiology should be compounded of roughly equal parts of invertebrate zoology, vertebrate zoology, and population biology. Figure 1 shows the schema with which I closed *The Insect Societies,* suggesting how the amalgam can be achieved.[5] Biologists have always been intrigued by comparisons between societies of invertebrates, especially insect societies, and those of vertebrates. They have dreamed of identifying the common properties of such disparate units in a way that would provide insight into all aspects of social evolution, including that of man. The goal can be expressed in modern terms as follows: when the same parameters and quantitative theory are used to analyze both termite colonies and troops of rhesus macaques, we will have a unified science of sociobiology. This may seem an impossibly difficult task. But as my own studies have advanced, I have been increasingly impressed with the functional similarities between invertebrate and vertebrate societies and less so with the structural differences that seem, at first glance, to constitute such an immense gulf between them. Consider for a moment termites and monkeys. Both are formed into cooperative groups that occupy territories. The group members communicate hunger, alarm, hostility, caste status or rank, and reproductive status among themselves by means of something on the order of 10 to 100 nonsyntactical signals.[6] Individuals are intensely aware of the distinction between groupmates and nonmembers. Kinship plays an important role in group structure and probably served as a chief generative force of sociality in the first place. In both kinds of society there is a well-marked division of labor, although in the insect society there is a much stronger reproductive component. The details of organization have been evolved by an evolutionary optimization process of unknown precision, during which some measure of added fitness was given to individuals with cooperative tendencies—at least toward relatives. The fruits of cooperativeness depend upon the particular conditions of the environment and are available to only a minority of animal species during the course of their evolution.[7]

---

[4] To emphasize his biological perspective, Wilson characterizes sociology as describing "phenotypes"—in other words, behavior is no more than the visible expression of genetic information. Just as Freud tried to unite the social sciences under his theory of psychoanalysis, Wilson states that the social sciences and humanities can be incorporated into the field of biology.

[5] *The Insect Societies,* published in 1971, was Wilson's exhaustive study of the behavior of ants. It was from his study of insects that he derived many of the insights he brought to his work in sociobiological theory.

[6] *Nonsyntactical signals:* nonlinguistic signals, or communications that are not language. Primate call systems, for example, are aural signals but not language.

[7] Wilson's focus on similarities between different species is typical of sociobiological studies. One could, no doubt, find more differences than similarities between termites and monkeys if one chose to look. It is probably no exaggeration to say that most anthropologists would find this list of similarities trivial and the differences one could think of profound. In fact, most cultural anthropologists probably believe that the sorts of behavior that sociobiologists study are relatively trivial and that any genetic universals underlying human behavior are limited and far less interesting than human cultural diversity.

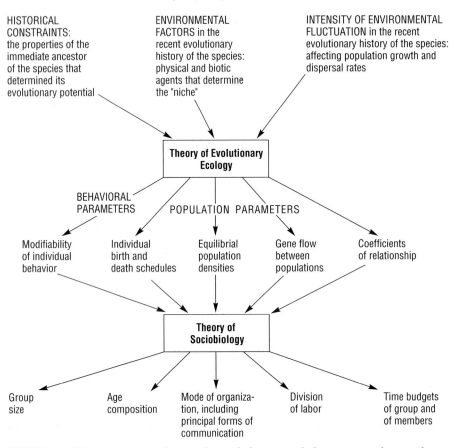

Evolutionary and Ecological Parameters

HISTORICAL CONSTRAINTS: the properties of the immediate ancestor of the species that determined its evolutionary potential

ENVIRONMENTAL FACTORS in the recent evolutionary history of the species: physical and biotic agents that determine the "niche"

INTENSITY OF ENVIRONMENTAL FLUCTUATION in the recent evolutionary history of the species: affecting population growth and dispersal rates

Theory of Evolutionary Ecology

BEHAVIORAL PARAMETERS

POPULATION PARAMETERS

Modifiability of individual behavior

Individual birth and death schedules

Equilibrial population densities

Gene flow between populations

Coefficients of relationship

Theory of Sociobiology

Group size

Age composition

Mode of organization, including principal forms of communication

Division of labor

Time budgets of group and of members

FIGURE 1 The connections that can be made between phylogenetic studies, ecology, and sociobiology. Reprinted by permission of the publisher from "The Morality of the Gene" in *Sociobiology: The New Synthesis* by Edward O. Wilson, pp. 3–6, Cambridge, Mass.: The Belknap Press of Harvard University Press. Copyright © 1975, 2000 by the President and Fellows of Harvard College.

This comparison may seem facile, but it is out of such deliberate oversimplification that the beginnings of a general theory are made. The formulation of a theory of sociobiology constitutes, in my opinion, one of the great manageable problems of biology for the next twenty or thirty years. The prolegomenon of Figure 1 guesses part of its future outline and some of the directions in which it is most likely to lead animal behavior research. Its central precept is that the evolution of social behavior can be fully comprehended only through an understanding, first, of demogra-

phy, which yields the vital information concerning population growth and age structure, and, second, of the genetic structure of the populations, which tells us what we need to know about effective population size in the genetic sense, the coefficients of relationship within the societies, and the amounts of gene flow between them. The principal goal of a general theory of sociobiology should be an ability to predict features of social organization from a knowledge of these population parameters combined with information on the behavioral constraints imposed by the genetic constitution of the species. It will be a chief task of evolutionary ecology, in turn, to derive the population parameters from a knowledge of the evolutionary history of the species and of the environment in which the most recent segment of that history unfolded. The most important feature of the prolegomenon, then, is the sequential relation between evolutionary studies, ecology, population biology, and sociobiology.[8]

In stressing the tightness of this sequence, however, I do not wish to underrate the filial relationship that sociobiology has had in the past with the remainder of behavioral biology. Although behavioral biology is traditionally spoken of as if it were a unified subject, it is now emerging as two distinct disciplines centered on neurophysiology and on sociobiology, respectively. The conventional wisdom also speaks of ethology, which is the naturalistic study of whole patterns of animal behavior, and its companion enterprise, comparative psychology, as the central, unifying fields of behavioral biology. They are not; both are destined to be cannibalized by neurophysiology and sensory physiology from one end and sociobiology and behavioral ecology from the other (see Figure 2).[9]

I hope not too many scholars in ethology and psychology will be offended by this vision of the future of behavioral biology. It seems to be indicated both by the extrapolation of current events and by consideration of the logical relationship behavioral biology holds with the remainder of science. The future, it seems clear, cannot be with the ad hoc terminology, crude models, and curve fitting that characterize most of contemporary ethology and comparative psychology. Whole patterns of animal behavior will inevitably be explained within the framework, first, of integrative neurophysiology, which classifies neurons and reconstructs their circuitry, and, second, of sensory physiology, which seeks to characterize the cellular transducers at the molecular level. Endocrinology will continue to play a peripheral role, since it is concerned with the cruder tuning devices of nervous activity. To pass from this level and reach the next really distinct discipline, we must travel all the way up to the society and the population. Not only are the phenomena best described by families of models different from those of cellular and molecular biology, but the explanations become largely evolutionary. There should be nothing surprising in this distinction. It is only a reflection of the larger division that separates the two greater domains of evolutionary biology and functional biology. As Lewontin[10] (1972a) has truly said: "Natural selection of the character states themselves is the essence of Darwinism. All else is molecular biology."[11]

---

[8] Since sociobiology focuses on natural selection and reproductive success as the mechanisms for determining behavior, such factors as population growth, gene flow, and demography are important to it. Behaviors must be analyzed in terms of these factors. Notice that Wilson sees the key issues as entirely within the traditional hard sciences. Anthropology, sociology, economics—not to mention the humanities—are not on the list. This is because sociobiologists, at the time this essay was written, perceived the subject materials of these disciplines as epiphenomenal: They were secondary manifestations of biologically based phenomena and therefore of no interest.

[9] Wilson was profoundly reductionist. He was in search of a few unifying principles that would explain all behavior. According to Wilson, even the fields that gave rise to sociobiology, such as psychology, were due to be subsumed by it or neurophysiology.

[10] Richard Lewontin (b. 1929) is a geneticist and evolutionary biologist.

[11] Wilson's worldview is evident in this passage. He invokes parsimony as one of his guiding principles—explanations must be neat, concise, and leave no loose ends. The vision behind this hearkens back to the science of the nineteenth century and the belief that the world is a rational and orderly place. This view is rejected by most current anthropologists and by many in the hard sciences as well, who see complexity at all levels.

Thirty years have passed since the publication of this essay, and the progress that Wilson predicted for "the next twenty or thirty years" has not taken place. Sociobiology may be a useful theoretical perspective for understanding some aspects of culture, but even its most fervent supporters probably no longer believe that it has the potential to replace the social sciences. By the mid-1980s, Wilson himself adopted a more moderate and sophisticated line on the distinction between evolutionary biology and culture. See, for example, his book *Biophilia* (1984).

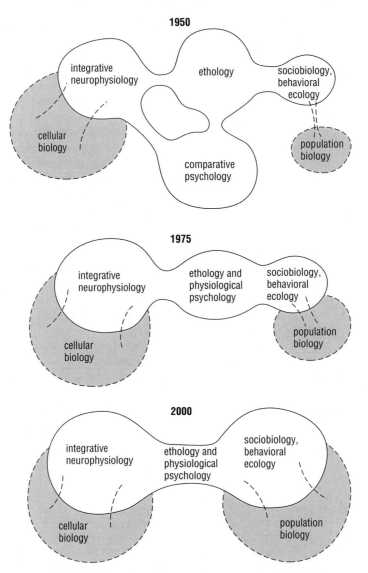

FIGURE 2   A subjective conception of the relative number of ideas in various disciplines in and adjacent to behavioral biology to the present time and as it might be in the future. Reprinted by permission of the publisher from "The Morality of the Gene" in *Sociobiology: The New Synthesis* by Edward O. Wilson, pp. 3–6, Cambridge, Mass.: The Belknap Press of Harvard University Press. Copyright © 1975, 2000 by the President and Fellows of Harvard College.

ACKNOWLEDGEMENT

Reprinted by permission of the publisher from "The Morality of the Gene" in *Sociobiology: The New Synthesis* by Edward O. Wilson, pp. 3–6, Cambridge, Mass.: The Belknap Press of Harvard University Press. Copyright © 1975, 2000 by the President and Fellows of Harvard College.

REFERENCE

Lewontin, R. C. 1972a. Testing the theory of natural selection. (Review of R. Creed, ed., *Ecological genetics and Evolution*. Blackwell Scientific Publications, Oxford, 1971.) *Nature*, London, 236 (5343): 181–182.

31. *The Hunting Handicap: Costly Signaling in Human Foraging Strategies*

REBECCA BLIEGE BIRD, ERIC ALDEN SMITH, AND DOUGLAS W. BIRD

INTRODUCTION

Human foragers often make decisions that lead them to bypass alternative activities with higher energy gain rates, provide widely shared goods without repayment, or incur an increased risk of injury. These decisions have often been explained by the benefits of a sexual division of labor in parental investment (e.g., Hurtado et al. 1992), the optimization of macronutrients (e.g., Hill 1988), or reduction of consumption variance (e.g., Smith 1988). In particular, the practice common to many hunter-gatherer societies of widespread or group-wide sharing of large prey captured by any subset of the group is conventionally explained as a form of risk reduction where all ultimately benefit from a reciprocal sharing of unpredictable harvests (reviews in Hawkes 1992; Winterhalder 1997).[1]

While some types of food seem to be distributed in ways that conform to delayed reciprocity

(2001)

(Gurven et al. 2000), recent studies (Hawkes 1993; Bliege Bird and Bird 1997) have challenged its ability to explain the wide variety of sharing patterns to which it has been claimed to apply. The cases that seem least congruent with strategies of delayed reciprocity are those associated with public distributions of food in which the acquirer does not control access to the harvest or its distribution, and may not even reserve a portion for him or herself (Wiessner 1996). Under these conditions, acquirers seem unlikely to be able to direct shares to reciprocators and withhold them from free riders, as is required to solve the collective action problem (e.g., prisoner's dilemma) associated with enforcing delayed reciprocity. Similar challenges to the primacy of reciprocal altruism (RA) on both theoretical and empirical fronts are also found in recent literature on nonhuman behavior (reviews in Dugatkin 1997; Pusey and Packer 1997). Many theorists have suggested the paradigm may require extensive

---

[1] In ecological and biological approaches to anthropology it is a fundamental tenet that cultural practices are best explained by underlying ecological reasons and that these are ultimately related to natural selection: Individuals who follow these practices are more likely to be reproductively successful than those who do not. Anthropologists are particularly interested in foraging peoples, reasoning that for most of human existence, people have survived by foraging. Gardening and agriculture appear relatively recently in the archaeological record. Thus, if people are adapted by natural selection to any form of food acquisition, it must be foraging. Given this perspective, the food choices of foraging peoples pose interesting problems. Ecological and biological anthropologists believe that such food choices must reflect the operation of underlying principles rather than historical

accident or taste preference. One powerful way of explaining such choices was optimal foraging theory (OFT). This was the idea that human foragers, like other animals, will choose foods that offer the maximal energy return for the minimal energy investment (Smith 1983; Hill, Kaplan, Hawkes, and Hurtado 1987; Nonaces and Dill 1993). Among some groups, OFT seems to model foraging behavior reasonably well, yet there are a great many deviations from it. This essay (as well as the ones mentioned in this paragraph) is an attempt to use ideas rooted in biology to explain those instances in which OFT fails.

revisions (Clements and Stephens 1995; Connor 1996; Dugatkin 1997; Roberts 1998).[2]

An alternative explanation for such "economically irrational" decisions is that under some circumstances they could serve as an honest signal of one or more dimensions of fitness-related quality (Neiman 1998; Boone 1998; Sosis 2000; Smith and Bliege Bird 2000). Costly signaling theory (CST) provides a powerful framework for explaining two paradoxical observations: the persistence of wasteful phenotypes when natural selection is assumed to create greater efficiency, and the evolution of honest communication despite the pervasive conflicts of interest underlying evolutionary processes (Zahavi 1975, 1977; Grafen 1990; Johnstone 1995, 1997; Getty 1998). CST proposes that communication between individuals with conflicting interests can be evolutionarily stable if the signal honestly advertises an underlying quality of interest to observers. Advertising is kept honest and thus mutually beneficial to both signaler and observer as long as the cost or benefit of advertisement is so closely tied to the quality of the signaler that faking it costs more than the signal is worth. If this holds, the correlation between the quality of a signaler and the quality or intensity of the signal will be maintained by differences in marginal cost or benefit, allowing recipients to reliably discriminate among competing signalers. When these conditions are met, honest signals and reliable communication will be evolutionarily stable, even when signaler and recipient are antagonists or competitors.[3]

The hypothesis that hunting might serve as a form of status competition among men interested in "showing off" to a public audience is not new (Hawkes 1990, 1991). Here, we recast the "show-off" model using a payoff structure compatible with CST (Smith and Bliege Bird 2000). We propose that individuals of high phenotypic quality might reap higher benefits or pay lower costs to acquire skill based resources or to unconditionally share their harvest. These benefits (material, political, and reproductive) flow from observers who find it in their interest to behave in ways that improve the relative advantage, status, or social dominance of signalers, ultimately enhancing signaler fitness. Analyzed according to CST, this is not delayed reciprocity involving an exchange of substance (to the observer) for social status (to the signaler), but rather a form of by-product mutualism. The payoff to the observer comes from the usefulness of the information inferred from the signal: he or she should be able to evaluate the signaler's suitability as a competitor, mate, or ally by attending to the signal rather than through more costly or unreliable means of assessing the signaler's abilities or hidden qualities. The high cost or low benefit of faking the signal guarantees that signalers will not engage in false advertising, and that observers will pay attention. Costly signaling can thus spread (by

---

[2] In other words, it's well known that in foraging groups hunters generally share their kill with all members of their group. If all hunters were equally good, then such sharing makes economic sense: Each should ultimately receive as much as he gives. However, all hunters are not equally good, hence those who provide large kills regularly sacrifice without receiving adequate compensation. The prisoner's dilemma is a classic problem in game theory. Here is a brief description: Imagine that two people are held in solitary confinement. They cannot see or talk to each other. The guards decide to play a little game with them: "If you choose to cooperate with the other prisoner, each of you will receive three candy bars. If one of you chooses to compete and the other to cooperate, the one who competes will receive five candy bars and the one who cooperates, none. If both of you choose to compete, each gets one candy bar. What will your choice be?" There is no real solution to the problem because maximizing one's return depends on guessing what one's fellow prisoner will do. A great deal has been written about the application of the prisoner's dilemma to evolution and economics. A good reference is Robert Axelrod's *The Evolution of Cooperation* (1984).

[3] So, what the authors propose to demonstrate is that, in some cases, hunters choose to pursue prey neither for their taste nor their nutritional value but rather because so doing demonstrates their ability to undertake difficult tasks successfully, and this tells others, especially potential mates, that they are particularly desirable. Note the authors' use of the term *phenotype* here and throughout this essay. An individual's behavior could conceivably be related to his or her personal psychology, history, culture, or any of a myriad of factors. A phenotype is the outward observable expression of a genetically based trait. By using *phenotype* to describe behaviors, the authors are proposing that these behaviors are ultimately rooted in some as yet undiscovered genotype. Thus, at root, they are biologically rather than culturally based.

natural selection or imitation) because of its mutual benefits to both signalers and observers.[4]

Here, we test the costly signaling hypothesis among the Meriam (a Melanesian people of Torres Strait, Australia). We evaluate two candidate foraging activities (spearfishing on the reef at low tide, and hunting turtle for public feasts), to determine whether these hunt types meet key criteria for costly signaling in being (1) differentially costly or beneficial in ways that are (2) honestly linked to signaler quality, and (3) designed to effectively broadcast the signal to the intended audience. We propose that accomplished spearfishers signal such qualities as hand-eye coordination, stealth, and patience, while successful turtle hunters signal strength, risk-taking, and (in the case of hunt leaders) a variety of cognitive and leadership abilities to potential allies, mates, and competitors.

METHODS[5]

Mer (a.k.a. Murray Island) is a small (1.6 × 2.2 km) island on the northern end of the Great Barrier Reef, 140 km from New Guinea in Australia's Torres Strait. The island's current population is 430 individuals of Torres Strait Islander descent, scattered in approximately 85 households. The Torres Strait as a whole is administered by the State of Queensland and the Commonwealth of Australia.

Prior to about 1975, when Australian welfare payments were first made available to all indigenous Australians, the Meriam were nearly full-time subsistence horticulturalists and marine foragers planting tropical yams, bananas, sugar cane, and introduced new world crops such as manioc, sweet potatoes, and corn, and harvesting marine fish, shellfish, and sea turtles. Today, fishing and shellfish collecting remain a critical component of Meriam subsistence economy: mean per capita after-sharing consumption rates average 630 kcal of meat and 40 g of protein. More than 80% of these calories are supplied by turtle when in season. For additional ethnographic description and previous work among the Meriam, see Haddon (1906), Beckett (1988), Sharp (1993), Bliege Bird et al. (1995), Bird and Bliege Bird (1997, 2000), Bliege Bird and Bird (1997), and Smith and Bliege Bird (2000).[6]

Observations of Meriam foraging choices, time allocation, and food-sharing strategies reported here were conducted over several periods totaling 27 months between January 1993 and July 1999. Much of this field research was specifically

---

[4] Several key concepts are found in this passage. Note first that the authors describe the behavior they observe as by-product mutualism. Mutualism in this sense refers to co-operation. There is mutualism when two individuals gain a benefit through cooperation. By-product mutualism is a special case. In by-product mutualism, one individual (A) benefits from the actions of another individual (B). But B would have done the action and gained the benefits regardless of A (Brown 1983). In the example presented here benefits are conferred on both the hunter who is signaling and the audience intended to receive the signal, but the hunter would signal even if there were no audience. In this essay, selection is assumed to be primarily at the level of the individual rather than the group. The emphasis throughout is on benefits received by individuals. Second, note that the authors suggest that traits are passed along through either natural selection, implying again a genetic basis for behavior, or through imitation or Lamarckian evolution, thus implying that some of what they observe is culturally rather than biologically based.

[5] In this section, the authors describe the site of their research and some of the basic techniques of hunting that

they observed. Note that the description owes much more to ethology, the study of animal behavior, than it does to anthropology. The focus is on the physical characteristics of the setting and on the actions that the people being studied actually performed. In this description we learn very little about Meriam culture or society. The methodology is entirely consistent with the theoretical position of the anthropologists. One of the fundamentals of behavioral ecology is to observe and analyze human behavior to the greatest extent possible as you would observe and analyze the behavior of any other animal. Pay close attention to the descriptions of the turtle hunts in the second half of this section; they are critical for understanding the rest of the essay.

[6] Of historical interest, note that the first reference on the Meriam that the authors cite is from Haddon. Mer was one of the sites investigated in the famous Torres Straits expeditions of the late nineteenth century (see the Introduction to Functionalism, pages 159–163, for more information on the Torres Straits expedition).

designed to test hypotheses related to the origin and maintenance of the human sexual division of labor, and to determine the nature of the tradeoffs affecting men's and women's foraging decisions.

Time allocation to intertidal activities (spearfishing, shellfish collecting) was measured through focal individual follows occurring during randomly selected days during the spring ebbing tide. Locations along the foreshore were observed from the midpoint of the ebbing tide, before the reef was fully exposed, for at least 2 h or until the last forager had left the reef. During the intertidal sampling period, we recorded the moment-by-moment behavior of at least one individual to arrive during the sample, and if the individual remained after the interval ended, we remained to completely record the episode. We observed the reef flat habitat for a total of 118.5 h over 41 spring ebb tide days, recording 338.1 forager hours of subsistence activity in 210 partial and full foraging follows of 94 men, women, and children entering the reef flat. We then analyzed the percentage of total foraging time each forager devoted to all potential intertidal activities during the follow.

We analyzed the reef as a bounded habitat within which there are "hunt types" sensu Smith (1991). All hunt types are simultaneously available options within the ecological habitat "reef flat at low tide": reef flat collecting, rocky shore harvesting, and spearfishing (Bird and Bliege Bird 1997, 2000). Reef flat collecting involves mobile search of shellfish, with in situ processing to increase the utility of the load (Bird and Bliege Bird 1997). Spearfishing involves search and travel across the reef looking for encounters with mobile prey (small fish and squid 250 g+) to the exclusion of all other prey; when prey are detected, the hunter stalks the prey and launches his spear from a distance. Both hunt types occur in the same patch during the same period of time, while the reef is exposed at low tide. The hunt types vary in how spatially exclusive they are within the habitat: spearfishing and shellfish collecting are the only two major hunt types in which the forager engaged in exclusive search for prey frequently encounters and ignores prey in the other hunt type. These are not the complete complement of hunt types simultaneously available, but they are the three in which adults spend more than 90% of their foraging

time while on the reef at low tide. Other minor hunt types are handline fishing from the reef edge and in deeper lagoons, netting sardines, hunting octopus, and diving from the reef edge to take underwater prey by hand. Gross foraging return rates for each hunt type (not including energetic expenditure assumed to be roughly equal for all reef hunt types) were calculated from the moment an individual stepped onto the exposed reef and began to engage in targeted search for particular prey types. The macronutrient content of finfish and shellfish was obtained through published sources and through individual analysis of samples collected on Mer (Hirth 1971; Sidwell 1981; Brand Miller et al. 1993).

For a detailed description of methods used to collect turtle hunting and sharing data see Bliege Bird and Bird (1997); the results presented here on turtle hunting and sharing are a reanalysis of those data. The acquisition of over 120 turtles was noted through daily sampling of the entire village during the nesting season (October–April) in 1994–1995, and ad lib sampling of the village during the 1994 and 1998 hunting seasons (May–September). Nearly every successful hunt or collection of turtle was recorded, with information obtained on acquirer(s), place acquired, method of acquisition, and subsequent distribution through informant interview.

There are two primary types of marine turtle acquisition on Mer: turtle hunting (*nam deraimer*) and turtle collection (*nam terpei*). Turtle hunting occurs throughout the year, but is the only way to acquire turtles between May and September (*Kob Kerker*), when green turtles (*Chelonia mydas*) feed and mate on shallow reefs about 16–20 km from Mer. Field observations indicate that turtles captured on hunts range from 100 to 150 kg live weight, with an average edible yield of 50.1 kg (Bliege Bird and Bird 1997). Hunters head out to the hunting grounds in open boats powered with outboard motors, often in cooperation with at least one other hunting boat. Among Meriam turtle hunters, there are three distinct roles: hunt leader (*ariemer-le*), jumper (*arpeir-le*), and driver, or tiller-man (*korizer-le*). Hunt leaders organize and direct the hunt; there is always only one leader per hunt, regardless of crew size. Hunt leaders bear the cost of organizing the hunt and ensuring boats and fuel to spare. They direct the crew to particular locations, decide whether prey encountered is worth pursuing, orchestrate the chase, and direct jumpers when to jump from the boat to secure the turtle. Hunt leaders are invested with public recognition and receive full credit for the kill regardless of whether or not they directly participate in capture.

The hunt proceeds as follows. While one man drives, the rest of the crew stands toward the bow scanning the reef for signs of turtle. The hunt leader directs the driver and coordinates with crews in other boats if present. When a turtle is spotted, the hunt leader makes a decision whether to pursue it based on its size (large turtles have more meat) and sex (female turtles have more fat). The boat(s) then give chase, keeping the turtle away from the reef edge. When the turtle tires, the hunt leader usually directs his jumper to launch himself from the bow of the boat with a rope attached to his upper arm. The jumper then attempts to secure the turtle by locking his arms around the flippers and, if successful, the crew then pulls him and the turtle on board.

Turtle hunting occurs primarily in the context of public feasting events: hunters choose to hunt in response to a request from feast organizers to provide turtles for consumption at a previously announced feast. The biggest and most elaborate Meriam feasts occur in the context of coming-of-age celebrations and funeral ceremonies (see Smith and Bliege Bird 2000 for further details). In contrast to turtle hunting, turtles are also collected ($n = 88$ events), primarily in the context of household provisioning, but also for feasts, by men of all ages, women, and children. This occurs only when

they can be harvested on beaches during the nesting season (*Nam Kerker:* October–April), although during these months some turtles are also hunted on nearby reefs. In the nesting season, turtles are collected at night or during the early morning hours as they crawl onto sandy beaches above the mean high water mark to lay their eggs. Turtles are acquired by flipping them onto their backs, trussing their flippers with ropes, and hauling them by boat back to the acquirer's household where they are kept alive until butchered. When butchered for "private" consumption, turtle shares are distributed in large, uncooked portions (10–11 kg) of meat, fat, organs, and eggs among nearby households, with the size of portions kept by the butchering household determined primarily by the number of demanders (hereafter termed "household consumption," sensu Bliege Bird and Bird (1997)). While hunting a turtle is a costly activity in which the benefit is acquired through the social value of the hunt, collecting a turtle is an activity which has little signaling potential and in which the benefit is primarily nutritional. However, there may be some signal value of displays of generosity among neighbors as turtle portions are shared according to the Meriam ethic of *debe tonar* ("the good way," which involves sharing without expectation of return).

All statistical analyses were performed using Statview (SAS). Large-sample means tests were performed after testing for normality and equality of variance using either one- or two-tailed *t*-tests depending upon the prediction tested, while tests on small samples and those violating the assumptions of parametric tests used two-tailed Mann-Whitney *U*-tests. All means are reported with associated SEs.[7]

---

[7] The authors of this essay take a scientific approach to anthropology. Some hallmarks of modern science are quantification, measurement, and hypothesis testing. The authors use statistical techniques, particularly *t*-tests and *U*-tests, to accomplish these tasks. *U*-tests and *t*-tests are basic statistical tests of the reliability of differences between two groups. Imagine that you can measure some attribute of two different groups, assigning an average to each. Of course, it is very unlikely that the averages of the groups will be identical, but what you would like to know is if the average is just the result of chance, or if it means there is a real difference between the groups. *U*-tests and *t*-tests help you figure this out by allowing you to calculate a probability that the difference between the averages is due to chance. If that probability is less than 5%, the results are deemed "significant." That is, it is considered unlikely that the differences are due to chance. The difference between a *t*-test and a *U*-test has to do with your expectations about the distribution of results. When the distribution of results for each group are "normal," that is, look like a bell curve, *t*-tests are used. If the results are a different shape, a *U*-test is used.

RESULTS

Spearfishing as Costly Signal

There are significant sex differences in time allocation to hunt types in the intertidal: on average, men spend 63% of their reef foraging time spearing, while for women this value is only 9% (t = 6.00, df = 66, p = 0.001), and women spend 76% and men 31% of their time shellfish collecting (t = 4.50, df = 66, p = 0.001).[8] The majority of men never collect shellfish at all, nor do they combine spearing with shellfish collecting in a single visit to the reef at low tide: 78.6% of 21 men in the time allocation sample spent *all* of their foraging time spearfishing.

Is spearfishing a signal? The decision men make to spear fish nearly exclusively (rather than collect shellfish) violates simple energy-maximizing prey choice models, because (1) on average, continuing to search for fish to spear (292 ± 135 kcal/h, n = 26) offers lower overall energy returns than shell fishing (1,492 ± 173 kcal/h, n = 47) while in the reef flat at low tide (t = 4.672, df = 71, p = 0.0001) and (2) on-encounter returns for the most skilled spearfisher (2,505 ± 2778 kcal/h) are equivalent to the on-encounter returns for the lowest-ranked shellfish prey still in the optimal diet breadth (2,214 ± 414 kcal/h) (see Table 1).[9] [Table 1 shows the mean calories obtained per encounter, the nutritional content, and the time allotted by men and women for reef collecting, reef spearing, and rocky shore harvesting. It shows

that reef spearing has poor returns compared with reef collecting and rocky shore harvesting.]

One explanation for this pattern might be that spearfishers are not maximizing calories, but other macronutrients. But this appears not to be the case: protein return rates from shellfish collecting at 284 ± 31 g/h are higher than from spearfishing at 6.6 ± 2.9 g/b (t = 6.78, df = 68, p = .0001). Fat return rates are also higher for shellfish collecting at 22 ± 3 g/h than for spearfishing at 1.6 ± 0.7 g/h (t = 4.808, df = 68, p = 0.0001).

Another possibility is that spearfishers prefer other benefits supplied by reef fish: they may be more valuable as trade goods than shellfish prey. But this seems unlikely: shellfish collecting produces larger harvests (1,962 ± 247 g, n = 44) than spearing (356 ± 100 g, n = 26) (t = 24.857, df = 68, p = 0.0001). Shellfish prey are also more likely to be shared: following a harvest of shellfish, on average 22% of the take is shared to another household, while only 7.5% of a spearing harvest is shared.

Finally, could choosing to spear fish instead of collecting shellfish as women do provide greater consumption benefits in the long-term? The short-term costs are inescapable: while women maximize their patch returns and the size of their meat harvests by stopping to take shellfish when encountered on the reef, male spearfishers take a large cut in protein, fat, and energy income by ignoring shellfish and continuing to search for fish to spear. There could be

---

[8] Results from t- and U-tests are generally given in the form (t or U =, df =, p =). In this expression, t or U refers to the t or U score (in general, the greater the number here, the more certain you are of a real difference between the two groups) and df stands for degrees of freedom, a complex concept related to the number of results that are free to vary and the number of variables in the experiment. In t- and U-tests generally, the larger your sample size, the larger the degrees of freedom and the smaller the t or U score needed to show differences between groups. Finally, p refers to the probability that the two groups are the same. In this case in the essay, p = 0.001, so there is only one chance in a thousand that the hunting and shellfish collecting behaviors of men and women are really the same.

[9] As this paragraph shows, spearfishing violates optimal foraging theory. If it has low caloric returns for the calories invested, then an economic fisher would not choose to do it. This makes the fact that most men spearfish an optimal test case for explanations other than OFT. In the next paragraphs, the authors discuss several possible explanations other than costly signaling, dismissing or minimizing the possibilities of each. These include the idea that spearfishers are maximizing fat and protein rather than calories, the idea that there are other economic benefits to spearfishing that are not gained through fish collecting, and that the practice of men spearfishing while women collect maximizes the long-term yield of the collection area.

long-term benefits of such specialization if by dividing labor and pooling harvests, male spearfishers and female shellfish collectors maintain long-term shellfishing productivity on the reef. This could happen if the cooperative pooling unit (the household) defended a reef territory, excluding other pooling units from foraging so that the future benefits of conservation could be realized. But they do not: while reef territories are owned, the group sharing use-rights to sections of reef is not equivalent to the pooling unit. Sections of reef are considered extensions of residential plots: use-rights to residential plots are shared by all members of a patriline. Only bounded clam gardens within reef territories are excludable and defendable by single households, and these gardens are approximately 2–4 m in diameter, not large enough to permit spearfishing. Any gains in long-term shellfish productivity would have to be shared by the entire patriline, and all men within the patriline would have to forgo shellfish collecting, which is unlikely since men do vary in the extent to which they collect shellfish. We cannot definitively exclude this possibility, only note that it seems unlikely.

Spearfishers interested in maximizing return rates should not ignore shellfish while foraging on the reef, but most of them do. The costs of choosing to spear fish do not appear to be balanced by benefits received through cooperative gender specialization in macronutrient harvesting, nor through reciprocal sharing. We propose that the benefits of spearfishing are gained through the honest signal value of acquiring the prey rather than through consumption, and that honesty is maintained through differential benefits: men of higher phenotypic quality benefit more than lower quality individuals because

they can signal more intensely each time they signal.

Prediction 1: *men who signal more frequently obtain greater benefits*[10]

If spearfishing is a competitive display, signalers should reap social benefits associated with more frequent spearfishing, such as the benefits from gaining status through building a reputation as a skilled spearfisher. In interviews with 33 Meriam men and women, none would nominate a slate of "the best shellfish collectors," claiming that "being better than others" (i.e., getting larger harvests) depends solely on working long hours, not on qualities intrinsic to the forager, and most nominated the most frequently observed woman on the reef as "hardest-working shellfish collector." Across individuals, shellfish-collecting harvest sizes are strongly contingent upon foraging time, whereas spearfishing harvest sizes are not. . . . [Figure 1 shows two graphs. The first compares harvest size with foraging time for spearfishing. The second makes the same comparison for reef shellfish collecting. Together they show that harvest increases with time for reef shellfish collecting, but not with spearfishing.] All interviewees were willing to nominate a slate of "the best spearfishers." Because there was little variance in signal frequency among the majority of men observed on the reef, we divided the signalers into the most frequent (1 man with 10 observed bouts) and the least frequent (14 men with 19 bouts total). The most frequent signaler obtained 23 out of 61 (37.7%) total nominations by the 32 respondents (who nominated as many as three individuals). More than 75% of respondents named the most frequent signaler as the best spearfisherman. None of the less frequent signalers in our sample obtained any nominations at all. The remainder of

---

[10] In this essay, perhaps more than any other in this book, the authors state general rules for the society they are studying. The essays that come close, those by Radcliffe-Brown, Gluckman, and White, state possible rules in very general terms. The literary technique of stating these principles as predictions is consistent with the scientific trope of the essay. However, the use of the term *prediction* is interesting. Normally, one would expect to make a prediction before collecting data. These predictions, however, seem to have been made after data collection and analysis. Thus, in this case, it is very difficult to tell if the reasoning is truly deductive (if the data were collected in order to test the predictions) or inductive (the predictions derived from data collected).

the nominations went to deceased individuals or those currently not active as spearfishers.[11]

Prediction 2: *signal intensity is linked to phenotypic quality*

For the qualities signaled by spearfishing to be honestly advertised, high quality spearfishers should signal more intensely, because they gain greater marginal benefits or endure lower marginal costs per unit signal. In addition to signal frequency (see above), good measures of signaling intensity are harvest size and success rate. The mean harvest size per bout (in kcal) of the most frequent spearfisher (680 ± 197, $n = 9$) was larger than that obtained by other spearfishers (209 ± 101, $n = 15$; $U = 32$, $p = 0.05$). His hunt type return rates were also higher at 616 ± 356 kg/h versus 137 ± 75 kg/h ($U = 32$, $p = 0.49$), although his bouts were of equal mean length as those of the less frequent signalers (106 ± 17.2 versus 102 ± 15.6 min). The most frequent signaler's return rates were still lower than he could achieve shellfish collecting ($U = 72$, $p = 0.002$). The "frequent signaler" also had a much lower bout failure rate than other men (failure rate per bout = 22.2% versus 66.7%; chi-squared 4.444, $p = 0.03$).[12]

Prediction 3: *the signal is designed to be perceived by the intended audience*

Since spearfishing is a solitary hunting activity that produces no large, widely consumed common good, the signal elements contained in spearfishing are subtle and difficult to observe. Yet reputations are still built in the absence of any overt boasting or tale-telling on the part of the forager himself, who when successful, displays the typical behavior of a male solitary hunter: he returns home carrying his catch quietly, albeit very visibly. The signal elements incorporated in spearfishing are conveyed to observers in three distinct ways. (1) Reef activities are highly visible to a large section of the village surrounding one's residence, which contributes to the ease of observer perception of bout frequency. (2) Spearfishermen make perception of harvest size easier by carrying their harvests openly in hand, rather than carrying them in a bucket, as line fishers and shellfish collectors do. (3) Although bout frequency is the signal element most easily observed, harvest size is usually made known to a large number of individuals through verbal communication. Hunts with large harvests are recounted many times over, and stories about such success become part of local legend.

Turtle Hunting as Costly Signal[13]

Turtle hunting could serve as a competitive display if foragers can distinguish themselves from others based on their skill. The signal(s) thus produced by turtle hunting would depend upon the kinds of costs incurred. If turtle hunting is associated with lower foraging returns than other options, signals of skill sent through hunting could honestly indicate the ability of the forager to expend time and energy in a wasteful pursuit. If hunting has a high return but is associated with wide, unconditional, and costly distributions of food, signals of skill could honestly indicate one's quality (prosocial tendencies, or ability to gain resource reserves through skill in other activities) by expending time and energy in providing goods for public consumption.

Hunting turtles is indeed a competitive pursuit, with a very different complement of participants than collecting. As the Meriam put it *anyone* can collect turtle in the nesting season, but only certain men have the ability to succeed at turtle

---

[11] Note the leap of faith demanded by the authors here. The authors show that there is a fairly high degree of agreement about who the best spearfishermen are (although there also seems to be quite a bit of variability about the rank of most of the men who fish). They suggest that being recognized as the best spearfisherman must, naturally, carry benefits. This is not an unreasonable thing to suggest, but the authors are weak about specifying exactly what those benefits are. Perhaps most Meriam women dislike the best spearfisherman because he is self-centered and always smells like fish.

[12] In other words, the best fisherman was able to get larger harvests with less time expended than other fishermen. Thus it "cost" him less to send a strong signal than it cost other spearfishermen who would have had to expend much more time and energy to bring home the same catch.

[13] In the section above the authors have discussed spearfishing as a costly signal. Now they perform the same task for turtle hunting, a separate and more complex case.

hunting. Older and younger men, children, and women of all ages participate in turtle *collecting* during the nesting season: 21% of turtle collections involve adult females. In contrast, for turtle *hunting*, the only participants are males between the ages of 16 and 47 (mean age = 31.6, n = 38). Though a substantial proportion of Meriam men participate in turtle hunting at some point in their lives, relatively few do so with regularity. In our sample of 37 turtle hunts extending over two periods (1994–1995 and 1998), there were a total of 102 man-days expended, or 2.76 hunters per hunt (all hunts last 1 day or less). For the 87 man-days where hunters are individually identified, there were a total of 40 unique individuals, or 2.18 hunts per hunter. But the 3 most active men participated a total of 16 times, or 18.4% of the hunter-days of known individuals. Thus, 44.4% of the 90 Meriam males aged 16–47 hunted at least once in the study period, but the 3 most active participants (3.3% of males) were over five times more likely to engage in a turtle hunt than the average Meriam male in this age range.[14]

Turtle hunting entails a variety of costs that could ultimately be linked to signaler quality in a way that ensures signals sent by hunting will remain honest (Smith and Bliege Bird 2000). Hunting may involve (1) high opportunity costs in the form of passing over opportunities to acquire other resources with a higher rate of return, (2) low consumption return rates (Bliege Bird and Bird 1997) as hunters distribute meat to non-hunters following the hunt, or (3) high energetic, monetary, or time investment costs of preparing for and conducting the hunt that reduce energetic return rates below that of other more easily acquired resources. There may be other costs or risks of a social nature that provide a link between turtle hunting and hunter quality, particularly the loss of social status should a hunter fail to deliver turtles to a feast (see below).[15]

Hunting Season Hunts

During the hunting season, between April and October, the goal of all hunts is to capture turtle for a previously arranged feast. During major feasts, all those who come must be fed by the feast-giving family and their allies, and the family can never predict precisely how many people will come to the feast itself. Theoretically, the entire population of the island (over 400 men, women, and children) plus many off-island visitors could attend, though attendance by 200 or fewer from both on and off the island is typical (mean = 174.9, range = 49–343, n = 54). Failure to provide turtle is a substantial cost to the hunter's status since all feast-goers will note the absence of turtle meat at the feast. Since hunts are only undertaken a day or two prior to a feast, there are only as many hunts as there are feasts during this season: in 1994 there were ten hunts for public feasts. During the hunting season, the turtle patch is more distant, encounters with turtle are less common, and turtles are more difficult to detect and follow under water that is often murky and broken by swells and whitecaps created by the nearly constant 20-knot southeast trade winds

---

[14] Interesting points sometimes lie hidden in the numbers. In the methods section above, the authors tell us that there are three different roles in the hunt: the leader, the jumper, and the tillerman. Further, their writing seems to imply that sometimes crews are quite large (for example, they talk about the leader directing jumpers rather than a single jumper). However, notice that the average crew size is only 2.76. That implies that on many hunts not all the roles were filled. In fact, the numbers suggest a few hunts with large crews and many hunts with very small crews. Did the most successful hunters frequently go out with a crew of one?

[15] One issue that the authors do not discuss but that readers might want to keep in mind is the inelastic nature of food demand. That is, the amount of food consumed by well-fed humans is relatively stable. A hunter who captures 100,000 calories can only eat around 2,000 in a day. As long as a hunter is assured of having enough to eat, whether he captures 1,000 or 100,000 might make little difference. Thus passing over rich resources or consuming a low percentage of a catch (points one and two in this paragraph) may not really be irrelevant. In a relatively lush environment like the one the Meriam live in, adequate food supply might be easy to get. This exposes a dilemma in ethological technique. The technique is designed to study nonhuman animals that engage in far less cooperation and planning than do humans. Can such a technique be appropriate to the study of human society?

during this season. After a successful hunt, hunters could expect to obtain a per capita net return of 4,653 kcal/h if they divided the turtle among themselves; however, all hunts during this season provision feasts, and hunters keep no share of the turtle they provide. Hunters deliver the turtle whole to the feasting location. Hunters thus obtain negative per capita consumption returns of −1,086 kcal/h, including the costs of traveling to the patch (see Bliege Bird and Bird 1997 for details of the method of calculating net returns from turtle hunting).

Nesting Season Hunts

During the remainder of the year, hunts are undertaken for two reasons: to provision previously arranged feasts ($n = 13$), and to provision households ($n = 9$). In this season, hunting is much easier and hunters take on fewer costs: turtles are found on nearby reefs waiting to crawl onto the beaches to lay eggs at night, the trade winds have largely ceased, and in between monsoon storms, the water is clear, calm, and visibility is excellent, allowing hunters to dog turtles more closely, to lose fewer, and to more finely discern size and sex. Considering only successful hunts, hunters in the nesting season could potentially obtain per capita returns of 8,061 kcal/h hunting for household consumption if they did not share the meet with others. But hunters share more widely than collectors during the same season, leaving their personal return rate from hunting for a feast at −1,633, and those from hunting for household consumption at 814 (Table 2). [Table 2 shows the mean returns for turtle hunting. It shows that many more turtles were acquired during nesting season than during hunting season. And for turtle hunters, the caloric returns were negative during both hunting and nesting seasons.] Hunts during the nesting season should not happen at all if hunters were interested solely in maximizing energetic return rates: during the nesting season, collected turtle offers higher after-sharing energetic returns than hunted turtle. In addition, other available resources are also more energetically productive: sardine netting provides 11,008 ± 1,705 ($n = 28$) kcal/h before sharing—sardine harvests are shared only 5% of the time, leaving

on average 10,864 kcal/h. If hunting turtle were solely about ensuring feast-goers can eat plenty of meat and fat, men should net 50 kg of sardines with no chance of failure rather than spending the entire day chasing turtle to risk coming back to the feast empty-handed.

Turtle hunting in both seasons thus satisfies two of our criteria for consideration as an honest and costly signal. Unlike turtle collecting, observers can distinguish skilled from unskilled individuals and participation is restricted to a subset of the community; second, hunting has the potential to generate high return rates among simultaneously available foraging alternatives (second only to sardine netting), but does not result in much consumption benefit to the hunters since they share widely and take no portion for themselves. As with spearfishing, we hypothesize that the benefits of hunting are gained through the honest-signal value of acquiring the prey, rather than through consumption, and that honesty is maintained through differential costs and benefits: men of higher phenotypic quality benefit more or pay less than lower-quality individuals per unit signal.

Prediction 1: *turtle hunting is differentially costly or beneficial*

The relative costs and benefits of hunting turtle vary with the season: hunts are less costly in the nesting season because the prey are found closer to home, but they are more ambiguous as a signal, since turtles may also be collected at this time. Since there is the potential for dishonest signaling (acquiring a turtle through collecting and passing it off as a hunted turtle), we predict that the benefits of hunting during the nesting season are lower as well. We would thus expect that more skilled hunters would be over-represented among hunting season hunts, which have the highest cost and the lowest signal ambiguity, while the least skilled hunters would be over-represented among nesting season hunts, when hunts are less costly as well as harder to discriminate from collecting. Among turtle hunt participants, age is usually a good proxy for skill, since hunt participants move up in the hierarchy of roles as they gain in skill over time, and since the skills necessary to be a good hunt leader are not dependent upon size and strength. We thus expect jumpers to make the move to become hunt leaders only during the nesting season. Hunt leaders during the hunting season ($n = 8$) are in fact an average of 7.9 years older than hunt leaders ($n = 22$) during the nesting season, a difference that is statistically significant ($U = 41.5$, $p = 0.05$). In contrast, there is no difference in age of jumper according to season ($df = 37$, $t = 0.253$, $p = 0.80$). Of the 17 known current hunt leaders, the 4 youngest (aged 18–22) were observed as hunt leaders only during the nesting season, and served only as jumpers during the hunting season.[16]

Prediction 2: *signal intensity is linked to phenotypic quality*

Turtle hunting provides evidence of skills that could honestly signal several relevant qualities: environmental and ethological knowledge, risk-taking, strength and agility, leadership and organizational abilities, and prosocial tendencies (e.g., expending time and energy in providing goods for public consumption at feasts). Such information is presumably of interest to potential female mates, their families, potential political alliance partners, or competitors for social status.

As detailed above, the most active hunters are a subset of the adult male population. The best turtle hunt leaders are well known to community members: in a series of 32 interviews we conducted with men and women in which informants were asked to nominate any three individuals of their choice for "best turtle hunters," 3 men (all ones we had observed as the most frequent hunt leaders) garnered 38 (39.6%) of the 96 nomina-

tions (a total of 30 men were nominated for "best hunter" out of a pool of 90 or more males aged 16 and older). While several deceased individuals or older men no longer active as hunt leaders were named among the "best hunters," no men currently active solely as jumpers were so named. Jumpers are rarely individually credited by others for acquiring a turtle, and drivers are rarely publicly credited with participation in the hunt. Feast-goers can readily name hunt leaders as providers of the turtle, even several years after the feast, but when pressed for the names of other hunt participants, lump all others together as "the boys." Jumpers may begin in this role as young as 15–17 years old; anecdotal evidence indicates that those who excel in this role and gain increasing knowledge and peer respect eventually become hunt leaders, while others remain jumpers or cease participating in turtle hunting.[17]

Prediction 3: *the signal is designed to be perceived by the intended audience*

Signals do little good if they are not perceived and the information contained is not deciphered. We propose that when signals are designed to acquire general social status or political dominance, broadcast efficiency will be increased by directing them at larger audiences, rather than small subsets of interested parties (as might be predicted if the signal elements of hunting were directed solely at potential mating partners). Thus, we predict that hunted turtles should be shared more widely than collected turtles; in other words, that individuals should choose to hunt for larger audiences, and to collect when audiences (the number

---

[16] Note the very strict adherence to an ethologically based research methodology. The researchers could easily have asked Meriam hunt leaders why they choose to hunt in the hunting or nesting season. They could have asked why they choose turtle hunting over sardine fishing, and the answers might have been enlightening. However, theoretical models built from animal behavior do not admit that type of questioning. They are built almost entirely on the observation of behavior and the assumption that observed behavior is, in some way, fitness enhancing.

[17] In the case of both spearfishing and turtle hunting, sexual selection is being implied. Although the authors do not state this directly, if these behaviors are to have any effect

on natural selection, men must be displaying turtle hunting or spearfishing abilities in much the same way that male peacocks display spectacular tail feathers. Peahens find large tail feather displays sexually attractive and, the authors suggest, human females find turtle hunting and spearfishing displays sexually attractive. If this is so, then over time, one would expect that the Meriam population would be genetically superior at the abilities involved in hunting to other populations not subject to the same pressures. We are not aware that this is indeed the case. However, perhaps all human populations were historically subject to conditions that selected for talents similar to those used in spearfishing and turtle hunting.

of households attracted to the turtle and consuming portions) are predicted to be smaller. Because turtles cannot be collected during the hunting season, we control for the effects of season. We thus predict that audience size should have a significant effect on acquisition method within the nesting season only: when larger audiences are available, men should prefer to hunt rather than collect. During the 1994–1995 nesting season, hunts for which the number of consumers were known ($n = 22$) averaged 26.7 ± 23.7 households, while collections ($n = 80$) averaged 18.7 ± 19.0 households consuming, a significant difference ($t = -1.649$, $df = 100$, $p = 0.05$).[18]

Individuals who acquire turtles for feasts have a large built-in audience; however, turtles acquired for household provisioning will be shared among a smaller number of households. If hunting serves as an honest signal and hunters wish to broadcast the signal widely, turtles acquired for household provisioning should also be shared more widely when hunted than when collected (controlling for season). During the 1994–1995 nesting season, there were 9 hunts and 44 collections to supply turtles for household consumption. . . . As predicted, hunted consumption turtles were shared to more households (7.5 ± 3.0) than collected consumption turtles (4.6 ± 2.5), and the statistical difference is strongly significant ($U = 64$, $p = 0.015$). Because the number of households receiving portions of a hunted turtle is larger than the number receiving portions of a collected turtle, portions shared to each household should be smaller, but they do not seem to be so, because hunters kept less for themselves and their own households than did collectors (mean portion kept (kcal) for hunters 7,780 ± 2,194 kcal, $n = 38$; for collectors = 14,387 ± 2,631 kcal, $n = 123$) although the difference is not significant (t-test on log-transformed kcal kept, $t = 0.682$, $df = 159$, $p = 0.50$).

DISCUSSION[19]

Although our sample of spearfishers is too small to define a continuum in level of skill, spearfishing does seem to exhibit strong potential for competitive signaling. The most frequent signaler obtains much higher gains per unit patch residence time than other spearfishers. Harvest size (the most easily observed indicator of return rates) is likely to be linked to phenotypic quality in the form of hand-eye coordination, stealth, and patience, and provides an immediate signal of forager quality. Success rate is a signal element contributing to the long-term reputation of the spear-fisher. High success rates in conjunction with large harvest size ensure that large harvests are more likely due to skill (forager-dependent variability) than to luck (forager-independent variability). As a result, the most active spearfisher gains the benefits of an enhanced spearing reputation that more infrequent signalers do not seem to enjoy. Spearing thus has the potential to serve as an honest signal of a spearfisherman's phenotypic quality.

Although we have demonstrated the potential for signaling, and the bias in men's foraging toward resources which have high competitive signaling potential, precisely how both signaler and observer ultimately benefit from the signal is not clear. We do know that good spearing men are widely recognized, and that this adds to their social status within the community. Potential competitors might also gain from knowing who is a better man with a spear, although the knowledge certainly would have been more useful in the past when spears were the major means of

---

[18] Remember that there is a difference between significant and meaningful. The results the authors mention above are significant because there is less than a 5% chance that the average number of people consuming hunted food at an occasion is the same as the number of people consuming gathered food. Notice that despite the statistically significant difference between the two groups, the plus and minus figures tell you that there is a great deal of overlap between them.

That doesn't mean that the authors' interpretation is incorrect. The difference between the two groups may be meaningful as well as significant, but it is left to the reader to judge whether the difference in size between the audience for hunting and the audience for collecting is really important.

[19] In this section, the authors recap the critical findings of their research and discuss several problems in it.

ambushing competitors. Spearing signals may not be designed to appeal to potential mates interested only in marrying provisioners. A man who demonstrates his intention to provision a household by collecting shellfish may be more attractive to such women than a man who demonstrates his intention to engage in a competitive, status-enhancing pursuit.[20]

Turtle hunters seem to have very different goals than turtle collectors. Compared to collecting, hunting is more costly (in time, energy, and risk), provides meat less efficiently, and is associated with wider distributions of meat and larger audiences to witness the hunters' prowess. Hunters keep no meat for themselves unless (quite rarely) hunting for household consumption, in which case they still keep less and share more than turtle collectors. Hunters take on a variety of costs for which they are not materially compensated: they expend more time and energy in hunting than they do collecting, they spend more money for fuel, they spend time organizing and preparing the hunting team and its equipment prior to the hunt, and they deliver the meat to be consumed by large audiences at feasts. The ability to bear such costs appears to be linked to hunter quality. Because a hunter is an organizer and decision-maker, his abilities peak as he gains skill and experience: those named as the best hunters are older than other hunt participants, such as jumpers. As we predicted, when hunting was less costly and more difficult to discriminate from collecting (i.e., during the nesting season), hunters were younger, in fact composed almost entirely of ambitious jumpers preparing to be hunt leaders themselves. Furthermore, the signals sent by hunting are efficiently broadcast: hunts were associated with larger numbers of consumers overall than collections during the nesting season and during household consumption

events. Most feast-goers (audience members), when quizzed, know the identity of hunters, but not the identity of jumpers.

Since the low take-home returns of hunters providing turtle for household consumption and the negative take-home returns of hunters providing turtle for a feast are due to widespread sharing, the argument could be made that the signal cost is eventually recovered in the form of meat or other goods or services returned as payback for the hunter's gift. In other words, perhaps RA[21] by the recipients of a hunter's largesse erases the cost of his signal (Sosis and Hill 1997). The stable maintenance of RA requires that the provisioning of a turtle be contingent upon the eventual receipt of counterbalancing benefits which compensate the hunter for the marginal cost of giving up turtle that could have been used in other fitness-enhancing ways. Previous tests of predictions based on RA in the form of risk reduction reciprocity for sharing of collected and hunted turtles combined received little support (Bliege Bird and Bird 1997). Further tests of alternative forms of reciprocity are being conducted to evaluate this line of explanation (R. Bliege Bird, G. Kushnik, E. A. Smith, D. Bird, C. Hadley, unpublished data), as will be detailed in future publications.

While we have measured the cost of hunting using direct material currencies such as time, energy, and money, there are additional social costs that, though difficult to measure, may be of equal or even greater importance. Turtles provided for feasts are needed by community elders (feast hosts) to enhance their own status by ensuring there is plenty of meat for guests. If successful hunting is a reliable signal of the hunter's underlying quality (as defined above), lower-quality individuals would be expected to fail on turtle hunts more often and thus pay a higher marginal

---

[20] Here the authors face but do not resolve the critical problem we identified earlier in the essay. They clearly show that spearfishing and turtle hunting have characteristics that could qualify them as costly signals. However, the theory can only work if these individuals really do receive benefits, particularly reproductive benefits. It is not unreasonable to suppose that they do, but the authors are unable to show it unambiguously. These passages demonstrate that they are well aware of this problem.

[21] Here the authors once again try to eliminate RA (reciprocal altruism, described in the opening paragraphs of this essay) as the cause of the wide sharing of hunted foods.

cost per turtle delivered to a feast (i.e., per unit signal). Failing to deliver a turtle to a feast also entails significant social costs, since the feast-holders are expected to serve turtle to their guests, and everyone will know when a hunter has failed. High-quality individuals should have a lower probability of failure and thus a high ratio of social benefits (from successful hunts) to costs (from failures). Low-quality individuals may face a large enough risk of failing to produce a net social deficit from their signaling attempts, and hence may avoid signaling at all, making it difficult to test this hypothesis. We do have anecdotal evidence that some men have attempted turtle hunting in the past, and given up when they found they were "no good at it." In addition, the facts (detailed above) that only certain men engage in turtle hunting, that only an older and more experienced subset of these become hunt leaders, and that hunt leader status is widely recognized in the community, all indicate that success in this endeavor is not equally available.[22]

To qualify as costly signaling, hunting must not only be honest, but must also reveal signaler quality. Given the three distinct roles played by hunt participants, we propose (but cannot currently test) that at least four distinct dimensions of underlying quality could be signaled through turtle hunting: (1) physical quality (such as strength, stamina, agility, and risk-taking); (2) cognitive skills (involving the ecological and ethological knowledge needed to successfully locate and capture turtles); (3) leadership skills (charisma and organizational abilities); and (4) generosity (ability and willingness to bear the high immediate cost in time, money, and energy of providing collective goods without direct compensation). We expect the first dimension to apply primarily to the younger men who serve as

"jumpers," whereas the other three dimensions refer primarily to hunt leaders.

The results of additional analysis in progress show that the display of such qualities is correlated with higher social status and higher age-specific reproductive success of hunters and their mates than other Meriam (E. A. Smith, R. Bliege Bird, D. Bird, unpublished data). As explained to us by Meriam hunters and their mates, the signals sent by hunters are likely to be part of both political strategies, in which hunters demonstrate to other men their honest intention to work for the public good, and reproductive strategies, in which hunters demonstrate their "willingness to work hard" in order to gain access to the "best girl" (Kaddy, personal communication; Passi, personal communication). Hunters know that spreading one's influence widely via the provisioning of collective goods at feasts increases social status over the long-term among the community as a whole, while less public-minded status enhancing activities (like stealing land or selfishly hoarding resources) provides narrow, short-term status in only a small pool of competitors.[23]

Implications for the Sexual Division of Labor

One intriguing result of our analysis are the gender differences in participation in those activities with high signaling potential. With spearfishing particularly, the differences were not consistent with the common notion that a sexual division of labor in humans functions to maximize the productivity of a cooperating male-female pair (see Bliege Bird 1999). We propose that the signaling benefits attached to certain foraging strategies may often change the valuation of certain prey items for some individuals. While foraging on the

---

[22] Here, again, is one of the most critical elements of the authors' argument: The system works because the signal is costly. That is, although it can be faked (for example, a poor hunter could do enough work to acquire turtles for a feast), the cost of faking it is so high in terms of time and energy expended, as well as risk of social embarrassment, that the good achieved (the social benefits of recognition as a good hunter) is not worth the costs incurred. We must

point out, however, that since the authors have not clearly specified the benefits that good hunters achieve, we have no method to judge how much they are worth.

[23] In this paragraph, the authors allow a rare bit of traditional ethnographic data into their essay in the form of interviews with Meriam men.

reef, males make choices that fail to maximize their macronutrient return rates. These choices appear to be due to the tradeoffs men face over foraging for highly productive resources which have little signaling value (shellfish) against foraging for less productive resources with high signaling value (speared fish). Likewise, choosing to hunt turtle for feasts provides much lower consumption benefits than collecting turtle for the household, but greater signaling benefits. Adult women only participate in cooperative turtle collection, comprising 21% of all participants, and do not hunt. These data suggest that foraging sex differences may not simply be a result of women preferring plants and men meat, or women preferring small harvests while men prefer large ones, or even women preferring prey which can be more easily harvested while children are present (shellfish are just as difficult as fish to collect with small children). Where there is a choice in foraging method, men seem to prefer to acquire meat through more risky methods that more easily differentiate the skill of individual foragers, while women seem to prefer less risky methods carrying little potential for discrimination of forager quality. We propose that sex-biased foraging preferences may arise due to the differing benefits each sex receives from investing in competition for status through signaling certain genotypic or phenotypic qualities.[24]

Foraging as Communication

As Hawkes (1990, 1991, 1992, 1993) first hypothesized, some kinds of hunting may persist in human populations because some foragers gain benefits from widely disseminating knowledge about their prowess relative to other individuals through the hunting of large and risky prey items. While Hawkes (1993) stressed the benefits that hunters obtain from providing collective goods (as with turtle hunting and unconditional sharing), our results show that benefits may also come in

the absence of any material good provided to observers (as with spearfishing) as a result of honestly revealing hidden information to interested parties. Differential costs and benefits for signalers of higher and lower quality serve to keep the information honest and valuable to observers.

Our results suggest that CST has the potential to account for many puzzling aspects of human foraging strategies, and to substantially modify received views about optimal foraging, food sharing, and other phenomena central to studies of human behavioral ecology in small-scale societies (Winterhalder and Smith 2000). CST may illuminate otherwise puzzling behaviors such as preference for prey and patch types which provide fewer energetic benefits than other possible choices and are more costly on other levels, if the costs (or benefits) incurred are linked to signaler quality, so that poorer-quality signalers cannot consistently maintain or reach the same level of signaling as higher-quality signalers. Signaling hypotheses have only just begun to be tested as a cause for variability in human foraging strategies. Sosis (2000) has suggested that the benefits of signaling may explain why Ifaluk men engage in energetically inefficient fishing methods associated with costly ritual preparations. Such benefits may also explain why Ache men prefer to hunt widely shared game even though palm starch collection would offer higher on-encounter energetic returns (Hill et al. 1987; Hawkes 1991).

We are not proposing that the signaling benefits provide the *only* motivation for hunters and meat recipients, but simply that they provide an additional factor of evolutionary and motivational significance shaping hunting and sharing decisions. Thus the social and political signaling benefits of at least certain forms of hunting may compensate for any economic "wastefulness," in the same way that Veblen (1899) explained both "conspicuous consumption" of material goods and "conspicuous leisure" as instances of "conspicuous expenditure" designed to gain or

---

[24] In this passage, the authors level another attack on economic models of forager behavior. Here they insist that the sexual division of labor in these societies occurs not because the group is trying to maximize its caloric return while min-

imizing its labor, as an economic model might have it. Instead they propose that the division of labor and the particular types of hunting performed by men are explained by competition for status and reproduction rather than calories.

maintain social benefits only indirectly related to economic advantage.[25] However, CST has the potential to explain not only "wasteful" foraging activities, but any behavior in which higher-quality individuals obtain higher marginal benefits because they can better absorb the cost of the behavior, and where such behavior is efficiently broadcast to the proper observers (potential mates, allies, or competitors).

ACKNOWLEDGEMENTS

We thank the Meriam community foremost, especially Chairman Ron Day for his foresight and tolerance, our Meriam families, particularly the Passis, and the turtle hunters who volunteered information or invited us on hunts. We also wish to acknowledge the invaluable field assistance of Andrew Passi, Rono "Sonny" Passi, Edna Kabere, Del Passi, and Craig Hadley. For many helpful discussions and comments on the manuscript, we thank Monique Borgerhoff Mulder, Thomas Getty, Craig Hadley, Polly Wiessner, Kristen Hawkes, Kim Hill, Frank Marlowe, Rich Sosis, Steven Siller, and Bruce Winterhalder. Research in 1998–1999 was supported by NSF grant SBR-9616096 to R.B.B. and E.A.S., NSF grant SBR-9616887 to D.W.B. and E.A.S., and research in 1994–1995 was supported by grants to R.B.B. and D.W.B. from AIATSIS, the L.S.B. Leakey Foundation, the Wenner Gren Foundation for Anthropological Research, and an NSF predoctoral fellowship to R.B.B. and an NSF Dissertation Improvement Grant to D.W.B.

REFERENCES

Beckett J. (1988). The Torres Strait Islanders: custom and colonialism. Cambridge University Press, Cambridge, UK.

Bird D. W., Bliege Bird R. (1997). Contemporary shellfish gathering strategies among the Meriam of the Torres Strait Islands, Australia: testing predictions of a central place foraging model. J Archaeol Sci 24:39–63.

Bird D. W., Bliege Bird R. (2000). The ethnoarchaeology of juvenile foragers: shellfishing strategies among Meriam children. J. Anthropol Archaeol 19:461–476.

Bliege Bird R. (1999). Cooperation and conflict: the behavioral ecology of the sexual division of labor. Evol Anthropol 8:65–75.

Bliege Bird R., Bird D. W. (1997). Delayed reciprocity and tolerated theft. Curr Anthropol 38:49–78.

Bliege Bird R., Bird D. W., Beaton J. (1995). Children and traditional subsistence on Mer (Murray Island), Torres Strait. Aust Aboriginal Stud 1:2–17.

Boone J. L. (1998). The evolution of magnanimity: when is it better to give than to receive? Hum Nat 9:1–21.

Brand Miller J., James K., Maggiore P. (1993). Tables of composition of Australian Aboriginal foods. Aboriginal Studies Press, Canberra.

Clements R., Stephens D. C. (1995). Testing models of non-kin cooperation—mutualism and the prisoner's dilemma. Anim Behav 50:527–535.

Connor R. C. (1996). Partner preferences in by-product mutualism and the case of predator inspection in fish. Anim Behav 51:451–454.

Dugatkin L. (1997). Cooperation among animals: an evolutionary perspective. Oxford University Press, New York.

Getty T. (1998). Handicap signaling: when fecundity and viability do not add up. Anim Behav 56:127–130.

Grafen A. (1990). Biological signals as handicaps. J Theor Biol 144:517–546.

Gurven M., Hill K., Hurtado A., Lyles R. (2000). Food transfers among Hiwi foragers of Venezuela: tests of reciprocity. Hum Ecol 28:171–218.

Haddon A. C. (1906). Sociology, magic and religion of the Eastern Islanders. Reports of the Cambridge Anthropological Expedition to Torres Straits, vol. 6. Cambridge University Press, Cambridge, UK.

Hawkes K. (1990). Why do men hunt? Some benefits for risky choices. In: Cashdan E. (ed.) Uncertainty in tribal and peasant economies. Westview, Boulder, pp. 145–166.

Hawkes K. (1991). Showing off: tests of another hypothesis about men's foraging goals. Ethol Sociobiol 12:29–54.

---

[25] Thorstein Veblen (1857–1929) was an economist and social theorist best known for his 1912 work, *The Theory of the Leisure Class*. In that work, he attempted to apply ideas about Darwinian evolution to economic life. In Veblen's analysis, the fundamental conflict and struggle in society is between making goods (the realm of factory workers and engineers) and making money (the realm of bankers and financiers). The goal of economic life in capitalism is "conspicuous consumption," a phrase that Veblen coined. He argued that the wealthy (particularly those who make money rather than goods) consumed conspicuously, buying obviously visible luxuries for the purposes of display rather than for any use value such objects might have. The notion that the most important part of consumption is display fits in well with the key points made in this essay.

Hawkes K. (1992). Sharing and collective action. In: Smith E. A., Winterhalder B. (eds.) Evolutionary ecology and human behavior. de Gruyter, Hawthorne, NY, pp. 269–300.

Hawkes K. (1993). Why hunter-gatherers work. Curr Anthropol 34:341–362.

Hill K. (1988). Macronutrient modifications of optimal foraging theory: an approach using indifference curves applied to some modern foragers. Hum Ecol 16:157–197.

Hill K., Kaplan H., Hawkes K., Hurtado A. M. (1987). Foraging decisions among Ache hunter-gatherers: new data and implications for optimal foraging models. Ethol Sociobiol 8:1–36.

Hirth H. (1971). Synopsis of biological data on the green turtle *Chelonia mydas* (Linnaeus).1758. FAO Fisheries Synopsis No 85. Food and Agriculture Organization of the United Nations, Rome.

Hurtado A. M., Hill K., Kaplan H., Hurtado I. (1992). Trade-offs between female food acquisition and child care among Hiwi and Ache foragers. Hum Nat 3:185–216.

Johnstone R. A. (1995). Sexual selection, honest advertisement and the handicap principle: reviewing the evidence. Biol Rev 70:1–65.

Johnstone R. A. (1997). The evolution of animal signals. In: Krebs J. R., Davies N. B. (eds.) Behavioural ecology: an evolutionary approach. Blackwell, Oxford, pp. 155–178.

Neiman F. D. (1998). Conspicuous consumption as wasteful advertising: a Darwinian perspective on spatial patterns in classic Maya terminal monument dates. In: Barton C. M., Clark G. A. (eds.) Rediscovering Darwin: evolutionary theory and archaeological explanation. Archaeological papers of the American Anthropological Association No 7, pp. 267–290.

Pusey A. E., Packer C. (1997). The ecology of relationships. In Krebs J. R., Davies N. B. (eds.) Behavioural ecology: an evolutionary approach. Blackwell, Oxford, pp. 254–283.

Roberts G. (1998). Competitive altruism: from reciprocity to the handicap principle. Proc R Soc Lond B 265:427–431.

Sharp N. (1993). Stars of Tagai: The Torres Strait Islanders. Aboriginal Studies Press, Canberra.

Sidwell V. (1981). Chemical and nutritional composition of finfishes, whales, crustaceans, mollusks, and their products. NOAA Technical Memorandum. National Marine Fisheries Services, Washington, DC.

Smith E. A. (1988). Risk and uncertainty in the "original affluent society": evolutionary ecology of resource sharing and land tenure. In: Ingold T., Riches D., Woodburn I. (eds.) Hunters and gatherers: history, evolution, and social change. Berg, Oxford, pp. 222–252.

Smith E. A. (1991). Inujjamiut foraging strategies: evolutionary ecology of an Arctic hunting economy. de Gruyter, Hawthorne, NY.

Smith E. A., Bliege Bird R. (2000). Turtle hunting and tombstone opening: public generosity as costly signaling. Evol Hum Behav 21:245–261.

Sosis R. (2000). Costly signaling and torch fishing on Ifaluk Atoll. Evol Hum Behav 21:223–244.

Sosis R., Hill K. (1997). Comment on Bliege Bird and Bird. Curr Anthropol 38:73–74.

Veblen T. (1899). Theory of the leisure class. Macmillan, New York.

Wiessner P. (1996). Leveling the hunter: constraints on the status quest in foraging societies. In: Wiessner P., Schiefenhovel W. (eds.) Food and the status quest. Berghahn, Providence, RI, pp. 171–192.

Winterhalder B. (1997). Gifts given, gifts taken: the behavioral ecology of nonmarket, intragroup exchange. J Archaeol Res 5:121–168.

Winterhalder B., Smith E. A. (2000). Analyzing adaptive strategies: human behavioral ecology at twenty-five. Evol Anthropol 9:51–72.

Zahavi A. (1975). Mate selection—a selection for handicap. J. Theor Biol 53:205–214.

Zahavi A. (1977). Reliability in communication systems and the evolution of altruism. In: Stonehouse B., Perrins C. M. (eds.) Evolutionary ecology. Macmillan, London, pp. 253–259.

Anthropology and Gender

Unlike many disciplines, in anthropology women have reached high levels of professional achievement and gained popular recognition for their work. In this century, women such as Ruth Benedict and Margaret Mead have become household names, whereas others such as Mary Douglas (b. 1921), Laura Bohannon (b. 1922), Sherry Ortner (b. 1941), Michelle Rosaldo (1944?–1981), Peggy Reeves Sanday (b. 1937), Louise Lamphere (b. 1940), Lila Abu-Lughod (b. 1952), and Marilyn Strathern (b. 1941) are widely known to scholars outside of anthropology.

Despite the achievements of women within anthropology, as Lamphere (2004:127) notes, even such seminal figures as Margaret Mead, Ruth Benedict, and Elsie Clew Parsons were marginalized, pigeonholed, and excluded from important aspects of the discipline. Until the mid-twentieth century, discussions of women in the anthropological literature were usually limited to introductory textbook chapters on marriage, family, and kinship. In the 1960s and 1970s, this situation began to change. The modern feminist movement in anthropology probably had its beginnings in the social upheavals of the 1960s—the civil rights movement, anti–Vietnam War activism, various consciousness-raising experiments and the wider "second-wave" feminist movement itself. By the early 1970s women anthropologists were incorporating these new perspectives into their research. Feminist anthropologists documented the discipline's neglect of women and gender as significant dimensions of social life (Morgen 1989:1), questioning anthropological assumptions they considered to be male centered. Since that time,

interest in the study of gender roles and focus on gender and sexuality in a cross-cultural perspective has increased, and some of the basic assumptions of anthropology have been called into question.

Much of the research by feminist anthropologists in the early 1970s was concerned with documenting women's lives and their roles in societies around the world. Assuming universal sexual asymmetry—that is, the worldwide subordination of women—virtually all of these early studies sought to explain this situation through various theoretical perspectives. For example, Friedl (1975) attempted to explain the position of women from a materialist perspective by focusing on women's subsistence roles. Chodorow (1974) examined the issue of subordination from a psychological view, emphasizing the role of childhood socialization in the formation of sex roles. Michelle Rosaldo and Louise Lamphere's 1974 volume, *Women, Culture, and Society*, and Reyna Reiter's 1975 anthology, *Toward an Anthropology of Women*, were two of the defining works in this era of feminist anthropology.

At the same time that feminist cultural anthropologists focused on gender inequality, research on women and gender by feminist archaeologists and physical anthropologists challenged the "man the hunter" version of human evolution. Work on this issue, such as the 1975 essay by physical anthropologist Sally Slocum (b. 1939) in this volume (essay 32), charged that women's roles in human evolution had been ignored because scholars focused on hunting rather than gathering. For instance, Slocum challenges the popular idea that hunting by men, because it implied toolmaking, communication, and the development of complex cognitive skills (Washburn and Lancaster 1968), played a pivotal role in our evolutionary past. She stresses that women's gathering and child care also demanded complex communication, cooperation, and toolmaking. Slocum argues that evidence indicates foraging, not hunting, was the principal economic strategy throughout most of human evolutionary history (Lamphere 1987:16). This "woman the gatherer" approach inspired scholars to revise the standard views on human evolution. One particularly significant study was Tanner and Zihlman's 1976 study of women's activities in economics and technology in relation to the roles that savanna living, foraging, and social organization played in human evolutionary selection.

By the 1980s, anthropological research into issues of gender had broadened substantially. Feminist researchers were increasingly joined by others whose interest in gender roles and sexuality was not necessarily linked to feminist concerns. Research and analysis in the 1980s moved away from the previous decade's blanket assumptions of gender asymmetry and followed three principal trends. The first of these focused on the social construction of gender. Researchers differentiated sex (a condition of biology) from gender (a social role assigned to an individual) and explored the many permutations of gender and sexuality among the different societies, a field pioneered by Margaret Mead in the 1930s. Good examples of this type of work are Herdt's 1984 examination of ritualized homosexuality among the Sambia of New Guinea and Nanda's examination of the Hijra, a group in India that cannot easily be classified as male or female (1990). Additionally, work such as Yanagisako and Collier's *Gender and Kinship* (1987) and Sanday and Goodenough's *Beyond the Second Sex* (1990), fall into this class of study.

Another direction in gender research and analysis explored a materialist perspective. Materialist scholars used cross-cultural analysis to explain differences in women's status, roles, and power. These researchers were relatively unconcerned with describing the ways in which gender is defined in different societies. They concentrated on research that analyzed gender-related activities using measures of social, economic, and political power (Morgen 1989:4). Many scholars in this area focused on gender as it relates to class, the social relations of power, and changes in modes of production. Essay 33, by Eleanor Leacock (1922–1987), fits this category of study. In this work, which appeared in 1983, Leacock argues that prior to Western contact, gender relations in Native American and Australian aboriginal societies were typically egalitarian because men and women participated equally in the processes of production. She argues that the unequal place of women in these societies today is the result of the subjugation of these societies by Europeans and the imposition of capitalist forms of production.

A third trend of this era concerned the range of variation of experiences of gender. As we noted above, feminist anthropology grew from the broader social movements of the 1960s. The feminist movement of that era was dominated by white, middle-class scholars and so largely concerned itself with issues of particular interest to that group. However, by the 1980s, women of different class and ethnic backgrounds were making feminist anthropologists increasingly aware that their interests did not necessarily coincide with those of the white middle-class women who had popularized feminism in anthropology. Micaela di Leonardo writes that feminist scholars were forced to confront "the question of 'difference'—the multiple racial, ethnic, class, sexual, age, regional, and national identities of women—as they noted their own restricted demographic representation and research interests" (1991:18).

Scholars following this third trend have emphasized the cultural specificity of gender identities. They have moved away from the earlier theorizing about "man" and "woman" as general concepts to focus on the different ways in which race, class, and gender structure cultural institutions. Essay 34, by Ann Stoler (b. 1949), is an example of this type of research. There she outlines the ways in which sexual behavior, rules sanctioning or forbidding sexual relationships and marriage between colonists and indigenous women, and laws prohibiting immigration of European women defined and enforced class and racial boundaries in the European colonies of Africa and Asia.

The work of anthropologists concerned with gender in the 1980s has produced a much greater multicultural focus in anthropology. These anthropologists have led the discipline in developing new, experimental forms of ethnographic writing. In particular, current feminist writing follows three new trends. First, feminist theorists have called the anthropological canon into question. In the introduction to *Women Writing Culture*, for example, Ruth Behar writes:

> Why is it that the legacy of what counts as social theory is traced back only to Lewis Henry Morgan, Karl Marx, Émile Durkheim, Max Weber, Michael Foucault and Pierre Bourdieu? Why is there not a parallel matrilineal genealogy taking off from say, the turn-of-the-century work of Charlotte Perkins Gilman? . . . Why is the culture concept in anthropology only traced through Sir Edward Tylor, Franz Boas, Bronislaw Malinowski, Claude Lévi-Strauss, and Clifford Geertz? Could the writing of culture not be traced, as the essays in this volume suggest, through Elsie Clews Parsons, Ruth Benedict, Margaret Mead, Ella Deloria, Zora Neale Hurston, Ruth Landes, and Barbara Myerhoff to Alice Walker? (1995:11–12)

Second, some feminist anthropologists have led the discipline in emphasizing multivocality—that is, giving voice to a variety of viewpoints in their ethnographic writing. They question the objectivity of science and argue that anthropologists are not uniquely qualified interpreters of culture. They claim that traditional anthropological writing distanced authors from their subjects. To counter this, feminist authors have encouraged women of color to write about their cultures for themselves and challenged anthropologists to take into account

"the discriminations of racism, homophobia, sexism, and classism" they claim are a part of traditional anthropology (Behar and Gordon 1995:7).

Finally, some feminist anthropologists have emphasized experimentation with nontraditional forms of anthropological writing. Claiming that all ways of knowing are subjective, these authors have offered works of poetry and fiction as new forms of ethnography. Others experiment with the epistemological assumptions of anthropology by introducing their own thoughts and experiences into their research. One form this work has taken is the "autoethnography"—works that combine autobiographical information with anthropological analyses. In "A Tale of Two Pregnancies" (essay 39 in this volume, published in 1995), for example, Lila Abu-Lughod discusses her experience of pregnancy and compares it with the pregnancies of Bedouin women with whom she conducted research.

The past twenty-five years has seen enormous growth in gender studies. Almost all major universities now have gender studies, or women's studies programs. Men still hold the majority of full professorships in anthropology, but women now make up half of most department faculties. Though all of these women do not necessarily have a particular interest in gender, it is probably true that the majority are sympathetic to gender-related concerns in university life in general and anthropology in particular. However, despite their success in the academy and after almost five decades of work in the areas of gender and sexuality, anthropologists have not successfully translated their findings to a wider culture beyond an academic context. The cultural clashes over women in the workplace, sexual harassment, marriage of same-sex couples, workplace and legal discrimination against homosexuals, to name a few, continue unabated in the United States more than seventy years after Margaret Mead's groundbreaking studies.

32. *Woman the Gatherer: Male Bias in Anthropology*

SALLY SLOCUM (b. 1939)

LITTLE SYSTEMATIC ATTENTION has been given in our discipline to an "anthropology of knowledge."[1] While some anthropologists have concerned themselves with knowledge in general, as seen through the varieties of human cultures, few have examined anthropological knowledge itself. An anthropology of knowledge would have several parts. First is what Peter Berger (1967: 1–18) has called "philosophical anthropology": a study of the nature of the human species. This has always been a legitimate concern of anthropology, but too often we become so concerned with minute differences that we forget we are studying a single species. Second is how we "know" anything—what is accepted as "proof," what is reality, what are the grounds for rationality (Garfinkel, 1960), what modes are used in gathering knowledge, what are the effects of differences in culture and world view on what we "know." Third is a close examination of the questions asked in anthropology, for questions always determine and limit answers.

It is the third point, the nature of anthropological questions, to which I wish to speak in this paper. We are human beings studying other human beings, and we cannot leave ourselves out of the equation. We choose to ask certain questions, *and not others.* Our choice grows out of the cultural context in which anthropology and anthropologists exist. Anthropology, as an academic discipline, has been developed primarily by white Western males, during a specific period in history. Our questions are shaped by the particulars of our historical situation, and by unconscious cultural assumptions.[2]

Given the cultural and ethnic background of the majority of anthropologists, it is not surprising that the discipline has been biased. There are signs, however, that this selective blindness is beginning to come under scrutiny. For example, in the exchange in the journal *Current Anthropology* (1968), anthropologists like Kathleen Gough and Gerald Berreman point out the unconscious efforts of American political and economic assumptions on our selection of problems and populations to be studied. Restive minority groups in this country are pointing to the bias inherent in anthropological studies of themselves through books such as Vine Deloria's *Custer Died for Your Sins.* We have always encouraged members of American minority groups, and other "foreigners," to take up anthropology because of the perspective on the world that they can supply. The invitation is increasingly being accepted. As we had both hoped and feared, repercussions from this new participation are being felt in theory, method, interpretation, and problem choice, shaking anthropology to the roots.[3]

(1975)

---

[1] The 1960s and 1970s were an era of radical rethinking within anthropology, with many strands contributing to a broad critique of positivist anthropology. The feminist critique was one of the most powerful, since it attacked what feminists viewed as fundamental biases in a field that prided itself on being relatively bias free. This essay is taken from one of several groundbreaking anthologies of feminist essays in anthropology to appear in the 1970s, *Toward an Anthropology of Women,* edited by Rayna Reiter (1975).

[2] One of the key questions of current anthropology is whether the fact that anthropology is generally done by a specific group of people fundamentally prejudices its results. Feminists were among the first to pose the question in these terms.

[3] The feminist critique was, of course, part of a broader revision of the social sciences and humanities that has continued in American intellectual culture. This change has been powerfully influenced by popular politics, especially the civil rights and women's movements of the 1960s. Several books aimed at popular rather than scholarly audiences were crucial. *Custer Died* (1969) was one of these. Dee Brown's 1971 *Bury My Heart at Wounded Knee* and Wallenchinsky and Wallace's 1975 *The People's Almanac* were others. All of these books became best sellers. *Bury My Heart,* first published in January 1971, had gone through thirteen printings by October of that year.

The perspective of women is, in many ways, equally foreign to an anthropology that has been developed and pursued primarily by males. There is a strong male bias in the questions asked, and the interpretations given. This bias has hindered the full development of our discipline as "the study of the human animal" (I don't want to call it "the study of man" for reasons that will become evident). I am going to demonstrate the Western male bias by reexamining the matter of evolution of Homo sapiens from our nonhuman primate ancestors. In particular, the concept of "Man the Hunter" as developed by Sherwood Washburn and C. Lancaster (1968) and others is my focus. This critique is offered in hopes of transcending the male bias that limits our knowledge by limiting the questions we ask.[4]

Though male bias could be shown in other areas, hominid evolution is particularly convenient for my purpose because it involves speculations and inferences from a rather small amount of data. In such a case, hidden assumptions and premises that lie behind the speculations and inferences are more easily demonstrated. Male bias exists not only in the ways in which the scanty data are interpreted, but in the very language used. All too often the word "man" is used in such an ambiguous fashion that it is impossible to decide whether it refers to males or to the human species in general, including both males and females. In fact, one frequently is led to suspect that in the minds of many anthropologists, "man," supposedly meaning the human species, is actually exactly synonymous with "males."

This ambiguous use of language is particularly evident in the writing that surrounds the concept of Man the Hunter.[5] Washburn and Lancaster make it clear that it is specifically males who hunt, that hunting is much more than simply an economic activity, and that most of the characteristics which we think of as specifically human can be causally related to hunting. They tell us that hunting is a whole pattern of activity and way of life: "The biology, psychology, and customs that separate us from the apes—all these we owe to the hunters of time past" (1968:303). If this line of reasoning is followed to its logical conclusion, one must agree with Jane Kephart when she says:

> Since only males hunt, and the psychology of the species was set by hunting, we are forced to conclude that females are scarcely human, that is, do not have built-in the basic psychology of the species: to kill and hunt and ultimately to kill others of the same species. The argument implies built-in aggression in human males, as well as the assumed passivity of human females and their exclusion from the mainstream of human development. (1970:5)

To support their argument that hunting is important to human males, Washburn and Lancaster point to the fact that many modern males still hunt, though it is no longer economically necessary. I could point out that many modern males play golf, play the violin, or tend gardens: these, as well as hunting, are things their culture teaches them. Using a "survival" as evidence to demonstrate an important fact of cultural evolution can be accorded no more validity when proposed by a modern anthropologist than when proposed by Tylor.

Regardless of its status as a survival, hunting, by implication as well as direct statement, is

---

[4] To some it seemed curious that anthropology should be accused of male bias. After all, several key early figures in anthropology had been women, and the best known anthropologist in America in the 1960s was Margaret Mead. However, statistically, anthropology was overwhelmingly dominated by men. Moreover, the institutions anthropologists frequently considered most worthy of study were those controlled by males.

[5] The feminist critique of the specific language used by anthropologists was particularly powerful because it referenced the Sapir-Whorf hypothesis that language shaped worldview, an idea that had been common since the 1930s and one to which most American anthropologists subscribed to one degree or another.

The idea of primitive "man" and "man" the hunter was a particularly apt target. Washburn and Lancaster had theorized that hunting was the most critical activity for early humans and that the most important human adaptations, bipedalism and language, arose as a result of it. This idea found its way into popular culture (where it is still common today). However, research in the 1960s had shown that male hunting played a relatively small role in supplying the nutritional needs of modern hunter-gatherers.

pictured as a male activity to the exclusion of females. This activity, on which we are told depends the psychology, biology, and customs of our species, is strictly male. A theory that leaves out half the human species is unbalanced. The theory of Man the Hunter is not only unbalanced; it leads to the conclusion that the basic human adaptation was the desire of males to hunt and kill.[6] This not only gives too much importance to aggression, which is after all only one factor of human life, but it derives culture from killing. I am going to suggest a less biased reading of the evidence, which gives a more valid and logical picture of human evolution, and at the same time a more hopeful one. First I will note the evidence, discuss the more traditional reading of it, and then offer an alternative reconstruction.

The data we have to work from are a combination of fossil and archaeological materials, knowledge of living nonhuman primates, and knowledge of living humans. Since we assume that the protohominid ancestors of Homo sapiens developed in a continuous fashion from a base of characteristics similar to those of living nonhuman primates, the most important facts seem to be the ways in which humans differ from nonhuman primates, and the ways in which we are similar. The differences are as follows: longer gestation period; more difficult birth; neoteny, in that human infants are less well developed at birth; long period of infant dependency; absence of body hair; year-round sexual receptivity of females, resulting in the possibility of bearing a second infant while the first is still at the breast or still dependent; erect bipedalism; possession of a large and complex brain that makes possible the creation of elaborate symbolic systems, languages, and cultures, and also results in most behavior being under cortical control; food sharing; and finally, living in families. (For the purposes of this paper I define families as follows: a situation where each individual has defined responsibilities and obligations to a specific set of others of both sexes and various ages. I use this definition because, among humans, the family is a *social* unit, regardless of any biological or genetic relationship which may or may not exist among its members.)

In addition to the many well-known close physiological resemblances, we share with nonhuman primates the following characteristics: living in social groups; close mother-infant bonds; affectional relationships; a large capacity for learning and a related paucity of innate behaviors; ability to take part in dominance hierarchies; a rather complex nonsymbolic communication system which can handle with considerable subtlety such information as the mood and emotional state of the individual, and the attitude and status of each individual toward the other members of the social group.[7]

The fossil and archaeological evidence consists of various bones labeled Ramapithecus, Australopithecus, Homo habilis, Homo erectus, etc.; and artifacts such as stone tools representing various

---

[6] In addition to Washburn and Lancaster, popular theory in ethology and evolution in the 1960s gave a very important place to aggression. Ethologist Konrad Lorenz's *On Aggression* (1966) and author Robert Ardrey's *African Genesis* (1961) were popular works that promoted this viewpoint. These works argued for the primacy of hunting and aggression in the evolutionary formation of humanity and more or less ignored the role played by women.

It is interesting to note that most of the primate ethology of the 1960s, particularly that on which Ardrey's popular works were based, was fundamentally flawed. It was derived largely from the work of Sir Solly Zuckerman (1904–1993) and Raymond Dart (1893–1988). Zuckerman drew his conclusions from watching an artificially assembled colony of hamadryas baboons in the London zoo in the 1920s. However, the behavior of these animals in the wild is very different from that of the London zoo colony. Dart, an anatomy professor and fossil hunter, on the basis of minimal evidence, proposed that early hominids had a murderous culture based on bone and wooden weaponry.

[7] Part of Slocum's argument comes from redefining differences between humans and nonhuman primates. In traditional anthropology and popular culture, the key differences between the two were brain size and language. She presents this image below. By 1970 it became clear that anatomical features such as bipedalism preceded language and increases in brain size, and thus were more important in differentiating between hominids and other primates. Notice that the first factors mentioned by Slocum in the previous paragraph all concern women exclusively. She places brain size and language well down the list.

cultural traditions, evidence of use of fire, etc. From this evidence we can make reasonable inferences about diet, posture and locomotion, and changes in the brain as shown by increased cranial capacity, ability to make tools, and other evidences of cultural creation. Since we assume that complexity of material culture requires language, we infer the beginnings of language somewhere between Australopithecus and Homo erectus.

Given this data, the speculative reconstruction begins. As I was taught anthropology, the story goes something like this. Obscure selection pressures pushed the protohominid in the direction of erect bipedalism—perhaps the advantages of freeing the hands for food carrying or for tool use. Freeing the hands allowed more manipulation of the environment in the direction of tools for gathering and hunting food. Through a hand-eye-brain feedback process, coordination, efficiency, and skill were increased. The new behavior was adaptive, and selection pressure pushed the protohominid further along the same lines of development. Diet changed as the increase in skill allowed the addition of more animal protein. Larger brains were selected for, making possible transmission of information concerned with tool making, and organizing cooperative hunting. It is assumed that as increased brain size was selected for, so also was neoteny—immaturity of infants at birth with a corresponding increase in their period of dependency, allowing more time for learning at the same time as this learning became necessary through the further reduction of instinctual behaviors and their replacement by symbolically invented ones.[8]

Here is where one may discover a large logical gap. From the difficult-to-explain beginning trends toward neoteny and increased brain size, the story jumps to Man the Hunter. The statement is made that the females were more burdened with dependent infants and could not follow the rigorous hunt. Therefore they stayed at a "home base," gathering what food they could, while the males developed cooperative hunting techniques, increased their communicative and organizational skills through hunting and brought the meat back to the dependent females and young. Incest prohibitions, marriage, and the family (so the story goes) grew out of the need to eliminate competition between males for females. A pattern developed of a male hunter becoming the main support of "his" dependent females and young (in other words, the development of the nuclear family for no apparent reason). Thus the peculiarly human social and emotional bonds can be traced to the hunter bringing back the food to share. Hunting, according to Washburn and Lancaster, involved "cooperation among males, planning, knowledge of many species and large areas, and technical skill" (1968:296). They even profess to discover the beginnings of art in the weapons of the hunter. They point out that the symmetrical Acheulian biface tools are the earliest beautiful man-made objects. Though we don't know what these tools were used for, they argue somewhat tautologically

---

[8] Despite the popular interest in the social and behavioral aspects of early humans, physical anthropology was, at the time this article was written, relatively unconcerned with it. Most physical anthropologists focused on recovering and identifying fossils. Although the version of evolution Slocum describes here was taught and generally accepted when she was writing, it was an area that had been relatively unstudied. Research since the 1970s has all but completely discredited this version of human evolution.

Slocum here is intentionally drawing a caricature of Washburn and Lancaster's position, presenting a version that can easily be demolished. Note the polemic tone of her writing. She both describes and ridicules Washburn and Lancaster's theory by using such phrases as "so the story goes" or "poor dependent females." Slocum's use of polemic language was, presumably, intentional. However, some of those she is critiquing, perhaps unintentionally, used language that seems equally polemic, which reinforces her point about bias in the literature. An example of this is an essay by Robin Fox that describes a theory by Chance, another researcher. According to Fox, Chance shows that "the whole process of enlarging the neo-cortex to take-off point was based on a competition between the dominant and sub-dominant males" (1972:373). Fox criticized Chance's view but was wildly condescending. In pointing out problems with the theory, he noted that it "would apply only to the male neo-cortex, and much as we may be mystified at the use made of this organ by the female of the species, she undoubtedly possesses it" (1972:373).

that the symmetry indicates they may have been swung, because symmetry only makes a difference when irregularities might lead to deviations in the line of flight. "It may well be that it was the attempt to produce efficient high-speed weapons that first produced beautiful, symmetrical objects" (1968:298).

So, while the males were out hunting, developing all their skills, learning to cooperate, inventing language, inventing art, creating tools and weapons, the poor dependent females were sitting back at the home base having one child after another (many of them dying in the process), and waiting for the males to bring home the bacon. While this reconstruction is certainly ingenious, it gives one the decided impression that only half the species—the male half—did any evolving. In addition to containing a number of logical gaps, the argument becomes somewhat doubtful in the light of modern knowledge of genetics and primate behavior.

The skills usually spoken of as being necessary to, or developed through, hunting are things like coordination, endurance, good vision, and the ability to plan, communicate, and cooperate. I have heard of no evidence to indicate that these skills are either carried on the Y chromosome, or are triggered into existence by the influence of the Y chromosome. In fact, on just about any test we can design (psychological, aptitude, intelligence, etc.) males and females score just about the same. The variation is on an individual, not a sex, basis.

Every human individual gets half its genes from a male and half from a female; genes sort randomly. It is possible for a female to end up with all her genes from male ancestors, and for a male to end up with all his genes from female ancestors. The logic of the hunting argument would have us believe that all the selection pressure was on the males, leaving the females simply as drags on the species. The rapid increase in brain size and complexity was thus due entirely to half the species; the main function of the female half was to suffer and die in the attempt to give birth to their large-brained male infants. An unbiased reading of the evidence indicates there was selection pressure on both sexes, and that hunting was not in fact the basic adaptation of the species from which flowed all the traits we think of as specifically human. Hunting does not deserve the primary place it has been given in the reconstruction of human evolution, as I will demonstrate by offering the following alternate version.

Picture the primate band: each individual gathers its own food, and the major enduring relationship is the mother-infant bond.[9] It is in similar circumstances that we imagine the evolving protohominids. We don't know what started them in the direction of neoteny and increased brain size, but once begun the trends would prove adaptive. To explain the shift from the primate individual gathering to human food sharing, we cannot simply jump to hunting. Hunting cannot explain its own origin. It is much more logical to assume that as the period of infant dependency began to lengthen, *the mothers would begin to increase the scope of their gathering to provide food for their still-dependent infants.* The

---

[9] The picture of the primate band that Slocum draws here is much closer to that held by current physical anthropologists than the version she presented and ridiculed above. It was, however, only one of several feminist versions of human evolution offered in the early 1970s. The version that was probably most popular with nonprofessionals at that time was the aquatic hypothesis. This view was presented by Elaine Morgan in her 1972 book *The Descent of Woman.* Like Ardrey (who was originally a playwright), Morgan was a writer rather than an anthropologist, and her book was aimed at a popular rather than a professional audience.

Morgan argued that the fundamental human characteristics of bipedalism, language, and tool use resulted from adaptation to living in coastal environments and that the crucial evolutionary pressures were on females rather than males. Morgan's original work was polemic in tone. She published a more technical version of it called *The Aquatic Ape* in 1982. The aquatic hypothesis enjoyed great popularity among feminists and some cultural anthropologists, but it has been rejected by physical anthropologists as incompatible with the fossil evidence.

Unlike Morgan or Ardrey, Slocum is a physical anthropologist; she did her doctoral work on rhesus monkeys. Thus, her argument comes from within physical anthropology and demonstrates a much greater technical command of the field than Morgan's or Ardrey's work. Despite her background, the essay is aimed at an audience of cultural rather than physical anthropologists.

already strong primate mother-infant bond would begin to extend over a longer time period, increasing the depth and scope of social relationships, and giving rise to the first sharing of food.

It is an example of male bias to picture these females with young as totally or even mainly dependent on males for food. Among modern hunter-gatherers, even in the marginal environments where most live, the females can usually gather enough to support themselves and their families. In these groups gathering provides the major portion of the diet, and there is no reason to assume that this was not also the case in the Pliocene or early Pleistocene. In the modern groups women and children both gather and hunt small animals, though they usually do not go on the longer hunts. So, we can assume a group of evolving protohominids, gathering and perhaps beginning to hunt small animals, with the mothers gathering quite efficiently both for themselves and for their offspring.

It is equally biased, and quite unreasonable, to assume an early or rapid development of a pattern in which one male was responsible for "his" females(s) and young. In most primate groups when a female comes into estrus she initiates coitus or signals her readiness by presenting. The idea that a male would have much voice in "choosing" a female, or maintain any sort of individual, long-term control over her or her offspring, is surely a modern invention which could have had no place in early hominid life. (Sexual control over females through rape or the threat of rape seems to be a modern human invention. Primate females are not raped because they are willing throughout estrus, and primate males appear not to attempt coitus at other times, regardless of physiological ability.) In fact, there seems to me no reason for suggesting the development of male-female adult pair-bonding until much later. Long-term monogamy is a fairly rare pattern even among modern humans—I think it is a

peculiarly Western male bias to suppose its existence in protohuman society. An argument has been made (by Morris, 1967, and others) that traces the development of male-female pair-bonding to the shift of sexual characteristics to the front of the body, the importance of the face in communication, and the development of face-to-face coitus. This argument is insufficient in the first place because of the assumption that face-to-face coitus is the "normal," "natural," or even the most common position among humans (historical evidence casts grave doubt on this assumption). It is much more probable that the coitus position was invented *after* pair-bonding had developed for other reasons.

Rather than adult male-female sexual pairs, a temporary consort-type relationship is much more logical in hominid evolution. It is even a more accurate description of the modern human pattern: the most dominant males (chief, headman, brave warrior, good hunter, etc.), mate with the most dominant females (in estrus, young and beautiful, fertile, rich, etc.), for varying periods of time. Changing sexual partners is frequent and common. We have no way of knowing when females began to be fertile year-round, but this change is not a necessary condition for the development of families. We need not bring in any notion of paternity, or the development of male-female pairs, or any sort of marriage in order to account for either families or food sharing.

The lengthening period of infant dependency would have strengthened and deepened the mother-infant bond; the earliest families would have consisted of *females and their children*. In such groups, over time, the sibling bond would have increased in importance also. The most universal, and presumably oldest, form of incest prohibition is between mother and son.[10] There are indications of such avoidance even among modern monkeys. It could develop logically from the mother-children family: as the

---

[10] Here, in passing, Slocum makes a stab at the origins of the incest taboo, one of the oldest problems in anthropology and one that is still not solved to general satisfaction. In fact, her case here is very weak, since females do not have to be fertile to have sex. However, just as theorists

such as Washburn tried to link the evolution of an enormous number of traits to male hunting, Slocum tries to link a wide range of characteristics to particular aspects of female-led evolution.

period of infant dependency lengthened, and the age of sexual maturity advanced, a mother might no longer be capable of childbearing when her son reached maturity. Another factor which may have operated is the situation found in many primates today where only the most dominant males have access to fertile females. Thus a young son, even after reaching sexual maturity, would still have to spend time working his way up the male hierarchy before gaining access to females. The length of time it would take him increases the possibility that his mother would no longer be fertile.

Food sharing and the family developed from the mother-infant bond. The techniques of hunting large animals were probably much later developments, after the mother-children family pattern was established. When hunting did begin, and the adult males brought back food to share, the most likely recipients would be first their mothers, and second their siblings. In other words, a hunter would share food *not* with a wife or sexual partner, but with those who had shared food with him: his mother and siblings.

It is frequently suggested or implied that the first tools were, in fact, the weapons of the hunters.[11] Modern humans have become so accustomed to the thought of tools and weapons that it is easy for us to imagine the first manlike creature who picked up a stone or club. However, since we don't really know what the early stone tools such as hand-axes were used for, it is equally probable that they were not weapons at all, but rather *aids in gathering.* We know that gathering was important long before much animal protein was added to the diet, and continued to be important. Bones, sticks, and hand-axes could be used for digging up tubers or roots, or to pulverize tough vegetable matter for easier eating. If, however, instead of thinking in terms of

tools and weapons, we think in terms of *cultural inventions,* a new aspect is presented. I suggest that two of the *earliest and most important* cultural inventions were containers to hold the products of gathering, and some sort of sling or net to carry babies.[12] The latter in particular must have been extremely important with the loss of body hair and the increasing immaturity of neonates, who could not cling and had less and less to cling to. Plenty of material was available—vines, hides, human hair. If the infant could be securely fastened to the mother's body, she could go about her tasks much more efficiently. Once a technique for carrying babies was developed, it could be extended to the idea of carrying food, and eventually to other sorts of cultural inventions—choppers and grinders for food preparation, and even weapons. Among modern hunter-gatherers, regardless of the poverty of their material culture, food carriers and baby carriers are always important items in their equipment.

A major point in the Man the Hunter argument is that cooperative hunting among males demanded more skill in social organization and communication, and thus provided selection pressure for increased brain size. I suggest that longer periods of infant dependency, more difficult births, and longer gestation periods also demanded more skills in social organization and communication—creating selective pressure for increased brain size without looking to hunting as an explanation. The need to organize for feeding after weaning, learning to handle the more complex social-emotional bonds that were developing, the new skills and cultural inventions surrounding more extensive gathering—all would demand larger brains. Too much attention has been given to the skills required by hunting, and too little to the skills required for gathering and the raising of dependent young. The techniques

---

[11] As Slocum attacked male bias in beliefs about evolution, she took on many commonly accepted themes in popular culture. The idea that early tools were offensive weapons came from Dart's work. Compare her analysis here to the story presented in Stanley Kubrick's *2001: A Space Odyssey,* an extremely popular film that appeared in the late 1960s. The opening scenes of the film show the discovery of tools: one apeman picks up a large bone, stares at it, and then uses it to beat a companion over the head.

[12] Here and later Slocum is engaging in pure speculation. Like the sociobiologists, she is arguing by analogy to modern hunting-gathering bands, using them as "living fossils"—a method that hearkens back to the nineteenth century.

required for efficient gathering include location and identification of plant varieties, seasonal and geographical knowledge, containers for carrying the food, and tools for its preparation. Among modern hunting-gathering groups this knowledge is an extremely complex, well-developed, and important part of their cultural equipment. Caring for a curious, energetic, but still dependent human infant is difficult and demanding. Not only must the infant be watched, it must be taught the customs, dangers, and knowledge of its group. For the early hominids, as their cultural equipment and symbolic communication increased, the job of training the young would demand more skill. Selection pressure for better brains came from many directions.

Much has been made of the argument that cooperation among males demanded by hunting acted as a force to reduce competition for females. I suggest that competition for females has been greatly exaggerated.[13] It could easily have been handled in the usual way for primates—according to male status relationships already worked out—and need not be pictured as particularly violent or extreme. The seeds of male cooperation already exist in primates when they act to protect the band from predators. Such dangers may well have increased with a shift to savannah living, and the longer dependency of infants. If biological roots are sought to explain the greater aggressiveness of males, it would be more fruitful to look toward their function as protectors, rather than any supposedly basic hunting adaptation. The only division of labor that regularly exists in primate groups is the females caring for infants and the males protecting the group from predators. The possibilities for both cooperation and aggression in males lies in this protective function.

The emphasis on hunting as a prime moving factor in hominid evolution distorts the data. It is simply too big a jump to go from the primate individual gathering pattern to a hominid cooperative hunting-sharing pattern without some intervening changes. Cooperative hunting of big game animals could only have developed *after* the trends toward neoteny and increased brain size had begun. Big-game hunting becomes a more logical development when it is viewed as growing out of a complex of changes which included sharing the products of gathering among mothers and children, deepening social bonds over time, increase in brain size, and the beginnings of cultural invention for purposes such as baby carrying, food carrying, and food preparation. Such hunting not only needed the prior development of some skills in social organization and communication, it probably also had to await the development of the "home base." It is difficult to imagine that most or all of the adult primate males in a group would go off on a hunting expedition, leaving the females and young exposed to the danger of predators, without some way of communicating to arrange for their defense, or at least a way of saying, "Don't worry, we'll be back in two days." Until that degree of communicative skill developed, we must assume either that the whole band traveled *and hunted* together, or that the males simply did not go off on large cooperative hunts.

The development of cooperative hunting requires, as a prior condition, an increase in brain size. Once such a trend is established, hunting skills would take part in a feedback process of selection for better brains just as would other cultural inventions and developments such as gathering skills. By itself, hunting fails to explain any part of human evolution and fails to explain itself.

Anthropology has always rested on the assumption that the mark of our species is our ability to *symbol*, to bring into existence forms of behavior and interaction, and material tools with which to adjust and control the environment. To explain human nature as evolving from the desire of males to hunt and kill is to negate most of

---

[13] Early theories about protohuman social organization tended to emphasize violent competition among males for essentially passive females. The popular image is of the caveman dragging the cavewoman off by the hair. More modern theory, however, tends to emphasize the role of females in sexual selection, diminishing the importance of male aggression.

anthropology.[14] Our species survived and adapted through the invention of *culture,* of which hunting is simply a part. It is often stated that hunting *must* be viewed as the "natural" species' adaptation because it lasted as long as it did, nine-tenths of all human history. However:

> Man the Hunter lasted as long as "he" did from no natural propensity toward hunting any more than toward computer programming or violin playing or nuclear warfare, but because that was what the historical circumstances allowed. We ignore the first premise of our science if we fail to admit that "man" is no more natural a hunter than "he" is naturally a golfer, for after symboling became possible our species left forever the ecological niche of the necessity of any one adaptation, and made all adaptations possible for ourselves. (Kephart, 1970:23)

That the concept of Man the Hunter influenced anthropology for as long as it did is a reflection of male bias in the discipline. This bias can be seen in the tendency to equate "man," "human," and "male"; to look at culture almost entirely from a male point of view; to search for examples of the behavior of males and assume that this is sufficient for explanation, ignoring almost totally the female half of the species; and to filter this male bias through the "ideal" modern Western pattern of one male supporting a dependent wife and minor children.[15]

The basis of any discipline is not the answers it gets, but the questions it asks. As an exercise in the anthropology of knowledge, this paper stems from asking a simple question: what were the females doing while the males were out hunting? It was only possible for me to ask this question after I had become politically conscious of myself as a woman. Such is the prestige of males in our society that a woman, in anthropology or any other profession, can only gain respect or be attended to if she deals with questions deemed important by men. Though there have been women anthropologists for years, it is rare to be able to discern any difference between their work and that of male anthropologists. Learning to be an anthropologist has involved learning to think from a male perspective, so it should not be surprising that women have asked the same kinds of questions as men. But political consciousness, whether among women, blacks, American Indians, or any other group, leads to reexamination and reevaluation of taken-for-granted assumptions. It is a difficult process, challenging the conventional wisdom, and this paper is simply a beginning. The male bias in anthropology that I have illustrated here is just as real as the white bias, the middle-class bias, and the academic bias that exist in the discipline. It is our task, as anthropologists, to create a "study of the human species" in spite of, or perhaps because of, or maybe even by means of, our individual biases and unique perspectives.[16]

REFERENCES

Berger, Peter, and T. Luckmann. 1967. *The Social Construction of Reality.* Garden City, N.Y.: Doubleday Anchor.

Current Anthropology. 1968. Social Responsibilities Symposium. Reprint from December 1968 issue.

---

[14] As you read these passages, recall again that this essay first appeared in 1971, close to the height of the movement protesting the Vietnam War. Slocum's suggestion that the hunting hypothesis negates most anthropology seems rash, but the idea that humans did not innately desire to kill was extremely popular in this era and, whether it followed logically or not, increased the emotional appeal of Slocum's argument.

[15] Slocum's suggestion that, even within anthropology, there was a tendency to equate man and human was certainly no exaggeration. Consider C. F. Hockett's 1973 anthropology text called *Man's Place in Nature,* with chapters titled "Man the Tinkerer," "Man the Chatterer," "Man the Worshiper," "Man the Owner," and so on.

[16] Notice the layering of political change, personal change, and theoretical perspective in this final paragraph. Slocum's perception that a change in her political consciousness caused a change in her theoretical position prefigures postmodern anthropology. Compare it to some of Renato Rosaldo's insights in essay 38 in this volume. However, Slocum is certainly no postmodernist, and feminist writers of this era did not make the leap to extreme relativism that characterizes some postmodern writing.

Garfinkel, Harold. 1960. "The Rational Properties of Scientific and Common Sense Activities." *Behavioral Science* 5, no. 1:72–83.

Kephart, Jane. 1970. "Primitive Woman as Nigger, or, The Origin of the Human Family as Viewed Through the Role of Women." M.A. Dissertation, University of Maryland.

Morris, Desmond. 1967. *The Naked Ape.* New York: McGraw-Hill.

Washburn, Sherwood, and Lancaster, C. 1968. "The Evolution of Hunting." In *Man the Hunter* edited by R. B. Lee and Irven DeVore. Chicago: Aldine.

---

33. *Interpreting the Origins of Gender Inequality: Conceptual and Historical Problems*

Eleanor Leacock (1922–1987)

For some time I have argued that the analysis of women's oppression and its origins calls for clarification along two lines, historical and conceptual.*[1] The historical dimension requires that the myth of the "ethnographic present" be totally eradicated, and that anthropologists deal fully with the fact that the structure of gender relations among the people they study does not follow from pre-capitalist production relations as such, but from the ways in which these have been affected by particular histories of colonization. The conceptual dimension requires a complete break with the tendency to interpret all cultures in terms of categories derived from capitalist society. Such categories distort the structure of primitive communist relations and thereby obscure the sources of hierarchy. Equally critical, as consistently pointed out by feminist scholars, is the need to root out the pervasive assumption that women are not actors on the scene of human history to the same degree as are men. There is still a widespread failure to recognize that correcting the anthropological distortion of women's roles in society has profound implications for the interpretation of social structure generally. In particular, the fact that the French Marxists have not launched a thorough-going criticism of Lévi-Strauss' assumption that the exchange of women by men inaugurated human society has served to weaken their analyses of pre-capitalist production modes.[2]

(1983)

---

[1] Leacock's original essay contained ninety-six notes. Space limitations prevent us from reproducing them here, but asterisks have been included to show where they were placed.

[2] Leacock's feminist Marxist perspective is immediately apparent in this opening paragraph. Here she touches on a number of issues that were central to feminists and Marxists in the late 1970s and early 1980s. These included a critique of the notion of the ethnographic present (see note 4) as well as a declaration that not only are women of equal importance to men in society but also relationships between men and women are fundamental elements that pattern society.

The notion of primitive communism is very important in this essay. Marx and Engels proposed that early societies were communistic. This idea was given force by Lewis Henry Morgan's description of early societies as having communistic living arrangements and possessing liberty and equality (1871, 1877). These descriptions provided data for Marx and Engels.

In the last sentence of the paragraph, Leacock refers to Lévi-Strauss' work *The Elementary Structures of Kinship,* in which he argues that the fact that women are commodities exchanged by men is one of the fundamental patterning elements of society. You can find a more thorough discussion of Lévi-Strauss' theory in the introduction to the "Structuralism" section in this book. Lévi-Strauss had a critical impact on the development of Marxist thought because many leading French Marxists of the 1960s and 1970s were his students.

ANTHROPOLOGY AND HISTORY

The importance of paying constant attention to history was impressed upon me as a graduate student at Columbia University when I was fortunate enough to take part in Wm. Duncan Strong's seminar on "Time Perspective and the Plains." Strong drew on archaeology and ethnohistory to demonstrate that "typical" Plains culture, as then conceived, was not aboriginal, but had developed in the 18th century when formerly diverse tribes, some agricultural, some hunting-gathering, took advantage of the horse and either moved out onto, or spent more of the year on the prairies. I would add that a greatly expanded market for buffalo hides plus land pressure resulting from European intrusion to the east and south were also important reasons for the move out onto the plains. In a fairly short time, social, ritual, and material traits were borrowed, developed, and/or elaborated upon by different peoples who integrated them into a relatively uniform culture.[3]

Strong's ethnohistorical orientation influenced a number of dissertations, some on Plains peoples,* and some on other areas.* Subsequently, extensive studies of native American social-economic organization and land use were undertaken in connection with the Indian Claims actions initiated in the 1950s.* This work revealed a fact of major significance for understanding the unstratified societies that existed in most of what was to become the United States: bands, villages, and towns were only loosely grouped into what are called tribes; politically, however, they functioned as fully autonomous units. The point was made explicit by Kroeber,* and it has been elaborated upon by Fried in his critique of the concept "tribe."* Kroeber wrote:

> The more we review aboriginal America, the less certain does any consistently recurring

phenomenon become that matches our usual conventional concept of tribe; and the more largely does this concept appear to be a White man's creation of convenience for talking about Indians, negotiation with them, administering them . . . It was infinitely more convenient and practicable for us to deal with representatives of one large group than with these of ten, twenty, or thirty tiny and shifting ones whose very names and precise habitat often were not known. This was equally so whether treaties were being negotiated for trade, traverse, settlement or resettlement, land cession, peace, subsidy or rationing, administration on a reservation, or abrogating and opening up a reservation. Generally we treated the nationality-"tribes" as if they were sovereign state-tribes, and by sheer pressure of greater strength forced the Indians to submit to our classification of them.*

Kroeber's point that tribes as commonly defined were a product of colonization requires the qualification that tribal organization and leadership were not only imposed from without. They also arose among native Americans as necessary for resisting white invasion. Such warfare as had existed in pre-colonial times usually took the form of petty raiding by young men (and such women as occasionally chose to participate) who tested their mettle in a coup-counting system that deemed it more prestigious to touch enemies than kill them. When warfare for survival became necessary, strong leaders emerged to unite one or more tribes and meet the need.

In any case, Kroeber wrote that the "larger nationalities," i.e., the culturally affiliated groups known as tribes, were "ethnic" but "non-political" in the sense that they held no power over their constituents. It was the "smaller units, whether they be called villages, bands, towns, tribelets, lineages, or something else . . . that were independent,

---

[3] The archaeologist William Duncan Strong (1899–1962) was a student of A. L. Kroeber and a classmate of Julian Steward. Strong was a major influence on Leacock during her years at Columbia. He conducted extensive research in the western United States, in Labrador, and with his student, Gordon R. Wiley (1913–2002) in Peru. Although not a Marxist, Strong emphasized the role of history in anthropology and critiqued both evolutionism without adequate his- torical research and functionalist approaches that ignored history, such as those of A. R. Radcliffe-Brown (Solecki and Wagley 1963). After Strong's death, Leacock edited the journals he kept during his fieldwork among the Naskapi Indi- ans. Although she began this project in the early 1960s, the resulting book, *Labrador Winter: The Ethnographic Journals of William Duncan Strong, 1927–1928,* was not published until 1994, seven years after her death.

sovereign, and held and used a territory."* However, these smaller units should not be considered miniature tribes in the sense of stable, bonded groups subject to the authority of a chief and/or council. Such a formulation violates the reality of communally organized societies, in which movement among groups was easy and frequent; rights to lands were not viewed as exclusive; decisions about individual activities were made by those who would carry them out; and decisions about group activities, arrived at through consensus, did not bind those who did not agree.* Such a formulation also distorts the working structure of relations among bands and villages and the complex social and ceremonial forms that affirmed cooperation and friendship or ritualized and contained potential animosity.

Kroeber's and Fried's discussions of changing political forms demonstrate how unjustifiable it is to consider the cultures that have been reconstructed from the memories of late 19th and early 20th century elders as "traditional" in the sense of pre-Columbian. To do so is to gloss over the active participation of native Americans in almost 500 years of post-colonial history. It is to present them as cardboard figures, living according to a congeries of "culture traits" within "culture areas," traits that did not change but were "lost" through "acculturation."*[4]

GENDER IN NATIVE NORTH AMERICA

With regard to the position of women, it is equally unjustifiable to make generalizations about one or another Indian culture without consideration of the historical dimension. During the colonial period, male authority was being encouraged by Euro-Americans in their political and military dealings with native Americans at the same time as Indian women were becoming dependent in individual households on wage-earning and trading husbands. For example, after documenting the full social equality of Cherokee women revealed by colonial accounts, Reid, an historian of law, wrote:

> The decline of hunting and the adoption of American ways during the nineteenth century, with the substitution of factory-made for homemade goods . . . freed the Cherokee woman from outdoor labor, placing her in the kitchen and her husband in the fields, but it also deprived her of economic independence, making her politically and legally more like her white sisters.*

A second example of changes in women's position following the colonization of native North America is afforded by the contrast between Lafitau and Morgan on the Iroquois.[5] In his 18th century account, Lafitau stated that Iroquois and/or Huron women were "the souls of the

---

[4] Throughout this section, Leacock shows her concern with the historical background of Native America and attacks the notion of the ethnographic present. Through the first half of the twentieth century, most ethnographies did not pay any particular attention to history. Societies were described either in their current state or as they were remembered by their elder members. For the purposes of their writing, many anthropologists assumed that the societies they studied were relatively isolated from external forces of change, and internally driven change was extremely slow. Thus, notions of history were largely irrelevant to ethnography. Additionally, two prominent schools of thought in the 1960s and 1970s were structuralism and ethnoscience (or new ethnography). Members of these schools focused on what they believed to be the fundamental ways in which members of a society understood their world. They held that the effects of history on such understandings were of little importance. Marxism, on the other hand, is fundamentally concerned with history: Marxists see societies developing as their internal con-

traditions are worked out. Thus, a feminist Marxist approach must be vitally concerned with showing the importance of history for understanding the position of women in society.

[5] In this section Leacock begins to build the case that the gender relations reported in most twentieth-century ethnographies are the result of contact with Europeans rather than structural elements of non-European society. Some of the important names Leacock mentions in this section are the Wyandot, Powell, and Lafitau. The Wyandot are better known as the Huron. Powell refers to John Wesley Powell (1834–1902), the founder of the Bureau of American Ethnology. Additional information on Powell can be found in the introduction to "Historical Particularism." Joseph-Francois Lafitau (1681–1746), author of *American Savages Compared with Those of Earliest Times* (1724), was a Jesuit missionary who worked among the Iroquois from 1711 to 1717. He wrote on Iroquois kinship systems one hundred years before Morgan.

Councils, the arbiters of peace and war," in whom "all real authority is vested."* In Morgan's 19th century description, despite reference to women's decision-making powers in Iroquois households, he wrote that Iroquois men considered women as "inferior, the dependent, and the servant of men," and that a woman, "from nurture and habit, . . . actually considered herself to be so."* Although the flatness of the latter statement can well be questioned, it was written at the time when Iroquois women had lost their role as major producers and the control over the products of their labor that had insured them personal autonomy and public authority. Their situation was no longer that of 1791, when elder Seneca women informed Colonel Proctor, an envoy from George Washington,

> you ought to hear and listen to what we, women, shall speak, as well as to the sachems; for we are the owners of this land—and it is ours. It is we that plant it for our and their use. Hear us, therefore, for we speak of things that concern us while our men shall say more to you; for we have told them.*

The changing relationship between women's economic role and their decision-making powers among the Iroquois and the Huron is further illuminated by a little known paper on the Wyandot by the early anthropologist Powell. Powell wrote:

> Cultivation is communal; that is, all of the able-bodied women of the gens take part in the cultivation of each household tract in the following manner:
> The head of the household sends her brother or son into the forest or to the stream to bring in game or fish for a feast; then the able-bodied women of the gens are invited to assist in the cultivation of the land, and when this work is done a feast is given.*

Powell stated that women were family heads among the Wyandot, and that four family heads, plus a man of their choosing, made up the clan council. The clan councils together made up the tribal council that was responsible for dividing Wyandot lands among the clans. The women councilors of each clan were in turn responsible for dividing it among the clan households, as well

as for matters such as giving personal names and discussing and consenting to marriages. Apparently the entire council, that is, including the male member, handled certain transgressions while others were brought before the tribal council. Warfare was the responsibility of the men; all "able-bodied men" made up what Powell called a "military council" headed by a "military chief." The fact that women were not members of these councils has led to a serious underestimation of their authority in societies organized, as many North American societies were, along lines roughly similar to the Wyandot Huron. First, accounts of military negotiations between the outsiders and "military councils" and "military chiefs" do not recognize the formal structure of women's power which can therefore be interpreted as indirect and "behind the scene."* Second, the imminence of conquest increased the responsibility and power of "military councils." Subsequent economic developments, along with policies such as the Dawes (General Allotment) Act of 1887 (designed to divide all Indian lands into family-owned plots), undercut the collective economic activities traditionally controlled by women. As among the Cherokee and the Iroquois, the egalitarian and reciprocal structure of decision-making among the Huron was destroyed.

CONCEPTUALIZING PRIMITIVE COMMUNISM AND ITS TRANSFORMATION

As the above discussion suggests, the egalitarian relations that obtained in most foraging and many horticultural societies around the world at the time of European expansion rested on the fact that all mature individuals participated directly in the full process of production. By "full process" I refer to Marx's concept of production, distribution, exchange, and consumption as "members of one entity, different aspects of one unit,"* as opposed to formulations that limit their emphasis to either work processes or the allocation of produce. The control that all individuals had over the conditions of their labor, over the skills as well as the resources necessary to perform it, and over the disposition and use of its products,

distinguishes egalitarian from hierarchically ordered structures.[6]

A Marxist conceptual baseline for analysing
egalitarian society, interpreted in these terms,
sharpens the fact that the transformation from
egalitarian to hierarchical relations was qualitative
and not merely quantitative. Such a view contrasts
with the common practice of describing egalitarian society in terms of the same features that characterize class society. In formulations of this type,
differential access to land and other resources,
hereditary authority, and social-economic hierarchies are treated as incipient—as weakly developed tendencies that only needed strengthening to
become predominant. Despite caveats to the contrary, history is thereby implied to be unilineal and
teleological, with Western society as its ultimate
purpose and measure. Alternatives for the future
are obscured by the implication that there was no
real alternative in the past.[7]

The widely held assumption that female subordination is a universal of human society derives
from, and in turn supports, the assumption that
primitive communal society was ultimately ordered by the same constraints and compulsions
that order class society.* Where institutionalized
hostility between the sexes exists, it is interpreted
as a variant of a universal battle between the
sexes, rather than as evidence of emerging status
differentiations among men and among women,
as well as between men and women. The critical

relationship between the development of ranking
and the attempt to subvert women's public and
autonomous status (such as in the so-called big
men societies of Melanesia) is seldom recognized. In sum, gender hierarchy is all too often
taken for granted, and both the structure of primitive communism and the basis for its transformation are thereby mystified.[8]

There is much talk of paradigms these days,
and much emphasis on process. Nonetheless,
cross-cultural analyses still rely heavily on states
or essences as categories, rather than processes or
relationships. The mid-century admission that the
regularities of social evolution as broadly outlined
by Engels and Morgan approximated historical reality, opened the way in anthropology for a dialectical analysis of human history in terms of basic
transformations in the ways people interrelated as
they reproduced themselves and their social structures. In particular, given the focus on relations
between individual and society that characterized
the personality and culture school, and its successors in psychological anthropology, the significance of Marx's sixth thesis on Feuerbach could
have been explored in terms of how individual behavior and societal processes interrelate.[9]

"The essence of man is no abstraction inherent
in each separate individual," Marx wrote. "In its reality it is the *ensemble* (aggregate) of social relations."* To Marx and Engels people did not have
an intrinsic nature apart from society, but neither

---

[6] In Marxist thought, there is a close link between production and power. Since social relations flow primarily from
relations of production, the greater the contribution of an individual to production, the greater that individual's power
should be. Leacock is arguing that her reading of the ethnography shows that women and men participated fully in production before their societies were profoundly affected by
Europeans. If they did so, then, from a Marxist viewpoint, it
would be a logical necessity that both men and women participated fully in political decision making as well.

[7] Although Leacock does not provide any references for
what she describes as a common practice—seeing egalitarian societies as incipient states—she is probably thinking of Morton Fried's *The Evolution of Political Society*
(1967). Fried's book was published several years before
this essay, and she cites it repeatedly later in the work.

[8] Many 1970s feminists understood female subordination as a human universal. Ortner, for example, says that

female subordination "exists within every type of social
and economic arrangement and in societies of every degree of complexity" (see essay 26). When a practice is universal, there is at least the strong suspicion that it is rooted
in human nature. However, for a Marxist, there can be no
such thing. Human nature is not fixed and universal, but
created in the process of production. Therefore, explanations that rely upon human nature cannot be sustained.
Leacock makes this point repeatedly in the next several
paragraphs.

[9] When Leacock refers to the midcentury admission that
Engels and Morgan were approximately correct, she is
probably thinking of Leslie White's work on cultural evolution and his editing of Morgan's work (see essay 18).
Marx's *Theses on Feuerbach* is a short work written in
1845. It was published as an appendix to Engels' *Ludwig
Feuerbach and the End of Classical German Philosophy*
(1949 [1888]). It consists of eleven brief points that, in

were they mere reflections of their society. In a number of oft-quoted passages, Marx and Engels stressed that "men make their own history,"* although the circumstances under which they do so are inherited from the past. Furthermore, the independent unfolding of social forces means that people's actions do not necessarily lead to the intended results. Instead the "simplest determinations," the relations of production, ways people relate to one another as they produce, distribute, exchange, and consume the necessities of life, set processes in motion that lie beyond the wills of the actors.* On the one hand, social structures are created by the behavior of individuals; "the social structure and the State are continually evolving out of the life-processes of definite individuals." On the other hand, however, these life-processes are themselves structured by production relations, as people "are effective, produce materially, and are active under definite material limits, presuppositions and conditions independent of their will."*[10]

Marxist dialectics, then, opened the way for examining the series of interlocking processes—the different levels of integration—that constitute human history. At the individual physiological level, human nature is not a given but a mix of potentials and propensities that are expressed differently under different conditions; at the societal level, social-historical processes are of an altogether different order; in between, mediating the two, at the individual psycho-social or behavioral level, the person operates as a nexus of social-economic relationships; and at the ideological level, people's perceptions of their relations to each other and to nature are patterned by traditional concepts, in part spontaneous and in part manipulated, and with a certain lawfulness of their own that arises from the nature of language as a symbol system.*

Such a line of thinking has been followed through only minimally. Instead, anthropology has been plagued by ever more radically reductionist and anti-historical formulations. In structuralist theory, and more recently in sociobiology, social determinants are defined in terms of behavioral outcomes and ultimately reduced to psychobiologically fixed entities. Whether these be such grotesque notions as Wilson's "conformer" and other behavior-specific genes, or Lévi-Strauss's more elegant, since undefined, deep structures, or Laughlin and d'Aquili's more scientifically couched, if less euphonious "neuroanatomical-neurophysiological relationships," their inventors all reduce human history and society to mere projections of individual biological propensities, with the environment the only independently interacting factor.*[11]

Marx's opinion, separated his own work from Feuerbach's. The sixth thesis, in its entirety, is

> Feuerbach resolves the religious essence into the human essence. But the human essence is no abstraction inherent in each single individual. In its reality it is the ensemble of the social relations. Feuerbach, who does not enter upon a criticism of this real essence, is consequently compelled: 1) To abstract from the historical process and to fix the religious sentiment as something by itself and to presuppose an abstract—isolated—human individual. 2) Essence, therefore, can be comprehended only as "genus," as an internal, dumb generality which naturally unites the many individuals.

In the following paragraph, Leacock explains the significance of Marx's point for her own argument.

[10] In this and the following paragraph, Leacock is describing a Marxist dialectic. She is saying that society is not simply a reflection of the structure of production (that is a position that Marxists call "vulgar materialism") but rather emerges from the relations of production and how people think about these relations.

[11] When this essay was written, French structuralism and sociobiology were extremely popular in the United States. In this paragraph, Leacock takes aim at both, particularly sociobiologist E. O. Wilson's *Sociobiology: The New Synthesis* (1975). (The introduction to Wilson's book is reprinted as essay 30.) Wilson's notion that genes were responsible for much of human nature was anathema to most anthropologists. Behind the notion of the "conformer gene" is the idea that hunting required a high degree of coordination and conformity. Laughlin (mentioned in this paragraph) called hunting the "master behavior pattern of the human species" (cited in Barash 1979:186). Thus, the tendency of humans to conform is genetically based—the result of the fact that, over the millennia, there was strong evolutionary pressure for conformity.

Leacock criticizes French structuralism as reductionist and antihistorical. For Lévi-Strauss, the underlying meaning of myths and other cultural phenomena involves a few universal themes such as resolving humans' relations to nature. The outward form of the stories and the historical circumstances that produced them have no meaning. This perspective is anathema to Leacock.

The result of ruling out a level of societal process entirely separate from individual propensities is like attempting to explain the movements of the solar system as flowing from the properties of the atomic particles (or processes) that make it up. To be sure, planetary movements are in a superficial sense the sum total of all movements of subatomic particles, just as social processes are in a trivial sense the sum total of individual behaviors. Scientifically, however, it would be absurd not to recognize that the lawful movements of planetary bodies have their own history of development, and operate at a level of integration independent from the internal processes that characterize their constituent parts. With respect to society, few would argue directly that social processes do not also operate at a level of their own. In effect, however, this is precisely what reductionist formulations imply.

Anthropologists have long been sensitive to biological reductionism with regard to physical variations of a racial order, and somewhat aware that reductionist formulations serve as ideological rationalizations of oppression. Unfortunately, this is not the case with respect to physical variations of a sexual order. Although the fact that physiological sex and social gender are far from isometric is well established and documented in anthropology, cross-cultural discussions of sex roles commonly fall into reductionism in their formulations.[12] Many Marxists, as well as other scholars, translate the gender structure of the hierarchical exploitative society with which they are familiar into innate predispositions and the practice is encouraged by the recent worldwide spread of Western norms, at least on a superficial level. The assumption remains prevalent that physiological differences between the sexes

embody hints of female subordination only slightly expressed in egalitarian cultures but that come to full flower in class-based state-organized urban societies. Instead of being treated as an historical development, hierarchy becomes written into human physiology. Despite much citation from Marx and Engels on the part of those who do this, they contradict a fully Marxist view of human nature as informed by the last hundred years of social science research. Their entanglement with male supremacist ideology feeds into and is fed by the failure to deal rigorously with both history and theory in the interpretation of primitive communist society and the source of its transformation.[13]

THE ORIGINS OF HIERARCHY

The two sets of relations defined by Marx and Engels as critical to the emergence of exploitation are: first, the loss of control over the production process (i.e., production, exchange, distribution, and consumption) through the division of labor beyond that by sex; and second, the emergence of dyadic relations[14] of dependency within individual families as a public/private dichotomy developed in economic and political life, making families separate economic units rather than parts of encompassing communal groups. The fundamental historical development analysed at length in Marx's opening section of *Capital* and central to Engels' reworking of Morgan's evolutionary hypothesis in *The Origin of the Family, Private Property and the State*, was the transformation from production for use to production for exchange. The emergence of production for exchange meant that value as an attribute of goods began to

---

[12] *Isometric:* of equal measure.

Here, Leacock says that although sex and gender are not equivalent, many scholars still believe that the physiological differences between men and women are the basis for gender inequality. One example of this type of work is Ortner's structural analysis in this volume (essay 26).

[13] In the paragraphs above, Leacock has condemned the sociobiologists and structuralists. Here she takes aim at unnamed Marxists who fail to fully apply Marxist analysis

to their subject because they accept the Western ideology of male supremacy. Neo-Marxist authors are well known for attacking one another's positions, and Leacock does not spare those who share her theoretical outlook.

[14] A dyadic relationship is one with two parts. Leacock argues here that the emergence of dyadic relations of dependency within individual families was a second factor explaining the origins of exploitation.

supersede use as the feature of primary social significance. As a consequence "abstract labor," the labor time represented in an exchangeable object, became separable from concrete work, a development that eventually made it possible for those who controlled exchange to regulate and exploit the productivity of others. Finally, money developed in various forms as a medium of exchange, as a pure commodity. Marx stressed that the money form allowed the fetishistic absurdity whereby relations among people appeared to them as relations among things; thus the structure of exploitation was mystified and the existence of class differences rationalized.[15]

In *The Evolution of Political Society,* Fried raised the question why people accepted control by others over the products of their work and allowed the loss of their independence.[16] Whatever the answer, Fried stated, people did not realize the magnitude of the changes they were bringing about.* To be sure, they did not, since, through exchange and the division of labor, people were simply enriching their lives and cementing interpersonal and intergroup bonds, innocent of the processes thereby set in motion. As Engels put it, "the more a social activity, a series of social processes . . . appears a matter of pure chance, then all the more surely within this chance the laws peculiar to it and inherent in it assert themselves." Commodity production and the division of labor that accompanied it slowly but inexorably led to class stratification; they raised up "incorporeal alien powers . . . too powerful for men's conscious control."*[17]

Simple barter does not separate the producer from control over exchange and distribution. As barter develops in importance, however, it leads to a contradiction between the material benefits to be derived from specialized production for trade and the structure of full egalitarianism. Fried suggested that the elaboration of redistribution was important to the emergence of ranking, the first form of stratification.* The focus should be sharpened and emphasis placed on the significance of redistribution for the emergence of commodity production with all its consequences. Goods produced for exchange rather than for use create new interest groups. For a long time, egalitarian relationships prevent persons in pivotal positions in networks of exchange and redistribution from exploiting the economic possibilities of their position. Nonetheless, the conflict between egalitarian relations sharpens and, in what are called ranking societies, people begin to accept dependent positions in relation to "big men" and other chiefly people in order to benefit from the handouts associated with them. Eventually, unequal appropriation among and within competitively structured lineages is institutionalized, and the conflict between egalitarian distribution and consumption on the one hand, and the potential

---

[15] In this paragraph, Leacock is trying to briefly recount Marx's theory of the origins of hierarchy. The first step is a movement from producing things simply to use them (for their "use value") to producing things as commodities that can be sold. Marx argues that this movement allows people in capitalist societies to think of the amount of labor that goes into the production of an object as equivalent to the value of that object. However, capitalist society makes a fetish of the commodity, valuing it over the labor that produced it. Marx's notion is sometimes referred to as the labor theory of value and is one of the most controversial aspects of his philosophy.

The Origin of the Family, Private Property, and the State (1972 [1884]) is a book that Engels wrote based on notes Marx had taken as he read Morgan's *Ancient Society* (1985 [1877]). Engels' analysis is based on Morgan's notion that families were originally matrilineal. He ties the historic shift from matrilineality to patrilineality to the emergence of private property. Leacock was very familiar with Engels' work. In fact, she wrote an introduction to the 1972 edition.

[16] In this section, Leacock leans heavily on the theory of stratification advanced by Morton Fried in *The Evolution of Political Society* (1967). The essay by Fried in this volume (essay 20), published seven years before his book, is a summary of the principal arguments he advanced there.

[17] In this section, "The Origins of Hierarchy," Leacock points out that social processes are qualitatively different from the actions of individuals. Here, individuals simply pursue their own benefit, but the net result is a social shift to hierarchy that results in their loss of independence. She argues that this same shift also results in the emergence of gender hierarchy.

afforded by exchange and increasing specialization of labor on the other, is partially resolved. New contradictions are already crystallizing, however, between the potentials created by increasingly farflung economic ties and social forms attuned to autonomous kin and village groupings, in turn to be resolved by full stratification and political organization and the familiar conflicts of class society.[18]

To return to the second component of exploitation and stratification, it is in conjunction with the above developments that a public/private dichotomy emerges and dyadic relations of dependence within families as economic units begin to take shape. Lévi-Strauss posits to the contrary, in egalitarian societies, women are not exchanged by men; instead they exchange goods and services with men.* Direct exchange between the sexes, like single barter, does not separate either sex from control over its own production. Instead, alienation develops in tandem with the development of exchange systems, as individuals use lineage and extended family units to compete for ranking positions in relation to control over the production and distribution of valued goods. Gender responsibilities for marketing and exchange vary according to how different environments and histories have patterned the sex division of labor, and women's position in decision-making structures varies correspondingly.* Yet the question remains: when ranking begins to undermine the equal prerogatives of people generally, why is it that the autonomy and authority of women as a sex are threatened rather than those of men? Aside from various formulations of male superiority, it is usually argued that the physical limitations of childbirth and suckling are critical. Yet these do not hinder women in egalitarian societies.* In keeping with my reading of dialectical materialist theory as outlined above, I would say that the significance of women's child-bearing ability is transformed by new social relations when they become the producers, not only of people as individuals, but also of what is becoming "abstract"—i.e., exploitable—labor. The origins of gender hierarchy, then, are inextricably meshed with the origins of exploitation and class stratification.*[19]

---

[18] In Marxist thinking, it is the resolution of conflict that creates change between social forms. However, each such resolution contains the germs of a new conflict and, hence, progress to new social forms. In this paragraph, Leacock points first to a conflict between egalitarian social forms and specialization. Since no two specializations are likely to be entirely equal, it is impossible to maintain egalitarian social relations once specialization begins. This problem is resolved in rank societies through a hierarchical ordering of kin groups. Such ranking, however, creates new contradictions because nonkin relations are now available through trade with distant people.

[19] Leacock argues that in egalitarian societies based on barter economics, gender relations are relations of equality. Making a fetish of commodities and making labor a commodity are part of the formation of hierarchical societies, and it is only when egalitarian societies become rank societies that women lose rights and men gain them. This leaves her with a difficult question: Why are women, rather than men, the ones who lose the rights? She rejects explanations rooted in either biology or "human nature" and instead asserts that women are disadvantaged because they are associated with the production of labor power rather than of commodities themselves. Thus, women produce labor, men produce commodities. Commodities are more valued in hierarchical societies than is labor; therefore men are more highly valued than women. Note that the accuracy of this claim rests wholly on acceptance of Marx's notion of the labor theory of value and the notion of making a fetish of the commodity. Without these ideas, there is no reason why producing labor should be intrinsically more or less valuable than producing commodities.

Interestingly, Leacock's analysis here bears a superficial resemblance to Ortner's notions in "Is Female to Male as Nature Is to Culture?" (essay 26). In that essay, Ortner contends that women are seen as inferior because nature is seen as inferior to culture. Women's production of children ties them to nature, whereas men's production of material ties them to culture. The critical difference between Ortner's structural analysis and Leacock's Marxist analysis is that Ortner sees the relative positions of nature and culture as fundamental features of human consciousness in all societies. Leacock, on the other hand, believes that the position of labor relative to its products is a specific, historical development in capitalist societies.

Engels posed a sharp contrast between the status of women among the egalitarian Iroquois and that in the patriarchal societies of the classical Middle East and Mediterranean where control over female sexuality was important for the inheritance of status and property. In his view, the family as an economic unit was of primary importance within the upper class although it had ramifications throughout society. It remained for mid-20th century Marxist-feminist scholarship to add a further dimension to these ramifications. Female subordination within the family as an economic unit also enabled an upper class to squeeze more surplus from workers, serfs and slaves. The fact that domestic work could be separated from a public sphere and assigned to women as the wards of men assured to an upper class the reproduction and maintenance of workers through socially unremunerated—i.e., slave—labor. This is not to say that the arrangement was thought through in advance any more than other major historical developments of the past. However, given the records of women's steady decline in legal and social rights in classical antiquity, it remains to trace some of the steps whereby the household subordination of women was buttressed by ideological and social sanctions as its economic advantages were realized.*[20]

All of this, however, pertains to the final stages of women's subordination. The majority of societies with which anthropology deals involve the most preliminary stages—points at which women's autonomy began to be threatened and a certain hostility between the sexes began to be institutionalized, but that were very far indeed from the legal and political reduction of women to the status of ward that accompanied full-scale stratification. I am suggesting that the structure of gender in such societies needs to be interpreted in relation to: the structure of exchange and the division of labor; the structure of ranking and the degree to which some sections of the society are gaining control over the labor of others; the structure of kinship and the extent to which lineages have become competing sodalities rather than the means for organizing production and distribution in communal villages; the degree to which the well-being of one segment of a society is not merely relative but is actually at the expense of other segments; and, in the light of all this, the structure of marriage in relation to control over children as exploitable labor or as exploiters of labor.[21]

In what are called ranking societies, women's position begins to shift from valued people who cement networks of reciprocal relations and who have access to various publically recognized mechanisms for adjudicating their interests as women, into that of service workers in the households of husbands and their kin groups. Bride wealth begins to take the form of purchasing a woman's children, rather than of gift exchange. Sacks has explored the relation of such developments to the emergence of status difference among women as well as between women and men.* She has demonstrated the

---

[20] Leacock is arguing that men were able to reproduce their superior social position by relying on the unpaid domestic work of women. Her argument comes substantially from Engels' *Origin of the Family*. In that work, Engels argues that property was key to marriage among the bourgeoisie, and he likened marriage to prostitution. Women in such marriages traded domestic and sexual service for economic support. Engels argued that after the communist revolution, marriage would be egalitarian since each partner would be equally involved in production.

[21] In this passage, Leacock cites two other prominent feminist anthropologists: Peggy Sanday (b. 1937) and Karen Sacks (b. 1941). When this essay was written, San-day had recently published *Female Power and Male Dominance: On the Origins of Sexual Inequality* (1981). There, she argued that in "inner oriented" societies—those with abundant food supplies and little threat of outside aggression—people lived in harmony with nature and each other. Gender relations were egalitarian. But in "outer oriented" societies, characterized by food scarcity and warfare, men dominated women. She reported that the number of "outer oriented" societies increased with colonialism. Karen Sacks is also concerned with issues of gender equality and, when this essay was written, had recently published *Sisters and Wives: The Past and Future of Sexual Equality* (1979).

usefulness of separating the status of women as wives from that as sisters in order to appreciate the extent to which women exercise publically recognized authority through the manipulation of kin ties in societies where economic stratification and gender hierarchy are emerging. Sanday has stressed the fact that women may protect and maintain their public authority well into the conditions of stratification, a fact attested to by extensive data on West African societies and suggested by the case of ancient Crete.* All told, a focus on the above developments and the particularities of their unfolding in different historical, cultural and environmental contexts, makes clear that changes in women's position are neither secondary phenomena, as some imply, nor prior to economic hierarchy, as argued by others. They are at the core of, and inseparable from, profound transformations that take place in conjunction with the development of exchange and the division of labor.

The social and economic subordination of women was established in some parts of the world millenia ago; it was unfolding in other parts of the world at the time of European exploration and conquest; and it has been developing in yet others in the context of Western colonialism and imperialism.* I am here arguing that in order to interpret this development correctly, it is essential, first: to have a clear concept of primitive communism, divested of stereotypical assumptions that female subordination is a natural rather than historical phenomenon, and second: to place any society under study clearly in the context of its particular history, pre- and post-colonial. I now return to the second point.

THE HISTORICAL CONTEXT OF ANTHROPOLOGICAL ANALYSIS

The actual people contemporary anthropologists study are not autonomous gatherer-hunters or horticulturalists or whatever. In one way or another the relations of capitalism have impinged upon them for a long time. Whatever the specific nature of a people's involvement with capitalism, the *ultimate* direction of change is the same: the individualization and alienation of labor, the individualization of the nuclear family, and the relegation of women both to unrecompensed domestic labor and to public labor as an unstable and underpaid work force. People lose what control over the process and products of their labor they previously had, and their labor itself becomes increasingly transformed into a commodity to be bought, if not outright commandeered. The responsibility for rearing the new generation is progressively transferred from some larger kin or band grouping to individual families. Idealized by missionary teachings as loving care for husband and children, women's labor in the household becomes for all practical purposes a gift to the plantation or mine owner, manufacturer or trader, who draws profits from the work of husbands and sons and then buys women's additional labor at a marginal price.*[22]

Untidy details like plantation labor and commercial transactions have too commonly been ignored when data on so-called traditional societies are codified and punched on IBM cards for cross-cultural comparison.[23] Not surprisingly, a recent analysis concludes that there are no consistent correlations between women's position in a society and other factors.* Luckily, however, ethnohistorical and archaeological reconstruction of

---

[22] Leacock's critical point is that women's domestic labor is essential to the reproduction of the workforce. Without domestic labor, families cannot be maintained and workers cannot be produced. However, the owners of capital (the factory owners or mine owners) pay their workers (usually male) but do not pay the women, whose work enables the production of these workers. Thus, from Leacock's perspective, women's domestic work is a gift to capitalists.

[23] Leacock is attacking George Peter Murdock's Human Relations Area Files project (see the section "The Reemergence of Evolutionary Thought"). Murdock's project was a descendant of the large-scale cross-cultural studies started by Herbert Spencer. Thus it has a history that places it squarely in the anti-Marxist camp. The "Outline of Cultural Materials" Murdock devised to code the HRAF is decidedly non-Marxist, giving little attention to conflict, imperialism, class consciousness, or other interests central to Marxist analysis.

pre-colonial and colonial culture histories is proceeding apace, and it is possible to throw light on puzzling cases where there seems to be little relation between female subordination and economic inequality.[24]

I have already made reference to North America, which, north of Mexico, constitutes the largest world area that was inhabited by egalitarian peoples at the time of European expansion. Ranking was elaborated in coastal areas, especially along the Gulf of Mexico and the northern Pacific, but the vast majority of native North Americans had retained egalitarian socio-economic structures. The Iroquois are the best known example of the gender equality common in North America, and, contrary to the opinion of Lévi-Strauss,* are not an anomaly. Instead, they afford a well-documented example of the economic and political reciprocity that accompanied the matrilineal-matrilocal organization widespread among North American horticulturalists.* Among hunting-gathering peoples, the Inuit (Eskimo) are commonly cited as an example of masculine brutality toward women in an otherwise egalitarian society, an example seemingly paralleled by accounts of female subordination among the Chipewyan.*

However, ethno-graphic accounts of women's independence and assertiveness among the Inuit indicate that ethno-historical analysis, long overdue, will reveal the latter-day character of male abusiveness as following from the demoralization and drunkenness suffered in many Inuit communities.* As for the Chipewyan case, it is based on an account of middlemen in the fur trade, the "gang" that collected around the unusually dedicated worker for the Hudson's Bay Company, and not on independent Chipewyan hunters. The quality of relations therein described contrasts sharply with the 17th century Jesuit accounts of gender equality among the Montagnais-Naskapi.*

Australia

Aboriginal Australia has furnished ample grounds for arguments that male dominance is a psychosocial or psychobiological universal rather than an historical development. Male control of women's marriage, male inheritance of land, virilocal residence, male brutality towards women, and male exclusion of women from important rituals in a non-stratified society form an imposing

---

[24] Leacock makes the point in the second half of this essay that European expansion, from the fifteenth century on, had critical effects on people throughout the world. In particular, as capitalist relations of production were imposed on indigenous groups, the social and political position of women suffered. Previously egalitarian societies, in which women enjoyed either full equality with men or very substantial rights, were subverted, and men came to dominate women. Leacock argues that most ethnographic writing simply fails to take the effects of European colonialism into account. Thus ethnographies that showed the oppression of women among indigenous peoples were generally in error. The authors of these monographs, writing in the ethnographic present, fail to realize that the practices they assume to be "traditional" date only from the transformation of these societies by capitalism. If these societies could be seen before the advent of European expansion, the equality of gender relations in egalitarian and early ranked societies would be apparent. In making this argument Leacock is strongly influenced by World System Theory, a popular neo-Marxist position of the 1960s and 1970s. Although notions of dependency have been around for a long time, World

System Theory was promoted by the work of Andre Gunder-Frank (b. 1929) and Immanuel Wallerstein (b.1930). In his most famous essay, "The Development of Underdevelopment" (1966), Gunder-Frank argued that the nations of Latin America were not poor because they failed to industrialize. Rather, the processes of the expansion of capitalism in the wealthy nations, particularly in North America and in northern Europe, had drawn wealth out of Latin America. Thus, the poverty of southern nations was directly linked to the wealth of northern capitalist societies. In 1974 Wallerstein published *The Modern World-System*, in which he traced the development of global capitalism from its origins in the early seventeenth century, emphasizing its deleterious effects on noncapitalist cultures around the world. As did Gunder-Frank, the principal thesis Wallerstein advanced was that the wealth of nations and the poverty of nations are interlinked. Today's wealthy nations became rich by expropriating the wealth of today's poor nations. Although Leacock focuses on gender relations rather than wealth, the fundamental argument is the same. She insists that it was the expansion of capitalist power that undermined the position of women in society after society.

package and have been documented again and again. To be sure, data modifying these generalizations are beginning to assert themselves. Older women have a say in marriages along with older men, while young men, like young women, have little say. Just as young women are commonly married the first time to elder men, so are young men often married to elder women. Women have clubs with which they not only defend themselves, but with which they beat men for misbehavior; they are not cowed by men. Furthermore, if wrongfully hit, a woman may simply leave, or may take up residence in the women's section of the camp, taboo to men. Women are important in the conduct of some male rituals, and are indifferent to their exclusion from others; their own, from which men are excluded, hold more interest for them.* Tindale has pointed out that among the Pitjandara of western Australia, women call male rituals to a close if they find themselves walking too far for food and wish to move camp.* Bell worked in a north-central Australian settlement where "the maintenance of law and order . . . is still a cooperative venture between men and women who turn to each other for assistance on some issues and assert their independent rights on others."*

However, while such data qualify the picture of male dominance claimed for Australian gatherer-hunters, the historical setting in which 20th century Aboriginal society has been functioning must be understood if this image is to be contradicted in its entirety. First and foremost, not to evaluate the effects of the brutal genocide native Australians have suffered is as unscientific as it is unethical. Brutality against native Australians has been practiced from the earliest forays by Malays; to the sporadic explorations by Europeans and the 1788 convict settlement at what is now Sydney; through the steady encroachment on Australian lands and the accompanying shooting, poisoning, beating and enslaving, along with disastrous disease; into the brutal policing and racist restrictions of the present. One cannot talk of men hitting women as if apart from a pattern of frontier violence where demoralization is compounded by alcohol.*

Second, it is—or should be—inexcusable to analyse land rights in Australia without considering the impact of forced movements away from coastal areas and the resulting land pressure in interior regions to which many Aborigines fled. Some early meetings between Europeans and Australians were friendly, but the Europeans were over-ready to use their guns, and apparently the Australians sometimes retaliated with the unambiguous act of treating their foes as food. For the most part, therefore, early explorers from Europe were glad to leave the Australians alone, once it was decided that there was no ready gold or other easy wealth on their lands. Then the arrival of the first merino sheep in New South Wales in 1797 was followed in 1813 by the discovery, west of the Blue Mountains, of the immense grasslands that were to make Australia the largest producer of fine wool in the world.* The push was on. The rich southeast, where 400 to 600 people were wont to gather at certain seasons to socialize and live on seafood and crayfish, was soon depopulated of Aborigines. Some were killed, some moved west, and a few married into the white community. The herders too pushed west, enslaving the Aborigines, or pressing them into labor, and brutally suppressing their resistance.* Driven westward and inland, away from expanding centers of white settlement and onto each other's traditional homelands, different peoples turned against each other, fighting and quarrelling. As among native Americans, the recognition of a common identity as Aborigines, with a common history and common struggle, took time to emerge. White Australians of course took advantage of and exacerbated divisiveness among the Aborigines, favoring "pacified" groups and using them to enslave or control others.

The demoralization found among displaced Aboriginal survivors is documented by Daisy Bates, who over a period of some forty years publicized the Aboriginal condition from her isolated camp in South Australia.* Despite the patronization and misinterpretations of her account, many incidents she reports parallel the macabre bitterness of collective suicide described by Turnbull for the Ik.* A particularly bizarre scene ensues when Bates accompanied Radcliffe-Brown to the grim hospital island where sick and fearful Aborigines, separated from their own people, are taken only to die. She describes Radcliffe-Brown asking the old men to sing ritual songs into his phonograph and playing them Tannhauser and Egmont in return.*[25]

By the 20th century, disease and genocide in its various forms had reduced an estimated 300,000 or more people of aboriginal Australia to less than 40,000.* By mid-century, with the "stabilization" of native reserves, and the dispensation of minimal food supplies and medical care by government or mission stations, the Aboriginal population began to rise again. Ritual life, too, began to revive and expand, although serving a new function as a focus for the assertion of identity and self-respect by a people robbed of their independence. Anthropologists also expanded in numbers, typically wishing to study the lives of pristine hunter-gatherers. They usually took care to interview people living a distance from mission stations or cattle ranches, rather than the service workers directly attached to such enterprises. Seldom, however, did they inquire deeply into a people's history, nor even inquire about existing official regulations for Aborigines, such as those that prohibit marriage off of a reserve.*

The point should be clear. To ignore the historical, economic, and political realities of Aboriginal life is to gloss over the effects of conquest and oppression, and therefore to misconstrue the social relations that obtained when Aborigines were autonomous gatherers and hunters in control of their own social world. With respect to relations between the sexes, when one scrapes the surface of ethnohistorical materials, one finds suggestions of women's former importance, such as Howitt's reference to influential elder women in southeastern Australia. Only recently, however, have these begun to be followed up.* As

long ago as a hundred years, Spencer and Gillin note a three-day women's section of an initiation ceremony among the Arunta and comment that "there was a time when women played a more important part in regard to such ceremonies than they do at the present time."* Unfortunately, they give no further information except that they personally find the ceremony boring. In his recently republished *Australian Religion*, Mircea Eliade makes ample reference to male high gods, but nowhere mentions the important mythological personage who keeps reappearing in the pages of Spencer and Gillin, the female Sun. Eliade writes that initiation for Australian girls is simpler than for boys, and flatly contradicts ethnographic fact by stating, "as everywhere in the world."*

Hart and Pilling raise the need for ethnohistorical work in their account of the Tiwi.* They describe how missionary influences as well as prostitution encouraged male control over women's sexuality in the early 20th century, and then go on to consider earlier influences on the politics of wife-trading. Archival research is needed, they write, to determine the extent of slave raiding by the Portuguese in the 18th century. Since it was probably the younger men who were taken off to Timor, they suggest the slaving may have encouraged the dominance of old Tiwi men and their monopolization of wives.

[*Leacock provides three additional ethnographic examples, but space considerations prevent us from reprinting them here. We summarize them below.*

In a 1,100-word section with 12 notes entitled "The Amazon," Leacock first divides Amazonian history into five periods. The first of these is

---

[25] This paragraph contains references to several notorious characters. Daisy Bates (1861–1951) was an Irishwoman who lived among the Aborigines for thirty years, beginning in about 1913. Bates wrote several books about her experience. It is impossible to doubt that horrific things happened to the Aborigines, but for their history Daisy Bates might not be the best source. Julia Blackburn, author of *Daisy Bates in the Desert: A Woman's Life Among the Aborigines* (1994), writes that Bates fabricated her life history and that she was unable to separate her experiences from her imagination.

Colin Turnbull was the author of *The Forest People* (1961) and *The Mountain People* (1972). The first of these describes the idyllic life of the Mbuti of the Ituri Forest and the second, the horrific life of the Ik of Uganda. Both portraits have been heavily critiqued as romantic (or antiromantic).

A. R. Radcliffe-Brown lived in Australia from 1926 to 1931. The image Bates and Leacock present here is a compelling one, and it may well have happened. It is clear that Radcliffe-Brown had little interest in history and believed that the social structures he studied had been relatively little affected by colonialism.

precolonial, but in the others she dwells on the effects of colonization. She then moves to a discussion of the Yanomamo, asserting that their portrayal as "the fierce people" serves to rationalize the destruction of the Amazon forests. Citing geographer William J. Smole (1976), Leacock argues that the Yanomamo studied by Chagnon were made fierce by their contacts with Portuguese and Spanish invaders. Smole also reports that the position of women among the highland Yanomamo he studied was very much better than that reported by Chagnon. Leacock concludes this section by claiming that Chagnon's failure to deal with the Yanomamo history and politics cast doubt on his portrayal of the male aggressiveness and dominance among a virtually pristine egalitarian people.

In an 830-word section with 6 notes entitled "Melanesia," Leacock suggests that the societies of New Guinea are often used as evidence for the subordination of women in egalitarian societies. This portrayal, however, is incorrect since ancient irrigation works and trade connections suggest that stratification had already begun in this area. Further, trade connections with Malays, Chinese, and Europeans may have badly compromised egalitarian relations. The hostility often expressed between men and women is highly suggestive of a society in which rank is being asserted and women are losing control over their production. The fact that in New Guinea women often respond to their subordination with open anger rather than passive acceptance is strongly suggestive of societies in which the process of stratification is only beginning. These relations may have been further exacerbated by European conquest, which increased conflict between tribes.

A 2,000-word section with 19 notes titled "Africa" includes a substantial critique of the work of French neo-Marxists Claude Meillassoux and Emanuel Terray. Their work was critical in the development of Marxist thought in anthropology during the 1960s and 1970s, and both worked in Africa. The French neo-Marxists broke from Soviet-style Marxist anthropology. Soviet ethnographers insisted on the primacy of the modes of production outlined by Marx and Morgan's scheme for the evolution of society. The French neo-Marxists expanded the notion of mode of production to include new modes germane to the societies anthropologists studied. They were also largely trained by Lévi-Strauss

and were deeply influenced by his notions on exchange and the role of women.

Leacock begins by noting that African history is extremely complex but often ignored. Despite some exceptions, the ethnography of African societies portrays women as firmly under male authority. Ethnohistorical work, however, shows that the position of African women deteriorated with the advent of colonial rule. Before colonialism, they often had important public political roles. Although in African hierarchical societies, women's autonomy was undermined, it was not destroyed, except in later Muslim states. Leacock faults the French neo-Marxists for failing to use Engels' notion that the subjugation of women was central to the development of hierarchy in analyzing the emergence of ranked societies in Africa. Because they agree with Lévi-Strauss on the universal subjugation of women, they tend to condense egalitarian and beginning rank societies into a single mode of production. This obscures the critical processes of the emergence of hierarchy. The problem is evident in Terray's work on the Gayman. Terray sees kin relations among the Gayman as exploiting women and youth. These relations were eventually dominated by relations based on slavery. Terray does not, however, look for a reason why women are exploited in the first place. Leacock, however, finds the answer in Terray's own work. She notes that he says the lineage structure is related to the political structure and did not come before it; further, "youth" was a rank that could include older men. Finally, captive labor was used in the lineage mode of production. Thus, Terray fails to realize that the exploitation of women and youth in the lineage mode of production is integral to the existence of hierarchical society and did not precede it. Terray also fails to consider that the ranked urban portion of society could have affected the more egalitarian rural part of society. His analysis is also weakened by failure to consider changes brought about by exposure to European slaving.]

CONCLUSION

Across the disciplines, research on the economic and social activities of women has been shaking up some established assumptions about society and history. I have argued that only when gender hierarchy is taken as an historical problematic, rather than a psycho-biological given, can the structure of primitive communist relations be properly understood, and the part played by exchange in the transformation of these relations clearly formulated. The need for an effective theory of exchange in pre-capitalist societies is well recognized by Marxist anthropologists,* but ironically it is associated, especially for those working in the structuralist tradition, with the wholly anti-Marxist concept of woman exchange as basic in primitive communist society.[26] Only when such a formulation is stringently challenged can the first phases of the process whereby women actually became exchanged be understood, for these were inseparable from initial steps in the transformation of use to value, work to abstract labor, and cooperative production to exploitation.

An effective theory of exchange is necessary both for analysing pre-capitalist societies and for interpreting the effects on these societies of colonization and imperialism. Only when the genders in primitive communist societies are understood as economically independent exchangers of goods and services, can the full force of capitalist relations in subverting the labor of women, and therefore transforming the entire structure of relationships in such societies, be appreciated. Until such time, the myth of the ethnographic present will continue to support the assumption, so prevalent in pop-science and the mass media, that the widespread normative ideal of men as household heads who provision dependent women and children reflects some human need or drive. And until such time, the unique and valued culture history and tradition of each Third World people will continue to be distorted, twisted to fit the interests of capitalist exploitation.

---

34. *Making Empire Respectable: The Politics of Race and Sexual Morality in Twentieth-Century Colonial Cultures*

ANN L. STOLER (b. 1949)

THE SHIFT AWAY from viewing colonial elites as homogeneous communities of common interest marks an important trajectory in the anthropology of empire, signaling a major rethinking of gender relations within it. More recent attention to the internal tensions of colonial enterprises has placed new emphasis on the quotidian[1] assertion of European dominance in the colonies, on imperial interventions in domestic life, and thus on the cultural prescriptions by which Euro-pean women and men lived (Callan and Ardener 1984; Knibiehler and Goutalier 1985; Reijs, et. al 1986; Callaway 1987; Strobel 1987). Having focused on how colonizers have viewed the indigenous Other, we are beginning to sort out how Europeans in the colonies imagined themselves and constructed communities built on asymmetries of race, class and gender—entities significantly at odds with the European models on which they were drawn.

(1989)

---

[26] Here, Leacock is once again attacking the French Marxists she has discussed in her analysis of Africa. We have edited this portion of the essay from the text, but be sure to read our condensation of it.

[1] *Quotidian:* daily. A quotidian assertion is an everyday assertion.

These feminist attempts to engage the gender politics of Dutch, French and British imperial cultures converge on some strikingly similar observations; namely that European women in these colonies experienced the cleavages of racial dominance and internal social distinctions very differently than men precisely because of their ambiguous positions, as both subordinates in colonial hierarchies and as active agents of imperial culture in their own right. Concomitantly, the majority of European women who left for the colonies in the late 19th and early 20th centuries confronted profoundly rigid restrictions on their domestic, economic and political options, more limiting than those of metropolitan Europe at the time and sharply contrasting the opportunities open to colonial men.

In one form or another these studies raise a basic question: in what ways were gender inequalities essential to the structure of colonial racism and imperial authority? Was the strident misogyny of imperial thinkers and colonial agents a byproduct of receiving metropolitan values ("they just brought it with them"), a reaction to contemporary feminist demands in Europe ("women need to be put back in their breeding place"), or a novel and pragmatic response to the conditions of conquest? Was the assertion of European supremacy in terms of patriotic manhood and racial virility an expression of imperial domination or a defining feature of it?[2]

In this paper I examine some of the ways in which colonial authority and racial distinctions were fundamentally structured in gendered terms. I look specifically at the administrative and medical discourse and management of European sexual activity, reproduction and marriage as it articulated with the racial politics of colonial rule. Focusing on French Indochina and the Dutch East Indies in the early 20th century, but drawing on other contexts, I suggest that the very categories of "colonizer" and "colonized" were secured through forms of sexual control which defined the domestic arrangements of Europeans and the cultural investments by which they identified themselves.*[3] Gender specific sexual sanctions demarcated positions of power by refashioning middle-class conventions of respectability, which, in turn, prescribed the personal and public boundaries of race.[4]

---

[2] In the 1970s and 1980s, feminist scholars tended to view women as a more or less homogenous group and focused their analysis on the social position of women in general. In the late 1980s and 1990s, the notion that women share common positions in society or face common problems came under sharp attack. Women from poor nations and from minority groups in wealthy nations led the charge. They argued that the feminist movement of the 1970s and 1980s was led by middle-class white scholars and reflected their concerns and opinions. The movement failed to recognize the privileged position of wealthy white women with respect to poor women of color. It failed to see that there were as many divisions among women as between women and men. Further, it failed to note that these divisions were often oppressive. Scholars in the late 1980s and 1990s moved to address this situation and often focused their work on the divisions among women and the ways in which the social positions and attitudes of wealthy women supported the social system and buttressed the oppression of poor women. Nowhere was this issue more apparent than in the anthropology of colonialism. In colonialism, women from colonizing societies, who were often quite brutally oppressed themselves, participated in and supported the oppression of women from colonized societies. Thus, examination of the colonial experience is ideal for exploring the complex ways in which notions of gender and ideas about class intersect and support one another.

[3] Stoler's original essay contained 29 notes totaling approximately 2,000 words. Space limitations prevent us from reproducing them here, but asterisks have been included to show where they were placed.

[4] Following a trend set in the 1980s (see Leacock, essay 33), Stoler argues that understanding the position of women in colonial society is central to any analysis of that society. Despite a myriad of different theoretical positions, a critical element that holds current feminist theorists together is the idea that gender relations are the fundamental, organizing principle of society.

Stoler's concern in this essay is understanding how men and women in colonial societies understood gender roles and classified the people around them. In one sense, this brings her close to the concerns of the ethnoscientists discussed in essays 27 and 28. However, Stoler's interests in history and in the relationship of systems of knowledge to systems of power clearly differentiate her from the ethnoscientists and show the influence of both Marx and Foucault.

Colonial authority was constructed on two powerful, but false, premises. The first was the notion that Europeans in the colonies made up an easily identifiable and discrete biological and social entity; a "natural" community of common class interests, racial attributes, political affinities and superior culture. The second was the related notion that the boundaries separating colonizer from colonized were thus self-evident and easily drawn (Stoler 1989). Neither premise reflected colonial realities (see for example, Cooper 1980; Drooglever 1980; Ridley 1983; Prochaska 1989; Comaroff (this volume)). Internal divisions developed out of conflicting economic and political agendas, frictions over appropriate methods for safeguarding European privilege and power, competing criteria for reproducing a colonial elite and for restricting its membership.[5]

This latter, the colonial politics of exclusion, was contingent on constructing categories, legal and social classifications designating who was "white," who was "native," who could become a citizen rather than a subject, which children were legitimate progeny and which were not. What mattered were not only one's physical properties but who counted as "European" and by what measure.* Skin shade was too ambiguous; bank accounts were mercurial; religious belief and

---

Michel Foucault (1926–1984), a French philosopher, was vitally concerned with the relationship between systems of knowledge and systems of power and social control. Foucault's early work (1965 [1961]) focused on the ways in which mental institutions create languages of inclusion and exclusion that reflect and support the social order. He characterized his later work as "genealogical." For Foucault, this meant tracing the histories of the systems of knowledge used by the powerful in order to understand the relationship between power and knowledge and its connection with actual practices. One place he tried to apply this method was in *The History of Sexuality* (1978). There, he argued that the notion that sexuality has been repressed in Western society is erroneous. In fact, a discussion of sexuality has been central to how Europeans understand their society as well as to defining membership in sexual minorities. In particular, Foucault argued that until the late eighteenth century, people who had sexual relations with members of their own sex were not considered homosexuals. However, in the eighteenth and nineteenth centuries, along with the emergence of science, the discourse on sexuality changed. Homosexuals began to be identified as a group possessing specific characteristics. In other words, homosexuality changed from something a person did to something a person was.

Although Stoler does not cite Foucault in this essay, his influence on her work is evident. Foucault saw discourse on sexuality as central to understanding social structure and power relations within Western society. Tracing the historical changes of this discourse was fundamental to his project. Stoler sees gender as essential in understanding power relations in colonial societies and tries to trace the history of gender-related discourse and actual practices.

While Stoler makes extensive use of Foucault's work, feminist thinkers have had a deeply ambivalent relationship with the work of Foucault. The ideas that our understandings are socially constructed discourses, that these are related to power structures, and that the meanings of sexuality are historically situated all have powerful resonances for feminists. However, feminists have also been critical of Foucault for what they see as his narrowly masculine vision, his pessimistic outlook, and his denial of the possibilities for political change (Sawicki 1991). Beyond this, Foucault has often been criticized for lacking interest in gender. Foucault's work focuses on the relationship of individuals to worlds of knowledge, but he was less interested in the relationship of people to one another. His work does not consider how "the deployment of sexuality has affected the relations between men and women" (Bell 1993:27), a central issue for feminists.

[5] Race is a critical item on the agenda for many contemporary feminists. Late nineteenth-century and early twentieth-century American anthropology was vitally concerned with the issue of race. There was fierce debate over the equality of races. For cultural anthropologists, the debate ended with Boas' insistence on the biopsychological equality of all humans. Human differences, most cultural anthropologists believed, were entirely cultural, and the issue of race could be disposed of altogether. The result of accepting this doctrine was that discussion of race as an important organizing principle of society is absent from most cultural anthropology between the time of Boas and the 1980s. However, as greater numbers of women and men of color became anthropologists, the issue of race began once again to be important. These anthropologists insisted that even though race was not viable as a biological concept, it had frequently been a major organizing principle of European-dominated society. Understanding how race could have no biological existence and yet be a fundamental element of society became central to their concerns.

education were crucial but never enough. Social and legal standing derived not only from color, but from the silences, acknowledgments, and denials of the social circumstances in which one's parents had sex (Martinez-Alier 1974; Ming 1983; Taylor 1983). Sexual unions in the context of concubinage, domestic service, prostitution or church marriage derived from the hierarchies of rule; but these were negotiated and contested arrangements, bearing on individual fates and the very structure of colonial society. Ultimately inclusion or exclusion required regulating the sexual, conjugal and domestic life of *both* Europeans in the colonies and their colonized subjects.[6]

Colonial observers and participants in the imperial enterprise appear to have had unlimited interest in the sexual interface of the colonial encounter (Malleret 1934:216; Pujarniscle 1931:106; Loutfi 1970:36). Probably no subject is discussed more than sex in colonial literature and no subject more frequently invoked to foster the racist stereotypes of European society. The tropics provided a site of European pornographic fantasies long before conquest was underway, but with a sustained European presence in colonized territories, sexual prescriptions by class, race and gender became increasingly central to the politics of rule and subject to new forms of scrutiny by colonial states (Loutfi 1971; Gilman 1985:79).*

While anthropologists have attended to how European, and particularly Victorian, sexual mores affected *indigenous* gendered patterns of economic activity, political participation and social knowledge, less attention has been paid to the ways in which sexual control affected the very nature of colonial relations themselves (Tiffany and Adams 1985). In colonial scholarship more generally, sexual domination has figured as a social metaphor of European supremacy. Thus, in Edward Said's treatment of orientalist discourse, the sexual submission and possession of Oriental women by European men "*stands for* the pattern of relative strength between East and West" (1979:6). In this "male power-fantasy," the Orient is penetrated, silenced and possessed (ibid:207). Sexuality illustrates the iconography of rule, not its pragmatics; sexual asymetries are tropes to depict other centers of power.[7]

Such a treatment begs some basic questions. Was sexuality merely a graphic substantiation of who was, so to speak, on the top? Was the medium the message, or did sexual relations always "mean" something else, stand in for other relations, evoke the sense of *other* (pecuniary, political, or some possibly more subliminal) desires? This analytic slippage between the sexual symbols of power and the politics of sex runs throughout the colonial record and contemporary commentaries upon it. Certainly some of

[6] In this passage, Stoler focuses on the intersection of race, class, and gender. Briefly, her point is that colonialism required maintaining the fiction that there was a clear racial difference between the colonized and the colonizer. Since the colonizers were more powerful than the subjects, this race difference was also a class difference. However, race is linked to sex and reproduction. Sex between members of different race/class groups creates progeny that are not easily classified and threaten the distinctions on which colonialism is based. Therefore, gender in general and control of sexuality in particular is a fundamental element of colonialism.

The notions of contested arrangements and negotiation appear in this passage as well. These ideas have become common in current anthropology. A contested arrangement is the idea that people are not satisfied with inferior social positions and invariably fight against them. Negotia-

tion covers the idea that individual or group identity is not a fixed essence but is determined by a process of give-and-take with other individuals and groups.

[7] Edward Said (pronounced "sa-*eed*") (b. 1935), a professor of comparative literature and cultural critic, has been an important figure in the development of current anthropology. Said's breakthrough book was *Orientalism* (1978). In this work, Said argues that scholars constructed an exotic, sensual Middle East that had little to do with the realities of the actual nations and powers of that region. However, since these exotic and sensual images were held and promoted by wealthy and powerful interests, they became widely accepted. Stoler is invoking the notion that the way the wealthy and powerful think, speak, and write about people and place has a critical influence on policies affecting those places and thus realities in them.

this is due to the polyvalent quality of sexuality; symbolically rich and socially salient at the same time. But sexual control was more than a "social enactment"—much less a convenient metaphor—for colonial domination (Jordan 1968:141); it was, as I argue here, a fundamental class and racial marker implicated in a wider set of relations of power (Ballhatchet 1980).

The relationship between gender prescriptions and racial boundaries still remains unevenly unexplored. While we know that European women of different classes experienced the colonial venture very differently from one another and from men, we still know relatively little about the distinct investments they had in a racism they shared (Van Helten and Williams 1983; Knibielher and Goutalier 1985; Callaway 1987). New feminist scholarship has begun to sort out the unique colonial experience of European women as they were incorporated into, resisted and affected the politics of their men. But the emphasis has tended to be on the broader issue of gender subordination and colonial authority, not more specifically on how sexual control figured in the construction of racial boundaries per se.*

The linkage between sexual control and racial tensions is both obvious and elusive at the same time. While sexual fear may at base be a racial anxiety, we are still left to understand why it is through sexuality that such anxieties are expressed (Takaki 1977). If, as Sander Gilman (1985) claims, sexuality is the most salient marker of Otherness, organically representing racial difference, then we should not be surprised that colonial agents and colonized subjects expressed their contests—and vulnerabilities—in these terms (see Chatterjee this volume).

An overlapping set of discourses has provided the psychological and economic underpinnings for colonial distinctions of difference, linking fears of sexual contamination, physical danger, climatic incompatibility, and moral breakdown to a European colonial identity with a racist and class-specific core. Colonial scientific reports and the popular press are laced with statements and queries varying on a common theme: "native women bear contagions"; "white women become sterile in the tropics"; "colonial men are susceptible to physical, mental and moral degeneration when they remain in their colonial posts too long." To what degree are these statements medically or politically grounded? We need to unpack what is metaphor, what is perceived as dangerous (is it disease, culture, climate, or sex?) and what is not.[8]

In the sections that follow I look at the relationship between the domestic arrangements of colonial communities and their wider political structures. Part I examines the colonial debates over European family formation, over the relationship between subversion and sex in an effort to trace how evaluations of concubinage, morality and white prestige more generally were altered by new tensions within colonial cultures and by new challenges to imperial rule.

Part II examines what I call the "cultural hygiene" of colonialism. Focusing on the early 20th century as a break point, I take up the convergent metropolitan and colonial discourses on health hazards in the tropics, race-thinking and social reform as they related to shifts in the rationalization of colonial management. In tracing how fears of "racial degeneracy" were grounded in class-specific sexual norms, I return to how and why biological and cultural distinctions were defined in gender terms.

THE DOMESTIC POLITICS OF COLONIALISM: CONCUBINAGE AND THE RESTRICTED ENTRY OF EUROPEAN WOMEN

The regulation of sexual relations was central to the development of particular kinds of colonial settlements and to the allocation of economic activity within them. Who bedded and wedded with whom in the colonies of France, England,

---

[8] The notion of unpacking is another common hallmark of current anthropology. To unpack an issue is to explore its various elements and levels of meaning. In this respect, the term updates Geertz's notion of "thick description," popular in the 1970s and 1980s.

Holland and Iberia was never left to chance. Unions between Annamite women and French men, between Javanese women and Dutch men, between Spanish men and Inca women produced offspring with claims to privilege, whose rights and status had to be determined and prescribed. From the early 1600s through the 20th century the sexual sanctions and conjugal prohibitions of colonial agents were rigorously debated and carefully codified. In these debates over matrimony and morality, trading and plantation company officials, missionaries, investment bankers, military high commands and agents of the colonial state confronted one another's visions of empire, and the settlement patterns on which it would rest.

In 1622 the Dutch East Indies Company (VOC) arranged for the transport of six poor but marriageable young Dutch women to Java, providing them with clothing, a dowry upon marriage and a contract binding them to five years in the Indies (Taylor 1983:12). Aside from this and one other short-lived experiment, immigration of European women to the East Indies was consciously restricted for the next 200 years. Enforcing the restriction by selecting bachelors as their European recruits, the VOC legally and financially made concubinage the most attractive domestic option for its employees (Blussé 1986:173; Ming 1983:69; Taylor 1983:16).

It was not only the VOC which had profited from such arrangements. In the 19th and early 20th centuries, salaries of European recruits to the colonial armies, bureaucracies, plantation companies and trading enterprises were kept artificially low because local women provided domestic services for which new European recruits would otherwise have had to pay. In the mid-1800s, such arrangements were *de rigueur* for young civil servants intent on setting up households on their own (Ritter 1856:21). Despite some clerical opposition, at the end of the century concubinage was the most prevalent living arrangement for European colonials in the Indies (Ming 1983:70; Taylor 1983:16; van Marle 1952:486).[9]

Referred to as *nyai* in Java and Sumatra, *congai* in Indochina, and *petite épouse* throughout the French empire, the colonized woman living as a concubine to a European man formed the dominant domestic arrangement in colonial cultures through the early 20th century. Unlike prostitution, which could and often did result in a population of syphilitic and therefore nonproductive European men, concubinage was considered to have a stabilizing effect on political order and colonial health—a relationship that kept men in their barracks and bungalows, out of brothels and less inclined to perverse liaisons with one another.[10]

In Asia and Africa corporate and government decision makers invoked the social services which local women supplied as "useful guides to the language and other mysteries of the local societies" (Malleret 1934:216; Cohen 1971:122). Handbooks for incoming plantation employees bound for Tonkin, Sumatra and Malaya urged men to find local "companions" as a prerequisite for quick acclimatization, as insulation from the ill-health that sexual abstinence, isolation and boredom were thought to bring (Butcher 1979:200, 202; Hesselink 1987:208; Braconier 1933:922; Dixon 1913:77). Although British and Dutch colonial governments officially banned concubinage in the early 20th century, such measures were only selectively enforced. It remained tacitly condoned and practiced long after (Hyam 1986; Callaway 1987:49). In Sumatra's plantation belt newly opened in the late 19th century, for example, Javanese and Japanese *huishoudsters* (householders) remained the rule rather than the exception through the 1920s (Clerkx 1961:87–93; Stoler 1985a:31–34; Lucas 1986:84).

---

[9] Note how Stoler draws attention to the fact that European colonials are not a homogenous group. They are divided not only by gender but also by social position. In this passage we learn that company owners encouraged the use of concubines because it allowed them to pay lower salaries and increase profits.

[10] In *The History of Sexuality* (1978), Foucault also links changing understandings of sexuality in the nineteenth century to ideas about health.

Concubinage was a contemporary term which referred to the cohabitation outside of marriage between European men and Asian women; in fact, it glossed a wide range of arrangements which included sexual access to a non-European woman as well as demands on her labor and legal rights to the children she bore (Pollman 1986:100; Lucas 1986:86).* Native women (like European women in a later period) were to keep men physically and psychologically fit for work, marginally content, not distracting or urging them out of line, imposing neither the time consuming nor financial responsibilities that European family life was thought to demand (Chivas-Baron 1929:103).*

To say that concubinage reinforced the hierarchies on which colonial societies were based is not to say that it did not make those distinctions more problematic at the same time. Grossly uneven sex ratios on North Sumatran estates made for intense competition among male workers and their European supervisors, with *vrouwen perkara* (disputes over women) resulting in assaults on whites, new labor tensions and dangerous incursions into the standards deemed essential for white prestige (Stoler 1985a:33; Lucas 1986:90–91). In the Netherlands Indies more generally an unaccounted number of impoverished Indo-European women moving between prostitution and concubinage further disturbed the racial sensibilities of the Dutch-born elite (Hesselink 1987:216). Metropolitan critics were particularly disdainful of such domestic arrangements on moral grounds— all the more so when these unions *were* sustained and personally significant relationships, thereby contradicting the racial premise of concubinage as an emotionally unfettered convenience.* But perhaps most important, the tension between concubinage as a confirmation and compromise of racial hierarchy was realized in the progeny that it produced, "mixed-bloods," poor "indos," and abandoned *"métis"* children who straddled the divisions of ruler and ruled and threatened to blur the colonial divide.[11]

[*In an 1,100-word conclusion to this section, with 3 notes, Stoler writes that although authors often claimed few European women lived in the colonies because of poor living conditions, in general, this was not true. European women were discouraged from emigrating. Concubinage remained the preferred form of relationship long after the colonies became stable, secure, and medically upgraded. One result of these policies was that European men far outnumbered European women in most colonies. Because they could control the immigration of European women and the sorts of sexual relations their employees were permitted, states and corporations could fix the conditions under which European populations and privileges could be reproduced. The involvement of states and corporations in intimate matters shows that sexuality was tightly tied to state security and corporate profit. Improper sexual relations were thought to subvert security and profit; "normal" relations supported them. Stoler demonstrates this principle using an example from northern Sumatra, where tobacco and rubber companies employed only single European workers. After the workers protested, the rule was changed and marriage permitted after five years' service. Some workers could get around this rule, but wages of new and low-level workers were kept too low to pay for a European family.*

Various considerations led government and company officials to pursue different policies in different places and at different times. Sometimes, as in Malaya in the 1920s, concubinage was favored because officials believed that allowing the immigration of European women would create a class of poor whites that would threaten European prestige. But earlier, in Java, concubinage itself was condemned as a source of poor whites, but the use of brothels was condoned. The difference between the two cases was political. Where European supremacy was clearly established, concubinage could be allowed. When European dominance was threatened, European women or prostitution were used to increase the distance between colonizer and colonized. In the next

---

[11] Thus, concubinage was a two-edged sword for European colonizers. On the one hand, the use of local women kept wages low and may have enabled rapid integration into local culture. On the other hand, it produced mixed-race children whose existence threatened the racial hierarchy on which colonialism rested.

sections, Stoler traces some common gendered is-
sues shared by different colonial societies, focusing
on how the positioning of European women pro-
moted racial distinctions and colonial control.]

RACIST BUT MORAL WOMEN: INNOCENT BUT IMMORAL MEN

Perhaps nothing is as striking in the sociological accounts of colonial communities as the extraordinary changes which are said to accompany the entry of European-born women. These adjustments shifted in one direction; toward European lifestyles accentuating the refinements of privilege and the etiquettes of racial difference. Most accounts agree that the presence of these women put new demands on the white communities to tighten their ranks, clarify their boundaries, and mark out their social space. The material culture of French settlements in Saigon, outposts in New Guinea, and estate complexes in Sumatra were retailored to accommodate the physical and moral requirements of a middle-class and respectable feminine contingent (Malleret 1934; Gordon and Meggitt 1985; Stoler 1989). Housing structures in Indochina were partitioned, residential compounds in the Solomon Islands enclosed, servant relations in Hawaii formalized, dress codes in Java altered, food and social taboos in Rhodesia and the Ivory Coast became more strict. Taken together, the changes encouraged new kinds of consumption and new social services catering to these new demands (Boutilier 1982; Spear 1963; Woodcock 1969; Cohen 1971).

The arrival of large numbers of European women thus coincided with an embourgeoisment of colonial communities and with a significant sharpening of racial lines. European women supposedly required more metropolitan amenities than men and more spacious surroundings to allow it; their more delicate sensibilities required

more servants and thus suitable quarters—discrete and enclosed. In short, white women needed to be maintained at elevated standards of living, in insulated social spaces cushioned with the cultural artifacts of "being European." Whether women or men set these new standards is left unclear. Who exhibited "overconcern" and a "need for" segregation (Beidelman 1982:13)? Male doctors advised French women in Indochina to have their homes built with separate domestic and kitchen quarters (Grall 1908:74). Segregationist standards were what women "deserved," and more importantly what white male prestige required that they maintain.[12]

Colonial rhetoric on white women was riddled with contradictions. At the same time that new female immigrants were chided for not respecting the racial distance of local convention, an equal number of colonial observers accused these women of being more avid racists in their own right (Spear 1963; Nora 1961). Allegedly insecure and jealous of the sexual liaisons of European men with native women, bound to their provincial visions and cultural norms, European women in Algeria, the Indies, Madagascar, India, and West Africa were uniformly charged with constructing the major cleavages on which colonial stratification rested (Spear 1963:140; Nora 1961:174; Mannoni 1964[1950]:115; Gan and Duignan 1978:242; Kennedy 1947:164; Nandy 1983:9).

What is most startling here is that women, otherwise marginal actors on the colonial stage, are charged with dramatically reshaping the face of colonial society, imposing their racial will on African and Asian colonies where "an iron curtain of ignorance" replaced "relatively unrestrained social intermingling" in earlier years (Vere Allen 1970:169; Cohen 1971:122). European women were not only the bearers of racist beliefs, but hardline operatives who put them into practice, encouraging class distinctions among whites while fostering new racial antagonisms, no longer

---

[12] Stoler's point in this section is that it is incorrect to believe that separation between natives and colonials increased because of the arrival of European women who required European surroundings. In fact, threatened by

challenges to European superiority, colonial leaders moved to increase the separation between rulers and subjects. The arrival of European women was the mechanism used to justify and enable the social disengagement of ruler and ruled.

muted by sexual access (Vere Allen 1970:168).* Are we to believe that sexual intimacy with European men yielded social mobility and political rights for colonized women? Or, even less likely, that because British civil servants bedded with Indian women, somehow Indian men had more "in common" with British men and enjoyed more parity? Colonized women could sometimes parlay their positions into personal profit and small rewards, but these were *individual* negotiations with no social, legal, or cumulative claims.[13]

Male colonizers positioned European women as the bearers of a redefined colonial morality. But to suggest that women fashioned this racism out of whole cloth is to miss the political chronology in which new intensities of racist practice arose. In the African and Asian contexts already mentioned, the arrival of large numbers of European wives, and particularly the fear for their protection, followed from new terms and tensions in the colonial encounter. The presence and protection of European women was repeatedly invoked to clarify racial lines. It coincided with perceived threats to European prestige (Brownfoot 1984:191), increased racial conflict (Strobel 1987:378), covert challenges to the colonial order, outright expressions of nationalist resistance, and internal dissension among whites themselves (Stoler 1989:147).

If white women were the primary force behind the decline of concubinage as is often claimed, they did so as participants in a broader racial realignment and political plan (Knibiehler and Goutalier 1985:76). This is not to suggest that European women were passive in this process, as the dominant themes in their novels attest (Taylor 1977:27). Many European women did oppose concubinage not because of their inherent jealousy of native women, but, as they argued, because of the double standard it condoned for European men (Clerkx 1961; Lucas 1986:94–95).* The voices of European women, however, had little resonance until their objections coincided with a realignment in racial and class politics.

DEALING WITH TRANSGRESSIONS: POLICING THE PERIL

The gender-specific requirements for colonial living, referred to above, were constructed on heavily racist evaluations which pivoted on the heightened sexuality of colonized men (Tiffany and Adams 1985). Although European women were absent from men's sexual reveries in colonial literature, men of color were considered to see them as desired and seductive figures. European women needed protection because men of color had "primitive" sexual urges and uncontrollable lust, aroused by the sight of white women (Strobel 1987:379; Schmidt 1987:411). In some colonies, that sexual threat was latent; in others it was given a specific name.

In southern Rhodesia and Kenya in the 1920s and 1930s, preoccupations with the "Black Peril" (referring to the professed dangers of sexual assault on white women by black men) gave rise to the creation of citizens' militias, ladies' riflery clubs and investigations as to whether African

---

[13] Stoler is arguing that colonial authorities were following a policy of blaming the victim. Immigration of European women was encouraged to increase the separation of ruler and subject. The attitudes of these same women were then blamed for misunderstandings between colonials and their subjects as well as for any new problems that resulted in increased social distance.

Stoler belittles the notion that concubinage had beneficial effects. However, the effects of concubinage are complex. If increased contact between colonials and their subjects or increased knowledge of local cultures by colonial officials was beneficial to the colonized, then concubinage had some positive effects. If colonial authorities did not at least believe that concubinage had some political benefit to their subjects, they would have no motivation to replace it. In other words, in order for colonial officials to feel threatened by concubinage (as Stoler argues they did), they must have believed that it increased the power of their subjects. On the other hand, it is also clear that concubinage relations were defined by structures of dominance and these assured that women and children were denied basic civil rights. Whatever benefits native women garnered, concubinage created a large population of illegitimate children, street orphans, a powerless and uneducated group with strong resentments.

female domestic servants would not be safer to employ than men (Kirkwood 1984:158; Schmidt 1987:412; Kennedy 1987:128–147). In New Guinea the White Women's Protection Ordinance of 1926 provided "the death penalty for any person convicted for the crime of rape or attempted rape upon a European woman or girl" (Inglis 1975:vi). And as late as 1934, Solomon Islands authorities introduced public flogging as punishment for "criminal assaults on [white] females" (Boutilier 1984:197).

What do these cases have in common? The rhetoric of sexual assault and the measures used to prevent it had virtually no correlation with the incidence of rape of European women by men of color. Just the contrary: there was often no evidence, *ex post facto* or at the time, that rapes were committed or that rape attempts were made (Schmidt 1987; Inglis 1975; Kirkwood 1984; Kennedy 1987; Boutilier 1984). This is not to suggest that sexual assaults never occurred, but that their incidence had little to do with the fluctuations in anxiety about them. Secondly, the rape laws were race-specific; sexual abuse of black women was not classified as rape and therefore was not legally actionable, nor did rapes committed by white men lead to prosecution (Mason 1958:246–247). If these accusations of sexual threat were not prompted by the fact of rape, what did they signal and to what were they tied?

Allusions to political and sexual subversion of the colonial system went hand in hand. Concern over protection of white women intensified during real and perceived crises of control—provoked by threats to the internal cohesion of the European communities or by infringements on their borders. While the chronologies differ, we can identify a patterned *sequence* of events in which Papuan, Algerian, and South African men heightened their demands for civil rights and refused the constraints imposed upon their edu-

cation, movements, or dress (Inglis 1975:8,11; Sivan 1983:178). Rape charges were thus based on perceived transgressions of political and social space. "Attempted rapes" turned out to be "incidents" of a Papuan man "discovered" in the vicinity of a white residence, a Fijian man who entered a European patient's room, a male servant poised at the bedroom door of a European woman asleep or in half-dress (Boutilier 1984:197; Inglis 1975:11; Schmidt 1987:413). With such a broad definition of danger, all colonized men of color were potential aggressors.

Accusations of sexual assault frequently followed upon heightened tensions within European communities—and renewed efforts to find consensus within them. In South Africa and Rhodesia, the relationship between reports of sexual assault and strikes among white miners and railway workers is well documented (van Onselen 1982:51; Kennedy 1987:138). Similarly, in the late 1920s when labor protests by Indonesian workers and European employees were most intense, Sumatra's corporate elite expanded their vigilante organizations, intelligence networks and demands for police protection to ensure their women were safe and their workers "in hand" (Stoler 1985b). In this particular context where the European community had been blatantly divided between low-ranking estate employees and the company elite, common interests were emphasized and domestic situations were rearranged.[14]

[*In an 800-word conclusion to this section, with 3 notes, Stoler notes that in Sumatra, in the 1920s, policies were enacted to favor European families. This undercut some European workers' opposition to colonial administration. New laws and policies curtailed native transgression of social and sexual boundaries, and women became responsible for guarding this separation. Despite this, European women were frequently blamed for overfamiliarity and provocation of native sexuality. They too were*

---

[14] In this section, Stoler continues to rely heavily on Foucault's notions about the meaning of discourse on sex. Foucault's main point is that when people discuss sexuality they are centrally concerned with society, relations of power, and defining group membership. Here, discussions of rape by native men and laws about it do not refer to actual instances of rape (though Stoler says these did occur) but to political fears. The fact that native men threatened the colonial system was discussed in terms of native men sexually threatening European women.

under constant surveillance and often had to obey rigid codes of chivalry. Nonetheless, women did frequently work in the colonies, but their work supported rather than contested colonial power structures. Some French feminists encouraged European women to go to the colonies, but in general, colonial administrators discouraged this. Colonial administrations feared that single or widowed working women would become a class of poor whites and their presence would damage European prestige. Stoler concludes that colonial policies were designed to exclude the many European women who fell outside of the rigorously assigned categories of custodians of family welfare and respectability. In the next section she aims to show "how a European family life and bourgeois respectability became increasingly tied to notions of racial survival, imperial patriotism and the political strategies of the colonial state."]

WHITE DEGENERACY, MOTHERHOOD AND THE EUGENICS OF EMPIRE

de-gen-er-ate (adj.) [L. *degeneratus*, pp. of *degenerare*, to become unlike one's race, degenerate < *degener*, not genuine, base < *de-*, from + *genus*, race, kind: see genus]. 1. having sunk below a former or normal condition, character, etc.; deteriorated. 2. morally corrupt; depraved n. (a degenerate person, esp. one who is morally depraved or sexually perverted) vi -at'ed, -at'ing 1. to decline or become debased morally, culturally, etc. 3. Biol. to undergo degeneration; deteriorate

[Webster's New World Dictionary 1972:371].

European women were essential to the colonial enterprise and the solidification of racial boundaries in ways that repeatedly tied their supportive and subordinate posture to community cohesion and colonial peace. These features of their positioning within imperial politics were powerfully reinforced at the turn of the century by a metropolitan bourgeois discourse (and an eminently anthropological one) intensely concerned with notions of "degeneracy" (Le Bras 1981:77). Middle-class morality, manliness and motherhood were seen as endangered by the intimately linked fears of "degeneration" and miscegenation in scientifically construed racist beliefs (Mosse 1978:82).* Due to environmental and/or inherited factors, degeneracy could be averted positively by eugenic selection, or negatively by eliminating the "unfit" (Mosse 1978:87; Kevles 1985:70–84). Eugenic arguments used to explain the social malaise of industrialization, immigration and urbanization in the early 20th century derived from the notion that acquired characteristics were inheritable and thus that poverty, vagrancy and promiscuity were class-linked biological traits, tied to genetic material as directly as nightblindness and blonde hair.[15]

Appealing to a broad political and scientific constituency at the turn of the century, eugenic societies included advocates of infant welfare programs, liberal intellectuals, conservative businessmen, Fabians,[16] and physicians with social concerns. By the 1920s, however, it contained an increasingly vocal number of those who called for and put into law, if not practice, the sterilization of significant numbers in the British, German and American working-class populations (Mosse 1978:87; 1982:122).* Negative eugenics never

---

[15] The notions of eugenics fit nicely with Spencer's idea of evolution. Recall that Spencer saw evolution occurring through struggle both between and within societies. Struggle for survival led to a constant bettering of a society's stock of people. Darwin's cousin, Sir Frances Galton (1822–1911), extended this argument to matters of intelligence. In his 1869 work *Hereditary Genius,* Galton proposed that intelligence is inheritable and that societies should take steps to assure the reproduction of their most fit members. He coined the term *eugenics* in *Inquiries into*

Human Faculty (1883) to describe the process of selectively breeding humans for intelligence and other forms of exceptionality. As Stoler reports, this notion became extremely popular in the late nineteenth and early twentieth centuries. Eugenics societies sprang up in many industrialized nations, including the United States.

[16] The Fabian society was an organization dedicated to establishing a democratic socialist state in England. It was the forerunner of the current British Labour Party.

gained the same currency in Holland as it did elsewhere, nevertheless, it seems clear from the Dutch and Dutch Indies scientific and popular press that concerns with hereditary endowment and with "Indo degeneracy" were grounded in a cultural racism that rivaled its French variant, if in a somewhat more muted form.*

Feminists attempted to appropriate this rhetoric for their own birth control programs, but eugenics was essentially elitist, racist and misogynist in principle and practice (Gordon 1976:395; Davin 1978; Hammerton 1979). Its proponents advocated a pronatalist policy toward the white middle and upper classes, a rejection of work roles for women that might compete with motherhood, and "an assumption that reproduction was not just a function but the purpose . . . of a woman's life" (Gordon 1976:134). In France, England, Germany, and the United States, positive eugenics placed European women of "good stock" as "the fountainhead of racial strength" (Ridley 1983:91), exalting the cult of motherhood while subjecting it to more thorough scientific scrutiny (Davin 1978:12).

As part of metropolitan class politics, eugenics reverberated in the colonies in predictable as well as unexpected forms. The moral, biological and sexual referents of the notion of degeneracy (distinct in the dictionary citation above) came together in how the concept was actually deployed. The "colonial branch" of eugenics embraced a theory and practice concerned with the vulnerabilities of white rule and new measures to safeguard European superiority. Designed to control the procreation of the "unfit" lower orders, eugenics targeted "the poor, the colonized, or unpopular strangers" (Hobsbawm 1987:253). It was, however, also used by metropolitan observers against colonials, and by colonial elites against "degenerate" members among themselves (Koks 1931:179–189). While studies in Europe and the U.S. focused on the inherent propensity of the poor for criminality, in the Indies delinquency among "European" children was biologically linked to the amount of *"native blood"* among children of poor Indo-Europeans (Braconier 1918:11). Eugenics provided not so much a new vocabulary as it did a medical and moral basis for anxiety over white prestige which reopened debates over segregated residence and education, new standards of morality, sexual vigilance and the rights of certain Europeans to rule.

Eugenic influence manifested itself, not in the direct importation of metropolitan practices such as sterilization, but in a translation of the political *principles* and the social values which eugenics implied. In defining what was unacceptable, eugenics also identified what constituted a "valuable life": "a gender-specific work and productivity, described in social, medical and psychiatric terms" (Bock 1984:274). Applied to European colonials, eugenic statements pronounced what kind of people should represent Dutch or French rule, how they should bring up their children and with whom they should socialize. Those concerned with issues of racial survival and racial purity invoked moral arguments about the national duty of French, Dutch, British, and Belgian colonial women to stay at home.[17]

If in Britain racial deterioration was conceived to be a result of the moral turpitude and the ignorance of working-class mothers, in the colonies, the dangers were more pervasive, the possibilities of contamination worse. Formulations to secure European rule pushed in two directions: on the one hand, away from ambiguous racial genres and open domestic arrangements, and on the other hand, toward an upgrading, homogenization, and a clearer delineation of European standards; away from miscegenation toward white endogamy, away from concubinage toward family formation and legal marriage; away from, as in the case of the Indies, mestizo customs and toward metropolitan norms (Taylor 1983; van Doorn 1985). As stated in the bulletin of the Netherlands Indies' Eugenic Society, "eugenics is

---

[17] Stoler's analysis of eugenics relies once again on Foucault's exposition of these ideas in *The History of Sexuality*. Foucault sees eugenics in terms of a discourse of degeneracy that becomes increasingly dominated by scientific themes (1978:118–19). In eugenics, issues of power and control are couched in the scientific language of breeding and genetics, purity and contamination.

nothing other than belief in the possibility of preventing degenerative symptoms in the body of our beloved *moedervolken,* or in cases where they may already be present, of counteracting them" (Rodenwaldt 1928:1).

Like the modernization of colonialism itself, with its scientific management and educated technocrats with limited local knowledge, colonial communities of the early 20th century were rethinking the ways in which their authority should be expressed. This rethinking took the form of asserting a distinct colonial morality, explicit in its reorientation toward the racial and class markers of "Europeanness," emphasizing transnational racial commonalities despite national differences—distilling a *homo europeaus* of superior health, wealth and intelligence as a white man's norm. As one celebrated commentator on France's colonial venture wrote: "one might be surprised that my pen always returns to the words *blanc* [white] or "European" and never to *"Français"*. . . in effect colonial solidarity and the obligations that it entails allies all the peoples of the white races" (Pujarniscle 1931:72; also see Delavignette 1946:41).

Such sensibilities colored imperial policy in nearly all domains with fears of physical contamination merging with those of political vulnerability. To guard their ranks, whites had to increase their numbers and to ensure that their members neither blurred the biological nor political boundaries on which their power rested.* In the metropole[18] the socially and physically "unfit," the poor, the indigent and the insane were either to be sterilized or prevented from marriage. In the British and Belgian colonies, among others, it was these very groups among Europeans who were either excluded from entry or institutionalized while they were there and when possible were sent home (Arnold 1979; see also Vellut 1987:97).

Thus, whites in the colonies adhered to a politics of exclusion that policed their members as well as the colonized. Such concerns were not new to the 1920s (Taylor 1983; Sutherland 1982). As early as the mid-18th century, the Dutch East Indies Company had already taken

"draconian measures" to control pauperism among "Dutchmen of mixed blood" (*Encyclopedie van Nederland-Indie* 1919:367). In the same period, the British East Indies Company legally and administratively dissuaded lower-class European migration and settlement, with the argument that it might destroy Indian respect for "the superiority of the European character" (quoted in Arnold 1983:139). Patriotic calls to populate Java in the mid-1800s with poor Dutch farmers were also condemned, but it was with new urgency that these possibilities were rejected in the following century as challenges to European rule were more profoundly felt.

Measures were taken both to avoid poor white migration and to produce a colonial profile that highlighted the vitality, colonial patriotism, and racial superiority of European men (Loutfi 1971:112–113; Ridley 1983:104).* Thus, British colonial administrators were retired by the age of 55, ensuring that "no Oriental was ever allowed to see a Westerner as he aged and degenerated, just as no Westerner needed ever to see himself . . . as anything but a vigorous, rational, ever-alert young Raj" (Said 1978:42). In the 20th century, these "men of class" and "men of character" embodied a modernized and renovated colonial rule; they were to safeguard the colonies against physical weakness, moral decay and the inevitable degeneration that long residence in the colonies encouraged and the temptations that interracial domestic situations had allowed.

Given this ideal, it is not surprising that colonial communities strongly discouraged the presence of nonproductive men. Dutch and French colonial administrators expressed a constant concern with the dangers of unemployed or impoverished Europeans. During the succession of economic crises in the early 20th century, relief agencies in Sumatra, for example, organized fund raisers, hill station retreats and small-scale agricultural schemes to keep "unfit" Europeans "from roaming around" (Kroniek 1917:49). The colonies were neither open for retirement nor tolerant of the public presence of poor whites. During the 1930s depression when tens of thousands of

---

[18] *The metropole* refers to the colonizing country.

Europeans in the Indies found themselves without jobs, government and private resources were quickly mobilized to ensure that they were not "reduced" to native living standards (Veerde 1931; Kantoor van Arbeid 1935). Subsidized health care, housing and education complemented a rigorous affirmation of European cultural standards in which European womanhood played a central role in keeping men *civilisé*.

[*In a 600-word section with 3 notes titled "On Cultural Hygiene: The Dynamics of Degeneration," Stoler reports that in twentieth-century Europe, medical and sociological work began to identify Europeans who stayed too long in the colonies as a distinct degenerate type. Colonials were believed to acquire physical and psychological faults from prolonged contact with native populations. Colonial medicine backed the notion that moral and cultural degeneracy produced by long stays in the colonies was associated with physical disease. Neurasthenia, a nervous disorder caused by exhaustion and overwork, was a common diagnosis. Whereas in Europe neurasthenia was associated with "modern civilization," in colonies it was believed to be caused by separation from civilization. One response to this was a proliferation of colonial "hill stations"—places that simulated European environments. Some doctors prescribed return to Europe; others insisted that a stable, European-style family life would reduce neurasthenia. They denounced the lifestyle of the "old colonists" as unhealthy.*]

CULTURAL CONTAMINATION, CHILDREN AND THE DANGERS OF METISSAGE

[Young colonial men] are often driven to seek a temporary companion among women of color; this is the path by which, as I shall presently show, contagion travels back and forth, contagion in all senses of the word [Maunier 1932:171].

Racial degeneracy was thought to have social causes and political consequences, both tied to the domestic arrangements of colonialism in specific ways. *Metissage* (interracial unions) generally, and concubinage in particular, represented the paramount danger to racial purity and cultural identity in all its forms. It was through sexual contact with women of color that French men "contracted" not only disease but debased sentiments, immoral proclivities and extreme susceptibility to decivilized states (Dupuy 1955:198).

By the early 20th century, concubinage was denounced for undermining precisely those things that it was charged with fortifying decades earlier. Local women who had been considered protectors of men's well-being, were now seen as the bearers of ill health and sinister influences; adaptation to local food, language, and dress, once prescribed as healthy signs of acclimatization, were now sources of contagion and loss of (white) self. The benefits of local knowledge and sexual release gave way to the more pressing demands of respectability, the community's solidarity and its mental health. Increasingly French men in Indochina who kept native women were viewed as passing into "the enemy camp" (Pujarniscle 1931:107). Concubinage became the source not only of individual breakdown and ill-health, but the biological and social root of racial degeneration and political unrest. Children born of these unions were "the fruits of regrettable weakness" (Mazet 1932:8), physically marked and morally marred with "the defaults and mediocre qualities of their [native] mothers" (Douchet 1928:10).[19]

Concubinage was not as economically tidy and politically neat as colonial policy makers had hoped. It concerned more than sexual exploitation and unpaid domestic work; it was about children—many more than official statistics often revealed—and who was to be acknowledged as a European and who was not. Concubine children posed a classification problem, impinging

---

[19] In this section on concubinage, Stoler makes a firm connection between race and gender. Mixed-race children were a special problem in colonial possessions because they blurred the definition of superior and inferior races on which colonial rule was based.

on political security and white prestige. The majority of such children were not recognized by their fathers, nor were they reabsorbed into local communities as authorities often claimed. Although some European men legally acknowledged their progeny, many repatriated to Holland, Britain or France and cut off ties and support to mother and children (Brou 1907; Ming 1983:75). Native women had responsibility for, but attenuated rights over, their own offspring. They could neither prevent their children from being taken from them nor contest paternal suitability for custody. While the legal system favored a European upbringing, it made no demands on European men to provide it; many children became wards of the state, subject to the scrutiny and imposed charity of the European-born community at large.

Concubine children were invariably counted among the ranks of the European colonial poor, but European paupers in the late 19th century Netherlands Indies came from a far wider strata of colonial society than that of concubines alone (Rapport der Pauperisme-Commissie 1903). Many Indo-Europeans had become increasingly marginalized from strategic political and economic positions in the early 20th century despite new educational opportunities encouraged at the turn of the century. In the 1920s and 1930s Indies-born and educated youth were uncomfortably squeezed between an influx of new colonial recruits from Holland and the educated *inlander* ("native") population with whom they were in direct competition for jobs (Mansvelt 1932:295).* At the turn of the century, volumes of official reports were devoted to documenting and alleviating the proliferation on Java of a "rough" and "dangerous pauper element" among (Indo) European clerks, low-level officials and vagrants (*Encyclopedie van Nederland-Indie* 1919:367).

European pauperism in the Indies reflected broad inequalities in colonial society, underscoring the social heterogeneity of the category "European" itself. Nonetheless, as late as 1917, concubinage was still seen by some as its major cause and as the principal source of *"blankenhaters"* (white-haters) (Braconier 1917:298). Concubinage became equated with a progeny of "malcontents," or "parasitic" whites, idle and

therefore dangerous. The fear of concubinage was carried yet a step further and tied to the political fear that such Eurasians would demand economic access, political rights and express their own interests through alliance with (and leadership of) organized opposition to Dutch rule (Mansvelt 1932; Blumberger 1939).*

Racial prejudice against *métis* was often, as in the Belgian Congo, "camouflaged under protestations of 'pity' for their fate, as if they were *'malheureux'* [unhappy] beings by definition" (Vellut 1982:103). As objects of charity, their protection in Indochina was a cause célèbre of European women—feminists and staunch colonial supporters—at home and abroad (Knibiehler and Goutalier 1985:37). European colonial women were urged to oversee their "moral protection," to develop their "natural" inclination toward French society, to turn them into "partisans of French ideas and influence" instead of revolutionaries (Chenet 1936:8; Sambuc 1931:261). The gender breakdown is clear: moral instruction reflected fears of sexual promiscuity in *métisse* girls and the political threat of *métis* boys turned militant men.

Orphanages for abandoned European and Indo-European children were not new features of 20th century colonial cultures; however, their importance increased vastly as an ever larger number of illegitimate children of mixed parentage populated grey zones along colonial divides. In the Netherlands Indies by the mid-18th century, state orphanages for Europeans were established to prevent "neglect and degeneracy of the many free-roaming poor bastards and orphans of Europeans" (quoted in Braconier 1917:293). By the 19th century, church, state and private organizations had become zealous backers of orphanages, providing some education but stronger doses of moral instruction. In India, civil asylums and charity schools cared for European and Anglo-Indian children in "almost every town, cantonment and hill-station" (Arnold 1979:108). In French Indochina in the 1930s virtually every colonial city had a home and society for the protection of abandoned *métis* youth (Chenet 1936; Sambuc 1931:256–272; Malleret 1934:220).

Whether these children were in fact "abandoned" by their Asian mothers is difficult to establish; the fact that *métis* children living in native homes were often *sought out* by state and private organizations and placed in these institutions to protect them against the "demoralised and sinister" influences of native kampung life suggests another interpretation (Taylor 1983). Public assistance in India, Indochina and the Netherlands Indies was designed not only to keep fair skinned children from running barefooted in native villages but to ensure that the proliferation of European pauper settlements was curtailed and controlled.* The preoccupation with creating a patriotic loyalty to French and Dutch culture among children was symptomatic of a more general fear; namely, that there were *already* patricides of the colonial fatherland in the making; that as adult women these children would fall into prostitution; that as adult men with emotional ties to native women and indigenous society they would join the enemies of the state, *verbasterd* (degenerate) and *décivilisé* (Braconier 1917:293; Pouvourville 1926; Sambuc 1931:261; Malleret 1934).[20]

EUROPEAN MOTHERHOOD AND MIDDLE-CLASS MORALITY

"A man remains a man as long as he is under the watch of a woman of his race" [George Hardy quoted in Chivas-Baron 1929:103].

Rationalization of imperial rule and safeguards against racial degeneracy in European colonies merged in the emphasis on particular moral themes. Both entailed a reassertion of European conventions, middle-class respectability, more frequent ties with the metropole and a restatement of what was culturally distinct and superior about how colonials ruled and lived. For those women who came to join their spouses or to find husbands, the prescriptions were clear. Just

as new plantation employees were taught to manage the natives, women were schooled in colonial propriety and domestic management. French manuals, such as those on colonial hygiene in Indochina, outlined the duties of colonial wives in no uncertain terms. As "auxiliary forces" in the imperial effort they were to "conserve the fitness and sometimes the life of all around them" by ensuring that "the home be happy and gay and that all take pleasure in clustering there" (Grall 1908:66; Chailley-Bert 1897). Practical guides to life in the Belgian Congo instructed (and indeed warned) *la femme blanche* that she was to keep "order, peace, hygiene and economy" (Favre 1938:217), "perpetuate a vigorous race," while preventing any "laxity in our administrative mores" (Favre 1938:256; Travaux du Groupe d'Etudes coloniales 1910:10).

This "division of labor" contained obvious asymmetries. Men were considered more susceptible to moral turpitude than women who were thus held responsible for the immoral states of men. European women were to create and protect colonial prestige, insulating their men from cultural and sexual contact with the colonized (Travaux . . . coloniales 1910:7). Racial degeneracy would be curtailed by European women charged with regenerating the physical health, the metropolitan affinities and the imperial purpose of their men (Hardy 1929:78).

At its heart was a reassertion of racial difference which harnessed nationalistic rhetoric and markers of middle-class morality to its cause (Delavignette 1946:47; Loutfi 1971:112; Mosse 1978:86). George Mosse describes European racism in the early 20th century as a "scavenger ideology," annexing nationalism and bourgeois respectability such that control over sexuality was central to all three (1985:10, 133–152). If the European middle class sought respectability "to maintain their status and self-respect against the

---

[20] Stoler's analysis of orphanages here bears resemblance to Foucault's analysis of insane asylums in *Madness and Civilization* (1965 [1961]). In that work he argued, among other things, that modern horror of madness is based on moral disapproval of the values implicit in it. He saw treatment of the insane as a way to bring

them back to bourgeois moral values. Stoler is arguing here that colonial Europeans in the twentieth century had a horror of the values implicit in children of mixed race. Orphanages were aimed at forcing the children to adopt the values of the colonizer rather than simply taking care of them.

lower-classes, and the aristocracy," in the colonies respectability was a defense against the colonized, and a way of more clearly defining themselves (Mosse 1985:5). Good colonial living now meant hard work, no sloth, and physical exercise rather than sexual release, which had been one rationale for condoning concubinage and prostitution in an earlier period. The debilitating influences of climate could be surmounted by regular diet and meticulous personal hygiene over which European women were to take full charge. Manuals on how to run a European household in the tropics provided detailed instructions in domestic science, moral upbringing and employer-servant relations. Adherence to strict conventions of cleanliness and cooking occupied an inordinate amount of women's time (Hermans 1925; Ridley 1983:77). Both activities entailed a constant surveillance of native nursemaids, laundrymen and live-in servants, while reinforcing the domestication of European women themselves (Brink 1920:43).

[*In a 1,200-word conclusion to this section, with 1 note, Stoler writes that it now became a European woman's duty to provide the happy family life seen as basic to colonial stability. The emphasis on women's duty to provide children and happy homes was also prevalent in Europe. This led to improvements in health care facilities but also to increased social control over reproduction.*

The belief that health conditions in the colonies were poor for women and children made childrearing a "conflicted endeavor" for colonial women. Doctors reported a wide range of grave medical conditions for women in the colonies, especially high infant mortality. In some cases doctors suggested that over generations, white women in the tropics would become sterile. In other cases prolonged residence would lead to reduced fertility or racial degeneration of offspring. Like the fear of degeneration, fears of sterility were linked to political issues. Such fears were greatest during the depression, when discussions about resettling poor whites in the colonies were often couched in terms of sex and the ability of white women to reproduce in the tropics.

Childrearing manuals used by colonial women warned against contact with natives. European children were perceived to be in danger

from both native caretakers and native children. Even where medical conditions were excellent, experts frequently claimed that European children could not thrive and should be sent back to Europe to be raised. Assuring the moral upbringing of children—that is, an upbringing free from contact with native people and ideas—became the principal focus of European women's associations. Women were caught between their responsibilities to raise their children in Europe and to be with their husbands in the colonies. These contrasting duties affected women's "social space" and economic possibilities.]

SHIFTING STRATEGIES OF RULE AND SEXUAL MORALITY

Though sex cannot of itself enable men to transcend racial barriers, it generates some admiration and affection across them, which is healthy, and which cannot always be dismissed as merely self-interested and prudential. On the whole, sexual interaction between Europeans and non-Europeans probably did more good than harm to race relations; at any rate, I cannot accept the feminist contention that it was fundamentally undesirable [Hyam 1986a:75].

The political etymology of colonizer and colonized was gender and class specific. The exclusionary politics of colonialism demarcated not just external boundaries but interior frontiers, specifying internal conformity and order among Europeans themselves. I have tried to show that the categories of colonizer and colonized were secured through notions of racial difference constructed in gender terms. Redefinitions of sexual protocol and morality emerged during crises of colonial control precisely because they called into question the tenuous artifices of rule *within* European communities and what marked their borders. Even from the limited cases we have reviewed, several patterns emerge. First and most obviously, colonial sexual prohibitions were racially asymetric and gender specific. Thus racial attributes were rarely discussed in nongendered terms; one was always a black *man*, an Asian *woman*. Secondly, interdictions against interracial unions were rarely a primary impulse in the strategies of rule. Interracial unions (as opposed to marriage) between European men and colonized women aided the long-term settlement of European men in the colonies while ensuring that colonial patrimony stayed in limited and selective hands. In India, Indochina and South Africa in the early centuries—colonial contexts usually associated with sharp social sanctions against interracial unions—"mixing" was systematically tolerated and even condoned.*

Changes in sexual access and domestic arrangements have invariably accompanied major efforts to reassert the internal coherence of European communities and to redefine the boundaries of privilege between the colonizer and the colonized. Sexual union in itself, however, did not automatically produce a larger population legally classified as "European." On the contrary, miscegenation signaled neither the absence nor presence of racial prejudice in itself; hierarchies of privilege and power were written into the *condoning* of interracial unions, as well as into their condemnation.

While the chronologies vary from one colonial context to another, we can identify some parallel shifts in the strategies of rule and in sexual morality. Concubinage fell into moral disfavor at the same time that new emphasis was placed on the standardization of European administration. While this occurred in some colonies by the early 20th century and in others later on, the correspondence between rationalized rule, bourgeois respectability and the custodial power of European women to protect their men seems strongest during the interwar years when Western scientific and technological achievements were then in question, and native nationalist and labor movements were hard pressing their demands.* Debates concerning the need to systematize colonial management and dissolve the provincial and personalized satraps of "the old-time *colon*" in the French empire invariably targeted and condemned the unseemly domestic arrangements in which they lived. British high colonial officials in Africa imposed new "character" requirements on their subordinates, designating specific class attributes and conjugal ties that such a selection implied (Kuklick 1979). Critical to this restruc-

turing was a new disdain for colonials too adapted to local custom, too removed from the local European community, and too encumbered with intimate native ties. As in Sumatra, this hands-off policy distanced Europeans in more than one sense: it forbade European staff both from personal confrontations with their Asian fieldhands and from the limited local knowledge they gained through sexual ties.

At the same time, medical expertise confirmed the salubrious benefits of European comradery and frequent home leaves, of a *cordon sanitaire*, not only around European enclaves, but around each home. White prestige became defined by this rationalized management and by the moral respectability and physical well-being of its agents, with which European women were charged. Colonial politics locked European men and women into a routinized protection of their physical health and social space in ways which bound gender prescriptions to class conventions, thereby fixing the racial cleavages between "us" and "them."

I have focused here on the multiple levels at which sexual control figured in the substance, as well as the iconography, of racial policy and imperial rule. But colonial politics was obviously not just about sex; nor did sexual relations reduce to colonial politics. On the contrary, sex in the colonies was about sexual access and reproduction, class distinctions and racial privileges, nationalism and European identity in different measure and not all at the same time. These major shifts in the positioning of women were not signaled by the penetration of capitalism per se but by more subtle changes in class politics, imperial morality and as responses to the vulnerabilities of colonial control. As we attempt broader ethnographies of empire, we may begin to capture how European culture and class politics resonated in colonial settings, how class and gender discriminations not only were translated into racial attitudes, but themselves reverberated in the metropole as they were fortified on colonial ground. Such investigations should help show that sexual control was both an instrumental image for the body politic, a salient part standing for the whole, and itself fundamental to how racial policies were secured and how colonial projects were carried out.[21]

REFERENCES

Abatucci. 1910. Le milieu africain consideré au point de vue de ses effets sur le système nerveux de l'européen. *Annales d'Hygiène et de Médecine Coloniale* 13:328–335.

Adas, Michael. 1989. *Machines as the Measure of Men: Scientific and Technological Superiority and Ideologies of Western Dominance.* Ithaca: Cornell University Press.

Arnold, David. 1979. European Orphans and Vagrants in India in the Nineteenth Century. *Journal of Imperial and Commonwealth History* 7:2:104–127.

———. 1983. White Colonization and Labour in Nineteenth-Century India. *Journal of Imperial and Commonwealth History* 11:2:133–158.

Bajema, Carl, ed. 1976. *Eugenics Then and Now.* Stroudsburg, PA: Dowden, Hutchinson & Ross.

Ballhatchet, Kenneth. 1980. *Race, Sex and Class under the Raj: Imperial Attitudes and Policies and Their Critics, 1793–1905.* New York: St. Martin's.

Baroli, Marc. 1967. *La vie quotidienne des Francais en Algérie.* Paris: Hachette.

Baudin, D. C. M. 1941 [1927]. *Het Indische Leven.* S'Gravenhage: H. P. Leopolds.

Beidelman, Thomas. 1982. *Colonial Evangelism.* Bloomington: Indiana University Press.

Berenger-Feraud, L. 1875. *Traité Clinique des Maladies des Europèens au Sénégal.* Paris: Adrien Delahaye.

Blumberger, J. Th. Petrus. 1939. *De Indo-Europeesche Beweging in Nederlandsch-Indie.* Haarlem: Tjeenk Willink.

Blussé, Leonard. 1986. *Strange Company: Chinese Settlers, Mestizo Women and the Dutch in VOC Batavia.* Dordrecht: Foris.

Bock, Gisela. 1984. Racism and Sexism in Nazi Germany: Motherhood, Compulsory Sterilization, and the State. In *When Biology Became Destiny: Women in Weimar and Nazi Germany,* pp. 271–296. New York: Monthly Review Press.

Boutilier, James. 1984. European Women in the Solomon Islands, 1900–1942. In *Rethinking Women's Roles: Perspectives from the Pacific,* Denise O'Brien and Sharon Tiffany, eds, pp. 173–199. Berkeley: University of California Press.

Braconier, A. de. 1913. Het Kazerne-Concubinaat in Ned-Indie. *Vragen van den Dag* 28:974–995.

———. 1917. *Het Pauperisme onder de in Ned. Oost-Indie levende Europeanen.* In *Nederlandsch-Indie* (1st yr.), 291–300.

———. 1918. *Kindercriminaliteit en de verzorging van misdadig aangelegde en verwaarloosde minderjarigen in Nederlandsch Indie.* Baarn: Hollandia-Drukkerij.

———. 1933. Het Prostitutie-vraagstuk in Nederlandsch-Indie. *Indisch Gids* 55:2:906–928.

Brink, K. B. M. Ten. 1920. *Indische Gezondheid.* Batavia: Nillmij.

Brou, A. M. N. 1907. Le Métis Franco-Annamite. *Revue Indochinois* (July):897–908.

Brownfoot, Janice N. 1984. Memsahibs in Colonial Malaya: A Study of European Wives in a British Colony and Protectorate 1900–1940. In *The Incorporated Wife,* Hilary Callan and Shirley Ardener, eds. London: Croom Helm.

Butcher, John. 1979. *The British in Malaya, 1880–1941: The Social History of a European Community in Colonial Southeast Asia.* Kuala Lumpur: Oxford University Press.

Callan, Hilary, and Shirley Ardener, eds. 1984. *The Incorporated Wife.* London: Croom Helm.

Callaway, Helen. 1987. *Gender, Culture and Empire: European Women in Colonial Nigeria.* London: Macmillan Press.

Chailley-Bert, M. J. 1897. L'Emigration des femmes aux colonies. Union Coloniale Francaise-conférence, 12 January. Paris: Armand Colin.

Chatterjee, Partha. 1989. Colonialism, nationalism, and colonialized women: the content in India. *American Ethnologist* 16(4):622–633.

Chenet, Ch. 1936. Le role de la femme française aux Colonies: Protection des enfants métis abandonnés. *Le Devoir des Femmes* (15 February):8.

Chivas-Baron, Clotide. 1929. *La femme française aux colonies.* Paris: Larose.

Clerkx, Lily. 1961. Mensen in Deli. Amsterdam: Sociologisch-Historisch Seminarium voor Zuidoost-Azie. Publication no. 2.

---

[21] Stoler presents a compelling argument; however, it is a point of view largely derived from her studies of historical documents and secondary analysis. The voices of the colonial subjects themselves are conspicuously absent. Given the current emphasis on multivocality in feminist anthropology, it is curious that Stoler does not allow colonial subjects, some of whom are still alive, to speak for themselves. We wonder what they would say.

Cock, J. 1980. *Maids and Madams.* Johannesburg: Raven Press.

Cohen, William. 1971. *Rulers of Empire: The French Colonial Service in Africa.* Stanford: Hoover Institution Press.

_____. 1980. *The French Encounter with Africans. White Response to Blacks, 1530–1880.* Bloomington: Indiana University Press.

Comaroff, John L. 1989. Images of Empire, Contests of Conscience: Models of Colonial Domination in South Africa. *American Ethnologist* 16(4):661–685.

Cool, F. 1938. De Bestrijding der Werkloosheidsgevolgen in Nederlandsch-Indie gedurende 1930–1936. *De Economist,* 135–147; 217–243.

Cooper, Frederick. 1980. *From Slaves to Squatters.* New Haven: Yale University Press.

Corneau, Grace. 1900. *La femme aux colonies.* Paris: Librairie Nilsson. Courtois, E.

_____. 1900. Des Régles Hygiéniques que doit suivre l'Europèen au Tonkin. *Revue Indo-chinoise* 83:539–541; 564–566; 598–601.

Davin, Anna. 1978. Imperialism and Motherhood. *History Workshop* 5:9–57.

Degler, Carl. 1971. *Neither Black nor White.* New York: Macmillan.

Delavignette, Robert. 1946. *Service Africain.* Paris: Gallimard.

Dixon, C. J. 1913. *De Assistent in Deli.* Amsterdam: J. H. de Bussy.

Douchet. 1928. Métis et congaies d'Indochine. Hanoi.

Dowd Hall, Jacquelyn. 1984. "The Mind that Burns in Each Body": Women, Rape, and Racial Violence. *Southern Exposure* 12:6:61–71.

Drooglever, P. 1980. *De Vaderiandse Club, 1929–42.* Franeker: T. Wever.

Dupuy, Aime. 1955. La personnalité du colon. *Revue d'Histoire Economique et Sociale* 33:1:77–103.

Encyclopedie van Nederland-Indie. 1919. S'Gravenhage Nijhoff and Brill.

Etienne, Mona, and Eleanor Leacock, eds. 1980. *Women and Colonization: Anthropological Perspectives.* New York: Praeger.

Fannon, Franz. 1967 [1952]. *Black Skin, White Masks.* New York: Grove Press.

Favre, J. L. 1938. *La Vie aux Colonies.* Paris: Larose.

Feuilletau de Bruyn, W. 1938. Over de Economische Mogelijkheid van een Kolonisatie van Blanken op Nederlandsch Nieuw-Guinea. In *Comptes Rendus du Congres International de Geographie, Amsterdam,* pp. 21–29. Leiden: Brill.

Fredrickson, George. 1981. *White Supremacy.* New York: Oxford University Press.

Gaitskell, Deborah. 1983. Housewives, Maids or Mothers: Some Contradictions of Domesticity for Christian Women in Johannesburg, 1903–39. *Journal of African History* 24:241–256.

Gann, L. H., and Peter Duignan. 1978. *The Rulers of British Africa, 1870–1914.* Stanford: Stanford University Press.

Gantes, Gilles de. 1981. *La population française au Tonkin entre 1931 et 1938. Memoire.* Aix-en-Provence: Institut d'Histoire des Pays d'Outre Mer.

Gartrell, Beverley. 1984. Colonial Wives: Villains or Victims? In *The Incorporated Wife,* H. Callan and S. Ardener, eds., pp. 165–185. London: Croom Helm.

Gilman, Sander L. 1985. *Difference and Pathology.* Ithaca: Cornell University Press.

Gordon, Linda. 1976. *Woman's Body, Woman's Right.* New York: Grossman.

Gordon, R., and M. Meggitt. 1985. *Law and Order in the New Guinea Highlands.* Hanover: University Press of New England.

Grall, Ch. 1908. *Hygiéne Coloniale Appliquée.* Paris: Bailliere. Grimshaw, Patricia

_____. 1983. Christian Woman, Pious Wife, Faithful Mother, Devoted Missionary: Conflicts in Roles of American Missionary Women in Nineteenth-Century Hawaii. *Feminist Studies* 9:3:489–521.

Hammerton, James. 1979. *Emigrant Gentlewomen.* London: Croom Helm. Hansen, Karen Tranberg

_____. 1986. Household Work as a Man's Job: Sex and Gender in Domestic Service in Zambia. *Anthropology Today* 2:3:18–23.

Hardy, George. 1929. *Ergaste ou la Vocation Coloniale.* Paris: Armand Colon.

Hartenberg. 1910. *Les Troubles Nerveux et Mentaux chez les coloniaux.* Paris.

Harwood, Dorothy. 1938. The Possibility of White Colonization in the Tropics. In *Comptes Rendu du Congrès Int'l de Géographie,* pp. 131–140. Leiden: Brill.

Hermans, E. H. 1925. *Gezondscheidsleer voor Nederlandsch-Indie.* Amsterdam: Meulenhoff.

Hesselink, Liesbeth. 1987. Prostitution: A Necessary Evil, Particularly in the Colonies: Views on Prostitution in the Netherlands Indies. In *Indonesian Women in Focus,* E. Locher-Scholten and A. Niehof, pp. 205–224. Dordrecht: Foris.

Het Pauperisme Commissie. 1901. *Het Pauperisme onder de Europeanen.* Batavia: Landsdrukkerij.

———. 1903. *Rapport der Pauperisme-Commissie.* Batavia: Landsdrukkerij.

Hobsbawn, Eric. 1987. *The Age of Empire, 1875–1914.* London: Weidenfeld and Nicholson.

Hunt, Nancy. 1988. Le bébé en brousse: European women, African Birth Spacing and Colonial Intervention in Breast Feeding in the Belgian Congo. *International Journal of African Historical Studies* 21:3.

Hyam, Ronald. 1986a. Empire and Sexual Opportunity. *Journal of Imperial and Commonwealth History* 14:2:34–90.

———. 1986b. Concubinage and the Colonial Service: The Crewe Circular (1909). *Journal of Imperial and Commonwealth History* 14:3:170–186.

Inglis, Amirah. 1975. *The White Women's Protection Ordinance: Sexual Anxiety and Politics in Papua.* London: Sussex University Press.

Jaurequiberry. 1924. *Les Blancs en Pays Chauds.* Paris: Maloine.

Jordan, Winthrop. 1968. *White over Black: American Attitudes Toward the Negro, 1550–1812.* Chapel Hill: University of North Carolina Press.

Joyeux, Ch., and A. Sice. 1937. *Affections exotiques du systéme nerveux. Précis de Médecine Coloniale.* Paris: Masson.

Kantoor van Arbeid. 1935. *Werkloosheid in Nederlandsch-Indie.* Batavia: Landsdrukkerij.

Kennedy, Dane. 1987. *Islands of White.* Durham: Duke University Press.

Kennedy, Raymond. 1947. *The Ageless Indies.* New York: John Day.

Kevles, Daniel. 1985. *In the Name of Eugenics.* Berkeley: University of California Press.

King, Anthony. 1976. *Colonial Urban Development.* London: Routledge & Kegan Paul.

Kirkwood, Deborah. 1984. Settler Wives in Southern Rhodesia: A Case Study. In *The Incorporated Wife,* H. Callan and S. Ardener, eds. London: Croom Helm.

Knibiehler, Y., and R. Goutalier. 1985. *La femme au temps des colonies.* Paris: Stock.

———. 1987. *Femmes et Colonisation: Rapport Terminal au Ministère des Relations Extérieures et de la Coopération.* Aix en-Provence: Institut d'Historie des Pays d'Outre-Mer.

Koks, Dr. J. Th. 1931. *De Indo.* Amsterdam: H. J. Paris.

Kroniek. 1917. *Oostkust van Sumatra-Instituut.* Amsterdam J. H. de Bussy.

Kuklick, Henrika. 1979. *The Imperial Bureaucrat: The Colonial Administrative Service in the Gold Coast, 1920–1939.* Stanford: Hoover Institution Press.

Le Bras, Hervé. 1981. Historie secrète de la fécondité. *Le Debat* 8:76–100.

Loutfi, Martine Astier. 1971. *Littérature et Colonialisme.* Paris: Mouton.

Lucas, Nicole. 1986. Trouwverbod, inlandse huishoudsters en Europese vrouwen. In *Vrouwen in de Nederlandse Kolonien,* J. Reijs, et al., eds., 78–97. Nijmegen: SUN.

Mackinnon, Murdoch. 1920. European Children in the Tropical Highlands. *Lancet* 199:944–945.

Malleret, Louis. 1934. *L'Exotisme Indochinois dans la Littérature Française depuis 1860.* Paris: Larose.

Mannoni, Octavio. 1964. *Prospero and Caliban.* New York: Praeger.

Mansvelt, W. 1932. De Positie der Indo-Europeanen. *Kolonial Studien,* 290–311.

Martinez-Alier, Verena. 1974. *Marriage, Class and Colour in Nineteenth Century Cuba.* Cambridge: Cambridge University Press.

Mason, Philip. 1958. *The Birth of a Dilemma: The Conquest and Settlement of Rhodesia.* New York: Oxford University Press.

Maunier, M. René. 1932. *Sociologie Coloniale.* Paris: Domat-Montchrestien.

Mazet, Jacques. 1932. *La Condition Juridique des Métis.* Paris: Domat-Montchrestien.

Mercier, Paul. 1965. The European Community of Dakar. In *Africa: Social Problems of Change and Conflict,* Pierre van den Berghe, ed., pp. 284–304. San Francisco: Chandler.

Ming, Hanneke. 1983. Barracks-Concubinage in the Indies, 1887–1920. *Indonesia* 35 (April):65–93.

Moore-Gilbert, B. J. 1986. *Kipling and "Orientalism."* New York: St. Martin's.

Mosse, George. 1978. *Toward the Final Solution.* New York: Fertig.

———. 1985. *Nationalism and Sexuality.* Madison: University of Wisconsin Press.

Muller, Hendrik. 1912. De Europeesche Samenleving. *Neerlands Indie.* Amsterdam: Elsevier: 371–384.

Nandy, Ashis. 1983. *The Intimate Enemy: Loss and Recovery of Self under Colonialism.* Delhi: Oxford University Press.

Nash, June. 1980. Aztec Women: The Transition from Status to Class in Empire and Colony. In *Woman and Colonization: Anthropological Perspectives,* Mona Etienne and Eleanor Leacock, eds., pp. 134–148. New York: Praeger.

Nieuwenhuys, Roger. 1959. *Tussen Twee Vaderlanden.* Amsterdam: Van Oorschot.

Nora, Pierre. 1961. *Les Français d'Algerie*. Paris: Julliard.

O'Brien, Rita Cruise. 1972. *White Society in Black Africa: The French in Senegal*. London: Faber & Faber.

Pollmann, Tessel. 1986. Bruidstraantjes: De Koloniale roman, de njai en de apartheid. In *Vrouwen in de Nederlandse Kolonien*, J. Reijs, et al., eds., pp. 98–125. Nijmegen: SUN.

Pourvourville, Albert de. 1926. Le Métis. Le Mal d'Argent. Paris: Monde Moderne, 97–114.

Price, Grenfell A. 1939. *White Settlers in the Tropics*. New York: American Geographical Society.

Prochaska, David. 1989. *Making Algeria French: Colonialism in Bone, 1870–1920*. Cambridge: Cambridge University Press.

Pujarniscle, E. 1931. *Philoxène ou de la litterature coloniale*. Paris.

Raptschinsky, B. 1941. *Kolonisatie van blanken in de tropen*. Den Haag: Bibliotheek van weten en denken.

Reijs, J., E. Kloek, U. Jansz, A. de Wildt, S. van Norden, and M. de Baar. 1986. *Vrouwen in de Nederlandse Kolonien*. Nijmegen: SUN.

Ridley, Hugh. 1983. *Images of Imperial Rule*. New York: Croom & Helm.

Ritter, W. L. 1856. *De Europeaan in Nederlandsch Indie*. Leyden: Sythoff.

Rodenwalt, Ernest. 1928. Eugenetische Problemen in Nederlandsch-Indie. *Ons Nageslacht*, 1–8.

Said, Edward W. 1978. *Orientalism*. New York: Vintage.

Sambuc. 1931. Les Métis Franco-Annamites en Indochine. *Revue du Pacifique*, 256–272.

Schmidt, Elizabeth. 1987. Ideology, Economics and the Role of Shona Women in Southern Rhodesia, 1850–1939. Ph.D. dissertation, University of Wisconsin.

Schneider, William. 1972. Toward the Improvement of the Human Race: The History of Eugenics in France. *Journal of Modern History* 54:269–291.

Schoevers, T. 1913. Het leven en werken van den assistant bij de Tabakscultuur in Deli. Jaarboek der Vereeniging "Studiebelangen." Wageningen: Zomer, 3–43.

Simon, Jean-Pierre. 1981. *Rapatriés d'Indochine*. Paris: Harmattan. Sivan, Emmanuel

_____. 1983. *Interpretations of Islam*. Princeton: Darwin Press.

Smith-Rosenberg, Carroll, and Charles Rosenberg. 1973. The Female Animal: Medical and Biological Views of Woman and Her Role in Nineteenth-Century America. *Journal of American History* 60(2):332–356.

Spear, Percival. 1963. *The Nabobs*. London: Oxford University Press.

Stepan, Nancy. 1982. *The Idea of Race in Science*. London: Macmillan.

Stoler, Ann. 1985a. *Capitalism and Confrontation in Sumatra's Plantation Belt, 1870–1979*. New Haven: Yale University Press.

_____. 1985b. Perceptions of Protest. *American Ethnologist* 12:4:642–658.

_____. 1989. Rethinking Colonial Categories: European Communities and the Boundaries of Rule. *Comparative Studies in Society and History* 13(1): 134–161.

Stoler, Ann Laura. 1995. *Race and the Education of Desire: Foucault's History of Sexuality and the Colonial Order of Things*. Chapel Hill: Duke University Press.

_____. 2002. *Carnal Knowledge and Imperial Power: Race and the Intimate in Colonial Rule*. Berkeley: University of California Press.

Strobel, Margaret. 1987. Gender and Race in the 19th and 20th Century British Empire. In *Becoming Visible: Women in European History*, R. Bridenthal et al., eds., pp. 375–396. Boston: Houghton Mifflin.

Stuurman, Siep. 1985. *Verzuiling, Kapitalisme en Patriarchaat*. Nijrnegen: SUN.

Sutherland, Heather. 1982. Ethnicity and Access in Colonial Macassar. In *Papers of the Dutch-Indonesian Historical Conference*, pp. 250–277. Leiden: Bureau of Indonesian Studies.

Takaki, Ronald. 1977. *Iron Cages*. Berkeley: University of California Press.

Taylor, Jean. 1977. The World of Women in the Colonial Dutch Novel. *Kabar Seberang* 2:26–41.

_____. 1983. *The Social World of Batavia*. Madison: University of Wisconsin Press.

Tiffany, Sharon, and Kathleen Adams. 1985. *The Wild Woman: An Inquiry into the Anthropology of an Idea*. Cambridge, MA: Schenkman.

Tirefort, A. 1979. 'Le Bon Temps': La Communauté Francaise en Basse Cote d'Ivoire pendant L'Entre-Deux Guerres, 1920–1940. Troisième Cycle, Centre d'Etudes Africaines, Paris.

Travaux du Groupe d'Etudes Coloniales. 1910. *La Femme Blanche au Congo*. Brussels: Misch & Thron.

Van Doom, Jacques. 1983. *A Divided Society: Segmentation and Mediation in Late-Colonial Indonesia*. Rotterdam: CASPA.

_____. 1985. Indie als Koloniale Maatschappy. In *De Nederlandse samenleving sinds 1815*, F. L. van Holthoon, ed. Assen: Maastricht.

Van Helten, J., and K. Williams. 1983. 'The Crying Need of South Africa': The Emigration of Single

British Women in the Transvaal, 1901–1910. *Journal of South African Studies* 10:1:11–38.

Van Heyningen, Elizabeth B. 1984. The Social Evil in the Cape Colony 1868–1902: Prostitution and the Contagious Disease Acts. *Journal of Southern African Studies* 10:2:170–197.

Van Marle, A. 1952. De group der Europeanen in Nederlands-Indie. *Indonesie*, 5:2:77–121; 5:3:314–341; 5:5:481–507.

Van Onselen, Charles. 1982. *Studies in the Social and Economic History of the Witwatersrand 1886–1914.* Vol. I. New York: Longman.

Veerde, A. G. 1931. Onderzoek naar den omvang der werkloosheid op java, November 1930–Juni 1931. *Koloniale Studien*, 242–273; 503–533.

Vellut, Jean-Luc. 1982. Materiaux pour une image du Blanc dans la société coloniale du Congo Belge. In *Stéréotypes Nationaux et Préjudés Raciaux aux XIXe et XXe Siècles*, Jean Pirotte, ed. Leuven: Editions Nauwelaerts.

Vere Allen, J. de. 1970. Malayan Civil Service, 1874–1941: Colonial Bureaucracy Malayan Elite. *Comparative Studies in Society and History* 12:149–178.

Wanderken, P. 1943. Zoo leven onze kinderen. In *Zoo Leven Wij in Indonesia*, pp. 172–187. Deventer: Van Hoever.

Wertheim, Willem. 1959. *Indonesian Society in Transition.* The Hague: Van Hoeve.

Winckel, Ch. W. F. 1938. The Feasibility of White Settlements in the Tropics: a Medical Point of View. In *Comptes Rendus de Congrès International de Géographie Amsterdam*, pp. 345–356. Leiden: Brill.

Woodcock, George. 1969. *The British in the Far East.* New York: Atheneum.

Symbolic and Interpretive Anthropology

Beginning in the 1960s and reaching its fullest expression in the 1970s, symbolic or interpretive anthropology was part of a general reevaluation of cultural anthropology as a scientific enterprise. Materialists insisted that the analysis of culture focus on empirical material phenomena. Ethnoscientists and cognitive anthropologists argued that culture was a mental phenomenon that could be modeled following principles similar to mathematics or formal logic. Symbolic anthropologists agreed with the ethnoscientists and cognitive anthropologists that culture was a mental phenomenon but rejected the notion that culture could be modeled like mathematics or logic. Instead they used a variety of analytical tools drawn from psychology, history, and literature to study symbolic action within culture. Their fundamental interest was in examining how people formulated their reality. Dolgin, Kemnitzer, and Schneider (1977), for example, write: "Our concern is not with whether or not the views a people hold are accurate in any 'scientific' sense of the term. . . . In social action, that which is thought to be real is treated as real" (quoted in Lett 1987:111).

The development of symbolic analysis was influenced by the work of Benjamin L. Whorf and Edward Sapir in linguistics and ethnoscientific studies, which gained popularity in the 1950s. Symbolic anthropologists argue that, like language, symbols are a shared system of meaning that can only be understood within a particular historical and social context. Culture, they believe, lies in people's interpretations of the events and the things around them. In other words, symbolic anthropologists believe we construct our cultural reality. Consequently, they take a semiotic approach focusing on the analysis of meaning. As Geertz writes;

> Believing, with Max Weber, that man is an animal suspended in webs of significance he himself has spun, I take cultures to be those webs, and the analysis of it to be therefore not an experimental science in search of law but an interpretive one in search of meaning. (1973:5)

The term *symbolic anthropology* covers a variety of forms of analysis, but two dominant trends in the field are represented by the work of Clifford Geertz (1926–2006) and Victor Turner (1920–1983). Although both are concerned with the interpretation of symbolic action, their approaches are very different. Geertz's emphasis on culture as an organized collection of symbolic systems is typically American in flavor. Turner's work, on the other hand, is in the British structural-functionalist style and is concerned with the operation of symbols in the maintenance of society.

Geertz argues that "Whatever sense we have of how things stand with someone else's inner life, we gain it through their expressions, not through some magical intrusion into their consciousness" (1986:373). Thus, cultures are embodied in public symbols and actions.

To Geertz, symbols are means of transmitting meaning. His focus is on how symbols affect the way people think about their world, how "symbols operate as vehicles of culture" (Ortner 1984:129). For example, in "Deep Play: Notes on the Balinese Cockfight" (see essay 37), Geertz describes and analyzes the various symbolic meanings of the cockfight for the Balinese who engage in the sport and how these various levels of meaning influence their lives. Ultimately, he argues that the cockfight does not have any function in the sense of maintaining social solidarity, reinforcing societal norms or filling Malinowskian biopsychological needs. Instead, the cockfight enables the Balinese to share experiences and create meaning from their lives, much in the same way that sports or religious rituals may be organizing experiences for those in the West.

Geertz's type of analysis is focused at the level of the individual participant in society. Although he acknowledges that it is impossible to get inside the head of native informants, he wants to provide his readers with a sense of what it might feel like to be a member of the culture he is describing. He does this using a technique he calls "thick description." Geertz assumes that important symbols and actions have many layers of meaning and that their power derives from this fact. In thick description, the anthropologist attempts to analyze each layer of meaning. Geertz compares doing thick description to peeling an onion. There is layer after layer after layer, but no reward at the center. The onion is its layers; similarly, culture is its meanings (see Geertz 1973:6–10). As the article reprinted here shows, this actor-centered perspective is fundamental to Geertz's form of analysis.

Victor Turner approached symbolic analysis from a different angle. Trained in British structural functionalism, he examined symbols as mechanisms for the maintenance of society. Turner viewed symbols as "operators in the social process, things that, when put together in certain arrangements in certain contexts (especially rituals), produce essentially social transformations" (Ortner 1984:131). Turner argued that social solidarity had to be continually maintained. Ritual symbols, in his view, were the primary tools through which social order was renewed. Turner also made a major contribution to the conceptual vocabulary of symbolic analysis by outlining various properties of symbols such as multivocality, condensation, the unification of disparate significata, and polarization of meaning (Turner 1967b:28). These terms are discussed in essay 36.

Unlike Geertz's "thick description," Turner followed a more formal program of symbolic analysis. He believed that the interpretation of ritual symbols could be derived from three classes of data: (1) external form and observable characteristics, (2) the interpretations of specialists and laypeople

within the society, and (3) deduction from specific contexts by the anthropologist.

Turner viewed his work as a contrast to Levi-Strauss' structuralism and to the psychoanalytic analysis of cultural symbols. In particular, he emphasized study of the context in which symbols were expressed. He wrote:

> I found that I could not analyze ritual symbols without studying them in a time series in relation to other "events," for symbols are essentially involved in social process. I came to see performances of rituals as distinct phases in the social process whereby groups became adjusted to internal changes and adapted to their external environment. From this standpoint the ritual symbol becomes a factor in social action, a positive force in an activity field. (Turner 1967:20)

One of the great shortcomings of symbolic analysis is that it is primarily descriptive and does not lend itself to general theoretical or methodological formulations. Symbolic anthropologists claim to search for universals of human understanding through the collection of locally particular data. However, much of what symbolic anthropologists know is derived through imaginative insight into particular cultures or events within those cultures. As a result, their knowledge does not provide a theoretical basis for understanding culture as a universal phenomenon.

Mary Douglas (b. 1921) is one symbolic anthropologist whose work defies this generalization. She has attempted to analyze universal patterns of symbolism, focusing on beliefs about pollution and hygiene as they are expressed in religions. In her two most famous works—*Purity and Danger* (1966) and *Natural Symbols* (1970)—Douglas contends that universal patterns of purity-pollution symbolism exist and are based on reference to the human body. She argues her case from a Durkheimian perspective, suggesting that shared symbols "create a unity in experience" (1966:2) and that religious ideas about purity and pollution symbolize beliefs about social order. In the introduction to *Purity and Danger* she writes:

> I believe that some pollutions are used as analogies for expressing a general view of the social order. For example, there are beliefs that each sex is a danger to the other through contact with sexual fluids. . . . Such patterns of sexual

danger can be seen to express symmetry or hierarchy. It is implausible to interpret them as suggesting something about the actual relation of the sexes. I suggest that many ideas about sexual dangers are better interpreted as symbols of the relation between parts of society, as mirroring designs of hierarchy or symmetry which apply in the larger social system. . . . Sometimes bodily orifices seem to represent points of entry or exit to social units, or bodily perfection can symbolise an ideal theocracy. (1966:3–4)

Symbolic anthropology is concerned with studying the process by which people give meaning to their world and how this world is expressed in cultural symbols. Geertz writes that "Cultural analysis is (or should be) guessing at meanings, assessing the guesses, and drawing explanatory conclusions from the better guesses" (1973:20).

However, symbolic anthropologists have never specifically explained a methodology for "guessing at meaning." Anthropologists who do not share Geertz's views often believe that this is a fundamental flaw. Critics claim that the credibility of symbolic interpretation is based on the explanatory skills of the anthropologist and argue that such anthropology often seems closer to literary criticism than social science. In fact, much of the work that characterized the symbolic analyses of the 1970s and 1980s was incorporated into the postmodern movement of the 1990s. Today it is rare to see analytical work such as that conducted by Turner and Geertz. Rather than being concerned with what a symbol "means," contemporary symbolic analyses are much more likely to be concerned with the postmodern issues of agency, power, and positioning.

35. *External Boundaries*

Mary Douglas (b. 1921)

THE IDEA OF society is a powerful image. It is potent in its own right to control or to stir men to action. This image has form; it has external boundaries, margins, internal structure. Its outlines contain power to reward conformity and repulse attack. There is energy in its margins and unstructured areas. For symbols of society any human experience of structures, margins or boundaries is ready to hand.[1]

Van Gennep shows how thresholds symbolise beginnings of new statuses. Why does the bridegroom carry his bride over the lintel? Because the step, the beam and the door posts make a frame which is the necessary everyday condition of entering a house. The homely experience of going through a door is able to express so many kinds of entrance. So also are cross roads and arches, new seasons, new clothes and the rest. No experience is too lowly to be taken up in ritual and given a lofty meaning. The more personal and intimate the source of ritual symbolism, the more telling its message. The more the symbol is drawn from the common fund of human experience, the more wide and certain its reception.[2]

From *Purity and Danger* (1966)

---

[1] Trained by Evans-Pritchard at Oxford in the British structural-functionalist school, Mary Douglas was influenced by Durkheim's notions of society and social cohesion. Durkheim argued that religion was essentially a model of society that served to promote social cohesion (see essay 6); Douglas believes that shared symbols promote social solidarity and provide mechanisms for social control. She opens this article with a powerful image of society as a coherently organized whole. Her comment that human experiences of structures or boundaries can serve as symbols of society hints at one of her fundamental ideas—that the human body is a symbol of society.

[2] Douglas, interested in discovering universals of symbolism, suggests that the most potent symbols are found in the realm of the mundane. Because the form of the human body may be the most common human experience, her analysis centers on the body and its products.

The structure of living organisms is better able to reflect complex social forms than door posts and lintels. So we find that the rituals of sacrifice specify what kind of animal shall be used, young or old, male, female or neutered, and that these rules signify various aspects of the situation which calls for sacrifice. The way the animal is to be slaughtered is also laid down. The Dinka cut the beast longitudinally through the sexual organs if the sacrifice is intended to undo an incest; in half across the middle for celebrating a truce; they suffocate it for some occasions and trample it to death for others. Even more direct is the symbolism worked upon the human body. The body is a model which can stand for any bounded system. Its boundaries can represent any boundaries which are threatened or precarious. The body is a complex structure. The functions of its different parts and their relation afford a source of symbols for other complex structures. We cannot possibly interpret rituals concerning excreta, breast milk, saliva and the rest unless we are prepared to see in the body a symbol of society, and to see the powers and dangers credited to social structure reproduced in small on the human body.[3]

It is easy to see that the body of a sacrificial ox is being used as a diagram of a social situation. But when we try to interpret rituals of the human body in the same way the psychological tradition turns its face away from society, back towards the individual. Public rituals may express public concerns when they use inanimate door posts or animal sacrifices: but public rituals enacted on the human body are taken to express personal and private concerns. There is no possible justification for this shift of interpretation just because the rituals work upon human flesh. As far as I know the case has never been methodically stated. Its protagonists merely proceed from unchallenged assumptions, which arise from the strong similarity between certain ritual forms and the behavior of psychopathic individuals. The assumption is that in some sense primitive cultures correspond to infantile stages in the development of the human psyche. Consequently such rites are interpreted as if they express the same preoccupations which fill the mind of psychopaths or infants.[4]

Let me take two modern attempts to use primitive cultures to buttress psychological insights. Both stem from a long line of similar discussions, and both are misleading because the relation between culture and individual psyche are not made clear.

Bettelheim's *Symbolic Wounds* is mainly an interpretation of circumcision and initiation rites. The author tries to use the set rituals of Australians and Africans to throw light on psychological phenomena. He is particularly concerned to show that psychoanalysts have overemphasized girls' envy of the male sex and overlooked the importance of boys' envy of the female sex. The idea came to him originally in studying groups of schizophrenic children approaching adolescence. It seems very likely that the idea is sound and important. I am not at all claiming to criticize his insight into schizophrenia. But when he argues that rituals which are explicitly designed to produce genital bleeding in males are intended to express male envy of female reproductive processes, the anthropologist should protest that this is an inadequate interpretation of a public rite. It is inadequate because it is merely descriptive. What is being carved in human flesh is an image of society. And in the moiety- and section-divided tribes he cites, the Murngin and Arunta, it seems more likely that the public rites are concerned to

---

[3] Douglas treats the symbolism of blood, breast milk, and other products of the human body as symbols of society. Ultimately, this argument is based on the organic analogy, a nineteenth-century model of society generally associated with Spencer. But whereas Spencer argued by direct analogy—telegraph wires are the nerves of society, for instance—Douglas' argument is symbolic—society is not a body, but it can be symbolically represented by a body. In the next essay, on Ndembu symbolism, Victor Turner makes a similar point.

[4] Douglas here criticizes psychological interpretations of symbolism, particularly psychoanalytic interpretations, which have tended to treat non-Western peoples as childlike or mentally ill. One line of psychoanalytic thought equates the trancing of shamans or other religious specialists in primitive societies with the acts of psychiatric patients in Western hospitals. See, for example, Kroeber's "Psychotic Factors in Shamanism" (1940) or Devereux's "Shamans as Neurotics" (1961).

create a symbol of the symmetry of the two halves of society.[5]

The other book is *Life Against Death,* in which Brown outlines an explicit comparison between the culture of "archaic man" and our own culture, in terms of the infantile and neurotic fantasies which they seem to express. Their common assumptions about primitive culture derive from Roheim (1925): primitive culture is autoplastic, ours is alloplastic.[6] The primitive seeks to achieve his desires by self-manipulation, performing surgical rites upon his own body to produce fertility in nature, subordination in women or hunting success. In modern culture we seek to achieve our desires by operating directly on the external environment, with the impressive technical results that are the most obvious distinction between the two types of cultures. Bettelheim adopts this summing up of the differences between the ritual and the technical bias in civilization. But he supposes that the primitive culture is produced by inadequate, immature personalities, and even that the psychological shortcomings of the savage accounts for his feeble technical achievements:

> If preliterate peoples had personality structures as complex as those of modern man, if their defenses were as elaborate and their consciences as refined and demanding; if the

dynamic interplay between ego, superego and id were as intricate and if their ego's were as well adapted to meet and change external reality—they would have developed societies equally complex, though probably different. Their societies have, however, remained small and relatively ineffective in coping with the external environment. It may be that one of the reasons for this is their tendency to try to solve problems by autoplastic rather than alloplastic manipulation. (p. 87)

Let us assert again, as many anthropologists have before, that there are no grounds for supposing that primitive culture as such is the product of a primitive type of individual whose personality resembles that of infants or neurotics. And let us challenge the psychologists to express the syllogisms on which such a hypothesis might rest. Underlying the whole argument is the assumption that the problems which rituals are intended to solve are personal psychological problems. Bettelheim actually goes on to compare the primitive ritualist with the child who hits his own head when frustrated. This assumption underlies his whole book.

Brown makes the same assumption, but his reasoning is more subtle.[7] He does not suppose that the culture's primitive condition is caused by individual personal traits: he allows very properly for the effect of cultural conditioning on the

---

[5] Bruno Bettelheim (1903–1990) was an Austrian student of Sigmund Freud who emigrated to the United States in 1939 and spent virtually his whole career at the University of Chicago. Bettelheim was best known for his work with emotionally disturbed children. He was also recognized for his psychoanalytic analysis of ethnographic material, particularly his 1955 work *Symbolic Wounds.*

[6] Geza Roheim (1892–1953) was a Hungarian anthropologist. Early in his career he became a follower of Freud. Roheim spent several years conducting fieldwork in Australia, Africa, and Melanesia and was one of the leading proponents of the psychoanalytic analysis of ethnographic material. When Malinowski attacked Freud's excursions into anthropology, Roheim was one of Freud's staunchest defenders. In his 1925 book *Australian Totemism,* he characterized primitive cultures as autoplastic and Western society as alloplastic. These are medical terms. *Autoplastic* refers to the surgical repair of defects with tissue from another part of the patient's body. *Alloplasty* is replacing a

diseased or damaged body part with synthetic material. Using Bettelheim's example from *Symbolic Wounds* that Douglas cites in the paragraph above, Australian Aborigines are autoplastic because a man performs a ritual subincision of his penis in order to simulate the flow of a woman's menstrual blood. Ritual use of a blood substitute, say a red vegetable dye, would be considered alloplastic.

[7] The Brown discussed here is the Oxford-educated American scholar Norman O. Brown (1913–2002), best known for his book *Life Against Death* (1959), a psychoanalytic reinterpretation of human history. Today, works such as *Life Against Death* and *Symbolic Wounds* are considered artifacts of a bygone era; even at the time of publication these works were never widely popular among American anthropologists. But Douglas is English, and Freudian theory was taken much more seriously by European anthropologists. When she wrote this book in 1966, she was attacking a view that was still popular among European scholars.

individual personality. But he proceeds to consider the total culture as if it, in its totality, could be compared to an infant or a retarded adult. The primitive culture resorts to bodily magic to achieve its desires. It is in a stage of cultural evolution comparable to that of infantile anal eroticism. Starting from the maxim: "Infantile sexuality is autoplastic compensation for the loss of the Other; sublimation is alloplastic compensation for loss of Self" (p. 170) he goes on to argue that "archaic" culture is directed to the same ends as infantile sexuality, that is, escape from the hard realities of loss, separation and death. Epigrams are, by their nature, obscure. This is another approach to primitive culture which I would like to see fully spelt out. Brown develops the theme only briefly, as follows:

> Archaic man is preoccupied with the castration complex, the incest taboo and the desexualisation of the penis, that is, the transference of the genital impulses into that aim-inhibited libido which sustains the kinship systems in which archaic life is embedded. The low degree of sublimation, corresponding to the low level of technology, means by our previous definitions, a weaker ego, an ego which has not yet come to terms (by negation) with its own pregenital impulses. The result is that all the fantastic wishes of infantile narcissism express themselves in unsublimated form so that archaic man retains the magic body of infancy. (p. 298–9)

These fantasies suppose that the body itself could fulfill the infant's wish for unending, self-replenishing enjoyment. They are a flight from reality, a refusal to face loss, separation and death. The ego develops by sublimating these fantasies. It mortifies the body, denies the magic of excrement and to that extent faces reality. But sublimation substitutes another set of unreal aims and ends by providing the self with another kind of false escape from loss, separation and death. This is how I understand the argument to run. The

more material that an elaborate technology imposes between ourselves and the satisfaction of our infantile desires, the more busily has sublimation been at work. But the converse seems questionable. Can we argue that the less the material basis of civilization is developed, the less sublimation has been at work? What precise analogy with infantile fantasy can be valid for a primitive culture based on a primitive technology? How does a low level of technology imply "an ego which has not yet come to terms (by negation) with its own pregenital impulses"? In what sense is one culture more sublimated than another?[8]

[*We have omitted a 1,000-word discussion in which Douglas refutes the psychoanalytic interpretation of excremental magic using an example of what she considers to be Brown's bias in his discussion of a Winnebago Indian trickster myth. She also cites an ethnographic example of how body substances such as blood and spittle may be considered as both polluting or sacred substances. Douglas concludes her discussion of what she calls "body dirt" with a reference to the ritual use of royal corpses. We rejoin the text at the beginning of her discussion of why products of the body are symbols of danger and power.*]

But now we are ready to broach the central question. Why should bodily refuse be a symbol of danger and of power? Why should sorcerers be thought to qualify for initiation by shedding blood or committing incest or anthropophagy?[9] Why, when initiated, should their art consist largely of manipulating powers thought to inhere in the margins of the human body? Why should bodily margins be thought to be specially invested with power and danger?

First, we can rule out the idea that public rituals express common infantile fantasies. These erotic desires which it is said to be the infant's dream to satisfy within the body's bounds are presumably common to the human race. Consequently body symbolism is part of the common

---

[8] Douglas' central argument is that bodily substances are symbols of danger or power because they symbolize relations within a society. Consequently, she strongly argues against the psychoanalytic notion that the ritualized use of body refuse, such as excrement, is a psychiatric phenomenon based on infantile fantasies.

[9] *Anthropophagy:* the eating of human flesh.

stock of symbols, deeply emotive because of the individual's experience. But rituals draw on this common stock of symbols selectively. Some develop here, others there. Psychological explanations cannot of their nature account for what is culturally distinctive.

Second, all margins are dangerous. If they are pulled this way or that the shape of fundamental experience is altered. Any structure of ideas is vulnerable at its margins. We should expect the orifices of the body to symbolise its specially vulnerable points. Matter issuing from them is marginal stuff of the most obvious kind. Spittle, blood, milk, urine, faeces or tears by simply issuing forth have traversed the boundary of the body. So also have bodily parings, skin, nail, hair clippings and sweat. The mistake is to treat bodily margins in isolation from all other margins. There is no reason to assume any primacy for the individual's attitude to his own bodily and emotional experience, any more than for his cultural and social experience. This is the clue which explains the unevenness with which different aspects of the body are treated in the rituals of the world. In some, menstrual pollution is feared as a lethal danger; in others not at all (see Chapter 9). In some, death pollution is a daily preoccupation; in others not at all. In some, excreta is dangerous, in others it is only a joke. In India cooked food and saliva are pollution-prone, but Bushmen collect melon seeds from their mouths for later roasting and eating (Marshall-Thomas, p. 44).[10]

Each culture has its own special risks and problems. To which particular bodily margins its beliefs attribute power depends on what situation the body is mirroring. It seems that our deepest fears and desires take expression with a kind of witty aptness. To understand body pollution we should try to argue back from the known dangers of society to the known selection of bodily themes and try to recognize what appositeness[11] is there.

In pursuing a last-ditch reduction of all behavior to personal preoccupations of individuals with their own bodies the psychologists are merely sticking to their last.

> The derisive remark was once made against psychoanalysis that the unconscious sees a penis in every convex object and a vagina or anus in every concave one. I find that this sentence well characterises the facts. (Ferenczi, *Sex in Psychoanalysis*, p. 227, quoted by Brown)[12]

It is the duty of every craftsman to stick to his last. The sociologists have the duty of meeting one kind of reductionism with their own. Just as it is true that everything symbolizes the body, so it is equally true (and all the more so for that reason) that the body symbolizes everything else. Out of this symbolism, which in fold upon fold of interior meaning leads back to the experience of the self with its body, the sociologist is justified in trying to work in the other direction to draw out some layers of insight about the self's experience in society.

If anal eroticism is expressed at the cultural level we are not entitled to expect a population of anal erotics. We must look around for whatever it is that has made appropriate any cultural analogy with anal eroticism. The procedure in a modest way is like Freud's analysis of jokes. Trying to find a connection between the verbal form and the amusement derived from it he laboriously reduced joke interpretation to a few general rules.

---

[10] At the start of this essay, Douglas referred to the work of Arnold van Gennep (1873–1957), a folklorist, and his influence is evident in this passage. His best known work is *Rites of Passage* (1960 [1909]). Every rite of passage marking a person's change from one status to another, in his view, was outlined by the stages of separation, transition, and incorporation. During the transition phase one is in a liminal state, outside the margins of society, no longer one thing, but not yet another. Thus, separation from the group is necessary because, in the stage of transition, one may be ritually impure or dangerous. Douglas applies this same principle to the human body. She writes that "all margins are dangerous" and that matter issuing from the body's orifices, because it has traversed the boundary of the body, may be dangerous. One of the classic discussions of liminal states in rites of passage is Victor Turner's "Betwixt and Between: The Liminal Period in Rites of Passage," first published in 1964 and then revised in 1967, in which he referred to this essay by Douglas.

[11] *Appositeness:* suitability or pertinence.

[12] Sandor Ferenczi was a professor of psychoanalysis and a colleague of Sigmund Freud.

No comedian script-writer could use the rules for inventing jokes, but they help us to see some connections between laughter, the unconscious, and the structure of stories. The analogy is fair for pollution is like an inverted form of humour. It is not a joke for it does not amuse. But the structure of its symbolism uses comparison and double meaning like the structure of a joke.[13]

Four kinds of social pollution seem worth distinguishing. The first is danger pressing on external boundaries; the second, danger from transgressing the internal lines of the system; the third, danger in the margins of the lines. The fourth is danger from internal contradiction, when some of the basic postulates are denied by other basic postulates, so that at certain points the system seems to be at war with itself. In this chapter I show how the symbolism of the body's boundaries is used in this kind of unfunny wit to express danger to community boundaries.[14]

The ritual life of the Coorgs (Srinivas) gives the impression of a people obsessed by the fear of dangerous impurities entering their system. They treat the body as if it were a beleaguered town, every ingress and exit guarded for spies and traitors. Anything issuing from the body is never to be re-admitted, but strictly avoided. The most dangerous pollution is for anything which has once emerged gaining re-entry. A little myth, trivial by other standards, justifies so much of their behavior and system of thought that the ethnographer has to refer to it three or four times. A Goddess in every trial of strength or cunning defeated her two brothers. Since future precedence depended on the outcome of these contests, they decided to defeat her by a ruse. She was tricked into taking out of her mouth the betel that she was chewing to see if it was redder than theirs and into popping it back again. Once she had realized she had eaten something which had once been in her own mouth and was therefore defiled by saliva, though she wept and bewailed she accepted the full justice of her downfall. The mistake canceled all her previous victories, and her brothers' eternal precedence over her was established as of right.

The Coorgs have a place within the system of Hindoo castes. There is good reason to regard them as not exceptional or aberrant in Hindoo India (Dumont and Peacock). Therefore they conceive status in terms of purity and impurity as these ideas are applied throughout the regime of castes. The lowest castes are the most impure and it is they whose humble services enable the higher castes to be free of bodily impurities. They wash clothes, cut hair, dress corpses and so on. The whole system represents a body in which by the division of labour the head does the thinking and praying and the most despised parts carry away waste matter. Each sub-caste community in a local region is conscious of its relative standing in the scale of purity. Seen from ego's position the system of caste purity is structured upwards. Those above him are more pure. All the positions below him, be they ever so intricately distinguished in relation to one another, are to him polluting. Thus for any ego within the system the threatening non-structure against which barriers must be erected lies below. The sad wit of pollution as it comments on bodily functions symbolizes descent in the caste structure by contact with faeces, blood and corpses.[15]

---

[13] Douglas is referring to Freud's *Jokes and Their Relation to the Unconscious* (1960 [1905]), which explored the relationship between dreams and jokes. In this book he outlined different types of jokes and the literary and psychological mechanisms that he believed made them amusing.

[14] Using the example of an Indian caste called the Coorgs, Douglas shows that the four types of bodily purity-pollution practices she outlines are symbolic models of larger social relationships.

[15] In the caste system of India, the purest individuals are leaders and priests; those who are most polluted have tasks dealing with the disposal of human waste and refuse. This association of pollution with human refuse is an extension of body symbolism, a key metaphor in Hindu belief. In the Vedas (sacred Hindu texts), the creation of the world is described as the result of the gods sacrificing a divine being named Purusha. From Purusha's mouth came the priests, from his arms the warriors, from his thighs the merchants, and from his feet the laborers. In other words, the caste divisions were created by the division of Purusha's body. This Hindu myth is a poetic example of the body-society symbolism with which Douglas began the essay.

The Coorgs shared with other castes this fear of what is outside and below. But living in their mountain fastness they were also an isolated community, having only occasional and controllable contact with the world around. For them the model of the exits and entrances of the human body is a doubly apt symbolic focus of fears for their minority standing in the larger society. Here I am suggesting that when rituals express anxiety about the body's orifices the sociological counterpart of this anxiety is a care to protect the political and cultural unity of a minority group. The Israelites were always in their history a hard-pressed minority. In their beliefs all the bodily issues were polluting, blood, pus, excreta, semen, etc. The threatened boundaries of their body politic would be well mirrored in their care for the integrity, unity and purity of the physical body.

The Hindoo caste system, while embracing all minorities, embraces them each as a distinctive, cultural sub-unit. In any given locality, any sub-caste is likely to be a minority. The purer and higher its caste status, the more of a minority it must be. Therefore the revulsion from touching corpses and excreta does not merely express the order of caste in the system as a whole. The anxiety about bodily margins expresses danger to group survival.[16]

That the sociological approach to caste pollution is much more convincing than a psychoanalytic approach is clear when we consider what the Indian's private attitudes to defecation are. In the ritual we know that to touch excrement is to be defiled and that the latrine cleaners stand in the lowest grade of the caste hierarchy. If this pollution rule expressed individual anxieties we would expect Hindoos to be controlled and secretive about the act of defecation. It comes as a considerable shock to read that slack disregard is their normal attitude, to such an extent that pavements, verandahs and public places are littered with faeces until the sweeper comes along.[17]

> Indians defecate everywhere. They defecate, mostly, beside the railway tracks. But they also defecate on the beaches—they defecate on the streets; they never look for cover. . . . These squatting figures—to the visitor, after a time, as eternal and emblematic as Rodin's Thinker—are never spoken of; they are never written about; they are not mentioned in novels or stories; they do not appear in feature films or documentaries. This might be regarded as part of a permissible prettifying intention. But the truth is that Indians do not see these squatters and might even with complete sincerity, deny that they exist. (Naipaul, chapter 3)

Rather than oral or anal eroticism it is more convincing to argue that caste pollution represents only what it claims to be. It is a symbolic system, based on the image of the body, whose primary concern is the ordering of a social hierarchy.

It is worth using the Indian example to ask why saliva and genital excretions are more pollution-worthy than tears. If I can reverently drink his tears, wrote Jean Genet, why not the so limpid drop on the end of his nose?[18] To this we can reply: first that nasal secretions are not so limpid as tears. They are more like treacle than water.

---

[16] Douglas suggests that anxiety about one's minority status in a society is typically reflected in rituals concerning the body's orifices. Just as Hindus must be careful about what goes into their body and the disposal of what comes out, the Coorgs, living isolated in the mountains, controlled who came into their communities and who left. The care taken to avoid pollution to their physical bodies is a symbolic manifestation of their desire to protect their political and social integrity as well. Note here that Douglas is outlining a principle she believes is universal; the Coorgs are simply an example.

[17] Douglas' comment that she was shocked to read that Indians defecate in public serves as a reminder that she is conducting cross-cultural comparative research in the tradition of Lévi-Strauss or Radcliffe-Brown. Though she does not make an issue of it, as Harris does in essay 21 on the uses of cattle in India, her interpretations are based on her reading of ethnographic material rather than personal field research.

[18] Jean Genet (1910–1986) was a French novelist, playwright, and protégé of the existentialist philosopher Jean-Paul Sartre. Genet was best known for his plays. His works are contributions to the theater of the absurd, a form of drama in which the impossible routinely happens in order to make philosophical points.

When a thick rheum oozes from the eye it is no more apt for poetry than nasal rheum.[19] But admittedly clear, fast-running tears are the stuff of romantic poetry: they do not defile. This is partly because tears are naturally preempted by the symbolism of washing. Tears are like rivers of moving water. They purify, cleanse, bathe the eyes, so how can they pollute? But more significantly tears are not related to the bodily functions of digestion or procreation. Therefore their scope for symbolizing social relations and social processes is narrower. This is evident when we reflect on caste structure. Since place in the hierarchy of purity is biologically transmitted, sexual behavior is important for preserving the purity of caste. For this reason, in higher castes, boundary pollution focuses particularly on sexuality. The caste membership of an individual is determined by his mother, for though she may have married into a higher caste, her children take their caste from her. Therefore women are the gates of entry to the caste. Female purity is carefully guarded and a woman who is known to have had sexual intercourse with a man of lower caste is brutally punished. Male sexual purity does not carry this responsibility. Hence male promiscuity is a lighter matter. A mere ritual bath is enough to cleanse a man from sexual contact with a low caste woman. But his sexuality does not entirely escape the burden of worry which boundary pollution attaches to the body. According to Hindoo belief a sacred quality inheres in semen, which should not be wasted. In a penetrating essay on female purity in India (1963) Yalman says:

> While caste purity must be protected in women and men may be allowed much greater freedom, it is, of course, better for the men not to waste the sacred quality contained in their semen. It is well-known that they are exhorted

not merely to avoid low-caste women, but all women (Carstairs 1956, 1957; Gough 1956). For the loss of semen is the loss of this potent stuff . . . it is best never to sleep with women at all.

Both male and female physiology lend themselves to the analogy with the vessel which must not pour away or dilute its vital fluids. Females are correctly seen as, literally, the entry by which the pure content may be adulterated. Males are treated as pores through which the precious stuff may ooze out and be lost, the whole system being thereby enfeebled.

A double moral standard is often applied to sexual offenses. In a patrilineal system of descent wives are the door of entry to the group. In this they hold a place analogous to that of sisters in the Hindoo caste. Through the adultery of a wife impure blood is introduced to the lineage. So the symbolism of the imperfect vessel appropriately weighs more heavily on the women than on the men.[20]

If we treat ritual protection of bodily orifices as a symbol of social preoccupations about exits and entrances, the purity of cooked food becomes important. I quote a passage on the capacity of cooked food to be polluted and to carry pollution (in an unsigned review article on Pure and Impure, *Contributions to Indian Sociology*, III, July 1959, p. 37).

> When a man uses an object it becomes part of him, participates in him. Then, no doubt, this appropriation is much closer in the case of food, and the point is that appropriation precedes absorption, as it accompanies the cooking. Cooking may be taken to imply a complete appropriation of the food by the household. It is almost as if, before being "internally absorbed" by the individual, food was, by cooking, collectively predigested. One

---

[19] *Limpid:* clear or transparent; *treacle:* molasses or syrup; *rheum:* a watery mucous discharge from the eyes or nose.

[20] Douglas says that rules of body purity and pollution are symbolic of a group's place in society as well as the preservation of that group. It follows that because caste membership is transmitted through women, the rules of sexual purity and pollution are more strict for women than

for men. Just as sexual restrictions can be symbolic of anxiety about caste membership, the polluting qualities of menstrual blood, semen, or other body products can be symbolic of lineage membership. Yalman's discussion of sexuality and male and female purity is actually a second issue—not the preservation of a social group such as a caste, but the maintenance of gender boundaries.

cannot share the food prepared by people without sharing in their nature. This is one aspect of the situation. Another is that cooked food is extremely permeable to pollution.

This reads like a correct transliteration of Indian pollution symbolism regarding cooked food. But what is gained by proffering a descriptive account as if it were explanatory? In India the cooking process is seen as the beginning of ingestion, and therefore cooking is susceptible to pollution, in the same way as eating. But why is this complex found in India and in parts of Polynesia and in Judaism and other places, but not wherever humans sit down to eat? I suggest that food is not likely to be polluting at all unless the external boundaries of the social system are under pressure.[21] We can go further to explain why the actual cooking of the food in India must be ritually pure. The purity of the castes is correlated with an elaborate hereditary division of labour between castes. The work performed by each caste carries a symbolic load: it says something about the relatively pure status of the caste in question. Some kinds of labour correspond with the excretory functions of the body, for example that of washermen, barbers, sweepers, as we have seen. Some professions are involved with bloodshed or alcoholic liquor, such as tanners, warriors, toddy tappers. So they are low in the scale of purity in so far as their occupations are at variance with Brahminic ideals. But the point at which food is prepared for the table is the point at which the interrelation of the purity structure and the occupational structure needs to be set straight. For food is produced by the combined efforts of several castes of varying degrees of purity: the blacksmith, carpenter, ropemaker, the peasant. Before being admitted to the body some clear symbolic break is needed to express food's separation from necessary but impure contacts. The cooking process, entrusted to pure hands, provides this ritual break. Some such break we would expect to find whenever the production of food is in the hands of the relatively impure.

These are the general lines on which primitive rituals must be related to the social order and the culture in which they are found. The examples I have given are crude, intended to exemplify a broad objection to a certain current treatment of ritual themes. I add one more, even cruder, to underline my point. Much literature has been expended by psychologists on Yurok pollution ideas (Erikson, Posinsky). These North Californian Indians who lived by fishing for salmon in the Klamath River, would seem to have been obsessed by the behavior of liquids, if their pollution rules can be said to express an obsession. They are careful not to mix good water with bad, not to urinate into rivers, not to mix sea and fresh water, and so on. I insist that these rules cannot imply obsessional neuroses, and they cannot be interpreted unless the fluid formlessness of their highly competitive social life be taken into account (Dubois).

To sum up. There is unquestionably a relation between individual preoccupations and primitive ritual. But the relation is not the simple one which some psychoanalysts have assumed. Primitive ritual draws upon individual experience, of course. This is a truism. But it draws upon it so selectively that it cannot be said to be primarily inspired by the need to solve individual problems common to the human race, still less explained by clinical research. Primitives are not trying to cure or prevent personal neuroses by their public rituals. Psychologists can tell us whether the public expression of individual anxieties is likely to solve personal problems or not. Certainly we must suppose that some interaction of the kind is probable. But that is not at issue. The analysis of ritual symbolism cannot begin until we recognize ritual as an attempt to create and maintain a particular culture, a particular set of assumptions by which experience is controlled.

---

[21] Douglas refers to the prohibition of eating beef in India, the principles of mana and taboo in traditional Polynesian societies, and the dietary rules about kosher food in Judaism. She suggests that if a society or class feels the need to protect itself from outsiders or foreign influences, this will be symbolized through rules of behavior and eating.

For example, in Polynesia, commoners were forbidden to touch anything associated with the noble classes because these objects contained mana, a power that could harm them. According to Douglas, protecting the body from pollution by guarding the orifices, in this case restricting the diet, symbolizes the protection of traditional beliefs.

Any culture is a series of related structures which comprise social forms, values, cosmology, the whole of knowledge and through which all experience is mediated. Certain cultural themes are expressed by rites of bodily manipulation. In this very general sense primitive culture can be said to be autoplastic. But the objective of these rituals is not negative withdrawal from reality. The assertions they make are not usefully to be compared to the withdrawal of the infant into thumb-sucking and masturbation. The rituals enact the form of social relations and in giving these relations visible expression they enable people to know their own society. The rituals work upon the body politic through the symbolic medium of the physical body.[22]

REFERENCES

Bettelheim, B. 1955. *Symbolic Wounds*. Glencoe, IL.

Brown, Norman O. 1959. *Life Against Death*. London.

Dubois, Cora. 1936. "The Wealth Concept as an Integrative Factor in Tolowa-Tututni Culture." Chapter in *Essays in Anthropology, Presented to A. L. Kroeber*.

Dumont, L. and Peacock, D. 1959. *Contributions to Indian Sociology*. Vol. III.

Marshall-Thomas, E. 1959. *The Harmless People*. New York.

Naipaul, V. S. 1964. *An Area of Darkness*. London.

Posinky. 1956. *Psychiatric Quarterly* XXX, p. 598.

Roheim, G. 1925. *Australian Totemism*.

Yalman, N. 1963. "The Purity of Women in Ceylon and Southern India." *Journal of the Royal Anthropological Institute*

---

[22] Douglas' conclusion reflects the strong influence of Durkheim on her work. Durkheim was concerned with demonstrating that society was a separate phenomenon from individual psychology and that social actions could not be reduced to the sum total of individual actions. In other words, he tried very hard to separate sociology from psychology. Douglas attempts to do the same thing. She insists that the rules of ritual and pollution are what Durkheim called *social facts*. They are not reducible to manifestations of individual psychology. Whatever effects they may have on the individual, they reflect the ways society maintains its structure and solidarity. The essay is profoundly symbolic—a materialist's analysis of the caste system, for example, would have focused on the political and economic inequalities inherent in it, which Douglas ignores. With some modification we could imagine this essay appearing as a chapter in Durkheim's *Elementary Forms of the Religious Life* (1965 [1912]). For example, in the last sentence of the paragraph above, she characterizes ritual as the attempt to create and maintain a particular culture.

---

36. *Symbols in Ndembu Ritual*

VICTOR TURNER (1920–1983)

AMONG THE NDEMBU of Zambia (formerly Northern Rhodesia), the importance of ritual in the lives of the villagers in 1952 was striking. Hardly a week passed in a small neighborhood without a ritual drum being heard in one or another of its villages.

By "ritual" I mean prescribed formal behavior for occasions not given over to technological routine having reference to beliefs in mystical beings or powers. The symbol is the smallest unit of ritual which still retains the specific properties of ritual behavior; it is the ultimate unit of specific structure in a ritual context. Since this essay is in the main a description and analysis of the structure and properties of symbols, it will be enough to state here, following the *Concise Oxford Dictionary*, that a "symbol" is a thing regarded by general consent as naturally typifying or representing or recalling something by possession of analogous qualities or by association in fact or thought. The symbols I observed in the field were, empirically, objects,

From *The Forest of Symbols* (1967)

activities, relationships, events, gestures, and spatial units in a ritual situation.[1]

Following the advice and example of Professor Monica Wilson, I asked Ndembu specialists as well as laymen to interpret the symbols of their ritual. As a result, I obtained much exegetic[2] material. I felt that it was methodologically important to keep observational and interpretative materials distinct from one another. The reason for this will soon become apparent.[3]

I found that I could not analyze ritual symbols without studying them in a time series in relation to other "events," for symbols are essentially involved in social process. I came to see performances of ritual as distinct phases in the social processes whereby groups became adjusted to internal changes and adapted to their external environment. From this standpoint the ritual symbol becomes a factor in social action, a positive force in an activity field. The symbol becomes associated with human interests, purposes, ends, and means, whether these are explicitly formulated or have to be inferred from the observed behavior.

The structure and properties of a symbol become those of a dynamic entity, at least within its appropriate context of action.[4]

STRUCTURE AND PROPERTIES OF RITUAL SYMBOLS

The structure and properties of ritual symbols may be inferred from three classes of data: (1) external form and observable characteristics; (2) interpretations offered by specialists and by laymen; (3) significant contexts largely worked out by the anthropologist.[5]

Here is an example. At *Nkang'a*, the girl's puberty ritual, a novice is wrapped in a blanket and laid at the foot of a *mudyi* sapling. The *mudyi* tree *Diplorrhyncus condylocarpon* is conspicuous for its white latex, which exudes in milky beads if the thin bark is scratched. For Ndembu this is its most important observable characteristic, and therefore I propose to call it "the milk tree" henceforward.[6] Most Ndembu women can attribute

---

[1] This essay, first presented as a paper at a professional meeting in 1958, is one of Turner's most famous works. In it he outlines some basic properties of symbols and contrasts his method of symbolic analysis with psychoanalytic thought using examples from his fieldwork with the Ndembu.

[2] *Exegetic:* the adjectival form of *exegesis,* an interpretation or explanation.

[3] Turner was a student of Monica H. Wilson (1908–1982), a Cambridge-educated South African social anthropologist. In the 1930s, most anthropologists in the structural-functionalist tradition were writing about African societies as static traditions. Wilson, however, focused on economic, political, and social change in African societies, particularly among the Nyakyusa. She is best known for her detailed fieldwork and ethnographies.

Turner speaks of keeping observational and interpretive materials separate from one another because he wrote this article at a time when symbolic interpretation was controversial and because of the training he received from Wilson. The care with which he outlines his argument is in part a reaction to the controversy caused by Freudian interpretations of ethnographic material. Psychoanalytic analysis relies heavily on the interpreter's explication of the unconscious meaning of a ritual or other symbols. In the British structural-functionalist tradition, Turner considers

symbols to be empirically verifiable units and is interested in the laws by which they are used.

[4] Contrary to the psychoanalytic approach, Turner maintains that because ritual symbols are a part of social action they must be analyzed within the social and temporal contexts in which they are expressed. Turner's structural-functionalist roots are also apparent in this paragraph in that he sees rituals as the mechanism by which groups adjust to changes in their social and external environment.

[5] Reacting to the ethnoscientists' critique of ethnography, Turner refuses to get drawn into a conflict over the validity of different forms of interpretation. Here he says that observed data, informants' interpretations, and the anthropologist's analysis are all legitimate. In the following paragraph he demonstrates how the symbolism of the *mudyi* tree can be viewed from all three perspectives.

[6] Turner says Ndembu women attribute several symbolic meanings to the *mudyi* tree. The fact that a single symbol can represent many things is called *multivocality,* and it is one of Turner's key ideas. He first defined the term in his article "Ritual Symbolism, Morality, and Social Structure among the Ndembu" (1965b). Note that Turner proposes to call the tree the milk tree, thus imposing a symbolic image of his own. What do the Ndembu call the *mudyi* tree? Is milk tree the English translation of *mudyi*?

several meanings to this tree. In the first place, they say that the milk tree is the "senior" (*mukulumpi*) tree of the ritual. Each kind of ritual has this "senior" or, as I will call it, "dominant" symbol. Such symbols fall into a special class which I will discuss more fully later. Here it is enough to state that dominant symbols are regarded not merely as means to the fulfillment of the avowed purposes of a given ritual, but also and more importantly refer to values that are regarded as ends in themselves, that is, to axiomatic values. Secondly, the women say with reference to its observable characteristics that the milk tree stands for human breast milk and also for the breasts that supply it. They relate this meaning to the fact that *Nkang'a* is performed when a girl's breasts begin to ripen, not after her first menstruation, which is the subject of another and less elaborate ritual. The main theme of *Nkang'a* is indeed the tie of nurturing between mother and child, not the bond of birth. This theme of nurturing is expressed at *Nkang'a* in a number of supplementary symbols indicative of the act of feeding and of foodstuff. In the third place, the women describe the milk tree as "the tree of a mother and her child." Here the reference has shifted from description of a biological act, breast feeding, to a social tie of profound significance both in domestic relations and in the structure of the widest Ndembu community. This latter meaning is brought out most clearly in a text I recorded from a male ritual specialist. I translate literally.

> The milk tree is the place of all mothers of the lineage (*ivumu*, literally "womb" or "stomach"). It represents the ancestress of women and men. The milk tree is where our ancestress slept when she was initiated. To initiate here means the dancing of women round and round the milk tree where the novice sleeps. One ancestress after another slept there down to our grand-

mother and our mother and ourselves the children. That is the place of our tribal custom (*muchidi*)[a] where we began, even men just the same, for men are circumcised under a milk tree.

This text brings out clearly those meanings of the milk tree which refer to principles and values of social organization. At one level of abstraction the milk tree stands for matriliny, the principle on which the continuity of Ndembu society depends. Matriliny governs succession to office and inheritance of property, and it vests dominant rights of residence in local units. More than any other principle of social organization it confers order and structure on Ndembu social life. Beyond this, however, "*mudyi*" means more than matriliny, both according to this text and according to many other statements I have collected. It stands for tribal custom (*muchidi wetu*) itself. The principle of matriliny, the backbone of Ndembu social organization, as an element in the semantic structure of the milk tree, itself symbolizes the total system of interrelations between groups and persons that makes up Ndembu society. Some of the meanings of important symbols may themselves be symbols, each with its own system of meanings. At its highest level of abstraction, therefore, the milk tree stands for the unity and continuity of Ndembu society. Both men and women are components of that spatiotemporal continuum. Perhaps that is why one educated Ndembu, trying to cross the gap between our cultures, explained to me that the milk tree was like the British flag above the administrative headquarters. "*Mudyi* is our flag," he said.[7]

When discussing the milk tree symbolism in the context of the girls' puberty ritual, informants tend to stress the harmonizing, cohesive aspects of the milk tree symbolism. They also stress the aspect of dependence. The child depends on its mother for nutriment; similarly, say the Ndembu, the tribesman drinks from the breasts of tribal

---

[7] Like Douglas, Turner inherited the Durkheimian perspective implicit in British structural functionalism. Here you see this perspective expressed in his statement that the *mudyi* tree represents not only breast milk, but at its most abstract level of meaning, Ndembu society. Turner was also influenced by Raymond Firth (1901–2002). A student of Malinowski, Firth was interested in linking the interpretation of symbolism to social structures and social events (Firth 1973:25). Note the symbolic tie between the *mudyi* tree and matrilineality. Here Turner makes the link between kinship and symbolism. In classic functionalist style, Turner focuses on the harmonious, integrative functions of symbols.

custom. Thus nourishment and learning are equated in the meaning content of the milk tree. I have often heard the milk tree compared to "going to school"; the child is said to swallow instruction as a baby swallows milk and *kapudyi*, the thin cassava gruel Ndembu liken to milk. Do we not ourselves speak of "a thirst for knowledge"? Here the milk tree is a shorthand for the process of instruction in tribal matters that follows the critical episode in both boys' and girls' initiation—circumcision in the case of the boys and the long trial of lying motionless in that of the girls. The mother's role is the archetype, of protector, nourisher, and teacher. For example, a chief is often referred to as the "mother of his people," while the hunter-doctor who initiates a novice into a hunting cult is called "the mother of huntsmanship *(mama dawuyang'a)*." An apprentice circumciser is referred to as "child of the circumcision medicine" and his instructor as "mother of the circumcision medicine." In all the senses hitherto described, the milk tree represents harmonious, benevolent aspects of domestic and tribal life.

However, when the third mode of interpretation, contextual analysis, is applied, the interpretations of informants are contradicted by the way people actually behave with reference to the milk tree. It becomes clear that the milk tree represents aspects of social differentiation and even opposition between the components of a society which ideally it is supposed to symbolize as a harmonious whole. The first relevant context we shall examine is the role of the milk tree in a series of action situations within the framework of the girls' puberty ritual. Symbols, as I have said, produce action, and dominant symbols tend to become focuses in interaction. Groups mobilize around

them, worship before them, perform other symbolic activities near them, and add other symbolic objects to them, often to make composite shrines. Usually these groups of participants themselves stand for important components of the secular social system, whether these components consist of corporate groups, such as families and lineages, or of mere categories of persons possessing similar characteristics, such as old men, women, children, hunters, or widows. In each kind of Ndembu ritual a different group or category becomes the focal social element. In *Nkang'a* this focal element is the unity of Ndembu women. It is the women who dance around the milk tree and initiate the recumbent novice by making her the hub of their whirling circle. Not only is the milk tree the "flag of the Ndembu"; more specifically, in the early phases of *Nkang'a*, it is the "flag" of Ndembu women. In this situation it does more than focus the exclusiveness of women; it mobilizes them in opposition to the men. For the women sing songs taunting the men and for a time will not let men dance in their circle. Therefore, if we are to take account of the operational aspect of the milk tree symbol, including not only what Ndembu say about it but also what they do with it in its "meaning," we must allow that it distinguishes women as a social category and indicates their solidarity.[8]

The milk tree makes further discriminations. For example, in certain action contexts it stands for the novice herself. One such context is the initial sacralization of a specific milk tree sapling. Here the natural property of the tree's immaturity is significant. Informants say that a young tree is chosen because the novice is young. A girl's particular tree symbolizes her new social personality as a mature woman. In the past and occasionally today,

---

[8] Anthropologist Max Gluckman (1911–1975) was a major influence on Turner. Gluckman, a structural-functionalist, focused on the socially integrative effects of ritual expressions of conflict (Gluckman 1956). Famous for his formulation of the concept of "rituals of rebellion," Gluckman proposed that the ritual enactment of conflict (such as that between women and men in the *Nkang'a* rite) is a form of catharsis that allows the expression of hostility without endangering the established social order. Having discussed the role that *mudyi* tree symbolism plays in tribal life, Turner tells us that the milk tree also represents differentiation

and opposition in a situation that should be harmonious. In the *Nkang'a* ritual the *mudyi* is the "flag" of Ndembu women as they highlight their opposition to men, taunting them and denying them access to their dance circle. This contradiction is explained in Gluckman's terms. Marxist analysts also placed emphasis on conflict, but used the concept very differently. For structural-functionalists, ritualized forms of conflict prevent social disruption and maintain a society's stability. For Marxists, conflict is the key force propelling revolution and, thus, social evolution.

the girl's puberty ritual was part of her marriage ritual, and marriage marked her transition from girlhood to womanhood. Much of the training and most of the symbolism of *Nkang'a* are concerned with making the girl a sexually accomplished spouse, a fruitful woman, and a mother able to produce a generous supply of milk. For each girl this is a unique process. She is initiated alone and is the center of public attention and care. From her point of view it is *her Nkang'a*, the most thrilling and self-gratifying phase of her life. Society recognizes and encourages these sentiments, even though it also prescribes certain trials and hardships for the novice, who must suffer before she is glorified on the last day of the ritual. The milk tree, then, celebrates the coming-of-age of a new social personality, and distinguishes her from all other women at this one moment in her life. In terms of its action context, the milk tree here also expresses the conflict between the girl and the moral community of adult women she is entering. Not without reason is the milk tree site known as "the place of death" or "the place of suffering," terms also applied to the site where boys are circumcised, for the girl novice must not move a muscle throughout a whole hot and clamant[9] day.

In other contexts, the milk tree site is the scene of opposition between the novice's own mother and the group of adult women. The mother is debarred from attending the ring of dancers. She is losing her child, although later she recovers her as an adult co-member of her lineage. Here we see the conflict between the matricentric family and the wider society which, as I have said, is dominantly articulated by the principle of matriliny. The relationship between mother and daughter persists throughout the ritual, but its content is changed. It is worth pointing out that, at one

phase in *Nkang'a*, mother and daughter interchange portions of clothing. This may perhaps be related to the Ndembu custom whereby mourners wear small portions of a dead relative's clothing. Whatever the interchange of clothing may mean to a psychoanalyst—and here we arrive at one of the limits of our present anthropological competence—it seems not unlikely that Ndembu intend to symbolize the termination for both mother and daughter of an important aspect of their relationship. This is one of the symbolic actions—one of very few—about which I found it impossible to elicit any interpretation in the puberty ritual. Hence it is legitimate to infer, in my opinion, that powerful unconscious wishes, of a kind considered illicit by Ndembu, are expressed in it.[10]

Opposition between the tribeswomen and the novice's mother is mimetically represented at the milk tree towards the end of the first day of the puberty ritual. The girl's mother cooks a huge meal of cassava and beans—both kinds of food are symbols in *Nkang'a*, with many meanings—for the women visitors, who eat in village groups and not at random. Before eating, the women return to the milk tree from their eating place a few yards away and circle the tree in procession. The mother brings up the rear holding up a large spoon full of cassava and beans. Suddenly she shouts: "Who wants the cassava of *chipwampwilu?*" All the women rush to be first to seize the spoon and eat from it. *"Chipwampwilu"* appears to be an archaic word and no one knows its meaning. Informants say that the spoon represents the novice herself in her role of married woman, while the food stands both for her reproductive power (*lusemu*) and her role as cultivator and cook. One woman told my wife: "It is lucky if the person snatching the spoon comes from the novice's own village.[11] Otherwise,

---

[9] *Clamant:* noisy.

[10] Elements of both Gluckman and Freud appear in this paragraph. First, Turner explains that the ritual allows the symbolic expression of hostility between the initiate's mother and the larger group of adult women in this matrilineal society. Then, because Turner was unable to elicit any explanation for a mother and daughter's exchange of apparel during the *Nkang'a* rite, he assumes the symbolism of the exchange indicates unconscious feelings that the Ndembu censor from conscious expression.

[11] Turner mentions the presence of his wife in this paragraph. Although she accompanied him into the field and helped him conduct research, Edith Turner (b. 1921) is rarely mentioned in his works. She is an accomplished anthropologist in her own right, with several books to her credit. Some of her works are *The Spirit and the Drum: A Memoir of Africa* (1987) and *Experiencing Ritual: A New Interpretation of African Healing* (1992).

the mother believes that her child will go far away from her to a distant village and die there. The mother wants her child to stay near her." Implicit in this statement is a deeper conflict than that between the matricentric family and mature female society. It refers to another dominant articulating principle of Ndembu society, namely virilocal marriage according to which women live at their husbands' villages after marriage. Its effect is sometimes to separate mothers from daughters by considerable distances. In the episode described, the women symbolize the matrilineal cores of villages. Each village wishes to gain control through marriage over the novice's capacity to work. Its members also hope that her children will be raised in it, thus adding to its size and prestige. Later in *Nkang'a* there is a symbolic struggle between the novice's matrilineal kin and those of her bridegroom, which makes explicit the conflict between virilocality and matriliny.

Lastly, in the context of action situation, the milk tree is sometimes described by informants as representing the novice's own matrilineage. Indeed, it has this significance in the competition for the spoon just discussed, for women of her own village try to snatch the spoon before members of other villages. Even if such women do not belong to her matrilineage but are married to its male members, they are thought to be acting on its behalf. Thus, the milk tree in one of its action aspects represents the unity and exclusiveness of a single matrilineage with a local focus in a village against other such corporate groups. The conflict between yet another subsystem and the total system is given dramatic and symbolic form.[12]

By this time, it will have become clear that considerable discrepancy exists between the interpretations of the milk tree offered by informants and the behavior exhibited by Ndembu in situations dominated by the milk tree symbolism. Thus, we are told that the milk tree represents the close tie between mother and daughter.

Yet the milk tree separates a daughter from her mother. We are also told that the milk tree stands for the unity of Ndembu society. Yet we find that in practice it separates women from men, and some categories and groups of women from others. How are these contradictions between principle and practice to be explained?

SOME PROBLEMS OF INTERPRETATION

I am convinced that my informants genuinely believed that the milk tree represented only the linking and unifying aspects of Ndembu social organization. I am equally convinced that the role of the milk tree in action situations where it represents a focus of specified groups in opposition to other groups, forms an equally important component of its total meaning. Here the important question must be asked, "meaning for whom?" For if Ndembu do not recognize the discrepancy between their interpretation of the milk tree symbolism and other behavior in connection with it, does this mean that the discrepancy has no relevance for the social anthropologist? Indeed some anthropologists claim, with Nadel (1954, 108), that "uncomprehended symbols have no part in social enquiry, their social effectiveness lies in their capacity to indicate, and if they indicate nothing to the actors, they are, from our point of view, irrelevant, and indeed no longer symbols (whatever their significance for the psychologist or psychoanalyst)."[13] Professor Monica Wilson (1957, 6) holds a similar point of view. She writes that she stresses "Nyakyusa interpretations of their own rituals, for anthropological literature is bespattered with symbolic guessing, the ethnographer's interpretations of the rituals of other people." Indeed, she goes so far as to base her whole analysis of Nyakyusa ritual on "the Nyakyusa translation or interpretation of the sym-

---

[12] Turner's analysis is clearly similar to the work on kinship conducted by Radcliffe-Brown a generation earlier (see essay 14). He states that the ritual actions refer to sociostructural elements of the society as well as express the conflict between matrilineality and virilocality.

[13] S. F. Nadel (1903–1956) received a doctoral degree in psychology and philosophy from the University of Vienna and studied anthropology at the London School of Economics with Malinowski and Seligman. He is best known for his work with the Nupe in northern Nigeria and the Nuba in Sudan.

bolism." In my view, these investigators go beyond the limits of salutary caution and impose serious, and even arbitrary, limitations on themselves. To some extent, their difficulties derive from their failure to distinguish the concept of symbol from that of a mere sign. Although I am in complete disagreement with his fundamental postulate that the collective unconscious is the main formative principle in ritual symbolism, I consider that Carl Jung (1949, 601) has cleared the way for further investigation by making just this distinction. "A sign," he says, "is an analogous or abbreviated expression of a *known* thing. But a symbol is always the best possible expression of a relatively *unknown* fact, a fact, however, which is none the less recognized or postulated as existing." Nadel and Wilson, in treating most ritual symbols as signs, must ignore or regard as irrelevant some of the crucial properties of such symbols.[14]

FIELD SETTING AND STRUCTURAL PERSPECTIVE

How, then, can a social anthropologist justify his claim to be able to interpret a society's ritual symbols more deeply and comprehensively than the actors themselves? In the first place, the anthropologist, by the use of his special techniques and concepts, is able to view the performance of a given kind of ritual as "occurring in, and being interpenetrated by, a totality of coexisting social entities such as various kinds of groups, sub-groups, categories, or personalities, and also barriers between them, and modes of interconnexion" (Lewin 1949, 200). In other words, he can place this ritual in its significant field setting and describe the structure and properties of that field. On the other hand, each participant in the ritual views it from his own

particular corner of observation. He has what Lupton has called his own "structural perspective." His vision is circumscribed by his occupancy of a particular position, or even of a set of situationally conflicting positions, both in the persisting structure of his society, and also in the role structure of the given ritual. Moreover, the participant is likely to be governed in his actions by a number of interests, purposes, and sentiments, dependent upon his specific position, which impair his understanding of the total situation. An even more serious obstacle against his achieving objectivity is the fact that he tends to regard as axiomatic and primary the ideals, values, and norms that are overtly expressed or symbolized in the ritual. Thus, in the *Nkang'a* ritual, each person or group in successive contexts of action, sees the milk tree only as representing her or their own specific interests and values at those times. However, the anthropologist who has previously made a structural analysis of Ndembu society, isolating its organizational principles, and distinguishing its groups and relationships, has no particular bias and can observe the real interconnections and conflicts between groups and persons, in so far as these receive ritual representation. What is meaningless for an actor playing a specific role may well be highly significant for an observer and analyst of the total system.[15]

On these grounds, therefore, I consider it legitimate to include within the total meaning of a dominant ritual symbol, aspects of behavior associated with it which the actors themselves are unable to interpret, and indeed of which they may be unaware, if they are asked to interpret the symbol outside its activity context. Nevertheless, there still remains for us the problem of the contradiction between the expressed meanings of the milk tree symbol and the meaning of the stereotyped forms of behavior closely associated with it.

---

[14] Here Turner attempts to deal with the argument that symbolic meaning not recognized by native informants is invalid. Although Turner does not use the terms, this is the same emic-etic debate that was conducted in the United States between ethnoscientists and materialists.

[15] Turner says that anthropologists are privileged observers without bias who can view symbolic actions in a wider social context than a ritual participant. Do you agree? Are

anthropologists really impartial observers with no particular bias, or do they have their "own particular corner of observation" too? This is a central question for the postmodernists, who claim that an observer cannot be impartial. But even if that is true, an important question remains: Can anthropologists accurately see some things invisible to a culture's participants?

Indigenous interpretations of the milk tree symbolism in the abstract appear to indicate that there is no incompatibility or conflict between the persons and groups to which it refers. Yet, as we have seen, it is between just such groups that conflict is mimed at the milk tree site.

THREE PROPERTIES
OF RITUAL SYMBOLS

Before we can interpret, we must further classify our descriptive data, collected by the methods described above. Such a classification will enable us to state some of the properties of ritual symbols.[16] The simplest property is that of *condensation*. Many things and actions are represented in a single formation. Secondly, a dominant symbol is a *unification of disparate significata*. The disparate *significata* are interconnected by virtue of their common possession of analogous qualities or by association in fact or thought. Such qualities or links of association may in themselves be quite trivial or random or widely distributed over a range of phenomena. Their very generality enables them to bracket together the most diverse ideas and phenomena. Thus, as we have seen, the milk tree stands for, *inter alia,* women's breasts, motherhood, a novice at *Nkang'a*, the principle of matriliny, a specific matrilineage, learning, and the unity and persistence of Ndembu society. The themes of nourishment and dependence run through all these diverse *significata*.

The third important property of dominant ritual symbols is *polarization of meaning*. Not only the milk tree but all other dominant Ndembu symbols possess two clearly distinguishable poles of meaning. At one pole is found a cluster of *significata* that refer to components of the moral and social orders of Ndembu society, to principles of social organization, to kinds of corporate grouping, and to the norms and values inherent in structural relationships. At the other pole, the *significata* are usually natural and physiological phenomena and processes. Let us call the first of these the "ideological pole," and the second the "sensory pole." At the sensory pole, the meaning content is closely related to the outward form of the symbol. Thus one meaning of the milk tree—breast milk—is closely related to the exudation of milky latex from the tree. One sensory meaning of another dominant symbol, the *mukula* tree, is blood; this tree secretes a dusky red gum.[17]

At the sensory pole are concentrated those *significata* that may be expected to arouse desires and feelings; at the ideological pole one finds an arrangement of norms and values that guide and control persons as members of social groups and categories. The sensory, emotional *significata* tend to be "gross" in a double sense. In the first place, they are gross in a general way, taking no account of detail or the precise qualities of emotion. It cannot be sufficiently stressed that such symbols are social facts, "collective representations," even though their appeal is to the lowest common denominator of human feeling. The second sense of "gross" is "frankly, even flagrantly, physiological." Thus, the milk tree has the gross meanings of breast milk, breasts, and the process of breast feeding. These are also gross in the sense that they represent items of universal Ndembu experience. Other Ndembu symbols, at their sensory poles of meaning, represent such themes as blood, male and female genitalia, semen, urine, and feces. The same symbols,

---

[16] Earlier, Turner defined "dominant symbols" as those referring to "axiomatic," or self-evident, values. In this section, he further explains dominant symbols and describes three of their most important properties: condensation, unification of disparate significata, and polarization of meaning. These principles help explain how symbols can have various and conflicting meanings.

[17] Turner here imposes a scheme of classification that strongly resembles Lévi-Strauss' nature-culture binary op-

position. The poles of meaning that Turner labels ideological and sensory could almost as easily be labeled culture and nature. Why, given that he considers these poles of meaning universal, did Turner not turn to structuralism? In the 1960s and 1970s a structural-functionalist interested in symbolic analysis could turn to Lévi-Strauss or Freud. Like Douglas, who studied the symbolism of body wastes and social boundaries, Turner chose to derive his symbolic meanings from Freud.

at their ideological poles of meaning, represent the unity and continuity of social groups, primary and associational, domestic, and political.[18]

[A 569-word section of Turner's article called "Reference and Condensation" has been omitted. In this section, Turner discusses Edward Sapir's discussion of the means by which ritual symbols stimulate emotional responses.]

DOMINANT AND INSTRUMENTAL SYMBOLS

Certain ritual symbols, as I have said, are regarded by Ndembu as dominant. In rituals performed to propitiate ancestor spirits who are believed to have afflicted their living kin with reproductive disorders, illness, or bad luck at hunting, there are two main classes of dominant symbols. The first class is represented by the first tree or plant in a series of trees or plants from which portions of leaves, bark, or roots are collected by practitioners or adepts in the curative cult. The subjects of ritual are marked with these portions mixed with water, or given them, mixed in a potion, to drink. The first tree so treated is called the "place of greeting" *(ishikenu)*, or the "elder" *(mukulumpi)*. The adepts encircle it several times to sacralize it. Then the senior practitioner prays at its base, which he sprinkles with powdered white clay. Prayer is made either to the named spirit, believed to be afflicting the principal subject of ritual, or to the tree itself, which is in some way identified with the afflicting spirit. Each *ishikenu* can be allotted several meanings by adepts. The second class of dominant symbols in curative rituals consists of shrines where the subjects of such rituals sit while the practitioners wash them with vegetable substances mixed with water and perform actions on their behalf of a symbolic or ritualistic

nature. Such shrines are often composite, consisting of several objects in configuration. Both classes of dominant symbols are closely associated with nonempirical beings. Some are regarded as their repositories; others, as being identified with them; others again, as representing them. In life-crisis rituals, on the other hand, dominant symbols seem to represent not beings but nonempirical powers or kinds of efficacy. For example, in the boys' circumcision ritual, the dominant symbol for the whole ritual is a "medicine" *(yitumbu)*, called *"nfunda,"* which is compounded from many ingredients, e.g., the ash of the burnt lodge which means "death," and the urine of an apprentice circumciser which means "virility." Each of these and other ingredients have many other meanings. The dominant symbol at the camp where the novices' parents assemble and prepare food for the boys is the *chikoli* tree, which represents, among other things, an erect phallus, adult masculinity, strength, hunting prowess, and health continuing into old age. The dominant symbol during the process of circumcision is the milk tree, beneath which novices are circumcised. The dominant symbol in the immediate postcircumcision phase is the red *mukula* tree, on which the novices sit until their wounds stop bleeding. Other symbols are dominant at various phases of seclusion. Each of these symbols is described as *"mukulumpi"* (elder, senior). Dominant symbols appear in many different ritual contexts, sometimes presiding over the whole procedure, sometimes over particular phases. The meaning-content of certain dominant symbols possesses a high degree of constancy and consistency throughout the total symbolic system, exemplifying Radcliffe-Brown's proposition that a symbol recurring in a cycle of rituals is likely to have the same significance in each. Such symbols also possess considerable autonomy with regard to the aims of the rituals in which they appear. Precisely because of these properties, dominant

---

[18] Turner is concerned not only with interpreting symbols but also with explaining why they affect people the way they do. He states that blood, genitals, semen, urine, and feces are all represented by basic Ndembu symbols at their sensory and ideological poles of meaning, thus relying on both Durkheim and Freud. He sees symbols as social facts and notes that at the ideological pole these symbols represent "unity and continuity of social groups," which draws on Durkheim. His identification of the sensory pole of meaning as being "flagrantly physiological" shows the influence of Freud, who believed that such physiological symbolism was universal because the experience of these elements in infancy was universal.

symbols are readily analyzable in a cultural framework of reference. They may be regarded for this purpose as what Whitehead would have called "eternal objects."[b] They are the relatively fixed points in both the social and cultural structures, and indeed constitute points of junction between these two kinds of structure. They may be regarded irrespective of their order of appearance in a given ritual as ends in themselves, as representative of the axiomatic values of the widest Ndembu society. This does not mean that they cannot also be studied, as we have indeed studied them, as factors of social action, in an action frame of reference, but their social properties make them more appropriate objects of morphological study than the class of symbols we will now consider.

These symbols may be termed "instrumental symbols." An instrumental symbol must be seen in terms of its wider context, i.e., in terms of the total system of symbols which makes up a given kind of ritual. Each kind of ritual has its specific mode of interrelating symbols. This mode is often dependent upon the ostensible purposes of that kind of ritual. In other words, each ritual has its own teleology.[19] It has its explicitly expressed goals, and instrumental symbols may be regarded as means of attaining those goals. For example, in rituals performed for the overt purpose of making women fruitful, among the instrumental symbols used are portions of fruit-bearing trees or of trees that possess innumerable rootlets. These fruits and rootlets are said by Ndembu to represent children. They are also thought of as having efficacy to make the woman fruitful. They are means to the main end of the ritual. Perhaps such symbols could be regarded as mere signs or referential symbols, were it not for the fact that the meanings of each are associated with powerful conscious and unconscious emotions and wishes. At the psychological level of analysis, I suspect that these symbols too would approximate to the condition of condensation symbols, but here we touch upon the present limits of competence of anthropological explanation, a problem we will now discuss more fully.

THE LIMITS OF ANTHROPOLOGICAL INTERPRETATION

We now come to the most difficult aspect of the scientific study of ritual symbolism: analysis. How far can we interpret these enigmatic formations by the use of anthropological concepts? At what points do we reach the frontiers of our explanatory competence? Let us first consider the case of dominant symbols. I have suggested that these have two poles of meaning, a sensory and an ideological pole. I have also suggested that dominant symbols have the property of unifying disparate *significata*. I would go so far as to say that at both poles of meaning are clustered disparate and even contradictory *significata*. In the course of its historical development, anthropology has acquired techniques and concepts that enable it to handle fairly adequately the kind of data we have classified as falling around the ideological pole. Such data, as we have seen, include components of social structure and cultural phenomena, both ideological and technological. I believe that study of these data in terms of the concepts of three major subdivisions of anthropology—cultural anthropology, structuralist theory, and social dynamics—would be extremely rewarding. I shall shortly outline how I think such analyses might be done and how the three frameworks might be interrelated, but first we must ask how far and in what respects is it relevant to submit the sensory pole of meaning to intensive analysis, and, more importantly, how far are we, as anthropologists, qualified to do so? It is evident, as Sapir has stated, that ritual symbols, like all condensation symbols, "strike deeper and deeper roots in the unconscious." Even a brief acquaintance with depth psychology is enough to

---

[19] What Turner means is that each ritual has its own design and purpose. An instrumental symbol must be analyzed in terms of the specific ritual context in which it occurs. Dominant symbols are "axiomatic," that is, self-evidently true. The implication here is that, within a culture, dominant symbols are constant in meaning, whereas the meaning of instrumental symbols is dependent on their context.

show the investigator that ritual symbols, with regard to their outward form, to their behavioral context, and to several of the indigenous interpretations set upon them, are partially shaped under the influence of unconscious motivations and ideas. The interchange of clothes between mother and daughter at the *Nkang'a* ritual; the belief that a novice would go mad if she saw the milk tree on the day of her separation ritual; the belief that if a novice lifts up the blanket with which she is covered during seclusion and sees her village her mother would die; all these are items of symbolic behavior for which the Ndembu themselves can give no satisfactory interpretation. For these beliefs suggest an element of mutual hostility in the mother-daughter relationship which runs counter to orthodox interpretations of the milk tree symbolism, in so far as it refers to the mother-daughter relationship. One of the main characteristics of ideological interpretations is that they tend to stress the harmonious and cohesive aspect of social relationships. The exegetic idiom feigns that persons and groups always act in accordance with the ideal norms of Ndembu society.

[*We have omitted a 700-word section of Turner's article called "Depth Psychology and Ritual Symbolism," in which he discusses the psychoanalytic interpretation of ritual symbols such as the work of Bruno Bettelheim, which was discussed in the previous essay, by Mary Douglas. In this section, Turner claims that psychoanalysts generally reject the ideological pole of meaning and focus on the sensory meanings. He writes that psychoanalysts regard indigenous explanations of symbols as identical to the justifications that neurotics provide for their behavior. Further, Turner says that psychoanalysts look on ritual symbols as being identical with symptoms of neurosis or psychosis or as dream symbols of Western Europeans. Turner, of course, disagrees with this point of view. He states that symbols are partly influenced by unconscious motivations and ideas, but his is not a psychoanalytic interpretation. He ends the section in an almost comic manner, referring to "hapless anthropologists" having to choose between competing psychoanalytic interpretations.*]

PROVINCES OF EXPLANATION

I consider that if we conceptualize a dominant symbol as having two poles of meaning, we can more exactly demarcate the limits within which anthropological analysis may be fruitfully applied. Psychoanalysts, in treating most indigenous interpretations of symbols as irrelevant, are guilty of a naive and one-sided approach. For those interpretations that show how a dominant symbol expresses important components of the social and moral orders are by no means equivalent to the "rationalizations," and the "secondary elaborations" of material deriving from endopsychic conflicts. They refer to social facts that have an empirical reality exterior to the psyches of individuals. On the other hand, those anthropologists who regard only indigenous interpretations as relevant, are being equally one-sided. This is because they tend to examine symbols within two analytical frameworks only, the cultural and the structural. This approach is essentially a static one, and it does not deal with processes involving temporal changes in social relations.

Nevertheless, the crucial properties of a ritual symbol involve these dynamic developments. Symbols instigate social action. In a field context they may even be described as "forces," in that they are determinable influences inclining persons and groups to action.[20] It is in a field context, moreover, that the properties we have described, namely, polarization of meanings, transference of affectual quality, discrepancy between meanings, and condensations of meanings, become most significant. The symbol as a unit of action, possessing these properties, becomes an object of

---

[20] The influence of Durkheim on Turner's analysis is strongly manifested in this section. Turner's description of symbols as forces that incline people to action is quite similar to Durkheim's description of social facts (see essay 5). Turner also refers to Durkheim's *The Elementary Forms of the Religious Life* (1965 [1912]) in this section, a portion of which is reprinted in essay 6.

study both for anthropology and for psychology. Both disciplines, in so far as they are concerned with human actions must conceptualize the ritual symbol in the same way.

The techniques and concepts of the anthropologist enable him to analyze competently the interrelations between the data associated with the ideological pole of meaning. They also enable him to analyze the social behavior directed upon the total dominant symbol. He cannot, however, with his present skills, discriminate between the precise sources of unconscious feeling and wishing, which shape much of the outward form of the symbol; select some natural objects rather than others to serve as symbols; and account for certain aspects of the behavior associated with symbols. For him, it is enough that the symbol should evoke emotion. He is interested in the fact that emotion is evoked and not in the specific qualities of its constituents. He may indeed find it situationally relevant for his analysis to distinguish whether the emotion evoked by a specific symbol possesses the gross character, say, of aggression, fear, friendliness, anxiety, or sexual pleasure, but he need go no further than this. For him the ritual symbol is primarily a factor in group dynamics, and, as such, its references to the groups, relationships, values, norms, and beliefs of a society are his principal items of study. In other words, the anthropologist treats the sensory pole of meaning as a constant, and the social and ideological aspects as variables whose interdependencies he seeks to explain.

The psychoanalyst, on the other hand, must, I think, attach greater significance than he now does to social factors in the analysis of ritual symbolism. He must cease to regard interpretations, beliefs, and dogmas as mere rationalizations when, often enough, these refer to social and natural realities. For, as Durkheim wrote (1954, 2–3), "primitive religions hold to reality and express it. One must learn to go underneath the symbol to the reality which it represents and which gives it its meaning. No religions are false, all answer, though in different ways, to the given conditions of human existence." Among those given conditions, the arrangement of society into structured groupings, discrepancies between the principles that organize these groupings, economic collaboration and competition, schism within groups and opposition between groups— in short, all those things with which the social aspect of ritual symbolism is concerned—are surely of at least equal importance with biopsychical drives and early conditioning in the elementary family. After all, the ritual symbol has, in common with the dream symbol, the characteristic, discovered by Freud, of being a compromise formation between two main opposing tendencies. It is a compromise between the need for social control, and certain innate and universal human drives whose complete gratification would result in a breakdown of that control. Ritual symbols refer to what is normative, general, and characteristic of unique individuals. Thus, Ndembu symbols refer among other things, to the basic needs of social existence (hunting, agriculture, female fertility, favourable climatic conditions, and so forth), and to shared values on which communal life depends (generosity, comradeship, respect for elders, the importance of kinship, hospitality, and the like). In distinguishing between ritual symbols and individual psychic symbols, we may perhaps say that while ritual symbols are gross means of handling social and natural reality, psychic symbols are dominantly fashioned under the influence of inner drives. In analyzing the former, attention must mainly be paid to relations between data external to the psyche; in analyzing the latter, to endopsychic data.[21]

For this reason, the study of ritual symbolism falls more within the province of the social anthropologist than that of the psychologist or psychoanalyst, although the latter can assist the

---

[21] Here Turner distinguishes between cultural symbols and individual psychological symbols. He argues that the former are the province of anthropology, the latter that of psychology. This concern with distinguishing anthropology and sociology from psychology is similar to that expressed by Durkheim at the turn of the century. Both Turner and Durkheim argued that collective phenomena are the subjects of anthropology and that individual consciousness belongs in psychology.

anthropologist by examining the nature and interconnections of the data clustered at the sensory pole of ritual symbolism. He can also, I believe, illuminate certain aspects of the stereotyped behavior associated with symbols in field contexts, which the actors themselves are unable to explain. For as we have seen, much of this behavior is suggestive of attitudes that differ radically from those deemed appropriate in terms of traditional exegesis. Indeed, certain conflicts would appear to be so basic that they totally block exegesis.

THE INTERPRETATION OF OBSERVED EMOTIONS

Can we really say that behavior portraying conflict between persons and groups, who are represented by the symbols themselves as being in harmony, is in the full Freudian sense unconscious behavior? The Ndembu themselves in many situations outside *Nkang'a*, both secular and ritual, are perfectly aware of and ready to speak about hostility in the relationships between particular mothers and daughters, between particular sublineages, and between particular young girls and the adult women in their villages. It is rather as though there existed in certain precisely defined public situations, usually of a ritual or ceremonial type, a norm obstructing the verbal statement of conflicts in any way connected with the principle and rules celebrated or dramatized in those situations. Evidences of human passion and frailty are just not spoken about when the occasion is given up to the public commemoration and reanimation of norms and values in their abstract purity.

Yet, as we have seen, recurrent kinds of conflict may be acted out in the ritual or ceremonial form. On great ritual occasions, common practice, as well as highest principle, receives its symbolic or stereotyped expression, but practice, which is dominantly under the sway of what all societies consider man's "lower nature," is rife with expressions of conflict. Selfish and factional interests, oath breaking, disloyalty, sins of omission as well as sins of commission, pollute and disfigure those ideal prototypes of behavior which in precept, prayer, formula, and symbol are held up before the ritual assembly for its exclusive attention. In the orthodox interpretation of ritual it is pretended that common practice has no efficacy and that men and women really are as they ideally should be. Yet, as I have argued above, the "energy" required to reanimate the values and norms enshrined in dominant symbols and expressed in various kinds of verbal behavior is "borrowed," to speak metaphorically in lieu at the moment of a more rigorous language, from the miming of well-known and normally mentionable conflicts. The raw energies of conflict are domesticated into the service of social order.[22]

I should say here that I believe it possible, and indeed necessary, to analyze symbols in a context of observed emotions. If the investigator is well acquainted with the common idiom in which a society expresses such emotions as friendship, love, hate, joy, sorrow, contentment, and fear, he cannot fail to observe that these are experienced in ritual situations. Thus, in *Nkang'a* when the women laugh and jeer at the men, tease the novice and her mother, fight one another for the "porridge of *chipwampwilu*," and so on, the observer can hardly doubt that emotions are really aroused in the actors as well as formally represented by ritual custom. ("What's Hecuba to him or he to Hecuba, that he should weep for her?")[23]

These emotions are portrayed and evoked in close relation to the dominant symbols of tribal cohesion and continuity, often by the performance of instrumentally symbolic behavior. However, since they are often associated with the mimesis[24] of interpersonal and intergroup conflict, such emotions

---

[22] For Turner, apparent conflict reinforces social order, once again illustrating Gluckman's perspective. Although he does not specifically call the *Nkang'a* a ritual of rebellion, it is clear that he has this in mind.

[23] Turner says that it is important for one to analyze symbols in the context of observed emotions. The quotation is from Hamlet, Act II, scene 2, where Hamlet, writing a play in which his father's murder will be re-created, comments on the power of emotion that can be expressed by an actor.

[24] *Mimesis:* imitation.

and acts of behavior obtain no place among the official, verbal meanings attributed to such dominant symbols.[25]

THE SITUATIONAL SUPPRESSION OF CONFLICT FROM INTERPRETATION

Emotion and praxis,[26] indeed, give life and coloring to the values and norms, but the connection between the behavioral expression of conflict and the normative components of each kind of ritual, and of its dominant symbols, is seldom explicitly formulated by believing actors. Only if one were to personify a society, regarding it as some kind of supra-individual entity, could one speak of "unconsciousness" here. Each individual participant in the *Nkang'a* ritual is well aware that kin quarrel most bitterly over rights and obligations conferred by the principle of matriliny, but that awareness is situationally held back from verbal expression: the participants must behave as if conflicts generated by matriliny were irrelevant.

[*Several paragraphs totaling about 560 words were omitted from the text. These contained a discussion of the situational suppression of conflict in the ritual expression of dominant symbols.*]

For example, in the frequently performed *Nkula* ritual, the dominant symbols are a cluster of red objects, notably red clay (*mukundu*) and the *mukula* tree mentioned previously. In the context of *Nkula*, both of these are said to represent menstrual blood and the "blood of birth," which is the blood that accompanies the birth of a child. The ostensible goal of the ritual is to coagulate the patient's menstrual blood, which has been flowing away in menorrhagia, around the fetus in order to nourish it. A series of symbolic acts are performed to attain this end. For example, a young *mukula* tree is cut down by male doctors and part of it is carved into the shape of a baby, which is then inserted into a round calabash medicated with the blood of a sacrificed cock, with red clay, and with a number of other red ingredients. The red medicines here, say the Ndembu, represent desired coagulation of the patient's menstrual blood, and the calabash is a symbolic womb. At the ideological pole of meaning, the *mukula* tree and the medicated calabash both represent (as the milk tree does) the patient's matrilineage and, at a higher level of abstraction, the principle of matriliny itself. This is also consistent with the fact that *ivumu*, the term for "womb," also means "matrilineage."[27] In this symbolism the procreative, rather than the nutritive, aspect of motherhood is stressed. However, Ndembu red symbolism, unlike the white symbolism of which the milk tree symbolism is a species, nearly always has explicit reference to violence, to killing, and, at its most general level of meaning, to breach, both in the social and natural orders. Although informants, when discussing this *Nkula* ritual specifically, tend to stress the positive, feminine aspects of parturition and reproduction, other meanings of the red symbols, stated explicitly in other ritual contexts, can be shown to make their influence felt in *Nkula*. For example, both red clay and the *mukula* tree are dominant symbols in the hunter's cult, where they mean the blood of animals, the red meat of game, the inheritance through either parent of hunting prowess, and the unity of all initiated hunters. It also stands for the hunter's power

---

[25] Turner's emphasis on interpreting behavior rather than thought appears repeatedly in this essay, highlighting the difference between him and the American ethnoscientists of this period. His focus on behavior largely collapsed the emic-etic distinctions so important in American anthropology.

[26] *Praxis:* practice, as distinguished from theory.

[27] Earlier in the article Turner stated that psychoanalytic interpretations typically focus on the sensory pole of meaning. Here, in his description of the *Nkula* ritual, the symbolism of the calabash as womb and red clay as menstrual blood is very Freudian. At the ideological pole of meaning the same symbols refer to the patient's matrilineage. This is a structural interpretation in the tradition of Radcliffe-Brown. The characteristics of symbols that Turner described earlier in this article—condensation, polarization of meaning, and the unification of disparate significata—allow him to reconcile these seemingly contradictory interpretations.

to kill.[28] The same red symbols, in the context of the *Wubanji* ritual performed to purify a man who has killed a kinsman or a lion or leopard (animals believed to be reincarnated hunter kin of the living), represent the blood of homicide. Again, in the boys' circumcision ritual, these symbols stand for the blood of circumcised boys. More seriously still, in divination and in antiwitchcraft rituals, they stand for the blood of witches' victims, which is exposed in necrophagous feasts.[29]

Most of these meanings are implicit in *Nkula*. For example, the female patient, dressed in skins like a male hunter and carrying a bow and arrow, at one phase of the ritual performs a special hunter's dance. Moreover, while she does this, she wears in her hair, just above the brow, the red feather of a lourie bird. Only shedders of blood, such as hunters, man-slayers, and circumcisers, are customarily entitled to wear this feather.[30] Again, after the patient has been given the baby figurine in its symbolic womb, she dances with it in a style of dancing peculiar to circumcisers when they brandish aloft the great *nfunda* medicine of the circumcision lodge. Why then is the woman patient identified with male blood-spillers? The field context of these symbolic objects and items of behavior suggests that the Ndembu feel that the woman, in wasting her menstrual blood and in failing to bear children, is actively renouncing her expected role as a mature married female. She is behaving like a male killer, not like a female nourisher. The situation is analogous, though modified by matriliny, to the following pronouncement in the ancient Jewish Code of Qaro: "Every man is bound to marry a wife in order to beget children, and he who fails of this duty is as one who sheds blood."

One does not need to be a psychoanalyst, one only needs sound sociological training, acquaintance with the total Ndembu symbolic system, plus ordinary common sense, to see that one of the aims of the ritual is to make the woman accept her lot in life as a childbearer and rearer of children for her lineage. The symbolism suggests that the patient is unconsciously rejecting her female role, that indeed she is guilty; indeed, "*mbayi,*" one term for menstrual blood, is etymologically connected with "*ku-baya*" (to be guilty). I have not time here to present further evidence of symbols and interpretations, both in *Nkula* and in cognate rituals, which reinforce this explanation. In the situation of *Nkula*, the dominant principles celebrated and reanimated are those of matriliny, the mother-child bond, and tribal continuity through matriliny. The norms in which these are expressed are those governing the behavior of mature women, which ascribe to them the role appropriate to their sex. The suppressed or submerged principles and norms, in this situation, concern and control the personal and corporate behavior deemed appropriate for man.

The analysis of *Nkula* symbolism throws into relief another major function of ritual. Ritual adapts and periodically readapts the biopsychical individual to the basic conditions and axiomatic values of human social life. In redressive rituals, the category to which *Nkula* belongs, the eternally rebellious individual is converted for a while into a loyal citizen. In the case of *Nkula*, a female individual whose behavior is felt to demonstrate her rebellion against, or at least her reluctance to comply with, the biological and social life patterns of her sex, is both induced and coerced by

---

[28] Earlier, Turner characterized instrumental symbols as those that have a ritually specific meaning; here he gives an example. The *mukula* tree represents menstrual blood and the matrilineage in the women's *Nkula* rite, but it also represents the blood of animals and the hunter's power to kill, among other meanings, in men's hunting rites.

[29] *Necrophagy* is the eating of the dead.

[30] The role reversals in the *Nkula* ceremony—women dressing in hunter's garb and dancing a hunter's dance—are other aspects of the rituals of rebellion that Gluckman

described in his research. See for example, his *Custom and Conflict in Africa* (1956). Gluckman's central idea was that while the ritualized reversing of established roles (the poor mock the wealthy, women dress as men) seemed to challenge the established order, in fact, these symbolic reversals reinforced it. (See essay 15.) Similarly, Turner identifies Ndembu women's ceremonial cross-dressing as a demonstration of male and female roles. He sees the ritual as a symbolic means of forcing women to accept their place as childbearers and not challenge male gender roles.

means of precept and symbol to accept her culturally prescribed destiny.[31]

MODES OF INFERENCE IN INTERPRETATION

Each kind of Ndembu ritual, like *Nkula*, has several meanings and goals that are not made explicit by informants, but must be inferred by the investigator from the symbolic pattern and from behavior. He is able to make these inferences only if he has previously examined the symbolic configurations and the meanings attributed to their component symbols by skilled informants, of many other kinds of ritual in the same total system. In other words, he must examine symbols not only in the context of each specific kind of ritual, but in the context of the total system. He may even find it profitable, where the same symbol is found throughout a wide culture area, to study its changes of meaning in different societies in that area.[32]

There are two main types of contexts, irrespective of size. There is the action-field context, which we have discussed at some length. There is also the cultural context in which symbols are regarded as clusters of abstract meanings. By comparing the different kinds and sizes of contexts in which a dominant symbol occurs, we can often see that the meanings "officially" attributed to it in a particular kind of ritual may be mutually consistent. However, there may be much discrepancy and even contradiction between many of the meanings given by informants, when this dominant symbol is regarded as a unit of the total symbolic system. I do not believe that this discrepancy is the result of mere carelessness and ignorance or variously distributed pieces of insight. I believe that discrepancy between

significata is a quintessential property of the great symbolic dominants in all religions. Such symbols come in the process of time to absorb into their meaning-content most of the major aspects of human social life, so that, in a sense, they come to represent "human society" itself.[33] In each ritual they assert the situational primacy of a single aspect or of a few aspects only, but by their mere presence they suffuse those aspects with the awe that can only be inspired by the human total. All the contradictions of human social life, between norms, and drives, between different drives and between different norms, between society and the individual, and between groups, are condensed and unified in a single representation, the dominant symbols. It is the task of analysis to break down this amalgam into its primary constituents.

[*The 350-word section called "The Relativity of Depth" was omitted from this text. In it, Turner criticizes the notion that psychoanalytic interpretations of symbolism are "deeper" than anthropological analyses and characterizes symbols as a "force in a field of social action."*]

CONCLUSION: THE ANALYSIS OF SYMBOLS IN SOCIAL PROCESSES

Let me outline briefly the way in which I think ritual symbols may fruitfully be analyzed. Performances of ritual are phases in broad social processes, the span and complexity of which are roughly proportional to the size and degree of differentiation of the groups in which they occur. One class of ritual is situated near the apex of a whole hierarchy of redressive and regulative institutions that correct deflections and deviations

---

[31] The paragraph concluding Turner's description of the *Nkula* rite highlights the structural-functionalist background that he brings to his analysis. Ritual compels a woman who rebels against her assigned role to "accept her culturally prescribed destiny," thus preserving the stability of Ndembu society.

[32] Note again Turner's view of the anthropologist as neutral omniscient observer—anthropologists can interpret, he

says, because they see the total system. The individual immersed in the system does not possess this clarity of vision. Compare this point of view with that of the postmodernists in essays 38 and 39.

[33] Remember Durkheim's contention that Australian Aboriginal religious beliefs were a model of their own society. Here Turner makes a similar claim, not just for Ndembu symbolism, but for the dominant symbols of any society.

from customarily prescribed behavior. Another class anticipates deviations and conflicts. This class includes periodic rituals and life-crisis rituals. Each kind of ritual is a patterned process in time, the units of which are symbolic objects and serialized items of symbolic behavior.

The symbolic constituents may themselves be classed into structural elements, or "dominant symbols," which tend to be ends in themselves, and variable elements, or "instrumental symbols," which serve as means to the explicit or implicit goals of the given ritual. In order to give an adequate explanation of the meaning of a particular symbol, it is necessary first to examine the widest action-field context, that, namely, in which the ritual itself is simply a phase. Here one must consider what kinds of circumstances give rise to a performance of ritual, whether these are concerned with natural phenomena, economic and technological processes, human life-crises, or with the breach of crucial social relationships. The circumstances will probably determine what sort of ritual is performed. The goals of the ritual will have overt and implicit reference to the antecedent circumstances and will in turn help to determine the meaning of the symbols. Symbols must now be examined within the context of the specific ritual. It is here that we enlist the aid of indigenous informants. It is here also that we may be able to speak legitimately of "levels" of interpretation, for laymen will give the investigator simple and esoteric meanings, while specialists will give him esoteric explanations and more elaborate texts. Next, behavior directed towards each symbol should be noted, for such behavior is an important component of its total meaning.[34]

We are now in a position to exhibit the ritual as a system of meanings, but this system acquires additional richness and depth if it is regarded as itself constituting a sector of the Ndembu ritual system, as interpreted by informants and as observed in action. It is in comparison with other sectors of the total system, and by reference to the dominant articulating principles of the total system, that we often become aware that the overt and ostensible aims and purposes of a given ritual conceal unavowed, and even "unconscious," wishes and goals. We also become aware that a complex relationship exists between the overt and the submerged, and the manifest and latent patterns of meaning. As social anthropologists we are potentially capable of analyzing the social aspect of this relationship. We can examine, for example, the relations of dependence and independence between the total society and its parts, and the relations between different kinds of parts, and between different parts of the same kind. We can see how the same dominant symbol, which in one kind of ritual stands for one kind of social group or for one principle of organization, in another kind of ritual stands for another kind of group or principle, and in its aggregate of meanings stands for unity and continuity of the widest Ndembu society, embracing its contradictions.[35]

THE LIMITS OF CONTEMPORARY ANTHROPOLOGICAL COMPETENCE

Our analysis must needs be incomplete when we consider the relationship between the normative elements in social life and the individual. For this

---

[34] Note Turner's comment that different people will interpret symbols differently. A decade later, postmodern writers emphasized this point. They used the term *positioning* and claimed that one's point of view was influenced by social, economic, and political factors. One important difference between Turner's view and that of the postmodernists was that these latter were more influenced by Marxism: They tended to see positioning in terms of conflict and domination of one group over another. Turner notes that positioning exists, but he does not question its effect. He insists that anthropologists occupy a privileged position and are impartial observers.

[35] In the two paragraphs above, Turner provides an outline of his methods of analysis. The sophistication that he brought to symbolic analysis becomes apparent when you compare his work with studies of ritual or religion from the first part of the century such as Sir James Frazer's *Golden Bough* (1911–1915 [1890]) and Freud's *Moses and Monotheism* (1939). Turner's analysis of the different types of symbols and their properties stands today as one of the seminal works in symbolic anthropology.

relationship, too, finds its way into the meaning of ritual symbols. Here we come to the confines of our present anthropological competence, for we are now dealing with the structure and properties of psyches, a scientific field traditionally studied by other disciplines than ours. At one end of the symbol's spectrum of meanings we encounter the individual psychologist and the social psychologist, and even beyond them (if one may make a friendly tilt at an envied friend), brandishing his Medusa's head, the psychoanalyst, ready to turn to stone the foolhardy interloper into his caverns of terminology.

We shudder back thankfully into the light of social day. Here the significant elements of a symbol's meaning are related to what it does and what is done to it by and for whom. These aspects can only be understood if one takes into account from the beginning, and represents by appropriate theoretical constructs, the total field situation in which the symbol occurs. This situation would include the structure of the group that performs the ritual we observe, its basic organizing principles and perdurable relationships, and, in addition, its extant division into transient alliances and factions on the basis of immediate interest and ambitions, for both abiding structure and recurrent forms of conflict and selfish interest are stereotyped in ritual symbolism. Once we have collected informants' interpretations of a given symbol, our work of analysis has indeed just begun. We must gradually approximate to the action-meaning of our symbol by way of what Lewin calls (1949, 149) "a stepwise increasing specificity"

from widest to narrowest significant action context. Informants' "meanings" only become meaningful as objects of scientific study in the course of this analytical process.[36]

NOTES

Read at a meeting of the Association of Social Anthropologists of the Commonwealth in London, March 1958. First published in *Closed Systems and Open Minds: The Limits of Naivety in Social Science*, M. Gluckman, ed. (Edinburgh: Oliver and Boyd, 1964).

[a] *Muchidi* also means "category," "kind," "species," and "tribe" itself.

[b] I.e., objects not of indefinite duration but to which the category of time is not applicable.

REFERENCES

Bettelheim, Bruno. 1954. *Symbolic Wounds: Puberty Rites and the Envious Male*. Glencoe, Ill: Free Press.

Durkheim, E. 1954. *Elementary Forms of the Religious Life*. London: Allen and Unwin.

Fenichel, Otto. 1946. *The Psychoanalytic Theory of Neuroses*. London: Routledge and Kegan Paul.

Jung, Carl G. 1949. *Psychological Types*. London: Routledge and Kegan Paul.

Lewin, K. 1949. *Field Theory in Social Science*. London: Tavistock Publications.

Nadel, S. F. 1954. *Nupe Religion*. London: Routledge and Kegan Paul.

Sapir, E. "Symbols," *Encyclopedia of the Social Sciences*, XIV. New York: Macmillan.

Wilson, M. 1957. *Rituals of Kinship Among the Nyakyusa*. London: Oxford University Press, for the International African Institute.

---

[36] The role of symbols in culture and individual psychology is a complex question that has defied definitive explication since it first arose at the turn of the century. In the final paragraphs, Turner, like Durkheim and Douglas, focuses on the intellectual division between anthropology-sociology and psychology.

37. *Deep Play: Notes on the Balinese Cockfight*

CLIFFORD GEERTZ (1926–2006)

THE RAID

Early in April of 1958, my wife and I arrived, malarial and diffident, in a Balinese village we intended, as anthropologists, to study.[1] A small place, about five hundred people, and relatively remote, it was its own world. We were intruders, professional ones, and the villagers dealt with us as Balinese seem always to deal with people not part of their life who yet press themselves upon them: as though we were not there. For them, and to a degree for ourselves, we were nonpersons, specters, invisible men.

We moved into an extended family compound (that had been arranged before through the provincial government) belonging to one of the four major factions in village life. But except for our landlord and the village chief, whose cousin and brother-in-law he was, everyone ignored us in a way only a Balinese can do. As we wandered around, uncertain, wistful, eager to please, people seemed to look right through us with a gaze focused several yards behind us on some more actual stone or tree. Almost nobody greeted us;

but nobody scowled or said anything unpleasant to us either, which would have been almost as satisfactory. If we ventured to approach someone (something one is powerfully inhibited from doing in such an atmosphere), he moved, negligently but definitely, away. If, seated or leaning against a wall, we had him trapped, he said nothing at all, or mumbled what for the Balinese is the ultimate nonword—"yes." The indifference, of course, was studied; the villagers were watching every move we made, and they had an enormous amount of quite accurate information about who we were and what we were going to be doing. But they acted as if we simply did not exist, which, in fact, as this behavior was designed to inform us, we did not, or anyway not yet.

This is, as I say, general in Bali. Everywhere else I have been in Indonesia, and more latterly in Morocco, when I have gone into a new village, people have poured out from all sides to take a very close look at me, and, often an all-too-probing feel as well. In Balinese villages, at least those away from the tourist circuit, nothing happens at all. People go on pounding, chatting, making

---

From *The Interpretation of Cultures* (1973)

---

[1] The work of symbolic anthropologists like Victor Turner and Mary Douglas was concerned with demonstrating what Devons and Gluckman (1964) called the "logic of the irrational." One motive underlying their work was to demonstrate how institutions that seemed irrational to the observer are actually rational, even if the natives themselves are unaware of the cultural logic behind their behavior. Turner and Douglas accounted for this hidden rationality by penetrating the surface behavior and explanations to look for concealed layers of meaning. This form of inquiry ultimately led analysts to resort to psychological explanations of behavior, or semimetaphysical concepts such as social facts or the collective conscience. Geertz, although he too is concerned with the interpretation of cultural symbolism, follows a very different approach: He wishes to provide the reader with an empathic understanding of another society. Geertz believes that culture is acted out in public symbols such as the cockfight and is the mechanism by which members of a society communicate their worldview. He is not trying to uncover the hidden symbolic meaning of the Balinese cockfight, for he believes the Balinese understand the symbolism of the contest as well as anyone. Instead, in this analysis Geertz attempts to situate readers of the essay within the Balinese system in order to facilitate their understanding of the meaning of the cockfight. This is not, in any sense, a scientific goal. His observations are not replicable. Someone else trying to do the same work might well have a very different set of insights.

Geertz's original article is accompanied by 43 voluminous footnotes, which space limitations do not allow us to reprint. Asterisks have been used to show readers the placement of his footnotes in the text.

offerings, staring into space, carrying baskets about while one drifts around feeling vaguely disembodied. And the same thing is true on the individual level. When you first meet a Balinese, he seems virtually not to relate to you at all; he is, in the term Gregory Bateson and Margaret Mead made famous, "away."* Then—in a day, a week, a month (with some people the magic moment never comes)—he decides, for reasons I have never quite been able to fathom, that you *are* real, and then he becomes a warm, gay, sensitive, sympathetic, though, being Balinese, always precisely controlled, person. You have crossed, somehow, some moral or metaphysical shadow line. Though you are not exactly taken as a Balinese (one has to be born to that), you are at least regarded as a human being rather than a cloud or a gust of wind. The whole complexion of your relationship dramatically changes to, in the majority of cases, a gentle, almost affectionate one—a low-keyed, rather playful, rather mannered, rather bemused geniality.

My wife and I were still very much in the gust-of-wind stage, a most frustrating, and even, as you soon begin to doubt whether you are really real after all, unnerving one, when, ten days or so after our arrival, a large cockfight was held in the public square to raise money for a new school.

Now, a few special occasions aside, cockfights are illegal in Bali under the Republic (as, for not altogether unrelated reasons, they were under the Dutch), largely as a result of the pretensions to puritanism radical nationalism tends to bring with it. The elite, which is not itself so very puritan, worries about the poor, ignorant peasant gambling all his money away, about what foreigners will think, about the waste of time better devoted to building up the country. It sees cockfighting as "primitive," "backward," "unprogressive," and generally unbecoming an ambitious nation. And, as with those other embarrassments—opium smoking, begging, or uncovered breasts—it seeks, rather unsystematically, to put a stop to it.

Of course, like drinking during Prohibition or, today, smoking marihuana, cockfights, being a part of "The Balinese Way of Life," nonetheless go on happening, and with extraordinary frequency. And, as with Prohibition or marihuana, from time to time the police (who, in 1958 at

least, were almost all not Balinese but Javanese) feel called upon to make a raid, confiscate the cocks and spurs, fine a few people, and even now and then expose some of them in the tropical sun for a day as object lessons which never, somehow, get learned, even though occasionally, quite occasionally, the object dies.

As a result, the fights are usually held in a secluded corner of a village in semisecrecy, a fact which tends to slow the action a little—not very much, but the Balinese do not care to have it slowed at all. In this case, however, perhaps because they were raising money for a school that the government was unable to give them, perhaps because raids had been few recently, perhaps, as I gathered from subsequent discussion, there was a notion that the necessary bribes had been paid, they thought they could take a chance on the central square and draw a larger and more enthusiastic crowd without attracting the attention of the law.

They were wrong. In the midst of the third match, with hundreds of people, including, still transparent, myself and my wife, fused into a single body around the ring, a superorganism in the literal sense, a truck full of policemen armed with machine guns roared up. Amid great screeching cries of "pulisi! pulisi!" from the crowd, the policemen jumped out, and, springing into the center of the ring, began to swing their guns around like gangsters in a motion picture, though not going so far as actually to fire them. The superorganism came instantly apart as its components scattered in all directions. People raced down the road, disappeared headfirst over walls, scrambled under platforms, folded themselves behind wicker screens, scuttled up coconut trees. Cocks armed with steel spurs sharp enough to cut off a finger or run a hole through a foot were running wildly around. Everything was dust and panic.

On the established anthropological principle, "When in Rome," my wife and I decided, only slightly less instantaneously than everyone else, that the thing to do was run too. We ran down the main village street, northward, away from where we were living, for we were on that side of the ring. About halfway down another fugitive ducked suddenly into a compound—his own, it turned out—and we, seeing nothing ahead of us but rice fields, open country, and a very high volcano, followed him. As the three of us came tumbling into the courtyard, his wife, who had apparently been through this sort of thing before, whipped out a table, a tablecloth, three chairs, and three cups of tea, and we all, without any explicit communication whatsoever, sat down, commenced to sip tea, and sought to compose ourselves.

A few moments later, one of the policemen marched importantly into the yard, looking for the village chief. (The chief had not only been at the fight, he had arranged it. When the truck drove up he ran to the river, stripped off his sarong, and plunged in so he could say, when at length they found him sitting there pouring water over his head, that he had been away bathing when the whole affair had occurred and was ignorant of it. They did not believe him and fined him three hundred rupiah, which the village raised collectively.) Seeing me and my wife, "White Men," there in the yard, the policeman performed a classic double take. When he found his voice again he asked, approximately, what in the devil did we think we were doing there. Our host of five minutes leaped instantly to our defense, producing an impassioned description of who and what we were, so detailed and so accurate that it was my turn, having barely communicated with a living human being save my landlord and the village chief for more than a week, to be astonished. We had a perfect right to be there, he said, looking the Javanese upstart in the eye. We were American professors; the government had cleared us; we were there to study culture; we were going to write a book to tell Americans about Bali. And we had all been there drinking tea and talking about cultural matters all afternoon and did not know anything about any cockfight. Moreover, we had not seen the village chief all day; he must have gone to town. The policeman retreated in rather total disarray. And, after a decent interval, bewildered but relieved to have survived and stayed out of jail, so did we.

The next morning the village was a completely different world for us. Not only were we no longer invisible, we were suddenly the center of all attention, the object of a great outpouring of warmth, interest, and most especially, amusement. Everyone in the village knew we had fled like everyone else. They asked us about it again and again (I must have told the story, small detail by small detail, fifty times by the end of the day), gently, affectionately, but quite insistently teasing us: "Why didn't you just stand there and tell the police who you were?" "Why didn't you just say you were only watching and not betting?" "Were you really afraid of those little guns?" As always, kinesthetically minded and, even when fleeing for their lives (or, as happened eight years later, surrendering them), the world's most poised people, they gleefully mimicked, also over and over again, our graceless style of running and what they claimed were our panic-stricken facial expressions. But above all, everyone was extremely pleased and even more surprised that we had not simply "pulled out our papers" (they knew about those too) and asserted our Distinguished Visitor status, but had instead demonstrated our solidarity with what were now our covillagers. (What we had actually demonstrated was our cowardice, but there is fellowship in that too.) Even the Brahmana priest, an old, grave, halfway-to-heaven type who because of its associations with the underworld would never be involved, even distantly, in a cockfight, and was difficult to approach even to other Balinese, had us called into his courtyard to ask us about what had happened, chuckling happily at the sheer extraordinariness of it all.

In Bali, to be teased is to be accepted. It was the turning point so far as our relationship to the community was concerned, and we were quite literally "in." The whole village opened up to us, probably more than it ever would have otherwise (I might actually never have gotten to that priest, and our accidental host became one of my best informants), and certainly very much faster. Getting caught, or almost caught, in a vice raid is perhaps not a very generalizable recipe for achieving that mysterious necessity of anthropological field work, rapport, but for me it worked very well. It led to a sudden and unusually complete acceptance into a society extremely difficult for outsiders to penetrate. It gave me the kind of immediate, inside-view grasp of an aspect of "peasant mentality" that anthropologists not fortunate enough to flee headlong with their subjects from armed authorities normally do not get. And, perhaps most important of all, for the other things might have come in other ways, it put me very quickly on to a combination emotional explosion, status war, and philosophical drama of central significance to the society whose inner nature I desired to understand. By the time I left I had spent about as much time looking into cockfights as into witchcraft, irrigation, caste, or marriage.[2]

OF COCKS AND MEN

Bali, mainly because it is Bali, is a well-studied place. Its mythology, art, ritual, social organization, patterns of child rearing, forms of law, even styles of trance, have all been microscopically examined for traces of that elusive substance Jane Belo called "The Balinese Temper."* But, aside from a few passing remarks, the cockfight has barely been noticed, although as a popular obsession of consuming power it is at least as important a revelation of what being a Balinese "is really like" as these more celebrated phenomena.* As much of America surfaces in a ball park, on a golf links, at a race track, or around a poker table, much of Bali surfaces in a cock ring. For it is only apparently cocks that are fighting there. Actually, it is men.

To anyone who has been in Bali any length of time, the deep psychological identification of Balinese men with their cocks is unmistakable. The double entendre here is deliberate. It works in exactly the same way in Balinese as it does in English, even to producing the same tired jokes, strained puns, and uninventive obscenities. Bateson and Mead have even suggested that, in line with the Balinese conception of the body as a set of separately animated parts, cocks are viewed as detachable, self-operating penises, ambulant genitals with a life of their own.* And while I do not have the kind of unconscious material either to confirm or disconfirm this intriguing notion, the fact that they are masculine symbols par excellence is about as indubitable, and to the Balinese about as evident, as the fact that water runs downhill.

The language of everyday moralism is shot through, on the male side of it, with roosterish imagery. *Sabung,* the word for cock (and one which appears in inscriptions as early as A.D. 922), is used metaphorically to mean "hero," "warrior," "champion," "man of parts," "political candidate," "bachelor," "dandy," "lady-killer," or "tough guy." A pompous man whose behavior presumes above his station is compared to a tailless cock who struts about as though he had a large, spectacular one. A desperate man who makes a last, irrational effort to extricate himself from an impossible situation is likened to a dying cock who makes one final lunge at his tormentor to drag him along to a common destruction. A stingy man, who promises much, gives little, and

---

[2] This is one of the most famous stories in anthropology and almost any anthropologist in the United States could tell it to you. Why? First, it is an adventure and a fieldworker's fantasy: Confused anthropologists find empathy and acceptance. Second, it highlights the strength of Geertz's writing style. Not only is it interesting because it is self-revealing, but Geertz was one of the finest writers in anthropology. The essay is full of action and humor. Interestingly, the essay was first published in *Daedalus,* a literary journal; it is aimed at a highly educated audience but not one composed exclusively of anthropologists.

Geertz's self-relevatory style was unusual for ethnographic writing at this time. (See the introduction to Evans-Pritchard's *The Nuer* [1940] for an early example of self-relevatory ethnographic writing.) Although the style is common now, compare his descriptions of the police raid with earlier ethnographic work. Can you imagine Kroeber or Radcliffe-Brown writing an account of their escape from the police? This story is not only fun to read, but Geertz's writing helps a reader visualize the events. He addresses the reader directly: "You have crossed, somehow, some oral or metaphysical shadow line. Though you are not exactly taken as Balinese . . . you are at least regarded as a human being" (1973:413).

The story with which Geertz begins this essay is crucial to his analysis as well. Due to a more or less chance occurrence, Geertz gained a particular position in Balinese society that enabled him to make certain kinds of observations. A decade before postmodernism became a serious endeavor within anthropology, Geertz, in this article, discussed his position within Balinese society and the insights it afforded him.

begrudges that, is compared to a cock which, held by the tail, leaps at another without in fact engaging him. A marriageable young man still shy with the opposite sex or someone in a new job anxious to make a good impression is called "a fighting cock caged for the first time."* Court trials, wars, political contests, inheritance disputes, and street arguments are all compared to cockfights.* Even the very island itself is perceived from its shape as a small, proud cock, poised, neck extended, back taut, tail raised, in eternal challenge to large, feckless, shapeless Java.*

But the intimacy of men with their cocks is more than metaphorical. Balinese men, or anyway a large majority of Balinese men, spend an enormous amount of time with their favorites, grooming them, feeding them, discussing them, trying them out against one another, or just gazing at them with a mixture of rapt admiration and dreamy self-absorption. Whenever you see a group of Balinese men squatting idly in the council shed or along the road in their hips down, shoulders forward, knees up fashion, half or more of them will have a rooster in his hands, holding it between his thighs, bouncing it gently up and down to strengthen its legs, ruffling its feathers with abstract sensuality, pushing it out against a neighbor's rooster to rouse its spirit, withdrawing it toward his loins to calm it again. Now and then, to get a feel for another bird, a man will fiddle this way with someone else's cock for a while, but usually by moving around to squat in place behind it, rather than just having it passed across to him as though it were merely an animal.

In the houseyard, the high-walled enclosures where the people live, fighting cocks are kept in wicker cages, moved frequently about so as to maintain the optimum balance of sun and shade. They are fed a special diet, which varies somewhat according to individual theories but which is mostly maize, sifted for impurities with far more care than it is when mere humans are going to eat it, and offered to the animal kernel by kernel. Red pepper is stuffed down their beaks and up their anuses to give them spirit. They are bathed in the same ceremonial preparation of tepid water, medicinal herbs, flowers, and onions in which infants are bathed, and for a prize cock just about as often. Their combs are cropped, their plumage dressed, their spurs trimmed, and their legs massaged, and they are inspected for flaws with the squinted concentration of a diamond merchant. A man who has a passion for cocks, an enthusiast in the literal sense of the term, can spend most of his life with them, and even those, the overwhelming majority, whose passion though intense has not entirely run away with them, can and do spend what seems not only to an outsider, but also to themselves, an inordinate amount of time with them. "I am cock crazy," my landlord, a quite ordinary *afficionado* by Balinese standards, used to moan as he went to move another cage, give another bath, or conduct another feeding. "We're all cock crazy."

The madness has some less visible dimensions, however, because although it is true that cocks are symbolic expressions or magnifications of their owner's self, the narcissistic male ego writ out in Aesopian terms, they are also expressions—and rather more immediate ones—of what the Balinese regard as the direct inversion, aesthetically, morally, and metaphysically, of human status: animality.

The Balinese revulsion against any behavior regarded as animal-like can hardly be overstressed. Babies are not allowed to crawl for that reason. Incest, though hardly approved, is a much less horrifying crime than bestiality. (The appropriate punishment for the second is death by drowning, for the first being forced to live like an animal.)* Most demons are represented—in sculpture, dance, ritual, myth—in some real or fantastic animal form. The main puberty rite consists in filing the child's teeth so they will not look like animal fangs. Not only defecation but eating is regarded as a disgusting, almost obscene activity, to be conducted hurriedly and privately, because of its association with animality. Even falling down or any form of clumsiness is considered to be bad for these reasons. Aside from cocks and a few domestic animals—oxen, ducks—of no emotional significance, the Balinese are aversive to animals and treat their large number of dogs not merely callously but with a phobic cruelty. In identifying with his cock, the Balinese man is identifying not just with his ideal self, or even his penis, but also, and at the same time, with what he most fears, hates, and ambivalence being what it is, is fascinated by—"The Powers of Darkness."

The connection of cocks and cockfighting with such Powers, with the animalistic demons that threaten constantly to invade the small, cleared-off space in which the Balinese have so carefully built their lives and devour its inhabitants, is quite explicit. A cockfight, any cockfight, is in the first instance a blood sacrifice offered, with the appropriate chants and oblations, to the demons in order to pacify their ravenous, cannibal hunger. No temple festival should be conducted until one is made. (If it is omitted, someone will inevitably fall into a trance and command with the voice of an angered spirit that the oversight be immediately corrected.) Collective responses to natural evils—illness, crop failure, volcanic eruptions—almost always involve them. And that famous holiday in Bali, "The Day of Silence" (*Njepi*), when everyone sits silent and immobile all day long in order to avoid contact with a sudden influx of demons chased momentarily out of hell, is preceded the previous day by large-scale cockfights (in this case legal) in almost every village on the island.

In the cockfight, man and beast, good and evil, ego and id, the creative power of aroused masculinity and the destructive power of loosened animality fuse in a bloody drama of hatred, cruelty, violence, and death. It is little wonder that when, as is the invariable rule, the owner of the winning cock takes the carcass of the loser—often torn limb from limb by its enraged owner—home to eat, he does so with a mixture of social embarrassment, moral satisfaction, aesthetic disgust, and cannibal joy. Or that a man who has

lost an important fight is sometimes driven to wreck his family shrines and curse the gods, an act of metaphysical (and social) suicide. Or that in seeking earthly analogues for heaven and hell the Balinese compare the former to the mood of a man whose cock has just won, the latter to that of a man whose cock has just lost.[3]

THE FIGHT

Cockfights (*tetadjen; sabungan*) are held in a ring about fifty feet square. Usually they begin toward late afternoon and run three or four hours until sunset. About nine or ten separate matches (*sehet*) comprise a program. Each match is precisely like the others in general pattern: there is no main match, no connection between individual matches, no variation in their format, and each is arranged on a completely ad hoc basis. After a fight has ended and the emotional debris is cleaned away—the bets have been paid, the curses cursed, the carcasses possessed—seven, eight, perhaps even a dozen men slip negligently into the ring with a cock and seek to find there a logical opponent for it. This process, which rarely takes less than ten minutes, and often a good deal longer, is conducted in a very subdued, oblique, even dissembling manner. Those not immediately involved give it at best but disguised, sidelong attention; those who, embarrassedly, are, attempt to pretend somehow that the whole thing is not really happening.[4]

A match made, the other hopefuls retire with the same deliberate indifference, and the selected cocks have their spurs (*tadji*) affixed—razor-sharp, pointed steel swords, four or five inches long.

---

[3] Although Geertz is attempting a very different kind of symbolic analysis than Freud or Lévi-Strauss, the influence of their work is apparent here. The symbolic link between the fighting birds, genitals, and male status is obviously Freudian. Although Geertz is not a structuralist, the binary constructions—man-beast, good-evil, creation-destruction—are based on Lévi-Strauss' nature-culture dichotomy. The human cultural world is repulsed by the animal-natural world, but the two spheres of existence meet in cocks and the cockfight.

[4] Geertz describes the cockfight and patterns of betting that take place in great detail. He attempts to re-create the context in which the action takes place in order that the reader may share, as much as possible, in the context in which Balinese cultural meaning is created. Geertz describes this form of analysis as "thick description" (1973:6), which he identifies as uncovering the layers of meaning surrounding an event.

This is a delicate job which only a small proportion of men, a half-dozen or so in most villages, know how to do properly. The man who attaches the spurs also provides them, and if the rooster he assists wins, its owner awards him the spur-leg of the victim. The spurs are affixed by winding a long length of string around the foot of the spur and the leg of the cock. For reasons I shall come to presently, it is done somewhat differently from case to case, and is an obsessively deliberate affair. The lore about spurs is extensive—they are sharpened only at eclipses and the dark of the moon, should be kept out of the sight of women, and so forth. And they are handled, both in use and out, with the same curious combination of fussiness and sensuality the Balinese direct toward ritual objects generally.

The spurs affixed, the two cocks are placed by their handlers (who may or may not be their owners) facing one another in the center of the ring.* A coconut pierced with a small hole is placed in a pail of water, in which it takes about twenty-one seconds to sink, a period known as a *tjeng* and marked at beginning and end by the beating of a slit gong. During these twenty-one seconds the handlers (*pengangkeb*) are not permitted to touch their roosters. If, as sometimes happens, the animals have not fought during this time, they are picked up, fluffed, pulled, prodded, and otherwise insulted, and put back in the center of the ring and the process begins again. Sometimes they refuse to fight at all, or one keeps running away, in which case they are imprisoned together under a wicker cage, which usually gets them engaged.

Most of the time, in any case, the cocks fly almost immediately at one another in a wing-beating, head-thrusting, leg-kicking explosion of animal fury so pure, so absolute, and in its own way so beautiful, as to be almost abstract, a Platonic concept of hate. Within moments one or the other drives home a solid blow with his spur. The handler whose cock has delivered the blow immediately picks it up so that it will not get a return blow, for if he does not the match is likely to end in a mutually mortal tie as the two birds wildly hack each other to pieces. This is particularly true if, as often happens, the spur sticks in

its victim's body, for then the aggressor is at the mercy of his wounded foe.

With the birds again in the hands of their handlers, the coconut is now sunk three times after which the cock which has landed the blow must be set down to show that he is firm, a fact he demonstrates by wandering idly around the ring for a coconut sink. The coconut is then sunk twice more and the fight must recommence.

During this interval, slightly over two minutes, the handler of the wounded cock has been working frantically over it, like a trainer patching a mauled boxer between rounds, to get it in shape for a last, desperate try for victory. He blows in its mouth, putting the whole chicken head in his own mouth and sucking and blowing, fluffs it, stuffs its wounds with various sorts of medicines, and generally tries anything he can think of to arouse the last ounce of spirit which may be hidden somewhere within it. By the time he is forced to put it back down he is usually drenched in chicken blood, but, as in prize fighting, a good handler is worth his weight in gold. Some of them can virtually make the dead walk, at least long enough for the second and final round.

In the climactic battle (if there is one; sometimes the wounded cock simply expires in the handler's hands or immediately as it is placed down again), the cock who landed the first blow usually proceeds to finish off his weakened opponent. But this is far from an inevitable outcome, for if a cock can walk, he can fight, and if he can fight, he can kill, and what counts is which cock expires first. If the wounded one can get a stab in and stagger on until the other drops, he is the official winner, even if he himself topples over an instant later.

Surrounding all this melodrama—which the crowd packed tight around the ring follows in near silence, moving their bodies in kinesthetic sympathy with the movement of the animals, cheering their champions on with wordless hand motions, shiftings of the shoulders, turnings of the head, falling back en masse as the cock with the murderous spurs careens toward one side of the ring (it is said that spectators sometimes lose eyes and fingers from being too attentive), surging forward again as they glance off toward another—is a vast body of extraordinarily elaborate and precisely detailed rules.[5]

These rules, together with the developed lore of cocks and cockfighting which accompanies them, are written down in palm-leaf manuscripts (*lontar; rontal*) passed on from generation to generation as part of the general legal and cultural tradition of the villages. At a fight, the umpire (*saja komong; djuru kembar*)—the man who manages the coconut—is in charge of their application and his authority is absolute. I have never seen an umpire's judgment questioned on any subject, even by the more despondent losers, nor have I ever heard, even in private, a charge of unfairness directed against one, or, for that matter, complaints about umpires in general. Only exceptionally well trusted, solid, and, given the complexity of the code, knowledgeable citizens perform this job, and in fact men will bring their cocks only to fights presided over by such men. It is also the umpire to whom accusations of cheating, which, though rare in the extreme, occasionally arise, are referred; and it is he who in the not infrequent cases where the cocks expire virtually together decides which (if either, for, though the Balinese do not care for such an outcome, there can be ties) went first. Likened to a judge, a king, a priest, and a policeman, he is all of these, and under his assured direction the animal passion of the fight proceeds within the civic certainty of the law. In the dozens of cockfights I saw in Bali, I never once saw an altercation about rules. Indeed, I never saw an open altercation, other than those between cocks, at all.

This crosswise doubleness of an event which, taken as a fact of nature, is rage untrammeled and, taken as a fact of culture, is form perfected, defines the cockfight as a sociological entity. A cockfight is what, searching for a name for something not vertebrate enough to be called a group and not structureless enough to be called a crowd, Erving Goffman has called a "focused gathering"—a set of persons engrossed in a common flow of activity and relating to one another in terms of that flow.* Such gatherings meet and disperse; the participants in them fluctuate; the activity that focuses them is discrete—a particulate process that reoccurs rather than a continuous one that endures. They take their form from the situation that evokes them, the floor on which they are placed, as Goffman puts it; but it is a form, and an articulate one, nonetheless. For the situation, the floor is itself created, in jury deliberations, surgical operations, block meetings, sit-ins, cockfights, by the cultural preoccupations—here, as we shall see, the celebration of status rivalry—which not only specify the focus but, assembling actors and arranging scenery, bring it actually into being.[6]

In classical times (that is to say, prior to the Dutch invasion of 1908), when there were no bureaucrats around to improve popular morality, the staging of a cockfight was an explicitly societal matter. Bringing a cock to an important fight was, for an adult male, a compulsory duty of citizenship; taxation of fights, which were usually held on market day, was a major source of public revenue; patronage of the art was [the] stated responsibility of princes; and the cock ring, or *wantilan*, stood in the center of the village near those other monuments of Balinese civility—the council house, the origin temple, the market-

---

[5] One criticism of Geertz's work is that his interpretation is intuitive, making it difficult for others to replicate. Indeed, one could say that the power of Geertz's analysis is based on his compelling writing style. For example, you may not have noticed that Geertz is not presenting us with a description of one cockfight but rather with a literary construct based on his experience of at least fifty-seven matches.

[6] In this paragraph, you get a sense of Geertz's definition of culture: a shared code of meaning that is acted out pub-

lically. Unlike the ethnoscientists, Geertz believes that culture is not a mental model, but exists between people, created by their social actions. Additionally Geertz was interested in the sociology of religion. His reference to Erving Goffman (1922–1982), an important sociologist of the 1960s, gives a clue to the sociological influence on his work. Goffman viewed individual actions as performances and was concerned with delineating the rules governing nonverbal interaction. You can see Goffman's influence in these paragraphs, as Geertz describes people's actions at cockfights.

place, the signal tower, and the banyan tree. Today, a few special occasions aside, the newer rectitude makes so open a statement of the connection between the excitements of collective life and those of blood sport impossible, but, less directly expressed, the connection itself remains intimate and intact. To expose it, however, it is necessary to turn to the aspect of cockfighting around which all the others pivot, and through which they exercise their force, an aspect I have thus far studiously ignored. I mean, of course, the gambling.

[*We have omitted a 2,200-word section with 7 footnotes called "Odds and Even Money," in which Geertz gives a detailed explanation of cockfight betting patterns. He identifies two types of bets in a cockfight, the main bet between the principals who own the fighting cocks and peripheral bets between members of the audience. The principal bets are large collective wagers involving coalitions of bettors; they are quietly arranged with the umpire in the center of the ring. The second type of bet is typically small and is arranged impulsively by individuals shouting back and forth across the ring.*

Because center bets are always for even money, participants typically arrange fair matches. The more evenly matched the cocks, the higher the center bets. The side bets vary wildly according to the odds individual bettors are willing to give. The larger the center bet, the more frenzied the side betting. These fights are considered more interesting because more is at stake in them. In a high-stakes fight, men are risking money and social prestige, as well as valuable fighting cocks. When a match ends, all bets are immediately paid.

We return to Geertz's narrative at the last paragraph in the section, where he introduces the notion of "depth" in the analysis of culture.]

The Balinese attempt to create an interesting, if you will, "deep," match by making the center

bet as large as possible so that the cocks matched will be as equal and as fine as possible, and the outcome, thus, as unpredictable as possible.[7] They do not always succeed. Nearly half the matches are relatively trivial, relatively uninteresting—in my borrowed terminology, "shallow"—affairs. But that fact no more argues against my interpretation than the fact that most painters, poets, and playwrights are mediocre argues against the view that artistic effort is directed toward profundity and, with a certain frequency, approximates it. The image of artistic technique is indeed exact: the center bet is a means, a device, for creating "interesting," "deep" matches, *not* the reason, or at least not the main reason, *why* they are interesting, the source of their fascination, the substance of their depth. The question of why such matches are interesting—indeed, for the Balinese, exquisitely absorbing—takes us out of the realm of formal concerns into more broadly sociological and social-psychological ones, and to a less purely economic idea of what "depth" in gaming amounts to.*

PLAYING WITH FIRE

Bentham's concept of "deep play" is found in his *The Theory of Legislation.** By it he means play in which the stakes are so high that it is, from his utilitarian standpoint, irrational for men to engage in it at all. If a man whose fortune is a thousand pounds (or ringgits) wages five hundred of it on an even bet, the marginal utility of the pound he stands to win is clearly less than the marginal disutility of the one he stands to lose. In genuine deep play, this is the case for both parties. They are both in over their heads. Having come together in search of pleasure they have entered into a relationship which will bring the participants, considered collectively, net pain rather than net pleasure. Bentham's conclusion was,

---

[7] For Geertz, the secret of decoding the cockfight lies in viewing it as a representation of Balinese society. The long discussion of cockfight betting in the next section leads to a discussion of how betting patterns recapitulate the divi-

sions of the larger society. This insight hearkens back to Durkheim and the structural functionalists, but Geertz does not use his analysis for their purposes.

therefore, that deep play was immoral from first principles and, a typical step for him, should be prevented legally.[8]

But more interesting than the ethical problem, at least for our concerns here, is that despite the logical force of Bentham's analysis men do engage in such play, both passionately and often, and even in the face of law's revenge. For Bentham and those who think as he does (nowadays mainly lawyers, economists, and a few psychiatrists), the explanation is, as I have said, that such men are irrational—addicts, fetishists, children, fools, savages, who need only to be protected against themselves. But for the Balinese, though naturally they do not formulate it in so many words, the explanation lies in the fact that in such play, money is less a measure of utility, had or expected, than it is a symbol of moral import, perceived or imposed.

It is, in fact, in shallow games, ones in which smaller amounts of money are involved, that increments and decrements of cash are more nearly synonyms for utility and disutility, in the ordinary, unexpanded sense—for pleasure and pain, happiness and unhappiness. In deep ones, where the amounts of money are great, much more is at stake than material gain: namely, esteem, honor, dignity, respect—in a word, though in Bali a profoundly freighted word, status.* It is at stake symbolically, for (a few cases of ruined addict gamblers aside) no one's status is actually altered by the outcome of a cockfight; it is only, and that momentarily, affirmed or insulted. But for the Balinese, for whom nothing is more pleasurable than an affront obliquely delivered or more painful than one obliquely received—particularly when mutual acquaintances, undeceived by surfaces, are watching—such appraisive drama is deep indeed.

This, I must stress immediately, is *not* to say that the money does not matter, or that the Balinese is no more concerned about losing five hundred ringgits than fifteen. Such a conclusion would be absurd. It is because money *does*, in this hardly unmaterialistic society, matter and matter very much that the more of it one risks, the more of a lot of other things, such as one's pride, one's poise, one's dispassion, one's masculinity, one also risks, again only momentarily but again very publicly as well. In deep cockfights an owner and his collaborators, and, as we shall see, to a lesser but still quite real extent also their backers on the outside, put their money where their status is.

It is in large part *because* the marginal disutility of loss is so great at the higher levels of betting that to engage in such betting is to lay one's public self, allusively and metaphorically, through the medium of one's cock, on the line. And though to a Benthamite this might seem merely to increase the irrationality of the enterprise that much further, to the Balinese what it mainly increases is the meaningfulness of it all. And as (to follow Weber[9] rather than Bentham) the imposition of meaning on life is the major end and primary condition of human existence, that access of significance more than compensates for the economic costs involved.* Actually, given the even-money quality of the larger matches, important changes in material fortune among those

---

[8] Jeremy Bentham (1748–1832) was an English philosopher and social theorist best known for his doctrine of Utilitarianism, the principles of which are outlined in his 1789 book *An Introduction to the Principles of Morals and Legislation*. Utilitarianism is the belief that the aim of society should be to create the greatest level of happiness for the greatest number of people. Bentham believed that correct conduct was determined by the balance of pleasure over pain that a given act would produce, and that pain and pleasure could be quantitatively measured. Thus legislative decision making could be reduced to a quasi-mathematical science. Among Bentham's best known intellectual followers were John Stuart Mill (1806–1873) and Herbert Spencer.

When Bentham died, his body was embalmed and his head removed and replaced with a wax replica. His corpse was then dressed and placed on display at University College, London, where it remains to this day.

[9] Geertz claims Max Weber as one of the major influences in his intellectual development. He was first exposed to Weber by one of his professors, Talcott Parsons (1902–1979), while a graduate student at Harvard University. For more information on Geertz's career and academic life, see Handler's 1991 interview with Geertz in *Current Anthropology*.

who regularly participate in them seem virtually nonexistent, because matters more or less even out over the long run. It is, actually, in the smaller, shallow fights, where one finds the handful of more pure, addict-type gamblers involved—those who *are* in it mainly for the money—that "real" changes in social position, largely downward, are affected. Men of this sort, plungers, are highly dispraised by "true cockfighters" as fools who do not understand what the sport is all about, vulgarians who simply miss the point of it all. They are, these addicts, regarded as fair game for the genuine enthusiasts, those who do understand, to take a little money away from—something that is easy enough to do by luring them, through the force of their greed, into irrational bets on mismatched cocks. Most of them do indeed manage to ruin themselves in a remarkably short time, but there always seems to be one or two of them around, pawning their land and selling their clothes in order to bet, at any particular time.*

This graduated correlation of "status gambling" with deeper fights and, inversely, "money gambling" with shallower ones is in fact quite general. Bettors themselves form a sociomoral hierarchy in these terms. As noted earlier, at most cockfights there are, around the very edges of the cockfight area, a large number of mindless, sheer-chance-type gambling games (roulette, dice throw, coin-spin, pea-under-the-shell) operated by concessionaires. Only women, children, adolescents, and various other sorts of people who do not (or not yet) fight cocks—the extremely poor, the socially despised, the personally idiosyncratic—play at these games, at, of course, penny ante levels. Cockfighting men would be ashamed to go anywhere near them. Slightly above these people in standing are those who though they do not themselves fight cocks, bet on the smaller matches around the edges. Next, there are those who fight cocks in small, or occasionally

medium matches, but have not the status to join in the large ones, though they may bet from time to time on the side in those. And finally, there are those, the really substantial members of the community, the solid citizenry around whom local life revolves, who fight in the larger fights and bet on them around the side. The focusing element in these focused gatherings, these men generally dominate and define the sport as they dominate and define the society. When a Balinese male talks, in that almost venerative way, about "the true cockfighter," the *bebatoh* ("bettor") or *djuru kurung* ("cage keeper"), it is this sort of person, not those who bring the mentality of the pea-and-shell game into the quite different, inappropriate context of the cockfight, the driven gambler (*potét,* a word which has the secondary meaning of thief or reprobate), and the wistful hanger-on, that they mean. For such a man, what is really going on in a match is something rather closer to an *affaire d'honneur* (though, with the Balinese talent for practical fantasy, the blood that is spilled is only figuratively human) than to the stupid, mechanical crank of a slot machine.[10]

What makes Balinese cockfighting deep is thus not money in itself, but what, the more of it that is involved the more so, money causes to happen: the migration of the Balinese status hierarchy into the body of the cockfight.[11] Psychologically an Aesopian representation of the ideal/demonic, rather narcissistic, male self, sociologically it is an equally Aesopian representation of the complex fields of tension set up by the controlled, muted, ceremonial, but for all that deeply felt, interaction of those selves in the context of everyday life. The cocks may be surrogates for their owners' personalities, animal mirrors of psychic form, but the cockfight is—or more exactly, deliberately is made to be—a simulation of the social matrix, the involved system of cross-cutting, overlapping, highly corporate

[10] The cockfight is not about winning or losing money; it is a simulation of the social interactions between various groups in the community. Geertz contends that this is why the matches are so "deep" to the Balinese.

[11] For Geertz, the cockfight is a symbolic key to Balinese personality because it is the ritual through which the

Balinese express their values. Geertz uses the phrase the "migration of the Balinese status hierarchy into the body of the cockfight" to characterize his idea that one can observe the stratification of Balinese society in the organization of people within and around the cockfight area.

groups—villages, kingroups, irrigation societies, temple congregations, "castes"—in which its devotees live.* And as prestige, the necessity to affirm it, defend it, celebrate it, justify it, and just plain bask in it (but not, given the strongly ascriptive character of Balinese stratification, to seek it), is perhaps the central driving force in the society, so also—ambulant penises, blood sacrifices, and monetary exchanges aside—is it of the cockfight. This ap-parent amusement and seeming sport is, to take another phrase from Erving Goffman, "a status bloodbath."*

The easiest way to make this clear, and at least to some degree to demonstrate it, is to invoke the village whose cockfighting activities I observed the closest—the one in which the raid occurred and from which my statistical data are taken.

Like all Balinese villages, this one—Tihingan, in the Klungkung region of southeast Bali—is intricately organized, a labyrinth of alliances and oppositions. But, unlike many, two sorts of corporate groups, which are also status groups, particularly stand out, and we may concentrate on them, in a part-for-whole way, without undue distortion.

First, the village is dominated by four large, patrilineal, partly endogamous descent groups which are constantly vying with one another and form the major factions in the village. Sometimes they group two and two, or rather the two larger ones versus the two smaller ones plus all the unaffiliated people; sometimes they operate independently. There are also subfactions within them, subfactions within the subfactions, and so on to rather fine levels of distinction. And second, there is the village itself, almost entirely endogamous, which is opposed to all the other villages round about in its cockfight circuit (which, as explained, is the market region), but which also forms alliances with certain of these neighbors against certain others in various supravillage political and social contexts. The exact situation is thus, as everywhere in Bali, quite distinctive; but the general pattern of a tiered hierarchy of status rivalries between highly corporate but various based groupings (and, thus, between the members of them) is entirely general.

Consider, then, as support of the general thesis that the cockfight, and especially the deep cockfight, is fundamentally a dramatization of status concerns, the following facts, which to avoid extended ethnographic description I shall simply pronounce to be facts though the concrete evidence, examples, statements, and numbers that could be brought to bear in support of them, is both extensive and unmistakable:[12]

1. A man virtually never bets against a cock owned by a member of his own kingroup. Usually he will feel obliged to bet for it, the more so the closer the kin tie and the deeper the fight. If he is certain in his mind that it will not win, he may just not bet at all, particularly if it is only a second cousin's bird or if the fight is a shallow one. But as a rule he will feel he must support it and, in deep games, nearly always does. Thus the great majority of the people calling "five" or "speckled" so demonstratively are expressing their allegiance to their kinsman, not their evaluation of his bird, their understanding of probability theory, or even their hopes of unearned income.

2. This principle is extended logically. If your kingroup is not involved you will support an allied kingroup against an unallied one in the same way, and so on through the very involved networks of alliances which, as I say, make up this, as any other, Balinese village.

---

[12] Geertz's discussion is reminiscent of Mauss' analysis of the potlatch (see essay 7). The potlatch was a competition for status between individuals representing their kin groups and communities. In the same way, the Balinese cockfight is a competition for status, with men always betting on the birds owned by kinsmen or men of their communities who are competing with people from other communities. A major difference between Geertz and Mauss, however, is that Mauss thought the potlatch was a real competition for status—a defeat in a potlatch meant the loss of a position of leadership. Geertz's point is that the cockfight does not really change anything. In fact, status in Bali is ascribed and cannot change. Although Geertz's analysis is interpretive, the discussion of betting and kin are structural-functionalist in tone. Durkheim or Radcliffe-Brown would have said that the function of the cockfight is to create and reinforce solidarity between these competing kin groups.

3. So, too, for the village as a whole. If an outsider cock is fighting any cock from your village, you will tend to support the local one. If, what is a rarer circumstance but occurs every now and then, a cock from outside your cockfight circuit is fighting one inside it, you will also tend to support the "home bird."

4. Cocks which come from any distance are almost always favorites, for the theory is the man would not have dared to bring it if it was not a good cock, the more so the further he has come. His followers are, of course, obliged to support him, and when the more grand-scale legal cockfights are held (on holidays, and so on) the people of the village take what they regard to be the best cocks in the village, regardless of ownership, and go off to support them, although they will almost certainly have to give odds on them and to make large bets to show that they are not a cheapskate village. Actually, such "away games," though infrequent, tend to mend the ruptures between village members that the constantly occurring "home games," where village factions are opposed rather than united, exacerbate.

5. Almost all matches are sociologically relevant. You seldom get two outsider cocks fighting, or two cocks with no particular group backing, or with group backing which is mutually unrelated in any clear way. When you do get them, the game is very shallow, betting very slow, and the whole thing very dull, with no one save the immediate principals and an addict gambler or two at all interested.

6. By the same token, you rarely get two cocks from the same group, even more rarely from the same subfaction, and virtually never from the same sub-subfaction (which would be in most cases one extended family) fighting. Similarly, in outside village fights two members of the village will rarely fight against one another, even though, as bitter rivals, they would do so with enthusiasm on their home grounds.

7. On the individual level, people involved in an institutionalized hostility relationship, called *puik,* in which they do not speak or otherwise have anything to do with each other (the causes of this formal breaking of relations are many: wife-capture, inheritance arguments, political differences) will bet very heavily, sometimes almost maniacally, against one another in what is a frank and direct attack on the very masculinity, the ultimate ground of his status, of the opponent.[13]

8. The center bet coalition is, in all but the shallowest games, *always* made up by structural allies—no "outside money" is involved. What is "outside" depends upon the context, of course, but given it, no outside money is mixed in with the main bet; if the principals cannot raise it, it is not made. The center bet, again especially in deeper games, is thus the most direct and open expression of social opposition, which is one of the reasons why both it and matchmaking are surrounded by such an air of unease, furtiveness, embarrassment, and so on.

9. The rule about borrowing money—that you may borrow *for* a bet but not *in* one—stems (and the Balinese are quite conscious of this) from similar considerations: you are never at the *economic* mercy of your enemy that way. Gambling debts, which can get quite large on a rather short-term basis, are always to friends, never to enemies, structurally speaking.

---

[13] The discussion of *puik* is a good place to make another point about Geertz's analysis. Because his work is interpretive, Geertz is often criticized by anthropologists who work in materialist traditions. However, some of Geertz's earlier work was concerned with economics, religion, and ecology. See, for example, his books *Agricultural Involution: The Processes of Ecological Change in Indonesia* (1963a) and *Peddlers and Princes: Social Development and Economic Change in Two Indonesian Towns* (1963b).

Here, in one of his most famous works, Geertz does not rule out materialist interpretations; he just is not interested in them. Geertz repeatedly insists that nothing really happens at a cockfight—the conflicts, alliances, wins, and losses are all symbolic of things that happen elsewhere. *Puik,* for example, are not caused by cockfight bets; rather, they signal deeper-level conflicts. In the cockfight, all action is symbolic. The real causes lie elsewhere, presumably in material circumstances.

10. When two cocks are structurally irrelevant or neutral so far as *you* are concerned (though, as mentioned, they almost never are to each other) you do not even ask a relative or a friend whom he is betting on, because if you know how he is betting and he knows you know, and you go the other way, it will lead to strain. This rule is explicit and rigid; fairly elaborate, even rather artificial precautions are taken to avoid breaking it. At the very least you must pretend not to notice what he is doing, and he what you are doing.

11. There is a special word for betting against the grain, which is also the word for "pardon me" (*mpura*). It is considered a bad thing to do, though if the center bet is small it is sometimes all right as long as you do not do it too often. But the larger the bet and the more frequently you do it, the more the "pardon me" tack will lead to social disruption.

12. In fact, the institutionalized hostility relation, *puik*, is often formally initiated (though its causes always lie elsewhere) by such a "pardon me" bet in a deep fight, putting the symbolic fat in the fire. Similarly, the end of such a relationship and resumption of normal social intercourse is often signalized (but, again, not actually brought about) by one or the other of the enemies supporting the other's bird.

13. In sticky, cross-loyalty situations, of which in this extraordinarily complex social system there are of course many, where a man is caught between two more or less equally balanced loyalties, he tends to wander off for a cup of coffee or something to avoid having to bet, a form of behavior reminiscent of that of American voters in similar situations.*

14. The people involved in the center bet are, especially in deep fights, virtually always leading members of their group—kinship, village, or whatever. Further, those who bet on the side (including these people) are, as I have already remarked, the more established members of the village—the solid citizens. Cockfighting is for those who are involved in the everyday politics of prestige as well, not for youth, women, subordinates, and so forth.

15. So far as money is concerned, the explicitly expressed attitude toward it is that it is a secondary matter. It is not, as I have said, of no importance; Balinese are no happier to lose several weeks' income than anyone else. But they mainly look on the monetary aspects of the cockfight as self-balancing, a matter of just moving money around, circulating it among a fairly well-defined group of serious cockfighters. The really important wins and losses are seen mostly in other terms, and the general attitude toward wagering is not any hope of cleaning up, of making a killing (addict gamblers again excepted), but that of the horse-player's prayer: "Oh, God, please let me break even." In prestige terms, however, you do not want to break even, but, in a momentary, punctuate sort of way, win utterly. The talk (which goes on all the time) is about fights against such-and-such a cock of So-and-So which your cock demolished, not on how much you won, a fact people, even for large bets, rarely remember for any length of time, though they will remember the day they did in Pan Loh's finest cock for years.

16. You must bet on cocks of your own group aside from mere loyalty considerations, for if you do not people generally will say, "What! Is he too proud for the likes of us? Does he have to go to Java or Den Pasar [the capital town] to bet, he is such an important man?" Thus there is a general pressure to bet not only to show that you are important locally, but that you are not so important that you look down on everyone else as unfit even to be rivals. Similarly, home team people must bet against outside cocks or the outsiders will accuse them—a serious charge—of just collecting entry fees and not really being interested in cockfighting, as well as again being arrogant and insulting.

17. Finally, the Balinese peasants themselves are quite aware of all this and can and, at least to an ethnographer, do state most of it in approximately the same terms as I have. Fighting cocks, almost every Balinese I have ever discussed the subject with has said, is like playing with fire only not getting burned. You activate village and kingroup rivalries and hostilities, but in "play" form, coming dangerously and entrancingly

close to the expression of open and direct inter-personal and intergroup aggression (something which, again, almost never happens in the normal course of ordinary life), but not quite, because, after all, it is "only a cockfight."

More observations of this sort could be advanced, but perhaps the general point is, if not made, at least well-delineated, and the whole argument thus far can be usefully summarized in a formal paradigm:

The more a match is . . .

1. Between near status equals (and/or personal enemies)
2. Between high status individuals

> *. . . the deeper the match.*

The deeper the match . . .

1. The closer the identification of cock and man (or, more properly, the deeper the match the more the man will advance his best, most closely-identified-with cock).
2. The finer the cocks involved and the more exactly they will be matched.
3. The greater the emotion that will be involved and the more the general absorption in the match.
4. The higher the individual bets center and outside, the shorter the outside bet odds will tend to be, and the more betting there will be overall.
5. The less an "economic" and the more a "status" view of gaming will be involved, and the "solider" the citizens who will be gaming.*

Inverse arguments hold for the shallower the fight, culminating, in a reversed-signs sense, in the coin-spinning and dice-throwing amusements. For deep fights there are no absolute upper limits, though there are of course practical ones, and there are a great many legend like tales of great Duel-in-the-Sun combats between lords and princes in classical times (for cockfighting has always been as much an elite concern as a popular one), far deeper than anything anyone, even aristocrats, could produce today anywhere in Bali.

Indeed, one of the great culture heroes of Bali is a prince, called after his passion for the sport, "The Cockfighter," who happened to be away at a very deep cockfight with a neighboring prince when the whole of his family—father, brothers, wives, sisters—were assassinated by commoner usurpers. Thus spared, he returned to dispatch the upstart, regain the throne, reconstitute the Balinese high tradition, and build its most powerful, glorious, and prosperous state. Along with everything else that the Balinese see in fighting cocks—themselves, their social order, abstract hatred, masculinity, demonic power—they also see the archetype of status virtue, the arrogant, resolute, honor-mad player with real fire, the *ksatria* prince.*[14]

FEATHERS, BLOOD, CROWDS, AND MONEY

"Poetry makes nothing happen," Auden says in his elegy of Yeats, "it survives in the valley of its saying … a way of happening, a mouth."[15] The cockfight too, in this colloquial sense, makes nothing happen. Men go on allegorically humiliating one another and being allegorically humiliated by one another, day after day, glorying quietly in the experience if they have triumphed, crushed only slightly more openly by it if they have not. *But no one's status really changes.* You cannot ascend the status ladder by winning cockfights; you cannot, as an individual, really ascend it at all. Nor can

---

[14] Despite the skill with which Geertz draws his picture of Balinese culture, the feminist critique of ethnographic writing applies here. In his footnote, Geertz writes that the cockfight is unusual in that it is a single-sex activity, yet he talks about cockfighting as a key to Balinese society. Perhaps it is a key only for male Balinese society.

[15] W. H. Auden (1907–1973) was a British-born American poet. William Butler Yeats (1865–1939) was an Irish poet and nationalist.

you descend it that way.* All you can do is enjoy and savor, or suffer and withstand, the concocted sensation of drastic and momentary movement along an aesthetic semblance of that ladder, a kind of behind-the-mirror status jump which has the look of mobility without its actuality.[16]

Like any art form—for that, finally, is what we are dealing with—the cockfight renders ordinary, everyday experience comprehensible by presenting it in terms of acts and objects which have had their practical consequences removed and been reduced (or, if you prefer, raised) to the level of sheer appearances, where their meaning can be more powerfully articulated and more exactly perceived. The cockfight is "really real" only to the cocks—it does not kill anyone, castrate anyone, reduce anyone to animal status, alter the hierarchical relations among people, or refashion the hierarchy; it does not even redistribute income in any significant way. What it does is what, for other peoples with other temperaments and other conventions, *Lear* and *Crime and Punishment* do; it catches up these themes—death, masculinity, rage, pride, loss, beneficence, chance—and, ordering them into an encompassing structure, presents them in such a way as to throw into relief a particular view of their essential nature. It puts a construction on them, makes them, to those historically positioned to appreciate the construction, meaningful—visible, tangible, graspable—"real," in an ideational sense. An image, fiction, a model, a metaphor, the cockfight is a means of expression; its function is neither to assuage social passions nor to heighten them (though, in its playing-with-fire way it does a bit of both), but, in a medium of feathers, blood, crowds, and money, to display them.

The question of how it is that we perceive qualities in things—paintings, books, melodies, plays—that we do not feel we can assert literally to be there has come, in recent years, into the very center of aesthetic theory.* Neither the sentiments of the artist, which remain his, nor those of the audience, which remain theirs, can account for the agitation of one painting or the serenity of another. We attribute grandeur, wit, despair, exuberance to strings of sounds; lightness, energy, violence, fluidity to blocks of stone. Novels are said to have strength, buildings eloquence, plays momentum, ballets repose. In this realm of eccentric predicates, to say that the cockfight, in its perfected cases at least, is "disquietful" does not seem at all unnatural, merely, as I have just denied it practical consequence, somewhat puzzling.

The disquietfulness arises, "somehow," out of a conjunction of three attributes of the fight: its immediate dramatic shape; its metaphoric content; and its social context. A cultural figure against a social ground, the fight is at once a convulsive surge of animal hatred, a mock war of symbolical selves, and a formal simulation of status tensions, and its aesthetic power derives from its capacity to force together these diverse realities. The reason it is disquietful is not that it has material effects (it has some, but they are minor); the reason that it is disquietful is that, joining pride to selfhood, selfhood to cocks, and cocks to destruction, it brings to imaginative realization a dimension of Balinese experience normally well-obscured from view. The transfer of a sense of gravity into what is in itself a rather blank and unvarious spectacle, a commotion of beating wings and throbbing legs, is effected by interpreting it as expressive of something unsettling in the way its authors and audience live, or, even more ominously, what they are.[17]

---

[16] In a 1991 interview (Handler 1991), Geertz stated that a weakness of anthropology before the 1960s was that anthropologists read only other anthropologists. His point was that intellectual development in anthropology is based on knowledge in a wide range of fields. As you read, look at the diversity of literature that Geertz ties into his work: Balinese sources, poetry, sociology, psychology, mythology, art, and philosophy, to name just a few, all have a place in his thought. Conversely, Geertz is one of the few anthropological theorists widely read by scholars of literature and history.

[17] Geertz views culture as shared codes of meaning that are publicly acted out, which makes his analysis a method of dramatic interpretation. The cockfight is like a play the Balinese perform for themselves, and its importance is artistic. Geertz says it has "aesthetic power" because it forces layers of significance, what he calls "diverse realities," together. It expresses what the Balinese are in a way that is "normally well obscured from view."

As a dramatic shape, the fight displays a characteristic that does not seem so remarkable until one realizes that it does not have to be there: a radically atomistical structure.* Each match is a world unto itself, a particulate burst of form. There is the matchmaking, there is the betting, there is the fight, there is the result—utter triumph and utter defeat—and there is the hurried, embarrassed passing of money. The loser is not consoled. People drift away from him, look around him, leave him to assimilate his momentary descent into nonbeing, reset his face, and return, scarless and intact, to the fray. Nor are winners congratulated, or events rehashed; once a match is ended the crowd's attention turns totally to the next, with no looking back. A shadow of the experience no doubt remains with the principals, perhaps even with some of the witnesses of a deep fight, as it remains with us when we leave the theater after seeing a powerful play well-performed; but it quite soon fades to become at most a schematic memory—a diffuse glow or an abstract shudder—and usually not even that. Any expressive form lives only in its own present—the one it itself creates. But, here, that present is severed into a string of flashes, some more bright than others, but all of them disconnected, aesthetic quanta. Whatever the cockfight says, it says in spurts.

But, as I have argued lengthily elsewhere, the Balinese live in spurts.* Their life, as they arrange it and perceive it, is less a flow, a directional movement out of the past, through the present, toward the future than an on-off pulsation of meaning and vacuity, an arrhythmic alternation of short periods when "something" (that is,

something significant) is happening, and equally short ones where "nothing" (that is, nothing much) is—between what they themselves call "full" and "empty" times, or, in another idiom, "junctures" and "holes." In focusing activity down to a burning-glass dot, the cockfight is merely being Balinese in the same way in which everything from the monadic encounters of everyday life, through the clanging pointillism of *gamelan*[18] music, to the visiting-day-of-the-gods temple celebrations are. It is not an imitation of the punctuateness of Balinese social life, nor a depiction of it, nor even an expression of it; it is an example of it, carefully prepared.*[19]

If one dimension of the cockfight's structure, its lack of temporal directionality, makes it seem a typical segment of the general social life, however, the other, its flat-out, head-to-head (or spur-to-spur) aggressiveness, makes it seem a contradiction, a reversal, even a subversion of it. In the normal course of things, the Balinese are shy to the point of obsessiveness of open conflict. Oblique, cautious, subdued, controlled, masters of indirection and dissimulation—what they call *alus*, "polished," "smooth"—they rarely face what they can turn away from, rarely resist what they can evade. But here they portray themselves as wild and murderous, with manic explosions of instinctual cruelty. A powerful rendering of life as the Balinese most deeply do not want it (to adapt a phrase Frye has used of Gloucester's blinding)[20] is set in the context of a sample of it as they do in fact have it.* And, because the context suggests that the rendering, if less than a straightforward description, is nonetheless more than an idle fancy; it is here that the disquietfulness—the

---

[18] *Gamelan* is a type of Southeast Asian music using chimes and gongs.

[19] Geertz has led us back from the details of the cockfight to his definition of culture. He stresses that culture does not exist apart from individuals; instead, it is created in people's interpretations of events around them and bound up in public symbols and communication (Applebaum 1987:485). Here he says the cockfight is not a depiction, expression, or example of Balinese life; rather, it *is* Balinese life.

[20] Northrop Frye (1912–1991) was an influential literary critic who was particularly concerned with the relationship of literature to myth and society. Gloucester's blinding occurs in Shakespeare's *King Lear,* where the Earl of Gloucester is punished for aiding Lear by having his eyes gouged out. Frye says that the audience does not want to see a real experience (a man's eyes put out); they want a vicarious experience from the point of view of the imagination. The fact that the blinding does not really happen is crucial to the psychological experience (Frye 1964:98–99).

disquietfulness of the *fight*, not (or, anyway, not necessarily) its patrons, who seem in fact rather thoroughly to enjoy it—emerges. The slaughter in the cock ring is not a depiction of how things literally are among men, but, what is almost worse, of how, from a particular angle, they imaginatively are.*

The angle, of course, is stratificatory. What, as we have already seen, the cockfight talks most forcibly about is status relationships, and what it says about them is that they are matters of life and death. That prestige is a profoundly serious business is apparent everywhere one looks in Bali—in the village, the family, the economy, the state. A peculiar fusion of Polynesian title ranks and Hindu castes, the hierarchy of pride is the moral backbone of the society. But only in the cockfight are the sentiments upon which that hierarchy rests revealed in their natural colors. Enveloped elsewhere in a haze of etiquette, a thick cloud of euphemism and ceremony, gesture and allusion, they are here expressed in only the thinnest disguise of an animal mask, a mask which in fact demonstrates them far more effectively than it conceals them. Jealousy is as much a part of Bali as poise, envy as grace, brutality as charm; but without the cockfight the Balinese would have a much less certain understanding of them, which is, presumably, why they value it so highly.

Any expressive form works (when it works) by disarranging semantic contexts in such a way that properties conventionally ascribed to certain things are unconventionally ascribed to others, which are then seen actually to possess them. To call the wind a cripple, as Stevens does, to fix tone and manipulate timbre, as Schoenberg does, or, closer to our case, to picture an art critic as a dissolute bear, as Hogarth does, is to cross conceptual wires;[21] the established conjunctions between objects and their qualities are altered, and phenomena—fall weather, melodic shape, or cultural journalism—are clothed in signifiers which normally point to other referents.* Similarly, to connect—and connect, and connect—the collision of roosters with the divisiveness of status is to invite a transfer of perceptions from the former to the latter, a transfer which is at once a description and a judgment. (Logically, the transfer could, of course, as well go the other way; but, like most of the rest of us, the Balinese are a great deal more interested in understanding men than they are in understanding cocks.)

What sets the cockfight apart from the ordinary course of life, lifts it from the realm of everyday practical affairs, and surrounds it with an aura of enlarged importance is not, as functionalist sociology would have it, that it reinforces status discriminations (such reinforcement is hardly necessary in a society where every act proclaims them), but that it provides a metasocial commentary upon the whole matter of assorting human beings into fixed hierarchical ranks and then organizing the major part of collective existence around that assortment. Its function, if you want to call it that, is interpretive: it is a Balinese reading of Balinese experience, a story they tell themselves about themselves.[22]

SAYING SOMETHING OF SOMETHING

To put the matter this way is to engage in a bit of metaphorical refocusing of one's own, for it shifts the analysis of cultural forms from an endeavor

---

[21] Wallace Stevens (1879–1955) was an American poet, Arnold Schoenberg (1874–1951) an Austrian composer, and William Hogarth (1697–1764) an English painter and lithographer.

[22] Although rarely discussed in this light, Geertz's article is an attack on structural functionalism. A young generation of American anthropologists, including Geertz, David Schneider, and Eric Wolf, butted heads with a group of British anthropologists, including Max Gluckman and Meyer Fortes, at a conference in Cambridge, England, in 1963. In this essay, Geertz has performed an analysis that could have come straight from the pen of a British structural-functionalist ethnographer. In the last few sections, however, he turns the structural-functionalist position upside down, saying that functionalist conclusions are meaningless for the Balinese. Instead he points to an existentialist conclusion. That is, the cockfight is not about social divisions, it is about understanding what it means to be human in Bali and the being and nothingness that are its temporary results.

in general parallel to dissecting an organism, diagnosing a symptom, deciphering a code, or ordering a system—the dominant analogies in contemporary anthropology—to one in general parallel with penetrating a literary text. If one takes the cockfight, or any other collectively sustained symbolic structure, as a means of "saying something of something" (to invoke a famous Aristotelian tag), then one is faced with a problem not in social mechanics but social semantics.* For the anthropologist, whose concern is with formulating sociological principles, not with promoting or appreciating cockfights, the question is, what does one learn about such principles from examining culture as an assemblage of texts?[23]

Such an extension of the notion of a text beyond written material, and even beyond verbal, is, though metaphorical, not, of course, all that novel. The *interpretatio naturae* tradition of the middle ages, which, culminating in Spinoza, attempted to read nature as Scripture, the Nietzschean effort to treat value systems as glosses on the will to power[24] (or the Marxian one to treat them as glosses on property relations), and the Freudian replacement of the enigmatic text of the manifest dream with the plain one of the latent, all offer precedents, if not equally recommendable ones.* But the idea remains theoretically undeveloped; and the more profound corollary, so far as anthropology is concerned, that cultural forms can be treated as texts, as imaginative works built out of social materials, has yet to be systematically exploited.*

In the case at hand, to treat the cockfight as a text is to bring out a feature of it (in my opinion, the central feature of it) that treating it as a rite

or a pastime, the two most obvious alternatives, would tend to obscure: its use of emotion for cognitive ends. What the cockfight says it says in a vocabulary of sentiment—the thrill of risk, the despair of loss, the pleasure of triumph. Yet what it says is not merely that risk is exciting, loss depressing, or triumph gratifying, banal tautologies of affect, but that it is of these emotions, thus exampled, that society is built and individuals are put together. Attending cockfights and participating in them is, for the Balinese, a kind of sentimental education. What he learns there is what his culture's ethos and his private sensibility (or, anyway, certain aspects of them) look like when spelled out externally in a collective text; that the two are near enough alike to be articulated in the symbolics of a single such text; and—the disquieting part—that the text in which this revelation is accomplished consists of a chicken hacking another mindlessly to bits.

Every people, the proverb has it, loves its own form of violence. The cockfight is the Balinese reflection on theirs: on its look, its uses, its force, its fascination. Drawing on almost every level of Balinese experience, it brings together themes—animal savagery, male narcissism, opponent gambling, status rivalry, mass excitement, blood sacrifice—whose main connection is their involvement with rage and the fear of rage, and, binding them into a set of rules which at once contains them and allows them play, builds a symbolic structure in which, over and over again, the reality of their inner affiliation can be intelligibly felt. If, to quote Northrop Frye again, we go to see *Macbeth* to learn what a man feels like after he has gained a kingdom and lost his soul, Balinese go to cockfights to find out what a man,

---

[23] In this final section, Geertz summarizes his argument and explains how the cockfight attains personal significance for Balinese participants. Up to now the analysis has been very particular, but his conclusions try to say something universal about the nature of culture: that cultures are a form of text.

[24] Baruch Spinoza (1632–1677) was an influential philosopher in the rationalist tradition. In one of his best known works, *Ethics,* he set out a geometrical program of definitions, axioms, postulates, and theorems that he proposed was a systematic procedure for the perfection of human nature. His work influenced many later scholars, including Georg Wilhelm Friedrich Hegel.

Friedrich Nietzsche was a German philosopher whose work was influential in the development of existentialism. His book, *The Birth of Tragedy* (1956 [1871]), was important to the work of Ruth Benedict and is discussed in essay 16. Geertz's comment concerning the "will to power" refers to a concept Nietzsche developed in his most famous work, *Thus Spake Zarathustra* (1954 [1883–1885]).

usually composed, aloof, almost obsessively self-absorbed, a kind of moral autocosm, feels like when, attacked, tormented, challenged, insulted, and driven in result to the extremes of fury, he has totally triumphed or been brought totally low. The whole passage, as it takes us back to Aristotle (though to the *Poetics* rather than the *Hermeneutics*), is worth quotation:

> But the poet [as opposed to the historian], Aristotle says, never makes any real statements at all, certainly no particular or specific ones. The poet's job is not to tell you what happened, but what happens: not what did take place, but the kind of thing that always does take place. He gives you the typical, recurring, or what Aristotle calls universal event. You wouldn't go to *Macbeth* to learn about the history of Scotland—you go to it to learn what a man feels like after he's gained a kingdom and lost his soul. When you meet such a character as Micawber in Dickens, you don't feel that there must have been a man Dickens knew who was exactly like this: you feel that there's a bit of Micawber in almost everybody you know, including yourself. Our impressions of human life are picked up one by one, and remain for most of us loose and disorganized. But we constantly find things in literature that suddenly coordinate and bring into focus a great many such impressions, and this is part of what Aristotle means by the typical or universal human event.*

It is this kind of bringing of assorted experiences of everyday life to focus that the cockfight, set aside from that life as "only a game" and reconnected to it as "more than a game," accomplishes, and so creates what, better than typical or universal, could be called a paradigmatic human event—that is, one that tells us less what happens than the kind of thing that would happen if, as is not the case, life were art and could be as freely shaped by styles of feeling as *Macbeth* and *David Copperfield* are.

Enacted and re-enacted, so far without end, the cockfight enables the Balinese, as, read and reread, *Macbeth* enables us, to see a dimension of his own subjectivity. As he watches fight after fight, with the active watching of an owner and a bettor (for cockfighting has no more interest as a pure spectator sport than does croquet or dog racing), he grows familiar with it and what it has to say to him, much as the attentive listener to string quartets or the absorbed viewer of still life grows slowly more familiar with them in a way which opens his subjectivity to himself.*

Yet, because—in another of those paradoxes, along with painted feelings and unconsequenced acts, which haunt aesthetics—that subjectivity does not properly exist until it is thus organized, art forms generate and regenerate the very subjectivity they pretend only to display. Quartets, still lifes, and cockfights are not merely reflections of a pre-existing sensibility analogically represented; they are positive agents in the creation and maintenance of such a sensibility. If we see ourselves as a pack of Micawbers, it is from reading too much Dickens (if we see ourselves as unillusioned realists, it is from reading too little); and similarly for Balinese, cocks, and cockfights. It is in such a way, coloring experience with the light they cast it in, rather than through whatever material effects they may have, that the arts play their role, as arts, in social life.*

In the cockfight, then, the Balinese forms and discovers his temperament and his society's temper at the same time. Or, more exactly, he forms and discovers a particular facet of them. Not only are there a great many other cultural texts providing commentaries on status hierarchy and self-regard in Bali, but there are a great many other critical sectors of Balinese life besides the stratificatory and the agonistic that receive such commentary. The ceremony consecrating a Brahmana priest, a matter of breath control, postural immobility, and vacant concentration upon the depths of being, displays a radically different, but to the Balinese equally real, property of social hierarchy—its reach toward the numinous[25] transcendent. Set not in the matrix of the kinetic emotionality of animals, but in that of the static passionlessness of divine mentality, it expresses tranquillity not disquiet. The mass festivals at the village temples, which mobilize the whole lo-

---

[25] *Numinous:* mysterious, surpassing comprehension.

cal population in elaborate hostings of visiting gods—songs, dances, compliments, gifts—assert the spiritual unity of village mates against their status inequality and project a mood of amity and trust.* The cockfight is not the master key to Balinese life, any more than bullfighting is to Spanish. What it says about that life is not unqualified nor even unchallenged by what other equally eloquent cultural statements say about it. But there is nothing more surprising in this than in the fact that Racine and Moliere were contemporaries, or that the same people who arrange chrysanthemums cast swords.*26

The culture of a people is an ensemble of texts, themselves ensembles, which the anthropologist strains to read over the shoulders of those to whom they properly belong. There are enormous difficulties in such an enterprise, methodological pitfalls to make a Freudian quake, and some moral perplexities as well. Nor is it the only way that

symbolic forms can be sociologically handled. Functionalism lives, and so does psychologism. But to regard such forms as "saying something of something," and saying it to somebody, is at least to open up the possibility of an analysis which attends to their substance rather than to reductive formulas professing to account for them.

As in more familiar exercises in close reading, one can start anywhere in a culture's repertoire of forms and end up anywhere else. One can stay, as I have here, within a single, more or less bounded form, and circle steadily within it. One can move between forms in search of broader unities or informing contrasts. One can even compare forms from different cultures to define their character in reciprocal relief. But whatever the level at which one operates, and however intricately, the guiding principle is the same: societies, like lives, contain their own interpretations. One has only to learn how to gain access to them.27

---

26 This paragraph is important because it shows that Geertz was moving away from the popular image of culture as an organic whole toward the postmodern vision of culture as the intersection of competing views and interests. Geertz emphasizes that rather than presenting a consistent, integrated message, culture is full of competing voices and messages that are at odds with each other. Jean Racine (1639–1699) and Jean-Baptiste Molière (1622–1673) were French playwrights: the first a great writer of tragedies, the latter famous for his comedies. The last line of the paragraph refers to Ruth Benedict's study of Japanese national character, *The Chrysanthemum and the Sword* (1946).

27 The notion that a culture is a collection of texts that anthropologists read over the shoulders of those who live

them had a powerful impact on the next generation of anthropological theorists. In particular, this idea led anthropologists to borrow some of the tools of textual analysis from literary criticism. Geertz's work provided part of the foundation for postmodernism, which is dealt with in the next section.

This essay was published at a time when the works of modern French critical thinkers such as Roland Barthes (1915–1980) and Jacques Derrida (1930–2004) were becoming available in English. Among their critical insights is the notion that texts are systems of symbols that reveal the assumptions of particular cultures at particular times. As Geertz was writing this essay, the whole idea of deconstructing texts, or culture, was transforming the field of literary criticism. This essay is a critical bridge between literature and anthropological theory.

Postmodernism and Its Critics

McGee: "I'm having trouble getting started on this introduction to postsmodernism."
Warms: "Why don't you write about the process of writing the introduction?"

Rich Warms responded to Jon McGee's difficulty starting this introduction in a classic postmodernist fashion, trying to convince him to write it in a postmodern style. We hope that what makes Warms' (unsuccessful) response postmodern will become clear as you read.

Modernism is a term drawn from the study of literature and art as well as the history of science. In general, it reflects the epistemological notion that the world is knowable. People can use the techniques of science, philosophy, and rational inquiry to analyze and understand their world. Proper use of these tools can lead us to a thorough understanding of any subject material to which they are applied. In anthropology, modernism broadly refers to the time period stretching from the early twentieth century until the mid-1970s (Manganaro 1990). Analysts suggest that some of the attributes of modernist writing in anthropology were detachment, the assumption of a position of scientific neutrality, and rationalism (Rabinow 1986).

Postmodernists challenge the assertion that science and rationalism can lead to full and accurate knowledge of the world. They argue that these are specific historically constituted ways of knowing. Therefore, they can create only specific historically constituted sorts of truths. Since the ideas and practices that we usually refer to when we talk about science and rationality had their historical origin at a certain time and among a certain class within Western European and North American society, the truths they generate are appropriate to (or empowering of) that group.

Such truths are limited. They do not transcend time and space. Further, the methods of science and rationality, when applied to other cultures (or other groups within Western culture) are more likely to produce gross distortions than anything else. Other peoples have their own ways of knowing, and, since all knowledge is historically constituted, these are just as valid (or just as invalid) as any other. The postmodernist challenge has led anthropologists to examine the basis of their discipline and led to a rancorous debate between proponents of the two points of view.

Although the authors represented in this section are all Americans, the roots of the postmodern approach to anthropology lie in Europe, particularly in the work of the hermeneutic philosophers and post–World War II French social theorists Jacques Derrida (1930–2004) and Michel Foucault (1926–1984).

Hermeneutics, the study of the interpretation of meanings, has been an intellectual concern in Europe for most of this century, but it was largely ignored by American anthropologists until the cognitive research of the 1960s and 1970s. Hermaneuticists, following the philosopher Martin Heidegger (1889–1976), believe that humans cannot have knowledge about the world that is not tinged by a particular perspective or bias. Knowledge is conditioned by culture, context, and history. Hermeneuticist Hans-Georg Gadamer (1900–2002), for example, wrote that the sciences did not allow humans to see beyond their culturally shaped contexts (Applebaum 1987:486). According to this philosophy, because we cannot separate our ways of knowing from our language and culture, it is impossible for us to interpret the world in a truly detached, objective manner. We all interpret the world around us in our own way, based on our language, cultural background, and personal experiences.

Layton divides the European postmodernists into two groups, the "hard" or extreme postmodernists such as Derrida, and the "soft" or moderate postmodernists such as Foucault (1997: 186). Derrida is considered one of the fathers of deconstruction in European thought (Lilla 1998:36). He argued that all cultures construct autonomous self-contained worlds of meaning. Thus ethnographic descriptions distort native understandings by forcing them into our own society's ways of conceptualizing the world. In other words, meaning can never be accurately translated.

Foucault is best known in the United States for his discussion of "discourses of power." He argued that social relations between people are characterized by dominance and subjugation. Dominating people or classes control the ideological conditions under which knowledge, truth, and reality are defined. "Because modernity is viewed, alongside other configurations of knowledge, as the product of power, the objective character of scientific knowledge is shown to be an historical construct" (Erickson 1998:142). In the United States, anthropologists such as George Marcus (b. 1946), Michael Fischer (b. 1946), Steven Tyler (b. 1932), and James Clifford (b. 1945) were profoundly affected by Derrida and Foucault.

Throughout the history of our discipline, anthropologists positioned themselves as authorities on other cultures. They fortified this claim by providing convincing written descriptions of other cultures and emphasizing the importance of their individual experiences of fieldwork. The hermeneutic and deconstructionist approaches encouraged anthropologists to examine the ways in which the authority of anthropologists is established and maintained. This led to questions about the nature and credibility of that authority. Some of the most important of these issues involve the conduct of fieldwork, the literary techniques used in the writing of ethnographies, and the validity of the author's interpretations over competing alternatives.

The conduct of fieldwork is a critical issue to postmodernists because traditionally most ethnography has contained very little information on the actual process of research. Postmodernists argue that it is precisely this process that is crucial in the creation of ethnographic texts. They believe that anthropologists can never be unbiased observers of all that goes on in a culture. Fieldworkers must, of necessity, be in specific places at specific times. As a result, they see some things and not others. The particular circumstances of fieldwork—the political context in which it occurs, the investigator's preferences and predilections, and the people met by chance or design—all critically condition the understanding of society that results. Ethnography has traditionally been written as if the anthropologist was a neutral, omniscient observer. Postmodernists claim, however, that because the collection of anthropological data is subjective, it is not possible to analyze the data objectively. The Rosaldo essay in this section dramatically illustrates this point. In "Grief and a Headhunter's Rage," Renato Rosaldo (b. 1941) describes his almost unbearable sorrow after the accidental death of his wife in the field. He then tells us how this experience led him to a visceral understanding of why Ilongot men go head-hunting after the death of loved ones, something he could not comprehend through intellectual study of the custom.

Writing ethnography is the primary means by which anthropologists convey their interpretations of other cultures, and ethnographies have traditionally followed some basic literary conventions, which Marcus and Cushman (1982) have described in detail. Even if you are not a student of ethnographic writing, you will immediately recognize several of these forms. One of the most obvious characteristics of ethnographic writing is that rather than saying, "I am writing my interpretation of what the natives were doing," authors claim to represent the native point of view. Of course, an anthropologist cannot possibly present the point of view of everyone in a society; he or she works with selected informants. So the anthropologist chooses who speaks for the society and in his or her translation of the native language decides what words are presented to the audience.

Another common rhetorical device of Anglo-American ethnography is that writers claim to completely describe other cultures or societies even though anthropologists actually know only the part of a culture that they personally experience. One of the more insidious writing conventions is that of the omniscient narrator, the authoritative third-person observer who replaces the fallible first person. Instead of writing, "I saw my informant pour ketchup on his ice cream," which is the result of direct observation, many ethnographies contain statements like "The people of San Marcos pour ketchup on their ice cream." The use of the omniscient narrator heightens the sense of scientific objectivity projected by the text, but it also severs the relationship between what the ethnographer knows and how he or she came to know it (Marcus and Cushman 1982:32).

One result of these understandings was the more revealing style in which some anthropologists began to write ethnographies. There has always been some self-revelation in ethnography, but in the late 1960s and early 1970s, anthropologists such as Chagnon (1968), Brigs (1970), Geertz (1973), and Rabinow (1977) began to write ethnographies in which their recounting of their own experiences and feelings takes a prominent role. For postmodern writers in the 1980s and 1990s, this self-reflexiveness is not simply a more straightforward form of reportage. The recounting of field experiences can become the narrative device by which anthropological understanding is conveyed. Rosaldo, for example, says that the writing of his article was an act of catharsis that helped him deal with his grief as well as giving him new insight into the Ilongot custom of head-hunting.

A second issue that underlies almost all postmodern writing lies in the area of interpretation. Postmodernists maintain that if a text is an author's interpretation and if that author's work is taken as an authoritative account, then all other voices and interpretations are silenced. Because everything is an interpretation in the postmodern view, the only way authors can generate an interpretation that is accepted as true is to "delicense"

all others. But can one person's interpretation be more valid than another's? Postmodernists maintain that it cannot. They insist that the acceptance of an interpretation is ultimately an issue of power and wealth. Historically, they say, the interpretations voiced by white Protestant males in Western industrialized nations have delicensed all others and silenced them. They ask why the Anglo-American view of events is the only acceptable interpretation and claim that deconstructing the work of this mainstream allows other opinions to be expressed. Postmodernists assert that in history, literature, and politics, the voices of women, minorities, and the poor are finally being heard.

A final form of postmodern scholarship deals with textual analysis (and this, in fact, informs most other sorts of postmodern thinking). Postmodernists argue that data are, of themselves, mute. Data are just data. Anthropologists (and all others) construct meaning from the data through the process of writing. Because one must write according to certain literary conventions (tense, voice, and so on), the finished text is of necessity a literary construction of its author. Readers in turn, impose their own interpretation on the author's text. In other words, the written word can never be adequate to represent reality. Instead, writing involves the piling up of layer upon layer of convention and interpretation. Similarly, reading involves its own conventions and each reader brings their own histories and understandings to the act of reading. Thus, a finished text is a thing unto itself. It can not be an accurate representation of the reality it claims to portray, for this is impossible. Neither can it be understood as accurately reflecting the mind and understandings of its author (since these must be filtered through the conventions of reading and the reader's experience). So, what's a postmodernist to do? Well, the answer is that the postmodernist deconstructs the ways in which the devices and conventions of writing and reading are exploited in the text, explores the sorts of meanings that are promoted by the text as well as those that are delegitimized, and examines what this may tell us about the current or historical nature of the society in which the text is written and read. Of course, a text can tell us very little of the "reality" of its purported subject. Further, since any form of deconstruction and analysis is itself a literary process, all deconstruction is subject to further deconstruction. There can be no end.

The issues of reflexivity, desconstruction, and interpretation are all important elements that inform the work of Lila Abu-Lughod. Abu-Lughod issued a call for new forms of ethnographic writing in her 1991 essay "Writing Against Culture." There, she argued that the writing of ethnography is inherently an expression of Western power because the concept of culture necessarily contains an element of hierarchy, and ethnographic writing is based on the textual construction of the "other." In other words, the subject of the text is not real people in the context of their lives but a fictional composite people constructed by the author and removed from the reality of the particulars of individually lived lives. Thus she advocates for "writing against culture," and proposes strategies for dealing with these textual forms of oppression. In particular, Abu-Lughod proposes that anthropologists write "ethnographies of the particular" (1991:149). By this she means that instead of writing broad generalizations of a whole group, anthropologists should write ethnographies of particular people in specific times and places. Abu-Lughod's essay in this volume, "A Tale of Two Pregnancies," is this type of experimental form of ethnography. It contrasts Abu-Lughod's experiences when pregnant with those of Kareema, an Egyptian Bedouin woman who had been pregnant during Abu-Lughod's fieldwork in her community. This essay is an excellent example of Abu-Lughod's notion of an ethnography of the particular because she is the principal subject of her essay. There is very little Bedouin "other" in the essay, most of which consists of specific descriptions of specific events during Abu-Lughod's fieldwork and the period in which she was trying to and eventually succeeded in becoming pregnant. On the one hand, the essay is a good read. Abu-Lughod comments on her experiences, the nature of fertility medicine in the United States, her experiences in Egypt, and various other aspects of modernity. On the other hand, the thoughtful reader might ask what separates this sort of anthropology from the literary essay.

During the postmodern section of our theory class one year, a student fell into a nihilistic funk. "Why should I have spent all this time and money getting an anthropology degree," he asked, "if it is all just interpretations of interpretations and there is no objective knowledge to be gained in anthropology? Why shouldn't I just go be an English major?" Good questions.

No doubt, taken to its logical extreme, postmodernism comes very close to turning anthropology into a subfield of literature. However, understanding the postmodern critique encourages anthropologists to be aware of issues of rhetoric, power, voice, and perspective. This awareness can inform and enrich our own writing and help us evaluate both our own and other's claims to objectivity. Beyond this, hermeneutic philosophers remind us that ethnographies are literary creations, so it becomes possible to think of cultures as the poetic interplay of voices and performances. Cultures, instead of being read as texts, can be viewed as performances in which the anthropologist participates. This understanding can allow ethnographers greater insight into the complexities of cultures and invites them to consciously consider their specific effect on those they study. It may also aid them in seeing individual differences, conflict, and fragmentation within cultures. Rather than throwing anthropology into a relativistic black hole, as imagined by our student, the postmodern critique demands that we ask new and challenging questions and thus opens new realms for ethnographic research. For example, anthropologists must now ask how new forms of authority and voices other than their own can be included in ethnography. As Marcus (1992) asks, "who is to be included or excluded from having a voice in the development of knowledge about society and culture?" Furthermore, anthropologists must determine what kind of information can be counted as knowledge.

However, postmodernism has received extensive criticism within anthropology. Many scholars vigorously defend the idea that anthropology is or should be an empirical science. They argue that although some aspects of ethnographic data collection are subjective, it is possible to do empirically objective anthropology.

O'Meara (1989), for example, systematically explores and refutes the primary arguments that postmodernists give to support their claim that anthropology is not a science. Additionally, many scholars critical of the postmodernist view argue that this position, pursued to its logical extreme, must result in nihilism. If all voices should be heard, they say, are fascist voices, the voices of white supremacists or neo-Nazis, less worthy of respect than others? As Todorov, a key postmodern thinker, has pointed out, "It is not possible without inconsistency, to defend human rights on one hand and deconstruct the idea of humanity with the other" (1987:190). Current-day postmodernists argue that power constructs truth. They use this argument, they claim, to recover the voices and agendas of the powerless. Many, perhaps most, postmodernists are politically liberal and care deeply about issues of oppression and exploitation. However, not all postmodernists have opted to side with the powerless. Some writers have made the choice to work with the powerful and create the truth they desire. Indeed, during World War II, hermaneuticist Martin Heidegger was an apologist for the Nazis and Paul de Man, who later became a prominent deconstructionist, was a Nazi journalist (Lehman 1992).

The final essay in this section, by Roy D'Andrade (b. 1931), is a strong critique of the postmodernist perspective. Arguing that postmodernists have misrepresented the notion of objectivity, D'Andrade presents a defense of objectivity and science. He asserts that science has advanced knowledge and that the postmodern critique of anthropology is based on an implicit moral, rather than objective, model of the world. D'Andrade contends that the postmodernist critique of science—that it has led to oppression and Western hegemony—are moral claims not supported by any data and that the difference between moral and objective models should be recognized.

Postmodernism has been one of the most controversial developments in anthropology in recent times. In the last decade several prominent departments of anthropology have been torn apart by the conflicts between faculty who held a postmodern viewpoint and those who did not, particularly archaeologists and biological anthropologists. Bitter departmental infighting has led to the breakup of departments. In some cases, biological anthropologists have been encouraged to join programs in biology, and frustrated archaeologists have called for their own separate departments of archaeology. Teaching in a department that is committed to a four-field approach and in which many faculty work together across the subdisciplines of anthropology, we believe this fragmentation of anthropology is a profoundly disheartening trend. First, as we noted above, the value of postmodernist research largely depends on the sorts of questions a researcher wishes to ask, what the scholar believes the goals of anthropology should be. As this volume shows, there has never been any real agreement on this issue. There should be room for more than one type of anthropology within a major university department. If there is not, we risk producing students whose thinking is narrow and rigid.

Second, since the days of Boas, anthropology has been a holistic discipline. Many of the central figures of early twentieth-century anthropology worked in more than one subdiscipline. Boas wrote in biological anthropology, Kroeber and Steward worked in archaeology, as did many others. Acknowledging that today few anthropologists do research and publish in more than one of the subdisciplines, nonetheless, we believe that multidisciplinary training enhances our understanding of the human condition. Human societies are the result of biology, history, and culture. We ignore that fact at our own peril.

Our third and final concern is practical. Most of the big fights in anthropology have occurred in large departments. These programs train a relatively high percentage of the anthropologists in this country, and their members (and former students) hold many of the important positions in organizations such as the American Anthropological Association. Such departments are probably large enough to survive should anthropology break down into its constituent subdisciplines. However, most anthropology programs in the United States are small, consisting of fewer than ten professors and instructors. If large departments encourage intolerance and their students pursue policies of division in the smaller departments that hire them, our existence as a discipline may be threatened. In a small department, if the biological anthropologists go off and join biology programs and the archaeologists move to history or establish their own institutes, there won't be much left. The remaining cultural anthropologists will likely be swallowed by English literature, history, and sociology departments.

Postmodernism, in and of itself, is no threat to anthropology. It is simply one more flavor in the stew of anthropological theory. Many of its key elements have been broadly incorporated into much of cultural anthropology. Some of its more radical elements have been widely repudiated. Postmodernism can do us no harm. Departmental infighting certainly can.

---

38. *Grief and a Headhunter's Rage*

RENATO ROSALDO (b. 1941)

IF YOU ASK an older Ilongot man of northern Luzon, Philippines, why he cuts off human heads, his answer is brief, and one on which no anthropologist can readily elaborate: He says that rage, born of grief, impels him to kill his fellow human beings. He claims that he needs a place "to carry his anger." The act of severing and tossing away the victim's head enables him, he says, to vent and, he hopes, throw away the anger of his bereavement. Although the anthropologist's job is to make other cultures intelligible, more questions fail to reveal any further explanation of this man's pithy statement.[1] To him, grief, rage, and headhunting go together in a self-evident manner. Either you understand it or you don't. And, in fact, for the longest time I simply did not.

In what follows, I want to talk about how to talk about the cultural force of emotions.[a] The *emotional force* of a death, for example, derives less from an abstract brute fact than from a particular intimate relation's permanent rupture. It refers to the kinds of feelings one experiences on learning, for example, that the child just run over by a car is one's own and not a stranger's. Rather than speaking of death in general, one must consider the subject's position within a field of social relations in order to grasp one's emotional experience.[b]

My effort to show the force of a simple statement taken literally goes against anthropology's classic norms, which prefer to explicate culture through the gradual thickening of symbolic webs of meaning. By and large, cultural analysts use

From *Culture and Truth* (1989)

---

[1] From the opening, it is evident that Rosaldo is writing a different sort of anthropology than most of the authors in this book. Most anthropological writing has been built on a scientific model. Essays are written as reports, almost always in the third person. This essay, on the other hand, is conversational in tone, and much of it is in the first and second person. Beyond this, Rosaldo seems, in his opening, to deny the possibility of meaningful anthropological explanation of Ilongot headhunting. The idea of emotional force is not so much explanation as a statement that no further description or explanation is possible.

not *force* but such terms as *thick description, multivocality, polysemy, richness,* and *texture.*[2] The notion of force, among other things, opens to question the common anthropological assumption that the greatest human import resides in the densest forest of symbols and that analytical detail, or "cultural depth," equals enhanced explanation of a culture, or "cultural elaboration." Do people always in fact describe most thickly what matters most to them?

THE RAGE IN ILONGOT GRIEF

Let me pause a moment to introduce the Ilongots, among whom my wife, Michelle Rosaldo, and I lived and conducted field research for thirty months (1967–69, 1974). They number about 3,500 and reside in an upland area some 90 miles northeast of Manila, Philippines.[c] They subsist by hunting deer and wild pig and by cultivating rain-fed gardens (swiddens) with rice, sweet potatoes, manioc, and vegetables. Their (bilateral) kin relations are reckoned through men and women. After marriage, parents and their married daughters live in the same or adjacent households. The largest unit within the society, a largely territorial descent group called the *bertan*, becomes manifest primarily in the context of feuding. For themselves, their neighbors, and their ethnographers, headhunting stands out as the Ilongots' most salient cultural practice.

When Ilongots told me, as they often did, how the rage in bereavement could impel men to headhunt, I brushed aside their one-line accounts as too simple, thin, opaque, implausible, stereotypical, or otherwise unsatisfying. Probably I naively equated grief with sadness. Certainly no personal experience allowed me to imagine the powerful rage Ilongots claimed to find in bereavement. My own inability to conceive the force of anger in grief led me to seek out another level of analysis that could provide a deeper explanation for older men's desire to headhunt.[3]

Not until some fourteen years after first recording the terse Ilongot statement about grief and a headhunter's rage did I begin to grasp its overwhelming force. For years I thought that more verbal elaboration (which was not forthcoming) or another analytical level (which remained elusive) could better explain older men's motives for headhunting. Only after being repositioned through a devastating loss of my own could I better grasp that Ilongot older men mean precisely what they say when they describe the anger in bereavement as the source of their desire to cut off human heads. Taken at face value and granted its full weight, their statement reveals much about what compels these older men to headhunt.

In my efforts to find a "deeper" explanation for headhunting, I explored exchange theory, perhaps because it had informed so many classic ethnographies. One day in 1974, I explained the

---

[2] By invoking the concepts of thick description and multivocality, Rosaldo is referring especially to Clifford Geertz and Victor Turner. The important difference between Rosaldo and Geertz can be seen in two different possible interpretations of the following story recounted by Geertz: "There is an Indian story—at least I heard it as an Indian story—about an Englishman who, having been told that the world rested on a platform which rested on the back of an elephant which rested in turn on the back of a turtle, asked (perhaps he was an ethnographer; it is the way they behave), what did the turtle rest on? Another turtle. And that turtle? 'Ah, Sahib, after that it is turtles all the way down.'" (1973:28–29).

Geertz goes on to say that "cultural analysis is intrinsically incomplete"—meaning that there is always another

layer of meaning. His parable can also be interpreted to mean that there is no meaning other than that expressed. It is all just turtles and nothing beyond that. This, perhaps, is the meaning that Rosaldo would prefer.

[3] Rosaldo and other postmodern authors share a great deal of concern with the idea of the privileged position. In social science, to privilege a position is to give special credence to certain types of explanation and discount others. Postmodernists argue that Western social science has privileged a particular type of analysis: that which follows the model used in the physical sciences. The closer an explanation is to this model, the more "true" the information it generates, and the higher the prestige of the field that uses it.

anthropologist's exchange model to an older Ilongot man named Insan. What did he think, I asked, of the idea that headhunting resulted from the way that one death (the beheaded victim's) canceled another (the next of kin). He looked puzzled, so I went on to say that the victim of a beheading was exchanged for the death of one's own kin, thereby balancing the books, so to speak. Insan reflected a moment and replied that he imagined somebody could think such a thing (a safe bet, since I just had), but that he and other Ilongots did not think any such thing.[4] Nor was there any indirect evidence for my exchange theory in ritual, boast, song, or casual conversation.[d]

In retrospect, then, these efforts to impose exchange theory on one aspect of Ilongot behavior appear feeble.[5] Suppose I had discovered what I sought? Although the notion of balancing the ledger does have a certain elegant coherence, one wonders how such bookish dogma could inspire any man to take another man's life at the risk of his own.

My life experience had not as yet provided the means to imagine the rage that can come with devastating loss. Nor could I, therefore, fully appreciate the acute problem of meaning that Ilongots faced in 1974. Shortly after Ferdinand Marcos declared martial law in 1972, rumors that firing squads had become the new punishment for headhunting reached the Ilongot hills. The men therefore decided to call a morato-rium on taking heads. In past epochs, when headhunting had become impossible, Ilongots had allowed their rage to dissipate, as best it could, in the course of everyday life. In 1974, they had another option; they began to consider conversion to evangelical Christianity as a means of coping with their grief.[6] Accepting the new religion, people said, implied abandoning their old ways, including headhunting. It also made coping with bereavement less agonizing because they could believe that the deceased had departed for a better world. No longer did they have to confront the awful finality of death.

The force of the dilemma faced by the Ilongots eluded me at the time. Even when I correctly recorded their statements about grieving and the need to throw away their anger, I simply did not grasp the weight of their words. In 1974, for example, while Michelle Rosaldo and I were living among the Ilongots, a six-month-old baby died, probably of pneumonia. That afternoon we visited the father and found him terribly stricken. "He was sobbing and staring through glazed and bloodshot eyes at the cotton blanket covering his baby."[e] The man suffered intensely, for this was the seventh child he had lost. Just a few years before, three of his children had died, one after the other, in a matter of days. At the time, the situation was murky as people present talked both about evangelical Christianity (the possible renunciation of taking

---

[4] The "deeper" explanation of head-hunting for which Rosaldo searched was some sort of accounting modeled on a natural law (here, a mathematical formula, one death cancels another). However, in describing this theory to the Ilongot, Rosaldo faces a problem: Even if the theory explains observed behavior, how can Rosaldo grant it any explanatory power when the idea is utterly unintelligible to the Ilongot themselves?

[5] In some ways, the idea of privileged position is a recasting of the emic-etic dichotomy. A principal source of postmodern thought is ethnoscience and cognitive anthropology, but there is a powerful difference between postmodern thought and ethnoscience. Earlier debate on emics and etics was about the privileging of one or the other of these two positions. Postmodernism con-fronts the specific interests and positioning of both the anthropologists and their informants. Part of the reason for Rosaldo's misunderstanding of Ilongot head-hunting comes from his attempt to apply a Western scientific model to it.

[6] Although postmodern anthropology draws on ethnoscience, it is critically different in many ways, one of which is shown here. Ethnoscientists viewed culture as a more or less unchanging mental template. For postmodernists, culture is always historically contingent. The actions of individuals and the derivation of meaning within cultures cannot be explained without reference to specific sociohistorical circumstances.

heads) and their grudges against lowlanders (the contemplation of headhunting forays into the surrounding valleys).[7]

Through subsequent days and weeks, the man's grief moved him in a way I had not anticipated. Shortly after the baby's death, the father converted to evangelical Christianity. Altogether too quick on the inference, I immediately concluded that the man believed that the new religion could somehow prevent further deaths in his family. When I spoke my mind to an Ilongot friend, he snapped at me, saying that I had missed the point: what the man in fact sought in the new religion was not the denial of our inevitable deaths but a means of coping with his grief. With the advent of martial law, headhunting was out of the question as a means of venting his wrath and thereby lessening his grief. Were he to remain in his Ilongot way of life, the pain of his sorrow would simply be too much to bear.[f] My description from 1980 now seems so apt that I wonder how I could have written the words and nonetheless failed to appreciate the force of the grieving man's desire to vent his rage.

Another representative anecdote makes my failure to imagine the rage possible in Ilongot bereavement all the more remarkable. On this occasion, Michelle Rosaldo and I were urged by Ilongot friends to play the tape of a headhunting celebration we had witnessed some five years before. No sooner had we turned on the tape and heard the boast of a man who had died in the intervening years than did people abruptly tell us to shut off the recorder. Michelle Rosaldo reported on the tense conversation that ensued:[8]

> As Insan braced himself to speak, the room again became almost uncannily electric. Backs straightened and my anger turned to nervousness and something more like fear as I saw that Insan's eyes were red. Tukbaw, Renato's Ilongot "brother," then broke into what was a brittle silence, saying he could make things clear. He told us that it hurt to listen to a headhunting celebration when people knew that there would never be another. As he put it: "The song pulls at us, drags our hearts, it makes us think of our dead uncle." And again: "It would be better if I had accepted God, but I still am an Ilongot at heart; and when I hear the song, my heart aches as it does when I must look upon unfinished bachelors whom I know that I will never lead to take a head." Then Wagat, Tukbaw's wife, said with her eyes that all my questions gave her pain, and told me: "Leave off now, isn't that enough? Even I, a woman, cannot stand the way it feels inside my heart."[g]

From my present position, it is evident that the tape recording of the dead man's boast evoked powerful feelings of bereavement, particularly rage and the impulse to headhunt. At the time I could only feel apprehensive and diffusely sense the force of the emotions experienced by Insan, Tukbaw, Wagat, and the others present.

The dilemma for the Ilongots grew out of a set of cultural practices that, when blocked, were agonizing to live with.[9] The cessation of headhunting

---

[7] A key source of the emphasis on history in postmodernism is Marxism, particularly as filtered by the French Marxist anthropologists and political radicals of the 1960s and 1970s (when most postmodernists were doing their graduate training). Marxists, of course, see culture as part of a historical process that will ultimately result in communism. Postmodernists do not see any end to history, but they do view cultural action as dependent on historical circumstances. It is, for example, critical to the story Rosaldo is telling here that the action takes place in 1974, when head-hunting was made impossible and evangelical Christianity was available as an alternative.

[8] This extended quotation, presumably originally from field notes, is typical of the self-revealing style of postmodernism. Michelle Rosaldo's *Knowledge and Passion* (1980) makes extensive use of such quotations. In traditional ethnography, information from the field is presented in abstract, scientific fashion. Names are rarely mentioned; in fact, pains are sometimes taken to ensure the anonymity of the speakers. Here the opposite is done. Since all knowledge is contingent on the positioning of observers and informants, the fact that specific people are speaking is critical.

[9] Another aspect of Marxist theory absorbed by postmodernists is the emphasis on conflict. Functionalists and ethnoscientists looked for logically consistent systems. Postmodernists believe society to be beset by conflict between social groups (here, the Ilongot versus the government) or between theory and practice (the Calvinist example that follows). The contradictions are not abnormalities that would be eliminated in a smoothly functioning society, but rather a fundamental part of any social system.

called for painful adjustments to other modes of coping with the rage they found in bereavement. One could compare their dilemma with the notion that the failure to perform rituals can create anxiety.[h] In the Ilongot case, the cultural notion that throwing away a human head also casts away the anger creates a problem of meaning when the headhunting ritual cannot be performed. Indeed, Max Weber's classic problem of meaning in *The Protestant Ethic and the Spirit of Capitalism*[10] is precisely of this kind.[i] On a logical plane, the Calvinist doctrine of predestination seems flawless: God has chosen the elect, but his decision can never be known by mortals. Among those whose ultimate concern is salvation, the doctrine of predestination is as easy to grasp conceptually as it is impossible to endure in everyday life (unless one happens to be a "religious virtuoso"). For Calvinists and Ilongots alike, the problem of meaning resides in practice, not theory. The dilemma for both groups involves the practical matter of how to live with one's beliefs, rather than the logical puzzlement produced by abstruse doctrine.

HOW I FOUND THE RAGE IN GRIEF

One burden of this introduction concerns the claim that it took some fourteen years for me to grasp what Ilongots had told me about grief, rage, and headhunting. During all those years I was not yet in a position to comprehend the force of anger possible in bereavement, and now I am. Introducing myself into this account requires a certain hesitation both because of the discipline's

taboo and because of its increasingly frequent violation by essays laced with trendy amalgams of continental philosophy and autobiographical snippets. If classic ethnography's vice was the slippage from the ideal of detachment to actual indifference, that of present-day reflexivity is the tendency for the self-absorbed Self to lose sight altogether of the culturally different Other. Despite the risks involved, as the ethnographer I must enter the discussion at this point to elucidate certain issues of method.[11]

The key concept in what follows is that of the positioned (and repositioned) subject.[j] In routine interpretive procedure, according to the methodology of hermeneutics, one can say that ethnographers reposition themselves as they go about understanding other cultures. Ethnographers begin research with a set of questions, revise them throughout the course of inquiry, and in the end emerge with different questions than they started with. One's surprise at the answer to a question, in other words, requires one to revise the question until lessening surprises or diminishing returns indicate a stopping point. This interpretive approach has been most influentially articulated within anthropology by Clifford Geertz.[k]

Interpretive method usually rests on the axiom that gifted ethnographers learn their trade by preparing themselves as broadly as possible. To follow the meandering course of ethnographic inquiry, field-workers require wide-ranging theoretical capacities and finely tuned sensibilities. After all, one cannot predict beforehand what one will encounter in the field. One influential anthropologist, Clyde Kluckhohn, even went so far as to recommend a double initiation: first, the ordeal

---

[10] The book by Weber to which Rosaldo refers in this paragraph was extremely influential in anthropology and sociology. In it, Weber argued that the beliefs encouraged by Calvinist theology, particularly individualism and the work ethic, contributed directly to the rise of capitalism.

[11] The fundamental implication of Rosaldo's position is that the accounts produced by ethnographers depend upon their positioning, that is, the vantage point from which they view and analyze society. Their positioning is, in turn, contingent on their life experiences rather than be-

ing derived from any uniform application of scientific method. The logical extension of this is that postmodern ethnographies are often highly introspective. They become tales about the ethnographer's experiences. The subject of such work is generally the ethnographer's increasing understanding of himself or herself and the people with whom he or she is living. Rather than writing conventional anthropological reports, postmodernists tend to write about the process of doing fieldwork. Although Rosaldo criticizes the worst excesses of this sort of ethnography, he uses this approach himself.

of psychoanalysis, and then that of fieldwork. All too often, however, this view is extended until certain prerequisites of field research appear to guarantee an authoritative ethnography. Eclectic book knowledge and a range of life experiences, along with edifying reading and self-awareness, supposedly vanquish the twin vices of ignorance and insensitivity.[12]

Although the doctrine of preparation, knowledge, and sensibility contains much to admire, one should work to undermine the false comfort that it can convey. At what point can people say that they have completed their learning or their life experience? The problem with taking this mode of preparing the ethnographer too much to heart is that it can lend a false air of security, an authoritative claim to certitude and finality that our analyses cannot have. All interpretations are provisional; they are made by positioned subjects who are prepared to know certain things and not others.[13] Even when knowledgeable, sensitive, fluent in the language, and able to move easily in an alien cultural world, good ethnographers still have their limits, and their analyses always are incomplete. Thus, I began to fathom the force of what Ilongots had been telling me about their losses through my own loss, and not through any systematic preparation for field research.

My preparation for understanding serious loss began in 1970 with the death of my brother,

shortly after his twenty-seventh birthday. By experiencing this ordeal with my mother and father, I gained a measure of insight into the trauma of a parent's losing a child. This insight informed my account, partially described earlier, of an Ilongot man's reactions to the death of his seventh child. At the same time, my bereavement was so much less than that of my parents that I could not then imagine the overwhelming force of rage possible in such grief. My former position is probably similar to that of many in the discipline. One should recognize that ethnographic knowledge tends to have the strengths and limitations given by the relative youth of field-workers who, for the most part, have not suffered serious losses and could have, for example, no personal knowledge of how devastating the loss of a long-term partner can be for the survivor.

In 1981 Michelle Rosaldo and I began field research among the Ifugaos of northern Luzon, Philippines. On October 11 of that year, she was walking along a trail with two Ifugao companions when she lost her footing and fell to her death some 65 feet down a sheer precipice into a swollen river below. Immediately on finding her body I became enraged. How could she abandon me? How could she have been so stupid as to fall? I tried to cry. I sobbed, but rage blocked the tears. Less than a month later I described this moment in my journal: "I felt like in a nightmare, the whole world around me expanding and

---

[12] Anthropologists in the 1960s were very concerned with the methodology of data gathering. Ethnoscientists and cognitive anthropologists, reacting to the lack of preparation of most fieldworkers, prescribed very specific types of training and interviewing, such as controlled eliciting, to attempt to produce scientifically valid, replicable results. If, on the other hand, anthropology is about the interpretation of culture, then it is dependent on the life experiences of the anthropologist, and training can never be adequate and can never produce scientific, replicable results. Postmodernists insist on good training in language and ethnography, but they do not believe that such skills will result in a scientific anthropology.

[13] Rosaldo's argument is that interpretation changes with positioning. To understand Ilongot head-hunting, he had to experience grief and loss himself. In this paragraph and

later, he describes those personal experiences. Personal revelation is very rare in traditional ethnography but has become commonplace in recent ethnographic accounts. Traditional ethnography does contain occasional glimpses of the fieldworker. For example, Evans-Pritchard, in the introduction to *The Nuer* (1940), tells about his personal experience of Nuer land and his problems living there. However, the reader learns nothing of his background or family life. Here, and later, Rosaldo touches on experiences that are so personal they may make the reader uneasy (because of our own positioning, Michelle Rosaldo is a real person to us in a way that the dead Ilongot uncle described earlier is not). The difference is that Evans-Pritchard did not believe that his background had a critical bearing on his understanding of the Nuer. Rosaldo is convinced that only his personal experiences allow him to understand the Ilongot.

contracting, visually and viscerally heaving. Going down I find a group of men, maybe seven or eight, standing still, silent, and I heave and sob, but no tears." An earlier experience, on the fourth anniversary of my brother's death, had taught me to recognize heaving sobs without tears as a form of anger. This anger, in a number of forms, has swept over me on many occasions since then, lasting hours and even days at a time. Such feelings can be aroused by rituals, but more often they emerge from unexpected reminders (not unlike the Ilongots' unnerving encounter with their dead uncle's voice on the tape recorder).

Lest there be any misunderstanding, bereavement should not be reduced to anger, neither for myself nor for anyone else.[1] Powerful visceral emotional states swept over me, at times separately and at other times together. I experienced the deep cutting pain of sorrow almost beyond endurance, the cadaverous cold of realizing the finality of death, the trembling beginning in my abdomen and spreading through my body, the mournful keening that started without my willing, and frequent tearful sobbing. My present purpose of revising earlier understandings of Ilongot headhunting, and not a general view of bereavement, thus focuses on anger rather than on other emotions in grief.

Writings in English especially need to emphasize the rage in grief. Although grief therapists routinely encourage awareness of anger among the bereaved, upper-middle-class Anglo-American culture tends to ignore the rage devastating losses can bring.[14] Paradoxically, this culture's conventional wisdom usually denies the anger in grief at the same time that therapists encourage members of the invisible community of the bereaved to talk in detail about how angry their losses make them feel. My brother's death in combination with what I learned about anger from Ilongots (for them, an emotional state more publicly celebrated than denied) allowed me immediately to recognize the experience of rage.[m]

Ilongot anger and my own overlap, rather like two circles, partially overlaid and partially separate. They are not identical. Alongside striking similarities, significant differences in tone, cultural form, and human consequences distinguish the "anger" animating our respective ways of grieving. My vivid fantasies, for example, about a life insurance agent who refused to recognize Michelle's death as job-related did not lead me to kill him, cut off his head, and celebrate afterward. In so speaking, I am illustrating the discipline's methodological caution against the reckless attribution of one's own categories and experiences to members of another culture. Such warnings against facile notions of universal human nature can, however, be carried too far and harden into the equally pernicious doctrine that, my own group aside, everything human is alien to me. One hopes to achieve a balance between recognizing wide-ranging human differences and the modest truism that any two human groups must have certain things in common.

Only a week before completing the initial draft of an earlier version of this introduction, I rediscovered my journal entry, written some six weeks after Michelle's death, in which I made a vow to myself about how I would return to writing anthropology, if I ever did so, "by writing Grief and a Headhunter's Rage . . . ." My journal went on to reflect more broadly on death, rage, and headhunting by speaking of my "wish for the Ilongot solution; they are much more in touch with reality than Christians. So, I need a place to carry my anger—and can we say a solution of the imagination is better than theirs? And can we condemn them when we napalm villages? Is our

---

[14] Rosaldo's understanding is conditioned not only by his experiences but by his own culture. Here, he points to the "Anglo-American" understanding of grief. One of the principal motivations for postmodern interpretive anthropology is culture critique. For the postmodernist, anthropology allows the opportunity to reflect upon and analyze the culture of our own society as much as it allows for the analysis of the other. Here and later, in order for Rosaldo to examine and explain Ilongot practices, he must also examine and explain American practices. Anthropology then becomes a dialogue—a negotiation of interpretation between ethnographers and the cultures they purport to study.

rationale so much sounder than theirs?" All this was written in despair and rage.[15]

Not until some fifteen months after Michelle's death was I again able to begin writing anthropology. Writing the initial version of "Grief and a Headhunter's Rage" was in fact cathartic, though perhaps not in the way one would imagine.[16] Rather than following after the completed composition, the catharsis occurred beforehand. When the initial version of this introduction was most acutely on my mind, during the month before actually beginning to write, I felt diffusely depressed and ill with a fever. Then one day an almost literal fog lifted and words began to flow. It seemed less as if I were doing the writing than that the words were writing themselves through me.

My use of personal experience serves as a vehicle for making the quality and intensity of the rage in Ilongot grief more readily accessible to readers than certain more detached modes of composition. At the same time, by invoking personal experience as an analytical category one risks easy dismissal. Unsympathetic readers could reduce this introduction to an act of mourning or a mere report on my discovery of the anger possible in bereavement. Frankly, this introduction is both and more. An act of mourning, a personal report, *and* a critical analysis of anthropological method, it simultaneously encompasses a number of distinguishable processes, no one of which cancels out the others. Similarly, I argue in what follows that ritual in general and Ilongot headhunting in particular form the intersection of multiple coexisting social processes.[17] Aside from revising the ethnographic record, the paramount claim made here concerns how my own mourning and consequent reflection on Ilongot bereavement, rage, and headhunting raise methodological issues of general concern in anthropology and the human sciences.

DEATH IN ANTHROPOLOGY

Anthropology favors interpretations that equate analytical "depth" with cultural "elaboration."[18] Many studies focus on visibly bounded arenas where one can observe formal and repetitive events, such as ceremonies, rituals, and games. Similarly, studies of word play are more likely to focus on jokes as programmed monologues than on the less scripted, more free-wheeling improvised interchanges of witty banter. Most ethnographers prefer to study events that have definite locations in space with marked centers and outer edges. Temporally, they have middles and endings. Historically, they appear to repeat identical structures by seemingly doing things today as they were done yesterday. Their qualities of fixed definition liberate such events from the untidiness of everyday life so that they can be "read" like articles, books, or, as we now say, *texts*.

Guided by their emphasis on self-contained entities, ethnographies written in accord with

---

[15] Notice the important role that empathy plays in Rosaldo's analysis. He warns against false attribution of our character traits to the other, but his essential insight into Ilongot headhunting occurs only after he has personal experiences that allow him to identify with them in a visceral way.

[16] Postmodernists remind us that most of what anthropologists do, we do for our own purposes. Here, Rosaldo's anthropological insights come either as revelation or therapy. As he reports later, writing this essay was a cathartic act and an enormously personal one.

[17] Turner's idea of multivocality runs deeply through Rosaldo's work. Just as symbols do not necessarily have single meanings, cultural action does not have discrete, unique causes. Instead, causation is always multiple. Rosaldo's essay is no exception: It is "an act of mourning, a personal report, and an analysis of anthropological method."

[18] Rosaldo's analysis of anthropological interpretations of mourning is actually a general attack on traditional anthropological method. In some ways, it is an extension of the reasoning of ethnoscience. Ethnoscientists and cognitive anthropologists criticized traditional anthropologists for using their own systems of classification rather than those of the natives. Rosaldo suggests that the problem goes further: The way ethnography is written—the way it delimits events by time, actors, physical location, and so on—is, in itself, the imposition of a certain sort of reality upon ethnographic material. To postmodernists, such boundaries are artificial, the products of specific observers or specific individuals involved. To report on an event, the ethnographer draws discrete boundaries around it. The type of boundary drawn around the event critically influences its interpretation.

classic norms consider death under the rubric of ritual rather than bereavement. Indeed, the subtitles of even recent ethnographies on death make the emphasis on ritual explicit. William Douglas's *Death in Murelaga* is subtitled *Funerary Ritual in a Spanish Basque Village;* Richard Huntington and Peter Metcalf's *Celebrations of Death* is subtitled *The Anthropology of Mortuary Ritual;* Peter Metcalf's *A Borneo Journey into Death* is subtitled *Berawan Eschatology from Its Rituals.*[n] Ritual itself is defined by its formality and routine; under such descriptions, it more nearly resembles a recipe, a fixed program, or a book of etiquette than an open-ended human process.

Ethnographies that in this manner eliminate intense emotions not only distort their descriptions but also remove potentially key variables from their explanations. When anthropologist William Douglas, for example, announces his project in *Death in Murelaga,* he explains that his objective is to use death and funerary ritual "as a heuristic device with which to approach the study of rural Basque society."[o] In other words, the primary object of study is social structure, not death, and certainly not bereavement. The author begins his analysis by saying, "Death is not always fortuitous or unpredictable."[p] He goes on to describe how an old woman, ailing with the infirmities of her age, welcomed her death. The description largely ignores the perspective of the most bereaved survivors, and instead vacillates between those of the old woman and a detached observer.

Undeniably, certain people do live a full life and suffer so greatly in their decrepitude that they embrace the relief death can bring. Yet the problem with making an ethnography's major case study focus on "a very easy death"[q] (I use Simone de Beauvoir's title with irony, as she did) is not only its lack of representativeness but also that it makes death in general appear as routine for the survivors as this particular one apparently was for the deceased. Were the old woman's sons and daughters untouched by her death? The case study shows less about how people cope with death than about how death can be made to appear routine, thereby fitting neatly into the author's view of funerary ritual as a mechanical programmed unfolding of prescribed acts.[19] "To the Basque," says Douglas, "ritual is order and order is ritual."[r]

Douglas captures only one extreme in the range of possible deaths. Putting the accent on the routine aspects of ritual conveniently conceals the agony of such unexpected early deaths as parents losing a grown child or a mother dying in childbirth. Concealed in such descriptions are the agonies of the survivors who muddle through shifting, powerful emotional states. Although Douglas acknowledges the distinction between the bereaved members of the deceased's domestic group and the more public ritualistic group, he writes his account primarily from the viewpoint of the latter. He masks the emotional force of bereavement by reducing funerary ritual to orderly routine.[20]

Surely, human beings mourn both in ritual settings *and* in the informal settings of everyday life. Consider the evidence that willy-nilly spills over the edges in Godfrey Wilson's classic anthropological account of "conventions of burial" among the Nyakyusa of South Africa:[21]

> That some at least of those who attend a Nyakyusa burial are moved by grief it is easy to

---

[19] Rosaldo here shows an example of how the preconceptions of the investigator can exert a powerful influence over the ethnography produced. Notice that Rosaldo is not accusing Douglas of misreporting but rather of choosing a point of view within Basque society that confirms his own understanding of that society.

[20] One element of Rosaldo's critique of anthropology is a recurring theme first expressed in Boas' attack on the evolutionists. According to Rosaldo, Douglas is not producing ethnography driven by observation but using specific case examples to back his theoretical position. To some degree, this is also true of the symbolic anthropologists, with whom Rosaldo has great sympathy. Symbolic anthropologists tended to concentrate on the analysis of ceremony and other symbolically complex behavior. They saw these events as the points at which culture displays its greatest richness, therefore making interpretive analysis more productive.

[21] Godfrey Wilson (?–1944), whom Rosaldo quotes here, was the husband of Monica Wilson. The Wilsons worked together in Tanganyika (now Tanzania) and Northern Rhodesia (now Zambia) in the 1930s and 1940s. Victor Turner was a student of Monica Wilson and refers extensively to her work in essay 36 in this volume.

establish. I have heard people talking regret-
fully in ordinary conversation of a man's death;
I have seen a man whose sister had just died
walk over alone towards her grave and weep
quietly by himself without any parade of grief;
and I have heard of a man killing himself because of his grief for a dead son.[s]

Note that all the instances Wilson witnesses or
hears about happen outside the circumscribed
sphere of ormal ritual. People converse among
themselves, walk alone and silently weep, or more
impulsively commit suicide. The work of grieving,
probably universally, occurs both within obligatory
ritual acts and in more everyday settings where
people find themselves alone or with close kin.

In Nyakyusa burial ceremonies, powerful
emotional states also become present in the ritual itself, which is more than a series of obligatory acts. Men say they dance the passions of
their bereavement, which includes a complex mix
of anger, fear, and grief:

> "This war dance (*ukukina*)," said an old man, "is
> mourning, we are mourning the dead man. We
> dance because there is war in our hearts. A pas-
> sion of grief and fear exasperates us (*ilyyojo liku-
> tusila*)."... *Elyojo* means a passion or grief, anger
> or fear; *ukusila* means to annoy or exasperate
> beyond endurance. In explaining *ukusila* one
> man put it like this: "If a man continually insults
> me then he exasperates me (*ukusila*) so that I
> want to fight him." Death is a fearful and griev-
> ous event that exasperates those [men] nearly
> concerned and makes them want to fight.[t]

Descriptions of the dance and subsequent quarrels, even killings, provide ample evidence of the
emotional intensity involved. The articulate testimony by Wilson's informants makes it obvious
that even the most intense sentiments can be
studied by ethnographers.

Despite such exceptions as Wilson, the general rule seems to be that one should tidy things
up as much as possible by wiping away the tears
and ignoring the tantrums. Most anthropological
studies of death eliminate emotions by assuming
the position of the most detached observer.[u]
Such studies usually conflate the ritual process
with the process of mourning, equate ritual with
the obligatory, and ignore the relation between
ritual and everyday life. The bias that favors formal ritual risks assuming the answers to questions that most need to be asked. Do rituals, for
example, always reveal cultural depth?[22]

Most analysts who equate death with funerary
ritual assume that rituals store encapsulated wisdom as if it were a microcosm of its encompassing
cultural macrocosm. One recent study of death
and mourning, for example, confidently begins by
affirming that rituals embody "the collective wisdom of many cultures."[v] Yet this generalization
surely requires case-by-case investigation against
a broader range of alternative hypotheses.[23]

At the polar extremes, rituals either display
cultural depth or brim over with platitudes. In
the former case, rituals indeed encapsulate a culture's wisdom; in the latter instance, they act as
catalysts that precipitate processes whose unfolding occurs over subsequent months or even
years. Many rituals, of course, do both by combining a measure of wisdom with a comparable
dose of platitudes.

---

[22] The notion that great symbolic complexity does not
necessarily indicate great meaning to the people involved
is critical to Rosaldo's concept of force. If this is true, exhaustive interpretive treatments of ceremony may not aid
much in understanding culture. Great cultural depth may
be present in the Nyakyusa ceremonies described in this
passage, but as Rosaldo notes later, despite great symbolism there was little depth in the ceremonies he attended
for his brother and wife.

[23] Cultural force, though it may not be present in ritual,
frequently appears where powerful emotional states such
as rage, anger, fear, or love are expressed. However, traditional ethnography, modeled on scientific writing, deals
only very poorly with these. The scientific trope in writing
demands that reporting be dispassionate and that writers
adopt an emotionally neutral stance toward their subjects.
Paul Stoller (b. 1947) contends that "vivid descriptions of
the sensoria of ethnographic situations have been largely
overshadowed by a dry analytic prose" (1989:8). Although
it may be relatively easy to describe a ritual in such prose,
Stoller claims that characterizations of others as they lead
their social lives are lost in this sort of writing. He argues
for an anthropology that relies more on descriptions of
nonvisual sensory information.

My own experience of bereavement and rituals fits the platitudes and catalyst model better than that of microcosmic deep culture. Even a careful analysis of the language and symbolic action during the two funerals for which I was a chief mourner would reveal precious little about the experience of bereavement.[w] This statement, of course, should not lead anyone to derive a universal from somebody else's personal knowledge. Instead, it should encourage ethnographers to ask whether a ritual's wisdom is deep or conventional, and whether its process is immediately transformative or but a single step in a lengthy series of ritual and everyday events.

In attempting to grasp the cultural force of rage and other powerful emotional states, both formal ritual and the informal practices of everyday life provide crucial insight. Thus, cultural descriptions should seek out force as well as thickness, and they should extend from well-defined rituals to myriad less circumscribed practices.

GRIEF, RAGE, AND ILONGOT HEADHUNTING

When applied to Ilongot headhunting, the view of ritual as a storehouse of collective wisdom aligns headhunting with expiatory sacrifice.[24] The raiders call the spirits of the potential victims, bid their ritual farewells, and seek favorable omens along the trail. Ilongot men vividly recall the hunger and deprivation they endure over the days and even weeks it takes to move cautiously toward the place where they set up an ambush and await the first person who happens along. Once the raiders kill their victim, they toss away the head rather than keep it as a trophy. In tossing away the head, they claim by analogy to cast away their life burdens, including the rage in their grief.

Before a raid, men describe their state of being by saying that the burdens of life have made them heavy and entangled, like a tree with vines clinging to it. They say that a successfully completed raid makes them feel light of step and ruddy in complexion. The collective energy of the celebration with its song, music, and dance reportedly gives the participants a sense of well-being. The expiatory ritual process involves cleansing and catharsis.

The analysis just sketched regards ritual as a timeless, self-contained process. Without denying the insight in this approach, its limits must also be considered. Imagine, for example, exorcism rituals described as if they were complete in themselves, rather than being linked with larger processes unfolding before and after the ritual period. Through what processes does the afflicted person recover or continue to be afflicted after the ritual? What are the social consequences of recovery or its absence? Failure to consider such questions diminishes the force of such afflictions and therapies for which the formal ritual is but a phase. Still other questions apply to differently positioned subjects, including the person afflicted, the healer, and the audience. In all cases, the problem involves the delineation of processes that occur before and after, as well as during, the ritual moment.

Let us call the notion of a self-contained sphere of deep cultural activity the *microcosmic view,* and an alternative view *ritual as a busy intersection.* In the latter case, ritual appears as a place where a number of distinct social processes intersect. The crossroads simply provides a space for distinct trajectories to traverse, rather than containing them in complete encapsulated form. From this perspective, Ilongot headhunting stands at the confluence of three analytically separable processes.

The first process concerns whether or not it is an opportune time to raid. Historical conditions

---

[24] In this relatively brief section of the essay, Rosaldo gives an analysis of Ilongot head-hunting that is sensitive to the issues he raises throughout the paper. Rosaldo attempts to break through the boundaries imposed by the act of analysis. For many postmodernists, anthropology is, above all, the acts of observing and writing, which necessarily impose boundaries upon events. Because of this, anthropologists tend to write about self-contained events. To escape from this type of analysis, Rosaldo proposes instead that Ilongot head-hunting results from the intersection of three more or less independent processes.

determine the possibilities of raiding, which range from frequent to likely to unlikely to impossible.[25] These conditions include American colonial efforts at pacification, the Great Depression, World War II, revolutionary movements in the surrounding lowlands, feuding among Ilongot groups, and the declaration of martial law in 1972. Ilongots use the analogy of hunting to speak of such historical vicissitudes. Much as Ilongot huntsmen say they cannot know when game will cross their path or whether their arrows will strike the target, so certain historical forces that condition their existence remain beyond their control. My book *Ilongot Headhunting, 1883–1974* explores the impact of historical factors on Ilongot headhunting.

Second, young men coming of age undergo a protracted period of personal turmoil during which they desire nothing so much as to take a head. During this troubled period, they seek a life partner and contemplate the traumatic dislocation of leaving their families of origin and entering their new wife's household as a stranger. Young men weep, sing, and burst out in anger because of their fierce desire to take a head and wear the coveted red hornbill earrings that adorn the ears of men who already have, as Ilongots say, arrived (*tabi*). Volatile, envious, passionate (at least according to their own cultural stereotype of the young unmarried man [*buintaw*]), they constantly lust to take a head. Michelle and I began fieldwork among the Ilongots only a year after abandoning our unmarried youths; hence our ready empathy with youthful turbulence. Her book on Ilongot notions of self explores the passionate anger of young men as they come of age.

Third, older men are differently positioned than their younger counterparts. Because they have already beheaded somebody, they can wear the red hornbill earrings so coveted by youths. Their desire to headhunt grows less from chronic adolescent turmoil than from more intermittent acute agonies of loss. After the death of somebody to whom they are closely attached, older men often inflict on themselves vows of abstinence, not to be lifted until the day they participate in a successful headhunting raid. These deaths can cover a range of instances from literal death, whether through natural causes or beheading, to social death where, for example, a man's wife runs off with another man. In all cases, the rage born of devastating loss animates the older men's desire to raid. This anger at abandonment is irreducible in that nothing at a deeper level explains it. Although certain analysts argue against the dreaded last analysis, the linkage of grief, rage, and headhunting has no other known explanation.[26]

My earlier understandings of Ilongot headhunting missed the fuller significance of how older men experience loss and rage. Older men prove critical in this context because they, not the youths, set the processes of headhunting in motion. Their rage is intermittent, whereas that of youths is continuous. In the equation of headhunting, older men are the variable and younger men are the constant. Culturally speaking, older men are endowed with knowledge and stamina that their juniors have not yet attained, hence they care for (*saysay*) and lead (*bukur*) the younger men when they raid.

In a preliminary survey of the literature on headhunting, I found that the lifting of mourning prohibitions frequently occurs after taking a head. The notion that youthful anger and older men's rage lead them to take heads is more

---

[25] The idea of positioning is again crucial. Rosaldo has spoken earlier of the positioning of the anthropologist; here the positioning of the Ilongot becomes the main object of analysis. Rosaldo does not see Ilongot society as timeless, harmonious, and undifferentiated (as Durkheim, for example, might) but as fixed in historical time and composed of diverse individuals and groups with different interests. Head-hunting happens when historical circumstances make it possible and when the emotional states of young and old men coincide.

[26] In analyzing the head-hunting of the older men, Rosaldo applies his notion of force. He insists that there is no meaningful way to analyze Ilongot rage other than to record it. His insistence that there can be no other explanation of the linkage of grief, rage, and head-hunting is extremely provocative. Many anthropologists find it difficult to accept.

plausible than such commonly reported "explanations" of headhunting as the need to acquire mystical "soul stuff" or personal names.[x] Because the discipline correctly rejects stereotypes of the "bloodthirsty savage," it must investigate how headhunters create an intense desire to decapitate their fellow humans. The human sciences must explore the cultural force of emotions with a view to delineating the passions that animate certain forms of human conduct.

SUMMARY

The ethnographer, as a positioned subject, grasps certain human phenomena better than others. He or she occupies a position or structural location and observes with a particular angle of vision. Consider, for example, how age, gender, being an outsider, and association with a neocolonial regime influence what the ethnographer learns.[27] The notion of position also refers to how life experiences both enable and inhibit particular kinds of insight. In the case at hand, nothing in my own experience equipped me even to imagine the anger possible in bereavement until after Michelle Rosaldo's death in 1981. Only then was I in a position to grasp the force of what Ilongots had repeatedly told me about grief, rage, and headhunting. By the same token, so-called natives are also positioned subjects who have a distinctive mix of insight and blindness. Consider the structural positions of older versus younger Ilongot men, or the differing positions of chief mourners versus those less involved during a funeral. My discussion of anthropological writings on death often achieved its effects simply by shifting from the position of those least involved to that of the chief mourners.

Cultural depth does not always equal cultural elaboration. Think simply of the speaker who is filibustering. The language used can sound elaborate as it heaps word on word, but surely it is not deep. Depth should be separated from the presence or absence of elaboration. By the same token, one-line explanations can be vacuous or pithy. The concept of force calls attention to an enduring intensity in human conduct that can occur with or without the dense elaboration conventionally associated with cultural depth. Although relatively without elaboration in speech, song, or ritual, the rage of older Ilongot men who have suffered devastating losses proves enormously consequential in that, foremost among other things, it leads them to behead their fellow humans. Thus, the notion of force involves both affective intensity and significant consequences that unfold over a long period of time.

Similarly, rituals do not always encapsulate deep cultural wisdom. At times they instead contain the wisdom of Polonius.[28] Although certain rituals both reflect and create ultimate values, others simply bring people together and deliver a set of platitudes that enable them to go on with their lives. Rituals serve as vehicles for processes that occur both before and after the period of their performance. Funeral rituals, for example, do not "contain" all the complex processes of bereavement. Ritual and bereavement should not be collapsed into one another because they neither fully encapsulate nor fully explain one another. Instead, rituals are often but points along a number of longer processual trajectories; hence, my image of ritual as a crossroads where distinct life processes intersect.[y]

The notion of ritual as a busy intersection anticipates the critical assessment of the concept of culture developed in the following chapters. In contrast with the classic view, which posits culture as a self-contained whole made up of coherent patterns, culture can arguably be conceived as a more porous array of intersections where distinct

---

[27] Postmodern anthropology collapses many of the distinctions upon which more traditional anthropology is based. There is no longer an observer and an observed. Instead there are individuals prepared to know certain things and not others. These are both anthropologists and members of the cultures the anthropologists are analyz-

ing. Accepting Rosaldo's critique renders the distinction between emic and etic meaningless.

[28] Polonius, a character in *Hamlet*, is minister to the king and Ophelia's father. Although he is the king's advisor, he dispenses greeting-card wisdom.

processes crisscross from within and beyond its borders. Such heterogeneous processes often derive from differences of age, gender, class, race, and sexual orientation.

This book argues that a sea change in cultural studies has eroded once-dominant conceptions of truth and objectivity. The truth of objectivism—absolute, universal, and timeless—has lost its monopoly status. It now competes, on more nearly equal terms, with the truths of case studies that are embedded in local contexts, shaped by local interests, and colored by local perceptions. The agenda for social analysis has shifted to include not only eternal verities and lawlike generalizations but also political processes, social changes, and human differences. Such terms as *objectivity, neutrality,* and *impartiality* refer to subject positions once endowed with great institutional authority, but they are arguably neither more nor less valid than those of more engaged, yet equally perceptive, knowledgeable social actors. Social analysis must now grapple with the realization that its objects of analysis are also analyzing subjects who critically interrogate ethnographers—their writings, their ethics, and their politics.[29]

NOTES

An earlier version of this chapter appeared as "Grief and a Headhunter's Rage: On the Cultural Force of Emotions," in *Text, Play, and Story: The Construction and Reconstruction of Self and Society,* ed. Edward M. Bruner (Washington, D.C.: American Ethnological Society, 1984), pp. 178–95.

[a] In contrasting Moroccan and Javanese forms of mysticism, Clifford Geertz found it necessary to distinguish the "force" of cultural patterning from its "scope" (Clifford Geertz, *Islam Observed* [New Haven, Conn: Yale University Press, 1968]). He distinguished force from scope in this manner: "By 'force' I mean the

thoroughness with which such a pattern is internalized in the personalities of the individuals who adopt it, its centrality or marginality in their lives" (p. 111). "By 'scope,' on the other hand, I mean the range of social contexts within which religious considerations are regarded as having more or less direct relevance" (p. 112). In his later works, Geertz developed the notion of scope more than that of force. Unlike Geertz, who emphasizes processes of internalization within individual personalities, my use of the term force stresses the concept of the positioned subject.

[b] Anthropologists have long studied the vocabulary of the emotions in other cultures (see, e.g., Hildred Geertz, "The Vocabulary of Emotion: A Study of Javanese Socialization Processes," *Psychiatry* 22 [1959]: 225–37). For a recent review essay on anthropological writings on emotions, see Catherine Lutz and Geoffrey M. White, "The Anthropology of Emotions," *Annual Review of Anthropology* 15 (1986):405–36.

[c] The two ethnographies on the Ilongots are Michelle Rosaldo, *Knowledge and Passion: Ilongot Notions of Self and Social Life* (New York: Cambridge University Press, 1980), and Renato Rosaldo, *Ilongot Headhunting, 1883–1974: A Study in Society and History* (Stanford, Calif: Stanford University Press, 1980). Our field research among the Ilongots was financed by a National Science Foundation predoctoral fellowship, National Science Foundation Research Grants GS–1509 and GS–40788, and a Mellon Award for junior faculty from Stanford University. A Fulbright Grant financed a two-month stay in the Philippines during 1981.

[d] Lest the hypothesis Insan rejected appear utterly implausible, one should mention that at least one group does link a version of exchange theory to headhunting. Peter Metcalf reports that, among the Berawan of Borneo, "Death has a chain reaction quality to it. There is a considerable anxiety that, unless something is done to break the chain, death will follow upon death. The logic of this is now plain: The unquiet soul kills, and so creates more unquiet souls" (Peter Metcalf, *A Borneo Journey into Death: Berawan Eschatology from Its Rituals* [Philadelphia: University of Pennsylvania Press, 1982], p. 127).

[29] In closing his essay, Rosaldo makes several important points. He refers to the fact that in a world where education in Western languages is increasingly widespread, people who were traditionally the subjects of ethnography are increasingly reading it, and sometimes writing their own. A traditional anthropologist such as Evans-Pritchard did not have to worry about how the Nuer were going to react to his description of them. Current anthropologists write with the knowledge that some of their informants will read and critique their work. This approach has changed the nature of anthropology.

More controversially, Rosaldo asserts that the interpretations of anthropologists must be judged as neither more nor less valid than those of other astute observers. By extension, this implies that anthropological training confers no particular authority. If this is the case, what should be the role of the "human sciences," among which Rosaldo has included anthropology?

[e] R. Rosaldo, *Ilongot Headhunting, 1883–1974,* p. 286.

[f] Ibid., p. 288.

[g] M. Rosaldo, *Knowledge and Passion,* p. 33.

[h] See A. R. Radcliffe-Brown, *Structure and Function in Primitive Society* (London: Cohen and West, Ltd., 1952), pp. 133–52. For a broader debate on the "functions" of ritual, see the essays by Bronislaw Malinowski, A. R. Radcliffe-Brown, and George C. Homans, in *Reader in Comparative Religion: An Anthropological Approach* (4th ed.), ed. William A. Lessa and Evon Z. Vogt (New York: Harper and Row, 1979), pp. 37–62.

[i] Max Weber, *The Protestant Ethic and the Spirit of Capitalism* (New York: Charles Scribner's Sons, 1958).

[j] A key antecedent to what I have called the "positioned subject" is Alfred Schutz, *Collected Papers,* vol. 1, *The Problem of Social Reality,* ed. and intro. Maurice Natanson (The Hague: Martinus Nijhoff, 1971). See also, e.g., Aaron Cicourel, *Method and Measurement in Sociology* (Glencoe, Ill.: The Free Press, 1964) and Gerald Berreman, *Behind Many Masks: Ethnography and Impression Management in a Himalayan Village,* Monograph No. 4 (Ithaca, N.Y.: Society for Applied Anthropology, 1962). For an early anthropological article on how differently positioned subjects interpret the "same" culture in different ways, see John W. Bennett, "The Interpretation of Pueblo Culture," *Southwestern Journal of Anthropology* 2 (1946):361–74.

[k] Clifford Geertz, *The Interpretation of Cultures* (New York: Basic Books, 1974) and *Local Knowledge: Further Essays in Interpretive Anthropology* (New York: Basic Books, 1983).

[l] Although anger appears so often in bereavement as to be virtually universal, certain notable exceptions do occur. Clifford Geertz, for example, depicts Javanese funerals as follows: "The mood of a Javanese funeral is not one of hysterical bereavement, unrestrained sobbing, or even of formalized cries of grief for the deceased's departure. Rather, it is a calm, undemonstrative, almost languid letting go, a brief ritualized relinquishment of a relationship no longer possible" (Geertz, *The Interpretation of Cultures,* p. 153). In cross-cultural perspective, the anger in grief presents itself in different degrees (including zero), in different forms, and with different consequences.

[m] The Ilongot notion of anger (*liget*) is regarded as dangerous in its violent excesses, but also as life-enhancing in that, for example, it provides energy for work. See the extensive discussion in M. Rosaldo, *Knowledge and Passion.*

[n] William Douglas, *Death in Murelaga: Funerary Ritual in a Spanish Basque Village* (Seattle: University of Washington Press, 1969); Richard Huntington and Peter Metcalf, *Celebrations of Death: The Anthropology of Mortuary Ritual* (New York: Cambridge University Press, 1979); Metcalf, *A Borneo Journey into Death.*

[o] Douglas, *Death in Murelaga,* p. 209.

[p] Ibid., p. 19.

[q] Simone de Beauvoir, *A Very Easy Death* (Harmondsworth, United Kingdom: Penguin Books, 1969).

[r] Douglas, *Death in Murelaga,* p. 75.

[s] Godfrey Wilson, *Nyakyusa Conventions of Burial* (Johannesburg: The University of Witwatersrand Press, 1939), pp. 22–23. (Reprinted from Bantu Studies.)

[t] Ibid., p. 13.

[u] In his survey of works on death published during the 1960s, for example, Johannes Fabian found that the four major anthropological journals carried only nine papers on the topic, most of which "dealt only with the purely ceremonial aspects of death" (Johannes Fabian, "How Others Die: Reflections on the Anthropology of Death," in *Death in American Experience,* ed. A. Mack [New York: Schocken, 1973], p. 178).

[v] Huntington and Metcalf, *Celebrations of Death,* p. 1.

[w] Arguably, ritual works differently for those most afflicted by a particular death than for those least so. Funerals may distance the former from overwhelming emotions whereas they may draw the latter closer to strongly felt sentiments (see T. J. Scheff, *Catharsis in Healing, Ritual, and Drama* [Berkeley: University of California Press, 1979]). Such issues can be investigated through the notion of the positioned subject.

[x] For a discussion of cultural motives for headhunting, see Robert McKinley, "Human and Proud of It! A Structural Treatment of Headhunting Rites and the Social Definition of Enemies," in *Studies in Borneo Societies: Social Process and Anthropological Explanation,* ed. G. Appell (DeKalb, Ill.: Center for Southeast Asian Studies, Northern Illinois University, 1976), pp. 92–126; Rodney Needham, "Skulls and Causality," *Man* 11 (1976): 71–88; Michelle Rosaldo, "Skulls and Causality," *Man* 12 (1977):168–70.

[y] Pierre Bourdieu, *Outline of a Theory of Practice* (New York: Cambridge University Press, 1977), p. 1.

39. *A Tale of Two Pregnancies*

LILA ABU-LUGHOD (b. 1952)

ENTERING MY TWENTY-fourth week. Heartburn woke me up this morning, and I turned to my favorite of the three pregnancy guidebooks I keep near my bed—the one organized around anxieties. In the section titled "Heartburn and Indigestion," sandwiched between "Losing Your Figure" and "Food Aversions and Cravings," I read: "It's nearly impossible to have an indigestion-free nine months; it's just one of the less pleasant facts of pregnancy."[1]

I closed my eyes. This was, I thought, what my friend Kareema must have felt.[a] She was the mother of eleven whom I'd seen through two pregnancies in the 1980s. Like all but one of her others, her last pregnancy, at an age closer to my current age than I liked to imagine, had proceeded without the benefit of medical care. She had suffered terrible indigestion, and I remembered those many evenings when, by the light of a kerosene lantern, I had prepared her the fizzy orange drink she swore relieved the pain: effervescent tablets of vitamin C purchased at the local pharmacy, dissolved in a glass of water.[2]

In those days I understood little about what Kareema and the other Awlad 'Ali Bedouin women I lived with in Egypt were experiencing. Caught up in my own world and my research,

first in my mid-twenties and later in my thirties, I claimed to be, and was, very interested in women's experiences. But I barely noticed anything about their pregnancies except protruding bellies artfully hidden by large red belts. The women worked hard, lifting heavy cooking pots, carrying their other children on their backs, washing clothes, and walking long distances to visit friends and relatives. Pregnancy hardly seemed to interfere. At the end, with the help of a local midwife, their mothers, or their mothers-in-law, these women suddenly produced infants who, by the time I would see them, were lovingly swaddled and lying close to them. Or so it seemed. Except that every older woman who told me her life story mentioned a miscarriage or a stillbirth.

My pregnancy, in contrast, was the ultimate late-capitalist U.S. achievement: assisted by the most recent advances in reproductive technology, monitored from egg production to fetal heartbeats with the help of ultrasound and hormonal analysis, and expensive. I was one of the fortunate women in her late thirties for whom in vitro fertilization had succeeded on the first try. I began the pregnancy with a mix of scientific knowledge, common sense, and holistic medical

From *Women Writing Culture* (1995)

---

[1] Like the opening to Geertz's analysis of the Balinese cockfight, Abu-Lughod starts this essay with a personal account that immediately draws the reader into her story. Unlike Geertz, who abandon's his personal account for a more formal analysis, Abu-Lughod focuses on the personal experience of her pregnancy and writes completely in a personal, reflexive, style. She embraces the postmodern view that ethnography is the creation of the writer, arguing that because ethnographers know things within a personal context, what they write are partial and positioned truths (1991:141). Consequently, in writing about her pregnancy, Abu-Lughod tries to place the reader within her frame of reference as an anthropologist and a woman pregnant with twins.

[2] In her critique of ethnography "Writing Against Culture," Abu-Lughod criticizes the practice of making ethnographic generalizations. She says that generalization is a part of a language of power used by those who stand apart from and outside of those they study (1991:150). She argues that one way to combat generalization is to write "ethnographies of the particular" (1991:149), and indeed her essay is an outstanding example of this approach: She is writing about her pregnancy and her experiences with one specific Egyptian Bedouin woman; she does not try to discuss pregnancy for Bedouin women in general.

advice: warned by my books about preeclampsia, prevented from carrying heavy objects by my husband, pampering myself by lying down to allow blood to flow to my placenta, counting my calcium milligrams, balancing my green and yellow vegetables, and studying with some despair the undecipherable diagrams that promise to guide pregnant women through proper exercise regimens.[3]

If I had not known Kareema and the other women in Egypt who had shared their lives with me, I would not have been able to shake my head and laugh at myself for the fuss I was making. I also might not have felt so lucky. My personal experience of the pregnancy was shaped by the double (or hybrid, in Kirin Narayan's view) life I lived as an anthropologist.[b] I moved between the world of "home" in the United States, with my network of friends and family and the resources of feminist scholarship on reproduction to help me think about the facts of life, and "the field" in Egypt, where I was surrounded by women who became pregnant, gave birth, lived with children, and talked to me and to each other about why things sometimes went wrong. I looked to both places for help in understanding what was happening to me, just as I had sought this pregnancy in both places.[4]

SEARCHING FOR CHILDREN

Living in what is known as the Western Desert of Egypt, with only a substandard clinic not close enough for easy access, the Bedouin women I knew could not take advantage of the superb doctors and excellent hospital facilities available in Egypt's major cities, Cairo and Alexandria. They gave each other advice, told stories about their pregnancies and those of others, and complained—of headaches, fevers, aches, swelling. That did not stop them from feeling sorry for me, their anthropologist friend, still childless long after their own daughters, who had kept me company on the long winter evenings of my first stay in the late 1970s, had married and given birth to one, two, sometimes three children.[5]

Even though I did not yet want children, they sympathetically told me stories about women who were "searching for children" too. They explained the theory of "blocking"—how conception could be blocked by a sudden fright, by being confronted with someone who has come back from a funeral, or by a donkey who has just given birth. They scared me by offering to take me to healers to have a string sewn through my back or an amulet made. They told me how a second

---

[3] In "Grief and a Headhunter's Rage" (essay 38), published just two years before this essay, Rosaldo argues that how one understands events depends on one's positioning and that interpretations change as one's positioning changes. Although Abu-Lughod noticed that women were pregnant and had babies, it was not until she became pregnant that these events took on new significance for her. In Rosaldo's terminology, as Abu-Lughod's position changed her Egyptian friends' pregnancies became events with "force." McGee had a similar experience. It was not until McGee's wife, pregnant with their first child, went with him into the field that he thought to ask Lacandon Maya women about pregnancy and childbirth. Like Abu-Lughod he discovered that most women had lost babies or their own daughters in childbirth (McGee 2002:67–70).

Preeclampsia is a condition that occurs in 5 percent to 8 percent of pregnancies. It is characterized by high blood pressure and the presence of protein in the urine. It can be fatal to both mother and child.

[4] In this paragraph Abu-Lughod mentions Narayan's comment on anthropologists leading a "hybrid" life. In

other words, Abu-Lughod's viewpoint was created by the intersection of her multiple identities as a woman, anthropologist, wife, mother, her Palestinian background (Abu-Lughod is the daughter of the sociologist Janet Lippman and the political scientist Ibrahim Abu-Lughod), as well as years she spent as a child in Egypt. Through the course of the article she shows us some of these identities in the accounts she gives, as an anthropologist, a patient in an IVF clinic, Kareema's friend and confidant, and a mother.

[5] One of the many insights that postmodern anthropologists have contributed to cultural anthropology is a concern with generalization that Abu-Lughod has already mentioned. In part, avoiding generalizations may help anthropologists to avoid making claims that are beyond their knowledge. Note Abu-Lughod's wording in this paragraph. She is not making a claim to describe the behavior of all Bedouin women, rather she claims to present information from only "the Bedouin women I knew . . ."

fright could undo a blockage, or how bathing on successive Fridays with water in which a gold necklace had been soaked might counteract a different kind of blockage.

I eagerly scribbled all this in my notebooks; mostly it was material for my book on Bedouin women's stories. I wondered, occasionally, how these notions about flows and blockages fit with our medical narratives about hormones, eggs, sperm, and fallopian tubes. I had long been skeptical of images of how our bodies worked that relied on biological entities whose existence I had to take on faith. Emily Martin's analysis of the mechanical metaphors and bizarre implications of these scientific stories about women's bodies had confirmed my own ambivalence.[c,6]

Later, when I was back in Egypt in 1990 with my husband, I felt it was time to get pregnant. I did not yet know there was a serious problem, but other friends were generous with remedies for infertility. After appointments with the quiet and serious doctor at the Cairo Motherhood Center—where the equipment was sterilized, the sheets clean and white, the ultrasound machine shiny, and the receipts computer generated—I would fly south to the palm-draped village in Upper Egypt where my husband and I were then doing research. My new friend Zaynab, mother of five children conceived on annual visits of her migrant husband, took time from her busy schedule of working her small fields, collecting fodder for her animals, and pressing land claims against her paternal relatives to try to help me.

Zaynab knew of three treatments. First she took me to the ruins of the Pharaonic temple that dominated the small hamlet in which her mud-brick house stood. Calling out to the local guard that we were just going to the well, she saw to it that he waved us on, ignoring the fact that we had no entrance tickets. She took me around the temple and then down some steep steps to a pool of stagnant water. "It is good to bathe with this water," she said. Anticipating my modesty, she had brought with her an empty tin container. "You can do it back at the hotel," she explained as she filled the can with the water.

When we came out of the cool, dark shaft she steered me away from the entrance to the temple. "You have to leave by a different path from the one you used to enter," she said. Later, another old village woman told my husband that Zaynab should have had another woman there, hiding above the shaft, to drop a stone into the water just when I was looking in. This would have frightened me. Although they lived hundreds of miles from the Bedouin and shared little of their way of life, these village women seemed to be working with the same theory of blocking: a second fright undoes the effect of a first, and leaving by a different route literally opens up, or unblocks, a path to conception and birth.[d]

The next time I came to the village, still not pregnant, Zaynab decided to take me to the Coptic monastery nearby. "It's good," this Muslim woman explained, "to look at those Christian priests with their beards." When we had been admitted by a gentle nun, Zaynab whispered in the hush of the monastery, "Just look at the beautiful things, the velvet curtains, the pictures. The older things are, the better."

---

[6] Note in this paragraph that Abu-Lughod treats scientific medicine and the folktales of Egyptian infertility equally. She mentions Emily Martin's book *The Woman in the Body: A Cultural Analysis of Reproduction* (1987), in which Martin examines some American women's views of the medical science model of pregnancy and reproduction. As is shown more fully below, postmodernists frequently treat scientific models as the folktales of capitalist and technological society, granting them no more or less credibility than other folktales. The implication of Abu-Lughod's discussion is that rural Egyptian women have one truth, doctors in the IVF clinic another. Some postmodernists claim that because all ethnographic descriptions are the creation of the writer, one truth is as valid as another, and they point out that what is defined as true and who gets to impose that view is an issue of power. However, some issues lend themselves to empirical verification. Although Abu-Lughod may be skeptical of the images and mechanical metaphors by which Western physicians describe how our bodies work, the fact is, in purely practical terms, one form of therapy provided her with amulets and scraps of cloth, the other with twins. Abu-Lughod appears to acknowledge this point later in the essay when she says it is dangerous for feminists to reject science and technology and says, "So what if for two days a petri dish served as my fallopian tubes?"

Next we went to the monastery's cemetery. Zaynab kept calling out for someone. She seemed agitated and finally hailed a young boy who was riding by on his donkey. "Where is your father?" she asked. "Go get him. Tell them there's a woman here who wants him." Eventually a burly man with a huge grey mustache appeared. He was the undertaker. He led me around the cemetery, explaining so much that I couldn't tell if this was a guided tour meant for a tourist or something special to induce pregnancy.

I realized that he knew why I was there when he took me to a cloth-draped coffin, its cover half on, empty inside. He instructed me to take off my shoes and step back and forth over the casket seven times, using my right foot first each time. Later he took me down to some dusty vaults. Reaching inside, he tore a strip of green cloth off the top of another unused coffin. Zaynab had gone off. "Wrap it under your breasts and bathe three times with it," he said conspiratorially. "But don't tell the woman you're with about this."

Then he told me to climb into the vault. I started in but jumped back in fear as a lizard darted out. Scolding me for being afraid when he was there, he then instructed me to tear another strip of cloth from the cover of the empty coffin in the far corner. He wadded this up and told me to stuff it inside me when I had sex with my husband.

Just then Zaynab returned and reminded him that it was important for me to see the well. So we all walked on. With a key he opened a small structure housing a very old brick well. He told me to look down until I could see my own eye. It was a long way down and there was very little water at the bottom. He explained that the monastery had an electric pump for irrigation and that tanks of water were brought in from the pipeline for drinking. Zaynab and I finally left, she apologetically giving him a small sum (all I had brought with me), he saying he hoped God would grant me what I wanted.

A few weeks later Zaynab decided, with some encouragement from me, that she should take me to visit the local Muslim woman curer. This was an old woman who had married and had five children, spent years in Cairo, and returned to her father's village when her husband died. Her father, himself a religious figure with powers of healing, had appointed her his successor, and she was now famous throughout the area. It was rumored that people came from as far away as Kuwait to seek her help. I had heard about her and was curious.

We waited until the heat of the day had passed and then set off to her hamlet. In her courtyard we saw other women leaving. The healer herself sat in a dark room, a small and wrinkled blind woman with her knees drawn up and her feet tucked neatly under her black dress. Women with children in their laps sat waiting their turn to speak to her. After listening to them, she would talk quickly in a kind of rhyme while deftly winding green thread into small objects they were to take with them. When our turn came, Zaynab first discussed her land dispute. Then she explained my problem and answered questions for me. The old curer prescribed a concoction that my husband was to drink. Zaynab and I pressed some money into her hand and then walked home.

In the end the recipe was too complicated. I didn't know where to get many of the ingredients. I didn't even know what these spices and powders were. Their Arabic names meant nothing to me. And though surely I could have arranged to put the bowl of liquid out on the balcony to catch the starlight, as instructed, where would we get the glowing rod to douse in it, in our Cairo apartment?

The problem, of course, was that my husband and I didn't believe it would work. I had half-heartedly bathed with the water from the Pharaonic temple, wary enough of the dead insects floating in it not to splash sensitive parts of my body—the very parts that were supposed to receive this healing treatment. I had also dutifully stepped over the coffins in the Christian cemetery, feeling silly and hypocritical, but I never wrapped the cloth strips around my chest or stuffed them inside me. Oddly, though, I still have the strips of cloth in my dresser drawer, somehow unable to bring myself to simply throw them away. I also don't quite know what to do with an old amulet I acquired from my Bedouin friends. I had wanted to see what was inside and had even photographed the contents. But then I could not help being awed by people's insistence that amulets were powerful and should never touch the ground or be thrown away. In matters mysterious, like religion and reproduction, one finds oneself uncertain enough about the truth to be half willing to "go native."[7]

INSIDE AND OUTSIDE THE BODY

When I returned home after a year in Egypt, I entered that new world that has become familiar to so many women of my generation and class in the U.S.—the world of laparoscopies, tubal adhesions, endometriosis, amniocentesis, and other such unpronounceables; the world of busy doctors in white coats who inspect and prod and shine lights at parts of you that you cannot see; the world of procedures that, they inform you absentmindedly, might cause slight cramping. I finally was allowed to graduate into the world of IVF, as in vitro fertilization is known. I joined well-dressed women with bags under their eyes who spent the early morning hours waiting their turn to have blood drawn from bruised veins and to lie back in darkened rooms with their legs in stirrups so their ovaries could be scanned on grainy black-and-white screens.

It was a world of sitting by the phone, waiting for your daily instructions. Of injections that quickly cured you of any squeamishness about large hypodermic needles. Sometimes, as you expertly drew from the small vials the correct dosages of Pergonal or Metrodin, or later, progesterone in a viscous base of sesame oil, you wondered if someone watching outside the apartment window might take you for a drug addict. This was, after all, New York.

"Our goal is to make you pregnant," the doctor had explained in our first visit. "Our success rates are the highest in the city. We average about thirty-three percent per three-month cycle." This kind of talk leads to a world of uneasy comparison. You look around the waiting room and wonder who will make the statistics. The woman next to you tells you she has fifteen eggs; yesterday you'd been told that you had five but that one was bigger than the others. "What does that mean?" you ask the busy doctor. "We'll see how they come along. If the others don't catch up, we'll have to cancel the cycle." You beg those little ones to grow.

Another woman tells you that this is her third try; last time she had to be hospitalized for ovarian enlargement. The next day someone tells you about her friend who had so many eggs she froze some. She became pregnant and had twins. Then her husband was killed in a car accident. Now she wants to thaw her other eggs and have another child by him. A tough young woman in blue jeans cheerfully jokes with the nurses as they take her blood. She's been coming for a year. You listen in dismay as another recounts how she got pregnant after four tries and then lost her triplets. She and her husband couldn't stand the strain, so they took a break for two years. You also look around at some of the women and think they're just too old.

All these women are surely bringing down the percentages. You think, with some secret pleasure, that this means your own odds as a first-timer are that much better. You keep talking to your friend and colleague, the one who told you about this clinic and who became pregnant on the first try. She barely seems to remember the anger and frustration you feel, or the uncertainty. She encourages you and tells you what will happen next. You compare notes about the waiting-room experience and tell her what an interesting anthropological study it would make, if only you didn't feel so much hostility to the money-making production line the clinic creates that all you

---

[7] In this essay Abu-Lughod describes herself as a "hybrid," with one foot in the Arab world and another in the West. She writes about how she undergoes the folk remedies of her Egyptian friends to get pregnant and then describes some of her experiences undergoing IVF procedures in New York City. She writes, "In matters mysterious, like religion and reproduction, one finds oneself uncertain enough about the truth to be half willing to 'go native.'" What crosses our minds when we read the last few pages of Abu-Lughod's essay is how Boasian it is. It is a classic telling of folklore much like Paul Radin's articles in the 1920s on Ojibwa folklore, but more personal.

want to do is escape—as soon as you no longer need their services so helplessly.

Retrieval is the clinical term for the procedure of removing your ripe eggs from the ovary to be fertilized outside your body. You go to the hospital for this, feeling perfectly healthy and afraid that when you wake up you won't be anymore. After being kept waiting, as usual, you are walked in your oversized nonskid slippers down corridors, into elevators, and then into an operating room. The room looks familiar from the slide show the nurse gave a few weeks earlier, and you feel less resentful at that two hours wasted in a session of elementary talk about IVF. (The session protects the IVF program by covering in simple language the complex material contained in the pile of consent forms you must sign.) The lights in the room are bright. It's a little cold. An intravenous feeder is put in your wrist, and the nurses talk to you reassuringly. You disappear. You wake up in the recovery room, people groaning all around you, some quite frightening with tubes in their noses. You want to get away but are too groggy to move.

As we were leaving the hospital, my husband and I bumped into one of the doctors. She asked how it had gone. I said no one had told us. Surprised, she went off to telephone the lab. She gave us the first good news: they had retrieved six eggs. She insisted that someone must have come to tell me in the recovery room but I had forgotten. I didn't believe her.

Then we waited for the telephone call our typed instructions said would come as soon as they knew the results. Five eggs had fertilized. One more success. As Sarah Franklin, one of the few feminist anthropologists to study IVF, has noted, the cultural narrative of conception has been rewritten by the infertility specialists so that conception is no longer the natural result of intercourse but a scientific and technological achievement. The road to pregnancy is a complex obstacle course in which hurdles are overcome, one by one.[e,8]

The next step was what they call "the transfer"—from dish to womb. Back at the hospital, I sat on a simple wooden bench with the same women who had been in the surgical waiting room on the day of the retrieval. Everyone was a little nervous, but cheerful. This part wasn't supposed to hurt. To pass the time we chatted. One of the women asked if I remembered the blonde woman who had been there with us three days earlier. Yes. "Well," she whispered, "her husband was in there for an hour and a half and couldn't do it. So they had to rush me ahead of her in line for the retrieval." We giggled in a mixture of relief that our husbands had performed efficiently and embarrassment at the others' humiliation.

Finally, my turn. I entered the familiar operating room and climbed onto the table. The doctor was joking with the embryologist in the adjoining room. It had been a long day. Suddenly I saw something come into focus on the elevated television screen to my right. My name was typed on the screen, and there were my four fertilized eggs. The fifth, the doctor explained, had disintegrated. An assistant printed out the image on two polaroid snapshots, a general view and a close-up. I had imagined test-tube babies as little fetuses in jars, but these were just cells, clusters of overlapping circles sitting in a petri dish, like illustrations from a biology textbook.

The transfer only took a minute, with some joking about not dropping the catheter as the embryologist rushed from the lab to the table. I was moved onto a trolley and wheeled out, like the women who went before me, clutching my Polaroids.

Abandoned together in a small, otherwise empty ward, we made conversation. One woman's companion helped us exchange our "baby pictures," all we might get for the $8,000 we had had

---

[8] Comparing the descriptions of the IVF procedures with the treatments she received from her Egyptian friends it is clear that Abu-Lughod found the IVF procedures unpleasant. In this paragraph she cites Sarah Franklin's work on IVF, in which Franklin concludes that "the cultural narrative of conception has been rewritten by the infertility specialists so that conception is no longer the natural result of intercourse but a scientific and technological achievement." If all truths are positioned truths, then the truths of physicians who are fertility specialists are naturally influenced by their position as doctors, just as the truths of Bedouin women are affected by their positions as women in Egypt.

to pay up front (I was counting the days until my insurance company would reimburse me; most of the women had no insurance coverage for IVF). The doctor had told us we could leave after fifteen minutes, but we all insisted on staying for forty-five—superstitious that if we stood up our precious embryos might slide out. One by one, we gingerly climbed out of bed and dressed. I took a taxi home, not wanting to risk the subway.

The month during which I underwent IVF was also the month in which the copyedited manuscript of my book on Bedouin women's stories arrived in the mail.[f] I read over the chapter called "Reproduction," written before I'd entered that strange world of reproductive technology. I could have longed for the more natural character of these women's experiences of becoming pregnant and having babies. I could have viewed pregnancy as an alienation of my body by the medical establishment. But I thought of Donna Haraway, the feminist historian of science, who keeps insisting that it is dangerous for feminists, nostalgic for an organic wholeness, to condemn and reject science and technology. Such associations of the natural with the feminine have been essential to women's confinements to the body and the home; and such rejections of science leave it in the hands of others who may not have women's interests at heart.[g] In the late twentieth century the boundaries between inside and outside our bodies are more fluid. Are glasses to be rejected because they are not our natural eyes? So what if for two days a petri dish served as my fallopian tubes?[9]

Still, I refused to believe the nurse who telephoned twelve days later to say my blood test was positive. I thought the IVF staff would fudge the results so they could publish articles in the medical journals and claim to be the best clinic in the city. Then they'd accuse you, the incompetent female body, of having lost the baby. I didn't believe I was pregnant until two weeks later, when I saw, on that familiar black-and-white television screen, the image of those tiny sacs, each with a twinkling star in it. Fetal heartbeats. Multiple gestation, as they call it in the business.[10]

Kareema, on the other hand, knew the other signs of pregnancy. Her period stopped. She began to feel sick. She threw up. She felt fatigued. She couldn't bear to smoke. Some women have cravings; others have aversions to certain foods. Some Bedouin women claim to have aversions to their husbands.

My menstrual cycle had been suppressed by drugs, and it was too early for the other signs. I was dependent on the ultrasound scanner for my knowledge of pregnancy. I recalled Rosalind Petchesky's classic work on fetal imaging and the politics of reproduction. Rather than condemning, along with other feminists, the panoptic gaze the ultrasound technologies afford the male medical establishment or even the disembodiment of the fetus from the mother, demoted to a mere environment for this rights-bearing entity, she drew attention to the possibility that women might experience this technology positively. "How different women," she wrote, "see fetal images depends on the context of the looking and the relationship of the viewer to the image and what it signifies."[h] I couldn't help finding it reassuring to see on the screen to my right what was supposed to be inside

---

[9] Here we reach the passage mentioned in note 6 above. However, consider carefully what Abu-Lughod is saying. Is she saying that it is dangerous for women to reject science because, in so doing, they reject an accurate method of understanding and interacting with the physical empirical world? Or, alternatively, is she saying that it is dangerous for women to reject science because in so doing they confirm their position on the nature side of the nature/culture dichotomy (see Ortner's discussion in essay 26) and leave a powerful discourse "in the hands of others who may not have women's interests at heart" (men, of course).

This might be a false dichotomy. Perhaps she is making both points at once.

[10] How is the reader to understand this paragraph? Is it comic relief, or is Abu-Lughod so deeply suspicious of medicine and capitalism that her first response to good news is to assume that she is simply being manipulated for the benefit of the clinic? Although it is certainly conceivable that a clinic could do that, it is a bit surprising that a patient who came to a clinic by choice would react to good news by first assuming it was not only incorrect but guided by immoral purposes as well.

me. I was so unsure of my babies that I worried about their having disappeared if I didn't see them every two weeks or so.[11]

COMMUNITIES OF WOMEN

Now, months later, when I have heartburn and the amazement of feeling the babies move in a part of me that had never even existed before, I feel closer to Kareema. The belly I rub with almond oil and look down at is here, not on the screen. It looks the way Kareema's did. My pregnancy book had told me I'd first feel the babies' movements as butterflies or fish swimming around, but the book was wrong. It was a definite thumping—like a heartbeat in the wrong place. I wondered what else the book might be wrong about and instead tried to remember every detail of what the Bedouin women had said and done. How would I cope when the babies came? I tried to remember how these women had managed. How had they breastfed? It had all seemed so natural and easy. How had they coped at night? I don't remember Kareema's babies crying. I realized I hadn't paid much attention to things that now mattered enormously to me. I also understood now that Kareema had probably been feeling that same thumping inside her as she kindly told me folktales to record for my book.

When you are pregnant for the first time, you suddenly see other women you know in a different light. My mother began to tell stories about her pregnancies, and I loved seeing her soften as she reminisced about how exquisite it was to hold an infant. My mother-in-law seemed remarkable for having had seven children. I asked my sister about her experience of giving birth alone in India. She said she had never read a book on the subject and had no idea what was going on. My friends with children began to seem more important. I felt I was crossing a threshold I hadn't noticed before.

This experience of recognizing a commonality among women led me to think back to an article I had begun writing five years earlier about the possibilities for feminist ethnography.[i] I had argued that women ethnographers who studied women unsettled the central divide between Self and Other on which anthropology usually rested. This was not because of any essential, cross-cultural sameness of women but because feminist anthropologists had to recognize that womanhood was only a partial identity. In the abstract language of academic life I wrote, "By working with the assumption of difference in sameness, of a self that participates in multiple identifications, and an other that is also partially the self, we might be moving beyond the impasse of the fixed self/other or subject/object divide."[j] I also noted, however, that there was often a perceived kinship, albeit limited, between women anthropologists and their women subjects that made seeking knowledge of their situations more of a political project that had implications for "home." The kinship Zaynab and other women in Egypt felt for me was apparent in their sisterly concerns about my childless state and their efforts to help me. My feelings for them had led me both to friendships there and to explorations in my anthropological work back home about ways to represent them that might make the complexity of their lives and individual personalities— forms of complexity we recognize in the Self, not the Other—more apparent.[12]

[11] *Panoptic* means "all-encompassing." When Abu-Lughod refers to the "panoptic gaze" the ultrasound technology provided the medical professionals caring for her, she means that her fetuses were completely revealed inside her.

[12] This essay, published in 1995, is in many ways the companion of an essay Abu-Lughod wrote in 1991, called "Writing Against Culture." In the earlier essay Abu-Lughod writes at length about the divide between self and other, or between writers and their subjects, on which ethnography rests. She says anthropology's avowed goal may be "the study of man [sic]," but it is a discipline built on the historically constructed divide between the West and the non-West. It has been and continues to be primarily the study of the non-Western other by the Western self, ". . . And the relationship between the West and the non-West, at least since the birth of anthropology, has been constituted by Western domination." One of the remedies Abu-Lughod suggests to combat this process of "othering" is to write ethnographies of the particular—exactly what she has done in the essay.

What I did not explore then was another process that could occur: that one's own constructions of personal experience would be shaped by knowledge of these women's lives and even by particular women one had come to know.[k] In being pregnant, I was finding that the cultural resources I had at my disposal to think about what I was experiencing and to fill in gaps in my knowledge of an uncertain terrain included both those from "home" and those from "the field," often juxtaposed. From "home" I had my own family background, the biomedical discourse with which so many white middle-class women feel comfortable, feminist critiques of this same discourse as well as of the popular cultural representations in media and books, and a patchy familiarity with women who had given birth.[l] From Kareema and the other women I knew in Egypt I had notebooks full of beliefs about reproduction, stories about reproduction, and, most important of all, years' worth of vivid memories of an everyday world rich in pregnancies, births, and children. I now thought and felt with all these resources.[13]

As I begin to gain confidence that the pregnancy really will last, I have started to worry about the birth. I sometimes skip ahead to the later chapters of my pregnancy books and frighten myself with those glossy photographs that seem to have nothing to do with the reassuring text about positions, helpers, and water births. I look at my husband and wonder about my new dependency—will he mop my brow as they show husbands doing in the photographs, will he comfort me, will he find the birth disgusting, will he help me? When I dare look beyond the birth, I am excited. My husband, always more optimistic than I am, reminds me that this is a new adventure for us. When he compliments me for being so brave I swell with pride.

Yet when I think ahead to the days and weeks just after the birth, I envy Kareema. Like most professional women I have good friends, but they don't live nearby. My family too is scattered. My sister, whom I saw every day for more than a month because she gave me my injections, won't be around. I look forward to the new intimacy with my husband, and I'm counting on him; but I've been warned about the strains. As an academic I think of books as companions, but will they really give me the advice I need? So much is unknown: I don't know how long I'll be in the hospital; whether I'll have a caesarian section; who will deliver me; whether the babies will be in incubators.

When Kareema gave birth, as usual the women in her community dropped everything to come help. She had her baby in the room she likes best for this—a warm room away from the rest of the house. Her cousin and her best friend, women she has known nearly all her life, were there to hold her. Along with some other women and all her children, they stayed with her for a week, busily cooking, doing her laundry for her, and talking. They had all been through this experience. They knew she would be there when it was their turn. They joked and gossiped and told stories late into the night. They made her soothing teas. No men came near, and few demands were made on them. It was a sort of holiday. Kareema's only responsibility was to rest, to nurse and change her new infant, and to receive her women visitors, who came bringing chickens, eggs, bars of soap, and little hand-sewn dresses.

At my wedding four years ago, I missed my Bedouin friends. To bring them in, I recited some songs they would have sung to celebrate my wedding had they been there. It will be harder to find a substitute for the busy companionship they provide to the mother of a newborn. They say a new mother should not be left alone. I expect I will be, from time to time. They say she is vulnerable. We call it postpartum depression. Perhaps I'll wear my Bedouin silver bracelet.

---

[13] Many anthropologists have discovered that lessons they learned in the field can have unexpected applications at home. Although Abu-Lughod makes the point more eloquently, what she describes in this paragraph is what introductory cultural anthropology textbooks call the *process of becoming bicultural*.

They say it is good for a new mother to wear silver; it protects her.[14]

NOTES

I am grateful to the women like Kareema and Zaynab in Egypt who taught me about infertility, among other things. A fellowship from the National Endowment for the Humanities through the American Research Center in Egypt enabled me to come to know Zaynab in 1990. Since 1978 I have had generous support for my research among the Awlad 'Ali Bedouin; my most recent extended stay with Kareema and her family was made possible by a Fulbright award. Ruth Behar's insightful suggestions made the essay richer.

[a] All the names used in this essay are pseudonyms.

[b] In a sensitive and sensible rethinking of the misnomer of "native" or "indigenous" anthropologist, Kirin Narayan has drawn attention to the complex and shifting identifications all anthropologists have and has proposed hybridity as a more appropriate characterization of anthropologists' identities. She has also suggested that their texts should embody the enactment of that hybridity. See Kirin Narayan, "How Native Is a 'Native' Anthropologist?" *American Anthropologist* 95 (1993): 671–86.

[c] Emily Martin, *The Woman in the Body: A Cultural Analysis of Reproduction* (Boston: Beacon Press, 1987).

[d] For more on Awlad 'Ali theories of infertility, see Lila Abu-Lughod, *Writing Women's Worlds: Bedouin Stories* (Berkeley: University of California Press, 1993), chap. 3. See also Marcia Inhorn, *Quest for Conception: Gender, Infertility, and Egyptian Medical Traditions* (Philadelphia: University of Pennsylvania Press, 1994), especially its rich descriptions of Egyptian infertility treatments.

[e] Sarah Franklin, "Making Sense of Missed Conceptions: Anthropological Perspectives on Unexplained Infertility," in *Changing Human Reproduction*, ed. Meg Stacey (London: Sage Publications, 1992), 75–91; and "Postmodern Procreation: A Cultural Account of Assisted Reproduction," in *Conceiving the New World Order: The Global Politics of Reproduction*, ed. Faye D. Ginsburg and Rayna Rapp (Berkeley: University of California Press, 1995), 323–45.

[f] Abu-Lughod, *Writing Women's Worlds*.

[g] Among the articles in which Donna Haraway makes this sort of argument, "A Cyborg Manifesto," in her *Simians, Cyborgs, and Women* (New York: Routledge, 1991), 149–81, is probably the most powerful.

[h] Rosalind Pollack Petchesky, "Fetal Images: The Power of Visual Culture in the Politics of Reproduction," *Feminist Studies* 13, no. 2 (Summer 1987): 280.

[i] Lila Abu-Lughod, "Can There Be a Feminist Ethnography?" *Women and Performance* 5, no. 1 (1990): 7–27.

[j] Ibid., 25.

[k] It is difficult for anthropologists to reflect on the ways their sense of self or their experience of life events might have been shaped by the people and ideas encountered in the field. It can be done, however, as exemplified by Dorinne Kondo, "Dissolution and Reconstitution of Self: Implications for Anthropological Epistemology," *Cultural Anthropology* I (1986): 74–88; Renato Rosaldo, "Introduction: Grief and a Headhunter's Rage," in his *Culture and Truth* (Boston: Beacon Press, 1989), 1–21; and Paul Riesman, *Freedom in Fulani Life: An Introspective Ethnography* (Chicago: University of Chicago Press, 1977).

[l] This greater acceptance by middle-class women of the biomedical discourse on reproduction is documented by Martin, *Woman in the Body*, and by Rayna Rapp, "Constructing Amniocentesis: Maternal and Medical Discourses," in *Uncertain Terms: Negotiating Gender in American Culture*, ed. Faye Ginsburg and Anna Lowenhaupt Tsing (Boston: Beacon Press, 1990), 28–42.

---

[14] You have now completed Abu-Lughod's story about pregnancy. Her topic is interesting, her writing style engaging, but stop for a moment and reflect on what you have learned by reading the essay. Do you come away better informed about Egyptian women's ideas on pregnancy and childbirth or in vitro fertilization? The purpose of the essay is for Abu-Lughod to discuss her feelings and experiences, not tell us about Egyptian women (though Abu-Lughod certainly does this in other publications). For many postmodernists ethnography is not really a descriptive or analytical account of life in another culture, it is a narrative created by the author, little different from a novel. This essay was printed in a volume called *Women Writing Culture*, but Abu-Lughod is telling us much more about herself than about Bedouin culture. One implication of a strong postmodern position is that anthropologists cannot tell us about another culture. They can only tell us about their own experiences.

40. *Moral Models in Anthropology*

Roy D'Andrade (b. 1931)

For over a decade there have been concerted attacks in anthropology on objectivity (Rosaldo 1989), science (Scheper-Hughes 1991), the notion of truth (Tyler 1986), making generalizations of any kind (Abu-Lughod 1991), doing ethnography (Dwyer 1982), and anthropology itself as a type of Western colonialism (Asad 1973). These attacks come not from some fringe group but from well-known and established anthropologists. Why should so many anthropologists attack the very foundations of their discipline? Originally, I thought these attacks came from people who had the same agenda I did, just different assumptions about how to accomplish that agenda. I now realize that an entirely different agenda is being proposed—that anthropology be transformed from a discipline based upon an *objective* model of the world to a discipline based upon a *moral* model of the world.

By a "model" I mean a set of cognitive elements used to understand and reason about something. The term "moral" is used here to refer to the primary *purpose* of this model, which is to identify what is *good* and what is *bad* and to allocate *reward* and *punishment*. In the usual language of philosophy, goodness and badness, like beauty and taste, are considered subjective, not objective things; the beauty of a human baby may not be beauty to an ostrich and the badness of killing one's lover may not be badness to a praying mantis. An objective description tells about the thing described, not about the agent doing the description, while a subjective description tells how the agent doing the description *reacts* to the object. "He is a good guy" is a subjective description of someone; "He helps his friends" would be a more objective description of the same person.

The distinction between object and subject is one of the basic human cognitive accomplishments. Normal people are expected to be able to recognize the difference between their response to an object and the object itself. Despite the cognitive salience of the objective/subjective distinction, in ordinary talk the two are often blended. To say someone is a "crook" is to refer to more than the objective fact that something was intentionally taken by someone who had no legal right to it; part of the meaning of "crook" is that the person who did this did something *bad* and is a *bad person*. Many of the terms of natural language blend the way the world is and our reaction to it, perhaps because in this way we can tell others how we want them to respond also ("respond as *I* do"). Although it may be impossible to present an entirely objective account, when we want to understand something outside ourselves we use terms that, so far as possible, tell about *that thing* so we can understand *that thing*, rather than our *response* to that thing. One tries to be objective if one wants to tell others about the *object*, not about oneself.[1]

It should be noted that an objective account is not necessarily value-free. For example, the

(1995)

[1] D'Andrade opens his essay with a seemingly common-sensical account of the difference between objectivity and subjectivity. But common sense is not so common, and there may be no such thing as sense. Much of the postmodern anthropology of the 1980s and 1990s has been aimed at dissolving the distinction between the objective and subjective. Postmodernists typically claim that because observations can never exist independently of the observer, all observations are necessarily subjective. Thus, the claim of Western physical and social scientists that they produce objective observations is inaccurate. It reflects the privileged position of science rather than anything "real" about the world. To a postmodernist, D'Andrade's claim that objective science exists seems anachronistic, possibly even quaint.

statement "X cures cancer" is not free of positive value for most people. Nor are objective accounts necessarily unbiased. One well-known way of producing a biased account is to report only those facts which reflect badly on something. As used here, *objectivity* refers just to the degree to which an account gives information about the object being described. Finally, it should be noted that trying to be objective does not preclude investigating other people's subjective worlds. One can be as objective about what people think as one can be about the crops they grow.[2]

One result of the attempt to be objective—to talk about the thing, not oneself—is that it is more likely that what one says can be tested to see if it is true or false. And because it is more likely that an objective account can be tested, an objective account can be attempted again by someone else and the replicability of the account assessed. For knowledge to accumulate, accounts must be objective, but they must also be testable and replicable. What Pons and Fleischmann said about cold fusion was objective enough, but unfortunately what they described seems to be unreplicable.[3]

In contrast to an objective model, which tries to describe the object, the aim of a moral model is to identify what is good and bad, to allocate praise and blame, and also to explain how things not in themselves good or bad come to be so. Typically, this is done using words that Kenneth Burke (1945) calls "god" terms, words that stand for things that are an *ultimate* good or an *ultimate* evil and which are the source of further good or evil.[4] Thus, in the current moral model in anthropology, *oppression* is an ultimate evil; nothing can make oppression good, and it is assumed that most of the bad things in the world are the result of oppression. The truth of the badness of *oppression* is not an empirical matter. If you lack moral sense, no recounting of the facts can explain it to you. And given the ultimate badness of oppression, anything that creates or maintains oppressions must also be bad. Thus colonialism is bad because it necessarily involves the use of oppression. Power is bad because it is an instrument of oppression. The hegemony of Western culture is bad because it supports and maintains Western colonialist oppression. Silencing and violence are bad because they are typical means of oppression. And so on.[a]

Every moral model must contain at least partially objective terms if it is to apply to things in the world. Thus "oppression" is not totally subjective; like the term "crook," it refers to something objective—the use of power by some individuals

---

[2] D'Andrade defines objectivity as "the degree to which an account gives information about the object being described." By defining objectivity this way, he tries to avoid the postmodern critique that objectivity is impossible to achieve because ethnographic writing reflects the background of the author. D'Andrade claims that an objective account does not have to be value free.

[3] The allusion to Pons and Fleischmann and cold fusion refers to a scientific controversy in 1989–1990. B. Stanley Pons and Martin Fleischmann are two chemists. Pons was at the University of Utah and Fleischmann at the University of Southampton in England. In March 1989 they held a news conference and announced that they had successfully initiated a cold fusion nuclear reaction in a tabletop device they had constructed for a few thousand dollars. Their announcement triggered a frenzy of activity. Scientists in physics labs all over the world rushed to replicate Pons and Fleischmann's experiment. The two were called to Washington to make a presentation before members of the House Committee on Science, Space, and Technology.

However, when all attempts to replicate their work failed or were inconclusive, the accuracy of Pons and Fleischmann's work was challenged and their professional reputations called into question. They resigned their university posts and went to work in a privately funded research facility in France.

[4] Kenneth Burke (1897–1993) was a poet, literary theorist, and critic whose major philosophical and critical work was concerned with the nature of knowledge and his view of literature as symbolic action. Burke attempted to integrate scientific and philosophical concepts with his perspectives on literature. This resulted in numerous scholarly publications, including the 1945 volume *A Grammar of Motives* cited here by D'Andrade. Burke had an incredibly diverse career. He worked for the New York Bureau of Social Hygiene, was a music critic for the *Nation,* and held a variety of academic posts at such institutions as the New School for Social Research, University of Chicago, Princeton, Indiana University, and Pennsylvania State University.

or groups to affect other individuals or groups in ways not to their liking. The subjective part of the term "oppression" is the evaluation built into it that defines this use of power as something bad and as something that brings about things that are bad.[5]

In most moral models there is some way to correct evil. In the current moral model in anthropology this is done by unmasking the symbolic hegemony that hides and legitimates oppression. The morally corrective act is *denunciation*. One can also act morally by giving voice to those who resist oppression; this at least identifies the oppression and the oppressors. Nowadays, one can have a moral career in anthropology; having a moral career in anthropology is being known for what one has denounced.[6]

Nancy Scheper-Hughes' "Hungry Bodies, Medicine, and the State: Toward a Critical Psychological Anthropology" (1992*a*) is a good illustration of the use of the current moral model in anthropology.[7] In her paper, Scheper-Hughes explicitly says that she wants to redirect psychological anthropology toward the new model. According to Scheper-Hughes (1992*a*:229):

> The essential insight, derived from European critical theory, is that the given world or the "commonsense reality" may be false, illusory, and oppressive. It is an insight shared with all contemporary critical epistemologies including modern psychoanalysis, feminism and Marxism.

All variants of modern critical theory work at the essential task of stripping away the surface forms of reality in order to expose concealed and buried truths. Their aim, then, is to "speak truth" to power and domination, both in individuals and submerged social groups or classes.

Demystification—"exposing concealed and buried truths"—is thus seen as a necessary remedy for the domination of individuals, groups, and classes. And the "critical theories" which do this are different from "objective" theories.

> [Critical theories] are reflexive rather than objective epistemologies. Critical theories differ radically in their epistemology from positivist theories derived from the natural sciences. All theories in the "natural" sciences presuppose an "objective" structure of reality knowable by minds that are likewise understood as sharing uniform cognitive structure. Critical theories assert the subjectivity of knowable phenomena and propose "reflection" as a valid category and method of discovery.[8]

The problem Scheper-Hughes is addressing here, I think, involves the term "truth." Immediately before, she has said that the goal is to "speak truth to power." But isn't finding out the truth what science—old-fashioned anthropology—does? She claims that "critical theories" do something else—they know in a "subjective" way, not just an "objective" way, by "reflection." Scheper-Hughes is not explicit about how reflection works as a

---

[5] D'Andrade believes that even subjective judgments have an objective foundation that can be exposed to empirical examination. Thus he is able to answer the postmodernist claim that there is no such thing as objectivity.

[6] Although D'Andrade's tone here sounds sarcastic, the call to fight oppression and give a voice to oppressed peoples has long been a goal for many anthropologists. Boas, for example, was an outspoken pacifist and supporter of human rights. More recently, Harvard anthropologist David Maybury-Lewis (b. 1929) founded he organization Cultural Survival in 1972, with the specific goal of campaigning for the rights of indigenous peoples and oppressed ethnic minorities around the world.

[7] D'Andrade's essay is one of a pair of works featured in a 1995 issue of *Current Anthropology* under the title "Objectivity and Militancy: A Debate." Nancy Scheper-Hughes

(b. 1944), who features so prominently in D'Andrade's essay, is the author of the second essay—the "militancy" side of the debate. Scheper-Hughes is currently a professor of anthropology at the University of California–Berkeley. Two of her best known works are *Saints, Scholars, and Schizophrenics: Mental Illness in Rural Ireland* (1979) and *Death Without Weeping: The Violence of Everyday Life in Brazil* (1992).

[8] Critical theory is a broad term generally used to designate neo-Marxist, post-structuralist, and deconstructionist theories. A principal aspect of critical theory is that it is overtly political. Epistemology, which is of central concern to postmodernists, is the investigation of the origin and nature of knowledge. What Scheper-Hughes is saying in this paragraph is that critical theories are reflexive rather than objective ways of knowing.

method of discovery, but she is clear that it is different from "positivism" and "natural science." In her view, "The objectivity of science and of medicine is always a phantom objectivity, a mask that conceals more than it reveals" (p. 229). Thus, positivistic natural science is a *bad* way to find out about the world because it is part of the process of mystification. Objectivity turns out to be a mask for domination. One of the most salient characteristics of the current moral model is exactly this attack on objectivity.

Scheper-Hughes continues (p. 229):

> At the heart of all critical theories and methods is a critique of ideology and power. Ideologies (whether political, economic, or religious) can mystify reality, obscure relations of power and domination, and prevent people from grasping their situation in the world. Specific forms of consciousness may be called ideological when they are invoked to sustain or legitimate particular institutions or social practices. When these institutional arrangements reproduce inequality, domination, and human suffering, the aims of critical theory are broadly emancipatory.

This repeats some of the ideas already presented: reality gets mystified to obscure relations of domination; the goal is to emancipate by revealing the ideologies which mystify such relations (pp. 229–30):

> The process of liberation is complicated, however, by the unreflexive complicity and identification of people with the very ideologies and practices that are their own undoing. Here is where Antonio Gramsci's notion of hegemony is useful. Gramsci . . . recognized that the

dominant classes exercised power both directly and forcefully through the state, and also indirectly by merging with the civil society and identifying their own class-based interests with broad cultural ideas and aims, making them appear indistinguishable from each other.

Here Scheper-Hughes begins to specify how mystification works—by the identification of the interests of the dominant classes with "broad" cultural ideas and aims. The state is the power that acts to create this mystification (p. 230):

> Increasingly in modern bureaucratic states technicians and professionals—laboratory scientists, geneticists, doctors, psychologists, teachers, social workers, sociologists, criminologists and so forth—come to play the role of the "traditional intellectuals" in sustaining "common sense" definitions of reality through their highly specialized and validating forms of discourse. Gramsci anticipated Foucault (see Foucault 1972) in his understanding of the diffuse power circuits in modern states and of the role of "expert" forms of power/knowledge in sustaining the "common sense" order of things.[9]

Scheper-Hughes makes the case that in Northeast Brazil people suffer from a disorder called *nervos* that involves weakness, sleeplessness, heart palpitations, shaking, headache, fainting, etc., and that this disorder "is a primary idiom through which hunger and hunger-anxiety are expressed" (1992*a*:231). For this disorder, minor tranquilizers are considered by the Brazilian medical establishment to be an appropriate treatment. This treatment, according to Scheper-Hughes, by *not* recognizing the problems of hunger that

---

[9] Strongly influenced by the work of Michel Foucault, Scheper-Hughes cites his 1972 text *The Archaeology of Knowledge*. In this work, Foucault argues that all knowledge is conditioned by its historical context. Further, critical symbols and ideas serve the purposes of the powerful, thereby controlling and dominating people's understanding of the world. Foucault's ideas are described more fully in footnote 4 of essay 34.

Antonio Gramsci (1891–1937) was an Italian scholar and politician who founded the Italian Communist party in 1921, then left to spend two years in Russia. When he returned to Italy, he was elected head of the Communist Party and was elected to the Italian parliament. In 1926 his party

was outlawed; Gramsci was then arrested and imprisoned for eleven years. Gramsci's health deteriorated badly while in prison, and he died in a Roman hospital soon after his release. He is best known for the series of letters he wrote from prison, which were published posthumously in 1947 as *Lettere dal carcere* or *Prison Notebooks* (1994). Although a Communist, Gramsci turned away from Marx's emphasis on materialism and focused on the concept of symbolic hegemony. That is to say, the political and intellectual leaders of a society create a system of beliefs and ideas that are accepted by the common people and that help maintain the power of the ruling class. Additional information on Gramsci can be found in essay 42, footnote 11.

underlie *nervos,* deflects the underlying rage against domination and mystifies the source of the problem (p. 230):

> In the context of this discussion, doctors occupy the pivotal role of "traditional" intellectuals whose function is, in part, to fail to see the secret indignation of the hungry poor expressed in their inchoate folk idiom of *"nervos."* But anthropologists, too, often play the role of the "traditional" intellectual in their unconscious collusions with hegemonic interpretations of social reality fostered by powerful local interests.[10]

The specification of the immoral agents moves from the state to bureaucracy technicians to doctors to teachers and social workers and finally to anthropologists. All are in complicity with oppression, although they may not know it. So— "What is to be done?" According to Scheper-Hughes (p. 229),

> As social scientists (and not social revolutionaries) critical practice implies an epistemological struggle in which the contested domain is anthropology itself. The struggle concerns the way knowledge is generated, the class interests that it serves, and the challenge is to make our discipline more relevant and non-oppressive to the people we study. Finally, it is addressed to clinical practitioners as a challenge to reintegrate the social and political dimension in their practice so as to put themselves squarely on the side of human suffering.

The call to action is clear. Anthropology has been part of the process of mystification, serving interests that oppress others. The moral thing to do is to denounce those who maintain this mystification and transform anthropology from an objective natural science, which is just a charade and a means of continuing oppression, into a *critical anthropology* which will help change the world.

It is important to keep in mind that one can also use an objective model for moral purposes, as for example, in investigating the biochemical basis of schizophrenia in order to make possible better medicine for schizophrenics. The separation between moral models and objective models is not based on the motives or biases of the investigator. In most scientific fields which aim to help people, there are both moral and objective models, linked together. For example, in medicine, there is an objective language of physiology and biochemistry that describes what various pathogens do and how the body reacts to them. This biological model describes how things work, not whether viruses or antibodies are good or bad. Linked to this objective model is a less formal model concerning what is healthy, what is safe, what is medically ethical, etc., in which, for example, melanoma is considered a *bad* cancer while warts are usually considered *benign*. This language of health and ethics is carefully kept separate from the objective language of biological processes. One of my colleagues calls this the "separation of church and state." You can have both, but they should be kept separate and distinct.

The separation of moral models and objective models is a crucial issue. It is exactly this separation that is explicitly attacked by anthropology's current moralists. For example, Rabinow[11] (1983:68–70, emphasis added) offers what he calls a "schematization of relations of truth and power" as follows:

> In the first position, that represented by Boas, the role of the anthropologist as a scientist was to speak truth to power. Boas was a profoundly political man: a typical secular, emancipated, German, Jewish liberal with a strong faith in

---

[10] It is hard to read the works of Scheper-Hughes and not be moved by her call to action. As a young woman in the mid-1960s, Scheper-Hughes worked as a Peace Corps volunteer among the urban poor of northeastern Brazil. She later returned to the same area to conduct fieldwork that resulted in a number of publications (1989, 1992). In these she vividly describes the horrible conditions under which children and adults live and die.

[11] Paul Rabinow (b. 1944), like Scheper-Hughes, is a professor in the Department of Anthropology at the University of California–Berkeley. Rabinow was one of the early voices in the postmodern movement in anthropology. In *Reflections on Fieldwork in Morocco* (1977), Rabinow discusses the process of doing fieldwork and the ways in which his position as a young outsider anthropologist affected the people he talked to and the data he collected. The book is widely considered a classic of reflexive ethnography.

the force of reason as a functional tool of political emancipation and as an absolute value in its own right. The calling of the intellectual, for Boas, consisted of the advancement of reason through science and the conquest of tradition, irrationality, and injustice.

The dignity and achievements of Boas and his students are not in question—they were centrally responsible for making antiracism an accepted part of the American academic agenda—but neither are their limits and contradictions. The position of speaking truth to power, opposing humanism to nihilism, is still with us; and it is by no means the worst alternative. But ultimately *this position has not proved sufficiently hardy,* either intellectually or politically, to have spawned a science or politics which lives up to the standards of coherence and efficacy by which these individuals wished to be judged.

In an important sense, the second position, that represented by Geertz, *has no politics at all.* The ascetic imperative of Boas or Weber, who sought to separate truth and politics, still entailed an active vigilance lest these two realms fuse. It never occurred to these European intellectuals that political concerns were not central to the life of an intellectual—they saw them as so central they had to be kept in check. The sacrifice demanded of the scientist was not the loss of political passions but only that they be kept clearly distinct from scientific activities qua science. Over the time of two generations, the tension between these two callings, and hence the potential threat they posed for each other's autonomy, was gradually dissipated. In its place an ethics of scientific comportment became a code of civility. As this code took center stage, the more directly political concerns were weakened.

I am not advocating that we jettison the moral and intellectual achievements of the aggressively antiracist anthropology of Boas, nor that we discard what has been constructed and made to function as a civility which allows

for dispute within a community of shared discourse. The main conclusion I draw from the analysis presented in this paper is that *it is the dogged separation of truth and power in order to construct a science which has had the most deleterious effects on anthropology;* it is the conception of a humanist activity which has unwittingly pushed these anthropologists into a kind of nihilism which is the exact opposite of their intent.

Rabinow is clear that in his opinion the separation of moral models from objective models is a mistake resulting in an anthropology without morality ("politics" is a code word for "morality"). He presumes that anthropology *should* be moral and that the failure of anthropologists to maintain Boas's moral passion condemns the idea of separating moral and objective models; Geertz has failed us because he has no politics.[b]

Rabinow asserts that all anthropologists must have Boas's moral passion. I do not agree. In my moral universe, one can be an anthropologist simply because one is interested in human life and still be a good person. However, whether or not one has politics, or believes that all anthropologists should have politics, I argue that anthropology's claim to moral authority rests on knowing *empirical* truths about the world and that moral models should be kept separate from objective models because moral models are counterproductive in discovering how the world works. This is not an argument that anthropologists should have no politics; it is an argument that they should keep their politics separate from the way they do their science.

Without attempting to meet all attacks, I will first take up some of the most egregious arguments against objectivity.

1. *Objective models are dehumanizing.*

According to Rorty[12] (1983:164), "Foucault is doubtless right that the social sciences have

---

[12] Richard Rorty (b. 1931) is a prominent American philosopher. In his breakthrough work, *Philosophy and the Mirror of Nature* (1979), he promoted a style of thinking he called pragmatism. Rorty argued that philosophy cannot be a science and that the scientific method itself was invalid. Instead, beliefs about the world are supported by appeals to the conventional means through which a culture justifies its beliefs. Such a system of justification does not have any necessary foundation in empirical reality. Apart from specific social and cultural traditions of justification, there can be no general account of what makes a proposition true.

coarsened the moral fiber of our rulers. Something happens to politicians who are exposed to endless tabulations of income levels, rates of recidivism, cost-effectiveness of artillery fire, and the like—something like what happens to concentration camp guards." Here is complete fantasy. No evidence besides a mention of Foucault is cited. Certainly I know of no research that shows that social science research findings have a dehumanizing effect on people. What seem to be operating here are the assumptions of the current moral model; objectivity is part of science, science is used in the domination of others, domination is the inhuman treatment of others, hence objectivity is dehumanizing. All this follows from first principles and need not be proved.[13]

2. *The distinctions between objectivity and subjectivity, fact and language, knowledge and opinion, depend on a realist conception of the world and the correspondence theory of truth. This theory is flawed, and therefore the distinctions which grow out of it are confusing and unnecessary.*

The realist conception of science argues that science "works" because it corresponds in some degree and in some manner to the "way the world really is." That is, science tries to find out the "truth," and "truth" consists of statements that correspond to "reality." It is this correspondence to reality that explains why science is successful at prediction and control. The argument of Rorty (1991) and others, who call themselves "relativists," or "antirealists" or "antirationalists," is that the "correspondence" between statements and the world is not an obvious matter. Various conventions about what counts as evidence are needed in order to decide the truth or falsity of statements; in a mature science these conventions are quite complex. For example, in psychology, the value of experimental evidence depends on a variety of statistical considerations involving reliability, control cases, proportion of the variance accounted for, type 1 and type 2 errors, etc. But where do these conventions come from?

They are conventions agreed upon by a community. Thus truth depends on the consensus of the community, and objectivity reduces to social solidarity (Rorty 1991:22).

This argument has also been put forward by a number of individuals working in the history of science and the sociology of knowledge. Latour (1988), Latour and Woolgar (1979), Shapin and Schaffer (1985), and others have presented specific case histories which they argue show that scientific debate is determined not by the winners' being closer to some abstract truth but by their having more social and cultural power. Philip Kitcher, a philosopher of science who is a vigorous defender of the rationality of science, summarizes the position of the antirationalists, among whom he explicitly includes Feyerabend, Barnes, Bloor, Shapin, Schaffer, Collins and Latour, as follows (1993:198):

[1] The community decision is reached when sufficiently many sufficiently powerful subgroups within the community have arrived at decisions (possibly independent, possibly coordinated) to modify their practices in a particular way.

[2] Scientists are typically moved by nonepistemic as well as epistemic goals.

[3] There is significant cognitive variation within scientific communities, in terms of individual practices, underlying propensities, and exposure to stimuli.

[4] During all phases of scientific debate, the processes undergone by the ultimate victors are no more well designed for promoting cognitive progress than those undergone by the ultimate losers.

[5] Scientific debates are closed when one group musters sufficient power to exclude its rival(s) from the community; the subsequent articulation and development of the successful modification of practice absorb all available resources, so that later comparisons can be made between a highly developed tradition and an underdeveloped rival. . . .

---

[13] D'Andrade refers to arguments from *first principles*. Such an argument starts with a basic, universal, verifiable statement with which everybody can agree and goes on to produce larger truths such as the existence of God, or the scientific method.

Kitcher points out that the first three points are not central to the antirationalist argument; the crucial points are 4 and 5, which deny that, over the long term, correspondence with the "truth," or with "the way the world really is," tips the battle so that scientific knowledge progresses. All five points are empirical generalizations; if they are true it is a matter not of first principles but of fact. Kitcher argues that a more empirically accurate characterization would modify points 4 and 5 as follows:

> [4] During the early phases of scientific debate, the processes undergone by the ultimate victors are (usually) no more well designed for promoting cognitive progress than those undergone by the ultimate losers.
>
> [5] Scientific debates are closed when, as a result of conversations among peers and encounters with nature that are partially produced by early decisions to modify individual practices, there emerges in the community a widely shared argument, encapsulating a process for modifying practice which, when judged by [an external standard] is markedly superior in promoting cognitive progress than other processes undergone by protagonists in the debate: power accrues to the victorious group principally in virtue of the integration of this process into the thinking of members of the community and recognition of its virtues.[14]

There is probably no "knock-down" argument from first principles to demonstrate that the correspondence theory of truth is right (or wrong) or that scientific knowledge has advanced (or not advanced). Whether the correspondence theory of truth is right and whether scientific knowledge has advanced are empirical questions, and I think that the empirical answers are reasonably clear. As Gellner (1992:60–61) has said:

> One particular style of knowledge [scientific knowledge] has proved so overwhelmingly powerful, economically, militarily, administratively, that all societies have had to make their peace with it and adopt it. Some have done it more successfully than others, and some more willing or more quickly than others; but all of them have had to do it, or perish. Some have retained more, and some less, of their previous culture.

That is, the empirical support for the hypothesis that science advances is simply the strong evidence that scientific knowledge about the world *has* advanced. Whether, on balance, scientific knowledge has been used for good or evil is another question. My own unoriginal conclusion is that, on balance, the world is considerably better off because of science. However, those who disagree on this point would, I believe, still have to agree that scientific *knowledge* has advanced. Given the obvious success of science as a way of finding out about the world, it is remarkable that many anthropologists are attracted to philosophers and historians who flirt with the idea that there is no true progress in scientific knowledge and no way of knowing what is true.[c,15]

The antirationalists further argue that there are no independent criteria for explaining the success of science (Rorty 1991). My own opinion is that the success of science is due primarily

---

[14] The difference between D'Andrade's argument and that of the critical theorists is well summed up in the comparison of this version of point 5 with the version above. In the first version, the critical issue is not how well a theory maps reality but whether those who promote the theory have political and economic power. If a theory is promoted by the powerful, it is accepted. In the version of point 5 presented here, it is the degree of explanatory power of a theory that determines its acceptance. If a theory is a powerful device to explain empirical reality, then it will be accepted by members of the scientific community. Both of these positions are extreme, but how you feel about them is probably a good

indication of your own position in the debate between postmodernists and their detractors. If you lean toward the first point 5, you favor postmodern interpretations. If you prefer the second, you will be more comfortable in the empiricist camp.

[15] Although D'Andrade makes a strong case for the advancement of knowledge through science, it is also true that other ways of knowing may be equally valid. If one's goal is to describe the world or the cultural understandings of members of a society, then art, literature, myth, and other modes of interpretation may offer insights as powerful as those generated by science.

both to the norm of presenting generalizations in a form that makes it possible to dispute them with evidence and to the norm of carrying out extensive tests of other people's generalizations. The testability of statements and the constant testing of statements ward off the very strong tendency of humans to believe what they *want* to believe. It is these two norms that give the scientific enterprise its power.[16]

Finally, there is something inconsistent about the statements made by Rorty and others about the badness of the subject/object, language/fact, and knowledge/opinion distinctions. For example, according to Rorty (1991:41, emphasis added);

> On the pragmatist view, the contrast between "relations of ideas" and "matters of fact" is a special case of the bad seventeenth-century contrasts between being "in us" and being "out there," between subject and object, between our beliefs and what those beliefs (moral, scientific, theological, etc.) are trying to get right. . . . [The pragmatist] is suggesting that instead of invoking anything like the idea-fact, or language-fact, or mind-world, or subject-object distinctions to explicate our intuition that *there is something out there to be responsible to*, we just drop the intuition.

Imagine a lazy student in one of Rorty's classes who complains that he only got a D. Professor Rorty says, "That is what you deserve." The student replies, "You are invoking the intuition that there is something out there [my performance, objectively viewed] *to be responsible to.* You should drop that intuition. Subjectively, I *feel* I did quite well, and although I said that I would turn in a paper, the *fact* that I did not simply reinvokes the language/fact distinction, which depends on the flawed correspondence theory of truth." Of course, Rorty would explain that he bases his judgments on the normal consensus about what counts as true (the professor's judg-

ment) rather than some ultimate correspondence of the professor's judgment with reality. What Rorty means by "objectivity" and "truth" is not what the student means; Rorty is talking about ultimate truth and complete objectivity, not ordinary judgments about course performance and broken promises. Rorty does not mean (I think) that in ordinary life the distinctions between object and subject, mind and world, idea and fact, etc., should be dispensed with (that would make an odd world). It is only in certain kinds of philosophic discourse that these distinctions are not to be made. However, in my opinion this speaks badly for such kinds of philosophic discourse.

3. *The idea that people can be objective is illusory; people construct the reality that suits them best. Hence an objective model is impossible, and any pretense that such a model can be achieved is simply hegemonic mystification.*

Scheper-Hughes's statement "The objectivity of science and of medicine is always a phantom objectivity, a mask that conceals more than it reveals" (1992:229) is one example of this position. It should be noted that the meaning of "objective" in these arguments is shifted from "an account which describes the object, not the describer" to "an account given without bias or self-interest." This is a secondary sense of the term; literally, "objective" glosses as "pertaining to the object." The secondary sense of the term "unbiased" is an extension based on the notion that those who have no axe to grind give a more objective account. By shifting from the primary sense to the secondary sense one can make the case that, since people are always biased to some degree, an "objective" account is impossible. Then, since "objectivity" (not having any interests) is impossible, any claim to objectivity must be a "mask," a mystification. However, the accusation

---

[16] Note the shift of style in this paragraph. D'Andrade shies away from making a bold statement about the reasons for the success of science. Instead he offers us his opinion, which may be right or wrong, but in any event is only an opinion. He is wise in doing this, since he is entering an area where there is much disagreement, and he has told us just above that there is no way to argue from first principles to scientific truth. Nonetheless, what he suggests here is far from radical. The notion that the strength of science comes from public attempts to falsify hypotheses comes primarily from the work of Karl Popper and is widely accepted.

depends on the trick of substituting a secondary for a primary meaning. Besides, who ever claimed that scientists are unbiased? A brief acquaintanceship with the history of science would certainly dis-abuse anyone of that notion. Science works not because it produces unbiased accounts but because its accounts are objective enough to be proved or disproved no matter what anyone wants to be true.[17]

While I am objecting to the rhetorical tricks that are used to identify objectivity and science with badness, I should also note that similar tricks are used to identify objectivity and science with goodness. The methods of science and the use of objective accounts are the best way to find out about the world (I would argue), but the method has no *guarantee* of working. Employment of the term "science" as an honorific to give weight to unreplicated and often unsound generalizations, sometimes constructed with considerable bias, is a continuing abuse. One could even argue that there is so much positive mystification around the term "science" that some negative mystification is needed as a balance. Fine, if the result is intellectual balance—the recognition that, on both sides, rhetoric is not evidence and that "fact" is always a probability, not an absolute.[18]

It might be thought that I am claiming that science should be value-free and outside politics. This is not the case. Science is an institutionalized activity—a means, not an end. It can be used for all sorts of ends—to create engines of war, to make new products, to cure physical and mental ills, and even just to discover things. The determination of the ends of scientific activity in the United States has long been a political matter in which Congress and a variety of interest groups, including those who want to do science just for the sake of enlightenment, contend for the money. Science demystified is not intrinsically good or bad.

4. *Objectivity is part of the general hegemony of Western culture, and is authoritarian and oppressive.*

Abu-Lughod (1991:150–51) writes:

Generalization, the characteristic model of operation and style of writing of the social sciences, can no longer be regarded as neutral description. . . . There are two reasons for anthropology to be wary of generalization. The first is that, as part of a professional discourse of "objectivity" and expertise, it is inevitably a language of power. On the one hand, it is the language of those who seem to stand apart from and outside of what they are describing. . . . On the other hand, even if we withhold judgment on how closely the social sciences can be associated with the apparatuses of management, we have to recognize how all professional discourses by nature assert hierarchy.

Here the contagious badness-of-oppression continues to spread like a plague; oppression's badness infects power, power's badness infects objectivity ("standing apart"), and objectivity's badness infects generalizations. Again, the badness is asserted on the basis of first principles, not demonstrated. In opposition to Abu-Lughod, I claim that it is *not* bad to make generalizations about people and that ethnographic generalizations do *not* damage people. *Nor does objectivity. Nor do power*

---

[17] The distinction D'Andrade makes here is important. It is clear that the types of questions scientists ask and the reasons for which they ask them are set by their personal backgrounds, cultures, histories, and desires. Scientific questions are always in this sense subjective, and scientific observers are human and always have axes to grind. However, does that necessarily mean their results are invalid? D'Andrade says observers don't have to be objective in order for observations to be objective.

[18] Here D'Andrade discusses the use of *science* as an honorific. In so doing he is acknowledging that in our society, to designate a field of study as science is to privilege it. When he talks about using the term *science* to support unsound generalizations, he is probably thinking of "creation science," or Erik Von Daniken's theory that archaeological remains can only be explained by extraterrestrial landings, and other such pseudoscientific endeavors. In these cases, the term *science* is clearly used to lend an air of legitimacy to otherwise nonscientific investigations.

D'Andrade calls for intellectual balance—that identifying science with goodness or badness is equally absurd. He says rhetoric is not evidence and "fact" is always probability.

differences. This is another fantasy. What damages people is the way power is *used* and the way generalizations are *used*. And what *helps* people is the way power is *used* and the way generalizations are *used*. It is irrational to hold that power as such is bad. The result is a spreading pollution that makes it bad to say that the Bedouin are polygynous (Abu-Lughod 1991:153).[19]

One effect of the current ban on objectivity is the substitution of stories and narratives for generalizations. Abu-Lughod says, "For these reasons I propose that we experiment with *narrative ethnographies of the particular* in a continuing tradition of fieldwork-based writing" (1991:153, emphasis added). By telling a story about someone, the ethnographer does not have to make any generalizations and thereby appears to avoid the danger of hegemonic discourse. However, the appearance is deceptive; quite the reverse happens in fact. It is a natural assumption of the reader that any narrative is, in some important sense, typical of what happens in that place, unless told otherwise. Kenneth Burke (1945) calls this rhetorical strategy that of the "reductive anecdote"—the world is "summarized by" and "reduces to" the story one tells about it. *Presenting an anecdote is just as essentializing and totalizing as stating a generalization.* Consider, for example, the well-known anecdote about George Washington and the cherry tree: it acts just like the generalization "Washington was honest" but hides the claim. Hence Burke's comment on the rhetorical use of anecdotes: beware of people just telling stories.[20]

It is striking that these attacks on objective models do not present any evidence of the damage done by objectivity. In the same vein, evidence about the good done by science is ignored. A major reason for the unimportance of evidence, I believe, is what is being asserted is not a set of empirical facts but whether one's first allegiance is to morality or to truth. My hypothesis that what is being expressed is allegiance to a set of moral principles explains another rather odd aspect of many of the attacks—their loose adherence to the laws of logic. A number of scholars who have critiqued various postmodernist positions (e.g., Spiro 1986, Bailey 1991, Gellner 1992) have commented on the internal contradictions, principle begging, and appeals to authority found in much of this writing. These objections have not been answered; the usual response I have heard is that they are "beside the point." And, if the point is that relativism is the correct *moral* response to cultural differences, then, indeed, logic and evidence are not relevant.

One might say, "Well, some of these moral concerns may be overdone, but why not use the current moral model? Isn't it a reasonable model of reality as well as a model which shows what is right? Can't one blend together objectivity and morality in a single model?" So far as I know, a mixed model would not violate any principle of logic. However, there are reasonably well-understood problems with trying to graft moral and objective models together if one wants to find out about the world. It may need to be repeated that the argument here is not against

---

[19] D'Andrade's use of Abu-Lughod's work is particularly apt. An important feminist anthropologist and postmodernist, Abu-Lughod has led the field in presenting narrative accounts of women she worked with in her study of Bedouin society. However, it is important to point out that although Abu-Lughod is a radical postmodernist who has pioneered the use of genres such as "auto-ethnography" (she writes extensively about her own pregnancy, for example—see essay 39), she is not quite as radical as D'Andrade portrays her. In the passage he cites here, she does not say that all anthropology should become narrative stories, but that such stories should "complement rather than replace a range of other types of anthropological projects. . . ." She does not say we should completely avoid the use of the term *polygyny* but

rather discuss the ways in which particular individuals "live the 'institution' that we call polygyny."

[20] In this passage, D'Andrade makes an ironic point, turning one of the basic insights of the postmodernists against them. The notion that authors build authority through the conventions and styles of writing is fundamental to deconstructionist theory. D'Andrade notes that postmodern attempts to discuss the particular through narrative stories are doomed because, whether they desire it or not, such stories are bound to be understood as generalizations. He backs his point with a quote from Burke, but it could easily be supported with reference to Derrida or other postmodern philosophers.

anthropologists' having moral models. Indeed, I believe that anthropologists should work to develop more coherent, clearly articulated moral models. These moral models should, I think, describe both the anthropologist's responsibilities and a vision of what the good society and the good culture would look like. The point has often been made that if anthropologists do not try to influence the ends to which the knowledge they produce is used, others will do it for them. But—the point I am arguing—these moral models should be kept separate from the objective models with which we debate what is.

The first problem with blended models is *identification*. To use the current moral model, with its emphasis on the badness of oppression, to understand the world, one must be able to identify when something is or is not oppression. But what makes something oppression? Is taking away the freedom of serial murderers oppression? Most people would say that it is not—that they deserve to have their freedom taken away, and that it is prudent to do so as well. It is not oppression, then, if the people being dominated deserve to be dominated or need to be dominated for the common good. But who is to say who deserves to be dominated? And who is to say what the common good is? Serbs believe that Croats should be dominated for a variety of reasons. Badness and goodness are not simple properties of things but complex interactions between events and human intentions and welfare. It becomes very difficult to define what oppression is except by one's *reaction* to the situation—whenever it seems to be a bad use of power call it "oppression," and whenever it is a good use call it "justice" or something else. This is a central doctrine of subjectivity; what one truly feels is bad is bad. Of course, one can say that this is just quibbling, and that everyone—or almost everyone—can tell a good from a bad use of power. However, because of the complexity of human life we often find ourselves vehemently disagreeing even with people we respect about exactly this. The experience of people trying to find out about how the world works is that you find out more when you avoid the use of evaluative terms—otherwise you spend all your time arguing about the use of these terms, trying to make the bad things get the bad words and the good things get the good words.

A second problem in trying to meld together moral and objective models is that the objective world comes in many shades of grey but the moral world tends toward black and white. Oppression, for example, is not an all-or-none state; it varies in degree. Not every use of power is equally bad. To make a model account for what happens in the world, one usually needs to distinguish *more* from *less*. But morality does not seem to like to do this; each case of oppression must be treated as an equal horror because they are all *wrong*. Sin is sin, and if one sets up a scale of greater and lesser sins one quickly finds out that lesser sins are no longer considered *real* sins. Thus the pragmatics of morality and the pragmatics of finding out about the world pull in different directions.

A third problem is the powerful tendency to believe that good things produce good results and bad things produce bad results: "By their fruits ye shall know them." But the complexities of causality do not respect our human wish for the good to produce good and the bad to produce bad. Furthermore, the pragmatics of morality tend strongly toward a unicausal view of events; for every bad event there is a single bad thing that caused it. This makes assignment of blame much easier. But the world tends to be strongly multicausal. When a fire burns down a building, who is to blame? Why, the man who threw the match in the wastepaper basket. But for a physicist the match would not have lit the material in the wastepaper basket if it had a higher combustion point or if there had been no oxygen in the air or if the building had been made entirely of stone. We *blame* a knowing and intentional agent, but almost always what happens is the result not *just* of a knowing intentional act but a complex web of causes. Use of the notion that "bad causes bad" results in the kind of conclusion that Abu-Lughod reaches about generalizations: power brings about oppression, therefore power is bad. Science gives people power, therefore science is bad. Objectivity is part of science, therefore objectivity is bad. Generalizations are produced by objective science, therefore generalizations are bad. And some would take it further: generalizations are based on fieldwork, therefore fieldwork is, if not bad, at least a situation that places one in very grave moral jeopardy.[21]

A fourth pragmatic problem in trying to meld moral and objective models is that whereas an objective model can—at least sometimes—be changed by new data, new arguments, new theories, moral models are very hard to change. The history of the current moral model is interesting in this regard. So far as I have been able to ascertain, the present moral model was first outlined by Jeremy Bentham, a late-18th-century English philosopher and one of the founders of utilitarianism. Bentham said that those who govern use symbols which serve the interests of the governing class. These symbols are fictions; there is no such thing as the "Crown" or the "Church," for example. Bentham's interest was in revealing the rhetorical fictions and phantoms used to hide what he termed "sinister interests" (Bentham 1952). His goal was explicitly moral: to demystify and thereby denounce these fictions so that there could be clarification of the "common good."[22]

Marx, who read Bentham and commented on his notions of sinister interests and fictions, added Bentham's ideas about mystification to his own model of social conflict and its resolution through socialism. He disclaimed ethical and humanitarian reasons for preferring socialism. For him it was historically determined that socialism would overthrow capitalism. The important causal machinery in Marx's model concerns class conflict and material conditions. Symbolic hegemony might have

some effect in slowing down the revolution, since false consciousness could interfere temporarily with the necessary recognition of class interests on the part of workers, but it was not a primary force. The Benthamite model was, however, often used by Marxists in their intellectual battles with other political philosophies and in their battles with each other. The standard argument was that the ideas of other philosophies were nothing more than expressions of class interests and attempts at symbolic hegemony; Marxism alone had an "objective" basis. Later, in Gramsci's writings, the complex machinery of the Marxist model, involving forces of production, relations of production, material conditions, etc., was replaced by the role of symbols, culture, and intellectuals in the maintenance and legitimation of the status quo (Femia 1981). The material parts of the Marxist model were eliminated, and what remained was the claim that governments were able to stay in power because the state controlled ideology which became part of the common sense of the common culture. The model moved back from Marx to Bentham, except that the state remained the primary source of oppression.[23]

By the late 1960s the current oppression model was a well-entrenched part of the ideology of the American intellectual radical left in the social sciences and the humanities. The main outlines of this model were presented in a collection of essays, edited by Dell Hymes, titled *Reinventing Anthropology*.[24] Much of the moral stirring in anthropology at that time was a result

---

[21] This is probably D'Andrade's weakest point. Although it is certainly true that since the early 1970s anthropologists have often condemned fieldwork as supporting oppression (see footnote 24), it is less clear that they believe there is a single cause for evil in the world. In fact, it would probably be more accurate to say that postmodernists emphasize complexity of both cause and effect.

[22] Jeremy Bentham is less well noted for these positions than for the utilitarian principle that good can be defined as that which provides the greatest benefit to the greatest number of people. A more complete note on Bentham can be found in essay 37, footnote 8.

[23] D'Andrade's interpretation of Gramsci is extreme. Although Gramsci does give a more prominent place to the power of ideology (which he terms hegemony) than Marx, he never completely abandons materialism.

[24] In the 1970s, anthropologists started to cast a critical eye on their discipline. First, anthropologists who worked for government agencies or received government funding were severely criticized because of popular sentiment against U.S. government actions in Southeast Asia. Second, because many anthropologists worked in countries that were former colonial possessions of European nations, and worked with the approval of those governments in a context of coercion, their research was seen as supporting the colonial oppression of those governments. Dell Hymes' 1972 book *Reinventing Anthropology* and Talal Asad's *Anthropology and the Colonial Encounter* (1973) were particularly vigorous in their condemnation of the discipline. A more recent critique of anthropology in this vein is Faye Harrison's *Decolonizing Anthropology: Moving Further Toward an Anthropology for Liberation*, published in 1991.

of the Vietnam war, and *Reinventing Anthropology* reflects the conflicts of that time. But beyond discussion of issues relating to Vietnam, the contributors were clear that anthropology should be permanently changed. In the essays in this volume (Hymes 1972), Berreman called for an end to the pervasive hypocrisy of academic anthropology, William Willis defined anthropology as the study of dominated people done in aid of imperialism, Minna Caulfield discussed cultural exploitation in terms of its effect on the colonialized culture and individuals sharing it, Richard Clemmer discussed the development of resistance among American Indians, Norman Klein speculated about the effect of the 1960 counterculture on American cultural hegemony, Robert Jay described how he had come to feel that anthropological theory and anthropological fieldwork involve serious moral problems because of their dehumanizing effects on society and on anthropologists, and Bob Scholte presented an agenda for anthropology based on a reflexive and critical epistemology in contrast to "value-free" social science.

All of this was stated clearly in the 1960s. However, unlike the current moralists, the moralists of the 1960s and 1970s were, with some exceptions, young and relatively unknown and also not epistemological relativists. What seems to have happened next is that this model went "tacit" and then reemerged in full voice in the 1980s as a part of the postmodernist movement.[d] Postmodernism, with its concerns about the authority of representation and its interest in the deconstruction of the verities, gave the

moral model a much more resplendent vocabulary and greater epistemological bite. *Writing Cultures* (Clifford and Marcus 1986) was ostensibly about a new way of writing ethnography. Behind the discussion of modes of presentation was the presupposition that the old way of writing was the expression of the old objective (realist/hegemonic) model and therefore had to be replaced. The language used in the essays in *Writing Cultures* made strong claims to upper-middle-class sensibility in esthetic matters but did not modify the basics of the moral model. It did, however, make it possible to claim that concern with writing and representation counted as a serious moral pursuit. In any case, the moral model, as developed during the later part of the 18th century, has changed very little because, I believe, of its usefulness in moral argument by intellectuals against other intellectuals.[25]

So far, I have discussed four general problems with the use of moral models as a means of finding out about the world: the difficulty in getting reliable identifications for basic terms, the tendency towards all-or-none thinking, the tendency towards monocausality and evaluative contagion, and the difficulty of changing a moral model. There are also a number of problems with the *particular* moral model of oppression current in anthropology.

First, in my opinion, this particular moral model is not a very good representation of the way the world is. As an explanation of what is happening globally, the model in its Gramscian form made most sense in the 1950s and '60s,

---

[25] Clifford and Marcus' 1986 volume *Writing Culture: The Poetics and Politics of Ethnography* was a decisive volume, bringing together a collection of essays by several leading American postmodernists, including James Clifford, Vincent Crapanzano, Renato Rosaldo, Stephen Tyler, Talal Asad, George Marcus, Michael Fischer, and Paul Rabinow. The point of *Writing Culture* was to argue that ethnographic writing was a cross between fiction, memoir, scientific report, and travelogue. Therefore, anthropological writing should be subjected to literary and political analysis.

Ironically, this volume was severely attacked by feminist anthropologists for the lack of women authors in the work (there is only one—a literary critic named Pratt) and

for Clifford's dismissal of feminist anthropology in the volume's introduction. Clifford wrote,

> Feminist ethnography has focused either on setting the record straight about women or revising anthropological categories (for example the nature/culture opposition). It has not produced either unconventional forms of writing or a developed reflection on ethnographic textuality as such. (1986: 20–21)

Behar and Gordon edited a volume in 1995 called *Women Writing Culture* specifically in response to Clifford's challenge.

when the cold war was at its height. At that time two powerful empires, one capitalist, the other communist, held sway over much of the world. The difference between the two empires was not a matter of material conditions; both were modern industrial economies. What happened to make the difference was ideology. That is, to explain how the world could be so divided, it made sense to postulate that the division was due to differences in belief and that the commitment to belief was the result of the rhetoric produced by mystifiers who managed the flow of symbols and information that created the common sense of ordinary people. The Gramscian worldview is clearly inadequate, however, to account for the breakup of the Soviet Union and the current world disorder in which nation-states are unable to contain ethnic conflicts. The present problem for any macro-social theory is not identifying oppression but accounting for the failure of current governments to maintain order.[26]

It can be argued that the moral model still has some representational adequacy in accounting for oppression within particular countries. However, in my opinion, oppression in China, Brazil, or the United States can be better understood by recourse to theoretical models about the privileged access of special-interest groups to governmental functions, the operation of political parties, the lack of civil society, and other standard kinds of political analysis than by explanation based on a model of mass mystification. The only situation to which the oppression/mystification/denunciation model seems to have a reasonable degree of fit is to discrimination—racism and sexism. However, even with respect to racism and sexism the moral model does not explain much; it simply condemns discrimination as oppression. It does not tell us why discrimination is worse at some times and in some places.

A number of other problems with the current moral model may be considered briefly. The moral model has no theory of *good* power or *good* inequality and so must simply condemn without understanding much of the operation of any social system. Also, the model is almost entirely negative in character; it creates a climate of denunciation and rage. Further, while those who use the model are reflexive in asking, "Am *I* acting oppressively?" they are not at all reflexive on other points; they do not ask, "What is there about *me* that makes *me* see oppression as bad?" or "Why should others believe *my* assertions when *I* do not believe theirs?" or "Why have *I* been blessed with the knowledge of good and evil that *others* do not seem to have?" Overall, there is the unreflexive assumption that one is a member of an elect that by natural grace knows what is right, and this elect consists of those who hold the current moral model. All others are to be driven out of anthropology by "epistemological struggle," as Scheper-Hughes puts it.

Another limitation of the current model is that it does not seem likely that it will bring about very much good in the world. It does not lead one to do

---

[26] Note that once again, D'Andrade shifts to a writing style that emphasizes opinion. Here he argues that Gramscian notions are ill-suited to account for the breakup of the Soviet Union and the problems of the maintenance of order in the world today. However, this relies on a gross oversimplification of Gramsci's work consistent with D'Andrade's notion that Gramsci was not a materialist. Gramsci did not propose that hegemony existed devoid of material circumstances or opposition. In fact, he proposed the existence of counterhegemonies within societies and saw politics as a battleground between economic forces and contesting hegemonic and counterhegemonic systems. As a result, followers of Gramsci do not have any particular difficulty accounting for recent events. However, it does not follow that Gramsci's model is the best one, and D'Andrade is certainly entitled to his opinions.

The idea that the fundamental problem for current theories is to account for the failure of current governments to maintain order is a popular notion promoted in the works of Robert Kaplan. Kaplan sees understanding the collapse of state authority as basic to any appreciation of the world's current condition or its future. He has written frequently on this subject. One of his most important essays, "The Coming Anarchy," appeared in early 1994.

D'Andrade argues that the moral model is ill-equipped to deal with current conditions. Below he issues a scathing condemnation of the postmodern viewpoint, arguing that this moral model has no explanatory value, is good for little but condemnation with no understanding, and is unlikely to bring about the positive change it seeks.

anything positive about bad conditions. Instead it leads to denunciations of various social practitioners, such as social workers, doctors, psychiatrists, economists, civil servants, bureaucrats, etc., and especially other anthropologists. Isn't it odd that the true enemy of society turns out to be that guy in the office down the hall? But the intellectual destruction of these mystifiers, however desirable within the framework of the model, is unlikely to help the truly oppressed very much. Steven Sangren, in his article "Rhetoric and the Authority of Anthropology" (1988), pointed to the will to power expressed by postmodernist advocates of the moral model. The current moral model is a good instrument for intellectual battle within the university; it hardly seems likely, even on its own terms, to accomplish much else. This is what Bentham created it for, and this has been its most important use in Marxist thought.

The best part of the model is the analysis of different kinds of mystification; these do tell us something about the world. Much weaker is the assertion that these mystifications are effective in maintaining oppression—that ordinary people do not rise to overthrow the capitalists or colonialists or sexists because of the power of these mystifications. This is undemonstrated though in some cases plausible. More often it appears to be the case that people do not revolt either because (1) they face overwhelming force, (2) they are receiving satisfaction from their lives as lived, or (3) the persons, groups, or institutions that the social scientist has identified as the source of the oppression are not the true source of oppression—the source being more diffuse and less amenable to solution than the social scientist thinks and the social scientist's explanation in fact being the one that is mystifying.

Finally, the current moral model is ethnocentric. It is strong for equality (the escape from inequality) and freedom (the release from oppression). In my opinion these are not bad values, but they are very American. These are not the predominant values of modern Japan, India, China, the Middle East, or Southeast Asia, but they are the predominant values in the United States and much of Europe. It is ironic that these moralists should be so colonialist in their assumption about what is evil.

However, even if the moral model were a more adequate representation of what is going on in the world, included a theory of good power and good inequality, were less negative in character, more reflexive about matters of moral belief, and more oriented toward doing something positive in the world, gave better explanations for why people do not revolt, and were much less ethnocentric, it would still be a mistake to try to make such a model also serve as the model for understanding how things work. The driving force of a moral model is the allocation of praise and blame, reward and punishment, and this goal *will* shape its cognitive character. The driving force of an objective model is the goal of obtaining a surer understanding of how things work, of what is happening "out there." It is nice to believe that one can have both in a single model, but the evidence is strong that one cannot. The current moral model is a case in point.

It comes down to a choice: whatever one wants in the way of political change, will the first priority be to understand how things work? That would be my choice. I believe that anthropology can maintain its moral authority only on the basis of empirically demonstrable truths. But I am afraid that my choice may be in the minority. A large and growing number of American anthropologists appear to believe that the moral agenda of anthropology should take priority over the scientific agenda. An even larger number appear to believe that the scientific agenda of anthropology is in deservedly bad repute because of its association with oppression. "Science" has become a bad word in anthropology.[e] Can we at least hold on to "objectivity?"

I do not know how this will turn out. Perhaps after another few years of continued moral suasion, the internal bickering of the moralists will begin to be more interesting than their message, and the current wave of moral righteousness will be followed by a period of cynicism and disillusionment. This seems to be what happened after the French Revolution, after Cromwell in England, and after Stalin in Russia. In five or ten years the New Young Turks will probably flaunt their cynicism and find the moral pretensions of their elders unbearably hypocritical. In any case, let us hope that anthropology, as a science, will survive.

As estheticized journalism and moralistic pamphleteering it can easily be replaced.[27]

NOTES

[a] A reviewer of an earlier draft of this article disagreed with my characterization of the "oppression model" as moral, arguing that the current "postmodern" position derives from the work of Nietzsche, Derrida, DeMan, and Foucault, all in the reviewer's opinion "amoral relativists." Whatever the merits of this reviewer's position, it is nevertheless the case that the anthropologists cited here—Rosaldo, Scheper-Hughes, Rabinow, Dwyer, Abu-Lughod, and others—are principled moralists who wish to make this world better.

[b] In his Distinguished Lecture to the American Anthropological Association "Anti Anti-Relativism," Geertz (1984) protests Rabinow's characterization. Geertz makes the point that *his* politics of tolerance and understanding—of fighting against provincialism and ethnocentrism—are just as moral as other positions and that it is unfair to be labeled "without politics" by those who have *other* politics.

[c] Bruno Latour (1993) appears to have moved to a realist position not substantially different from that of Kitcher. For example, in discussing Shapin and Schaffer's account of the controversy between Boyle and Hobbes about vacuum pumps and the role of experimentation, Latour (1993:28 emphasis added) says, "Boyle . . . invents the laboratory within which artificial machines create phenomena out of whole cloth. Even though they are artificial, costly, and hard to reproduce, and despite the small number of trained reliable witnesses, *these facts indeed represent nature as it is. . . . Scientists are scrupulous representatives of the facts.* Who is speaking when they speak? The facts themselves beyond all question, but also their authorized spokespersons."

[d] A reviewer of an earlier draft points out that during this period there were extensive criticisms by feminist, Third World, and minority scholars of the biases in social science writing and research. The influence of these critiques on anthropology has been very powerful, and in many cases they have been used to support a blanket rejection of objectivity and a commitment to the kind of moral model described here. However, many feminist, minority, and Third World scholars do not reject the idea of objectivity and in fact find that the epistemological relativism typical of much postmodernist writing undercuts attempts to identify what has actually happened in the world and what needs to be changed.

[e] Laura Nader has a good point with respect to the conception of "science." She says, "One question that should interest all of us has to do with clarifying the meaning of the *human* sciences qua science. In order to do this there needs to be recognition of plurality in science. . . . A recognition of many kinds of science as applied to anthropology forces us to consider that the study of the human condition requires a division of labor in the research process. . . . how do anthropologists escape from dogmatic orthodoxy? They are driven by the research question" (Nader 1989:154).

---

[27] In his final comments D'Andrade issues a devastating critique of the moral model upon which postmodernism is based and turns the postmodern attack upon itself. He concludes:

1. The moral model is good for intellectual fighting but little else.
2. The postmodern focus on oppression may, in fact, obscure the real reasons people do not attempt to change their lives.
3. The moral model is ethnocentric, assuming Western moral values and goals.
4. The objective model attempts to discover how things work, but the moral model focuses on assigning blame and punishment.

Like much anti-postmodernist writing, D'Andrade's conclusion is alarmist in tone. He positions himself as a minority voice arguing against an overwhelming tide of antiscience and irrationality. In the last line, he goes as far as to suggest that if the forces of darkness—the postmodernists—win, the existence of the discipline of anthropology itself will be threatened. But it is important to note that the debate between those who view anthropology as the description of culture and those who view it as a science of culture designed to produce generalizable laws is as old as the discipline itself and unlikely to abate . . . ever.

It is not much of an exaggeration to say that this debate is one of the basic forces that drives anthropological theory. To grossly oversimplify: In American anthropology, Boas' inductive methodology was a reaction to the generalizations of nineteenth-century thinkers. Steward's and White's generalizations about cultural evolution were a reaction to the Boasians' insistence on the *sui generis* nature of culture. Ethnoscientists produced highly particularistic accounts of culture in reaction to cultural ecology. Ecological and cultural-materialists, in their turn, reacted to the accounts of ethnoscientists, urging a generalizable, empirically based anthropology; and postmodernists, reacting to this, call for highly particular, narrative accounts of culture. What's next?

REFERENCES

Abu-Lughod, Lila. 1991. "Writing against culture," in *Recapturing Anthropology.* Edited by Richard G. Fox, pp. 37–62. Santa Fe: School of American Research Press.

Asad, Talal. 1973. *Anthropology and the colonial encounter.* London: Ithaca Press.

Bailey, F. G. 1991. *The prevalence of deceit.* Ithaca: Cornell University Press.

Bentham, Jeremy. 1952. *Bentham's handbook of political fallacies.* Baltimore: Johns Hopkins Press.

Burke, Kenneth. 1945. *A grammar of motives.* New York: Prentice-Hall.

Clifford, James, and George Marcus. 1986. *Writing culture: The poetics and politics of ethnography.* Berkeley: University of California Press.

Dwyer, Kevin. 1986. *Moroccan dialogues: Anthropology in question.* Baltimore: Johns Hopkins University Press.

Femia, Joseph V. 1981. *Gramsci's political thought: Hegemony, consciousness, and the revolutionary process.* Oxford: Clarendon Press.

Geertz, Clifford. 1984. Anti anti-relativism. *American Anthropologist.* 86: 263–78.

Gellner, Ernest. 1992. *Postmodernism, reason, and religion.* New York: Routledge.

Hymes, Dell. 1972. *Reinventing anthropology.* New York: Random House.

Kitcher, Philip. 1993. *The advancement of science.* Oxford: Oxford University Press.

Latour, Bruno. 1988. *The Pasteurization of France.* Cambridge: Harvard University Press.

––––––. 1993. *We have never been modern.* Cambridge: Harvard University Press.

Latour, Bruno, and Steve Woolgar. 1979. *Laboratory life.* Princeton: Princeton University Press.

Nadar, L. 1989. Post-interpretive anthropology. *Anthropological Quarterly* 62: 149–59.

Rabinow, Paul. 1983. "Humanism as nihilism: The bracketing of truth and seriousness in American cultural anthropology," in *Social science as moral inquiry.* Edited by R. Bellah, P. Rabinow, and W. Sullivan, pp. 33–51. New York: Columbia University Press.

Rorty, Richard. 1983. "Method and morality," in *Social science as moral inquiry.* Edited by R. Bellah, P. Rabinow, and W. Sullivan, pp. 52–75. New York: Columbia University Press.

––––––. 1991. *Objectivity, relativism, and truth: Philosophical papers.* Vol. 1. Cambridge: Cambridge University Press.

Rosaldo, Renato. 1989. *Culture and truth: The remaking of social analysis.* Boston: Beacon Press.

Scheper-Hughes, Nancy. 1992. "Hungry bodies, medicine, and the state: Toward a critical psychological anthropology," in *New directions in psychological anthropology.* Edited by T. Schwartz, G. White, and C. Lutz, pp. 221–47. New York: Cambridge University Press.

Shapin, Steven, and Simon Schaffer. 1982. *Leviathan and the air-pump.* Princeton: Princeton University Press.

Spiro, Melford E. 1986. Cultural relativism and the future of anthropology. *Cultural Anthropology* 1259–89.

Tyler, Stephen A. 1986. "Post-modern ethnography: From the document of occult to occult document," in *Writing cultures.* Edited by J. Clifford and G. Marcus, pp. 122–40. Berkeley: University of California Press.

Globalization, Power, and Agency

Samuel Goldwyn, or Yogi Berra, or Casey Stengle once said "never make predictions, especially about the future." In true postmodern fashion, the quote is attributed to all three, and many others besides. We'll never know who really said it first, and there is a website dedicated to tracking claims for its authorship: http://www.larry.denenberg.com/predictions.html. It's impossible to really know the directions anthropological theory will move in the next ten years. However, based on the tendencies of the last decade or so, it seems that work having to do with globalization, power, and agency will probably play an important role in the discipline. In this concluding chapter, we offer three examples of this sort of work from the 1990s.

To some degree, interest in globalization is probably driven by facts on the ground. Today, almost all anthropologists would accept the notion that cultures are constantly changing. Authors such as Wolf, Leacock, Stoller, and others, have pointed out that most societies studied by anthropologists were deeply affected by the experience of the expansion of Western societies, the emergence of capitalism, colonization, and other external forces. Often, when anthropologists thought they were looking at "primitive" societies and "stone age" peoples, they were, in fact, looking at societies that owed their origin to the policies of European governments.

Despite this, when Napoleon Chagnon went to do research among the Yanomamo in 1964, for example, he could be excused if he believed that they were relatively untouched by the outside world and living in more or less the same way they had for countless generations. This is what they looked like. They had relatively few material goods from outside, had only rarely seen others who did not look like them, and behaved in ways clearly alien to Venezuelan and Brazilian societies. In the past forty years, the Yanomamo have been the subject of endless controversy. Their land has been invaded by gold miners, they have been at the center of disputes about national parks and the rights of native peoples. They have been the subject of both documentary and fiction films. Their leaders have been frequent presences at universities and government hearings. Yanomamo crafts can be purchased on the Internet. We have no wish to take sides in any of the controversies surrounding the Yanomamo. We do wish to point out that, whatever you can say about them, you can't say they have been unaffected by the rest of the world.

The Yanomamo are an extreme (and largely tragic) example. However, what is true of them is also the case just about everywhere else in the world. Almost anywhere you go, at least some people have access to the rest of the world. Television is ubiquitous, and it no longer feels terribly strange to be sitting in a small African village watching American sitcoms. In 2005 *USA Today* reported that about one in nine Africans had a cell phone. No doubt, the distribution of these phones is affected by geography, class, ethnicity, and many other factors, but the numbers are impressive nonetheless. The trappings of consumer society are visible virtually everywhere in the world. Globalization is simply one of the most obvious and powerful phenomena in the world. This is particularly clear to anthropologists who (like McGee) have worked in a single location for several decades.

Globalization anthropology has numerous critical theoretical sources. Among the most important of these is surely the work of Eric Wolf.

Wolf's contribution is discussed more fully in Part 3, essay 23. Briefly, Wolf, strongly influenced by Marx, argued that the societies anthropologists examined must be seen in their historical contexts. In the past several hundred years, the most critical component of this context was the expansion of power of Europe and the incorporation of societies across the globe in an economic system dominated by capitalism. Globalization theorists do not generally share Wolf's interest in the long-term history of the societies they study. Rather, they tend to focus on the present and the past couple of decades in analyzing the ways in which societies are articulated with the world economy in general and with capitalist enterprises in particular. Critical foci of their studies include the effects of the expansion of multinational corporations, the outsourcing of production and labor, and the ability to move goods and information around the globe.

Although Wolf was concerned largely with large-scale economic and social processes, globalization theorists tend to be interested in specific local effects of economic incorporation. Guided by the work of Antonio Gramsci and Michel Foucault (both of whom have been discussed earlier in this book), they seek to understand the ways in which both the powerful and the powerless perceive and manipulate symbols and comprehend their position in the world; how they choose which objects and activities are desirable; and how they view the goals of society. Gramsci and Foucault were both interested in the relationship between ideas and power. Foucault in particular explored the ways in which knowledge, rather than being abstract and universal, is created and used by powerful people and institutions. For Foucault, there is no truth, in an abstract and absolute sense. Rather there are "regimes of truth," conditions and processes under which what counts as "truth" in a given society is established and used. Essentially, globalization theorists attempt to describe the truths of capitalist society and elucidate the processes by which they are both established and challenged.

A third influence in globalization theory is the thought of the French sociologist Pierre Bourdieu (1930–2002), in particular his ideas regarding *habitus* and *multiple forms of capital*. Bourdieu expands upon the notion of habitus found in the work of Marcel Mauss and Norbert Elias (1897–1990). Habitus is a complex concept, and there is much debate in anthropology over what exactly it means. For Bourdieu, it seems to have the sense of largely unconscious aspects of social life that are inscribed in the body, including dispositions, habits of perception, and action. Habitus is distinct from the notion of a habit. For example, I like to walk my dog at 8:00 in the evening. It's a habit that I've developed over the past several years. It would be habitus if it went without saying that, in my society, if one had a dog, one always walked it at 8 P.M. and if it would not occur to me to walk the dog at any other time. From this description you can see the clear connection between the idea of habitus and Durkheim's notions of social fact and collective conscience. Habitus refers to those aspects of culture of which participants in the culture are not fully conscious.

Economic capital is wealth that can be invested in ownership of the means of production with the goal of increase. Bourdieu points out that in addition to economic capital, individuals in society also manipulate social, cultural, and symbolic capital. Social capital refers to membership in networks of individuals and positions within such networks. An individual with a wide social network can activate it to pursue economic or other goals. Cultural capital refers to the possession of education, special knowledge, and skills. Symbolic capital refers to the possession of prestige and honor (as well as to the actual symbols of those things), which possession determines the degree to which a person's words are likely to be taken seriously. For Bourdieu, these forms of capital inform, along with habitus, what he refers to as a *field*, a complex interplay of social, physical, economic, and communicatory connections.

The three essays in this section capture much of the flavor of the globalization approach. The first, by Arjun Appadurai, shows a particularly deep debt to French postmodern scholars. In addition to Foucault and Bourdieu, Appadurai also refers to the work of Lacan and Derrida, among others. The world, Appadurai argues, is probably best described as a series of "scapes": ethnoscapes, mediascapes, technoscapes, financescapes, and ideoscapes. He asks us to contemplate the global structure of each of these as well as the relationships between them. Appadurai's notion of a "scape" is clearly similar to Bourdieu's idea of a field.

The second essay, by Philippe Bourgois, is closer to neo-Marxist thinking than the first. Bourgois focuses his attention on the poor of New York and the ways in which they are ensnared in a battle against a system of ideas that justifies the economic order. Bourgois relies heavily on the thinking of Antonio Gramsci, who, within a Marxist framework, emphasized the importance of ideas and symbols in maintaining control of society, and on the work of cultural-production theorists, who stressed the meanings and practices that individuals acquire as a result of their structural position in society as well as the ways they respond to these positions and create new, counter-hegemonic meanings.

Our final essay comes from Aihwa Ong, who examines the ways in which business and political elites in Asia attempt to mold the public perceptions of both the nation and the economy. Such elites create images of proper or desirable behaviors that, although they do not reflect individuals' economic reality (particularly that of women), they are nonetheless powerful influences on the ways in which people behave and understand their own lives. Ong's work shows particularly strong influence from Foucault and Bourdieu.

To some degree, globalization theory represents a synthesis between the materialism and attempted empiricism of the neofunctionalists and neo-Marxists and the more idealist approaches of the cognitive and the symbolic and interpretive anthropologists. Like materialists, they are concerned with people's behaviors and choices. They see these as influenced by economic pressures and economic rationales and set within systems of relations of production. Like symbolic and interpretive anthropologists, they are particularly concerned with the ways in which people create and contest meaning and morality within these structures. Despite this apparent rapprochement, the work of many globalization theorists is more likely to be appreciated by those sympathetic to literary and interpretivist approaches to anthropology than by those who would like to see a natural science of anthropology.

---

41. *Disjuncture and Difference in the Global Cultural Economy*

Arjun Appadurai (b. 1949)

It takes only the merest acquaintance with the facts of the modern world to note it is now an interactive system in a sense that is strikingly new. Historians and sociologists, especially those concerned with translocal processes (Hodgson 1974) and the world systems associated with capitalism (Abu-Lughod 1989; Braudel 1981–4; Curtin 1984; Wallerstein 1974; Wolf 1982), have long been aware that the world has been a congerie of large-scale interactions for many centuries. Yet today's world involves interactions of a new order and intensity. Cultural transactions between social groups in the past have generally been restricted, sometimes by the facts of geography and ecology, and at other times by active resistance to interactions with the Other (as in China for much of its history and in Japan before the Meiji Restoration). Where there have been sustained cultural transactions across large parts of the globe, they have usually involved the long-distance journey of commodities (and of the merchants most concerned with them) and of travelers and explorers of every type (Helms 1988; Schafer 1963). The two main forces for sustained cultural interaction before this century have been warfare (and the large-scale political systems sometimes generated

(1990)

by it) and religions of conversion, which have sometimes, as in the case of Islam, taken warfare as one of the legitimate instruments of their expansion. Thus, between travelers and merchants, pilgrims and conquerors, the world has seen much long-distance (and long-term) cultural traffic. This much seems self-evident.[1]

But few will deny that given the problems of time, distance, and limited technologies for the command of resources across vast spaces, cultural dealings between socially and spatially separated groups have, until the past few centuries, bridged at great cost and sustained over time only with great effort. The forces of cultural gravity seemed always to pull away from the formation of large-scale ecumenes, whether religious, commercial, or political, toward smaller-scale accretions of intimacy and interest.

Sometime in the past few centuries, the nature of this gravitational field seems to have changed. Partly because of the spirit of the expansion of western maritime interests after 1500, and partly because of the relatively autonomous developments of large and aggressive social formations in the Americas (such as the Aztecs and the Incas), in Eurasia (such as the Mongols and their descendants, the Mughals and Ottomans), in island Southeast Asia (such as the Buginese), and in the kingdoms of precolonial Africa (such

as Dahomey), an overlapping set of ecumenes began to emerge, in which congeries of money, commerce, conquest, and migration began to create durable cross-societal bonds. This process was accelerated by the technology transfers and innovations of the late eighteenth and nineteenth centuries (e.g., Bayly 1989), which created complex colonial orders centered on European capitals and spread throughout the non-European world. This intricate and overlapping set of Euro-colonial worlds (first Spanish and Portuguese, later principally English, French, and Dutch) set the basis for a permanent traffic in ideas of peoplehood and selfhood, which created the imagined communities (Anderson 1983) of recent nationalisms throughout the world.

With what Benedict Anderson[2] has called "print capitalism," a new power was unleashed in the world, the power of mass literacy and its attendant large-scale production of projects of ethnic affinity that were remarkably free of the need for face-to-face communication or even of indirect communication between persons and groups. The act of reading things together set the stage for movements based on a paradox—the paradox of constructed primordialism. There is, of course, a great deal else that is involved in the story of colonialism and its dialectically generated nationalisms (Chatterjee 1986), but the

---

[1] In the nineteenth and twentieth centuries, anthropologists tended to understand the object of their study as more or less bounded tribes, ethnic groups, or communities. Though connections among communities or between the communities studied by anthropologists and the worlds from which the anthropologists came were sometimes noted, these were treated as recent and not particularly important. The anthropologists' job was to see beyond them to the original, precontact, pristine community. In the 1970s and 1980s World Systems theorists such as those mentioned in this paragraph argued that this perception was incorrect. The communities anthropologists studied were not bounded and traditional but rather connected to and conditioned by international flows of trade and by wealth. Appadurai follows and extends this argument. In this paragraph and below, he points out that although interaction between cultures has been the rule rather than the exception, the difficulty and expense of communication historically militated against a world system. Over the

past several centuries these factors have steadily diminished in importance until, by the end of the twentieth century (when this piece was written) the transmission of information and transportation of people is both low cost and relatively simple. This has important implications for cultures and the ways in which they are studied.

[2] Benedict Anderson (b. 1936) is a scholar of international studies. In his 1983 book *Imagined Communities* he argued that the technology of print and the use of the vernacular were essential to the idea of nationhood in Europe. Latin had been universal in Europe. The printing of works in vernacular languages allowed people to conceive of themselves as members of specific language communities. This became one of the building blocks of nationalism. Anderson's notion that nations are the results of very particular—rather than natural and inevitable—historical processes and types of understandings underpins Appadurai's ideas in this essay.

issue of constructed ethnicities is surely a crucial strand in this tale.

But the revolution of print capitalism and the cultural affinities and dialogues unleashed by it were only modest precursors to the world we live in now. For in the past century, there has been a technological explosion, largely in the domain of transportation and information, that makes the interactions of a print-dominated world seem as hard-won and as easily erased as the print revolution made earlier forms of cultural traffic appear. For with the advent of the steamship, the automobile, the airplane, the camera, the computer, and the telephone, we have entered into an altogether new condition of neighborliness, even with those most distant from ourselves. Marshall McLuhan, among others, sought to theorize about this world as a "global village," but theories such as McLuhan's appear to have overestimated the communitarian implications of the new media order (McLuhan and Powers 1989). We are now aware that with media, each time we are tempted to speak of the global village, we must be reminded that media create communities with "no sense of place" (Meyrowitz 1985). The world we live in now seems rhizomic (Deleuze and Guattari 1987), even schizophrenic, calling for theories of rootlessness, alienation, and psychological distance between individuals and groups on the one hand, and fantasies (or nightmares) of electronic propinquity on the other. Here, we are close to the central problematic of cultural processes in today's world.[3]

Thus, the curiosity that recently drove Pico Iyer[4] to Asia (1988) is in some ways the product of a confusion between some ineffable McDonaldization of the world and the much subtler play of indigenous trajectories of desire and fear with global flows of people and things. Indeed, Iyer's own impressions are testimony to the fact that, if a global cultural system is emerging, it is filled with ironies and resistances, sometimes camouflaged as passivity and a bottomless appetite in the Asian world for things western.

Iyer's own account of the uncanny Philippine affinity for American popular music is rich testimony to the global culture of the hyperreal, for somehow Philippine renditions of American popular songs are both more widespread in the Philippines, and more disturbingly faithful to their originals, than they are in the United States today. An entire nation seems to have learned to mimic Kenny Rogers and the Lennon sisters, like a vast Asian Motown chorus. But Americanization is certainly a pallid term to apply to such a situation, for not only are there more Filipinos singing perfect renditions of some American songs (often from the American past) than there are Americans doing so, there is also, of course, the fact that the rest of their lives is not in complete synchrony with the referential world that first gave birth to these songs.

In a further globalizing twist on what Fredric Jameson[5] has recently called "nostalgia for the present" (1989), these Filipinos look back to a world they have never lost. This is one of the central ironies of the politics of global cultural flows, especially in the arena of entertainment and leisure. It plays havoc with the hegemony of Eurochronology. American nostalgia feeds on

---

[3] Marshall McLuhan (1911–1980) was a seminal thinker in media studies. In his 1962 book *The Guttenberg Galaxy,* McLuhan argued that advances in communications technology were turning the world into a "global village" in which all people were connected to one another and the transfer of information was instantaneous. McLuhan promoted a theory of technological determinism, arguing that changes in culture are driven by changes in the technology of communication. Although McLuhan's ideas have been very influential, they are also frequently criticized and deeply controversial. Appadurai clearly appreciates McLuhan's work but argues that the global village is a gross oversimplification.

[4] Pico Iyar (b. 1957) is a travel writer and journalist. A multicultural individual himself (British born of Indian descent), Iyer's writing focuses on the ironies and paradoxes of globalization. An often-cited quote from him is, "I am a multinational soul on a multinational globe on which more and more countries are as polyglot and restless as airports (in London 1996)."

[5] Frederic Jameson (b. 1934) is an American philosopher and literary critic. He is best known for his Marxist critique of postmodernism, which he argues is a feature of corporate capitalism. Jameson's best known work is *Postmodernism: Or the Cultural Logic of Late Capitalism* (1991).

Filipino desire represented as a hypercompetent reproduction. Here, we have nostalgia without memory. The paradox, of course, has its explanations, and they are historical; unpacked, they lay bare the story of the American missionization and political rape of the Philippines, one result of which has been the creation of a nation of make-believe Americans, who tolerated for so long a leading lady who played the piano while the slums of Manila expanded and decayed.[6] Perhaps the most radical postmodernists would argue that this is hardly surprising because in the peculiar chronicities of late capitalism, pastiche and nostalgia are central modes of image production and reception. Americans themselves are hardly in the present anymore as they stumble into the megatechnologies of the twenty-first century garbed in the film-noir scenarios of sixties' chills, fifties' diners, forties' clothing, thirties' houses, twenties' dances, and so on ad infinitum.

As far as the United States is concerned, one might suggest that the issue is no longer one of nostalgia but of a social *imaginaire*[7] built largely around reruns. Jameson was bold to link the politics of nostalgia to the postmodern commodity sensibility, and surely he was right (1983). The drug wars in Colombia recapitulate the tropical sweat of Vietnam, with Ollie North and his succession of masks—Jimmy Stewart concealing John Wayne concealing Spiro Agnew and all of them transmogrifying into Sylvester Stallone, who wins in Afghanistan—thus simultaneously fulfilling the secret American envy of Soviet imperialism and the rerun (this time with a happy ending) of the Vietnam War. The Rolling Stones, in their fifties, gyrate before eighteen-year-olds who do not appear to need the machinery of nostalgia to be sold on their parents' heroes. Paul McCartney is selling the Beatles to a new audience by hitching his oblique nostalgia to their desire for the new that smacks of the old. *Dragnet* is back in nineties drag, and so is *Adam-12*, not to speak of *Batman* and *Mission Impossible*, all dressed up technologically but remarkably faithful to the atmospherics of their originals.

The past is now not a land to return to in a simple politics of memory. It has become a synchronic warehouse of cultural scenarios, a kind of temporal central casting, to which recourse can be taken as appropriate, depending on the movie to be made, the scene to be enacted, the hostages to be rescued. All this is par for the course, if you follow Jean Baudrillard or Jean-Francois Lyotard[8] into a world of signs wholly unmoored from their social signifiers (all the world's a Disneyland). But I would like to suggest that the apparent increasing substitutability of whole periods and postures for one another, in the cultural styles of advanced capitalism, is tied to larger global forces, which have done much to show Americans that the past is usually another country. If your present is their future (as in much modernization theory and in many self-satisfied tourist fantasies), and their future is your past (as in the case of the Filipino virtuosos of American popular music), then your own past can be made to appear as simply a normalized modality of your present. Thus, although some

---

[6] Appadurai refers to Imelda Marcos (b. 1929), wife of former Philippine dictator Ferdinand Marcos (1917–1989).

[7] Here Appadurai refers to the work of the French psychoanalytic Marxist Jacques Lacan (1901–1981). Lacan argued that a critical realization for children is their existence as an entity seen by others (he calls this the mirror stage). This gives children a way of understanding and imagining themselves. To create this understanding, children begin to assemble a story of what it is they are like. But, ultimately, they can not truly see themselves. Rather, they compose their self-image out of partial glimpses of themselves, understandings of other children, stories they are told, pictures they see, and so on. This collection is the *imaginaire*, and, by definition, it is not accurate. Lacan had a genius for and love of puns. *Imaginaire* is an example, connoting both "imaginary" and "made up of images." In another wonderful pun (that doesn't translate as easily), Lacan calls the child with an *imaginaire* an *homme-lette*. In French, this has the connotation of both a "little man" and an omelet—something made out of broken eggs. Appadurai in this passage speaks of America as an *imaginaire*, an idea composed of bits and pieces, of images that are other than reality.

[8] Jean Baudrillard (b. 1929) and Jean-Francois Lyotard (1924–1998) are both well-known postmodern theorists.

anthropologists may continue to relegate their Others to temporal spaces that they do not themselves occupy (Fabian 1983), postindustrial cultural productions have entered a postnostalgic phase.

The crucial point, however, is that the United States is no longer the puppeteer of a world system of images but is only one node of a complex transnational construction of imaginary landscapes. The world we live in today is characterized by a new role for the imagination in social life. To grasp this new role, we need to bring together the old idea of images, especially mechanically produced images (in the Frankfurt School sense);[9] the idea of the imagined community (in Anderson's sense); and the French idea of the imaginary (*imaginaire*) as a constructed landscape of collective aspirations, which is no more and no less real than the collective representations of Emile Durkheim, now mediated through the complex prism of modern media.

The image, the imagined, the imaginary— these are all terms that direct us to something critical and new in global cultural processes: the imagination as a social practice. No longer mere fantasy (opium for the masses whose real work is elsewhere), no longer simple escape (from a world defined principally by more concrete purposes and structures), no longer elite pastime (thus not relevant to the lives of ordinary people), and no longer mere contemplation (irrelevant for new forms of desire and subjectivity), the imagination has become an organized field of social practices, a form of work (in the sense of both labor and culturally organized practice), and a form of negotiation between sites of agency (individuals) and globally defined fields of possibility. This unleashing of the imagination links the play of pastiche (in some settings) to the terror and coercion of states and their competitors. The imagination is now central to all forms of agency, is itself a social fact, and is the key component of the new global order. But to make this claim meaningful, we must address some other issues.

HOMOGENIZATION AND HETEROGENIZATION

The central problem of today's global interactions is the tension between cultural homogenization and cultural heterogenization. A vast array of empirical facts could be brought to bear on the side of the homogenization argument, and much of it has come from the left end of the spectrum of media studies (Hamelink 1983; Mattelart 1983; Schiller 1976), and some from other perspectives (Gans 1985; Iyer 1988). Most often, the homogenization argument subspeciates into either an argument about Americanization or an argument about commoditization, and very often the two arguments are closely linked. What these arguments fail to consider is that at least as rapidly as forces from various metropolises are brought into new societies they tend to become indigenized in one or another way: this is true of music and housing styles as much as it is true of science and terrorism, spectacles and constitutions. The dynamics of such indigenization have just begun to be explored systemically (Barber 1987; Feld 1988; Hannerz 1987, 1989; Ivy 1988; Nicoll 1989; Yoshimoto 1989), and much more needs to be done. But it is worth noticing that for the people of Irian Jaya, Indonesianization may be more worrisome than Americanization, as Japanization may be for Koreans, Indianization for Sri Lankans, Vietnamization for the Cambodians, and Russianization for the people of Soviet Armenia and

---

[9] The Frankfort School was a group of scholars who examined the Western philosophical tradition and Marxism in light of twentieth-century history. One influential member was Walter Benjamin (1892–1940). In "The Work of Art in the Age of Mechanical Reproduction," Benjamin argued that in traditional societies art had an "aura"; that is, its originality and creativity inspired feelings of awe and respect in those who viewed it. In the modern era, mechanical reproduction has subverted the uniqueness of works of art, and therefore their power was diminished. Benjamin looked upon this as an ambiguous but generally positive development. It meant that people could observe and analyze art free from the mysticism of power. Benjamin believed that media such as radio and film had the potential to liberate, creating alternatives to the high culture of elites. Appadurai refers again to Benjamin later in this essay.

the Baltic republics. Such a list of alternative fears to Americanization could be greatly expanded, but it is not a shapeless inventory: for polities of smaller scale, there is always a fear of cultural absorption by polities of larger scale, especially those that are nearby. One man's imagined community is another man's political prison.

This scalar dynamic, which has widespread global manifestations, is also tied to the relationship between nations and states, to which I shall return later. For the moment let us note that the simplification of these many forces (and fears) of homogenization can also be exploited by nation-states in relation to their own minorities, by posing global commoditization (or capitalism, or some other such external enemy) as more real than the threat of its own hegemonic strategies.

The new global cultural economy has to be seen as a complex, overlapping, disjunctive order that cannot any longer be understood in terms of existing center-periphery models (even those that might account for multiple centers and peripheries). Nor is it susceptible to simple models of push and pull (in terms of migration theory), or of surpluses and deficits (as in traditional models of balance of trade), or of consumers and producers (as in most neo-Marxist theories of development). Even the most complex and flexible theories of global development that have come out of the Marxist tradition (Amin 1980; Mandel 1978; Wallerstein 1974; Wolf 1982) are inadequately quirky and have failed to come to terms with what Scott Lash and John Urry have called disorgan-

ized capitalism (1987). The complexity of the current global economy has to do with certain fundamental disjunctures between economy, culture, and politics that we have only begun to theorize.[10]

I propose that an elementary framework for exploring such disjunctures is to look at the relationship among five dimensions of global cultural flows that can be termed (a) *ethnoscapes*, (b) *mediascapes*, (c) *technoscapes*, (d) *financescapes*, and (e) *ideoscapes*.[a] The suffix -scape allows us to point to the fluid, irregular shapes of these landscapes, shapes that characterize international capital as deeply as they do international clothing styles. These terms with the common suffix -scape also indicate that these are not objectively given relations that look the same from every angle of vision but, rather, that they are deeply perspectival constructs, inflected by the historical, linguistic, and political situatedness of different sorts of actors: nation-states, multinationals, diasporic communities, as well as subnational groupings and movements (whether religious, political, or economic), and even intimate face-to-face groups, such as villages, neighborhoods, and families. Indeed, the individual actor is the last locus of this perspectival set of landscapes, for these landscapes are eventually navigated by agents who both experience and constitute larger formations, in part from their own sense of what these landscapes offer.[11]

These landscapes thus are the building blocks of what (extending Benedict Anderson) I would like to call imagined worlds, that is, the multiple worlds that are constituted by the historically

---

[10] Here Appadurai introduces a critical element of his thinking as represented by this essay: that the patterns of economy and culture in the world are far more complex than existing theories suggest. He introduces the term *disjuncture* to characterize this complexity. A disjuncture is a separation, a disconnection, a disunion. Appadurai uses the term to signify ideas that are in some sort of relationship to one another but where that relationship is cannot be specified because it is characterized by gaps and irregularity. You will recall that much of anthropological theory from the time of Herbert Spencer on envisioned societies and cultures as more or less organic. That is, they understood societies as being composed of a series of elements that stood in certain relations to each other. Together, these elements created the pattern of the culture. This vision of

culture received its maximal expression in functionalism but is also present in Boasian anthropology, cultural ecology, and neofunctionalism. It was, to some degree, challenged by Neo-Marxists, who saw cultures as consisting of elements that conflicted and clashed rather than cooperated. Appadurai extends this argument, envisioning culture as characterized by elements that combine, conflict, cooperate, and separate in ways that seem largely chaotic.

[11] This passage draws the reader to a critical aspect of the essay. Appadurai is describing phenomena that exist at many different levels of scale. We can talk of financescape and ideoscape at the level of the nation, the village, or perhaps the individual. This is an idea he returns to again at the end of the essay.

situated imaginations of persons and groups spread around the globe (see Appadurai 1996: ch. 1). An important fact of the world we live in today is that many persons on the globe live in such imagined worlds (and not just in imagined communities) and thus are able to contest and sometimes even subvert the imagined worlds of the official mind and of the entrepreneurial mentality that surround them.[12]

By *ethnoscape,* I mean the landscape of persons who constitute the shifting world in which we live: tourists, immigrants, refugees, exiles, guest workers, and other moving groups and individuals constitute an essential feature of the world and appear to affect the politics of (and between) nations to a hitherto unprecedented degree. This is not to say that there are no relatively stable communities and networks of kinship, friendship, work, and leisure, as well as of birth, residence, and other filial forms. But it is to say that the warp of these stabilities is everywhere shot through with the woof of human motion, as more persons and groups deal with the realities of having to move or the fantasies of wanting to move. What is more, both these realities and fantasies now function on larger scales, as men and women from villages in India think not just of moving to Poona or Madras but of moving to Dubai and Houston, and refugees from Sri Lanka find themselves in South India as well as in Switzerland, just as the Hmong are driven to London as well as to Philadelphia. And as international capital shifts its needs, as production and technology generate different needs, as nation-states shift their policies on refugee populations, these moving groups can never afford to let their imaginations rest too long, even if they wish to.

By *technoscape,* I mean the global configuration, also ever fluid, of technology and the fact that technology, both high and low, both mechanical and informational, now moves at high speeds across various kinds of previously impervious boundaries. Many countries now are the roots of multinational enterprise: a huge steel complex in Libya may involve interests from India, China, Russia, and Japan, providing different components of new technological configurations. The odd distribution of technologies, and thus the peculiarities of these technoscapes, are increasingly driven not by any obvious economies of scale, of political control, or of market rationality but by increasingly complex relationships among money flows, political possibilities, and the availability of both un- and highly skilled labor. So, while India exports waiters and chauffeurs to Dubai and Sharjah, it also exports software engineers to the United States—indentured briefly to Tata-Burroughs or the World Bank, then laundered through the State Department to become wealthy resident aliens, who are in turn objects of seductive messages to invest their money and know-how in federal and state projects in India.

The global economy can still be described in terms of traditional indicators (as the World Bank continues to do) and studied in terms of traditional comparisons (as in Project Link at the University of Pennsylvania), but the complicated technoscapes (and the shifting ethnoscapes) that underlie these indicators and comparisons are further out of the reach of the queen of social sciences than ever before.[13] How is one to make a meaningful comparison of wages in Japan and the

---

[12] Appadurai owes a critical debt to the Italian Marxist Antonio Gramsci (1897–1931) and notions of hegemony and counter-hegemony. Gramsci focused on understanding ideology within a Marxist framework. He emphasized that power elites set the general rules of understanding and debate within a society. He referred to this as the hegemony of the ruling classes. However, hegemony is negotiated as intellectuals and oppressed classes create counter-hegemonies to challenge elite ideas. In this passage, Appadurai notes that individuals are able to challenge and subvert the "official mind." Additional information on Gramsci can be found in note 11 in the next essay.

[13] Founded in 1968 by Nobel prize–winning economist Lawrence Klein and supported by the United Nations, Project LINK attempts to create a comprehensive global econometric model. From relatively small beginnings LINK now includes more than 70 different models. It has moved from the University of Pennsylvania to the University of Toronto and the United Nations in New York. The "queen of the social sciences" refers, of course, to economics.

United States or of real-estate costs in New York and Tokyo, without taking sophisticated account of the very complex fiscal and investment flows that link the two economies through a global grid of currency speculation and capital transfer?

Thus it is useful to speak as well of *financescapes,* as the disposition of global capital is now a more mysterious, rapid, and difficult landscape to follow than ever before, as currency markets, national stock exchanges, and commodity speculations move megamonies through national turnstiles at blinding speed, with vast, absolute implications for small differences in percentage points and time units. But the critical point is that the global relationship among ethnoscapes, technoscapes, and financescapes is deeply disjunctive and profoundly unpredictable because each of these landscapes is subject to its own constraints and incentives (some political, some informational, and some technoenvironmental), at the same time as each acts as a constraint and a parameter for movements in the others. Thus, even an elementary model of global political economy must take into account the deeply disjunctive relationships among human movement, technological flow, and financial transfers.

Further refracting these disjunctures (which hardly form a simple, mechanical global infrastructure in any case) are what I call *mediascapes* and *ideoscapes,* which are closely related landscapes of images. Mediascapes refer both to the distribution of the electronic capabilities to produce and disseminate information (newspapers, magazines, television stations, and film-production studios), which are now available to a growing number of private and public interests throughout the world, and to the images of the world created by these media. These images involve many complicated inflections, depending on their mode (documentary or entertainment), their hardware (electronic or preelectronic), their audiences (local, national, or transnational), and the interests of those who own and control them. What is most important about these mediascapes is that

they provide (especially in their television, film, and cassette forms) large and complex repertoires of images, narratives, and ethnoscapes to viewers throughout the world, in which the world of commodities and the world of news and politics are profoundly mixed. What this means is that many audiences around the world experience the media themselves as a complicated and interconnected repertoire of print, celluloid, electronic screens, and billboards. The lines between the realistic and the fictional landscapes they see are blurred, so that the farther away these audiences are from the direct experiences of metropolitan life, the more likely they are to construct imagined worlds that are chimerical, aesthetic, even fantastic objects, particularly if assessed by the criteria of some other perspective, some other imagined world.

Mediascapes, whether produced by private or state interests, tend to be image-centered, narrative-based accounts of strips of reality, and what they offer to those who experience and transform them is a series of elements (such as characters, plots, and textual forms) out of which scripts can be formed of imagined lives, their own as well as those of others living in other places. These scripts can and do get disaggregated into complex sets of metaphors by which people live (Lakoff and Johnson 1980) as they help to constitute narratives of the Other and protonarratives of possible lives, fantasies that could become prolegomena to the desire for acquisition and movement.[14]

Ideoscapes are also concatenations of images, but they are often directly political and frequently have to do with the ideologies of states and the counterideologies of movements explicitly oriented to capturing state power or a piece of it. These ideoscapes are composed of elements of the Enlightenment worldview, which consists of a chain of ideas, terms, and images, including freedom, welfare, rights, sovereignty, representation, and the master term democracy. The master narrative of the Enlightenment (and its many variants in Britain, France, and the United States) was constructed with a certain internal logic and

---

[14] *Prolegomena:* an introduction or introductory comments.

presupposed a certain relationship between reading, representation, and the public sphere. (For the dynamics of this process in the early history of the United States, see Warner 1990.) But the diaspora of these terms and images across the world, especially since the nineteenth century, has loosened the internal coherence that held them together in a Euro-American master narrative and provided instead a loosely structured synopticon of politics, in which different nation-states, as part of their evolution, have organized their political cultures around different keywords (e.g., Williams 1976).

As a result of the differential diaspora of these keywords, the political narratives that govern communication between elites and followers in different parts of the world involve problems of both a semantic and pragmatic nature: semantic to the extent that words (and their lexical equivalents) require careful translation from context to context in their global movements, and pragmatic to the extent that the use of these words by political actors and their audiences may be subject to very different sets of contextual conventions that mediate their translation into public politics. Such conventions are not only matters of the nature of political rhetoric: for example, what does the aging Chinese leadership mean when it refers to the dangers of hooliganism? What does the South Korean leadership mean when it speaks of discipline as the key to democratic industrial growth?

These conventions also involve the far more subtle question of what sets of communicative genres are valued in what way (newspapers versus cinema, for example) and what sorts of pragmatic genre conventions govern the collective readings of different kinds of text. So, while an Indian audience may be attentive to the resonances of a political speech in terms of some keywords and phrases reminiscent of Hindi cinema, a Korean audience may respond to the subtle codings of Buddhist or neo-Confucian rhetoric encoded in a political document. The very relationship of reading to hearing and seeing may vary in important ways that determine the morphology of these different ideoscapes as they shape themselves in different national and transnational contexts. This globally variable synaesthesia[15] has hardly even been noted, but it demands urgent analysis. Thus democracy has clearly become a master term, with powerful echoes from Haiti and Poland to the former Soviet Union and China, but it sits at the center of a variety of ideoscapes, composed of distinctive pragmatic configurations of rough translations of other central terms from the vocabulary of the Enlightenment. This creates ever new terminological kaleidoscopes, as states (and the groups that seek to capture them) seek to pacify populations whose own ethnoscapes are in motion and whose mediascapes may create severe problems for the ideoscapes with which they are presented. The fluidity of ideoscapes is complicated in particular by the growing diasporas (both voluntary and involuntary) of intellectuals who continuously inject new meaning-streams into the discourse of democracy in different parts of the world.[16]

---

[15] *Synesthesia:* an association of sensation, in this case reading, with other sensations. In Appadurai's example, he is discussing the association of reading with hearing and seeing.

[16] Appadurai here employs a fundamental element of postmodern thinking particularly shaped by the work of Jacques Derrida (1930–2004). Derrida argued that authors lose control of their text. Readers understand text based on their own histories and contexts. Thus, meaning can never be fixed. Here Appadurai notes that the lexicon of modern political debate was largely generated by the historical experiences and meanings of Enlightenment Europe. It is now used freely throughout the world and, because of this, takes on meanings its authors could not even imagine let alone control. So, for example, the authors of the Declaration of Independence did not intend for any of its wording to resonate with either Buddhist or Confucian thinking, which they were not particularly aware of either. Yet, passages of that document may take on special meaning for individuals in those traditions because, by chance, they do so resonate. These meanings may, or may not have anything to do with what the authors intended. From a postmodern perspective, loss of authorial control is an aspect of all text. Appadurai points out that this is much more the case when text (and movies and advertisement and all other forms of communication) move among people of radically different cultures and histories.

This extended terminological discussion of the five terms I have coined sets the basis for a tentative formulation about the conditions under which current global flows occur: they occur in and through the growing disjunctures among ethnoscapes, technoscapes, financescapes, mediascapes, and ideoscapes. This formulation, the core of my model of global cultural flow, needs some explanation. First, people, machinery, money, images, and ideas now follow increasingly non-isomorphic paths; of course, at all periods in human history, there have been some disjunctures in the flows of these things, but the sheer speed, scale, and volume of each of these flows are now so great that the disjunctures have become central to the politics of global culture. The Japanese are notoriously hospitable to ideas and are stereotyped as inclined to export (all) and import (some) goods, but they are also notoriously closed to immigration, like the Swiss, the Swedes, and the Saudis. Yet the Swiss and the Saudis accept populations of guest workers, thus creating labor diasporas of Turks, Italians, and other circum-Mediterranean groups. Some such guest-worker groups maintain continuous contact with their home nations, like the Turks, but others, like high-level South Asian migrants, tend to desire lives in their new homes, raising anew the problem of reproduction in a deterritorialized context.

Deterritorialization, in general, is one of the central forces of the modern world because it brings laboring populations into the lower-class sectors and spaces of relatively wealthy societies, while sometimes creating exaggerated and intensified senses of criticism or attachment to politics in the home state. Deterritorialization, whether of Hindus, Sikhs, Palestinians, or Ukrainians, is now at the core of a variety of global fundamentalisms, including Islamic and Hindu fundamentalism. In the Hindu case, for example, it is clear that the overseas movement of Indians has been exploited by a variety of interests both within and outside India to create a complicated network

of finances and religious identifications, by which the problem of cultural reproduction for Hindus abroad has become tied to the politics of Hindu fundamentalism at home.

At the same time, deterritorialization creates new markets for film companies, art impresarios, and travel agencies, which thrive on the need of the deterritorialized population for contact with its homeland. Naturally, these invented homelands, which constitute the mediascapes of deterritorialized groups, can often become sufficiently fantastic and one-sided that they provide the material for new ideoscapes in which ethnic conflicts can begin to erupt. The creation of Khalistan, an invented homeland of the deterritorialized Sikh population of England, Canada, and the United States, is one example of the bloody potential in such mediascapes as they interact with the internal colonialisms of the nation-state (e.g., Hechter 1975). The West Bank, Namibia, and Eritrea are other theaters for the enactment of the bloody negotiation between existing nation-states and various deterritorialized groupings.

It is in the fertile ground of deterritorialization, in which money, commodities, and persons are involved in ceaselessly chasing each other around the world, that the mediascapes and ideoscapes of the modern world find their fractured and fragmented counterpart. For the ideas and images produced by mass media often are only partial guides to the goods and experiences that deterritorialized populations transfer to one another. In Mira Nair's brilliant film *India Cabaret*,[17] we see the multiple loops of this fractured deterritorialization as young women, barely competent in Bombay's metropolitan glitz, come to seek their fortunes as cabaret dancers and prostitutes in Bombay, entertaining men in clubs with dance formats derived wholly from the prurient dance sequences of Hindi films. These scenes in turn cater to ideas about western and foreign women and their looseness, while they provide tawdry career alibis for these women. Some of these women come from Kerala, where

---

[17] *India Cabaret* (1985) is a made-for-TV documentary that details the lives and expectations of two aging strippers at a run-down Bombay night club.

cabaret clubs and the pornographic film industry have blossomed, partly in response to the purses and tastes of Keralites returned from the Middle East, where their diasporic lives away from women distort their very sense of what the relations between men and women might be. These tragedies of displacement could certainly be replayed in a more detailed analysis of the relations between the Japanese and German sex tours to Thailand and the tragedies of the sex trade in Bangkok, and in other similar loops that tie together fantasies about the Other, the conveniences and seductions of travel, the economics of global trade, and the brutal mobility fantasies that dominate gender politics in many parts of Asia and the world at large.

While far more could be said about the cultural politics of deterritorialization and the larger sociology of displacement that it expresses, it is appropriate at this juncture to bring in the role of the nation-state in the disjunctive global economy of culture today. The relationship between states and nations is everywhere an embattled one. It is possible to say that in many societies the nation and the state have become one another's projects. That is, while nations (or more properly groups with ideas about nationhood) seek to capture or co-opt states and state power, states simultaneously seek to capture and monopolize ideas about nationhood (Baruah 1986; Chatterjee 1986; Nandy 1989). In general, separatist transnational movements, including those that have included terror in their methods, exemplify nations in search of states. Sikhs, Tamil Sri Lankans, Basques, Moros, Quebecois—each of these represents imagined communities that seek to create states of their own or carve pieces out of existing states. States, on the other hand, are everywhere seeking to monopolize the moral resources of community, either by flatly claiming perfect co-evality between nation and state, or by systematically museumizing and representing all the groups within them in a variety of heritage politics that seems remarkably uniform throughout the world (Handler 1988; Herzfeld 1982; McQueen 1988).

Here, national and international mediascapes are exploited by nation-states to pacify separatists or even the potential fissiparousness[18] of all ideas of difference. Typically, contemporary nation-states do this by exercising taxonomic control over difference, by creating various kinds of international spectacle to domesticate difference, and by seducing small groups with the fantasy of self-display on some sort of global or cosmopolitan stage. One important new feature of global cultural politics, tied to the disjunctive relationships among the various landscapes discussed earlier, is that state and nation are at each other's throats, and the hyphen that links them is now less an icon of conjuncture than an index of disjuncture. This disjunctive relationship between nation and state has two levels: at the level of any given nation-state, it means that there is a battle of the imagination, with state and nation seeking to cannibalize one another. Here is the seedbed of brutal separatisms—majoritarianisms that seem to have appeared from nowhere and microidentities that have become political projects within the nation-state. At another level, this disjunctive relationship is deeply entangled with the global disjunctures discussed throughout this chapter: ideas of nationhood appear to be steadily increasing in scale and regularly crossing existing state boundaries, sometimes, as with the Kurds, because previous identities stretched across vast national spaces or, as with the Tamils in Sri Lanka, the dormant threads of a transnational diaspora have been activated to ignite the micropolitics of a nation-state.

In discussing the cultural politics that have subverted the hyphen that links the nation to the state, it is especially important not to forget the mooring of such politics in the irregularities that now characterize disorganized capital (Kothari 1989; Lash and Urry 1987). Because labor, finance, and technology are now so widely separated, the volatilities that underlie movements for nationhood (as large as transnational Islam on the one hand, or as small as the movement of the Gurkhas for a separate state in Northeast

---

[18] *Fissiparousness:* the tendency of things to break into pieces.

India) grind against the vulnerabilities that characterize the relationships between states. States find themselves pressed to stay open by the forces of media, technology, and travel that have fueled consumerism throughout the world and have increased the craving, even in the non-western world, for new commodities and spectacles. On the other hand, these very cravings can become caught up in new ethnoscapes, mediascapes, and, eventually, ideoscapes, such as democracy in China, that the state cannot tolerate as threats to its own control over ideas of nationhood and peoplehood.[19] States throughout the world are under siege, especially where contests over the ideoscapes of democracy are fierce and fundamental, and where there are radical disjunctures between ideoscapes and technoscapes (as in the case of very small countries that lack contemporary technologies of production and information); or between ideoscapes and financescapes (as in countries such as Mexico or Brazil, where international lending influences national politics to a very large degree); or between ideoscapes and ethnoscapes (as in Beirut, where diasporic, local, and translocal filiations are suicidally at battle); or between ideoscapes and mediascapes (as in many countries in the Middle East and Asia) where the lifestyles represented on both national and international TV and cinema completely overwhelm and undermine the rhetoric of national politics. In the Indian case, the myth of

the law-breaking hero has emerged to mediate this naked struggle between the pieties and realities of Indian politics, which has grown increasingly brutalized and corrupt (Vachani 1989).

The transnational movement of the martial arts, particularly through Asia, as mediated by the Hollywood and Hong Kong film industries (Zarilli 1995) is a rich illustration of the ways in which long-standing martial arts traditions, reformulated to meet the fantasies of contemporary (sometimes lumpen) youth populations, create new cultures of masculinity and violence, which are in turn the fuel for increased violence in national and international politics.[20] Such violence is in turn the spur to an increasingly rapid and amoral arms trade that penetrates the entire world. The worldwide spread of the AK-47 and the Uzi, in films, in corporate and state security, in terror, and in police and military activity, is a reminder that apparently simple technical uniformities often conceal an increasingly complex set of loops, linking images of violence to aspirations for community in some imagined world.[21]

Returning then to the ethnoscapes with which I began, the central paradox of ethnic politics in today's world is that primordia (whether of language or skin color or neighborhood or kinship) have become globalized. That is, sentiments, whose greatest force is in their ability to ignite intimacy into a political state and turn locality into a staging ground for identity, have become spread

---

[19] When the first version of this essay was published in 1991, China had recently put down a very widely publicized mass pro-democracy demonstration. In May 1989 hundreds of thousands of students demanded democracy by protesting in Beijing's Tiananmen Square. The movement was crushed by the Chinese Army in late May of that year. The number who died is still unknown, but estimates vary from under 100 to as many as 3,000.

[20] *Lumpen* is a term from Marxist vocabulary. It generally refers to the underclass, particularly dispossessed and displaced individuals; the very lowest social strata. See also note 10 in essay 42 by Bourgois, where Marx's term *lumpenproletariat* is discussed.

[21] Over the past several paragraphs Appadurai has presented a powerful historical argument. Until perhaps the time of World War II, the various *scapes* that Appadurai

characterizes existed in greater or lesser synchrony. Nation-states, capital, media, and so on, overlapped. Firms were tied to national interests and the result was a world characterized by the hegemony of Western wealth, power, and ideas. In the past fifty years or so, these ties have come loose from their moorings, which has radically affected the interests of nations and capitalist firms. The result is a profoundly disjunctive world. On the other hand, Appadurai may be extending his argument a bit too far. In the paragraph you just read, he argues that the international popularity of Kung-fu films is a causative factor in the rise in the international arms trade. Appadurai's ideas have been very productive in inspiring research about the ways in which nationalism, capitalism, the media and other aspects of modernity articulate, but it's difficult to imagine exactly what data would show the connection between things such as Kung-fu films and the arms trade.

over vast and irregular spaces as groups move yet stay linked to one another through sophisticated media capabilities. This is not to deny that such primordia are often the product of invented traditions (Hobsbawm and Ranger 1983) or retrospective affiliations, but to emphasize that because of the disjunctive and unstable interplay of commerce, media, national policies, and consumer fantasies, ethnicity, once a genie contained in the bottle of some sort of locality (however large), has now become a global force, forever slipping in and through the cracks between states and borders.

But the relationship between the cultural and economic levels of this new set of global disjunctures is not a simple one-way street in which the terms of global cultural politics are set wholly by, or confined wholly within, the vicissitudes of international flows of technology, labor, and finance, demanding only a modest modification of existing neo-Marxist models of uneven development and state formation. There is a deeper change, itself driven by the disjunctures among all the landscapes I have discussed and constituted by their continuously fluid and uncertain interplay, that concerns the relationship between production and consumption in today's global economy. Here, I begin with Marx's famous (and often mined) view of the fetishism of the commodity and suggest that this fetishism has been replaced in the world at large (now seeing the world as one large, interactive system, composed

of many complex subsystems) by two mutually supportive descendants, the first of which I call production fetishism and the second, the fetishism of the consumer.[22]

By *production fetishism* I mean an illusion created by contemporary transnational production loci that masks translocal capital, transnational earning flows, global management, and often faraway workers (engaged in various kinds of high-tech putting-out operations) in the idiom and spectacle of local (sometimes even worker) control, national productivity, and territorial sovereignty. To the extent that various kinds of free-trade zones have become the models for production at large, especially of high-tech commodities, production has itself become a fetish, obscuring not social relations as such but the relations of production, which are increasingly transnational. The locality (both in the sense of the local factory or site of production and in the extended sense of the nation-state) becomes a fetish that disguises the globally dispersed forces that actually drive the production process. This generates alienation (in Marx's sense) twice intensified, for its social sense is now compounded by a complicated spatial dynamic that is increasingly global.[23]

As for the *fetishism of the consumer*, I mean to indicate here that the consumer has been transformed through commodity flows (and the mediascapes, especially of advertising, that accompany them) into a sign, both in Baudrillard's

---

[22] Commodity fetishism is a critical idea introduced by Marx in *Capital* (1930 [1867]). Marx argues that in capitalism (as distinct from other modes of production) commodities are removed from the conditions of their production through the medium of money. This disjuncture makes it possible to think of a market consisting only of items that are traded against each other and especially against money. Economists focus on this market, but in doing so they fetishize commodities, making them magical items that seem to have wills and values of their own, separate from either their uses or their conditions of production. Because of this fetishism, so Marx argues, bourgeois economists misunderstand the true nature of both value (which is tied to the amount of labor in things) and economic relations themselves. Fetishizing the commodity thus acts to disguise or obscure the true nature of the

relation of production that created it. In the next paragraphs, Appadurai argues that a similar process has happened for both production and consumption. They have become terms that mask rather than reveal processes and understanding.

[23] Alienation in Marx's sense refers to removal. Recall that Marx believed that workers were alienated to the extent that ownership of the means of production was taken away from them. Here they are doubly alienated because not only are the means of production (the factory) removed from the worker but, despite its physical presence, it is removed from the nation as well. The factory may be physically located nearby, but virtually all aspects of its control, operation, and economic benefits may be managed from afar.

sense of a simulacrum[24] that only asymptotically approaches the form of a real social agent, and in the sense of a mask for the real seat of agency, which is not the consumer but the producer and the many forces that constitute production. Global advertising is the key technology for the worldwide dissemination of a plethora of creative and culturally well-chosen ideas of consumer agency. These images of agency are increasingly distortions of a world of merchandising so subtle that the consumer is consistently helped to believe that he or she is an actor, where in fact he or she is at best a chooser.

The globalization of culture is not the same as its homogenization, but globalization involves the use of a variety of instruments of homogenization (armaments, advertising techniques, language hegemonies, and clothing styles) that are absorbed into local political and cultural economies, only to be repatriated as heterogeneous dialogues of national sovereignty, free enterprise, and fundamentalism in which the state plays an increasingly delicate role: too much openness to global flows, and the nation-state is threatened by revolt, as in the China syndrome; too little, and the state exits the international stage, as Burma, Albania, and North Korea in various ways have done. In general, the state has become the arbitrageur of this *repatriation of difference* (in the form of goods, signs, slogans, and styles). But this repatriation or export of the designs and commodities of difference continuously exacerbates the internal politics of majoritarianism and homogenization, which is most frequently played out in debates over heritage.

Thus the central feature of global culture today is the politics of the mutual effort of sameness and difference to cannibalize one another and thereby proclaim their successful hijacking of the twin Enlightenment ideas of the triumphantly universal and the resiliently particular. This mutual cannibalization shows its ugly face in riots, refugee flows, state-sponsored torture, and ethnocide (with or without state support). Its brighter side is in the expansion of many individual horizons of hope and fantasy, in the global spread of oral rehydration therapy and other low-tech instruments of well-being, in the susceptibility even of South Africa to the force of global opinion, in the inability of the Polish state to repress its own working classes, and in the growth of a wide range of progressive, transnational alliances.[25] Examples of both sorts could be multiplied. The critical point is that both sides of the coin of global cultural process today are products of the infinitely varied mutual contest of sameness and difference on a stage characterized by radical disjunctures between different

---

[24] *Baudrillard's sense of simulacrum:* A simulacrum is an image or a representation. Baudrillard (1994) argued that advanced capitalism and, in particular, the media, have detached the image from the real. As we are bombarded with images, we are exposed to models of objects and behaviors that have no counterparts in our actual lives. The notions of masculinity and femininity seen on TV, the homes portrayed on TV and in glossy magazines, and so on, are frequently held up as perfectly desirable. Thus consumerism is fired by an attempt to purchase and create in reality a simulacrum or model that has no origin in reality. Efforts to model reality on such a simulacrum are ultimately doomed and lead to a collapse of meaning. Appadurai, following Baudrillard, argues for a fetishism of the consumer. He claims that analysts focus on consumer behavior, but such a focus misunderstands the true dynamics of the situation. The consumer is buffeted and controlled by elements of capitalism that structure the nature of desire and the possibilities available to satisfy it.

[25] Appadurai, referring to South Africa and Poland here, is commenting on the politics of the 1980s. Between the early years of the twentieth century and the early 1990s, South Africa had a legal system of discrimination called apartheid. It was eventually brought to an end by a combination of civil disobedience in South Africa and sanctions and diplomatic pressure from the rest of the world. In Poland, a communist nation after World War II, an anticommunist trade union, Solidarity, was founded in 1980. Despite several attempts, the government was unable to suppress the union and by 1989, a Solidarity-led government was in place and union leader Lech Walesa (b. 1943) had been elected president. Note that the collapse of apartheid, the success of Solidarity, and the fall of communism in Eastern Europe and Russia were titanic events that had just happened when Appadurai wrote this essay.

sorts of global flows and the uncertain landscapes created in and through these disjunctures.

THE WORK OF REPRODUCTION IN AN AGE OF MECHANICAL ART

I have inverted the key terms of the title of Walter Benjamin's famous essay (1969) to return this rather high-flying discussion to a more manageable level. There is a classic human problem that will not disappear however much global cultural processes might change their dynamics, and this is the problem today typically discussed under the rubric of reproduction (and traditionally referred to in terms of the transmission of culture). In either case, the question is, how do small groups, especially families, the classical loci of socialization, deal with these new global realities as they seek to reproduce themselves and, in so doing, by accident reproduce cultural forms themselves? In traditional anthropological terms, this could be phrased as the problem of enculturation in a period of rapid culture change. So the problem is hardly novel. But it does take on some novel dimensions under the global conditions discussed so far in this chapter.[26]

First, the sort of transgenerational stability of knowledge that was presupposed in most theories of enculturation (or, in slightly broader terms, of socialization) can no longer be assumed. As families move to new locations, or as children move before older generations, or as grown sons and daughters return from time spent in strange parts of the world, family relationships can become volatile; new commodity patterns are negotiated, debts and obligations are recalibrated, and rumors and fantasies about the new setting are maneuvered into existing repertoires of knowledge and practice. Often, global labor diasporas involve immense strains on marriages in general and on women in particular, as marriages become the meeting points of historical patterns of socialization and new ideas of proper behavior. Generations easily divide, as ideas about property, propriety, and collective obligation wither under the siege of distance and time. Most important, the work of cultural reproduction in new settings is profoundly complicated by the politics of representing a family as normal (particularly for the young) to neighbours and peers in the new locale. All this is, of course, not new to the cultural study of immigration.

What is new is that this is a world in which both points of departure and points of arrival are in cultural flux, and thus the search for steady points of reference, as critical life choices are made, can be very difficult. It is in this atmosphere that the invention of tradition (and of ethnicity, kinship, and other identity markers) can become slippery, as the search for certainties is regularly frustrated by the fluidities of transnational communication. As group pasts become increasingly parts of museums, exhibits, and collections, both in national and transnational spectacles, culture becomes less what Pierre Bourdieu would have called a habitus (a tacit realm of reproducible practices and dispositions) and more an arena for conscious choice, justification, and representation, the latter often to multiple and spatially dislocated audiences.[27]

---

[26] Though he phrases it partially as the anthropological issue of enculturation, Appadurai also locates his argument squarely in neo-Marxist thought. For Marx, every society both produces and reproduces. It produces its livelihood and it reproduces the mode of production. Societies provide their members sufficient resources to reproduce their own living conditions and relations of production as they promulgate ideologies that justify these conditions and relations. Social reproduction is the force that drives society forward in time. Appadurai, punning on the title of Walter Benjamin's most famous essay "The Work of Art in the Age of Mechanical Reproduction," points to the difficulties of social reproduction in an age of global flow.

[27] Habitus has become a common idea in current anthropology and is most frequently associated with Pierre Bourdieu. It refers to the common daily practices and beliefs of an individual as a member of a social group that form the basic assumptions about the nature of social life and the world. Two key characteristics of habitus are, first, that its elements are so basic to individuals' understandings that they cannot be thought of directly without

The task of cultural reproduction, even in its most intimate arenas, such as husband-wife and parent-child relations, becomes both politicized and exposed to the traumas of deterritorialization as family members pool and negotiate their mutual understandings and aspirations in sometimes fractured spatial arrangements. At larger levels, such as community, neighborhood, and territory, this politicization is often the emotional fuel for more explicitly violent politics of identity, just as these larger politics sometimes penetrate and ignite domestic politics. When, for example, two offspring in a household split with their father on a key matter of political identification in a transnational setting, preexisting localized norms carry little force. Thus a son who has joined the Hezbollah group in Lebanon may no longer get along with parents or siblings who are affiliated with Amal or some other branch of Shi'i ethnic political identity in Lebanon. Women in particular bear the brunt of this sort of friction, for they become pawns in the heritage politics of the household and are often subject to the abuse and violence of men who are themselves torn about the relation between heritage and opportunity in shifting spatial and political formations.

The pains of cultural reproduction in a disjunctive global world are, of course, not eased by the effects of mechanical art (or mass media), for these media afford powerful resources for counternodes of identity that youth can project against parental wishes or desires. At larger levels of organization, there can be many forms of cultural politics within displaced populations (whether of refugees or of voluntary immigrants), all of which are inflected in important ways by media (and the mediascapes and ideoscapes they

offer). A central link between the fragilities of cultural reproduction and the role of the mass media in today's world is the politics of gender and violence. As fantasies of gendered violence dominate the B-grade film industries that blanket the world, they both reflect and refine gendered violence at home and in the streets, as young men (in particular) are swayed by the macho politics of self-assertion in contexts where they are frequently denied real agency, and women are forced to enter the labor force in new ways on the one hand, and continue the maintenance of familial heritage on the other. Thus the honor of women becomes not just an armature of stable (if inhuman) systems of cultural reproduction but a new arena for the formation of sexual identity and family politics, as men and women face new pressures at work and new fantasies of leisure.[28]

Because both work and leisure have lost none of their gendered qualities in this new global order but have acquired ever subtler fetishized representations, the honor of women becomes increasingly a surrogate for the identity of embattled communities of males, while their women in reality have to negotiate increasingly harsh conditions of work at home and in the nondomestic workplace. In short, deterritorialized communities and displaced populations, however much they may enjoy the fruits of new kinds of earning and new dispositions of capital and technology, have to play out the desires and fantasies of these new ethnoscapes, while striving to reproduce the family-as-microcosm of culture. As the shapes of cultures grow less bounded and tacit, more fluid and politicized, the work of cultural reproduction becomes a daily hazard. Far more could, and should, be said about the work of

---

difficulty. They are the things that not only go without saying but are extremely difficult to say. Second, in at least some of its expressions, habitus is a physical thing. It is expressed in people's bodies and the ways in which these are held and used in social interaction. Appadurai here points out that the global economy has the effect of making culture a conscious attribute and a series of choices rather than a habitus, something that is inscribed in our consciousness and our bodies in ways that we can only partially recognize.

[28] In this passage, Appadurai modifies Benjamin's argument. Benjamin was optimistic about mass culture because he saw it as demystifying art and giving it as a tool to the masses. Appadurai, however, sees the media as providing images of violence and sexuality that encourage street and household-level violence by individuals (particularly men) who are denied any meaningful agency in the world at large. Thus, mechanical art becomes not a tool of the people but an avenue to power and profit by the capitalist elite at the expense of the poor.

reproduction in an age of mechanical art: the preceding discussion is meant to indicate the contours of the problems that a new, globally informed theory of cultural reproduction will have to face.

SHAPE AND PROCESS IN GLOBAL CULTURAL FORMATIONS

The deliberations of the arguments that I have made so far constitute the bare bones of an approach to a general theory of global cultural processes. Focusing on disjunctures, I have employed a set of terms (*ethnoscape, financescape, technoscape, mediascape,* and *ideoscape*) to stress different streams or flows along which cultural material may be seen to be moving across national boundaries. I have also sought to exemplify the ways in which these various flows (or landscapes, from the stabilizing perspectives of any given imagined world) are in fundamental disjuncture with respect to one another. What further steps can we take toward a general theory of global cultural processes based on these proposals?

The first is to note that our very models of cultural shape will have to alter, as configurations of people, place, and heritage lose all semblance of isomorphism.[29] Recent work in anthropology has done much to free us of the shackles of

highly localized, boundary-oriented, holistic, primordialist images of cultural form and substance (Hannerz 1989; Marcus and Fischer 1986; Thornton 1988). But not very much has been put in their place, except somewhat larger if less mechanical versions of these images, as in Eric Wolf's work on the relationship of Europe to the rest of the world (1982). What I would like to propose is that we begin to think of the configuration of cultural forms in today's world as fundamentally fractal, that is, as possessing no Euclidean boundaries, structures, or regularities. Second, I would suggest that these cultural forms, which we should strive to represent as fully fractal, are also overlapping in ways that have been discussed only in pure mathematics (in set theory, for example) and in biology (in the language of polythetic classifications). Thus we need to combine a fractal metaphor for the shape of cultures (in the plural) with a polythetic account of their overlaps and resemblances. Without this latter step, we shall remain mired in comparative work that relies on the clear separation of the entities to be compared before serious comparison can begin. How are we to compare fractally shaped cultural forms that are also polythetically overlapping in their coverage of terrestrial space?[30]

Finally, in order for the theory of global cultural interactions predicated on disjunctive flows to have any force greater than that of a mechanical

---

[29] *Isomorphism:* sharing the same or similar form.

[30] In this last section of the essay, Appadurai refers to ideas from mathematics and biology. Chaos mathematics was an extremely popular notion of the late 1980s and 1990s. Enthusiasm for it was fired, in part, by James Gleick's popular 1987 account: *Chaos: Making a New Science.* The notion of a fractal is central to chaos theory. A fractal is, technically, a complex figure that can be represented by a mathematical equation. The key characteristic of a fractal is that its pattern repeats itself on both larger and smaller scales. For example, the pattern of a coastline is repeated in the pattern of a smaller section of that coastline, and repeated again in a still smaller section, and so on and so on. Thus, fractals are said to be self-referential. It is not clear that this definition is quite the same as "as possessing no Euclidean boundaries, structures, or regularities," which raises at least two inter-

esting questions: First, is Appadurai simply using *fractal* as a synonym for *chaotic* (and thus mischaracterizing both fractals and the idea of chaos math, which does both seek and find complex patterns)? Second, is the nature of culture properly fractal—that is, are the patterns of global culture reiterated at many different levels: the state, nation, community, individual and so on?

Appadurai also invokes the idea of *polythetic set.* A group is polythetic if all its members share a number of traits but there is no one identifying trait that is shared by all members. The philosopher Wittgenstein (1889–1951) provides an example. He challenges us to come up with a single trait shared by all games. This is an impossible task, but Wittgenstein (2001) argues that our failure at it is not the result of our lack of understanding the true nature of games but rather indicates that games form a polythetic group and have a family resemblance rather than a single defining characteristic.

metaphor, it will have to move into something like a human version of the theory that some scientists are calling chaos theory. That is, we will need to ask not how these complex, overlapping, fractal shapes constitute a simple, stable (even if large-scale) system, but to ask what its dynamics are: Why do ethnic riots occur when and where they do? Why do states wither at greater rates in some places and times than in others? Why do some countries flout conventions of international debt repayment with so much less apparent worry than others? How are international arms flows driving ethnic battles and genocides? Why are some states exiting the global stage while others are clamoring to get in? Why do key events occur at a certain point in a certain place rather than in others? These are, of course, the great traditional questions of causality, contingency, and prediction in the human sciences, but in a world of disjunctive global flows, it is perhaps important to start asking them in a way that relies on images of flow and uncertainty, hence chaos, rather than on older images of order, stability, and systematicness. Otherwise, we will have gone far toward a theory of global cultural systems but thrown out process in the bargain. And that would make these notes part of a journey toward the kind of illusion of order that we can no longer afford to impose on a world that is so transparently volatile.[31]

Whatever the directions in which we can push these macrometaphors (fractals, polythetic classifications, and chaos), we need to ask one other old-fashioned question out of the Marxist paradigm: is there some pre-given order to the relative determining force of these global flows? Because I have postulated the dynamics of global cultural systems as driven by the relationships among flows of persons, technologies, finance, information, and ideology, can we speak of some structural-causal order linking these flows by analogy to the role of the economic order in one version of the Marxist paradigm? Can we speak of some of these flows as being, for a priori structural or historical reasons, always prior to and formative of other flows? My own hypothesis, which can only be tentative at this point, is that the relationship of these various flows to one another as they constellate into particular events and social forms will be radically context-dependent. Thus, while labor flows and their loops with financial flows between Kerala and the Middle East may account for the shape of media flows and ideoscapes in Kerala, the reverse may be true of Silicon Valley in California, where intense specialization in a single technological sector (computers) and particular flows of capital may well profoundly determine the shape that ethnoscapes, ideoscapes, and mediascapes may take.[32]

This does not mean that the causal-historical relationship among these various flows is random or meaninglessly contingent but that our current theories of cultural chaos are insufficiently developed to be even parsimonious models at this point, much less to be predictive theories, the golden fleeces of one kind of social science. What I have sought to provide in this chapter is a reasonably economical technical vocabulary and a rudimentary model of disjunctive flows, from which something like a decent global analysis might emerge. Without some such analysis, it will be difficult to construct what John Hinkson calls a "social theory of postmodernity" that is adequately global (1990:84).

---

[31] In this passage, Appadurai seems to call for a predictive science of anthropology. Invoking chaos mathematics seems to suggest that we could apply some sort of mathematical formula to either predict or explain major geopolitical events with a degree of certainty. It is far from clear that we've made any progress in this direction. A critical problem is that ideas such as ethnoscapes are powerful metaphors and useful tools for thinking about the nature of modernity. However, it is not apparent how such ideas could be quantified in ways that might make rigorous prediction or explanation possible.

[32] In concluding, Appadurai returns again to Marx. In Marxist thought, production and ideology both play important roles, but forces and relations of production are held to be prior to and more important than ideology. Here, Appadurai suggests that no such relationship will hold true for the *scapes* he identifies. Rather, their relationships will need to be determined afresh for each instance of analysis.

NOTES

[a]One major exception is Fredric Jameson, whose work on the relationship between postmodernism and late capitalism has in many ways inspired this essay. The debate between Jameson and Aijaz Ahmad in *Social Text*, however, shows that the creation of a globalizing Marxist narrative in cultural matters is difficult territory indeed (Ahmad 1987; Jameson 1986). My own effort in this context is to begin a restructuring of the Marxist narrative (by stressing lags and disjunctures) that many Marxists might find abhorrent. Such a restructuring has to avoid the dangers of obliterating difference within the Third World, eliding the social referent (as some French postmodernists seem inclined to do), and retaining the narrative authority of the Marxist tradition, in favor of greater attention to global fragmentation, uncertainty, and difference.

REFERENCES

Abu-Lughod, J. L. (1989). *Before European Hegemony: The World System AD 1250–1350*. New York: Oxford University Press.

Ahmad, A. (1987). Jameson's Rhetoric of Otherness and the "National Allegory," *Social Text* 17: 3–25.

Amin, S. (1980). *Class and Nation: Historically and in the Current Crisis*. New York and London: Monthly Review Press.

Anderson, B. (1983). *Imagined Communities: Reflections on the Origin and Spread of Nationalism*. London: Verso.

Appadurai, A. (1996). *Modernity at Large: Cultural Dimensions of Globalization*. Minneapolis: University of Minnesota Press.

Barber, K. (1987). Popular Arts in Africa, *African Studies Review* 30(3) (September): 1–78.

Baruah, S. (1986). Immigration, Ethnic Conflict and Political Turmoil, Assam 1979–1985, *Asian Survey* 26(11) (November): 1184–206.

Bayly, C. A. (1989). *Imperial Meridian: The British Empire and the World, 1780–1830*. London and New York: Longman.

Benjamin, W. (1969). The Work of Art in the Age of Mechanical Reproduction [1936]. In H. Arendt (ed.) *Illuminations*. H. Zohn (trans.). New York: Schocken Books.

Braudel, F. (1981–4). *Civilization and Capitalism, 15th–18th Century* (3 vols.) London: Collins.

Chatterjee, P. (1986). *Nationalist Thought and the Colonial World: A Derivative Discourse?* London: Zed Books.

Curtin, P. (1984). *Cross-Cultural Trade in World History*. Cambridge: Cambridge University Press.

Deleuze, G., and F. Guattari (1987). *A Thousand Plateaus: Capitalism and Schizophrenia*. B. Massumi (trans.). Minneapolis: University of Minnesota Press.

Fabian, J. (1983). *Time and the Other. How Anthropology Makes Its Object*. New York: Columbia University Press

Feld, S. (1988). Notes on World Beat, *Public Culture* 1(1): 31–7.

Gans, E. (1985). *The End of Culture: Toward a Generative Anthropology*. Berkeley: University of California Press.

Hamelink, C. (1983). *Cultural Autonomy in Global Communications*. New York: Longman.

Handler, R. (1988). *Nationalism and the Politics of Culture in Quebec*. Madison: University of Wisconsin Press.

Hannerz, U. (1987). The World in Creolization, *Africa* 57(4): 546–59.

———. (1989). Notes on the Global Ecumene, *Public Culture* 1(2) (Spring): 66–75.

Hechter, M. (1975). *Internal Colonialism: The Celtic Fringe in British National Development, 1536–1966*. Berkeley: University of California Press.

Helms, M. W. (1988). *Ulysses' Sail: An Ethnographic Odyssey of Power, Knowledge, and Geographical Distance*. Princeton, NJ: Princeton University Press.

Herzfeld, M. (1982). *Ours Once More: Folklore, Ideology and the Making of Modern Greece*. Austin: University of Texas Press.

Hinkson, J. (1990). Postmodernism and Structural Change, *Public Culture* 2(2) (Spring): 82–101.

Hobsbawm, E., and T. Ranger (eds.) (1983). *The Invention of Tradition*. New York: Cambridge University Press.

Hodgson, M. (1974). *The Venture of Islam. Conscience and History in a World Civilization* (3 vols). Chicago: University of Chicago Press.

Ivy, M. (1988). Tradition and Difference in the Japanese Mass Media, *Public Culture* 1(1): 21–9.

Iyer, P. (1988). *Video Night in Kathmandu*. New York: Knopf.

Jameson, F. (1983). Postmodernism and Consumer Society. In H. Foster (ed.) *The Anti-Aesthetic: Essays on Postmodern Culture*. Port Townsend, WA: Bay Press.

———. (1986). Third World Literature in the Era of Multi-National Capitalism, *Social Text* 1 (Fall): 65–88.

———. (1989). Nostalgia for the Present, *South Atlantic Quarterly* 88(2) (Spring): 517–37.

Kothari, R. (1989). *State against Democracy: In Search of Humane Governance*. New York: New Horizons.

Lakoff, G., and M. Johnson (1980). *Metaphors We Live By*. Chicago and London: University of Chicago Press.

Lash, S., and J. Urry (1987). *The End of Organized Capitalism*. Madison: University of Wisconsin Press.

Mandel, E. (1978). *Late Capitalism*. London: Verso.

Marcus, G., and M. Fischer (1986). *Anthropology as Cultural Critique: An Experimental Moment in the Human Sciences*. Chicago: University of Chicago Press.

Manttelart, A. (1983). *Transnational and the Third World: The Struggle for Culture*. South Hadley, MA: Bergin and Garvey.

McLuhan, M., and B. R. Powers (1989). *The Global Village: Transformations in World Life and Media in the 21st Century*. New York: Oxford University Press.

McQueen, H. (1988). The Australian Stamp: Image, Design and Ideology, *Arena* 84 (Spring): 78–96.

Meyrowitz, J. (1985). *No Sense of Place: The Impact of Electronic Media on Social Behavior*. New York: Oxford University Press.

Nandy, A. (1989). The Political Culture of the Indian State, *Daedalus* 118(4): 1–26.

Nicoll, F. (1989). My Trip to Alice, *Criticism, Heresy and Interpretation* 3: 21–32.

Schafer, E. (1963). *Golden Peaches of Samarkand: A Study of T'ang Exotics*. Berkeley: University of California Press.

Schiller, H. (1976). *Communication and Cultural Domination*. White Plains, NY: International Arts and Sciences.

Thornton, R. (1988). The Rhetoric of Ethnographic Holism, *Cultural Anthropology* 3(3) (August): 285–303.

Vachani, L. (1989). *Narrative, Pleasure and Ideology in the Hindi Film: An Analysis of the Outsider Formula*. MA thesis, Annenberg School of Communication, University of Pennsylvania.

Wallerstein, L. (1974). *The Modem World System* (2 vols.) New York and London: Academic Press.

Warner, M. (1990). *The Letters of the Republic: Publication and the Public Sphere in Eighteenth-Century America*. Cambridge, MA: Harvard University Press.

Williams, R. (1976). *Keywords*. New York: Oxford University Press.

Wolf, E. (1982). *Europe and the People without History*. Berkeley: University of California Press.

Yoshimoto, M. (1989). The Postmodern and Mass Images in Japan, *Public Culture* 1 (2): 8–25.

Zarilli, P. (1995). Repositioning the Body: An Indian Martial Art and its Pan-Asian Publics. In C. A. Breckenridge (ed.), *Consuming Modernity: Public Culture in a South Asian World*. Minneapolis: University of Minnesota Press.

---

42. *From Jíbaro to Crack Dealer: Confronting the Restructuring of Capitalism in El Barrio*

PHILIPPE BOURGOIS (b. 1956)

FOLLOWING HIS YEAR and a half of field work in a rural coffee-growing country in the central highlands of Puerto Rico from 1948 through 1949, Eric R. Wolf warned that even the small farmers and coffee pickers in the most isolated and traditional rural barrio that he was studying "in the future will supply many hundreds of hands to the coast, to the towns, and to the United States" (Wolf 1956*b*, 231). Macroeco-nomic and political forces proved Wolf's warning to be an understatement. American industrial capital was provided with extraordinary incentives and local agricultural development in Puerto Rico atrophied at the same time that emigration to the factories of New York City was actively promoted. The ensuing exodus over the next three and a half decades of almost a third of Puerto Rico's total population resulted proportionally

(1995)

in one of the larger labor migrations in modern history.[1]

STRUCTURAL CONSTRAINTS OF THE NUYORICAN EXPERIENCE

The majority of the immigrants found employment in New York City's most vulnerable subsector of light manufacturing. They arrived precisely on the eve of the structural decimation of factory production in urban North America. Indeed, the post-World War II Puerto Rican experience provides almost a textbook illustration of what Wolf in his later work refers to as "the growth of ever more diverse proletarian diasporas" that "capitalist accumulation . . . continues to engender" as it spreads across the globe (1982a, 383). Perhaps most interesting and relevant for understanding Nuyorican ethnicity—that is, the experience of New York City-born and raised Puerto Ricans—are the contradictory ways that the "changing needs of capital . . . continuously produce and recreate symbolically marked 'cultural' distinctions" among "the new working classes" who have criss-crossed oceans and continents in their struggle for survival and dignity (Wolf 1982a, 379–380).[2]

Depending upon one's formal definition, over the past three or four generations, the Puerto Rican people—especially those living in New York—have passed through almost a half dozen distinct modes of production: (1) from small land-owning semisubsistence peasantry or hacienda peons; (2) to export agricultural laborers on foreign-owned, capital-intensive plantations; (3) to factory workers in urban shantytowns; (4) to sweatshop workers in ghetto tenements; (5) to service sector employees in high-rise inner-city housing projects; (6) to underground economy entrepreneurs homeless on the street.[3]

This marathon sprint through economic history onto New York City's streets has been compounded ideologically by an overtly racist

---

[1] This essay first appeared in Articulating Hidden Histories (Schneider and Rapp 1995), a collection of essays dedicated to exploring the legacy of Eric R. Wolf. Wolf (1923–1999) is generally considered one of the most important Marxist-influenced anthropologists of the midcentury. He is particularly interested in the ways in which the expansion of capitalism has affected cultures throughout the world. He explores this theme at length in *Europe and the People Without History* (1982), a book widely considered a classic of the neo-Marxist approach. As you read the essays in this section you will see that they are clearly a synthesis of Marxist and interpretive approaches. Globalization theory provides an intersection between capitalism, power, and meaning. An analysis like Bourgois' illustrates the economic pressures and relations between different elements in an economic system while at the same time illustrating the ways in which people create and contest meaning within these economic structures. In this essay Bourgois discusses how the economic opportunities for young working-class Puerto Rican men have evaporated in the last twenty years as the New York City economy has changed. He shows how these young men attempt to negotiate their way through an unfamiliar cultural landscape in which they are ill-equipped to succeed.

[2] One of Wolf's key contentions is that the histories of oppressed peoples and minority groups are fundamental to understanding culture and ourselves (Schneider and Rapp 1995:7). Wolf sees such people as fundamental actors driving culture change—a theme he explores in *Peasant Wars of the Twentieth Century* (1969). Bourgois, in dealing with people from the slums of New York, is acting very much in the tradition of Wolf.

[3] The *mode of production* is a fundamental Marxist concept. Unfortunately, Marx never provided a concise definition of it. Briefly, a mode of production is a pattern that combines labor, the machines and raw materials that workers use, and the social and technical relations under which they use them (Suchting 1983:76–77). Marx analyzed the history of Europe as a series of successive modes of production. His modes were Asiatic, ancient, feudal, and modern bourgeois (Lichtheim 1973:151). Traditional Marxist analysis demanded that societies belong to one of these four modes. One of the neo-Marxists' critical innovations was to expand the mode of production concept to include many societies that did not fit easily into Marx's original modes. This, however, tended to result in a great proliferation of new modes of production. Here Bourgois delineates a number of modes of production, none of which are found in the works of Marx, but each of which describes a pattern of labor, material, equipment, social, and technical relationships that is found in the modern world.

"cultural assault." Literally overnight the new immigrants—many of whom were enveloped in a *jíbaro* (hillbilly)-dominated culture emphasizing interpersonal webs of patriarchal *respeto*—found themselves transformed into "racially" inferior cultural pariahs. Ever since their arrival they have been despised and humiliated with that virulence so characteristic of America's history of polarized race relations in the context of massive labor migrations. Even though the Puerto Rican experience is extreme, it is by no means unique. On the contrary, peoples all through the world and throughout history have been forced to traverse multiple modes of production and have suffered social dislocation.[4]

The historic structural transformations imposed upon the Puerto Rican jíbaro translate statistically into a tragic profile of unemployment, substance abuse, broken families, and devastated health in U.S. inner cities. No other ethnic group except perhaps Native Americans fares more poorly in the official statistics than do mainland U.S. Puerto Ricans. This is most pronounced for the majority cohort living in New York City where Puerto Ricans have the highest welfare dependency and poverty rates, the lowest labor force participation rates, and the fastest growing HIV infection rates of any group (Falcon 1992; Lambert 1990).

THE ETHNOGRAPHIC SETTING

These contemporary expressions of historical dislocation formed the backdrop for my five years of participant-observation fieldwork on street culture in the "crack economy" during the late 1980s and early 1990s. For a total of approximately three and a half years I lived with my wife and young son in an irregularly heated, rat-filled tenement in East Harlem, better known locally as El Barrio or Spanish Harlem. This two-hundred-square-block neighborhood is visibly impoverished yet it is located in the heart of the richest city in the western hemisphere. Its vacant lots and crumbling abandoned tenements are literally a stone's throw from multimillion-dollar condominiums. Although one in three families survives on public assistance, the majority of El Barrio's 130,000 Puerto Rican and African-American residents comprise the ranks of the "working poor." They eke out an uneasy subsistence in entry-level service and manufacturing jobs in a city with one of the highest costs of living in the world.[5]

In my ethnographic research, I explored the ideologies (i.e., the power-charged belief systems) that organize "common sense" on the street—what I call "street culture." Consequently, over the years, I interacted with and befriended the addicts, thieves, dealers, and con artists who comprise a minority proportion of El Barrio residents but who exercise hegemony over its public space. Specifically, I focused on a network of some twenty-five street-level crack dealers who operated on and around my block.

On the one hand, such an intensive examination of street participants risks exoticizing the neighborhood and may be interpreted as reinforcing violent stereotypes against Puerto Ricans. On the other hand, case studies of the "worthy poor" risk "normalizing" the experience of class

---

[4] The Boasian tradition in anthropology has often emphasized the unique characteristics of cultures. Ethnoscientists (essays 27, 28) as well as some postmodernists (essays 38, 39) claimed that cultures were essentially incommensurate and no attempt should be made to compare them. Marxism, on the other hand, is a universalizing theory. Marxists claim that fundamental hidden processes underlie all societies. As a result, these societies pass through similar stages and take similar forms. Thus, while much of anthropology emphasizes cultural variation, Marxist anthropologists tend to be more concerned with cultural similarities.

[5] Note that while Bourgois' essay is an analysis of Nuyorican culture, it is also a scathing critique of American capitalism. It is impossible to read this essay without asking yourself, "What kind of system allows this waste of human talent?" Marx, of course, held that capitalism was inherently oppressive and that it would inevitably give way to socialism and communism. In other words, he thought the rise of communism to be a scientific certainty. Most modern Marxists reject this theological notion. However, they generally continue to be harsh critics of capitalism. Bourgois continues to critique American capitalism throughout this essay. He is particularly caustic in its final paragraphs.

and racial segregation and can mask the depths of human suffering that accompanies rapid economic restructuring. Furthermore, the legally employed majority of El Barrio residents has lost control of the streets and has retreated from daily life in the neighborhood. To understand the experience of living in the community, the ideologies of violence, opposition, and material pursuit which have established hegemony over street life—much to the dismay of most residents—have to be addressed systematically. Furthermore, on a subtle theoretical level, the "caricatural" responses to poverty and marginalization that the dealers and addicts represent provide privileged insight into processes that may be experienced in one form or another by major sectors of any vulnerable working-class population experiencing rapid structural change anywhere in the world and at any point in history.[6] Once again, there is nothing structurally exceptional about the Puerto Rican experience except that the human costs involved are more clearly visible given the extent and rapidity with which Puerto Rican society has been absorbed by the United States and the particularly persistent virulence of American ideologies around "race" and culture.[7]

My central concern is the relationship of the street dealers to the worlds of work—that is, the legal and illegal labor markets—that employ them and give meaning to their lives. The long-term structural transformation of New York from a manufacturing to a service economy is crucial to understanding this experience. Although economists, sociologists, and political scientists have argued extensively over the details of the statistics, most recognize that the dislocations caused by the erosion of the manufacturing sector are a driving force behind the economic polarization of urban America (Wilson 1987). They also specifically recognize that Puerto Ricans are the most vulnerable group in New York's structural adjustment because of their over-concentration in the least dynamic subsector within light manufacturing and because of their fragile incipient foothold in public sector and service employment (Rodriguez 1989).

Through my ethnographic data I hope to show the local-level implications of the global-level restructuring of capital and, in the process, give voice to some unrepentant victims. In a nutshell, I am arguing that the transformation from manufacturing to service employment—especially in the professional office work setting—is much more culturally disruptive than the already revealing statistics on reductions in income, employment, unionization, and worker's benefits would indicate. Low-level service sector employment engenders a humiliating ideological—or cultural—confrontation between a powerful corps of white office executives and their assistants versus a mass of poorly educated, alienated, "colored" workers.[8]

---

[6] Bourgois says that his focus on dealers and addicts provides insight into processes that may be experienced by segments of *any* [emphasis ours] vulnerable population experiencing rapid change. This statement gains credibility as you read accounts of other people dislocated by rapid social and economic change. In essay 43, you will read Ong's description of Chinese working-class girls who move to cities in search of employment and end up working as prostitutes. As you do so, consider whether or not Bourgois' style of analysis is applicable in their case too.

[7] This passage expresses several key concerns of current anthropology. The first is the notion of "exoticizing." To exoticize a group of people is to make them appear strange, foreign, and, ultimately, to diminish their humanity. A group that is exotic doesn't have to be taken seriously. A second key concept is "privilege." A privileged in-

sight is one that is to be taken more seriously because of the position of those who offer it. The use of privilege in this manner is often derogatory. Thus, white males of European extraction are held to have privileged positions. That is, for historical reasons, they are the ones whose voices and interpretations are granted the most credibility. Much current anthropology makes an issue of resisting the privileged voices of these people. Here, Bourgois speaks of the privileged voice of the crack dealers, an extremely unprivileged group of people. They are to be taken more seriously because their control of public spaces in the neighborhood and their position in society gives them special insight.

[8] Notice two critical Marxist concerns in the previous two paragraphs. The first is the relationship of work and meaning. Marxists take production as the most basic patterning

SHATTERED WORKING-CLASS DREAMS

All the crack dealers and addicts whom I have interviewed worked at one or more legal jobs in their early youth. In fact, most entered the labor market at a younger age than the typical American. Before they were twelve years old they were bagging groceries at the supermarket for tips, stocking beer off-the-books in local *bodegas,* or shining shoes. For example, Julio, the night manager at a video games arcade that sells five-dollar vials of crack on the block where I lived, pursued a traditional working-class dream in his early adolescence. With the support of his extended kin who were all immersed in a working-class "common sense," he dropped out of junior high school to work in a local garment factory:

> I was like fourteen or fifteen playing hooky and pressing dresses and whatever they were making on the steamer. They was cheap, cheap clothes.
>
> My mother's sister was working there first and then her son, my cousin Hector—the one who's in jail now—was the one they hired first, because his mother agreed: "If you don't want to go to school, you gotta work."
>
> So I started hanging out with him. I wasn't planning on working in the factory. I was supposed to be in school; but it just sort of happened.

Ironically, little Julio actually became the agent who physically moved the factory out of the inner city. In the process, he became merely one

more of the 445,900 manufacturing workers in New York City to lose their jobs as factory employment dropped 50 percent from 1963 to 1983 (Romo and Schwartz 1993). Of course, instead of understanding himself as the victim of a structural transformation, Julio remembers with pleasure and even pride the extra income he earned for clearing the machines out of the factory space:

> Them people had money, man. Because we helped them move out of the neighborhood. It took us two days—only me and my cousin, Hector. Wow! It was work. They gave us seventy bucks each.[9]

Almost all the crack dealers had similar tales of former factory jobs. For poor adolescents, the decision to drop out of school and become a marginal factory worker is attractive. It provides the employed youth with access to the childhood "necessities"—sneakers, basketballs, store-bought snacks—that sixteen-year-olds who stay in school cannot afford. In the descriptions of their first forays into legal factory-based employment, one hears clearly the extent to which they and their families subscribed to mainstream working-class ideologies about the dignity of engaging in "hard work" versus education.

Had these enterprising, early-adolescent workers from El Barrio not been confined to the weakest sector of manufacturing in a period of rapid job loss their teenage working-class dream might have stabilized. Instead, upon reaching their mid-twenties they discovered themselves to be

---

element of society. Marx (in this volume) wrote that ". . . [people] begin to distinguish themselves from animals as soon as they begin to produce their means of subsistence. . . ." Here, Bourgois takes it as axiomatic that people's lives are given meaning by their work, rather than, as might be possible, people choose their jobs because of meanings they acquire from religion or other aspects of social life. The second is the notion of conflict. Conflict is central to Marxist analysis. All societies (except the future communist utopia) are riven by conflicts. History and progress are the inexorable working out of these conflicts and the generation of new conflict. You will notice however, that in addition to this focus on production,

Bourgois also discusses how young men try to negotiate their worldview within a dominate corporate model, contest that model, and negotiate their own meanings of the world outside the corporate context.

[9] In Marxist analysis, the structural factors that drive cultural change are often hidden from cultural participants. In this passage we see Julio actively participating in the change that will lead to poverty for the people around him. In his study of poverty in America Shipler (2004) discovered that because of their day-to-day focus on survival, the working poor find long-term planning virtually impossible.

unemployable high school dropouts. This painful realization of social marginalization expresses itself generationally as the working-class values of their families conflict violently with the reality of their hard-core lumpenization.[10] They are constantly accused of slothfulness by their mothers and even by friends who have managed to maintain legal jobs. They do not have a regional perspective on the dearth of adequate entry-level jobs available to "functional illiterates" in New York City and they begin to suspect that they might indeed be "vago bons" (lazy bums) who do not *want* to work hard and help themselves. Confused, they take refuge in an alternate search for career, meaning, and ecstasy in substance abuse.[11]

Formerly, when most entry-level jobs were found in factories the contradiction between an oppositional street culture and traditional working-class, shop-floor culture was less pronounced—especially when the worksite was protected by a union. Factories are inevitably rife with confrontational hierarchies; nevertheless, on the shop floor, surrounded by older union workers, high school dropouts who are well versed in the latest and toughest street-culture styles function effectively. In the factory, being tough and violently macho has high cultural value; a certain degree of opposition to the foreman and the "bossman" is expected and is considered appropriately masculine.

In contrast, this same oppositional street identity is nonfunctional in the service sector that has burgeoned in New York's finance-driven economy because it does not allow for the humble, obedient, social interaction—often across gender lines—that professional office workers impose on their subordinates. A qualitative change characterizes the tenor of social interaction in office-based service sector employment. Workers in a mailroom or behind a photocopy machine cannot publicly maintain their cultural autonomy. Most concretely, they have no union; more subtly, there are few fellow workers

---

[10] The word *lumpenization* comes from Marx's notion of the *lumpenproletariat*. Marx described the lumpenproletariat as comprising "ruined and adventurous off-shoots of the bourgeoisie, vagabonds, discharged soldiers, discharged jail-birds . . . pickpockets, brothel keepers, rag-pickers, beggars," etc. (Bottomore 1991:327). Thus, the lumpenproletariat are the disinherited dregs of society. Their significance is twofold. First, since workers fear lumpenization, they will accept high levels of exploitation. Second, the lumpenproletariat are politically volatile. Since they are disaffected, they are easily drawn to political radicals and can be mobilized to challenge the power structure.

[11] The work of Antonio Gramsci (1891–1937) has been critical for many modern Marxists, and his effect is felt throughout this essay. Gramsci was a founder of the Italian Communist Party. Imprisoned from 1926 to 1937, he was released because of ill health and died shortly thereafter. Gramsci's key works are his prison notebooks which, since they were written in part to avoid detection by prison censors, are extremely difficult to understand. Gramsci's most important contribution to Marxism is the concept of hegemony, which he does not define with any precision. He most consistently uses *hegemony* to refer to a system of political and moral leadership. It describes the use by the leadership of a society of "intellectual devices to infuse its ideas of morality to gain the support of those who resist or may be neutral, to retain the support of those who consent to its rule . . ." (Kurtz 1996:106). In other words, hegemony is a system of ethical and political ideas propounded by a broad alliance of political and intellectual leaders and believed as "common sense" by the masses. The hegemony of a dominant class is created and reinforced in the institutions, social relations, and dominant ideas of a society (Sassoon 1991:230). In proposing a primary role for hegemony and intellectual leadership, Gramsci provides a counterbalance to the traditional Marxist emphasis on the fundamental importance of economic relations of production. The notion of hegemony has been attractive to Marxist anthropologists because it gives critical importance to the cultural realm. Gramsci's influence has been particularly felt in Cultural Studies and cultural-production theory (see footnote 23).

The concept of hegemony plays a crucial role in this essay. In this passage, the working-class families of the crack dealers accept the hegemonic ideology of America's power elites: "common sense" about "hard work." The dealers themselves are at least partially accepting of these same ideologies and suspect that they are "vago bons."

surrounding them to insulate them and to provide them with a culturally based sense of class solidarity.[a] Instead they are besieged by supervisors and bosses from the alien, hostile, and obviously dominant culture. When these office managers are not intimidated by street culture, they ridicule it. Workers like Willie and Julio appear inarticulate to their professional supervisors when they try to imitate the language of power in the workplace and instead stumble pathetically over the enunciation of unfamiliar words. They cannot decipher the hastily scribbled instructions—rife with mysterious abbreviations—that are left for them by harried office managers. The "common sense" of white-collar work is foreign to them; they do not, for example, understand the logic for filing triplicate copies of memos or for postdating invoices. When they attempt to improvise or show initiative they fail miserably and instead appear inefficient—or even hostile—for failing to follow "clearly specified" instructions.

Their "social skills" are even more inadequate than their limited professional capacities. They do not know how to look at their fellow co-service workers—let alone their supervisors—without intimidating them. They cannot walk down the hallway to the water fountain without unconsciously swaying their shoulders aggressively as if patrolling their home turf. Gender barriers are an even more culturally charged realm. They are repeatedly reprimanded for harassing female co-workers.

The cultural clash between white "yuppie" power and inner-city "scrambling jive" in the service sector is much more than a difference of style. Service workers who are incapable of obeying the rules of interpersonal interaction dictated by professional office culture will never be upwardly mobile. In the high-rise office buildings of midtown Manhattan, newly employed inner-city high school dropouts suddenly realize that they look like idiotic buffoons to the men and women they work for. Once again, a gender dynamic exacerbates the confusion and sense of insult experienced by young, male inner-city employees because most supervisors in the lowest reaches of the service sector are women. Street culture does not allow males to be subordinate across gender lines.[12]

"GETTIN' DISSED"

On the street, the trauma of experiencing a threat to one's personal dignity has been frozen linguistically in the commonly used phrase "to diss" which is short for "to disrespect." Significantly, back in the coffee-hacienda highlands of Puerto Rico in 1949, Wolf had noted the importance of the traditional Puerto Rican concept of *respeto:* "The good owner 'respects' [*respeta*] the laborer." Wolf pointed specifically to the role "respect" plays in controlling labor power: "It is probably to the interest of the landowner to make concessions to his best workers, to deal with them on a respect basis, and to enmesh them in a network of mutual obligations" (Wolf 1956b, 235; see also Lauria 1964).[13]

---

[12] This passage points up a crucial issue in Marxist analysis, and in much of anthropology. The individuals in Bourgois' study seem to be in "the iron grip of culture." Bourgois' subjects are frightening but somewhat attractive. This comes from the sense that they might be decent individuals trapped by forces beyond their control. In this paragraph, workers are "incapable" of obeying the rules of office culture and forbidden by Puerto Rican street culture from being subordinate to women. Does culture really compel us to this degree?

[13] The theme of this section is the clash of cultures: the "street culture" of the crack dealers versus the office culture in which they seek employment. Although the subjects of his study are Puerto Rican Americans, Bourgois says their experience is not unique and has been re-enacted all over the world throughout history. In this, he is focusing his analysis on class and economic conflict rather than race or ethnicity. Notice also that while Bourgois is sympathetic to his crack-dealer subjects, the cultures in question are not equal. The critical dimension of the relationship of crack-dealer culture to office culture is that the members of office-worker culture have power, and despite their demands for respect, crack dealers have none.

Puerto Rican street dealers do not find "respect" in the entry-level service sector jobs that have increased twofold in New York's economy since the 1950s. On the contrary, they "get dissed" in their new jobs. Julio, for example, remembers the humiliation of his former work experiences as an "office boy," and he speaks of them in a race- and gender-charged idiom:

> I had a prejudiced boss. She was a fucking "ho'," Gloria. She was white. Her name was Christian. No, not Christian, Kirschman. I don't know if she was Jewish or not. When she was talking to people she would say, "He's illiterate."
>
> So what I did one day was, I just looked up the word, "illiterate," in the dictionary and I saw that she's saying to her associates that I'm stupid or something!
>
> Well, I am illiterate anyway.

The most profound dimension of Julio's humiliation was being obliged to look up in the dictionary the word used to insult him. In contrast, in the underground economy, he is sheltered from this kind of threat:

> Big Pete [the crack house franchise owner], he would never disrespect me that way. He wouldn't tell me that because he's illiterate too. Plus I've got more education than him. I got a GED.

To succeed at Gloria Kirschman's magazine publishing company, Julio would have had to submit wholeheartedly to her professional cultural style but he was unwilling to compromise his street identity. He refused to accept her insults and he was unable to imitate her culture; hence, he was doomed to a marginal position behind a photocopy machine or at the mail meter. The job requirements in the service sector are largely cultural—that is, having a "good attitude"—therefore they conjugate powerfully with racism:

> I wouldn't have mind that she said I was illiterate. What bothered me was that when she called on the telephone, she wouldn't want me to answer even if my supervisor who was the receptionist was not there. [Note how Julio is so low in the office hierarchy that his immediate supervisor is a receptionist.]
>
> When she hears my voice it sounds like she's going to get a heart attack. She'd go, "Why are you answering the phones?"
>
> That bitch just didn't like my Puerto Rican accent.

Julio's manner of resisting this insult to his cultural dignity exacerbated his marginal position in the labor hierarchy:

> And then, when I did pick up the phone, I used to just sound *Porta'rrrican* on purpose.

In contrast to the old factory sweatshop positions, these just-above-minimum-wage office jobs require intense interpersonal contact with the middle and upper-middle classes. Proximal contact across class lines and the absence of a working-class autonomous space for eight hours a day in the office can be a claustrophobic experience for an otherwise ambitious, energetic, young inner-city worker.

Willie interpreted this requirement to obey white, middle-class norms as an affront to his dignity that specifically challenged his definition of masculinity:

> I had a few jobs like that [referring to Julio's "telephone diss"] where you gotta take a lot of shit from bitches and be a wimp.
>
> I didn't like it but I kept on working, because "Fuck it!" you don't want to fuck up the relationship. So you just be a punk [shrugging his shoulders dejectedly].

One alternative for surviving at a workplace that does not tolerate a street-based cultural identity is to become bicultural: to play politely by "the white woman's" rules downtown only to come home and revert to street culture within the safety of one's tenement or housing project at night. Tens of thousands of East Harlem residents manage this tightrope, but it often engenders accusations of betrayal and internalized racism on the part of neighbors and childhood friends who do not have—or do not want—these bicultural skills.

This is the case, for example, of Ray, a rival crack dealer whose black skin and tough street demeanor disqualify him from legal office work. He quit a "nickel-and-dime messenger job downtown" to sell crack full-time in his project stairway shortly after a white woman fled from him shrieking down the hallway of a high-rise office building. Ray and the terrified woman had ridden the elevator together and coincidentally Ray had stepped off on the same floor as her to make a delivery. Worse yet, Ray had been trying to act like a "debonair male" and suspected the contradiction between his inadequate appearance and his "chivalric" intentions was responsible for the woman's terror:

> You know how you let a woman go off the elevator first? Well that's what I did to her but I may have looked a little shabby on the ends. Sometime my hair not combed. You know. So I could look a little sloppy to her maybe when I let her off first.

What Ray did not quite admit until I probed further is that he too had been intimidated by the lone white woman. He had been so disoriented by her tabooed, unsupervised proximity that he had forgotten to press the elevator button when he originally stepped on after her:

> She went in the elevator first but then she just waits there to see what floor I press. She's playing like she don't know what floor she wants to go to because she wants to wait for me to press my floor. And I'm standing there and I forgot to press the button. I'm thinking about something else—I don't know what was the matter with me. And she's thinking like, "He's not pressing the button; I guess he's following me!"

As a crack dealer, Ray no longer has to confront this kind of confusing humiliation. Instead, he can righteously condemn his "successful" neighbors who work downtown for being ashamed of who they were born to be:

> When you see someone go downtown and get a good job, if they be Puerto Rican, you see them fix up their hair and put some contact lens in their eyes. Then they fit in. And they do it! I seen it.

> They turnovers. They people who want to be white. Man, if you call them in Spanish, it wind up a problem.
>
> When they get nice jobs like that, all of a sudden, you know, they start talking proper.

SELF-DESTRUCTIVE RESISTANCE

Third- and second-generation Spanish Harlem residents born into working-class families do not tolerate high levels of "exploitation." In the new jobs available to them, however, there are no class-based institutions to channel their resistance. They are caught in a technological time warp. They have developed contemporary mainstream American definitions of survival needs and emotional notions of job satisfaction. In short, they are "made in New York"; therefore, they are not "exploitable" or "degradable." Both their objective economic needs as well as their personal cultural dignities have to be satisfied by their jobs. They resist inadequate working conditions. Finally, they are acutely aware of their relative depravation vis-à-vis the middle-level managers and wealthy executives whose intimate physical proximity they cannot escape at work.

At the same time that young men like Julio, Willie, and Ray recognize how little power they have in the legal labor market, they do not accept their domination passively. They are resisting exploitation from positions of subordination. They are living the unequal power struggle that a growing body of anthropological and ethnographic literature is beginning to address (Bourgois in press; Foley 1990; Fordham 1988; Willis 1977; Wolf 1990*b*, 590).

Unfortunately, for people like Julio and Willie, the traditional modes of powerless resistance— footdragging, disgruntlement, petty theft, and so forth—which might be appropriate in traditional peasant or even proletarian settings (see Scott 1985) contradict the fundamental "technological" requirement for enthusiastic "initiative" and "flexibility" that New York's finance-driven service sector demands. In manufacturing, resistance can be channeled through recognized institutions— unions—that often reinforce class consciousness.

In fact, oppositionally defined cultural identities are so legitimate on the shop floor that they even serve to ritualize management/worker confrontation.[14]

In the service sector, however, there is no neutral way to express cultural nonconformity. Scowling on the way to brewing coffee for a supervisor results in an unsatisfactory end-of-year performance evaluation. Stealing on the job is just cause for instant job termination. Indeed, petty theft is the avenue for "powerless revenge" most favored by Willie and Julio. They both were skilled at manipulating the Pitney-Bowes postage meter machines and at falsifying stationery inventory to skim "chump change."

More subtle, however, was the damage to Julio's work performance due to his constant concern lest Gloria Kirschman once again catch him off guard and "disrespect" him without his being immediately aware of the gravity of the insult. Consequently, when he was ordered to perform mysteriously specific tasks such as direct mailings of promotional materials that required particular combinations of folding, stuffing, or clipping, he activated his defense mechanisms. Julio had rarely received direct mail advertisements in his project apartment mailbox; consequently, the urgency and the precision with which his supervisor oversaw the logistics of these mailings appeared overbearingly oppressive and insulting. Gloria appeared almost superstitious in the rigor and anxiety with which she supervised each detail and Julio refused to accept the "flexibility" that these delicate mailings required—that is, late-night binges of collating

and recollating to make bulk-rate postage deadlines coincide with the magazine's printing and sales deadlines. Furthermore, to Julio, it was offensive to have to bring over the assembled promotional packets to Gloria's home for a last-minute late-night inspection:

It would be late and I would be at the office to do these rush jobs: collate them, staple them, fold them in the correct way . . . whatever way she said. It was always different. And it had to be just the way she wanted it. I'd stuff them just the right way [making frantic shuffling motions with his hands] and then seal the shit.

I used to hate that. I would box it and take it to the 38th Street Post Office at 10:30 at night.

But then sometimes she would call me from home and I would have to bring papers up to her house on 79th Street and 3rd Avenue [Manhattan's silk stocking district] to double check.

And she would try to offer me something to eat and I would say, "No, thank you," because she would try to pay me with that shit. 'Cause she's a cheap bitch.

She'd say, "You want pizza, tea, or cookies?" She had those Pepperidge Farm cookies [wrinkling his face with disgust].

But I wouldn't accept anything from her. I wasn't going to donate my time, man.

She thought I was illiterate. She thought I was stupid. Not me boy, charge *every penny*. From the moment I leave the office that's overtime all the way to her house. That's time and a half.

I used to exaggerate the hours. If I worked sixteen, I would put eighteen or twenty to see if I could get away with it. And I would get away

---

[14] Here Bourgois focuses on class conflict, a fundamental theme in Marxist analysis. Whereas Durkheim and the functionalist thinkers saw society as fundamentally cooperative, Marx saw it as riven by conflict. This is illustrated in Bourgois' descriptions of factory workers. The functionalist approach to inequality, often credited to sociologists Kingsley Davis and Wilbert Moore, suggests that people work cooperatively at their level of competence and are rewarded appropriately for their efforts. The center of this model is consensus. We all work together, each doing his or her job, to produce a final product. In Marxist analysis, on the other hand, factory production seems almost secondary to the struggle between workers and overseers on

the factory floor. Workers are in conflict with managers and owners. Unable, in most circumstances, to openly rebel, they protest their condition by theft and small acts of sabotage. If these are not excessive, such acts are tolerated by owners as a cost of doing business. In fact, tolerating small amounts of theft is one way owners can keep wages low. The critical issue for Bourgois' crack dealers is that in a factory, there is separation of the classes. Management and workers rarely meet face-to-face. This makes small acts of resistance possible. On the other hand, in an office, service workers are in constant contact with management. This means that they must suppress all insubordination or develop subtle ways of showing it.

with it. I'm not going to do that kind of shit
for free.

And that bitch was crazy. She used to eat
baby food. I know cause I saw her eating it with
a spoon right out of the jar.

If Julio appeared to be a scowling, ungrateful,
dishonest worker to Gloria, then Gloria herself
looked almost perverted to Julio. What normal
middle-aged woman would invite her twenty-
year-old employee into her kitchen late at night
and eat baby food in front of him?[15]

Julio's victories over his employer, Gloria, were
Pyrrhic.[16] In the cross-cultural confrontation taking place in the corridors of high-rise office buildings there is no ambiguity over who wields power.
This unequal hierarchy is constantly reasserted
through the mechanisms of cultural capital so foreign to participants in street culture. For example,
when someone like Willie, Julio, or Ray is "terminated" for suspicion of theft, the personnel report
registers an insulting notation: "lack of initiative,"
"inarticulate," or "no understanding of the purpose of the company." Julio correctly translates
this information into street-English: "She's saying
to her associates that I'm stupid!"

Willie and Julio have no frame of reference to
guide them through service employment because
their social network only has experience with factory work. In their first factory jobs, both Willie
and Julio were guided by older family members
who were producing the very same products they
were making. Still today, for example, Julio's
mother is a sweatshop/homework seamstress
and Willie's uncle is a factory foreman in the
Midwestern town where his metal-chroming
company relocated. In contrast, the only socialization available to Willie and Julio in the service

sector comes from equally isolated and alienated
fellow workers. Willie, for example, who has always been precocious in everything he has done
in life—from dropping out of school, to engaging
in street violence, to burglarizing, to selling drugs,
to abusing women, to becoming a crack addict—
immediately understood the impossibility of his
supervisor's maintaining an objective quality control in the mailroom where he worked prior to
being hired by Julio at the crack house:

I used to get there late, but the other workers
wasn't never doing shit. They was *lazy* mother-
fuckers—even the supervisor.

They all be sitting, asking each other questions over the phone, and fooling with video
games on the computer. And that's all you do at
a place like that. My boss, Bill, be drinking on
the sneak cue, and eating this bad-ass sausage.

Finally, the precarious tenure of entry-level
jobs in the service sector was the immediate pre-
cipitating factor in Willie's and Julio's retreat from
the legal labor market. When they were not fired
for "bad attitude," they were laid off due to economic retrenchment. The companies employing
them fluctuated with the unpredictable whims of
rapidly changing "yuppie fashions." Julio, for example, lost two different positions in fragile companies that folded: (1) Gloria Kirschman's trendy
magazine, and (2) a desktop publishing house.

Surprisingly, in his accounts of being laid off
Julio publicly admitted defeat and vulnerability.
On repeated occasions I had seen Julio brave
violence on the streets and in the crack house. I
knew him capable of deliberate cruelty, such as
refusing to pay for his fifteen-year-old girlfriend's
abortion or of slowly breaking the wrist of an
adolescent who had played a prank on him.[17]

---

[15] Like the story above about Ray and the elevator, this
story emphasizes the overlap between class and culture. In
both stories, attempts to show respect or friendship are misinterpreted. In the first story, Ray's attempt to show respect
to a woman on an elevator goes awry when she interprets
his actions as those of an assailant. In this story, Gloria almost certainly understands herself as proffering a minimal
degree of friendship. Julio interprets this as an insult.

[16] A *Pyrrhic victory* is a victory at a cost so great it harms
the victor.

[17] To his credit, Bourgois does not romanticize the central
characters in this essay. They are capable of great cruelty
and violence. However, in the logic of Marxist analysis,
they are victims of economic forces beyond their control.
More specifically, their surroundings have made them
who they are. Thus, despite their actions, these young men
are depicted in a sympathetic light. Still, many thousands
of people are subjected to the same conditions and virtually none of them sell drugs or break the wrists of children.
Bourgois' argument is compelling, but is it complete?

Downtown, however, behind the computer terminal where he had held his last job "in printing," he had been crushed psychologically by the personnel officers who fired him. Ironically, I registered on my tape recorder his tale of frustration, humiliation, and self-blame for losing his last legal job as a printer only a week after recording with him a bravado-laced account of how he mugged a drunken Mexican immigrant in a nearby housing project:

> I was with Rico and his girl, Daisy. We saw this Mexican. . . . He was just probably drunk. I grabbed him by the back of the neck, and put my 007 [knife] in his back [making the motion of holding someone in a choke hold from behind]. Right here [pointing to his own lower back]. And I was jigging him *HARD* [grinning for emphasis at me and his girlfriend, who was listening, rapt with attention]!
>
> I said: *"No te mueve cabron o te voy a picar como un pernil* [Don't move motherfucker or I'll stick you like a roast pork]." [More loud chuckles from Julio's girlfriend.] Yeah, yeah, like how you stab a pork shoulder when you want to put all the flavoring in the holes.
>
> I wasn't playing, either, I was serious. I would have jigged him. And I'd regret it later, but I was looking at that gold ring he had. [Chuckle.]
>
> The Mexican panicked. So I put him to the floor, poking him hard, and Rico's girl started searching him.
>
> I said, "Yo, take that asshole's fucking ring too!"
>
> After she took the ring we broke out. We sold the ring and then we cut-out on Daisy. We left her in the park, she didn't get even a cent. She helped for nothing. [More chuckling.]

As a knife-wielding mugger on the street, Julio could not contrast more dramatically with the panic-stricken employee begging for a second chance that legal employment had reduced him to:

> I was more or less expecting it. But still, when I found out, I wanted to cry, man. My throat got dry, I was like . . . [waves his hands, and gasps as if struck by a panic attack].
>
> They called me to the office, I was like, "Oh *shit!*"
>
> I couldn't get through to them. I even told them, "I'll let you put me back to messenger; I will take less pay; just keep me employed. I need the money; I need to work. I got a family."
>
> But they said, "Nope, nope, nope." I left.
>
> I just stood right outside the building; I was fucked, man. All choked up. *Me jodieron* [They jerked me].[18]

THE NEW IMMIGRANT ALTERNATIVE

The flooding of cocaine and then crack onto America's streets during the 1980s infused new energy into the underground economy, making drug dealing the most vibrant equal opportunity employer for Harlem youths. Normally, in order to fill jobs adequately in the expanding service sector, New York's legal economy should have to compete for the hearts and minds of the growing proportion of the inner city's "best and brightest" who are choosing to pursue more remunerative and culturally compatible careers in the underground economy. A wave of cheaper, more docile and disciplined new immigrant workers, however, is altering this labor power balance. These immigrants—largely undocumented—are key agents in New York's latest structural economic adjustment. Their presence allows low-wage employment to expand while social services retrench.

---

[18] These two stories are important because they demonstrate that, at some level, Julio understands the true nature of power. Julio is a violent and abusive individual capable of injuring another person without remorse. He is, however, easily defeated by people such as Gloria Kirschman, who would probably be terrified of him were they to meet on the streets of the barrio. The point is that ultimately power does not stem from the ability of individuals to threaten physical violence, but from the relations of production in which they are enmeshed. Management is able to demolish Julio because he realizes that, despite his bravado, they hold enormous power and he holds almost none. For Marxists, although physical violence may be terrible, the worst sort of violence is structural—that is, the violence done to human beings that stems from exploitative and oppressive relationships of production.

This helps explain, for example, how the real value of the minimum wage could have declined by one-third in the 1980s while the federal government was able to decrease the proportion of its contribution to New York City's budget by over 50 percent (Berlin 1991, 10; Rosenbaum 1989, A1). The breakdown of the inner city's public sector is no longer an economic threat to the expansion of New York's economy because the labor force that these public subsidies maintain is increasingly irrelevant.[19]

Like the parents and grandparents of Julio and Willie, many of New York's newest immigrants are from remote rural communities or squalid shantytowns where meat is eaten only once a week, and where there is no running water or electricity. In downtown Manhattan many of these new immigrants are Chinese, but in East Harlem the vast majority are Mexicans from the rural states of Puebla and Guerrero. To them, New York's streets are still "paved in gold" if one works hard enough.

Half a century ago Julio's mother fled precisely the same living conditions these new immigrants are only just struggling to escape. Her reminiscences about childhood in her natal village reveal the trajectory of improved material conditions, cultural dislocation, and crushed working-class dreams that is propelling her second-generation son into a destructive street culture:

> I loved that life in Puerto Rico, because it was a healthy, healthy, healthy life.
>
> We always ate because my father always had work, and in those days the custom was to have a garden in your patio to grow food and everything that you ate.
>
> We only ate meat on Sundays because everything was cultivated on the same little parcel of land. We didn't have a refrigerator, so we ate *bacalao* [salted codfish], which can stay outside, and a meat that they call old-meat, *carne de vieja,* and sardines from a can. But thanks to God, we never felt hunger. My mother made a lot of cornflour.
>
> Some people have done better by coming here, but many people haven't. Even people from my barrio, who came trying to find a better life [*buen ambiente*] just found disaster. Married couples right from my neighborhood came only to have the husband run off with another woman.
>
> In those days in Puerto Rico, when we were in poverty, life was better. Everyone will tell you life was healthier and you could trust people. Now you can't trust anybody.
>
> What I like best was that we kept all our traditions . . . our feasts. In my village, everyone was either an Uncle or an Aunt. And when you walked by someone older, you had to ask for their blessing. It was respect. There was a lot of respect in those days. [Original in Spanish][20]

Ironically, at sixty, Julio's monolingual Spanish-speaking mother is the only one of her family who can still compete effectively with the new immigrants who are increasingly filling Manhattan's entry-level labor market. She ekes out a living on welfare in her high-rise housing-project apartment by taking in sewing from undocumented garment industry subcontractors.

Rather than bemoaning the structural adjustment which is destroying their capacity to survive on legal wages, street-bound Puerto Rican youths celebrate their "decision" to bank on the underground economy and to cultivate their street identities. Willie and Julio repeatedly assert their pride in their street careers. For example, one Saturday night after they finished their midnight shift at

---

[19] The principle underlying this passage is the notion that in a capitalist society an individual's value is his or her contribution to capitalist production. Individuals who make no contribution have no value. Because they can be easily replaced by new immigrants, Julio and those like him have very little value, and society need not expend much on their support.

[20] Marxists hold that capitalism is a system of maximal exploitation because under capitalism, the individual is stripped of everything except his or her labor. This has sometimes led Marxists to romanticize noncapitalist systems of production. In this passage, Julio's mother reminisces about the beauty of life in Puerto Rico, forgetting for the moment that it was most likely the crushing poverty and misery of that life that caused her family to emigrate to New York City. Bourgois uses this rather long quote as a rhetorical device to emphasize the misery of relations of production in New York.

the crack house, I accompanied them on their way to purchase "El Sapo Verde" (The Green Toad), a twenty-dollar bag of powder cocaine, sold by a reputable outfit three blocks away. While waiting for Julio and Willie to be "served" by the coke seller, I engaged three undocumented Mexican men drinking beer on a neighboring stoop in a conversation about finding work in New York. One of the new immigrants was already earning five hundred dollars a week fixing deep-fat-fry machines. He had a straightforward racist explanation for why Willie—who was standing next to me—was "unemployed":

> OK, OK, I'll explain it to you in one word: Because the Puerto Ricans are brutes! [pointing at Willie] Brutes! Do you understand?
>
> Puerto Ricans like to make easy money. They like to leech off the other people. But not us Mexicans! No way! We like to work for our money. We don't steal. We came here to work and that's all. [Original in Spanish]

Instead of physically assaulting the employed immigrant for insulting him, Willie turned the racist tirade into the basis for a new, generational-based "American-born," urban cultural pride. In fact, in his response, he ridiculed what he interpreted to be the hillbilly naivete of the Mexicans who still believe in the "American Dream." He spoke slowly in street-English as if to mark sarcastically the contrast between his "savvy" Nuyorican identity versus the limited English proficiency of his detractor:

> That's right, m'a man! We is real vermin lunatics that sell drugs. We don't want no part of society. "Fight the Power!"[b]
>
> What do we wanna be working for? We rather live off the system. Gain weight, lay women.

When we was younger, we used to break our asses too. [Gesturing toward the Mexican men who were straining to understand his English] I had all kinds of stupid jobs too . . . advertising agencies . . . computers.

But not no more! Now we're in a rebellious stage. We rather evade taxes, make quick money and just survive. But we're not satisfied with that either. Ha![21]

CONCLUSION: ETHNOGRAPHY AND OPPRESSION

America was built on racial hierarchy and on blame-the-victim justifications for the existence of poverty and class distinctions. This makes it difficult to present ethnographic data from inner-city streets without falling prey to a "pornography of violence" or a racist voyeurism. The public "common sense" is not persuaded by a structural economic understanding of Willie's and Julio's "self-destruction." Even the victims themselves psychologize their unsatisfactory lives. Most concretely, political will and public policy ignore the fundamental structural economic facts of marginalization in America (see Romo and Schwartz 1993). Instead the first priority of federal and local social "welfare" agencies is to change the psychological—or at best the "cultural"—orientations of misguided individuals (Katz 1989).[22]

Unfortunately researchers in America have allowed the gap to grow between their hegemonically "liberal" intellectual community and an over-whelmingly conservative popular political culture. From the late 1970s through most of the 1980s, inner-city poverty was simply ignored by

---

[21] Gramsci believed that subaltern populations, that is, those who are subordinate or held in positions of oppression and exploitation, produce intellectuals who develop counter-hegemonic ideas. In other words, the oppressed develop new notions of morality and leadership, as well as new alliances that redefine the cultural worlds in which they live. In Gramsci's thought, the organization of a counter-hegemony is critical to developing the revolutionary potential of the masses. In this passage the recent Mexican immigrants echo the hegemonic ideas of bourgeois

American society. Willie, in ridiculing these ideas and defying the "hard work makes success" logic of the Mexicans, offers a counter-hegemonic response.

[22] In other words, social institutions serve to reinforce the hegemonic ideas of the power elites. The "cure" for Willie's radicalism, for instance, is to be found in social service organizations that will convince him of the virtues of "common sense" and "hard work."

all but right-wing academics who filled a popular vacuum with scientifically flawed "best sellers" on the psychological and cultural causes of poverty in order to argue against the "poisonous" effect of public sector intervention (cf. Gilder 1982; Murray 1984). Their analyses coincide with the deep-seated individualistic, blame-the-victim values so cherished in American thought.

There is a theoretical and methodological basis for anthropology's reticence to confront devastating urban poverty in its front yard. Qualitative researchers prefer to avoid tackling taboo subjects such as personal violence, sexual abuse, addiction, alienation, self-destruction, and so forth, for fear of violating the tenets of cultural relativism and of contributing to popular racist stereotypes. Even the "new advocacy ethnography" which is confronting inner-city social crises—homelessness, AIDS, teen pregnancy—in an engaged manner tends to present its "subjects" in an exclusively sympathetic framework (Dehavenon n.d.). The pragmatic realities of a new advocacy anthropology require published data to be politically crafted. A complex critical perspective therefore is often stifled by the necessity of contributing effectively and responsibly to a "policy debate." Defining policy as a political arena for engagement can demobilize both theory and practice.

Regardless of the political, scholarly, or personal motivations, anthropology's cautious and often self-censored approaches to social misery have obfuscated an ethnographic understanding of the multifaceted dynamics of the experience of oppression and ironically sometimes even have served to minimize the depths of human suffering involved. At the same time, there is a growing body of ethnographic literature at the intersection of education and anthropology—sometimes referred to as cultural production theory—which provides insight into how contradictory and complicated forms of resistance often lead to personal self-destruction and community trauma (Foley 1990; Fordham 1988; MacLeod 1987; Willis 1977). Nevertheless, perhaps even these more self-consciously theoretical attempts to grapple with an unpleasant reality tend to glorify—or at least to overidentify with—the resistance theme in order to escape a "blame-the-victim" insinuation (see Bourgois 1989).[23]

Much of the problem is rooted in the nature of the ethnographic endeavor itself. Engulfed in an overwhelming whirlpool of personal suffering it is often difficult for ethnographers to see the larger relationships structuring the jumble of human interaction around them. Structures of power and history cannot be touched or talked to. Empirically this makes it difficult to identify the urgent political economy relationships shaping everyday survival—whether they be public sector breakdown or economic restructuring. For my own part, in the heat of daily life on the street in El Barrio, I often experienced a confusing anger with the victims, the victimizers, and the wealthy industrialized society that generated

---

[23] Cultural-production theory is part of the Cultural Studies approach to anthropology and sociology that is closely identified with the work of the Birmingham Centre for Contemporary Cultural Studies and French Marxist Louis Althusser. Cultural Studies scholars focus on studying popular culture expressed in the styles adopted by subcultures as well as in cinema and television aimed at mass audiences. Following Althusser, they believe popular culture expresses the structural relationships between classes and social groups. In addition to expressing this relationship, culture is an ideology that defines the relationship of individuals and groups to the world. This is similar to Gramsci's notion of hegemony and counter-hegemony (see footnotes 11 and 21).

Paul Willis is perhaps the best known cultural-production theorist. He locates his notion of cultural production within the general field of Cultural Studies. However, while Cultural Studies stresses the meanings and practices that individuals acquire as a result of their structural position in society, Willis emphasizes the meanings that individuals create in response to these positions. He claims that individuals are "active appropriators who produce meanings and cultural forms" (1983:114) and sees the production of culture as the active creation, by individuals, of new forms and styles that allow them to occupy (and often challenge) the structural positions capitalist society forces them into. Willis' theory has been widely criticized for political pessimism and romanticization of the oppressed (Walker 1986), hence Bourgois' attempt in the last sentence of this paragraph to distance himself from this theory.

such a record toll of unnecessary human suffering. For example, when confronted with a pregnant friend frantically smoking crack—and condemning her fetus to a postpartum life of shattered emotions and dulled brain cells—it was impossible for me to remember the history of her people's colonial terror and humiliation or to contextualize her position in New York's changing economy. Living the inferno of what America calls its "underclass," I—like my neighbors around me and like the pregnant crack addicts themselves—often blamed the victim. To overcome such a partial perspective when researching painful human contexts it is especially important to develop a sensitive political economy analysis that "articulates the hidden histories" of the peoples raking themselves over the coals of the latest forms of capitalism.

NOTES

The author would like to thank the following institutions for their support: The Russel Sage Foundation, the Harry Frank Guggenheim Foundation, the Social Science Research Council, the National Institute on Drug Abuse, the Wenner-Gren Foundation for Anthropological Research, the United States Bureau of the Census, and San Francisco State University. Helpful critical comments by Jane Schneider and Rayna Rapp changed the shape of the article. Finally, none of this could have been written without Harold Otto's moral support and typing, as well as final work on the keyboard by Henry Ostendorf and Charles Pearson.

[a] Significantly, there are subsectors of the service industry that are relatively unionized—such as hospital work and even custodial work—where there is a limited autonomous space for street culture and working-class resistance.

[b] "Fight for Power" is a song composed by the rap group Public Enemy.

REFERENCES

Berlin, Gordon. 1991. "The Poverty among Families: A Service Decategorization Response." Photocopied report, Manpower Demonstration Research Corporation, New York.

Bourgois, Philippe. 1989. "Crack in Spanish Harlem: Culture and Economy in the Inner City." *Anthropology Today* 5:6–11.

———. In press. *In Search of Respect: Selling Crack in Spanish Harlem.* New York: Cambridge University Press.

Dehavenon, Anna Lou, ed. n.d. *There Is No Place Like Home: The Anthropology of United States Homelessness and Housing.* Unpublished manuscript.

Falcon, Angelo. 1992. "Puerto Ricans and Other Latinos in New York City Today: A Statistical Profile." Pamphlet, Institute for Puerto Rican Policy, New York.

Foley, Doug. 1990. *Learning Capitalist Culture: Deep in the Heart of Tejas.* Philadelphia: University of Pennsylvania.

Fordham, Signithia. 1988. "Racelessness as a Factor in Black Students' School Success: Pragmatic Strategy or Pyrrhic Victory?" *Harvard Educational Review* 53: 257–293.

Gilder, George. 1982. *Wealth and Poverty.* New York: Bantam.

Katz, Michael. 1989. *The Undeserving Poor: From the War on Poverty to the War on Welfare.* New York: Pantheon Press.

Lambert, Bruce. 1990. "AIDS Travels New York-Puerto Rico 'Air Bridge,'" *New York* Times (15 June):B1.

Lauria, Anthony, Jr. 1964. "'Respeto,' 'Relajo,' and Inter-Personal Relations in Puerto Rico." *Anthropological Quarterly* 37(2):53–67.

MacLeod, Jay. 1987. *Ain't No Makin' It: Leveled Aspirations in Low-Income Neighborhood.* Boulder, Colo.: Westview Press.

Murray, Charles. 1984. *Losing Ground: American Social Policy 1950–1980.* New York: Basic Books.

Rodriguez, Clara E. 1989. *Puerto Ricans: Born in the U.S.A.* Winchester, Mass.: Unwin Hyman.

Romo, Frank, and Michael Schwartz. 1993. "The Coming of Post-Industrial Society Revisited: Manufacturing and the Prospects for a Service Based Economy." In *Explorations in Economic Sociology*, Richard Swedburg, ed., 335–373. New York: Russell Sage Foundation.

Rosenbaum, David E. 1989. "Bush and Congress Reach Accord Raising Minimum Wage to $4.25." New York Times (1 November):A1–A2.

Scott, James C. 1985. *Weapons of the Weak: Everyday Forms of Peasant Resistance.* New Haven: Yale University Press.

Willis, Paul. 1977. *Learning to Labor: How Working Class Kids Get Working Class Jobs.* New York: Columbia University Press.

Wilson, William Julius. 1987. *The Truly Disadvantaged: The Inner City, the Underclass, and Public Policy.* Chicago: University of Chicago Press.

Wolf, Eric R. 1956b. "San Jose: Subcultures of a Traditional Coffee Municipality." In *The People of Puerto*

Rico: A Study in Social Anthropology, by Julian Steward et al., pt. 7, 171–264. Urbana: University of Illinois Press.

———. 1982a. *Europe and the People without History.* Berkeley, Los Angeles, London: University of California Press. (Translations: German, Italian, Spanish.)

———. 1990b. "Distinguished Lecture: Facing Power—Old Insights, New Questions." *American Anthropologist* 92:586–596.

43. *The Family Romance of Mandarin Capital*

AIHWA ONG (b. 1950)

COSMOPOLITICS AND THE SUBALTERN UNCONSCIOUS

In *Anthropology and Politics,* Joan Vincent[1] identifies the 1980s as the era of "cosmopolitics."[a] She sees the cosmopolitical turn as most promising for ethnographic research on the political economies of third-world countries. Vincent's remarkable contribution to anthropology has been grounded in intensive fieldwork in Zanzibar, Uganda, and Ulster and archival research on Ireland and the Philippines. Clearly, anthropology is the discipline to track down, delineate, and expose the complex politics of colonial imperialism and capitalism inside and outside the European homeland. Less well known, perhaps, is Vincent's extensive influence among students (graduates of Barnard College, Columbia University, and other institutions), who have been inspired, encouraged, and guided to study the cosmopolitics of subaltern classes, peasantries, and women "confronting global capital" in communities around the world.[b] I was one of those privileged students, and my work has always shown the

traces, I hope, of Vincent's political sensibility. In this chapter, I want to recast some of Vincent's ideas about the strategic importance of "men in motion," in the "moving frontier" of colonial capitalism, as well as the question of class consciousness in late-twentieth-century capitalisms.[c]

In her study of British rule in colonial Uganda, Vincent wondered what factors in colonial capitalism accounted for the lack of class consciousness among subaltern groups.[d] Influenced, perhaps, by Marx's comparison of French peasants to "a sack of potatoes"—"they cannot represent themselves, they must be represented"[e]—Vincent suggested that the mobility of capitalist agents disguised the class character of imperial capital, leaving local groups unconnected to each other even as they were objectively exploited by the same system. By arguing that the mobility of capital and its agents was dialectically linked to the fixity of subaltern groups, in both geographical and ideological senses, Vincent identified the critical process whereby transnational capital reinforces the mobility of some at the expense of many, a power

(1999)

---

[1] Joan Vincent (b. 1928) is a distinguished political anthropologist. She was a professor at Barnard College of Columbia University from 1968 until her retirement in 1995. Since then, she has remained extremely active in the field. Most of her research has been conducted in Uganda and other locations in East Africa. She has been particularly interested in issues of colonialism, power elites, and cultural change. Ong's footnotes (which appear at the end of the essay) provide important background information on Vincent as well as brief discussion of her key ideas. Be sure to read these notes.

mechanism that is especially significant in the era of late capitalism.[f,2]

The ideological murkiness of traveling agents of capitalism, and the "class unawareness" of subaltern groups, are complex ethnographic questions that challenge us to move beyond a class-centered analysis. While other scholars of colonial and postcolonial societies have dealt with issues of class consciousness in relatively stable situations of class exploitation,[g] Vincent's focus on the moving frontiers of capitalism vividly problematizes analytical linkages between capitalist mobility and the political (un)conscious of subaltern groups. Indirectly, her work on Teso poses the question, How does one account for political consciousness when the material links to capital are so attenuated as to seem invisible to the dominated?[h] This question suggests the obverse, that is, What happens when the material relations of exploitation are keenly felt and yet are not symbolically linked to a politics of class identity? This is an especially important theme in the contemporary world, where so much of what we take to be reality is complexly mediated by the dynamic flows of images that make all systems of referents highly fragmented, destabilized, and not directly connected to the structure of production.[i] While it is fashionable among orthodox Marxists to reject such observations as "postmodernist," I maintain that the days are over for calmly plotting a structural relationship between the "objective" and the "subjective" aspects of (class) consciousness. Capital remains fundamental to our understanding of contemporary social life, and it is sensible to think of capital as highly sped-up, constantly mutating sets of material, technological, and discursive relations, of production and consumption, in which everything is reduced to an exchange value. Donald Lowe refers to this phenomenon in the United States, where accelerated production/consumption has annihilated use values, as "the hegemony of exchangist practices."[j] Even when we move away from the centers of global capitalism, subaltern groups in the new transnational publics shaped by capital, travel, and mass media cannot develop political consciousness in a way that escapes the mediations of ethnic identifications, mass culture, and national ideologies. Indeed, transnational capitalism in Asia has been linked not so much to the rise of class hostility but to other forms of cultural struggle that privilege gender, family, ethnicity, and nationality.[k,3]

---

[2] Marx insisted that ultimately the most important divisions in society, and the most important identification for individuals, was class. This left a problem: If the association of individual with class was so important, why did people not seem to experience class consciousness (and hence rise up and overthrow their oppressors)? One answer was that ruling elites used a variety of physical and ideological mechanisms to prevent this from happening.

The Italian Marxist Antonio Gramsci identified oppressed groups (particularly in Southen Italy), as "subalterns" and proposed that the job of the intelligentsia was to raise the class consciousness of Subaltern groups and allow them to escape that status.

In the 1980s, the notion of subaltern studies became popular in social science. It was largely developed by Ranajit Guha, an Indian historian, in the context of the analysis of colonialism and the independence movement in India. Guha and others argued that the dominant narrative of colonialism and independence was heavily biased toward the roles played by elite members of Indian society. Guha proposed, instead, to focus on peasants and those peripheralized by the state. Although the 1980s Subaltern scholars focused largely on Asia, by the 1990s the term *subaltern* was widely used to refer to any oppressed or marginalized group. Of course, who is oppressed depends upon what the comparison group is. Within a nation, economic, ethnic, and religious minorities may be subaltern. Among nations, even elites of poor nations may be subaltern; they play subordinate roles in a global economy dominated by elites from wealthy nations.

[3] In this complex paragraph, Ong seems to argue that in a landscape of high-speed travel, complex media images, and destabilized polities, the connections between exploitation and class consciousness are difficult to untangle. Though the dynamics of capitalism are critical to any analysis, class consciousness does not seem an important factor in Asia. Following Lowe (1995:102), she suggests that one cause of this may be that in postindustrial economies (specifically, capitalist economies) everything is reduced to an "exchange value." For Marx, the "real" value of anything was its use value—what purpose it

The problem of subaltern consciousness, then, is not merely one of the "invisibility" of dominant relations to subalterns or the impossibility of the "authentic" representation of subalterns by nonsubalterns;[1] rather, it is also one of linking "subaltern" imagination not to the structure of production but to what Foucault calls "knowledge power." In the contemporary world, where so much of everyday consciousness is mediated by "print (and electronic) capitalism," discursive knowledges constitute a field of power that defines entities such as the family, gender, ethnicity, race, and nationality and thus constitutes the political consciousness of class-differentiated subjects.[m] How are social identities rooted in objective class differences shaped not by an ideology of class exploitation but by the corporatist hegemony of exchangist values? I find Fredric Jameson's notion of "the political unconscious" especially useful for unmasking ideological messages embedded in cultural narratives about the traveling subject of contemporary Asian capitalism.[n] Although Jameson is interested in uncovering the political unconscious—a structure of psyche that is historical—in literary works, I wish here to uncover the political unconscious in commercialized cultural and political forms linked to mobile Chinese families that have recently dominated public cultures in Southeast Asia. What are the ideological messages in the figuration of traveling masculine subjects and entrepreneurial families? What do they tell us about the popular imagination of power, authority, and desires in the brave new Asian world of authoritarian states and free-flowing capitalism?[4]

THE GOVERNMENTALITY OF FAMILY ROMANCES

This rise of Chinese corporate forms in the Southeast Asian public landscape has been sudden and quite startling. I remember visiting Malaysia in 1992 on Chinese New Year and being amazed by the huge commercial displays of Chinese words, figures, and banners on major hotels and stores. Despite Malaysia's large Chinese minority, the public display of Chinese symbols had been muted throughout the 1970s and 1980s, when Malaysianization policies established Malay language, personalities, and cultural icons as the appropriate vehicles for public prestige and pageantry. The new prominence of Chinese iconography outside "Chinatown," I was told, was a sign of welcome for Taiwanese businessmen, who have become the main investors in Malaysia, overtaking the Japanese. Ironically, while blatant displays of Chinese artifacts in public culture have been suppressed for fear of inciting local ethnic-Chinese chauvinism, commercial images of Chineseness as symbols

---

served. By emphasizing the buying and selling of commodities, the capitalist market "fetishized" them, removing them from the conditions of their production. Ong and Lowe suggest that in current-day economies, everything is fetishized, and this effectively camouflages the relations of production (and the oppression they entail), both retarding the development of class consciousness and promoting the development of alternative forms of identification.

[4] Given the complexity of the world, Ong argues that the critical intellectual task is not piercing through the obfuscation caused by the media to unmask the true nature of the relations of production (postmodern insights tell us these can't have any true nature) but rather to understand the specific relationships between power and knowledge. Here, she relies on Foucault, who, as we have seen earlier, argues that the nature of what counts as knowledge is conditioned by the historical development of political power

in certain classes and institutions. Thus, for example, it is critical to understand the ways in which the discourse of family is used as a culturally constructed signifier of nostalgia and longing. As an element of capitalism, it can be used to sell anything from political platforms to burgers (Lowe 1995, Gillis 2000). As Ong notes, the ideology is shaped not by notions of class, exploitation, and oppression but rather by a sort of capitalism based on values such as nostalgia, longing, and dreams of wealth and glamour. In a world of "exchangist values" people believe that such intangibles can be acquired through the purchase of material goods, memberships, and experiences. These notions (dreams of wealth and glamour and so on) form Jameson's "political unconscious" (see note 5 in essay 41 by Appadurai). Ong's goal in this essay is to explore the nature of this political unconscious among wealthy and mobile Chinese families.

are permitted and even encouraged for their links to transnational capital and entrepreneurs, in effect casting them as "'thoroughly modern' Asians."[o,5]

This flamboyant display of Chinese corporatism indexes a new accommodation between translocal capital and the developmental state, an alliance that enables cosmopolitan Chinese iconography to dominate public culture. These, however, are not apolitical images of culture and consumption but are imbued with messages about the stereotypical "Asian" family order, gender hierarchy, and subscription to a particular state vision of communitarian capitalism. Indeed, just as the world of Walt Disney disseminates capitalist ideology,[p] the new Asian public culture creates a realm where cosmopolitan images promote a kind of ideological conformity that is especially powerful because it is cast in the language of family romance and modern adventure.[q]

Embedded in these public cultural forms are political messages about power, masculinity, and a mobile economic liberalism. As Foucault has reminded us, economic liberalism is not simply a theory of political and economic behavior but "a style of thinking quintessentially concerned with the art of governing."[r] The objective of political economy resituates "governmental reason within a newly complicated, open and unstable politico-epistemic configuration."[s] One can say that a kind of laissez-faire governmentality infuses the market behavior of overseas Chinese, among whom a premium is placed on norms that allow the free play of market forces, flexible activities, and the self-discipline of the profit maximizer. In Adam Smithian thinking, the state is ideally a solicitous institution that makes corrective adjustments to open channels to free trade, but its interventions should be limited so as not to hamper the workings of market rationality. Indeed, while nation-states such as Singapore, Malaysia, and Indonesia may be politically repressive now and again, the state ensures the freedom of economic activities across the region. Prime Minister Mahathir Mohamad of Malaysia calls such a combination of "not-so-liberal democracy" and government intervention into the economy "communitarian capitalism."[t] These ideas about the inseparable links between economic liberalism and authoritarian rule are disseminated through public cultures that recast capitalist strategies and state control as family romances.[6]

The new Asian publics are increasingly contexts through which, in Lynn Hunt's words, "private

---

[5] Ong's comments here are important because ethnic identity, and in particular Chinese ethnic identity, is an important topic in Malaysia. There are nearly 7 million ethnic Chinese in Malaysia (out of a total population of about 24 million). The Chinese community has been relatively isolated from the ethnic Malay community, in part because most Malays are Muslim and most Chinese are not. Important, since at least the mid-twentieth century, the Chinese community has also controlled much of the economy. Chinese economic control resulted in high tensions between the Chinese and Malay community, and in 1969 anti-Chinese riots left at least 200 people dead. This unrest resulted in the New Economic Policy (NEP) of 1971, an ambitious economic program that systematically favored ethnic Malays over the Chinese. Though Malaysia has prospered in the past two decades, the NEP has had limited success. In 2002, ethnic Chinese controlled more than 40 percent of the shares of Malaysian companies, compared to only 20 percent controlled by ethnic Malays (*Economist* 2005). Given this background, open displays of Chinese economic power are extremely interesting. You should note as well that Ong herself grew up in Malaysia.

[6] This is an interesting passage viewed from the perspective of American politics. In the United States, politicians often make a link between American-style capitalism and the spread of democracy. Adam Smith (see essay 1, footnote 3) believed in economic freedom. He proposed that society as a whole would benefit if individuals pursued their economic self-interest. Governments, in a Smithian world, exist in order to assure that individuals are free to do this. Governments should provide security from external or internal violence, administer justice in an equitable fashion, and undertake public works that, by their nature, cannot be undertaken profitably by any individual or corporation (traditionally, things like road construction were believed to fall into this category). But it was not clear to Smith that any of these governmental obligations are necessarily linked to democracy. Here Ong notes the connection between economically liberal and the politically authoritarian policies of Asian governments.

sentiments and public politics" are interwoven and struggled over by different class, ethnic, and nationality groups.[u] Following Hunt, I use the construct of family romance(s) to mean the collective and unconscious images of family order that underlie public politics.[v] Narratives of affluent Chinese families provide a kind of structure to political imaginaries, which (like nationalism) can crosscut and neutralize the interpellations of class, gender, and ethnicity.[w] Family romances do not operate in an apolitical manner but inform the way people imagine the operations of power between individuals and the state, between different ethnic groups, and of course between men and women. Below, I suggest that family romances—as articulated in public displays, images, and narratives—are vehicles that variously encode political messages about (1) a fraternal tribal capitalism; (2) Chinese-native elite alliances; (3) the moral economy of the state; and (4) working-class women's dreams. These are different facets of "the family model of politics,"[x] and they speak to the differing notions of authority and legitimacy among transnational capitalists, their bureaucratic partners, and the new middle classes; they also shape the notions of authority and legitimacy of subaltern subjects in Asian modernity.[7]

THE ROMANCE OF FAMILY EMPIRES OVER THE PAST TWO DECADES

Southeast Asia has seen the emergence of about a dozen major Chinese business families whose multinational holdings place them among the world's richest people. Chinese-owned companies that enjoy the patronage of politicians have become "larger than all but the biggest local branches of the global MNCS [multinational corporations] which proliferated throughout the region" in the 1980s.[y] Their owners include Robert Kuok and the Kwek brothers of Malaysia and Hong Kong, Liem Sioe Liong and William Soeryadjaya of Indonesia, and the late Chin Sophronphanich and the Lamsam family of Thailand.[z] Taken together, overseas-Chinese corporate families and professionals are the new economic elite in Asia (outside Japan); their activities, mobility, and stories are the stuff of a regional thinking about "communitarian capitalism."

The symbolic qualities of Chinese corporate families—interpersonal relations based on fraternity and mandarin ideals—are key elements in a political imaginary of regional development and interethnic dependence between rulers and capitalists. This Chinese capitalist triumphalism arose in the context of a sustained economic boom that began in the 1970s, when Singapore and Hong Kong joined South Korea as the new "dragons" in Asia. In the next decade, as Malaysia, Thailand, and Indonesia won the label "minidragons," ethnic-Chinese business groups began to exercise their critical role in forming economic linkages that supplemented and went beyond the strategies of the developmental states. In 1991, the Singapore Chinese Chamber of Commerce held the first global meeting of Chinese chambers of commerce from all over the world, inviting participants from seventy-five countries. This meeting of business interests was represented as a model of postcolonial fraternal bonds that overcame regional and political differences. A leader of the Singapore Chamber of Commerce told me that there was no language barrier at the gathering because the Chinese entrepreneurs were all bound by kinship, in the double sense of having both blood and fictive fraternal bonds.[aa] As I mentioned in chapter 2,[8] this rediscovered

---

[7] Lynn Hunt (b. 1948) is an eminent historian of the French Revolution who has been particularly concerned with issues of gender and human rights.

[8] Ong refers to chapter 2 of *Flexible Citizenship* from which this essay has been reprinted. Chapter 2, titled "A Momentary Glow of Fraternity," concerns the ways in which "culture and race have become critical raw materials in competing imaginaries of modernity" (1999:55) in contemporary Asia.

brotherhood in the context of transnational capitalism has been dubbed a "momentary glow of fraternity"; it asserts a transnational autonomy vis-à-vis the less-flexible patriarchal authority of the state.[bb]

Emboldened by their successes in forming transnational networks, overseas entrepreneurs boast of using fraternal links to bypass or do without political and legal regulations. In an interview, a member of the Singapore Chamber of Commerce recalled for me: "Overseas Chinese grew more confident and more concerned about their identity. Globalization requires going beyond just national identity in enlarging our scope and permutations of what we're trying to do. Although investments are directed by our government regionalization policy, most important linkages are made through company levels, and again at the local level through human relations."[cc],[9]

Ethnic-Chinese solidarity based on male bonding and networks has created what Joel Kotkin calls "the most economically important of the Asian global tribes" and has made the "old government ideology of nation-states . . . outmoded."[dd] This use of the term tribe to refer to traveling ethnic businessmen constructs an essentialist concept of cultural difference and brings to mind the band of brothers who ritually sacrificed the original father figure in Freud's *Totem and Taboo*.[ee] Fraternal networks are represented as the modern Asian way of doing business man to man, usurping the paternalistic role

of the government in economic activities. The familial morality of Chinese capitalism, then, is not that of the autocratic father but rather the fraternal flexibility that forms alliances across ideological, political, and ethnic borders.[10]

The oxymoron Confucian merchant is a sign of the extravagance of Chinese capitalism.[ff] That Confucian philosophy puts traders at the bottom of the occupational hierarchy and regards their singular pursuit of wealth as the very antithesis of Confucian values has not been an obstacle to business-news images of capitalists as reborn Confucians. In narratives of East Asian triumphalism, Chinese merchants are likened to mandarins whose high status stems not only from their fortunes but also from their representation of a reworked Confucianism of the "all-men-are-brothers" sort.

The merchant mandarin par excellence is Robert Kuok,[11] a Malaysian-born tycoon who has been called "the embodiment of a Confucian gentleman" in the region's authoritative business magazine, the *Far Eastern Economic Review*.[gg] The cover of the issue in which this assessment appears displays Kuok dressed in an emperor's yellow dragon robes in the regal pose of an ancestor figure. His spectacular economic success has been attributed not only to his masterful cultivation of relationships with capitalists and politicians but also to his loyalty to business subordinates and to his sense of business discretion. The family romance behind this merchant prince

---

[9] Note Ong's style here and throughout. Influenced by issues of positioning and voice raised by postmodernists, Ong injects herself into the essay by writing in the first person. In this case she says an official "recalled for me" rather than simply, an official "recalled." By doing so, she reminds you that the author is a presence in the work, not an omniscient observer.

[10] Ong here references Freud's key contribution to anthropology: *Totem and Taboo* (1950 [1913]). In that work, Freud imaginatively reconstructs the "primal family," the original human group, which supposedly consisted of a man, his wives, and their offspring. Freud argued that the sons of such a family were consumed with desire for their mothers and both love and sexual jealousy for the father. The sons banded together, killed and ate the father, and had sex with the mothers. Later, overcome with remorse,

they elevated the memory of the father and worshiped him and forbade sex with mothers (and sisters). Thus, from this story, Freud derives both the origin of totemic religious practices and the incest taboo. Overwhelmingly, anthropologists, both of Freud's time and the current day, reject this reconstruction of history. Ong is, of course, not supporting it either. Rather, she uses it as an analogy: The businessmen band together as brothers and subvert their government's authority through their kin ties.

[11] A self-made man, Robert Kuok (b. 1923) is reputed to be the richest person in Malaysia. Forbes estimates his current fortune at about 5 billion dollars, which places him among the world's 125 richest people (but not in the top 100). He is the head of the Kuok Group, whose economic interests range from shipping and food processing to hotels (*Forbes* 2006).

celebrates the values of discipline, pragmatism, and economic success; it opposes political idealism and the impractical goals of the anticolonial revolutionary. The trader and the revolutionary are key figures in overseas-Chinese history.[hh] The story of Robert Kuok and his younger brother Willie is presented as a morality tale of overseas Chinese who are torn between a foolish anti-imperialist struggle (Willie) and practical adjustments to imperial rule and global capitalism (Robert). The sensible influence is represented by Kuok's mother, a "very austere, very religious" and "old-fashioned" woman, that is, an authentic Chinese parental figure of piety and moral uprightness.[ii] It is instructive that maternal, rather than paternal, influence is constructed as the key influence on sons in this diasporan-Chinese family. Emigration from China breaks with the traditional patriarchal power associated with the lineages and the ancestral temples of the home culture.

The Kuok brothers were educated in elite colonial British schools (where Robert's classmates included future politicians such as Lee Kuan Yew).[12] The Second World War, which precipitated the process of decolonization, set the brothers off on radically different paths. While Robert worked with the occupying Japanese forces and learned from their rice trade, his younger brother, Willie, entered the jungle to join the anti-imperialist Communist Party of Malaysia as a propagandist. By the end of the war, both brothers had gained fame. Willie's death at the hands of British troops was announced in the British House of Commons.[13] A few years later, Robert Kuok established a major sugar mill and, through rapid expansion, soon became the "sugar king" of Southeast Asia. Expanding his strategic ties to overseas-Chinese traders and indigenous politicians, Robert Kuok has built an empire based on commodities, shipping, banking, and property development, with offices in Hong Kong, Beijing, Paris, and Santiago.

This story, which has been reported in the international press and circulates among overseas Chinese, contrasts "good" and "bad" overseas-Chinese male subjects. Robert Kuok is the reassuring image of a new diasporan masculine ideal—open to all kinds of advantageous alliances, tempered by an astute judgment of human relations, and always nurturing social relations with associates. This mandarin image was further promoted by Forbes, the world's leading business magazine: "Nearly all the first-generation tycoons, such as Indonesia's Liem [Sioe Liong], Malaysia's Kuok, and Hong Kong's Li Ka-shing, have the same image: trustworthy, loyal, humble, gentlemanly, skilled at networking and willing to leave something on the table for partners."[jj]

In his study of the intertwining of nationalism and sexuality in Nazi Germany and Great Britain, George Mosse[14] notes that bourgeois manhood was often represented by values of restraint and self-control. "Manliness was not just a matter of courage, it was a pattern of manners and morals" that appealed to the middle classes as virtue and respectability, or the control of passion.[kk] In Chinese dynastic romances, the manly virtues of the new bourgeoisie are a mix of restrained flamboyance and benevolence toward those who are less well endowed. This vision of a gentrified tycoon culture—a world away from the hubbub of Chinese commercial streets—appeals to the new middle classes, who have been keeping up with global "middling" norms of the good life.[ll]

---

[12] Lee Kwan Yew (b. 1923) Served as first prime minister of Singapore (1959–1990). He continues to hold a cabinet-level position in the Singaporean government.

[13] Though Ong doesn't mention it, a third brother, Philip Kuok (1921–2003), became an important diplomat. He served as Malaysian ambassador to Belgium and Luxemburg in the 1960s and West Germany in the 1970s. In 1975, he became chairman of the Malaysian Tourist Development Corporation.

[14] George Mosse (1918–1999) was an eminent historian who focused primarily on the history of fascism in Nazi Germany. He was particularly concerned with the ways in which authoritarian regimes manipulated symbols to maintain power and control. Mosse was from an extremely wealthy German Jewish family that owned newspapers, including the eminent *Berliner Tagesblatt*. He fled Germany in 1933.

Such images of family morality—restraint, fraternity, princeliness—both represent and resonate with the fantasies of Chinese families, with their nostalgia for a remembered glorious culture, and with the ways they understand economic and political experiences. There is growing evidence that the middle classes in Southeast Asia now look to (Chinese) business families rather than to the families of sultans or kings as models for appropriate modern Asian masculine conduct, practices, and values. Chinese communities in Malaysia take great pride in the Kuoks, who are viewed as homegrown sons who have become global empire builders. They closely follow the business decisions and property acquisitions of the Kuoks (that is, of Robert, the surviving brother, and both brothers' children), seeking clues as to how to conduct themselves and attain economic success. Furthermore, the media prominence of the Kuoks, together with that of the Lis of Hong Kong, the Liems of Indonesia, and so on, has given ethnic-Chinese minorities in Southeast Asia a new respectability; spurred by the new political tolerance toward Chinese business, even the assimilated are "coming out of the closet" as "Chinese." For instance, with the end of military rule, more and more Sino-Thais are asserting their Chinese origins, and culture in Bangkok has become "more openly Chinese."[mm] In visits to Singapore or Hong Kong, ethnic Chinese from ASEAN countries can discard their batik or Thai-silk shirts, drop their indigenous names, and speak Chinese dialects and perform kinship rituals, especially around business banquets. More and more, in cities such as Kuala Lumpur and Bangkok, and in trips back to the mainland, corporate power is stamped with Chinese business practices and rituals.[nn,15]

Even indigenous ASEAN leaders, long suspicious of ethnic-Chinese business, now strategically position themselves as closer to Chinese corporate practices. Malaysian and Singaporean leaders use the category "East Asian" to refer to their own countries, seeking to link their "minidragon" status to the economic boom in China. Malay businessmen are taking up Mandarin to do business and learn from ethnic-Chinese entrepreneurs. Recently, the Malaysian deputy prime minister invoked the Chinese sage Lao Tse to urge "the youth of East Asia" to combine spiritual with material success. He said that they should struggle for both free trade (against Western protectionist policies) and ethical values (against the complacency that comes with affluence).[oo] This yoking of free trade with reified Chinese values is one example of attempts by Malaysian leaders to proclaim that theirs is "a noncapitalist market economy" that is founded on the communitarian but flexible relations of the "bamboo network."

CROSS-ETHNIC AND CROSS-NATIONAL FRATERNITIES

What do these images of fraternal capitalism and economic dynasties tell us about the ways elite power sharing is imagined? In postcolonial Southeast Asian nation-states, whether monarchist or republican, discussion of dynastic rule is often tightly controlled, if not banned outright. In Thailand, subjects are forbidden to discuss the power and authority of the monarchy, while in Indonesia and Singapore, the state does not tolerate any commentary about the political and economic privileges of ruling families. In recent years, Lee Kuan Yew has sued foreign scholars and newspapers for writing about alleged nepotism in Singapore's political system.[pp] While any discussion of patriarchal political rule is suppressed, there has been an explosion of stories about business dynasties.

Economic dynasties and alliances, not dynastic politics, are the narratives of elite power. Even as stories celebrate the restraint of the merchant princes, they also valorize the extravagance of their corporate networks. As is clear from the above, this fascination with Asian business empires is often

---

[15] ASEAN, the Association of Southeast Asian Nations, includes Brunei, Cambodia, Indonesia, Laos, Malaysia, Myanmar, Philippines, Singapore, Thailand, and Vietnam. Originally created in 1967 to act as a counterbalance to communism in Vietnam, today it is an organization that serves to promote economic and cultural cooperation.

fed by Western publications such as the *Far Eastern Economic Review,* which is owned by Dow Jones and Company, the Wall Street firm. In many ways, the family model of Asian capitalism is also a creation of Western media barons and reflects a mix of orientalist fantasy, business instrumentalism, and an American spin on economic opportunities and contacts in Asia. *The Review* has a new series called "Family Ties," devoted to "Asia's family-held business groups." One such story, about a Hong Kong beverage entrepreneur, is sub-titled "Grandson of Indentured Servant in Malaysia Epitomizes the Overseas Chinese Success Story."qq This rags-to-riches story is repeated many times because "probably at no point in history have so many families accumulated so much wealth in a single generation."rr These stories are an endorsement and a celebration of the transnational expansion of business families beyond their host countries and beyond even the region. More fundamentally, they constitute a regime of truth about the ascent of a new kind of transnational fraternal alliance in the new Southeast Asia. They also note the role of strategic links to officials and the importance of cross-ethnic relations—business partnerships, marriages, kinship relations—in the rise of the new Asian tycoons.[16]

The image of merchant princes has helped legitimize the new moral order of capitalist-state alliances. Although Islamic leaders in Indonesia have for years criticized the links between Chinese bosses (*cukong*) and the Soeharto family, the fortunes of the Indonesian ruling class are intertwined with and dependent on their contacts with Chinese businessmen.ss Under the *cukong* system,

Chinese bosses bankroll and otherwise support Indonesian politicians in exchange for patronage and protection from excessive attacks on the Chinese. The biggest *cukong* is Liem Sioe Liong,[17] whose great fortune has been tied to that of President Soeharto's family. Their partnership began during the Second World War, when Soeharto was an army man in the provinces and Liem was a commodities trader and suspected gunrunner.tt The rise of Soeharto as president and the growth of Liem's Salim Group of companies are intertwined events that have led to many suspicions among the indigenous (*pribumi*) business community. The economic fortunes of the Soeharto family have also expanded as a result of the *cukong* connection that won the late Madam Hartinah Tien Soeharto the nickname "Mrs. Ten Percent" in reference to commissions she gathered through wielding nepotistic influence. The Soeharto children are partners in many of the Salim Group ventures. While the Soeharto government has suppressed Western press reports about Soeharto family business interests, such *cukong* arrangements have aided in the rise of many Chinese firms, which, with their ability to attract foreign investments, have led Indonesia's economic resurgence.uu

Across the water, Malay-Chinese business alliances, called Ali-Baba partnerships,vv have also been a key to the rise of powerful companies. For instance, one top Malay stockbroker not only has his de rigueur Chinese business partner but also a Chinese wife (Robert Kuok's daughter);[18] in addition, he has access to top Malay government officials.ww Someone else who participates in an Ali-Baba partnership is Francis Yeoh.[19]

---

[16] The notion of "regime of truth" comes from Foucault. In "Truth and Power" he argues that each society creates its "regime of truth"—the fashions, mechanisms, and structures through which what is accepted as truth is generated and propagated. Here Ong is specifically concerned with the generation of truth in the Malaysian and Singaporean political context. Certain kinds of truths are permissible and authorized (the truths of Chinese business families). Certain kinds of truths are de-authorized and punishable (the truths of the same families when they are directly involved in politics). Ong mentions Orientalism (see note 7, in essay 34), but note that this isn't a simple imposition of Western imagination on an Asian subject. It is the active

appropriation of Western imagination by Asian political and economic actors with their own purposes in mind.

[17] Liem Sioe Liong (b. 1919) is an Indonesian businessman with an estimated net worth of more than 750 million dollars. Forbes rated Liem Sioe Liong as the twenty-third wealthiest person in Asia in 2005. Liong is chairman of the Salim Group, a highly diversified organization dealing in everything from banking to cloves and cement.

[18] Rashid Hussain is married to Sue Kuok.

[19] Francis Yeoh (b. 1954) is a construction and utilities tycoon with an estimated worth of 1.1 billion dollars.

Despite being an ethnic-Chinese Christian in a predominantly Muslim, Malay-chauvinist state, he has been called "the master builder of Malaysia [who] thrives with a little help from his friends."[xx] Indeed, like virtually every successful corporate heavyweight here, he is a familiar presence in the halls of political power and is an intimate of Prime Minister Mahathir.[20] That symbiosis of political power and entrepreneurial energy is a phenomenon that has spread throughout much of Southeast Asia and helps explain the region's economic dynamism. These stories suggest that fraternal alliances between (Chinese) businessmen and (indigenous) bureaucrats are partnerships that thrive because fraternal business links are meshed with authoritarian political structures.

But in a globalized economy, such business-government fraternizing is not limited to Southeast Asian countries. The overseas-Chinese corporate practice of providing credit and payoffs in exchange for political favors and protection has spread to the United States. Liem's banking partner, Mocthar Riady, was caught up in a recent uproar over giving "soft money" to the Democratic Party (see chapter 6).[21] But precisely because the alliances between Chinese financiers and politicians in Southeast Asia have their limits in attracting capital from overseas, and because Chinese firms have become modern transnational corporations, they are moving beyond their own governments to seek relations with politicians in a number of countries. In transnational business fraternities, governments are resources that can be made to share power through capitalism.

Although indigenous communities in Southeast Asia continue to be suspicious of Chinese traders, their gentrification as merchant princes casts a glow of respectability and modernity onto generals and politicians often suspected of economic incompetence and corruption. The wider acceptance of Chinese business by political elites is reflected in the number of Beijing-bound trade delegations from ASEAN countries that are composed of ethnic-Chinese businessmen. Government-business partnerships are touted in the Malaysian press as the new vehicles for strengthening the national economy through the expansion of transnational contacts that build on Chinese networks. Ethnic Chinese in partnership with state enterprises are viewed as less disloyal, especially if, like Liem, they are careful to invest in their home country while exploring other opportunities abroad.

Another feather in the cap of the Chinese tycoon is his new image as a multicultural leader who is an effective mediator for governments, and not only between, say, Kuala Lumpur or Jakarta and Beijing. As their operations expand overseas, the press celebrates their ideologically indiscriminate flexibility in doing business: "Robert Kuok appears to blend just as easily with Cuban leader Fidel Castro and Chinese Premier Li Peng as he does with Malaysian Prime Minister Datuk Seri Mahathir Mohamad and Indonesian President Soeharto. . . . 'Robert Kuok has funded the entire world,' a Malaysian broker points out. 'He is everyone's friend.'"[yy] Overseas-Chinese entrepreneurs are the new heroes, glad-handing world leaders while spreading fraternal friendship and business to any spots that remain resistant to global capitalism.

THE FAMILY ROMANCE OF THE STATE

The romance of Chinese families is also deployed by academics and government officials to organize popular understanding of political morality. Since the 1980s, states such as Taiwan and Singapore have undertaken Confucianizing campaigns as a way to shape the cultural imagination

---

[20] And opera superstar Luciano Pavarotti (b. 1935).

[21] Chapter 6 is titled "A Better Tomorrow? The Struggle for Global Visibility" and is concerned with "circulating images, narratives, and information." The Riady family was heavily (and scandalously) involved with the Clintons and their associates. Mochtar Riady's son James made more than twenty visits to the Clinton Whitehouse. The Riadys contributed over $700,000 to the Democratic Party, of which $450,000 was returned as possibly illegal (*Washington Post,* 1998). According to Bob Woodward, (1998) the Riadys had a long-term relationship with a Chinese intelligence agency.

of citizenship. These discourses allow the state to produce disciplinary knowledges and ideologically align family and state interests along a single moral continuum. In Singapore, an educational campaign was launched to promote religious knowledge and moral education through the systematic introduction of Confucian studies into the school curriculum. This strategy reached beyond the school gates through the promotion of research to support these Confucianizing claims.[22]

In Singapore in 1994, a book on Chinese pioneers in capitalism was published to great fanfare—"They are selling like hotcakes," a scholar told me. Drawing on the life stories of forty-seven Chinese businessmen, *Stepping Out: The Making of Chinese Entrepreneurs* was presented as a collective morality tale of Singapore's success. The authors claimed that these businessmen's Confucian morality had been essential to their capitalist success, which in turn, had contributed to national strength. These rags-to-riches Singaporeans were constructed as paragons of Confucian virtue—self-sacrificing, honest, trustworthy, respectful—who were impelled by a moral ethos of "doing life . . . with others, for others, because of others." These capitalist pioneers were defined as examples of a Singapore Everyman, benevolent patriarchs who treated their business partners and workers "like brothers." The authors claimed that the "Confucian merchant" of contemporary Singapore was formed in a moral order that emphasized trust, confidentiality, and the social control of subordinates.[zz] This relentlessly male vision of society—one that traces family genealogies from fathers to sons, who are construed as male-to-male partners—excludes women from the public sphere; women are constructed, almost by omission, as exclusively creatures of the private sphere, who never step out. Sociologist Claire Chiang, one of the authors of *Stepping Out*, seems quite content with this romantic picture she has helped produce. In an interview, she confided that in the course of her research among the business families, "there is no mention of the daughters holding the [reins]. But daughters are often on the cashier's side, holding the purse."[aaa] This rigid public/private division along gender lines, with female power being relegated to the realm of the domestic budget, conjures up a fantasy about "traditional" Chinese gender roles, in which women remain fixed within the household. The book received the imprimatur of Goh Keng Swee, the architect of Singapore's modern economy, who maintained in a foreword that Singapore's economic affluence is proof that the moral basis of entrepreneurial success in Singapore was "founded on the Confucian ethic" of these male pioneers.[bbb]

Such a scenario makes public masculinity and private femininity the foundation of state. Indeed, there is a clear attempt to coordinate what I have called "the moral economy of the family" with the moral economy of the state (see chapter 2). For besides constructing the Confucianized family as the backbone of economic development, the state reiterates its policies of strengthening the family by providing guarantees of social security and order.[ccc] A Singapore official describes Singapore as a capitalist society built upon "socialist" families: "For many East Asian societies, it is not only the family that is socialist, it is the extended family and sometimes the extended clan."[ddd] The fact that women are an important part of the workforce, that divorce rates are rising, and that government campaigns promoting marriage among the professional elite fail to make a big dent in the number of unmarried

---

[22] In this and the following paragraphs, Ong, heavily influenced by Foucault, lays out in considerable detail how the power elites in Malaysian and Singaporean society create a particular "regime of truth," depicting extremely wealthy merchant families as displaying Confucian values. However, as Ong noted above, much of Confucian thinking portrayed merchants in an extremely poor light. For example, the Confucian philosopher Han Fei-zi (280–233 B.C.E.) wrote that merchants accumulated wealth by exploiting farmers and were parasites on the state. It is also interesting to note that although Ong claims Chinese businessmen use images of traditional family and religious values to supercede or avoid state-level control, in this paragraph she focuses on government promotion of Confucian values to maintain control, much like the focus on "family values" by American politicians.

women does not deter such profamily claims. On the contrary, it is the very anxiety engendered by such trends that accounts for the twinned ideologies of feminine domesticity and masculine public life.

The romance of the invented Confucian family is an ideological expression of the state's promotion of extended family formation through its housing, educational, and savings schemes.[eee] These themes, which integrate the family romance with state policy, are further developed in profamily campaigns that encourage marriage and reproduction among professional women; these women are urged to return home, almost as a patriotic duty, to make babies who are deemed to be of a higher "quality" than those of lower-class women. By providing ideological and institutional supports to families threatened with individualism and fragmentation, the state restores faith that the moral power of Confucian ideology can forge a successful alliance with capitalism so that fraternal power can flourish in the public sphere without the threat of bad mothers undoing gender difference and hierarchy in the home. Geraldine Heng and Janadas Devan have coined the term "state fatherhood" to describe the state engineering of racial demographics, family, gender, and class relations in Singapore.[fff]

WORKING WOMEN'S DREAMS OF TRAVELING ROMANCE

Thus far, I have discussed how different romances of the Chinese family express messages about fraternal power, interethnic alliances, and the gendered public-private division that betray unifying themes of an emerging political imagination in Southeast Asia, which is grappling with the forces of late capitalism. In what ways do these masculinist imaginaries resonate with the consciousness of working-class women, who, after all, form the bulk of the labor force in Asia?[23] In his study of petit bourgeois and working-class Malaysian Chinese, Don Nonini identifies a dialectic of mobility and location that is highly gendered. He observes that their familial strategies send men overseas for education and work, while women are required to stay at home and care for the remaining family members.[ggg] How, one may ask, does the family romance resonate with working-class women who also migrate but whose experiences are different from those of traveling men? Do men in charge of mobility represent a kind of symbolic capital working women may identify with? I turn to the experiences of working-class women in south China, a region undergoing major transformations as a result of economic activities by ethnic Chinese from Southeast Asia.

In the fall of 1993, I visited China's most successful special economic zones, which are based in coastal cities such as Shenzhen, Xiamen, Guangzhou (Canton), and Shantou, where tens of thousands of young women from the inland provinces have descended to work in factories that are mainly financed and operated by overseas-Chinese capital. For instance, in Shenzhen, the roaring metropolis of China's future, right across the water from Hong Kong, 80 percent of the investors are Chinese from Hong Kong and the Asia Pacific region. These "Chinese from overseas," who are so vaunted in the mass media, are viewed in an intensely ambivalent way by local women (see chapter 1). In their workaday world, female workers in Shenzhen want to maintain distance from Hong Kong and overseas-Chinese managers, visitors, and businessmen. According to Ching Kwan Lee, young migrant women from

---

[23] In this passage, Ong makes a critical point that resonates strongly with our discussion in the introduction to this section. Interest in globalization is driven significantly by "facts on the ground." Ong has explained above that governments and business elites promote the notion of Confucian values, which assign women to the domestic sphere or to a subsidiary role to men in supporting the family. However, the reality is that women make up the majority of the industrial work force, so their own interests and goals are critical. Women are not passive recipients of the ideology of the government and power elites. Rather, they contest this ideology through the actual conditions under which they labor and their understanding of those conditions.

the impoverished interior consider overseas Chinese to be outsiders who do not share their culture or appreciate their own very different backgrounds.[hhh] Furthermore, as Lee's research has shown, overseas managers enjoy enormous discretionary power over the treatment of workers on the shop floor, as well as over their chances of remaining in the cities. Many female workers prefer to be supervised by their own kinsmen or townsfolk who work in the same factory. Indeed, regimes of control based on kinship and localistic ties are pervasive throughout the manufacturing industry, for personalistic relations increase workers' compliance and also lift the burden of direct confrontation from overseas-Chinese bosses. The cultural divide is deepened because female workers feel that their foreign bosses are unable to empathize with their problems and their very limited options in the labor force. There is also the image of overseas-Chinese men as uncontrollable agents of sexual exploitation, now made more flexible and invasive by the flows of capital.

In the Women's Federation (Funu Lianhehui) office of Shenzhen, the director told me that Hong Kong and overseas-Chinese men were perceived as good catches by local women, although "their cultural standards are not so high." This was her way of saying that for young women, these men are chiefly attractive because of their money and mobility "Hong Kong visitors are bad for public morality. There are about ten thousand truck drivers coming into Shenzhen each day, and they contribute to prostitution."[iii] The booming mistress trade is sparked by the Hong Kong men's "railroad policy" of keeping a mistress at each stop on their circuit, and there is a "concubine village" near a container-truck border crossing where many Hong Kong men have set up a home away from home, sometimes with children.[jjj] Some of these women may take second jobs as agents for their patrons' businesses in China. Such practices recall the early days of Chinese sojourning in Southeast Asia, when families were left in different sites in the diaspora. It is one of the many ironies of late capitalism that premodern family forms and female exploitation, which the communist state had largely erased in the cities, are being resurrected.[24]

In the Deng era,[25] the mass-entertainment industry has redefined the passive and self-sacrificing young woman, an icon of the precommunist era, as a cultural ideal. After having viewed *Yearnings*, a phenomenally popular TV series about family upheavals in post-Tiananmen China, Lisa Rofel notes that the family and female self-sacrifice have become new symbols of national unity. She argues that an underlying theme in the melodrama is the emergence of a strong and controlled masculinity that may lead the battered nation into the future.[kkk] We must note, however, that the urban population in coastal China seems to favor foreign programs beamed from the Star TV satellite network, which has created a whole new trans-Asian public through its bewildering variety of Asian and Western offerings, including MTV, talk shows, movies, and so forth. In Shenzhen, working women watch Hong Kong soap operas for cultural scripts on how to be independent modern women. I visited a beauty parlor set up by three enterprising female migrants in one of the hastily built workers' apartment complexes to serve the increasing demand for personal grooming. While attending to the customers, the hair-dressers watched Hong Kong soaps on television and made a running

---

[24] Ong's discussion of the rise of prostitution in the newly capitalizing Chinese cities is strongly reminiscent of Philippe Bourgois' analysis of Puerto Rican drug dealers in a New York City barrio [essay 42]. In each case, nonlegitimate forms of commerce develop as a result of people struggling to survive in rapidly changing economic circumstances.

[25] Deng Xiaoping (1904–1997) emerged as the most powerful single leader in China after the 1976 death of Mao

Zedong. He was critical in repudiating many of the policies of Mao's era, allowing the emergence of capitalism and opening China to overseas investors. The Deng era can be dated from about 1978 until 1997.

Yearnings was first broadcast in 1990. It was a fifty-part, hour-long television melodrama—the first of its kind in China.

commentary on what they imagined to be women's greater choices and strategies in overseas-Chinese communities. For these young women, who had left their rural villages for the bright city lights and begun the difficult climb toward middle-class status, the lure of capitalism lay in the possibility for self-reliance, not self-sacrifice. They were preoccupied with figuring out strategies and networks for crossing into this brave new world. While young women routinely rely on family, neighbors, and friends to leave their villages and survive in the industrial cities, many are now seeking new relations that are not based on already constituted kinship or social bonds. Among Shenzhen's female working class, most kinship and hometown networks lead straight back to the village; at best, they prove to be only a weak source of coercion and support in the work-place.[lll] Women who desire wealth and travel to rich places outside China answer to a different family romance.

For these women, overseas-Chinese men represent a vision of capitalist autonomy and a source of new "network capital."[mmm] In an interesting reformulation of Pierre Bourdieu's concept of symbolic capital,[nnn] Siu-lun Wong and Janet Salaff use network capital to mean acquired personal networks based on friendship, school ties, and professional contacts (rather than networks formed from links based on family, family name, and hometown).[ooo] They argue that the accumulation of network capital has been a critical practice of well-to-do Hong Kongers in their emigration strategies.[26] Working-class women in coastal China are less well positioned to build on professional contacts, but many depend on personal charms to create new personal connections. So even a road-trip Romeo from Hong Kong can be an irresistible catch because

he literally and figuratively embodies the guanxi (ideally through marriage) that will lead to the dazzling world of overseas-Chinese capitalism.[27] Marriage to a traveling man enables one to expand one's accumulation of network capital and can also benefit the members of one's family, who eventually may also emigrate to the capitalist world, where their desires for wealth and personal freedom can be met.

So mobility, wealth, and an imagined metropolitan future, rather than love or class solidarity, account for the lure of family romances. Feelings of regional, cultural, and class differences from overseas-Chinese men may remain, but not sufficiently to deter working women from marrying them to "develop a bridge to leave China," a common expression used by the women I met. One of the three hairdressers I visited was corresponding with a Chinese Canadian and a white American she met in a bar. I later learned that she had begun a courtship with a male cousin who had emigrated to California, and she eventually flew to San Francisco to marry him.[ppp] Hers was a particularly creative weaving of acquired and created networks in a successful emigration strategy. Another young woman I met, who is considered a classic north China beauty, has a faithful, perfectly respectable Chinese boyfriend who works in the government. This beauty, however, frequents bars; she hopes to meet an overseas-Chinese man who can help her leave China.

That karaoke bars are the sites of mobility and new wealth is apparent from their video equipment and their clientele of foreign businessmen, hustlers, and upwardly mobile women. Indeed, the bar has taken over from the work-place, where worker politics have become too contaminated by Communist Party and capitalist interests to protect the collective interests of workers.

---

[26] Symbolic capital plays a substantial role in Bourdieu's thought. He argued that there were several different sorts of capital (or wealth). Symbolic capital refers to honor or prestige (or the symbols of these things) that cause a person's words to be taken seriously. Symbolic capital can easily lead to economic capital. Wong and Salaff's notion of network capital seems to correspond more closely to Bourdieu's idea of social capital, the possession of, or ac-

cess to, social networks. This is an idea that has been widely publicized (in particular, see Putnam 2000).

[27] *Guanxi:* an important concept in Chinese society, referring to social relationships that are mutually supportive and in which partners can be prevailed upon to perform favors or services for one another.

Instead, many working women prefer the "state-free" arena of bars and discos to work out individual strategies of eluding economic exploitation, at least of the factory kind. The romance of mobile capitalism, then, conjures up a felicitous brew of imagined personal freedom and wealth, a heady mix that young women imagine traveling men can provide the passports to. This particular conjunction of working women's middle-class dreams and mobile men has reinforced conditions ripe for the masculinist thrust and scope of sexual and class exploitation throughout Asia.

CONCLUSION

I have traced the different family romances between corporate brothers, state and capital, and men and women that have proliferated in the public cultures of the new Asia. These unifying themes indicate that the family imaginary both expresses and normalizes the tensions between fluidity and rigidity, the public and the private, economic power and political power, exploitation and romance, and domination and subordination. David Harvey notes that the flexible operation of late capitalism is exceptionally creative in its destruction of rigidities. But he has not considered how cultural messages that romanticize mobile capital can also reinforce, ramify, and reinstall various relations of inequality and thus promote a new kind of conformity to flexible accumulation and state authority. Cultural forms labeled Chinese or Confucian in modern state regimes, corporate networks, and individual practices express and shape a political unconscious that construes male corporate power as benevolent, enlightened, and progressive for individuals and for the state.

While capitalism has increased female employment at most levels of the labor market, its institutions and family metaphors have also made more mobile, more extensive, and more complex the sexual and class exploitation of women and the working population. The romance of merchant mandarins and the Confucian family defines men to be in charge of both wealth and mobility, while women are localized in domestic situations or workplaces commanded by men. These visions of social and family order resonate with aspirations of different classes and underlie the sense of a distinctive transnational Asian publicness that obscures the divisions of class and gender. Such family romances reinforce the dark secrets of family, nation-state, and global capitalism that promise wealth, security, and escape but deliver exploitation, despair, and entrapment. By stripping off the veil of romance, we reveal that the mobile forces of capitalism, as Joan Vincent has documented and theorized in her life's work, are alternately destructive and creative of the class, ethnic, and gender relations that constitute the very transnational networks that have developed within and alongside global capitalism.[28]

NOTES

[a] Joan Vincent, *Anthropology and Politics* (Tucson: University of Arizona Press, 1990), 329–99. Vincent traces this theoretical destination back to the 1950s, when

---

[28] The ending passages of this essay present a good example of the way in which globalization studies mix the symbolic and ideological aspects of anthropological inquiry with more economic and materialist concerns. Ong has outlined the way she believes the state and business operate together to create a convincing system of symbols (the family, Confucianism, the heroic entrepreneur, and so on). She shows how female workers accept some of these but reject others (such as self-sacrifice for family), creating their own symbolic world. Ong argues these symbols have very important economic effects and implications. They permit and justify the exploitation of workers (as Ong notes above), but they also create a world in which men and women struggle, sometimes successfully, to improve their economic and material lives. According to the Chinese government, by 2003, 19 percent of Chinese were "middle class." This number is almost certainly exaggerated, but it is undoubtedly true that tens of millions of Chinese have greatly improved their economic lot in the past decade. Whether or not the family imagery Ong discusses really has the economic effects she claims is not really demonstrated in this essay. However, it is a marvelous example of the marriage of materialist and postmodern analysis and demonstrates the direction that many anthropologists have taken in the last decade.

Eric Wolf and Sydney Mintz, under the supervision of Julian Steward (*The People of Puerto Rico* [Urbana: University of Illinois Press, 1956]), reworked the community-study approach within hierarchical systems of political economies. In the 1970s, Immanuel Wallerstein (*The Modern World-System*) explained the world system in rather taxonomic terms. In the following decade, Wolf (Europe) and Mintz (*Sweetness and Power*) in different ways plotted the cultural histories of conquest, colonialism, the division of labor, trade, and consumption in making diverse political economies that were also contexts of cultural making. By then, many anthropologists of different persuasions, including Marxists and symbolic analysts, had come to assume a global-local axis (which Vincent called "Europe and the Third World in a single paradigm") as background and frame for their ethnographies.

[b] *Vincent, Anthropology and Politics,* 409.

[c] In her first book, *African Elite: The Big Men of a Small Town* (Chicago: University of Chicago Press, 1971), Vincent drew critical attention to the strategic importance of "men in motion" circulating through small towns in East Africa as agents in the expansion of British capital; the movements of these indigenous men became inseparable from the "moving frontier" of imperial capitalism. See Vincent, *Teso in Transformation: The Political Economy of Peasant and Class in Eastern Africa* (Berkeley and Los Angeles: University of California Press, 1982), 9–n.

[d] Vincent, *Teso in Transformation,* 259–62.

[e] Karl Marx, *The Eighteenth Brumaire of Louis Bonaparte* (1869; reprint, New York: International Publishers, 1963), 124. Marx described the nineteenth-century French peasantry as atomized household units that did not enter into social relations with each other. Unaware of the wider relations that exploited them as a collectivity, they were incapable of enforcing class interests in their own name.

[f] This insight was later echoed in Massey, "Power Geometry."

[g] There is a huge literature on this topic, but among the more innovative are Wolf, *Peasants* (Englewood Cliffs, N.J.: Prentice Hall, 1996); Scott, *Weapons of the Weak;* and Ranajit Guha and Gayatri Chakravorty Spivak, eds., *Selected Subaltern Studies* (New York: Oxford University Press, 1988).

[h] To Marx, the "stupefied seclusion" of the French peasantry under the Bonaparte dynasty was compounded by the priest—"the anointed bloodhound of the earthly police"—as the ideological instrument of the government (Marx, *Eighteenth Brumaire,* 125, 129–30). Marxist approaches to the problems of cultural consciousness among third-world peasants are dominated by notions of ideological mystification, as, for example, in Eric

Wolf, *Peasants,* and a variant of ideological mystification that incorporates the concept of a resistant peasant subculture, as, for example, in Scott, *Moral Economy.*

[i] For cultural approaches to relations of production and consumption in our highly technologized, late-capitalist world see Harvey, *Condition of Postmodernity;* Jameson, *Postmodernism;* and Donald M. Lowe, *The Body in Late-Capitalist USA* (Durham, N.C.: Duke University Press, 1995).

[j] Lowe, *Body in Late-Capitalist USA,* 15. See also Jameson, *Postmodernism.*

[k] See Ong, "Gender and Labor Politics."

[l] As Gayatri C. Spivak has claimed in 1988 (Spivak, "Can the Subaltern Speak?"). She maintains that subalterns can neither be depicted by nor spoken for by elites whose relations of domination prevent them from portraying the "real" interests of subalterns.

[m] Lowe, *Body in Late-Capitalist USA,* 8. Like Donald Lowe, I do not see a problem in combining both Marxist and Foucauldian approaches as a way to better grasp the constitution of contemporary social consciousness. See, for example, Ong, *Spirits of Resistance.*

[n] See Fredric Jameson, *The Political Unconscious: Narrative as a Socially Symbolic Act* (Ithaca, N.Y.: Cornell University Press, 1981).

[o] Cristina S. Blanc, "The Thoroughly Modern 'Asian': Capital, Culture, and Nation in Thailand and the Philippines," in Ong and Nonini, *Ungrounded Empires,* 261–86.

[p] See Ariel Dorfman and Armand Mattelart, *How to Read Donald Duck: Imperialist Ideology in the Disney Comic,* trans. David Kunzie (New York: I. G. Editions, 1975).

[q] Of course, American popular culture continues to be widespread throughout the region, and Japanese mass culture is growing in appeal among young Taiwan and Hong Kong Chinese. Nevertheless, I maintain that whatever cultural forms are used and borrowed from the United States or Japan, they are often deployed and woven within cultural scripts about Chinese ethnicity or national identity, depending on the particular programs.

[r] Gordon, "Governmental Rationality," 14.

[s] Ibid., 16.

[t] See Mahathir Mohamad and Shintaro Ishihara, "Will East Beat West?" *World Press Review,* December 1995, 6–11. For a fuller discussion of this idea see Aihwa Ong, "Strategic Sisterhood or Sisters in Solidarity? Questions of Communitarianism and Citizenship in Asia," *Indiana Journal of Global Legal Studies* 4, no. 1 (1997): 1–29.

ᵘLynn Hunt, *The Family Romance of the French Revolution* (Berkeley and Los Angeles: University of California Press, 1992), 4.

ᵛIbid., viii.

ʷHall, "Toad in the Garden."

ˣHunt, *Family Romance*, 1.

ʸJamie Mackie, "Changing Patterns of Chinese Big Business in Southeast Asia," in *Southeast Asian Capitalists*, ed. Ruth McVey (Ithaca, N.Y.: South East Asia Program, Cornell University, 1992), 161. Most of the international financing for this elite Chinese minority came from the wider network of overseas Chinese investments, and the increased mobility of capital has served to decrease Chinese leeway vis-à-vis local governments.

ᶻIbid.; see other chapters in McVey, *Southeast Asian Capitalists*.

ᵃᵃInterview by author, Singapore, August 1994.

ᵇᵇ*Business Week*, 29 November 1993.

ᶜᶜInterview by author, Singapore, August 1994.

ᵈᵈJoel Kotkin, "Family Ties in the New Global Economy," *Los Angeles Times Magazine*, 17 January 1993, 21–22.

ᵉᵉSigmund Freud, *Totem and Taboo: Some Points of Agreement between the Mental Lives of Savages and Neurotics*, in *The Standard Edition of the Complete Psychological Works*, vol. 13, trans. James Strachey (London: Hogarth Press, 1958). See Hunt, *Family Romance*, 1–16, for a fascinating analysis of Freud's "primal scene" and its subthemes.

ᶠᶠ"Confucian capitalist" has also been used to describe the South Korean founder of Hyundai, one of Asia's wealthiest industrialists, but it has been used more to refer to his "stern domination" and even "autocratic predilections" than to the positive fraternal values that have been attributed to Chinese capitalists (*Far Eastern Economic Review*, 22 June 1995, 60).

ᵍᵍJonathan Friedland, "Kuok the Kingpin," *Far Eastern Economic Review*, 7 February 1991, 46.

ʰʰIn Southeast Asia, whereas contemporary scholarly and media discussions about the rise of entrepreneurs are becoming ever more common, there is a deafening silence on the history of anti-imperialist struggles and the patriots who fought and died for national independence.

ⁱⁱJonathan Friedland, "Friends of the Family," *Far Eastern Economic Review*, 7 February 1991, 48–49.

ʲʲForbes, 18 July 1994, 12.

ᵏᵏGeorge L. Mosse, *Nationalism and Sexuality: Middle-Class Morality and Sexual Norms in Modern Europe* (Madison: University of Wisconsin Press, 1985), 10–13.

ˡˡI borrow the term "middling" from Paul Rabinow. Rabinow (*French Modem*) talks about the "middling modernity" of middlebrow expertise in shaping social knowledges, norms, and sensibilities in modern society.

ᵐᵐWilliam Barnes, "Chinese Out of Thais' Closet," *South China Morning Post*, 26 February 1994, 4.

ⁿⁿSee Ong and Nonini, *Ungrounded Empires*, chaps. 5, 9.

ᵒᵒ"Anwar: Be Committed to Ethical Values," *New Straits Times*, 7 August 1994, A1.

ᵖᵖSee "Singapore Charges Scholar, Herald Tribune," *San Francisco Chronicle*, 19 November 1994, 8.

�q�q Mark Clifford, "Profile K. S. Lo: Milk for the Millions," *Far Eastern Economic Review*, 9 June 1994, 78.

ʳʳMark Clifford, "Heir Force," *Far Eastern Economic Review*, 17 November 1994, 78.

ˢˢSee Richard Robison, *Indonesia: The Rise of Capital* (Sydney: Allen and Unwin, 1986), for a discussion of the state-private capital alliances in Indonesia.

ᵗᵗSee Adam Schwarz, A Nation in Waiting: Indonesia in the 1990s (Sydney: Allen and Unwin, 1994), 109–14, for an account of Liem's vast family business and long-term links with Soeharto.

ᵘᵘIbid., 108.

ᵛᵛAh is a common Malay name and Baba refers to the Straits Chinese men who under colonialism often played the role of comprador to British concerns.

ʷʷS. Jayasankaran, "Taking Stock: Malaysia's Rashid Hussain: At the Crossroads," *Far Eastern Economic Review*, 20 April 1995, 76–77.

ˣˣEdward A. Gargan, "The Master Builder."

ʸʸ*Far Eastern Economic Review*, S February 1991, 47.

ᶻᶻChan and Chiang, *Stepping Out*, 15, 98, 354.

ᵃᵃᵃClaire Chang, interview by *Asian Wall Street Journal*, 25 November 1993, 5.

ᵇᵇᵇJoh Keng Swee, foreword to Chan and Chiang, *Stepping Out*, viii–ix.

ᶜᶜᶜJim Scott maintains that in Southeast Asian peasant societies, the unequal exchanges between peasants and their clients are morally justified in terms of the patrons' guarantees of their social and economic security (see Scott, *Moral Economy*).

ᵈᵈᵈ*International Herald Tribune*, 22 June 1994, 4.

ᵉᵉᵉSee Chua Beng Huat, *Communitarian Ideology and Democracy in Singapore* (London: Routledge, 1995).

ᶠᶠᶠSee Heng and Devan, "State Fatherhood."

ᵍᵍᵍNonini, "Shifting Identities."

ʰʰʰLee, "Factory Regimes."

ⁱⁱⁱInterview by author, Shenzhen, P.R.C., November 1993.

jjj See Nora Lee, "Duplicitous Liaisons," *Far Eastern Economic Review,* 20 April 1995, 64–65.

kkk See Lisa Rofel,"'Yearnings': Televisual Love and Melodramatic Politics in Contemporary China," *American Ethnologist* 21, no. 4 (1994): 700–722.

lll See Lee, "Factory Regimes."

mmm This term was first used in Mayfair Yang, "The Gift Economy and State Power in China," *Comparative Studies in Society and History* 31 (1989): 25–54, where the author comments on the practice of accumulating network capital in contemporary China as a way to by-pass and subvert state regulations. See also Yang, *Gifts, Favors, and Banquets.*

nnn See Bourdieu, *Outline,* 171–83.

ooo See Siu-lun Wong and Janet W. Salaff, "Network Capital: Emigration from Hong Kong" (paper presented at the conference "The Transnationalization of Chinese Capitalism," National University of Singapore, 8 August 1994).

ppp I am grateful to Connie Clark, a graduate student in anthropology at the University of California, Berkeley, for keeping me abreast of developments in these women's lives. Clark, who was conducting dissertation research in Shenzhen, introduced me to these women and, together with Ching Kwan Lee, showed me various aspects of working women's lives during my field trip.

BIBLIOGRAPHY

GENERAL REFERENCES

A wide variety of reference works were used to fill in definitions, dates, and details of biography. The following four books were among the most useful.

Edwards, Paul, ed. 1967. *The Encyclopedia of Philosophy.* New York: Macmillan.

Gacs, Ute, and Aisha Khan, Jerry McIntyre, and Ruth Weinberg, eds. 1989. *Women Anthropologists: Selected Biographies.* Chicago: University of Illinois Press.

Sills, David L. 1968. *International Encyclopedia of the Social Sciences.* New York: Macmillan.

Winters, Christopher, ed. 1991. *International Dictionary of Anthropologists.* New York: Garland.

REFERENCES CITED

Abu-Lughod, Lila. 1991. Writing Against Culture. In *Recapturing Anthropology: Working in the Present,* Richard G. Fox, ed., pp. 137–162. Santa Fe: SAR Press.

———. 1995. A Tale of Two Pregnancies. In *Women Writing Culture,* Ruth Behar and Deborah A. Gordon, eds., pp. 339–349. Berkeley: University of California Press.

Adams, R. M. 1966. *The Evolution of Urban Society.* Chicago: Aldine.

Agar, Michael H. 1980. *The Professional Stranger: An Informal Introduction to Ethnography.* New York: Academic Press.

Applebaum, Herbert, ed. 1987. *Perspectives in Cultural Anthropology.* Albany: State University of New York Press.

Ardrey, Robert. 1961. *African Genesis.* New York: Atheneum Publishers.

Asad, Talal. 1973. *Anthropology and the Colonial Encounter.* London: Ithaca Press.

Atkinson, J. J. 1903. *Primal Law.* London, New York, and Bombay: Longman, Green.

Axelrod, Robert. 1984. *The Evolution of Cooperation.* New York: Basic Books.

Bachofen, Johann Jakob. 1992 [1861]. *Das Mutterrecht.* In *Myth, Religion and Mother Right: Selected Writings of J. J. Bachofen,* Ralph Manheim, trans. Princeton, NJ: Princeton University Press.

Barash, D. 1979. *The Whisperings Within.* New York: Harper and Row.

Barnes, Harry E. 1960. Foreword. In *Essays in the Science of Culture in Honor of Leslie A. White,* Gertrude E. Dole and Robert L. Carneiro, eds., pp. xi–xvi. New York: Crowell.

Bateson, Gregory. 1958 [1936]. *Naven.* Palo Alto, CA: Stanford University Press.

Bateson, Gregory, and Margaret Mead. 1942. *Balinese Character: A Photographic Analysis.* New York: New York Academy of Sciences.

Bateson, M. C. 1984. *With a Daughter's Eye: A Memoir of Margaret Mead and Gregory Bateson.* New York: William Morrow.

Bauer, Bruno. 1974 [1841–42]. *Kritik der Evangelischen Geschichte der Synoptiken.* New York: Hildesheim.

Beardsley, Richard K. 1976. An Appraisal of Leslie A. White's Scholarly Influence. *American Anthropologist* 78(3):617–620.

Behar, Ruth, and Deborah A. Gordon. 1995. *Women Writing Culture.* Berkeley: University of California Press.

Behar, Ruth. 1995. Introduction: Out of Exile. In *Women Writing Culture,* Ruth Behar and Deborah A. Gordon, eds., pp. 1–29. Berkeley: University of California Press.

Bell, V. 1993. *Interrogating Incest: Feminism, Foucault, and the Law.* London: Routledge.

Benedict, Ruth Fulton. 1930. Psychological Types in the Cultures of the Southwest. In *Proceedings of the Twenty-Third International Congress of Americanists* (held at New York, September 17–22, 1928), pp. 572–581. Lancaster, PA: Science Press Printing.

———. 1934a. Anthropology and the Abnormal. *Journal of General Psychology* 10(2):59–82.

———. 1934b. *Patterns of Culture.* Boston, New York: Houghton Mifflin.

———. 1946. *The Chrysanthemum and the Sword: Patterns of Japanese Culture.* Boston: Houghton Mifflin.

———. 1948. Anthropology and the Humanities. *American Anthropologist* 50:585–593.

Benedict, Ruth Fulton, and Gene Weltfish. 1943. *The Races of Mankind.* New York: Public Affairs Committee.

Benjamin, Walter. 1969 [1936]. The Work of Art in the Age of Mechanical Reproduction. In *Illuminations,* H. Arendt, ed., pp. 217–252.

Bentham, Jeremy. 1789. *An Introduction to the Principles of Morals and Legislation.* London.

Berlin, Brent O., Dennis Breedlove, and Peter Raven. 1974. *Principles of Tzeltal Plant Classification.* New York: Academic Press.

Bettelheim, Bruno. 1955. *Symbolic Wounds: Puberty Rites and the Envious Male.* London: Thames and Hudson.

Blackburn, J. 1994. *Daisy Bates in the Desert*: *A Woman's Life Among the Aborigines.* London: Secker & Warburg.

Boas, Franz. 1896. The Limitations of the Comparative Method in Anthropology. *Science,* n.s., 4: 901–908.

———. 1901. The Mind of Primitive Man. *The Journal of American Folklore* 14(52):1–11.

———. 1911. *Handbook of American Indian Languages,* Part 1. Smithsonian Institution, Washington DC, Bureau of American Ethnology, Bulletin 40.

———. 1912. Changes in the Bodily Form of Descendants of Immigrants. *American Anthropologist* 14(3): 530–562.

———. 1974. [1938]. *The Background of My Early Thinking: The Shaping of American Anthropology 1883–1911: A Franz Boas Reader.* G. Stocking, ed. New York, Basic Books: 41–42.

Bock, Phillip K. 1988. *Rethinking Psychological Anthropology.* New York: W. H. Freeman.

Borofsky, Robert, ed. 1994. *Assessing Cultural Anthropology.* New York: McGraw-Hill.

Bottomore, T. 1991. Lumpenproletariat. In *A Dictionary of Marxist Thought,* T. Bottomore, ed., p. 327. Oxford: Basil Blackwell.

Bourdieu, Pierre. 1977 *Outline of a Theory of Practice.* Richard Nice, trans. Cambridge: Cambridge University Press.

Bourgois, Philippe. 1995. From Jíbaro to Crack Dealer: Confronting the Restructuring of Capitalism in El Barrio. In *Articulating Hidden Histories: Exploring the Influence of Eric R. Wolf,* Jane Schneider and Rayna Rapp, eds., pp. 125–141. Berkeley: University of California Press.

Boyne, Roy. 1966. Structuralism. In *The Blackwell Companion to Social Theory,* Bryan S. Turner, ed., pp. 194–220. Oxford: Blackwell.

Briggs, Jean L. 1970. *Never in Anger: Portrait of an Eskimo Family.* Cambridge, MA: Harvard University Press.

Brillouin, Leon. 1956. *Science and Information Theory.* New York: Academic Press.

Brown, Dee. 1971. *Bury My Heart at Wounded Knee.* New York: Holt, Rinehart, and Winston.

Brown, D. E. 1991. *Human Universals.* New York: McGraw-Hill.

Brown, Jerram L. 1983. Cooperation—A Biologist's Dilemma. *Advances in the Study of Behavior* 13:1–37.

Brown, Norman O. 1959. *Life Against Death: The Psychoanalytical Meaning of History.* Middletown, CT: Wesleyan University Press.

Bucher, Bernadette, and Claude Lévi-Strauss. 1985. An Interview with Claude Lévi-Strauss 30 June 1982. *American Ethnologist* 12(2):360–368.

Bücher, Carl. 1968 [1901]. *Industrial Evolution.* New York: Augustus M. Kelley.

Buffon, Georges Louis Leclerc. 1752–1799. *Histoire naturelle, générale et particulier.* Paris: De l'Imprimerie Royale.

Carneiro, Robert L. 1970. A Theory of the Origin of the State. *Science* 169:733–738.

———. 1981. "Leslie White." In *Totems and Teachers: Perspectives on the History of Anthropology.* New York: Columbia University Press.

Carneiro, Robert L., ed. 1967. *The Evolution of Society: Selections from Herbert Spencer's Principles of Sociology.* Chicago: University of Chicago Press.

Caspari, Rachel. 2003. From Types to Populations: A Century of Race, Physical Anthropology, and the American Anthropological Association. *American Anthropologist* 105(1):65–76.

Casson, Ronald W. 1983. Schemata in Cognitive Anthropology. *Annual Reviews of Anthropology.* 12: 429–462.

Chagnon, Napoleon. 1968. *The Fierce People.* New York: Holt, Rinehart, and Winston.

Chayanov, Aleksandr V. 1966. *The Theory of Peasant Economy.* Daniel Thorner, Basile Kerblay, and R. E. F. Smith, eds. Homewood, IL: R. D. Irwin.

Childe, V. Gordon. 1942. *What Happened in History.* Baltimore: Penguin.

Chodorow, Nancy. 1974. Family Structure and Feminine Personality. In *Woman, Culture, and Society,* Michelle Rosaldo and Louise Lamphere, eds., pp. 43–66. Palo Alto, CA: Stanford University Press.

Clifford, James, and George E. Marcus, eds. 1986. *Writing Culture: The Poetics and Politics of Ethnography.* Berkeley: University of California Press.

Cole, Douglas. 1983. "'The Value of a Person Lies In His Herzensbildung,' Franz Boas' Baffin Island Letter-Diary, 1883–1884. In *Observers Observed: Essays on Ethnographic Fieldwork,* George Stocking, ed., pp. 13–52. Madison: University of Wisconsin.

Collier, Jane F. 1974. Women in Politics. In *Woman, Culture, and Society,* Michelle Rosaldo and Louise Lamphere, eds., pp. 89–96. Palo Alto, CA: Stanford University Press.

Collier, Jane F., and Sylvia Yanagisako, eds. 1987. *Gender and Kinship.* Palo Alto, CA: Stanford University Press.

Comte, August. 1975 [1922]. Plan of the Scientific Operations Necessary for Reorganizing Society. In *Auguste Comte and Positivism: The Essential Writings,* Gertrud Lenzer, ed., pp. 9–69. New York: Harper Torchbooks.

Condorcet, Jean-Antoine-Nicholas. 1902 [1794]. *Esquisse d'un tableau historique des progrès de l'esprit humain.* Paris: Bibliothèque Nationale.

Conkey, Margaret, and Janet Spector. 1984. Archaeology and the Study of Gender. *Advances in Archaeological Method and Theory* 7:1–38.

Copeland, Lennie. 1985. *Going International: How to Make Friends and Deal Effectively in the Global Marketplace.* New York: Random House.

Coquery-Vidrovitch, Catherine. 1978. Researches on an African Mode of Production. In *Relations of Production: Marxist Approaches to Economic Anthropology,* David Sedden, ed., pp. 261–288. London: Frank Cass.

Cosmides, L., and J. Tooby. 1997. *Evolutionary Psychology: A Primer.* http://www.psych.ucsb.edu/research/cep/primer.htm, retrieved October 20, 1998.

Crapo, Richley H. 1993. *Cultural Anthropology: Understanding Ourselves and Others.* Guilford, CT: Dushkin Publishing Group.

Crocker, J. Christopher. 1977. My Brother the Parrot. In *The Social Use of Metaphor: Essays on the Anthropology of Rhetoric,* J. David Sapir and J. Christopher Crocker, eds., pp. 164–192. Philadelphia: University of Pennsylvania Press.

Crosby, Alfred W. 1989. *America's Forgotten Pandemic: The Influenza of 1918.* Cambridge: Cambridge University Press.

D'Andrade, Roy. 1995a. *The Development of Cognitive Anthropology.* Cambridge: Cambridge University Press.

———. 1995b. Moral Models in Anthropology. *Current Anthropology* 36(3):399–408.

Darnell, Regna. 2001. *Invisible Genealogies: A History of Americanist Anthropology.* Lincoln: University of Nebraska Press.

Darwin, Charles. 1858. On the tendency of species to form varieties; and on the perpetuation of varieties and species by natural means of selection. *Journal of the Linnean Society* 3:45–62.

———. 1871. *The Descent of Man and Selection in Relation to Sex.* London: John Murray.

———. 1883 [1868]. *The Variation of Animals and Plants Under Domestication,* 2nd ed. New York: D. Appleton.

———. 1952 [1839]. *Journal of Researches* (reprint). New York: Hafner.

———. 1988 [1859]. *On the Origin of Species.* New York: New York University Press.

Davis, K. and Wilbert Moore. 1945. Some Principles of Stratification. *American Sociological Review* 10: 242–249.

———. 1953. Replies to Tumin. *American Sociological Review* 18:394–396.

Dawkins, Richard. 1976. *The Selfish Gene.* New York: Oxford University Press.

de Beauvoir, Simone. 1952. *The Second Sex,* H. M. Parshley, ed. and trans. New York: Knopf.

Delegorgue, Adulphe. 1847 [1990]. *Travels in Southern Africa.* Durbin: Killie Campbell Africana Library; Pietermaritzburg: University of Natal Press.

Deloria, Vine, Jr. 1969. *Custer Died for Your Sins: An Indian Manifesto.* New York: Macmillan.

Devereux, G. 1961. Shamans as Neurotics. *American Anthropologist* 63:1088–1090.

Devons, Ely, and Max Gluckman. 1964. Conclusion: Modes and Consequences of Limiting a Field of Study. In *Closed Systems and Open Minds,* Max Gluckman, ed., pp. 254–259. Chicago: Aldine.

Diamond, Stanley, ed. 1960. *Culture in History: Essays in Honor of Paul Radin.* New York: Columbia University.

di Leonardo, Micaela. 1991. Introduction to Gender, Culture, and Political Economy: Feminist Anthropology in Historical Perspective. In *Gender at the Crossroads of Knowledge,* Micaela di Leonardo, ed., pp. 1–48. Berkeley: University of California Press.

Dolgin, Janet L., David S. Kemnitzer, and David M. Schneider. 1977. *Symbolic Anthropology.* New York: Columbia University Press.

Douglas, Mary. 1966. *Purity and Danger: An Analysis of the Concepts of Pollution and Taboo.* London: Routledge and Kegan Paul.

———. 1970. *Natural Symbols: Explorations in Cosmology.* New York: Pantheon Books.

Durkheim, Émile. 1933 [1893]. *The Division of Labor in Society,* George Simpson, trans. New York: Macmillan.

———. 1951 [1897]. *Suicide: A Study in Sociology,* Jon A. Spaulding and George Simpson, trans. New York: Free Press.

———. 1965 [1912]. *The Elementary Forms of the Religious Life,* Joseph Swain, trans. New York: Free Press.

Durkheim, Émile, and Marcel Mauss. 1963 [1903]. *Primitive Classification,* Rodney Needham, trans. Chicago: University of Chicago Press.

Economist. 2005. Race in Malaysia: Failing to Spread the Wealth. *The Economist* April 25, 2005. http://www.economist.com/world/asia/displayStory.cfm?story_id=4323219

Eiseley, Loren. 1961. *Darwin's Century: Evolution and the Men Who Discovered It.* New York: Anchor Books.

Elkin, A. P. 1941. Native Languages and the Field Worker in Australia. *American Anthropologist* 43(1): 89–94.

Engels, Friedrich. 1949 [1888]. *Ludwig Feuerbach and the End of Classical German Philosophy.* Moscow, Foreign Languages Publishing House.

———. 1972 [1884]. *The Origin of the Family, Private Property, and the State.* New York: Pathfinder Press.

Erickson, P. A. W., and L. D. Murphy. 1998. *A History of Anthropological Theory.* Ontario: Broadview Press.

Evans-Pritchard, E. E. 1940. *The Nuer: A Description of the Modes of Livelihood and Political Institutions of a Nilotic People.* Oxford: Oxford University Press.

———. 1951a. *Kinship and Marriage Among the Nuer.* Oxford: Clarendon Press.

———. 1951b. *Social Anthropology.* New York: Free Press.

———. 1956. *Nuer Religion.* Oxford: Clarendon Press.

Fagan, Brian M. 1989. *People of the Earth: An Introduction to World Prehistory.* Glenview, IL: Scott, Foresman.

Fessler, Daniel. 1995. *A Small Field With a Lot of Hornets: An Exploration of Shame, Motivation, and Social Control.* Ph.D. dissertation, University of California, San Diego.

Firth, Raymond. 1964. The Place of Malinowski in the History of Economic Anthropology. In *Man and Culture: An Evaluation of the Work of Bronislaw Malinowski,* Raymond Firth, ed., pp. 209–227. New York: Harper and Row.

———. 1973. *Symbols, Public and Private.* Ithaca, NY: Cornell University Press.

Flannery, Kent V. 1972. The Cultural Evolution of Civilizations. *Annual Review of Ecological Systems* 3:399–426.

Forbes. 2006. Lists, Billionaires, #114 Robert Kuok. http://www.forbes.com/lists/2006/10/ARHN.html.

Fortes, Meyer, and E. E. Evans-Pritchard. 1967 [1940]. *African Political Systems.* London: Oxford University Press.

Foucault, Michel. 1965 [1961]. *Madness and Civilization.* New York: Pantheon.

———. 1972. *The Archaeology of Knowledge,* A. M. Sheridan Smith, trans. New York: Harper Colophon.

———. 1978. *The History of Sexuality,* vol. 1, *An Introduction.* New York: Pantheon.

———. 1980. Truth and Power. In *Power/Knowledge: Selected Interviews and Other Writings, 1972–1977 by Michel Foucault.* Colin Gordon, ed., pp. 109–133. New York: Pantheon.

Fox, Robin. 1972. In the Beginning: Aspects of Hominid Behavorial Evolution. In *Perspectives on Human Evolution,* Sherwood L. Washburn and Phyllis Dolhinow, eds., pp. 358–381. New York: Holt, Rinehart, and Winston.

Frake, Charles. 1962. The Ethnographic Study of Cognitive Systems. In *Anthropology and Human Behavior,* Thomas Gladwin and William D. Sturtevant, eds., pp. 72–85. Washington: Anthropological Society of Washington.

Frank, G. 1997. Jews, Multiculturalism, and Boasian Anthropology. *American Anthropologist* 99(4):731–745.

Frazer, James George. 1911–1915 [1890]. *The Golden Bough: A Study in Magic and Religion,* 3rd ed. London: Macmillan.

Freeman, Derek. 1983. *Margaret Mead and Samoa: The Making and Unmaking of an Anthropological Myth.* Cambridge: Harvard University.

Freidl, Ernestine. 1975. *Women and Men: An Anthropologist's View.* New York: Holt, Rinehart, and Winston.

Freud, Sigmund. 1939. *Moses and Monotheism,* Katherine Jones, trans. London: Hogarth Press.

———. 1950 [1913]. *Totem and Taboo: Some Points of Agreement Between the Mental Lives of Savages and Neurotics,* James Strachey, trans. New York: W. W. Norton.

———. 1960 [1905]. *Jokes and Their Relation to the Unconscious,* James Strachey, trans. New York: W. W. Norton.

———. 1961 [1930]. *Civilization and Its Discontents,* James Strachey, trans. New York: W. W. Norton.

———. 1961 [1928]. *The Future of an Illusion,* James Strachey, trans. New York: W. W. Norton.

———. 1963 [1900]. *On Dreams,* James Strachey, trans. New York: W. W. Norton.

Fried, Morton. 1967. *The Evolution of Political Society.* New York: Random House.

Friedman, Jonathan. 1974. Marxism, Structuralism, and Vulgar Materialism. *Man* 9(3):444–469.

Frye, Northrop. 1964. *The Educated Imagination.* Bloomington: Indiana University Press.

Gadamer, Hans-Georg. 1975. *Truth and Method,* Garren Burden and John Cumming, trans. New York: Seabury Press.

Galton, F., Sir. 1869. *Hereditary Genius: An Inquiry into its Laws and Consequences.* London: Macmillan.

———. 1883. *Inquiries into Human Faculty and Its Development.* New York: Macmillan.

Garbarino, Merwyn S. 1977. *Sociocultural Theory in Anthropology.* New York: Holt, Rinehart, and Winston.

Geertz, Clifford. 1963a. *Agricultural Involution: The Processes of Ecological Change in Indonesia.* Berkeley: University of California Press.

———. 1963b. *Peddlers and Princes: Social Development and Economic Change in Two Indonesian Towns.* Chicago: University of Chicago Press.

———. 1973. *The Interpretation of Cultures.* New York: Basic Books.

———. 1975. On the Nature of Anthropological Understanding. *American Scientist* 63:1, 47–53.

———. 1986. Making Experience Authoring Selves. In *The Anthropology of Experience,* Victor W. Turner and Edward M. Bruner, eds., pp. 373–380. Urbana: University of Illinois Press.

Gennep, Arnold van. 1960 [1909]. *The Rites of Passage,* Monica Vizedom and Gabrielle L. Caffee, trans. Chicago: University of Chicago Press.

Gerth, H. H., and C. Wright Mills. 1946. Introduction: The Man and His Work. In *From Max Weber: Essays in Sociology,* H. H. Gerth and C. Wright Mills, eds., pp. 1–74. New York: Oxford University Press.

Gibbon, Edward. 1942 [1776–1788]. *The Decline and Fall of the Roman Empire.* New York: E. P. Dutton.

Gillis, John R. 2000. *Our Virtual Families: Toward a Cultural Understanding of Modern Family Life.* Working Paper No. 2, The Emory Center for Myth and Ritual in American Life Department of History, Rutgers University, New Brunswick, NJ.

Gleick, James. 1987. *Chaos: Making a New Science.* New York: Viking.

Gluckman, Max. 1947. Malinowski's Contribution to Social Anthropology. *African Studies* 6:57–76.

———. 1949. *Malinowski's Sociological Theories.* Rhodes-Livingstone Paper 16. Livingstone, Northern Rhodesia: Rhodes-Livingstone Institute.

———. 1954. *Rituals of Rebellion in South-East Africa.* The Frazer Lecture 1952. Manchester: Manchester University Press.

———. 1956. *Custom and Conflict in Africa.* Glencoe, IL: Free Press.

———. 1967 [1956]. "The Peace in the Feud." In *Custom and Conflict in Africa,* pp. 2–26. New York: Barnes and Noble.

Goldenweiser, Alexander. 1910. Totemism: An Analytical Study. *Journal of American Folklore* 23:179.

———. 1917. The Autonomy of the Social. *American Anthropologist* 19(3):447–449.

Goodenough, Ward. 1956. Componential Analysis and the Study of Meaning. *Language* 32:195–216.

Goody, Jack. 1977. *The Domestication of the Savage Mind.* Cambridge: Cambridge University Press.

———. 1995. *The Expansive Moment: Anthropology in Britain and Africa 1918–1970.* Cambridge: Cambridge University Press.

Gorer, Geoffrey, and John Rickman. 1962 [1949]. *The People of Great Russia: A Psychological Study.* New York: W. W. Norton.

Gould, Stephen Jay. 1981. *The Mismeasure of Man.* New York: W. W. Norton.

———. 1989. *Wonderful Life: The Burgess Shale and the Nature of History.* New York: W. W. Norton.

———. 1994. Cabinet Museums Revisited. *Natural History* 103(1):12–20.

Graebner, F. 1911. *Die Methode der Ethnologie.* Heidelberg: C. Winter.

Gramsci, Antonio. 1994. *Letters From Prison,* Frank Rosengarten, ed.; Raymond Rosenthal, trans. New York: Columbia University Press.

Graves, Robert. 1948. *The White Goddess.* New York: Vintage Books.

Gross, Feliks. 1986. Young Malinowski and His Later Years. *American Ethnologist* 13(3):556–570.

Gunder-Frank, A. 1966. "The Development of Underdevelopment." *Monthly Review* 18(4):17–31.

Handler, Richard. 1991. An Interview with Clifford Geertz. *Current Anthropology* 32(5):603–613.

Hardin, Garrett. 1968. The Tragedy of the Commons. *Science* 162(13 December):1243–1248.

Harris, Marvin. 1968. *The Rise of Anthropological Theory.* New York: Thomas Y. Crowell.

———. 1974. *Cows, Pigs, Wars and Witches: The Riddles of Culture.* New York: Random House.

———. 1977. *Cannibals and Kings: The Origins of Culture.* New York: Random House.

———. 1979. *Cultural Materialism: The Struggle for a Science of Culture.* New York: Random House.

———. 1981. *America Now: The Anthropology of a Changing Culture.* New York: Simon and Schuster.

———. 1985. *Good to Eat: Riddles of Food and Culture.* New York: Simon and Schuster.

———. 1994. Cultural Materialism is Alive and Well and Won't Go Away Until Something Better Comes Along. In *Assessing Cultural Anthropology,* R. Borofsky, ed., pp. 62–76. New York: McGraw-Hill.

Harrison, Faye V., ed. 1991. *Decolonizing Anthropology: Moving Further Toward an Anthropology for Liberation.* Washington, DC: American Anthropological Association, Association of Black Anthropologists.

Harrison, Lawrence E. 1992. *Who Prospers?: How Cultural Values Shape Economic and Political Success.* New York: Basic Books.

Harrison, Lawrence E., and Samuel Huntington, eds. 2001. *Culture Matters: How Values Shape Human Progress.* New York: Basic.

Herdt, Gilbert. 1984. *Ritualized Homosexuality in Melanesia.* Berkeley: University of California.

Herskovits, Melville. 1957. Some Further Notes on Franz Boas' Arctic Expedition. *American Anthropologist* 59:112–116.

Hertz, Robert. 1973 [1909]. The Pre-eminence of the Right Hand: A Study in Religious Polarity. In *Right and Left: Essays on Dual Symbolic Classification,* Rodney Needham, ed., pp. 3–31. Chicago: University of Chicago Press.

Hill, K. 1988. Macronutrient Modifications of Optimal Foraging Theory: An Approach Using Indifference Curves Applied to Some Modern Foragers. *Human Ecology* 16:157–197.

Hill, K., H. Kaplan, K. Hawkes, A. M. Hurtado. 1987. Foraging Decisions Among Ache Hunter-Gatherers: New Data and Implications for Optimal Foraging Models. *Ethnology and Sociobiology.* 8:1–36.

Hobbes, Thomas. 1983 [1651]. *Leviathan.* London: Dent.

Hockett, Charles F. 1973. *Man's Place in Nature.* New York: McGraw-Hill.

Hoebel, E. Adamson. 1949. *Man in the Primitive World: An Introduction to Anthropology.* New York: McGraw-Hill.

Hoernle, Agnes Winnifred. 1925. The Social Organization of the Nama Hottentots of Southwest Africa. *American Anthropologist* 27(1):1–24.

Holland, Dorothy, and Debra Skinner. 1987. Prestige and Intimacy, the Cultural Models Behind Americans' Talk about Gender Types. In *Cultural Models in Language and Thought,* D. Holland and N. Quinn, eds., pp. 78–111. New York: Cambridge University Press.

Holmes, G. 1914. Areas of American Culture Characterization Tentatively Outlined as an Aid in the Study of Antiquities. *American Anthropologist* 16:413–416.

Hsu, Francis L. K. 1980. Margaret Mead and Psychological Anthropology. *American Anthropologist* 82(2):349–353.

Humboldt, Alexander von. 1874 [1845–1862]. *Kosmos.* Stuttgart: J. G. Cotta.

Humboldt, Wilhelm von. 1963. *Humanist Without a Portfolio: An Anthology of the Writings of Wilhelm von Humboldt,* Marianne Cowen, trans. Detroit: Wayne State University Press.

Hutchins, Edwin. 1994. *Cognition in the Wild.* Cambridge: MIT Press.

Hyatt, Marshall. 1990. *Franz Boas, Social Activist: The Dynamics of Ethnicity.* New York: Greenwood Press.

Hymes, Dell. 1972. *Reinventing Anthropology.* New York: Pantheon.

Jacknis, Ira. 2002. The First Boasian: Alfred Kroeber and Franz Boas, 1896–1905. *American Anthropologist* 104(2):520–529.

Jameson, Fredric. 1991. *Postmodernism, or, The Cultural Logic of Late Capitalism*. Durham, NC: Duke University.

Jung, Carl Gustave. 1971 [1923]. *Psychological Types*. Princeton, NJ: Princeton University Press.

Kaplan, David, and Robert A. Manners. 1972. *Cultural Theory*. Englewood Cliffs, NJ: Prentice-Hall.

Kaplan, Robert. 1994. The Coming Anarchy. *Atlantic Monthly* 273(2):44–76.

Karp, Ivan, and Kent Maynard. 1983. Reading the Nuer. *Current Anthropology* 24(4):481–503.

Kenyatta, Jomo. 1979 [1938]. *Facing Mount Kenya: The Traditional Life of the Gikuyu*. London: Heinemann.

Keys, Ancel. 1943. Physical Performance in Relation to Diet. *Federation Proceedings* 2:164–187.

———. 1946. Nutrition and Capacity for Work. *Occupational Medicine* 2:536–545.

Kirchhoff, Paul. 1935 [1955]. Principles of Clanship in Human Society. *Davidson Journal of Anthropology* 1:1–10.

Kormondy, E. J., and D. E. Brown. 1998. *Fundamentals of Human Ecology*. Upper Saddle River: Prentice Hall.

Kottak, Conrad Phillip. 1994. *Cultural Anthropology*. New York: McGraw-Hill.

Kroeber, A. L. 1901. Decorative Symbolism of the Arapaho. *American Anthropologist* 3:308–336.

———. 1917. The Superorganic. *American Anthropologist* 19:163–213.

———. 1925. *Handbook of the Indians of California*. Bulletin of the Bureau of American Ethnology, 78.

———. 1939. *Cultural and Natural Areas of Native North America*. Berkeley: University of California Press.

———. 1940. Psychotic Factors in Shamanism. *Character and Personality* 8:204–215.

———. 1959. The History of Personality in Anthropology. *American Anthropologist* 61(3):398–404.

Kuhn, Thomas S. 1962. *The Structure of Scientific Revolutions*. Chicago: University of Chicago Press.

Kuklick, H. 1991. *The Savage Within: The Social History of British Anthropology, 1885–1945*. Cambridge: Cambridge University Press.

Kurtz, Donald V. 1996. Hegemony and Anthropology: Gramsci, Exegesis, Reinterpretations. *Critique of Anthropology* 16(2):103–135.

La Capra, Dominick. 1972. *Emile Durkheim: Sociologist and Philosopher*. Ithaca: Cornell University.

Lacoste, Yves. 1984. *Ibn Khaldoun: The Birth of History and the Past of the Third World*. London: Verso.

Lafitau, Joseph-Francois. 1724. *Mœurs des Sauvages Ameriquains*. Paris: Saugrain.

Lamphere, Louise. 1987. The Struggle to Reshape Our Thinking About Gender. In *The Impact of Feminist Research in the Academy*, Christie Farnham, ed., pp. 11–33. Bloomington: Indiana University Press.

———. 2004. Unofficial Histories: A Vision of Anthropology from the Margins. *American Anthropologist* 106(1):126–139.

Langness, L. L. 1987. *The Study of Culture*. Novato, CA: Chandler and Sharp.

Lavery, David. 2001. The Imagination of Insurance: Wallace Stevens and Benjamin Lee Whorf at The Hartford. *Legal Studies Forum* 24(3–4):481–492.

Layton, Robert. 1997. *An Introduction to Theory in Anthropology*. Cambridge: Cambridge University Press.

Le Bon, Gustave. 1977 [1895]. *The Crowd: A Study of the Popular Mind*. New York: Penguin Books.

Leach, Edmund R. 1954. *Political Systems of Highland Burma: A Study of Kachin Social Structure*. London: London School of Economics and Political Science.

———. 1976. *Claude Lévi-Strauss*. New York: Penguin Books.

———. 1984. Glimpses of the Unmentionable in the History of British Social Anthropology. In *Annual Review of Anthropology*, Bernard Siegel, Alan Beals, and Stephen Tyler, eds., Vol. 13, pp. 1–23. Palo Alto, CA: Annual Reviews.

Leacock, Eleanor. 1983. Interpreting the Origins of Gender Inequality: Conceptual and Historical Problems. *Dialectical Anthropology* 7(4):263–284.

Leaf, Murray J. 1979. *Man, Mind, and Science: A History of Anthropology*. New York: Columbia University Press.

Lehman, David. 1992. Paul de Man: The Plot Thickens. *New York Times Book Review*, May 24.

Lesser, Alexander. 1981. Franz Boas. In *Totems and Teachers: Perspectives on the History of Anthropology*, Sydel Silverman, ed., pp. 1–31. New York: Columbia University Press.

Lett, James. 1987. *The Human Enterprise: A Critical Introduction to Anthropological Theory*. Boulder, CO: Westview Press.

———. 1997. *Science, Reason and Anthropology: The Principles of Rational Inquiry.* Lanham, MD: Rowman & Littlefield.

Lévi-Strauss, Claude 1951 "Language and the Analysis of Social Laws." *American Anthropologist.* 53(2): 155–163.

———. 1963. The Effectiveness of Symbols. In *Structural Anthropology,* pp. 186–205. New York: Basic Books.

———. 1963. Structural Analysis in Linguistics and in Anthropology. In *Structural Anthropology,* pp. 31–54. New York: Basic Books.

———. 1969 [1949]. *The Elementary Structures of Kinship,* rev. ed. Boston: Beacon Press.

———. 1969. *The Raw and the Cooked.* New York: Harper and Row.

———. 1973. *From Honey to Ashes.* Chicago: University of Chicago Press.

Levy-Bruhl, Lucien. 1966 [1910]. *How Natives Think,* Lillian A. Clare, trans. New York: Washington Square Press.

Lewis, Herbert S. 2001. The Passion of Franz Boas. *American Anthropologist* 103(2):447–467.

Lichtheim, G. 1973. Marx and the "Asiatic Mode of Production." In *Karl Marx,* T. Bottomore, ed., pp. 151–171. Englewood Cliffs, Prentice Hall.

Lilla, Mark. 1998. The Politics of Jacques Derrida. *The New York Review of Books* 45(11):36–41.

Locke, John. 1939 [1690]. An Essay Concerning the True Original Extent and End of Civil Government. In *The English Philosophers from Bacon to Mill,* Edwin A. Burtt, ed. New York: Modern Library.

Lorenz, Konrad. 1952. *King Solomon's Ring: New Light on Animal Ways,* Marjorie Kerr Wilson, trans. New York: Crowell.

———. 1966. *On Aggression.* Harcourt, Brace and World.

Lounsbury, Floyd. 1956. A Semantic Analysis of the Pawnee Kinship Usage. *Language* 32:158–194.

Lowe, Donald. 1995. *The Body in Late-Capitalist USA.* Durham, NC: Duke University Press.

Lowie, Robert H. 1913. Military Societies of the Crow Indians. *Anthropological Papers of the American Museum of Natural History* 11:145–217.

———. 1920. *Primitive Society.* New York: Liveright.

———. 1937. *The History of Ethnological Theory.* New York: Holt, Rinehart, and Winston.

———. 1946. Review of a Scientific Theory of Culture and Other Essays by Bronislaw Malinowski. *American Anthropologist* 48(1):118–119.

Lubbock, Sir John. 1865. *Prehistoric Times: As Illustrated by Ancient Remains and the Manners and Customs of Modern Savages.* London: William and Norgate.

———. 1870. *Origin of Civilization and the Primitive Condition of Man: Mental and Social Condition of Savages.* London: Longman, Green.

Lucy, John A. 1997. Linguistic Relativity, *Annual Reviews of Anthropology* 26:291–312.

Lutkehaus, N. C. 1995. Margaret Mead and the "Rustling-of-the-Wind-in-the-Palm-Trees-School" of Ethnographic Writing. In *Women Writing Culture,* R. Behar and D. A. Gordon, eds., pp. 186–201. Berkeley: University of California Press.

Lyell, Sir Charles. 1834. *Principles of Geology.* London: J. Murray.

———. 1863. *The Geological Evidences of the Antiquity of Man.* Philadelphia: G. W. Childs.

MacCormack, Carol P. 1980. Nature, Culture, and Gender: A Critique. In *Nature, Culture, and Gender,* Carol P. MacCormack and Marilyn Strathern, eds., pp. 1–24. Cambridge: Cambridge University Press.

McDowell, Nancy. 1980. The Oceanic Ethnography of Margaret Mead. *American Anthropologist* 82(2): 278–303.

Macintosh, Sir James. 1828 [1799]. *A Discourse on the Study of the Law of Nature and Nations.* London: H. Goode.

McLennan, John Ferguson. 1865. *Primitive Marriage: An Inquiry into the Origin of the Form of Capture in Marriage Ceremonies.* Edinburgh: A. and C. Black.

Maillet, Benoit de. 1748. *Telliamed, ou, Entretiens d'un philosophe indien avec un missionaire françois sur le diminution de la mer, la formation de la terre, l'origine de l'homme, etc.* Amsterdam: L'honore.

Maine, H. S. 1963. *Ancient Law: Its Connection with the Early History of Society and Its Relation to Modern Ideas.* Boston: Beacon Press.

Malefijt, Annemarie de Waal. 1989. *Religion and Culture: An Introduction to Anthropology of Religion.* Prospect Heights: Waveland Press.

———. 1974. *Images of Man: A History of Anthropological Thought.* New York: Alfred A. Knopf.

Malinowski, Bronislaw. 1922. *Argonauts of the Western Pacific.* New York: E. P. Dutton.

————. 1955 [1927]. *Sex and Repression in Savage Society.* New York: Harcourt, Brace.

————. 1929a. Practical Anthropology. *Africa* 2:22–38.

————. 1929b. *The Sexual Life of Savages in Northwestern Melanesia.* London: Routledge.

————. 1935. *Coral Gardens and Their Magic.* New York: American Book Company.

————. 1939. The Group and the Individual in Functional Analysis. *American Journal of Sociology* 44: 938–964.

————. 1954 [1925]. *Magic, Science and Religion and Other Essays.* New York: Doubleday.

————. 1967. *A Diary in the Strict Sense of the Term.* New York: Harcourt, Brace and World.

Malotki, Ekkehart. 1983. *Hopi Time: A Linguistic Analysis of the Temporal Concepts in the Hopi Language.* (Trends in Linguistics, Studies and Monographs, 20.) Berlin: Mouton.

Malthus, Thomas Robert. 1926 [1798]. *An Essay on the Principles of Population as It Affects the Future Improvement of Society with Remarks on the Speculations of Mr. Godwin, M. Condorcet, and Other Writers.* London: Macmillan.

Manganaro, Marc, ed. 1990. *Modernist Anthropology: From Fieldwork to Text.* Princeton, NJ: Princeton University Press.

Manners, David. 1973. Obituary of Julian Steward. *American Ethnologist,* 75:886–903.

Marcus, George. 1992. Cultural Anthropology at Rice since the 1980s. Provost Lecture, February 17, 1992. http://www.ruf.rice.edu/~anth/research/marcus-provost-lecture.htm

Marcus, George E., and Dick Cushman. 1982. Ethnographies as Texts. *Annual Reviews of Anthropology* 11:25–69.

Marx, Karl. 1930 [1867]. *Capital: A Critique of Political Economy,* 4th ed., Paul Eden and Paul Ceder, trans. New York: E. P. Dutton.

————. 1963 [1844]. On the Jewish Question. In *Karl Marx: Early Writings,* T. B. Bottomore, ed., pp. 3–40. New York: McGraw-Hill.

Marx, Karl, and Freidrich Engels. 1970 [1846]. *The German Ideology: Part One with Selections From Parts Two and Three, Together with Marx's Introduction to A Critique of Political Economy,* C. J. Arthur, ed. New York: International Publishing.

————. 1972 [1848]. The Communist Manifesto. In *Karl Marx: Essential Writings,* Fredrick L. Bender, ed., pp. 240–263. New York: Harper and Row.

————. 1975 [1845]. *The Holy Family: Or, Critique of Critical Criticism: Against Bruno Bauer and Company.* Moscow: Progress Publishers.

Mason, Otis. 1895. Similarities in Culture. *American Anthropologist* 8:101–117.

Mauss, Marcel. 1967 [1925]. *The Gift: Forms and Functions of Exchange in Archaic Societies,* Ian Cunnison, trans. New York: W. W. Norton.

Mayer, Jean, and Beverly Bullen. 1960. Nutrition and Athletic Performance. *Physiological Reviews* 40(3): 369–397.

McGee, R. Jon. 2002. *Watching Lacandon Maya Lives.* Boston: Allyn and Bacon.

Mead, Margaret. 1928. *Coming of Age in Samoa: A Psychological Study of Primitive Youth for Western Civilization.* New York: William Morrow.

————. 1930. *Growing Up in New Guinea: A Comparative Study of Primitive Education.* New York: William Morrow.

————. 1935. *Sex and Temperament in Three Primitive Societies.* New York: William Morrow.

————. 1939. Native Languages as Field-Work Tools. *American Anthropologist* 41(2):189–205.

————. 1949. *Male and Female: A Study of the Sexes in a Changing World.* New York: William Morrow.

Metzger, Duane and G. Williams. 1966. Some Procedures and Results in the Study of Native Categories: Tzeltal "Firewood." *American Anthropologist* 68: 389–407.

Modell, Judith Schachter. 1983. *Ruth Benedict: Patterns of a Life.* Philadelphia: University of Pennsylvania Press.

Montagu, Ashley. 1980. *Sociobiology Examined.* Oxford: Oxford University Press.

Morgan, Elaine. 1972. *The Descent of Woman.* New York: Stein and Day.

————. 1982. *The Aquatic Ape.* New York: Stein and Day.

Morgan, Lewis Henry. 1871. Systems of Consanguinity and Affinity of the Human Family. Smithsonian Contributions to Knowledge no. 218, vol. 17. Washington: Smithsonian.

————. 1966 [1851]. *League of the Ho-dé-no-sau-nee or Iroquois.* New York: B. Franklin.

————. 1985 [1877]. *Ancient Society.* Tucson: University of Arizona Press.

Morgen, Sandra. 1989. Gender and Anthropology: Introductory Essay. In *Gender and Anthropology—Critical*

Reviews for Research and Teaching, Sandra Morgen, ed., pp. 1–20. Washington, DC: American Anthropological Association.

Morton, Samuel G. 1839. *Crania Americana*. Philadelphia: J. Dobson.

———. 1844. *Crania Aegyptica*. Philadelphia: J. Penington.

Müller, F. Max. 1977 [1856]. *Comparative Mythology*. New York: Arno Press.

Murdock, George Peter. 1951. British Social Anthropology. *American Anthropologist* 53:465–473.

Murdock, George P. 1959. Evolution in Social Organization. In *Evolution and Anthropology*, B. Meggers, ed., pp. 126–145. Washington: Anthropological Society of Washington.

———. 1960 [1949]. *Social Structure*. New York: Macmillan.

Murphy, R. F. 1994. The Dialectics of Deeds and Words. In *Assessing Cultural Anthropology*, R. Borofsky, ed., pp. 55–61. New York: McGraw Hill.

Murray, Margaret Alice. 1921. *The Witch-Cult in Western Europe: A Study in Anthropology*. Oxford: Clarendon Press.

Nadel, S. F. 1954. *Nupe Religion*. London: Routledge and Kegan Paul.

Nanda, Serena. 1990. *Neither Man nor Woman: The Hijras of India*. Belmont, CA: Wadsworth.

National Cyclopedia of American Biography. 1967. William Graham Sumner, vol. 25, pp. 8–9. Clifton, NJ: J. T. White.

Nietzsche, Friedrich. 1954 [1883–1885]. *Thus Spake Zarathustra*. New York: Modern Library.

———. 1956 [1871/1887] *The Birth of Tragedy and the Genealogy of Morals*. Garden City, NY: Doubleday.

Nonacs, P., and L. M. Dill. 1993. Is Satisficing an Alternative to Optimal Foraging Theory? *Oikos* 24: 371–375.

Northrup, F. S. C. 1947. *The Logic of the Sciences and the Humanities*. New York: McMillan.

Obeyesekere, Gananath. 1981. *Medusa's Hair: An Essay on Personal Symbols and Religious Experience*. Chicago: University of Chicago Press.

O'Laughlin, Bridget. 1975. Marxist Approaches in Anthropology. In *Annual Review of Anthropology*, Bernard Siegel, Alan Beals, and Stephen Tyler, eds., vol. 4, pp. 341–370. Palo Alto, CA: Annual Reviews.

O'Meara, J. Tim. 1989. Anthropology as Empirical Science. *American Anthropologist* 91:354–369.

Ong, Aihwa. 1999. *Flexible Citizenship: The Logic of Transnationality*. Durham, NC: Duke.

Ong, Walter J. 1982. *Orality and Literacy: The Technologizing of the Word*. New York: Methuen.

Oppenheimer, Franz. 1914. *The State: Its History and Development Viewed Sociologically*, John M. Gitterman, trans. Indianapolis: Bobbs-Merrill.

Orlove, Benjamin S. 1980. Ecological Anthropology. In *Annual Review of Anthropology*, Bernard Siegel, Alan Beals, and Stephen Tyler, eds., vol. 9, pp. 235–273. Palo Alto, CA: Annual Reviews.

Ortner, Sherry B. 1973. On Key Symbols. *American Anthropologist* 75:1338–1346.

———. 1975. Gods' Bodies, Gods' Food: A Symbolic Analysis of Sherpa Ritual. In *The Interpretation of Symbolism*, Ray Willis, ed., pp. 133–167. New York: John Wiley and Sons.

———. 1984. Theory in Anthropology since the Sixties. *Comparative Studies in Society and History* 26(1): 126–166.

Ortner, Sherry B., and Harriet Whitehead. 1981 [1974]. *Sexual Meanings: The Cultural Construction of Gender and Sexuality*. Cambridge: Cambridge University Press.

Ortner, Sherry B., and Harriet Whitehead. 1981. Introduction: Accounting for Sexual Meanings. In *Sexual Meanings: The Cultural Construction of Gender and Sexuality*, pp. 1–27. Cambridge: Cambridge University Press.

Pathe, R. A. 1988. Gene Weltfish. In *Women Anthropologists: A Biographical Dictionary*, U. Gacs, A. Khan, J. McIntyre, and R. Weinberg, eds., pp. 372–381. New York: Greenwood Press.

Paulme, Denise. 1960. *Femmes d'Afrique Noire*. Paris: Mouton.

Peace, W. J. 1998. "Bernhard Stern, Leslie A. White, and an Anthropological Appraisal of the Russian Revolution." *American Anthropologist* 100(1):84–93.

Peace, William, and David H. Price. 2001. The Cold War Context of the FBI's Investigation of Leslie A. White. *American Anthropologist* 103(1):164–167.

Pike, Kenneth. 1954. *Language in Relation to a Unified Theory of the Structure of Human Behavior*, vol. 1. Glendale, CA: Summer Institute of Linguistics.

Pinker, Steven. 1994. *The Language Instinct: How the Mind Creates Language*. New York: HarperCollins.

Plato. 1993. *Republic*, Robin Waterfield, trans. Oxford: Oxford University Press.

Polanyi, Karl. 1944. *The Great Transformation*. Boston: Beacon.

Polanyi, Karl, Conrad M. Arensberg, and Harry W. Pearson. 1957. *Trade and Market in the Early Empires: Economies in History and Theory*. Glencoe, IL: Free Press.

Price, David H. 2004 [1960]. *Threatening Anthropology: McCarthyism and the FBI's Harassment of Activist Anthropologists*. Durham, NC: Duke University Press.

Putnam, Robert D. 2000. *Bowling Alone: The Collapse and Revival of American Community*. New York: Simon & Schuster.

Quetelet, Adolphe. 1848. *Du Système Sociale et des Lois qui le Régissent*. Paris: Guillaumin.

———. 1968 [1835]. *A Treatise on Man and the Development of His Faculties*. New York: B. Franklin.

Rabinow, Paul. 1977. *Reflections on Fieldwork in Morocco*. Berkeley: University of California Press.

———. 1986. Representations Are Social Facts: Modernity and Postmodernity in Anthropology. In *Writing Culture: The Poetics and Politics of Ethnography*, James Clifford and George Marcus, eds., pp. 234–261. Berkeley: University of California Press.

Radcliffe-Brown, A. R. 1924. The Mother's Brother in South Africa. *South African Journal of Science* 21: 542–555.

———. 1964 [1922]. *The Andaman Islanders*. New York: Free Press.

———. 1965a. [1940]. On Joking Relationships. In *Structure and Function in Primitive Society*, pp. 90–104. New York: Free Press.

———. 1965b [1935]. On the Concept of Function in Social Science. In *Structure and Function in Primitive Society*, pp. 178–187. New York: Free Press.

Radin, Paul. 1911. Description of a Winnebago Funeral. *American Anthropologist* 13(3):437–444.

———. 1924. Ojibwa Ethnological Chit Chat. *American Anthropologist* 26(4):491–530.

———. ed. 1926. *Crashing Thunder: The Autobiography of an American Indian*. New York: Appleton.

———. 1957 [1927]. *Primitive Man as Philosopher*, 2nd ed. New York: Dover Publications.

Rappaport, Roy A. 1967. *Pigs for the Ancestors*. New Haven: Yale University Press.

———. 1984. *Pigs for the Ancestors*, 2nd ed. New Haven: Yale University Press.

———. 1994. Humanity's Evolution and Anthropology's Future. In *Assessing Cultural Anthropology*, R. Borofsky, ed., pp. 153–167. New York, McGraw Hill.

Reiter, Rayna, ed. 1975. *Toward an Anthropology of Women*. New York: Monthly Review Press.

Resek, Carl. 1960. *Lewis Henry Morgan: American Scholar*. Chicago: University of Chicago Press.

Ritzer, George. 1992. *Sociological Theory*, 3rd ed. New York: McGraw-Hill.

Rivers, W. H. R. 1900. A Genealogical Method of Collecting Social and Vital Statistics. *Journal of the Anthropological Institute*, n.s., 3:74–82.

———. 1910. The Genealogical Method of Anthropological Inquiry. *Sociological Review* 3:1–12.

Roheim, Geza. 1971 [1925]. *Australian Totemism: A Psychoanalytic Study in Anthropology*. New York: Humanities Press.

Romanucci-Ross, Lola. 2001. Celebrants and the Celebrity: Biography as Trope. *American Anthropologist* 103(4):1174–1178.

Rosaldo, Michelle, and Louise Lamphere, eds. 1974. *Women, Culture, and Society*. Palo Alto, CA: Stanford University Press.

Rosaldo, Michelle. 1974. Women, Culture, and Society: A Theoretical Overview. In *Women, Culture, and Society*, Michelle Rosaldo and Louise Lamphere, eds., pp. 14–42. Palo Alto, CA: Stanford University Press.

———. 1980. *Knowledge and Passion: Ilongot Notions of Self and Social Life*. Cambridge: Cambridge University Press.

Rorty, Richard. 1979. *Philosophy and the Mirror of Knowledge*. Princeton: Princeton University Press.

Rousseau, Jean-Jacques. 1974 [1762]. *Émile*, Barbara Foxley, trans. New York: E. P. Dutton.

Rylko-Bauer, Barbara, Merrill Singer, and John van Willigen. 2006. Reclaiming Applied Anthropology: Its Past, Present, and Future. *American Anthropologist* 108(1):178–190.

Sacks, K. 1979. *Sisters and Wives: The Past and Future of Sexual Equality*. Westport, CT: Greenwood Press.

Sahlins, Marshall D. 1964. Culture and Environment: The Study of Cultural Ecology. In *Horizons of Anthropology*, Sol Tax, ed., pp. 132–147. Chicago: Aldine.

———. 1968. *Tribesmen*. Englewood Cliffs, NJ: Prentice Hall.

———. 1972. *Stone Age Economics*. Chicago: Aldine.

———. 1976. *The Use and Abuse of Biology: An Anthropological Critique of Sociobiology*. Ann Arbor: University of Michigan Press.

Sahlins, Marshall D., and Elman R. Service. 1960. *Evolution and Culture*. Ann Arbor: University of Michigan Press.

Said, E. 1978. *Orientalism*. New York: Pantheon.

Sanday, Peggy Reeves. 1980. Margaret Mead's View of Sex Roles in Her Own and Other Societies. *American Anthropologist* 82(2):340–348.

———. 1981. *Female Power and Male Dominance: On the Origins of Sexual Inequality.* New York: Cambridge University Press.

Sanday, Peggy Reeves, and Ruth Gallagher Goodenough eds. 1990. *Beyond the Second Sex: New Directions in the Anthropology of Gender.* Philadelphia: University of Pennsylvania Press.

Sangren, Steven P. 1988. Rhetoric and the Authority of Ethnography. *Current Anthropology* 29(3):405–435.

Sapir, Edward. 1924. Culture, Genuine and Spurious. *American Journal of Sociology* 29:401–429.

Sassoon, A. S. 1991. Hegemony. In *A Dictionary of Marxist Thought,* T. Bottomore, ed., pp. 229–231. Oxford: Basil Blackwell.

Sawicki, J. 1991. *Disciplining Foucault: Feminism, Power, and the Body.* New York: Routledge.

Scheper-Hughes, Nancy. 1979. *Saints, Scholars, and Schizophrenics: Mental Illness in Rural Ireland.* Berkeley: University of California Press.

———. 1989. Death Without Weeping. *Natural History* 98:8–16.

———. 1992. *Death Without Weeping: The Violence of Everyday Life in Brazil.* Berkeley: University of California Press.

———. 1995. The Primacy of the Ethical: Propositions for a Militant Anthropology. *Current Anthropology* 36 (3):409–420.

Schneider, Jane, and Rayna Rapp eds. 1995. *Articulating Hidden Histories: Exploring the Influence of Eric R. Wolf.* Berkeley: University of California Press.

Seligman, Charles G. 1910. *The Melanesians of British New Guinea.* Cambridge: Cambridge University Press.

Service, Elman R. 1962. *Primitive Social Organization: An Evolutionary Perspective.* New York: Random House.

———. 1976. Leslie Alvin White, 1900–1975. *American Anthropologist* 78(3):612–617.

Service, Elman. 1988. Morton Herbert Fried (1923–1986). *American Anthropologist* 90(1):148–152.

Shannon, Claude. 1948. A Mathematical Theory of Communication. *Bell System Technical Journal* 27:379–423.

Shankman, Paul, and Angela Thieman Dino. 2001. The FBI File of Leslie A. White. *American Anthropologist* 103(1):161–164.

Shapiro, Lawrence. 2004. *The Mind Incarnate.* Cambridge: MIT Press.

Shipler, David K. 2004. *The Working Poor: Invisible in America.* New York: Knopf.

Shipp, E. R. 1980, August 5. Prof. Gene Weltfish Dead at 78; Was a Target of Anti-Red Drives. *New York Times,* p. B101.

Silverman, J. 1967. Shaminism and Acute Schizophrenia. *American Anthropologist* 69:21–31.

Sloan, Richard P. 2006. Trivializing the Transcendant: What Can Science Really Tell Us About Faith? *Christianity Today.*

Smith, Adam. 1976 [1776]. *An Inquiry into the Nature and Causes of the Wealth of Nations.* Oxford: Clarendon Press.

Smith, E. A. 1983. Anthropological Applications of Optimal Foraging Theory: A Critical Review. *Current Anthropology* 24:625–651.

Smith, Grafton Elliot. 1928. *In the Beginning: The Origin of Civilization.* New York: Morrow.

Solecki, R., and C. Wagley. 1963. William Duncan Strong (1899–1962). *American Anthropologist* 65(5):1102–1111.

Spencer, Herbert. 1859. What Knowledge Is of Most Worth? *Westminster Review* 72:1–41.

———. 1860. The Social Organism. *Westminster Review,* n.s., 17:51–68.

———. 1873–1934. *Descriptive Sociology,* 13 vols. New York: Appleton-Century-Crofts.

———. 1898 [1864]. *Principles of Biology.* New York: D. Appleton.

———. 1961 [1873]. *The Study of Sociology.* Ann Arbor: University of Michigan Press.

———. 1967. *The Evolution of Society: Selections from Herbert Spencer's Principles of Sociology,* Robert L. Carneiro, ed. Chicago: University of Chicago Press.

———. 1969 [1851]. *Social Statics: The Conditions Essential to Human Happiness Specified, and the First of them Developed.* New York: A. M. Kelley.

———. 1975 [1885]. *The Principles of Sociology.* Westport, CN: Greenwood Press.

Spier, Leslie, A. Irving Hallowell, and Stanley S. Newman, eds. 1941. *Language, Culture, and Personality: Essays in Memory of Edward Sapir.* Menasha, WI: Sapir Memorial Publication Fund.

Spinoza, Baruch. 1930 [1677]. *Ethics.* London: Oxford University Press.

Spradley, James P. 1980. *Participant Observation*. New York: Holt, Rinehart, and Winston.

Spradley, James P., ed. 1987. *Culture and Cognition*. New York: Waveland Press.

Steward, Julian. 1955. *Theory of Culture Change: The Methodology of Multilinear Evolution*. Urbana: University of Illinois Press.

Stirner, Max. 1918 [1844]. *The Ego and Its Own*. Steven T. Byington, trans. New York: Boni and Liveright.

Stocking, G. 1968. The Scientific Reaction Against Cultural Anthropology, 1917–1920. In *Race, Culture, and Evolution: Essays in the History of Anthropology*, G. Stocking, ed., pp. 270–307. New York: Free Press.

———. 1974. *The Shaping of American Anthropology 1883–1911*. New York: Basic Books.

———. 1987. *Victorian Anthropology*. New York: Free Press.

———. 1992. Ideas and Institutions in American Anthropology: Thoughts Toward a History of the Interwar Years. The Ethnographer's Magic and Other Essays. In *The History of Anthropology*, G. Stocking, ed., pp. 114–177. Madison, University of Wisconsin.

———. 1995. *After Tylor: British Social Anthropology 1888–1951*. Madison: University of Wisconsin Press.

Stoler, Ann Laura. 1989. Making Empire Respectable: The Politics of Race and Sexual Morality in 20th-Century Colonial Cultures. *American Ethnologist* 16(4):634–660.

———. 1995. *Race and the Education of Desire: Foucault's History of Sexuality and the Colonial Order of Things*. Chapel Hill: Duke University Press.

———. 2002. *Carnal Knowledge and Imperial Power: Race and the Intimate in Colonial Rule*. Berkeley: University of California Press.

Stoller, Paul. 1989. *The Taste of Ethnographic Things: The Senses in Anthropology*. Philadelphia: University of Pennsylvania Press.

Strauss, Claudia. 1992. What Makes Tony Run: Schemas as Motives Reconsidered. In *Human Motives and Cultural Models*, Roy D'Andrade and Claudia Strauss, eds., pp. 197–224. Cambridge: Cambridge University Press.

Strauss, Claudia, and Naomi Quinn. 1994. A Cognitive/Cultural Anthropology. In *Assessing Cultural Anthropology*, Robert Borofsky, ed., pp. 284–300. New York: McGraw Hill.

Strauss, David Friedrich. 1892. *The Life of Jesus*, 2nd ed., George Eliot, trans. London: Swan and Sonnenschein.

Strong, W. D. 1994. *Labrador winter : The Ethnographic Journals of William Duncan Strong, 1927–1928*, Eleanor Leacock, ed. Washington DC: Smithsonian Institution.

Sturtevant, William C. 1964. Studies in Ethnoscience. *American Anthropologist* 66:99–131.

———. 1987. Studies in Ethnoscience. In *Culture and Cognition*, James P. Spradley ed., pp. 129–167. New York: Waveland.

Suchting, W. A. 1983. *Marx: An Introduction*. New York: New York University Press.

Sumner, William Graham. 1963 [1914]. The Concentration of Wealth: Its Economic Justification. In *The Challenge of Facts and Other Essays*, Albert G. Keller, ed., pp. 79–90. New Haven: Yale University Press.

Sumner, William Graham, and Albert G. Keller. 1927. *The Science of Society*. New Haven: Yale University Press.

Tanner, Nancy, and Adrienne Zihlman. 1976. Women in Evolution, Part I: Innovation and Selection in Human Origins. *Signs* 2(3):585–608.

Taylor, Charles. 1979. Interpretation and the Sciences of Man. In *Interpretive Social Science: A Reader*, Paul Rabinow and W. M. Sullivan, eds., pp. 25–71. Berkeley, University of California Press.

Taylor, William Cooke. 1840. *The Natural History of Society in the Barbarous and Civilized State*. New York: Appleton.

Tax, Sol. 1958. The Fox Project. *Human Organization* 17:17–19.

———. 1960. Action Anthropology. In *Documentary History of the Fox Project, 1948–1959*. Fred Gearing, Robert McC. Netting, and Lisa R. Peattie, eds., pp. 167–171. Chicago: University of Chicago Press.

Thomas, David C., and Kerr Inkson. 2004. *Cultural Intelligence: People Skills for Global Business*. San Francisco: Berrett-Koehler.

Todorov, Tzvetzn. 1987. *Literature and Its Theorists: A Personal View of Twentieth-Century Criticism*, Catherine Porter, trans. Ithaca, NY: Cornell University Press.

Tönnies, Ferdinand Julius. 1957 [1887]. *Gemeinschaft und Gesellschaft, Community and Society*. East Lansing: Michigan State University Press.

Tooker, Elizabeth. 1992. Lewis H. Morgan and His Contemporaries. *American Anthropologist* 94(2):357–375.

Turgot, Anne-Robert-Jacques. 1973 [1750]. *Turgot on progress, sociology and economics: A philosophical review of the successive advances of the human mind,*

On universal history (and) Reflections on the formation and the distribution of wealth, Roland L. Meek, trans. Cambridge: Cambridge University Press.

Turnbull, C. 1961. *The Forest People.* New York: Simon and Schuster.

———. 1972. *The Mountain People.* New York: Simon and Schuster.

Turner, Bryan S., ed. 1966. *The Blackwell Companion to Social Theory.* Oxford: Blackwell.

Turner, Edith. 1987. *The Spirit and the Drum: A Memoir of Africa.* Tucson: University of Arizona Press.

———. 1992. *Experiencing Ritual: A New Interpretation of African Healing.* Philadelphia: University of Pennsylvania Press.

Turner, Jonathon H., Leonard Beeghley, and Charles H. Powers. 1989. *The Emergence of Sociological Theory.* Belmont: Wadsworth.

Turner, Victor. 1967a. Betwixt and Between: The Liminal Period in Rites of Passage. In *The Forest of Symbols: Aspects of Ndembu Ritual,* pp. 93–111. Ithaca, NY: Cornell University Press.

———. 1967b. Ritual Symbolism, Morality, and Social Structure among the Ndembu. In *African Systems of Thought,* M. Fortes and G. Dieterlen, eds., pp. 48–58. London: Oxford University Press.

Tyler, Stephen. 1969. *Cognitive Anthropology.* New York: Holt, Rinehart, and Winston.

———. 1978. *The Said and the Unsaid: Mind, Meaning, and Culture.* New York: Academic Press.

Tylor, Sir Edward Burnett. 1861. *Anahuac: Or Mexico and the Mexicans, Ancient and Modern.* London: Longman, Green, Longman and Roberts.

———. 1871. *Primitive Culture.* London: John Murray.

———. 1889. On a Method of Investigating the Development of Institutions; Applied to Laws of Marriage and Descent. *Journal of the Royal Anthropological Institute* 18:245–269.

———. 1920. *Primitive Culture,* 2nd ed. London: John Murray.

Veblen, Thorstein. 1912 [1899]. *The Theory of the Leisure Class: An Economic Study of Institutions.* New York: Viking Press.

Vico, Giambattista. 1984 [1774]. *The New Science of Giambattista Vico,* Thomas Goddard Bergin and Max Harold Fisch, trans. Ithaca, NY: Cornell University Press.

Walker, J. C. 1986. Romanticizing Resistance, Romanticizing Culture: Problems in Willis's Theory of Cultural Production. *British Journal of Sociology of Education* 7(1):59–80.

Wallenchinsky, David, and Irving Wallace, eds. 1975. *The People's Almanac.* Garden City, NY: Doubleday.

Wallerstein, I. 1974. *The Modern World-System; Capitalist Agriculture and the Origins of the European World-Economy in the Sixteenth Century (by) Immanuel Wallerstein.* New York: Academic Press.

Washburn, Sherwood, and C. Lancaster. 1968. The Evolution of Hunting. In *Man the Hunter,* R. B. Lee and Irven DeVore, eds., pp. 293–303. Chicago: Aldine.

Washington Post. 1998. *Campaign Finance Key Players: The Riady Family* http://www.washingtonpost.com/wp-srv/politics/special/campfin/players/riady.htm

Weber, Max. 1958 [1930]. *The Protestant Ethic and the Spirit of Capitalism,* Talcott Parsons, trans. New York: Charles Scribner's Sons.

———. 1993 [1920]. *The Sociology of Religion.* Boston: Beacon Press.

———. 1978. *Economy and Society: An Outline of Interpretive Sociology,* Guenther Roth and Claus Wittich, eds., Ephraim Fischoff, trans. Berkeley: University of California Press.

White, Leslie A. 1943. Energy and the Evolution of Culture. *American Anthropologist* 43:335–356.

———. 1949. Ikhnaton: The Great Man vs. the Culture Process. In *The Science of Culture: A Study of Man and Civilization,* pp. 233–281. New York: Farrar, Strauss.

———. 1959. *The Evolution of Culture.* New York: McGraw-Hill.

———. 1975. *The Concept of Cultural Systems: A Key to Understanding Tribes and Nations.* New York: Columbia University Press.

Whorf, Benjamin Lee. 1956. *Language Thought and Reality.* Cambridge, MA, M.I.T. Press.

Wierzbicka, Anna. 2005. Empirical Universals of Language as a Basis for the Study of Other Human Universals and as a Tool for Exploring Cross-Cultural Differences. *Ethos* 33(2):256–291.

Willis, P. 1983. Cultural Production and Theories of Reproduction. In *Race, Class and Education,* L. Barton and S. Walker, eds., pp. 107–138. London: Croom Helm.

Wilson, Edward O. 1971. *The Insect Societies.* Cambridge, MA: Harvard University Press.

———. 1975. *Sociobiology: The New Synthesis.* Cambridge, MA: Belknap Press of Harvard University Press.

———. 1984. *Biophilia*. Cambridge, MA: Harvard University Press.

Wissler, Clark. 1917. *The American Indian: An Introduction to the Anthropology of the New World*. New York: D. C. McMurtrie.

———. 1926. *The Relation of Nature to Man in Aboriginal America*. New York: Oxford University Press.

Wolf, Eric R. 1959. *Sons of the Shaking Earth*. Chicago: University of Chicago Press.

———. 1966. *Peasants*. Englewood Cliffs, NJ: Prentice-Hall.

———. 1969. *Peasant Wars of the Twentieth Century*. New York: Harper and Row.

Wittgenstein, Ludwig. 2001. *Philosophical Investigations*. 3rd ed. Oxford: Blackwell.

———. 1981. *Totems and Teachers: Perspectives on the History of Anthropology*, Sydel Silverman, ed. New York: Columbia University Press.

———. 1982. *Europe and the People Without History*. Berkeley: University of California Press.

Wolf, Eric R., and Joseph G. Jorgensen. 1970, November 19. Anthropology on the Warpath in Thailand. *New York Review of Books*, pp. 26–35.

Woodward, Bob. 1998. Findings Link Clinton Allies to Chinese Intelligence. *Washington Post*. Tuesday, February 10, 1998; Page A01.

Wundt, Wilhelm Max. 1904 [1874]. *Principles of Physiological Psychology*, Edward Bradford Titchener, trans. New York: Macmillan.

———. 1916 [1912]. *Elements of Folk Psychology: Outlines of a Psychological History of the Development of Mankind*. New York: Macmillan.

Yanagisako, Sylvia, and Jane Collier. 1987. Toward a Unified Analysis of Gender and Kinship. In *Gender and Kinship: Essays Toward a Unified Analysis*, pp. 14–50. Palo Alto, CA: Stanford University Press.

CREDITS

Lila Abu-Lughod, "A Tale of Two Pregnancies" from *Women Writing Culture,* edited by Ruth Behar and Deborah Gordon. Copyright © 1995 by The Regents of the University of California, University of California Press. Reprinted by permission.

Arjun Appadurai, "Disjuncture and Difference in the Global Cultural Economy" from *Public Culture,* vol. 2, no. 2, (Spring 1990): pp. 1–24. Published by Duke University Press.

Jerome H. Barkow, "The Elastic Between Genes and Culture." Reprinted from *Ethnology and Sociobiology,* vol. 10 (1989): pp. 111–129. Copyright © 1989 by Elsevier Science, Inc. Reprinted with permission from Elsevier.

Rebecca Bliege Bird, Eric Alden Smith, and Douglas W. Bird, "The Hunting Handicap: Costly Signaling in Human Foraging Strategies" from *Behavioral Ecology and Sociobiology,* vol. 50 (2001): pp. 9–19. Copyright © 2001 Springer-Verlag. Reprinted by permission of Springer-Verlag GmbH.

Philippe Bourgois, "From Jíbaro to Crack Dealer: Confronting the Restructuring of Capitalism in El Barrio" from *Articulating Hidden Histories: Exploring the Influence of Eric R. Wolf,* edited by Jane Schneider and Rayna Rapp (Berkeley: University of California Press, 1995), 125–141. Reprinted by permission.

Harold C. Conklin, "Hanunoo Color Categories" from *Southwestern Journal of Anthropology,* vol. 11 (1955): pp. 339–344. Reproduced with permission of the *Journal of Anthropological Research.*

Roy D'Andrade, "Moral Models in Anthropology" from *Current Anthropology,* vol. 36, no. 3 (June 1995): pp. 399–408. Copyright © 1995 by the Wenner-Gren Foundation for Anthropological Research, Inc. Reprinted by permission of the University of Chicago Press.

Mary Douglas, "External Boundaries" from *Purity and Danger: An Analysis of the Concepts of Pollution and Taboo* by Mary Douglas. (London: Routledge & Kegan Paul, 1966), pp. 114–128. Copyright © 1966 by Mary Douglas. Reproduced by permission of Taylor & Francis Books UK.

Emile Durkheim, "What Is a Social Fact?" Reprinted with the permission of The Free Press, a division of Simon & Schuster Adult Publishing Group from *The Rules of Sociological Method* by Emile Durkheim, translated by Sarah A. Solovay and John H. Mueller, edited by George E. G. Catlin. Copyright © 1938 by George E. G. Catlin. Copyright © renewed 1966 by Sarah A. Solovay, John H. Mueller, George E. G. Catlin. All rights reserved.

Emile Durkheim, "The Cosmological System of Totemism and the Idea of Class," from *The Elementary Forms of the Religious Life,* translated by Joseph Ward Swain (London: George Allen & Unwin, 1915), pp. 141–156. Reproduced by permission of Taylor & Francis Books UK.

E. E. Evans-Pritchard, "The Nuer of the Southern Sudan" from *African Political Systems,* edited by Myers Fortes and E. E. Evans-Pritchard. (London: Oxford University Press, 1940), pp. 272–296. Reprinted by permission of the International African Institute.

Morton H. Fried, "On the Evolution of Social Stratification and the State" from *Culture in History: Essays in Honor of Paul Radin,* edited by Stanley Diamond, pp. 713–731. Copyright © 1960 Columbia University Press. Reprinted with permission of the publisher.

Clifford Geertz, "Deep Play: Notes on the Balinese Cockfight" from *Daedalus,* 101:1 (Winter, 1972): pp. 1–38. Copyright © 1972 by the American Academy of Arts and Sciences. Reprinted with permission of MIT Press.

Max Gluckman, "The License in Ritual" from *Custom and Conflict in Africa* by Max Gluckman. (Oxford: Basil Blackwell, 1956), pp. 109–136. Reprinted with permission from Blackwell Publishing Limited.

Marvin Harris, "The Cultural Ecology of India's Sacred Cattle" from *Current Anthropology,* vol. 7, no. 1 (1966): pp. 51–59. Copyright © 1966 by the Wenner-Gren Foundation for Anthropological Research, Inc. Reprinted by permission of the University of Chicago Press.

Eleanor Leacock, "Interpreting the Origins of Gender Inequality: Conceptual and Historical Problems" from *Dialectical Anthropology,* vol. 7, no. 4 (1983):

INDEX